Morally Sensitive Issues and Cross-Border Movement in the EU

SCHOOL OF HUMAN RIGHTS RESEARCH SERIES, Volume 72

The titles published in this series are listed at the end of this volume.

Morally Sensitive Issues and Cross-Border Movement in the EU

The cases of reproductive matters and legal recognition of same-sex relationships

Nelleke Koffeman

intersentia

Cambridge – Antwerp – Portland

Intersentia Ltd
Sheraton House | Castle Park
Cambridge | CB3 0AX | United Kingdom
Tel.: +44 1223 370 170 | Email: mail@intersentia.co.uk

Nelleke Koffeman
Morally Sensitive Issues and Cross-Border Movement in the EU. The cases of reproductive matters and legal recognition of same-sex relationships

ISBN 978-1-78068-349-2
D/2015/7849/134
NUR 828

British Library Cataloguing in Publication Data. A catalogue record for this book is available from the British Library.

Acknowledgements

There must be a correlation between the number of pages of a dissertation and the number of people whom the author would like to include in the acknowledgments, as there is indeed a considerable number of people whose names I would like to mention here.

Evidently I would like to start with my supervisors, my '*Doktoreltern*', Prof. Janneke Gerards and Prof. Rick Lawson, a golden team. Rick, thank you first of all for opening the doors to academia to me by hiring me as your student assistant, ten years ago, and for being my mentor since. I have learned so much from your great expertise, your impressive analytical skills and your captivating writing style (in aqua blue!). I am also very grateful to you for your feedback and advice and for the enthusiasm with which you introduced me to many knowledgeable and inspiring people. Thank you also for the personal notes, the warm hospitality I received from you and Mielle at the Kloksteeg, and for the positive energy that you radiate.

Janneke, there are many reasons for which I admire you and I feel so privileged that you have been one of my supervisors. Not only are you a respected expert in the area of European (human rights) law, you are also – and to me even more importantly – an incredibly nice person and an outstanding supervisor. You are most reliable and you have (with no exceptions!) always provided me – quicker than I could dream or even think of – with clear, detailed and stimulating feedback. Thank you for all those meetings without any time pressure and for creating opportunities for me. Also, there has always been warm personal contact, and that has made me count my blessings even more.

In the course of my PhD research I have had the occasion and privilege to engage in cross-border movement myself, something for which I am very grateful. It has brought me new horizons, confronted me with new ideas and many inspiring people have crossed my path, both during international conferences and in the course of research visits to distinguished foreign universities. In Ireland I would like to thank NUI Galway, in particular Prof. Donncha O'Connell, as well as Dr. Ciara Smyth and Conor Hanly for hosting me twice, both in 2009 and 2013. You have been so hospitable and the insights into the Irish legal system and political debates you provided me with have been incredibly helpful. I am furthermore very grateful to Dublin-based Prof. Fergus Ryan and Fiona Duffy for the dedicated way in which they each kept me informed about the – often fast-moving – developments in those areas of Irish law that were relevant to my research.

At the Humboldt-Universität zu Berlin, where I spent six months in 2011, it is first and foremost Prof. Susanne Baer to whom I would like to express my sincere gratitude. Thank you for welcoming me at your chair and for helping me to reflect upon my research by posing spot-on, thought-provoking questions. Many thanks also to Sophie Rosenbuch for being such a kind and helpful host, to Dr. Sarah Elsuni and to the German Academic Exchange Service (DAAD) for making it possible by means of a scholarship. I would further like to thank Jerzy Szczesny at the Bundestag, for keeping me updated so enthusiastically about German developments in the area of LGBT rights. It was also in Berlin that I met the lovely and unequalled Prof. Nora Markard, and it was such a joy to find our friendship flourish during our time in New York. There have been others who made those months in Berlin such a dear time and that made, and make, me come back over and over again: Octavio Gonzalez Segovia, Pablo Rojas, Laura Ledesma, Beatriz Torres, Eyob Mulatu, Carlos Vallejos and Philip Mehls. I look forward to seeing you again, wherever that may be.

I am furthermore very grateful to Fordham Law School in New York, in particular to Dean Toni Fine, for hosting me in the spring of 2013, and to the Leiden University Fund for awarding me a grant that made it possible. My research time in the Big Apple has been very important for defining the ultimate direction of my book. Also, another metropolis was thereby enclosed in my heart.

There are a number of individual experts whom I would like to mention here, as I am grateful to them for taking the time to discuss my research with me. These are CJEU Judge Prof. Koen Lenaerts in Luxembourg, Dr. Jacco Bomhoff in London, and Prof. Richard Storrow, Prof. Susanne Goldberg, Prof. Arthur Leonard and Prof. Evan Wolfson in New York. Many thanks also to the colleagues from the *Rights on the Move* project for the highly interesting meetings. At Leiden University I would like to mention Prof. Kees Waaldijk, whose passion for LGBT rights has been contagious and who has furthermore put me in touch with many experts in the field. Prof. Aart Hendriks has, with great enthusiasm, shown a continuous interest in my research, and the ZONmW project that we did together with Janneke was a sheer joy. Thank you.

At the Europa Institute I would like to thank Prof. Stefaan Van den Bogaert for managing the department with devotion and expertise and for his confidence in me. I would further like to mention my (former) 'roomies' Bas van Bockel, Jorrit Rijpma and Armin Cuyvers whose humour, good company and helpful feedback I much appreciate. Armin, I am delighted that you accepted my invitation to be my *paranimf* and I look forward to all our future legal and non-legal reflections. There have been many other great EI colleagues over the years whom have contributed enormously to me having very much enjoyed working there. These are, amongst others (!), Barbara Cooreman, Yvonne van der Vlugt, Vestert Borger, Narin Tezcan, Elsbeth Beumer, Vicky Kosta, Jasmina Mačkić, Meehea Park, Darinka Piqani, Moritz Jesse, Agis Karpetas, Christa Tobler, Alison McDonnell, Wendy Rodger, Melanie Fink, and so many more. Then there were the ladies from '*het promoclubje*' and the '*Renkum posse*' (Vestert Borger, Ingrid Leijten and Ruben Zandvliet) with whom I spent those both most productive and enjoyable weeks in villa 'Molenbeke' in the summer of 2014. It has been such a pleasure and privilege to work with many other great colleagues at Leiden Law School, for example the members of the Leiden Court Watchers, as well as outside Leiden, for example in '*het leesclubje*' and in the Netherlands School of Human Rights Research.

A big thank you to Lara Rudnik for assisting me with finalising the references in the footnotes which care and precision, and to Joost Abbel and Rosan Dekker from Studio Hudson for the apt cover illustration.

Turning to the private sphere, there are many sweet and inspiring people in my circle of friends whom I would like to thank for their committed friendship and support during the PhD writing process. Whether we met through our studies (Anna Gouwenberg and Karima Hara), our student association (Nicole Janse, Marijke Kuiper, Maartje Beekman, and too many others to mention all by name here), sports or other shared interests (Camille Tonino and Joyce Dreessen), or during times abroad (Tonje Røland, Daniiela Kroemer, Stefan Mayr and Andrea Gruber), thank you all. Then there are three friends who have been there from my very first day in respectively primary school, secondary school and university, namely Lieke Buitink, Thessa Wong and Vera van Voorst. You are all very dear to me; I hope we stay as close during all other phases in life that may follow.

I would like to thank my parents, Leo and Greetje Koffeman, for all their confidence, support, inspiration, advice and love. Kees and Nico, it is simply great to have you on board in the family. Ide, my big brother, thank you for your care, your humour and creativity and your reflections upon life. My sweet sister Eva, my rock, thank you for being there for me always, for teaching me so many things (not least how to read and write!), and for sharing in the PhD writing process. Gijs, thank you for being you. I am so happy that we met again and I am very much looking forward to all that lies ahead of us.

CONTENTS

Introduction

Chapter 1
Introduction

1.1. Object of study and research questions

Within the European Union (EU) considerable diversity exists in respect of morally sensitive issues like abortion, assisted human reproduction (AHR), surrogacy and legal recognition of same-sex relationships. The EU Member States have made diverging choices in respect of these matters and followed different tracks in their regulation of these areas. States often expressly claim recognition of such national specificities at the European level. While the twentieth century has witnessed an increased intergovernmental cooperation between States as well as an increased transferral of state powers to supranational organisations such as the EU, certain competences have traditionally remained with the States. The aforementioned morally sensitive issues are areas of law *par excellence* where standards are primarily set at State level. It is usually considered that it should be left to each State to decide whether, for example, abortion is available on social grounds, whether couples can become parents with the involvement of a surrogate mother and whether same-sex couples can marry and/or adopt children.

While there is no strong degree of European regulation in these areas, and while diversity is generally respected at European level, there is nonetheless a certain body of European law applicable in these fields. The EU has competences in respect of issues that are strongly related to, and at times intertwined with, reproductive matters and legal recognition of same-sex relationships. Here, one may think of competences in the areas of health and equal treatment.[1] In addition, several of these morally sensitive issues come within the scope of the European Convention on Human Rights (ECHR), for instance by means of the right to respect for private life under Article 8 ECHR.[2] That raises the question whether such European standard-setting (potentially and indirectly) affects the room for States to regulate in these areas and thus whether this has implications for the existing diversity in the European Union in morally sensitive issues.

Cross-border movement within the EU adds a new dimension to this already complex picture. Cross-border movement is a given within the EU; people move around in the EU for various reasons and purposes, not uncommonly pursuing economic

---

1 Arts. 168 and 19 TFEU. See more elaborately Ch. 3, section 3.1.3.1 and Ch. 9, section 9.3.

2 See more elaborately Ch. 2 and Ch. 8.

objectives.[3] Such mobility is enabled and stimulated by the EU free movement rules that, *inter alia*, protect the free movement of persons and the freedom to receive services in another EU Member State.[4] Diverging regimes in the aforementioned morally sensitive matters may, however, create obstacles to such cross-border movement; they may hinder or deter persons from making use of their free movement rights. For instance, same-sex couples may be discouraged from moving to an EU Member State where they have no possibility of having their relationship legally recognised by means of a civil partnership or marriage. Differences in regimes in morally sensitive issues may, by contrast, also be the direct impetus for cross-border movement within the EU as people from Member States with less permissive regimes may wish to enjoy the possibilities, rights and benefits of more permissive regimes of other States. For example, in Member States with restrictive abortion regimes, women who wish to have their pregnancy terminated may want to travel to Member States with more liberal regimes.

Such cross-border movement and the existing obstacles thereto do not only highlight existing diversity, they also imply, among other things, that States are increasingly more confronted with (the consequences and effects of) other States' regimes. For example, same-sex couples residing in one EU Member State may claim recognition of their marriage concluded in another Member State, while women or couples who had a certain type of AHR treatment in another State that is outlawed under the law of their own State, may claim reimbursement of the costs involved in that treatment under the national health system of their State. Such confrontation may require a reaction from the States involved, whether they function as country of origin or as country of destination or both. That raises the question of how national and European law respond to such cross-border movement. Are States receptive to cross-border movement in respect of morally sensitive issues, or do they (try to) ward it off? Also, it may be asked how much room do EU law and the ECHR actually leave States to respond to such cross-border movement in different ways? A related question is whether and to what extent such cross-border movement, and the legal responses thereto, impact national standard-setting in these morally sensitive issues, and, consequently, how they influence both the existing diversity and the legal development regarding these matters in Europe.

The present research explores this cross-border dimension of morally sensitive issues within the European Union. It aims to provide an overview of trends and developments in national law and European law, as well as to give insight into the interests that are at stake both in internal and in cross-border situations. Such an overview allows for taking stock of the situation and it enables further analysis of the various interests involved in this multi-level picture. Thus, this research may assist legislatures and judiciaries in answering the question how the relevant interests

[3] See, for example, Statistics of Eurostat, as online available at www.ec.europa.eu/eurostat/statistics-explained/index.php/EU_citizenship_-_statistics_on_cross-border_activities, visited February 2015. More elaborately, see Ch. 9, section 9.5.

[4] *Inter alia* Arts. 21, 45 and 56 TFEU and Art. 45 CFR. More elaborately, see Ch. 3, section 3.5 and Ch. 9, section 9.6.

should be balanced and at what level (e.g. European or national) that balance should be struck. Importantly, this research does not aim to take any normative stance towards the issues it focuses on. Instead it wants to observe, clarify and typify an existing dynamic, whereby various areas and levels of law interact, and in doing so it aims to reveal the analytical framework for decision-making regarding these issues.

1.2. Approach and Methodology

The basic ingredients of the present research are two thematic case studies – one on reproductive matters (Case Study I) and one on legal recognition of same-sex relationships (Case Study II) – which focus on five jurisdictions. The latter encompass three national jurisdictions – Germany, Ireland and the Netherlands – and two European jurisdictions or systems, namely the EU and the ECHR. Justification of this selection of jurisdictions, as well as further definition of the two case studies is given below in sections 1.3 and 1.4, while an outline of the present volume is provided in section 1.5 below.

The two thematic case studies investigate for the three national jurisdictions as well as for the relevant European jurisdictions what – if any – standard-setting is in place in respect of reproductive matters and legal recognition of same-sex relationships respectively, and how this developed over time. This analysis, *inter alia*, provides insight into what considerations and interests play, or have played, a role in legislative debates and case law and how change was, or may be, brought about. It also makes clear in what respects the regimes studied differ and how European law has influenced, or may influence, national standard-setting in these areas. Apart from providing insight into these matters, and apart from substantiating the claim that considerable diversity indeed exists within the EU in morally sensitive issues, this analysis of the internal picture per jurisdiction provides the basis for the subsequent analysis of the cross-border picture per jurisdiction.

After briefly indicating the scale at which cross-border movement takes place, both case studies subsequently involve further examination for each of the five jurisdictions of how they have dealt and deal with cross-border situations in these areas and how they interact in this regard. Thereby, *inter alia*, Private International Law regimes and (national implementation of) the EU free movement rules are studied, in order to answer questions like whether foreign marriages and civil partnerships of same-sex couples are recognised or whether women who wish to have an abortion in another country have a right to access to information about such foreign abortion services, as well as a right to follow-up treatment upon return.

The analysis provided in the two case studies makes it possible to discern trends in standard-setting and in judicial and legislative processes regarding these morally sensitive issues. Also, various legal responses to cross-border movement in respect of these issues can be identified. The analysis further allows for observations about what interests and considerations have informed the relevant legal responses, what implications these responses have for the individuals involved in the cross-border movement and how the various legal responses interrelate. Finally, it allows for some conclusions to be drawn as to the extent to which cross-border movement impacts national standard-setting.

The methodology adopted in this research has consisted first and foremost of a doctrinal approach. The current book presents a systematic analysis of applicable standards in two areas of law in five jurisdictions and provides insight in how these interact. This descriptive legal analysis[5] includes binding or 'positive' law (legislation, case law), as well as legal doctrine and academic literature. Further, in order to provide for a more complete picture, non-binding documents (so-called 'soft law'), such as policy documents, reports of government appointed committees, guidelines of the medical profession and resolutions of the European Parliament have been studied. This is only different for the chapters on the ECHR (Chapters 2 and 8). Given that when it comes to the ECHR, it is the case law of the European Court of Human Rights (ECtHR) that sets the relevant framework, these chapters contain first and foremost a case law analysis, and only incidentally refer to legal doctrine and academic literature. Also, non-binding standard-setting in these areas in the context of the Council of Europe (CoE) more broadly is not separately discussed.

The research not only describes the positive law, however, but also the development of the relevant law. Moreover, it aims to provide some insight in the preceding and accompanying political and public debates. In that sense, the research fits in with the 'law in context' approach.[6] Concretely this means that also parliamentary documents, pre-legislative initiatives that did not make it into law and sometimes references to newspaper articles are included in the analysis in the case studies. Further, while for the present research no empirical legal science was carried out, incidentally reference is made to existing sociological studies, for instance to studies based on surveys amongst services recipients involved in cross-border reproductive care (CBRC), as these studies gave insight into the implications of certain legal responses to cross-border movement in these areas. Also, reference is made to statistics on the actual scale at which cross-border movement in respect of morally sensitive issues takes place within the European Union and to and from the States studied in this research. With respect to these figures the research relies completely on secondary sources.

---

5 Smits describes descriptive legal science as '[...] the systematic description of the law in a certain field.' The author notes that it is '[...] usually seen as a synonym for a legal doctrinal approach or for legal systematization [...]'. J.M. Smits, *The Mind and Method of the Legal Academic* (Cheltenham, Elgar 2012) p. 11.

6 Nelken has described 'law in context' as '[...] learning to think of law in terms of larger processes – bringing out, for example, the similarities between decision-making in legal and other settings. It suggests that we configure law as one stage, aspect, or method, of dealing with wider processes of disputing or social regulation, and that we treat these processes as related in some way to the needs, (social) problems and conflicts of social groups.' D. Nelken, *Beyond law in context: developing a sociological understanding of law* (London, Ashgate 2009) pp. xii-xiii. Nelken refers (at p. xii (in footnote 4) and at p. xxvii) to Twining as 'one of the founders of the law in context approach'. See also W. Twining, *Law in context, enlarging a discipline* (Oxford, Clarendon Press 1997).

The subject-matters of the present research have turned out to be 'moving targets'. Legislation and case law on the issues discussed are in a constant state of flux and the topics are characterised by fast-moving social and scientific developments. Even since 2009, the year this research was commenced, important changes have occurred, both at national level and at European level. The continuous succession of developments rendered it inescapable to choose a clear cut-off date, which was set at 31 July 2014. The case studies cover developments until that date[7] and the observations and conclusions, while also reflecting upon possible future developments, are based on that analysis.

Selection of the 'starting point' of the relevant analysis has appeared more naturally, as the discussion of the relevant national and European standard-setting begins with the first steps of regulation in the respective jurisdictions. As generally fairly 'new' topics are concerned,[8] at least when it comes to the regulation thereof by European States, this generally concerns the 1960s for liberalisation of abortion laws, the 1980s for AHR treatment and surrogacy and the 1990s for legal recognition of same-sex relationships. Evidently, as further explained in the respective chapters, sometimes much older developments lay at the basis of this standard-setting.

1.3. The two case studies

The case studies on reproductive matters and legal recognition of same-sex relationships respectively have been chosen because they concern pre-eminently morally sensitive issues and, consequently, politically controversial matters, in respect of which EU Member States have long take different positions, and still did so at the time this research was commenced (i.e., in 2009). For example, in respect of abortion it has been observed:

> 'It is difficult to imagine a more controversial and divisive topic around which opinions as to the associated penumbra of moral/legal issues are so radically and conclusively polarised than that of abortion.'[9]

In respect of equality for lesbian, gay, bisexual, transgender and intersexual persons (LGBTIs) the following was observed as recently as 2013 by a Member of the European Parliament: 'Next to abortion, it is the single most sensitive issue to work on. Politicians just prefer to stay away from it [...].'[10]

---

7 While there have been further interesting developments after 31 July 2014, particularly in respect of surrogacy (e.g. ECtHR 27 January 2015, *Paradiso and Campabello*, no. 25358/12; *M.R. and D.R. (suing by their father and next friend O.R.) & ors* v. *An t-Ard-Chláraitheoir & ors* [2014] IESC 60 and BGH 10 December 2014, Az XII ZB 463/13) these have thus not been included in this research.

8 Evidently, the themes as such are not necessarily new, as for instance same-sex relationships and surrogacy (the low-technological form, see 1.3.1 below) have been held to have taken place since the birth of mankind.

9 D. Curtin, 'Case note to CJEU C-159/90', 29 *CML Rev* (1992), p. 585.

10 Dutch Liberal MEP Sophie in 't Veld as quoted in: H. Mahoney, 'Reding should 'stick neck out' on gay rights', *euobserver.com* 7 May 2013, www.euobserver.com/lgbti/119977, visited 10 July 2014.

Moreover, the issues covered by the two case studies are not 'just' morally sensitive issues, they also concern areas in which fundamental rights claims can be made. While this implies that there is room for European influence, this has been the case to a limited extent only. Particularly when this research was commenced (i.e., in 2009) there was, and in fact there is still, limited European standard-setting in these areas.[11] This makes these case studies all the more interesting for investigating the interaction and interrelationship between European law and national law.

Further, and importantly given the focus of this research, these also concern areas that have a demonstrable cross-border dimension. Not only has cross-border movement for abortion – in the past often referred to as 'abortion tourism' – been much reported on,[12] but cross-border reproductive care (CBRC) has also become a widely recognised phenomenon.[13] Further, it is self-evident that same-sex couples (often referred to as 'rainbow families', particularly where they have children) cross borders within the EU, even though exhaustive statistics on the scale at which they do so are lacking.[14] Over the years there has been increasingly more academic and political attention for the free movement of rainbow families within the EU.[15]

1.3.1. Definition of Case Study I

Case Study I on reproductive matters covers three subjects, namely abortion, assisted human reproduction (AHR) and surrogacy. In the discussion of regulation of AHR a number of issues that may occur in the course of AHR treatment are included. Firstly, AHR may involve the donation of gametes (both sperm (semen) and egg cells (ovum)) and embryos. In the discussion of the relevant standard-setting in Case Study I, attention is paid to the question of whether, and if so, under what circumstances, donors can remain anonymous.[16] Further, standard-setting in respect of preimplantation genetic diagnosis (PGD) is explored. PGD '[...] involves checking the genes and/or chromosomes of embryos created through [*in vitro* fertilisation (IVF treatment)].'[17] It '[...] enables people with an inheritable condition in their family to

---

11 As set out more elaborately in Ch. 2, Ch. 3, Ch. 8 and Ch. 9.

12 See, *inter alia*, Ch. 5, section 5.4.

13 See, *inter alia*, A.P. Ferraretti et al., 'Cross-border reproductive care: a phenomenon expressing the controversial aspects of reproductive technologies', 20 *Reproductive BioMedicine Online* (2010), p. 261. See also Ch. 3, section 3.4.2.

14 More elaborately, see Ch. 9, section 9.5.

15 For instance, 'freedom of movement for LGBT people' is one of the five priorities of the European Parliament's Intergroup on LGBT rights. See www.lgbt-ep.eu/work/priority-1, visited January 2015. More elaborately, see Ch. 9, section 9.6.

16 In the context of high-technological surrogacy (see below) a distinction can be made between the biological mother (the woman who carries and gives birth to the child) and the genetic mother (the woman whose egg-cell is used in creation of the embryo). Evidently no such distinction can be made between biological and genetic fathers. For purposes of clarity, however, the choice has been made in this research to use the terms 'genetic parents' and also 'genetic father' in most cases. Only where the term 'biological' has been referred to expressly in regulations or case law, this may be different.

17 Website of the UK Human Fertilisation and Embryology Authority (HFEA) www.hfea.gov.uk/preimplantation-genetic-diagnosis.html, visited 12 March 2015.

avoid passing it on to their children.'[18] A related issue that is addressed is whether gender selection in the course of IVF treatment is allowed for under the national law. Also addressed is the vitrification of egg cells (also referred to as oocyte freezing), whereby egg cells are frozen and stored for use in future treatment.[19] Lastly, surrogacy, a highly divisive topic which may include AHR treatment, is included in the case study. Surrogacy concerns the situation where another woman carries and gives birth to a child for an individual or couple who want(s) to have a child. There are two types of surrogacy: so-called low-technological surrogacy, where the surrogate mother is also the genetic mother of the child; while high-technological surrogacy refers the situation where the surrogate mother is not genetically related to the child, because the child that she carries and to which she gives birth was conceived during IVF treatment with the use of the gametes of donors (often, but not necessarily the intended parents).

For each of these topics, Case Study I first of all sets out whether the relevant reproductive service is at all legalised and if so under what conditions access to these services is provided. Also, the financing of abortion and AHR treatment under each State's national health system is briefly addressed. Thereby only State regulation is discussed, since that gives the clearest expression of a State's (moral) position on the matter. Private regulation (i.e., private insurance) is thus excluded. In the discussion of national regulation of surrogacy, the possibilities (if they exist at all) for intended parents to establish parental links with a child born following a surrogacy arrangement are also discussed.

Because the focus lies on reproductive treatment, scientific biomedical research and cloning fall outside the scope of the case study. Also, Case Study I does not cover adoption. While a means of family building as well, it has been considered too remote from the issue of reproduction. Further, this Case Study concentrates on the rights and interests of services recipients, not on care providers and intermediaries. For that reason, areas of law like EU competition law, state aid rules and public procurement rules in respect of (cross-border) health care are not included in the analysis.[20]

---

18 *Idem.*

19 The website of the UK Human Fertilisation and Embryology Authority (HFEA) explains this method as follows: 'The use of frozen eggs in treatment is a relatively new development. [...]. [...] vitrification (a new method for egg storage) has recently been shown to improve the chance of eggs surviving the freeze-thaw process and therefore increase the success rate. To help boost egg production, fertility drugs are used to stimulate the ovaries to produce follicles (which contain the eggs). The developing follicles are monitored and when they are large enough, they are carefully emptied to collect the eggs that they have produced. [...] To freeze the eggs, they are placed in storage in liquid nitrogen.' See www.hfea.gov.uk/46.html, visited 12 March 2015.

20 See, *inter alia*, J.W. van de Gronden et al. (eds.), *Health care and EU law* (The Hague, T.M.C. Asser Press 2011) pp. 265–359 and L. Hancher and W. Sauter, 'One step beyond? From Sodemare to Docmorris: The EU's freedom of establishment case law concerning healthcare', 47 *CMLRev* (2010) p. 117.

1.3.2. Definition of Case Study II

Case Study II explores what the various jurisdictions provide in respect of legal recognition of same-sex relationships. Thereby a first focal point is whether same-sex couples have (a right to) access to a registration form – civil partnership or marriage – under the relevant jurisdictions and, if so, what these entail. The discussion thus focuses on special institutes; other forms of granting of certain rights or benefits to unmarried (stable) couples, such as housing benefits for cohabiting couples, are not discussed separately. The Case Study aims not so much to provide an exhaustive comparative overview of all public and private effects of these institutes, but mainly to give insight into the differences between the protection that same-sex couples enjoy under the law of the relevant regimes if compared to different-sex couples. Hence, the public effects of these institutes in areas like taxes and pensions are discussed in some detail where there have been noteworthy developments in this regard in case law or legislation in the various jurisdictions. The applicable property regimes and rules concerning private law aspects like name and inheritance, are not included in the research, although developments in this regard are sometimes noted where they appear to be highly relevant for the overall picture. Also, while briefly addressed, no detailed assessment of the regulation of divorce and separation is included in Case Study II.

Secondly, especially since this has proven a controversial matter in many EU Member States, the case study also covers the question of parental rights for same-sex couples. Thereby various forms of adoption are discussed, namely second-parent adoption,[21] successive adoption[22] and joint adoption. Also, legal parenthood by operation of the law and access to AHR treatment for same-sex couples are addressed.

Case Study II, in the same vein as Case Study I, focuses on services recipients, thereby concentrating on the rights and interests of same-sex couples and rainbow families. Standard-setting regarding third parties, such as civil servants, is not included in the case study.[23]

1.4. The five jurisdictions

As noted above, the present book presents an in-depth study of the moral choices of three EU Member States, namely Germany, Ireland and the Netherlands. Thereby the deliberate choice has been made to study three national jurisdictions in-depth, instead of covering a wider array of States more superficially. Only such an in-depth study provides a true insight into the development of the relevant legal frameworks, in legislative and judicial processes and in the relevant legal dynamics.

---

21 The term second-parent adoption concerns the adoption of a child by the partner of the child's legal and genetic parent.

22 Successive adoption concerns the situation where a partner adopts the child of an adoptive parent.

23 Hence, the issue of conscientious objections of civil servants against concluding marriages or civil partnerships between same-sex couples is not discussed separately.

In selecting three States, it was first of all ensured that these States cover a certain range in approaches in respect of reproductive matters and legal recognition of same-sex relationships; that they are, so to speak, on different sides of the moral spectrum. Generally speaking, although one must be very careful with such generalisations, one could say that Ireland represents the more traditional approach in Europe, or at least did so at the time the research was commenced (in 2009). The Netherlands, on the other hand, belongs to the more progressive, liberal tradition, while Germany may – or in any case could – be seen as representing the middle ground.

Further, the three States selected have different (constitutional) profiles. While Germany and Ireland have a strong Constitution, whereby the German Constitutional Court and the Irish Supreme Court can review the constitutionality of legislation,[24] in the Netherlands the Constitution is comparatively 'weak', and Dutch courts cannot review the constitutionality of Acts of Parliament.[25] Also, the relationship with European law differs or has differed amongst the three States. For example, the Irish Constitution is strongly dualist[26] and implementation the ECHR[27] has appeared to be a lengthy and rather arduous process, while in respect of EU law various reservations and opt-outs apply.[28] The Dutch legal order, by contrast, is very open to European and International Law, as self-executing International Law standards, have direct effect in the Dutch legal order.[29] The German legal order has its own

---

24 The German Constitutional Court may rule upon the formal or substantive compatibility of Federal Law or Land law with the Basic Law (Art. 94(2) Basic Law). This Court also has jurisdiction to rule upon constitutional complaints from individuals, who are alleging that one of their basic rights has been infringed by a public authority (Arts. 93(2) and 93 (4a) Basic Law). In Ireland, the President may, after consultation with the Council of State, refer a bill passed by both Houses of Parliament to the Supreme Court for a decision on the question of whether such a bill or any specified provision or provisions of such a bill is or are repugnant to this Constitution or to any provision thereof (Art. 26.1.1° Irish Constitution). Although some type of bills are excluded, the President has total discretion in referring any bill (see B. McCracken, 'The Irish Constitution – an overview', in: J. Sarkin and W. Binchy (eds.), *Human Rights, the Citizen and the State. South African and Irish Approaches* (Dublin, Round Hall Sweet & Maxwell 2001) p. 52 at pp. 56–57). The President shall not sign any bill which is the subject of a reference to the Supreme Court pending the pronouncement of the decision of the Court (Art. 46.3° Irish Constitution). The Court has to give a ruling within 60 days. If the Supreme Court decides that any provision of a bill is repugnant to the Constitution or to any provision thereof, the President must decline to sign such a bill.

25 Art. 94 of the Dutch Constitution reads: 'Statutory regulations in force within the Kingdom shall not be applicable if such application is in conflict with provisions of treaties or of resolutions by international institutions that are binding on all persons.' Translation taken from www.government.nl/documents-and-publications/regulations/2012/10/18/the-constitution-of-the-kingdom-of-the-netherlands-2008.html, visited 12 March 2015.

26 Art. 29 Irish Constitution.

27 See, *inter alia*, D. O'Connell, 'Ireland', in: R. Blackburn and J. Polakiewicz (eds.), *Fundamental Rights in Europe. The ECHR and its Member States 1950–2000* (Oxford, Oxford University Press 2001) p. 425 and S. Besson, 'The Reception Process in Ireland and the United Kingdom', in: H. Keller and A. Stone Sweet (eds.), *A Europe of Rights. The impact of the ECHR on National Legal Systems* (Oxford, Oxford University Press 2008) p. 31 at p. 52.

28 See more elaborately Ch. 5, section 5.2.

29 Art. 93 of the Dutch Constitution. In practice, Dutch Courts tend to examine the compatibility of statutory law with International Treaty law, with the general effect that the European Convention has come to serve as a kind of shadow constitution. J.H. Gerards and M. Claes, 'National report – The Netherlands', in: J. Laffranque (ed.), *The Protection of Fundamental Rights Post-Lisbon: The Interaction*

relationship with European law,[30] and the German Constitutional Court in particular has been both an important generator of European integration and has at the same time applied the brakes on various occasions.[31]

Lastly, language considerations have also played a role in the selection of these three national jurisdictions. Given the aim of making an in-depth analysis of the laws of the various jurisdictions, it is considered important to study them in their original language, without needing to rely on secondary sources or translations. It is for that reason that jurisdictions like Poland or Greece – even though highly interesting for the present research and even though they concern non-Western European systems – have not been included in the present research.

The two European jurisdictions studied are EU law and the ECHR. The standard-setting in these jurisdictions gives context to and sets limits to national standard-setting in these areas. It requires little explanation that EU law is included in this research, which concentrates on the legal dynamics within the EU. Also, EU law standards are binding upon the Member States and have primacy over conflicting national standards,[32] and many EU law provisions are directly applicable in the legal orders of the Member States.[33] The ECHR, for its part, sets the context for any State or Union action in these areas, as not only all EU Member States are High Contracting Parties to the Convention, but the fundamental rights as guaranteed under the ECHR also constitute general principles of EU law.[34]

International standards, such as human rights standards other than the ECHR or (non-binding) standard-setting within the Hague Conference on Private International Law,[35] or the International Commission on Civil Status,[36] are not separately discussed in this study. There are only few applicable binding international standards, and such

between the Charter of Fundamental Rights of the European Union, the European Convention on Human Rights and National Constitutions, Reports of the XXV FIDE Congress Tallinn, Vol. 1 (Tartu, Tartu University Press 2012) p. 613.

30 Following Art. 25 German Basic Law, the general rules of international law form an integral part of and take precedence over German Federal Law and directly create rights and duties for the inhabitants of the federal territory. The Basic Law furthermore contains a particular provision concerning the European Union (Art. 23). It provides that the Federal Republic of Germany shall '[...] participate in the development of the European Union that is committed to democratic, social and federal principles, to the rule of law, and to the principle of subsidiarity, and that guarantees a level of protection of basic rights essentially comparable to that afforded by this Basic Law.' To this end the Federation may transfer sovereign powers. The establishment of the European Union, as well as changes in its treaty foundations and comparable regulations that amend or supplement the German Basic Law, or make such amendments or supplements possible, are subject to the procedure for amendment of the German Basic Law (Art. 23(1) in combination with Art. 79(2) and (3) German Basic Law).

31 For example, BVerfG 29 May 1974, Az. 2 BvL 52/71, *NJW* 1974 p. 1697 (*Solange I*); BVerfG 22 October 1986, Az. 2 BvR 197/83, *NJW* 1987 p. 577 (*Solange II*); BVerfG 14 October 2004, Az. 2 BvR 1481/04, *NJW* 2004 p. 3407 and BVerfG 30 June 2009, Az. 2 BvE 2/08 a.o., *NJW* 2009 p. 2267 (*Lissabon Urteil*).

32 Case 6/64 *Costa/ENEL* [1964] ECR 585, ECLI:EU:C:1964:66 and Case C-399/11, *Melloni* [2013] ECR 0000, ECLI:EU:C:2013:107.

33 Case 26/62 *Van Gend en Loos* [1963] ECR 0001, ECLI:EU:C:1963:1.

34 Art. 6(3) TEU.

35 See www.hcch.net/index_en.php, visited June 2014.

36 See www.ciecl.org, visited June 2014.

standards as exist have often been integrated in standard-setting in one or more of the jurisdictions studied.[37] Hence, where relevant, international standards are covered by the discussion of the relevant standard-setting in the jurisdictions studied.

1.5. Outline

The two case studies introduced above, form the backbone of this volume. Each one consists of six chapters, five describing the standard-setting in the five selected jurisdictions, and one drawing conclusions for the case study.

Each of the ten substantive chapters of the two case studies first sets out the development of the law in respect of reproductive matters, respectively legal recognition of same-sex relationships in the five jurisdictions, as well as their current state of affairs. For a better understanding of the relevant standard-setting and – where relevant – the debates in politics and legal scholarship concerning these often controversial matters, a general (constitutional) framework is sketched first. A brief introduction is given to very prominent rights in the relevant jurisdictions (e.g. the protection of the unborn on the Irish jurisdiction and the protection of marriage under the German Basic Law), as well as to a selection of themes and – in the case of the EU – competences that are key in the respective case studies. Subsequently, the chapters sketch both the internal picture and the cross-border picture. The analysis of the internal picture addresses matters like whether, and if so under what conditions, (a right to) access to a certain reproductive treatment is in place under the law of the respective jurisdictions or what parental rights same-sex couples enjoy under the respective regimes. The relevant discussions of the cross-border picture, start – where available – with some statistics on the scale of cross-border movement in the context of the respective case study. Thereafter there is discussion of what the various jurisdictions provide in respect of issues like access to information about foreign reproductive treatment options and the recognition of parental links established abroad.

On the basis of the analysis provided in the various substantive chapters, conclusions are drawn per case study (Chapters 7 and 13). The concluding chapter, Chapter 14, provides a synthesis of the relevant findings of Chapters 7 and 13, as well as a number of observations about morally sensitive issues and cross-border movement within the EU more generally.

---

37 For example, as further explained in Ch. 12, section 12.4.2, Dutch Private international law is firmly rooted in international Treaty law. In respect of marriage, the applicable law was for 70 years, the Hague Convention relating to the settlement of the conflict of the laws concerning marriage of 1902.

Case Study I – Reproductive Matters

CHAPTER 2
ECHR

2.1. REPRODUCTIVE MATTERS UNDER THE ECHR

2.1.1. A right to respect for the decision (not) to become a genetic parent

When it comes to reproduction both Articles 8 and 12 ECHR have played a role in the case law of the ECtHR. While 'the right to found a family' ex. Article 12 ECHR may seem the most obvious provision to base any claim in this respect on, it has in fact been the right to respect for private and family life (Article 8 ECHR) on the basis of which the most substantive case law in this field has been decided.[1] This has everything to do with the narrow wording and interpretation of Article 12, which reads:

> 'Men and women of marriageable age have the right to marry and to found a family, according to the national laws governing the exercise of this right.'

With the wording 'this right' at the end of the provision, the right to marry and the right to found a family are firmly bracketed together.[2] The Court has repeatedly held that the right to marry under Article 12 ECHR refers to the 'traditional marriage between persons of opposite biological sex' (see also Chapter 8, section 8.2).[3] In the 1950s, when the Convention was drafted, the founding of a family may well have been considered to be the primary function of the institution of marriage. The Court has, however, since observed 'major social changes in the institution of marriage since the adoption of the Convention'[4] and held that '[...] the inability of any couple to conceive or parent a child cannot be regarded as *per se* removing their right to enjoy the first limb of this provision.'[5] Thereby also different-sex couples who do not wish to or are unable to found a family may exercise the right to marry. Still, Article 12 offers no protection to unmarried couples who wish to found a family; the right to found a family within the meaning of Article 12 exists only

---

1 Various judges held in a dissenting opinion of 2011 that Art. 8 of the Convention by then appeared to play 'an enhanced role [...] regarding questions related to procreation and reproduction.' Joint dissenting opinion of Tulkens, Hirvelä, Lazarova Trajkovska and Tsotsoria to ECtHR [GC] 3 November 2011, *S.H. a.o.* v. *Austria*, no. 57813/00, para. 3.

2 Compare C.A. White and C. Ovey, *Jacobs, White and Ovey, The European Convention on Human Rights* (Oxford, Oxford University Press 2010) p. 354.

3 *Inter alia* ECtHR 24 June 2010, *Schalk and Kopf* v. *Austria*, no. 30141/04.

4 ECtHR 11 July 2002, *Christine Goodwin* v. *the United Kingdom*, no. 28657/95, para. 100.

5 *Inter alia* ECtHR 11 July 2002, *Christine Goodwin* v. *the United Kingdom*, no. 28657/95, para. 100. See also ch. 8, section 8.2.1.

within marriage.[6] In other words, only married different-sex couples can claim a right to found a family under Article 12.[7] Besides, as is clear from its wording, the exercise of this right is subjected to the national laws of the Contracting Parties to the ECHR. Article 12 furthermore primarily entails a negative obligation; States must refrain from interfering with the having of children within marriage. In exceptional circumstances, an interference with this right may be justified, for example if a person is detained.[8] The primary negative reading of Article 12 is affirmed by the Court's explicit finding that this provision 'or any other Article of the Convention'[9] does not guarantee a right to procreation.[10]

The right to found a family ex. Article 12 is furthermore closely interlinked with the right to respect for family life under Article 8 ECHR. As the Court has explained:

> 'The exercise of the right to marry and found a family gives rise to personal, social and legal consequences as a result of which there is a close affinity between the rights under Articles 8 and 12 of the Convention [...].'[11]

Whilst the concept of 'family' in Article 12 is limited to the circle of parents and children,[12] the notion 'family life' within the meaning of Article 8 ECHR has been given a much broader reading.[13] This notion is not confined to blood relationships or marriage-based relationships and may encompass other *de facto* family ties where

6 See Harris et al., *Law of the European Convention on Human Rights* (Oxford, Oxford University Press 2009) p. 554 and H.L. Janssen, 'Commentaar op art. 12 EVRM, para. C.1.8', ['Commentary to Art. 12 ECHR, para. C.1.8'], in: *Sdu Commentaar EVRM, Deel 1 – Materiele* bepalingen ['Sdu Commentary to the ECHR, Part 1 – Material provisions'] (Den Haag, Sdu Uitgevers 2013).

7 Compare White and Ovey 2010, *supra* n. 2, at p. 354 and Harris et al. 2009, *supra* n. 6, at p. 554.

8 In *Dickson* the Court held that the Convention did not require States to allow for conjugal visits. ECtHR [GC] 4 December 2007, *Dickson* v. *the United Kingdom*, no. 44362/04, para. 81. In 1975 the Commission had held the right to found a family to be absolute. See ECmHR 21 May 1975 (dec.), *X.* v. *the United Kingdom*, no. 6564/74.

9 ECtHR 6 March 2003 (dec.), *Margarita Šijakova and Others* v. *"the former Yugoslav Republic of Macedonia"*, no. 67914/01.

10 *Idem* and ECtHR 15 November 2007 (dec.), *S.H. and others* v. *Austria*, no. 57813/00. In the latter case the ECtHR declared Art. 12 inapplicable to a complaint about an Austrian prohibition of the use of donated gametes in AHR treatment. The Court reiterated that '[...] the right to procreation [was] not covered by Art. 12'. On the basis of this decision Harris et al. concluded that '[...] there is no positive obligation on the State to facilitate the having of children within marriage by legislation to permit artificial insemination or, a fortiori, by providing for it through state funded medical institutions.' Harris et al. 2009, *supra* n. 6, at p. 555. On this question see also section 2.3.1 below. See furthermore M. Eijkholt, 'The right to found a family as a stillborn right to procreate?', 18 *Medical Law Review* (2010) p. 127.

11 ECtHR 8 November 2011, *V.C.* v. *Slowakia*, no. 18968/07, para. 159, referring to ECtHR 5 January 2010, *Frasik* v. *Poland*, no. 22933/02, para. 90. In this case about the forced sterilisation of a woman of Roma origin, the Court found a violation of Art. 8 and therefore considered it not necessary to examine separately the applicant's complaint under Art. 12 of the Convention (para. 160).

12 P. van Dijk et al. (eds.), *Theory and Practice of the European Convention on Human Rights* (Antwerpen, Intersentia 2006) p. 856. The right to found a family does not extend to having grandchildren. ECtHR 6 March 2003 (dec.), *Sijakova and others* v. *"The former Yugoslav Republic of Macedonia"*, no. 67914/01.

13 Compare White and Ovey 2010, *supra* n. 2, at p. 354.

the parties are living together outside of marriage.[14] The Court has, furthermore, held that the relationship of a cohabiting same-sex couple living in a stable *de facto* partnership also falls within the notion of 'family life'.[15] Still, also this right does not grant a right to procreate. The Court has held that

> '[...] the right to respect for family life presupposes the existence of a family and does not safeguard the mere desire to found a family.'[16]

The Court has recognised, however, that the notion 'private life' (Article 8 ECHR) includes a right to respect for the decision to become a parent.[17] The first judgment in which the Court accepted this to be so was *Evans* v. *the UK* (GC, 2007).[18]

The applicant in the *Evans* case claimed that the provisions of the UK Human Fertilisation and Embryology Act 1990 which required her former partner's consent before embryos made with their joint genetic material could be implanted in her uterus, violated her rights under Article 8 (in conjunction with Article 14, the prohibition of discrimination) of the Convention.[19] In the course of fertility treatment Ms. Evans was diagnosed with a pre-cancerous condition of her ovaries and was offered one cycle of *in vitro* fertilisation (IVF) treatment prior to the surgical removal of her ovaries. Before the embryos created could be implanted into Ms. Evans' uterus, the relationship between her and her partner broke down. Subsequently her former partner did not consent to Ms. Evans using the embryos alone nor did he consent to their continued storage. Ms. Evans' claims before the domestic courts, seeking an injunction against her former partner to give his consent, were rejected. After exhaustion of domestic remedies she lodged a complaint with the ECtHR.[20] The Grand Chamber of the ECtHR noted that the applicant did not complain that she was in any way prevented from becoming a mother in a social, legal, or even physical sense, since there was no rule of domestic law or practice to stop her from adopting a

14 *Inter alia* ECtHR 24 June 2010, *Schalk and Kopf* v. *Austria*, no. 30141/04, para. 91 and ECtHR 8 November 2011, *V.C.* v. *Slowakia*, no. 18968/07, para. 142.

15 ECtHR 24 June 2010, *Schalk and Kopf* v. *Austria*, no. 30141/04, para. 94.

16 ECtHR 26 February 2002, *Fretté* v. *France*, no. 36515/97, para. 32, where the Court referred to ECtHR 13 June 1979, *Marckx* v. *Belgium*, no. 6833/74, para. 31 and ECtHR 28 May 1985, *Abdulaziz, Cabales and Balkandali* v. *the United Kingdom*, nos. 9214/80 a.o., para. 62.

17 ECtHR [GC] 4 December 2007, *Dickson* v. *the United Kingdom*, no. 44362/04, para. 66. The Court referred to ECmHR 22 October 1997 (dec.), *E.L.H. and P.B.H.* v. *the United Kingdom*, no. 32568/96; ECtHR 18 September 2001 (dec.), *Kalashnikov* v. *Russia*, no. 47095/99; ECtHR 29 April 2003, *Aliev* v. *Ukraine*, no. 41220/98, paras. 187–189; ECtHR 7 March 2006, *Evans* v. *the United Kingdom*, no. 6339/05, paras. 71–72 and ECtHR 30 October 2012, *P. and S.* v. *Poland*, no. 57375/08, para. 111. The Court has also spoken of 'the right to respect for both the decisions to have and not to have a child'. ECtHR 8 November 2011, *V.C.* v. *Slovakia*, no. 18968/07, para. 138.

18 ECtHR [GC] 10 April 2007, *Evans* v. *the United Kingdom*, no. 6339/05. The Chamber judgment in this case dates from 7 March 2006.

19 Ms. Evans furthermore claimed that the legislation violated the embryos' right to life under Article 2 ECHR, but that claim will not be discussed here.

20 The application in this case was lodged on 11 February 2005. On 7 March 2006 a Chamber delivered its judgment in the case. On 5 June 2006 the applicant requested the referral of the case to the Grand Chamber, which delivered its judgment on 10 April 2007. ECtHR 7 March 2006, *Evans* v. *the United Kingdom*, no. 6339/05 and ECtHR [GC] 10 April 2007, *Evans* v. *the United Kingdom*, no. 6339/05.

child or even giving birth to a child originally created *in vitro* from donated gametes. Her complaint was, more precisely, that the consent provisions of the respective UK law prevented her from using the embryos that she and her former partner had created together, and thus, given her particular circumstances, from ever having a child to whom she was genetically related. The Grand Chamber considered that this more limited issue, concerning the right to respect for the decision to become a parent in the genetic sense, fell within the scope of Article 8 since

> '[...] "private life", which is a broad term, encompassing, *inter alia,* aspects of an individual's physical and social identity including the right to personal autonomy, personal development and to establish and develop relationships with other human beings and the outside world [...], incorporates the right to respect for both the decisions to become and not to become a parent.'[21]

After the recognition of this right in *Evans*, the Court has in some – but not all relevant – later cases based this right on both the notion of private life and of family life.[22] Also, the Court has spoken of 'a right to respect for [the] decision to become a *genetic* [emphasis added] parent'.[23] The Court has furthermore – albeit incidentally – considered this choice to be 'a particularly important facet of an individual's existence or identity'.[24]

In the case of *Ternovsky* v. *Hungary* (2010),[25] concerning the choice of giving birth in one's home, the Court also recognised a right to decide upon circumstances of becoming a parent.[26] States have, further, an obligation under the Convention to protect the reproductive health of women.[27] Lastly, important for the present case study is that the Court has held that the right of a couple to conceive a child includes a right to make use of medically assisted procreation for that purpose.[28] The relevant ruling and its implications are discussed more elaborately in section 2.3 below.

21 ECtHR 7 March 2006, *Evans* v. *the United Kingdom*, no. 6339/05, para. 57 and ECtHR [GC] 10 April 2007, *Evans* v. *the United Kingdom*, no. 6339/05, para. 71.

22 ECtHR [GC] 4 December 2007, *Dickson v. United Kingdom*, no. 44362/04, para. 66 and ECtHR 28 August 2012, *Costa and Pavan* v. *Italy*, no. 54270/10.

23 *Idem.*

24 ECtHR [GC] 4 December 2007, *Dickson* v. *United Kingdom*, no. 44362/04, para. 78. As discussed below (section 2.3), the Court has not expressly repeated this in later case-law.

25 ECtHR 14 December 2010, *Ternovsky* v. *Hungary*, no. 67545/09.

26 The Court held: '"Private life" [...] incorporates the right to respect for both the decisions to become and not to become a parent [...]. The notion of a freedom implies some measure of choice as to its exercise. The notion of personal autonomy is a fundamental principle underlying the interpretation of the guarantees of Article 8 [...]. Therefore the right concerning the decision to become a parent includes the right of choosing the circumstances of becoming a parent. The Court is satisfied that the circumstances of giving birth incontestably form part of one's private life for the purposes of this provision [...]'. The Court found that legislation which arguably dissuades health professionals who might otherwise be willing from providing the requisite assistance in giving birth in one's home constituted an interference with the exercise of the right to respect for private life by prospective mothers. ECtHR 14 December 2010, *Ternovsky* v. *Hungary*, no. 67545/09, para. 22.

27 The Court has ruled so in several cases about forced sterilisation of Roma women, e.g. ECtHR 8 November 2011, *V.C.* v. *Slovakia*, appl. no. 18968/07, para. 145.

28 ECtHR [GC] 3 November 2011, *S.H. a.o.* v. *Austria*, no. 57813/00, para. 78.

2.1.2. The status of the unborn under the ECHR

When it comes to the rights of the unborn child, the ECtHR has never taken a strong position. In *X* v. *the United Kingdom* (1980)[29] the Commission considered that the general usage of the term 'everyone' ('*toute personne*') in the Convention and the context in which it was used in its Article 2 (the right to life) did not include the unborn. The Commission noted a '[...] divergence of thinking on the question of where life begins', and took a clear stance in holding that the unborn did not enjoy an absolute right to life, as '[...] the "life" of the foetus is intimately connected with, and it cannot be regarded in isolation of, the life of the pregnant woman.'

This early decision was later confirmed in the case of *Vo* v. *France* (2004),[30] where the Court observed that '[...] if the unborn [did] have a "right" to "life", it [was] implicitly limited by the mother's rights and interests.'[31] The Court did not rule out the possibility that in certain circumstances safeguards may be extended to the unborn child,[32] but considered it neither desirable, nor even possible, to answer in the abstract the question whether the unborn child is a person for the purposes of Article 2 ECHR.[33] In the absence of any European consensus on the scientific and legal definition of the beginning of life, the issue of when the right to life begins came within the margin of appreciation that States enjoyed in this sphere.

The term 'unborn' usually refers to an embryo *in vivo*, that is, an embryo in the woman's body. In respect of *in vitro* embryos there is even less case law. In *Evans* (2007),[34] a Chamber of the Court referred to both the *Vo* judgment and to national law, when it held that the embryos created in the course of the IVF treatment as commenced by Ms. Evans and her former partner did not enjoy the right to life under Article 2 ECHR.[35] Remarkably, in *Costa and Pavan* v. *Italy* (2012, see also section 2.3.4 below) the Court stressed that 'the concept of "child" [could] not be put in the same category as that of "embryo"',[36] without explaining this finding further.[37]

---

29 ECmHR 13 May 1980 (dec.), *X* v. *The United Kingdom*, no. 8416/79.

30 ECtHR [GC] 8 July 2004, *Vo* v. *France*, no. 53924/00.

31 *Idem*, para. 80.

32 *Idem*, para. 80.

33 *Idem*, para. 85.

34 See section 2.1.1 above and section 2.3.2 below.

35 ECtHR [GC] 10 April 2007, *Evans* v. *the United Kingdom*, no. 6339/05, para. 56, confirming ECtHR 7 March 2006, *Evans* v. *the United Kingdom*, no. 6339/05, para. 46. The subsequent case *Knecht* (2012) did not address the question as to the status of (frozen) embryos. The case concerned a complaint lodged by a woman who lost access to her frozen embryos when they were taken from the clinic storing them and transferred to the Romanian Institute of Forensic Medicine in connection with a criminal investigation. According to the statement of facts in the case the complaint was originally also based on Art. 2 of the Convention, but it was ultimately phrased and examined under Art. 8 ECHR only. The Court did not find a violation of that provision, as the breach of the applicant's rights had yet been expressly acknowledged and redressed at national level. ECtHR 2 October 2012, *Daniela Knecht* v. *Romania*, no. 10048/10.

36 ECtHR 28 August 2012, *Costa and Pavan* v. *Italy*, no. 54270/10, para. 62.

37 Possibly the Grand Chamber of the Court will give more clarification on the matter in a pending case on donation of *in vitro* embryos for scientific research. In *Parrillo* v. *Italy*, a woman who wished to donate embryos created in the course of AHR treatment for scientific research, complained that she was

2.1.3. The rights of the (future) child under the ECHR

The ECHR does not contain a specific Article on the rights of the child, but all its provisions also apply to children. Further, the rights of the child have been given an increasingly more prominent role in the ECtHR's case law. This is first and foremost underlined by the fact that the Court has held that in judicial decisions where the rights under Article 8 ECHR of parents and those of a child are at stake, the rights of the child must be the paramount consideration. If any balancing of interests is necessary, the interests of the child must prevail.[38] The Court has held such in the context of adoption of a child, parental authority and child care,[39] in immigration cases[40] and in cases concerning child abduction.[41] This means, for example, that recognition of paternity cannot take place if such recognition is not in the child's interest.[42] The principle has also increasingly been recognised in cases where children claimed a right to know their genetic origins, although there the Court has still allowed States to balance the rights of the child against those of the parents concerned and the public interest (see section 2.1.4 hereafter).

The Court has further strengthened the protection of the rights of the child by interpreting the notion 'family life' under Article 8 ECHR extensively. In the ground breaking *Marckx* judgment of 1979, the Court for the first time held that *de facto* family life was also worthy of protection under Article 8 ECHR.[43] Consequently, States may not discriminate between children born within marriage and children born outside marriage, as such discrimination based on birth cannot be justified. The Court furthermore recognised that family life includes not only social, moral or cultural relations, but also comprises interests of a material kind such as inheritance rights.[44] Interpreting Article 8 in light of the Convention on the Rights of the Child,[45]

---

banned from doing so because of an Italian law prohibiting such scientific research. The fact that the Chamber relinquished jurisdiction in favour of the Grand Chamber in this case, may be an indication that the Court will set out more general principles in this case. ECtHR 28 May 2013 (dec.), *Parrillo* v. *Italy*, no. 46470/11. On 28 January the Chamber relinquished jurisdiction in favour of the Grand Chamber in this case. The Grand Chamber held a hearing in the case in June 2014. See press release ECHR 173 (2014).

38 ECtHR 5 November 2002, *Yousef* v. *the Netherlands*, no. 33711/96, para. 73.

39 E.g. ECtHR 10 June 2006, *Schwizgebel* v. *Switzerland*, no. 25762/07; ECtHR 21 December 2010, *Anayo* v. *Germany*, no. 20578/07 and ECtHR [GC] 13 July 2000, *Scozzari and Giunta* v. *Italy*, nos. 39221/98 and 41963/98, para. 148.

40 E.g. ECtHR [GC] 18 October 2006, *Üner* v. *the Netherlands*, no. 46410/99, para. 58 and ECtHR 23 June 2008, *Maslov* v. *Bulgaria*, no. 1638/03.

41 E.g. ECtHR [GC] 6 July 2010, *Neulinger and Shuruk* v. *Switzerland*, no. 41615/07, paras. 135–136 and ECtHR [GC] 26 November 2013, *X* v. *Latvia*, no. 27853/09, paras. 93–108.

42 ECtHR 5 November 2002, *Yousef* v. *the Netherlands*, no. 33711/96, para. 73.

43 ECtHR 13 June 1979, *Marckx* v. *Belgium*, no. 6833/74, para. 31.

44 It is not, as such, a requirement of Art. 8 that a child should be entitled to some share in the estates of his parents, as such an entitlement is not indispensable in the pursuit of a normal family life. However, once States grant such rights, they must, again, do so without discriminating on grounds of birth. ECtHR 13 June 1979, *Marckx* v. *Belgium*, no. 6833/74, paras. 52–53.

45 ECtHR 28 June 2007, *Wagner and J.M.W.L.* v. *Luxembourg*, no. 76240/01, para. 120, under reference to ECtHR 26 June 2003, *Maire* v. *Portugal*, no. 48206/99, para. 72.

the Court has, moreover, held that States have a positive obligation to protect children's family ties:

> '[...] where the existence of a family tie with a child has been established, the State must act in a manner calculated to enable that tie to be developed and legal safeguards must be established that render possible, from the moment of birth or as soon as practicable thereafter, the child's integration in his family [...]'.[46]

The child's right to personal identity, which is an aspect of the right to respect for private life under Article 8 ECHR, has proven key in parent-child relations. In the cases of *Mennesson* v. *France* and *Labassee* v. *France* (2014), for example, the Court ruled that establishment of parentage for a child born through surrogacy affected the establishment of the essence of his or her identity. As further explained in section 2.4.2 below, in these cases a refusal to recognise parental links between the intended and genetic father of the children concerned, has been found to violate these children's rights.

2.1.4. The right to know one's genetic origins

As far as the present author is aware, there has not been any case before the ECtHR in which a donor-conceived child claimed that he or she had a right to access to information about his or her genetic parent(s). In a case of the late 1990s, however, which indirectly touched upon the matter, the Court observed that there was no consensus amongst the member States of the Council of Europe on the question of whether the interests of a child conceived in such a way were best served by preserving the anonymity of the donor of the sperm or whether the child should have the right to know the donor's identity.[47]

The Court has furthermore examined several cases where children born out of wedlock or children who were given up for adoption anonymously relied on Article 8 in their claim that they had a right to know whom their natural parent(s) were.[48] The Court's rulings in these cases have proven indicative for the situation of children conceived by means of AHR or through surrogacy.

---

46 ECtHR 22 April 1997, *X, Y and Z* v. *the United Kingdom*, no. 21830/93, para. 43. See also ECtHR 28 June 2007, *Wagner and J.M.W.L.* v. *Luxembourg*, no. 76240/01, para. 119, under reference to ECtHR 27 October 1994, *Kroon and Others* v. *the Netherlands*, no. 18535/91, para. 32.

47 ECtHR 22 April 1997, *X, Y and Z* v. *the United Kingdom*, no. 21830/93, para. 44. See also ECtHR [GC] 3 November 2011, *S.H. a.o.* v. *Austria*, no. 57813/00, para. 83; C. Lind, 'Perceptions of sex in the legal determination of fatherhood – X, Y and Z v UK', 9 *Child & Fam. L. Q.* (1997) p. 401.

48 The Court has also examined cases in which a man wished to institute proceedings to contest his paternity of a child born in wedlock or, alternatively, to have his putative biological paternity recognised. ECtHR 24 November 2005, *Shofman* v. *Russia*, no. 74826/01, para. 30; ECtHR 19 October 1999 (dec.), *Yildirim* v. *Austria*, no. 34308/96; ECtHR 28 November 1984, *Rasmussen* v. *Denmark*, no. 8777/79, para. 33 and ECtHR 18 May 2006, *Różański* v. *Poland*, no. 55339/00, para. 62.

In *Mikulic* (2002),[49] the ECtHR ruled that there is 'a direct link' between the establishment of paternity and a child's private life. The Court recognised that each individual has a vital interest, protected by Article 8 of the Convention, in receiving the information necessary to uncover the truth about an important aspect of one's personal identity.[50] The Court has confirmed the right to know one's origins and the child's vital interest in its personal development in later cases. Birth, and in particular the circumstances in which a child was born, form part of a child's private life guaranteed by Article 8 ECHR.[51] The Court has held that '[...] an individual's interest in discovering his or her parentage does not disappear with age, quite the reverse'.[52] It has furthermore recognised that the process of ascertaining the identity of one's parents may imply mental and psychological suffering.[53]

On the other hand, the Court has also explicitly recognised the rights of the parents in this context. In *Godelli* (2012), a case concerning a woman who had been given up for adoption anonymously after her birth, the Court noted that the expression 'everyone' in Article 8 ECHR applies to both the child and the mother: '[o]n the one hand, the child has a right to know its origins [...] [o]n the other hand, a woman's interest in remaining anonymous in order to protect her health by giving birth in appropriate medical conditions cannot be denied.'[54] The Court has, furthermore, held that the protection of third persons may preclude their being compelled to make themselves available for medical testing of any kind, including DNA testing. Also, there may be a general interest at stake. For example in the cases concerning anonymous adoption, the Court accepted this to be the general interest '[...] to protect the mother's and child's health during pregnancy and birth [...] and to avoid illegal abortions and children being abandoned other than under the proper procedure.'[55]

The Court has never ruled *in abstracto* whose interests should prevail in situations where these rights collide, except for when the parent is already deceased. In the latter situation, the deceased no longer enjoys a right to private life and the right of the child enjoys full protection.[56] In all other situations, the national system must, as a minimum, provide for an independent authority that can decide about access to

49 ECtHR 4 September 2002, *Mikulic* v. *Croatia*, no. 53176/99.

50 *Idem*, paras. 55 and 64.

51 ECtHR [GC] 13 February 2003, *Odièvre* v. *France*, no. 42326/98. As Bonnet has observed, in establishing a right to knowledge of one's identity the Court mobilised a complexity of different but interconnected elements of the right to respect for private life: relations with the outside world, personal development and mental health are all coalescing in the vital interest of obtaining information concerning the identity of one's natural parents. V. Bonnet, 'L'accouchement sous X et la Cour Européenne des Droits de l'Homme (à propos de l'arrêt *Odièvre c. la France* du 13 février 2003)', 58 *Revue trimestrielle des droits de l'homme* (2004) p. 405 at p. 413.

52 ECtHR 25 September 2012, *Godelli* v. *Italy*, no. 33783/09, para. 56.

53 *Idem*.

54 *Idem*, para. 50. Earlier ECtHR [GC] 13 February 2003, *Odièvre* v. *France*, no. 42326/98, para. 44.

55 ECtHR 4 September 2002, *Mikulic* v. *Croatia*, no. 53176/99, para. 64.

56 ECtHR 13 July 2006, *Jäggi* v. *Switzerland*, no. 58757/00, para. 42.

information about one's genetic origins.[57] The Court has – in any case initially – left States a wide margin of appreciation when it comes to the actual balancing of the rights at stake. Exemplary in this regard is the French case *Odièvre* (2003)[58] in which a woman who had been given up for adoption anonymously when she was a child claimed a right to knowledge about their personal history. Ms. Odièvre had been able to obtain non-identifying information about her natural family, but her request for disclosure of details about the identity of her brother was refused as it would entail a breach of confidence. The ECtHR observed that there were two competing interests in the case before it: on the one hand, the right to know one's origins and the child's vital interest in its personal development; and, on the other, a woman's interest in remaining anonymous in order to protect her health by giving birth in appropriate medical conditions.[59] The Court considered that those interests were not easily reconciled, as they concerned two adults, each endowed with free will. Furthermore, the Court noted, the rights of third parties – essentially the adoptive parents, the father and the other members of the natural family – and the general interest to avoid (illegal) abortions and children being abandoned other than under the proper procedure, were at issue. The Court left the respondent state a wide margin of appreciation '[...] in view of the complex and sensitive nature of the issue of access to information about one's origins, an issue that concern[ed] the right to know one's personal history, the choices of the natural parents, the existing family ties and the adoptive parents.'[60] It found that France had sought to strike a balance and to ensure sufficient proportion between the competing interests and concluded that the national authorities had not overstepped their wide margin of appreciation.

The seven dissenters to this judgment were of the opinion that the relevant French law had not provided for any balancing of interests, but merely '[...] accepted that the mother's decision constituted an absolute defence to any requests for information by the applicant, irrespective of the reasons for or legitimacy of that decision.'[61] The dissenters stressed that the right to respect for private life[62] included the right to personal development and to self-fulfilment, and underlined that the issue of access to information about one's origins concerned the essence of a person's identity and therefore constituted an essential feature of private life protected by Article 8 ECHR.[63] The dissenting judges linked personal identity to personal autonomy, more expressly than the majority of the Court had done, when considering that '[...] being given access to information about one's origins and thereby acquiring the ability

57 ECtHR 4 September 2002, *Mikulic* v. *Croatia*, no. 53176/99, para. 64. This also holds for access to information about one's childhood ECtHR [GC] 7 July 1989, *Gaskin* v. *the United Kingdom*, no. 10454/83, para. 49.

58 ECtHR [GC] 13 February 2003, *Odièvre* v. *France*, no. 42326/98.

59 *Idem*, para. 44.

60 *Idem*, para. 49.

61 Joint dissenting opinion of Judges Wildhaber, Sir Nicolas Bratza, Bonello, Loucaides, Cabral Barreto, Tulkens and Pellonpää to ECtHR [GC] 13 February 2003, *Odièvre* v. *France*, no. 42326/98, para. 7.

62 *Idem*. Literally the dissenting opinion here speaks of 'familiy life', however from the context one can distract that this was a mistake.

63 *Idem*, para. 3.

to retrace one's personal history [was] a question of liberty and, therefore, human dignity that lie[d] at the heart of the rights guaranteed by the Convention.'[64]

The Court subsequently accorded more weight to the child's interests in *Kalacheva* v. *Russia* (2009),[65] where a mother of a child born out of wedlock complained that unsuccessful court proceedings against the putative father of the child in order to establish his paternity had violated her Article 8 rights. The Court considered that establishment of paternity of the applicant's daughter was a matter related to her private life. Importantly, the Court held that the best interest of the child implicated an unambiguous answer on whether or not the putative father was indeed the father.[66] It concluded that the domestic authorities' approach in handling the applicant's case had fallen short '[...] of the State's positive obligation to strike a fair balance between competing interests of the parties to the proceedings with due regard to the best interests of the child'. The Court thus took the child's best interests – *inter alia,* the child's right to personal identity and personal autonomy – into account in finding a violation of the Article 8 rights of the mother.

Moreover, in *Godelli* (2012) – a case already briefly discussed (see section 2.1.4 above) – the Court found that the competing interests had not been adequately balanced at national level. In this case the Court accorded a fairly narrow margin of appreciation to the State, basing itself on a reasoning which resembled that of the dissenters to the *Odièvre* judgment. That is, the Court considered that the right to an identity, which includes the right to know one's parentage, was an integral part of the notion of private life and held that in such cases, 'particularly rigorous scrutiny' was called for when balancing the competing interests. The Court subsequently distinguished the case at hand from *Odièvre* on the point that the applicant in *Godelli* did not have access to any information about her mother and birth family, not even non-identifying information.[67] The Court found a violation of Article 8 on the ground that there was no machinery in place enabling the applicant's right to learn about her genetic origins to be balanced against the mother's interests in remaining anonymous. The *Godelli* judgment did not grant children an unqualified right to know all details about their genetic origins, however. After all, if non-identifying information had been made available, possibly no violation may have been found in this case. The fact that the Court has shifted from according a wide margin of appreciation in these matters, to according a narrow one, is proof, however, of the Court's increased attention to, and protection of, the rights of the child.

2.2. Abortion under the ECHR

Abortion is and has always been a delicate issue within the Council of Europe. Views on the circumstances under which an abortion may be permissible, differ widely

64 *Idem.*
65 ECtHR 1 May 2009, *Kalacheva* v. *Russia*, no. 3451/05.
66 *Idem*, para. 36.
67 ECtHR 25 September 2012, *Godelli* v. *Italy*, no. 33783/09, para. 55.

between the High Contracting parties to the ECHR. Obviously, what makes abortion such a delicate matter is the fact that primarily two (conflicting) rights are at stake: those of the mother and arguably those of the unborn child.[68] Further, the (future) father may also claim certain rights. As observed by the Court:

> '[...] the issue has always been determined by weighing up various, and sometimes conflicting, rights or freedoms claimed by a mother or a father in relation to one another or *vis-à-vis* the foetus.'[69]

Because of the lack of consensus on the issue, the Court – as earlier the Commission did – left and still leaves states a wide margin of appreciation in abortion issues. It finds that in such a delicate area the Contracting States must have a certain discretion.[70] The Court considers abortion issues to be up to national courts particularly because '[...] the central issue requires a complex and sensitive balancing of equal rights to life and demands a delicate analysis of country-specific values and morals.'[71] Consequently, the Court has been hesitant to recognise a right to abortion as such. However, already in the early case of *Brüggeman and Scheuten* (1976) the former Commission recognised that Article 8 is applicable to abortion issues:

> '[...] legislation regulating the interruption of pregnancy touches upon the sphere of private life, since whenever a woman is pregnant her private life becomes closely connected with the developing foetus.'[72]

The Court confirmed this finding in later case law. In *R. R.* v. *Poland* (2011)[73] it spoke of '[...] the right to decide on the continuation of pregnancy'[74] and ruled that:

> '[...] the decision of a pregnant woman to continue her pregnancy or not belongs to the sphere of private life and autonomy.'[75]

Incidentally, the Court has spoken of 'the right to decide on the termination of a pregnancy', but at the same time stressed that this right was not absolute.[76] Also, this phrasing has not been repeated in later case law. In fact, in that very same ruling the Court confirmed that Article 8 cannot be interpreted as conferring a right to abortion.[77] In other cases the ECtHR considered it not to be its task to examine

---

68 As yet discussed (see section 2.1.2 above), the Court has considered it neither desirable, nor even possible to answer in the abstract the question whether the unborn child is a person for the purposes of Art. 2 of the Convention (the right to life). ECtHR [GC] 8 July 2004, *Vo* v. *France*, no. 53924/00, para. 85.

69 ECtHR 26 May 2011, *R. R.* v. *Poland*, no. 27617/04, para. 181, referring to ECtHR [GC] 8 July 2004, *Vo* v. *France*, no. 53924/00, para. 82.

70 E.g. ECmHR 19 May 1992 (dec.), *Hercz* v. *Norway*, no. 17004/90.

71 ECtHR 27 June 2006 (dec.), *D.* v. *Ireland*, no. 26499/02, para. 90.

72 ECmHR 19 May 1976 (dec.), *Brüggeman and Scheuten* v. *Germany*, no. 6959/75.

73 ECtHR 26 May 2011, *R. R.* v. *Poland*, no. 27617/04.

74 *Idem*, para. 188.

75 ECtHR 26 May 2011, *R. R.* v. *Poland*, no. 27617/04, para. 181.

76 ECtHR 30 October 2012, *P. and S.* v. *Poland*, no. 57375/08.

77 *Idem*. See earlier ECtHR [GC] 16 December 2010, *A, B and C* v. *Ireland*, no. 25579/05, para. 214.

whether the Convention guarantees a right to have an abortion.[78] The Court thus seems very reluctant to give a principled ruling on the matter.

The following subsections discuss the ECtHR's case law on abortion in chronological order. Not surprisingly, a considerable number of cases originate from Ireland. The fact that Ireland is one of the national jurisdictions included in this research, justifies a somewhat more extensive discussion of the facts of these cases. Also, exactly because of Ireland's very restrictive abortion regime, many Irish women have gone, and still go, abroad for an abortion.[79] The ECtHR has accordingly heard various cases from Ireland containing cross-border elements. For example, the first Irish case relating to abortion before the Strasbourg Court, *Open Door* v. *Ireland* (1992)[80] concerned not so much the question of a right to abortion in itself, but the issue of the provision of information about foreign abortion services. This case is, like particular cross-border aspects of the other relevant abortion cases, (further) discussed in section 2.4.1 below. The second Irish abortion case before the ECtHR, *D.* v. *Ireland* (2006),[81] could have resulted in a more substantial ruling of the Court on the scope of Article 8 in abortion matters, had the case not been declared inadmissible on grounds of non-exhaustion of domestic remedies.

2.2.1. The case of *D.* v. *Ireland* (2006)

Ms. D. complained before the ECtHR about the need to travel abroad to have an abortion in the case of a lethal foetal abnormality and about the restrictions for which the 1995 Regulation of Information (Services outside the State for Termination of Pregnancies) Act provided.[82] She thereby invoked Articles 3, 8 and 10 of the Convention. Ms. D. submitted that she was obliged to research abortion options in the United Kingdom and to travel abroad to be treated by unknown medical personnel in an unknown hospital, without the involvement of her treating doctor. She pointed out that certain follow-up matters were not available in Ireland following an abortion abroad and, with two children in Ireland, she could not remain in the UK for counselling there. She held that the State placed an unduly harsh burden on the few women in her situation, by denying them an abortion in Ireland, and claimed that Irish law was 'arbitrary and draconian'.[83]

In its decision of 27 June 2006, the ECtHR declared her application inadmissible for non-compliance with the requirement to exhaust domestic remedies as regards the availability of abortion in Ireland in the case of fatal foetal abnormality.[84] In the absence of a domestic decision, the ECtHR held it impossible to establish that

---

78 E.g. ECtHR 20 March 2007, *Tysiąc* v. *Poland*, no. 5410/03, para. 103.

79 See also ch. 5, section 5.4.

80 ECtHR 29 October 1992, *Open Door and Dublin Well Woman* v. *Ireland*, nos. 14234/88 and 14235/88. See also ch. 5, section 5.2.

81 ECtHR 27 June 2006 (dec.), *D.* v. *Ireland*, no. 26499/02.

82 See ch. 5, section 5.2.3.

83 ECtHR 27 June 2006 (dec.), *D.* v. *Ireland*, no. 26499/02, para. 59.

84 *Idem*, paras. 103–104.

Article 40.3.3° clearly excluded an abortion in the applicant's situation in Ireland and that no effective remedies were available to request an exemption.[85] The Court acknowledged that Article 40.3.3° had to be understood as excluding a liberal abortion regime, but considered that the Irish courts were, nonetheless, unlikely to interpret the provision with remorseless logic, particularly when the facts were exceptional. The Court held it possible that an Irish court might, in fact, have allowed for her abortion to be carried out, through a further interpretation of the term 'unborn'. If it had been established that there was no realistic prospect of the foetus being born alive, then there was 'at least a tenable' argument which would be seriously considered by the domestic courts to the effect that the foetus was not an 'unborn' for the purposes of Article 40.3.3° or that, even if it was an 'unborn', its right to life was not actually engaged as it had no prospect of life outside the womb.[86] It has been suggested that by taking this approach the Court basically sought, and found, a way out of this case.[87] For one thing, the Court's suggestion that abortion on grounds of lethal foetal abnormality could potentially form a ground for a legal abortion in Ireland has not materialised (see Chapter 5).

While the *D.* case thus stranded in the admissibility stage, the case of the Polish Ms. Tysiąc was the first case in which the Court can be said to have given a more substantive answer to the question of whether the Convention provides for a right to abortion. The issue of needing to travel abroad for an abortion, as put forward in the *D.* case, was addressed in the subsequent ruling *A, B and C* v. *Ireland* (2010), as discussed thereafter in section 2.2.3.

2.2.2. The case of *Tysiąc* v. *Poland* (2007)

The applicant in *Tysiąc* (2007) suffered, for many years, from severe myopia, a disability of medium severity whereby her eyesight had severely deteriorated. When in February 2000 she discovered that she was pregnant for the third time, she decided to consult several doctors as she was concerned that her pregnancy could have an impact on her health. Various medical experts concluded that there would be a serious risk to her eyesight if she carried the pregnancy to term. However, the head of the gynaecology and obstetrics department of a public hospital in Warsaw, found that there were no medical grounds for performing a therapeutic abortion. Ms. Tysiąc was therefore unable to have her pregnancy terminated and gave birth to her third child in November 2000. Following the delivery, the applicant's eyesight deteriorated considerably as a result of what was diagnosed as a retinal haemorrhage. A panel of doctors concluded that her condition required treatment and daily assistance and declared her to be significantly disabled. Her criminal complaint against the head of the gynaecology and obstetrics department was unsuccessful.

85 *Idem*, para. 69.

86 ECtHR 27 June 2006 (dec.), *D.* v. *Ireland*, no. 26499/02, para. 69.

87 B. Daly, '"Braxton Hick's" or the Birth of a New Era? Tracing the Development of Ireland's Abortion Laws in Respect of European Court of Human Rights Jurisprudence', 18 *European Journal of Health Law* (2011) p. 375 at p. 386.

Before the ECtHR, Ms. Tysiąc claimed, *inter alia*, that she satisfied the Polish statutory conditions for access to abortion on therapeutic grounds. She maintained that the fact that she was not allowed to terminate her pregnancy in spite of the risks to which she was exposed, amounted to a violation of Article 8.[88] She further complained that no procedural and regulatory framework had been put in place to enable a pregnant woman like herself to assert her right to a therapeutic abortion, thus rendering that right ineffective.

The Court reiterated that 'private life' was a broad term, encompassing, *inter alia*, aspects of an individual's physical and social identity, including the right to personal autonomy, personal development and to establish and develop relationships with other human beings and the outside world. Furthermore, the Court referred to previous case law in which it had held that private life included a person's physical and psychological integrity and that the State was under a positive obligation to secure to its citizens their right to effective respect for this integrity. The Court noted expressly that in the case before it 'a particular combination of different aspects of private life' was concerned. It found that, apart from balancing the individual's rights against the general interest in the case of a therapeutic abortion the national regulations on abortion also had to be assessed against the positive obligations of the State to secure the physical integrity of mothers-to-be.[89] The ECtHR further held explicitly that it did not consider it to be its task to examine whether the Convention guaranteed a right to have an abortion.[90] Instead, the Court chose a procedural approach and formulated the central question of this case as:

> '[...] whether, having regard to the particular circumstances of the case and notably the nature of the decisions to be taken, an individual has been involved in the decision-making process, seen as a whole, to a degree sufficient to provide her or him with the requisite protection of their interests.'[91]

Having chosen this approach, the conclusion of the Court was that '[...] once the legislature decides to allow abortion, it must not structure its legal framework in a way which would limit real possibilities to obtain it.'[92] With respect to the specific case at hand, the Court concluded that Polish law, as applied to Ms. Tysiąc's case, did

---

88 Ms. Tysiąc also complained under Arts. 3 (prohibition of inhuman and degrading treatment) and 13 (right to an effective remedy). As regards her complaint under Art. 3, the Court found that the facts did not reveal a breach of that provision and considered that it was more appropriate to examine Ms. Tysiąc's complaints under Art. 8. Relying on Art. 14, Ms. Tysiąc furthermore alleged that she had been discriminated against on the grounds of her sex and her disability. Having regard to its reasons for finding a violation of Art. 8, however, the Court did not consider it necessary to examine the applicant's complaints separately under Art. 14 ECHR.

89 ECtHR 20 March 2007, *Tysiąc* v. *Poland*, no. 5410/03, paras. 107–108.

90 *Idem*, para. 103. In his dissenting opinion to the judgment, Judge Bonello considered: 'In this case the Court was neither concerned with any abstract right to abortion, nor, equally so, with any fundamental human right to abortion lying low somewhere in the penumbral fringes of the Convention.' Dissenting Opinion of Judge Bonello to ECtHR 20 March 2007, *Tysiąc* v. *Poland*, no. 5410/03, para. 1.

91 ECtHR 20 March 2007, *Tysiąc* v. *Poland*, no. 5410/03, para. 113.

92 *Idem*, para. 116.

not contain any effective mechanism capable of determining whether the conditions for obtaining a lawful abortion had been met.[93]

2.2.3. The case of *A, B and C* v. *Ireland* (2010)

A fresh application against Ireland lodged in 2005 challenged the ECtHR's line of case law as regards abortion once again. Three women residing in Ireland claimed that, given their financial situation and/or their state of health, they had to be allowed to have an abortion *within* Ireland, instead of being forced to travel to the United Kingdom to procure one.[94]

The first applicant, referred to as '*A*', was an unmarried and unemployed mother of four children, all of whom had been placed in foster care. She was a former alcoholic struggling with depression and living in poverty. In 2005 she unintentionally became pregnant again. She decided to have an abortion to avoid jeopardising her health and her chances of reuniting her family. She paid for the abortion in a private clinic in the UK by borrowing money from a money lender. She travelled back to Ireland by plane the day after the abortion for her contact visit with her youngest child. On the train returning from Dublin she began to bleed profusely, and an ambulance met the train. At a nearby hospital she underwent a dilation and curettage. The applicant claimed she experienced pain, nausea and bleeding for weeks thereafter but did not seek further medical advice.

The second applicant ('*B*') became pregnant unintentionally. She had taken the 'morning-after pill' and was advised by two different doctors that there was therefore a substantial risk of an ectopic pregnancy, a condition which could not be diagnosed until six to ten weeks of pregnancy. Since she could not care for a child on her own at that time of her life, the applicant decided to have an abortion. Believing that she was not entitled to an abortion in Ireland, the applicant travelled to England for an abortion when she was seven weeks pregnant. By that time it had been confirmed that it was not an ectopic pregnancy. The applicant had had difficulty meeting the costs of the travel and, not having a credit card, had used a friend's credit card to book the flights.

Lastly '*C*', the third applicant, was suffering from a rare form of cancer for which she had been treated with chemotherapy since 2002. Before the treatment she had discussed with her doctor the implications of her illness as regards her desire to have children. She had been advised that it was not possible to predict the effect of pregnancy on her cancer and that, if she did become pregnant, it would be dangerous for the foetus if she were to have chemotherapy during the first trimester. In 2005, while in remission from the cancer, the applicant had become pregnant without being aware of it. In the mean time, she underwent a series of tests for cancer for which

[93] *Idem*, para. 124.

[94] As explained in Ch. 5, under Irish law abortion is prohibited safe in the exceptional circumstance that the life of the mother is endangered by the pregnancy.

pregnancy is a contraindication. When she discovered her pregnancy, she consulted various medical practitioners and searched the Internet, as she was concerned about the impact of the pregnancy on her health and life and about the risks the prior tests for cancer posed to the health foetus. *C* alleged that the information she had received from Irish medical experts was insufficient and unclear. Given the uncertainty about the risks involved, she decided to travel to England for an abortion. As her pregnancy was at an early stage, the applicant wished to have a medical abortion, whereby drugs would be administered to induce a miscarriage. She could not, however, find a clinic which would provide this treatment as she was a non-resident and because of the need for follow-up care. According to *C*, she consequently had to wait a further eight weeks until a surgical abortion was possible. After having returned to Ireland after the abortion, she suffered complications of an incomplete abortion, including prolonged bleeding and infection, allegedly without receiving adequate medical care.

All three applicants complained that the impossibility for them to have an abortion in Ireland placed an excessive burden on them, making their abortion procedures unnecessarily expensive, complicated and traumatic. They asserted that the restriction on abortion stigmatised and humiliated them and entailed the risk of damaging their health in breach of Article 3 of the Convention. Relying on Article 8, the applicants argued that the fact that it was open to women – provided they had sufficient resources – to travel outside Ireland to have an abortion, defeated the aim of the restriction. They also alleged that fact that abortion was available in Ireland only in very limited circumstances was disproportionate and excessive. The third applicant furthermore complained that the restriction on abortion, and the lack of clear legal guidelines regarding the circumstances in which a woman could have an abortion to save her life, infringed upon her right to life under Article 2 ECHR.[95]

In 2009 the Chamber relinquished jurisdiction in this case in favour of the Grand Chamber, which issued its judgment a year later, in December 2010.[96] The Court explicitly determined the scope of the case. In this regard it stressed that it did not consider it its role '[...] to examine submissions which do not concern the factual matrix of the case before it'.[97] Rather, the Court held it to be its task to assess

> '[...] the impugned legal position on abortion in Ireland in so far as it directly affected the applicants, in so far as they belonged to a class of persons who risked being directly affected by it or in so far as they were required to either modify their conduct or risk prosecution [...].'[98]

Before addressing this question on the merits, the Court first had to examine the admissibility of the case.

95 The applicants furthermore invoked Arts. 13 (right to an effective remedy) and 14 (prohibition of discrimination) of the Convention.

96 ECtHR [GC] 16 December 2010, *A, B and C* v. *Ireland*, no. 25579/05.

97 *Idem*, para. 123.

98 *Idem*, para. 123.

2.2.3.1. *Admissibility*

Contrary to the *D* case as discussed above, the applications of *A*, *B* and *C* were not declared inadmissible for non-exhaustion of domestic remedies, even though that point was raised by the respondent government. The government claimed that the applicants could and should have started a constitutional action. In this context, they underlined 'the interpretative potential of Article 40.3.3 of the Constitution'. The government suggested that there was potential that the claim of *C* would have been accepted, as '[...] the domestic courts would be unlikely to interpret Article 40.3.3° with "remorseless logic"', as the ECtHR itself had held in the *D* decision (see above). It was, however, acknowledged that this Article 'on no analysis' permitted abortion in Ireland for social reasons. Particularly the latter acknowledgment was ground for the Court to consider it not demonstrated '[...] that the first and second applicants had an effective domestic remedy available to them as regards their complaint about a lack of abortion in Ireland for reasons of health and/or well-being.'[99] With the respect to the third applicant's complaint, the Court joined the examination of this objection to examination of the merits of her complaint (see section 2.2.3.5 below).[100]

2.2.3.2. *Assessment of the complaints under Articles 2 and 3*

The third applicant was the only one to also rely on Article 2 (the right to life). She maintained that even in a life-threatening situation abortion was not available in Ireland, because there was no legislation implementing Article 40.3.3° of the Irish Constitution and providing clarity as to the circumstances under which an abortion could be legally performed in Ireland. All three applicants furthermore complained that the impact of the restrictions on abortion in Ireland and of travelling abroad for an abortion constituted treatment which breached Article 3 of the Convention. According to the applicants the criminalisation of abortion was '[...] discriminatory (crude stereotyping and prejudice against women), caused an affront to women's dignity and stigmatised women, increasing feelings of anxiety'. Women in their situation only had two options; '[...] overcoming taboos to seek an abortion abroad and aftercare at home or maintaining the pregnancy in their situations'. These options were 'degrading and a deliberate affront to their dignity'.[101] The government, for its part, argued that no issue arose under Article 2 of the Convention and denied the stigma and taboo effect of the criminalisation of abortion.[102]

The Court declared the Article 2 complaint manifestly ill-founded. It held that there was 'no evidence of any relevant risk' to *C*'s life, as there was no legal impediment to her travelling for an abortion abroad, and she had not submitted that possible post-abortion complications concerned a risk to her life.[103] By adopting this reasoning, the Court thus did not give a conclusive answer to the question whether the provision

99 *Idem*, para. 152.
100 *Idem*, para. 155.
101 *Idem*, para. 162.
102 *Idem*, para. 161.
103 *Idem*, para. 158.

of abortion in case of a real threat to the life of the mother is required as a minimum level of protection offered to the pregnant woman under Article 2 of the Convention.

The complaints of the applicants under Article 3 (prohibition of degrading treatment), were likewise rejected. The Court considered it evident that travelling abroad for an abortion was '[...] both psychologically and physically arduous for each of the applicants' and that it was financially burdensome for the first applicant. Still – without further explaining this point – the Court did not consider that these circumstances disclosed a level of severity falling within the scope of Article 3 of the Convention.[104]

2.2.3.3. Assessment of the complaints under Article 8

The applicants accepted that the restrictive Irish abortion legislation pursued the aim of protecting foetal life, but they questioned whether the laws were effective in achieving that aim. They also questioned how the State could maintain the legitimacy of that aim '[...] given the opposite moral viewpoint espoused by human rights bodies worldwide'. In this regard they furthermore argued that '[...] there was evidence of greater support for broader access to legal abortion', within Ireland itself. Also, they asserted that the restrictive nature of the legal regime in Ireland disproportionately harmed women and therefore urged the Court '[...] to express the minimum requirements to protect a woman's health and well-being under the Convention'.

The Irish government, for its part, adduced that the protection accorded under Irish law to the right to life of the unborn was '[...] based on profound moral values deeply embedded in the fabric of society in Ireland and the legal position was defined through equally intense debate' and that this had been a 'long, complex and delicate process'. They, *inter alia*, argued that the Court had to respect 'a diversity of traditions and values' amongst the Contracting States and that the Court was not to scrutinise or measure the moral validity, legitimacy or success of this aim pursued with the Irish abortion laws, namely the protection of morals and the rights and freedoms of others including the protection of pre-natal life. The government denied the existence of a consensus in Europe in favour of greater access to abortion, including on social grounds. In any case, so they warned, it was difficult to determine the scope of fundamental rights based on any such consensus. Also, the protection of ECHR rights was not to be made dependent upon popular will. In conclusion the government claimed that it would be inappropriate for the ECtHR '[...] to attempt to balance the competing interests where striking that balance domestically has been a long, complex and delicate process, to which a broad margin of appreciation applied and in respect of which there was plainly no consensus in member States of the Council of Europe'.[105]

---

104 *Idem*, paras. 163–164.

105 ECtHR [GC] 16 December 2010, *A, B and C* v. *Ireland*, no. 25579/05, para. 191.

The Court started its assessment of the complaints under Article 8 with a repetition of its previous finding that this provision could not be interpreted as conferring a right to abortion.[106] At the same time it found in the case at hand that the prohibition of the termination of the first and second applicant's pregnancies sought for reasons of health and/or well-being amounted to an interference with their right to respect for their private lives:

> 'While Article 8 cannot [...] be interpreted as conferring a right to abortion, the Court finds that the prohibition in Ireland of abortion where sought for reasons of health and/ or well-being about which the first and second applicants complained, and the third applicant's alleged inability to establish her qualification for a lawful abortion in Ireland, come within the scope of their right to respect for their private lives and accordingly Article 8.'[107]

The implications of this important and new ruling were played down, however, as subsequently the Court effectively accepted even the most far-reaching interference with this right. The ECtHR held a complete prohibition on abortions for health and/ or well-being reasons, to constitute no violation of Article 8, but to fall within the State's margin of appreciation.

2.2.3.4. A wide margin of appreciation, no violation

The Court considered that the Irish abortion prohibition was based on '[...] profound moral values concerning the nature of life which were reflected in the stance of the majority of the Irish people against abortion during the 1983 referendum and which had [...] not been demonstrated to have changed significantly since then.'[108] The Irish choice had thus emerged from 'the lengthy, complex and sensitive debate in Ireland'.[109] The Court was not convinced by evidence such as opinion polls, which the applicants had put forward, as proof that the views of the Irish people in respect of abortion had changed. It held that this could not displace the State's opinion to the Court on the exact content of the requirements of morals in Ireland.[110]

The Court ruled that Ireland enjoyed a wide margin '[...] in determining the question whether a fair balance had been struck between the protection of the public interest, notably the protection accorded under Irish law to the right to life of the unborn, and the conflicting rights of the applicants to respect for their private lives under Article 8 of the Convention.'[111] Such a wide margin of appreciation was accorded, because of 'the acute sensitivity of the moral and ethical issues raised by the question of abortion'.[112] Although the Court observed a consensus amongst a substantial majority

106 *Idem*, para. 214.
107 *Idem*, para. 214.
108 *Idem*, para. 226.
109 *Idem*, para. 239.
110 *Idem*, para. 226.
111 *Idem*, para. 233.
112 *Idem*, para. 233.

of the Contracting States of the Council of Europe towards allowing abortion on broader grounds than accorded under Irish law,[113] the Court did not consider this consensus to decisively narrow the broad margin of appreciation of the State:

> 'Of central importance is the finding in the [...] *Vo* case [...] that the question of when the right to life begins came within the States' margin of appreciation because there was no European consensus on the scientific and legal definition of the beginning of life, so that it was impossible to answer the question whether the unborn was a person to be protected for the purposes of Article 2. Since the rights claimed on behalf of the foetus and those of the mother are inextricably interconnected [...], the margin of appreciation accorded to a State's protection of the unborn necessarily translates into a margin of appreciation for that State as to how it balances the conflicting rights of the mother. It follows that, even if it appears from the national laws referred to that most Contracting Parties may in their legislation have resolved those conflicting rights and interests in favour of greater legal access to abortion, this consensus cannot be a decisive factor in the Court's examination of whether the impugned prohibition on abortion in Ireland for health and well-being reasons struck a fair balance between the conflicting rights and interests, notwithstanding an evolutive interpretation of the Convention [...].'[114]

The margin of appreciation was not unlimited, however, the Court clarified. A prohibition of abortion to protect unborn life was '[...] not automatically justified under the Convention on the basis of unqualified deference to the protection of pre-natal life or on the basis that the expectant mother's right to respect for her private life is of a lesser stature.'[115]

The Court attached considerable, if not decisive, weight to the fact that under Irish abortion law women who wished to have an abortion for health and well-being reasons were allowed the option of lawfully travelling to another State to do so.[116] The Court did not underestimate the serious impact of the impugned restriction on the first and second applicant and accepted that the process of travelling abroad for an abortion was 'psychologically and physically arduous for the first and second applicants, additionally so for the first applicant given her impoverished circumstances'.[117] The Court even did not exclude, as the first two applicants had argued, that the impugned prohibition on abortion was to a large extent ineffective in protecting the unborn in the sense that a substantial number of women took the option open to them in law

---

113 *Idem*, para. 235. In particular, the Court noted that the first and second applicants could have obtained an abortion on request (according to certain criteria including gestational limits) in some 30 Contracting States. The first applicant could have obtained an abortion justified on health and well-being grounds in approximately 40 Contracting States and the second applicant could have obtained an abortion justified on well-being grounds in some 35 Contracting States. The Court further noted that only three States had 'more restrictive access to abortion services than in Ireland namely, a prohibition on abortion regardless of the risk to the woman's life' and that certain States had in recent years extended the grounds on which abortion could be obtained.

114 ECtHR [GC] 16 December 2010, *A, B and C* v. *Ireland*, no. 25579/05, para. 237.

115 *Idem*, para. 238.

116 *Idem*, para. 239.

117 *Idem*, para. 239.

of travelling abroad for an abortion not available in Ireland. It held it, however to be '[...] not possible to be more conclusive, given the disputed nature of the relevant statistics provided to the Court [...].'[118] With a view to the wide margin of appreciation accorded to the Irish State, the Court concluded that Article 8 had not been violated in respect of the first and the second applicant:

> '[...] having regard to the right to lawfully travel abroad for an abortion with access to appropriate information and medical care in Ireland, the Court does not consider that the prohibition in Ireland of abortion for health and well-being reasons, based as it is on the profound moral views of the Irish people as to the nature of life [...] and as to the consequent protection to be accorded to the right to life of the unborn, exceeds the margin of appreciation accorded in that respect to the Irish State. In such circumstances, the Court finds that the impugned prohibition in Ireland struck a fair balance between the right of the first and second applicants to respect for their private lives and the rights invoked on behalf of the unborn.'[119]

Six dissenting judges strongly disagreed with the approach of the majority.[120] They argued that the margin should have been significantly reduced on grounds of the existing consensus on the balancing of the right to life of the foetus with the right to health and well-being of the mother. The dissenters considered the fact that the Court for the first time had disregarded the existence of a European consensus on the basis of 'profound moral views' to be a dangerous development:

> 'Even assuming that these profound moral views are still well embedded in the conscience of the majority of Irish people, to consider that this can override the European consensus, which tends in a completely different direction, is a real and dangerous new departure in the Court's case-law.'[121]

The dissenters were also very critical that the majority referred in its reasoning to the right to lawfully travel abroad for an abortion. They argued that the majority based its reasoning on the 'disputable' premise that '[...] the fact that Irish law allows abortion for those who can travel abroad suffices to satisfy the requirements of the Convention concerning applicants' right to respect for their private life'.[122] According to the dissenters, the position taken by the Court on the matter did '[...] not truly address the real issue of unjustified interference in the applicants' private life as a result of the prohibition of abortion in Ireland'.[123]

The Court's approach in respect of the margin of appreciation doctrine was unprecedented. It has been qualified as an '[...] unwelcome new approach that

118 *Idem*, para. 239.
119 *Idem*, para. 241.
120 Joint dissenting opinion of judges Rozakis, Tulkens, Fura, Hirvelia, Malinverni and Poalelungi to ECtHR [GC] 16 December 2010, *A, B and C* v. *Ireland*, no. 25579/05.
121 *Idem*, para. 9.
122 *Idem*, para. 8.
123 *Idem*, para. 8.

threaten[ed] to undermine the evolutive nature of the Convention's obligations'.[124] Others acknowledged that the approach was new and 'from an argumentative perspective at least remarkable', but nevertheless welcomed the Court's reluctance in taking a firm stance in controversial moral issues.[125] In (Irish) legal scholarship critique was also issued on how the ECtHR had established the position of the Irish people. It was held that the Court had too easily accepted that the Irish Protocols to the EU Treaties and the results of the Irish abortion referenda were sufficient to determine the views of the Irish people.[126] More fundamentally, the question was raised whether such an internal consensus could and should indeed trump an existing European consensus.[127]

2.2.3.5. Procedural approach; violation in respect of third applicant

The third applicant – who was suffering from a rare form of cancer – furthermore claimed that there was no legal framework in place '[...] through which the relevant risk to her life and her entitlement to an abortion in Ireland could have been established'. This point was supported by third party interveners *Doctors for Choice, Ireland* and the British Pregnancy Advisory Service, who submitted:

> 'Irish medical professionals were in an unclear position and unable to provide adequate medical services. Doctors advising a patient on the subject faced criminal charges, on the one hand, and an absence of clear legal, ethical or medical guidelines, on the other. The Medical Council Guidelines were of no assistance. They had never heard of any case where life-saving abortions had been performed in Ireland. Irish doctors did not receive any training on abortion techniques and were not therefore equipped to carry out an abortion or to provide adequate post-abortion care.'[128]

---

124 E. Wicks, '*A, B, C v Ireland*: Abortion Law under the European Convention on Human Rights', 11 *HRLR* (2011) p. 556 at p. 562. According to Wicks '[t]he margin of appreciation is controversial enough already without the Court choosing to depart from its previous practice of restricting the margin on the rare occasions when a moral consensus can be identified.' The author also claimed (at p.565) that the explicit recognition of an emerging consensus hinted at 'a more interventionist Court in future abortion cases'.

125 J.H. Gerards, 'Case note to ECtHR [GC] 16 December 2010, *A, B and C* v. *Ireland*, no. 25579/05', 12 *European Human Rights Cases* 2011/40 (in Dutch).

126 For example, McGuinness held: 'The Court seems to rely on [...] Protocol [17] and Protocol 35 of the Lisbon Treaty (which is essentially cut and pasted from Maastricht) as evidence against the argument that the will of the people had changed. This is at best a questionable argument which provides a shaky foundation for an already shaky application of the margin of appreciation.' S. McGuinness, 'Commentary A, B, and C leads to D (for Delegation!)', 19 *Medical Law Review* (2011) p. 476 at p. 486. De Londras and Dzehtsiarou held: 'The Court accepted that the net result in these referenda could be read as communicating accurately the position of the Irish people, i.e. that they were happy with the abortion regime as it stands in Ireland. However, a closer mining of the materials relied upon by the Court tells a somewhat more complex story.' They observed that '[...] perhaps the best course of action for the Court is not to read any meaning into these results at all outside of their role in determining the current legal position.' F. de Londras and K. Dzehtsiarou, 'Grand Chamber of the European Court of Human Rights, A, B & C v Ireland', 62 *International and Comparative Law Quarterly* (2013) p. 250 at pp. 260 and 261.

127 De Londras and Dzehtsiarou 2013, *supra* n. 126, at p. 257.

128 ECtHR [GC] 16 December 2010, *A, B and C* v. *Ireland*, no. 25579/05, para. 207.

The government had maintained that effective and accessible medical and judicial procedures existed whereby a woman could establish her entitlement to a lawful abortion in Ireland. The Court however, had 'a number of concerns' as to the effectiveness of the existing medical consultation procedure as a means of establishing the third applicant's eligibility for a lawful abortion in Ireland.[129] The ground upon which a woman could seek a lawful abortion in Ireland was expressed in broad terms and the Irish professional medical guidelines did not give sufficiently precise guidance for doctors to assess whether the life of the pregnant woman was at risk. Also, there was

> '[...] no framework whereby any difference of opinion between the woman and her doctor or between different doctors consulted, or whereby an understandable hesitancy on the part of a woman or doctor, could be examined and resolved through a decision which would establish as a matter of law whether a particular case presented a qualifying risk to a woman's life such that a lawful abortion might be performed.'[130]

'Against this background of substantial uncertainty', the Court considered it 'evident' that the provisions of the Irish Criminal Code on abortion constituted '[...] a significant chilling factor for both women and doctors in the medical consultation process.'[131]

Furthermore, the ECtHR did not accept that the litigation options relied on by the government constituted effective and accessible procedures which allowed the third applicant to establish her right to a lawful abortion in Ireland. The government had submitted that the third applicant could have initiated a constitutional action in which she could have obtained mandatory orders requiring doctors to terminate her pregnancy. The ECtHR did not consider constitutional courts to be the appropriate forum for such determinations, however, and it was not clear how the courts would enforce a mandatory order requiring doctors to carry out an abortion.

The Court accordingly rejected the government's submission that the third applicant had failed to exhaust domestic remedies. It concluded that Article 8 ECHR had been violated as the Irish authorities had failed to comply with their positive obligation to secure to the applicant's effective respect for her private life '[...] by reason of the absence of any implementing legislative or regulatory regime providing an accessible and effective procedure by which [she] could have established whether she qualified for a lawful abortion in Ireland in accordance with Article 40.3.3° of the Constitution.'[132] Because of this finding, the Court found it not necessary to address the parties' additional submissions concerning the timing, speed, costs and confidentiality of the domestic proceedings.[133]

[129] *Idem*, para. 252.
[130] *Idem*, para. 252.
[131] *Idem*, para. 254.
[132] *Idem*, para. 267.
[133] *Idem*, para. 263.

The Court noted in conclusion that Ireland had failed to implement Article 40.3.3° of the Irish Constitution and that the government had not given convincing explanations for this failure. In respect of the burden of such implementation it noted:

> 'As to the burden which implementation of Article 40.3.3 would impose on the State, the Court accepts that this would be a sensitive and complex task. However, [...] it is not for this Court to indicate the most appropriate means for the State to comply with its positive obligations [...]. Equally, implementation could not be considered to involve significant detriment to the Irish public since it would amount to rendering effective a right already accorded, after referendum, by Article 40.3.3 of the Constitution.'

The – more pragmatic – procedural approach taken by the court in respect of the complaint of the third applicant originated from the *Tysiąc* case.[134] It was further developed by the Court in the subsequent abortion case law, which is discussed hereafter.

2.2.4. Consolidation of the procedural approach in abortion cases

The most prominent abortion case law of the ECtHR since the *A, B and C* judgment originates from complaints against Poland, another Council of Europe Member State with more restrictive abortion laws. *R. R.* v. *Poland* (2011)[135] is an important case in this regard, in which the Court also made important observations in respect of genetic screening (see section 2.3.4 below). The applicant in this case was 18 weeks pregnant when her family doctor estimated in February 2002 that it could not be ruled out that the foetus was affected with some malformation. *R. R.* informed her doctor that she wished to have an abortion if this suspicion proved true. Two further ultrasound scans confirmed that her foetus was probably malformed. *R. R.* was advised to have an amniocentesis, but all doctors she turned to refused to carry this out. When requesting an abortion, she was repeatedly refused. As a result of this hindrance to access to prenatal genetic screening, the statutory time limit for a legal abortion on the grounds of foetal abnormality passed. Subsequently, in July 2002, *R. R.* gave birth to a child suffering from Turner syndrome.

In 2004, *R. R.* lodged a complaint with the ECtHR. Relying on Articles 3, 8 and 13 ECHR, she complained that she was denied access to the prenatal genetic tests to which she was entitled when pregnant due to her doctors' lack of proper counselling, procrastination and confusion. The Court found that her suffering reached the minimum threshold of severity under Article 3, calling it '[...] a matter of great regret that the applicant was so shabbily treated by the doctors dealing with her case.' The Court noted that she was in a situation of great vulnerability, deeply distressed as she was by the information that the foetus could be affected with some malformation. She had to endure weeks of painful uncertainty concerning the health of the foetus

---

134 McGuinness considered the *A,B and C* v. *Ireland* judgment 'a logical and conservative follow-on from the decision in *Tysiac v Poland*'. McGuinness 2011, *supra* n. 126, at p. 483.

135 ECtHR 26 May 2011, *R. R.* v. *Poland*, no. 27617/04.

and she suffered acute anguish through having to think about how she and her family would be able to ensure the child's welfare, happiness and appropriate long-term medical care. Her concerns were not properly acknowledged and addressed by the health professionals dealing with her case and no regard was had to the temporal aspect of her predicament. This suffering could be said to have been aggravated by the fact that the diagnostic services which she had requested early on at all times had been available and that she had been entitled as a matter of domestic law to avail herself of them. In conclusion, the Court found a violation of Article 3, which was the first time it had done so in an abortion case.[136]

In its examination of the complaint under Article 8, the Court once again confirmed that the matter before it fell within the scope of this provision. Like in the case of *A, B and C* v. *Ireland*, the ECtHR observed a consensus amongst a substantial majority of the Contracting States of the Council of Europe towards allowing abortion.[137] And again, the Court chose a procedural approach. Referring to the *A, B and C* case, the Court reiterated:

> 'While a broad margin of appreciation is accorded to the State as regards the circumstances in which an abortion will be permitted in a State, once that decision is taken the legal framework devised for this purpose should be "shaped in a coherent manner which allows the different legitimate interests involved to be taken into account adequately and in accordance with the obligations deriving from the Convention" [...].'[138]

The Court held that the State's positive obligation to secure to their citizens their right to effective respect for their physical and psychological integrity could include an obligation to adopt regulations concerning access to information about an individual's health. It added:

> 'While the State regulations on abortion relate to the traditional balancing of privacy and the public interest, they must – in case of a therapeutic abortion – be also assessed against the positive obligations of the State to secure the physical integrity of mothers-to-be [...].'[139]

The Court underlined that these positive obligations had to be assessed on the basis of the rule of law, which presupposed that domestic law had to provide for legal protection against arbitrary interferences by public authorities with the rights safeguarded by the Convention.[140] The Court furthermore reiterated that the Convention was intended to guarantee rights that were practical and effective.[141] This meant that the relevant decision-making process had to be fair and it had to

136 See also S. Donoghue and C.-M. Smyth, 'Abortion for Foetal Abnormalities in Ireland; The Limited Scope of the Irish Government's Response to the A, B and C Judgment', 20 *European Journal of Health Law* (2013) p. 117 at p. 133.
137 ECtHR 26 May 2011, *R. R.* v. *Poland*, no. 27617/04, para. 186.
138 ECtHR 26 May 2011, *R. R.* v. *Poland*, no. 27617/04, para. 187.
139 *Idem*, para. 188.
140 *Idem*, para. 190.
141 The Court referred to ECtHR 9 October 1979, *Airey* v. *Ireland*, no. 6289/73, para. 24.

afford due respect for the interests safeguarded by it. Having regard to the particular circumstances of the case, and notably the nature of the decisions to be taken, it had to be examined if an individual had been involved in the decision-making process, seen as a whole, to a degree sufficient to provide her or him with the requisite protection of his or her interests.[142] The Court continued:

> 'The Court has already held that in the context of access to abortion a relevant procedure should guarantee to a pregnant woman at least a possibility to be heard in person and to have her views considered. The competent body or person should also issue written grounds for its decision [...].'[143]

Apart from a right to be heard in person, the Court also recognised a right to timely access to information about one's health. In the context of pregnancy, this included information about the foetus' health, as 'during pregnancy the foetus' condition and health constitute an element of the pregnant woman's health'.[144] The Court considered the effective exercise of this right to relevant information on the mother's and foetus' health to be 'directly relevant' and 'often decisive' for the possibility of exercising personal autonomy, also covered by Article 8 of the Convention'.[145]

In the case before it, the Court observed 'a striking discordance' between the theoretical right to a lawful abortion in Poland and the reality of its practical implementation.[146] It found that the relevant Polish law did not contain any effective mechanisms which would have enabled *R. R.* to seek access to a diagnostic service, decisive for the possibility of exercising her right to take an informed decision as to whether to seek an abortion or not.[147] The Court concluded that Article 8 was violated, because the Polish State had not complied with its positive obligations to safeguard the applicant's right to respect for her private life '[...] in the context of controversy over whether she should have had access to, firstly, prenatal genetic tests and subsequently, an abortion, had the applicant chosen this option for her'.[148] This aspect of the case, concerning genetic testing, is further discussed below under 2.3.4.

The *R. R.* judgment by some has been read as containing another indication that a right to abortion on medical grounds could be read into the Convention.[149] While later case law has not shown this to be the case, the principles as established in the *R. R.* case as regards the procedure allowing for a timely decision that must be in place, have been subsequently confirmed in the Strasbourg case law.[150]

---

142 The Court referred to *mutatis mutandis* ECtHR 8 July 1987, *W. v. the United Kingdom*, no. 9749/82, paras. 62 and 64.

143 ECtHR 26 May 2011, *R. R.* v. *Poland*, no. 27617/04, para. 191.

144 *Idem*, para. 197.

145 *Idem*, para. 197.

146 *Idem*, para. 210.

147 *Idem*, para. 208.

148 ECtHR 26 May 2011, *R. R.* v. *Poland*, no. 27617/04, para. 211.

149 E.g. Donoghue and Smyth 2013, *supra* n. 136, at p. 133, referring to para. 159 of the *R. R.* judgment.

150 For instance, in *P. and S.* v. *Poland*, concerning a minor pregnant girl, the Court ruled that in such a situation, the interests and life prospects of the mother of the girl were also involved in the decision

2.2.5. The rights of the father-to-be in abortion cases

There have been a few claims before the ECtHR by fathers-to-be who opposed to an intended abortion by the mother-to-be. They were however not very successful, as the Court found the interference with the father's rights justified in order to protect the rights of the mother-to-be, whose pregnancy was terminated 'in accordance with her wish' and '[...] in order to avert the risk of injury to her physical or mental health'.[151] In *Boso* (2002) the Court held that:

> '[...] any interpretation of a potential father's rights under Article 8 of the Convention when the mother intends to have an abortion should above all take into account her rights, as she is the person primarily concerned by the pregnancy and its continuation or termination.'[152]

The interests of fathers-to-be can thus only be defined by taking account of the mother's rights to physical integrity and personal autonomy.

2.3. Assisted human reproduction and surrogacy under the ECHR

As to date there have been relatively few cases on AHR before the ECtHR, but the fast-moving scientific developments in this field may well lead to a growing number of cases in the future. So far, there have been cases about IVF treatment and the use of donated gametes during such treatment as well as cases concerning prenatal or preimplantation genetic screening. There have not been any cases concerning the commensurability of surrogacy or gender selection brought before the Court, but there have been cases on the question of the recognition of parentage of intended (commissioning) parents who engaged in a surrogacy arrangement in a foreign country. All these cases – that are discussed in more detail in the subsequent sections – were decided on the basis of Article 8 ECHR (the right to respect for private and family life).

---

whether to carry the pregnancy to term or not. This implied that there had to be a procedure in place '[...] for the determination of access to a lawful abortion whereby both parties [could] be heard and their views fully and objectively considered, including, if necessary, the provision of a mechanism for counselling and reconciling conflicting views in favour of the best interest of the minor.' The Court once again stressed that '[...] effective access to reliable information on the conditions for the availability of lawful abortion, and the relevant procedures to be followed, [was] directly relevant for the exercise of personal autonomy' and underlined that the time factor was of critical importance. ECtHR 30 October 2012, *P. and S.* v. *Poland*, no. 57375/08, para.111.

151 E.g. ECmHR 13 May 1980 (dec.), *X.* v. *the United Kingdom*, no. 8416/79 (by some this case is referred to as '*Paton* v. *UK*', see J. McHale, 'Fundamental rights and health care', in: E. Mossialos et al. (eds.), *Health Systems Governance in Europe: The Role of European Union Law and Policy* (Cambridge, Cambridge University Press 2010) p. 282 at p. 289, online available at www.euro.who.int/en/who-we-are/partners/observatory/studies/health-systems-governance-in-europe-the-role-of-eu-law-and-policy, visited June 2014) and ECmHR 19 May 1992 (dec.), *Hercz* v. *Norway*, no. 17004/90.

152 ECtHR 5 September 2002 (dec.), *Boso* v. *Italy*, no. 50490/99.

In the case of *Dickson* (2007) – which concerned the refusal of facilities for artificial insemination to a prisoner and his wife – the Court found that Article 8 was applicable and that the artificial insemination facilities at issue concerned the private and family life of the applicants which notions incorporated the right to respect for their decision to become genetic parents.[153] Subsequently – under reference to this paragraph of the *Dickson* judgment – the Grand Chamber of the Court in *S.H. and Others* v. *Austria* (2011) held for the first time that:

> '[...] the right of a couple to conceive a child and to make use of medically assisted procreation for that purpose is also protected by Article 8, as such a choice is an expression of private and family life. Article 8 of the Convention therefore applies to the present case.'[154]

This finding may give the impression that the Court recognised an enforceable right to conceive a child and to make use of medically assisted procreation to that end, and has thus defined positive obligations for the State to enable such access.[155] This reading has, however, been refuted by the Court itself. The *S.H. and Others* case was about an Austrian prohibition on the use of donated gametes in the course of AHR treatment. The Chamber, ruling first in the case in 2010, had already emphasised that there was 'no obligation on a State to enact legislation of the kind and to allow artificial procreation'.[156] After the case was referred to it, the Grand Chamber acknowledged that the matter before it could be seen as '[...] raising an issue as to whether there exist[ed] a positive obligation on the State to permit certain forms of artificial procreation using either sperm or ova from a third party.' It however chose to approach the case as one involving an interference with the applicants' right to avail themselves of techniques of artificial procreation as a result of the operation of the relevant sections of the Austrian Artificial Procreation Act. The outcome of this assessment is discussed in further detail below (see 2.4.3). For now it suffices to say that the most plausible reading of the above quoted paragraph is that it confirms that there is a right to *respect for the decision* to conceive a child and for the decision to resort to assisted human reproduction techniques to that end. The wording 'such a choice' also affirms that the Court had a somewhat narrow interpretation of this right in mind.[157]

A further and related question is how important the words 'a couple' are in the above quoted paragraph. The question is whether it includes individuals who wish

---

153 ECtHR [GC] 4 December 2007, *Dickson* v. *the United Kingdom*, no. 44362/04, para. 66.

154 ECtHR [GC] 3 November 2011, *S.H. a.o.* v. *Austria*, no. 57813/00, para. 82. Subsequently confirmed in, *inter alia*, ECtHR 2 October 2012, *Daniela Knecht* v. *Romania*, no. 10048/10, para. 54.

155 This wording was used by Brems in her case note to the 2006 Chamber judgment in *Evans*. E. Brems, 'Case note to *Evans* v. *the United Kingdom* (2006)', 7 *European Human Rights Cases* 2006/47 (in Dutch).

156 ECtHR 4 April 2010, *S.H. a.o.* v. *Austria*, no. 57813/00, para. 74.

157 This approach was also taken by the respondent government. In accepting that Art. 8 ECHR was applicable to the case it referred to the judgment of the Austrian Constitutional Court in the case which had held that the decision of spouses or a cohabiting couple to conceive a child and to make use for that end of medically assisted procreation techniques fell within the sphere of protection of Art. 8.

to become a genetic parent and who need help from a third party to that end. From cases like *Evans*, it follows that Article 8 grants *individuals* a right to respect for the decision to become a genetic parent. In *Costa and Pavan* (2012, see section 2.3.4 below), the Court held – under reference to *Dickson* – that it had acknowledged a right to respect for the decision to become genetic parents and that it had concluded in *S.H. and Others* as referred to above that Article 8 applies to heterologous insemination techniques for *in vitro* fertilisation.[158] On the basis of this phrasing it has been suggested that the Court acknowledged in *Costa and Pavan* that individuals also enjoy the right to conceive a child and to make use of medically assisted procreation for that purpose.[159] It is true that the Court referred to the more neutral term 'parents' and not to a 'couple', and to heterologous insemination, which – other than homologous insemination – involves a third party. Still, future case law will have to show if the right to make use of medically assisted procreation is also enjoyed by individuals. Also, it remains to be seen if the term 'couple' in this context will be held to include same-sex couples (see also Chapter 8, section 8.2.4.3).

The following subsections discuss the ECtHR's case law in the field of AHR on a thematic basis, starting with the question of access to such treatment. There are no separate subsections on gender selection, vitrification of egg cells, post-mortem reproduction or public funding for AHR treatment, as there has so far simply not been any case law of the Strasbourg Court on these matters. From this discussion it will become clear that once States introduce possibilities for AHR, they are bound by certain obligations under the Convention. For example, they must create a transparent system of procedural safeguards and they must respect the principle of non-discrimination when offering such services.

2.3.1. Access to AHR treatment

To date there have been few cases brought before the ECtHR concerning a complaint about limited or obstructed access to AHR treatment. The only case decided by the Court where this matter was at stake, concerns *Gas and Dubois* (2012).[160] A same-sex couple in a French civil partnership (PACS), *inter alia*, complained that they did not have access to IVF treatment involving anonymous donor insemination. As further explained in Chapter 8, section 8.2.4.3, the Court rejected this complaint, first of all because the applicants had not challenged the legislation in question before the national courts. The Court further noted that such treatment was available in France only for different-sex couples and '[...] for therapeutic purposes only, with a view in particular to remedying clinically diagnosed infertility or preventing the transmission of a particularly serious disease'. Without explaining this further, the Court concluded that the applicants' situation was not comparable to that of infertile

158 ECtHR 28 August 2012, *Costa and Pavan* v. *Italy*, no. 54270/10, para. 49.

159 A. Hendriks, 'Case-note to ECtHR 2 October 2012, *Daniela Knecht* v. *Romania*, no. 10048/10', 13 *European Human Rights Cases* 2012/228 (in Dutch).

160 EHRM 15 March 2012, *Gas and Dubois* v. *France*, no. 25951/07.

heterosexual couples and held that they were therefore no victim of a difference in treatment.[161]

Given that various Council of Europe Member States – including the three States studied in this research[162] – have set conditions for access to AHR treatment, for instance in respect of civil status or age, it is not unlikely that more ECtHR case law on the question will develop in the future. This may also involve questions as to the positive obligations of the States in this area, for instance in relation to funding of AHR treatment.

2.3.2. Balancing the rights of parties to AHR treatment

The *Evans* case – as discussed in section 2.1.1 above – concerned the question whether IVF treatment could be continued if one of the parties withdrew his or her consent. The crux of the matter was that the Article 8 rights of two private individuals, Ms. Evans and her former partner, were in conflict. Moreover, as the Grand Chamber of the ECtHR underlined in its judgment, each person's interest was entirely irreconcilable with the other's, since if Ms. Evans was permitted to use the embryos, her former partner would be forced to become a father, whereas if his refusal or withdrawal of consent was upheld, Ms. Evans would be denied the opportunity of becoming a genetic parent. In the difficult circumstances of the case, whatever solution the national authorities adopted would result in the interests of one of the parties being wholly frustrated.[163] In addition, so the ECtHR observed, the case did not involve simply a conflict between individuals: the legislation in question also served a number of wider public interests for instance in upholding the principle of the primacy of consent and promoting legal clarity and certainty.[164]

The Grand Chamber acknowledged that the issues raised by the case before it were undoubtedly of a morally and ethically delicate nature and that there was no uniform European approach in the field.[165] It considered it relevant that the relevant domestic law was the culmination of an exceptionally detailed examination of the social, ethical and legal implications of developments in the field of human fertilisation and embryology, and the fruit of much reflection, consultation and debate.[166]

As regards the balance struck between the conflicting Article 8 rights of the parties to the IVF treatment, the Court had great sympathy for Ms. Evans, who clearly desired a genetically-related child above all else. However, it did not consider that her right to respect for the decision to become a parent in the genetic sense was to be accorded greater weight than her former partner's right to respect for his decision not

161 *Idem*, para. 63.
162 See Ch. 4, section 4.3.3, Ch. 5, section 5.3.3 and Ch. , section 6.3.2.
163 ECtHR [GC] 10 April 2007, *Evans* v. *the United Kingdom*, no. 6339/05, para. 73.
164 *Idem*, para. 74.
165 *Idem*, paras. 78–79.
166 *Idem*, para. 86.

to have a genetically-related child with her.[167] Given the lack of European consensus, the fact that the domestic rules had been clear and had been brought to the attention of Ms. Evans and the fact that they had struck a fair balance between the competing interests, the ECtHR concluded that there was no violation of Article 8.[168] The absolute nature of the rules '[...] served to promote legal certainty and to avoid the problems of arbitrariness and inconsistency inherent in weighing, on a case-by-case basis, [...] "entirely incommensurable" interests [...].'[169]

The four dissenters on the contrary did not consider that the domestic legislation had struck a fair balance in the special circumstances of the case.[170] While they agreed with the majority that, in particular where an issue was of a morally and ethically delicate nature, a bright-line rule could best serve the various – often conflicting – interests at stake, in the particular circumstances of the case, however, the bright-line rule had been too absolute in nature.[171] The dissenters argued that the fact that the legislation in place effectively deprived Ms. Evans from ever again being able to decide to become a genetic mother inflicted a disproportionate moral and physical burden that could '[...] hardly be compatible with Article 8 and the very purposes of the Convention protecting human dignity and autonomy.'[172]

2.3.3. Donation of gametes

The question as to whether a prohibition on gamete donation was in violation of the Convention was put before the Court in *S.H. and Others* v. *Austria* (2011), by

167 ECtHR [GC] 10 April 2007, *Evans* v. *the United Kingdom*, no. 6339/05, para. 90. Earlier the Chamber had regarded it not self-evident that in the process of IVF treatment the balance of interests would always tip decisively in favour of the female party. The Chamber had not been persuaded that the situation of the male and female parties to IVF treatment could not be equated. It held that '[...] while there [was] clearly a difference of degree between the involvement of the two parties in the process of IVF treatment, the Court [did] not accept that the Article 8 rights of the male donor would necessarily [have been] less worthy of protection than those of the female [...]'. The Grand Chamber did not examine this specific question in detail, but it also did not refute this finding. ECtHR 7 March 2006, *Evans* v. *the United Kingdom*, no. 6339/05, para. 66. Ben-Naf'tali and Canor acknowledged that Ms. Evans could well have had a fundamental human right to be a mother to a genetically related child, but they did not think that she had a human right to be the genetically related mother of her former partner's child. In their view her desire, or 'human aspiration' to that effect did not rise to the level of a human right. O. Ben-Naf'tali and I. Canor, 'Case note to Evans v. United Kingdom (2007)', *American Journal of International Law* (2008), p. 132. See also R. Thorton, 'European Court of Human Rights: Consent to IVF treatment', in*: International journal of Constitutional Law* 2008, p. 325 and Brems 2006, *supra* n. 155.

168 ECtHR [GC] 10 April 2007, *Evans* v. *the United Kingdom*, no. 6339/05, para. 92.

169 *Idem*, para. 89. The Chamber had noted in this regard that '[...] strong policy considerations underlay the decision of the legislature to favour a clear or "bright line" rule which would serve both to produce legal certainty and to maintain public confidence in the law in a sensitive field.' As paraphrased in ECtHR [GC] 10 April 2007, *Evans* v. *the United Kingdom*, no. 6339/05, para. 60.

170 Joint dissenting opinion by Judges Türmen, Tsatsa-Nikolovska, Spielmann and Ziemele to ECtHR [GC] 10 April 2007, *Evans* v. *the United Kingdom*, no. 6339/05.

171 *Idem*, para. 6.

172 *Idem*, para. 13.

two Austrian married couples who wanted a child but suffered from infertility.[173] Owing to their medical conditions only *in vitro* fertilisation with the use donor gametes would allow the couples to have a child of whom one of them would be the genetic parent. The one couple was in need of sperm of a donor, whereas the other couple wished to use donor ova in the *in vitro* fertilisation process. The applicable Austrian Artificial Procreation Act of 1992, allowed for certain assisted procreation techniques, in particular *in vitro* fertilisation with ova and sperm from the spouses or cohabitating partners themselves (homologous methods) and, in exceptional circumstances, the donation of sperm when introduced into the reproductive organs of a woman. *In vitro* fertilisation techniques with the use of donated sperm or ova from a third party, as requested by the applicants in this case, were, however, prohibited under Austrian law. With this prohibition the Austrian legislature aimed to avoid the forming of unusual personal relationships such as a child having 'more than one biological mother (a genetic one and one carrying the child)'.[174] The prohibition also aimed to avoid the risk of the exploitation of women, as pressure might be put on a woman from an economically disadvantaged background to donate ova, who otherwise would not be in a position to afford an *in vitro* fertilisation in order to have a child of her own. In 1998 the two women lodged an application with the Austrian Constitutional Court for a review of the constitutionality of the prohibition. This Court ruled that the legislature had not overstepped its margin of appreciation when it established the permissibility of homologous methods as a rule and insemination using donor sperm as an exception.

The couples subsequently lodged a complaint with the ECtHR in 2000.[175] They alleged in particular that the provisions of the Austrian Artificial Procreation Act prohibiting the use of ova from donors and sperm from donors for *in vitro* fertilisation, the only medical techniques by which they could successfully conceive children, violated their rights under Article 8 of the Convention read alone and in conjunction with Article 14 (the prohibition of discrimination). The Austrian government claimed in response that States enjoyed a wide margin of appreciation in the area and had to decide for themselves what balance had to be struck between the competing interests 'in the light of the specific social and cultural needs and traditions of their countries.'[176] They pointed out that in Austria unease existed '[...] among large sections of society about the role and possibilities of modern reproductive medicine.'[177] Ovum donation entailed a risk of exploitation and humiliation of women involved. Also, it raised questions of divided motherhood and the child's right to know its genetic origins.[178] Because there was, furthermore, a risk of selective reproduction involved, the matter

173 ECtHR [GC] 3 November 2011, *S.H. a.o.* v. *Austria*, no. 57813/00.

174 In the terminology of this research these concern the genetic mother and the biological mother (the birth mother).

175 Both the Chamber, and later the Grand Chamber rejected the government's preliminary objections that the two husbands had failed to exhaust domestic remedies their personal situation was intrinsically linked to that of their spouses. ECtHR [GC] 3 November 2011, *S.H. a.o.* v. *Austria*, no. 57813/00, para. 47.

176 *Idem*, para. 63.

177 *Idem*, para. 64.

178 *Idem*, para. 66.

raised '[...] fundamental questions regarding the health of children thus conceived and born, touching essentially upon the general ethical and moral values of society.'[179] The Austrian legislature had 'after thorough preparation', balanced the interests at stake and had come to a law that took into account human dignity, the well-being of the child and the right to procreation.[180]

In 2010 the Chamber of the ECtHR, by a majority, found a violation of Article 8 in conjunction with Article 14.[181] It held that the applicants were subject to an unjustified difference in treatment,[182] *vis-à-vis* other couples who, owing to their medical condition, did not need egg cell donation or sperm donation for *in vitro* fertilisation. The Chamber was not persuaded that a complete prohibition was the only or the least intrusive means to prevent the risks associated with egg cell donation.[183] It saw no insurmountable obstacles to bringing family relations which would result from a successful use of the artificial procreation techniques at issue into the general framework of family law and other related fields of law. The Chamber considered that the various arguments advanced by the government in order to justify the prohibition of egg cell donation were of little relevance for the examination of the prohibition on the use of donor sperm. The government had asserted that non-*in vitro* artificial insemination had been in use for some time, that it was easy to handle and that its prohibition would therefore have been hard to monitor. Balancing this argument of 'mere efficiency' against the interests of the applicants, the Chamber found that the difference in treatment at issue was not justified. It therefore concluded, by six votes to one, that there had been a violation of Article 14 in conjunction with Article 8 ECHR.

Not surprisingly, the Austrian government requested the case to be referred to the Grand Chamber. This was accepted, and by judgment of 3 November 2011 the Grand Chamber overturned the Chamber judgment, ruling that the Convention had not been violated. The Grand Chamber assessed the matter on the basis of Article 8 only.[184] It accepted that the issue fell within the scope of this Article, that the measure at issue was provided for by law, and that it pursued the legitimate aims of the protection of

---

179 *Idem*, para. 65.

180 *Idem*, para. 65.

181 ECtHR 4 April 2010, *S.H. a.o.* v. *Austria*, no. 57813/00.

182 *Idem*, para. 63.

183 *Idem*, paras. 77–78. The Court considered the risk that women might be exploited and that the technique might be used for selective reproduction, an argument directed against artificial procreation in general. In this respect the Court observed that under Austrian law remuneration of ova and sperm donation was prohibited. Further, the risks to the health of the mother were not any different from those in the case of ova taken from the woman aspiring to be a mother herself, an *in vitro* fertilisation technique allowed in Austria. In response to the government's argument concerning unusual family relationships, the Court noted that family relationships which do not follow the typical parent-child relationship based on a direct biological link, were nothing new.

184 Initially, the Grand Chamber did not justify this decision, but after having found no violation of Art. 8 ECHR, it considered that that the substance of this complaint had been sufficiently taken into account in examination of the applicants' complaints under Art. 8 of the Convention. There was therefore no cause for a separate examination of the same facts from the standpoint of Art. 14 read in conjunction with Art. 8 of the Convention. ECtHR [GC] 3 November 2011, *S.H. a.o.* v. *Austria*, no. 57813/00, para. 120.

health or morals and the protection of the rights and freedom of others.[185] The Court stressed that it was not its task to review the Austrian legislation or practice in the abstract, but that it had to confine itself, 'without overlooking the general context', to an examination of the issues raised by the case before it.[186]

In respect of the margin of appreciation to be accorded to the State when deciding any case under Article 8 of the Convention, the Grand Chamber reiterated its standing case law concerning the various factors that influenced the width of the margin to be accorded. It first considered that where a particularly important facet of an individual's existence or identity was at stake, the margin allowed to the State would normally be restricted. The Court did not make explicit, however, whether it considered the matter at hand to concern such a particularly important facet of an individual's existence or identity.[187] Still, this was not the only factor influencing the width of the margin, as the Court continued by repeating its standing case law:

> 'Where, however, there is no consensus within the member States of the Council of Europe, either as to the relative importance of the interest at stake or as to the best means of protecting it, particularly where the case raises sensitive moral or ethical issues, the margin will be wider [...]. By reason of their direct and continuous contact with the vital forces of their countries, the State authorities are, in principle, in a better position than the international judge to give an opinion, not only on the "exact content of the requirements of morals" in their country, but also on the necessity of a restriction intended to meet [...]. There will usually be a wide margin of appreciation accorded if the State is required to strike a balance between competing private and public interests or Convention rights [...].'[188]

The Court observed a clear trend in the legislation of the Contracting States towards allowing gamete donation for the purpose of *in vitro* fertilisation, reflecting an emerging European consensus. The Court, however, did not consider this emerging consensus sufficient to narrow the margin of appreciation of the State for the following reasons:

> 'That emerging consensus is not, however, based on settled and long-standing principles established in the law of the member States but rather reflects a stage of development within a particularly dynamic field of law and does not decisively narrow the margin of appreciation of the State. Since the use of IVF treatment gave rise then and continues to

---

185 ECtHR [GC] 3 November 2011, *S.H. a.o.* v. *Austria*, no. 57813/00, para. 90.

186 *Idem*, para. 92.

187 *Idem*, para. 82. In its earlier judgment in ECtHR [GC] 4 December 2007, *Dickson* v. *the United Kingdom*, no. 44362/04, the Court had held that the choice to become a genetic parent indeed concerned such a matter.

188 ECtHR [GC] 3 November 2011, *S.H. a.o.* v. *Austria*, no. 57813/00, para. 94, referring to: ECtHR [GC] 10 April 2007, *Evans* v. *the United Kingdom*, no. 6339/05, para. 77; ECtHR [GC] 22 April 1997, *X, Y and Z* v. *the United Kingdom*, no. 21830/93, para. 44; ECtHR 26 February 2002, *Fretté* v. *France*, para. 41; ECtHR [GC] 11 July 2002, *Christine Goodwin* v. *the United Kingdom*, no. 28957/95, para. 85; ECtHR [GC] 16 December 2010, *A, B and C* v. *Ireland*, no. 25579/05, para. 232 and ECtHR [GC] 4 December 2007, *Dickson* v. *the United Kingdom*, no. 44362/04, para. 78.

> give rise today to sensitive moral and ethical issues against a background of fast-moving medical and scientific developments, and since the questions raised by the case touch on areas where there is not yet clear common ground amongst the member States, the Court considers that the margin of appreciation to be afforded to the respondent State must be a wide one [...]. The State's margin in principle extends both to its decision to intervene in the area and, once having intervened, to the detailed rules it lays down in order to achieve a balance between the competing public and private interests [...]. However, this does not mean that the solutions reached by the legislature are beyond the scrutiny of the Court. It falls to the Court to examine carefully the arguments taken into consideration during the legislative process and leading to the choices that have been made by the legislature and to determine whether a fair balance has been struck between the competing interests of the State and those directly affected by those legislative choices.'[189]

The four dissenting judges were very critical in respect of this approach. They found that instead a narrow margin had to be accorded as the right at stake was crucial to the individual's effective enjoyment of intimate or key rights. They furthermore held that the Court was overextending the margin of appreciation:

> 'The Court [...] takes the unprecedented step of conferring a new dimension on the European consensus and applies a particularly low threshold to it, thus potentially extending the States' margin of appreciation beyond limits. The current climate is probably conducive to such a backward step. The differences in the Court's approach to the determinative value of the European consensus and a somewhat lax approach to the objective indicia used to determine consensus are pushed to their limit here, engendering great legal uncertainty.'[190]

The majority of the Grand Chamber found that 'concerns based on moral considerations or on social acceptability' were to be taken seriously in a sensitive domain like artificial procreation. Given the fact that 'the field of artificial procreation is developing particularly fast both from a scientific point of view and in terms of the development of a legal framework for its medical application',[191] the Court was sympathetic to States acting with particular caution in the field of artificial procreation, also because the consequences of legislative measures could well become apparent only after a considerable length of time.[192] At the same time, it held that moral concerns were not in themselves sufficient reasons for a complete ban on a specific artificial procreation technique; the State had to provide for a legal framework concerning AHR '[...] which allow[ed] the different legitimate interests involved to be adequately taken into account.'[193] Thereby it was not, however, required that legislation governing important aspects of private life provided for the weighing of competing interests in the circumstances of each individual case.

---

189 ECtHR [GC] 3 November 2011, *S.H. a.o.* v. *Austria*, no. 57813/00, paras. 96–97.

190 Joint dissenting opinion of Judges Tulkens, Hirvelä, Lazarova Trajkovska and Tsotsoria to ECtHR [GC] 3 November 2011, *S.H. a.o.* v. *Austria*, no. 57813/00, para. 8.

191 *Idem*, para. 103.

192 *Idem*, para. 103.

193 *Idem*, para. 100.

Where such important aspects were at stake, the legislature could adopt rules of an absolute nature which served to produce legal certainty (see also section 2.3.2 on the weighing of interests in reproduction matters).[194]

The Court examined the situation of the two couples, the first and second applicants and the third and fourth applicants respectively, separately. In respect of the prohibition on egg cell donation, the Court attached weight to the fact that the Austrian legislature had not completely ruled out artificial procreation, since it allowed the use of homologous techniques. It also noted that the Austrian Artificial Procreation Act provided for specific safeguards and precautions, which intended to prevent potential risks of eugenic selection and their abuse and to prevent the risk of exploitation of women in vulnerable situations as ovum donors.[195] According to the Court, the Austrian legislature could theoretically have adopted a legal framework satisfactorily regulating the problems arising from ovum donation, such as the creation of relationships in which the social circumstances deviated from the biological ones. At the same time, however, the Court was mindful of '[...] the fact that the splitting of motherhood between a genetic mother and the one carrying the child differs significantly from adoptive parent-child relations and has added a new aspect to this issue.'[196] The Court emphasised that the central question in terms of Article 8 of the Convention was not '[...] whether a different solution might have been adopted by the legislature that would arguably have struck a fairer balance, but whether, in striking the balance at the point at which it did, the Austrian legislature exceeded the margin of appreciation afforded to it under that Article.'[197] By a majority of 13 out of 17 judges, the Grand Chamber concluded that it had not. Thereby it attached some importance to the fact that there was no sufficiently established European consensus in respect of the use of donated egg cells in AHR treatment.

The Court assessed the Austrian prohibition on sperm donation against the background of the wider context of the legislative framework of which it formed a part.[198] The Court took into account that the prohibition of the donation of gametes was a controversial issue in Austrian society, '[...] raising complex questions of a social and ethical nature on which there was not yet a consensus in the society and which had to take into account human dignity, the well-being of children thus conceived and the prevention of negative repercussions or potential misuse.'[199] According to the Court, the Austrian legislature had adopted a careful and cautious approach in seeking to reconcile social realities with its approach of principle in this field. The Court observed in this respect:

194 *Idem*, para. 110.

195 *Idem*, para. 105. The Court noted that the use of artificial procreation techniques was reserved to specialised medical doctors who had particular knowledge and experience in this field and were themselves bound by the ethical rules of their profession. Also the remuneration of ovum and sperm donation was statutorily prohibited.

196 *Idem*, para. 105.

197 *Idem*, para. 106.

198 *Idem*, para. 112.

199 *Idem*, para. 113.

> '[...] that there [was] no prohibition under Austrian law on going abroad to seek treatment of infertility that uses artificial procreation techniques not allowed in Austria and that in the event of a successful treatment the Civil Code contain[ed] clear rules on paternity and maternity that respect the wishes of the parents (see, *mutatis mutandis*, *A. B. and C. v. Ireland*, cited above, § 239).'[200]

The four dissenting judges considered this argument 'particularly problematical'. They held:

> 'In our view, the argument that couples can go abroad (without taking into account the potential practical difficulties or the costs that may be involved) does not address the real question, which is that of interference with the applicants' private life as a result of the absolute prohibition in Austria; it totally fails to satisfy the requirements of the Convention regarding the applicants' right to compliance with Article 8. Furthermore, by endorsing the Government's reasoning according to which, in the event that treatment abroad is successful, the paternity and maternity of the child will be governed by the Civil Code in accordance with the parents' wishes, the Grand Chamber considerably weakens the strength of the arguments based on "the unease existing among large sections of society as to the role and possibilities of modern reproductive medicine", particularly concerning the creation of atypical family relations [...]. Lastly, if the concern for the child's best interests – allegedly endangered by recourse to prohibited means of reproduction – disappear as a result of crossing the border, the same is true of the concerns relating to the mother's health referred to several times by the respondent Government to justify the prohibition.'[201]

These judges were, furthermore, critical of the Court's dealing with the time-aspect in the case. They held that the majority should have taken account of developments since 1999, when the Austrian Constitutional Court had dismissed the application lodged by the applicants. They found this approach '[...] all the more problematical in that the main thrust of the Grand Chamber's reasoning [was] based on the European consensus regarding gamete donation [...] [had] evolved considerably.[202]

The Grand Chamber concluded its ruling with noting that this area – which was subject to a particularly dynamic development in science and law – was to be kept under review by the Contracting States.[203] Thereby the Court referred to its own case law in the field of legal recognition of transsexuality in which the Court had repeatedly issued similar warnings, before changing its position, on the basis of evolved European consensus.[204]

---

200 *Idem*, para. 114.

201 Joint Dissenting Opinion of Judges Tulkens, Hirvelä, Lazarova Trajkovska and Tsotsoria to ECtHR [GC] 3 November 2011, *S.H. a.o.* v. *Austria*, no. 57813/00, para. 13.

202 *Idem*, paras. 4–6.

203 ECtHR [GC] 3 November 2011, *S.H. a.o.* v. *Austria*, no. 57813/00, para. 118.

204 ECtHR [GC] 17 October 1986, *Rees* v. *the United Kingdom*, no. 9532/81, para. 47 and ECtHR [GC] 11 July 2002, *Christine Goodwin* v. *the United Kingdom*, no. 28957/95, para. 74.

The *S.H and Others* case thus set some general principles in respect of AHR, the wide margin of appreciation granted to States in such matters being the most prominent. On the matter of donation of gametes in particular, there have been no further cases decided by the Court since *S.H. and Others.*[205]

2.3.4. Preimplantation genetic diagnosis

The ECtHR has firstly ruled upon cases concerning prenatal screening. The first case in which it did so, albeit indirectly, concerned a situation where compensation was claimed for the birth of children with severe disabilities which had not been detected during pregnancy on account of negligence in establishing a prenatal diagnosis. The applicants in the French cases of *Draon* and *Maurice* (2005)[206] were parents who had brought proceedings against hospitals because of such negligence, but while these proceedings were pending, a new law on medical liability was introduced in France. This new law no longer provided for a possibility to claim compensation from the hospital or doctor responsible for life-long 'special burdens' resulting from the child's disability. Consequently the applicants were not awarded compensation for such special burdens. The ECtHR found that the law in question violated their right to protection of property (Article 1 of Protocol No. 1 ECHR). The Court did not find it necessary to examine, '[...] whether the measures taken by the respondent State in relation to disabled persons [had] anything to do with the applicants' right to lead a normal family life'.[207] The Court thus left undecided whether Article 8 was applicable to the case, but nonetheless considered that – even supposing it was applicable – the situation complained of by the applicants did not constitute a breach of that provision.[208] The Court noticed that the new rules were '[...] the result of comprehensive debate in Parliament, in the course of which account [had been] taken of legal, ethical and social considerations', and concerns relating to the proper organisation of the health service and the need for fair treatment for all disabled persons.[209] They at least pursued the legitimate aim of the protection of health or morals.[210] The Court left the State a wide margin of appreciation in 'this difficult social sphere'[211] and concluded that by deciding to reorganise the system of compensation for disability in France, the French legislature had not overstepped its margin of appreciation.[212]

Another important case on the issue of prenatal screening concerned *R. R.* v. *Poland* (2011),[213] as discussed in section 2.2.4 above. In that case, the Court found a violation

205 See, however, the pending case *Parrillo* v. *Italy*, no. 46470/11.
206 ECtHR 16 October 2005, *Draon* v. *France*, no. 1513/03 and ECtHR 16 October 2005, *Maurice* v. *France*, no. 11810/03.
207 ECtHR 16 October 2005, *Maurice* v. *France*, no. 11810/03, para. 119.
208 *Idem*, para. 120.
209 *Idem*, para. 121.
210 *Idem*, para. 121.
211 *Idem*, para. 123.
212 *Idem*, para. 124.
213 ECtHR 26 May 2011, *R. R.* v. *Poland*, no. 27617/04.

of Article 3 ECHR, but also concluded that Article 8 ECHR had been violated, because the relevant Polish law did not contain any effective mechanisms which would have enabled *R. R.* to seek access to a diagnostic service, decisive for the possibility of exercising her right to take an informed decision as to whether to seek an abortion or not.[214] It was also in this case that the Court explicitly recognised a right to timely access to information about the foetus' health (see section 2.2.4 above).[215]

In *Costa and Pavan* (2012)[216] the Court assessed whether a legal prohibition on preimplantation genetic diagnosis (PGD) was in violation of the Convention. The applicants in this case were a couple who had found in 2006, when their daughter was born, that they were healthy carriers of cystic fibrosis. In 2010 the woman had fallen pregnant again and a prenatal test had shown that the unborn child had also been affected by the disease. They had decided to have the pregnancy terminated on medical grounds. The couple subsequently wished to have access to AHR treatment including PGD but had been denied such access as there was a blanket ban on the use of PGD in place in Italy. That same year they lodged a complaint with the ECtHR, who decided to give priority to the case.

The Court was not convinced by the government's argument that the case did not come within the scope of the Convention because the applicants in fact claimed 'a right to have a healthy child'. The Court held that Article 8 ECHR was applicable to the case before it as '[...] the applicants' desire to conceive a child unaffected by the genetic disease of which they are healthy carriers and to use [AHR treatment] and PGD to this end [...] [was] a form of expression of their private and family life.'[217] There had been an interference with these Article 8 rights, because the applicants had had no access to AHR under Italian law, in particular to PGD, as the relevant law had imposed a blanket ban on access to this technique. The Court accepted that this interference was in accordance with the law and that it could be regarded as pursuing the legitimate aims of protecting morals and the rights and freedoms of others. The interference was, however, disproportionate.

The government's arguments that the interference was justified because of '[...] concern to protect the health of "the child" and the woman, the dignity and freedom of conscience of the medical professions and the interest in precluding a risk of eugenic selection'[218] were not persuasive to the Court. It considered the Italian legislation incoherent and inconsistent:

> 'While stressing that the concept of "child" cannot be put in the same category as that of "embryo", [the Court] fails to see how the protection of the interests referred to by the

214 *Idem*, para. 208. A violation of the procedural limb of Art. 8 ECHR in a case concerning prenatal screening was also found in ECtHR 24 June 2014, *A.K.* v. *Latvia*, no. 33011/08.

215 ECtHR 26 May 2011, *R. R.* v. *Poland*, no. 27617/04, para. 197.

216 ECtHR 28 August 2012, *Costa and Pavan* v. *Italy*, no. 54270/10.

217 *Idem*, para. 50.

218 *Idem*, para. 54.

> Government can be reconciled with the possibility available to the applicants of having an abortion on medical grounds if the fœtus turns out to be affected by the disease, having regard in particular to the consequences of this both for the fœtus, which is clearly far further developed than an embryo, and for the parents, in particular the woman […]. […] Furthermore, the Government have failed to explain how the risk of eugenic selection and affecting the dignity and freedom of conscience of the medical professions would be averted in the event of an abortion being carried out on medical grounds. […] The Court cannot but note that the Italian legislation lacks consistency in this area. On the one hand it bans implantation limited to those embryos unaffected by the disease of which the applicants are healthy carriers, while on the other hand it allows the applicants to abort a fœtus affected by the disease […].'

As a result of this incoherent and inconsistent legislation, so the Court continued, the couple had been left with only one choice, which, moreover, brought anxiety and suffering, namely to start a pregnancy by natural means and terminate it if prenatal tests showed the foetus to have the disease, a situation which involved anxiety for the woman particularly. The applicants had already terminated one earlier pregnancy for that reason.

The Court distinguished the case from *S.H. and Others* v. *Austria* (2011), in which it, as discussed above, had held a ban on gamete donation not to violate the Convention. The case before it namely concerned homologous insemination instead of heterologous insemination. Also, the Italian ban on PGD had to be assessed in the light of the Italian abortion legislation.[219] The Court subsequently noted that while PGD raised sensitive moral and ethical questions, the national 'solutions' were not beyond the scrutiny of the Court.[220] The Court did not explicitly address the government's argument that there was no consensus on the matter, but noted and stressed that this concerned a specific case, which affected apart from Italy only two more High Contracting Parties. Unanimously the Court concluded that the interference with the applicants' right to respect for their private and family life had been disproportionate.[221]

2.3.5. Surrogacy

To date there have been no cases before the ECtHR where the Court was asked to rule on the compatibility of surrogacy with the Convention. The Court has, however, examined – and will in future cases examine – complaints about the non-recognition of parental links that were established abroad in cross-border surrogacy cases. Because of their cross-border aspects, these judgments are discussed below in section 2.4.2. The Court noted in these judgments that surrogacy concerns a delicate ethical issue in respect of which no consensus exists in Europe. The Court also

219 *Idem*, para. 62.
220 *Idem*, para. 61.
221 ECtHR 28 August 2012, *Costa and Pavan* v. *Italy*, no. 54270/10, paras. 63–64. The judgment became final in February 2013 when a request for referral to the Grand Chamber was dismissed.

importantly held that establishment of parentage for a child born through surrogacy affects the establishment of the essence of his or her identity, as protected by the right to respect for private life.

2.3.6. Establishment of parental links after AHR treatment

The Court's case law on the right to respect for family life under Article 8 ECHR is elaborate. There have been, however, only few cases where this right was relied upon to claim legal recognition of family ties with a child that was conceived in the course of AHR treatment with the use of donor gametes and/or a surrogate mother.

In a case of the early 1990s the Commission held that the situation in which a person donates sperm only to enable a woman to become pregnant through artificial insemination does not of itself give the donor a right to respect for family life with the child.[222] In this case a refusal to grant him visitation rights to the child was held not to be in violation of Article 8 ECHR, as the Commission was of the opinion that the applicant's contact with the child, both in itself and together with his donorship, formed an insufficient basis for the conclusion that as a result thereof such close personal ties had developed between them that their relationship fell within the scope of 'family life' as referred to in Article 8.

Mere genetic parenthood has thus not been held to be sufficient for protection of the right to respect for family life under Article 8 ECHR. This has been confirmed by case law outside the area of gamete donation, for example in situations where a woman who had given her children up for adoption after birth, claimed a right to contact with and information about her genetic children.[223] There have also been various cases before the Court where a man unsuccessfully tried to challenge the paternity of another man's paternity of his (presumed) genetic child.[224] The Court accepted in those cases that a decision to reject a request to legally establish paternity of a (presumed) genetic child interfered with the right to respect for private life under Article 8 ECHR. However, such an interference could be justified so long as there was no close personal relationship between the (presumed) genetic father and the respective child.

Hence, for genetic parents it may not be sufficient to rely on their genetic parenthood in order to establish parental links with their child. The actual existence of family life is what counts under the right to respect for family life. This is not to say that genetic parenthood does not play a role in the Court's case law on reproductive matters. In fact, in the French cross-border surrogacy cases to which already reference was made in section 2.1.3 above, genetic parenthood can be held to have played a decisive role. As discussed in more detail below in section 2.4.2, the Court ruled that where the legal parent-child relationship is concerned, an essential aspect of the

222 ECmHR 8 February 1993 (dec.), *J.R.M.* v. *the Netherlands*, no. 16944/90.
223 ECtHR 5 June 2014, *I. S.* v. *Germany*, no. 31021/08.
224 ECtHR 22 March 2012, *Ahrens* v. *Germany*, no. 45071/09.

identity of individuals is at stake and stressed the importance of biological parentage as a component of identity, as protected under the right to respect for private life (Article 8 ECHR).[225]

There have, further, been cases before the Strasbourg Court where a person claimed the recognition of parenthood of a child conceived with the use of donor gametes, and to whom he or she was thus not genetically related. The first time the Court was confronted with such a question was in 1997 in the *X, Y and Z* case. A female-to-male post-operative transsexual was not permitted under UK law to marry a woman and could therefore not be regarded as the father of the child born with his female partner. The child had been conceived by artificial insemination, using sperm from an anonymous donor. The Grand Chamber of the Court noted that until then it had been called upon to consider only family ties existing between genetic parents and their offspring, while the case at hand 'raised different questions'.[226] The Court continued:

> '[...] it has not been established before the Court that there exists any generally shared approach amongst the High Contracting Parties with regard to the manner in which the social relationship between a child conceived by AID ['artificial insemination by donor'] and the person who performs the role of father should be reflected in law. Indeed, according to the information available to the Court, although the technology of medically assisted procreation has been available in Europe for several decades, many of the issues to which it gives rise, particularly with regard to the question of filiation, remain the subject of debate. For example, there is no consensus amongst the member States of the Council of Europe on the question whether the interests of a child conceived in such a way are best served by preserving the anonymity of the donor of the sperm or whether the child should have the right to know the donor's identity. [...] In conclusion [...], the Court is of the opinion that Article 8 cannot, in this context, be taken to imply an obligation for the respondent State formally to recognise as the father of a child a person who is not the biological father.'[227]

The fact that this case concerned a transsexual, while there was at the time no European consensus on transsexuality, has unmistakably been an important, if not crucial, factor in the Court's conclusion in this case. One must therefore be careful not to disentangle this ruling from the particular factual circumstances of the case at hand. Still, the finding that Article 8 would not imply an obligation for States to formally recognise as the father of a child a person who was not the biological father is interesting. The Court adopted a similar line of reasoning in later case involving a same-sex couple who had a child after resorting to AHR treatment. Here a clear overlap with Case Study II is visible. As further explained in Chapter 8, section 8.2.4.2, in *Boeckel and Gessner-Boeckel* (2013),[228] the Court declared manifestly ill-founded the complaint of two women in a civil partnership, who wished to be both registered as parents in the birth certificate of the child to whom one of them had given birth.

225 ECtHR 26 June 2014, *Mennesson* v. *France*, no. 65192/11, para. 100.

226 ECtHR [GC] 22 April 1997, *X, Y and Z* v. *the United Kingdom*, no. 21830/93, para. 43.

227 *Idem*, paras. 44 and 52.

228 ECtHR 7 May 2013 (dec.), *Boeckel and Gessner-Boeckel* v. *Germany*, no. 8017/11.

The Court held that it could be ruled out '[...] on biological grounds that the child descended from the other partner.' It accepted that, under these circumstances, there was '[...] no factual foundation for a legal presumption that the child descended from the [...] partner [of the woman who had given birth to the child]'.[229]

2.4. Cross-border cases and the ECHR

The ECtHR has decided a couple of interesting cross-border cases involving either abortion or surrogacy. While there have been no cases on travel bans as such or on refusals to reimburse the costs of treatment obtained abroad, there have been cases on access to and provision of information about foreign treatment options. Also, the matter of after care, after abortions abroad has been addressed in the case law. Lastly, the Court has decided cases about the recognition of parental links with a child born after surrogacy in a foreign country. These three limbs of case law are discussed in the three following subsections.

2.4.1. Information about foreign treatment options and follow-up treatment

In *Open Door* (1992) an injunction had been granted restraining the Irish counselling agencies *Open Door Counselling* and *Dublin Well Woman Centre* from assisting pregnant women in seeking legal abortion services abroad (see also Chapter 5, section 5.2.2). In its report of March 1991 the European Commission on Human Rights had held that this injunction was not prescribed by law and therefore violated their right to freedom of expression (Article 10 ECHR).[230] While the Commission had thus not decided the nub of the matter before it, the Court instead addressed the proportionality of the injunction.[231]

The Court firstly noted that there was no doubt that the injunction constituted an interference with the applicants' freedom to impart and receive information.[232] The

229 *Idem*, para. 30. At the time this research was concluded (i.e. 31 July 2014) there was another (potentially) relevant case pending (*Francine Bonnaud and Patricia Lecoq* v. *France*, no. 6190/11), where two women who live as a couple and who both had a child following AHR treatment complain about the rejection of the their requests to be granted parental authority each in respect of the other's child. In May 2013 the Court invited the Government to submit observations 'in the light of the judgments in *Gas and Dubois v. France* and *X and Others v. Austria*, and the adoption in France of the law of 17 May 2013 opening marriage to same sex couples.' ECtHR, *Factsheet Sexual Orientation Issues*, edn. April 2015.

230 ECmHR 7 March 1991 (report), *Open Door and Dublin Well Woman* v. *Ireland*, nos. 14234/88 and 14235/88. By decision of 15 May 1990 the ECmHR had already declared the complaint admissible. After the delivery of this report, both the Commission and the Irish government decided to bring the case before the ECtHR.

231 See also D. Cole, '"Going to England": Irish Abortion Law and the European Community', 17 *Hastings Int'l & Comp. L. Rev.* (1993–1994) p. 113 at p. 135.

232 ECtHR 29 October 1992, *Open Door and Dublin Well Woman* v. *Ireland*, nos. 14234/88 and 14235/88, para. 50.

Court furthermore held that the restriction was prescribed by law[233] and pursued the legitimate aim of '[...] the protection of morals of which the protection in Ireland of the right to life of the unborn [was] one aspect'.[234] It acknowledged that since it was not possible to find in the legal and social orders of the Contracting States a uniform European conception of morals, '[...] national authorities enjoy[ed] a wide margin of appreciation in matters of morals, particularly in an area such as [abortion] which touche[d] on matters of belief concerning the nature of human life.'[235] However, the restriction was disproportionate to the aims pursued. The Court was struck by 'the absolute nature of the Supreme Court injunction which imposed a "perpetual" restraint on the provision of information to pregnant women concerning abortion facilities abroad, regardless of age or state of health or their reasons for seeking counselling on the termination of pregnancy'.[236]

In assessing the proportionality of the restriction, the Court took into consideration a number of other factors. First, it assessed that the link between the provision of information and the destruction of unborn life was not as definite as contended;[237] and that information could be obtained from other sources in Ireland.[238] The restriction was further ineffective in protecting the right to life of the unborn since it did not prevent large numbers of Irish women from continuing to obtain abortions in Great Britain.[239] Also, the injunction created a risk to the health of those women seeking abortions at a later stage in their pregnancy due to the lack of proper counselling and had adverse effects on women who were not sufficiently resourceful or did not have the necessary level of education to have access to alternative sources of information.[240] The Court accordingly found a violation of Article 10 ECHR. Having regard to this finding, the Court – like the Commission earlier – considered it unnecessary to examine the case under Articles 8 (right to respect for private life) and 14 (prohibition of discrimination) ECHR.[241]

Later, in *A, B and C* v. *Ireland*, the Court – as discussed above – set access to information about foreign abortion services as an element of the minimum level of protection that States with a restrictive abortion regime had to offer under Article 8. The Court held that Ireland had met that minimum standard because:

> '[...] the Thirteenth and Fourteenth Amendments to the Constitution removed any legal impediment to adult women travelling abroad for an abortion and to obtaining information in Ireland in that respect. Legislative measures were then adopted to ensure the provision of information and counselling about, *inter alia*, the options available including abortion services abroad, and to ensure any necessary medical treatment before, and

233 *Idem*, para. 60.
234 *Idem*, para. 63.
235 *Idem*, para. 68.
236 *Idem*, para. 73.
237 *Idem*, para. 75.
238 *Idem*, para. 76.
239 *Idem*, para. 76.
240 *Idem*, para. 77.
241 *Idem*, para. 83.

> more particularly after, an abortion. The importance of the role of doctors in providing information on all options available, including abortion abroad, and their obligation to provide all appropriate medical care, notably post abortion, is emphasised in CPA work and documents and in professional medical guidelines [...]. The Court has found that the first two applicants did not demonstrate that they lacked relevant information or necessary medical care as regards their abortions [...].'[242]

The ECtHR concluded that *because* Ireland had provided for '[...] the right to travel abroad lawfully for an abortion with access to appropriate information and medical care in Ireland', the prohibition in Ireland of abortion for health and well-being reasons had not exceeded the margin of appreciation accorded in that respect to the Irish State.[243]

A somewhat different, but nonetheless much connected, question was at issue in the case of *Women on Waves* (2009). In 2004 the 'abortion boat' of the Dutch foundation *Women on Waves* set sail to Portugal to campaign in favour of the decriminalisation of abortion (see also Chapter 6, section 6.4.1.3). The ship was, however, blocked from entering Portuguese territorial waters by a Portuguese warship acting on the basis of a ministerial order banning such entry. After being unsuccessful in challenging the ban before the national courts, *Women on Waves* and two Portuguese organisations who had invited the foundation to come to Portugal, filed a complaint with the ECtHR. They based their complaints on a number of Convention provisions, including Article 2 of Protocol No. 4 (freedom of movement). The Court decided to examine the case on the basis of Article 10 (the freedom of expression) only and found a violation of this provision. The Strasbourg Court accepted that the measure pursued the legitimate aims of the prevention of disorder and the protection of health, but also noted that these had affected the very substance of the ideas and information imparted. It further took into account that the case did not involve private land or publicly owned property but the territorial waters of the respondent State, and that it had not been shown that the applicant associations had intended to deliberately breach Portuguese legislation on abortion. The Court reiterated that freedom to express opinions in the course of a peaceful assembly was so important that it could not be restricted in any way, so long as the person concerned did not commit any reprehensible acts. Lastly, the Portuguese authorities could have resorted to other means of preventing disorder and protecting health than taking such a radical measure as dispatching a warship, with a serious deterrent effect. The Court unanimously found a violation of Article 10 ECHR in this case.

2.4.2. Legal recognition of parental links established abroad

The issue of legal recognition of parental links established in another country, has, incidentally, come before the Strasbourg court. Until the *Mennesson* and *Labassee*

242 *Idem*, para. 239.
243 *Idem*, para 241.

judgments (as discussed in greater detail below) were issued, cross-border adoption cases like *Wagner* and *Negrepontis-Giannisis*[244] were the most cited authorities in relation to this question. The applicants in the *Wagner* case were a Luxembourg national and her adoptive child, who has been born in Peru. They had unsuccessfully applied to the Luxembourg Courts to have the adoption decision pronounced in Peru declared enforceable in Luxembourg. The Luxembourg courts had dismissed the application because the Luxembourg Civil Code made no provision for full adoption by a single woman. The ECtHR found a violation of Article 8 ECHR (to right to respect for private and family life) in this case. While the Court accepted that the refusal pursued the legitimate aim of protecting the 'health and morals' and the 'rights and freedoms' of the child,[245] the Court found that the failure of the Luxembourg courts to recognise the family ties created by the judgment of full adoption delivered in Peru, was disproportionate. The Court stressed the importance of carrying out an actual examination of the situation[246] and held:

> 'The Court considers that the decision refusing enforcement fails to take account of the social reality of the situation. Accordingly, since the Luxembourg courts did not formally acknowledge the legal existence of the family ties created by the Peruvian full adoption, those ties do not produce their effects in full in Luxembourg. The applicants encounter obstacles in their daily life and the child is not afforded legal protection making it possible for her to be fully integrated into the adoptive family. Bearing in mind that the best interests of the child are paramount in such a case [...], the Court considers that the Luxembourg courts could not reasonably disregard the legal status validly created abroad and corresponding to a family life within the meaning of Article 8 of the Convention.'[247]

The Court also found a violation of Article 14 (prohibition of discrimination) taken in conjunction with Article 8 ECHR. While it again could not exclude that the aim invoked by the government could be considered legitimate, the unequal treatment of the applicant,[248] was disproportionate. The Court considered:

> 'The consequence of this refusal to order enforcement is that the second applicant suffers on a daily basis a difference in treatment by comparison with a child whose full adoption is recognised in Luxembourg. It is an inescapable finding in this case that the child's ties with her family of origin have been severed but that no full and entire substitute tie exists with her adoptive mother. The second applicant is therefore in a legal vacuum which has not been remedied by the fact that simple adoption has been granted in the meantime [...] It follows in particular that, not having acquired Luxembourg nationality, the second applicant does not have the advantage of, for example, Community preference;

244 ECtHR 28 June 2007, *Wagner and J.M.W.L.* v. *Luxembourg*, no. 76240/01 and ECtHR 3 May 2011, *Negrepontis-Giannisis* v. *Greece*, no. 56759/08.

245 ECtHR 28 June 2007, *Wagner and J.M.W.L.* v. *Luxembourg*, no. 76240/01, para. 126.

246 *Idem*, para. 135.

247 *Idem*, paras. 131–132.

248 The Court considered the applicant to be in a similar situation to that of '[...] any child who ha[d] been the subject in Peru of a full adoption judgment entailing the severance of the ties with his or her family of origin and whose adoptive parent ha[d] sought to have that judgment enforced under Luxembourg law.' *Idem*, para. 151.

> if she wished to serve an occupational apprenticeship she would not obtain a work permit unless it were shown that an equivalent candidate could not be found on the European employment market. Next, and above all, for more than ten years the minor child has had to be regularly given leave to remain in Luxembourg and has had to obtain a visa in order to visit certain countries, in particular Switzerland.'[249]

The mother was held to indirectly suffer, on a daily basis, the obstacles experienced by her child and therefore also to be discriminated against. The Court did not find any ground in the present case to justify such discrimination of the applicants.[250] In any event, the child could not be blamed for circumstances for which she was not responsible.[251]

This line of reasoning was pursued in two recent judgments that come within the scope of this case study. In June 2014, the Court decided two important cases against France on international surrogacy.[252] The applicants in *Mennesson* and *Labassee* were two couples who had engaged in heterologous surrogacy in the United States of America (USA), as well as their children whom were consequently born in California and Minnesota respectively. In both cases the couple had had recourse to *in vitro* fertilisation using a donated ovum and the sperm of Mr. Mennesson and Mr. Labassee respectively. The embryos thus obtained were subsequently implanted into the uterus of a surrogate mother. The surrogate mother for the Mennesson couple gave birth to twins in October 2001, while the surrogate mother for the Labassee couple gave birth to a daughter in November 2001.

In both cases the couples had been legally recognised as the parents of the children by Court order in the relevant US State. In the case of the Mennessons this was done before the birth of the twins and the Californian Court had yet recognised Mrs. Mennesson, the intended non-genetic mother, as legal mother of the child. Subsequently, in both cases a birth certificate had been drafted, stating that the couple (the intended parents) were the parents of the child. Upon return to France, the couples unsuccessfully sought to have these birth certificates entered in the French register of births, marriages and deaths. The French authorities refused such entries, because they suspected that the cases involved surrogacy arrangements, surrogacy being unlawful under French law. In the *Mennesson* case, the public prosecutor instructed that the birth certificates be, nevertheless, entered in the register and subsequently brought proceedings against the couple with a view to having the entries annulled. The Labassee couple instead obtained an '*acte de notoriété*', a document issued by a judge attesting to the existence of a *de facto* parent-child relationship. However, the public prosecutor refused to enter this in the French register, after which the couple appealed the case to the courts.

---

249 *Idem*, paras. 155–156.
250 *Idem*, para. 157.
251 *Idem*, para. 158.
252 ECtHR 26 June 2014, *Mennesson* v. *France*, no. 65192/11 and ECtHR 26 June 2014, *Labassee* v. *France*, no. 65941/11.

Both domestic proceedings ended before the Court of Cassation, which ruled on 6 April 2011 that recording such entries in the register would give effect to a surrogacy agreement that was null and void on public policy grounds under the French Civil Code. This Court ruled that the right to respect for private and family life had not been infringed now that the annulment of the entries had not prevented children from living in France with the intended parents. Also, the legal parenthood of the parents was still recognised under the laws of California and Minnesota respectively. That very same day the couples filed a complaint with the ECtHR. Mr. Mennesson also lodged an application with the Paris District Court for a certificate of French nationality for the twins. In March 2014 he was informed that the request was still being processed.[253]

Before the Strasbourg Court, the applicants in both cases invoked Article 8 ECHR (the right to respect for private and family life) and complained of the fact that, to the detriment of the children's best interests, they were unable to obtain recognition in France of legal parent-child relationships that had been lawfully established abroad as the result of a surrogacy agreement.

In *Mennesson*, the Court found that the refusal of the French authorities to legally recognise the family tie between the applicants constituted an interference with Article 8, of both its private life aspect and its family life aspect. The Court referred in this regard to its approach in *Wagner* and *Negrepontis-Giannisis* (see above). The Court furthermore accepted that this interference had a sufficient legal basis in domestic law, which was foreseeable and accessible.[254] Also, the interference pursued a legitimate aim, but the Court did not accept all aims put forward by the French government. The government had claimed that the refusals to record the American birth certificates in the French register, were based on '[...] ethical and moral principles according to which the human body could not become a commercial instrument and the child be reduced to the object of a contract.'[255] The Court did not accept that the interference pursued the legitimate aim of the prevention of disorder or crime, as the government had not established that where French nationals had recourse to a surrogacy arrangement in a country in which such an agreement was legal this amounted to an offence under French law. The Court understood, however, that the government sought '[...] to deter its nationals from having recourse to methods of assisted reproduction outside the national territory that [were] prohibited on its own territory and aim[ed], in accordance with its perception of the issue, to protect children and [...] surrogate mothers'. Accordingly, the Court accepted that the interference pursued the legitimate aims of the protection of health and the protection of the rights and freedoms of others.[256] The Court did not further elaborate on the first legitimate aim, but basically focused on the latter in its subsequent assessment of the necessity of the measure, in particular on the protection of the child.

253 ECtHR 26 June 2014, *Mennesson* v. *France*, no. 65192/11, para. 28.
254 *Idem*, paras. 57–58.
255 *Idem*, para. 60.
256 *Idem*, paras. 61–62.

The French government had pointed out that to authorise entry in the register of births, marriages and deaths of the details of foreign civil-status documents of children born as the result of a surrogacy agreement performed outside France, would have been '[...] tantamount to tacitly accepting that domestic law had been circumvented and would have jeopardised the consistent application of the provisions outlawing surrogacy.'[257] The Court acknowledged that the community had an interest '[...] in ensuring that its members conform to the choice made democratically within that community',[258] but found that it had to be verified whether the domestic courts had duly taken account of the need to strike a fair balance between this interest and '[...] the interest of the applicants – the children's best interests being paramount – in fully enjoying their rights to respect for their private and family life.'[259]

The Court defined the interests of the child in this case in the context of the right to personal identity. It held in this regard:

> 'Respect for private life requires that everyone should be able to establish details of their identity as individual human beings, which includes the legal parent-child relationship. [...] an essential aspect of the identity of individuals is at stake where the legal parent-child relationship is concerned [...].'[260]

This was also reason for the Court to reduce the margin of appreciation, despite the fact that surrogacy raised sensitive ethical questions and the fact that there was accordingly no consensus in Europe on the lawfulness of surrogacy arrangements or the legal recognition of the relationship between intended parents and children thus conceived abroad.[261]

The Court noted that the children concerned were in a position of legal uncertainty, about their lineage and their nationality, and this uncertainty was liable to have negative repercussions on the definition of their personal identity. Although aware that the children had been identified in the USA as the children of Mr. and Mrs. Mennesson, France nonetheless denied them that status under French law. The Court considered that this 'contradiction' undermined the children's identity within French society.[262] The non-recognition of the legal parenthood of the French couple also had implications for the children's inheritance rights. All together 'a serious question' arose as to the compatibility of this situation with the child's best interests:

> 'The Court can accept that France may wish to deter its nationals from going abroad to take advantage of methods of assisted reproduction that are prohibited on its own territory [...]. [...] [H]owever, the effects of non-recognition in French law of the legal parent-child relationship between children thus conceived and the intended parents are not limited to the

257 *Idem*, para. 83.
258 *Idem*, para. 84.
259 *Idem*, para. 84.
260 *Idem*, para. 80.
261 *Idem*, paras. 78 and 80.
262 *Idem*, para. 96.

> parents alone, who have chosen a particular method of assisted reproduction prohibited by the French authorities. They also affect the children themselves, whose right to respect for their private life – which implies that everyone must be able to establish the substance of his or her identity, including the legal parent-child relationship – is substantially affected. Accordingly, a serious question arises as to the compatibility of that situation with the child's best interests, respect for which must guide any decision in their regard.'[263]

The Court, moreover, found that this analysis took on 'a special dimension' where one of the intended parents was also the child's genetic parent. It stressed the importance of biological parentage 'as a component of identity' and continued:

> '[...] it cannot be said to be in the interests of the child to deprive him or her of a legal relationship of this nature where the biological reality of that relationship has been established and the child and parent concerned demand full recognition thereof. Not only was the relationship between the third and fourth applicants and their biological father not recognised when registration of the details of the birth certificates was requested, but formal recognition by means of a declaration of paternity or adoption or through the effect of *de facto* enjoyment of civil status would fall foul of the prohibition [on attribution of the status of father or mother by contract and on giving effect to a parent-child relationship provided for in a surrogacy agreement] established by the Court of Cassation in its case-law in that regard [...]. The Court considers, having regard to the consequences of this serious restriction on the identity and right to respect for private life of the third and fourth applicants, that by thus preventing both the recognition and establishment under domestic law of their legal relationship with their biological father, the respondent State overstepped the permissible limits of its margin of appreciation. [...] Having regard also to the importance to be given to the child's interests when weighing up the competing interests at stake, the Court concludes that the right of the third and fourth applicants to respect for their private life was infringed.'[264]

While the Court thus found a violation of the right to respect for private life of the children, the Court found no violation of the right to respect for family life of the parents and the children. The Court accepted that this right had been interfered with, but held that a fair balance had been struck between the interests of the applicants and those of the State. The applicants had put forward that on account of the lack of recognition in French law of the legal parent-child relationship, the children did not have French civil-status documents or a French family record book, and were therefore obliged to produce – non-registered – US civil documents accompanied by an officially sworn translation each time access to a right or a service required proof of the legal parent-child relationship. They were sometimes met with '[...] suspicion, or at the very least incomprehension, on the part of the person dealing with the request'. Moreover, the children had not been granted French nationality, which complicated travel as a family and raised concerns about the stability of the family unit.[265] The Court noted it was not established that it was impossible to

---

263 *Idem*, para. 99.
264 *Idem*, paras. 100–101.
265 *Idem*, paras. 88–89.

overcome these practical difficulties. Also, the inability to obtain recognition of the legal parent-child relationship under French law had not prevented the applicants from enjoying in France their right to respect for their family life. The family had been able to settle in France shortly after the birth of the children and had been in a position to live there together '[...] in conditions broadly comparable to those of other families [...]'. There was nothing to suggest that they were at risk of being separated by the authorities on account of their situation under French law.[266]

In the case of the Labassee family, the Court adopted the same approach as in *Mennesson*, finding that there had been no violation of Article 8 concerning the applicants' right to respect for their family life, and a violation of Article 8 concerning the right of the child concerned to respect for her private life. The Chamber was unanimous in both cases, and both judgments became final in September 2014.

In legal scholarship it was noted that the fact that the Court had examined the issue (also) from the perspective of the right of the child to personal identity, made this judgment widely applicable, including in international surrogacy cases where no family life had yet been established between the intended – and genetic – parent(s) and the child. In this regard, the question was posed whether or not the personal identity of the intended (genetic) parents was also at stake.[267] Further, the question was raised regarding what the Court would have ruled if none of the intended parents were also genetic parents of the child.[268]

A month after the *Mennesson* and *Labassee* judgments, the Court decided another international surrogacy case, which concerned the length of a procedure for the issuing of travel documents for a child born via heterologous surrogacy in the Ukraine. The applicants in *D and Others*[269] were a Belgian married couple who had entered into a surrogacy agreement in the Ukraine, following which a child was born in February 2013. The intended father was also the genetic father of the child, while the genetic mother was the woman who had donated the egg cell. In accordance with Ukrainian law, the Belgian couple had been recorded on the child's birth certificate as the parents of the child. When they subsequently applied to the Belgian embassy in Ukraine for a passport, this was denied, because they failed to prove that they were the genetic parents of the child. The couple subsequently had started proceedings before the Belgian courts in order to obtain emergency travel documents (a '*laissez-passer*'). The competent court had given the case priority, but had refused the issuing of the travel documents, so long as the genetic parenthood of the intended father was not established. It took four months and 12 days before the Belgian court found it established in August 2013 that the intended father was

266 *Idem*, para. 92.

267 N.R. Koffeman, 'Case-note to ECtHR 26 June 2014, *Mennesson* v. *France*, no. 65192/11 and ECtHR 26 June 2014, *Labassee* v. *France*, no. 65941/11', 15 *European Human Rights Cases* 2014/222 (in Dutch), referring to ECtHR 22 March 2012, *Ahrens* v. *Germany*, no. 45071/99, para. 60, where the Court held that: '[...] establishment of paternity concern[s] that man's private life under Article 8, which encompasses important aspects of one's personal identity [...].'

268 *Idem*.

269 ECtHR 8 July 2014 (dec.), *D. a.o.* v. *Belgium*, no. 29176/13.

also the genetic father of the child and ordered the issuing of the required travel documents. While the proceedings were pending, the child remained in the Ukraine, while the parents had to go back to Belgium, because their visas had expired. They visited the child twice for a duration of one month in total. Since August 2013 the couple and the child lived together in Belgium.

The legal situation of the applicants had thus significantly changed since their lodging of a complaint with the ECtHR in April 2013. The Court accordingly struck down their complaint about the Belgian authorities' refusal to authorise the child's entry to the national territory. This had been adequately and sufficiently remedied and the dispute was to be considered as resolved.

The applicants had further alleged that their effective separation from the child, on account of the Belgian authorities' refusal to issue a travel document, had been contrary to the best interests of the child and in breach of their right to respect for family life under Article 8 ECHR. The Court found the duration of the temporary separation, for the duration of the proceedings, not unreasonable. The Court held that States were under no obligation under the Convention to authorise the entry of a child born with a foreign surrogate mother, without first subjecting the case to some form of legal examination.[270] It further took into account that the Belgian couple – who had sought legal advice of both a Belgian and a Ukrainian lawyer – could have reasonably foreseen that a court procedure was required, before they could bring the child to Belgium. The Belgian State could not be held responsible for the fact that the couple had not been granted a visa in the Ukraine for an extended period. Furthermore, while their case had been pending before the Belgian court, the couple had been enabled to spend time with the child in the Ukraine, without any interference from the authorities. Also, the Belgian court had given the case priority. The Court concluded that the Belgian state had not exceeded the margin of appreciation and declared the complaint manifestly ill-founded.

The Court thus did not hold, in *D and Others*, that States were under no obligation under the Convention to authorise the entry of a child born with a foreign surrogate mother, but it accepted that the authorities first subjected the case to some form of legal examination.[271] Even more fundamental questions in respect of international surrogacy may be addressed in an Italian case that was still pending before the Court at the time this research was concluded (i.e., 31 July 2014).[272] In that international surrogacy case, the child had been placed for adoption by the Italian authorities after it had become clear that the intended parents were not the genetic parents of the child.

---

270 *Idem*, para. 59.

271 N.R. Koffeman, 'Case-note to ECtHR 8 July 2014 (dec.), *D. a.o.* v. *Belgium*, no. 29176/13', 15 *European Human Rights Cases* 2014/269 (in Dutch).

272 *Paradiso and Campanelli* v. *Italy*, no. 25358/12, lodged on 27 April 2012. This application was communicated to the Italian Government on 9 May 2012.

2.5. Conclusions

The ECtHR's case law with regard to reproductive matters, while still fairly limited, is steadily expanding. The overall first impression that arises from the case law discussed in this chapter is that of a rather reluctant, sometimes evasive and overall pragmatic Court when it comes to reproduction matters. Having regard to the wide variety of views in this ethically and morally sensitive field and the fast-moving scientific developments, the Court has left many reproductive matters up to the national authorities to decide. It has not, for example, taken a strong stance on the status of the unborn life. The Court generally leaves States a wide margin of appreciation in dealing with as morally and ethically sensitive issues as reproductive matters, which involve a complex balancing of various individual and general interests, and upon which generally no European consensus exists. As a result, even far-reaching interferences, such as an absolute prohibition on abortion on social and medical grounds or on the use of donated gametes in the course of IVF treatment, have been held not to violate the Convention.

The Court has, furthermore, introduced some variations on its well-established margin of appreciation doctrine, especially in the context of reproductive rights. In *S. H. and Others,* the Court seemed to set the barrier higher than it had done previously in its case law, by holding that for a common ground to decisively narrow the margin, it had to be 'based on settled and long-standing principles established in the law of the member States'. The Court's approach in defining the issue on which consensus had to exist in *A, B and C* – whereby an existing consensus on allowing for abortion on social and medical grounds was outweighed by a lack of European consensus in respect of the right to life of the unborn – was also unprecedented. These variations on the margin of appreciation doctrine illustrate that the Court is generally reluctant to intervene in reproductive matters. States are left much room to introduce change at their own pace, as long as the competing interests have been weighed in the national legislative process, and as long as they keep this area under review.[273]

Although the life, physical integrity and personal autonomy of pregnant women enjoy protection as rights under the ECHR, the ECtHR has repeatedly held that neither Article 8 ECHR, nor any other Convention Article, can be interpreted as conferring a right to abortion. Nonetheless, it has found that a prohibition on abortion for reasons of health and/or well-being amounted to an interference with the right to respect for private life. Further, it has held that the right to respect for private life incorporates the right to respect for the decision not to become a (genetic) parent. From the *A, B and C* case it follows that a State may completely ban abortion on such grounds, as long as it allows women the option of lawfully travelling to another State to undergo an abortion and as long as women have access to appropriate information

[273] ECtHR [GC] 3 November 2011, *S.H. a.o.* v. *Austria*, no. 57813/00, paras. 103 and 118. The Court accepted that States adopt rules in this area which do not provide for the weighing of competing interests in the circumstance of each individual case.

and medical care before and after the abortion. The burden of travelling as such was not considered in violation of the Convention.

On the other hand, it must be borne in mind that the Convention only sets a minimum standard and that States are free to offer a higher level of protection to the Convention rights. Also, there has been an increasingly greater impact of the ECHR on national abortion regimes through the Court's procedural approach in these matters. Apart from violations of the right to respect for private life (Article 8), this has even resulted in the finding of a violation of Article 3 ECHR (the prohibition of inhuman and degrading treatment). A similar impact of the ECtHR's case law is visible in the area of AHR. States must shape their legal frameworks in the area of reproductive matters '[...] in a coherent manner which allows the different legitimate interests involved to be adequately taken into account.'[274] In *Costa and Pavan* this resulted in an obligation for Italy to legalise PGD. States must, furthermore, provide for an independent authority that can decide about access to information about one's genetic origins (see section 2.1.4 above).

Hence, while principled choices in reproductive matters are left to the States, the fact that reproductive matters fall within the scope of the Convention means that, as soon as a State regulates this area of law, certain general obligations resulting from the Convention apply. As the discussed case law shows, these entail that the right or entitlement granted at national level must be effective, and that the relevant legislation must be coherent and allow for the different legitimate interests involved to be adequately taken into account. In abortion situations this means concretely that the pregnant woman has the right to be heard in person, that the competent body or person should issue written grounds for its decision and the woman must be given timely access to information about her and the foetus' health. The right or entitlement must, furthermore, be granted in a non-discriminatory manner,[275] although the Court has also held a same-sex couple as not being in a similar situation to infertile different-sex couples with regard to access to AHR treatment (see section 2.3.1 above).

The ECtHR's case law has also had an impact on the States' standard-setting in cross-border situations. In respect of cross-border abortions, States must ensure that women can freely travel to another country, that they have access to information about foreign abortion options and that they have access to follow-up treatment upon return to their home countries. These minimum requirements were, at the same time, considered sufficient to justify very restrictive national abortion legislation (see section 2.2.3). In cross-border surrogacy cases, States must recognise parental links

274 *Idem*, para. 100.

275 The Chamber judgment in the case of *S.H. and Others* v. *Austria* (2010)(see sections 2.3 and 2.3.3 above) illustrated this approach well. While the Convention does not guarantee a right to access to assisted human reproduction, the Chamber held that the prohibition of discrimination entailed that an Austrian prohibition on IVF treatment with the use of donor gametes could not be justified. This judgment was, however, overruled by the Grand Chamber, and such reasoning has since not been repeated by the Court.

established abroad between a genetic intended father and a child born with a surrogate mother in a foreign country. Here, the Court based its reasoning completely on the right to personal identity of the child, and this was, in *Mennesson* and *Labassee*, also ground for narrowing the margin of appreciation.

All in all, it seems that the Court's case law in reproductive matters, particularly in the field of assisted human reproduction and surrogacy, is not yet crystallised. The Court has stressed that this area needs to be kept under review by the Contracting States, and at the time of conclusion of this research (i.e., 31 July 2014) various cases were still pending, which could potentially challenge the Court to tackle (more) substantive claims.

CHAPTER 3
EU

3.1. CONSTITUTIONAL FRAMEWORK

3.1.1. The status of the unborn under EU law

A common conception of the status of the unborn does not exist in EU law. The beginning of life has not been defined in any EU legislative instrument, nor in any ruling of the Court of Justice of the European Union (CJEU). It is not, for example, decided how the term 'everyone' under Article 2(1) Charter ('Everyone has the right to life') is to be defined.[1] This matter is – so it can be concluded – left to the discretion of the Member States.

Two CJEU rulings have, nevertheless, indirectly touched upon this sensitive issue. The cases *Sabine Mayr* (2008)[2] and *Brüstle* (2011)[3] concerned the interpretation of terms and concepts in EU Directives which have a (remote) connection to the unborn. While these judgments give some clues with regard to the CJEU's approach to the unborn, it must be underlined that it remains impossible to draw any substantive conclusions as to the status of the unborn in EU law from these rulings. This has everything to do with the fact that the definitions given by the CJEU were strictly confined to the context of the relevant Directives, which concerned employment law and patent law respectively.

The case of *Sabine Mayr* (2008) concerned the question whether a female worker who was undergoing *in vitro* fertilisation treatment was protected against dismissal under EU law.[4] The Grand Chamber of the Court ruled that the prohibition of dismissal of pregnant workers in Article 10(1) of Council Directive 92/85/EEC,[5] did not extend

---

1 The explanations to the Charter provide no clarification on this point. Guiding is therefore the case law of the ECtHR on this point. As set out in Ch.2, the ECtHR left this matter to the States to decide upon. It is, furthermore, noted that the European Parliament held in a Resolution of 1989 that there was a need ' to protect human life from the moment of fertilization'. Resolution of the European Parliament on artificial insemination *in vivo* and in vitro of 16 March 1989, Preamble under C, [1989] OJ C96/127, p. 172.

2 Case C-506/06 *Sabine Mayr* [2008] ECR I-1017, ECLI:EU:C:2008:119.

3 Case C-34/10 *Oliver Brüstle* v. *Greenpeace eV* [2011] ECR I-9821, ECLI:EU:C:2011:669.

4 The preliminary reference, *inter alia*, concerned the interpretation of Council Directive 92/85/EEC of 19 October 1992 on the introduction of measures to encourage improvements in the safety and health of pregnant workers, workers who have recently given birth and women who are breastfeeding [1992] OJ L348/1.

5 Council Directive 92/85/EEC of 19 October 1992 on the introduction of measures to encourage improvements in the safety and health of pregnant workers, workers who have recently given birth and women who are breastfeeding [1992] OJ L348/1.

to a female worker who was undergoing *in vitro* fertilisation treatment where, on the date she was given notice of her dismissal, her ova had already been fertilised by her partner's sperm, so that *in vitro* fertilised ova existed, but they had not yet been transferred into her uterus.[6] Such dismissal was, however, precluded by EU law if the woman was in 'an advanced stage' of IVF treatment and inasmuch as it was established that the dismissal was essentially based on the fact that the woman had undergone such treatment.[7] The Court defined an 'advanced stage' of IVF treatment as '[...] between the follicular puncture and the immediate transfer of the *in vitro* fertilised ova into [the woman's] uterus'.[8]

Hence, apparently the CJEU considered an advanced stage of IVF treatment to come so close to pregnancy that the protection against dismissal as afforded by the Directive to pregnant women had to be extended to this situation. To infer from this ruling any finding in respect of the beginning of life or the status of the unborn under EU law, would not, however, be possible without resorting to speculation.

In *Brüstle* (2011)[9] the German Federal Court of Justice had made a preliminary reference to the CJEU concerning the patentability of biotechnological inventions in which human embryos were used. The CJEU gave an autonomous interpretation of the term 'human embryo' within the meaning of Directive 98/44/EC on the legal protection of biotechnological inventions ('the Biotechnology Directive').[10] The Court underlined that such a uniform definition was desired, to avoid the '[...] risk of the authors of certain biotechnological inventions being tempted to seek their patentability in the Member States which [had] the narrowest concept of human embryo and [were] accordingly the most liberal as regards possible patentability, because those inventions would not be patentable in the other Member States.' According to the Court such a situation would have adversely affected the smooth functioning of the internal market which was the aim of the Directive.[11] The Court also underlined the following:

---

6 Case C-506/06 *Sabine Mayr* [2008] ECR I-1017, ECLI:EU:C:2008:119, para. 53.

7 *Idem*, para. 54. The Court based its finding on Arts. 2(1) and 5(1) of Council Directive 76/207/EEC of 9 February 1976 on the implementation of the principle of equal treatment for men and women as regards access to employment, vocational training and promotion, and working conditions.

8 *Idem*, para. 54.

9 Case C-34/10 *Oliver Brüstle* v. *Greenpeace eV* [2011] ECR I-9821, ECLI:EU:C:2011:669; see also S. Henette-Vauchez, 'L'embryon de l'Union', 48 *RTD eur.* (2012) pp. 355–368.

10 Directive 98/44/EC of the European Parliament and of the Council of 6 July 1998 on the legal protection of biotechnological inventions [1998] OJ L213/13.

11 Case C-34/10 *Oliver Brüstle* v. *Greenpeace eV* [2011] ECR I-9821, ECLI:EU:C:2011:669, para. 28. For critique in this respect, see H. Somsen, 'Brüstle: embryonale fout met grote gevolgen' ['Brüstle: embroynic mistake with major consequences'], *Nederlands Tijdschrift voor Europees Recht* (2012) p. 33 at p. 37 and F.M. Fleurke, 'Case note to Case C-34/10 (*Brüstle*)', 13 *European Human Rights Cases* 2012/54 (in Dutch). Spranger held it to be 'hardly comprehensible' how the Court could arrive at this 'unambiguous evaluation'. The author held that the existing divergences in patent law 'in no way' needed necessarily to be aligned in the direction of a wide embryo-concept. T.M. Spranger, 'Case C-34/10, Oliver Brüstle v. Greenpeace e.V., Judgment of the Court (Grand Chamber) of 18 October 2011', 49 *CLMRev.* (2012) p. 1197 at 1202.

> '[...] although, the definition of human embryo is a very sensitive social issue in many Member States, marked by their multiple traditions and value systems, the Court is not called upon, by the present order for reference, to broach questions of a medical or ethical nature, but must restrict itself to a legal interpretation of the relevant provisions of the Directive.'[12]

Hence, the Court confined itself to the legal interpretation of the concept of 'human embryo' within the meaning of the Biotechnology Directive, i.e., within the context of patent law.[13] According to the Court this concept was to be understood in a wide sense however, as the 'context and aim'[14] of the Directive showed that the European Union legislature intended to exclude any possibility of patentability where respect for human dignity could be affected.[15] The Court held that any human ovum after fertilisation, any non-fertilised human ovum into which the cell nucleus from a mature human cell had been transplanted, and any non-fertilised human ovum whose division and further development had been stimulated by parthenogenesis constituted a 'human embryo' within the meaning of the Directive.[16] The CJEU left it for the referring court to ascertain, in the light of scientific developments, whether this also held for a stem cell obtained from a human embryo at the so-called blastocyst stage (i.e., approximately five days after fertilisation).[17]

Precisely because the Court stressed that it only gave a 'legal interpretation' of the term 'human embryo' and only within the context of the Biotechnology Directive, one has to be very careful in making any inferences from this judgment in respect of the status of the unborn in EU law in a broader sense,[18] such as the question as

---

12 Case C-34/10 *Oliver Brüstle* v. *Greenpeace eV* [2011] ECR I-9821, ECLI:EU:C:2011:669, para. 30. The Court referred to Case C-506/06 *Sabine Mayr* [2008] ECR I-1017, ECLI:EU:C:2008:119, para. 38.

13 Art. 6(2)(c) of Directive 98/44/EC.

14 Remarkably, the Court did not refer to the EU Charter of Fundamental Rights, nor to the European Convention on Human Rights. See also Fleurke 2012, *supra* n. 11.

15 Case C-34/10 *Oliver Brüstle* v. *Greenpeace eV* [2011] ECR I-9821, ECLI:EU:C:2011:669, para. 34.

16 *Idem*, para. 38. Spranger observed that this definitely was '[...] not only extremely broad, but also open towards further extension, with further developments of modern life sciences.' Spranger 2012, *supra* n. 11, at p. 1203. AG Cruz Villalón has held in a case of a later date that an ovum whose development has been stimulated without fertilisation and which was not capable of becoming a human being could not be considered a human embryo. However, if this ovum was genetically manipulated in such a way that it could develop into a human being, it had to be regarded as a human embryo and as such excluded from patentability, the AG held. Case C-364/13 *International Stem Cell Corporation* v. *Comptroller General of Patents, nyr,* ECLI:EU:C:2014:2104, Opinion of AG Cruz Villalón.

17 Case C-34/10 *Oliver Brüstle* v. *Greenpeace eV* [2011] ECR I-9821, ECLI:EU:C:2011:669, para. 38. At the blastocyst stage, embryonic stem cells are pluripotent, which means that there are able to develop into various organs and tissues, but not into a complete individual.

18 Advocate General Bot had also warned that from the 'legal definition' as chosen by him, no inferences could be drawn 'for other areas which relate to human life, but which are on an entirely different level and fall outside the scope of Union law.' For that reason, Bot considered that the reference made at the hearing to judgments delivered by the European Court of Human Rights on the subject of abortion was, 'by definition', outside the scope of the *Brüstle* case. He held it not to be possible to compare the question of the possible use of human embryos for industrial or commercial purposes 'with national laws which seek to provide solutions to individual difficult situations.' Case C-34/10 *Oliver Brüstle* v. *Greenpeace eV* [2011] ECR I-9821, ECLI:EU:C:2011:138, Opinion of AG Bot, para. 49.

from which developmental stage an embryo is an independent bearer of rights.[19] In the words of Spranger '[...] all attempts to ascribe a general legal significance to the decision of the Court of Justice going beyond the realm of patent law must be emphatically opposed.'[20] The author underlined 'the limited relevance of patent law', which understood itself '[...] basically as a value-neutral subject matter and [was], also for systematic reasons, not the right place for the establishment of all-purpose new standards for the entire European legal order.'[21] Nevertheless, some have argued that the approach taken by the Court presupposed a certain bio-ethic vision, that was however not made explicit.[22]

For one thing, the cases of *Sabine Mayr* and *Brüstle* confirmed the observation that the CJEU shows considerable judicial restraint in cases which touch upon such sensitive and ethical issues such as the status of the unborn. Furthermore, the interpretation of Union law that the CJEU gave was in both these cases confined to the very specific subject matter at stake.

3.1.2. (Potentially) relevant Charter rights

Several Articles of the Charter of Fundamental Rights of the European Union (CFR)[23] relate in one way or another to reproductive rights.[24] The CJEU's case law on these provisions is, however, still fairly limited and therefore provides little guidance in respect of application of these Articles in the context of the present case study. It is recalled in this regard, that the CFR also has a limited scope of application; its provisions '[...] are addressed to the institutions, bodies, offices and agencies of the

19 T. Groh, 'Anmerkung zu C-34/10 (*Brüstle*)' ['Case note to Case C-34/10 (*Brüstle*)'], 23 *Europäische Zeitschrift für Wirtschaftsrecht* (2011) p. 910 at p. 910.

20 Spranger 2012, *supra* n. 11, at p. 1205.

21 *Idem*.

22 B. van Beers, 'Het Europese Hof van Justitie over de vermarkting van menselijke embryo's. Van economische naar ook bio-ethische integratie binnen de EU?' ['The European Court of Justice on the commercialisation of human embryos. From economic to also bio-ethical integration in the EU?'], 37 *NTM/NJCM-Bull.* (2012) p. 242 at pp. 255–256. Without substantiating this with references, Spranger held that '[a]lready shortly after the publication of the decision, the opinion that the Court of Justice has delivered a complete embryo definition for all areas of European Law or that this complete, or all-purpose, definition should at least be indirectly derived from the decision in the interest of a consistent legal order, has actually been expressed by various stakeholders. The author held '[t]hese attempts at interpretation', to be 'falsified by the remarks of the Court of Justice itself'. He furthermore held that they misjudged the 'scope' which the CJEU and the ECtHR had so far, 'and with good reasons' attributed to the Member States, ' in view of the concretization of ethically problematic or socially controversial concepts of the modern life sciences'. Spranger 2012, *supra* n. 11, at p. 1205. See also at pp. 1208–1209.

23 Charter of fundamental rights of the European Union [2000] OJ C364/1.

24 Yet in 1989 – hence much before the Charter of Fundamental Rights even existed – the European Parliament had held in a Resolution that the main criteria governing the area were '[...] the mother's right to self-determination and the respect of the rights and interests of the child, i.e. the right to life and physical, psychological and existential integrity, the right to a family, the right to be looked after by its parents and to grow up in a suitable family environment and the right to its own genetic identity. Resolution of the European Parliament on artificial insemination in vivo and in vitro of 16 March 1989, Preamble under D [1989] OJ C96/127, p. 172.

Union with due regard for the principle of subsidiarity and to the Member States only when they are implementing Union law'.[25]

Article 1 CFR, to start with, contains a fundamental right to human dignity.[26] While there is little case law on this specific Charter Article, the right to human dignity was already recognised by the CJEU as part of Union law in 2001.[27] Also, it has been upheld as a justification for restrictive measures in free movement cases.[28] The CJEU, furthermore, considered it 'not indispensable' in that regard for the restrictive measure issued by the authorities of a Member State to correspond to a conception shared by all Member States as regards the precise way in which the fundamental right or legitimate interest in question was to be protected.[29]

The right to life and the right to integrity of the person are codified in Articles 2 and 3 CFR, respectively. The latter Article provides that in the fields of medicine and biology the free and informed consent of the person concerned; the prohibition of eugenic practices; the prohibition on making the human body and its parts, as such, a source of financial gain;[30] as well as the prohibition of the reproductive cloning of human beings, must be respected in particular.[31]

---

25 Art. 51 TFEU. See also, *inter alia*, Case C-617/10 *Åkerberg Fransson* [2013] ECR 0000, ECLI:EU:C:2013:105; K. Lenaerts, 'The EU Charter of Fundamental Rights: Scope of Application and Methods of Interpretation', in: V. Kronenberger et al. (eds.), *De Rome à Lisbonne: les juridictions de l'Union européenne à la croisée des chemins: mélanges en l'honneur de Paolo Mengozzi* (Bruxelles, Bruylant 2013) p. 107 and W.B. van Bockel and P.J. Wattel, 'New Wine into Old Wineskins: the Scope of the Charter of Fundamental Rights of the EU after Åkerberg Fransson', 38 *European law review* (2013) p. 866.

26 Art. 1 CFR reads: 'Human dignity is inviolable. It must be respected and protected.'

27 Case C-377/98 *Netherlands* v. *European Parliament and Council* [2001] ECR I-7079, ECLI:EU:C:2001:523, paras. 70–77.

28 In *Omega* (2004), the Court held that there was no doubt that the objective of protecting human dignity was compatible with EU law. Case C-36/02 *Omega* [2004] ECR I-9609, ECLI:EU:C:2004:614.

29 *Idem*, para. 37.

30 As McHale has pointed out, the prohibition on making (parts of) the human body a source of financial gain is also recognised in the Tissue and Cells Directive (see also section 3.3.2 below). J. McHale, 'Fundamental rights and health care', in: E. Mossialos et al. (eds.), *Health Systems Governance in Europe: The Role of European Union Law and Policy* (Cambridge, Cambridge University Press 2010) p. 282 at p. 300, online available at www.euro.who.int/en/who-we-are/partners/observatory/studies/health-systems-governance-in-europe-the-role-of-eu-law-and-policy, visited June 2014.

31 The official explanation to this Article reads:

'1. In its judgment of 9 October 2001 in Case C-377/98 *Netherlands* v *European Parliament and Council* [2001] ECR-I 7079, at grounds 70, 78 to 80, the Court of Justice confirmed that a fundamental right to human integrity is part of Union law and encompasses, in the context of medicine and biology, the free and informed consent of the donor and recipient.

2. The principles of Article 3 of the Charter are already included in the Convention on Human Rights and Biomedicine, adopted by the Council of Europe (ETS 164 and additional protocol ETS 168). The Charter does not set out to depart from those principles, and therefore prohibits only reproductive cloning. It neither authorises nor prohibits other forms of cloning. Thus it does not in any way prevent the legislature from prohibiting other forms of cloning.

3. The reference to eugenic practices, in particular those aiming at the selection of persons, relates to possible situations in which selection programmes are organised and implemented, involving campaigns for sterilisation, forced pregnancy, compulsory ethnic marriage among others, all acts

A related Charter provision that may potentially prove of relevance for the status and development of reproductive rights within EU law is Article 35 CFR. Following this Article '[e]veryone has the right of access to preventive health care and the right to benefit from medical treatment under the conditions established by national laws and practices.'[32] This provision thus '[...] does not recognize *per se* a right to health assured by EU law, but rather a principle of access to health based on national legislation'.[33] The Article has been categorised amongst the Charter rights which in fact merely constitute 'pure objectives' of the Union[34] and it has been questioned whether it will make a practical difference in terms of litigation.[35]

Article 7 of the Charter contains a right to respect for private and family life which corresponds to Article 8 ECHR.[36] Article 9 CFR lays down the right to found a family, a right that is disconnected from the right to marry, that is also provided for in Article 9.[37] The Commentary to the Charter by the EU Network of Independent Experts on Fundamental Rights of 2006 noted – without specifying this further – that the right to found a family provided '[...] for some aspects of reproductive choice including the use of new procreative technologies'.[38] At the same time, it was noted that there was 'a diversity of domestic legislation on this subject'.[39] This diversity is implied in the fact that this right – like under Article 12 ECHR on which it is

deemed to be international crimes in the Statute of the International Criminal Court adopted in Rome on 17 July 1998 (see its Article 7(1)(g)).'

Explanations relating to the Charter of Fundamental Rights [2007] OJ C303/17, p.18.

32 Art. 35 CFR further provides that '[a] high level of human health protection shall be ensured in the definition and implementation of all Union policies and activities.'

33 S. De la Rosa, 'The directive on cross-border healthcare or the art of codifying complex case law', 49 *CML Rev.* (2012) p. 15 at p. 35, footnote 75. The Explanations to this Article also speak of 'principles' that are set out in this Article, which are based on Art. 168 TFEU and Arts. 11 and 13 of the European Social Charter.

34 T. K. Hervey, 'We don't see a Connection: the "Right to Health" in the EU Charter and European Social Charter', in: G. De Búrca et al. (eds.), *Social rights in Europe* (Oxford, Oxford University Press) p. 305 at p. 318.

35 J. McHale, 'Fundamental rights and health care', in: E. Mossialos et al. (eds.), *Health Systems Governance in Europe: The Role of European Union Law and Policy* (Cambridge, Cambridge University Press 2010) p. 282 at pp. 304 and 306–307, online available at www.euro.who.int/en/who-we-are/partners/observatory/studies/health-systems-governance-in-europe-the-role-of-eu-law-and-policy, visited June 2014. McHale refers (in footnote 98), to T. Hervey, 'The right to health in European Union law', in: T. Hervey and J. Kenner (eds.), *Economic and social rights under the EU Charter of Fundamental Rights: a legal perspective* (Oxford, Hart 2003) p. 193 at p. 210.

36 Explanations relating to the Charter of Fundamental Rights [2007] OJ C303/17, p. 20.

37 EU Network of Independent Experts on Fundamental Rights, *Commentary of the Charter of Fundamental Rights of the European Union*, June 2006, online available at www.ec.europa.eu/justice/fundamental-rights/files/networkcommentaryfinal_en.pdf, visited June 2014. In this Commentary it was observed (at p. 103): 'Article 9 of the Charter approaches the rights at stake, i.e. the right to found a family and the right to marry as two different and separate rights, suggesting that the former is not necessarily connected with the latter. Apparently, it seems from the wording, i.e., the usage of the plural form 'these rights', that a disconnection between the right to marry and to found a family has been envisaged. In other words, a marriage does not necessarily imply procreation.'

38 EU Network of Independent Experts on Fundamental Rights, *Commentary of the Charter of Fundamental Rights of the European Union*, June 2006, p. 104, online available at www.ec.europa.eu/justice/fundamental-rights/files/networkcommentaryfinal_en.pdf, visited June 2014.

39 *Idem.*

based[40] – is guaranteed in accordance with the national laws governing the exercise of this right. The right to found a family under Article 9 CFR has never been referred to in a CJEU judgment, let alone interpreted by the Court.

Article 33(1) CFR is also related to the family and provides that the family shall enjoy 'legal, economic and social protection'.[41] Further, other than the ECHR, the Charter provides expressly for the rights of the child, which is based on the UN Convention on the Rights of the Child.[42] Its Article 24(2) provides that '[...] in all actions relating to children, whether taken by public authorities or private institutions, the child's best interests must be a primary consideration.' Following the third paragraph of Article 24, every child has the right '[...] to maintain on a regular basis a personal relationship and direct contact with both his or her parents, unless that is contrary to his or her interests.'[43]

Article 21 CFR lays down a prohibition on discrimination. Contrary to Article 14 ECHR this is a self-standing right that can be invoked independently from other Charter rights. The provision is not intended to introduce 'a sweeping ban of discrimination' that covers any Member States' action and private action, but, like all Charter rights, addresses the institutions and the Member States when they are implementing Union law.[44] According to the Explanations to the Charter, this Article draws, *inter alia*, on Article 11 of the Convention on Human Rights and Biomedicine which contains a prohibition on discrimination on the basis of genetic heritage.

Lastly, Article 45 EU Charter grants every EU citizen the right to move and reside freely within the territory of the Member States.[45] While this right is thus granted to those with EU citizenship only, it is provided that such freedom of movement and residence may be granted to third-country nationals who are legally resident in the territory of a Member State.[46]

---

40 See Explanations relating to the Charter of Fundamental Rights [2007] OJ C303/17.

41 This Article has not been applied in CJEU case law. It has only been briefly mentioned in Case C-147/08 *Jürgen Römer* v. *Freie und Hansestadt Hamburg* [2011] ECR I-3591, ECLI:EU:C:2010:425, Opinion of AG Jääskinen, para. 174.

42 Explanations relating to the Charter of Fundamental Rights [2007] OJ C303/17, p. 25.

43 The explanations to the Charter explain that this paragraph of Art. 24 '[...] takes account of the fact that, as part of the establishment of an area of freedom, security and justice, the legislation of the Union on civil matters having cross-border implications, for which Article 81 of the Treaty on the Functioning of the European Union confers power, may include notably visiting rights ensuring that children can maintain on a regular basis a personal and direct contact with both of their parents.' Explanations relating to the Charter of Fundamental Rights [2007] OJ C303/17, p. 25.

44 Explanations relating to the Charter of Fundamental Rights [2007] OJ C303/17, p. 24.

45 The Explanations to the Charter clarify that this right is guaranteed by Arts. 20(2)(a) and 21 TFEU as well as Case C-413/99 *Baumbast* [2002] ECR I-7091, ECLI:EU:C:2002:493.

46 Art. 45(2) CFR. According to the Explanations to the Charter this second paragraph refers to the power granted to the Union by Arts. 77, 78 and 79 TFEU. Explanations relating to the Charter of Fundamental Rights [2007] OJ C303/17, p. 29.

Whether the Charter supports the 'right to reproduce discourse'[47] is as yet an open question. The explanations to the Charter and the CJEU case law as they currently stand do not provide sufficient ground for such a conclusion. McHale has pointed out that in developing health policies or in litigation, use of the Charter may prove problematic because it has a limited scope, because it does not make clear how to balance conflicting rights and because it contains concepts, such as dignity, which are very broad and therefore difficult to enforce. The author has also warned that there are '[...] differing religious, cultural and ethical perspectives regarding certain fundamental rights questions' within the EU and that '[r]espect for equality and diversity of cultural and religious viewpoints does not sit easily with a single "EU" approach to fundamental human rights in health care.'[48]

3.1.3. Relevant EU competences

The EU Treaties provide for various Union competences that apply or may apply in the context of the present case study. The most general one for cross-border situations is of course the EU's competence in respect of the internal market.[49] The application of the EU's free movement rules to cross-border health care cases, and cross-border abortions and AHR treatment in particular, is discussed in more detail in sections 3.5 and 3.6.2 below. Another general competence that may be of relevance for the present case study concerns the EU's competence to adopt (harmonising) legislation to combat certain forms of discrimination.[50] The coming into being of this competence and its general application are discussed more extensively in Chapter 9,[51] while its (potential) application in respect of reproductive matters in particular is discussed in sections 3.3.3 and 3.3.4 below.

The present section briefly sets out four more specific EU competences. Most of these concern primarily the present case study, namely public health, social security and criminal law. The EU's competence in respect of civil matters (including family law) having cross-border implications, as discussed in section 3.1.3.3 below, is also relevant for Case Study II.

---

47 T.K. Hervey and J.V. McHale, *Health Law and the European Union* (Cambridge: Cambridge University Press 2004) p. 145, referring (in footnote 219) to S. Millns, 'Reproducing inequalities; assisted conception and the challenge of legal pluralism', 24 *Journal of Social Welfare and Family Law* (2002) p. 19 at p. 32.

48 J. McHale, 'Fundamental rights and health care', in: E. Mossialos et al. (eds.), *Health Systems Governance in Europe: The Role of European Union Law and Policy* (Cambridge, Cambridge University Press 2010) p. 282 at pp. 312–313, online available at www.euro.who.int/en/who-we-are/partners/observatory/studies/health-systems-governance-in-europe-the-role-of-eu-law-and-policy, visited June 2014.

49 Art. 114 TFEU.

50 Art. 19 TFEU.

51 In particular in section 9.3.

3.1.3.1. Public health

Public health is generally considered a '[...] particularly sensitive area of national competence involving complex, costly, and important political and social choices'.[52] The Union's competences in respect to public health have therefore always been, and still are, rather limited. Under the Treaty of Rome (the EEC Treaty) of 1957 there was no Community competence in this field. Public health was only referred to as a ground for derogation from the free movement rules.[53] The Maastricht Treaty (1992)[54] was the first to provide for a limited Union competence regarding public health. Article 129 EC Treaty provided that the (then) European Community was to '[...] contribute towards ensuring a high level of human health protection by encouraging Member States, and if necessary, by lending support to their action'. The Lisbon Treaty (2009), as presently still in force, changed little in this regard. On the basis of Article 168 TFEU the European Union has a coordinating competence in respect of the 'protection and improvement of human health'.[55] This means that the Union may support, coordinate or supplement the actions of the Member States in this field. Following Article 168(7) TFEU Union action in the field of public health must respect the responsibilities of the Member States '[...] for the definition of their health policy and for the organisation and delivery of health services and medical care'. The responsibilities of the Member States include the '[...] management of health services and medical care and the allocation of the resources assigned to them'. The Union has the task of encouraging cooperation between the Member States, especially to improve the complementarity of the Member States' health services in cross-border areas.[56] New is that Article 9 TFEU expressly provides that the EU has the duty to protect human health in all its policies and activities.[57] Even though this 'multi-sector social clause'[58] is no basis for any EU competence, some have argued that it shows the 'social commitment' of the Union.[59]

3.1.3.2. Social security

The picture in respect of the regulation of social security is fairly similar. By way of Article 118 Maastricht Treaty (1992) the Commission was given the task of promoting close cooperation between Member states in respect of social security. Following the present Article 153 TFEU the Union supports and complements the activities of the Member States in the field of social security. It is emphasised that

---

52 S. O'Leary, 'Free movement of persons and services', in: P. Craig and G. de Búrca, *The Evolution of EU law* (Oxford: Oxford University Press 2011) p. 499 at p. 522.

53 Art. 36 EEC Treaty.

54 Treaty of the European Union, together with the complete text of the Treaty establishing the European Community [1992] OJ C224/1.

55 Art. 6(a) TFEU. Shared competence between the Union and the Member States are confined only to 'common safety concerns in public health matters, for the aspects defined in this Treaty'. Art. 4(2)(k) TFEU.

56 Art. 168(2) TFEU.

57 Art. 9 TFEU however reads that 'in defining and implementing its policies and activities, the Union takes into account requirements linked to the [...] protection of human health'.

58 De la Rosa 2012, *supra* n. 33 at p. 35.

59 *Idem.*

Member States retain the right '[...] to define the fundamental principles of their social security systems'.[60] The CJEU has repeatedly affirmed that EU law '[...] does not detract from the powers of the Member States to organise their social security systems'.[61] It is well-established case law that in the absence of harmonisation at EU level, it is for the legislature of each Member State to determine the conditions concerning the right or duty to be insured with a social security scheme[62] and the conditions for entitlement to benefits.[63]

3.1.3.3. Civil matters (including family law) having cross-border implications

In principle, the EU has no competences in respect of family law, however, Article 81(3) TFEU, confers on the Council the power to adopt 'measures concerning family law having cross-border implications'. This forms part of the Union's competence to develop '[...] judicial cooperation in civil matters having cross-border implications, based on the principle of mutual recognition of judgments and of decisions in extrajudicial cases.'[64] Article 81 TFEU explicitly provides that '[s]uch cooperation may include the adoption of measures for the approximation of the laws and regulations of the Member States', such as measures aimed at ensuring '[...] the compatibility of the rules applicable in the Member States concerning conflict of laws'.[65]

This legal basis for judicial cooperation in cross-border civil matters was first introduced by the Treaty of Amsterdam (1999).[66] The Presidency Conclusions of the Tampere European Council of 1999 had held that mutual recognition had to become '[...] the cornerstone of judicial co-operation in both civil and criminal matters within the Union.'[67] At the time, it was provided under the then Article 65 EC Treaty that measures could only be adopted 'insofar as necessary for the proper functioning of the internal market'. The Lisbon Treaty (2009) changed this into 'particularly when necessary for the proper functioning of the internal market', thus making Article 81

---

60 Art. 153(4) TFEU.

61 Case 238/82 *Duphar and Others* v. *Netherlands* [1984] ECR 523, ECLI:EU:C:1984:45, para.16 and Case C-70/95 *Sodemare and Others* v. *Regione Lombardia* [1997] ECR I-3395, ECLI:EU:C:1997:301, para. 27.

62 Case 110/79 *Una Coonan* v. *Insurance Officer* [1980] ECR 1445, ECLI:EU:C:1980:112, para. 12, and Case C-349/87 *Paraschi* v. *Landesversicherungsanstalt Württemberg* [1991] ECR I-4501, ECLI:EU:C:1991:372, para. 15.

63 Joined Cases C-4/95 and C-5/95 *Stöber and Piosa Pereira* v. *Bundesanstalt für Arbeit* [1997] ECR I-511, ECLI:EU:C:1997:44, para. 36 and Case C-158/96 *Kohll* [1998] ECR I-1931, ECLI:EU:C:1998:171, para. 18.

64 Art. 81(1) TFEU. Storskrubb has questioned whether this cross-border limitation '[...] is still able to stem the dynamism of the policy area'. The author furthermore posed questions as to the exact implications of the inclusion of the principle of mutual recognition in this Article. E. Storskrubb, 'Civil Jusitice – A newcomer and an unstoppable wave?', in: P. Craig and G. De Búrca, *The evolution of EU Law*, 2nd edn. (Oxford, Oxford University Press 2011) p. 307.

65 Art. 81(2)(c) TFEU.

66 Art. 65 EC (old).

67 Tampere European Council 15 and 16 October 1999 Presidency Conclusions, para. VI, online available at www.europarl.europa.eu/summits/tam_en.htm, visited June 2014.

TFEU a more independent legal basis.[68] In the subsequent Stockholm Programme (2010–2014)[69] it was held that mutual recognition had to be extended '[...] to fields that [had] not yet [been] covered but [were] essential to everyday life [...] while taking into consideration Member States' legal systems, including public policy, and national traditions in this area.'[70]

If 'measures concerning family law with cross-border implications' are concerned, the Council can only act in accordance with a special legislative procedure; it has to consult the European Parliament first and can only adopt measures with a unanimous vote. Exceptionally, acts concerning family law with cross-border implications may be adopted by the ordinary legislative procedure. That requires a proposal from the Commission, after which the Council has to act unanimously after consulting the European Parliament.[71] Unique to this 'PIL passerelle' clause is that national parliaments must be notified of a Commission proposal and any national parliament can in principle block the adoption of the proposal by the Council.[72] This has been held to demonstrate '[...] the balance between the political desire to move forward in the area of family law and the politically sensitive nature of the area.'[73] Further, since the Treaty of Lisbon national courts may request preliminary rulings in respect of this provision.[74]

3.1.3.4. Criminal law

The Union has little competences with respect to criminal law. Possible approximation of substantive criminal laws is limited to narrowly defined '[...] areas of particularly serious crime with a cross-border dimension resulting from the nature or impact of such offences or from a special need to combat them on a common

68 It has therefore been concluded that '[t]he position that Article 81 TFEU is but merely a lex specialis of Article 114 TFEU can no longer be maintained.' G.-R. de Groot and J.-J. Kuipers, 'The New provisions on Private international law in the Treaty of Lisbon', 15 *Maastricht Journal of European and Comparative Law* (2008) p. 109 at p. 112. But see in respect of the old Art. 65 EC Treaty: R. Baratta, 'Problematic elements of an implicit rule providing for mutual recognition of personal and family status in the EC', *IPRax* (2007) p. 4 at p. 5 and J. Meeusen et al., 'General Report', in J. Meeusen et al. (eds.), *International family law for the European Union* (Antwerpen, Intersentia 2007) p. 1 at p. 13.

69 The Stockholm Programme – An open and secure Europe serving and protecting citizens [2010] OJ C115/1.

70 *Idem*, para. 3.1.2.

71 Art. 81(3) TFEU reads: 'Notwithstanding paragraph 2, measures concerning family law with cross-border implications shall be established by the Council, acting in accordance with a special legislative procedure. The Council shall act unanimously after consulting the European Parliament.
The Council, on a proposal from the Commission, may adopt a decision determining those aspects of family law with cross-border implications which may be the subject of acts adopted by the ordinary legislative procedure. The Council shall act unanimously after consulting the European Parliament.
The proposal referred to in the second subparagraph shall be notified to the national Parliaments. If a national Parliament makes known its opposition within six months of the date of such notification, the decision shall not be adopted. In the absence of opposition, the Council may adopt the decision.'

72 See also Groot, de and Kuipers 2008, *supra* n. 68, at pp. 112–114, who sketch three scenarios in which they consider the passerelle clause likely to be used.

73 Storskrubb 2011, *supra* n. 64, at p. 307.

74 Art. 267 TFEU.

basis', none of which appears relevant for the present case study.[75] The Union may, however, take measures for coordination and cooperation between police and judicial authorities and other competent authorities.[76] There is, furthermore, foreseen in mutual recognition of judgments in criminal matters.[77] It has been in this context that the European Arrest Warrant (EAW) was drafted. The (potential) application of that instrument in the context of the present case study is discussed in section 3.6.4 below.

3.2. Absence of EU standards on abortion

As the Council has acknowledged '[t]he Treaties do not provide a basis for the Union to adopt measures with respect to questions related to abortion.'[78] As explained in section 3.1.3 above, the Union's competences in the field of health care, social security law and criminal law are generally limited. The only case that came before the CJEU which had to do with abortion was the *Grogan* case (see section 3.5.2.1 below). While – as explained below – the CJEU took a much debated approach in deciding this free movement case, no substantive conclusion in respect of abortion can be drawn from this judgment. The substantive legal regulation of abortion has always been, is, and is anticipated to remain in the near future, a matter for the Member States.

The issue of abortion has nonetheless incidentally been debated at EU level. As explained in section 3.5.1 below, particularly cross-border movement that has taken place for this purpose has caught the attention of the EU institutions. EU institutions have, however, been very hesitant to take any position in respect of substantive regulation of abortion. By way of exception, in 2013 the European Parliament's Committee on Women's Rights and Gender Equality invited the European Parliament to take a strong stance in favour of abortion, when it tabled a motion for a resolution on Sexual and Reproductive Health and Rights.[79] The Resolution held that women

[75] Art. 83(1) TFEU limits these areas of crime to the following: terrorism, trafficking in human beings and sexual exploitation of women and children, illicit drug trafficking, illicit arms trafficking, money laundering, corruption, counterfeiting of means of payment, computer crime and organised crime. On the basis of developments in crime, the Council may – unanimously and after obtaining the consent of the European Parliament – adopt a decision identifying other areas of crime that meet the criteria specified in this paragraph.

[76] Art. 67(3) TFEU.

[77] Arts. 67(3) and 82 TFEU.

[78] Answer of the Council of 15 March 2010 to written question by Magdi Cristiano Allam (PPE) to the Council: Member States' autonomy and the right to life, P-6267/09 of 9 December 2009, www.europarl.europa.eu/sides/getAllAnswers.do?reference=P-2009-6267&language=HU, visited July 2014. In a similar vein the Commission held back in 1989 that it '[...] did not consider the approximation of national rules concerning the prevention and termination of pregnancy to be necessary for the completion of the internal market.' A. Sherlock, 'The Right to life of the unborn and the Irish Constitution', 24 *Irish Jurist* (1989) p. 13, referring (in footnote 29) to European Parliament – Written Questions with Answer [1989] OJ C111/1, p. 16.

[79] Motion for a European Parliament Resolution on Sexual and Reproductive Health and Rights (2013/2040(INI)), online available at www.europarl.europa.eu/sides/getDoc.do?pubRef=-//EP//NONSGML+REPORT+A7-2013-0306+0+DOC+PDF+V0//EN, visited 24 July 2014.

had '[...] the right to decide freely and responsibly the number, timing and spacing of their children' and recommended that high-quality abortion services were made legal and accessible to all women, including non-resident women.[80] The motion was rejected and the very brief Resolution that was adopted instead in Parliament merely noted that the formulation and implementation of policies on sexual and reproductive health and rights was a competence of the Member States.[81]

3.3. (Limited) EU standards related to assisted human reproduction and surrogacy

There are very few EU law standards relating to assisted human reproduction (AHR). Various of the existing standards in this regard, are, moreover, non-binding. For example, in a Resolution of 1989 the European Parliament (EP) took a clearly directive stance on assisted human reproduction.[82] The EP, *inter alia*, called on Member States to limit the number of egg cells fertilised by *in vitro* fertilisation to the number that could actually be implanted. The Parliament also called for a prohibition on 'any form of genetic experiments on embryos outside the womb' and considered that the storage of frozen embryos was only to be permitted if the woman's state of health temporarily prevented her from having the embryo implanted and she had stated that she was willing to have it implanted at a later date. Heterologous insemination was, moreover, considered 'not desirable'. The Resolution set out a number of conditions that States had to meet if they did not accept the latter principles, including, *inter alia*, that only altruistic donation of gametes would be allowed.

Other examples of non-binding EU instruments and documents relating to AHR are the Opinion of the European Group on Ethics in Science and New Technologies (EGE)[83] on ethical aspects of prenatal diagnosis (PND) of the year 1996[84] and a 2008

80 *Idem*, paras. 28, 30 and 38.

81 European Parliament Resolution of 10 December 2013 on Sexual and Reproductive Health and Rights (2013/2040(INI)), online available at www.europarl.europa.eu/sides/getDoc.do?type=TA&reference=P7-TA-2013-0548&language=EN&ring=A7-2013-0426, visited 24 July 2014.

82 Resolution of the European Parliament on artificial insemination in vivo and in vitro of 16 March 1989, [1989] OJ C96/127, p.171.

83 The European Group on Ethics in Science and New Technologies (EGE) advises the European Commission on ethical questions relating to sciences and new technologies, either at the request of the Commission or on its own initiative. Commission Decision 2010/1/EU of 23 December 2009 on the renewal of the mandate of the European Group on Ethics in Science and New Technologies [2010] OJ L1/8. The Group of advisers to the European Commission on the ethical implications of biotechnology (GAEIB) as established in 1991 (see Commission, 'Promoting the competitive environment for industrial activities based on biotechnology within the Community' (Communication), SEC(91) 629 final), was followed-up by the present EGE in 1998. See also H. Bubsby et al., 'Ethical EU law? The influence of the European Group on Ethics in Science and New Technologies', 33 *European Law Review* (2008) p. 803.

84 Opinion of the group of advisers on the ethical implications of biotechnology to the European Commission, *Ethical aspects of prenatal diagnosing*, Opinion no. 6, 20 February 1996, online available at www.ec.europa.eu/archives/european_group_ethics/docs/opinion6_en.pdf, visited 5 June 2012. The Opinion only dealt with PND which was defined as allowing '[...] the examination of pregnancies at high risk of fetal anomaly or genetic disease to rule out or confirm the presence of such an anomaly or

Resolution on the demographic future of Europe, in which the European Parliament called on Member States '[...] to ensure the right of couples to universal access to infertility treatment'.[85] Furthermore, the European Institutions have commissioned and financed various research studies in the field. An example concerns a 2008 Comparative Analysis of Medically Assisted Reproduction in the EU by the European Society of Human Reproduction and Embryology (ESHRE), which was commissioned and financed by the Directorate-General for Health and Consumers of the European Commission.[86] This and other studies are referred to throughout this chapter, particularly in section 3.4, concerning statistics on CBRC.[87]

Only few binding EU standards on AHR exist. The EU has very limited competences in this field, which has everything to do with the sensitivity of the matter. This sensitivity was underlined by the CJEU in its judgment in the *Sabine Mayr* case (2008), which, as noted above (see section 3.1.1), revolved around the question of whether women who are in an advanced stage of IVF treatment are also protected against dismissal under EU law.[88] Using a wording comparable to the equally yet discussed *Brüstle* case (also section 3.1.1), the Court held that it was not called upon to broach medical or ethical questions:

> '[...], although, [...], artificial fertilisation and viable cells treatment is a very sensitive social issue in many Member States, marked by their multiple traditions and value systems, the Court is not called upon, by the present order for reference, to broach questions of a medical or ethical nature, but must restrict itself to a legal interpretation of the relevant provisions of Directive 92/85 taking account of the wording, the broad logic and the objectives of that directive.'[89]

---

disease using invasive techniques: amniocentesis, chorionic villus sampling or fetal blood sampling.' It did not deal with prenatal screening, neither preconceptional testing or screening, nor preimplantation diagnosis. It was held that these techniques introduced 'additional ethical issues which would require separate consideration.' The EGE advised that the use of PND relied on the free and informed consent of the woman or couple concerned. It stressed the importance of careful non-directive genetic counselling. In this respect, the EGE held that '[*i*]n accordance with the subsidiarity principle, the European Union [had] strive to achieve a high and comparable level of quality of the training of the professionals, namely concerning the genetic counselling, and of the services provided in different Member States.' The EGE furthermore held that PND had to always be offered on the basis of specific medical indications. It considered the choice of sex or other characteristics for nonmedical reasons an ethically unacceptable indication for PND and held that it therefore had to be prohibited. The present author is not aware of any follow-up to this EGE-Opinion.

85 European Parliament Resolution of 21 February 2008 on the demographic future of Europe, Resolution 2007/2156 INI9, P6_TA(2008)0066, www.europarl.europa.eu/sides/getDoc.do?pubRef=-//EP//TEXT+TA+P6-TA-2008-0066+0+DOC+XML+V0//EN, visited July 2014.

86 ESHRE, *Comparative Analysis of Medically Assisted Reproduction in the EU: Regulation and Technologies*, SANCO/2008/C6/051, online available at www.ec.europa.eu/health/blood.../study_eshre_en.pdf, visited July 2014.

87 Another example concerns A. Coverleyn et al., *Pre-implantation Genetic Diagnosis in Europe* (Joint Research Centre of the European Commission, January 2007), online available at www.ftp.jrc.es/EURdoc/eur22764en.pdf, visited 24 July 2014.

88 Case C-506/06 *Sabine Mayr* [2008] ECR I-01017, ECLI:EU:C:2008:119, para. 53–54.

89 *Idem*, para. 38.

Hence, from this judgment, no normative position on the issue of (access to) AHR treatment can be inferred. The judgment nonetheless had some impact on national policies in this field, as States from then on had to protect women who were in an advanced stage of IVF treatment against dismissal.

No normative stance was taken either in the *In vitro* diagnostic medical devices Directive (1998) and the EU Tissues and Cells Directive (2004) which set safety and quality requirements for *in vitro* diagnostic medical devices and AHR treatments for those Member States in which such devices are legally on the market, or in which such treatment is provided. The following subsections discuss these Directives. As yet no case law exists in which any of these Directives has been applied in a manner that has direct (substantive) relevance to the present case study.

3.3.1. The EU In vitro diagnostic medical devices Directive (1998)

Following a Commission Proposal of 1995,[90] Directive 98/79/EC on *in vitro* diagnostic medical devices was adopted in 1998.[91] It provides for harmonisation of national provisions governing the placing on the market of *in vitro* diagnostic medical devices,[92] including *in vitro* fertilisation and assisted reproduction technologies products.[93] Such harmonisation was considered desired as disparities as regards '[...] the content and scope of the laws, regulations and administrative provisions in force in the Member States with regard to the safety, health protection and performance, characteristics and authorisation procedures for *in vitro* diagnostic medical devices' were considered to create barriers to trade.[94] Such harmonisation was, however, not to affect the ability of the Member States to manage the funding of public health and sickness insurance schemes relating directly or indirectly to *in vitro* diagnostic medical devices.[95] On the basis of the Directive, Member States

90 Proposal for a European Parliament and Council Directive on in vitro diagnostic medical devices [1995] OJ C172/21.

91 Directive 98/79/EC of the European Parliament and of the Council of 27 October 1998 on in vitro diagnostic medical devices [1998] OJ L331/1 amended by Regulation (EC) No 1882/2003 of the European Parliament and of the Council of 29 September 2003.

92 Art. 1(2)(b) of the Directive defines the term '*in vitro* diagnostic medical device' as: '[...] any medical device which is a reagent, reagent product, calibrator, control material, kit, instrument, apparatus, equipment, or system, whether used alone or in combination, intended by the manufacturer to be used *in vitro* for the examination of specimens, including blood and tissue donations, derived from the human body, solely or principally for the purpose of providing information: concerning a physiological or pathological state, or concerning a congenital abnormality, or to determine the safety and compatibility with potential recipients, or to monitor therapeutic measures.'

93 European Commission, DG Health and Consumer Protection, *Guidelines for conformity assessment of including In Vitro Fertilisation (IVF) and Assisted Reproduction Technologies (ART) products*, Guidance Document Meddev 2.2/4, January 2012, p. 2, www.ec.europa.eu/health/.../meddev/2_2_4_ol_en.pdf, visited July 2014.

94 Recital No. 2 Directive 98/79/EC. Accordingly, the legal basis of the Directive was Art. 95 EC Treaty (old), concerning the approximation of laws in respect of the internal market. The harmonisation of national legislation was considered 'the only means of removing such barriers to free trade and of preventing new barriers from arising' (Recital No. 3 Directive 98/79/EC).

95 Recital 4 Directive 98/79/EC.

must monitor the security and quality of *in vitro* diagnostic medical devices, which may be placed on the market and/or put into service only if they comply with certain (design and manufacturing) requirements, when duly supplied and properly installed, maintained and used in accordance with their intended purpose.[96] Member States may not create any obstacle to the placing on the market or the putting into service within their territory of devices which meet these requirements.[97] Hence, the objective of this Directive was, and is, primarily the optimisation of trade in *in vitro* diagnostic medical devices, and not to regulate AHR treatment substantively. This purely economic objective fits in with the broader internal market objectives of the EU.

While Member States may thus not create any obstacle to the placing on the market or the putting into service within their territory of *in vitro* diagnostic medical devices which meet the above-described requirements, they may, nevertheless, regulate – or even prohibit – the *use* of such devices within their territory, probably including on moral grounds. Such a regulation or prohibition would hinder market access,[98] but could possibly be justified on grounds of protection of public morals or protection fundamental rights such as human dignity, or on grounds of public order, public health or consumer protection. This only holds, of course, as long as the national measure would also be appropriate for securing the attainment of the objective pursued and would not go beyond what would be necessary in order to attain it.[99]

3.3.2. The EU Tissues and Cells Directive (2004)

The EU Tissues and Cells Directive (2004)[100] provides for a unified framework in order to ensure high standards of safety and quality with respect to the procurement,

---

96 Art. 3 Directive 98/79/EC.

97 Art. 5(1) Directive 98/79/EC.

98 Compare Case C-110/05 *Commission* v. *Italy* [2009] ECR I-519, ECLI:EU:C:2009:66, para. 56, where the Court held that '[...] a prohibition on the use of a product in the territory of a Member State has a considerable influence on the behaviour of consumers, which, in its turn, affects the access of that product to the market of that Member State.'

99 E.g. Case C-110/05 *Commission* v. *Italy* [2009] ECR I-519, ECLI:EU:C:2009:66, para. 59.

100 The Tissues and Cells Directive is made up of three Directives: the parent Directive 2004/23/EC of the European Parliament and of the Council of 31 March 2004 on setting standards of quality and safety for the donation, procurement, testing, processing, preservation, storage and distribution of human tissues and cells [2004] OJ L102/48, which provides the framework, and two technical directives: Directive 2006/17/EC of 8 February 2006 implementing Directive 2004/23/EC of the European Parliament and of the Council as regards certain technical requirements for the donation, procurement and testing of human tissues and cells [2006] OJ L38/40 and Directive 2006/86/EC of 24 October 2006 implementing Directive 2004/23/EC of the European Parliament and of the Council as regards traceability requirements, notification of serious adverse reactions and events and certain technical requirements for the coding, processing, preservation, storage and distribution of human tissues and cells [2006] OJ L294/32. Directive 2006/17/EC was amended by Commission Directive 2012/39/EC (Commission Directive 2012/39/EU of 26 November 2012 amending Directive 2006/17/EC as regards certain technical requirements for the testing of human tissues and cells [2012] OJ L327/24), which, *inter alia*, amended one of the selection criteria and laboratory tests required for donors of reproductive cells, as set out in Annex III to Directive 2006/17/EC. As a complement to the Tissues and Cells Directive the European Society of Human Reproduction and Embryology (ESHRE) issued a revised

testing, processing, storage and distribution of tissues and cells across the EU and to facilitate exchanges thereof.[101] Such EU standards are supposed to reassure the public that tissues and cells procured in other Member States carry the same guarantees as those in their own Member States.[102] The Directive explicitly covers gametes, foetal tissue and embryonic stem cells.[103] Hence, as observed in a report of 2008:

> '[...] implementation of this Directive requires clinics in all [...] EU Member States, specialized in Medically Assisted Reproductive (MAR) technologies, including fertility treatment and pre-implantation genetic diagnosis, to adapt to stringent measures and to implement systems and operating procedures concerning accreditation, designation, authorization, licensing, inspection and registration of MAR-treatments.'[104]

Both third party gametes donors and individuals or couples from whom gametes are taken in the course of an IVF cycle are considered 'donors' within the meaning of this Directive.[105] The Directive provides that Member States must 'endeavour to ensure' voluntary and unpaid donations.[106] Donors may receive compensation, but this is '[...] strictly limited to making good the expenses and inconveniences related to the donation procedure.' Member States define the conditions under which the compensation may be granted.[107] Furthermore, as a matter of principle, donation must be anonymous.[108] In respect of donation of gametes in particular, Article 14(3) provides that

> 'Member States shall take all necessary measures to ensure that the identity of the recipient(s) is not disclosed to the donor or his family and vice versa, without prejudice to legislation in force in Member States on the conditions for disclosure, notably in the case of gametes donation.'

Following Article 9 of the Directive, Member States '[...] shall take all necessary measures to ensure that all imports of tissues and cells from third countries are undertaken by tissue establishments accredited, designated, authorised or licensed for the purpose of those activities, and that imported tissues and cells can be traced

---

version of its guidelines for good Practices in IVF clinics. These guidelines were published in 23 *Human Reproduction* (2008) p. 1253.

101 Recital 4 Directive 2004/23/EC.

102 *Idem.*

103 Recital 7 Directive 2004/23/EC.

104 ESHRE 2008, *supra* n. 86, at p. 1.

105 Following Art. 3(c) a 'donor' means 'every human source, whether living or deceased, of human tissues and cells'. 'Donation' is defined as donating human tissues or cells intended for human application (Art. 3(d)). ESHRE explained in its position paper on the Directive that in a couple, man and woman are considered donors to each other (see Annex 9 to the study).

106 Art. 12(1) and Preamble under 18 Directive 2004/23/EC.

107 Art. 12(1) Directive 2004/23/EC. The Commission considered the paying of substantial fees to obtain human egg cells to be against the principles expressed in Directive 2004/23/EC. See European Commission, Health & Consumer Protection Directorate-General, *Report on the Regulation of Reproductive Cell Donation in the European Union*, February 2006, p. 2, online available at www.ec.europa.eu/health/archive/ph_threats/human_substance/documents/tissues_frep_en.pdf, visited 23 June 2014.

108 Art. 15(1) and Preamble under 18 Directive 2004/23/EC.

from the donor to the recipient and vice versa [...]'.[109] States are free to introduce more stringent protective measures.[110] For example, they may prohibit the donation, processing or procurement of gametes, they may prohibit or restrict the import of gametes and they are free to introduce requirements for voluntary unpaid donation.[111] Lastly, the Directive is not to interfere '[...] with provisions of the Member States defining the legal term 'person' or 'individual'.'[112]

The European Society of Human Reproduction and Embryology (ESHRE) considered execution of some of the areas in the Directive problematic, due to its wide coverage in comparison to the 'very specific nature' of AHR, '[...] including numerous repeated procedures on the same patient and the usually long duration of treatments at the clinics/units.'[113] To complement the Directive, the *ESHRE Guidelines for good practice in IVF laboratories* were drafted, '[...] to promote assurance of good laboratory practice and to define the concept of qualified embryologists.'[114]

While anonymous donation is thus clearly the point of departure of the Directive,[115] it nevertheless seems to leave some room for States to give prevalence to protection of the future child's interest in knowing his or her genetic parents, by prohibiting anonymous donation within their territory.[116] Whether this also holds in the case of IVF clinics importing gametes from other States, is less clear.[117] Another open question in this regard is if it would be an 'import' within the meaning of the Directive if a woman receives a donated gametes in the course of treatment in a third country and then travels back to her home Member State. It was observed in 2006

109 Following Art. 8(4) Directive 2004/23/EC data required for full traceability shall be kept for a minimum of 30 years after clinical use.

110 Art. 4(2) Directive 2004/23/EC.

111 Art. 4(2) and (3) Directive 2004/23/EC.

112 Recital No. 12 Directive 2004/23/EC. This sentence was yet included in Recital No. 7 of the original Commission proposal for the Directive. The explanatory Memorandum to this Proposal does not give any further clarification on this point, rendering it difficult to draw any conclusions in respect of the interpretation of this consideration. Commission, 'Proposal for a Directive of the European Parliament and of the Council on setting standards of quality and safety for the donation, procurement, testing, processing, storage, and distribution of human tissues and cells', COM (2002) 319 final.

113 ESHRE position paper on the EU Tissues and Cells Directive EC/ 2004/23, November 2007, Annex 9 to ESHRE 2008, *supra* n. 86.

114 M.C. Magli et al., 'Revised guidelines for good practice in IVF laboratories', 23 *Human Reproduction* (2008) at p. 1253.

115 Art. 15(1) and Recital No. 18 of the Preamble to Directive 2004/23/EC.

116 See also Health & Consumer Protection Directorate-General of the European Commission, *Report on the Regulation of Reproductive Cell Donation in the European Union – Results of Survey -, Directorate C – Public Health and Risk Assessment C6 – Health measures*, February 2006, p. 3, online available at www.ec.europa.eu/health/archive/ph_threats/human_substance/documents/tissues_frep_en.pdf, visited June 2014.

117 While Art. 9 holds that States 'shall take all necessary measures to ensure' that the donor can be traced back, Art. 4(3) holds that the Directive 'does not affect the decisions of the Member States prohibiting the donation, procurement, testing, processing, preservation, storage, distribution or use of any specific type of human [...] cells or cells from any specified source, *including where those decisions also concern imports of the same type of human [...] cells* (emphasis added).'

that in any case not many Member States appeared to have regulated the import and export of gametes.[118]

All in all, the Directive leaves considerable room to Member States to regulate gamete donation. In a Resolution of 2005, the European Parliament called on the Commission to assess national legislations governing gamete donation.[119] The resulting Report of 2006 showed that national approaches in respect of '[...] confidentiality, anonymity and non-remuneration in the donation of reproductive cells, as well as donor compensation, consent for egg cell donations and the importation and exportation of reproductive cells' varied greatly.[120] This supports the conclusion that in respect of reproductive treatment the Tissues and Cells Directive has – in any case until that time – had little to no harmonising effect. At the same time, this is a particularly dynamic field of law and as a consequence the situation may have changed since 2006.

3.3.3. EU non-discrimination law and access to AHR treatment

Various EU Member States – including the three EU Member States included in this research[121] – restrict access to AHR treatment on grounds of age, civil status or combined gender of the couple that wishes to have access to it. Even though this may be perceived as discrimination, EU non-discrimination law as it stands provides no ground for challenging such national regulations and it seems unlikely that this will change in the near future. Under the present EU legal framework, discrimination based on age and sexual orientation is prohibited in employment, occupation and vocational training only.[122] While in 2008 a broader Equal Treatment Directive was proposed,[123] which was intended to expand the reach of EU non-discrimination law to matters like social protection, health care and access to goods and services which are available to the public,[124] reproductive rights were explicitly excluded from the

---

118 European Commission, Health & Consumer Protection Directorate-General, *Report on the Regulation of Reproductive Cell Donation in the European Union*, February 2006, p. 5, online available at www.ec.europa.eu/health/archive/ph_threats/human_substance/documents/tissues_frep_en.pdf, visited 23 June 2014. At p. 6 of this report it was held that '[f]or reproductive cells in general, no serious report or suspicion of unauthorised, illegal or otherwise suspect import/export of these human cells [had] been detected in any of the Member States.'

119 European Parliament Resolution on the trade in human egg cells (P6_TA(2005)0074).

120 European Commission, Health & Consumer Protection Directorate-General, *Report on the Regulation of Reproductive Cell Donation in the European Union*, February 2006, p. 2, online available at www.ec.europa.eu/health/archive/ph_threats/human_substance/documents/tissues_frep_en.pdf, visited 23 June 2014.

121 See Ch. 4, section 4.3.3, Ch. 5, section 5.3.3 and Ch. 6, section 6.3.2.

122 Council Directive 2000/43/EC of 29 June 2000 implementing the principle of equal treatment between persons irrespective of racial or ethnic origin [2000] OJ L180/22 and Council Directive 2000/78/EC of 27 November 2000 establishing a general framework for equal treatment in employment and occupation [2000] OJ L303/16.

123 Commission, 'Proposal for a Council Directive on implementing the principle of equal treatment between persons irrespective of religion or belief, disability, age or sexual orientation', COM (2008) 426 final. For further discussion of this proposal for a Directive, see Ch. 9, section 9.3.4.1.

124 Proposed Recital No. 17 and Art. 3(2) of COM (2008) 426 final.

scope of the Directive as proposed by the Commission. The European Economic and Social Committee (EESC) was very critical on this point, holding that access to reproductive services was an integral part of health services, in respect of which under both EU law and national law there was to be no discrimination on any grounds.[125] The EESC accordingly proposed that the Directive should apply to national laws relating to reproductive rights.[126] The European Parliament, for its part, amended the relevant proposed Article 3(2) from '[t]his Directive is without prejudice to national laws on marital or family status and reproductive rights', to the more neutral '[t]his Directive does not alter the division of competences between the European Union and its Member States.'[127] The legislative process stagnated in 2011 and it is therefore yet to be seen to what extent the Directive – if ever adopted[128] – will have a bearing on Member States' legislative choices in respect of access to reproductive care.

3.3.4. EU law and surrogacy

As matters stand today, no EU standards on surrogacy exist.[129] This, again, has everything to do with a lack of EU competences in this field. In 2011, the Commission, in answering a question by a Member of Parliament who claimed that the sensitive issue of surrogacy warranted a coordinated stance within the EU, put it as follows:

> 'The Treaty on European Union and the Treaty on the Functioning of the European Union do not give the European Union powers to adopt legislation on harmonisation of national laws on methods of reproduction with the help of surrogate mothers. It is therefore incumbent on individual Member States to regulate this matter in the light of their social and cultural traditions.'[130]

---

125 The EESC held there to be evidence of discrimination in relation to reproductive services on grounds of sexual orientation, disability and age. Opinion of the European Economic and Social Committee on the 'Proposal for a Council directive on implementing the principle of equal treatment between persons irrespective of religion or belief, disability, age or sexual orientation', para. 3.2.2.4 [2009] OJ C182/19, p. 21.

126 Opinion of the European Economic and Social Committee on the 'Proposal for a Council directive on implementing the principle of equal treatment between persons irrespective of religion or belief, disability, age or sexual orientation', para. 3.2.2.5 [2009] OJ C182/19, p. 21.

127 Accordingly, Recital No. 17 was proposed to be amended from 'This Directive is without prejudice to national laws on marital or family status, including on reproductive rights' to 'This Directive does not alter the division of competences between the European Union and its Member States, including in the area of marital and family law and health law.' European Parliament legislative resolution of 2 April 2009 on the proposal for a Council directive on implementing the principle of equal treatment between persons irrespective of religion or belief, disability, age or sexual orientation (COM (2008) 0426 – C6-0291/2008 – 2008/0140(CNS)) [2010] OJ C137E/68, pp. 75 and 81.

128 See Ch. 9, section 9.3.4.1.

129 It is reminded that this study was concluded on 31 July 2014.

130 Answer by the Commission of 10 March 2011, to written question no. 42 to the Commission by Ivo Belet (PPE) of 21 February 2011, H-000096/2011, online available at www.europarl.europa.eu/sides/getDoc.do?type=CRE&reference=20110310&secondRef=ANN-01&language=EN&detail=H-2011-000096&query=QUESTION, visited June 2014.

The Commission at the time made clear that it had no plans to explore coordination of the issue of surrogate motherhood within the EU. Instead, it referred to the work of the Hague Conference on Private International Law, of which the EU is a full member. It is in this context that the Commission follows developments on surrogate motherhood at international level (see also section 3.6.1 below).[131]

Surrogacy has incidentally been debated in European Parliament. In a Resolution of 1989, the European Parliament considered that in in general, any form of surrogate motherhood had to be rejected and that the procuring of surrogate mothers for gain had to be punishable by law.[132] While the matter was subsequently not on the table for decades, more recently the European Parliament Committee on Legal Affairs took on the issue again, thereby focussing mainly on its cross-border aspects (see 3.6.3 below). In 2013 a study came out that had been ordered by this Committee,[133] which gave a comparative overview of the Member States' legal situations in respect of surrogacy. The question was also addressed if this matter called for regulation at EU level. In this regard the conclusion was drawn that prohibiting the conception of a child through surrogacy under EU law was impossible, because no consensus on this issue consisted among the EU Member States. The report concluded that 'a global response' to surrogacy was most desirable, as 'a purely intra-EU regime' had territorial limitations.[134] In respect of possible EU action in the field, the report observed that this would have to respect the different (moral) attitudes towards surrogacy across the Member States:

> '[...] what seems clear in thinking about the future competency of the EU in this area is that Member States will retain the competency to decide on what moral grounds to act and what policy decisions to make on the permissibility of surrogacy. If an action or a legislative act was adopted, the instrument in which any harmonised response would be delivered would be required to recognise the wide spectrum of domestic law attitudes to surrogacy across states: if, as a matter of policy, a given legal system does not admit surrogacy in its domestic law, it would be inappropriate to impose on it a (European) structure of cross-border surrogacy regulation.'[135]

The report made a number of recommendations in respect of cross-border surrogacy that are discussed in section 3.6.3.2 below.

---

131 *Idem* and Answer given by Mrs Reding on behalf of the Commission on 5 May 2011, to question for written answer by Ivo Belet (PPE) to the Commission of 21 March 2011, E-002642/2011, online available at www.europarl.europa.eu/sides/getAllAnswers.do?reference=E-2011-002642&language=EN, visited June 2014.

132 Resolution of the European Parliament on artificial insemination in vivo and in vitro of 16 March 1989 [1989] OJ C96/127, p. 173.

133 For the relevant terms of reference, see www.europarl.europa.eu/tenders/2012/20120423/ANNEX%20I%20Global%20terms%20of%20reference.pdf, visited June 2014.

134 L. Brunet et al., *A Comparative Study on the Regime of Surrogacy in EU Member States*, 2013, PE 474.403, pp. 157 and 194, online available at www.europarl.europa.eu/RegData/etudes/etudes/join/2013/474403/IPOL-JURI_ET(2013)474403_EN.pdf, visited 31 March 2014.

135 *Idem*, at p. 195.

The only existing CJEU case law that relates to surrogacy concerned two joined employment cases decided by the Grand Chamber of the CJEU in 2014. In both *C.D.* and *Z.* the question was raised whether EU law provided for entitlements for female employees who, as an intended mother[136] had a child through a surrogacy agreement to paid leave equivalent to maternity leave or adoption leave.[137]

In *C.D.* the woman concerned, Ms. D., was a UK national who had concluded a surrogacy agreement in accordance with UK law. Ms D.'s partner (the intended father) provided the sperm, but the egg cell was not Ms. D.'s. Right after the child was born, Ms. D. began to mother and breastfeed the child and some months later a UK court granted her and her partner full and permanent parental responsibility for the child. Yet before the baby was born Ms. D., had made an application to her employer for paid leave under its adoption policy, but was informed that there was 'no legal right to paid time off for surrogacy'. Ms. D. subsequently brought an action before the Employment Tribunal claiming that she had been the subject of discrimination on the grounds of sex and/or pregnancy and maternity. This Tribunal made a preliminary reference to the CJEU, asking the Court whether the Pregnant Workers' Directive (Directive 92/85)[138] provided a right to receive maternity leave to an intended mother who had a baby through a surrogacy arrangement, and who was breastfeeding the child. The Tribunal also wondered whether a refusal to grant such leave constituted discrimination in breach of the Equal Treatment Directive (Directive 2006/54).[139] The CJEU joined this case with another case raising similar questions, namely the *Z.* case.

The *Z.* case concerned Irish school teacher, Ms. Z., who, together with her husband, had entered into a surrogacy agreement in California. Ms. Z. had a rare condition which had the effect that, although she had healthy ovaries and was fertile, she had no uterus and could not support a pregnancy. The child born with the surrogate mother was genetically related to both Ms. Z. and her husband, and in accordance with Californian law the child's birth certificate provided that they were the child's parents. Ms. Z. applied to the government department for leave equivalent to adoptive leave, but the department refused that application on the ground that she did not satisfy the requirements laid down by the relevant maternity or adoptive leave schemes. Ms. Z. subsequently brought an action against the government department before the Equality Tribunal, claiming that she was discriminated against on the grounds of gender, family status and disability. The Equality Tribunal stayed the proceedings and referred preliminary questions to the CJEU. It, *inter alia*, asked the

---

136 The CJEU employed the term 'commissioning mother' instead of 'intended mother' in these cases.

137 Case C-167/12 *C.D.* v. *S.T.*, *nyr*, ECLI:EU:C:2014:169 and Case C-363/12, *Z.*, *nyr*, ECLI:EU:C:2014:159.

138 Council Directive 92/85/EEC of 19 October 1992 on the introduction of measures to encourage improvements in the safety and health at work of pregnant workers and workers who have recently given birth or are breastfeeding (tenth individual Directive within the meaning of Article 16(1) of Directive 89/391/EEC) [1992] OJ L348/1.

139 Directive 2006/54/EC of the European Parliament and of the Council of 5 July 2006 on the implementation of the principle of equal opportunities and equal treatment of men and women in matters of employment and occupation (recast) [2006] OJ L204/23.

Court whether such a refusal to grant leave constituted discrimination on the ground of sex within the meaning of Directive 2006/54 and/or discrimination on grounds of disability within the meaning of the Employment Equality Framework Directive (Directive 2000/78).[140]

In both cases an Opinion was delivered by an Advocate General (AG). In *C.D.* AG Kokott held that an intended mother who had a baby through a surrogacy arrangement and who took the child into her care following birth – irrespective of whether she was also breastfeeding her child – had a right to receive maternity leave under the Pregnant Workers' Directive, as this leave was not intended solely to protect the health of workers, but also '[...] to protect the special relationship between a woman and her child over the period which follows pregnancy and childbirth'.[141] In practical terms the AG suggested that the leave of the intended mother was to amount to at least two weeks and that any other maternity leave taken by the surrogate mother had to be deducted. Kokott found no discrimination or unfavourable treatment in breach of the Equal Treatment Directive (Directive 2006/54) in the *C.D.* case. AG Wahl, who gave an Opinion in the *Z.* case,[142] even held that this Directive did not apply at all, as the differential treatment of which Ms. Z complained was not based on sex, so he held, '[...] but on the refusal of national authorities to equate the situation of a commissioning mother with that of either a woman who [had] given birth or an adoptive mother.'[143] Wahl, furthermore, found that the inability to have a child by conventional means was not linked to the capacity of the person concerned to work, and thus did not constitute 'disability' within the meaning of Directive 2000/78. The AG concluded his opinion with the following remark:

> '[...] I have considerable sympathy with the difficulties that [intended] parents undoubtedly face because of the legal uncertainty surrounding surrogacy arrangements in a number of Member States. However, I do not believe that it is for the Court to substitute itself for the legislature by engaging in constructive interpretation that would involve reading into Directives 2006/54 and 2000/78 (or, indeed Directive 92/85) something that is simply not there.'[144]

These words must have found an audience at CJEU, as the Court subsequently ruled in both cases that there was no breach of EU law. In respect of the Pregnant Workers' Directive the Court held that its objective was to encourage improvements in the health and safety at work of pregnant workers and workers who had recently given birth or who were breastfeeding. Maternity leave aimed to protect the health of the mother of the child in the particularly vulnerable situation arising from her pregnancy.[145] The

140 Council Directive 2000/78/EC of 27 November 2000 establishing a general framework for equal treatment in employment and occupation [2000] OJ L303/16.

141 Case C-167/12 *C.D.* v. *S.T.*, *nyr*, ECLI:EU:C:2013:600, Opinion of AG Kokott of 26 September 2013, para. 45.

142 Case C-363/12 *Z.*, *nyr*, ECLI:EU:C:2013:604, Opinion of AG Wahl of 26 September 2013.

143 AG Wahl used the term 'commissioning mother' instead of 'intended mother' as the CJEU would later also do. For the sake of consistency, this chapter only employs the term 'intended' in this context.

144 Case C-363/12 *Z.*, *nyr*, ECLI:EU:C:2013:604, Opinion of AG Wahl of 26 September 2013, para. 120.

145 Case C-167/12 *C.D.* v. *S.T.*, *nyr*, ECLI:EU:C:2014:169, paras. 29 and 35.

CJEU acknowledged, as AG Kokott had called to mind, that maternity leave was also intended '[...] to ensure that the special relationship between a woman and her child is protected', but held that this objective concerned only the period after pregnancy and childbirth.[146] This implied that the grant of maternity leave pursuant to the Directive presupposed that the worker concerned had been pregnant and had given birth to a child. The Court therefore concluded that Directive 92/85 did not apply to a female worker who as an intended mother had had a baby through a surrogacy arrangement, even in circumstances where she was (to be) breastfeeding the baby following the birth. The Court noted that States were not, of course, precluded by the Directive from allowing intended mothers to take maternity leave.

The CJEU further ruled that there was no discrimination on grounds of sex in breach of Directive 2006/54. There was no direct discrimination because under the applicable national legislation intended fathers were treated in the same way as intended mothers, in that they were not entitled to paid leave equivalent to maternity leave either.[147] The Court held that there was, furthermore, nothing that established that the refusal of leave at issue put female workers at a particular disadvantage compared with male workers.[148] Lastly, because an intended mother who had a baby through a surrogacy arrangement had not been pregnant, she could not, by definition, be subject to less favourable treatment related to her pregnancy. The Court thus did not equate any unfavourable treatment that is related to pregnancy with sex discrimination.[149] It furthermore did not at all refer to the general principle of equal treatment.

The question of whether the refusal to grant Ms. Z. leave constituted discrimination on grounds of disability in breach of Directive 2000/78 was also answered in the negative. In line with AG Wahl's Opinion, the Court found that the inability to have a child by conventional means did not constitute 'disability' within the meaning of the Directive, as this concept presupposed that the limitation from which the person suffered, in interaction with various barriers, could hinder that person's full and effective participation in professional life on an equal basis with other workers. This did not hold for Ms. Z., and the fact that she had been responsible for the care of the child from birth, was not such as to call that finding into question. The Court 'consequently' held it unnecessary to examine the validity of Directive 2000/78 in the light of Article 10 TFEU[150] and the Charter,[151] as the referring Tribunal had asked. It held such an examination in the light of the UN Convention on the Rights of Persons with Disabilities (the CRPD) not even possible, as the provisions of that

---

146 *Idem*, para. 36.

147 *Idem*, para. 47 and Case C-363/12 *Z.*, *nyr*, ECLI:EU:C:2014:159, para. 52.

148 Case C-167/12 C.D. v. S.T., nyr, ECLI:EU:C:2014:169, para. 49 and Case C-363/12 *Z.*, *nyr*, ECLI:EU:C:2014:159, para. 54.

149 Compare and contrast Case C-177/88 *Dekker* [1990] ECR I-3941, ECLI:EU:C:1990:383.

150 Art. 10 TFEU reads: 'In defining and implementing its policies and activities, the Union shall aim to combat discrimination based on sex, racial or ethnic origin, religion or belief, disability, age or sexual orientation.'

151 In particular Arts. 21, 26 and 34 CFR.

Convention had a programmatic character and were therefore not unconditional and sufficiently precise to have direct effect in EU law.

3.4. Cross-border movement for reproductive matters in the EU: some statistics

3.4.1. Statistics on cross-border abortions within the EU

On the basis of the existing studies, it is impossible to give a (complete) overview of the scale on which cross-border abortions take place within the EU. Not all Member States keep statistics of the number of abortions carried out within their territories on an annual basis, let alone the number of non-national or non-resident women involved in these abortions. An EU-wide study of 2011 has held that '[a] more consistent and coherent reporting of terminations of pregnancy is needed in the EU.'[152] The authors of this study explicitly underlined that data had to be collected '[...] to ascertain how often women [had] to cross country borders to access a termination of pregnancy.'[153]

It would go outside the scope of this legal study to examine whether statistics on cross-border abortions are kept for all 28 EU Member States and to analyse these statistics (if they exist at all). Such an exercise has been carried out, however, for the three jurisdictions selected for this research. Therefore, reference is made to Chapters 4, 5 and 6 where relevant statistics are discussed for Ireland, Germany and the Netherlands respectively. These three Member States have, or at least have had in the past, diverging abortion regimes, which can, to a certain extent, be considered representative of the entire EU. The statistics indicate that it is quite probable that cross-border abortions take place throughout the entire European Union. It is highly likely that all EU Member States function either as a country of origin, or a country of destination, or even both, in this respect. The existence of cross-border movement for abortions within the entire EU, can, it is submitted, therefore be presumed. The actual scale of this phenomenon can, however, only be estimated.

---

152 M. Gissler et al., 'Terminations of pregnancy in the European Union', 119 *BJOG An International Journal of Obstetrics and Gynaecology* (2012) p. 324 at p. 324.

153 *Idem*, at p. 330. The report furthermore held that '[*t*]he data for countries with restricted access to termination of pregnancy (Ireland, Malta, and Poland) did not cover terminations performed in other countries or illegal terminations, for example in private clinics. The true rates for these countries are likely to be much higher than those presented here. [...] National statistics on terminations of pregnancy in Romania, Ireland, Spain, and Greece have been reported to be too low according to national and international sources. The European statistical system should expand its quality reporting to data on terminations of pregnancy to get more detailed information on the coverage of the current reporting. [...] There are no clear guidelines for including temporary migrants and visitors in the national health information systems. For most countries, this did not affect the national figures on terminations of pregnancy. In Portugal, however, the termination rate decreased by more than one-sixth after taking out the terminations of pregnancy performed for non-resident women. The rate for the Netherlands, on the other hand, increases by one-sixth if non-residents are included in the national statistics.'

3.4.2. Statistics on CBRC within the EU

Although increasingly more comparative and international research is conducted in respect of cross-border reproductive care (CBRC),[154] no exhaustive statistics are available for the entire European Union in respect of such cross-border movement. This is so because for many States it holds that '[...] data are incomplete or not collected at all'.[155] It has been submitted that '[i]n practice, it is almost impossible to obtain an estimate of the proportion of patients exiting their own country, as no data are kept in countries of origin.'[156] The European Society of Human Reproduction and Embryology (ESHRE) nevertheless estimated in 2008 in its comparative analysis of medically assisted reproduction (MAR) in the EU that a minimum number of 11,000–14,000 services recipients were involved in CBRC within the EU every year.[157] As the ESHRE acknowledged, these numbers may be even higher in reality. Further, they may have increased since 2008 and may continue to increase in the future.

The relevant studies on CBRC in various EU Member States provide information in respect of origin, age and civil status of CBRC services recipients. They also show that reasons for crossing borders for AHR treatment vary between countries of origin and concern (predominantly) legal reasons as well as accessibility and quality of AHR treatment.[158]

3.4.3. Statistics on cross-border surrogacy within the EU

As is the case for cross-border abortions and CBRC, there are no complete or exhaustive EU-wide statistics in respect of cross-border surrogacy. As pointed out in a 2012 study commissioned by the European Parliament:

> 'Precise statistics relating to surrogacy are [...] hard to estimate. This is for a number of key reasons. First, traditional surrogacy does not necessarily require medical intervention and can thus be arranged on an informal basis between the parties concerned. Second, although gestational surrogacy does require medical intervention, officially reported statistics do not necessarily record the surrogacy arrangement but often only the IVF procedure. Third, in many countries there is simply no legal provision, regulation or licensing regime for either fertility treatment and/or surrogacy, to include commercial surrogacy in countries where such is not otherwise legally prohibited. This means that there are no formal reporting mechanisms, which can lead to a rather ad hoc collection of statistics by individual organisations, if indeed they are available at all. Finally, in

---

154 See for example F. Shenfield et al., 'Cross border reproductive care in six European countries', 25 *Human Reproduction* (2010) p. 1361 and G. Pennings et al., 'Cross-border reproductive care', 23 *Human Reproduction* (2008) p. 2182. See also Coverleyn et al. 2007, *supra* n. 87, at p. 80.

155 ESHRE 2008, *supra* n. 86, at p. 77.

156 *Idem*, Annex 6a, at p. 138.

157 *Idem*, at. p. 78.

158 *Idem*, Annex 6a, at pp. 136–137.

> countries where surrogacy is legally prohibited, those involved could potentially face criminal prosecution, thus exacerbating the difficulties of collecting relevant and accurate data.'[159]

Incidentally statistics as discussed in the previous section include reports of cases of surrogacy. Further incidental evidence proving the existence of this phenomenon can be found in case law from various (inter)national courts.[160] It must be noted, however, that such cross-border movement seems to take place primarily to States outside the EU, such as Ukraine and certain States of the United States of America, where (commercial) surrogacy is legalised.[161] Still, there is also cross-border movement taking place within Europe, for example to the UK and Greece, where surrogacy is legalised and regulated.

3.5. EU STANDARDS ON CROSS-BORDER HEALTH CARE

Even though the Treaties firmly hold that health care and social security are primarily Member State competences (see 3.2.3 above), national health care systems have not escaped considerable influence of EU law. This is mainly the result of the CJEU's internal market case law, which was triggered by the movement of workers and – later – patients throughout the Union.[162] In its case law, the CJEU has developed the '[...] basic components of a regulatory framework on cross-border healthcare services'.[163] In this exercise, the Court has always been aware of the Member States' discretion in this field:

> '[EU law] does not detract from the power of the Member States to organise their social security systems and to adopt, in particular, provisions intended to govern the organisation of health services [...]. In exercising that power, however, the Member States must comply with [EU law], in particular the provisions of the Treaty on the freedoms of movement, including freedom of establishment. Those provisions prohibit the Member States from introducing or maintaining unjustified restrictions on the exercise of those freedoms in the healthcare sector [...]. When assessing whether that obligation has been complied with, account must be taken of the fact that the health and life of humans rank foremost among the assets and interests protected by the Treaty and that it is for the Member States to determine the level of protection which they wish to afford to public health and the way in which that level is to be achieved. Since the level may vary from one Member State to another, Member States must be allowed discretion [...].'[164]

---

159 Brunet et al. 2013, *supra* n. 134, at p. 21.

160 See for example Ch.2, Ch. 4, Ch. 5 and Ch. 6.

161 Brunet et al. 2013, *supra* n. 134, at p. 2.

162 See J.W. van de Gronden, 'Richtlijn rechten van patiënten bij grensoverschrijdende gezondheidszorg: veel huiswerk voor de Nederlandse zorgwetgever?' ['Directive on rights of patients in cross-border health care: too much homework for the Dutch legislature on health?'], 59 *Tijdschrift voor Europees en economisch recht, SEW* (2001), p. 373.

163 O'Leary 2011, *supra* n. 52, at p. 522.

164 Joined Cases C-171/07 and C-172/07 *Apothekerkammer des Saarlandes a.o. and Helga Neumann-Seiwert* [2009] ECR I-4171, ECLI:EU:C:2009:316, paras. 18–19, referring to Case C-372/04

Primarily two EU law regimes, with different rationales,[165] apply to matters concerning access to, and reimbursement for, cross-border health care, of which cross-border abortions and cross-border reproductive care (CBRC) form a part. These are the Social Security Regulation[166] and the free movement rules.[167] The case law of the CJEU on the basis of the free movement rules has contributed considerably to the development of rights (and not merely privileges)[168] for patients who are crossing borders. Several of the principles as developed in the CJEU's case law on cross-border health care were subsequently codified in the Patient Mobility Directive of 2011,[169] which, in fact, now constitutes the third applicable regime. The Social Security Regulation has a primarily coordinating character: it contains no individual entitlements, but provides for equal access for services recipients from other EU Member States to entitlements provided at the national level. The Patient Mobility Directive, on the contrary, provides for (minimum) harmonisation. All in all, some have concluded that a process of 'EU competence creep' into the national health care systems is taking place.[170]

Watts [2006] ECR I-4325, ECLI:EU:C:2006:325, paras. 92 and 146; Case C-169/07 *Hartlauer* [2009] ECR I-1721, ECLI:EU:C:2009:141, paras. 29–30; Case C-322/01 *Deutscher Apothekerverband* [2003] ECR I-14887, ECLI:EU:C:2003:664, para. 103 and Case C-141/07 *Commission* v. *Germany* [2008] ECR I-6935, ECLI:EU:C:2008:492, para. 51.

165 As De la Rosa explains, the Regulation 'seeks to mitigate the negative consequences that may result from the coexistences of national systems of social protection that are rigidly different. By contrast, the system based on the freedom to provide services under the Treaty is based on a functional and finalist logic that [...] involves eliminating all obstacles "to intra-Community trade with a view to the merging of national markets into a single market".' De la Rosa 2012, *supra* n. 33, at p. 22, referring (in footnote 33) to Case 15/81 *Gaston Schul Douane Epediteur BV v. Inspecteur der Invoerrechten en Accijnzen, Roosendaal* [1982] ECR 1409, ECLI:EU:C:1982:135, para. 33.

166 Council Regulation (EEC) 1408/71 of 14 June 1971 on the application of social security schemes to employed persons and their families moving within the Community [1971] OJ L149/2, consolidated version OJ L28/1, accompanied by implementing Regulation (EEC) No 574/72. The 1971 Regulation was (partly) repealed by Regulation (EC) No 883/2004 of the European Parliament and of the Council of 29 April 2004 on the coordination of social security systems [2004] OJ L166/1, which in turn was accompanied by a 2009 implementation Regulation.

167 Arts. 28–39 and 45–66 TFEU. Palm and Glinos spoke of '[...] a dual system of access to cross-border care'. The authors discerned a third '[...] arrangement through which patient mobility takes place', namely 'the contractual route initiated bilaterally between actors in the field.' This matter will not be discussed here, as the present research focusses on State regulation in the area (see ch. 1, section 1.3.1). W. Palm and I.A. Glinos, 'Enabling patient mobility in the EU: between free movement and coordination', in: E. Mossialos et al. (eds.), *Health Systems Governance in Europe: The Role of European Union Law and Policy* (Cambridge, Cambridge University Press 2010) p. 509 at pp. 521 and 529, online available at www.euro.who.int/en/who-we-are/partners/observatory/studies/health-systems-governance-in-europe-the-role-of-eu-law-and-policy, visited June 2014.

168 Van der Mei observed that under the Regulation regime reimbursement for cross-border treatment was 'a privilege, not a right'. A.P. van der Mei, 'Zorg over de grens' ['Care across the border'], in: M. Faure and M. Peeters (eds.), *Grensoverschrijdend recht* [Cross-border law] (Antwerpen, Intersentia 2006) p. 49 at p. 49.

169 Directive 2011/24/EU of the European Parliament and of the Council of 9 March 2011 on the application of patients' rights in cross-border healthcare [2011] OJ L88/45, p. 46.

170 J. van de Gronden and E. Szyszczak, 'Conclusions: Constructing a 'Solid' Multi-Layered Health Care Edifice', in: J.W. van de Gronden et al. (eds.), *Health care and EU law* (The Hague, T.M.C. Asser Press 2011) p. 481 at p. 484.

This section sets out this general framework on cross-border health care. The relevant aspects of the EU Social Security Regulation are described in section 3.5.1. Subsequently, the case law in which the Court applied EU free movement rules to cases of cross-border health care is examined (section 3.5.2). The more recent important development in respect of cross-border health care, the Patient Mobility Directive, is discussed in section 3.5.3. As yet open questions as to the application of these regimes in cases of cross-border abortions and CBRC are raised – and to the extent possible – (tentatively) answered, in section 3.6.2.

3.5.1. The Social Security Regulation and cross-border health care

Since the early 1970s an EU regulation on the application of social security schemes to workers and their families who are moving within the European Union, has been in force.[171] Over the years it has been amended several times, most profoundly in 2004.[172] The present Regulation 883/2004 provides that EU citizens and residents, as well as their families, and, in certain cases, their survivors, may seek health care in other Member States, with the costs covered under the insurance of the State of affiliation, provided they have obtained authorisation from the competent institution.[173] The basic principle is that benefits in kind provided by the institution of one Member State on behalf of the institution of another Member State have to be fully refunded.[174]

Initially the Regulation provided that the required authorisation could not be refused where the treatment in question could not be provided for the person concerned within the territory of the Member State in which he or she resided. The CJEU interpreted this extensively by holding in *Pierik* (1978) that the duty to grant authorisation covered both cases where the treatment provided in another Member State was more effective than that which the person concerned could receive in the Member State where he or she resided and those situations in which the treatment in question could not be provided on the territory of the State of residence.[175] Out of dissatisfaction with this broad interpretation which opened the door widely to patient mobility, the EU Member States subsequently set limits to the duty to grant

171 Regulation 1408/71 [1971] OJ L149/1, consolidated version OJ L28/1, accompanied by implementing Regulation (EEC) No 574/72. Self-employed were included in the Regulation as of 1981. See H. Vollaard, 'Patiëntenmobiliteit in een Europese zorgruimte' ['Patient mobility in the European area of care'], in: A.C. Hendriks and H.-M. Th. D. ten Napel, *Volksgezondheid in een veellalige rechtsorde. Eenheid en verscheidenheid van norm en praktijk* [Public health in a multilevel jurisdiction. Unity and diversity in standards and practice] (Alphen aan de Rijn, Kluwer 2007) p. 291 at p. 296.

172 The 1971 Regulation was (partly) repealed by Regulation (EC) No 883/2004 of the European Parliament and of the Council of 29 April 2004 on the coordination of social security systems [2004] OJ L166/1, which in turn was accompanied by a 2009 implementation Regulation.

173 Arts. 2 and 22 Regulation (EC) No 883/2004. Hervey and McHale define the term 'benefits in kind' as 'health care services given free at the point of access'. Hervey and McHale 2004, *supra* n. 47, at p. 114.

174 Art. 36 Regulation (EC) No 883/2004.

175 Case 117/77 *Pierik (No.1)* [1978] ECR 825, ECLI:EU:C:1978:72, para. 22.

authorisation by amending the Regulation.[176] The present Article 22(2) of the present Regulation 883/2004 accordingly provides:

> 'An insured person who is authorised by the competent institution to go to another Member State with the purpose of receiving the treatment appropriate to his condition shall receive the benefits in kind provided, on behalf of the competent institution, by the institution of the place of stay, in accordance with the provisions of the legislation it applies, as though he were insured under the said legislation. The authorisation shall be accorded where the treatment in question is among the benefits provided for by the legislation in the Member State where the person concerned resides and where he cannot be given such treatment within a time-limit which is medically justifiable, taking into account his current state of health and the probable course of his illness.'[177]

As explained in section 3.5.2.3 below, the compatibility of this Regulation provision with the free movement rules has been questioned by some, but upheld by the CJEU.[178] Particularly important for the present case study is the rule that authorisation is to be accorded '[...] where the treatment in question is among the benefits provided for by the legislation in the Member State where the person concerned resides'.[179] Hence, if the national law has constrained or prohibited a certain treatment on ethical grounds and therefore does not provide for reimbursement under its national social security regime, no authorisation has to be accorded to an insured person who wishes to obtain such treatment abroad.[180] Accordingly, no costs have to be reimbursed either.

3.5.2. EU free movement law and cross-border health care

In the mid-1980s, the CJEU ruled that the freedom to provide services (presently Articles 56 and 57 TFEU) includes the freedom to receive medical treatment. In *Luisi and Carbone* (1984) the CJEU held:

176 Mei, van der 2006, *supra* n. 168, at. p. 53.

177 Art. 22(2) of Regulation (EC) No 883/2004.

178 Case C-56/01 *Inizan* [2003] ECR I-12403, ECLI:EU:C:2003:578. Critical in this respect was P. Cabral, 'The internal market and the right to cross border medical care', 29 *European Law Review* (2004) p. 673.

179 Art. 20(2) of Regulation (EC) No 883/2004.

180 In line herewith, already in *Pierik No. 2* (1979), the Commission emphasised in its submissions to the Court, that '[...] Member States retain certain powers in areas concerning morality. These powers could possibly be based on the reservations of sovereignty made by the Treaty in areas concerning public policy. Thus it can be accepted, on the basis of this principle that a competent institution can refuse the authorization where it concerns a treatment which is seriously contrary to the ethical rules prevailing in the Member State in question. However, since it is an exception to the Treaty, this principle must be very strictly construed, as meaning that the treatment in question must also be prohibited in the Member State in question. Thus a competent institution can refuse the authorization to undergo an abortion in another Member State only if abortion is prohibited in the competent institutions' own country.' Case 182/78 *Pierik (No.2)* [1979] ECR 1977, ECLI:EU:C:1979:142. See also Hervey and McHale 2004, *supra* n. 47, at p. 118.

> '[...] the freedom to provide services includes the freedom, for the recipients of services, to go to another Member State in order to receive a service there, without being obstructed by restrictions, even in relation to payments and that [...] persons receiving medical treatment [...] are to be regarded as recipients of services.'[181]

In this regard the Court does not distinguish between care provided in a hospital environment and care provided outside such an environment: all medical activities normally provided for remuneration constitute 'services' within the meaning of the Treaty.[182] This also holds for morally controversial, and in some Member States, even prohibited, medical activities such as AHR treatment[183] and abortion services, as follows from *Grogan* (1991).[184]

In *Grogan*, the Court did not accept that the termination of pregnancy could not be regarded as being a service, on the grounds that it was 'grossly immoral' and involved 'the destruction of the life of a human being, namely the unborn child'.[185] The CJEU considered:

> 'Whatever the merits of those arguments on the moral plane, they cannot influence the answer to the national court's first question. It is not for the Court to substitute its assessment for that of the legislature in those Member States where the activities in question are practised legally. Consequently, the answer to the national court's first question must be that medical termination of pregnancy, performed in accordance with the law of the State in which it is carried out, constitutes a service within the meaning of Article 60 [presently Article 56 TFEU] of the Treaty.'[186]

Hence, the fact that abortion was (and is) prohibited in Ireland in almost all situations, did (and does) not remove it from the scope of the free movement rules, because there were (and are) other Member States where abortion was (and is) legal.[187] Decisive

---

181 Joined Cases 286/82 and 26/83 *Luisi and Carbone* v. *Ministero del Tesoro* [1984] ECR 377, ECLI:EU:C:1984:35, para. 16.

182 Case C-368/98 *Vanbraekel* [2001] ECR I-5363, ECLI:EU:C:2001:400, para. 41; Case C-157/99 *Geraets-Smits and Peerbooms* [2001] ECR I-5473, ECLI:EU:C:2001:404, para. 53, referring to Joined Cases 286/82 and 26/83 *Luisi and Carbone* v. *Ministero del Tesoro* [1984] ECR 377, ECLI:EU:C:1984:35, para. 16, Case C-159/90 *Grogan* [1991] ECR I-4685, ECLI:EU:C:1991:378, para. 18, and Case C-158/96 *Kohll* [1998] ECR I-1931, ECLI:EU:C:1998:171, paras. 29 and 51.

183 See also Hervey and McHale 2004, *supra* n. 47, at p. 150, who conclude that all forms of assisted conception and the service of surrogate motherhood, if remunerated, fall within the scope of EU law. However, goods and services that are prohibited in *all* EU Member States are excluded from the scope of the free movement rules. Compare Case C-137/09 *Josemans* [2010] ECR I-13019, ECLI:EU:C:2010:774.

184 Case C-159/90 *Grogan* [1991] ECR I-4685, ECLI:EU:C:1991:378, paras. 20 and 21.

185 This argument was put forward by *the Society for the Protection of Unborn Children Ireland Ltd*, the plaintiff in the main proceedings. See subsection 3.6.2.1 below.

186 Case C-159/90 *Grogan* [1991] ECR I-4685, ECLI:EU:C:1991:378, paras. 20 and 21. Advocate General Van Gerven had come to the same conclusion, which he formulated as follows: 'The medical operation, normally performed for remuneration, by which the pregnancy of a woman coming from another Member State is terminated in compliance with the law of the Member State in which the operation is carried out is a (cross-border) service within the meaning of Article 60 of the EEC Treaty.' Case C-159/90 *Grogan* [1991] ECR I-4685, ECLI:EU:C:1991:378, Opinion of AG Van Gerven, para. 10.

187 *Idem*.

is, further, whether the activity is 'normally provided for remuneration'.[188] For the fulfilment of this requirement, the financing basis of the national health system does not matter.[189] From the perspective of the freedom to provide services, the Court has seen no reason to draw a distinction '[...] by reference to whether the patient pays the costs incurred and subsequently applies for reimbursement thereof or whether the sickness fund or the national budget pays the provider directly.'[190] As phrased by the CJEU in *Geraets-Smits and Peerbooms* (2001):

> 'It must be accepted that a medical service provided in one Member State and paid for by the patient should not cease to fall within the scope of the freedom to provide services guaranteed by the Treaty merely because reimbursement of the costs of the treatment involved is applied for under another Member State's sickness insurance legislation which is essentially of the type which provides for benefits in kind. Furthermore, the fact that hospital medical treatment is financed directly by the sickness insurance funds on the basis of agreements and pre-set scales of fees is not in any event such as to remove such treatment from the sphere of services within the meaning of Article 60 of the Treaty [now Article 57 TFEU].'[191]

While some criticised that this ruling was '[...] hard to reconcile with the traditional case law on the notion of remuneration within the meaning of the Treaty',[192] the Court pursued the approach taken in this case in later case law and has brought all sorts of national health systems within the scope of the free movement rules, such as a national social security framework,[193] a benefits-in-kind system,[194] and a reimbursement system. In *Watts* (2006) the Court also brought medical services provided under a national health service system, within the scope of EU law.[195]

Given that medical activities are 'services' within the meaning of the Treaty – and hence the free movement rules apply – the next question to be answered is to what extent States may restrict the freedom to receive and provide cross-border health services, for instance by subjecting access to, and reimbursement for, such treatment to certain conditions. The first question that needs to be answered in this regard is

188 More generally the Court has held that the '[...] special nature of certain services does not remove them from the ambit of the fundamental principle of freedom of movement'. Case C-158/96 *Kohll* [1998] ECR I-1931, ECLI:EU:C:1998:171, para. 20. See also Palm and Glinos 2010, *supra* n. 167, at p. 517.

189 *Inter alia* Case C-372/04 *Watts* [2006] ECR I-4325, ECLI:EU:C:2006:325. As Hervey and McHale explained '[...] remuneration need not come directly from the recipient of the services.' Hervey and McHale 2004, *supra* n. 47, at p. 120, referring (in footnote 64) to Case 352/85 *Bond van Adverteerders* [1988] ECR 2085, ECLI:EU:C:1988:196.

190 Case C-385/99 *Müller-Fauré and van Riet* [2003] ECR I-4509, ECLI:EU:C:2003:270, para. 103. See also Cabral 2004, *supra* n. 178, at p. 676.

191 Case C-157/99 *Geraets-Smits and Peerbooms* [2001] ECR I-5473, ECLI:EU:C:2001:404, paras. 55–56.

192 Cabral 2004, *supra* n. 178, at p. 677. The author alleged that 'treatment provided in the framework of a benefits-in kind system does not include the element of remuneration necessary to come within the scope of the Treaty's free movement of services provisions'. See also V. Hatzopoulos, 'Killing National Health and Insurance Systems but Healing Patients? The European Market for Health Care after the Judgments of the ECJ in Vanbraekel and Peerbooms', 39 *CMLRev.* (2002) p. 683 at pp. 705–720.

193 Case C-158/96 *Kohll* [1998] ECR I-1931, ECLI:EU:C:1998:171.

194 Case C-157/99 *Geraets-Smits and Peerbooms* [2001] ECR I-5473, ECLI:EU:C:2001:404, para. 55.

195 Case C-372/04 *Watts* [2006] ECR I-4325, ECLI:EU:C:2006:325.

whether there is indeed a restriction. While this test is generally a very generous one,[196] in the quoted *Grogan* case,[197] the Court answered this question in the negative. It concluded that the Irish prohibition on the distribution of information about foreign abortion services, constituted no restriction within the meaning of the Treaty, as it considered the link between the activity of the defendant student associations and medical terminations of pregnancies carried out in clinics in another Member State to be 'too tenuous'.[198] Because of its direct relevance for the present case study this judgment will be discussed more elaborately in the following sub-section.

3.5.2.1. A restriction of free movement? – The Grogan case

The *Grogan* case concerned a suit by *the Society for the Protection of Unborn Children Ireland Ltd* ('SPUC') against Stephen Grogan and 14 other officers of student associations who distributed free handbooks containing information about abortion services available in England.[199] The Irish High Court made a reference to the CJEU[200] for a preliminary ruling on three questions: (1) whether abortion was a 'service' within the meaning of the (then) EEC Treaty; (2) if so, whether the prohibition on distribution of information regarding those services constituted a restriction within the meaning of Article 59 of the Treaty; and (3) if so, whether such a restriction could be justified under Community law.

After having established that the termination of pregnancy was a service within the meaning of the Treaty (see above), the CJEU answered the second question in the negative. It concluded that the link between the activity of the defendant student associations and medical terminations of pregnancies carried out in clinics in another Member State was 'too tenuous' for the prohibition on the distribution of information to be capable of being regarded as a restriction within the meaning of (then) Article 59 of the Treaty.[201] The Court noted that the information concerning foreign abortion providers was '[…] not distributed on behalf of an economic operator established in another Member State.' The Court concluded that, on the contrary, the information constituted a manifestation of freedom of expression and of the freedom to impart and receive information which was independent of the economic activity carried on by clinics established in another Member State.[202] Despite this finding, the Court did not assess the claim of the student associations that the prohibition interfered with their freedom of expression (Article 10 ECHR), as the Court considered itself not to

196 T.K. Hervey, 'The Current Legal Framework on the Right to Seek Health Care Abroad in the European Union', 9 *The Cambridge Yearbook of European Legal Studies* (2007) p. 261 at p. 270. As Hervey explained, '[t]he essence of the Court's approach is to consider the potential for the restriction to inhibit inter-Member State provision of services.'

197 Case C-159/90 *Grogan* [1991] ECR I-4685, ECLI:EU:C:1991:378.

198 *Idem*, para. 24.

199 See also Ch. 5.

200 At the time, the Court of Justice of the European Communities.

201 Presently Art. 56 TFEU.

202 Case C-159/90 *Grogan* [1991] ECR I-04685, ECLI:EU:C:1991:378, para. 26.

have jurisdiction '[…] with regard to national legislation lying outside the scope of Community law'.[203] In conclusion the Court ruled:

> '[…] it is not contrary to Community law for a Member State in which medical termination of pregnancy is forbidden to prohibit students associations from distributing information about the identity and location of clinics in another Member State where voluntary termination of pregnancy is lawfully carried out and the means of communicating with those clinics, where the clinics in question have no involvement in the distribution of the said information.'[204]

Advocate General Van Gerven had earlier taken another approach in his Opinion in this case. He had argued that the right to receive services in another Member State encompassed the right to receive, unimpeded, information in one's own Member State about providers of services in another Member State and about how to communicate with them. Van Gerven had considered that the Irish prohibition on distribution of abortion information constituted a restriction of this freedom.[205] Accordingly he had examined if this restriction could be justified. Firstly he had held it to be 'undeniable' that the prohibition had been promoted by an objective which had been regarded in Ireland as an imperative requirement of public interest:

> 'The protection of the unborn enshrined in the national Constitution (and the prohibition of abortion inherent therein) and likewise the resultant need to prevent abortions – naturally only within the jurisdiction of the Member State concerned – by prohibiting the distribution of information thereon in its territory are regarded in that Member State as forming part of the basic principles of society.'[206]

Van Gerven had accepted such an objective to be justified under Community law, since it related '[…] to a policy choice of a moral and philosophical nature the assessment of which [was] a matter for the Member States' and in respect of which they were entitled to invoke the ground of public policy referred to in the Treaty. He had continued:

> 'Although the scope of the concept of public policy "cannot be determined unilaterally by each Member State without being subject to control by the institutions of the Community", nevertheless, as "the particular circumstances justifying recourse to the concept of public policy may vary from one country to another", it is necessary "to allow the competent national authorities an area of discretion within the limits imposed by the Treaty and the provisions adopted for its implementation". There can, in my estimation, be no doubt that values which, in view of their incorporation in the Constitution, number among "the fundamental values to which a nation solemnly declares that it adheres" fall within the

---

203 *Idem*, para. 31.

204 *Idem*, para. 32.

205 Van Gerven considered that although the national measure was not discriminatory, it could overtly or covertly, actually or potentially, impede intra-Community trade in services. Case C-159/90 *Grogan* [1991] ECR I-4685, ECLI:EU:C:1991:249, Opinion of AG Van Gerven, para. 21.

206 *Idem*, para. 26.

> sphere in which each Member State possesses an area of discretion "in accordance with its own scale of values and in the form selected by it".'[207]

Having accepted that there was a public interest pursued with the measure, Van Gerven next had assessed if the Irish prohibition had been proportionate. He had found that the Irish prohibition had not banned all information but only information which assisted pregnant women to terminate unborn life. Therefore, Van Gerven had considered the restriction not disproportionate.[208] He had noted that his conclusion would have been different however, in respect of, for example, a ban on pregnant women going abroad or a rule under which they would be subjected to unsolicited examinations upon their return from abroad.

The Court's ruling in the *Grogan* case met with both considerable critique and comprehension in legal scholarship. It has been held that the judgment led to '[...] a great deal of speculation with respect to the extent to which the (essentially economic) principles of EU law [had to] be permitted to undermine ethical principles, especially those enshrined in national constitutions.'[209] By some, it was argued that the CJEU had unjustifiably made market freedoms triumph over human rights,[210] but others disagreed.[211] It was often argued that the judgment was at variance with the at the time existing line of case law.[212] Possibly the Court's restrained approach was influenced by the sensitivity of the subject concerned.[213] At the same time, as pointed out by many, and as feared by the Irish government, it followed from the judgment that if a direct link with the abortion providers could be established in a different case, Community law (now EU law) could potentially override the relevant Article 40.3.3° of the Irish Constitution.[214] Hence, it was argued that '[...] the message

---

207 *Idem*, para. 26, referring (in footnote 41) to Case 30–77 *Regina* v. *Bouchereau* [1977] ECR 1999, ECLI:EU:C:1977:172, paras. 33 and 34; Case 41/74 *Van Duyn* v. *Home Office* [1974] ECR 1337, ECLI:EU:C:1974:133; Case C-379/87 *Groener* v. *Minister of Education* [1989] ECR 3967, ECLI:EU:C:1989:197, Opinion of AG Darmon, para. 21, and Case 121/85 *Conegate Limited* v. *HM Customs & Excise* [1986], ECR 1007, ECLI:EU:C:1986:114, para. 14.

208 *Idem*, para. 35. According to De Búrca this conclusion could well have represented 'his [...] substantive reconciliation within Community law of competing moral choices and human rights'. G. de Búrca, 'Fundamental Human Rights and the Reach of EC law', 13 *Oxford Journal of Legal Studies* (1993) p. 283 at p. 300.

209 Hervey and McHale 2004, *supra* n. 47, at p. 152. The authors held that this debate went 'to the heart of matters central to the EU's "constitutional" law [...].'

210 A.L. Young, 'The Charter, Constitution and Human Rights: is this the Beginning or the End for Human Rights Protections by Community Law?', 11 *European Public Law* (2005) p. 219 at p. 227, referring (in footnote 51) to, *inter alia*, D.R. Phelan, 'Right to life of the Unborn v Promotion of Trade in Services: The European Court of Justice and the Normative Shaping of the European Union', 55 *Modern Law Review* (1992), pp. 670–689.

211 E.g. De Búrca 1993, *supra* n. 208, at pp. 299–300.

212 E.g. S. O'Leary, 'The Court of Justice as reluctant constitutional adjudicator: an examination of the abortion information case', 17 *European Law Review* (1992) p. 138, particularly at p. 146.

213 Lawson pointed out that 'virtually all commentators of the judgment' noted that the CJEU had 'evaded giving a substantive ruling on a sensitive issue'. R.A. Lawson, 'The Irish Abortion Cases: European Limits to National Sovereignty?', 1 *European Journal of Health Law* (1994) p. 167 at p. 173.

214 See A.-M.E.W. Sterling, 'The European Union and Abortion Tourism: Liberalizing Ireland's Abortion Law', 20 *Boston College International & Comparative Law Review* (1997) p. 385 at p. 392; B. Mercurio, 'Abortion in Ireland: An Analysis of the Legal Transformation Resulting from Membership in the

left to Ireland as to the future acceptability of restrictions on abortion-related mobility was nevertheless clear'.[215] By some *Grogan* was even perceived as a triumph for the woman to choose.[216]

As elucidated in Chapter 5 after the *Grogan* case, the Irish government successfully lobbied for the adoption of Protocol 17 to the Maastricht Treaty. This Protocol provided:

> 'Nothing in the Treaty on the European Union or in the Treaties establishing the European Communities or in the Treaties or Acts modifying or supplementing those Treaties shall affect the application in Ireland of Article 40.3.3° of the Constitution of Ireland.'[217]

Because of consternation following the so-called *X Case* (see Chapter 5, section 5.2.2),[218] the Irish government, soon after the adoption of the Protocol, settled for a Solemn Declaration to the effect that Protocol 17 would not '[...] limit freedom either to travel between Member States or [...] to obtain or make available in Ireland information relating to services lawfully available in Member States'.[219] Some argued that consequentially, it seemed that the status of EU law *vis-à-vis* Irish abortion law had not changed very much at all.[220] The same text as in Protocol 17

European Union', 11 *Tulsa Journal of International and Comparative Law* (2003) p. 141 at p. 160; B. Moriarty and A.-M. Mooney Cotter (eds.), *Human rights law* (Oxford, Oxford University Press 2004) p. 18 and F. Fabbrini, *Fundamental rights in Europe, Challenges and Transformations of a Multilevel System in Comparative Perspective* (F. Fabrinni © 2012) p. 213. See also Ch. 5, section 5.2.1.1.

215 C. Hilson, 'The Unpatriotism of the Economic Constitution? Rights to Free Movement and their Impact on National and European Identity', 14 *European Law Journal* (2008) p. 186 at p. 189.

216 Young 2005, *supra* n. 210, at p. 230.

217 Protocol Annexed to the Treaty On European Union, signed at Maastricht on 7 February 1992 [1992] OJ C191/1, p. 94.

218 See, *inter alia*, F. Murphy, 'Maastricht: implementation in Ireland', 19 *European Law Review* (1994) p. 94 at pp. 94–95.

219 Declaration of the High Contracting Parties to the Treaty on European Union Treaty on European Union, signed at Maastricht on 7 February 1992 [1992] OJ C191/1, p. 109. The relevant part of the Declaration reads: 'That it was and is their intention that the Protocol shall not limit freedom to travel between Member States or, in accordance with conditions which may be laid down, in conformity with Community law, by Irish legislation, to obtain or make available in Ireland information relating to services lawfully available to Member States.' Some uncertainty as to the legal status of this declaration existed. Sterling held that it neither appeared to be legally binding on the CJEU, nor to serve as anything more than an interpretive guide for the courts (Sterling 1997, *supra* n. 214, at p. 396, referring to A. Eggert and B. Rolston, 'Ireland', in B. Rolston and A. Eggert (eds.), *Abortion in the new Europe, A comparative handbook* (Westport, Greenwood Press 1994) p. 168 and D. Curtin, 'Case note to ECJ C-159/90', 29 *CML Rev* (1992) p. 585 at pp. 602–03). Buckley called it 'nothing more than a statement of political intent' (A.M. Buckley, 'The primacy of democracy over natural law in Irish abortion law: an examination of the C case' 9 *Duke Journal of Comparative & International law* (1998) p. 275 at p. 289). Lawson observed that to the extent that the Protocol had legal effect, it only related to the application *in Ireland* of Art. 40.3.3° (Lawson 1994, *supra* n. 213, at p. 181). See D.A. MacLean, 'Can the EC kill the Irish unborn?; An investigation of the European Community's ability to impinge on the moral sovereignty of Member States', 28 *Hofstra Law Review* (1999) p. 527 at p. 560; G. Hogan and G. Whyte, *J.M. Kelly, The Irish Constitution* (Dublin, LexisNexis Butterworths 2003) p. 1506 and Mercurio 2003, *supra* n. 214, at pp. 164–165.

220 Fabbrini 2012, *supra* n. 214, at p. 214 referring to C. Forder, 'Abortion: A Constitutional Problem in European Perspective', 1 *Maastricht Journal of European and Comparative Law* (1994) p. 56 at p. 64.

was annexed to the defeated Treaty establishing a Constitution for Europe[221] and is now annexed as Protocol 35 to the Lisbon Treaty.[222] By virtue of Article 51 TEU the Protocols and Annexes to the Treaties form an integral part thereof and consequently the CJEU has jurisdiction to interpret them. As yet, the Irish Protocol has not been invoked in any proceedings before the CJEU and it remains to be seen whether it ever will be invoked.[223]

In cross-border health care cases of a later date and of a morally less controversial nature than the *Grogan* case, the Court had less difficulty in finding a restriction of free movement. In the ground-breaking cases of *Kohll* and *Decker* (both 1998) the CJEU ruled that refusal to reimburse treatment obtained abroad and a requirement of prior authorisation for such treatment, constituted a restriction of the freedom to receive services.[224] The Court held that:

> '[...] such rules deter insured persons from approaching providers of medical services established in another Member State and constitute, for them and their patients, a barrier to freedom to provide services.'[225]

Hence, any refusal to reimburse treatment obtained abroad and any requirement of prior authorisation for such treatment constitutes a restriction of the freedom to receive services. The fact that the treatment is not legal in the state of affiliation, or not among the benefits provided for by the legislation of that State, has no bearing on this finding.

3.5.2.2. Justification of restrictions of free movement

It is recalled that restrictions of the freedom to receive services can be justified if they fulfil the four so-called *Gebhard* conditions: (1) they must be applied in a non-discriminatory manner; (2) they must be justified by imperative requirements in the general interest; (3) they must be suitable for securing the attainment of the objective which they pursue; and (4) they must not go beyond what is necessary in order to attain it.[226]

---

221 Protocol 31 on Art. 40.3.3 of the Constitution of Ireland, to the (never adopted) Treaty establishing a Constitution for Europe and to the Treaty establishing the European Atomic Energy Community [2004] OJ C310/1, p. 377.

222 Protocol 35 on Art. 40.3.3 of the Constitution of Ireland to the Treaty on European Union and to the Treaty on the Functioning of the European Union and to the Treaty establishing the European Atomic Energy Community. Protocols [2008] OJ C115/201, p. 321.

223 By contrast, Joined Cases C-411/10 and C-493/10 *N.S.* v. *Secretary of State for the Home Department* [2011] ECR I-13905, ECLI:EU:C:2011:865, on Protocol (No 30) on the application of the Charter to Poland and to the United Kingdom (Protocols [2010] OJ C83/201, p. 313).

224 Case C-158/96 *Kohll* [1998] ECR I-1931, ECLI:EU:C:1998:171 and Case C-120/95 *Decker* [1990] ECR I-3941, ECLI:EU:C:1990:383. The German Minister of Health, for example, reportedly declared not to follow-up *Decker* and *Kohll*. Vollaard 2007, *supra* n. 171, at p. 298.

225 Case C-158/96 *Kohll* [1998] ECR I-1931, ECLI:EU:C:1998:171, para. 35.

226 Case C-55/94 *Gebhard* [1995] ECR I-4165, ECLI:EU:C:1995:411, para. 37.

The first *Gebhard* criterion is often fulfilled.[227] Further, in free movement cases, it is a matter of EU law, not national law, whether a justifiable public interest worthy of protection is present.[228] In cross-border health care cases, the CJEU has accepted various overriding (imperative or mandatory) reasons in the general interest capable of justifying a barrier to the principle of freedom to provide services. This goes, for example, for the possible risk of seriously undermining a social security system's financial balance.[229] The objective of maintaining a balanced medical and hospital service open to all – even if it is intrinsically linked to the method of financing the social security system – may also fall under grounds of public health under the present Article 52 TFEU,[230] in so far as it contributes to the attainment of a high level of health protection.[231] The Court has further held that Article 52 TFEU permits Member States to restrict the freedom to provide medical and hospital services, in so far as the maintenance of treatment capacity or medical competence on national territory is essential for the public health, and even the survival of the population.[232]

Until today, there has not been a case before the CJEU in which a Member State refused patients from other Member States access to treatment for reasons of overburdening of its national health services. Therefore it cannot be conclusively answered (yet) if the Court would accept such a ground for restriction of free movement rights.[233]

The following subsections discuss the conditions under which the Court has accepted prior authorisation requirements and reimbursement refusals as justified restrictions of free movement rules. Except for the above-discussed *Grogan* case – in which the CJEU concluded that the freedom to receive and provide services was not restricted – there is to date no case law in which the free movement rules have been applied to cases concerning abortion services or AHR treatment, in particular.

227 Measures which are discriminatory on grounds of nationality can be justified only under the grounds set out in the Treaty (e.g. in Art. 52 TFEU). In the case of non-discriminatory measures, public grounds may be based on the Treaty provisions, or on other objective public interests, as accepted by the CJEU under its *rule of reason* doctrine.

228 Hervey 2007, *supra* n. 196, at p. 273.

229 Case C-158/96 *Kohll* [1998] ECR I-1931, ECLI:EU:C:1998:171, para. 41; Case C-157/99 *Geraets-Smits and Peerbooms* [2001] ECR I-5473, ECLI:EU:C:2001:404, para. 72; and Case C-385/99 *Müller-Fauré and Van Riet* [2003] ECR I-4509, ECLI:EU:C:2003:270, para. 73.

230 Art. 56 EC Treaty (*old*).

231 Case C-158/96 *Kohll* [1998] ECR I-1931, ECLI:EU:C:1998:171, para. 50; Case C-157/99 *Geraets-Smits and Peerbooms* [2001] ECR I-5473, ECLI:EU:C:2001:404, para. 73; and Case C-385/99 *Müller-Fauré and Van Riet* [2003] ECR I-4509, ECLI:EU:C:2003:270, para. 67.

232 Case C-158/96 *Kohll* [1998] ECR I-1931, ECLI:EU:C:1998:171, para. 51; Case C-157/99 *Geraets-Smits and Peerbooms* [2001] ECR I-5473, ECLI:EU:C:2001:404, para. 74; and Case C-385/99 *Müller-Fauré and Van Riet* [2003] ECR I-4509, ECLI:EU:C:2003:270, para. 67.

233 Here, an argument in the affirmative could be made by applying with analogy the *Bressol* judgment. In this case the CJEU ruled that a limitation on enrolment by non-resident students in certain university courses in the public health field is, in principle, precluded by EU law. It held such a limitation to be compatible with EU law, however, if proved justified with regard to the protection of public health. Case C-73/08 *Bressol and Others* [2010] ECR I-2735, ECLI:EU:C:2010:181.

3.5.2.3. Conditions for authorisation requirements in respect of scheduled care

Initially the finding of a restriction in *Kohll* (1998) appeared difficult to reconcile with the Social Security Regulation under which prior authorisation is a basic principle (see above). The Court tried to alleviate this tension, by interpreting the relevant Regulation provisions in line with the free movement rules.[234] Put differently, the Court has '[...] cleverly facilitated the coexistence of the two systems by emphasizing their complementary nature as much as possible'.[235] It held the relevant Article 22 of the Regulation in itself to be compatible with the free movement rules. National authorisation systems based on Article 22 of the Regulation were, however, subject to certain conditions.[236]

Firstly, the Court has made a distinction between hospital and non-hospital care.[237] Restrictions of the freedom to provide and receive services in the form of prior authorisation requirements cannot be justified for non-hospital care.[238] This is, however, different in respect of hospital care, which, by nature, requires planning:

> '[...] by comparison with medical services provided by practitioners in their surgeries or at the patient's home, medical services provided in a hospital take place within an infrastructure with, undoubtedly, certain very distinct characteristics. It is thus well known that the number of hospitals, their geographical distribution, the mode of their organisation and the equipment with which they are provided, and even the nature of the medical services which they are able to offer, are all matters for which planning must be possible.'[239]

The nucleus of this ruling is thus the 'planning' aspect and not so much the exact place where the treatment takes place.[240] What is crucial is whether the objects of ensuring sufficient and permanent access to a balanced range of high-quality and up-to-date treatment, while controlling costs and avoiding, so far as possible, any waste of

---

[234] Case C-56/01 *Inizan* [2003] ECR I-12403, ECLI:EU:C:2003:578.

[235] De la Rosa 2012, *supra* n. 33, at p. 22.

[236] Cabral 2004, *supra* n. 178, at pp. 679–680.

[237] Hospital care may include private hospitals. In *Stamatelaki* (2007) the Court held an absolute exclusion of reimbursement by a national social security institution of the costs occasioned by treatment of persons insured with it in private hospitals in another Member State, to be incompatible with the freedom to provide and receive services. According to the CJEU less restrictive measures could be adopted, such as a prior authorisation scheme which complies with the requirements imposed by Union law and, if appropriate, the determination of scales for reimbursement of the costs of treatment. Case C-444/05 *Stamatelaki* [2007] ECR I-3185, ECLI:EU:C:2007:231.

[238] Both *Kohll* and *Decker* concerned so-called extramural care. *Kohll* concerned dental care, while *Decker* concerned the purchase of a pair of spectacles with corrective lenses.

[239] Case C-157/99 *Geraets-Smits and Peerbooms* [2001] ECR I-5473, ECLI:EU:C:2001:404, para. 76.

[240] In *Müller-Fauré and van Riet* the Court emphasised how difficult it is to distinguish 'hospital services' from 'non-hospital services' and pointed out that services provided in a hospital environment that could also be provided by a practitioner in his surgery or in a health centre could, for that reason, be placed on the same footing as non-hospital services. Case C-385/99 *Müller-Fauré and van Riet* [2003] ECR I-4509, ECLI:EU:C:2003:270, para. 75. In *Commission* v. *France*, the Court confirmed that planning considerations may also prove relevant for medical treatment provided outside a hospital setting. Case C-512/08 *Commission* v. *France* [2010] ECR I-8833, ECLI:EU:C:2010:579, para. 34.

financial, technical and human resources can be guaranteed.[241] Therefore, it is more appropriate to speak of 'scheduled' (generally hospital) care and 'unscheduled' care. For scheduled care a prior authorisation requirement may, in principle, be justified. However, it is nevertheless necessary that the conditions attached to the grant of such authorisation are justified in light of the relevant public imperatives, that they do not exceed what is objectively necessary for that purpose and that the same result cannot be achieved by less restrictive rules.[242]

In the *Geraets-Smits en Peerbooms* (2001)[243] and *Müller-Fauré* (2003)[244] cases the Court subjected national systems which set a prior authorisation requirement for hospital care to certain conditions.[245] Authorisation can be refused on the ground of lack of medical necessity only if the same or equally effective treatment can be obtained without undue delay within the insured person's own health care system. Hence, foreign treatment options may alleviate the burden of long waiting lists. Further, if national legislation subjects reimbursement for medical treatment obtained abroad to the condition that the treatment is regarded as 'normal in the professional circles concerned', authorisation cannot be refused on that ground where it appears that the treatment concerned is sufficiently tried and tested by international medical science.[246] Prior administrative authorisation schemes must, furthermore, provide for certain procedural guarantees. For example, the national authorities' discretion must be based on 'objective, non-discriminatory criteria which are known in advance'.[247] Further, a procedural system must be in place, '[...] which is easily accessible and capable of ensuring that a request for authorisation will be dealt with objectively and impartially within a reasonable time'. Refusals to grant authorisation must be capable of being challenged in judicial or quasi-judicial proceedings.[248]

241 Case C-512/08 *Commission* v. *France* [2010] ECR I-8833, ECLI:EU:C:2010:579, para. 33, referring to Case C-157/99 *Geraets-Smits and Peerbooms* [2001] ECR I-5473, ECLI:EU:C:2001:404, paras. 76–81; Case C-385/99 *Müller-Fauré and van Riet* [2003] ECR I-4509, ECLI:EU:C:2003:270, paras. 76–81, and Case C-372/04 *Watts* [2006] ECR I-4325, ECLI:EU:C:2006:325, paras. 108–110.

242 E.g. Case C-173/09 *Elchinov* [2010] ECR I-8889, ECLI:EU:C:2010:581, para. 44.

243 Case C-157/99 *Geraets-Smits and Peerbooms* [2001] ECR I-5473, ECLI:EU:C:2001:404, para. 54. See Hatzopoulos 2002, *supra* n. 192, at pp. 705–720.

244 Case C-385/99 *Müller-Fauré and Van Riet* [2003] ECR I-4509, ECLI:EU:C:2003:270.

245 As Cabral explained: 'While prior authorisation systems for hospital care are thus in principle compatible with Community law, Member States must, however, comply with a certain number of conditions with regard to the way these systems are organised and operated in practice.' Cabral 2004, *supra* n. 178, at p. 683.

246 Hervey and McHale argued that '[p]articularly with relatively new treatments', there was 'likely to be considerable room for difference among professional opinion'. The authors warned that patients were likely to exploit this. Hervey and McHale 2004, *supra* n. 47, at pp. 136–137.

247 Case C-173/09 *Elchinov* [2010] ECR I-8889, ECLI:EU:C:2010:581, para. 44.

248 *Inter alia*, Case C-157/99 *Geraets-Smits and Peerbooms* [2001] ECR I-5473, ECLI:EU:C:2001:404, para. 90; Case C-385/99, *Müller-Fauré and van Riet* [2003] ECR I-4509, ECLI:EU:C:2003:270, para. 85 and Case C-372/04 *Watts* [2006] ECR I-4325, ECLI:EU:C:2006:325, para. 116.

3.5.2.4. *The amount and the kind of costs to be reimbursed*

Under the Social Security Regulation the amount to be reimbursed is determined on the basis of the legislation of the Member State in which the treatment is provided.[249] Even if the country of affiliation provides for a higher amount to be reimbursed, no more than the actual costs of treatment is reimbursed. On the basis of the free movement rules, the CJEU has ruled, however, that if the reimbursement of costs incurred for hospital services provided in a Member State of stay, calculated under the rules in force in that State, is less than the amount which application of the legislation in force in the Member State of affiliation would afford to a person receiving hospital treatment in that State, additional reimbursement covering that difference must be granted to the insured person by the competent institution.[250] An exception is made for so-called 'unscheduled' hospital treatment, obtained by an insured person '[...] whose travel to another Member State is for reasons relating to tourism or education, for example, and not to any inadequacy in the health service to which he is affiliated'.[251] In that situation, so the CJEU has ruled, the rules of the Treaty on freedom of movement offer '[...] no guarantee that all hospital treatment services which may have to be provided to him unexpectedly in the Member State of stay will be neutral in terms of cost'.[252]

Apart from the actual care costs, additional costs involved in foreign medical treatment, such as costs for board, lodging, travel, visitors' tax and the production of a final medical report, may also be claimed for reimbursement, to the extent that such costs would also be reimbursed had the treatment taken place in the country of affiliation.[253] Although such costs are not medical in character, and are not as a rule paid to health care providers, the CJEU nonetheless considers them to be inextricably

---

249 Art. 22(1)(c) Regulation 1408/71, as interpreted in Case C-368/98 *Vanbraekel* [2001] ECR I-5363, ECLI:EU:C:2001:400, para. 33. On the basis of Art. 36 Regulation 1408/71 the competent institution remains responsible for subsequently reimbursing the institution of the place of stay.

250 Case C-368/98 *Vanbraekel* [2001] ECR I-5363, ECLI:EU:C:2001:400. Under certain circumstances also treatment obtained in a non-EU-Member State must be reimbursed. Case C-145/03 *Keller* v. *Instituto Nacional de Gestion Sanitaria (Ingesa)* [2005] ECR I-2529, ECLI:EU:C:2005:211.

251 Case C-211/08 *Commission* v. *Spain* [2010] ECR I-5267, ECLI:EU:C:2010:340, para. 61. In para. 58, the Court held that '[...] with regard at least to hospital care, [...] cases of 'unscheduled treatment', as referred to in Art. 22(1)(a) of Regulation 1408/71 [...] must be distinguished [...] from cases of 'scheduled treatment', as referred to in Art. 22(1)(c) of that Regulation.

252 Case C-211/08 *Commission* v. *Spain* [2010] ECR I-5267, ECLI:EU:C:2010:340, para. 61. The CJEU held (in para. 79) that to impose on Member States the obligation to guarantee to persons insured under the national system that the competent institution will provide complementary reimbursement whenever the level of cover applicable in the Member State of stay in respect of the unscheduled hospital treatment in question proves to be lower that that applicable under its own legislation 'would ultimately undermine the very fabric of the system which Regulation No 1408/71 sought to establish'. Critical in this respect: A.P. van der Mei, 'Cross-border access to healthcare and entitlement to complementary "Vanbraekel reimbursement"', 36 *European Law Review* (2011) p. 431.

253 Case C-8/02 *Ludwig Leichtle* v. *Bundesanstalt für Arbeit* [2004] ECR I-2641, ECLI:EU:C:2004:161. See Mei, van der 2006, *supra* n. 168, at pp. 68–69.

linked to the cure itself.[254] Any conditions set for the reimbursement of such costs have to be justified on imperative grounds and have to meet the proportionality test.[255]

3.5.3. The EU Patient Mobility Directive (2011)

As a result of the increased number of CJEU judgments in respect of access to and reimbursement for cross-border health care, the Commission and the Member States felt the need to codify – and to a certain extent to clarify[256] – the relevant principles resulting from this case law in a new legislative instrument.[257] In 2011, this finally resulted in the adoption of a separate Directive on the application of patients' rights in cross-border health care.[258] The adoption of this instrument was, however, preceded by intense debates.

In June 2002 the Council considered that there was '[...] a need to strengthen cooperation in order to promote the greatest opportunities for access to health care of high quality while maintaining the financial sustainability of healthcare systems in the European Union'.[259] Subsequently the Commission convened a 'High-Level Process of Reflection on Patient Mobility and Healthcare Developments in the EU'. This resulted, in April 2004, in a Commission Communication on patient mobility.[260] The Commission considered a European strategy needed to ensure that citizens could exercise their rights to seek care in other Member States if they wished, and to ensure that European cooperation could help systems to work together to better meet the challenges they faced.[261] The Commission held that for citizens, the first step was '[...] to provide them with a clearer overview of the existing EU legal framework regarding access to healthcare and the reimbursement of the costs incurred in another Member State.'[262] The Services Directive draft of 2004 had included health care services.[263] However, because of its sensitivity and public finance implications,

254 *Idem*, para. 35.

255 See A. den Exter, 'Access to Health Care in the Netherlands: The Influence of (European) Treaty Law', 33 *Journal of Law, Medicine & Ethics* (2005) p. 698 at p. 703.

256 Following Art. 1(1) Directive 2011/24/EU, the Directive aims at clarifying its relationship with the existing framework on the coordination of social security systems, i.e. Regulation (EC) No 883/2004. Further, following Recital 8 of the Preamble, the Directive is intended to achieve a more general, and also effective, application of principles developed by the Court of Justice on a case-by-case basis.

257 De la Rosa call this codification exercise unique for the fact that it intervenes in a particularly sensitive area. De la Rosa 2012, *supra* n. 33, at p. 17.

258 Directive 2011/24/EU of the European Parliament and of the Council of 9 March 2011 on the application of patients' rights in cross-border healthcare[2011] OJ L88/45, p. 46.

259 2440th Council meeting, Health, Luxembourg, 26 June 2002, 10090/02 (Presse 182) of 26 June 2002, p. 11, online available at www.consilium.europa.eu/ueDocs/cms_Data/docs/pressData/en/lsa/71383.pdf, visited June 2014.

260 Commission, 'Follow-up to the high level reflection process on patient mobility and healthcare developments in the European Union', COM (2004) 301 final.

261 *Idem*, at p. 2.

262 *Idem*.

263 Commission, 'Proposal for a Directive on services in the Internal Market', COM (2004) 2 final. Proposed Art. 23 provided for the assumption of health care costs.

this sector was excluded from the final Services Directive of 2006.[264] The Council and the European Parliament proffered a sector-specific instrument. In 2006 a public consultation on the issue was run,[265] after which a Commission proposal followed in 2008.[266] On first reading this was rejected by the Council, the prior authorisation requirement for hospital care and the legal basis of the Directive, being just some of the issues in respect of which no agreement could be reached.[267] Extensive debates and various amendments followed, resulting, at a certain point in time, in a 'political and legislative limbo'.[268] Nevertheless, in 2011 all negotiations resulted in the adoption of Directive 2011/24/EU on the application of patients' rights in cross-border healthcare ('the Patient Mobility Directive').[269] The Directive has a dual legal basis: Article 114 TFEU (internal market) and Article 168 TFEU (health).[270] The latter was allegedly chosen to secure the Member States' competences in respect of public health.[271] The deadline for implementation of the Directive by the Member States was set at October 25th 2013.

The Patient Mobility Directive '[...] provides rules for facilitating the access to safe and high-quality cross-border healthcare and promotes cooperation on healthcare between Member States, in full respect of national competencies in organising and delivering healthcare.'[272] The term 'health care' is broadly defined as '[...] health services provided by health professionals to patients to assess, maintain or restore their state of health, including the prescription, dispensation and provision of medicinal products and medical devices'.[273]

---

264 Directive 2006/123/EC of the European Parliament and of the Council of 12 December 2006 on services in the internal market [2006] OJ L376/36. See also O'Leary 2011, *supra* n. 52, at p. 522.

265 Commission, 'Consultation regarding Community action on health services' (Communication), SEC (2006) 1195/4. See also Commission, 'Summary report of the responses to the consultation regarding "Community action on health services"', SEC (2006) 1195/4.

266 Commission, 'Proposal for a Directive of the European Parliament and of the Council on the application of patients' rights in cross-border healthcare', COM (2008) 414 final.

267 De la Rosa 2012, *supra* n. 33, at p. 26. See also T. Hervey, 'Cooperation between health care authorities in the proposed Directive', in: J.W. van de Gronden et al. (eds.), *Health care and EU law* (The Hague, T.M.C. Asser Press 2011) p. 161 at pp. 163–164.

268 G. Davies, 'Legislating for Patient's Rights', in: J.W. van de Gronden et al. (eds.), *Health care and EU law* (The Hague, T.M.C. Asser Press 2011) p. 191 at p. 191.

269 Directive 2011/24/EU of the European Parliament and of the Council of 9 March 2011 on the application of patients' rights in cross-border healthcare [2011] OJ L88/45. The Patient mobility Directive was approved by the European Parliament on 19 January 2011 and entered into force on 24 April 2011 (Art. 22 Directive 2011/24/EU).

270 Recital No. 2 of the Preamble to the Directive explains: 'Article 114 TFEU is the appropriate legal basis since the majority of the provisions of this Directive aim to improve the functioning of the internal market and the free movement of goods, persons and services. Given that the conditions for recourse to Article 114 TFEU as a legal basis are fulfilled, Union legislation has to rely on this legal basis even when public health protection is a decisive factor in the choices made. In this respect, Article 114(3) TFEU explicitly requires that, in achieving harmonisation, a high level of protection of human health is to be guaranteed taking account in particular of any new development based on scientific facts.'

271 De la Rosa 2012, *supra* n. 33, at p. 27.

272 Art. 1(1) Directive 2011/24/EU.

273 Art. 3(a) Directive 2011/24/EU. Recital 6 to the Preamble furthermore holds that '[a]s confirmed by the [CJEU] on several occasions, while recognising their specific nature, all types of medical care fall within the scope of the TFEU.'

The Directive explicitly claims not to affect '[...] laws and regulations in Member States relating to the organisation and financing of healthcare in situations not related to cross-border healthcare.'[274] Further, following Recital No. 4 of the Preamble, the transposition of the Directive into national legislation and its application was not intended to result in '[...] patients being encouraged to receive treatment outside their Member State of affiliation.'[275] Recital No. 7 adds to this:

> 'This Directive respects and is without prejudice to the freedom of each Member State to decide what type of healthcare it considers appropriate. No provision of this Directive should be interpreted in such a way as to undermine the fundamental ethical choices of Member States.'[276]

By many, the Patient Mobility Directive has been perceived as a 'Citizenship Directive'[277] and as a reflection of the Union's 'rebalancing of its action in a more social direction'.[278] Before its adoption in amended form, Davies called mobile patients the 'winners' under the Directive.[279] Van de Gronden and Szyszczak later pointed out, however, that those provisions of the Patient Mobility Directive giving patients generous entitlements to cross-border hospital care were heavily amended before the Directive was finally adopted.[280] They concluded that respect for Member States' competences was still '[...] one of the underpinning principles of how EU law deals with health care'. Critique has been issued that the Directive is '[...] primarily aimed at individuals or groups of individuals who have the cognitive and social resources to engage in a process of mobility'.[281] De la Rosa described the Directive in the following words:

> '[The Patient Mobility Directive] displays an original combination of the codifying solutions derived from the free provision of services; the facilitation of the exercise of

---

274 Art. 2(4) Directive 2011/24/EU.

275 The 'Member State of affiliation' is the Member State that is competent to grant to the insured person a prior authorisation to receive appropriate treatment outside the Member State of residence. Art. 3(c) Directive 2011/24/EU.

276 Recital No. 7 of the Preamble to Directive 2011/24/EU. Recital No. 5 adds to this that '[...] decisions about the basket of healthcare to which citizens are entitled and the mechanisms used to finance and deliver that healthcare [...] must be taken in the national context.'

277 Davies 2011, *supra* n. 268, at p. 207.

278 De la Rosa 2012, *supra* n. 33, at p. 16.

279 According to Davies mobile patients were the 'winners', 'provided they get what they expect and treatment abroad does not turn out to be more different and less satisfactory than they had hoped.' According to the author, the facilitation measures are at the heart of whether the Directive will be a success or not. Davies, furthermore, observes that the EU is also potentially a winner, as mobility of patients will tend to lead to a greater health care integration, which, he thinks, will ultimately strengthen the EU's position in the global health industry. The author furthermore held that: 'The rights in the Directive [...], like other free movement rights, are a form of substantive constitution building, harnessing the needs and wishes of individuals to re-constitute the European space.' Davies 2011, *supra* n. 268, at pp. 207–208.

280 Gronden, van de and Szyszczak 2011, *supra* n. 170, at p. 488, referring to Davies 2011, *supra* n. 268.

281 De la Rosa 2012, *supra* n. 33, at pp. 38–39. On the other hand, the national information points for which the Directive provides (see section 3.5.3.2 below) may assist in making cross-border health care accessible for a wider public.

patient mobility by highlighting information in relation to such mobility; the promotion of cooperation between States in connection with Article 168 TFEU; and, to head the entire undertaking, the incessant reminder of the essentially national character of health policy.'[282]

3.5.3.1. Authorisation and reimbursement for cross-border health care

By way of codification of the CJEU's case law, Article 7 of the Patient Mobility Directive provides that the Member State of affiliation shall ensure that the costs incurred by an insured person who receives cross-border healthcare are reimbursed, if the healthcare in question is among the benefits to which the insured person is entitled in the Member State of affiliation. It is for the Member State of affiliation to determine, whether at a local, regional or national level, the healthcare for which an insured person is entitled to assumption of costs and the level of assumption of those costs, regardless of where the healthcare is provided.[283] Hence – as is the case under Article 22 of the Social Security Regulation – a State does not have to reimburse treatment obtained abroad, if such treatment is prohibited under the domestic law, or if the relevant national scheme does not provide for reimbursement for that kind of treatment.

The costs of cross-border healthcare are reimbursed or paid directly by the Member State of affiliation up to the level of costs that would have been assumed by the Member State of affiliation, had this healthcare been provided in its territory without exceeding the actual costs of healthcare received.[284]

Prior authorisation may be required under certain conditions. It is allowed if health care is concerned that is made subject to planning requirements relating to the object of ensuring sufficient and permanent access to a balanced range of high-quality treatment, but only if it involves overnight hospital accommodation for the patient in question for at least one night, or requires the use of highly specialised and cost-intensive medical infrastructure or medical equipment.[285] Prior authorisation may also be required if the care is provided by a health care provider that, on a case-by-case basis, could give rise to serious and specific concerns relating to the quality or safety of the care, with the exception of healthcare which is subject to Union legislation ensuring a minimum level of safety and quality throughout the Union.[286] This provision is difficult to reconcile with the weight attached to mutual recognition by the CJEU in its case law.[287] Following Article 8(6) the Member

282 *Idem,* at p. 18.

283 Art. 7(4) Directive 2011/24/EU.

284 Art. 7(4) Directive 2011/24/EU. It is furthermore stressed in Art. 1(4) that nothing in the Directive obliges a Member State to reimburse costs of healthcare provided by healthcare providers established on its own territory if those providers are not part of its social security system or public health system.

285 Art. 8(2)(a) Directive 2011/24/EU.

286 Art. 8(2)(c) Directive 2011/24/EU.

287 E.g. Case C-444/05 *Stamatelaki* [2007] ECR I-3185, ECLI:EU:C:2007:231, para. 37, where the Court held that the Greek authorities had to recognise that private hospitals located in other Member States were also subject, in those Member States, to quality controls and that doctors established in those

State of affiliation may refuse to grant prior authorisation if, according to a clinical evaluation, the patient will be exposed, with reasonable certainty, to a patient-safety risk that cannot be regarded as acceptable, taking into account the potential benefit to the patient of the sought after cross-border healthcare.[288] Prior authorisation may also be refused if the healthcare concerned can be provided on the territory of the Member State of affiliation within a time limit which is medically justifiable, taking into account the current state of health and the probable course of the illness of each patient concerned.[289]

Where medical follow-up proves necessary after a patient has received cross-border health care, the State of affiliation must ensure that the same medical follow-up is available '[...] as would have been if that healthcare had been provided on its territory.'[290]

3.5.3.2. Information rights

The Patient Mobility Directive has introduced considerable rights to information for patients involved in cross-border care.[291] Appropriate information 'on all essential aspects of cross-border healthcare' was considered '[...] necessary in order to enable patients to exercise their rights on cross-border healthcare in practice.'[292] The Directive, *inter alia*, provides for the establishment of national contact points in each Member State.[293] These are to deliver information to patients involved in cross-border care concerning healthcare providers; information on the relevant standards and guidelines; information on patients' rights, complaints procedures and mechanisms for seeking remedies, as well as the legal and administrative options available to settle disputes, including in the event of harm arising from cross-border healthcare.[294] Furthermore, in the Member State of affiliation, mechanisms have to be put in place to provide patients, on request, with information on their rights and entitlements relating to receiving cross-border healthcare, '[...] in particular as regards the terms and conditions for reimbursement of costs [...] and procedures for accessing and determining those entitlements and for appeal and redress if patients consider that

States who operate in those establishments provided professional guarantees equivalent to those of doctors established in Greece. See also Case C-255/09 *Commission* v. *Portugal* [2011] ECR I-10547, ECLI:EU:C:2011:695, para. 83, where the Court ruled that a requirement of prior authorisation for reimbursement of the medical expenses in question could not be justified on public health grounds relating to the need to control the quality of healthcare services provided abroad.

288 Art. 8(6)(a) Directive 2011/24/EU.

289 Art. 8(6)(d) Directive 2011/24/EU.

290 Art. 5(c) Directive 2011/24/EU.

291 Palm and Baeten considered that the revolutionary nature of the Directive lied in the inclusion of these '"new" patient rights'. W. Palm and R. Baeten, 'The quality and safety paradox in the patients' rights Directive', 21 *Eur J Public Health* (2011) p. 272 at p. 272.

292 Recital No. 48 of the Preamble to Directive 2011/24/EU.

293 The Directive makes a distinction between responsibilities of the Member State of treatment (Art. 4) and responsibilities of the Member State of affiliation (Art. 5). It is, however, inescapable that all Member States have to meet all requirements, as they may function both as States of treatment and States of affiliation.

294 Arts. 4(2)(a) and 6(3) Directive 2011/24/EU.

their rights have not been respected [...].'[295] Healthcare providers in the State where the treatment takes place, for their part, have to '[...] provide relevant information to help individual patients to make an informed choice, including on treatment options, on the availability, quality and safety of the healthcare they provide in the Member State of treatment and that they also provide clear invoices and clear information on prices, as well as on their authorisation or registration status, their insurance cover or other means of personal or collective protection with regard to professional liability.'[296] The Directive does not oblige Member States to deliver information in other languages than their official languages.[297]

3.6. Cross-border movement in reproductive matters under EU law

3.6.1. Political attention for cross-border movement in reproductive matters

Cross-border movement for reproductive matters has occasionally been discussed at the EU level. Particularly cross-border abortions have caught the attention of the EU institutions.[298] For instance, in the early 1980s when abortion was much debated in most (then) EC Member States, the European Parliament adopted a non-binding Resolution on the position of women in the European Community in which cross-border abortions were also addressed.[299] The Resolution noted '[...] the problems caused by the fact that women seeking abortions frequently [had] to seek the termination in another country and requested the Commission to press the Council for decisions at national level to obviate the need for such journeys and ensure that every woman who [found] herself in difficulty could obtain the necessary assistance in her own state.'[300] It has been noted that this was particularly controversial in a Member State like Ireland, as it '[...] gave rise to concern in certain quarters that this was the beginning of Community pressure to liberalise Ireland's abortion legislation.'[301]

---

295 Art. 5(b) Directive 2011/24/EU.

296 Art. 4(2)(b) Directive 2011/24/EU.

297 Art. 4(5) Directive 2011/24/EU. See also Palm and Baeten 2011, *supra* n. 291, at p. 273, who furthermore point out that '[t]he level of information provided and the way in which the contact points will work in the different Member States is likely to reflect cultural and organizational differences [...].'

298 See also the Resolution of the European Parliament of 12 March 1990 on reports of gynaecological examinations by the German Federal Frontier Police [1991] OJ C106/102, pp. 103, 113 and 135, as discussed in Ch. 4, section 4.4.1.1.

299 European Parliament resolution of 11 February 1981 on the situation of women in the European Community, [1981] OJ C50/24, p. 34. The Resolution followed a Report of the Ad Hoc Committee on Women's Rights on the position of women in the European Community, A1-0829/80. See also Sherlock 1989, *supra* n. 78.

300 As paraphrased by Sherlock 1989, *supra* n. 78, referring (in footnote 29) to [1989] OJ C111/1, p. 16.

301 *Idem*. The author stressed that the Resolution was not legally binding and that the Parliament lacks the power to initiate legislation.

In 2004, when the Portuguese authorities refused to allow the ship of the Dutch organisation *Women on Waves* to enter Portuguese territorial waters (see Ch. 6, section 6.4.1.3; and Ch. 2, section 2.4.1), this also caught the attention of the European institutions. It caused a 'lively, controversial and important debate' in the European Parliament[302] and made the Commission get involved in the matter. Upon receiving a complaint by *Women on Waves* about the refusal, the Commission inquired with the Portuguese authorities. It thereby made clear that Member States could restrict the fundamental right of free movement '[...] solely where it [was] justified on grounds of public policy, public security and public health and that where a Member State adopt[ed] a measure refusing entry to its territory based on one of these grounds, it [had to] respect the general principles of Community law and in particular the proportionality principle, and fundamental rights, including the right to freedom of information and expression.'[303] The present author is not aware of any subsequent action from the side of the Commission in this case;[304] there has not been a case before the CJEU resulting from any infringements proceedings initiated by the Commission in this matter.[305]

On another occasion, in 2006, the Council declined to give its opinion on a report that citizens of other EU Member States went to a Spanish clinic for late abortions (i.e., after 30 weeks of pregnancy).[306] The Council answered that this matter did not fall within the Union's competences.[307]

---

302 Contribution of Commissioner Wallström to the debate in European Parliament of 16 September 2004, www.europarl.europa.eu/sides/getDoc.do?pubRef=-%2f%2fEP%2f%2fTEXT%2bCRE%2b20040916%2bITEM-001%2bDOC%2bXML%2bV0%2f%2fEN&language=EN, visited June 2014.

303 Letter of the Commission to the Portuguese authorities on 14 October 2004 to request further information, as referred to in Answer of the Commission to oral Parliamentary Question No. 69 by Anne Van Lancker to the Commission, of 26 November 2004 (H-0450/04), online available at www.europarl.europa.eu/sides/getDoc.do?pubRef=-//EP//TEXT+CRE+20041216+ANN-01+DOC+XML+V0//LV&query=QUESTION&detail=H-2004-0450, visited June 2014.

304 On 23 November 2004, the Commission received a reply from the Portuguese authorities who justified their decision on the United Nations Convention on the Law of the Sea and on the need to protect public health, safeguard the legal order and prevent abuse of rights. Three days later the Commission informed Parliament that it planned to decide on the follow-up to this official complaint in its next meeting on infringements. Answer of the Commission to oral Parliamentary Question No. 69 by Anne Van Lancker to the Commission, of 26 November 2004 (H-0450/04), online available at www.europarl.europa.eu/sides/getDoc.do?pubRef=-//EP//TEXT+CRE+20041216+ANN-01+DOC+XML+V0//LV&query=QUESTION&detail=H-2004-0450, visited June 2014.

305 The matter has, however, been decided by the ECtHR on the basis of Art. 10 ECHR. See Ch. 2, section 2.4.1.

306 See also Ch.6, section 6.4.1.2.

307 The Representative of the Council held that the European Union Treaties had not bestowed on the Community or the Union the competence whereby the Union could regulate on abortions. The Member States thus had the competence to regulate on this and ensure compliance in their territory with the laws that they passed. The EU could not interfere '[...] in unsatisfactory states of affairs due to differences in the legislation of Member States when it [came] to areas that [were] not within its competence.' When a Member of Parliament submitted that this concerned a European problem of a cross-border nature, the representative of the Council answered that the free mobility of people was 'one of the European Union's basic concerns'. It was held that if there were 'illegal goings-on in Member States', it was their responsibility and duty to monitor them and intervene. In this case it was incontrovertibly clear that big differences between the laws in Member States led to very different practices around Europe. Answer of the Council to oral Parliamentary Question No. 69 by B. Belder to the Council, of 7 November 2006

The motion for a resolution on Sexual and Reproductive Health and Rights,[308] as tabled by the European Parliament's Committee on Women's Rights and Gender Equality in 2013 (see 3.2 above), deplored the fact that the restrictive abortion laws of certain countries resulted in a divide between those who could afford to travel, and those who could not and were forced to seek clandestine abortions. It called on Member States to '[...] refrain from preventing pregnant women seeking abortion to travel to other Member States or jurisdictions where the procedure is legal'.[309] As explained above, the motion was not, however, adopted.[310]

Cross-border surrogacy has also received attention at the EU level. For instance, as noted in section 3.3.4 above, in 2012 the European Parliament issued a call for tender for a comparative study on the regime of surrogacy in the EU Member States, whereby the question to be addressed was also whether solutions to existing problems could be better achieved on the EU level. The findings of the ensuing study in respect of cross-border cases are discussed in section 3.6.3 below.

In international surrogacy cases, often third countries (non-EU Member States), such as Ukraine, Russia, India or the United States of America, are involved. The EU has not adopted specific foreign policies in respect of international surrogacy. For instance, the issue is not addressed in specific country strategy papers. In relation to India, the Commission stressed, in 2013, in response to Parliamentary questions, that the EU had '[...] engaged with the Government of India and Indian civil society organisations since the early 1990s, on improvement of maternal health, reducing child mortality and protecting women's rights', but that there was '[...] no funding available for the creation of information, monitoring systems or to produce and publish data with regard to the phenomenon of business of surrogate motherhood in India.'[311] The EU follows the developments on surrogate motherhood at international level through the Hague Conference on Private International Law, of which it has been a member since 2007.[312]

(H-0983/06), online available at www.europarl.europa.eu/sides/getDoc.do?type=CRE&reference=20061213&secondRef=ITEM-021&language=EN#3-429, visited June 2014.

308 Motion for a European Parliament Resolution on Sexual and Reproductive Health and Rights (2013/2040(INI)), online available at www.europarl.europa.eu/sides/getDoc.do?pubRef=-//EP//NONSGML+REPORT+A7-2013-0306+0+DOC+PDF+V0//EN, visited June 2014.

309 *Idem*, paras. 28, 30 and 38.

310 See section 3.2 above.

311 Answer given by Mr. Piebalgs on behalf of the Commission (22 March 2013) to Question No E-001081/13, no. P7_QE(2013)001081.

312 See 3.3.4 above. The Hague Conference decided in 2011 that issues surrounding cross-border surrogacy arrangements required further examination, and in 2013 a study on the matter came out. The study concluded that further international work was desired with a view to ensuring legal certainty and security of legal status for children and families in international surrogacy situations and to protecting the '[...] rights and welfare of children, parents and other parties involved with the conception of children in international situations, in line with established global human rights standards.' Following this study, the General Council of the Hague Conference invited the Permanent Bureau to continue information gathering and postponed any decision on the establishment of an Experts' Group on the matter to its meeting in 2015. Permanent Bureau Hague Conference on Private international law, *The desirability and feasibility of further work on the parentage / surrogacy project*, Preliminary Document No 3 B of April 2014 for the attention of the Council of April 2014 on General Affairs and Policy of

3.6.2. Open questions regarding the application of cross-border health care standards

There are various open questions concerning the application the EU law standards on cross-border health care, as described in section 3.5 above, to cross-border abortions, cross-border reproductive care and cross-border surrogacy. With the exception of the *Grogan* case, none of CJEU judgments and legislative instruments as discussed in section 3.5 dealt explicitly with these matters. Consequently, application of these standards to situations of cross-border abortions, CBRC and cross-border surrogacy raises questions, which as yet, have not been explicitly addressed by the EU legislature, nor by the CJEU. This section identifies these open questions and endeavours to formulate tentative answers where possible.

For one thing, abortion and AHR treatment fall within the definition of 'services' within the meaning of the TFEU, and 'health care' within the meaning of the Patient Mobility Directive,[313] as long as they are not outlawed by all Member States and as long and normally provided for remuneration. Only if a certain type of AHR treatment or abortion would be outlawed by *all* Member States, could this specific treatment be excluded from the scope of the EU free movement rules.[314] While for abortion such a situation is in any case not anticipated in the near future, it is conceivable that all EU Member States could explicitly prohibit practices like gender selection in the course of AHR treatment for reasons other than medical ones. In that scenario, the EU free movement rules could not provide a basis for any claim as regards access to, or reimbursement for, such treatment.

Surrogacy is in itself not a medical activity, and the Patient Mobility Directive and specific cross-border health care case law do not, therefore, apply. In high-technological surrogacy AHR treatment is, however, involved and that type of medical treatment evidently comes within the scope of the EU standards on cross-border health-care. Surrogacy itself could possibly be considered a service within the meaning of the Treaties,[315] as a result of which the general Treaty rules (Articles 56 and 57 TFEU) apply. This certainly holds for the services that surrogacy intermediaries offer.

Even though abortion, (common types of) AHR treatment and possibly also surrogacy thus qualify as (health care) services within the meaning of the Treaty, the freedom to receive such services may be restricted. A full restriction on cross-border

---

the Conference; Permanent Bureau Hague Conference on Private international law, *A study of legal parentage and the issues arising from international surrogacy arrangements,* Preliminary Document No 3 C of March 2014 for the attention of the Council of April 2014 on General Affairs and Policy of the Conference and Conclusions and Recommendations adopted by the Council on General Affairs and Policy of the Conference (8–10 April 2014). All three documents are online available at www.hcch.net/index_en.php?act=text.display&tid=183, visited June 2014.

313 See Case C-159/90 *Grogan* [1991] ECR I-4685, ECLI:EU:C:1991:378, as discussed in section 3.5.2.1 above.

314 Case C-137/09 *Josemans* [2010] ECR I-13019, ECLI:EU:C:2010:774.

315 Brunet et al. 2013, *supra* n. 134, at pp. 142–143.

movement for reproductive matters by means of a ban on travelling may be very hard to justify under EU law, however. A restriction by means of criminal prosecution after return to the home state may also not be easily justified. In most cases the double criminality rule under the European Arrest Warrant will prevent such prosecution anyhow (see section 3.6.4 below). Such measures are not, furthermore, very likely to be imposed, as the chapters on Ireland, Germany and the Netherlands for this case study have shown.[316] It is more likely that restrictions on free movement consist of refusals of reimbursement;[317] prior authorisation requirements; bans or limitations on information about foreign treatment options or refusals to provide follow-up care after treatment has been obtained abroad. Restrictive regimes concerning abortion, AHR treatment and/or surrogacy may also in themselves constitute an obstacle to free movement. All these possible restrictions are addressed in the various subsections below.

3.6.2.1. Reimbursement for treatment obtained abroad

The basic and most relevant rule for the present case study in respect of reimbursement is that States do not have to reimburse treatment obtained abroad, if such treatment is prohibited under the domestic law, or if its national scheme does not provide for reimbursement for that kind of treatment.[318] Additional costs, such as costs for board, lodging, travel, visitors' tax and the production of a final medical report, can also not be claimed in this situation.[319]

While this, at first sight, seems to be a clear-cut rule, to determine if the treatment in question is '[...] among the benefits provided for by the legislation in the Member State where the person concerned resides' may sometimes prove problematic, because entitlements to medical benefits may be phrased in rather broad terms in national (private) social security regulations.[320] For example, it may be provided under the social security scheme of Member State *A* that a couple is entitled to reimbursement for 'three IVF cycles'. Suppose that, in that State IVF treatment with the use of donated gametes is lawfully available only if such donation is altruistic and if the donor is known to the woman or couple involved in the IVF treatment. Could reimbursement be claimed for IVF treatment obtained in Member State *B*, where

316 An exception forms the (withdrawn) prosecution in the Netherlands for abortion in Spain. See Ch. 6, section 6.4.1.2.

317 It has also been pointed out, however, that most of cross-border AHR treatment takes place in the context of private treatment, '[...] and so public interest justifications with respect to the burdens on the public purse, the organisation of national health (insurance) schemes and the need for planning, management and capacity building, that are at issue in the general litigation on free movement of patients do not apply with the same force.' Hervey and McHale 2004, *supra* n. 47, at p. 152.

318 Art. 22 Regulation 883/2004 and Art. 7 Directive 2011/24/EU.

319 Case C-8/02 *Ludwig Leichtle* v. *Bundesanstalt für Arbeit* [2004] ECR I-2641, ECLI:EU:C:2004:161. Mei, van der 2006, *supra* n. 168, at pp. 68–69.

320 See Case C-173/09 *Elchinov* [2010] ECR I-8889, ECLI:EU:C:2010:581, para. 59, where the Court considered that '[...] it is for each Member State to decide which medical benefits are reimbursed by its own social security system. To that end, the Member State concerned is entitled to list precisely treatments or treatment methods or to state more generally the categories or types of treatments or treatment methods.'

commercial and anonymous donation of gametes is legal and common practice? The answer is most likely in the negative, as such treatment would not have been reimbursed if obtained in Member State *A*, the State of affiliation. In other words, it is not among the benefits provided for by the legislation in Member State *A*. Whether this is indeed the correct reading of the law has not been confirmed at EU level.[321]

Another question is, where a new type of AHR treatment has become available that is not (yet) available in Member State *A*, and therefore also not (yet) explicitly provided for or prohibited in the State of affiliation, whether it should be reimbursed by the latter state. On the basis of the existing case law there is no definite answer to this question (yet). Some guidance may be found in the case of *Elchinov* (2010) where the CJEU ruled that:

> '[...] where the list of medical benefits reimbursed does not expressly and precisely specify the treatment method applied but defines types of treatment [...] it is for the competent institution of the Member State of residence of the insured person to assess, applying the usual principles of interpretation and on the basis of objective and non-discriminatory criteria, taking into consideration all the relevant medical factors and the available scientific data, whether that treatment method corresponds to benefits provided for by the legislation of that Member State.'[322]

It must be noted that the *Elchinov* case did not concern morally controversial treatment. It seems very likely that in cases concerning such controversial treatment, the national authorities would rule that foreign treatment options do not correspond to treatment available in the state of affiliation. If the authorities nevertheless come to the conclusion that the treatment methods do correspond, prior authorisation – so the Court has ruled – may not be refused on the ground that such a treatment method is not available in the Member State of affiliation.[323] That brings us to the question of whether States may restrict access to, and reimbursement for, abortions and AHR treatment that has been provided in another EU Member State, for example, by setting prior authorisation requirements.

3.6.2.2. Prior authorisation requirements and refusal of authorisation

Two issues warrant particular attention when the EU rules in respect of prior authorisation are applied in the present case study. These are the questions of whether abortions and AHR treatment qualify as 'scheduled treatment',[324] and whether safety and quality concerns may be accepted as a ground for the refusal of authorisation for such treatment.

321 Dutch courts have in any case taken different views in this regard. See Ch. 6, section 6.5.2.

322 Case C-173/09 *Elchinov* [2010] ECR I-8889, ECLI:EU:C:2010:581.

323 *Idem*, para. 62, where the Court ruled that '[...] such a ground, if it were accepted, would imply a restriction on the scope of the second subparagraph of Article 22(2) of Regulation No 1408/71.'

324 From the CJEU's case law it follows that in this regard, not so much the hospital environment, but the planning element is decisive (see 3.5.2.3 above).

Under the Patient Mobility Directive a prior authorisation requirement for scheduled treatment can only be set if the treatment involves overnight hospital accommodation for the patient in question for at least one night, or if it requires use of highly specialised and cost-intensive medical infrastructure or medical equipment.[325] As a rule, no hospital accommodation is required for abortion and AHR treatment.[326] Whether any of these types of treatment involve 'highly specialised and cost-intensive medical infrastructure or medical equipment', within the meaning of the Directive, is less obvious.[327] The CJEU has so far given only limited guidance on the interpretation of this condition for authorisation. In *Commission* v. *France* (2010)[328] the Court accepted a prior authorisation requirement for treatment requiring the use of 'major medical equipment'[329] available outside hospital infrastructures, because the conditions for the installation, operation and use of this equipment were 'especially onerous', while both its purchase and its installation and use represented high costs of 'hundreds of thousands, even millions, of euro'.[330] The Court held that the planning endeavours of the national authorities and the financial balance of the supply of up-to-date treatment would be jeopardised, if persons insured in one Member State could, freely and in any circumstances, obtain at the expense of the competent institution, from service providers established in other Member States, treatment involving the use of major medical equipment.[331] It is submitted that generally medical equipment for abortion does not qualify as 'major medical equipment'. Presumably this also holds for equipment for most – if not all – (common) types of AHR treatment. New medical and technological developments may, nevertheless, lead to different conclusions in this regard. Hence, it cannot be ruled out that (certain types of) AHR treatment qualify as scheduled treatment, on the grounds of which a prior authorisation requirement in principle may be set. Generally, however, it is concluded that abortion and AHR treatment are not made subject to planning requirements, and that therefore no prior authorisation requirements may be set on that ground.

---

325 Art. 8(2)(a) Directive 2011/24/EU.

326 Within the EU practices vary as to the place where abortions and AHR treatment take place; this may be in (special clinics within) hospitals or in private clinics. In Ireland, for example, only private AHR clinics exists, whereas in the Netherlands all AHR-clinics are accommodated in public hospitals. In Germany both private and public clinics provide AHR treatment. Generally, also in situations where the treatment is carried out in a hospital, no accommodation for the night is required.

327 Art. 8(2)(a) Directive 2011/24/EU.

328 Case C-512/08 *Commission* v. *France* [2010] ECR I-8833, ECLI:EU:C:2010:579.

329 In the relevant case, under national (French) law the term 'major medical equipment' was held to include: a 'PET scanner'; a nuclear magnetic resonance imaging or spectrometry apparatus for clinical use; a medical scanner; a hyperbaric chamber and a cyclotron for medical use. See Case C-512/08 *Commission* v. *France* [2010] ECR I-8833, ECLI:EU:C:2010:579, para. 9.

330 *Idem*, para. 39. Advocate General Sharpston had proposed that 'highly specialised and cost-intensive medical infrastructure or medical equipment' could concern 'major medical equipment' that is very expensive to acquire, that may need to be installed in a specific setting and may need to be used and maintained by suitably qualified and trained personnel. Opinion of Advocate General Sharpston delivered on 15 July 2010, Case C-512/08 *Commission* v. *France* [2010] ECR I-8833, ECLI:EU:C:2010:579, para. 73.

331 Case C-512/08 *Commission* v. *France* [2010] ECR I-8833, ECLI:EU:C:2010:579, para. 40.

The rule that safety and quality issues can provide grounds for setting a prior authorisation requirement[332] may prove particularly relevant in the present case study.[333] For example, Dutch genealogists have expressed their concerns about the safety and quality of AHR treatment in Spanish clinics, where various fertilised egg cells are implanted in one cycle.[334] Could such concerns constitute ground for Dutch insurers to refuse to authorise women to have AHR treatment in Spain?[335] The answer is most likely in the negative, as the Patient Mobility Directive provides that an authorisation requirement is not allowed for types of healthcare that are subject to Union legislation ensuring a minimum level of safety and quality throughout the Union.[336] As explained in section 3.3.2 above, this is indeed the case in respect of IVF treatment, by means of the EU Tissues and Cells Directive. This minimum harmonisation therefore seems to bar the setting of prior authorisation requirements for AHR treatment such as IVF treatment. In respect of abortion there is, on the other hand, no such harmonisation in place.[337]

The foregoing conclusions render it less imperative to apply the CJEU's case law and the rules under the Patient Mobility Directive in respect of refusal of authorisation to the present case study. After all, there seems to be little ground for the setting of such authorisation requirements in the first place. Still, it may be worth examining the rule that authorisation can be refused if the same or equally effective treatment can be provided on the territory of the Member State of affiliation within a time limit which is medically justifiable, taking into account the current state of health and the probable course of the illness of each patient concerned.[338] This rule – which concerns remedying the disadvantageous consequences of waiting lists – is relevant only in situations where the treatment concerned is, in principle, legally available in the State of affiliation.

---

332 Art. 8(2)(c) Directive 2011/24/EU, as discussed in section 3.5.3.1 above.

333 A further question is if the conditions concerning quality and safety could also be interpreted in a moral sense. Could the (moral or psychological) effects of certain types of treatment – such as abortion – be considered to be an unacceptable patient-safety risk, justifying a prior authorisation requirement? While, again, no final answer to this question can be given as no CJEU ruling has been made on this particular question, it is submitted that this would stretch the interpretation of these rules – which concern integrity, quality and safety of the health care provider – too far.

334 *Nieuwsuur* 9 September 2010, www.nieuwsuur.nl/onderwerp/183384-spanje-is-hoop-voor-onvruchtbare-vrouwen.html, visited January 2011.

335 Under the Patient Mobility Directive, prior authorisation may also be required (1) if the care is provided by a health care provider that could give rise to serious and specific concerns relating to the quality or safety of the care, or (2) if the patient will be exposed with reasonable certainty to a patient safety risk. Art. 8(2)(c) Directive 2011/24/EU.

336 Art. 8(2)(c) Directive 2011/24/EU.

337 As Palm and Baeten explained in respect of the Patient Mobility Directive: 'The idea that the Directive would impose Member States to define clear quality and safety standards and to establish mechanisms to ensure that providers would have to meet these standards and could be sanctioned if they did not, was considered by the Member States a bridge too far, as it would touch upon their freedom and competence to organize and deliver health care according to national principles and priorities.' Palm and Baeten 2011, *supra* n. 291, at p. 273.

338 Case C-157/99 *Geraets-Smits and Peerbooms* [2001] ECR I-5473, ECLI:EU:C:2001:404 and Art. 8(6)(d) Directive 2011/24/EU.

In various EU countries, waiting lists exist for donated gametes, which reportedly are reason for couples to go abroad.[339] This raises the question of whether the time limits involved in such waiting lists can be considered 'medically justifiable'. The answer may depend on the question if infertility – which often constitutes ground for people to wish to resort to (certain types of) AHR treatment – is considered an illness. This concerns a sensitive question, which has not (yet) been conclusively answered at EU level and may not be easily done so either. It may also depend on the age of the couple involved in the AHR treatment and the age limits that national law has set for access to AHR treatment.

Another as yet undecided issue concerns the question of whether certain types of AHR treatment or abortion can be held to be 'sufficiently tried and tested by international medical science', in which case authorisation for reimbursement cannot be refused.[340]

3.6.2.3. Medical follow-up after cross-border treatment

There are some open issues in respect of the obligation on the State of affiliation to provide the necessary medical follow-up in the context of the present case study. In principle, the State of affiliation must ensure that the same medical follow-up is available 'as would have been if that healthcare had been provided on its territory.'[341] It is insufficiently clear how this provision must be interpreted in situations where the respective treatment is prohibited in the country of affiliation. Can an Irish medical practitioner or psychologist thus refuse to treat an Irish woman who had an abortion on therapeutic or social grounds in England? Are those Dutch genealogists who refuse to treat women who underwent AHR treatment in Spain acting in breach of EU law?[342] The literal text of the Directive does not give a conclusive answer and the primary free movement rules do not give much guidance either. It may be assumed that any refusal to give a medical follow-up to a medical service received abroad constitutes a barrier to the freedom to receive services. After all, the prospect of such a refusal may withhold certain services recipients from even making use of their free movement rights. Whether such a restriction could be justified is, however, an open question. The protection of the reputation (and credibility) of the medical profession may possibly constitute an overriding public interest in such situations. Next the proportionality of the restriction must be assessed. A refusal of life-saving treatment in case of a bleeding after an abortion appears evidently disproportional, but in respect of psychological treatment after an abortion on social grounds, this disproportionality may be less evident. There are thus many open questions here.

---

339 E.g. Shenfield et al. 2010, *supra* n. 154.

340 Hervey and McHale argued that '[p]articularly with relatively new treatments', there was 'likely to be considerable room for difference among professional opinion'. The authors warned that patients were likely to exploit this. Hervey and McHale 2004, *supra* n. 47, at pp. 136–137.

341 Art. 5(c) Directive 2011/24/EU.

342 See Ch. 6, section 6.5.3.

3.6.2.4. Information about foreign abortion and AHR services and surrogacy

There is nothing to indicate that the provisions of the Patient Mobility Directive in respect of information rights, as set out in section 3.5.3.2 above, would not apply in respect of cross-border abortions or reproductive care. Hence, national information points should also provide information about these types of treatment. As noted above, surrogacy does not in itself come within the scope of the Patient Mobility Directive, however. There is consequently no obligation on Member States to actively provide information about such services in other Member States. Whether they may, on the other hand, restrict access to such information, is another question that must be assessed on the basis of the Treaty free movement rules. As yet, this issue has not been addressed by the CJEU.

3.6.2.5. Different regimes as an obstacle to free movement?

EU citizens may be deterred from making use of their free movement rights under Article 21 TFEU, if the host State prohibits abortion (on certain grounds), surrogacy or (certain types of) AHR treatment. This may even be the case if the conditions for access to such treatment are stricter under the law of the host state, than under the law of the state of origin. For example, a same-sex couple may be deterred from moving to a State where access to IVF treatment is limited to (married) different-sex couples. While this matter has never been decided by the CJEU, it cannot be ruled out that the CJEU would accept that such (more) restrictive regimes constitute a restriction on free movement rights. The next question is then whether such a restriction could be justified. Various possible justification grounds are conceivable, such as the protection of public health, the protection of morals, public order grounds, protection of the unborn child, and the interests of the (future) child. The assessment of the proportionality depends on the justification ground and on the particular circumstances of the case and in this regard there are, again, various open questions.[343]

3.6.3. Recognition of parental links established abroad

There is, as matters stand, no provision of EU law that requires expressly that Member States must recognise parental links that have been established in another country in a cross-border surrogacy situation. As explained in section 3.1.3.3 above, the EU has a competence to develop judicial cooperation within the EU in civil matters with cross-border implications. None of the instruments that have been adopted on this legal basis are applicable to cross-border surrogacy cases and it is consequently the Private International Law regimes of States that are primordially decisive. For example, (non-)contractual obligations arising out of family relationships are excluded from the scope of the so-called Rome Regulations that provide for uniform rules for

[343] One factor which may be of relevance is the internal consistency of the national law. For example, in case a Member State prohibits surrogacy, it may be taken into account whether surrogacy intermediaries that collaborate with foreign surrogacy agencies are also prohibited.

determining the law applicable to contractual and non-contractual obligations in the European Union.[344] Further, the so-called *Brussels I* Regulation of 2000[345] provides for rules governing the jurisdiction of courts and the recognition and enforcement of judgments in civil and commercial matters in EU Member States, but it does not apply to 'the status or legal capacity of natural persons'.[346] The *Brussels II bis* Regulation (2003)[347] provides for automatic recognition of all judgments issued by courts of other Member States relating to parental responsibility without any intermediary procedure being required.[348] However, it is made very clear that the Regulation '[...] does not apply to the establishment of parenthood, since this is a different matter from the attribution of parental responsibility, nor to other questions linked to the status of persons.'[349] Apart from 'the establishment or contesting of a parent-child relationship' also 'judgments on adoption and the related preparatory measures, and annulment or revocation of adoption' are excluded from the scope of the Regulation.[350]

There is, moreover, as yet no EU instrument that provides for mutual recognition of birth certificates within the EU, although the first explorative steps in this regard have been taken by the European Commission, as explained hereafter.[351] A study of 2013 commissioned by the European Parliament also made suggestions for possible EU approaches to the issue (see section 3.6.3.2 below).

Whether a refusal by one Member State to recognise parental links as established in another EU Member State would constitute a violation of the free movement rules is a question that has never been conclusively answered by the CJEU. Intended parents who are EU citizens may rely on their free movement rights and if the child has EU-citizenship, they may also invoke the EU-citizenship rights of the child (Article 21 TFEU). A refusal by an EU Member State to give recognition to a birth certificate issued in another Member State may consequently well be considered a restriction of the latter right, but whether such a restriction could be upheld on public

---

344 See Art. 1(2)(b) Regulation (EC) No 593/2008 ('Rome I') and Art. 1(2)(a) Regulation (EC) No 864/2007 ('Rome II'). See Brunet et al. 2013, *supra* n. 134, at p. 148.

345 Council Regulation (EC) No 44/2001 of 22 December 2000 on jurisdiction and the recognition and enforcement of judgments in civil and commercial matters. The Regulation superseded the Brussels Convention of 1968, which was applicable between the EU countries before the Regulation entered into force.

346 Art. 1(2)(a). This is not different in the new version of the Regulation, European Parliament and Council Regulation 1215/2012/EU of 12 December 2012 on jurisdiction and the recognition and enforcement of judgments in civil and commercial matters [2012] OJ L351/1.

347 Council Regulation 2201/2003/EC of 27 November 2003 concerning jurisdiction and the recognition and enforcement of judgments in matrimonial matters and the matters of parental responsibility, repealing Regulation 1347/2000/EC [2003] OJ L338/1.

348 Recognition may be refused if such recognition is manifestly contrary to public policy, but only if it is in the best interests of the child. Art. 23 Regulation 2201/2003.

349 Recital 10 Regulation 2201/2003.

350 Art. 3(a) and (b) Regulation 2201/2003.

351 Commission, 'Green Paper 'Less bureaucracy for citizens: promoting free movement of public documents and recognition of the effects of civil status records', COM (2010) 747 final.

order grounds is as yet another open question.[352] Some guidance may be found in the *Dafeki* case (1997), where the Court held that:

> '[...] the exercise of the rights arising from freedom of movement for workers [was] not possible without production of documents relative to personal status, which [were] generally issued by the worker's State of origin.'[353]

Therefore, Member States were obliged to accept such documents, unless their accuracy was seriously undermined in an individual case. Cross-border surrogacy cases generally do not concern the free movement of workers, and it is therefore to be awaited if a similar reasoning would be applied in this context.[354]

3.6.3.1. Green Paper on recognition of civil status records (2010)

In the year 2010 the Commission published a Green Paper on the free movement of public documents and recognition of the effects of civil status records.[355] For the present research – both for this case study as well as for Case Study II – particularly the issue of recognition of the effects of civil status records is relevant. Civil status records were defined in the Green Paper as:

> '[...] records executed by an authority in order to record the life events of each citizen such as birth, filiation, adoption, marriage, recognition of paternity, death and also a surname change following marriage, divorce, a registered partnership, recognition, change of sex or adoption.'[356]

The fact that this definition thus includes records concerning birth, filiation and adoption, renders the Green Paper also relevant for cross-border surrogacy situations.

---

352 States will presumably invoke public policy grounds and possibly also national identity. The CJEU has proven respectful for national identity arguments in cases concerning the spelling of names, which case-law may be relevant for the present case. However, it is uncertain if such a case would pass the proportionality test. Forceful counter-arguments would be the rights of the child and the right to respect for family life, which States have to protect when they act within the scope of EU law. Thereby note must be taken of the ECtHR judgments in the *Mennesson* and *Labassee* cases (ch. 2). See also Ch. 9, section 9.6.3.

353 Case C-336/94 *Dafeki* [1997] ECR I-6761, ECLI:EU:C:1997:579, para. 19.

354 Possibly another avenue could be via the right to receive services (Art. 56 TFEU), if surrogacy can indeed be qualified as a service. The non-recognition of parental links with a child born through surrogacy in another Member State could then possibly be seen as discouraging and thus restricting the right to receive services.

355 COM (2010) 747 final. In the so-called Stockholm programme (OJ C115/1, p. 13), the European Council had yet invited the Commission to: '[...] follow up on the recent study on the possible problems encountered with regard to civil status documents and access to registers of such documents.' It was held that '[i]n the long term, it might be considered whether mutual recognition of the effects of civil status documents could be appropriate, at least in certain areas. Work developed by the International Commission on Civil Status should be taken into account in this particular field.'

356 According to the Green paper, civil status records are '[...] records executed by an authority in order to record the life events of each citizen such as birth, filiation, adoption, marriage, recognition of paternity, death and also a surname change following marriage, divorce, a registered partnership, recognition, change of sex or adoption.' See COM (2010) 747 final, para. 4.1.

The Commission's main policy objectives were: (1) to reduce obstacles to the free movement of citizens; (2) to guarantee the continuity and permanence of the civil status situation to European citizens exercising their right to free movement and (3) to increase legal certainty in relation to civil status matters.[357] It was held that it had to be possible to guarantee the continuity and permanence of a civil status situation to all European citizens exercising their right of freedom of movement:

> '[...] the legal status acquired by the citizen in the first Member State [...] should not be questioned by the authorities of the second Member State since this would constitute a hindrance and source of objective problems hampering the exercise of citizens' rights.'[358]

The Commission saw three policy options in regard of recognition of the effects of civil status records: (1) assisting national authorities to cooperate more effectively 'until there is greater convergence of MS' substantive family law'; (2) automatic recognition 'of civil status situations established in other Member States' or (3) harmonisation of conflict-of-laws rules.[359]

The second option was the most far-reaching, as it implied that once parental links had been established in one Member States, all other Member States had to accept these – even if surrogacy had been involved. The various contributions by national authorities in the public consultation process showed that such automatic recognition, if indeed proposed by the Commission, is not very likely to meet with unanimity in the Council. The German Federal Government, for example, put forward that in cases concerning issues like 'the filiation of a child in the case of a "surrogate mother"' and 'the introduction of presumptions of filiation in favour of the mother's registered female partner', the EU could not require a Member State's legislature '[...] to place its family law at the disposal of the [...] other Member States without restriction, allowing the persons concerned to have a family law relationship that exist[ed] under the law of another Member State to be registered in that State even though they [had] no close ties with that state's legal order.'[360] According to the German government,

> '[i]n such a case there would be no justification for this legal order, which is purely fortuitous or chosen comparatively freely by the persons concerned, to take precedence over the assessments of legal orders which – on the basis, say, of the nationality of the persons concerned or where they actually live – have an objectively closer connection with the facts and hence a greater claim to be applied.'[361]

---

357 COM (2010) 747 final.

358 *Idem*, para. 4.1.

359 The Green Paper made clear that the Commission had 'neither the power nor the intention [...] to modify the national definition of marriage.' *Idem*, para. 4.3.

360 Federal Government observations on COM (2010) 747 final, pp. 12–13, online available at www.ec.europa.eu/justice/newsroom/civil/opinion/files/110510/public_authorities/germany_minjust_en.pdf, visited June 2014.

361 *Idem*.

The option of harmonisation of conflict-of-laws rules received more support during the public consultation, but met with critique as well. It therefore seems more realistic to anticipate that only the first policy option – i.e., closer cooperation between Member States – could receive the required unanimity in the Council. Such cooperation, by nature, does not affect the Member States' possibilities to uphold and apply their own national standards in cross-border situations, for instance by means of public policy exceptions.

The public consultation was closed in May 2011. Both the EESC[362] and the Committee of the Regions have published an Opinion on the matter.[363] In a Resolution of 2012, the European Parliament called on the Commission to propose measures to mutually recognise the effects of civil status documents on the basis of the principle of mutual recognition.[364] In the subsequent year the Commission published a proposal for a regulation on the free movement of public documents, which aimed to abolish requirements of proof of the genuineness of public documents, or the signatures of national officials on such documents, as issued by public authorities in other Member States.[365] The question of the recognition of the effects of civil status records was not, however, addressed in this proposal.[366] On that point so far no further legislative initiative has been taken.[367]

3.6.3.2. EP study on surrogacy in the EU (2013)

The European Parliament Committee on Legal Affairs has in recent years expressed a particular interest in surrogacy in the European Union. In 2010 at the request of this Committee a note was published on mutual recognition of surrogacy agreements. The note proposed

362 European Economic and Social Committee, 'Opinion on the Communication from the Commission to the European Parliament, the Council, the European Economic and Social Committee and the Committee of the Regions on Reinforcing sanctioning regimes in the financial services sector', COM (2010) 716 final. The EESC considered that, in connection with civil status records, the Commission had to: (1) establish a *supra*national optional system for the European civil status record; (2) start the work needed to harmonise rules concerning conflicts of law, and (3) '[...] establish mutual recognition by identifying the minimum requirements to be met by civil status records and consensus on the presumption of their general validity within the EU, once it has been verified that the relevant authority has issued them lawfully.'

363 Committee of the Regions, 'Opinion on Green Paper 'Less bureaucracy for citizens: Promoting free movement of public documents and recognition of the effects of civil status records', [2012] OJ C54/23.

364 European Parliament Resolution of 24 May 2012 on the fight against homophobia in Europe (2012/2657(RSP)) P7_TA(2012)0222). In a Resolution of November 2010 the European Parliament had yet welcomed the Commission's efforts to empower citizens to exercise their free movement rights and 'strongly' supported plans to enable the mutual recognition of the effects of civil status documents. European Parliament Resolution on civil law, commercial law, family law and Private international law aspects of the Action plan implementing the Stockholm Programme, 23 November 2010, P7_TA(2010)0426.

365 Commission, 'Proposal for a Regulation of the European Parliament and of the Council on promoting the free movement of citizens and businesses by simplifying the acceptance of certain public documents in the European Union and amending Regulation (EU) No 1024/2012', COM (2013) 228 final.

366 It was stressed in the proposal (at p. 7) that the draft Regulation did '[...] not deal with the recognition of the content of public documents issued by the authorities of the Member States.'

367 It is noted that this research was concluded on 31 July 2014.

> '[...] concerted efforts at the level of the EU and the Hague Conference for Private International Law in two directions: (i) to study cross-border surrogacy (its nature, magnitude and personal experiences) and (ii) to produce an international Convention on private international aspects of surrogacy arrangements following the model of the Hague Intercountry Adoption Convention.'[368]

Subsequently, in 2013 a comparative study on surrogacy regimes of the EU Member States came out, which also addressed the question of whether there was a need for a common EU approach to the issue (see also 3.4.4 above). The authors of the report alleged that leaving the free movement rules to operate as they did amounted to 'an implicit authorisation of surrogacy'. They also observed that '[...] mutual recognition within the EU (mostly via national laws and not EU law) allow[ed] the desired civil and parental status of children born though surrogacy to be recognised in their State of residence.'[369] Because '[...] a fragile consensus [...] in relation to the acknowledgment of the child's civil status and legal parenthood' could perhaps be identified, the authors of the report held it imaginable that EU law 'authorised' what they called 'ex-post mechanisms of recognition'.[370] The report made no specific proposals for possible EU law instruments to enable such recognition, but merely held '[...] a harmonisation of conflict-of-law rules or a mutual recognition' on the basis of Articles 67(4) and 81 TFEU imaginable and '[t]he deepening of civil status mutual recognition [...] a good solution'.[371] When no unanimity could be found for such an EU response to surrogacy, the enhanced cooperation procedure was considered 'an interesting one'.[372] Another possible approach suggested in the report was that the EU could join a (to be drafted) international instrument on surrogacy.[373] The report concluded that further research was needed in respect of, *inter alia*, 'the EU legal basis and their potential to frame surrogacy'.[374] The report was presented by the Committee on Legal Affairs in July 2013, but has not resulted in any legislative action at EU level in this field.

3.6.4. The European Arrest Warrant and reproductive matters

Following the adoption of the Council Framework Decision on the European Arrest Warrant (EAW) in 2002, the then existing complex and time-consuming formal European extradition system, was replaced by a system of surrender between judicial

368 European Parliament, Policy Department C, Citizen's rights and constitutional affairs, *Recognition of parental responsibility: biological parenthood v. legal parenthood, i.e. mutual recognition of surrogacy agreements: What is the current situation in the MS? Need for EU action?* Note PE 432–738, 2010, p. 9.

369 Brunet et al. 2013, *supra* n. 134, at p. 197.

370 *Idem*, at p. 197.

371 *Idem*, at p. 198–199.

372 *Idem*, at p. 198.

373 *Idem*, at p. 199.

374 *Idem*, at p. 199.

authorities.[375] This was seen as '[...] the first concrete measure in the field of criminal law implementing the principle of mutual recognition which the European Council referred to as the "cornerstone" of judicial cooperation.'[376]

On the basis of Article 2 of the Framework Decision a European Arrest Warrant may be issued for acts punishable by the law of the issuing Member State by a custodial sentence or a detention order for a maximum period of at least 12 months or, where a sentence has been passed or a detention order has been made, for sentences of at least four months.

Under the old extradition system every extradition request was tested on the basis of the principle of double-criminality following which the acts for which extradition was requested constituted an offence under the law of both the extraditing and the executing Member State. Because this was a time-consuming assessment, the Commission proposed to abolish this principle. This was not, however, acceptable to many Member States, including the Netherlands and Germany. *Inter alia*, concerns were expressed that in some States abortion was perceived as murder or grievous bodily injury and that consequently States with a more liberal regime would risk needing to surrender citizens to States where abortion was criminalised.[377] The Netherlands pled for the drafting of a 'negative' list of offences that would be excluded from the scope of application of the EAW.[378] Such list was to include issues like euthanasia, abortion and certain drugs offences.[379]

A compromise was found by the drawing-up of a list of certain offences in respect of which States have to surrender pursuant to a European Arrest Warrant, without verification of the double criminality of the act. This is the case only if the offences are punishable in the issuing Member State by a custodial sentence or a detention order for a maximum period of at least three years. The list includes, *inter alia*, murder,

---

375 Council Framework Decision 2002/584/JHA of 13 June 2002 on the European Arrest Warrant and the surrender procedures between Member States, amended by Council Framework Decision 2009/299/JHA of 26 February 2009 amending Framework Decisions 2002/584/JHA, 2005/214/JHA, 2006/783/JHA, 2008/909/JHA and 2008/947/JHA, thereby enhancing the procedural rights of persons and fostering the application of the principle of mutual recognition to decisions rendered in the absence of the person concerned at the trial [2009] OJ L81/24.

376 Recital 6 in the Preamble to Council Framework Decision 2002/584/JHA.

377 Sections 58 and 59 of the Irish Offences Against the Person Act 1861.

378 The implementation of the EAW Framework Decision in the Netherlands involved extensive parliamentary debates, in which concerns were expressed this endangered the Dutch legislation concerning abortion, drugs and – in particular – euthanasia. Other than is the case concerning euthanasia (Art. 13 Overleveringswet [Act on the surrender of persons]) the Dutch implementation Act does not provide for a special regulation in respect of abortion.

379 The Irish Minister of Justice supported the inclusion of list with offences to which the double criminality principles would not apply, but he was against the Dutch proposal. D. Staunton, 'Disagreements slow plans for anti-terrorism laws in EU; A proposed European arrest warrant has caused clashes among states, writes Denis Staunton', *The Irish Times* 17 October 2001, p. 13. Ireland, furthermore, protested as it had to amend its Constitution in order to provide for surrender of its nationals to other EU Member States. 'Euthanasie ongewild hoger op EU-agenda', *NRC Handelsblad* 17 October 2001, pp. 1–2. Compare F. Kools, 'Gedoogbeleid onder vuur EU; Europees strafrecht', *Trouw* 18 October 2001, p. 4.

grievous bodily injury and illicit trade in human organs and tissue.[380] For all other offences, not listed in the relevant Article 2(2), the principle of double criminality applies; surrender may be subject to the condition that the acts for which the EAW has been issued constitute an offence under the law of the executing Member State, whatever the constituent elements or however it is described.[381] Following Article 4(7)(a), the executing judicial authority may refuse to execute the EAW where it relates to offences which are regarded by the law of the executing Member State as having been committed in whole or in part in the territory of the executing Member State.[382]

Article 2(3) provides for a possibility for the Council to extend or amend the list of categories of offence as contained in Article 2(2). It may do so in the light of reports submitted by the Commission on the operation of the Framework Decision.[383] In its 2006 review of the application of the EAW, the Commission observed that some Member States had indeed expressed the intention to review the list of crimes in respect of which the double criminality requirement was lifted '[...] in particular due to concerns in relation to abortion, euthanasia and possession of drugs.'[384] The present author is not, however, aware of any follow-up in this respect.[385] In an annex to its 2011 report, the Commission noted that the Netherlands had stated that it would not surrender a national for the prosecution '[...] for an offence that [was] not an offence under Dutch law, because it [was] impossible under the relevant treaties and the national law to transfer a person where the requirement of double criminality

380 Art. 2(2) Framework Decision 2002/584/JHA.

381 Arts. 2(4) and 5(1) Framework Decision 2002/584/JHA. On the basis of Art. 2 of the Framework Decision a European Arrest Warrant may be issued for acts punishable by the law of the issuing Member State by a custodial sentence or a detention order for a maximum period of at least 12 months or, where a sentence has been passed or a detention order has been made, for sentences of at least four months.

382 As Blekxtoon and Van Ballegooij explain, this provision respects the interests of the requested state might have '[...] in the case *not* being prosecuted, at least in not being obliged to arrest and surrender the requested person, because the act is not punishable under its law and is in that state perhaps even valued positively instead of being condemned.' The authors give 'the obvious example' of ''murder' committed by a physician who has ended the life of an incurable patient (at his/her sincere request) whose severe suffering could no be relieved (euthanasia)'. R. Blekxtoon and W. van Ballegooij, *Handbook on the European Arrest Warrant* (The Hague, T.M.C. Asser Press 2005) p. 161. Under Art. 4(7)(b) such refusal is also permitted if the EAW relates to offences which have been committed outside the territory of the issuing Member State and the law of the executing Member State does not allow prosecution for the same offences when committed outside its territory.

383 Arts. 2(2) and 34(3) Framework Decision 2002/584/JHA.

384 Commission, 'Staff Working Document annexed to the Report from the Commission based on Art. 34 of the Council Framework Decision of 13 June 2002 on the European Arrest Warrant and the surrender procedures between Member States (revised version)', COM (2006) 8 final, p. 6. The Commission held the fact that Belgian legislation provided that abortion and euthanasia were not covered by 'murder or grievous bodily harm', to be contrary to the Framework Decision, since it is the law of the issuing state and not the executing state which determines whether an offence is within the list.

385 The 2009 amendment (*supra* n. 375), did not provide for any such change. A 2011 Commission working documents notes in respect of Belgium: 'The limitation of the list of offences with regard to euthanasia and abortion was made at the time of the legislative adoption of the Belgian implementing legislation. There is no political will to change it.' Commission, 'Staff working document to the 2011 report of the Commission Report from the Commission to the European Parliament and the Council on the implementation since 2007 of the Council Framework Decision of 13 June 2002 on the European arrest warrant and the surrender procedures between Member States', COM (2011) 175 final.

ha[d] not been met.' The Netherlands reportedly did not see a contradiction with the Framework Decision, since the Framework Decision did not regulate return but left that to the Member State. The Commission held it nevertheless to be '[...] clear that one of the principal advantages of this Framework Decision compared with previous extradition arrangements [was] the removal of the double criminality requirement in relation to the Article 2(2) list of categories of offences.' It held that the Dutch position 'obviously' ran counter to this.'[386]

Under the EAW Framework as currently in force, it is, in theory, possible that Member States with restrictive abortion laws, such as Ireland, can issue an EAW in a case where a national had an abortion in a Member State with more permissive abortion regimes. For such an EAW to escape the double criminality requirement, the issuing Member State would have to qualify the offences as any of the offences enlisted in Article 2(2) of the Framework Decision, for example 'murder' or 'grievous bodily injury'.[387] While the minimum requirement of three years of Article 2(2) may have been met in some cases,[388] it is not, from a language perspective a foregone conclusion that the aforementioned qualifications would indeed be employed by the issuing State. The requested State can, furthermore, refuse to execute the EAW if the abortion has taken place on its territory (Article 4(7)(a) of the Framework Decision). Moreover, it may not be very likely that States would indeed proceed to issue such an EAW, not only from a diplomatic viewpoint, considering the sensitivity of the matter in Europe, but also considering the low prosecution practice of most States.[389] Hence, the practical relevance of the EAW for abortion cases may after all prove to be limited.

In respect of AHR treatment or surrogacy no specific concerns were expressed in the process towards adoption of the EAW and the present author is not aware of any such discussions since. It is therefore equally uncertain whether the EAW regime could possibly and would ever be applied to matters related to AHR or surrogacy. As yet open questions are, for example, if trade in gametes could be qualified as 'illegal trade in human cells and tissue', in some circumstances,[390] and whether certain types of AHR treatment could be considered as 'grievous bodily injury' within the meaning of Article 2(2). So far, the CJEU has not given any ruling on these matters.

---

386 COM (2011) 175 final, pp. 131–132.

387 Douglas-Scott considered abortion to be indeed 'capable of falling within Art. 2(2). S. Douglas-Scott, 'The rule of law in the European Union – putting the security into the area of freedom, security and justice', 29 *European Law Review* (2004) p. 219 at p.225.

388 See for example Ch. 5, section 5.2.8.

389 See for example Ch. 5, section 5.2.9 and ch. 6, section 6.2.4.

390 Blekxtoon and Van Ballegooij have put forward that even if the conduct described in the arrest warrant is not illicit under the law of the state where the arrest warrant is meant to be executed, surrender is not barred 'as the illicit trafficking as such falls within the category and consequently double criminality is not to be verified.' Blekxtoon and Ballegooij, van 2005, *supra* n. 382, at p. 161.

3.7. Conclusions

EU law contains little to no substantial standard-setting in respect of abortion, AHR treatment or surrogacy. These matters have not gone unnoticed at the EU political level, but the EU legislature has been quite firm in stressing that there is no EU competence to regulate for these sensitive issues substantively. EU law only sets certain quality and safety standards for AHR services and for the placing in the market of *in vitro* diagnostic medical devices. While these contain certain rules on the donation of gametes, States are given much discretion in this regard (section 3.3.2 above). The EU's non-discrimination law, furthermore, has only limited implications for Member States' regulation of this area. States must provide for protection of women who are in an advanced stage of IVF treatment against dismissal, but there is no obligation under EU law to grant paid leave to intended mothers who had a child through a surrogacy agreement and restrictions on access to AHR treatment cannot be challenged on the basis of EU non-discrimination law (sections 3.3.3 and 3.3.4).

If one thing, the present chapter shows that as a result of EU (free movement) law EU citizens and residents of EU Member States have a broader range of choice when it comes to medical treatment.[391] Although exhaustive statistics are lacking, it is obvious that such cross-border movement in reproductive matters indeed takes place within the EU (section 3.4). Once treatment can be qualified as a 'medical service' – which is the case when it is lawful in at least one Member State and normally provided for remuneration – the EU regime on cross-border health care as set out in section 3.5 applies. This means that people have access to medical services, including abortion and AHR treatment, that may not be available or even prohibited in their home country. States remain free, however, to decide what treatment they wish to regulate or to prohibit within their own jurisdictions.[392]

While EU law has thus increased access to medical treatment, free movement can, nevertheless, be restrained. For instance, States are under no obligation to reimburse treatment obtained abroad, if that treatment is not among the benefits provided for by their national legislation (section 3.6.2.1). Whether they can set prior authorisation requirements in cases concerning abortion and AHR treatment, can not be said with absolute certainty (section 3.6.2.2). There are equally questions as to the obligations of States under EU law to provide medical follow-up care after a patient has had an abortion or has obtained AHR treatment in another Member State (section 3.6.2.3). It furthermore remains to be seen if the CJEU will some day rule that different regimes

[391] Compare Van de Gronden and Szyszczak who held that '[...] the freedom of choice (of medical treatment) of individuals is a value that is protected in the case law of the EU Courts.' Gronden, van de and Szyszczak 2011, *supra* n. 170, at p. 487. De la Rosa observed that '[t]hrough [the] facilitation of access to care, citizens can access forms of care that, in the State in which they are insured, are either non-existent or rare, and thereby benefit from the various structures and health facilities found in different States.' De la Rosa 2012, *supra* n. 33, at p. 23.

[392] Presumably, it is for that reason that Hervey and McHale observed in 2004 that until that time, 'little concrete success' could be reported in cases where parties had, by relying on EU law, sought to undermine national legal standards on human reproduction, including those enshrined in national constitutions. Hervey and McHale 2004, *supra* n. 47, at p. 153.

in respect of abortion, AHR treatment and/or surrogacy may in themselves constitute an obstacle to free movement (section 3.6.2.5). What seems established, however, is that States must actively provide information about foreign abortion services and AHR treatment options through national contact points (section 3.6.2.4). This does not hold for surrogacy, however, as that does not qualify as health care under the Patient Mobility Directive.

In respect of surrogacy there is certainly nothing provided at EU level. Intended mothers are not protected under EU employment law (section 3.3.4) and none of the existing EU PIL instruments provides for the recognition of parental links established in another Member State (section 3.6.3). The latter issue has, however, caught the attention of EU institutions and the first careful initiatives have been taken that could lead to the adoption of EU instruments in the future. Whether this indeed materialises, yet remains to be seen, particularly now that unanimity in the Council is required. In any case, any possible EU instrument could only regulate for cross-border surrogacy cases within the EU, while in many international surrogacy cases third countries are involved.

All in all, while EU law may potentially have even more impact on the reproductive matters that are central to this case study, it may well be that this potential will not be exploited, exactly because of the sensitivity of the matter at stake.

Chapter 4
Germany

4.1. Constitutional framework

The relevant constitutional framework for the German law on reproductive issues relates to various provisions of the German Basic Law. Prominent and important rights that are involved in reproductive matters are the right to human dignity (Article 1(1) Basic Law), the right to free development of the personality (Article 2(1) Basic Law) and the special protection of the family (Article 6(1) Basic Law).[1] This section firstly gives a brief introduction to the first two Articles. The special protection of the family is closely intertwined with the special protection of marriage and is therefore set out elaborately in Chapter 10.[2] Subsection 4.1.3 explains how a right to procreate has been held to follow from these rights. Next, three interrelated issues concerning the rights of the (future) child are discussed, namely; the status of the unborn, the best interests of the child and the right to access to information about one's genetic origins.

4.1.1. Human dignity (Article 1(1)) as guiding principle under the German Basic Law

With the atrocities of World War II freshly in mind, the drafters of the German Basic Law (1949) wanted the new constitution to provide an answer to the totalitarian contempt of the individual by the National Socialistic regime.[3] Human dignity (*'die Würde des Menschen'*) was therefore taken as the basic and guiding principle of the Basic Law.[4] It was included in its first provision, Article 1(1), which reads:

> 'Human dignity shall be inviolable. To respect and protect it shall be the duty of all state authority.'[5]

Illustrative of its fundamental significance in German law is the fact that this provision is protected from amendment (the so-called eternity clause

1 Art. 6(1) Basic Law reads: 'Marriage and the family shall enjoy the special protection of the state.'

2 The right to equal treatment as protected under Art. 3 of the German Basic Law is also discussed in Ch. 10.

3 H. Dreier, 'Art. 1', in H. Dreier (ed.), *Grundgesetz-Kommentar, Band 1, Präambel, Artikel 1–19* [Commentary to the Basic Law, Volume 2, Preamble, Articles 1–19], 2nd edn. (Tübingen, Mohr Siebeck 2004) p. 39 at p. 161.

4 *Idem*, at p. 154.

5 English translation by C. Tomuschat and D.P. Currie, online available at: www.gesetze-im-internet.de/englisch_gg/index.html, visited June 2014.

('*Ewigkeitsgarantie*'[6])).[7] Over the years, human dignity – interpreted by the German Federal Constitutional Court (*Bundesverfassungsgericht*, BVerfG) as the supreme value ('*obersten Wert*') of the Basic Law[8] – has come to serve as an interpretative and guiding principle ('*Grundnorm*'[9]) for the other provisions of the Basic Law.[10] Next to this '*Fundierungscharakter*', human dignity is also a right of its own ('*Norm des objektiven Verfassungsrecht*'). While an exact definition is difficult to find, the Constitutional Court held in 2009 that the protection of human dignity was based '[…] on the idea of Man as a spiritual and moral being which [had] the capabilities of defining himself, and of developing, in freedom.'[11] The common denominator of the protection of Article 1(1) has accordingly been held to be to prevent the human being from being downgraded to a simple means ('*der konkrete Mensch* [*wird*] *zum Objekt, zu einem Bloßen Mittel, zur vertretbaren Größe herabgewuridgt*').[12]

Numerous individual rights have been brought under the scope of this first and fundamental provision of the German Basic Law. Authors who have been critical of the frequent invocation of human dignity in all sorts of contexts have warned against inflation ('*Trivialisierung*' and '*Inflationierung*') of the principle.[13] It is disputed in German legal scholarship whether it follows from the fundamental character of the right to human dignity of Article 1(1) Basic Law that it is absolute, i.e., that no balancing against other fundamental rights is allowed.[14]

4.1.2. Article 2: personal freedoms

Article 2 of the German Basic Law contains a number of personal freedoms that are relevant for the present case study on reproductive matters. Its first paragraph provides for a general personality right (*das allgemeine Persönlichkeitsrecht*) and reads:

> 'Every person shall have the right to free development of his personality insofar as he does not violate the rights of others or offend against the constitutional order or the moral law.'

---

6 Dreier 2004, *supra* n. 3, at p. 163.

7 On the basis of Art. 79(3) Basic Law, the principles of Arts. 1 and 20 Basic Law cannot be amended.

8 *Inter alia* BVerfG 16 January 1957, Az. 1 BvR 253/56, *NJW* 1957 p. 297 and BVerfG 16 July 1969, Az. 1 BvL 19/63, *NJW* 1969 p. 1707. See Dreier 2004, *supra* n. 3, at p. 161, footnote 125.

9 Dreier 2004, *supra* n. 3, at p. 161.

10 *Idem*, at p. 155.

11 BVerfG 30 June 2009, Az. 2 BvE 2/08 a.o., *NJW* 2009 p. 2267, para. 364.

12 Dreier 2004, *supra* n. 3, at p. 167, referring to 'G. Dürig, *AöR* 81 (1956)'.

13 Dreier 2004, *supra* n. 3, at pp. 164–166.

14 Dreier for instance argues that such balancing is not possible. Dreier 2004, *supra* n. 3, at p. 163, referring to BVerfG 10 October 1995, Az. 1 BvR 1476/91 a.o., *NJW* 1995 p. 3303 and BVerfG 11 March 2003 (dec.), Az. 1 BvR 426, *NJW* 2003 p. 1303.

This right is considered one of the most fundamental rights in the German Constitution,[15] as underlined by its position in the Basic Law, directly after the first Article on human dignity.[16] No exhaustive definition of this personality right exists,[17] but it in any case contains a right to respect for the private and intimate sphere, a right to personal autonomy, as well as a right to free development of the personality.[18] As explained further in the subsequent subsection, the latter right, *inter alia*, includes a right to procreate.

Further, on the basis of the second paragraph of Article 2, every person has the right to life and physical integrity. As explained in more detail below, the right to life has been held to apply from the moment of nidation.[19] The right to free development of the personality in combination with the right to physical integrity has also been understood as to contain a right to bio-ethical self-determination.[20]

4.1.3. The fundamental right to procreate

German legal scholarship generally accepts that a fundamental right to procreate (*'Recht auf Fortpflanzung'*) exists. This right is also referred to as right to reproductive autonomy (*'Recht auf reproduktive Autonomie'*) or right to have offspring (*'Recht auf Nachkommenschaft'*).[21] The foundation of the right to procreate in the German Basic Law, however, is debated. Some hold that a right to procreate can be derived from the right to free development of the personality (*'das allgemeine Persönlichkeitsrecht'*) of Article 2(1) in combination with Article 1(1) Basic Law.[22] It was also Article 2(1) from which the Federal Financial Court (*Bundesfinanzhof*, BFH) derived a right for women to bear children. According to the BFH, this includes a right to make use of

---

15 H. Lang, 'BeckOK GG Art. 2' ['Beck online Commentary to Art. 2 GG'], in: V. Epping and C. Hillgruber (eds.), *Beck'scher Online-Kommentar GG* [Beck Online Commentary to the German Basic Law], 22nd edn. (München, Verlag Beck 2014) Rn. 31.

16 U. Di Fabio, 'GG Art. 2' ['Art. 2 German Basic Law'], in: R. Herzorg et al. (eds.) *Maunz und Dürig Grundgesetz-Kommentar* [Maunz and Dürig Commentary to the Basic Law], 71st edn. (München, Verlag C.H. Beck 2014) Rn. 127–131.

17 *Idem*, Rn. 147–148.

18 *Idem*, Rn. 204.

19 See section 4.1.4.

20 Di Fabio 2014, *supra* n. 16, Rn. 204.

21 See R. Müller-Terpitz, 'Das Recht auf Fortpflanzung – Vorgaben der Verfassung und der EMRK' ['The right to procreate – guidelines of the German Constitution and the ECHR'], in: H. Frister and D. Olzen (eds.), *Reproduktionsmedizin, Rechtliche Fragestellungen. Dokumentation der Tagung zum 10-jährigen Bestehen des Instituts für Rechtsfragen der Medizin Düsseldorf* [Reproduction medicine, legal questions. Proceedings of the Conference for the 10 year anniversary of the Düsseldorf institute for medical legal issues] (Düsseldorf, Düsseldorf University Press 2010) p. 9 at p. 11 and M. Reinke, *Fortpflanzungsfreiheit und das Verbot der Fremdeizellspende* [Freedom of reproduction and the prohibition of egg-cell donation] (Berlin, Duncker & Humblot 2008) p. 190. Reinke refers to R. Badinter, 'Menschenrechte gegenüber de Fortschritten in der Medizin, der Biologie und der Biochemie – Wie soll sich die Rechtspolitik gegenüber der Humangenetik verhalten?', *RuP* 1985, p. 196; to T. Ramm, 'Die Fortpflanzung – ein Freiheitsrecht?', *JZ* 1989, p. 866 and to H. Kliemt, 'Normative Probleme der künstlichen Geschlechtsbestimmung und des Klonens', *ZRP* 1979, pp. 165 and 168.

22 Reinke 2008, *supra* n. 21, at p. 190, footnote 349.

medical methods to initiate a pregnancy, to the extent to which such measures are legal:

> 'Das Recht, Kinder zu gebären, gehört bei verheirateten wie bei unverheirateten Frauen zwar zum Kernbereich des Grundrechts auf freie Entfaltung der Persönlichkeit [...] und schließt das Recht ein, ärztliche Maßnahmen zur Herbeiführung einer Schwangerschaft vornehmen zu lassen, soweit diese rechtlich erlaubt sind.'[23]

Others base a right to procreate on the (right to) special protection of the family of Article 6(1) Basic Law.[24] Müller-Terpitz, for instance, argues that Article 6(1) protects a right to personal development within the family. This right, the author holds, necessarily also includes the foundation of such a family and thus the right to procreate.[25] A third view sees Article 6(1) Basic Law as a reinforcement of the right to free development of the personality.[26]

The right to procreate is not absolute and various German regulations concerning reproductive matters – as discussed more extensively in section 4.3 – have been regarded as (justified) interferences with the right to procreate.[27] Here, one may think of the prohibition on egg cell donation (see section 4.3.4.1 below) and the (former) prohibition on preimplantation genetic diagnosis (PGD, see 4.3.6 below).[28]

4.1.4. The status of the unborn under German law

The question as from what stage of development the (constitutional) protection of unborn life begins is subject to debate in German legal scholarship.[29] Views differ from a strict negation of any protection of unborn life, to a multistage ascent protection whereby the intensity of the protection is made dependent on the stage of development of the unborn life, to a full protection of all forms of human life.[30] In its abortion judgment of 1975 (see section 4.2.2 below) the Constitutional Court held that the right to life ex Article 2(2) Basic Law extends to the unborn life from the

23 The Court held: 'The right to bear children forms part of the core essence of the right to free development of the personality of both unmarried and married women [...] and includes the right to undergo medical treatment to procure a pregnancy, to the extent that such treatment is lawful.' BFH 28 July 2005, Az. III R 30/03, *NJW* 2005 p. 3517, para. 47. The BFH also held that no right to state finance or tax deduction for the costs of such AHR treatment can be derived from the right to free development of the personality.

24 As noted above, this right is discussed in more detail in Ch. 10, section 10.1.2.

25 Müller-Terpitz 2010, *supra* n. 21, at p. 12.

26 Reinke 2008, *supra* n. 21, at p. 190, footnote 350.

27 See Müller-Terpitz 2010, *supra* n. 21, at p. 15.

28 Other examples, that are not extensively discussed in this chapter are the limitation of the fertilisation of a maximum of three egg-cells per cycle (Art. 1(1)(4) ESchG) and the limitation of the implantation of embryos to a maximum of three per cycle (Art. 1(1)(3) ESchG).

29 M. Herdegen, ‚GG Art. 1 Abs 1' ['Art. 1 para. 1 GG'], in: R. Herzorg et al. (eds.), *Maunz und Dürig Grundgesetz-Kommentar* [Maunz and Dürig Commentary to the Basic Law], 55th ed (München, Verlag Beck 2011) Rn. 60.

30 Herdegen 2011, *supra* n. 29, Rn. 60.

moment of nidation, i.e., from the 14th day after conception.[31] The starting point of an entitlement to the constitutional right to life, is not, however, necessarily the same point in time, as the starting point of the protection of other constitutional rights. The more broadly defined right to human dignity may for instance extend to life before nidation, a view that is widely supported in legal scholarship.[32] In its 1975 judgment the Court left this question open,[33] and the BVerfG has never conclusively ruled on the matter. In legal scholarship, it has been argued that even if it is accepted that human dignity extends to the pre-nidative life, it cannot automatically be said that all biotechnological practices are in violation of Article 1(1) Basic Law.[34]

The question whether the embryo *in vitro* (i.e., outside the woman's body) also enjoys subjective rights to human dignity, life and physical integrity, has been subject of debate in legal scholarship.[35] In this respect again a distinction has been made between different stages of development of the *in vitro* unborn life, whereby the constitutional protection increases in force in accordance with its stage of development.[36] When drafting the Embryo Protection Act (*Embryoschutzgesetz*, ESchG) by the end of the 1980s (see 4.3.1 below), the German legislature took as a starting point that human life begins with '*Kernverschmelzung*', i.e., with the fertilisation of a human egg cell.[37] Accordingly, any processing of human embryos, even in the earliest cell stage, must be in conformity with the protection of human dignity ex Article 1(1) Basic Law, the legislature held.[38]

4.1.5. The best interests of the child

Even though the German Basic Law contains no specific Article on the rights of the child in general,[39] the best interests of the child ('*Kindeswohl*'), is also under German law an important notion. It has been held to find its constitutional foundation in

31 BVerfG 25 February 1975, Az. 1 BvF 2/74, *NJW* 1975 p. 573, para. 136.

32 Compare Herdegen 2011, *supra* n. 29, Rn. 61 and Dreier 2004, *supra* n. 3, at pp. 173 and 181.

33 The Court held that where human life exists, it is entitled to human dignity.

34 Dreier 2004, *supra* n. 3, at p. 186.

35 See Müller-Terpitz 2010, *supra* n. 21, at pp. 16 and 18.

36 Herdegen 2011, *supra* n. 29, Rn. 60 and 68. In 2014 the Administrative Court of Appeal of Münster ruled that the protection of children under Art. 42 of the Social Act, Book VIII did not apply to a cryopreserved embryo, but only applied to children from the moment of birth. OVG Münster 15 January 2014 (dec.), Az. 12 A 2078/13, paras. 12–18.

37 *BT-Drs.* XI/5460, p. 6. See also the Explanatory memorandum to the ESchG Bill, as printed in M. Lanz-Zumstein (ed.), *Embryonenschutz und Befruchtungstechnik, Seminarbericht und Stellungnahmen aus der Arbeitsgruppe "Gentechnologie" des deutschen Juristinnenbundes* [Protection of embryos and fertilisation techniques, Seminar report and statements of the working group "Genetic Engineering" of the German Women Lawyers' Association], (München, J. Schweitzer Verlag 1986) Annex 1, p. 155.

38 Lanz-Zumstein 1986, *supra* n. 37, at p. 156. The legislature typified the protection of human dignity as one of the primary aims pursued with the introduction of the Embryoschutzgezetz (EschG) [Embryo Protection Act] and the later Stamzellgesetz (StZG) [Stemm Cell Act]. *BT-Drs.* 11/5460, p. 6 and Art. 1 StZG, *BGBl. I*, p. 2277, last amended by *BGBl. I*, p. 1708.

39 Art. 6 Basic Law contains three paragraphs that concern rights of children in particular, namely paras. 2, 3 and 5.

a combination of rights, namely the right to free development of the personality (Article 2(1) in combination with Article 1(1)) as well as the parental responsibility of Article 6(2) Basic Law.[40]

4.1.6. The right to know one's genetic origins

In 1988 the BVerfG ruled for the first time that a child has a right to know about its lineage or genetic origins ('*Recht auf Kenntnis der Abstammung*').[41] In the relevant case, which concerned a child conceived in an extramarital affair, the Court based its finding on Article 6(5) (equal treatment of children born outside marriage)[42] in combination with Article 2(1) Basic Law (the general right to personality).[43] Shortly thereafter the Court grounded a right to know about one's genetic origins on Article 2(1) in connection with Article 1(1) Basic Law (the right to human dignity).[44]

In 2008 a new Article 1598a was included in the Civil Code, on the basis of which father, mother and child may each bring proceedings to claim consent to a genetic examination to clarify natural parentage.[45] If one of the family members refuses to give such consent, the family court can substitute that consent and order acquiescence

[40] Müller-Terpitz 2010, *supra* n. 21, at p. 19 and R. Müller-Terpitz, 'GG Art. 6 [Ehe, Familie, nicht eheliche Kinder]' ['Marriage, family, children born out of wedlock'], in: A. Spickhoff, *Medizinrecht* [Medical Law], 2nd edn. (München, Verlag Beck 2014) Rn. 12.

[41] BVerfG 18 January 1988 (dec.), Az. 1 BvR 1589/87, *NJW* 1988 p. 3010. See also R. Ratzel ,Beschränkung des Rechts auf Fortpflanzung durch das ärztliche Berufsrecht' ['Limitation of the right to procreate by means of the law on the medical profession'], in: H. Frister and D. Olzen (eds.), *Reproduktionsmedizin, Rechtliche Fragestellungen. Dokumentation der Tagung zum 10-jährigen Bestehen des Instituts für Rechtsfragen der Medizin Düsseldorf* [Reproduction medicine, legal questions. Proceedings of the Conference for the 10 year anniversary of the Düsseldorf institute for medical legal issues] (Düsseldorf, Düsseldorf University Press 2010) p. 43 at pp. 51–52.

[42] Art. 6(5) Basic Law reads: 'Children born outside of marriage shall be provided by legislation with the same opportunities for physical and mental development and for their position in society as are enjoyed by those born within marriage.' Translation from www.gesetze-im-internet.de/englisch_gg, visited June 2014.

[43] Art. 2(1) Basic Law reads: 'Every person shall have the right to free development of his personality insofar as he does not violate the rights of others or offend against the constitutional order or the moral law.' Translation from www.gesetze-im-internet.de/englisch_gg, visited June 2014.

[44] BVerfG 31 January 1989, Az. 1 BvL 17/87, *NJW* 1989 p. 891 and BVerfG 13 February 2007, Az. 1 BvR 421/05, *NJW* 2007 p. 753. See also J. Young Lee, *Unterhaltsverpflichtungen bei Leihmutterschaft* [Maintenance obligations in the case of surrogacy] (Baden-Baden, Nomos Verlagsgesellschaft 1996) pp. 91–108.

[45] Art. 1598a (1) BGB. This provision was inserted in the Civil Code following a 2007 BVerfG judgment in which the Constitutional Court found that a secret paternity test could not be used in court proceedings and commissioned the legislature to provide for proceedings in which paternity could be established. BVerfG 13 February 2007, Az. 1 BvR 421/05, *NJW* 2007 p. 753. See F. Klinkhammer, 'Der Scheinvater und sein Kind – Das Urteil des BVerfG vom 13.2.2007 und seine gesetzlichen Folgen' ['The ostensible father and his child – The judgment of the German Constitutional Court of 12 February 2007 and its legal consequences'], *Forum Familienrecht* 4/2007, pp. 128–131, online available at www.forum-familienrecht.de/neu/dateien/0407/128–131.pdf, visited March 2011. See also BGH 25 June 2008 (dec.), Az. XII ZB 163/06, *NJW* 2008 p. 3429 and BVerfG 13 October 2008 (dec.), Az. 1 BvR 1548/03, *NJW* 2009 p. 423.

in the taking of a sample.[46] The court has to suspend the proceedings '[...] if and as long as the clarification of the natural parentage would result in a considerable adverse effect on the best interests of the minor child which would be unreasonable for the child even taking into account the concerns of the person entitled to clarify.'[47]

The first case on the implications of the right to know one's genetic origins in the context of heterologous insemination was decided in 2013 by the Court of Appeal (*Oberlandesgericht*, OLG) of Hamm.[48] This Court ruled that the interests of a child conceived with donated sperm, to get information about its genetic origins had precedence over the rights of the sperm donor and the doctor involved to keep such information confidential. This implied an obligation for the doctor involved to provide information about the donor to the child.[49] The Court held that knowledge about 'constitutive factors' such as descent was important for the free development of the personality. It gave important information about one's genes, formed the personality and was a key factor in the development of the personal identity. The Court acknowledged that personal freedoms of the donor were also concerned, but ruled that the rights of the donor-conceived child were to be given more and decisive weight.[50] A year later another OLG ruled, that sperm donors in turn have a right to be informed about the birth of children following their donation.[51]

4.2. German abortion legislation

While nowadays abortion is no longer a hot topic in Germany,[52] it was definitely so in the 1970s and 1980s. In the former Federal Republic of Germany (FRG, 'West Germany') in particular, abortion was a highly controversial topic. While in the former German Democratic Republic (GDR, 'East Germany') rather liberal abortion laws were adopted and enacted, the FRG chose a considerably more restrictive path. These FRG abortion laws were, to a large extent, the result of an ongoing dialogue between the legislature and the Federal Constitutional Court. This also goes for the German abortion laws as currently in force in the unified Germany. The latest

---

46 Art. 1598a (2) BGB.

47 Art. 1598a (3) BGB. Translation taken from www.gesetze-im-internet.de/englisch_bgb/englisch_bgb.html#p5357, visited June 2014.

48 OLG Hamm 6 February 2013, Az. I-14 U 7/12, *NJW* 2013 p. 1167.

49 See also M. Wellenhoffer, 'Die Samenspende und ihre (späten) Rechtsfolgen' ['Sperm donation and its (late) legal consequences'], *Zeitschrift für das gesamte Familienrecht, FamRZ* (2013) p. 825 and A. Jorzig, 'Anspruch auf Kenntnis der genetischen Abstammung eines durch eine heterologe Insemination gezeugten Kindes' ['The right to information on the genetic descent of a child born through heterologous insemination'], *jurisPR-MedizinR* (2013) Anm. 1.

50 OLG Hamm 6 February 2013, Az. I-14 U 7/12, *NJW* 2013 p. 1167, para. 52.

51 OLG Karlsruhe 7 February 2014 (dec.), Az. 16 UF 274/13, *NJW* 2014 p. 2050.

52 Ulsenheimer observes that since the year 2000 the discussions about abortions have diminished considerably. Further, in legal praxis, the criminal prohibition of abortion plays at present a marginal role, with less and less, to almost no criminal convictions on the basis of this provision. K. Ulsenheimer, 'Schwangerschaftsabbruch' ['Termination of pregnancy'], in: A. Laufs and B.R. Kern (eds.), *Handbuch des Arztrechts* [Handbook of medical law], 4th edn. (München, Verlag Beck 2010) Rn. 6.

substantial amendment to the present German abortion laws dates back to 2009 and concerned so-called late abortions (see 4.2.6 below).

This section gives a – mainly chronological – overview of the coming into existence of the various abortion regimes in former West Germany, former East Germany, as well as present (unified) Germany. To the extent that these are available, relevant statistics concerning criminal prosecutions and convictions on the basis of these laws are provided.[53] This sketch of the different German abortion regimes gives an insight in the possible causes for cross-border movement for abortions from (as well as within) Germany, a topic that will be discussed in section 4.4 below.

4.2.1. Early German abortion legislation

The Prussian Criminal Code of 1851[54] and the subsequent Criminal Code of 1871 (*Reichsstrafgesetzbuch*) fully criminalised abortion.[55] A pregnant woman who wilfully terminated her pregnancy risked a penalty of a minimum of six months and a maximum of five years imprisonment.[56] These provisions remained in force for approximately 50 years. From the first decade of the 20th century onwards, several proposals for legalisation of abortion were introduced,[57] but none was followed-up by actual legislation. Only the penalties to be imposed in case of abortion were made less severe in 1926.[58] Further, in 1927, the *Reichsgericht* – at that time the highest German court – ruled that abortion in cases of grave danger to the life and health of the mother was an 'extra-statutory necessity' and accordingly could not be considered a crime.[59]

Under the national-socialist regime, abortions were regarded as 'attacks on the life force of the nation' and laws regulating the matter were held to serve the 'protection of the nation's strength'.[60] Penalties for abortions were seriously augmented and

53 Other than in Ch. 5 and Ch. 6, these statistics on prosecutions are not discussed in a separate subsection, but are integrated in the main text. This choice has been made deliberately, because the German legal situation has been more complex, particularly because of the two separate and simultaneous regimes before the 1990 reunification.

54 Arts. 181 and 182 Strafgesetzbuch für die Preußischen Staaten [Criminal Code for the Prusian State] of 14 April 1851, as referred to in BVerfG 25 February 1975, Az. 1 BvF 2/74 a.o., *NJW* 1975 p. 573, para. 32.

55 Strafgesetzbuch für das Deutsche Reich [Criminal Code for the German Reich] of 15 May 1871, *RGBl.* p. 127, as referred to BVerfG 25 February 1975, Az. 1 BvF 2/74 a.o., *NJW* 1975 p. 573, para. 32.

56 Art. 218 StGB (*old*). See BVerfG 25 February 1975, Az. 1 BvF 2/74 a.o., *NJW* 1975 p. 573, paras. 33–35.

57 See BVerfG 25 February 1975, Az. 1 BvF 2/74 a.o., *NJW* 1975 p. 573, para. 32, where the Court referred to 'Gustav Radbruchs Entwurf eines Allgemeinen Deutschen Strafgesetzbuches (1922), Tübingen 1952, p. 28, § 225' and 'Grotjahn-Radbruch, *Die Abtreibung der Leibesfrucht*, 1921'.

58 Gesetz zur Abänderung des Strafgesetzbuchs [Act on the Amendment of the Criminal Code] of 18 May 1926, *RGBl. I* p. 239 as cited in BVerfG 25 February 1975, Az. 1 BvF 2/74 a.o., *NJW* 1975 p. 573, para. 7.

59 Reichsgericht 11 March 1927, 61 RGst 242 (1937), as cited in BVerfG 25 February 1975, Az. 1 BvF 2/74 a.o., *NJW* 1975 p. 573, para. 6.

60 BVerfG 25 February 1975, Az. 1 BvF 2/74 a.o., *NJW* 1975 p. 573, para. 9.

included even the death penalty.[61] At the same time a policy was adopted whereby 'unworthy lives' were aborted for eugenic reasons.[62]

After World War II the abortion laws of the Federal Republic of Germany (FRG, 'West Germany') and the German Democratic Republic (GDR, 'East Germany') developed in different directions. The FRG re-enacted the general prohibition on abortion of the pre Nazi era laws. Further, the Basic Law was adopted which included the rights to human dignity, the right to life and the right to bodily integrity, of which, in any case, the right to life would later be held applicable to unborn life by the Constitutional Court (see 4.2.2). In the GDR, instead, the emancipation and self-determination of the woman were central and accordingly more liberal abortion laws were enacted.[63] Initially the different states (*Länder*) of the GDR had different abortion laws, all allowing for abortion on the basis of a criminological or medical indication and some additionally allowing for abortion on social, medical-social or eugenetic grounds.[64] In 1950 an abortion regime for the entire GDR was adopted, following which abortion was allowed if a special Committee had judged that the life or the health of the pregnant women was seriously endangered.[65] As Lammich explained, some of these Committees included social grounds in their judgments. This was reason for the Minister of Health to issue an instruction in 1965, following which a serious deterioration of the woman's physical or mental health constituted legitimate ground for an abortion.[66]

In West Germany, in the 1960s, various bills seeing at the liberalisation of the abortion laws were tabled in the FRG Parliament.[67] While none of the proposals to legalise abortion under certain conditions was adopted, the sentences to be imposed were again lowered in 1969.[68] Further, a considerable decline is visible in prosecutions

61 Verordnung zur Durchführung der Verordnung zum Schutz von Ehe, Familie und Mutterschaft [Regulation on the Introduction oft he Regulation on the Protection of Marriage, Family and Maternity] of 18 March 1943, *RGBl. I* p. 169.

62 A. Eser, 'Reform of German abortion law: first experiences', 34 *The American Journal of Comparative Law* (1986) p. 369 at p. 371, footnote 13, referring to 1935 *RGBl. I* p. 773.

63 See also A. Laufs, 'Schwangerschaftsabbruch' ['Termination of pregnancy'], in A. Laufs et al., *Arztrecht* [Medical law] 6th edn. (München, Verlag Beck 2009) Rn. 27–58. In Rn. 45, footnote 77 the author refers to Arts. 153–155 StGB-DDR, Act of 12 January 1968, revised version of 14 December 1988, *GBl. I* 1989, No. 3, p. 33 with the amendment of 29 June 1990, *GBl. I*, No. 39, p. 526; Art. 1(2) and Art. 3(1) Gesetz über die Unterbrechung der Schwangerschaft [Act on the Termination of Pregnancy] of 9 March 1972, *GBl. I*, No. 5, p. 89. Laufs explains that after 12 weeks of pregnancy an indication model applied.

64 See S. Lammich, 'Landesbericht Deutsche Demokratische Republik' ['National report German Democratic Republic'], in A. Eser and H.-G. Koch, *Schwangerschaftsabbruch im internationalen Vergleich, Rechtlichen Regelungen – Soziale Rahmenbedingungen – Empirische Grunddaten, Teil 1: Europa* [Abortion in international comparison, legal regulation – social framework – empirial basic data, part 1: Europe] (Baden-Baden, Nomos Verlagsgesellschaft 1988) p. 326 at pp. 337–338.

65 Gesetz über den Mutter- und Kinderschutz und die Rechte der Frau [Act on the protection of Mother and child and the rights of the woman] of 27 September 1950, *GBl. der DDR* 1950, p. 1037.

66 Instruction of the Minister of Health of 15 March 1965, as referred to by Lammich 1988, *supra* n. 64, at p. 339, footnote 29.

67 *BR-Drs.* 270/60, pp. 38 and 278; *BR-Drs.* 200/62, pp. 35–36 and 38 and *BT-Drs.* V/32.

68 Erste Gesetz zur Reform des Strafrechts (1. StrRG) [First Act on the Reform of the Criminal Law] Act of 25 June 1969, *BGBl. I* p. 645.

based on the abortion laws in force at that time: between 1960 and 1969 the number of registered cases dropped with approximately 75 per cent from 4,195 in 1960 to 1,150 in 1969.[69] In that same period the number of convictions dropped from 1,809 to 596. There are no reliable numbers of abortions carried out in the FRG in the 1960s, but estimates lie between 400,000 and one million abortions a year in the mid-1960s.[70] An increasing number of women in the FRG went abroad for an abortion (relevant statistics are discussed in greater detail in section 4.4 below). Under influence of the liberalisation of the abortion legislation of various West European countries, campaigns aimed at the legalisation of abortion intensified in the FRG. At the time, a group of German and Swiss professors made suggestions for improvements to the then existing Criminal Code.[71] The group agreed that some relaxation of the criminal prohibition on abortion was desirable. The group was, however, divided in respect of how to achieve this; while the majority proposed a so-called 'periodic model' or 'stipulation model'[72] (whereby the stage of the pregnancy is primarily decisive for the question whether abortion is permitted or not), a minority favoured an 'indications model' (whereby the penalisation depends on the ground ('indication') for the intended abortion).

In the meantime, in East Germany, the Pregnancy Termination Act (*Gesetz über die Unterbrechung der Schwangerschaft*) entered into force in 1972.[73] This act implemented a periodic model: women in the GDR had the right to have an abortion in an obstetric/gynaecological institution within 12 weeks from the beginning of the pregnancy.[74] At a later stage of the pregnancy an abortion could be performed only if an expert medical commission estimated that continuation of the pregnancy would endanger the life of the woman or if there were other grave reasons.[75] Abortions were prohibited where they could lead to gravely injurious or life-threatening

---

69 H.-G. Koch, 'Bundersrepublik Deutschland' ['Federal Republic of Germany'], in: A. Eser and H.-G. Koch, *Schwangerschaftsabbruch im internationalen Vergleich, Rechtlichen Regelungen – Soziale Rahmenbedingungen – Empirische Grunddaten, Teil 1: Europa* [Abortion in international comparison, legal regulation – social framework – empirial basic data, Part 1: Europe] (Baden-Baden, Nomos Verlagsgesellschaft 1988) p. 17 at p. 249.

70 Koch 1988, *supra* n. 69, at p. 234.

71 J.J. Darby, Alternative Draft of a Penal Code for The Federal Republic of Germany (New York, South Hackensack 1977).

72 K.L. Belew, 'Stem Cell Division: Abortion Law and Its Influence on the Adoption of Radically Different Embryonic Stem Cell Legislation in the United States, the United Kingdom and Germany', 39 *Texas international Law Journal* (2003–2004) p. 479 at p. 508.

73 Gesetz über die Unterbrechung der Schwangerschaft [Act on the Termination of Pregnancy] of 9 March 1972, *GBl. I*, No. 5, p. 89 and the related implementing regulations of the same date (*GBl. II*, p. 149). See BVerfG 28 May 1993, Az. 2 BvF 2/90 a.o., *NJW* 1993 p. 1751 and S. Halliday, 'A comparative analysis of some of the legal parameters of the right to life and the right to privacy in the regulation of abortion', in: J. MacEldowney and G. Weick, *Human rights in transition* (Frankfurt am Main, Lang 2003) p. 85 at p. 93.

74 Art. 1(2) Gesetz über die Unterbrechung der Schwangerschaft 1972 [Pregnancy Termination Act 1972] (*old*).

75 Art. 2 Gesetz über die Unterbrechung der Schwangerschaft 1972 [Pregnancy Termination Act 1972] (*old*).

complications[76] or if less than six months had elapsed since the last pregnancy termination.[77]

Two years later, in 1974, after intense debate, the Parliament of the FRG finally passed the Abortion Reform Act.[78] Similar to the abortion laws of the GDR, this Act introduced a periodic model (the so-called '*Fristenregelung*'). Abortion was not liable to punishment if it was performed in a medical clinic within the first 12 weeks of pregnancy and after the woman underwent counselling.[79] Between the 12th and the 22nd week, abortion was not punishable if the woman's life or health was seriously endangered by the pregnancy or if there was a substantial ground to believe that the child would be born with such a serious birth defect that the woman could not be expected to carry the pregnancy to full term.[80] After the 22nd week, abortion would only be permitted if the pregnancy constituted a danger to the life of the pregnant woman.[81] Further, the State was under a duty to keep statistics of abortions carried out.[82] The Act never entered into force, however, as the Christian Democrats in Parliament, together with various States,[83] successfully lodged a complaint with the Federal Constitutional Court.

4.2.2. The first BVerfG abortion judgment and subsequent legislation

By judgment of 25 February 1975, the First Senate of the Constitutional Court by a majority[84] declared the 1974 Abortion Reform Act partly unconstitutional.[85] Using historical, systematic and textual interpretation,[86] the Court considered that the right to life ex. Article 2(2) Basic Law extended to the unborn life from the moment of nidation, i.e., from the 14th day after conception.[87] The BVerfG held that

76 Art. 3(1) Gesetz über die Unterbrechung der Schwangerschaft 1972 [Pregnancy Termination Act 1972] (*old*).

77 Art. 3(2) Gesetz über die Unterbrechung der Schwangerschaft 1972 [Pregnancy Termination Act 1972] (*old*).

78 Fünftes Gesetz zur Reform des Strafrechts (5. StrGZ) [Fifth Act on the Reform of the Criminal law], 1974 *BGBl. I*, No. 63, p. 1297.

79 Arts. 218 and 218a StGB.

80 Art. 218b StGB.

81 Art. 218b (1) StGB.

82 Art. 4 5. StrGZ, 1974 *BGBl.* I, pp. 1298–1299.

83 Namely the *Länder* Baden-Württemberg, Bavaria, Rheinland-Pfalz, Saarland and Schleswig-Holstein. BVerfG 25 February 1975, Az. 1 BvF 2/74 a.o., *NJW* 1975 p. 573, para. 18.

84 The exact voting rate falls under the secrecy of the chambers of the Court. In literature it has been presumed that the judgment was passed with a five to three vote. Koch 1988, *supra* n. 69, at p. 82, footnote 415.

85 BVerfG 25 February 1975, Az. 1 BvF 2/74 a.o., *NJW* 1975 p. 573. For a critical case note to this judgment see W. Brugger, 'Abtreibung – ein Grundrecht oder ein Verbrechen? Ein Vergleich der Urteile des United States Supreme Court und des BVerfG' ['Abortion – a fundamental right or a criminal act? A comparison of the case law of the United States Supreme Court and the German Constitutional Court'], *NJW* (1986) p. 896. See also M.A. Case 2009, 'Perfectionism and Fundamentalism in the Application of the German Abortion Laws', in S.H. Williams, *Constituting equality: gender equality and comparative constitutional rights* (New York, Cambridge University Press 2009) p. 93 at p. 95.

86 See Brugger 1986, *supra* n. 85, at p. 898.

87 BVerfG 25 February 1975, Az. 1 BvF 2/74 a.o., *NJW* 1975 p. 573, para. 136.

the constitutional right to life entailed not only a duty for the State to refrain from direct interference in the life of the unborn, but also a State obligation to protect and support such life, by guarding it against illegal interference by third parties, including the mother. The Court considered that from the Basic Law it followed that the law had to express a clear disapproval of abortion. Although the legislature was free to express such disapproval by other means than by the threat of criminal punishment, the total sum of relevant legal norms had to protect the right to life of the unborn sufficiently.[88] The Court held that the periodic model as proposed by the 1974 Act did not meet that requirement, inasmuch as it exempted pregnancy termination from punishment '[...] even if there were no grounds that were of lasting duration in the face of the order of values of the Basic Law'.[89] As Eser observed, with this 'somewhat sibylline expression' the Court in fact held that the unborn life could only be adequately protected on the basis of an indications model.[90]

The BVerfG considered that the legislature was entitled to leave abortion free of punishment in those exceptional situations where the woman was subject to burdens which demanded such a degree of sacrifice of her own existential values that one could no longer expect her to carry the pregnancy to full term. The Court mentioned four indications that could, in principle, justify an abortion: a medical indication (i.e., when the life and/or the health of the mother is endangered by the pregnancy); a criminological indication (i.e., if the pregnancy has been brought about by means of a criminal offence); an embryopathic indication (i.e., in the case that a non-curable genetic abnormality of the embryo is suspected so that a continuation of the pregnancy cannot be expected from the mother) and 'other situations of general necessity' (i.e., social reasons). While the Court did not give any further interpretation of these indications, for all of them it applied that there was an interest equally worthy of protection, which was so pressing that it could not be required under all circumstances that precedence was given to the rights of the unborn.

The Constitutional Court left it to the legislature to lay down in law the exact boundaries between indicated and non-indicated abortions. The argument in defence of the 1974 Act that other Western democratic States had recently adopted even more liberalised or 'modern' abortion laws than foreseen by the challenged Act, was rejected by the Court.[91] Not only did the Court find those laws to be 'highly controversial', but it also held that the FRG legislature was bound by fundamentally different standards than the foreign legislatures. As a response to the National Socialistic laws, the German Basic Law constituted a legal order whereby human

---

88 See Eser 1986, *supra* n. 62, at pp. 373–374.

89 BVerfG 25 February 1975, Az. 1 BvF 2/74 a.o., *NJW* 1975 p. 573, para. 68 and para. 21 of the English translation of this judgment as online available at www.bverfg.de, visited 23 June 2014. The original formulation in German was: 'Es ist mit der dem Gesetzgeber obliegenden Lebensschutzpflicht unvereinbar, daß Schwangerschaftsabbrüche auch dann rechtlich nicht mißbilligt und nicht unter Strafe gestellt werden, wenn sie aus Gründen erfolgen, die vor der Wertordnung des Grundgesetzes keinen Bestand haben.' Compare Eser 1986, *supra* n. 62, at p. 374.

90 Eser 1986, *supra* n. 62, at p. 374.

91 BVerfG 25 February 1975, Az. 1 BvF 2/74 a.o., *NJW* 1975 p. 573, para. 206.

dignity was the central value reference point for all legislation to be enacted by the legislature.

To the judgment a joint dissenting opinion by judges Rupp-von Brünneck and Simon was attached, who held that the Court should have displayed more judicial self-restraint.[92] They disagreed with the majority's 'rigorism'[93] that under the Basic Law the legislature was obliged to protect constitutional rights, like the unborn's right to life, by means of penalisation. The dissenting judges maintained that – despite certain deficiencies – the regulation of abortion by means of social regulations, as introduced by the challenged Act, was more in line with the spirit of the Basic Law than the model based on penalisation as advocated by the majority of the Court.[94]

The judgment, eagerly awaited by legal scholars, was received as a rejection of the '*Fristenlösung*' (the periodic model), requiring the legislature to undertake further action.[95] The FRG legislature indeed developed an indications model, which was enacted by law of 1976.[96] The new Act was intended to take sufficient account of the emergencies in which a pregnant woman may find herself as well as to prevent illegal abortions. It was further intended 'to ensure that, "in cases where the law guarantees exemption from punishment", pregnant women would not be placed at a disadvantage because of their financial situations'.[97] Abortion was criminalised, but an abortion carried out within the first 12 weeks of pregnancy was not punishable in case an indication justifying the abortion existed. Two doctors needed to certify that according to medical knowledge either a medical,[98] an embryopathic,[99] a criminological[100] or a 'general crisis'[101] indication existed. While the medical indication could exempt an abortion from penalisation throughout the entire duration of the pregnancy, for the embryopathic indication a time limit was set at 22 weeks, and for the criminological and the general crisis indications this time limit was set at 12 weeks. It was, furthermore, required that the abortion was carried out in a hospital or expressly authorised facility; that the pregnant woman had undergone counselling; that she consented to the abortion and that she had observed a three-day

92 *Idem*, para. 222.
93 *Idem*, para. 260.
94 *Idem*, para. 269.
95 Koch 1988, *supra* n. 69, at p. 82, with useful references in footnote 417. For a critical reflection upon the 1975 abortion judgment, see Brugger 1986, *supra* n. 85, at pp. 896–901.
96 Fünfzehnte Strafrechtsänderungsgesetz [Fifteenth Act on Amendment of the Criminal Law] Act of 18 May 1976, 1976 *BGBl. I*, p. 1213. Compare Case 2009, *supra* n. 85, at p. 95 and Halliday 2003, *supra* n. 73, at p. 94.
97 As quoted by the German Constitutional Court in BVerfG 28 May 1993, Az. 2 BvF 2/90 a.o., *NJW* 1993 p. 1751, para. 20.
98 The medical indication concerned both the physical and mental health of the pregnant woman. Art. 218a (1) StGB (*old*).
99 Art. 218a (2) I StGB (*old*).
100 Art. 218a (2) II StGB (*old*).
101 The German term is '*algemeine Notlagenindikation*'. Art. 218a (2) III StGB (*old*).

reflection period.[102] Doctors were not required to assist an abortion, except in case of a life-threatening or serious health-threatening situation.[103]

Statistics show that in the period 1975–1985 the number of registered prosecutions on the basis of Article 218 StGB declined from 639 to 92 per year, while the number of criminal convictions on grounds of this provision dropped from 87 to 10 per year.[104] The total number of officially registered abortions for these years rose from 19,076 in the year 1975 to 91,064 in the year 1982, and subsequently went down to 83,538 for the year 1985. It is widely accepted that due to a registration deficit, the actual abortions numbers exceed these official numbers.[105]

4.2.3. German reunification and abortion controversy

When East and West Germany reunited to form one sovereign state in 1990, the reconciliation of the two former countries' abortion laws proved to be one of the most difficult and controversial issues. For a while the abortion discussion even jeopardised the signing of the Reunification Treaty.[106] Ultimately, a compromise was reached, whereby – for a period of two years – the abortion laws of both regimes remained in effect simultaneously.[107] Hence, in the two years between reunification and the entry into force of new legislation, women from the former FRG were able to have an abortion in the former GDR without fear of criminal prosecution or punishment (see also section 4.4.1.1 below). The legislature of reunified Germany was called upon to enact, at the latest by December 31 1992, laws which ensured better protection of unborn life and provided a better solution in conformity with the Basic Law for conflict situations faced by pregnant women, than was at the time the case in both parts of Germany.[108] After two years of heated and emotional debates, this objective was fulfilled by virtue of the adoption of a compromise regime in the shape of the Pregnancy and Family Assistance Act of 1992.[109]

---

102 Art. 218b StGB (*old*).

103 Art. 2 5. StrGZ.

104 Koch 1988, *supra* n. 69, at p. 249.

105 *Idem*, at p. 235, footnote 6.

106 M.G. Mattern, 'German Abortion Law: The Unwanted Child of Reunification', 13 *Loyola of Los Angeles International and Comparative Law Review* (1990–1991) p. 643 at p. 651.

107 Unification Treaty of 31 August 1990 in conjunction with the Act on the Unification Treaty of 23 September 1990, *BGBl. II*, p. 885; *cf.* Appendix II, Chapter III, Subject Area C, Section I, No. 1.

108 Art. 31(4) of the Unification Treaty of 31 August 1990, as referred to in BVerfG 28 May 1993, Az. 2 BvF 2/90 a.o., *NJW* 1993 p. 1751. See also the English translation of the text as provided on the website of the German History Institute germanhistorydocs.ghi-dc.org/pdf/eng/Unification_Treaty.pdf, visited 24 June 2014.

109 Gesetz zum Schutz des vorgeburtlichen/werdenden Lebens, zur Förderung einer kinderfreundlicheren Gesellschaft, für Hilfen im Schwangerschaftskonflikt und zur Regelung des Schwangerschaftsabbruchs (Schwangeren- und Familienhilfegesetz) [Act to Protect Unborn/Gestating Life, Promote a Society More Hospitable Toward Children, Provide Assistance in Pregnancy Conflicts and Regulate Pregnancy Termination (Pregnancy and Family Assistance Act)] Act of 27 July 1992, *BGBl. I*, p. 1398.

4.2.4. The Pregnancy and Family Assistance Act (1992)

The Pregnancy and Family Assistance Act of 1992 consisted of a package of acts, including the Pregnancy Conflict Act (*Schwangerschaftskonfliktgesetz*, SchKG),[110] which related to the counselling procedure to be followed in case an abortion was desired. The unified legislature took as a starting point that, '[...] in light of the significance of the gestating life as a legal value and the constitutional guarantee of it, penal protection [was] indispensable.'[111] Accordingly, abortion was criminalised and punishable with imprisonment of up to three years or a fine.[112] Acts of which the effects occurred before completion of the nidation of the fertilised egg in the uterus were not considered to be pregnancy terminations within the meaning of the Criminal Code. Under certain conditions abortion would be not illegal or would be exempted from punishment. Within 12 weeks of conception, an abortion was not illegal if performed by a physician with the consent of the pregnant woman and if the woman received counselling at least three days prior to the carrying out of the abortion.[113] Abortion was also not illegal if the existence of certain legal indications was ascertained. The new system differed from the old FRG regime, to the extent that the previous statutory definitions of the criminological indication and the general emergency indication were abolished. Only medical and embryopathic indications could constitute grounds for justification of a pregnancy termination. The first required that according to medical knowledge the abortion was necessary to remove a threat to the life of the pregnant woman or a threat of grave physical or mental distress on the part of the woman, inasmuch as this threat could not be removed in another way which could be exacted of the woman, the abortion was not illegal.[114] The embryopathic indication required the existence of compelling grounds for assuming that, due to heredity or detrimental influences, the child would suffer from irreversible injury to its health so grave that a continuation of the pregnancy could not be exacted of the woman.[115]

These exemptions to the criminal prohibition on abortion were based on the idea that only the pregnant woman herself could assess the conflict situation in which she found herself. The Act was considered a compromise solution taking 'both the high value of unborn life and the self-determination of the woman into account'.[116] The degree in which the Criminal Code was to be used to protect unborn life was made dependent on the existence of other provisions offering true effective

[110] Gesetz zur Vermeidung und Bewältigung von Schwangerschaftskonflikten (Schwangerschaftskonfliktgesetz – SchKG) [Act on prevention of and the overcoming of pregnancy conflicts, Pregnancy Conflict Act] of 27 July 1992, *BGBl. I*, p. 1398.

[111] BVerfG 28 May 1993, Az. 2 BvF 2/90 a.o., *NJW* 1993 p. 1751, para. 38 (in the English translation of the judgment this is para. 37).

[112] In aggravated cases the term of imprisonment could be increased to a maximum of five years (Art. 218(2) StGB). In case the pregnant woman committed the offence herself, she was liable to punishment up to one year or a fine.

[113] Art. 218a (1) StGB.

[114] Art. 218a (2) StGB.

[115] Art. 218a (3) StGB.

[116] BVerfG 28 May 1993, Az. 2 BvF 2/90 a.o., *NJW* 1993 p. 1751, para. 38 (in the English translation this is para. 37).

protection of gestating life. The law therefore provided for various socio-political measures to protect unborn life, such as sex education; a legal right to counselling through licensed counselling centres;[117] reimbursement for the costs of (advice about) contraceptives;[118] as well as state-funded assistance in the care for children.[119] Compulsory counselling for women considering an abortion was introduced to ensure that the woman would not make '[...] her responsible decision of conscience regarding a pregnancy termination in isolation from the fundamental decision for the protection of the gestating life that is prescribed by the Basic Law.'[120] During the counselling the woman was offered '[...] advice and assistance in her conflict as well as sufficient information about governmental assistance as the basis for thorough reflection on her situation'.[121] It was thought that '[...] preparedness to decide in favour of gestating life [was] greatest when the woman [did] not have the feeling that she [had to] subjugate herself to the verdict of others, but rather [was] able, after receiving qualified counselling and carefully considering the situation, to decide for herself whether to continue the pregnancy.'[122]

The 1992 Act did not contain an obligation on the State to keep federal statistics on abortions, as had been required until the old FRG regime.[123] It further provided for a right to benefits for insured persons in the event of a legal abortion performed by a physician in a hospital or in another institution recognised by the law.[124]

The State of Bavaria and the Christian Democrats in the German Federal Parliament, petitioned to the Federal Constitutional Court to challenge the 1992 Pregnancy and Family Assistance Act. By judgment of 4 August 1992, the Federal Constitutional Court temporarily enjoined[125] the coming into force of the substantial provisions

---

117 Gesetz über Aufklärung, Verhütung, Familienplanung und Beratung (BeratungsG) [Act on sex education, contraception, family planning and counselling] as introduced by Art. 1 Schwangeren- und Familienhilfegesetz. The information that the state is required to provide under this Act includes sex education, information about contraception and family planning, benefits for promoting families and assistance to children and families, social and economic assistance for pregnant women, pregnancy termination methods and the related risks as well as possible solutions for psycho-social conflicts in connection with pregnancy.

118 Art. 2 Schwangeren- und Familienhilfegesetz [Pregnancy and Family Assistance Act].

119 Art. 5 Schwangeren- und Familienhilfegesetz [Pregnancy and Family Assistance Act].

120 BVerfG 28 May 1993, Az. 2 BvF 2/90 a.o., *NJW* 1993 p. 1751, para. 38 (in the English translation this is para. 37).

121 *Idem.*

122 *Idem.*

123 Art. 4 5. StrGZ. In the GDR under the Anweisung sur Erfassung der vorzeitigen Schwangerschaftbeendigung [Instruction registration of premature pregnancy termination] of 21 March 1972 there was a duty to report legally carried out abortions, but not many statistics are available. See Lammich 1988, *supra* n. 64, at pp. 358 and 369–370.

124 Art. 2 Schwangeren- und Familienhilfegesetz [Pregnancy and Family Assistance Act], introducing the new Arts. 24a, 24b of the Sozialgesetzbuch Fünftes Buch (SGB V) [Fifth Volume of the Code of Social Security Law].

125 *Inter alia*, Art. 32 BVerfGG [Federal Constitutional Court Act].

(Articles 13(1)[126] and 16[127]) of the Act.[128] Subsequently, the State of Bavaria and the Christian Democrats petitioned the Constitutional Court for abstract judicial review[129] of the provisions on the consultation and indication ascertainment procedure and health insurance benefits in the event of pregnancy terminations on the basis of the general emergency indication.[130] Consequently, on 28 May 1993 the BVerfG delivered its second abortion judgment.[131]

4.2.5. The second BVerfG abortion judgment (1993)

By judgment of 28 May 1993, the second Senate of the BVerfG held that the concept of counselling during the first 12 weeks of pregnancy was in itself not in violation of the Basic Law, but that the counselling regulation, as foreseen by the challenged Act, did not fulfil the State's duty to effectively protect unborn life (Article 1(1) read together with Article 2(2) Basic Law). By reference to its first abortion judgment of 1974, the Court reiterated that unborn human life was accorded human dignity and that Articles 1(1) and 2(2) of the Basic Law required that the State protects human life, including that of the unborn. It held the obligation to protect unborn human life to be related to the individual life and to not human life in general. The BVerfG further reiterated that the unborn was entitled to legal protection, even *vis-à-vis* its mother.[132] Such protection was only possible if the legislature fundamentally forbade the mother to terminate her pregnancy and thus imposed on her the fundamental

126 Art. 13(1) Schwangeren- und Familienhilfegesetz [Pregnancy and Family Assistance Act] replaced the at that time existing substantial abortion provisions (Arts. 218–219d of the Criminal Code in the version promulgated on 10 March 1987, *BGBl. I*, p. 945 at p. 1160) with new Arts. 218 -219b.

127 Art. 16 Schwangeren- und Familienhilfegesetz [Pregnancy and Family Assistance Act] revoked the provisions of the laws of the GDR that were still in force on the basis of the Unification Treaty.

128 See BVerfG 28 May 1993, Az. 2 BvF 2/90 a.o., *NJW* 1993 p. 1751, para. 98.

129 Art. 93(1)(2) Basic Law and Art. 13(6) BVerfGG.

130 Art. 218b (1) first sentence and (2); Art. 219(1) first sentence StGB in the version of the Fifteenth Act on Amendment of the Criminal Law and Arts. 200f, and 200g of the Reichsversicherungsordnung (RVO) [Reich Insurance Code]. The petitioners argued that the proposed abortion provisions providing for benefits from the statutory health insurance in the event of abortions, on the basis of a general emergency indication, contravened the State's obligation to protect unborn life. The State of Bavaria held for the same reason that the obligation on States to provide for abortion facilities (Art. 15(2) Schwangeren- und Familienhilfegesetz [Pregnancy and Family Assistance Act] and the provision in Art. 24b SGB V in the version of Art. 2 Schwangeren- und Familienhilfegesetz [Pregnancy and Family Assistance Act]) was unconstitutional. Moreover, the State of Bavaria argued that the Federal government had no legislative authority in such matters as the regulation of abortion.

131 BVerfG 28 May 1993, Az. 2 BvF 2/90 a.o., *NJW* 1993 p. 1751. See G. Hermes and S. Walther, 'Schwangerschaftsabbruch zwischen Recht und Unrecht – Das zweite Abtreibungsurteil des BVerfG und seine Folge' ['Pregnancy termination between right and wrong – The second judgment on abortion of the German Constitutional Court and its consequences'], *NJW* (1993) p. 2337; A. Zimmerman, 'Verbreitung von Informationen über Schwangerschaftsunterbrechungen und Europäische Menschenrechtskonvention' ['Dissemination of information on the termination of pregnancies and the European Convention on Human Rights'], *NJW* 1993, p. 2966 and E. Deutsch, 'Neues Verfassungszivilrecht: Rechtswidriger Abtreibungsvertrag gültig – Unterhaltspflicht aber kein Schaden' ['New Constitutional civil law: unlawful abortion convention in force – Maintenance obligation but no damages'], *NJW* (1993) p. 2361.

132 The Court referred to BVerfG 25 February 1975, Az. 1 BvF 2/74 a.o., *NJW* 1975 p. 573.

legal obligation to carry the child to term.[133] The Court emphasised that the fundamental prohibition on pregnancy termination and the fundamental obligation to carry the child to term were two integrally connected elements of the protection mandated by the Basic Law. The extent of the obligation to protect unborn life had to be determined with a view to competing legal values, including the right to life and physical inviolability of the pregnant woman (Article 2(2) of the Basic Law) and her right to personal development (Article 2(1) of the Basic Law). The State had to undertake sufficient normative and practical measures to the attainment of appropriate and, as such, effective protection, thereby combining elements of preventative and repressive protection.[134]

The BVerfG accepted that in exceptional situations it would be permissible, 'perhaps even mandatory', not to impose upon a pregnant woman a legal obligation to carry the child to term.

The Court left it up to the legislature to determine in detail on the basis of the criterion of 'non-exactability' what constituted an exceptional situation. This criterion meant that the woman had to be subject to burdens which demanded such a degree of sacrifice of her own existential values that one could no longer expect her to go through with the pregnancy.[135] Abortions performed without ascertainment of the existence of an indication pursuant to the counselling regulation, could not be declared to be justified ('not illegal'). The Court held that a justification for abortion could only be considered where there was an emergency situation, which had to be ascertained and clearly defined. Because under the challenged Act no such emergency situation was required for the justification of an abortion during the first 12 weeks of pregnancy abortion, the Court declared the relevant provision of the Act (the new Article 218a (1) Criminal Code) unconstitutional and thus invalid. It held that this provision contravened Article 1(1) in conjunction with Article 2(2) of the Basic Law, inasmuch as the provision declared an abortion under the preconditions set forth in the respective provision to not be illegal.

The Court further ruled that the regulation of counselling for a pregnant woman in an emergency and conflict situation, as foreseen by the challenged Act,[136] failed to satisfy the constitutional requirements of Article 1(1) in conjunction with Article 2(2) Basic Law. The goal of counselling in pregnancy conflict situations had to be the protection of the unborn child and the counsellors had to try to encourage the woman

---

133 *Idem.*

134 This has also been referred to as the *Untermaßverbot* ['prohibition on too little protection']. See BVerfG 1993, para. 166 (English translation, para. 154), referring to 'Isensee in: *Handbuch des Staatsrechts*, Volume V, 1992, § 111 marginal note No. 165 et seq'. The important finding of the Court in this case (in para. 258) that characterisation in law of the existence of a child as a source of injury is excluded on constitutional grounds (Art. 1(1) Basic Law), will not be discussed in further detail here. For discussion of that matter, see *inter alia* E. Deutsch, 'Neues Verfassungszivilrecht: Rechtswidriger Abtreibungsvertrag gültig – Unterhaltspflicht aber kein Schaden', *NJW* 1993 pp. 2361–2363 and *Der Spiegel*, ‚Drama in der Kantine', 52/1997, pp. 22–25.

135 The Court referred to BVerfG 25 February 1975, Az. 1 BvF 2/74 a.o., *NJW* 1975 p. 573.

136 The new Art. 219 StGB.

to continue her pregnancy and show her opportunities for a life with the child.[137] In the Court's opinion, this goal and content of counselling did not find sufficiently clear expression in the new Article 219 Criminal Code. Further, there were not enough state powers and duties to guarantee the organisation and supervision of the counselling institutions. The legislature had failed to lay down, to a sufficient extent, the special duties of the physician whom the woman asked to perform a termination, and the special duties of the people in the pregnant woman's circle. Further, it had not made certain breaches of duty punishable.[138] The Court employed its competence to specify the method of execution of its decisions[139] and dictated alternative provisions in respect of the counselling procedure, that were to supplement the relevant provisions of the challenged Act.[140] These supplementary provisions underlined that counselling was to be '[...] guided by the effort to encourage the woman to continue the pregnancy' and had to make the woman aware of the fact that abortion could only be considered in exceptional circumstances '[...] where bearing the child to term would place the woman under a burden which [...] [was] so severe and exceptional that it exceed[ed] the limits of exactable sacrifice.' The supplementary provisions further, *inter alia*, provided for more detailed regulations concerning the setting up of counselling centres and the keeping of records by counsellors.[141]

The Court further held that the legislature was under an obligation to ascertain at reasonable intervals whether the law really was having the protective effect that could be expected on the basis of its duty to protect unborn human life.[142] The Court therefore considered it essential to have reliable abortion statistics with sufficient information.[143] Accordingly, the Court declared the respective provision of the new Act, removing the obligation to keep federal abortion statistics,[144] irreconcilable with Article 1(1) read together with Article 2(2) of the Basic Law.

In respect of reimbursement for abortions, the Court held that the Basic Law did not permit the granting of a right to benefits from the statutory health insurance for an abortion whose legality had not been established according to the constitutional standards, i.e., abortions carried out without having followed the statutory counselling

137 BVerfG 28 May 1993, Az. 2 BvF 2/90 a.o., *NJW* 1993 p. 1751, para. 228 (in the English translation this is para. 217).

138 *Idem*, para. 305 (English translation, para. 294).

139 Art. 35 BVerfGG (Federal Constitutional Court Act) reads: 'In its decision the Federal Constitutional Court may state by whom it is to be executed; in individual instances it may also specify the method of execution.'

140 See BVerfG 28 May 1993, Az. 2 BvF 2/90 a.o., *NJW* 1993 p. 1751, under II.

141 *Idem*.

142 *Idem*, para. 308 (in the English translation this is para. 298b).

143 The Court considered it essential to have statistics '[...] on the total number of pregnancy terminations, on the number of pregnancy terminations as compared to the whole population, on the total number of pregnancy terminations as compared to the number of women of childbearing age, on the total number of pregnancy terminations as compared to the number of pregnancies, on the total number of pregnancy terminations as compared to the total number of live or dead births, and finally on the total number of pregnancy terminations as compared to the number of terminations not subject to punishment because of extenuating legal reasons.' BVerfG 28 May 1993, Az. 2 BvF 2/90 a.o., *NJW* 1993 p. 1751, para. 310 (in the English translation this is para. 299c).

144 Art. 15(2) Schwangeren- und Familienhilfegesetz [Pregnancy and Family Assistance Act].

procedure. In other words, the abortion had to be indicated and the counselling process that had been followed had to be in conformity with the constitutional requirements as set out by the Court.[145]

Three judges dissented. Judge Böckenforde concurred with the essential points in the majority judgment, but disagreed with the majority's ruling that ruled out social security benefits for abortions for non-indicated abortions during the first 12 weeks of pregnancy. The Judge held it to be for the legislature to decide on that point.[146] In their joint opinion, Judges Mahrenholz and Sommer claimed that the new Article 218a (1) was constitutional. In their opinion the majority judgment had failed to achieve a balance between the human dignity of the unborn on the one hand, and the dignity of the pregnant woman on the other. They felt that from a constitutional perspective the unique comparative problem raised by the 'joined twosomeness' of the pregnant woman and the unborn child could not be dealt with 'by simply juxtaposing the two'.[147] The judges were of the opinion that the developmental process of pregnancy implied a developmental element in the pregnant woman's constitutional status and required the legislature to provide different kinds of State protection during the early and late phases of pregnancy. They agreed with the majority judgment that the regulation of counselling as provided by the challenged Act contained deficiencies and was therefore unconstitutional. Lastly, they did not hold the payment of social insurance benefits for pregnancy terminations carried out by a physician during the first 12 weeks following conception, to contravene the Basic Law.

In legal scholarship, the judgment met with considerable critique. Many authors pointed out that the Court's reasoning was not entirely consistent and contained various value contradictions.[148] Tröndle argued that the protection concept, as developed by the BVerfG, contained a serious contradiction, as it on the one hand put the State under obligation to protect unborn life, but, on the other hand, left only the counselled pregnant woman answerable to the question of whether an abortion was to take place or not.[149] The author was further critical of the fact that the BVerfG had taken up the role of quasi-legislature and had exempted abortion from the criminal law domain under certain circumstances.[150] Hermes and Walther have shown themselves to be critical of the 'judicial activism' of the BVerfG, and contended that the Court's attempt to find a compromise solution for the abortion controversy had failed. The authors claimed that the legislature had yet found the necessary compromise with

145 On the other hand, the Court considered the granting of social assistance benefits in cases of economic hardship for pregnancy terminations which are not punishable by law according to the counseling regulation, 'just as unobjectionable from a constitutional point of view as continued payment of salary or wages is.'

146 Dissenting opinion of Judge Böckenforde to BVerfG 28 May 1993, Az. 2 BvF 2/90 a.o., *NJW* 1993 p. 1751.

147 Joint dissenting opinion of Judges Mahrenholz and Sommer to BVerfG 28 May 1993, Az. 2 BvF 2/90 a.o., *NJW* 1993 p. 1751, para. I. 1.

148 See Ulsenheimer 2010, *supra* n. 52, Rn. 5.

149 H. Tröndle, 'Das Schwangeren- und Familienhilfeänderungsgesetz' [The Pregnancy and Family Assistance Revision Act'], *NJW* (1995) p. 3009 at p. 3010.

150 *Idem*, at p. 3011.

exceptional thoroughness and conscious of the competing constitutional values and moral views, after which the Court had set foot on the – avoidable – path to the '*verfassungsgerichtlichen Juridiktionsstaat*' ('a Constitutional order ruled by the judiciary').[151]

The 1993 BVerfG judgment put the difficult task before the German legislature of drafting new abortion legislation.[152] New heated parliamentary debates were the result,[153] and various bills were drafted.[154] This finally resulted in the adoption of the Pregnancy and Family Assistance Revision Act (*Schwangeren- und Familienhilfeänderungsgesetz, SFHÄndG*) in August 1995.[155] This compromise Act not only responded to the BVerfG judgment, but also finally brought an end to the discrepancies between Eastern and West German abortion laws.[156]

4.2.6. The Pregnancy and Family Assistance Revision Act (1995) and subsequent amendments

The entry into force of the Pregnancy and Family Assistance Revision Act at 1 October 1995 introduced the abortion regime that is still in force today in Germany. Basic principle of this regime is – following the 1993 BVerfG abortion decision – the criminal prohibition of abortion (Article 218 Criminal Code). Acts, the effects of which occur before the conclusion of the nidation, are not deemed to be an abortion within the meaning of the Criminal Code. Advertising for abortion[157]

151 Hermes and Walther 1993, *supra* n. 131, at p. 2346.

152 Tröndle claimed that the judgment was of little assistance and its content unfit to offer the legislature any normative guidance in this process. Tröndle 1995, *supra* n. 149, at p. 3012. Eser spoke of the BVerfG as having left behind a 'Torso mit Reparaturvorgaben'. A Eser, 'Schwangerschaftsabbruch: Reformversuche im Umsetzung des BVerfG-Urteils', *JZ* (1994) p. 503.

153 Tröndle 1995, *supra* n. 149, at pp. 3009–3010.

154 *BT-Drs.* 12/6643; *BT-Drs.* 12/6669 and *BT-Drs.* 12/6944. A. Eser, 'Schwangerschaftsabbruch: Reformversuche im Umsetzung des BVErfG-Urteils' ['Termination of pregnancy: reform efforts in the implementation of the judgment of the German Constitutional Court'], *JZ* (1994) pp. 503–510 at p. 504; Ulsenheimer 2010, *supra* n. 52, Rn. 5 and Tröndle 1995, *supra* n. 149, at pp. 3012–3013.

155 Act of 28 August 1995 *BGBl. I* p. 1050.

156 Art. 16 of the 1992 Pregnancy and Family Assistance Act foresaw in the revocation of the provisions of the laws of the GDR that were still in force on the basis of the Unification Treaty. However, by judgment of 4 August 1992, the Federal Constitutional Court temporarily enjoined the coming into force of this provision of the Act and by judgment of 28 May 1993 the Court declared the Act invalid, for being irreconcilable with the Basic Law. The result was that until the entering into force of the 1995 Act, the former FRG and GDR abortion regimes were still in force. BVerfG 28 May 1993, Az. 2 BvF 2/90 a.o., *NJW* 1993 p. 1751. See also above.

157 Art. 219a Criminal Code reads:
'(1) Whosoever publicly, in a meeting or through dissemination of written materials (section 11(3)), for material gain or in a grossly inappropriate manner, offers, announces or commends
1. his own services for performing terminations of pregnancy or for supporting them, or the services of another; or
2. means, objects or procedures capable of terminating a pregnancy with reference to this capacity,or makes declarations of such a nature shall be liable to imprisonment of not more than two years or a fine.

and for bringing abortion means into circulation is also prohibited.[158] Nobody can be forced to assist in an abortion, except for in cases of acute and serious danger to the life or health of the pregnant woman.[159]

Following Article 218 '[w]hosoever terminates a pregnancy is liable to imprisonment of not more than three years or a fine'.[160] If the abortion is committed by the pregnant woman herself, the maximum penalty is imprisonment of one year or a fine.[161] There are, however, exceptions to liability for abortion. Under certain circumstances, the defining elements of the offence of abortion under Article 218 are considered not to be fulfilled and the abortion is accordingly not punishable (*'nicht rechtswidrig'*, Article 218a Criminal Code).[162] This is the case if, during the first 12 weeks of pregnancy, an abortion is performed by a physician at the request of a pregnant woman who can show to the physician a certificate that she had counselling at least three days before the operation.[163] Further, if the requirements for a medical-social[164] or a criminological indication[165] have been fulfilled and the woman has given informed consent, an abortion may also be exempted from punishment. The medical-social indication is present if, '[...] considering the present and future living conditions of the pregnant woman, the termination of the pregnancy is medically necessary to avert a danger to the life or the danger of grave injury to the physical or mental health of the pregnant woman and if the danger cannot reasonably be averted in another

(2) Subsection (1) No 1 above shall not apply when physicians or statutorily recognised counselling agencies provide information about which physicians, hospitals or institutions are prepared to perform a termination of pregnancy under the conditions of section 218a (1) to (3).

(3) Subsection (1) No 2 above shall not apply if the offence was committed with respect to physicians or persons who are authorised to trade in the means or objects mentioned in subsection (1) No 2 or through a publication in professional medical or pharmaceutical journals.'

Translation taken from www.gesetze-im-internet.de/englisch_stgb/englisch_stgb.html#StGBengl_000P219b, visited June 2014. See, *inter alia*, Ulsenheimer 2010, *supra* n. 52, Rn. 62–65.

158 Art. 219b Criminal Code reads:

'(1) Whosoever with intent to encourage unlawful acts under section 218 distributes means or objects which are capable of terminating a pregnancy shall be liable to imprisonment of not more than two years or a fine.

(2) The secondary participation by a woman preparing the termination of her own pregnancy shall not be punishable under subsection (1) above.

(3) Means or objects to which the offence relates may be subject to a deprivation order.'

Translation taken from www.gesetze-im-internet.de/englisch_stgb/englisch_stgb.html#StGBengl_000P219b, visited June 2014.

159 Art. 12 SchKG. See also Ulsenheimer 2010, *supra* n. 52, Rn. 53–54.

160 In especially serious cases – e.g. if the offender acts against the will of the pregnant woman; or if the offender through gross negligence causes a risk of death or serious injury to the pregnant woman – the penalty may be increased to five years' imprisonment (Art. 218(2) StGB).

161 Art. 218(3) StGB.

162 Note the difference in formulation when compared to the 1992 version of the Act which spoke of abortions being 'not illegal' (nicht rechtswidrig') if certain conditions were met. This formulation was declared unconstitutional by the Constitutional Court in BVerfG 28 May 1993, Az. 2 BvF 2/90 a.o., *NJW* 1993 p. 1751.

163 Art. 218a (1) StGB.

164 Art. 218a (2) StGB.

165 Art. 218a (3) StGB.

way from her point of view.'[166] While an abortion on the basis of the criminological indication can only be exempted from punishment if the abortion is performed within the first 12 weeks of pregnancy, the medical-social indication is not subject to a time limitation.

Within the first 22 weeks of pregnancy the pregnant woman is, furthermore, exempted from punishment if the abortion was performed by a physician after counselling in an emergency or conflict situation. This exception to liability does not hold for the physician or any other person committing the offence of abortion.[167] If the pregnant woman was in exceptional distress, the court may also dispense with punishment under the general abortion prohibition of Article 218 Criminal Code.[168] In addition, the pregnant woman is not liable for attempt to terminate her pregnancy.[169]

The requirements for a counselling procedure for women in an emergency or conflict situation have been laid down in Articles 219ff Criminal Code, whereby the legislature aimed to put the 1993 BVerfG abortion judgment into effect. The first paragraph of Article 219 provides that:

> 'The counselling serves to protect unborn life. It should be guided by efforts to encourage the woman to continue the pregnancy and to open her to the prospects of a life with the child; it should help her to make a responsible and conscientious decision. The woman must thereby be aware, that the unborn child has its own right to life with respect to her at every stage of the pregnancy and that a termination of pregnancy can therefore only be considered under the legal order in exceptional situations, when carrying the child to term would give rise to a burden for the woman which is so serious and extraordinary that it exceeds the reasonable limits of sacrifice. The counselling should, through advice and assistance, contribute to overcoming the conflict situation which exists in connection with the pregnancy and remedying an emergency situation. [...].'[170]

Hence, the primary object of counselling is the protection of unborn life and counselling must contribute to overcoming the conflict situation. The counselling must take place through a recognised pregnancy conflict counselling agency.[171] After conclusion of the counselling on the subject, the counselling agency must issue the pregnant woman a certificate. The physician who intends to perform the termination of the pregnancy is excluded from being a counsellor.[172] This counselling regulation has been criticised for being practically unusable for the attainment of the goal

166 Art. 218a (2) StGB. Translation taken from www.gesetze-im-internet.de/englisch_stgb/englisch_stgb.html#StGBengl_000P218a, visited June 2014. This has been held to cover also those situations that were covered by the previously existing 'general crisis' indication of Art. 218a (2) III StGB (*old*). See Ulsenheimer 2010, *supra* n. 52, Rn. 37 and Laufs 2009, *supra* n. 63, Rn. 40.

167 Art. 218a (4) StGB.

168 *Idem.*

169 Art. 218(4) StGB.

170 Art. 219(1) StGB. Translation taken from www.iuscomp.org/gla, visited June 2014.

171 Art. 219(2) StGB.

172 *Idem.*

of effective protection of the unborn life,[173] as well as dogmatically unfortunate fashioned and not providing sufficient legal clarity.[174]

The present German abortion law no longer provides for a separate embryopathic indication. Even though such an indication was not considered unconstitutional – in fact it was even expressly suggested – by the BVerfG,[175] the legislature wanted to express in the law of 1995 that also the disabled life is worthy of constitutional protection. At the same time, the legislature accepted that this indication was in fact covered by the medical-social indication.[176] It is now required that the (future) disability of the unborn constitutes a burden which demands such a degree of sacrifice of the pregnant woman's own existential values that one could no longer expect her to go through with the pregnancy.[177] While the exemption of punishment from an abortion on the basis of a criminological indication was made subject to a time limit set at 12 weeks after conception, the medical-social indication of Article 218a (2) was not subjected to any time limit in the 1995 Act. This implied that the previously existing time limit of 22 weeks for abortions on embryopathic grounds[178] had been lifted. Further, it implied that for abortions on embryopathic grounds no longer a counselling obligation existed; abortions on grounds on a medical indication after 12 weeks of pregnancy were left to the appraisal of the medical expert.[179] Both these implications of the new regulation have been criticised in legal scholarship[180] and politics. The call for an amendment of the law on this point grew particularly after reports of allegedly increasing numbers of late abortions (i.e., after the 23rd week of

173 Tröndle 1995, *supra* n. 149, at p. 3009.

174 R. Eschelbach, 'BeckOK StGB § 218' ['Beck online Commentary to StGB § 218'], in: B. von Heintschel-Heinegg (ed.), *Beck'scher Online-Kommentar StGB* [Beck Online Commentary to the StGB], 15th ed (München, Beck Verlag 2011) Rn. 24.

175 BVerfG 25 February 1975, Az. 1 BvF 2/74 a.o., *NJW* 1975 p. 573 and BVerfG 28 May 1993, Az. 2 BvF 2/90 a.o., *NJW* 1993 p. 1751.

176 *BT-Drs.* 13/1850, p 26. See also Ulsenheimer 2010, *supra* n. 52, Rn. 37; Eschelbach 2011, *supra* n. 174, Rn.1 and Laufs 2009, *supra* n. 63, Rn. 51.

177 W. Gropp, 'StGB § 218 Schwangerschaftsabbruch' ['§ 218 StGB Termination of pregnancy'], in W. Joeks and K. Miebach (eds.), *Münchener Kommentar zum StGB* [*Münchener Commentary to the StGB*], 2nd edn. (München, Verlag C.H. Beck 2012), Rn. 61. See also Ulsenheimer 2010, *supra* n. 52, Rn. 39.

178 See 4.2.2 above. See also Ulsenheimer 2010, *supra* n. 52, Rn. 38.

179 *BT-Drs.* 16/12970, p. 5.

180 R. Beckmann, 'Der „Wegfall" der embryopathischen Indikation' ['The „abolition" of de embryopatic indication'], *MedR* (1998) p. 155; E. Deutsch, 'Die Spätabtreibung als juristisches Problem' ['Late abortions as a legal problem'], *ZRP* (2003) p. 332 and F. Czerner, ‚Reform der Reform: Wiedereinführung der embryopathischen Indikation bei Spätabtreibungen?' ['Reform of the reform: reintroduction of the embryopathic indication for late abortions?'], *ZRP* (2009) p. 233. Czerner argues for the re-introduction of a separate embryopathic indication.

pregnancy) on embryopathic grounds.[181] After long discussions,[182] by Act of 2009[183] an extra counselling obligation was introduced for abortions on the basis of the social-medical indication.[184] Under the current law, the physician who has diagnosed an abnormality ('*Behinderung*') with the foetus is obliged to offer the pregnant woman counselling, which includes, *inter alia*, the dissemination of information about life with a disabled child. Further, a reflection period of three days after the diagnosis has to be observed, before an abortion can be performed.[185]

Since the year 2001 the annual abortion numbers in Germany have decreased every year, in total with more than 20 per cent, to an annual number of 102,802 in 2013.[186] The number of criminal convictions for illegal abortions has for a long time been and still is very low.[187]

4.2.7. Abortion and public funding

On the basis of Article 24b (1) and (2) SGB V,[188] women who are insured under the statutory health insurance, the so-called *Gesetzliche Krankenversicherung* (*GKV*), have a right to reimbursement of the costs of an abortion if this abortion is not against the law ('*nicht rechtswidrig*'),[189] and if it is performed by a physician in an institution that meets the requirements of Article 13(1) SchKG. Aims of this regulation are to

181 See, *inter alia*, *BT-Drs.* 16/12664; *BT-Drs.* 16/11330; *BT-Drs.* 16/11106; *BT-Drs.* 16/11347; *BT-Drs.* 16/11377 and *BT-Drs.* 16/11342. The official numbers of the *Statistisches Bundesamt Deutschland* [German Statistics] give a multifaceted picture. While in the period 1997–2009 the number of abortions carried out after the 23rd week of pregnancy had risen from 190 to 237 (with a lowest point in the year 2000 with 154 abortions), the percentage of abortions carried out on grounds of the medical indication had dropped from 3.5 in 1997 to 2.9 in the year 2009 (with a lowest percentage of 2.5 per cent in the year 2002). Statistisches Bundesamt Deutschland, *Schwangerschaftsabbrüche – FS12 R. 3 2010*, online available at www.destatis.de, visited June 2011.

182 See *supra* n. 181. See also Ulsenheimer 2010, *supra* n. 52, Rn. 40 and Czerner 2009, *supra* n. 180, at p. 233.

183 Gesetz zur Änderung des Schwangerschaftskonfliktgesetzes (SchKGÄndG) [Act on the Amendment of the Pregnancy Conflict Act] of 26 August 2009, *BGBl. I*, No. 58, p. 2990. The Act entered into force on 1 January 2010.

184 Art. 2 SchKG. See critical C. von Dewitz, 'Diskriminierung ungeborener Kinder mit Behinderungen durch die gesetzliche Regelung zum Schwangerschaftsabbruch' ['Discrimination of unborn children with disabilities by way of the regulation on termination of pregnancy'], *Zfl* (2009) p. 74.

185 In case of non-observance of the reflection period, a fine of maximum €5,000- can be imposed. See Ulsenheimer 2010, *supra* n. 52, Rn. 40.

186 Ulsenheimer 2010, *supra* n. 52, Rn. 6, footnote 18, referring to '*DÄBl* 2001, A 2065'. The exact figures per year are: 1996: 130,889; 1997: 130,890; 1998: 131,795; 1999: 130,471; 2000: 134,609; 2001: 134,964; 2002: 130,387; 2003: 128,030; 2004: 129,650; 2005: 124,023; 2006: 119,710; 2007: 116,781; 2008: 114,484; 2009: 110,694; 2010: 110,431, 2011: 108,867; 2012: 106,815 and 2013: 102,802. Statistisches Bundesamt Deutschland, *Schwangerschaftsabbrüche – FS12 R. 3 2010*, online available at www.destatis.de, visited June 2011.

187 For the years 1960–1985 statistics on prosecutions and criminal convictions are available. See Koch 1988, *supra* n. 69, at p. 249. For the period after 1985, the present author is only aware of a few incidental statistics, such as eight convictions in 1990 and ten in 1991. Ulsenheimer 2010, *supra* n. 52, Rn. 6, footnote 18, referring to '*DÄBl* 2001, A 2065'.

188 Previously Art. 200 f Reichsversicherungsordnung (RVO) [Reich Insurance Code].

189 See also BVerfG 28 May 1993, Az. 2 BvF 2/90 a.o., *NJW* 1993 p. 1751, as discussed above.

prevent illegal abortions with their inherent risks for the health and the life of the pregnant woman, to protect pregnant women from social disadvantage and to ensure their sustenance.[190] The constitutionality of this regulation and its predecessors have been questioned,[191] but the regulation has been upheld by the Constitutional Court.[192] It is safe to say that abortions on the basis of a medical or a criminological indication are not against the law and thus qualify for statutory reimbursement.[193] Whether this also counts for abortions on the basis of an embryopathic indication (that is held to be covered by the medical-social indication of Article 218a (2), see above), is more controversial.[194] Abortions that are exempted from punishment on the basis of Article 218a (1) qualify for recovery from the statutory scheme to a limited extent only.[195]

4.3. German legislation on assisted human reproduction and surrogacy

The German legal framework concerning AHR is somewhat fragmented. It consists of both the Federal Embryo Protection Act (*Embryoschutzgesetz*, ESchG),[196] as well as regulations of the German Medical Association ('*Bundesärztekammer*'). Further, for certain matters, for instance concerning public funding, provisions of the German Social Code are relevant too. Germany is no party to the CoE Biomedicine Convention.[197] Allegedly, the main reason for this is that Germany regarded the Biomedicine Convention's regulation of research on persons who cannot give consent (i.e., embryos), for the benefit of others, as ethically problematic.[198]

190 K. Höfler, ‚SGB V § 24b Schwangerschaftsabbruch und Sterilisation' [§ 24b SGB V Pregnancy Termination and Sterilisation'], in: S. Leitherer (ed.), *Kasseler Kommentar, Sozialversicherungsrecht* [Kasseler Commentary social insurance law], 69th ed (München, Verlag Beck 2011).

191 For example J. Isensee, ‚Abtreibung als Leistungstatbestand der Sozialversicherung und der grundgesetzliche Schutz des ungeborenen Lebens' ['Abortion as an element of offence under social insurance law and the constitutional protection of the life of the unborn child'], *NJW* (1986) p. 1645 and F. Hoffmann-Klein, 'Zur Verfassungsmäßigkeit der Abtreibungsfinanzierung', *ZfL* (2010) p. 82.

192 BVerfG 18 April 1984 (dec.), Az. 1 BvL 43/81, *NJW* 1984 p. 1805 and BVerfG 28 May 1993, Az. 2 BvF 2/90 a.o., *NJW* 1993 p. 1751, See also W. Esser, 'Die Rechtswidrigkeit des Aborts' ['The unlawfulness of abortions'], *MedR* (1983) p. 57.

193 See Höfler 2011, *supra* n. 190, Rn. 15b-c.

194 Generally it is accepted that such is the case if the genetic abnormality of the embryo can be expected to constitute a danger to a grave impairment of the physical or emotional state of health of the pregnant woman. See Höfler 2011, *supra* n. 190, Rn. 15 d.

195 Art. 24b (3) and (4) SGB V.

196 Gesetz zum Schutz von Embryonen (Embryonenschutzgesetz – ESchG) [Act on the Protection of Embryos (Embryo Protection Act)] of 13 December 1990, *BGBl. I* p. 2746, amended by Art. 22 Act of 23 October 2001, *BGBl. I* p. 2702.

197 Convention for the protection of Human Rights and Dignity of the Human Being with regard to the Application of Biology and Medicine: Convention on Human Rights and Biomedicine, CETS No. 164 (entry into force 1 December 1999). Germany has signed nor ratified this Convention (state of affairs 31 July 2014).

198 Dreier 2004, *supra* n. 3, at p. 157.

Hereafter first a brief outline of the coming into force of the Embryo Protection Act is given, after which the relevant substantive legal norms concerning AHR treatment are discussed thematically in greater detail.

4.3.1. Early (legislative) developments

Rapid technical developments in the field of biomedicine in the 1970s and 1980s[199] intensified public and political debate about AHR. At the time an embryo created outside the body of the woman enjoyed no legal protection: Article 218 ff StGB (concerning abortion, see 4.1.4 above) only protected embryos that were already transferred into the woman's body.[200] In the beginning of the 1980s various advisory committees from the legal profession, such as the German Women Lawyers Association (*'Deutscher Juristinnenbund'*) and the German (*'Deutscher Richterbund'*), issued studies and statements on assisted human reproduction.[201] In 1985, the so-called 'Benda Commission'[202] – a working party on genome analysis and gene therapy appointed by the Federal Minister of Justice and the Federal Minister of Research and Technology jointly – made recommendations to the legislature on AHR issues.[203] The Commission, *inter alia*, recommended prohibiting the anonymous donation of gametes and sterilising the donors of gametes after ten

199 For example the birth of the first IVF baby, Louise Brown in England in 1978.

200 Art. 218 StGB reads: 'Acts, the effects of which occur before the conclusion of the nesting of the fertilised egg in the uterus, shall not qualify as termination of pregnancy within the meaning of this law.' See R. Keller et al., *Embryonenschutsgesetz, Kommentar zum Embryonenschutzgesetz* [Embryo Protection Act, Commentary to the Embryo Protection Act] (Stuttgart, W. Kolhammer GmbH 1992) p. 57. See also Lanz-Zumstein 1986, *supra* n. 37.

201 E.g. 'Thesen einer Arbeitsgruppe des Deutschen Juristinnenbundes zu künstlichen Befruchtungen' [Statements of a working group of the German Women Lawyers Association on artificial insemination] and 'Thesen des Deutschen Richtersbundes zur Fortpflanzungsmedizin und zur Humangenetik' [Statements of the German Judges Association on reproductive medicine and on human genetics], as published in Lanz-Zumstein 1986, *supra* n. 37.

202 The Commission was named after its chair, Professor Ernst Benda. As Fuchs explains, its composition was '[...] based on the principle of interdisciplinarity, with certain important organisations and associations also being represented: it included scientists and medical experts from various learned societies and research foundations, representatives of the major churches, a philosopher, representatives of a variety of legal disciplines of the German Medical Association, the Federal Employers' Association and the German Trades Union Congress.' M. Fuchs, *National ethics councils. Their backgrounds, functions and modes of operation compared* (Berlin, German National Ethics Council 2005) p. 41, online available at: www.ethikratorg/_english/publications/Fuchs_International_Ethics_Councils.pdf, visited March 2011. See also E. Deutsch, 'Des Menschen Vater und Mutter. Die künstliche Befruchtung beim Menschen – Zulässigkeit und zivilrechtliche Folgen' ['A man's father and mother. Artificial insemination with human beings – Permissibility and civil law effects'], *NJW* (1986) p. 1971.

203 Bundesminister für Forschung und Technologie (ed.) [Federal Minister for Research and Technology], *In-vitro-Fertilisation, Genomanalyse und Gentherapie, Bericht der gemeinsamen Arbeitsgruppe des Bundesministers für Forschung und Technologie und des Bundesministers für Justiz ('Benda-Bericht')* [In vitro fertilisation, genome anlysis and gene therapy, report of the joint working group of the Federal Minister for Research and Technology and the Federal Minister of Justice] No. 6 in the series *Gentechnologie – Chancen und Risiken* [Gene technology – Opportunities and Risks] (München, Schweitzer 1985). See also Deutsch 1986, *supra* n. 202, at p. 1972 and Keller et al. 1992, *supra* n. 200, at pp. 67–68.

successful AHR treatments; prohibiting surrogacy and the donation of embryos; and prohibiting *in vitro* fertilisation for unmarried couples and single persons. That same year, the German Medical Association adopted a regulation on the matter,[204] which for years was the only existing regulatory measure in the field of reproductive care. In the meantime, various German States (*'Länder'*), drafted their own legislation concerning AHR issues.[205] All together the need for federal legislation on the matter was felt even more strongly.

Following the recommendations of the aforementioned 'Benda-Commission', the Minister of Justice tabled a 'discussion bill' (*'Diskussionsentwurf'*) for an act on the protection of embryos in 1986.[206] After relevant advisory bodies had given their reaction to this discussion bill,[207] the Federal Minister for Finance issued a so-called 'work bill' (*'Arbeitsentwurf'*)[208] in 1988. In the mean time, some – impatient[209] – states (*'Länder* and political parties') and political parties also tabled bills.[210] It was, however, the government bill that finally made it into law: in 1990 the Embryo Protection Act (*Embryoschutzgesetz*, ESchG) was adopted by the *Bundestag*.[211] It entered into force on 1 January 1991.[212]

4.3.2. The Embryo Protection Act (1991)

The Embryo Protection Act is first of all a penal act.[213] This has to do with the division of Federal and State competences in Germany. At the time of its coming into force there was no explicit federal competence for AHR issues. Instead, the federal legislature could only enact federal law in the field of civil and criminal law (Article 75(1) Basic Law) or with respect to diseases which posed a danger to the public or were communicable (Article 74(19) Basic Law).[214] Regulations concerning the professional medical practice fell – and still fall – within exclusive

204 Richtlinien zur Durchführung von In-vitro Fertilisation (IVF) und Embryotransfer (ET) als Behandlungsmethode der menschlichen Sterilität [Guidelines on implementation of *in vitro* fertilisation (IVF) and Embryo transfer (ET) as treatment for human infertility] of 1985 as printed in Keller et al. 1992, *supra* n. 200, at pp. 273–282.

205 See Keller et al. 1992, *supra* n. 200, at pp. 73–76.

206 *BT-Drs.* 11/5460. For a critique on this bill see *inter alia* Deutsch 1986, *supra* n. 202, at p. 1971.

207 See Keller et al. 1992, *supra* n. 200, at pp. 69–71.

208 See Keller et al. 1992, *supra* n. 200, at pp. 76–77.

209 *Idem*, at pp. 77.

210 See Keller et al. 1992, *supra* n. 200, at pp. 77–80.

211 *BR-Drs.* 745/90.

212 Art. 13 ESchG.

213 For a discussion of the pro and cons concerning the use of penal law for the regulation of reproductive matters, see Keller et al. 1992, *supra* n. 200, at pp. 81–97.

214 See also H. Seibert, 'Gesetzgebungskompetenz und Regelungsbefugnis im Bereich der Befruchtungstechniken' ['Legislative power and regulatory power in the area of fertilization techniques'], in: M. Lanz-Zumstein, *Embryonenschutz und Befruchtungstechnik, Seminarbericht und Stellungnahmen aus der Arbeitsgruppe "Gentechnologie" des deutschen Juristinnenbundes* [Protection of embryos and fertilisation techniques, seminar report and statements from the working group "Genetic Engineering" of the German Women Lawyers Association] (München, J Schweitzer Verlag 1986) p. 142.

State competence.[215] Since 1994 a (concurrent) competence for issues concerning human artificial insemination exists,[216] although thus far this competence has not been used by the federal legislature.[217] Consequently there is no coherent legal framework concerning AHR in German law: relevant provisions can be found in the Criminal Code, in the Civil Code as well as in Regulations drawn up by the German Medical Association (see below). This fragmentary character of the ESchG and of the regulation of AHR in general has been criticised repeatedly.[218]

The ESchG aims to prevent possible abuse of new reproduction techniques and resorts to penal law only where it is considered essential for the protection of particularly fundamental rights. According to its Explanatory Memorandum, the Act aimed to protect the constitutional values of human dignity and human life and the best interests of the child in particular.[219] The ESchG, therefore, *inter alia*, prohibits gender selection in the course of AHR (section 4.3.5 below);[220] *in vitro* fertilisation of more egg cells than can be transferred into the woman's body within one cycle;[221] as well as any processing of human embryos that does not serve the purpose of the preservation ('*Erhaltung*') of the embryo.[222]

The Act was further intended to prevent 'divided motherhood', a term which refers to the situation whereby the woman giving birth to the child is different from the woman genetically related to the child. For that reason, the Act further prohibits egg cell donation (see section 4.3.4.1 below);[223] the fertilisation of human egg cells with a view to embryo donation or for the purpose of the transferral of the embryo to a surrogate mother ('*Ersatzmutter*');[224] and the fertilisation of the egg cells of a woman who has declared her intention to place her child into the care of third parties after birth (see section 4.3.9 below).[225]

---

215 Ratzel 2010, *supra* n. 41, at p. 43 under reference to BVerfG 16 February 2000, Az. 1 BvR 420/97, *NJW* 2000 p. 857.

216 Art. 74 (26) Basic Law. *BT-Drs.* 16/813, p. 14, *BGBl. I* p. 3146. See also the textual amendment of this provision of 28 August 2006 (*BGBl. I* p. 2034), whereby 'künstliche Befruchtung beim Menschen' ['artificial insemination of human beings'] was replaced by 'medizinisch unterstützte Erzeugung menschlichen Lebens' ['medically assisted reproduction of human life'].

217 See Ratzel 2010, *supra* n. 41, at p. 43.

218 For example Keller et al. 1992, *supra* n. 200, at p. 89.

219 *BT-Drs.* 11/5460, p. 6. See also the previous Explanatory memorandum to the ESchG Bill, as printed in Lanz-Zumstein 1986, *supra* n. 37, Annex 1, pp. 153–164.

220 Art. 3 ESchG.

221 Art. 1(1)(3) ESchG. This was later set at a maximum of three egg cells.

222 Art. 2 ESchG. Other practices that are prohibited are: the creation of human embryos for research purposes (Art. 1(2) ESchG); gen transfers in human 'Keimbahnzellen'; the splitting of totipotent cells of a human embryo; human cloning (the purposefully creation of genetically identical human beings) (Art. 6 ESchG); any purposefully creation of hybrids ('Chimaren und Hybridwesen') of human beings and animals (Art. 7 ESchG).

223 Art. 1(1)(1) ESchG.

224 Art. 1(1)(2) ESchG.

225 Art. 1(1)(5) ESchG.

The Embryo Protection Act was not intended to concern the protection of the embryo from the moment of nidation, as from that point in time the provisions of Article 218ff of the Criminal Code (concerning abortion) apply.[226]

To date, only a few prosecutions have been instituted on the basis of the ESchG.[227] Nevertheless, the fairly rigid regulations of the Act and its chilling effect[228] have been prominent in the societal and political debate, for instance in respect of the (longtime) highly controversial topic of preimplantation genetic diagnosis (PGD, see 4.3.6 below).[229] The most substantive amendment to the Embryo Protection Act was adopted in 2011, when the prohibition on PGD was indeed mitigated (see 4.3.6 below).[230] As will become clear throughout this chapter, in respect of the controversial and sensitive AHR matters, it has often been case law that gave the impetus for further development of the law. In this regard, often a consistency of law argument – i.e., a claim that the AHR legislation was inconsistent with abortion legislation – has been made and accepted.[231]

4.3.3. Access to AHR treatment

Under German law access to AHR is regulated in professional codes and regulations, both at federal and at state level. The Medical Associations of most States follow the regulations of the Federal German Medical Association, following which the actual access to AHR treatment is limited to specific groups in society. Para. 3.1.1 of the Regulations of the German Medical Association concerning assisted human reproduction (‘*(Muster-)Richtlinie zur Durchführung der assistierten Reproduktion*’) restricts access to heterologous insemination,[232] to married women or women in a stable partnership with a man who has declared himself willing to accept parental responsibility for the child conceived through the AHR procedure.[233] It has been concluded that single women and women with a same-sex partner are thus excluded

---

226 *BT-Drs.* 11/5460, p. 7. On the scope of the Act, see also R. Neidert, ‘Das überschätzte Embryonenschutzgesetz – was es verbietet und nicht verbietet’ [‘The overestimated law Embryo Protection Act – what it prohibits and does not prohibit’], *ZRP* (2002) p. 467.

227 R. Müller-Terpitz, ‘Gesetz zum Schutz von Embryonen (Embryonenschutzgesetz – ESchG)’ [Act on the protection of embryos (Embryo Protection Act – ESchG)’], in: A. Spickhoff, *Medizinrecht* [Medical Law], 1st edn. (München, Verlag Beck 2011), no. 190, Rn. 1(4).

228 *Idem.*

229 *Idem.*

230 Art. 1 Gesetz zur Regelung der Präimplantationsdiagnostik (Präimplantationsdiagnostikgesetz – PräimpG) [Act on the Regulation of preimplantation genetic diagnosis] Act of 21 November 2011, *BGBl.* I, p. 2228. Earlier amendments were not substantive.

231 As will be explained in the various sections below, considerable critique has been issued on the alleged inconsistency between the ESchG and the German abortion laws. See for instance Keller et al. 1992, *supra* n. 200 and Ulsenheimer 2010, *supra* n. 52, Rn. 8.

232 The term ‘heterologous insemination’ refers to insemination with donated sperm.

233 (Muster-)Richtlinie zur Durchführung der assistierten Reproduktion [(Model) Regulations on the implementation of medically assisted reproduction] as published in *Deutsches Ärzteblatt* 103 (2006), no. 20, 19 May 2006, pp. A1392–1403, online available at www.bundesaerztekammer.de/downloads/Kuenstbefrucht_pdf.pdf, visited June 2011.

from access to such AHR treatment.[234] These restrictions have been criticised; some have pointed out that by virtue of the general right to the free development of the personality (Article 2 Basic Law) persons in a same-sex partnership also enjoy protection of their desire to have children. Since this right is an individual right, so it has been argued, its protection or implementation cannot be made dependent on the actual partnership nor the sexual orientation of the individual concerned.[235] The *Lesben- und Schwulenverbands in Deutschland* (the Gay Federation in Germany (LSVB)) has taken the viewpoint that the fact that the Regulations do not provide for access to AHR for women in a civil partnership, does not mean that access for this group is prohibited.[236] However, only the Medical Associations of the States of Berlin and Hamburg allow for access to assisted human reproduction for women in civil partnerships.[237]

4.3.4. Donation of gametes and embryos

The German law on donation of gametes and embryos is mixed. Firstly, heterologous sperm donation is not prohibited,[238] but not extensively regulated either. Article 1600(5) of the German Civil Code provides that if a child is conceived with donated sperm and the male partner of the mother has agreed to this, the mother and the man cannot challenge the man's paternity. Further, as explained in section 4.1.6 above, the OLG of Hamm ruled in 2013 that a child that has been conceived with sperm from a donor has a right to know about its genetic origins. It has been noted that sperm donation therefore implies considerable financial risks for the sperm donor, as a child conceived with his sperm and raised by a single mother or by two women in a registered partnership can in theory make a claim for maintenance and inheritance rights.[239] On the other hand, these groups are often excluded from

---

[234] *Idem.* See also the Commentary to this Regulation as published in 103 *Deutsches Ärzteblatt* (2006) p. A 1400. In the latest version of the Regulation this limitation is no longer included in the text itself, but is still foreseen for in the Explanatory Memorandum to the Regulation.

[235] Ratzel 2010, *supra* n. 41, at pp. 54–55, footnote 43.

[236] See www.lsvd.de/newsletters/newsletter-2011/insemination-ist-nicht-verboten/index.html and www.lsvd.de/recht/andere-rechtsgebiete/kuenstliche-befruchtung/index.html, both visited June 2013.

[237] See www.lsvd.de/recht/andere-rechtsgebiete/kuenstliche-befruchtung.html#c7732, visited June 2014. In Hamburg these women first have to consult a special committee. Richtlinien zur assistierten Reproduktion der Ärztekammer Hamburg [Guidelines on assisted reproduction of the Medical Council of Hamburg], Annex to Art.13(2) of the Berufsordnung [Professional Code], under 3.2.3, online available at www.aerztekammer-hamburg.de/berufsrecht/richtlinien_zur_assistierten_reproduktion.pdf, visited June 2014.

[238] Yet in 1908 there was a case of sperm insemination before the highest Federal Court at that time, the Reichsgericht. A woman hat inseminated herself with the sperm of her husband, without his knowledge. The Court rejected the husband's claim that he could not be the father because of the self-insemination. RG JW 1908, p. 485f. See also W. Küppers, *Die zivilrechtlichen Folgen der entgeltlichen Tragemutterschaft* [The civil consequences of commercial surrogacy] (Frankfurt am Main, Peter Lang 1988) p. 8.

[239] H. Kreß. 'Samenspende und Leihmutterschaft – Problemstand, Rechtsunsicherheiten, Regelungsansätze' ['Sperm donation and surrogacy – Problems, legal uncertainty, regulatory approaches'], *FPR* (2013), *supra* n. 49.

AHR treatment on the basis of the (non-binding) Regulations of the German Medical Association concerning assisted human reproduction (see above).

While sperm donation is thus allowed for under German law, egg cell donation is prohibited. This also holds for post-mortem fertilisation of an egg cell, as explained in more detail in section 4.3.4.2 below. Embryo donation is not explicitly provided for under German law. It has been held that it is therefore not outlawed, apart from in surrogacy situations (see 4.3.9 below).[240]

4.3.4.1. Prohibition on egg cell donation

By virtue of Article 1(1) ESchG the transplant of an unfertilised egg cell of another woman (in other words: heterologous donation of egg cells) is prohibited.[241] It is the act of transplantation that is punishable: the woman from whom the donated egg cell originates, and the woman into whom the donated egg cell is implanted, are explicitly exempted from punishment.[242]

The prohibition on egg cell donation first of all aims to protect the child's best interests[243] by preventing the division of motherhood between a biological and a genetic mother.[244] Pursuant to Article 1591 Civil Code, the woman who gives birth to the child, is the mother. Divided motherhood and the inherent uncertainty about the motherhood were considered by the legislature to endanger the development of the child into a responsible personality.[245] Account was also taken of the risk that the biological mother would distance herself from the child should the child be disabled or suffer from a serious hereditary disease, for which she would hold the donating woman responsible.[246] Other arguments put forward to justify the prohibition on egg cell donation were the possible commercial exploitation of women and health risks for women. In a 2010 third party intervention by the German government in an Austrian case before the European Court of Human Rights (ECtHR) concerning the donation of gametes, the German position on egg cell donation was summarised as follows:

> 'The prohibition [on egg cell donation] was supposed to protect the child's welfare by ensuring the unambiguous identity of the mother. Biologically, only women were capable of carrying a child to term. Splitting motherhood into a genetic and a biological mother

240 Müller-Terpitz 2011, *supra* n. 227, '§ 1 Mißbräuchliche Anwendung von Fortpflanzungstechniken', Rn. 8.

241 This prohibition is further laid down in a Regulation of the German Medical Association *(Muster-) Berufsordnung für die deutschen Ärztinnen und Ärzte* [(Model) regulations for German medical practitioners] (MBO-Ä 1997), Part D.IV. No. 15I2. See Müller-Terpitz 2011, *supra* n. 227, Rn. 5.

242 Art. 1(3)(1) ESchG.

243 Art. 2(1) in combination with Art. 1(1) Basic Law as well as Art. 6(2) Basic Law.

244 Abschlußbericht der Bund/Länder-Arbeitsgruppe 'Fortpflanzungsmedizin' [Final report of the Federal/State working group reproductive medicine] published in the *Bundesanzeiger* [Government Gazette] of 6 January 1989. See Keller et al. 1992, *supra* n. 200, at p. 147.

245 *BT-Drs.* 11/1856, p. 9 and *BT-Drs.* 11/5460, pp. 6–7. See also Keller et al. 1992, *supra* n. 200, at pp. 121–122 and Reinke 2008, *supra* n. 21, at pp. 151–152.

246 See Keller et al. 1992, *supra* n. 200, at p. 149.

> would result in two women having a part in the creation of a child. This would be an absolute novelty in nature and in the history of mankind. In legal, historical and cultural terms, the unambiguousness of motherhood represented a fundamental and basic social consensus and, for this reason alone, was considered indispensable by German legislators. In addition, the relationship with the mother was assumed to be important for the child's discovery of identity. As a result, the child would have extreme difficulties in coping with the fact that in biological terms two women had a part in his or her existence. Split motherhood and the resulting ambiguousness of the mother's identity might jeopardise the development of the child's personality and lead to considerable problems in his or her discovery of identity. It was therefore contrary to the child's welfare. Another danger was that the biological mother, being aware of the genetic background, might hold the egg donor responsible for any illness or handicap of the child and reject him or her. A conflict of interests between the genetic and biological mother could unfold to the detriment of the child. For the donor, making ova available was a complicated and invasive procedure which might result in a physical and psychological burden and a medical risk for the donor. Another conflict which might arise and strain the genetic and biological mothers' relationships with the child was that a donated egg might result in the recipient getting pregnant while the donor herself failed to get pregnant by means of in vitro fertilisation. For the aforementioned reasons, split motherhood was considered to be a serious threat to the welfare of the child which justified the existing prohibitions under the Embryo Protection Act.'[247]

The prohibition on heterologous egg cell donation has often received considerable criticism in German legal scholarship. The provision has been considered an unjustified interference with the constitutional right to procreate.[248] Further, the child's best interests argument has been questioned, as it is in this context in fact used as an argument for not at all letting a child come into existence.[249] It was further held that the risk of exploitation of women could be reduced by a prohibition on remuneration for egg cell donation and through the monitoring of AHR clinics.[250] Besides, it has been argued that the health risks involved in egg cell donation are not considerably greater than when artificial insemination with the use of the woman's own egg cell is employed.[251]

The fact that, on the contrary, heterologous sperm donation is not illegal has increased the criticism of the egg cell donation prohibition. This discrepancy has been held to be in violation of the prohibition on discrimination (Article 3 Basic Law).[252] Others,

---

247 ECtHR 4 April 2010, *S.H. a.o.* v. *Austria*, no. 57813/00, paras. 52–55. A shorter – and therefore less insightful – summary can be found in paras. 70–71 of the Grand Chamber judgment in this case, dating from 3 November 2011.

248 Art. 2 in combination with Art. 6(1) Basic Law. See also Reinke 2008, *supra* n. 21.

249 Müller-Terpitz 2011, *supra* n. 227, Rn. 7.

250 *Idem.*

251 *Idem.*

252 *Idem.* Compare the claim made by the applicants before the ECtHR in the case of *S.H. a.o.* v. *Austria* ECtHR [GC] 3 November 2011, no. 57813/00. See Ch. 2, section 2.3.3.

however, have seen relevant biological differences between divided motherhood and fatherhood that justify the difference made.[253]

4.3.4.2. Post-mortem reproduction

Following Article 5(1)(3) of the Embryo Protection Act, it is prohibited to intentionally fertilise an egg cell with the sperm of a man who has passed away. While the person carrying out the fertilisation risks a maximum punishment of three years' imprisonment or a fine, the woman who is involved in the insemination, will not be subject to punishment.[254] The Article aims both to protect the man's right to personal autonomy, including his right to procreate, as well as to serve the best interests of the child.[255] Post-mortem fertilisation of an egg cell is prohibited under Article 1(1)(2) ESchG for similar reasons. It is thus the act of post-mortem fertilisation that is outlawed. The implantation of an embryo that was created with the gametes of a man before he passed away is not prohibited under the ESchG.[256] In a case where a woman wished to have her cryopreserved egg cells implanted, the OLG Rostock held such implantation of those egg cells that had been fertilised with the semen (sperm) of her late husband before his death, not to be against the best interests of the child, because the husband had expressly informed his wife of his child wish before he died.[257]

4.3.5. Gender selection

Article 3 ESchG prohibits the artificial fertilisation of an egg cell with a sperm cell after selection of the gender chromosomes.[258] With this prohibition the legislature intended to refrain from entering into the ethically and legally unjustifiable area of positive eugenics.[259] The prohibition was held to comply with the State's positive obligation to protect human dignity (Article 1 Basic Law).[260]

The selection of gender chromosomes by a physician is exempted from punishment if it serves to prevent the child from suffering from Duchenne muscular dystrophy or

---

253 D. Prütting and W. Höfling, *Fachanwaltskommentar Medizinrecht* [Lawyers' commentary to medical law], 1st edn. 2010, Rn. 10.

254 Art. 4(2) EschG.

255 R. Müller-Terpitz, 'Gesetz zum Schutz von Embryonen (Embryonenschutzgesetz – ESchG). § 4 Eigenmächtige Befruchtung, eigenmächtige Embryoübertragung und künstliche Befruchtung nach dem Tode' [Act on the protection of embryos (Embryo Protection Act – ESchG) § 4 Self-insemination, embryo transfer and artificial insemination after decease'], in: A. Spickhoff, *Medizinrecht* [Medical Law], 2nd edn. (München, Verlag Beck 2014) Rn. 1.

256 OLG Rostock 7 May 2010, Az. 7 U 67/09 and Müller-Terpitz 2014, *supra* n. 255.

257 OLG Rostock 7 May 2010, Az. 7 U 67/09. See also M. Schafhausen, 'Herausgabe von imprägnierten Eizellen nach dem Tode des Mannes' ['Release of fertilised egg cells after decease of the man'], *jurisPR-MedizinR* (9/2010) Anm. 1 and A. Prehn, 'Die Strafbarkeit der post-mortem-Befruchtung nach dem Embryonenschutzgesetz' ['The punishability of post-mortem fertilisation under the Embryo Protection Act'], *MedR* (2011) p. 559.

258 The penalty that may be imposed is imprisonment for the maximum duration of one year or a fine.

259 *BT-Drs.* 11/5460, p. 10. See also Keller et al. 1992, *supra* n. 200, at p. 215 and Müller-Terpitz 2011, *supra* n. 227, Rn. 3(1).

260 Müller-Terpitz 2011, *supra* n. 227, Rn. (3)(1).

a similar serious gender related hereditary disease.[261] With this exception, account is taken of the difficult conflict situation in which parents involved may find themselves and the exception aims to prevent the developing embryo from suffering from a serious hereditary disease.[262]

4.3.6. Preimplantation genetic diagnosis (PGD)

While prenatal genetic diagnosis is allowed under German law and can in serious cases even justify an abortion on the basis of a medical-social indication (see 4.2.6 above), preimplantation genetic diagnosis (PGD)[263] has been controversial for a long time. Only in July 2011, the *Bundestag* adopted a law allowing for PGD under strict conditions.

At the time of the entering into force of the ESchG, PGD was not yet practiced in Germany, but only abroad. It is probably for that reason that PGD was not explicitly prohibited by nor provided for in the ESchG. Consequently, from the moment PGD became technically possible, it has been heavily debated whether it was prohibited under German law.[264] Those who argued it was relied primarily on Article 2(1) ESchG (prohibition on abusive use of extra corporal embryos)[265] and – sometimes – on Article 1(1)(2) (prohibition on abusive use of AHR techniques). Article 2(1) ESchG prohibits the abusive use of and sale ('*Veraußerung*'[266]) of human embryos[267] that have been created outside the human body, or that have been taken from the woman's body before the moment of nidation. Abusive use is described as the sale ('*Abgabe*'),[268]

---

261 Art. 3, second sentence ESchG.

262 Müller-Terpitz 2011, *supra* n. 227, Rn. (3)(1), referring to *BT-Drs.* 11/8057, p. 15.

263 A possible source of confusion is the fact that in the German language this practice is known under the abbreviation 'PID'.

264 See for example E. Giwer, *Rechtsfragen der Präimplantationsdiagnostik: eine Studie zum rechtlichen Schutz des Embryos im Zusammenhang mit der Präimplantationsdiagnostik unter besonderer Berücksichtigung grundrechtlicher Schutzpflichten* [Legal questions on preimplantation genetic diagnosis: a study into the protection of embryos in relation to preimplantation genetic diagnosis taking particular account of constitutional obligations to protect] (Berlin, Duncker & Humblot 2001); P. Ferdinand, *Pränatal- und Präimplantationsdiagnistik aus verfassungsrechtlicher Sicht* [Prenatal and preimplantation genetic diagnosis from a constitutional perspective] (Frankfurt am Main, Peter Lang 2010) and Neidert 2002, supra n. 226.

265 Keller et al. 1992, *supra* n. 200, at pp. 208–209.

266 For an explanation of this term, see G. Pelchen and P. Häberle, 'E 100. Gesetz zum Schutz von Embryonen (Embryonenschutzgesetz – ESchG) – § 2 Missbräuchliche Verwendung menschlicher Embryonen' [E.100. Act on the protection of embryos (Embryo Protection Act) – § 2 Abusive use of human embryos], in: G. Erbs and M. Kohlhaas, *Strafrechtliche Nebengesetze* [Ancillary criminal laws] (München: Verlag C.H. Beck 2011) Rn. 3. The autors refer to *BR-Drs.* 417/89.

267 Human embryos are defined in Art. 8(1) ESchG as: ‚[...] die befruchtete, entwicklungsfähige menschliche Eizelle vom Zeitpunkt der Kernverschmelzung an, ferner jede einem Embryo entnommene totipotente Zelle, die sich bei Vorliegen der dafür erforderlichen weiteren Voraussetzungen zu teilen und zu einem Individuum zu entwickeln vermag.' '[...] the fertilised human ovum which is capable of development after the nuclei have merged, also any totipotent cell extracted from an embryo capable – under the right circumstances – of dividing and developing into an individual.'].

268 See also Pelchen and Häberle 2011, *supra* n. 266, Rn. 4.

purchase ('*Erwerb*')[269] or use ('*Verwendung*'),[270] for a purpose that does not serve the preservation ('*Erhaltung*') of the embryo. This means, *inter alia*, that acts that deteriorate the embryo's chances of survival are prohibited.[271] Some qualified PGD as such abusive use of the embryo within the meaning of Article 2 ESchG.[272]

This discussion and legal uncertainty, in combination with the perceived prohibition on PGD, caused German women and couples to go abroad to obtain such testing (see also 4.4.2 below, for (limited) statistics). This cross-border practice in itself fuelled the discussion in Germany even more.[273] The prohibition on PGD was considered to imply a conflict of values ('*Wertungswiderspruch*') within the German legal order in various respects. In other words, the law was held to be internally inconsistent.[274] Firstly, many argued that a prohibition on PGD was inconsistent with German abortion laws: contraceptive measures before nidation were not prohibited, as a result of which the embryo *in vitro* – while at the same stage of development – enjoyed stronger protection than the embryo *in vivo*. The fact, in particular, that German law was permissive in respect of prenatal genetic diagnosis, which could, in serious cases, even justify an abortion, while PGD was prohibited, received heavy criticism in (international) legal scholarship.[275] It was claimed that access to PGD could in certain situations contribute to the prevention of abortions at a later stage of the pregnancy. Further, it was argued that the prohibition of PGD was at variance with the fact that a physician was exempted from punishment if he carried out gender

---

269 *Idem*, Rn. 5.

270 *Idem*, Rn. 6.

271 Keller et al. 1992, *supra* n. 200, at p. 206.

272 *Idem*, at pp. 208–209. This line of reasoning was initially also accepted by the KG which ruled by judgment of 2008 that the provision of PGD to three couples constituted an offence in violation of Art. 1(1)(2) ESchG. KG 9 October 2008 (dec.), Az. 3 Ws 139/08. This judgment was however later overruled (see below). Pelchen and Häberle also considered it controversial whether the actual diagnostic measures involved in PGD could be qualified as abusive use of the embryo. They identified two other possible ways in which PGD could be held to be in violation of Art. 2(1) ESchG. Firstly, they pointed out that if a physician wants to eliminate 'unsuitable' embryos after PGD, the question is raised whether these embryos were created for another purpose than their preservation within the meaning of Art. 2(1) ESchG. They further raised the question if the destruction of 'unsuitable' embryos after a preimplantation genetic test gave a negative result, is a punishable abuse of the embryo. Pelchen and Häberle 2011, *supra* n. 266, Rn. 6.

273 See for example S. Kunz-Schmidt, 'Präimplantationsdiagnostik (PID) – der Stand des Gesetzgebungsverfahrens und der aktuellen Diskussion' ['Preimplantation genetic diagnosis (PGD) – the current legislative procedure and debate'], *NJ* (2011) p. 231 at p. 235 and Deutsche Akademie der Naturforscher Leopoldina et al., *Ad-hoc statement Preimplantation genetic diagnosis (PGD). The effects of limited approval in Germany*, January 2011, p. 4, online available at: www.leopoldina.org/fileadmin/user_upload/Politik/Empfehlungen/Nationale_Empfehlungen/stellungnahme_PID_2011_final_a4ansicht_EN.pdf visited June 2011.

274 See T. Henking, *Wertungswidersprüche zwischen Embryonenschutzgesetz und den Regelungen des Schwangerschaftsabbruchs? Am Beispiel des Verbots der Präimplantationsdiagnostik* [Contradictory values between the Emrbyo Protection Act and the Regulations on termination of pregnancy. The prohibition on preimplantation genetic diagnosis as an example] (Baden-Baden, Nomos Verlagsgesellschaft 2010).

275 E.g. A. Coverleyn et al., *Pre-implantation Genetic Diagnosis in Europe'* (Joint Research Centre of the European Commission, January 2007) p. 80, online available at www.ftp.jrc.es/EURdoc/eur22764en.pdf, visited July 2014.

selection in order to prevent that the future child would suffer from Duchenne muscular dystrophy or a similar serious gender related hereditary disease (see above).

Based on such criticism, ever more voices advocated a (limited) legalisation of PGD. In 2000, the German Medical Association framed a discussion paper that took the lawfulness of PGD as a starting point, but also proposed to subject access to PGD to strict conditions.[276] This view was supported by a majority of the German Ethics Council.[277] Nevertheless, a bill to this effect did not meet the required majority in Parliament.[278] Finally, it was case law that gave the decisive impetus for legislative change in the field of PGD.

In May 2009 the District Court (*Landesgericht*) of Berlin acquitted a gynaecologist who stood trial for having provided PGD to three couples with a child wish, while tests had established that of each couple, one of the parents had a serious hereditary defect.[279] The Court held that PGD with the aim of discovering serious genetic deficiencies was not criminal. The Public Prosecutor appealed the case to the German Supreme Court (*Bundesgerichtshof*, BGH), which confirmed by judgment of 6 July 2010 that PGD with the aim of discovering serious genetic deficiencies was not illegal.[280] The BGH held that from Article 1(1)(2) ESchG (prohibition on abusive use of AHR techniques) and Article 2(1) ESchG (prohibition on abusive use of human embryos) no prohibition on PGD could be deduced that would be in conformity with Article 103(2) Basic Law. According to the latter constitutional provision an act may be punished only if it has been defined by a law as a criminal offence before the act was committed. Basing itself on the wording as well as the objective of the ESchG (namely the protection of the embryo against abuse), the BGH held that the acts of the accused did not constitute criminal offence. The Court considered that the ESchG did not expressly prohibit PGD and that it was not evident that the legislature would have prohibited PGD had it been yet available at the time of the drafting of the ESchG. This was, furthermore, held to be in line with the value judgment contained

---

276 Bundesärztekammer [German Medical Association], 'Diskussionsentwurf zu einer Richtlinie zur Präimplantationsdiagnostik of 3 March 2000, *Dtsch. Ärztebl.* (DA) 97 (2000), p. A525-A528.

277 Nationalen Ethikrat (German Ethics Council), *Stellungnahme Genetische Diagnostik vor und während der Schwangerschaft* [Position paper genetic diagnosis before and during pregnancy] (Nationaler Ethikrat, Berlin 2003) online available at www.ethikrat.org/dateien/pdf/Stellungnahme_ Genetische-Diagnostik.pdf, visited June 2011. See also *BT-Drs.* 14/9020, p. 86.

278 *BT-Drs.* 15/1234.

279 In the indictment this conduct was qualified as abusive use of reproduction techniques (Art. 1(1)(2) ESchG) and abusive use of human embryos (Art. 2(1) ESchG). LG Berlin 14 May 2009, Az. (512) 1 Kap Js 1424–06 KLs (26/08), *NJW* 2010 p. 2672. See R. Beckman 'Präimplantationsdiagnostik und Embryonenschutzgesetz, Zugleich Besprechung von LG Berlin' ['Preimplantation genetic diagnosis and the Embryo Protection Act, as well as case-note to LG Berlin'], *ZfL* (2009) p. 125.

280 BGH 6 July 2010, Az. 5 StR 386/09, *NJW* 2010 p. 2672 and H.-G Dederer,' Zur Straflosigkeit der Präimplantationsdiagnostik, Anmerkungen zu BGH, Urt. v. 6.7.2010 – 5 StR 386/09' ['To the impunity of preimplantation genetic diagnosis, Commentary to the BGH judgment of 6.7.2010 – 5 StR 386/09'], *MedR* (2010) p. 819. See also 'PID Grundsatzurteil. Koalition streitet um Gentests an Embryonen', *Spiegel online* 11 July 2010, online available at: www.spiegel.de/wissenschaft/ medizin/0,1518,705898,00.html, visited September 2011 and U. Bahnsen, 'Um Leid zu verhindern; Gentests an Embryonen: Die Abwehrfront im Parlament beginnt zu bröckeln', *Die Zeit* 21 October 2010, p. 37.

in Article 3 ESchG, which provided that in case of serious hereditary diseases, an exception to the prohibition on gender selection could be made. The Court pointed at the considerable risks involved in the criminalisation of the transferral of embryos into a woman's body without diagnostic testing, even in cases where the parents carried a hereditary effect. In particular in a later stage of the pregnancy, permissive prenatal diagnostic testing could lead to results that constituted grounds for an abortion. The Court again made a comparison with the exception on the prohibition of gender selection, which also aimed to prevent abortions in a later phase of the pregnancy. The press release issued by the BGH on this judgment underlined that only PGD with the aim of discovering serious genetic deficiencies was not prohibited and that the judgment had not opened the way to an unlimited selection of embryos on the basis of genetic characteristics.[281]

The BGH judgment – which to some came as a surprise[282] – evoked a heated debate in legal scholarship, politics and society in general on the question how this ruling was to be implemented in law.[283] Numerous non-governmental actors issued opinions and statements on the matter. The German Academy of Sciences Leopoldina, for example, recommended that PGD be permitted by law under restricted and defined conditions,[284] which would have the same implications for the embryo as prenatal genetic diagnosis and abortion.[285] Leopoldina judged positively the potential contribution of limited legalisation of PGD to the avoidance of abortions[286] and

281 Press release Bundesgerichtshof of 6 July 2010, no 137/2010, online available at www.juris.bundesgerichtshof.de/cgi-bin/rechtsprechung/document.py?Gericht=bgh&Art=pm&Datum=2010&Seite=3&nr=52539&pos=112&anz=249, visited September 2011.

282 U. Schroth, 'Präimplantationsdiagnostik zur Feststellung genetischer Schäden eines extrakorporal erzeugten Embryos' ['Preimplantation genetic diagnosis to determine genetic disorders of *in vitro* embryos'], *NJW* (2010) p. 2676–2677.

283 E.g. Beckmann 2009 *supra* n. 279; Dederer 2010, *supra* n. 280; B. Ruso and M. Thöni, 'Quo vadis Präimplantationsdiagnostik?' ['Quo vadis preimplantation genetic diagnosis?'], *MedR* (2010) p. 74; H. Kreß, 'Präimplantationsdiagnostik und Fortpflanzungsmedizin angesichts des ethischen Pluralismus. Rechtspolitische Gesichtspunkte nach dem Urteil des BGH' ['Preimplantation genetic diagnosis in the light of ethical pluralism. Legal political considerations after the judgment of the German Federal Court of Justice'], *ZRP* (2010) p. 201 and A.B. Lungstras, 'Die Präimplantationsdiagnostik verbieten oder erlauben?' ['To allow or to prohibit preimplantation genetic diagnosis'], *NJ* (2010) p. 485.

284 Deutsche Akademie der Naturforscher Leopoldina et al. 2011, *supra* n. 273 at p. 2. The report held that the stance that PGD was prohibited under the ESchG warranted review. The authors pointed at 'new research findings and the availability of modified examination techniques' that had been developed to remove non-totipotent cells beyond the fourth day of gestation, without exposing the embryo to an increased risk of injury or a reduction in implantation frequency. The authors were further of the opinion that 'the issue of selection decision by women within the context of PGD has not yet received the necessary legal recognition in Germany.'

285 The report held that this equalisation should be restricted to limited PGD approval for non-totipotent *in vitro* embryonic cells. 'The investigation should [...] only be carried out for couples whose future children have, from an objective medical view-point, a high risk of a known and serious monogenic disease, or a hereditary chromosomal aberration, or in cases where death or miscarriage is expected. No age limit for disease-onset should be specified in determining the legitimacy of PGD. PGD must not be used for legally or socially defined goals which do not directly concern the welfare of the affected couple.'

286 Deutsche Akademie der Naturforscher Leopoldina et al. 2011, *supra* n. 273, at p. 3.

the death of unaffected embryos[287] as well as cross-border medical tourism.[288] The German Medical Association pleaded for the drafting of a comprehensive act on assisted reproduction in which the regulation of PGD would be provided for.[289] The Association set itself the task of drafting a guideline on PGD (*'(Muster-)Richtlinie zur Durchführung der Präimplantationsdiagnostik'*), allowing for PGD only in cases in which the couple involved in the AHR ran an increased risk of passing on certain hereditary diseases and under strict conditions such as counselling and approval by an ethics committee.[290] The German Bar Association, on the contrary, saw no need for such a separate examination by a committee.[291] The German Ethics Council (*'Deutscher Ethikrat'*) was strongly divided on the topic;[292] only a small majority of 13 out of 24 Council members pleaded for restricted legalisation of PGD. Some saw this division in the scholarly and professional world as a reflection of opinions in society.[293]

Within Parliament, various bills were tabled, of which three were debated. In line with the public debate, the proposed regulations varied from a strict prohibition on PGD[294] to legalisation of PGD under certain (limited) circumstances.[295] During the first reading in April 2011, none of the bills received the necessary majority vote in Parliament.[296] A middle-ground solution, providing for PGD only under very restrictively defined conditions,[297] stalled during the second reading.[298] As a result, during the final vote two completely opposite solutions were on the table in July 2011, when a final decision by Parliament was expected. Opponents of legalisation of PGD in fact wanted to undo the effects of the BGH judgment. They argued that it would be difficult to define the circumstances under which PGD would be allowed and warned that the creation of exceptions carried the risk that other illnesses or genetic features would also be accepted as grounds for the selection of future life.[299] While this approach received considerable support in Parliament, the possibility of

---

287 *Idem*, at p. 4.

288 *Idem.*

289 *Bundesärztekamme* [German Medical Association], Memorandum of 17 February 2011, online available at www.bundesaerztekammer.de, visited September 2011.

290 *Idem.*

291 Stellungnahme des Deutschen Anwaltvereins durch den Medizinrechtsausschuss zu den Gesetzentwürfen zur Präimplantationsdiagsnostik [Position paper of the working group on medical law of the German bar association on the draft bill on preimplantation genetic diagnosis], no. 12/2011, March 2011, online available at www.anwaltverein.de, visited September 2011.

292 Deutscher Ethikrat [German Ethics Council], *Präimplantationsdiagnostik Stellungnahme* [Position on preimplantation genetic diagnosis], Berlin 8 March 2011, online available at www.ethikrat.org/dateien/pdf/stellungnahme-praeimplantationsdiagnostik.pdf, visited September 2011.

293 See also Redaktion beck-aktuell, 'Hauchdünne Mehrheit im Ethikrat für Embryonentests', *Becklink* 1011054 (Verlag C.H. Beck 2011).

294 *BT-Drs.* 17/5440.

295 *BT-Drs.* 17/5451.

296 Redaktion beck-aktuell, 'Anhörung zur Präimplantationsdiagnostik: Befürworter und Gegner des PID-Verbots untermauern ihre Ansicht jeweils unter Verweis auf Grundrechte', 26 May 2011, *Becklink* 1013490.

297 *BT-Drs.* 17/5452.

298 Redaktion beck-aktuell, 'Bundestag stimmt für begrenzte Zulassung der Präimplantationsdiagnostik', *Becklink* 1014650 (Verlag C.H. Beck 2011).

299 *Idem.*

resorting to PGD only in exceptionally serious cases received even more support. Therefore, but only after lengthy and emotive debates,[300] the Bill legalising PGD under limited conditions finally gained the required majority vote in Parliament in July 2011.[301] Subsequently, in September 2011, the Senate (*Bundesrat*) approved the Act on preimplantation genetic diagnosis (*Präimplantationsdiagnostikgesetz* (PräimpG)).[302, 303]

According to the new legislation, PGD is punishable with imprisonment of up to one year or a fine of a maximum of 50,000 euros.[304] PGD is only allowed if there is a high risk that a genetic disorder on the side of the parents will cause the embryo to suffer from a defect from which a miscarriage will follow or that implies that the future child will suffer from a serious hereditary disease.[305] Access to such lawful PGD is subject to conditions. Written consent of the woman whose egg cell is being used, medical and psychosocial counselling, as well as approval of use of the diagnosis by an interdisciplinary ethics committee, are all mandatory. Further, only licensed institutions can carry out PGD.[306]

4.3.7. Vitrification of egg cells

The Embryo Protection Act does not prohibit vitrification of gametes and embryos (‘*Kryokonservierung*’). This practice has nonetheless been held to be controversial from a legal-political perspective, because it may negatively impact the quality of the egg cells or embryos and may therefore raise questions as to the rights of the unborn – *in vitro* – life.[307] Vitrification of gametes is not reimbursed under the

300 *Idem.*

301 The Bill received a ‘suprisingly clear’ majority of 326 votes. The Bill providing for a full prohibition obtained 260 votes. Redaktion beck-aktuell, ‘Bundestag stimmt für begrenzte Zulassung der Präimplantationsdiagnostik’, *Becklink* 1014650 (Verlag C.H. Beck 2011).

302 Gesetz zur Regelung der Präimplantationsdiagnostik (Präimplantationsdiagnostikgesetz – PräimpG) [Act on the Regulation of preimplantation genetic diagnosis], Art. 1 of Act of 21 November 2011, *BGBl. I*, p. 2228. The Act is complemented by a Decree of 2013, Verordnung zur Regelung der Präimplantationsdiagnostik (Präimplantationsdiagnostikverordnung – PIDV) of 21 February 2013, *BGBl. I* p. 323, which entered into force on 1 February 2014. For a critical note, see C. Pestalozza, ‘Eine späte und mißliche Geburt: Die Verordnung zur Regelung der Präimplantationsdiagnostik’, *MedR* 2013 pp. 343–250.

303 *BR-Drs.* 480/11. See also www.bundesrat.de/cln_171/nn_6898/DE/presse/pm/2011/132-2011.html?__nnn=true, visited September 2012.

304 The new Art. 3a (1) ESchG.

305 The new Art. 3a (2) ESchG. A high risk is defined as a 25 to 50 per cent probability. *BT-Drs.* 17/5451, p. 10.

306 The new Art. 3a (3) ESchG.

307 A. Laufs, ‘§ 129 Fortpflanzungs- und Genmedizin’ [‘§ 129 Reproduction and gene medicine’] in: A. Laufs and B.R. Kern (eds.), *Handbuch des Arztrechts* [Handbook of Medical Law], 4th edn. (München, Verlag C.H. Beck 2010) Rn. 26–27 and M. Quaas et al., ‘§ 68 Einzelfelder der Biomedizin, b) Kryokonservierung’ [‘§ 68 Individual areas of Biomedicine, b) cryopreservation’], in: M. Quaas et al., *Medizinrecht* [Medical law] 2nd edn. (München, Verlag C.H. Beck 2008) Rn. 67.

statutory health insurance (see also 4.3.8 below),[308] but it qualifies for certain tax deductions.[309]

4.3.8. AHR treatment and public funding

Since 1990, Article 27a of the German Social Act (*Socialgesetzbuch*, SGB) sets certain conditions for AHR treatment[310] to qualify for reimbursement from the statutory health insurance (*Gesetzliche Krankenversicherung*, GKV).[311] Firstly, an entitlement to reimbursement only exists for AHR treatment that is deemed medically necessary.[312] This means that the couple's desire to have children must be unfulfilled and that the cause for the infertility of the couple together cannot be cured by medical treatment.[313] A further condition is set in respect of age: only insured women between 25 and 40 years old and insured men between 25 and 50 years old may claim reimbursement for the costs of AHR treatment on the basis of the statutory insurance scheme.[314] Also, only three treatment cycles are eligible for reimbursement[315]; any further attempts to initiate a pregnancy will have to be paid for by the insured couple themselves.[316]

Further and importantly, only homologous insemination, whereby the gametes of the couple involved are used, is reimbursed.[317] The couple must, moreover, be married.

---

308 BSG 22 March 2005, Az. B 1 KR 11/03 R, *NJW* 2005 p. 2476.

309 FG Niedersachsen 14 March 2013, Az. 5 K 9/11.

310 Apart from IVF treatment this may also concern other types of treatment, such as vitrification of tissue of the ovaries (BSG 17 February 2010, Az. B 1 KR 10/09 R), provided the criteria of the Article are met.

311 Art. 2(2) Act of 26 June 1990, *BGBl. I*, p. 1211. This provision was amended by Article 1 (14) Gesetz zur Modernisierung der gesetzlichen Krankenversicherung (GKV-Modernisierungsgesetz – GMG) [Act on the modernisation of the National Health Scheme] Act of 14 November 2003, *BGBl. I* p. 2190. See also Richtlinien des Bundesausschusses der Ärzte und Krankenkassen über ärztliche Maßnahmen zur künstlichen Befruchtung ('Richtlinien über künstliche Befruchtung') [Guidelines of the Federal Commission of Doctors and Health Insurance on medically assisted reproduction] of 14 August 1990, *Bundesarbeitsblatt* 1990, No. 12, and *Bundesanzeiger* 2010; No. 182, p. 4003, online available at www.kbv.de/39321.html, visited August 2011. See also B. Schmeilzl and M. Krüger, 'Künstliche Befruchtung: Wer trägt die Kosten? Eine Übersicht nach Fallgruppen' ['Artificial insemination: who bears the costs? An overview according to categories of cases'], *NZS* (2006) p. 630.

312 Art. 27a (1) SGB.

313 BSG 22 March 2005, Az. B 1 KR 11/03 R, *NJW* 2005 p. 2476. See also Ulsenheimer 2010, *supra* n. 52, Rn. 63.

314 Art. 27a (3) SGB. See BSG 19 September 2007, Az. B 1 KR 6/07 R and BSG 3 March 2009, Az. B 1 KR 7/08 R, in which the Federal Social Court held these age restrictions to be legitimate. Critical were H. Kentenich and K. Pietzer, 'Überlegungen zur gesetzlichen Nachbesserung in der Reproduktionsmedizin' ['Thoughts on legislative improvements in the field of reproduction medicine'], in: H. Frister and D. Olzen, *Reproduktionsmedizin, Rechtliche Fragestellungen. Dokumentation der Tagung zum 10-jährigen Bestehen des Instituts für Rechtsfragen der Medizin Düsseldorf* [Reproduction medicine, legal questions. Proceedings of the Conference for the 10 year anniversary of the Düsseldorf institute for medical legal issues] (Düsseldorf, Düsseldorf University Press 2010) p. 59 at p. 70.

315 Before the amendments of the year 2004 (*BGBl. I*, p. 2190), this number was set at four.

316 Art. 27b (1)(2) SGB.

317 See section 4.3.4 above and BSG 9 October 2001, Az. B 1 KR 33/00 R, *NJW* 2002 p. 1517. This is different in respect of tax deduction. Since 2010 also heterologous insemination qualifies for tax deduction. BFH 16 December 2010, Az. VI R 43/10 *NJW* 2011 p. 2077.

The latter limitation has been set from the very beginning.[318] The legislature justified this limitation on grounds of its obligation to give special protection to marriage and the family under Article 6(1) Basic Law.[319] In February 2007, the Constitutional Court ruled that this limitation of reimbursement for AHR treatment to married couples was not unconstitutional.[320] The Court held that the general principle of equality of Article 3(1) Basic Law would have been violated if AHR treatment were considered to serve the purpose of curing a disease. The legislature had not, however, assigned medical treatment with the purpose of causing a pregnancy as 'treatment of a disease' ('*Krankenbehandlung*'), but as so-called 'performance' ('*Leistung*').[321] The Court considered this choice to fall within the legislature's freedom to set conditions for reimbursement on the basis of the statutory health insurance regulations, particularly in the grey area between diseases and those physical and mental affections of a person that cannot necessarily be dispelled or cured by means of medical services on the basis of the statutory health insurance.[322] The Court considered that the legislature had sufficient objective grounds to relate the reimbursement for AHR treatment to marriage, particularly as this served the child's best interests. Further, Article 6(1) was not violated: from the special protection of marriage and the family, no claim on the State could be derived to enable the creation of a family by means of State-funded AHR treatment. Although the Court saw no constitutional objection against the reimbursement of AHR treatment for unmarried couples, it saw no constitutional obligation to that effect either. Kentenich and Pietzer questioned, in 2010, whether this fixation on the marital status still would be tenable, given that in 2005 one third of all children born in Germany were born out of wedlock.[323] While unmarried women cannot have their AHR treatment reimbursed under the statutory health insurance, they may claim tax deduction.[324] Tax deduction is also available

---

318 Art. 27a (1)(3) SGB. As noted above (in section 4.3.3), the Regulations of the German Medical Association also provide for access to AHR for women in a stable partnership with a man who has declared to accept parental responsibility for the child conceived through the AHR procedure.

319 RegE KOV-AnpG 1990, *BR-Drs.* 65/90, p. 35. See also R. Brandts, 'Artikel 27a SGB V' ['Article 27a Social Law Act part V'] in: S. Leitherer, *Kasseler Kommentar zum Socialversicherungsrecht* [Kasseler Commentary to Social security law], 69st edn. (München Verlag H.C. Beck 2011), Rn. 27. Müller-Terpitz has argued that from Art. 6(1) Basic Law no entitlement to claim financial support for reproductive treatment follows; instead the State has a protective and stimulating role. Müller-Terpitz 2010, *supra* n. 21, at p. 13.

320 BVerfG 28 February 2007, Az. 1 BvL 5/03, *NJW* 2007 p. 1343. The judgment was adopted with a seven to one vote. The dissenting judge did however not write a dissenting opinion. This judgment is also referred to in BVerfG 21 July 2010 (dec.), Az. 1 BvR 2464/07, *NJW* 2010 p. 2783.

321 In 2009 the Constitutional Court held that the term ‚illness' did not cover the desire for successful family planning within marriage ('Vor allem kann der Begriff der Krankheit, der grundsätzlich die Leistungen der gesetzlichen Krankenversicherung auslöst, nicht durch Auslegung dahingehend erweitert werden, dass er auch den Wunsch nach einer erfolgreichen Familienplanung in einer Ehe umfasst.') BVerfG 27 February 2009 (dec.), Az. 1 BvR 2982/07, *NJW* 2009 p. 1733, para. 10. See also BSG 3 April 2001, Az. B 1 KR 40/00 R, *NJW* 2002 p. 1598. Critical on this point is S. Huster, 'Die Leistungspflicht der GKV für Maßnahmen der künstlichen Befruchtung und der Krankheitsbegriff' ['The obligation of the GKV to reimburse artificial insemination and the definition of illness'], *NJW* (2009) p. 1713.

322 See also Huster 2009, *supra* n. 321, at p. 1713.

323 Kentenich and Pietzer 2010, *supra* n. 314, at p. 70.

324 BFH 10 May 2007, Az. III R 47/05, *NJW* 2007 p. 3596. See F. Grube, 'Aufwendungen einer unverheirateten Frau für künstliche Befruchtung als außergewöhnliche Belastung' ['Expenses of an

to certain other groups of recipients of AHR treatment.[325] For instance, since 2010, heterologous insemination also qualifies for tax deduction.[326]

In 2004, the full reimbursement for AHR treatment was subjected to a 50 per cent cut.[327] The legislature did not explain this reduction, but most likely it was introduced in order to cut expenses.[328] It has been reported that since this change in the law the number of AHR treatments in Germany has dropped considerably.[329] Two individuals lodged a constitutional complaint against this new rule, alleging, *inter alia*, that the 50 per cent cut violated the general principle of equality (Article 3(1) Basic Law) and the Social State principle (Article 20(1) Basic Law).[330] They were, however, unsuccessful, as the Constitutional Court in 2009 refused to accept their complaint.[331] Referring to its aforementioned 2007 ruling concerning the limitation of reimbursement for AHR treatment to married couples, the Court repeated that there was no obligation on the legislature to fund the creation of a family by means of statutory health insurance. The Court considered that reimbursement for AHR treatment concerned a 'performance' ('*Leistung*') that fell within the legislature's discretionary freedom. AHR treatment, the Court held, concerned no therapeutically necessary medical treatment, but merely the desire of the insured to live the life he or she wished to live.[332]

4.3.9. Surrogacy

German law shows – and has always shown – a clear disapproval of both commercial and altruistic surrogacy and provides for its penalisation under certain circumstances. Surrogacy is held to be against the values of the Basic Law and it is considered to

unmarried woman for artificial insemination as extraordinary financial burden'], *juris Praxis Report SteuerRecht* 45 (2007) Anm. 5.

325 There is also tax deduction for the vitrification of egg cells when after a successful first pregnancy, these are maintained for further pregnancies (FG Niedersachsen 14 March 2013, Az. 5 K 9/11). The question of whether tax deduction also applies when no fertility treatment is taking place or is actually planned, was pending before the Federal Financial Court (Az. XI R 23/13) by the time this research was concluded (i.e. 31 July 2014).

326 BFH 16 December 2010, Az. VI R 43/10, *NJW* 2011 p. 2077. In 1999 this court had ruled to the contrary (BFH 18 May 1999, Az. III R 46/97, *NJW* 1999 p. 2767).

327 Art. 1 (14) GKV-Modernisierungsgesetz – GMG. See also *BT-Drs.* 15/1525 S 83.

328 Brandts 2011, *supra* n. 319, Rn. 27.

329 Huster 2009, *supra* n. 321, p. 1713, footnote 3, under reference to 'Wilke et al., *Gesundheitsökonomie und Qualitätsmanagement*, 2008, p. 149'. See also Kentenich and Pietzer 2010, *supra* n. 314, at p. 69, footnote 18, under reference to 'Deutsches IVF-Register, *DIR-Jahrbuch Ärztekammer Schleswig-Holstein*, 2007'.

330 The complainants also (unsuccesfully) relied on Arts. 1(1); 2(1) and 6(1) Basic Law.

331 The BVerfG may refuse complaints on the basis of Art. 93b BVerfGG. BVerfG 27 February 2009 (dec.), Az. 1 BvR 2982/07, *NJW* 2009 p. 1733.

332 The Court spoke of 'die Wünsche eines Versicherten für seine individuelle Lebensgestaltung' ['the desire of an insured person for his individual way of living']. See also E. Beckhove,'Die Kostenübernahme für künstliche Befruchtungen – Fallgruppen' ['Reimbursement of artificial insemination – categories of cases'], *NJOZ* (2009) p. 1465.

result in difficult psychological and social conflicts for all parties involved.[333] As for the prohibition on heterologous egg cell donation, the legislature wanted to prevent situations of divided motherhood. Further, it is considered unethical to make a child the object of a legal act.[334] By prohibiting surrogacy the legislature aimed to protect the human dignity of both surrogate mothers and children.[335]

In respect of surrogacy, German law makes a distinction between '*Ersatzmutterschaft*' (the situation where the surrogate mother gives birth to a genetically related child) and '*Leihmutterschaft*' (the situation where the surrogate mother is not genetically related to the child).[336] In this research both situations are referred to with the English term 'surrogacy'. The difference in terminology can be explained by the fact that different regimes each with a somewhat different focus apply to surrogacy situations.[337]

Surrogacy was first prohibited in the framework of adoption legislation. This was initially the result of court rulings to that effect.[338] Later, by amendment of 1989, a prohibition on surrogacy mediation was included in the Adoption Mediation Act (1976) (*Adoptionsvermittlungsgesetz*, AdVermiG).[339] Surrogacy mediation with financial

---

333 V. Wache, '§ 13a AdVermiG nr. 1' ['§ 13a AdVermiG no. 1'], in: G. Erbs and M. Kohlhaas (eds.), *Strafrechtliche Nebengesetze* [Ancillary criminal laws] (München, Verlag C.H. Beck 2011) and K. Boele-Woelki et al., *Draagmoederschap en illegale opneming van kinderen* [Surrogacy and unlawful placement of children] (Utrecht, Utrecht Centre for European research into Family Law 2011) pp. 224–225, Annex to *Kamerstukken II* 2010/11, 32500-VI no. 83 and online available at www.wodc.nl/onderzoeksdatabase/draagmoederschap.aspx?cp=44&cs=6837, visited June 2014.

334 Boele-Woelki et al. 2011, *supra* n. 333, at p. 224.

335 KG 1 August 2013, Az. 1 W 413/12, *NJW* 2015 p. 479, referring to *BT-Drs.* 11/4154, p. 6 and *BT-Drs.* 11/5460, p. 6.

336 See Boele-Woelki et al. 2011, *supra* n. 333, at p. 225. The terminoglogy is not entirely consistently applied. Other terms used are: 'Mietmutterschaft', 'Tragemutterschaft' and 'übernommene Mutterschaft'. See T. Rauscher, '§ 1591 Mutterschaft' ['§ 1591 Maternity'] in: *J. von Staudingers Kommentar zum Bürgerlichen Gezetzbuch mit Einführungsgesetz und Nebengesetzen. Buch 4. Familienrecht, §§ 1589, 1600d (Abstammung)* [J. von Staudinger's Commentary to the Civil Code, with the Introductory Act and anciliary acts, Volume 4, Family law, §§ 1589, 1600d (descent)] Rn. 6. For a general overview of German legislation concerning surrogacy, see V. Bokelmann and M. Bokelmann, *Zur Lage der für andere übernommen Mutterschaft in Deutschland, Rechtsvergleich mit Reformvorschlägen* [On the situation of surrogate motherhood in Germany, Comparitive legal research with proposals for reform] (Frankfurt am Main, Peter Lang 2003).

337 For a discussion of the difference in terminology, see Boele-Woelki et al. 2011, *supra* n. 333, at pp. 225 and 227–228, footnote 49, referring *inter alia* to S. Liermann, 'Der Begriff ‚Ersatzmutter' im Embryonenschutzgesetz' ['The notion of 'surrogate mother' in the Embryo Protecion Act'], *Zeitschrift für das gesamte Familienrecht, FamRZ* (1991) p. 1403.

338 E.g. OLG Hamm 7 April 1983 (dec.), Az. 3 Ss OWi 2007/82, *NJW* 1985 p. 2205; OLG Hamm 2 December 1985 (dec.), Az. 11 W 18/85, *NJW* 1986 p. 781; AG Gütersloh 17 December 1985, Az. 5 XVI 7/85 and LG Freiburg 25 March 1987, Az. 8 O 556/86, *NJW* 1987 p. 1486.

339 Since that date the Adoption Mediation Act has been called Gesetz über die Vermittlung der Annahme als Kind und über das Verbot der Vermittlung von Ersatzmüttern (Adoptionsvermittlungsgesetz – AdVermiG) [Act on adoption mediation and on the prohibition oof surrocay mediation (Adoption Mediation Act)]. See A A. Lüderitz, ‚Verbot von Kinderhandel und Ersatzmuttervermittlung durch Änderung des Adoptionsvermittlungsgesetzes' ['Prohibition of child trafficking and of surrogacy mediation by means of amendment of the German adoption Act'], *NJW* (1990) p. 1633.

gain is punishable by two years' imprisonment or a fine.[340] The intended parents and the surrogate mother are exempted from punishment.[341] Further, Articles 1(1)(6) and (7) of the subsequent Embryo Protection Act (ESchG) prohibit the use of AHR techniques with the aim of providing for a surrogacy agreement. Punishable with imprisonment up to three years or a fine is anyone who removes an embryo from a woman before the completion of implantation in the uterus, in order to transfer it to another woman or to use it for another purpose not serving its preservation.[342] This also goes for anyone who attempts to carry out an artificial insemination of a woman who is prepared to give up her child permanently after birth (surrogate mother).[343] The woman from whom the egg cell or embryo originated and the surrogate mother are exempted from punishment.[344] This also holds for the person who wishes to take long-term care of the child (the intended parent).[345]

In 1998 a new Article 1591 was included in the Civil Code that also contributes to the prevention of surrogacy.[346] It provides that the mother of a child is the woman who gave birth to them. Hence, even if a woman gives birth to a child that is not genetically related to her, she, as the birth mother, is considered the mother in terms of the law. This is based on the *mater semper certa est* principle. Motherhood cannot even be challenged by the child if it claims to be genetically related to another woman (i.e., an egg cell donor).[347] Intended parents – including the woman who donated an egg cell – can only become the legal parents of the child if they adopt the child.[348] In that case, the surrogate mother and the legal father[349] must consent to the adoption. Such adoption furthermore requires court approval and may only be approved if it is in the best interests of the child.[350] Whether surrogacy automatically stands in the way of a lawful adoption is controversial.[351] In general, both commercial and altruistic surrogacy agreements are held to be void for violating a statutory prohibition (Article 134 BGB) and/or for being contrary to public policy (Article 138(1) BGB).[352]

There have been several international surrogacy cases before the German courts in which the Courts confirmed the German prohibition on surrogacy. The relevant case

340 Art. 14b (2)(1) AdVermiG. If no financial gain is involved in the surrogacy mediation, the maximum penalty is one year imprisonment or a fine (Art. 14b (1) AdVermiG. If the mediator acts by virtue of his or her profession, the imprisonment may be three years, maximum.

341 Art. 14b (3) AdVermiG.

342 Art. 1(1)(6) ESchG.

343 Art. 1(1)(7) ESchG.

344 Art. 1(3)(1) ESchG.

345 Art. 1(3)(2) ESchG.

346 *BT-Drs.* 13/4899, p. 51 f. See Rauscher 2011, *supra* n. 336, Rn. 10 and Boele-Woelki et al. 2011, *supra* n. 333, at p. 225.

347 Rauscher 2011, *supra* n. 336, Rn. 16.

348 See, *inter alia*, Rauscher 2011, *supra* n. 336, Rn. 7 and 17.

349 If the surrogate mother was married at the time the child was born, her husband is automatically the legal father (Art. 1592(1) BGB). The husband may, however, contest his paternity on the basis of Art. 1600 ff BGB.

350 Art. 1741(1)(1) BGB.

351 See the judgment AG Hamm 19 March 2007 (dec.), Az. XVI 23/06, as discussed in section 4.5.3 below and Boele-Woelki et al. 2011, *supra* n. 333, at p. 229.

352 For a critical discussion of this matter, see Boele-Woelki et al. 2011, *supra* n. 333, at pp. 226 and 229–231.

law concerning the implications of such cross-border surrogacy agreements – *inter alia*, the question of the civil registration of children concerned – is discussed below, in section 4.5.3.

4.4. Statistics on cross-border movement

4.4.1. Statistics on cross-border abortions

4.4.1.1. Cross-border movement from Germany

The restrictive abortion laws of the FRG and the liberalisation of abortion laws in other Western European States caused West German women to go abroad for an abortion in large numbers.[353] Not surprisingly, no official statistics have been kept by the German authorities of the total number of German women who had abortions abroad. There are only limited statistics available which show the total numbers of registered abortions per year within (former West, former East and unified) Germany.

For an idea of the total number of German women who have had an abortion abroad in recent decades, one must resort to and add up the official statistics from other European States, where the State of origin of the women undergoing an abortion is registered. Not all European States keep statistics and even less break the numbers down on the basis of the country of residence of the woman. It is therefore impossible to set an exact number of abortions undergone by German women abroad. From the UK Health Department and the Dutch Health Inspection ('*Inspectie voor de Gezondheidszorg*') some statistics in this respect are available, however, giving at least some impression of the scale of cross-border movement in this respect.

For the year 1971 (i.e., at a time when in the FRG very restrictive abortion laws were in force), statistics kept by the UK Health Department show that of the total number of 126,777 abortions performed in England and Wales, 32,207 were performed on women not residing in England and Wales, with 13,560 abortions performed on women residing in (West) Germany, hence more than 10 per cent of the total abortions carried out in England and Wales in 1971.[354] The total number of abortions performed within West Germany itself in that year was 7,043. For the year 1971, there are no statistics available for the Netherlands, nor for East Germany.[355]

353 See, *inter alia*, Eser 1986, *supra* n. 62, at p. 377. The author was critical of the fact that the law tolerated such abortion tourism '[...] which benefits only those who can afford it'.

354 The report notes: 'For the period 1971–90, figures for East Germany, West Germany and Germany NOS have been combined to produce totals for unified Germany.' Office of population censuses and surveys, *Abortion Statistics, Legal abortions carried out under the 1967 Abortion Act in England and Wales*, 1991, Series AB, no. 18 (London, HMSO 1993) p. 8, online available at www.statistics.gov.uk/downloads/theme_health/AB18_1991/ab18_1991.pdf, visited 1 April 2011.

355 For 1972, however, a total number of 114,000 is reported for the GDR. Lammich 1988, *supra* n. 64, at p. 369, footnote 93 under reference to 'Wolff, *DÄBl.* 1981, 1055'.

Not surprisingly, the more the German abortion laws were liberalised, the numbers of women in the FRG going abroad for abortions declined. Also, the figures indicate that women went to neighbouring countries more often than to other (European) countries. It was, for instance, estimated that in the 1980s annually approximately 5,000 women from South Germany had an abortion in neighbouring Austria.[356] Up until 1977, the number of women from the FRG having abortions in England and Wales and in the Netherlands exceeded the officially registered numbers of abortions within the FRG itself.[357] In 1975, for example, 19,076 abortions were registered in the FRG, while 3,404 women from the FRG had abortions in England and Wales and no less than 61,000 women from the FRG were registered as having abortions in the Netherlands. The abortion statistics for the FRG show a clear rise in the total number of abortions registered within the FRG for the following years: 21,371 for 1976; 54,309 for 1977; 73,548 for 1978; and up to 91,064 for 1982.[358] In the subsequent years this number slowly declined to an annual number of 84,274 in 1986. In the meantime, the numbers of abortions that women from the FRG had in England and Wales and the Netherlands, gradually decreased.[359] This may have been linked to the entering into force of the more liberal FRG abortions laws of 1976.[360]

The number of German women having abortions in the Netherlands decreased even further when more permissive abortion laws were adopted after reunification. In the period after reunification of East and West Germany, but before the entering into force of the Pregnancy and Family Assistance Revision Act of 1995, still considerable cross-border movement took place. For the year 1990, for example, Dutch statistics give a number of 6,517 women residing in Germany who underwent abortions in the Netherlands.[361] It must be noted that at that time West German women also had

356 Koch 1988, *supra* n. 69, at p. 237, footnote 16, referring to E. Ketting and P. van Praag, *Schwangerschaftsabbruch, Gesetz und Praxis im internationalen Vergleich* [Termination of pregnancy, law and practice in international comparison] (Tübingen, DGVT 1985) p. 80, at. pp. 134 f. As Koch explains, exact numbers are not available as in Austria no official abortion statistics are kept.

357 It must be noted, however, that for 1973 and 1974 this cannot be concluded with certainty, as no official numbers from the Netherlands for those years are known.

358 Koch 1988, *supra* n. 69, at p. 235. For the period 1970–1986, the exact numbers are: 1970: 4,882; 1971: 7,043; 1972: 9,829; 1973:13,021; 1974: 17,814; 1975: 19,076; 1976: 21,371; 1977: 54,309; 1978: 73,548; 1979: 82,788; 1980: 87,702; 1981: 87,535; 1982: 91,064; 1983: 86,529; 1984: 86,298; 1985: 83,538; 1986: 84,274.

359 *Idem*. For England and Wales the exact numbers of abortions performed on women from the FRG are: 1970: 3,621; 1971: 13,560; 1972: 17,531; 1973: 11,326; 1974: 5,991; 1975: 3,404; 1976: 2,384; 1977: 1,705; 1978: 1,171; 1979: 722; 1980: 584; 1981: 514; 1982: 365; 1983: 298; 1984: 250. For the Netherlands statistics are available from the year 1975. According to these statistics the number of women from the FRG having an abortion in the Netherlands per year was: 1975: 61,000; 1976: 60,000; 1977: 56,500; 1978: 42,000; 1979: 32,000; 1980: 26,200; 1981: 20,900; 1982: 17,800; 1983: 14,600; 1984: 11,300 and 1985: 8,297. The number for the year 1985 comes from: Inspectie voor de Gezondheidszorg, Ministerie van Volksgezondheid, Welzijn en Sport [The Dutch Health Care Inspectorate], *Jaarrapportage 2009 van de Wet afbreking zwangerschap* [Annual Report under the Pregnancy Termination Act 2010], December 2010, Annex 2, online available at www.igz.nl/Images/2010-12percent20Jaarrapportage%20WAZ%20 2009_tcm294-292695.pdf visited June 2011.

360 Fünfzehnte Strafrechtsänderungsgesetz [Fifteenth Act on Amendment of the Criminal Law] Act of 18 May 1976, 1976 *BGBl. I*, p. 1213.

361 Inspectie voor Gezondheidszorg [The Dutch Health Care Inspectorate], *Jaarrapportage 2008 van de Wet afbreking zwangerschap* [Annual Report under the Pregnancy Termination Act 2008], The Hague

the opportunity to go to East Germany for an abortion. The present author is not, however, aware of any statistics in this respect.

In 1991 it was reported that the German Federal Frontier Police (*Bundesgrenzschutz*) obliged German women to undergo gynaecological examinations.[362] The European Parliament (EP) adopted a Resolution on the matter,[363] in which reference was made to its own Resolution on abortion of 12 March 1990 (see Chapter 3, section 3.6.1).[364] The EP shared 'the concern reportedly already expressed in German Parliament' about the behaviour of the German Federal Frontier Police[365] and called on the German authorities to cease the practice concerned. It believed that the internal borders of the (then) Community were not to be used '[...] to threaten citizens with prosecution for activities that are perfectly legal in some Member States but not in others'. The European Parliament condemned the 'humiliating practice' of the German Federal Frontier Police, which it held to be 'contrary to the aim of free movement of persons between the Member States of the Community' and a 'violation of the fundamental right of every individual to physical integrity'.[366] Later the edges were taken off these reports,[367] but it remains unclear if any criminal prosecutions were initiated following the searches.[368]

After the entry into force of the Pregnancy and Family Assistance Revision Act in 1995 for the unified Germany, the statistics kept in the Netherlands and England and

---

December 2009, Annex 2, p. 29, online available at www.igz.nl, visited June 2011.

362 S.F. Kreimer, 'But Whoever Treasures Freedom…: The Right to Travel and Extraterritorial Abortions', 91 *Michigan Law Review* (1993) p. 907 at p. 908, referring (in footnote 5) to 'EUR. PARL. DEB. (3–403) 202–05 (Mar. 14, 1991) (debate on resolutions condemning compulsory gynaecological examinations by German officials of returning German women at the Dutch-German border); id. at 203 (statement of Rep. Van Den Brink) (stating that over 6000 German women have had abortions in the Netherlands); id. at 204 (statement of Rep. Keppelhoff- Wiechert) (defending searches on the ground that officials 'are required by the code of criminal procedure to investigate illegal abortions of this kind carried out abroad'); Nina Bernstein, Germany Still Divided on Abortion, NEWSDAY, Mar. 11, 1991, at 5, 13 (reporting an account of a German woman returning from the Netherlands who was forced to submit to a vaginal examination at a Catholic hospital near the border and was charged with having an illegal abortion; noting that German Interior Ministry acknowledges the practice; citing a study by the Max Planck Institute in Freiburg that found such 'inquisition[s]' to be 'standard practice'); Karen Y. Crabbs, The German Abortion Debate: Stumbling Block to Unity, 6 FLA. J. INTL. L. 213, 222–23 (1991) (describing prosecutions and searches).' See also J.M. Bik, 'Duitse vrouwen na abortus verplicht tot onderzoek', *NRC Handelsblad* 4 maart 1991, p. 11 and Case 2009, *supra* n. 85, at p. 96 referring to T. Jones. 'Social Policy; Wall still divides Germany on the Abortion Question', *Los Angeles Times* 19 October 1991, p. A4.

363 Resolution of the European Parliament of 12 March 1990 on reports of gynaecological examinations by the German Federal Frontier Police [1991] OJ C106/102, pp. 103, 113 and 135.

364 Resolution of the European Parliament on artificial insemination in vivo and in vitro of 16 March 1989, [1989] OJ C96/127.

365 Para. 5 of the 1990 Resolution, *supra* n. 363. The EP Resolution does not refer to any parliamentary documents of the German *Bundestag*.

366 The present author is not aware of any follow-up of this EP Resolution in German Parliament.

367 'Duitsers doen geen abortus-onderzoek', *NRC Handelsblad* 20 March 1991, p. 7.

368 A Dutch newspaper reported that the one of the German Max Planck Institutes had statistics showing that approximately 60 per cent of the German women who had an abortion in the Netherlands was prosecuted. 'Europarlement veroordeelt 'abortuscontrole' aan grens', *NRC Handelsblad* 15 March 1991, p. 3. It has proven impossible for the present author however, to verify this report.

Wales of abortions undergone by women residing in Germany, show a considerable decrease in numbers. For instance, for 1995 a total number of 2,982 abortions performed on women residing in Germany were registered by the Dutch Health Inspection, compared to 6,517 abortions five years earlier, in 1990. Of the total number of 179,522 abortions performed in England and Wales in 1991, only 109 involved women residing in Germany.[369]

Since the year 2000, the registered number of German women having abortions abroad stabilised around an annual figure of approximately 1,100 for the Netherlands[370] and less than 20 in England and Wales.[371] In 2008, 79 per cent of those women residing in Germany who had abortions in the Netherlands were more than 12 weeks pregnant.[372] After 12 weeks of pregnancy, German law subjects access to abortion to stricter conditions (see 4.2.6 above). The introduction of an extra counselling obligation for abortions on the basis of the social-medical indication in 2009[373] may have triggered women in Germany to have abortions abroad, but the present author is not aware of any research studies or statistics in this respect.[374]

---

369 Office of population censuses and surveys, *Abortion Statistics, Legal abortions carried out under the 1967 Abortion Act in England and Wales 1991*, Series AB, no. 18 (London, HMSO 1993) p. 8, online available at www.statistics.gov.uk/downloads/theme_health/AB18_1991/ab18_1991.pdf, visited April 2011. The British perspective has been described as follows by the British Medical Association: 'In the early 1970s a large number of abortions were carried out for non-residents of England and Wales reaching a peak of 56,581 in 1973 representing a third of all abortions carried out in that year. In the early 1980s the number was around 34,000 (20 per cent of the total) and from 1995 the number has been around 9,500 representing 5 per cent of the total number of abortions.' British Medical Association, *Abortion statistics and trends, a briefing paper from the BMA*, 17 June 2005, p. 5, online available at www.bma.org.uk/images/Abortiontimelimits_tcm41-20443.pdf, visited 30 March 2011.

370 The exact figures were as follows: 2000: 1,603; 2005: 1,148; 2006: 1,092; 2007: 1,193; 2008: 1,171; 2009: 1,123. Annex 2 to Inspectie voor de Gezondheidszorg, Ministerie van Volksgezondheid, Welzijn en Sport [The Dutch Health Care Inspectorate], *Jaarrapportage 2009 van de Wet afbreking zwangerschap* [Annual Report under the Pregnancy Termination Act 2010] December 2010, online available at www.igz.nl/Images/2010-12%20Jaarrapportage%20WAZ%202009_tcm294-292695.pdf, visited 30 March 2011.

371 The exact numbers for England and Wales are 2002: 46; 2003: 25; 2004: 16; 2005: 19; 2006: 18; 2007: 12; 2008: 16; 2009: 17 and 2010: 12. The annual abortion statistics for England and Wales are available at the website of the UK Department of Health. For instance, the statistics for 2010 can be found in Table 12a to UK Department of Health, *Abortion Statistics, England and Wales: 2010*, May 2011, online available at www.dh.gov.uk/en/Publicationsandstatistics/Publications/PublicationsStatistics/DH_126769, visited 19 July 2011.

372 See www.rutgersnissogroep.nl/productenendiensten/onderzoekspublicaties/onderzoekspublicaties-1/downloadbare-publicaties-in-pdf/rapport-lar-2008.pdf, visited 30 March 2011, p. 35.

373 Gesetz zur Änderung des Schwangerschaftskonfliktgesetzes (SchKGÄndG) [Act on the Amendment of the Pregnancy Conflict Act] of 26 August 2009, *BGBl. I*, No. 58, p. 2990. See section 4.2.6 above.

374 The number of women from Germany going to the Netherlands has not changed significantly in the subsequent years. For example in 2010, 1,112 women of the total number of 30,577 women having an abortion in the Netherlands was resident in Germany. Inspectie voor Gezondheidszorg, *Jaarrapportage 2012 van de Wet afbreking zwangerschap,* Utrecht December 2013, Annex 2, p. 37, online available at: www.igz.nl, visited June 2014.

4.4.1.2. *Cross-border movement to Germany*

The statistics kept on the basis of Article 15 Pregnancy Conflict Act (see 2.4.2 above)[375] show that abortions undergone by foreign women in Germany make up only a very small portion of the total number of abortions carried out in Germany. It is interesting to note, however, that while the total number of abortions performed in Germany on an annual basis dropped from 134,964 in 2001 to 102,802 in 2013, the number of abortions undergone by women residing abroad rose considerably from 501 in 2001, to 1,092 in 2013.[376] These German statistics are not, however, accompanied by any interpretation, rendering it impossible to identify any cause for this change in numbers.

4.4.2. Statistics and reported cases on cross-border reproductive care

As has been stressed repeatedly throughout this study, no reliable and exhaustive overview exists of the actual prevalence of cross-border reproductive care in Europe (see also Chapter 3, section 3.4). Nevertheless, there are strong indications that such cross-border movement takes place, also to and from Germany, as various (European) research studies and court proceedings prove.

The prohibition on PGD, which was only partly lifted in 2011, has for many years been reason for women and couples from Germany with a child wish to go abroad to have such genetic tests carried out. The 2007 study into preimplantation genetic diagnosis (PGD) across Europe of the Joint Research Centre of the European Commission reported that for German residents the main reason for going abroad for treatment was that PGD was not permitted in Germany.[377] In various news reports estimates have been reported of approximately 100 German women undergoing PGD abroad, predominantly in Belgium, Spain and the Czech Republic.[378] It is thus widely

375 On the basis of Art. 15 SchKG the German State has an obligation to keep statistics in respect of abortions carried out in Germany.

376 The exact number of abortions undergone in Germany by women residing in a foreign country, compared to the total number of abortions undergone in Germany per year (between brackets), for the period 2001–2013 is as follows: 2013: 1,092 (102,802); 2012: 1,088 (106,815); 2011: 1,006 (108,867); 2010: 925 (110,431); 2009: 657 (110,694); 2008 720 (114,484); 2007: 556 (116,871); 2006: 509 (119,710); 2005: 517 (124 023); 2004: 483 (129 650); 2003: 531 (128,030); 2002: 462 (130,387) and 2001: 501 (134,964). Statistisches Bundesamt Deutschland, *Schwangerschaftsabbrüche – FS12 R. 3 2008* and *FS12 R. 3 2013*, online available at www.destatis.de, visited June 2014. See also K. Zabrzynski, 'Zur Abtreibung über die Grenze, Immer mehr Polinnen lassen einen Schwangerschaftsabbruch in Berlin, Prenzlau oder Schwedt vornehmen', *Berliner Zeitung* 30 October 2010, p. 24.

377 PGD is neither allowed in Switzerland and Italy. Also for residents of these countries the main reason to go abroad for this type of treatment is the non-availability of it in the home country. Additional reasons for travelling that this research has revealed include the quality of the treatment, test availability, financial resources and manpower. Coverleyn et al. 2007, *supra* n. 275, at p. 79.

378 W.-M. Catenhusen, 'POSITION; Mit Embryonen verantwortlich umgehen Der Gesetzgeber muss der Präimplantationsdiagnostik klare Grenzen setzen', *Der Tagesspiegel* 9 July 2010, p. 17; 'PID-Tourismus; Wenn Eltern ihre schlechten Gene fürchten müssen', *Berliner Morgenpost Online* 19 October 2010, www.morgenpost.de/web-wissen/article1426581/Wenn-Eltern-ihre-schlechten-Gene-fuerchten-muessen.htm; K. Elger and V. Hackenbroch, 'Schwere Schäden', *Der Spiegel* 25 October 2010, p. 180 and

acknowledged that this cross-border movement takes place – a phenomenon that has been referred to as '*PID-Tourismus*' ('PGD tourism').[379, 380] The 2011 PGD regulation will presumably have reduced the number of Germans going abroad for PGD. There is, however, also a possibility that because of the great stigma that surrounded the matter for many years, some couples and individuals still prefer to go abroad for PGD.

Another issue in respect of which German laws are more restrictive than the laws of certain other European states, concerns egg cell donation. A research study published in 2010 concerning six European countries (Belgium, Czech Republic, Denmark, Slovenia, Spain and Switzerland), showed that 14.4 per cent of the cross-border 'patients' participating in the study, came from Germany. For these German patients 'legal reasons' were the predominant reasons for travelling (80.2 per cent)[381] and almost half of the German women concerned (44.6 per cent) travelled abroad to obtain egg cell donation.[382] The study also showed that most of the German patients travelled to the Czech Republic (67.2 per cent).

4.4.3. Statistics on cross-border surrogacy

The case law concerning cross-border surrogacy, as discussed in section 4.5.3 below, shows that there have been – particularly over the past five years – growing numbers of cases in which couples or individuals from Germany have gone abroad with the aim of arranging a surrogacy agreement under a more permissive jurisdiction, mainly non-EU Member States, such as India, Ukraine and the USA. While such cross-border movement is thus certainly taking place, there is too little data available to draw any conclusions in respect of the actual scale of this cross-border movement.

4.5. German abortion and AHR legislation and cross-border movement

This section discusses the implications of German law for those who go abroad for an abortion, AHR treatment or surrogacy. Contrary to the other chapters in this case study, information about foreign treatment and follow-up care after treatment abroad

A Müller-Lissner, 'Eingeschränkt erlauben; Deutsche Wissenschaftsakademien befürworten Präimplantationsdiagnostik', *Der Tagesspiegel* 19 January 2011, p. 39. See, as an illustration, also the below discussed case concerning a claim for reimbursement for preimplantation genetic diagnosis (PGD) treatment obtained in Belgium (see section 4.5.2 below). SG Berlin 23 March 2007, Az. S 86 KR 660/04.

379 *Inter alia*, E. Schwinger, 'Ende einer Farce. Der Embryonenschutz soll Leben schützen, aber er kann Menschen schaden', *Der Spiegel* 12 July 2010, p. 116; Berliner Morgenpost Online 2010, *supra* n. 378; Elger and Hackenbroch, *supra* n. 378, at p. 180 and Kunz-Schmidt 2011, *supra* n. 273, at p. 235.

380 Deutsche Akademie der Naturforscher Leopoldina et al. 2011, *supra* n. 273, at p. 23. See also Deutscher Ethikrat 2011, *supra* n. 292 at pp. 93–95.

381 F. Shenfield et al., 'Cross border reproductive care in six European countries', 25 *Human Reproduction* (2010) p. 1361.

382 *Idem*, at p. 1365.

are not discussed separately here. As far as the present author is aware, German law does not provide for any particular rules in this regard, nor have these topics been the subject of extensive debate in Germany.

4.5.1. Criminal liability for abortions and AHR treatment obtained abroad

Under GDR law, the territoriality and the personality principle applied in respect of the scope of applicability of the Criminal Code. In exceptionally serious cases and only after permission had been granted by the Public Prosecutor, could proceedings be brought for illegal abortions performed abroad.[383] Besides, special internal regulations existed concerning abortions performed on foreign women on GDR territory.[384]

In the FRG the territoriality principle applied to all offences, including that of Article 218ff Criminal Code.[385] On the basis of Article 5(9) Criminal Code, an abortion performed abroad could be prosecuted in the FRG, irrespective of the law of the country in which the abortion was performed, if the perpetrator was FRG national ('*Deutscher*') at the time of the offence and if his/her livelihood fell within the scope of the FRG law. Further, Article 7(1) Criminal Code provided that crimes committed against a FRG national in a foreign state could be prosecuted in the FRG if the abortion laws of that foreign state were similar to, or stricter than, that of the FRG. The unborn life was considered to be a 'FRG national' within the meaning of this law. As Koch has explained, this meant that all pregnant women with FRG nationality who went abroad for abortions that were not allowed for under FRG law, were just as punishable abroad under FRG law, as they would have been if the abortions had taken place on FRG territory.[386] Doctors domiciled in the FRG who performed abortions that were illegal under FRG law, were punishable irrespective of the nationality of the pregnant women or the laws of the States where the abortions were performed. Further, aiding or abetting the performance of an illegal abortion – through mediation by agencies or by the financing of travel expenses – constituted an independent crime under Article 9(2) Criminal Code.

Article 5(9) Criminal Code, as currently in force in the unified Germany, still provides that abortions undergone abroad can be prosecuted in Germany, if the victim (the unborn child) is a German citizen or if the offender (the pregnant woman or the doctor involved) at the time of the abortion is German and has her or his main livelihood in the territory of the Federal Republic of Germany.[387] Hence, the

383 Lammich 1988, *supra* n. 64, at p. 347, referring to Art. 80 of the 1968 StGB. The present author is not aware of any statistics in respect of proceedings brought on the basis of this provision.

384 As Lammich explains, prosecution was possible if the woman worked in the GDR or followed education there and if diplomatic relations existed between her country of nationality and the GDR. Lammich 1988, *supra* n. 64, at pp. 352–353.

385 Koch 1988, *supra* n. 69, at pp. 108–109.

386 Compare *Idem*, at p. 109.

387 Art. 7 I StGB and Art. 5(9) StGB. See also Laufs 2009, *supra* n. 63, Rn. 30. Art. 5(9) only sees at Art. 218 StGB, Art. 218b and 219 a and b are not covered. H. Satzger et al. (eds.), *StGB, Strafgesetzbuch*

regulation is based on the passive personality principle (protection of unborn life) that is complemented with, as well as delimited by, the active personality principle and the principle of domicile.[388] This provision was included in the Criminal Code by law of 1995, as a direct response to the cross-border movement for abortions which existed at the time.[389] Two aims were to be achieved by the provision: (1) to prevent German medical practitioners living close to the border from performing abortions abroad; and (2) to prevent pregnant German women from having abortions abroad free from punishment.[390] Some argued that this provision furthermore contributed to the preservation of the German people,[391] but this idea has been strongly rejected by others.[392]

No particular arrangements were made in respect of cross-border AHR treatment. Consequently, the general principles concerning punishability of cross-border offences and crimes under Article 7 of the German Criminal Code apply. This means, *inter alia*, that a requirement of double criminality applies and that either the offender or the victim or both of them must be German nationals. The present author is not aware of cases in which prosecutions were initiated in cross-border cases on grounds of criminal prohibitions of any of the types of AHR treatment as discussed in this chapter.[393]

4.5.2. Public funding for treatment obtained abroad

Insured persons are in principle entitled to reimbursement for medical treatment received abroad, to the extent that the treatment also qualifies for reimbursement on the basis of the German statutory health insurance (*Gesetzliche Krankenversicherung*, GKV) if it would have been received in Germany.[394] The fact that the treatment is legal in the country where it is carried out is not relevant in this regard.[395] Accordingly, in 2007 the District Court Berlin rejected a woman's claim for reimbursement for preimplantation genetic diagnosis (PGD) treatment obtained in Belgium, on

Kommentar [StGB, Commentary to the Criminal Code] (Köln, Heymann 2009) Rn. 21 and Laufs 2009, *supra* n. 63, Rn. 21.

388 M. Böse 'StGB § 5 Auslandstaten gegen inländische Rechtsgüter' ['Criminal Code § 5 Acts committed abroad against domestic legal interests'] in: U. Kindhauser, *Strafgesetzbuch: Lehr- und Praxiskommentar* [Criminal Code: Commentary for studies and legal practice] (Baden-Baden, Nomos 2010) p. 332.

389 *Idem*, at p. 332 and Müller-Terpitz 2011, *supra* n. 227, Rn. 40.

390 See G. Werle and F. Jeßberger, 'Rn 132' ['Rn. 132'], in: H.W. Laufhütte et al., *Leipziger Kommentar, Großkommentar zum Strafgesetzbuch* [Leipziger Commentary, Commentary to the Criminal Code] (Berlin, De Gruyter Recht 2007) under reference to *BR-Drs.* 200/62, p. 111 and *BT-Drs.* V/4095, p. 5.

391 Böse 2010, *supra* 388, at p. 332, referring to 'M.K.-Ambos, Rn. 29'.

392 Werle and Jeßberger 2007, *supra* n. 390, Rn. 137.

393 See also G. von Dannecker, 'Können europäische Vorgaben ein Tätigwerden des nationalen Strafgesetzgebers auf dem Gebiet des Biostrafrechts erzwingen?' ['Can European guidelines exact action of national criminal law legislatures in the area of bio criminal law?'], in: E. Hilgendorf and S. Beck, *Biomedizinische Forschung in Europa* [Biomedical research in Europe], IUS Europaeum 49 (Baden-Baden, Nomos 2010) p. 161.

394 Art. 13(4) SGB V.

395 See BSG 9 October 2001, Az. B 1 KR 33/00 R, *NJW* 2002 p. 1517, para. 12.

the ground that no entitlement to reimbursement for such treatment existed under German law at the time.[396] Tax deduction for treatment obtained abroad, that is not legally available in Germany, may also be problematic.[397]

4.5.3. Cross-border surrogacy under German law

German couples or individuals who have made surrogacy arrangements in foreign countries may encounter considerable difficulties in establishing their legal parenthood of the child in Germany. They may also encounter difficulties in obtaining travel documents for the child. The case law on the matter is, however, diverse, and it may also depend on the specific legal documents on which the intended parents rely.

As explained above in section 4.4.8, a foreign surrogacy agreement is considered void under German law because it violates a statutory prohibition and is against public policy, within the meaning of Articles 134 and 138 of the German Civil Code.[398] The fact that surrogacy is not prohibited in the country where the surrogacy agreement is concluded has no bearing on this finding.[399] Intended parents can thus not rely directly on a foreign surrogacy agreement, but they may instead apply for recognition of a foreign judgment recognising them as the child's legal parents or on a foreign birth certificate on which they are stated as the child's legal parents.

Foreign judgments in family matters are in principle recognised under German law,[400] unless such recognition is considered manifestly incompatible with fundamental principles of German law, in particular when it is incompatible with fundamental rights.[401] In a case of 2007 a German couple that had arranged a surrogacy agreement with a Turkish family, was for this reason faced with a refusal by the German Court to enforce the judgment of a Turkish court awarding the adoption rights over the child to the German intended parents. The German Court held this Turkish judgment to be against the child's best interests, as the child had only been given birth to with the aim of handing it over to the German intended parents.[402] Another example dates from 2013,[403] when the Appeals Court of Berlin refused to recognise a judgment by a Californian judge which recognised the legal parenthood of an intended co-father in a surrogacy situation, because surrogacy was considered incommensurable with

396 SG Berlin 23 March 2007, Az. S 86 KR 660/04, p. 54.

397 In respect of treatment in the course of a surrogacy arrangement in California, see FG München 21 February 2000 (dec.), Az. 16 V 5568/99 and FG Düsseldorf 9 May 2003, Az. 18 K 7931/00 E.

398 AG Hamm 22 February 2011 (dec.), Az. XVI 192/08, para. 15.

399 *Idem*, para. 20.

400 Art. 108 Gesetz über das Verfahren in Familiensachen und in den Angelegenheiten der freiwilligen Gerichtsbarkeit (FamFG) [Act on the Procedure in Family Matters and in Matters of Non-contentious Jurisdiction], Act of 7 December 2008, *BGBl. I* p. 2586.

401 Art. 109(4) FamFG. See also B. Heiderhoff, 'Rechtliche Abstammung im Ausland geborener Leihmutterkinder' ['The legal descent of surrogate children born abroad'], *NJW* (2014) p. 2673 at p. 2674.

402 AG Hamm 19 March 2007 (dec.), Az. XVI 23/06. See also LG Dortmund 13 August 2007 (dec.), Az. 15 T 87/07.

403 KG 1 August 2013, Az. 1 W 413/12, *NJW* 2015 p. 479.

the German legal order, in particular with the human dignity of surrogate mother and child.[404]

By contrast, there also have been German courts that have held that recognition of a foreign judgment recognising the intended parents as legal parents of the child was required with a view to the best interests of the child. In 2013 the Administrative Court of Friedberg ruled that the best interests of the child required the recognition of such a foreign judgment, where the child would otherwise become stateless and the care for the child would not be guaranteed, because the surrogate mother and her husband refused to take the child into care.[405] There have been more cases where Administrative Courts have held the recognition of a foreign judgment granting legal parenthood to an intended father in a surrogacy situation to be compatible with the fundamental principles of German law and fundamental rights in particular.[406] Also, various academic authors have held that the rights and interests of the child had to be given priority, which in most international surrogacy cases entailed that the legal parenthood of the intended parents had to be recognised.[407]

It has generally been even more difficult for intended parents to rely directly on the birth certificate of the child as proof of its descent. In this situation German Private International Law applies, as laid down in the Second Chapter of the Introductory Act to the Civil Code (*Einführungsgesetz zum Bürgerlichen Gesetzbuche*, EGBGB). The Third Section of this Chapter concerns Family Law and its Article 19 focuses on descent. The EGBGB also contains a general public order provision, namely Article 6, which provides that '[a] provision of the law of another country shall not be applied where its application would lead to a result which is manifestly incompatible with the fundamental principles of German law.' The Article adds to this that inapplicability ensues, in particular, if the application of foreign law 'would be incompatible with civil rights.'[408]

Incompatibility with German public order has been a ground for some German Courts to refuse to issue a passport to a child born to a surrogate mother in a foreign country.[409] In a case of 2012 concerning the Ukraine, the Administrative Court of Berlin ruled that the relevant provision in Ukrainian family law that provided that in

404 The Court noted that the situation would be different if the intended father had recognised the child with the consent of the surrogate mother. See C. Benicke, 'Kollisionsrechtliche Fragen der Leihmutterschaft' ['Conflict-of-laws questions in respect of surrogacy'], *StAZ* (2013) p. 101 at p. 111.

405 AG Friedberg 1 March 2013, Az. 700 F 1142/12, para. 32, as subsequently confirmed in AG Gießen 7 November 2013, Az. 22 III 9/13. See also B. Heiderhoff, 'Der gewöhnliche Aufenthalt von Säuglingen', *IPRax* (2012) p. 523 at p. 526.

406 AG Frankfurt 7 May 2013 (dec.), Az. 464 F 10402/12 (concerning intended fathers in a registered partnership) and AG Neuss 13 May 2013 (dec.), Az. 45 F 74/13 (concerning a single father).

407 Heiderhoff 2014A, *supra* n. 401, at p. 2674 and D. Baetge, 'Art. 6 EGBGB, Öffentliche Ordnung (ordre public)', in: M. Herberger et al., *Juris Praxis Kommentar BGB*, 7th edn. (Saarbrücken, juris GmbH 2014), Rn. 112. For a different point of view see Benicke 2013, *supra* n. 404, at p. 111.

408 Translation taken from www.gesetze-im-internet.de/englisch_bgbeg/index.html, visited June 2014.

409 VG Berlin 5 September 2012 (dec.), Az. 23 L 283/12. Yet in 2009 had this Court refused to issue a visum for family reunification for a child that was born abroad with a surrogate mother. See VG Berlin 26 November 2009 (dec.), Az. VG 11 L 396.09.

surrogacy cases the genetic parents were considered as the legal parents of the child, was manifestly incompatible with the fundamental principles of German law within the meaning of Article 6 EGBGB.[410]

Secondly, once arrived in Germany, intended parents who engaged in international surrogacy may encounter difficulties in establishing legal parenthood of the child. Following Article 36(1) PStG, only children with German nationality can be registered in the Register of Births. Article 19 EGBGB provides that the descent of a child is governed by the law of the place where the child has his or her habitual residence.[411] If the child has his or her habitual residence in Germany, German law thus applies. Under German law, a child may acquire German nationality if one or both of the parents have German nationality. This often does not hold, however, for a child born to a foreign surrogate mother, because, as explained above in section 4.3.9, under German law the birth mother is recognised as the legal mother (Article 1591 BGB). If she is married, her husband is the legal father of the child (Article 1592(1) BGB), and not the intended father, even if he is the child's genetic father. This may thus stand in the way of registration of a child born to a foreign surrogate mother in the German Register of Births.[412]

There are two possible courses that can be taken, nonetheless, to establish legal parenthood in cross-border surrogacy cases. The first is recognition of paternity by the intended father ('*Anerkennung*' within the meaning of Article 1592(2) BGB). Such recognition is only possible if the surrogate mother consents and if she is unmarried.[413] If the surrogate mother is married, her husband first has to contest his paternity, before the intended father can have his paternity of the child recognised. This approach has indeed been approved of by some German Courts in international surrogacy cases. For instance, in a case of 2009 the District Court of Nürnberg held the recognition of paternity by a German man in respect of a child born to a Russian citizen not to be against German public order, even while there was a suspicion of surrogacy involved in the case.[414] Heiderhoff has nonetheless called

410 VG Berlin 5 September 2012 (dec.), Az. 23 L 283/12, para. 10. See also C. Mayer, 'Sachwidrige Differenzierungen in internationalen Leihmutterschaftsfällen' ['Improper differentiations in international surrogacy cases'], *IPRax* (2014) p. 57. In an earlier Indian case where there was a suspicion of surrogacy, this same Court had held it not for the Court to decide on the child's citizenship in the course of an application for a passport. VG Berlin 15 April 2011 (dec.), Az. 23 L 79/11.

411 This Article, furthermore, provides that in relation to each parent the descent can also be determined by the law of the country of this parent's nationality. This has not, however, been applied by any German court in an international surrogacy case. For a critical note in this respect, see M. Steinbeis, 'Mater überhaupt nicht semper certa est' ['*Mater semper certa est* does not hold at all'], blog of 2 November 2012, online available at: www.verfassungsblog.de/mater-uberhaupt-nicht-semper-certa-est/#.VGDYgxYeDCF, visited 10 November 2014.

412 OLG Stuttgart 7 February 2012 (dec.), Az. 8 W 46/12, *NJW-RR* 2012 p. 389. See also J. Rieck, 'Nachbeurkunding einer Auslandsgeburt bei Leihmutterschaft', *Zeitschrift für das gesamte Familienrecht, FamFR* 2012 p. 166. This case was referred to the BVerfG but refused by this Court (see below).

413 VG Berlin 26 November 2009 (dec.), Az. 11 L 396/09; VG Berlin 15 April 2011 (dec.), Az. 23 L 79/11 and VG Köln 13 November 2013, Az. 10 K 2043/12.

414 AG Nürnberg 14 December 2009 (dec.), Az. UR III 0264/09. For another, more recent example, see OLG Düsseldorf 26 April 2013 (dec.), Az. I-3 Wx 211/12. See also Mayer 2014, *supra* n. 410.

such '*Anerkennung*' by the intended father an unsatisfactory solution, as it does not provide sufficient legal certainty for the intended parent(s). She has furthermore pointed out that this course cannot be taken by single women or women in a civil partnership.[415]

Intended parents can also become legal parents by adopting the child. Some German courts have made very explicit that adoption is the only possible way for intended parents in international surrogacy situations to be registered as the legal parents of the child under German law.[416] Article 22 EGBGB provides that the adoption of a child is governed by the law of the country of which the adopter is a national at the time of the adoption.[417] In most cases originating from Germany, this is thus German law. Further, as Heiderhoff has explained, for adoption it is required that the child is resident/present in Germany, a requirement which may not always be easily met in international surrogacy cases.[418] Further, and importantly, any adoption order can only be granted if such adoption is considered to be in the interests of the child.

There have been German courts that refused to grant an adoption order for an intended parent in a cross-border surrogacy situation, because the foreign surrogacy agreement was void (see above).[419] There have, however, also been courts that held the granting of an adoption order in international surrogacy situations to be in the interests of the child. In a case of 2012, the Frankfurt District Court held, in this regard, that considerations aiming at the general prevention of surrogacy could not outweigh the individual interests of the child, including its right not to be discriminated against.[420]

The German case law in respect of cross-border surrogacy cases is thus somewhat ambiguous, and there are still various open questions. This is particularly so now that all relevant judgments are issued by lower or regional courts; the matter has not been decided by for example the Federal Administrative Court or the Constitutional Court. In 2012 the latter Court refused to accept a constitutional complaint about a refusal to register intended (and genetic) parents who had gotten twins after entering into a surrogacy agreement under Californian law, for lack of fundamental constitutional significance (Article 93a (2)(a) BVerfGG).[421] The Constitutional Court found that the complainants should have provided the Court with more factual and

415 Heiderhoff 2014A, *supra* n. 401, at p 2676.

416 OLG Stuttgart 7 February 2012, Az. 8 W 46/12, *NJW-RR* 2012 p. 389, para. 12.

417 Art. 23 EGBGB further provides that '[t]he necessity and the granting of the consent of the child, and of a person who is related to the child under family law, to a declaration of descent, to conferring a name, or to an adoption are additionally governed by the law of the country of which the child is a national.' However, where the best interest of the child so requires, German law is applied instead.

418 Heiderhoff 2014A, *supra* n. 401, at p. 2675. As Heiderhoff explains adoption in the country where the child was born is often impossible, because under the law of that country the intended are yet automatically recognised as parents.

419 AG Hamm 22 February 2011 (dec.), Az. XVI 192/08, paras. 20 and 26. Critical in this respect: P. Friederici, 'Unzulässigkeit der Adoption auf Grund eines Leimuttervertrags' ['Inadmissibility of adoption on the basis of a surrogacy agreement'], *FamFR* (2011) p. 551.

420 LG Frankfurt a.M. 3 August 2012 (dec.), Az. 2–09 T 51/11.

421 BVerfG 22 August 2012 (dec.), Az. 1 BvR 573/12, *NJW-RR* 2013 p.1. See Steinbeis 2012, *supra* n. 411.

legally relevant information, such as the nationality of the surrogate mother, her civil status and whether the intended father had yet recognised the child.[422]

The existing legal uncertainty and the implications of some of the less permissive rulings for the intended parents and children concerned, have been reason for some to call for a change of German family law on the matter.[423] So far, however, no action has been taken by the German legislature in this respect. The German government has, furthermore, been hesitant in respect of any regulation of the matter at European or international level.[424]

4.6. Conclusions

The German legislature has been very careful in respect of the drafting of legislation concerning abortion and AHR treatment. Fear for eugenetics has been a compelling argument for the initial absolute prohibition on Prenatal Genetic Diagnosis (PGD) and for the still existing prohibition on gender selection. The protection of human dignity that extends to the unborn has also constituted a compelling argument against such practices. At the same time, the right to free development of the personality of Article 2(1) enjoys strong protection under the German Basic Law, too. From this right, a right to self-determination for the pregnant woman follows (see section 4.1.2 above). Consequently, the German legislature has constantly had to search for a careful balance between all rights and values at stake. In respect of AHR, human dignity arguments on behalf of the (future) child have often been read into the principle of the best interests of the child. The best interests of the child have, for instance, been accepted as a justification for the prohibitions on surrogacy and egg cell donation (see 4.3.3.1 and 4.3.9 above). All in all, in making decisions in this sensitive area of law, the German legislature and courts are bound by the value system of the German Basic Law, to which great significance is attached. The general reluctance to legislate on AHR matters of the German legislature can also be explained by (uncertainty over the effects of) fast-moving medical developments. For example, long lasting uncertainty about legality of PGD followed from the fact that at the time of the drafting of the Embryo Protection Act, PGD was not yet practiced in Germany.

422 *Idem*, para. 15.

423 Heiderhoff 2014A, *supra* n. 401, at p. 2677.

424 In the Public Consultation on the EU Green Paper on the recognition of the effects of civil status records (see more elaborately Ch. 3, section 3.6.3.1) the German Federal Government put forward that in respect of the filiation of a child in the case of a surrogate mother, the EU could not require a Member State's legislature 'to place its family law at the disposal of the [...] other Member States without restriction, allowing the persons concerned to have a family law relationship that exists under the law of another Member State to be registered in that State even though they have no close ties with that state's legal order.' Federal Government observations on COM (2010) 747 final, pp. 12–13, online available at www.ec.europa.eu/justice/newsroom/civil/opinion/files/110510/public_authorities/germany_minjust_en.pdf, visited June 2014.

Legislative change has often been instigated by federal courts' judgments. This goes for the amendment of the abortion regimes of 1975 (in respect of the former FRG) and 1992 (in respect of the unified Germany), as well as for the lifting of the absolute prohibition on PGD in 2011. The courts have at the same time shown deference to political and societal sensitivities and have given the legislature discretion to regulate matters, for instance in respect of reimbursement for AHR treatment.

Clearly, Germany's (fairly) restrictive laws have been – and to a limited extent still are – cause for cross-border movement in respect of abortion and AHR treatment. This was certainly the case in respect of the former FRG's abortion laws, as the statistics show. For some years in the beginning of the 1970s the number of women from the FRG having abortions abroad exceeded the number of FRG resident women who had abortions in their home country. When the German abortion laws gradually became more liberal, less cross-border movement from Germany took place. German residents, furthermore, actively sought, and seek, AHR treatment abroad. The lack of exhaustive statistics in this respect makes it impossible to draw any firm conclusions, but all reports show that restrictive German legislation, for instance on PGD, has been one of the – if not the main – reason(s) for couples from Germany searching for foreign alternatives. This has been certainly the case in respect of surrogacy, as that is outlawed under German law.

For sure, this cross-border activity has fuelled the debates at the national level, to which the German legislature has responded in various ways. In some cases the debate resulted in the relaxation of national law. This was undoubtedly the case in respect of abortion in the 1970s and in respect of the more recent phenomenon of '*PGD-Tourismus*'. At the same time, German standards have also been firmly upheld cross-border situations. The unique Criminal Code Article providing for the punishability of abortions performed abroad is a clear example, although the present author is not aware of any statistics concerning prosecution on the basis of this provision. Despite the penal law character of the ESchG, there is no equivalent to Article 5(9) Criminal Code in respect of AHR treatment and surrogacy. In regard of the latter, however, German Private International Law may discourage German residents from engaging in international surrogacy agreements. The much diversified approaches of the various German courts that have ruled in such cases render it difficult to draw firm conclusions on the state of the law in this respect. There is, however, an emerging trend visible in favour of recognising yet established parental links or enabling intended parents to establish parental links with the child, because the best interests of the child are held to require this.

Chapter 5
Ireland

5.1. Constitutional framework

Articles 40–44 of the Irish Constitution see at fundamental rights. Its Article 40 lays down a number of personal rights, ranging from freedom of expression to inviolability of dwellings and from liberty of the person to equal treatment before the law. No express provision is made for the right to respect for private life, but this right is covered by Article 40.3.1°, which protects more generally the 'personal rights'. Article 40.3.1° provides:

> 'The State guarantees in its laws to respect, and, as far as practicable, by its laws to defend and vindicate the personal rights of the citizen.'

As explained hereafter, this right includes a marital right to procreate. The third paragraph of Article 40.3 has been even more prominent in the Irish debate on reproductive matters, as it provides for a right to life for the unborn. An introduction to this right is given in section 5.1.2 below. Subsequently, the rights of the (future) child and the right to know one's genetic origins are discussed.

5.1.1. The marital right to procreate

Neither the Irish Constitution, nor any other Irish statutory act contains an explicit right to procreate. Such a right was however recognised by the Irish courts as an element of the right to marital privacy. The foundation for the recognition of this right was laid in *McGee* v. *Attorney General* (1973) concerning contraceptives.[1] In this case the Supreme Court recognised that the personal rights of Article 40.3.1° of the Irish Constitution implied a right to marital privacy. The Court held that therefore those provisions of the Criminal Law Amendment Act, 1935, which prohibited the sale or import of contraceptives[2] constituted an unjustified invasion of the woman's personal right to privacy in her marital affairs. The majority of the Court concluded that the impugned provisions were inconsistent with Article 40.3.1° of the Constitution and were therefore no longer in force.[3]

1 *McGee* v. *Attorney General & Anor* [1973] IESC 2; [1974] IR 284.

2 Section 17(3) of the Criminal Law Amendment Act, 1935.

3 The majority consisted of Judges Budd, Henchy and Griffin. Justice Walsh agreed that the relevant section of the Act was inconsistent with the Constitution, but he relied primarily on Art. 41 (on family rights) of the Constitution. Chief Justice Fitzgerald acknowledged that if the Act prohibited the use of contraceptives, it could have reasonably been held to contravene Art. 40 of the Constitution. As the contested section of the Criminal Law Amendment Act only concerned the sale and import of contraceptives, he did not find any unconstitutionality and proposed to dismiss the appeal. See also

In *Murray* v. *Ireland* (1991) – a case about imprisoned convicted criminals who were deprived of the ability to exercise their conjugal rights – Chief Justice Finlay confirmed the approach adopted by the majority in *McGee* and considered 'the right to beget children or further children of the marriage' a marital right.[4] The fact that a right to procreate has thus been expressly recognised for married couples,[5] does not necessarily *a contrario* mean that unmarried persons would not enjoy any such right. Until today, this has, however, simply not been expressly confirmed by any Irish court, nor in any piece of Irish legislation.[6]

5.1.2. The status of the unborn under Irish law

The unborn life enjoys distinct protection in the Irish Constitution. Following Article 40.3.3° '[t]he State acknowledges the right to life of the unborn and [...] guarantees in its laws to respect, and, as far as practicable, by its laws to defend and vindicate that right.'[7] When this right was included in the Irish Constitution in 1983 (see section 5.2 below), the term 'unborn'[8] was not defined, rendering its meaning uncertain.[9] It was correspondingly insufficiently clear from which moment in time unborn life begins; conception, implantation in the womb or some other point.[10] *Leitmotiv* in both the Irish abortion law history and the long existing – and at the moment of writing still existing – legal vacuum surrounding assisted human reproduction has been exactly this uncertainty as to the exact protection the Constitution offers to the unborn.

The Irish Constitution Review Group held in 1996 that a definition was needed as to when the 'unborn' acquires the protection of the law. 'Philosophers and scientists may continue to debate when human life begins but the law must define what it intends to protect', the Group's report read.[11] It added that 'unborn' seemed to imply 'on the way to being born' or 'capable of being born''.[12] This made some conclude

---

R. O'Connell, 'Natural Law: Alive and Kicking?: a Look at the Constitutional Morality of Sexual Privacy in Ireland', in: L. May, and J. Brown (eds), *Philosophy of law: classic and contemporary readings* (Chichester, Wiley-Blackwell 2010) p. 585 at p. 588.

4 Murray v. *Ireland* [1991] ILRM 465, Finlay CJ at 471–473.

5 See also Ch. 11, section 11.1.2.

6 See also section 5.3.3 below on access to AHR treatment under Irish law.

7 Eight Amendment of the Constitution Act, No. 8 (7 October 1983). This self-executing provision of the Constitution does not require legislation to give it effect.

8 '*Beo gan breith*' in the Irish version.

9 Commission on Assisted Human Reproduction, *Report of the Commission on Assisted Human Reproduction* (April 2005) Appendix III, p. 96, online available at www.dohc.ie/publications/pdf/cahr.pdf?direct=1, visited June 2014.

10 See, *inter alia*, A. Sherlock, 'The Right to life of the unborn and the Irish Constitution', 24 *Irish Jurist* (1989) p. 13 at p. 13; G. Whyte, 'The Moral Status of the Embryo', 12 *Medico-Legal Journal of Ireland* (2006), p. 72 at p. 82 and A. McMahon, 'The Legal Status of Embryos In Vitro in Ireland – A "Precarious" Position', 17 *Medico-Legal Journal of Ireland* (2011) p. 33.

11 The Constitution Review Group (Stationery Office, Dublin 1996), p. 252. The report is online available at www.archive.constitution.ie/publications/default.asp?UserLang=EN, visited 26 May 2014.

12 *Idem*, at p. 275.

that the embryo *in vitro* was not covered by Article 40.3.3°,[13] a reasoning that was later confirmed by the Irish Supreme Court.[14]

For a long time the legislature left the interpretation of the term 'unborn' to the courts.[15] While they gave some initial impetus to this exercise,[16] in respect of the fundamental question as to when life begins, the courts, however, turned the tables on the legislature. In a 2009 ruling the Supreme Court held:

> '[...] there is uncertainty or no consensus as to when human life begins. The choice as to how life before birth can be best protected, and therefore the point which in law that protection should be deemed to commence, is a policy choice for the Oireachtas.'[17]

The legislature eventually gave some further guidance on the matter in the 2013 Protection of life during pregnancy Act (as discussed in section 5.2.8 below). Under this act the term 'unborn' was held to mean '[...] following implantation until such time as it has completely proceeded in a living state from the body of the woman.'[18] Implantation was thus considered the decisive point in time at which the protection of Article 40.3.3° of the Constitution commenced. Whether this protection extends to other rights than the right to life only, such as the right to bodily integrity, is still an undecided matter.[19]

5.1.3. The rights of the (future) child

The rights of the child are not enumerated in the Irish Constitution, but several Articles refer to children. For example, Article 42.5, which permits the State to intervene in the family in certain circumstances, acknowledges the natural and imprescriptible rights of the child. In their case law, the Courts have recognised that children enjoy

---

13 D. Madden, 'In Vitro Fertilisation: The Moral and Legal Status of the Human Pre-Embryo', 3 *Medico-Legal Journal of Ireland* (1997) p. 12.

14 *Roche* v. *Roche & ors* [2009] IESC 82, Murray CJ. See also section 5.3.1 below.

15 See C.M. Colvin, 'Society for the Protection of unborn children (Ireland) Ltd v Grogan: Irish abortion law and the free movement of services in the European Community', 15 *Fordham International Law Journal* (1992) p. 476 at pp. 496–497 and S. Koegler, 'Ireland's Abortion Information Act of 1995', 29 *Vanderbilt Journal of Transnational Law* (1996) p. 1117 at p. 1126.

16 In a 1987 ruling, Chief Justice Hamilton held that the right to life of the unborn is afforded statutory protection from the date of its conception. *The Attorney General (Society for the Protection of the Unborn Children (Ireland Ltd)* v. *Open Door Counselling Ltd* [1988] IR 593, 598, [1987] ILRM 477, 480. Dissenting Judge Hederman held in *Attorney General* v. *X* [1992] 1 IR 1 at 12; [1992] ILRM 401 at 442: 'The right of life is guaranteed to every life born or unborn. One cannot make distinctions between individual phases of the unborn life before birth, or between unborn and born life.'

17 *Roche* v. *Roche & ors* [2009] IESC 82, Murray CJ. This judgment is discussed in further detail in section 5.3.1 below.

18 Section 2(1) Protection of life during pregnancy Act 2013.

19 In a ruling of 2009, the High Court suggested that the right to life of the unborn, as laid down in Art. 40.3.3° of the Irish Constitution, could in the future be held to include the inherent right to bodily integrity. *Ugbelese & Ors* v. *The Minister for Justice Equality and Law Reform* [2009] IEHC 598, paras. 65 and 74. See also I. Clissmann and J. Barrett, 'The Embryo in vitro after Roche v Roche: What Protection is Now Offered?', 18 *Medico-Legal Journal of Ireland* (2012) p. 13.

the protection provided by various Articles of the Constitution.[20] In *G.* v. *An Bord Uchtála* (1980)[21] the Supreme Court ruled that children have the right to be fed, to live, to be reared and educated, to have the opportunity of working and realising their full personality and dignity as a human being, and to have their welfare and health guarded and to be guarded against threats directed to their existence.[22] While some judges based the recognition of these rights on the personal rights as protected under Article 40.3.1° of the Constitution, others relied on Article 42.5.[23]

Over the years various calls for greater protection of children's rights in the Constitution were made.[24] In 2007 a Joint Parliamentary Committee on Constitutional Amendment on Children was established. In 2010 this Committee recommended amending the Constitution '[...] to enshrine and enhance the protection of the rights of children'.[25] This was followed up[26] and by referendum of November 2012 the Thirty-first Amendment to the Constitution was put before the people. It proposed to include a new Article 42A.1 in the Constitution, reading:

> 'The State recognises and affirms the natural and imprescriptible rights of all children and shall, as far as practicable, by its laws protect and vindicate those rights.'

The amendment was adopted by a 58 per cent majority; however, the referendum result became the subject of a legal challenge. This challenge was dismissed by the High Court,[27] but subsequently appealed to the Supreme Court. As the appeal was still pending, the envisaged amendment had not yet been implemented by the time this research was concluded (i.e., 31 July 2014).

While the amendment refers to 'all children', some concerns were expressed that by leaving Article 41 of the Constitution intact, 'the robust protection afforded to the marital family unit' would often 'tilt the balance away from the vindication of the individual children's rights.'[28] Such concerns were largely overcome by the 2014

---

20 UCD Constitutional Studies Group, *A Guide to the referendum on the 31st Amendment to the Constitution*, online available at www.ucd.ie/t4cms/Guide_to_the_31st_amendment.pdf, visited 9 July 2014.

21 *G.* v. *An Bord Uchtála* [1980] IR 32.

22 Joint Committee on the Constitutional Amendment on Children, *Third Report. Twenty-eighth Amendment of the Constitution Bill 2007 Proposal for a constitutional amendment to strengthen children's rights. Final Report*, February 2010, p. 35, online available at: www.oireachtas.ie/parliament/media/housesoftheoireachtas/contentassets/documents/JC-Constitutional-Amendment-on-Children-Final-Report.pdf, visited October 2011.

23 *Idem*, at p. 39.

24 As O'Shea has noted '[t]he need to amend the Constitution to provide greater protection for children was first highlighted in 1993 and since then numerous calls for constitutional reform from both the domestic and international levels have fallen on deaf ears.' O'Shea 2012, *supra* n. 11, at p. 87.

25 Joint Committee on the Constitutional Amendment on Children 2010, *supra* n. 22, at p. 14.

26 In September 2012 the Thirty-First Amendment of the Constitution (Children) Bill 2012 was presented.

27 'Challenge to Children's Referendum dismissed by High Court. A Dublin woman had taken a petition with an aim to quash the result in the November 2012 vote', *thejournal.ie* 18 October 2013, www.thejournal.ie/childrens-referendum-challenge-rejected-1135966-Oct2013, visited November 2013.

28 O'Shea 2012, *supra* n. 24, at pp. 92–93. The author observed: 'While the referendum's positive result may have symbolic value for the rights of the Irish child, any practical changes brought about by the

Children and Family Relationships Bill, as introduced in more detail in section 5.3.2 below. In this Bill the best interests of the child were a central focus. They were defined as follows:

> '[...] "best interests", in relation to a child, includes the physical, emotional, psychological, educational and social needs of the child including the child's need for stability having regard to the child's age and stage of development [...].'[29]

5.1.3. The right to know one's genetic origins

The right to know one's genetic origins is recognised under Irish law, but it does not enjoy very strong protection. The Supreme Court ruled in *I.O'T.* v. *B* (1998) that a child has an unenumerated constitutional right to know the identity of his or her natural parents.[30] It added, however, that this right is neither absolute nor unqualified; it must be balanced with the parent's constitutional right to privacy. *I.O'T.* v. *B* concerned an adoption case and the ruling was subsequently codified in adoption legislation.[31] As discussed more elaborately in section 5.3.4 below, there was, on the contrary, at the time of conclusion of this research[32] no specific legislation (yet) that regulated under what circumstances children born from a pregnancy involving gamete donation could have access to information about their genetic parents.

5.2. Irish abortion legislation

Abortion is not allowed under Irish law, safe for the exceptional situation that an abortion may save the life of the mother. Under sections 58 and 59 of the Offences Against the Person Act 1861, which was in force until 2014, both the attempt of a pregnant woman to procure a miscarriage and the supply of any poison or instrument to any woman with the intent to procure a miscarriage, were criminalised.[33] The

---

referendum are likely to be minimal, particularly as Art. 41 remains unchanged.'

29 Children and Family Relationships Bill, Revised version 26 September 2014, online available at: www.justice.ie/en/JELR/Pages/PB14000256, visited October 2014.

30 *I.O'T.* v. *B., The Rotunda Girls Aid Society & Father Doyle, and M. H.* v. *Father Doyle and The Rotunda Girls Aid Society* [1998] 2 IR 321. See M. Blair, 'Unveiling Our Heritage: A Comparative Examination of Access by Adopted Persons and Their Families to Identifying and Non–identifying Information', 3 *Irish Journal of Family Law* (2000) p. 10.

31 E.g. Art. 86 Adoption Act 2010 provides that the Civil Registry keeps an index '[t]o make traceable the connection between each entry in the Adopted Children Register and the corresponding entry in the register of births'. Information from this index can only be obtained by court order. The Court may not give access if it is not in best interests of any child concerned (Art. 88 Adoption Act 2010).

32 That is 31 July 2014.

33 The Irish Constitution of 1937 incorporated the common law prohibition on abortion and left the Offences Against the Persons Act intact. Both Section 58 and Section 59 of the Offences Against the Person Act 1861 were furthermore expressly upheld in Section 10 of the Health (Family Planning) Act 1979, No. 20/1979. See also Colvin 1992, *supra* n. 15, at pp. 491–92.

woman could in principle even face life imprisonment for an abortion attempt.[34] As explained below (in section 5.2.8), the maximum penalty was considerably lowered when new abortion legislation was adopted in 2013. Nonetheless, today a risk to the life of the mother is still the only ground for a lawful abortion in Ireland.

While the Irish Constitution of 1937 left the Offences Against the Persons Act intact,[35] developments in England and Wales and other Western countries influenced the Irish public debate on abortion. In *R. v. Bourne* (1939) the English Crown Court ruled that abortion to preserve the life of a pregnant woman was not unlawful and held that where a doctor was of the opinion that the probable consequence of a pregnancy was to render a woman a mental and physical wreck, he could properly be said to be operating for the purpose of preserving the life of the mother.[36] As a result of this judgment the Abortion Act 1967 was adopted in England and Wales permitting abortion, *inter alia*, to 'prevent grave permanent injury to the physical or mental health of the pregnant woman'.[37] Although Irish Courts held that the *R.* v. *Bourne* approach could not be adopted in the Irish jurisdiction,[38] these and similar developments in the United States of America[39] and in continental Europe[40] caused considerable concern in Ireland about the adequacy of existing provisions concerning abortion and the possibility of abortion being deemed lawful by judicial interpretation.[41] The Supreme Court decision in *McGee* (1973),[42] holding that the use of contraceptives fell within scope of the mother's private life, further fuelled the fear that abortion would also be legalised in Ireland.[43] Apparently this fear could not

[34] Before 1861 the UK Statute 43 Geo 3, ch 58 (1803) imposed the death penalty on anyone who administered poison with the intent to induce the miscarriage of a pregnant woman. In the 1861 Act this was changed to life imprisonment.

[35] J.A. Weinstein, '"An Irish solution to an Irish problem": Ireland's struggle with abortion law', 10 *Arizona Journal of International & Comparative Law* (1993) p. 165 at p. 170 and N. Klashtorny, 'Ireland's abortion law: an abuse of international law', 10 *Temple International & Comparative Law Journal* (1996) p. 419 at p. 421.

[36] *R.* v. *Bourne* [1939] 1 KB 687, [1938] 3 All ER 615. See also D. Curtin, 'Case note to ECJ C-159/90', 29 *CML Rev* (1992) p. 585 at pp. 585–586.

[37] Section 1(1)(b) Abortion Act 1967.

[38] *Society for the Protection of the Unborn Child* v. *Grogan and Others* (Unreported judgment of 6 March 1997) Keane J.

[39] *Roe* v. *Wade* 410 US 113 (1973), which had been preceded by *Griswold* v. *Connecticut*, 381 US 479 (1965) and *Eisenstadt* v. *Baird*, 405 US 438 (1972), were two cases similar to *McGee* v. *Attorney General & Anor* [1973] IESC 2; [1974] IR 284.

[40] See Colvin 1992, *supra* n. 15, at pp. 493–494 and Weinstein 1993, *supra* n. 35, at p. 171.

[41] See, *inter alia*, Colvin 1992, *supra* n. 15, at pp. 492–493; Koegler 1996, *supra* n. 15, at p. 422; L. Hamilton, 'Matters of life and death', 65 *Fordham Law Review* (1996) p. 543 at p. 548; A.-M.E.W. Sterling, 'The European Union and Abortion Tourism: Liberalizing Ireland's Abortion Law', 20 *Boston College International & Comparative Law Review* (1997) p. 385 at p. 388 and A.M. Buckley, 'The primacy of democracy over natural law in Irish abortion law: an examination of the C case' 9 *Duke Journal of Comparative & International law* (1998) p. 275 at p. 281.

[42] *McGee* v. *Attorney General & Anor* [1973] IESC 2; [1974] IR 284. See *inter alia* B. Mercurio, 'Abortion in Ireland: An Analysis of the Legal Transformation Resulting from Membership in the European Union', 11 *Tulsa Journal of International and Comparative Law* (2003) p. 141 at pp. 145–146.

[43] See, *inter alia*, Colvin 1992, *supra* n. 15, at p. 495; A. Thompson, 'International protection of women's rights: an analysis of *Open Door Counselling Ltd. and Dublin Well woman Centre v Ireland*',12 *Boston University International Law Journal* (1994) p. 371 at p. 374; P. Ward, 'Ireland: Abortion: X + Y = ?!', 33 *University of Louisville Journal of Family Law* (1994) p.385 at p. 389; Koegler 1996, *supra*

be remedied by the Court's explicit statement that the recognition of a marital right to privacy did not alter the prohibition on abortion,[44] as anti-abortion campaigners started a lobby to incorporate the right to life of the unborn in the Constitution.[45] This lobby resulted in a referendum held in September 1983 during which the Eighth Amendment of the Constitution was adopted.[46] Justice Finlay later referred to this referendum as '[...] a decision by the people to insert into the Constitution a specific guarantee and protection for a fundamental rights perceived to be threatened by developments in the societies of countries outside Ireland'.[47] The third subsection of Article 40.3, that was at the time newly introduced, is still in force, and reads:

> 'The State acknowledges the right to life of the unborn and, with due regard to the equal right to life of the mother, guarantees in its laws to respect, and, as far as practicable, by its laws to defend and vindicate that right.'[48]

Since the inclusion of this Article in the Constitution there have been many calls for the adoption of regulatory legislation. For instance in the *X Case*, which is discussed below in section 5.2.2, Supreme Court Justice McCarthy held that:

> 'The people, when enacting the Eighth Amendment, were entitled to believe that legislation would be introduced to regulate the manner in which the right to life of the unborn and the right to life of the mother could be reconciled.'[49]

---

n. 15, at pp. 1122–1123; D.A. MacLean, 'Can the EC kill the Irish unborn?; An investigation of the European Community's ability to impinge on the moral sovereignty of Member States', 28 *Hofstra Law Review* (1999) p. 527 at p. 552; J. Schweppe, 'Mothers, Fathers, Children and the Unborn – Abortion and the Twenty-Fifth Amendment to the Constitution Bill', 9 *Irish Student Law Review* (2001) p. 136 at pp. 138–139; M.C. McBrien, 'Ireland: balancing traditional domestic abortion law with modern reality and international influence', 26 *Suffolk Transnational Law Review* (2002) p. 195 at p. 204 and A.M. Clifford, 'Abortion in International waters off the coast of Ireland: avoiding a collision between Irish moral sovereignty and the European Community', 14 *Pace International Law Review* (2002) p. 385 at pp. 396–397. As Koegler pointed out, the Irish Court expressly relied on the U.S. Supreme Court decisions *Griswold* and *Eisenstadt* (see *supra* n.39).

44 *McGee* v. *Attorney General & Anor* [1973] IESC 2; [1974] IR 284 at. 335. As Hamilton observes, such observations were repeated in *G.* v. *An Bord Uchtála* [1980] IR 32 and *Norris* v. *Attorney General* [1983] IESC 3; [1984] IR 36. Hamilton 1996, *supra* n. 41, at p. 548.

45 In 1981 umbrella organisation *Pro Life Amendment Committee* was founded, which considered a constitutional amendment the best way to prevent the legalisation of abortion in Ireland. See Colvin 1992, *supra* n. 15, at pp. 495–496 and Koegler 1996, *supra* n. 15, at p. 1125.

46 53.67 per cent of the electorate voted with 841,233 votes in favour and 416,136 against.

47 T.A. Finlay, 'The Constitution of Ireland in a Changing Society', in: D. Curtin and D. O'Keeffe (eds.), *Constitutional Adjudication in European Community and National Law – Essays for the Hon. Mr. Justice T.F. O'Higgin* (Dublin, Butterworth 1992) p. 140. See also R.A. Lawson, 'The Irish Abortion Cases: European Limits to National Sovereignty?', 1 *European Journal of Health Law* (1994) p. 167 at p. 167.

48 Eight Amendment of the Constitution Act, No. 8 (7 October 1983). This self-executing provision of the Constitution does not require legislation to give it effect.

49 *Attorney General* v. *X* [1992] 1 IR 1; [1992] ILRM 401 at 451.

The Justice at the time called the legislature's failure to legislate 'inexcusable'.[50] Even though a call for legislation was repeated at many points in time since,[51] it was not until 2013, however, that any implementing legislation was adopted (see section 5.2.8 below).

Because of the strict Irish abortion laws, women and girls from Ireland have been, and are, travelling abroad for abortions (for statistics, see section 5.4 below). This cross-border movement has proven so deeply entrenched in the Irish abortion debate and has been so fundamental for the (development of) standard-setting in this area, that the present section 5.2 in setting out the Irish abortion legislation also addresses some cross-border elements. Section 5.5 below will subsequently single out a number of relevant cross-border issues, such as criminal liability for, public funding for and information about abortions obtained abroad.

5.2.1. The success of pro-life campaigners

After the successful 1983 referendum, the Irish pro-life (and thus anti-abortion) campaigners of the *Society for the Protection of the Unborn Children* (SPUC)[52] sought to stop women in Ireland from travelling abroad for abortions, and initiated a series of proceedings against the Irish counselling agencies *Open Door Counselling* and *Dublin Well Woman Centre*, who provided non-directive counselling about legal abortion services abroad.[53] The Irish Supreme Court granted an injunction restraining the two counselling agencies from assisting pregnant women '[...] to travel abroad to obtain abortions by referral to a clinic, by the making for them of travel arrangements, or by informing them of the identity and location and method of communication with a specified clinic or clinics or otherwise.'[54] The Supreme Court held that the agencies had no constitutional right to exercise their freedom of expression, as they were 'assisting in the ultimate destruction of the life of the unborn', whose right to life was expressly guaranteed by the Constitution.[55] The President of the Court, Chief Justice Finlay, held that '[...] no right could constitutionally arise to obtain information the purpose of [...] which was to defeat the constitutional right to life of

---

50 Compare *Roche* v. *Roche* as discussed in section 5.3.1 below.

51 See, *inter alia*, I. Bacik, 'Guest Editorial', 11 *Medico-Legal Journal of Ireland* 1997, p. 1.

52 In the below discussed *Grogan* case, the CJEU described SPUC as 'a company incorporated under Irish law whose purpose is to prevent the decriminalization of abortion and to affirm, defend and promote human life from the moment of conception.'

53 As Sherlock has explained, under the Censorship of Publications Act 1929 (Section 16), the printing, publishing, sell or distribution any book or periodical which advocated abortion was prohibited. Sherlock 1989, *supra* n. 10.

54 *The Attorney General (Society for the Protection of the Unborn Children (Ireland Ltd) v. Open Door Counselling Ltd* [1988] IR 593 at 598, [1987] ILRM 477 at 480. In Ireland injunctions apply to all those who have notice of them. Sterling therefore concludes that this ruling effectively forced abortion counselling to go underground. Sterling 1997, *supra* n. 41, at p. 390 referring to A.M. Hilbert, 'Notes, The Irish Abortion Debate: Substantive Rights and Affecting Commerce Jurisprudential Models', 26 *VanderBilt Journal of Transnational Law* (1994) p. 1117 at p. 1135.

55 *Idem*, at 624–625.

the unborn child'.[56] The counselling agencies, *Open Door Counselling* and *Dublin Well Woman Centre*, subsequently lodged a complaint with the European Court of Human Rights (ECtHR). Before this Court would issue its judgment in the case, the other European Court, the Court of Justice of the European Communities (now CJEU), gave a judgment in another case initiated by the Irish pro-life campaigners.

5.2.1.1. The Grogan case (1991) and its aftermath

SPUC also brought a suit against representatives of three Irish student associations who distributed free handbooks containing information about abortion services available in England. Referring to Articles 59 and 60 of the EEC Treaty (now 56 and 57 TFEU), the student associations – represented by one of their officers, Stephen Grogan – contended that Irish citizens had a right to receive and impart information about services lawfully available in other Member States. The High Court made a reference to the Court of Justice of the European Communities (now CJEU) for a preliminary ruling on three questions: (a) whether abortion was a 'service' within the meaning of the EEC Treaty; (b) if so, whether the prohibition on the distribution of information regarding those services constituted a restriction within the meaning of the Treaty; and (c) if so, whether such a restriction could be justified.[57] As discussed more elaborately in Chapter 3,[58] the Court held in its preliminary ruling that the links between the activities of the student associations and the providers of abortion services in the United Kingdom or elsewhere, were 'too tenuous', for the prohibition on the distribution of information to be regarded as a restriction within the meaning of the Treaty.[59] Accordingly, in August 1992 the High Court granted a permanent injunction.[60]

The Irish government was worried about the effect of the ruling of the Court of Justice in *Grogan*, as it implied that Irish abortion law could potentially conflict with

---

56 *Idem*, at 625. For critique of this ruling see also Hilbert 1994, *supra* n. 54, at p. 1134 and Thompson 1994, *supra* n. 43, at p. 382.

57 From *Campus Oil* v. *Minister for Industry* [1983] IESC 2; [1983] IR 82 it follows that under Irish law there is no appeal against a decision to refer a case to the CJEU. When the High Court did not grant an interlocutory injunction against the student associations while the CJEU's opinion was awaited, SPUC appealed to the Supreme Court against this inactivity. The Supreme Court unanimously granted the injunction, asserting that no Community law regarding services could outweigh the right to life of the unborn, as guaranteed by Ireland's Constitution. *The Society for the Protection of Unborn Children (Ireland) Ltd* v. *Grogan* [1989] IR 753 at 765; [1990] ILRM 350. According to Colvin this reflected a view contrary to the jurisprudence of the Court of Justice regarding the supremacy of Community law. Colvin 1992, *supra* n. 15, at p. 502. *Cf.* Case 11–70 *Internationale Handelsgesellschaft* [1970] ECR 1125, ECLI:EU:C:1970:114.

58 Ch. 3, section 3.5.2.1.

59 Case C-159/90 *The Society for the Protection of Unborn Children Ireland Ltd* v. *Stephen Grogan and others* [1991] ECR I-4685, ECLI:EU:C:1991:378, paras. 24–27.

60 *SPUC* v. *Grogan and others* [1993] 1 CMLR 197. Fletcher has explained that '[t]he Court's finding that the students' unions were not protected under EC law in their distribution of abortion information effectively meant that the injunction against their doing so continued to operate until it was lifted in March 1997, after the Abortion Information Act 1995 came into effect.' R. Fletcher, 'National crisis, supranational opportunity: the Irish construction of abortion as a European service', 8 *Reproductive Health Matters* (2000) p. 35 at p. 37.

Community law.[61] If a direct link with the abortion providers could be established in a different case, Community law could potentially override Article 40.3.3° of the Irish Constitution.[62] To avoid that possibility, the Irish government lobbied for a Protocol to the Maastricht Treaty.[63] This resulted in the adoption of Protocol 17 to the Treaty on European Union, which provided:

> 'Nothing in the Treaty on the European Union or in the Treaties establishing the European Communities or in the Treaties or Acts modifying or supplementing those Treaties shall affect the application in Ireland of Article 40.3.3° of the Constitution of Ireland.'[64]

While the Maastricht Treaty was signed by the Irish government on 7 February 1992, its ratification was subject to a referendum by the Irish electorate, which was due to take place in June 1992. This referendum would turn out to be significantly influenced by yet another stage in the Irish abortion debate, initiated by the highly controversial landmark case *Attorney General* v. *X*.[65]

5.2.2. The *X Case* (1992) and its aftermath

Ten days after the signing of the Treaty on European Union, the Irish Court had to interpret the Eighth Amendment in a case involving a 14-year-old girl – referred to as '*X*' – who was pregnant as a result of multiple rape and wished to travel to the United Kingdom (UK) with her parents to have an abortion. The girl claimed that she was suicidal at the thought of carrying her pregnancy to term. Prior to their leaving, the parents of the girl contacted the Irish police to inquire if DNA tests could be carried out on the foetus, in order to provide proof of paternity. The police contacted the Director of Public Prosecutions (DPP), who declared on 5 February 1992 that such evidence would be inadmissible.[66] The following day the family travelled to England to procure an abortion. The DPP in turn contacted the Attorney General who subsequently sought an injunction order seeking the immediate return of the girl and her parents to Ireland. The family returned and put evidence before the High Court that *X* would commit suicide if she were forced to carry her pregnancy to full term. The High Court held that an abortion could only be contemplated if it were established that an inevitable or immediate risk to the life of the mother existed. It balanced the right to life of the girl against that of her unborn child and concluded

61 Mercurio 2003, *supra* n. 42, at pp. 163 and 174. See also Hamilton 1996, *supra* n. 41, at p. 553.

62 See Sterling 1997, *supra* n. 41, at p. 392 and B. Moriarty and A.-M. Mooney Cotter (eds.), *Human rights law* (Oxford, Oxford University Press 2004) p. 18.

63 Treaty on European Union, signed at Maastricht on 7 February 1992 [1992] OJ C191/1.

64 Protocol Annexed to Treaty on European Union [1992] OJ C191/1, p. 94. As will be discussed below, the Protocol would later be partly revoked by the Irish government, under influence of domestic developments.

65 *Attorney General* v. *X* [1992] 1 IR 1; [1992] ILRM 401. Hogan and Whyte describe it as '[...] what must surely qualify as the most controversial case ever to come before an Irish court'. G. Hogan and G. Whyte, *J.M. Kelly, The Irish Constitution* (Dublin, LexisNexis Butterworths 2003) p. 1503. See also Buckley 1998, *supra* n. 41, at p. 285 and Mercurio 2003, *supra* n. 42, at p. 160.

66 See Ward 1994, *supra* n. 43, at p. 402.

that the risk that *X* would take her own life if an order would be made was 'much less' and 'of a different order of magnitude' than the certainty that the life of the unborn would be terminated if the order was not made.[67] Furthermore, the constitutional right to travel abroad[68] could not be invoked where the purpose of the travelling was to have an abortion.[69] The High Court accordingly granted an injunction preventing the girl from leaving Ireland for a period of nine months.

This judgment provoked unprecedented public reaction.[70] On the strong advice and with the financial support of the government, the family appealed the case to the Supreme Court.[71] In an *ex tempore* ruling of 26 February 1992, a four to one majority of the Supreme Court held that the injunction had to be lifted. Ten days later, on 5 March, the full judgments of the Court were handed down.[72] The majority of the Supreme Court held that the Constitution envisaged abortion being lawful in limited circumstances. Citing *McGee* (1973) Chief Justice Finlay noted that no interpretation of the Constitution was intended to be final for all time. He held this statement to be 'peculiarly appropriate and illuminating' in the interpretation of the Eighth Amendment, which dealt 'with the intimate human problem of the right of the unborn to life and its relationship to the right of the mother of an unborn child to her life.'[73] He recalled that by virtue of the amendment the State had a duty to have 'due regard' for the life of the mother. Chief Justice Finlay decided that the two rights at stake had to be interpreted harmoniously.[74] In Finlay's opinion the proper test to be applied in this case was:

> '[...] if it is established as a matter of probability that there is a real and substantial risk to the life, as distinct from the health, of the mother, which can only be avoided by the termination of her pregnancy, such termination is permissible, having regard to the true interpretation of Article 40, s.3, sub-s. 3 of the Constitution.'[75]

---

67 *Attorney General* v. *X* [1992] 1 IR 1, at 12; [1992] ILRM 401, at 410.

68 This unenumerated right was recognised for the first time in *State (KM)* v. *Minister for Foreign Affairs* [1979] IR 73, 80–81.

69 *Attorney General* v. *X* [1992] 1 IR 1, at 6–7; [1992] ILRM 401. See also Koegler 1996, *supra* n. 15, at p. 1126.

70 In the Netherlands, for example, parliamentary questions were posed about the *X Case*. *Kamerstukken II* 1991/92, no 398. See furthermore *inter alia* Weinstein 1993, *supra* n. 35, at p. 165 at p. 191; Klashtorny 1996, *supra* n. 35, at p. 419 at p. 428; Hamilton 1996, *supra* n. 41, at p. 554 and Buckley 1998, *supra* n. 41, at p. 286.

71 Sterling 1997, *supra* n. 41, at p. 393; Schweppe 2001, *supra* n. 43, at p. 141; S. Mullally, 'Debating Reproductive Rights in Ireland', in: B. Lockwood (ed.), *Women's Rights, A Human Rights Quarterly Reader* (Baltimore, Johns Hopkins University Press 2006) p. 613 at p. 626.

72 *Attorney General* v. *X* [1992] 1 IR 1; [1992] ILRM 401.

73 *Idem.*

74 Hogan and Whyte have defined the doctrine of harmonious interpretation as 'the principle that constitutional provisions should not be construed in isolation from all the other parts of the Constitution among which they are embedded but should be so construed as to harmonise with the other parts'. The authors held that this doctrine was 'no more than a presumption that the people who enacted the Constitution had a single scale of values, and wished those values to permeate their charter evenly and without internal discordance'. Hogan and Whyte 2003, *supra* n. 65, at p. 8.

75 *Attorney General* v. *X* [1992] 1 IR 1 at 53, [1992] ILRM 401 at 425.

The majority concluded that *in casu* this test was satisfied as it was established, as a matter of probability, that there was a real and substantial risk to the life of the mother by self-destruction which could only be avoided by termination of her pregnancy.[76] The exact standard of proof and the requirements needed to establish a sufficient risk were not, however, clarified in the majority judgment.[77] According to Hamilton no party foresaw the manner in which the Supreme Court interpreted the words of the Eight Amendment in the *X Case*.[78] Dissenting Judge Hederman deemed it possible to guard the mother against self-destruction and preserve the life of the unborn child at the same time. He held that

> '[...] no recognition of a mother's right of self determination can be given priority over the protection of the unborn life. The creation of a new life, involving as it does pregnancy, birth and raising the child, necessarily involves some restriction of a mother's freedom but the alternative is the destruction of the unborn life.'[79]

As Ward indicated, 'the most ironic consequence of the *X Case*' was that the judgment furthermore created an exception providing for lawful abortion to save the life of the mother *within* the Irish jurisdiction.[80] Because three out of five judges held that in this conflict of fundamental rights, the right to life of the unborn trumped the right to travel of the mother,[81] the case was decided on the theoretical basis of whether *X* would be allowed to have an abortion *in* Ireland, because if not, she did not have the right to travel to obtain one.[82] Thereby the Court's decision suggested that in other circumstances than a real and substantial risk to the life of the mother,

---

76 This same conclusion was later reached in the similar case of *A. and B.* v. *Eastern Health Board & C.* [1997] IEHC 176; [1998] 1 IR 464; [1998] 1 ILRM 460, often referred to as the *C case*. See also D.A. Cusack, 'Abortion – Conflicting Rights, Duties and Arguments', 3 *Medico-Legal Journal of Ireland* (1997) p. 82. Buckley observed that in the latter case the Court went further by permitting a state agency to fund and facilitate the young girl's abortion. According to the author as a result of this case it was unclear who had a right to an abortion in Ireland and who was able to receive government funding for such an abortion. Mercurio agreed with Buckley that Irish abortion law still failed to address the question of whether a woman who demonstrated a real and substantial risk to her life that qualified for an abortion was eligible to receive state-funded medical treatment. Both authors, furthermore, pointed out that the *C case* suggested that 'very little evidence [was] needed to prove a real and substantial risk of suicide'. Buckley 1998, *supra* n. 41, at pp. 302 and 304–305 and Mercurio 2003, *supra* n. 42, at p. 169.

77 Weinstein 1993, *supra* n. 35, at p. 193; Koegler 1996, *supra* n. 15, at pp. 1133–1134 and Klashtorny 1996, *supra* n. 35, at p. 429.

78 Hamilton 1996, *supra* n. 41, at p. 551.

79 *Attorney General* v. *X* [1992] 1 IR 1, at 72.

80 Ward 1994, *supra* n. 43, at p. 406. See also D. Cole, '"Going to England": Irish Abortion Law and the European Community', 17 *Hastings Int'l & Comp. L. Rev.* (1993–1994) p. 113 at p. 133; Hilbert 1994, *supra* n. 54, at p. 1141; Koegler 1996, *supra* n. 15, at p. 1133; Sterling 1997, *supra* n. 41, at p. 393; Buckley 1998, *supra* n. 41, at pp. 287–288; McBrien 2002, *supra* n. 43, at p. 211; Clifford 2002, *supra* n. 43, at p. 408; S.J. Johansen, 'Clearly Ambiguous: A Visitor's View of the Irish Abortion Referendum of 2002', 25 *Loyola of Los Angeles International & Comparative Law Review* (2003) p. 205 at p. 212 and Mercurio 2003, *supra* n. 42, at pp. 162–163.

81 Chief Justice Finlay, Justice Egan and Justice Hederman. Justice O'Flaherty and McCarthy disagreed. *Attorney General* v. *X* [1992] 1 IR 1 [1992] ILRM 401 at 453 and 456. See Hilbert 1994, *supra* n. 54, at p. 1142.

82 Buckley 1998, *supra* n. 41, at pp. 287–288, referring to Cole 1993–1994, *supra* n. 80, at p. 133; Hogan and Whyte 2003, *supra* n. 65, at p. 803 and Koegler 1996, *supra* n. 15, at p. 1134.

women could be restrained from travelling outside Ireland to procure an abortion.[83] This issue was later solved by the Thirteenth Amendment, that will be discussed in section 5.2.3 below.

Lastly, it should be pointed out that the Supreme Court decided the case – including its travel aspect – on the basis of national law only, thereby avoiding issues of European law.[84] Hilbert thinks that the fact that the Court in *X* characterised the issues raised on appeal as concerning Irish Constitutional law only, and no European Community law, revealed the Irish judiciary's 'overriding concern with defining domestic constitutional rights'.[85]

After the *X Case*, the Irish government feared that Irish voters disagreeing with the *X Case*, also disagreed with Protocol 17 and would therefore reject ratification of the Maastricht Treaty in a referendum which was scheduled for 12 June 1992.[86] The government therefore sought an amendment to Protocol 17, but the other EC Member States refused to reopen the debate on the Protocol. The Irish government subsequently settled for a Solemn Declaration to the effect that Protocol 17 would not '[...] limit freedom either to travel between Member States or [...] to obtain or make available in Ireland information relating to services lawfully available in Member States'.[87] In addition to the Declaration, the government promised that a separate referendum would be held regarding the right to travel abroad for an abortion and the right to receive information about foreign abortion clinics.[88] It seems that this promise had the desired effect; in June 1992 the ratification of the Maastricht Treaty was approved by the Irish people. Before the announced new abortion referendum would take place, the ECtHR delivered its judgment in *Open Door Dublin Well Woman* v. *Ireland*.[89] As discussed more in depth in Chapter 2,[90] the ECtHR found a violation of Article 10 in this case. Despite according a wide margin of appreciation in matters of morals '[...] particularly in an area such as the [one at stake] which touche[d] on matters of belief concerning the nature of human life',[91] the ECtHR considered the

---

83 Cole 1993–1994, *supra* n. 80, at p. 133. See also Koegler 1996, *supra* n. 15, at p. 1134 and Mercurio 2003, *supra* n. 42, at p. 166.

84 *Attorney General* v. *X* [1992] 1 IR 1, at 305–307. See also P. Fitzmaurice, '*Attorney General v X*: A lost opportunity to examine the limits of European integration', 26 *Brooklyn Journal of International Law* (2001) p. 1723 at p. 1750 and Lawson 1994, *supra* n. 47, at p. 175.

85 Hilbert 1994, *supra* n. 54, at p. 1143.

86 The Maastricht Treaty was signed by the Irish government on 7 February 1992. See Sterling 1997, *supra* n. 41, at pp. 394–95; Lawson 1994, *supra* n. 47, at p. 176; Klashtorny 1996, *supra* n. 35, at pp. 429–30 and Buckley 1998, *supra* n. 41, at p. 288. See F. Murphy, 'Maastricht: implementation in Ireland', 19 *European Law Review* (1994) p. 94.

87 Declaration of the High Contracting Parties to the Treaty on European Union [1992] OJ C191/1, p. 109. See also ch. 3, section 3.5.2.1, footnote 219.

88 See, *inter alia*, Klashtorny 1996, *supra* n. 35, at p. 430; P. Manners, 'Can governmental policy trump the freedom of speech? Access to information about abortion services in Ireland and the United States', 20 *Suffolk Transnational Law Review* (1996) p. 289 at p 295; Sterling 1997, *supra* n. 41, at p. 396 and Buckley 1998, *supra* n. 41, at p. 289.

89 ECtHR 29 October 1992, *Open Door and Dublin Well Woman* v. *Ireland*, nos. 14234/88 and 14235/88.

90 Ch. 2, section 2.4.1.

91 ECtHR 29 October 1992, *Open Door and Dublin Well Woman* v. *Ireland*, nos. 14234/88 and 14235/88, para. 68.

restriction to be disproportionate to the aims pursued. After the judgment from the ECtHR, *Open Door Counselling* and *Dublin Well Woman* applied to the Supreme Court to have the injunction restraining their activities lifted. This Court rejected their appeal,[92] as at the time Ireland was not required to follow the judgment, because rulings of the ECtHR did not override conflicting decisions of the Irish Court.[93]

5.2.3. The 1992 abortion referendum and the 1995 Abortion Information Act

A month after the ECtHR *Open Door* judgment, on 25 November 1992, the next abortion referendum was called. Three constitutional amendments were put before the electorate. The first proposal related to what has been described as the 'substantive' issue of the circumstances in which an abortion would be permissible within Ireland. By means of this proposal, the government tried to limit the effects of the *X Case*.[94] Abortion would be permitted where such was necessary to save the life, as distinct from the health of the mother, where such risk arose from an illness or disorder of the mother, other than a risk of suicide.[95] This proposal (the Twelfth Amendment) was defeated by both sides of the abortion debate and thus rejected in the vote.[96] The other two proposals concerning the freedom to travel abroad to obtain an abortion (the Thirteenth Amendment) and the provision of abortion information (the Fourteenth Amendment) were both adopted.[97] Although the Twelfth Amendment had been primarily intended as a correction of the *X Case*, the adoption of the Thirteenth Amendment also influenced the interpretation of that ruling. Any uncertainty as to whether women were only allowed to travel abroad where the

---

92 *Attorney General ex rel Society for the Protection of Unborn Children (Ireland) Ltd.* v. *Open Door Counselling & Dublin Well Woman Centre Ltd.* [1994] 1 ILRM 256. See also Ward 1994, *supra* n. 43, at pp. 396–397.

93 Sterling 1997, *supra* n. 41, at p. 398. More elaborately on the incorporation of the ECHR in the Irish jurisdiction, see D. O'Connell, 'Ireland', in: R. Blackburn and J. Polakiewicz (eds.), *Fundamental Rights in Europe. The ECHR and its Member States 1950–2000* (Oxford: Oxford University Press 2001) pp. 423–474.

94 See, *inter alia*, A. Eggert and B. Rolston, 'Ireland', in: B. Rolston and A. Eggert (eds.), *Abortion in the new Europe, A comparative handbook*, Westport (etc.): Greenwood Press 1994, pp. 157–172 at p. 169 and Ward 1994, *supra* n. 43, at p. 406. At the same time, as Eggert and Rolston observed, a vote in favour of this proposal would have allowed for therapeutic abortions, even within the confines of the Irish State.

95 The proposal read: 'It shall be unlawful to terminate the life of an unborn unless such termination is necessary to save the life, as distinct from the health, of the mother where there is an illness or disorder of the mother giving rise to a real and substantial risk to her life, not being a risk of self-destruction.'

96 The proposal was rejected with 1,079, 297 votes to 572,177. See also Buckley 1998, *supra* n. 41, at p. 290.

97 Thirteenth Amendment of the Constitution of Ireland, Act (23 December 1992) and Fourteenth Amendment of the Constitution of Ireland, Act (23 December 1992). The Thirteenth Amendment was adopted with 1,035,308 votes to 624,059. The Fourteenth Amendment was adopted with 992,833 votes to 665,106.

pregnancy posed a substantial risk to the life of the mother (see 5.2.2 above), was now removed.[98] The two new paragraphs to Article 40.3.3° provided:

> 'This subsection shall not limit freedom to travel between the State and another state.
>
> This subsection shall not limit freedom to obtain or make available, in the State, subject to such conditions as may be laid down by law, information relating to services lawfully available in another state.'[99]

For several years the government failed to adopt legislation clarifying the conditions under which information on foreign abortion services could be disseminated.[100] In 1995 the *Regulation of Information (Services outside the State for Termination of Pregnancies)* Bill was enacted.[101] The Act has been referred to as 'the culmination of years of litigation and controversy over abortion rights under Irish and EU law'.[102] It delineates how, and under what circumstances, publishers, organisations offering pregnancy counselling and the like can disseminate information concerning abortion. By virtue of this Act women in Ireland are entitled to receive information about abortion services, provided that such information does not advocate or promote the termination of a pregnancy.[103] Doctors and counsellors who make an appointment or any other arrangement for or on behalf of, a woman with a person who provides services outside Ireland for the termination of pregnancies, are guilty of an offence and can be convicted to a fairly moderate fine.[104]

The 1995 Act was referred by the President to the Supreme Court,[105] which held that the Bill did not constitute an unjust attack on the constitutional rights of the unborn or on the constitutional rights of the mother or any other person or persons, and concluded that a fair and reasonable balance between the various constitutional rights in question had been struck by the legislature.[106] The Supreme Court, *inter*

---

98 See Koegler 1996, *supra* n. 15, at p. 1136.

99 These amendments have been referred to as 'badly thought out and badly worded'. See B. McCracken, 'The Irish Constitution – an overview', in: J. Sarkin and W. Binchy (eds.), *Human Rights, the Citizen and the State. South African and Irish Approaches* (Dublin, Round Hall Sweet & Maxwell 2001) p. 52 at p. 60.

100 See Ward 1994, *supra* n. 43, at p. 407; Koegler 1996, *supra* n. 15, at p. 1136; Sterling 1997, *supra* n. 41, at p. 385; Buckley 1998, *supra* n. 41, at p. 290; Mercurio 2003, *supra* n. 42, at p. 166 and Mullally 2006, *supra* n. 71, at p. 629.

101 See Schweppe 2001, *supra* n. 43, at p. 145 and D. O'Connor, 'Limiting "public morality" exceptions to free movement in Europe: Ireland's role in a changing European Union', 22 *Brooklyn Journal of International Law* (1997) p. 695 at p. 708.

102 Sterling 1997, *supra* n. 41, at p. 386.

103 Sections 3 and 5 Regulation of Information (Services outside the State for Termination of Pregnancies) Act. See Schweppe 2001, *supra* n. 43, at p. 145 and Johansen 2003, *supra* n. 80, at p. 215.

104 Section 8 and 10 Regulation of Information (Services outside the State for Termination of Pregnancies) Act.

105 Pursuant to Art. 26 of the Irish Constitution the President may refer any bill to the Supreme Court for a determination of whether the bill is repugnant to any provision of the Constitution.

106 *Article 26 and the Regulation of Information (Services outside the State for Termination of Pregnancies) Bill* (1995) 2 ILRM 81, 107, [1995] 1 IR 1. See Schweppe 2001, *supra* n. 43, at p. 146. As various commentators have observed, this decision is significant, as for the first time the Court held

alia, held that once a woman had made an appointment with a foreign abortion clinic, the Act did not preclude Irish doctors and counsellors from communicating 'in the normal way' with the doctors from the foreign clinics with regard to the condition of their patients. Also, Irish doctors were free to give 'full information to a woman with regard to her state of health, the effect of the pregnancy thereon and the consequences to her health and life if the pregnancy continues', so as to enable her to make an informed decision about a pregnancy termination.

Following this ruling the 1995 Act became immune from future constitutional challenge.[107] A later challenge of (certain sections of) the Act before the ECtHR would prove unsuccessful (see section 5.2.6 below).

5.2.4. (Towards) the 2002 abortion referendum

In April 1995 a Constitution Review Group was established, with the task of establishing those areas where constitutional change could be necessary with a view to assisting the governmental committees in their constitutional review work. In its report of 1996 the Group considered that as a result of the *X Case* and the rejection of the Twelfth Amendment during the 1992 Referendum, the law on abortion in Ireland was unclear.[108] It therefore recommended the introduction of legislation to regulate the application of Article 40.3.3° within the terms of the *X Case*.[109] The report was followed-up by a *Green Paper on Abortion* (1999)[110] which gave seven possible constitutional and legislative solutions: (1) an absolute constitutional ban on abortion; (2) an amendment of the Constitution so as to restrict the application of the *X Case*; (3) the retention of the position applicable at the time; (4) the retention of the constitutional *status quo* with a legislative restatement of the prohibition of abortion; (5) legislation to regulate abortion as defined in the *X Case*; (6) a reversion to the pre-1983 position; and (7) permitting abortion beyond the grounds specified in the *X Case*. The Green Paper was referred to the all-party *Oireachtas* (Parliamentary) Committee on the Constitution. Despite a detailed process of consultation, this committee was unable to achieve consensus on any of the options set out in the paper.[111] In the meantime, the Supreme Court confirmed its ruling in the *X Case* in a very similar case, the so-called *C Case*.[112]

---

that amendments to the Constitution that violate natural law are acceptable. The Court considered that natural law was not antecedent and superior to the Constitution. O'Connor 1997, *supra* n. 101, at pp. 708–710; Buckley 1998, *supra* n. 41, at p. 291; Mullally 2006, *supra* n. 71, at p. 630 and A. O'Sullivan, 'Same-sex marriage and the Irish Constitution', 13 *The International Journal of Human Rights* (2009) p. 477 at p. 479.

107 Art. 34.3.3° of the Irish Constitution.

108 Report of the Constitution Review Group (1996, Pn 2632), p. 273–279.

109 *Idem.*

110 Office of the Taoiseach, *Green Paper on Abortion* (1999 Pn 7596), online available at www.taoiseach.gov.ie/upload/publications/251.rtf.

111 All Party Oireachtas Committee on the Constitution, *Fifth Report, Abortion* (2000) online available at www.taoiseach.gov.ie/attached_files/upload/publications/1434.pdf, visited 14 September 2010.

112 *A. and B.* v. *Eastern Health Board & C.* [1997] IEHC 176; [1998] 1 IR 464; [1998] 1 ILRM 460. See *supra* n. 76. See also Bacik 1997, *supra* n. 51.

The Government finally opted for amendment of the Constitution by taking away the threat of suicide as a ground for lawful abortion. It introduced the *Protection of Human Life in Pregnancy* Bill, which would from then on be the law on abortion in the State.[113] The proposed Bill provided for a definition of abortion,[114] and self-destruction was excluded as a ground for lawful abortion. If accepted, the new Act would thus overturn the *X Case*. As adoption of the Act required an amendment of the Constitution, the electorate was invited to a new Referendum, this time on the Twenty-Fifth Amendment of the Constitution. On 6 March 2002, a narrow majority – consisting of both pro-life and pro-choice supporters[115] – defeated the amendment.[116] Consequently the *X Case* remained the applicable abortion law.[117] Before this ruling could be codified in abortion legislation in 2013 (see section 5.2.8 below), its implications were challenged by new applications lodged with the ECtHR, as well as by a domestic procedure.

5.2.5. Abortion in case of lethal foetal abnormality? The cases of *D.* v. *Ireland* and *Miss D.*

In 2002 an application against Ireland was lodged with the ECtHR by a woman referred to as '*D.*' (see also Chapter 2, section 2.2.1). In late 2001 *D.* had become pregnant with twins. In early 2002 it became clear that one foetus had died in the womb and that the second foetus had a lethal abnormality. *D.* therefore decided that she could not carry the pregnancy to term. As she was informed in an Irish hospital that she had no right to an abortion in Ireland, she went to the United Kingdom for an abortion. She subsequently did not undertake any legal action in Ireland but immediately filed a complaint with the ECtHR.

Invoking Articles 3 and 8 ECHR, *D.* complained before the ECtHR about the need to travel abroad to have an abortion in the case of a lethal foetal abnormality. She held that the overall ban on abortion put an unduly harsh burden on women in her situation. She furthermore submitted that her right to receive information under

113 Explanatory Memorandum accompanying the Twenty-fifth Amendment of the Constitution (Protection of Human Life in Pregnancy Act 2002), Bill Number 48 of 2001. See also Schweppe 2001, *supra* n. 43, at pp. 136–162.

114 Section 1 of the Bill defined abortion as 'the intentional destruction by any means of unborn human life after implantation in the womb of a woman'.

115 Mercurio 2003, *supra* n. 42, at pp. 172–173. See also Johansen 2003, *supra* n. 80, at pp. 216–234, who explains that the wording of the Referendum was fraught with ambiguities.

116 50.42 per cent of those who voted, voted against the amendment, 49.58 per cent voted in favour of the amendment. As Mullally observes this proposal differed from the similar 1992 proposal, '[...] in that it protected the fetus' right to life only following implantation in the womb, thereby allowing for the use of contraceptives such as the morning-after pill.' Mullally 2006, *supra* n. 71, at p. 633. See also Johansen 2003, *supra* n. 80, at pp. 216 and 232–234. Schweppe criticised that '[...] putting a piece of technical legislation tot the people for approval [was] confusing'. Schweppe 2001, *supra* n. 43, at p. 156.

117 As confirmed in *Baby O.* v. *Minister for Justice, Equality and Law Reform* [2002] IESC 44; [2002] 2 IR 169. The possibility of termination of pregnancy when there is real and substantial risk to the life of the mother, was also explicitly recognised in Section 24.6 of the 2004 Medical Council's Guide to Ethical Conduct and Behaviour.

Article 10 ECHR had been violated in that the 1995 Abortion Information Act '[...] imposed unnecessary restraints on what a doctor could tell her and prohibited that doctor making proper arrangements, or a full referral, for an abortion abroad'.[118]

As also discussed in Chapter 2, in June 2006 the ECtHR declared the case inadmissible for non-exhaustion of domestic remedies. The government had asserted that a constitutional action had been available to the applicant and claimed that '[in] the absence of a domestic decision, it was impossible to foresee that Article 40.3.3° clearly excluded an abortion in the applicant's situation in Ireland.' They further argued that

> '[...] [if] it had been established that there was no realistic prospect of the foetus being born alive, then there was "at least a tenable" argument which would be seriously considered by the domestic courts to the effect that the foetus was not an "unborn" for the purposes of Article 40.3.3 or that, even if it was an "unborn", its right to life was not actually engaged as it had no prospect of life outside the womb.'

The Court indeed considered it arguable that an exception to the prohibition of abortion in Ireland could be made in cases of fatal foetal abnormality. In the Court's view there was '[...] a feasible argument to be made that the constitutionally enshrined balance between the right to life of the mother and of the foetus could have shifted in favour of the mother when the "unborn" suffered from an abnormality incompatible with life.' The Court accordingly found that at the time when *D.* lodged an application with the ECtHR, a legal constitutional remedy had in principle been available to her to obtain declaratory and mandatory orders with a view to obtaining a lawful abortion in Ireland.[119]

Soon after the ECtHR's inadmissibility decision – which inherently had no consequences for the Irish abortion legislation – a national case put the question of abortion in the case of lethal foetal abnormality back on the agenda.[120] The so-called 'Miss *D.* case' concerned a 17-year-old pregnant girl in the care of the Health Service Executive (HSE), who wished to have an abortion after she discovered that her foetus suffered from a lethal abnormality. When the HSE prevented her from travelling to the UK to obtain an abortion, the girl appealed to the High Court.[121] This Court did not decide the question of whether in situations of fatal foetal abnormality there was a right to abortion in Ireland, but simply ruled that there was no stay or

---

118 ECtHR 27 June 2006 (dec.), *D.* v. *Ireland*, no. 26499/02, para. 59.

119 *Idem*, para. 92.

120 As Donoghue and Smyth put it, the 'confidence of the European Court in the Irish judicial system [...] was soon dashed' by a subsequent national court case. S. Donoghue and C.-M. Smyth, 'Abortion for Foetal Abnormalities in Ireland; The Limited Scope of the Irish Government's Response to the A, B and C Judgment', 20 *European Journal of Health Law* (2013) p. 117 at p. 125.

121 *D (A Minor)* v. *District Judge Brennan, the Health Services Executive, Ireland and the Attorney General*, unreported judgment of the High Court of 9 May 2007. See *inter alia* www.ifpa.ie/node/396, visited June 2014 and B. Hewson, 'Ireland's Miss D: a 'bizarre dispute'', *Bpas Reproductive Review* (2007), online available at www.reproductivereview.org/index.php/rr/article/186, visited June 2014.

constitutional impediment which served to prevent Miss D. from travelling to the UK for terminating her pregnancy if she so wished.[122]

Late 2010, the ECtHR decided another Irish abortion case, a judgment which was highly relevant for cases like those of Miss D. In *A, B and C* v. *Ireland*, the Strasbourg Court addressed exactly the question whether the restrictive Irish abortion laws, implying that pregnant women have to go abroad for abortions on medical and social grounds, violated the Convention.

5.2.6. The ECtHR judgment in *A, B and C* v. *Ireland* (2010) and its follow-up in Ireland

As discussed more elaborately in Chapter 2, the ECtHR ruled in *A, B and C* v. *Ireland* that the Irish prohibition of abortion for health and well-being reasons '[...] based as it [was] on the profound moral views of the Irish people as to the nature of life and as to the consequent protection to be accorded to the right to life of the unborn', did not exceed the wide margin of appreciation accorded in that respect to Ireland.[123] The Court thereby had regard to 'the right to travel abroad lawfully for an abortion with access to appropriate information and medical care in Ireland'.[124] In respect of the complaint of the third applicant, who claimed that she did not have effective access to abortion in Ireland even though her pregnancy had posed a risk to her life, the Court instead found a violation of Article 8 ECHR. It held that Ireland had failed to provide for effective and accessible procedures which allowed her to establish her right to a lawful abortion in Ireland. It noted expressly that – as repeatedly pointed out at national level – the Irish government had failed to implement Article 40.3.3° and had not given any convincing explanations for this failure.[125]

Some called it 'bizarre' that until this ruling '[...] by refusing to enact any legislation concerning abortion successive Irish governments had managed to avoid the gaze of the European Court for a substantial period of time.'[126] Concretely the *A, B and C* judgment implicated that Ireland had to introduce legislation clarifying the circumstances under which a pregnancy posing a substantial risk to the life of the pregnant woman, could be terminated.[127] This has been qualified as 'more of a subtle change as opposed to a radical overhaul of the *status quo*.'[128] While it was argued by

122 O. Bowcott, 'Irish judge stirs up abortion debate by ruling 17-year-old can travel to UK for termination', *The Guardian* 10 May 2007, online available at www.theguardian.com/society/2007/may/10/health.frontpagenews, visited 29 April 2014.

123 ECtHR [GC] 16 December 2010, *A, B and C* v. *Ireland*, no. 25579/05, para. 226.

124 *Idem*, para. 241.

125 *Idem*, para. 265.

126 Donoghue and Smyth 2013, *supra* n. 120, at p. 140.

127 S. McGuinness, 'Commentary. A, B, and C leads to D (for Delegation!)', 19 *Medical Law Review* (2011) p. 476 at p. 476.

128 See, *inter alia*, J. Schweppe, 'Taking Responsibility for the "Abortion Issue": Some Thoughts on Legislative Reform in the Aftermath of A, B and C', 14 *Irish Journal of Family Law* (2011) p. 50 and B. Daly, '"Braxton Hick's" or the Birth of a New Era? Tracing the Development of Ireland's Abortion Laws in Respect of European Court of Human Rights Jurisprudence', *European Journal of Health*

some that there was no need at all to legislate and that the Irish people were entitled to determine future abortion policy,[129] it was widely acknowledged that as a result of the *A, B and C* ruling, the government could no longer refuse to legislate on the matter. However, some warned that, because of its 'long history of fudging the issue of abortion' no quick or direct response to the ruling could be expected from the Irish government.[130]

The government confirmed that it would study the ruling,[131] but did not act very speedily. Some politicians indicated that other political concerns, such as 'restoring sound political finances' had to be given priority and that a re-run of the abortion debates was not what the country needed at that point in time.[132] Nonetheless, in June 2011 the government submitted an action plan of the implementation of the *A, B and C* judgment to the Committee of Ministers of the Council of Europe. The action plan included the establishment of an expert group by November 2011 to make recommendations on such implementation.[133] There were, moreover, other international bodies at the time calling on Ireland to undertake action. The UN Special Rapporteur on the situation of human rights defenders recommended to implement the *X Case* and the *A, B and C* judgment by introducing the necessary legislation and medical guidelines regarding access to legal abortion.[134] Further, in its report on Ireland of September 2011 the Commissioner for Human Rights of the Council of Europe noted with concern that there was still no legislation in place to set a framework allowing for abortion in limited circumstances where a woman's life was deemed to be in danger because of pregnancy and expressed his hope that a 'coherent legal framework including adequate services' would be put in place without delay. The Commissioner reiterated his position that the lack of legislation adversely affected women who did not have the financial means to seek medical services outside the country and were therefore 'particularly vulnerable.'[135]

Law 18 (2011) pp. 375–395 at p. 394. See also S. Donnelly, 'A, B and C v Ireland: A Commentary', 17 *Medico-Legal Journal of Ireland* (2011) p. 43.

129 Opening statement by William Binchy to the Joint Committee on Health and Children, online available at www.oireachtas.ie/parliament/media/committees/healthandchildren/William-Binchy.pdf, visited June 2014.

130 McGuinness 2011, *supra* n. 127, at p. 488.

131 *Irish Times* 21 December 2010, www.irishtimes.com/newspaper/frontpage/2010/1221/1224285993635.html, visited 21 January 2011.

132 *Irish Times* 28 December 2010, www.irishtimes.com/newspaper/frontpage/2010/1228/1224286367982.html, visited 21 January 2011.

133 *ACTION Plan. A, B, and C v. Ireland, Application no 25579/2005, Grand Chamber judgment 16 December 2010*, Information submitted by the Government of Ireland on 30 November 2012, online available at www.health.gov.ie/wp-content/uploads/2014/03/Action_Plan_ABCvIreland_Nov2012.pdf, visited 2 March 2014.

134 Human Rights Council Twenty-second session Agenda item 3 Promotion and protection of all human rights, civil, political, economic, social and cultural rights, including the right to development, Report of the Special Rapporteur on the situation of human rights defenders, Margaret Sekaggya, Addendum, Mission to Ireland (19–23 November 2012), p. 21.

135 Report by the Commissioner for Human Rights of the Council of Europe, following his visit to Ireland 1- 2 June 2011, CommDH(2011)27, Strasbourg, 15 September 2011, p. 7. See also Report by the Commissioner for Human Rights on his visit to Ireland 26–30 November 2007, CommDH(2008)9, Strasbourg 30 April 2008, p. 23 ff.

In January 2012, the government submitted an Action Report to the Committee of Ministers in which it indicated that the expert group would complete its report within six months.[136] While in March the Committee of Ministers expressed its concerns and strongly encouraged the Irish authorities to ensure that the expert group completed its work as quickly as possible,[137] the report only came out in November 2012. Its completion may well have been prompted by the controversial death of a pregnant woman in a Galway hospital in October 2012.[138]

5.2.7. Towards abortion legislation

In November 2012 Irish (and subsequently international) media reported about the death of Savita Halappanavar.[139] This 31-year-old woman had been hospitalised in Galway in late October, where she was soon found to be miscarrying. During her hospitalisation Halappanavar repeatedly asked for an abortion, but the doctors refused to terminate the pregnancy as long as the foetus had a heartbeat. After three days in hospital, during which Halappanavar's condition had seriously deteriorated, the foetus' heartbeat stopped. A couple of days later Halappanavar passed away. Her death sparked public protests[140] and refuelled the Irish abortion debate.[141] An investigation into the case by the Health Service Executive revealed that '[t]he interpretation of the law related to lawful termination in Ireland, and particularly the lack of clear clinical guidelines and training [was] considered to have been a material contributory factor' to the death of Halappanavar.[142] The doctors had felt

136 DH-DD (2012)66, online available at www.wcd.coe.int/com.instranet.InstraServlet?command=com.instranet.CmdBlobGet&InstranetImage=2016427&SecMode=1&DocId=1848792&Usage=2, visited 15 May 2014.

137 DH-DD(2011)480, DH-DD(2012)66E, DH-DD(2011)645 and DH-DD(2011)628E, online available at www.wcd.coe.int/ViewDoc.jsp?Ref=CM/Del/Dec%282012%291136/12&Language=lanEnglish&Ver=original&Site=CM&BackColorInternet=C3C3C3&BackColorIntranet=EDB021&BackColorLogged=F5D383, visited 15 May 2014.

138 M.A. Rhinehart, 'Abortions in Ireland: Reconciling a History of Restrictive Abortion Practices with the European Court of Human Rights' Ruling in *A., B. & C.* v. *Ireland*', 117 *Penn State Law Review* (2012–2013) p. 959 at p. 973.

139 E.g. K. Holland, 'Woman 'denied a termination' dies in hospital', *The Irish Times* 14 November 2012, www.irishtimes.com/news/woman-denied-a-termination-dies-in-hospital-1.551412, visited 15 May 2014 and 'Woman dies after abortion request 'refused' at Galway hospital', BBC News 14 November 2012, online available at www.bbc.com/news/uk-northern-ireland-20321741, visited 15 May 2014.

140 'Ireland: Savita Halappanavar tragedy sparks public protests', Bpas reproductive review 19 November 2012, www.abortionreview.org/index.php/rr/article/1258, visited 15 May 2014.

141 See also A.A. Sheikh, 'Medico-Legal Aspects of the Savita Halappanavar Case', 18 *Medico-Legal Journal of Ireland* (2012) p. 58; M. Berer, 'Termination of pregnancy as emergency obstetric care: the interpretation of Catholic health policy and the consequences for pregnant women. An analysis of the death of Savita Halappanavar in Ireland and similar cases', 41 *Reproductive Health Matters* (2013) p. 9 and C. O'Sullivan et al., 'Article 40.3.3 and the Protection of Life During Pregnancy Bill 2013: The Impetus for, and Process of, Legislative Change', 3 *Irish Journal of Legal Studies* (2013) p. 1.

142 Health Service Executive of Ireland, *Investigation of Incident 50278 from time of patient's self referral to hospital on the 21st of October 2012 to the patient's death on the 28th of October, 2012, Final report,* June 2013, p. 73, online available at www.hse.ie/eng/services/news/nimtreport50278.pdf, visited 15 May 2014.

that under Irish law their hands were tied so long as there was a foetal heartbeat.[143] The investigation team was '[...] satisfied that concerns about the law, whether clear or not, impacted on the exercise of clinical professional judgement', and noted that there was '[...] an immediate and urgent requirement for a clear statement of the legal context in which clinical professional judgement [could] be exercised in the best medical welfare interests of patients'.[144]

The report on the implementation of *A, B and C* by the government appointed expert group, came out just after the Halappanavar case had become publicly known, which had refuelled the abortion debate.[145] The expert group had explored four options for implementation of the *A, B and C* judgment: (clinical) guidelines; statutory regulations; legislation alone; and legislation in combination with regulation. It was held that the adoption of non-statutory guidelines only, would not be sufficient.[146] After the CoE's Committee of Ministers had once again urged the Irish authorities to expedite the implementation of the *A, B and C* judgment,[147] the government announced in December 2012 the introduction of a combination of legislation and guidelines.[148]

Subsequently a Parliamentary Committee on Health and Children held public hearings with stakeholders on the matter.[149] This resulted in the publication of the *Protection of Life During Pregnancy Bill* 2013 in early May 2013.[150] The Bill prompted a divided response; while the Irish Prime Minister held that the Bill did not amount to a change in the law,[151] the Roman Catholic Church in Ireland reportedly called the legislation 'a dramatically and morally unacceptable change to Irish law'.[152] Some authors were very critical of the floodgate arguments that were voiced in the debates over the Bill, '[...] suggesting (either implicitly or expressly) that the introduction of abortion legislation within [the existing] constitutional boundaries

143 *Idem*, p. 33.

144 Health Service Executive of Ireland, Investigation of Incident 50278 from time of patient's self referral to hospital on the 21st of October 2012 to the patient's death on the 28th of October, 2012, Final report, June 2013, p. 73, online available at www.hse.ie/eng/services/news/nimtreport50278.pdf, visited 15 May 2014, pp. 69 and 74.

145 S. Ryan et al., *Report of the expert group on the judgment in A, B and C v Ireland*, Department of Health and Children, 2012, November 2012. The report is online available at www.ifpa.ie/sites/default/files/judgment_abc.pdf, visited 15 May 2014.

146 *Idem*, p. 45.

147 Council of Europe Committee of Ministers 1157th CDDH meeting, 6 December 2012, case No. 12, Case against Ireland, DH-DD(2011)480 a.o., www.wcd.coe.int/ViewDoc.jsp?id=2010979&Site=CM&BackColorInternet=C3C3C3&BackColorIntranet=EDB021&BackColorLogged=F5D383, visited 2 May 2014.

148 See www.ifpa.ie/Hot-Topics/Abortion/Abortion-in-Ireland-Timeline, visited 15 May 2014.

149 See also O'Sullivan et al. 2013, *supra* n. 141.

150 Bill no. 66 of 2013. By that time two Private Members Bills to implement the *X Case* had been rejected in the Parliament. See the IFPA website www.ifpa.ie/Hot-Topics/Abortion/Abortion-in-Ireland-Timeline, visited 15 May 2014.

151 'Abortion bill 'does not change' Irish law, says Kenny', BBC News 1 May 2013, www.bbc.com/news/world-europe-22363459, visited 15 May 2014.

152 D. Dalby, 'Irish Catholic Church Condemns Abortion Legislation', *The New York Times* 3 May 2013, www.nytimes.com/2013/05/04/world/europe/irish-catholic-church-condemns-abortion-legislation.html?_r=1&, visited 15 May 2014.

would only be a starting point, following which so-called "abortion on demand" would flow.'[153] They warned that the legislative process was in any case bound by the existing constitutional position.[154] As it was standing law since the *X Case* that a risk to the life of the mother could also consist of a suicide risk, '[...] much concern focused on the provision for pregnant women who [were] suicidal.'[155]

After an injunction aimed at preventing the Bill from being voted into law was refused,[156] it was adopted in Parliament ('*Dáil*') by a clear majority mid-July 2013.[157] During the day-long debates, the government had defeated 166 amendments.[158] On 30 July, a few days after the Senate ('*Seanad*') had passed the Bill, President Higgins signed off on the Act, without referring it to the Supreme Court.[159] The first Irish abortion act was thus enacted without a Court ruling and also without the Irish people having had a vote in a referendum.

5.2.8. The Protection of Life during Pregnancy Act (2014)

The Protection of life during Pregnancy Act entered into force 1 January 2014.[160] Following its Explanatory Memorandum, the main purpose of the Act is '[...] to restate the general prohibition on abortion in Ireland while regulating access to lawful termination of pregnancy in accordance with the *X Case* and the judgment of the European Court of Human rights in the *A, B and C* v. *Ireland* case.'[161] It is, furthermore, clarified that its purpose is '[...] to confer procedural rights on a woman who believes she has a life-threatening condition, so that she can have certainty as to whether she requires this treatment or not.'[162]

The Act repealed Sections 58 and 59 of the Offences Against the Person Act 1861.[163] Instead, the new Section 22 makes the intentional destruction of unborn human life an offence, liable on indictment to an unlimited fine or imprisonment for a term of

---

153 F. de Londras and L. Graham, 'Impossible Floodgates and Unworkable Analogies in the Irish Abortion Debate', 3 *Irish Journal of Legal Studies* (2013), p. 54.

154 *Idem*, at p. 59.

155 L. Smith-Spark and P. Taggart, 'Ireland's government puts forward draft abortion bill', CNN 1 May 2013, www.edition.cnn.com/2013/05/01/world/europe/ireland-abortion, visited 15 May 2014. On this issue, see F. de Londras, 'Suicide and Abortion: Analysing the Legislative Options in Ireland', 19 *Medico-Legal Journal of Ireland* 2013, p. 4.

156 'President of the High Court refuses abortion bill challenge', RTÉ news 17 July 2013, www.rte.ie/news/2013/0711/461938-abortion-court, visited 15 May 2014.

157 'Dáil votes in favour of abortion legislation', RTÉ News 12 July 2013, www.rte.ie/news/2013/0712/462013-abortion-law, visited 16 May 2014.

158 *Idem*.

159 M. O'Halloran, 'Seanad passes abortion legislation by 39 votes to 14', *Irish Times* 23 July 2013, www.irishtimes.com/news/politics/oireachtas/seanad-passes-abortion-legislation-by-39-votes-to-14-1.1472840 and 'President Higgins signs abortion Bill into law', *Irish Times* 30 July 2013, www.irishtimes.com/news/politics/president-higgins-signs-abortion-bill-into-law-1.1479519.

160 Protection of life during Pregnancy Act, No. 35/ 2013.

161 Explanatory Memorandum to the Protection of Life during Pregnancy Bill 2013, pp. 1–2.

162 *Idem*, p. 2.

163 Section 5 Protection of life during Pregnancy Act.

14 years at maximum, or both.[164] This implies that also the woman concerned may herself be prosecuted for having an abortion. Even though it was recognised that the potential criminalisation of a pregnant woman was 'a very difficult and sensitive matter', this provision was held to reflect 'the State's constitutional obligation arising from Article 40.3.3'.[165] The offence also applies to a body corporate.[166]

Interestingly and unprecedented in Ireland, the Act provides for a definition of the term 'unborn' within the meaning of the Act. It is clarified that:

> '[...] "unborn", in relation to a human life, is a reference to such a life during the period of time commencing after implantation in the womb of a woman and ending on the complete emergence of the life from the body of the woman'.[167]

This definition confirms and reflects the *Roche* v. *Roche* judgment of 2006, as discussed below in section 5.3.1, following which the protection of the unborn life is dependent on its presence in the woman's body. Also, this definition clearly excludes the preimplantation phase, implying that the prohibition on the destruction of unborn life does not cover medication like the morning after pill.[168]

The Act strictly defines the circumstances under which an abortion in Ireland may be lawful. Following Section 7 of the Act, this is so when

> '[...] two medical practitioners, having examined the pregnant woman, have jointly certified in good faith that (i) there is a real and substantial risk of loss of the woman's life from a physical illness, and (ii) in their reasonable opinion (being an opinion formed in good faith which has regard to the need to preserve unborn human life as far as practicable) that risk can only be averted by carrying out the medical procedure'.

The abortion must be carried out by an obstetrician at an appropriate institution.[169] In emergency situations a medical practitioner may carry out an abortion without involvement of another practitioner if he or she (1) believes in good faith that there is an immediate risk of loss of the woman's life from a physical illness; and (2) considers the abortion, in his or her 'reasonable opinion',[170] immediately necessary in order to save the life of the woman. In situations where there is a real and substantial risk of loss of the woman's life by way of suicide, three medical practitioners (two psychiatrists and one obstetrician) must give approval. Their decision can be

---

164 Section 22 Protection of life during Pregnancy Act. See De Londras and Graham 2013, *supra* n. 153, at p. 72.

165 General Scheme of the Protection of Life during Pregnancy Bill 2013, p. 31.

166 Section 23 Protection of life during Pregnancy Act.

167 Section 2(1) Protection of life during Pregnancy Act.

168 See also Schweppe 2001, *supra* n. 43, at p. 154.

169 Section 7(1)(b) Protection of life during Pregnancy Act. A list of 'appropriate institutions' is annexed to the Act.

170 This is described in Section 7(1)(a)(ii) Protection of life during Pregnancy Act as 'an opinion formed in good faith which has regard to the need to preserve unborn human life as far as practicable'.

appealed through a committee which must meet within seven days and give notice of its determination in writing to the woman and the Executive.[171]

Given that the Act only provides for situations where the life of the pregnant woman is at risk, no time limits are laid down in the Act.[172] The protection of medical practitioners, nurses and midwives with conscientious objections is provided for, save in emergency situations.[173] It is, furthermore, once again affirmed 'for the avoidance of doubt'[174] that the Act does not limit the freedom to travel to other States for an abortion and to obtain or make available in Ireland, 'in accordance with conditions for the time being laid down by law', information relating to abortion services lawfully available in another state.[175]

Following the entry into force of the Act, the Medical Council published an updated version of its Guidelines,[176] which, *inter alia*, provide that in exceptional circumstances a therapeutic intervention may be required during pregnancy, '[...] which may result in there being little or no hope of the baby surviving'.[177] Whether there is a real and substantial risk to the life of the pregnant woman which cannot be averted by other means, must be assessed 'in light of current evidence based best practice'.[178]

The new legislation has been criticised by Members of Parliament and campaigners from both sides in the abortion debate.[179]

5.2.9. Criminal prosecutions for abortions in Ireland

There have in the past '[...] been a number of prosecutions in Ireland under the provisions of the 1861 Act'.[180] However, statistics of Ireland's National Police

171 Section 13 Protection of life during Pregnancy Act.

172 See De Londras and Graham 2013, *supra* n. 153, at p. 61.

173 Section 17 Protection of life during Pregnancy Act.

174 General scheme of the Protection of Life during Pregnancy Bill 2013 (30 April 2013), p. 25, online available at www.static.rasset.ie/documents/news/protection-of-life-during-pregancy-bill.pdf, visited 16 May 2014.

175 Section 18 Protection of life during Pregnancy Act.

176 See www.medicalcouncil.ie/News-and-Publications/Publications/Information-for-Doctors/Medical-Council-Guide.html, visited 15 May 2014. The Guidelines are online available at www./bit.ly/RMPGuide. See also F. Gartland, 'Medical Council to bring out new guidelines following commencement of abortion law, *The Irish Times* 1 January 2014, online available at www.irishtimes.com/news/crime-and-law/medical-council-to-bring-out-new-guidelines-following-commencement-of-abortion-law-1.1641663, visited 15 May 2014 and M. Brennan, 'Delay in abortion guidelines not our fault, say medical professionals', *Independente.ie* 2 January 2014, www.independent.ie/irish-news/delay-in-abortion-guidelines-not-our-fault-say-medical-professionals-29882036.html, visited 16 May 2014.

177 *Idem*, Principle 21.2.

178 *Idem*, Principle 21.3.

179 'New abortion guidelines spark condemnation on all sides', *thejournal.ie* 4 July 2014, www.thejournal.ie/abortion-guidelines-ireland-1554267-Jul2014, visited 28 May 2014.

180 Sherlock 1989, *supra* n. 10.

Service show that prosecution practice has historically been very limited, in any case between the late 1940s and the early 1990s.[181] The annual reports that the National Police Service has published on its website for the years since then, only occasionally include statistics. The reports that do, namely those for the years 1998, 2000, 2003 and 2004, show that in those respective years no proceedings for the offence of procuring an abortion were commenced.[182] Further, only four abortion offences were reported to the Police in 2004, but these did not (in that year) result in the commencement of criminal proceedings.[183] Statistics in the annual reports of the Director of Public Prosecutions (DPP) for the past decade,[184] do not expressly provide for the offence of procuring a miscarriage, rendering it difficult to draw conclusions in this respect.[185] All in all, nonetheless, it seems safe to conclude that prosecution practice for abortion has been limited in Ireland. This is confirmed by the submission of the Irish government before the ECtHR in the *A, B and C* case that in respect of abortion '[t]here had been no criminal prosecution of a doctor in living memory'.[186]

5.2.10. Public funding for abortions in Ireland

Because abortion is only legally accessible in Ireland to save the life of the mother, it logically follows that this treatment is also covered by the national statutory health scheme. Abortions on any other ground are not legal in Ireland and are therefore also not reimbursed for under the Public Health Insurance.

---

181 The statistics on the website of Ireland's National Police Service go back to 1947. See www.garda.ie/Controller.aspx?Page=8824&Lang=1, visited 28 May 2014. As these statistics show, during the years 1947–1991 no reports of abortion offences were made to the police, with the exception of the years 1949–1951, 1958–1959, 1964 and 1968–1969. The number for these years are as follows: in 1949 two cases were reported and acquitted; in 1950 proceedings were commenced in two cases and in 1951 two cases were reported. In 1958 proceedings were commenced in one case, which resulted in an acquittal in 1958. In 1964 three cases were reported, resulting in one acquittal and two convictions. In 1968 in one reported case proceedings were commenced, which were still pending in 1969. The statistics for the subsequent years show no reports at all for the offence of procuring an abortion, rendering it unclear what the final outcome of the 1968 case was. Further, in 1948 and 1956 respectively a case was reported of a woman who died as the result of an abortion. In those cases charges were brought for murder. Report of the Commissioner of the Gárda Síochána on crime for the year 1948, p. 5, online available at www.garda.ie/Documents/User/2%201948%20Commissioners%20Report.pdf, visited 28 May 2014, and Report of the Commissioner of the Gárda Síochána on crime for the year 1956, p. 6, online available at www.garda.ie/Documents/User/3%201956%20Commissioners%20Report.pdf, visited 28 May 2014.

182 The respective reports are online available at www.garda.ie/Controller.aspx?Page=90&Lang=1, visited 28 May 2014.

183 See 'Year 2004 crime statistics, An Garda Síochána Annual Report 2004, p. 28, online availbale at www.garda.ie/Documents/User/Annual%20Report%202004%20-%20Stats.pdf, visited 28 May 2014.

184 Online available at www.dppireland.ie/publications/category/7/annual-reports/archive, visited 16 May 2014.

185 This also holds for statistics from the Central Statistics Office, as online available at www.cso.ie/Quicktables/GetQuickTables.aspx?FileName=cja01c1.asp&TableName=Homicide+Offences&StatisticalProduct=DB_CJ, visited 2 June 2014.

186 ECtHR [GC] 16 December 2010, *A, B and C* v. *Ireland*, no. 25579/05, para. 189.

5.3. (The absence of) Irish legislation on assisted human reproduction and surrogacy

While assisted reproductive technologies have existed in Ireland since the 1980s,[187] there is no specific legal framework in Ireland that regulates assisted human reproduction.[188] Consequently, procedures like IVF treatment involving gamete donation and surrogacy are not prohibited in Ireland, but are veiled in considerable legal uncertainty. This also holds for the family law implications of such treatment.[189]

The only form of regulation of the area has consisted of regulations transposing the EU Tissue and Cells Directives[190] and of guidelines by the medical profession, such as the Institute of Obstetricians and Gynaecologists (IOG) of the Royal College of Physicians of Ireland,[191] and more profoundly, the Irish Medical Council.[192] The latter's *Guide to professional conduct and ethics for registered medical practitioners* holds that '[...] assisted human reproduction treatments, such as In Vitro Fertilisation (IVF), should only be used after thorough investigation has shown that no other treatment is likely to be effective.'[193] Medical practitioners '[...] should ensure that appropriate counselling has been offered to the patient and that the patient has given informed consent before receiving any treatment.' The principles, furthermore, state that '[...] assisted reproduction services should only be provided by suitably qualified professionals, in appropriate facilities, and according to international best practice.' Thereby 'regular clinical audit and follow-up of outcomes should be the norm.'[194] No further guidance on AHR treatment is given in the guidelines.[195]

---

187 H. Coveney, 'Assisted Reproductive Technologies and the Status of the Embryo', 13 *Medico-Legal Journal of Ireland* (2007) p. 14 at p. 14. See also McMahon 2011, *supra* n. 10, at p. 33.

188 State of affairs on 31 July 2014.

189 In 2001 Madden observed the following: 'The vast array of permutations and combinations now possible in the creation of a child makes it extremely difficult to draw any broad principles as to legal parenthood. In Ireland these difficulties are exacerbated by the lack of legislation setting out parental rights and responsibilities in cases where sperm or egg donation is used or where a surrogate mother gives birth to another couple's genetic child.' D. Madden, 'Recent Developments in Assisted Human Reproduction: Legal and Ethical Issues', 7 *Medico-Legal Journal of Ireland* (2001) pp. 53–62.

190 European Communities (Quality and Safety of Human Tissues and Cells) Regulations, Statutory Instrument No. 158 of 2006. See also D. Madden, 'Guest Editorial: Assisted Reproduction in Ireland – Time to Legislate', 17 *Medico-Legal Journal of Ireland* (2011) p. 3. These Regulations are further discussed in section 5.3.4 below. On the Tissue and Cells Directives, see ch. 3, section 3.3.2.

191 See www.rcpi.ie, visited 28 May 2014. See also D. Dooley, 'Assisted Reproduction: the pursuit of consensus?', 5 *Medico-Legal Journal of Ireland* (1999) p. 65. In respect of research the Opinions of the Irish Council for Bioethics are authorative. See also Clissmann and Barrett 2012, *supra* n. 19.

192 By virtue of Section 7(2)(i) of the Medical Practitioners Act 2007 a task of the Medical Council is to give guidance on all matters related to professional conduct and ethics for registered medical practitioners. See www.citizensinformation.ie/categories/health/women-s-health/fertility_treatment, visited 28 May 2014.

193 Irish Medical Council, *Guide to professional conduct and ethics for registered medical practitioners*, 7th edition 2009, principle 20.1, p. 20.

194 *Idem*, Principle 20.2, p. 20.

195 Reportedly in 2011, Guidelines were drawn up in 2011 by the Irish Fertility Society. These Guidelines, which are not publicly available on the website of this Society, reportedly 'mirror most of the guidelines in the [...] 2005 Report [of the AHR Commission]'. Submission by Dr. Wingfield to the High Court in *M.R. & Another* v. *An t Ard Chláraitheoir* [2013] IEHC 91. On the report of the AHR Commission, see below.

AHR services are not provided by the public health services, but by private specialists and clinics only.[196] Because not all providers are registered medical practitioners, some '[...] fall outside of the remit of the Medical Council.'[197] In view of the existing legal vacuum, some private clinics set up their own rules. The Human Assisted Reproduction Ireland (HARI),[198] for example, provided on its website for 'rules and regulations', which included criteria that couples had to meet to qualify for an IVF treatment (see also the discussion on eligibility criteria below in section 5.3.3).[199] Other clinics expressly informed their clients about the persistent legal limbo and advised clients to obtain legal advice.[200]

As the (previous editions of the) Medical Council's guidelines were held to be '[...] insufficient because they [did] not have legal standing and many people involved in assisted human reproduction [were] not medical practitioners',[201] Senator Henry initiated a Bill in 1999 that provided for the regulation of providers of assisted human reproduction.[202] For unclear reasons, this Bill was, however, defeated and never made it into law. Soon thereafter, in March 2000, the Minister for Health and Children established a Commission on Assisted Human Reproduction (hereafter 'AHR Commission' or 'Commission'), with the following terms of reference:

> '[...] to prepare a report on the possible approaches to the regulation of all aspects of assisted human reproduction and the social, ethical and legal factors to be taken into account in determining public policy in the area.'[203]

One of the questions put before the Commission was whether legislation was necessary to regulate AHR or whether society had to continue to rely on voluntary regulation by the Irish Medical Council. In March 2005 the Commission published a report in which it made 40 recommendations.[204] The principal recommendation of the Commission was the drafting of a new Act to establish a regulatory body to regulate AHR services in Ireland.[205] 'In view of the major social, ethical and legal implications of assisted human reproduction for society in general as well as for the providers and users of services [...]', the AHR Commission believed that

196 See the website of the Health Service Executive www.hse.ie/eng/health/az/I/IVF, visited 16 May 2014.

197 B. Scannell, 'Brave New World? The Ethics of Pre-implantation Genetic Diagnosis in Ireland', 13 *Medico-Legal Journal of Ireland* (2007) pp. 27–35.

198 *Human Assisted Reproduction Ireland* (HARI) is based at the Rotunda Hospital campus in Dublin and is one of the largest centres for Assisted Reproductive Technology in Ireland.

199 Such couples are defined by HARI in its online rules and regulations as: 'A couple, aged 18 years and upwards who have been cohabiting on a permanent basis for a minimum of 2 years and who are committed to a long term relationship in which they can raise a child.' See www.hari.ie/index.php?section=hari&page=rules_and_regulations, visited September 2010.

200 See, for example, the website of the Irish *Sims IVF* clinic www.eggdonation.ie/, visited September 2010.

201 Dr Henry, Seanad Éireann – Volume 160 – 07 July, 1999. Regulation of Assisted Human Reproduction Bill, 1999: Second Stage. See also the Explanatory Memorandum to the Bill, p. 1.

202 Regulation of Assisted Human Reproduction Bill, Bill No. 7 of 1999. p. 1.

203 The Commission on Assisted Human Reproduction 2005, *supra* n. 9, pp. 32–33.

204 *Idem.*

205 *Idem*, p XV, Recommendation 1.

the guidelines from the Irish Medical Council on their own did not constitute a sufficient form of regulation.[206] Following the Commission's proposal the regulatory body had to be independent and publicly accountable to the government through the Department of Health and Children. It was to have: (1) the function of advising the government on all matters relating to AHR and associated procedures including research; (2) the authority to issue guidelines in relation to the provision of AHR services and associated procedures including research within the jurisdiction; (3) be authorised to issue licences for AHR procedures; and (4) have power to suspend or revoke a licence for stated reasons.[207]

In May 2005 the Minister for Health and Children referred the AHR Report to the *Oireachtas* Joint Committee on Health and Children for consideration. In November 2009 the Irish Minister for Health and Children informed the *Oireachtas* that her department was developing proposals for an appropriate regulatory framework, including legislation, in respect of AHR.[208] Thereto the approaches to regulation of AHR in other jurisdictions were examined and arising 'complex and profound' ethical, social and legal issues were considered. According to the Minister areas such as legal parentage; access to treatment services; donation of sperm, ova and embryos; and arrangements for consent, were explored and examined.[209] Only in 2014 did all this result in the initiation of a Bill dealing with certain issues pertaining to AHR, such as the establishment of paternity in donation cases (see 5.3.2 below). Until that time, the persisting lack of legislation inevitably resulted in issues concerning AHR being put before the judiciary. The courts, however, turned the tables on the legislature and held in the *Roche* v. *Roche* case that the *Oireachtas* had to be the first to act.[210]

5.3.1. The *Roche* v. *Roche* case (2006 and 2009)

The case of *Roche* v. *Roche* is the Irish equivalent of the *Evans* case which was decided by the ECtHR.[211] In 1994 Mrs. Roche underwent surgery for an ovarian cyst and she lost two thirds of her right ovary. In 2001 she and her husband commenced IVF treatment, which resulted in the creation of six viable embryos. Three were inserted into Mrs. Roche's uterus and the remaining three were frozen. Consequently Mrs. Roche became pregnant and in October 2002 she gave birth to a daughter. Towards the end of her pregnancy, marital difficulties arose between Mr. and Mrs. Roche. An attempt at reconciliation failed and the parties eventually entered into a judicial separation. Subsequently, Mrs. Roche wished to have the three frozen embryos implanted into her uterus, but Mr. Roche opposed. Mrs. Roche claimed to

206 *Idem*, at p.67. The Commission relied on a background research paper prepared by the Department of Foreign Affairs on relevant legislation in other countries of December 2001.

207 *Idem*, at p. 70.

208 Dáil Debate Vol. 693 No. 2 (4 November 2009) Answer of the Minister for Health and Children to question by deputy Liz McManus, question no. 86 [39291/09].

209 *Idem*.

210 *M. R.* v. *T. R. & Ors* [2006] IEHC 359, McGovern J.

211 See ch. 2, section 2.3.2.

be entitled to have the frozen embryos implanted into her womb against the wishes of her estranged husband. She asserted before the High Court that the embryos enjoyed the protection of Article 40.3.3° of the Irish constitution and that this provision required that their right to life would be vindicated by permitting her to have them implanted into her womb.

The High Court first dealt with the private law aspect of the case. In July 2006 Justice McGovern held that there was no agreement, either expressed or implied, as to what was to be done with the frozen embryos in the circumstances that had arisen. Accordingly, Mr. Roche had not entered into an agreement which required him to give his consent to the implantation of the three frozen embryos into Mrs. Roche's uterus.[212] Subsequently, in November 2006, Justice McGovern dealt with the question of whether the frozen embryos were 'unborn' for the purposes of Article 40.3.3° of the Irish Constitution. He held that it was not for the Courts to decide whether the word 'unborn' included embryos *in vitro*; holding it to be '[...] a matter for the Oireachtas, or for the people, in the event that a Constitutional Amendment [was] put before them'. Justice McGovern referred to the findings of the AHR Commission (see above) which had recommended that the embryo formed by IVF was not to attract legal protection until placed in the human body, at which stage it was to attract the same level of protection as the embryo formed *in vivo*.[213] McGovern came to the conclusion that the three frozen embryos were not 'unborn' within the meaning of Article 40.3.3° and were accordingly not given protection by the Irish Constitution. The Justice held it to be a matter for the Oireachtas 'to decide what steps should be taken to establish the legal status of embryos *in vitro*.'[214]

Mrs. Roche's appeal to the Supreme Court was dismissed in December 2009 as the highest judicial body in Ireland also deferred to the legislature. Chief Justice Murray held that the embryo had 'a moral status' and found that the creation and use of the human embryo could not be 'divorced from our concepts of human dignity'.[215] The Chief Justice held the point at which legal protection of the unborn life had to be deemed to commence, to be a policy choice for the Oireachtas:

> 'I do not consider that it is for a court of law, faced with the most divergent if most learned views in the discourses available to it from the disciplines referred to, to pronounce on the truth of when precisely human life begins. Absent a broad consensus or understanding on that truth, it is for legislatures in the exercise of their dispositive powers to resolve such issues on the basis of policy choices.'[216]

212 *R.* v. *R. & Ors* [2006] IEHC 221, McGovern J.
213 *Idem.*
214 *M. R.* v. *T. R. & Ors* [2006] IEHC 359, McGovern J.
215 *Roche* v. *Roche & ors* [2009] IESC 82, Murray CJ.
216 *Idem.*

Justice Fennelly found it 'disturbing' that 'no legislative proposal had even been formulated', some four years after the report of the AHR Commission.[217]

The judgment evoked concerns about the status and legal protection of the embryo *in vitro*.[218] It was held '[...] quite unusual for a constitution to give such strong protection to the in utero embryo while simultaneously giving none to the in vitro embryo'.[219] Many authors underlined that the case demonstrated (once more) the need for legislation in the area and were critical of the persisting legal limbo.[220]

5.3.2. Developments since *Roche* v. *Roche*

After the *Roche* v. *Roche* judgment, the Minister for Health reportedly '[...] accepted that it had a responsibility to introduce legislation in relation to AHR and that a legislative proposal would be brought before the Cabinet as soon as possible.'[221] Even though 'Legal Aspects of Human Reproduction' was one of the 37 projects of the Irish Law Reform Commission for the period 2008–2014,[222] this promise to act without further ado, was not kept. In 2011 Madden observed the following in respect of the Irish situation:

> 'Despite the availability of IVF and associated procedures in Ireland for many years, the clear need for legislative safeguards and oversight has not found its way into the statute books to date. This lacuna leaves Irish families and children, as well as clinicians working in this area, in a position fraught with difficulties and uncertainties. Lack of clarity about issues such as access to treatments, the status and parentage of children, the rights and responsibilities of genetic and birth parents, the legitimacy of payment for reproductive services, and the use of embryos for research purposes has left us in a complicated web of potential legal pitfalls which is the responsibility of Government to untangle.'[223]

---

217 *Roche* v. *Roche & ors* [2009] IESC 82, Fennelly J, para. 3. See also McMahon 2011, *supra* n. 10 and C. Hogan, 'JMcD v PL and BM Sperm Donor Fathers and De Facto Families', 13 *Irish Journal of Family Law* (2010) p. 83.

218 See Coveney 2007, *supra* n. 187; Madden 2011, *supra* n. 190 and G. Whyte,' The Moral Status of the Embryo', 12 *Medico-Legal Journal of Ireland* (2006) p. 77. See also A. Mulligan, 'Frozen Embryo Disposition In Ireland After *Roche v Roche*', 46 *The Irish Jurist* (2011) p. 202.

219 S. Mcguinness and S. Uí Chonnachtaigh, 'Implications of Recent Developments in Ireland for the Status of the Embryo, Special Section: Bioethics beyond Borders 2011', 20 *Cambridge Quarterly of Healthcare Ethics* (2011) p. 396 at p. 406.

220 E.g. Coveney 2007, *supra* n. 187, at p. 19; Hogan 2010, *supra* n. 217; McMahon 2011, *supra* n. 10; C. Power and G. Shannon, 'Practice and Procedure, Assisted reproduction in Ireland', 12 *Irish Journal of Family Law* (2009) p. 45 at p. 48 and Mcguinness and Uí Chonnachtaigh 2011, *supra* n. 219, at p. 406. See also C. Shanahan, 'Call to regulate assisted human reproduction', *irishexaminer.ie* 17 November 2010, www.irishexaminer.ie/ireland/call-to-regulate-assisted-human-reproduction-136703.html, visited March 2011.

221 Madden 2011, *supra* n. 190.

222 Law Reform Commission, *Report Third programme of law reform 2008–2014* (LRC 86 – 2007), December 2007, online available at www.lawreform.ie/_fileupload/Reports/ThirdProgramme.pdf, visited September 2010. See also Clissmann and Barrett 2012, *supra* n. 19.

223 Madden 2011, *supra* n. 190, at p. 5.

Some legislative action was finally taken in January 2014 with the publication of the Children and Family Relationship Bill (hereafter referred to as the '2014 Bill') by the then Minister for Justice, Equality and Defence. The Bill aimed to put in place a legal architecture which was intended to offer 'recognition and support to a wide range of different family structures.' The reforms envisaged focused 'more than ever before on the child at the centre of the family'.[224] The Bill – which has been referred to as 'truly historic'[225] and 'the most radical reform of Irish children's law in a century'[226] – was expected to be passed by the end of 2014.[227] For the present case study its parts 3 and 5 are of particular interest as they deal with parentage in cases of assisted reproduction and surrogacy arrangements respectively.

The following subsections of this section on Irish regulation in the field of AHR, discuss the existing (absence of) standard-setting for various types of AHR treatment. Thereby reference is made to both the recommendations of the AHR Commission on the specific matter, as well as (where applicable) to the relevant provisions of the 2014 Bill. First the issue of access to AHR treatment is discussed.

5.3.3. Access to AHR treatment

Access to AHR treatment has not been regulated at State level in Ireland. Certain requirements regarding civil status were, however, set by the medical profession, as well as by individual fertility clinics. Over the years they have softened their initially very strict conditions. For example, the 1994 edition of the Medical Council Guidelines limited the availability of AHR to married couples,[228] but subsequent editions of the Guidelines no longer included this condition.[229] *Human Assisted Reproduction Ireland* (HARI) made clear that it only provided IVF treatment to couples who were married or in a 'deemed stable relationship'.[230] Couples had to be able to demonstrate that 'an appropriate stable infrastructure' was in place which would 'maximise efficacy of therapy and safeguard the bringing up of a child.'[231] The Citizens' Information Board confirmed on its website that fertility services

224 Speech by the Minister for Justice, Equality and Defence, Alan Shatter TD, at the Children's Rights Alliance's Information Seminar on the Children and Family Relationships Bill, 10 April 2014, online available at www.justice.ie/en/JELR/Pages/SP14000104, visited 22 May 2014.

225 P. Duncan, 'New Bill 'won't devalue' traditional marital families', *Irishtimes.com* 10 April 2014, www.irishtimes.com/news/social-affairs/new-bill-won-t-devalue-traditional-marital-families-1.1757969, visited 21 May 2014.

226 F. Kelly, 'Bill to bring 'radical reform'', *Irishtimes.com* 17 April 2014, www.irishtimes.com/sponsored/ombudsman-for-children/bill-to-bring-radical-reform-1.1765188, visited 22 May 2014.

227 *Idem.*

228 See E.S. Sills and C.M. Healy, 'Building Irish families through surrogacy: medical and judicial issues for the advanced reproductive technologies', 5 *Reproductive Health* (2008), online available at www.reproductive-health-journal.com/content/5/1/9, visited September 2010. Reportedly also the guidelines laid down by the Institute of Obstetricians and Gynaecologists contained a similar restriction. Sherlock 1989, *supra* n. 10.

229 The Commission on Assisted Human Reproduction 2005, *supra* n. 9, at p. 32.

230 See *supra* n. 199.

231 Www.hari.ie/index.php?section=hari&page=rules_and_regulations, visited September 2010.

were generally available to applicants who were in a 'stable relationship', which was understood as to mean married and cohabiting opposite-sex couples. It was added that '[i]n practice, Irish clinics generally refuse[d] to make assisted reproduction available to cohabiting same-sex couples', while it had not yet been decided by an Irish court whether such a refusal amounted to discrimination on the grounds of sexual orientation under the Equal Status Act 2000 or the Equality Act 2004.[232]

Access to AHR was also discussed by the AHR Commission in its 2005 report. It was observed that practice was diverse. In general, obstetricians and gynaecologists did not discriminate between different-sex married couples and different-sex unmarried couples in a long-term relationship. They were, nevertheless, divided in their approach to single people, as only 53 per cent of the respondents to the survey conducted by the AHR Commission was prepared to offer AHR services to single people and relatively few (one in seven) were prepared to offer AHR services to same-sex couples.[233] The AHR Commission recommended that AHR services had to be available without discrimination on the grounds of gender, marital status or sexual orientation, 'subject to consideration of the best interests of any children that [were] born'.[234] This was '[...] generally viewed as taking a progressive step towards a socially diverse Ireland.'[235]

Requirements in respect of age have generally also been left to the medical profession. Madden observed in 1995 that '40 years would probably be the limit' for IVF treatment. She added that because practices like egg cell donation were not practised in Ireland, the limitations in this respect were primarily biological in character.'[236] As discussed below (see 5.3.9), the 2014 Bill initially set certain age limits for engaging in surrogacy.

5.3.4. Donation of gametes and embryos

Donation of gametes and embryos in the course of AHR treatment has long been, and is still today, mostly unregulated in Irish statutory legislation.[237] The Medical Guidelines are brief as regards the use of donor gametes from third parties in AHR treatment; those who offer donor programmes to patients, must consider the biological difficulties involved and pay particular attention to the source of the donated material. Such donations must be altruistic and non-commercial, and

232 Www.citizensinformation.ie/en/birth_family_relationships/cohabiting_couples/fertility_services_and_unmarried_couples.html, visited September 2010.

233 The Commission on Assisted Human Reproduction 2005, *supra* n. 9, at pp. 32–33.

234 *Idem*, at p. 34, Recommendation no. 17.

235 Sills and Healy 2008, *supra* n. 228.

236 D. Madden, 'Medico-Legal Aspects of In Vitro Fertilisation and Related Infertility Treatments', 1 *Medico-Legal Journal of Ireland* (1995) p. 13 ff.

237 This research was concluded on 31 July 2014. See also C. Power and G. Shannon, 'Practice and Procedure, Sperm donors and the legal recognition for same-sex couples', 11 *Irish Journal of Family Law* (2008) p. 44.

practitioners must keep accurate records for future reference.[238] The anonymous donation of gametes in the course of AHR treatment is at present legal in Ireland and it is taking place,[239] rendering it potentially difficult for a child born after such treatment to trace its genetic parents.[240]

The AHR Commission in principle had no objections to the use of donor gametes or embryos in AHR treatment to assist infertile people to conceive, but it recommended that such donation of sperm, ova and embryos was to be subject to regulation by the – to be established – regulatory body.[241] Furthermore, appropriate counselling to all donors of gametes and embryos by suitably qualified professionals was to be a pre-condition for informed consent by donors.[242] The Commission recommended in 2005 that appropriate guidelines were put in place '[...] to govern the selection of donors; to screen for genetic disorders and infectious disease; to set age limits for donors and to set an appropriate limit on the number of children to be born by the use of sperm or ova from a single donor.'[243]

Commercialisation and anonymity of donations were widely discussed within the AHR Commission. The Commission held financial inducements in AHR to be unacceptable. The regulatory body, as proposed by the Commission should therefore have power to prohibit any practice that could be deemed to constitute commercialisation of AHR.[244] It was recommended that donors were not to be paid nor were recipients to be charged for donations per se. Payment of reasonable expenses and payment for AHR services was not, however, precluded.[245]

As regards anonymity, the AHR Commission was receptive to the argument that 'having access to genetic origins is potentially of profound importance for people's understanding of their identity in a psychological, genetic and historical context.'[246] Avoidance of identity confusion could also be an argument in favour of disclosing the identity of the donor. The Commission concluded that the safeguarding of the best interests of the child born through AHR necessitated access for all children to information that would enable them to identify their genetic origins.[247] It recommended that '[...] any child born through use of donated gametes or embryos [had to], on maturity, be able to identify the donor(s) involved in his/her conception,[248] while donors were not be able to access the identity of children born through use of their

238 Irish Medical Council, *Guide to professional conduct and ethics for registered medical practitioners*, 7th edition 2009, Principle 20, p. 20. See also Clissmann and Barrett 2012, *supra* n. 19.

239 For example at the Sims IVF Clinic in Dublin, see www.egg.donation.ie, visited September 2010.

240 E.g. D. Madden, 'Legal Issues in Artificial Insemination', 2 *Medico-Legal Journal of Ireland* (1996) p. 11. See also section 5.1.4 above.

241 The Commission on Assisted Human Reproduction 2005, *supra* n. 9, at p. 45, Recommendation no. 19,.

242 *Idem*, at p. 45, Recommendation no. 20,.

243 *Idem*, at p. 45, Recommendation no. 21.

244 *Idem*, at p. 71.

245 *Idem*, at p. 46, Recommendation no. 23. See also 'Reproduction becomes a (baby) booming industry', *The Irish Examiner* 28 July 2005.

246 *Idem*, at p. 46.

247 *Idem*, at p. 46.

248 *Idem*, at p. 46, Recommendation no. 22.

gametes or embryos.'[249] The AHR Commission held that the main argument against the lifting of anonymity in donation centred on the fear that there would be no supply of sperm donors. According to the AHR Commission, however, countries where donor identification was permitted had found that reduced supply did not continue beyond a relatively brief period.[250]

In 2006 Regulations were adopted with a view to implementing the European Tissues and Cells Directives.[251] The Regulations, *inter alia*, set quality and safety standards for clinics who carry out AHR treatment involving the donation of gametes. Gamete donors must undergo certain medical tests and must give their informed consent to the donation.[252] While the Regulations endorse non-commercial donation, they are not very firmly phrased on this point. Following Article 13(1) of the Regulations, the Minister for Health and Children was to draw up national guidelines that would '[...] endeavour to ensure that the procurement of [gametes] is carried out on a non-profit basis', while AHR clinics for their part, must 'make every effort to ensure voluntary and unpaid donations' of gametes. The present author is not aware of the existence of any such guidelines.

AHR clinics must also ensure that all gametes '[...] can be fully identified and traced from donor to end user, or disposal, and vice versa'.[253] It is noted in Article 18(6) of the Regulations that the clinic must '[...] ensure that the identity of the recipient is not disclosed to the donor or his family and vice versa, without prejudice to any national law which may come into force on the conditions for disclosure, notably in the case of gametes donation'. Only in September 2014 such legislation was introduced (see below). Until that time there was only one relevant court case, dealing with the rights of a sperm donor.

In December 2009 in the case of *McD.* v. *L. & Anor*, the Supreme Court granted a sperm donor, who was the genetic father of a child born into a relationship between two women a right of access to his child.[254] The man and the lesbian couple had initially agreed that he would be a 'favourite uncle' in the life of the child, with access to the child at the couple's discretion. But when the child was born he sought a bigger role, including structured access. The lesbian couple refused. The dispute between the parties came to a head in 2007, when the couple wished to relocate to Australia with the child. The sperm donor and thus father requested guardianship

---

249 *Idem*, at p. 47, Recommendation no. 27.

250 *Idem*, at p. 45. While the report of the Commission on Assisted Human Reproduction based this conclusion exclusively on the Swedish example, developments in the United Kingdom and the Netherlands draw a different picture. See, *inter alia*, I. Turkmendag et al., 'The removal of donor anonymity in the UK: the silencing of claims by would-be parents', 22 *International Journal of Law, Policy and Family* (2008) p. 283.

251 European Communities (Quality and Safety of Human Tissues and Cells) Regulations, Statutory Instrument No. 158 of 2006.

252 Art. 13 and Schedule 3 to European Communities (Quality and Safety of Human Tissues and Cells) Regulations.

253 Art. 15(1) European Communities (Quality and Safety of Human Tissues and Cells) Regulations.

254 *McD* v. *L & Anor* [2009] IESC 81; [2010] 2 IR 199.

and joint custody[255] of his child, as well as an order regulating his access to the child. His claims were initially refused by the High Court after a 14-day long hearing.[256] On appeal he was, however, allowed access.[257] The Supreme Court considered the welfare of the child to be paramount; Justice Denham, *inter alia*, based her ruling on the 'benefit to a child, in general, to have the society of his father'. Contrary to the High Court's ruling, the Supreme Court ruled that there was no institution of a *de facto* family in Ireland. This Court thus held that the respondents were not a family under the Irish Constitution.[258] While the genetic mother of the child, had a natural right guaranteed by the Constitution to his custody and to look after his general care, his nurture, his physical and moral wellbeing and his education, in every respect, her lesbian partner had no legally or constitutionally recognisable family relationship with the child.[259]

The Supreme Court referred the case back to the High Court to determine how the father's access had to be exercised. In April 2010, this Court ruled that there was to be (direct) access, meaning that the father was to have personal contact with the child and the child was to have the society of the father.[260] Because the couple had in the meantime relocated to Australia, such access was to be established during trips of the father to Australia and during trips of the couple to Europe. The couple were, when appropriate, to encourage the child to communicate with his father and to establish friendly relations with him. The Court also ordered the opening up of e-mail contact between the father and the couple. The Court left it to the couple to reveal to the child, when it was age appropriate, that the father was his biological father. These orders were made conditional on the father to play the role of 'favourite uncle', not revealing his biological paternity, seeking no parental role in the child's upbringing and acknowledging and accepting the familial integrity of the couple and the child.

It was observed that the case exposed '[...] the pressing need for legislation to help provide some certainty for the adults and children involved.'[261] The 2014 Children and Family Relationship Bill initially did not provide for any right for the child to know its genetic origins.[262] *Inter alia*, the Irish Ombudsman for Children has been critical in this regard, and recommended in 2014 that provision was made '[...] for the gathering, retention and disclosure of information to people born through assisted reproduction and surrogacy regarding their birth and origins.'[263] This concern was

255 Section 11 of the Guardianship of Infants Act, 1964.

256 *McD.* v. *L. & Anor* [2008] IEHC 96.

257 *McD* v. *L & Anor* [2009] IESC 81; [2010] 2 IR 199. See also Hogan 2010, *supra* n. 217.

258 On this point see also ch. 11, section 11.3.5.1.

259 *McD* v. *L & Anor* [2009] IESC 81; [2010] 2 IR 199, Fenelly J, para. 115.

260 *McD* v. *L & Anor* [2010] IEHC 120.

261 Hogan 2010, *supra* n. 217, at p. 93.

262 The Children's Rights Alliance was concerned that the Bill did not provide for a right to know one's genetic parents. See P. Duncan, 'New Bill 'won't devalue' traditional marital families', *Irishtimes.com* 10 April 2014, www.irishtimes.com/news/social-affairs/new-bill-won-t-devalue-traditional-marital-families-1.1757969, visited 21 May 2014.

263 Advice of the Ombudsman for Children on the General Scheme of the Children and Family Relationships Bill 2014, May 2014, p. 16, online available at www.oco.ie/

addressed in the revised general scheme of the Children and Family Relationships Bill 2014 that the Minister for Justice and Equality published on 26 September 2014.[264] In the Revised Scheme a new Part was included to preserve a child's right to know its identity.[265] It provided for the creation of a national donor-conceived person register into which hospitals, clinics and medical services would be obliged to provide information. Future use of anonymous donor egg cells or sperm would be prohibited.[266]

The Bill further provided that donating gametes or an embryo, without the intention of using the material or the embryo for one's own reproductive use, would not confer parenthood on the donor.[267] Also, as noted below (see section 5.3.9), the *mater semper certa est* maxim was a basic principle of the Bill. It also applied when the birth mother was not genetically related to the child, for example when the embryo was created using a donor egg cell.[268] The husband, civil partner or cohabitant of the mother would be considered to be the other parent of the child '[...] if he or she had given a consent which remained valid at the time the procedure leading to implantation took place'.[269]

5.3.4.1. Post-mortem reproduction

Post-mortem reproduction is veiled in uncertainty in Ireland. In 1996 Madden observed that while there was '[...] no legislative prohibition in Ireland on a widow gaining access to her deceased husband's frozen sperm in an attempt to become pregnant', the legal status of a child born in such circumstances was uncertain.[270] While the 2014 Bill could have been a good occasion for the legislature to address the matter, it was expressly held not to provide for 'posthumous conception'.[271]

---

wp-content/uploads/2014/06/OCOAdviceonChildandFamilyRelBill2014.pdf, visited 21 May 2014. For other critique see B. Tobin, 'Surrogacy and identity: why Ireland needs its own sperm bank', *Irishtimes.com* 27 June 2014, www.irishtimes.com/news/health/surrogacy-and-identity-why-ireland-needs-its-own-sperm-bank-1.1846558, visited July 2014.

264 While this date strictly speaking falls outside the scope of this research (see ch. 1, section 1.2), this development was nonetheless included in the present research, as it proved highly important for various issues addressed in this case study.

265 The revised scheme is online at the website of the Department of Justice and Equality, www.justice.ie/en/JELR/Pages/PB14000256, visited September 2014. The revision was welcomed by the Children's Rights Alliance, see www.childrensrights.ie/resources/government-establish-new-donor-conceived, visited October 2014.

266 General Scheme of the Children and Family Relationships Bill, Summary of Provisions, online available at www.justice.ie/en/JELR/Note%20on%20the%20General%20Scheme%20of%20the%20Children%20and%20Family%20Relationships%20Bill.pdf/Files/Note%20on%20the%20General%20Scheme%20of%20the%20Children%20and%20Family%20Relationships%20Bill.pdf, visited October 2014.

267 Art. 8(2) of the Children and Family Relationship Bill in its version of January 2014.

268 Donation of gametes, without the intention of using the material or the embryo for ones own reproductive use, does not establish parenthood under the Children and Family Relationship Bill.

269 General Scheme of the Children and Family Relationship Bill, p. 22 and Art. 10 of the Children and Family Relationship Bill.

270 Madden 1996, *supra* n. 240.

271 General Scheme of the Children and Family Relationship Bill, p. 23.

5.3.5. Gender selection

Under Irish law nothing is provided in respect of gender selection in the course of AHR treatment. While it is correspondingly insufficiently clear if gender selection has taken or takes place in Ireland, there have been incidental reports of Irish couples going abroad for this purpose.[272] The AHR Commission at the time noted that 'public anxieties regarding slippery slopes towards the creation of children 'to order'' indicated 'a general disapproval of such techniques'.[273] The Commission felt that pre-conception sex selection had to be permitted 'only for the reliable prevention of serious sex linked genetic disorders but not for social reasons.'[274] This was not, however, followed-up by the legislature, also not when preimplantation genetic diagnosis (PGD) was introduced in Ireland.

5.3.6. Preimplantation genetic diagnosis (PGD)

Prenatal screening takes place in Ireland, be it unregulated.[275] Gestational age scans at around 18 weeks of pregnancy usually include screening for structural anomalies,[276] but genetic tests are not routinely offered and there is no national screening programme.[277] More importantly, termination of pregnancy for foetal anomaly is not permissible (see also section 5.2 above on Irish abortion laws).

Preimplantation genetic diagnosis (PGD) has long not been available in Ireland, because of the uncertain constitutional status of the embryo (see 5.1.2 above).[278] The question when life begins was qualified as '[...] the most astute ethical dilemma that PGD face[d] in Ireland [...].'[279]

The AHR Commission also addressed the issue of PGD in its 2005 report. A principled argument against it was voiced in the following terms:

> 'It could be argued that the application of PGD departs from the goals of preventive medicine and marks the start of the "slippery slope" to more eugenic objectives. There is

---

[272] See, for example, 'Jeff Steinberg: Irish Couples using Gender Selection', *RTÉ.ie* 3 March 2010, www.rte.ie/tv/theafternoonshow/2010/0303/jeffsteinbergirishcouplesusinggenderselection876.html, visited May 2014.

[273] The Commission on Assisted Human Reproduction 2005, *supra* n. 9, at p. 63.

[274] *Idem*, at p. 70, Recommendation no. 38.

[275] A. Coverleyn et al., *Pre-implantation Genetic Diagnosis in Europe'* (Joint Research Centre of the European Commission, January 2007) p. 66, online available at www.ftp.jrc.es/EURdoc/eur22764en.pdf, visited 24 July 2014.

[276] An example of a prenatal diagnosis concerns a test on sickle cell anaemia by the Irish National Centre for Medical Genetics. See www.genetics.ie/molecular, visited June 2014.

[277] Donoghue and Smyth 2013, *supra* n. 120, at pp. 139–140.

[278] The Commission on Assisted Human Reproduction 2005, *supra* n. 9, at p. 66. See also Coverleyn et al. 2007, *supra* n. 275, at p. 44.

[279] Scannell 2007, *supra* n. 197.

> a concern that therapeutic PGD that selects for "clinically" healthy embryos (disease free) may lead to enhancement PGD that selects for "socially" healthy embryos.'[280]

At the same time the AHR Commission was convinced that PGD could reduce the risk of serious genetic disorders. It therefore recommended, with one member dissenting, that PGD had to be allowed in Ireland, if regulated and monitored by the regulatory body.[281] This recommendation was not followed up by the Irish legislature; until today the issue has not been regulated for in law.

Despite the absence of statutory regulation in the field, in 2012, the Irish Medical Board licensed two Irish AHR clinics to offer PGD services.[282] The pro-life campaign qualified this as 'exploiting a gap in Irish laws'[283] and called for 'a detailed ethical debate on the issue of genetic screening'.[284] Such a debate has so far not taken place in Irish Parliament. Further, while clinics also provide for testing for gender related disorders, no express regulation seems to be in place for gender selection in case such a test is positive (see 5.3.5 above).[285]

5.3.7. Vitrification of egg cells

Vitrification of egg cells has not been debated Ireland to the same extent as it has been in the Netherlands, for example (see Chapter 5). The technique is offered by some of the Irish clinics,[286] but there are no particular statutory regulations in place.

---

280 The Commission on Assisted Human Reproduction 2005, *supra* n. 9, at p. 65.

281 *Idem*, at p. 73, Recommendation no. 40.

282 These are the Beacon CARE Fertility clinic in Dublin and at the Cork Fertility Centre. The clinics cooperate with a specialist genetics laboratory in the UK. See B. Roche, 'Two clinics to offer embryo screening', *Irishtimes.com* 13 November 2012, www.irishtimes.com/news/health/two-clinics-to-offer-embryo-screening-1.551312, visited May 2014 and B. Roche, 'First pregnancy in Ireland using new screening technique', *Irishtimes.com* 3 November 2013, www.irishtimes.com/news/ireland/irish-news/first-pregnancy-in-ireland-using-new-screening-technique-1.1582427, visited May 2014.

283 'IVF Clinics Exploit Gap in Irish Law', www.prolife.ie/prolife/ivf-clinics-exploit-gap-irish-law, visited 15 May 2013.

284 R. Riegel, 'First 'gene screened' Irish baby due in July', *Irish Independent* 4 November 2013, www.independent.ie/irish-news/first-gene-screened-irish-baby-due-in-july-29723997.html, visited 15 May 2014.

285 According to its website the Cork Fertility Centre offers PGD to couples at high risk of producing a child with a genetic disorder. The clinic carries out PGD for single gene disorders including; cystic fibrosis, fragile X syndrome, Duchenne muscular dystrophy and myotonic dystrophy, Tay-Sachs disease, beta-thalassemia, hemophilia A, and sickle cell disease. See www.corkfertilitycentre.com/Treatments, visited 22 May 2014. The list of disorders on the website of the Beacon CARE Fertility clinic is even longer. See www.carefertility.com/genetics-programme-sc2/what-is-pgd-what-is-genetic-diagnosis-sj1/, visited 22 May 2014.

286 See for example www.merrionfertility.ie/embryology/vitrification-.231.html, visited May 2014.

5.3.8. AHR treatment and public funding

As a general rule AHR services are not provided by public health services and their funding therefore primarily has to be carried for privately. For medical expenses, including IVF treatment, income tax relief may be claimed.[287] The Drugs Payment Scheme furthermore covers drugs used as part of fertility treatment.[288]

5.3.9. Surrogacy

Surrogacy is, like many other AHR issues, completely unregulated in the Irish jurisdiction. The matter has never been acknowledged by the Irish Medical Council in its guidelines[289] and statutory legislation was only proposed in 2014 by means of the Children and Family Relationship Bill (see below). However, this part of the Bill was taken out before the Bill could be tabled in Parliament. As a result, there remains today great legal uncertainty regarding surrogacy, particularly regarding the determination of legal parentage in situations involving surrogacy arrangements.

The absence of regulation, and for many years also of any case law on the matter, has left many questions unanswered. Some guidance has been given by the Citizen Information Board, which explained on its official website that '[…] traditionally, the surrogate mother is considered the legal mother of the child and the child's guardian, because she has given birth to the child.'[290] It was explained that if the surrogate mother was married her husband would be presumed by law to be the father of the child, unless the contrary was proven.[291] The intended parents – even if they were the genetic parents – would need to adopt the child in order to establish parental links with the child.[292] However, private adoptions are not allowed in Ireland and if the surrogate mother was married, it would not be possible for her to give up the child for adoption. Also there was no guarantee that the Irish Adoption Authority would place the child of a surrogate mother with the intended parent(s).[293] Further, because it is a criminal offence under Irish law to make or receive any payment or other reward

---

287 Between 2006 and 2009, tax relief for IVF treatment was provided for at the highest rate which was set at 41 per cent. As of 2009, this was reduced to 20 per cent. If the person or family concerned has taken out private health insurance cover, the insurance will take care of the expenses for AHR services, in which case the question of tax relief does not arise. See www.citizensinformation.ie/categories/money-and-tax/tax/income-tax-credits-and-reliefs/taxation_and_medical_expenses, visited 22 May 2014 and www.revenue.ie/en/tax/it/leaflets/it6.html, visited 22 May 2014.

288 See www.citizensinformation.ie/categories/health/women-s-health/fertility_treatment?printpreview=1, visited 22 May 2014. This webpage was last updated on 11 January 2012.

289 Sills and Healy 2008, *supra* n. 228.

290 See www.citizensinformation.ie/en/birth_family_relationships/adoption_and_fostering/surrogacy.html, visited 22 May 2014. It is thereby explained that '[l]egal maternity is important for birth registration, domicile and citizenship provisions, succession, childcare provisions, adoption, social welfare and educational provisions as many of these services and rights depend on the consent of the legal mother.'

291 Section 46 of the Status of Children Act 1987.

292 C. Palmer, 'Irish couples face an uphill struggle with surrogacy laws', *Independent.ie* 11 May 2009.

293 See www.citizensinformation.ie/en/birth_family_relationships/adoption_and_fostering/surrogacy.html, visited 22 May 2014.

in consideration of an adoption,[294] remuneration in a surrogacy arrangement could also be considered illegal.[295] An intended father who was genetically related to the child could alternatively apply for guardianship of the child under the Guardianship of Infants Act,[296] but his partner would not have such a right.[297]

Because of this lack of legal certainty in Ireland, it was also unclear if, and if so, at what scale, surrogacy took place within Ireland.[298] Reports were made that Irish couples engaged in surrogacy agreements abroad (see also 5.4.3 below).[299] In 2012, the then Minister for Justice, Equality and Defence therefore published a guidance document entitled 'Citizenship, parentage, guardianship and travel document issues in relation to children born as a result of surrogacy arrangements entered into outside the State'.[300] The document gave further guidance on the family law implications of surrogacy under Irish law. It was made clear that under Irish law the woman who gave birth to the child was the legal mother of the child, even if she was not herself the genetic mother of the child. It was furthermore explained that:

> 'Under the Guardianship of Infants Act 1964, the mother of a child born outside marriage is the child's sole guardian. Under Irish law, family relationships and the rights and responsibilities that flow from them cannot be subjected to the ordinary law of contract and cannot, in particular, be transferred to another person, bought, or sold. This means that, under Irish law, the surrogate mother and the child will have a life-long legal relationship with one another. [...] If the surrogate mother is married, then under section 46 of the Status of Children Act 1987, the surrogate mother's husband is presumed by law to be the father of the child, unless the contrary is proved on the balance of probabilities. The husband will also, along with the surrogate mother, be the joint guardian of the child. If the commissioning father is the genetic father of the child, it is possible to overcome the presumption of paternity in favour of the surrogate mother's husband, so as to allow the

294 Section 41(1) of the Adoption Act 1952. See also 'You'll have a baby in your arms within a year, NO questions asked.', *Daily Mirror* 16 January 2006 and C. O'Sullivan, 'More couples seeking British surrogate births', *The Irish Examiner* 9 August 2005.

295 Dr. D. Madden in Parliamentary debates Vol. no. 61, 15 September 2005. The Commission on Assisted Human Reproduction 2005, *supra* n. 9, at p. 51. See also Sills and Healy 2008, *supra* n. 228.

296 The AHR Commission pointed out in this respect that, '[...] alternatively, a commissioning man may apply for guardianship of the child under the Status of Children Act 1987 if he is the biological father of the child, but his partner would not have any right to make such an application.' The Commission on Assisted Human Reproduction 2005, *supra* n. 9, at p .51. See also Dr. D. Madden in Parliamentary debates Vol. no. 61, 15 September 2005.

297 See www.citizensinformation.ie/en/birth_family_relationships/adoption_and_fostering/surrogacy.html, visited September 2011.

298 R. de Brun, 'I've had eight babies for other people', *Independent.ie* 4 February 2008. See also 'You'll have a baby in your arms within a year, NO questions asked', *Daily Mirror* 16 January 2006 and C. Palmer, 'Irish couples face an uphill struggle with surrogacy laws', *Independent.ie* 11 May 2009.

299 See the submission of Dr. Wingfield to the High Court in *M.R. & Another* v. *An t Ard Chláraitheoir* [2013] IEHC 91 at 28.

300 'The Minister for Justice, Equality and Defence announces the publication of guidance for Irish couples on surrogacy arrangements made abroad', Press release on the website of the Department for Justice and Equality of 21 February 2012, www.justice.ie/en/JELR/Pages/PR12000035, visited 23 May 2014. The guidance document is online available at www.justice.ie, visited 23 May 2014, and is also published on the websites of each relevant Department. See also section 5.5.4 below.

> commissioning father to be recognised as the legal parent of the child. A guardianship order may also be sought by the commissioning father. [...] If the surrogate mother is not married, and the commissioning father is the genetic father of the child, then the Irish authorities may recognise his paternity of the child on receipt of reliable DNA evidence.'[301]

Surrogacy was also addressed by the AHR Commission in its 2005 report. The majority of the Commission recommended at the time that surrogacy and all issues pertaining thereto had to be permitted and had to be made subject to regulation by the regulatory body the Commission recommended to be established.[302] The Commission also recommended extending the remit of the Adoption Board to include surrogacy.[303] Acknowledging that both genetics and gestation played 'a necessary and equally important role in bringing the child into existence',[304] it further advised that the child born through surrogacy had to be presumed to be that of the commissioning couple.[305] The AHR Commission was of the view that payment of reasonable and legitimate expenses to the surrogate mother was not to be seen as contravening the Adoption Act.[306] In line with its recommendations as regards the use of donors in AHR procedures, it furthermore recommended that any child born through surrogacy, on reaching maturity, had to be entitled to access the identity of the surrogate mother and, where relevant, the genetic parents.[307]

None of the Commission's recommendations were followed up at the time, leaving the matter completely unregulated. It was therefore observed that:

> 'Until the Oireachtas passes a law specifically addressing surrogacy, Ireland will remain a blank slate leaving it to the judiciary to determine what rights either party in a surrogacy arrangement may have.'[308]

The judiciary indeed turned out to be the first needing to address the issue. The unprecedented, and for many, surprising, ruling of the High Court in *M R & Another* v. *An t Ard Chláraitheoir* (2013)[309] inevitably prompted the legislature to speed up the introduction of legislation, which it finally did in 2014.[310]

Applicants in *M R & Another* v. *An t Ard Chláraitheoir* were a married couple, referred to as '*OR*' and '*CR*'. Because *CR* was unable to give birth the natural way, the couple searched for alternative ways of having a child. The sister of *CR* volunteered

---

301 It was, furthermore, explained in the guidance document that in addition to such a declaration of parentage, a guardianship order was required for the genetic father to become also the guardian of the child.

302 The Commission on Assisted Human Reproduction 2005, *supra* n. 9, at p. 50, Recommendation No. 30.

303 Sills and Healy 2008, *supra* n. 228.

304 The Commission on Assisted Human Reproduction 2005, *supra* n. 9, at p. 51.

305 *Idem*, at p. 53, Recommendation No. 33.

306 *Idem*, at p. 50, Recommendation No. 31.

307 *Idem*, at p. 51, Recommendation No. 32.

308 Sills and Healy 2008, *supra* n. 228.

309 *M.R. & Another* v. *An t Ard Chláraitheoir* [2013] IEHC 91.

310 As explained below, the relevant part of the relevant Bill was, however, removed from the Bill that very same year.

to participate in a surrogacy arrangement, which progressed throughout 'in a very cooperative atmosphere'.[311] The ovum of *CR* was fertilised *in vitro* by the sperm of *OR* and implanted in the womb of the sister, who became pregnant of twins. After their birth, *CR*'s sister and *OR* attended the Registrar's office and were registered in the birth certificates as the parents of the children. *CR* and *OR* subsequently requested to have the Register corrected, holding that *CR*, being the genetic mother, should be registered as the mother.[312] They accompanied their request with DNA evidence. After this request was refused, the couple applied to the High Court, seeking a declaration that *CR* was the mother of the twins, that she was entitled to be registered as their mother, as well as a declaration that the continued failure to recognise *CR* and *OR* as the parents of the children was unlawful.

Referring to the *mater semper certa est* principle, the Respondents in this case, *An t Ard-Chláraitheoir* (the Chief Officer of the system of civil registration in Ireland) and the Attorney General, submitted that in Irish law, the mother of a child was the birth mother. The respondents claimed this to be a constitutional norm and 'an inherent and fundamental principle' of Irish law that was affirmed by Article 40.3.3° of the Irish Constitution. They further held it possible that the State would at some stage 'legislate to allow surrogacy', but stressed that this engaged 'a whole range of social and political issues', which were matters for the legislature.[313] It was furthermore submitted that if the Court were to accept the applicants' claims and make a declaration of parentage based on, *inter alia*, the DNA testing, it would bring about 'a seismic shift' in the manner in which the issue of motherhood was dealt with in the Irish jurisdiction.[314] Parenthood could not be a matter of intention, it was claimed. In the words of the Respondents:

> 'If we are to begin to look at genetics and not the birth then that raises a complex set of issues that is properly a matter for the legislature to deal with and is not something capable of being dealt with by the Court for the simple complexity of all that is involved.'[315]

High Court Judge Abbott was not convinced by these submissions. He observed that the central legal issue to be addressed in this case was who, in law, was entitled to be treated as the parents of the twins, in particular, who, in law, was to be treated as their mother.[316] Given that positive legislation on surrogacy was 'totally absent' in the Irish jurisdiction, the surrogacy contract in the case under examination was not illegal, it was just not enforceable.[317] Having heard a number of expert witnesses on the science of genetics versus the science of epigenetics, Judge Abbott held it to be 'most unlikely that epigenetics [would] ever trump the deterministic quality of chromosomal DNA'.[318] He was further of the opinion that the word 'mother' in

311 *M.R. & Another* v. *An t Ard Chláraitheoir* [2013] IEHC 91, at 96.
312 The applicants relied on Section 63 of the Civil Registration Act 2004.
313 *M.R. & Another* v. *An t Ard Chláraitheoir* [2013] IEHC 91, at 71.
314 *Idem*, at 91.
315 *Idem*, at 93.
316 *Idem*, at 2.
317 *Idem*, at 105.
318 *Idem*, at 98.

Article 40.3.3° had a meaning specific to the Article itself and that there was nothing in the Irish legislative context that positively affirmed the maxim of *mater semper certa est.* Judge Abbott held that this presumption had not survived the enactment of the Constitution insofar as it applied to the situation post IVF and considered that any alleged historic and European consensus on the *mater semper certa* principle was not to restrain the Court from making conclusions.[319] He accordingly held:

> 'To achieve fairness and constitutional and natural justice, for both the paternal and maternal genetic parents, the feasible inquiry in relation to maternity ought to be made by on a genetic basis and on being proven, the genetic mother should be registered as the mother under the [Civil Registration Act 2004].'[320]

The High Court accordingly granted the declarations sought by the applicants, holding that *CR* was the mother of the twins and that the continued failure to recognise *OR* and *CR* as their parents was unlawful.

As pointed out by many, this case highlighted the urgency with which legislation was required in this area.[321] Because the government was by that time eventually indeed in the process of preparing legislation on the issue, it subsequently appealed the case to the Supreme Court. It wished to ensure that the legislature's scope to legislate was 'absolutely clear' and wished to have 'a number of points of law of exceptional public importance' clarified.[322] After a four-day hearing in February 2014, the Supreme Court reserved judgment in the case.[323]

In the meantime the 2014 Children and Family Relationship Bill (see 5.3.2 above) was introduced. It initially also provided for a section on surrogacy. Had this not been taken out of the Bill at a later stage, it could have resulted in the introduction of the first statutory instrument in Ireland addressing the issue of surrogacy expressly. Even though the relevant provisions have thus not made it into law, they may still be indicative for possible future legislation in this area and that warrants a brief discussion of the relevant parts of the Bill here.

The Bill only focused on so-called gestational surrogacy involving AHR treatment as opposed to 'traditional surrogacy' whereby the surrogate mother is the genetic mother of the child she is carrying.[324] The making or receiving of payments in

319 *Idem*, at 105.

320 *Idem*, at 104.

321 E.g. A. Caffrey, 'Surrogacy – Genetics v Gestation: The Determination of "Mother" in Irish Law', 19 *Medico-Legal Journal of Ireland* (2013) p. 34 and A. Mulligan, 'Surrogacy in the Courts: The Definition of Motherhood', guest post at *humanrights.ie* of 30 January 2013, www.humanrights.ie/index.php/2013/01/30/surrogacy-in-the-courts-the-definition-of-motherhood, visited 21 May 2014.

322 Department of Social Protection, *Statement in relation to High Court judgment in the case of* MR, DR, OR and CR v An tÁrd Chlaraitheoir [Registrar General], Ireland & the Attorney General, 6 June 2013 online available at www.welfare.ie/en/pressoffice/Pages/pr060613a.aspx, visited 20 May 2014.

323 M. Carolan, 'Supreme Court reserves judgment in surrogacy case', *Irishtimes.com* 6 February 2014, www.irishtimes.com/news/crime-and-law/supreme-court-reserves-judgment-in-surrogacy-case-1.1682158, visited 22 May 2014.

324 General Scheme of the Children and Family Relationship Bill (version January 2014), p. 10.

relation to a surrogacy arrangement and advertisements for entering into a surrogacy arrangement were prohibited under the Bill. Those who engaged in commercial surrogacy could face a fine or imprisonment for a term not exceeding 12 months, or both.[325] Payment for the birth mother's reasonable costs, for legal advice and for AHR procedures involved in surrogacy agreements were not precluded. The Bill also set certain age requirements: the surrogate mother had to have attained the age of 24 years and had to have at least one child of her own, while the intended parents had to be between 21 and 45 years of age.[326]

The Bill set out the rule that the birth mother was always considered the mother whether or not she had a genetic connection to the child.[327] In respect of surrogacy in particular it was explained:

> 'The policy intention is that in a surrogacy case, the birth mother will be recorded as the child's mother. No surrogacy arrangement will be enforceable against her. However, on application to the court by the birth mother or the commissioning parents, or all of them, the court may legally assign parentage to the intending parents. The court may assign parentage on the basis of genetic connection to one of the intending parents and to the spouse, civil partner or cohabiting partner of that person. The consent of any surrogate is essential and she will be the legal mother of the child if she does not consent.'[328]

The Bill thus made it possible for the intending parents to establish parental links with the child, but at the same time reserved a decisive say for the surrogate mother. This was also reflected in the rule that an application to the court could be made no earlier than 30 days after the child's birth.[329] No presumptions as to parenthood in relation to the partner of a surrogate mother applied.[330] Lastly, the condition was set that before entering the arrangement the surrogate mother and the intended parents were to obtain legal advice from separate and independent legal practitioners.[331]

After the Bill had been published, the Children's Ombudsman was critical in respect of some of the proposed provisions on surrogacy. She, *inter alia*, held that provision had to be made for situations in which a surrogate consented to the assignment of legal parentage to the intended mother, but the latter refused to accept legal parentage.[332] The Children's Ombudsman in particular made recommendations in respect of cross-border surrogacy cases (see section 5.5.4 below). As noted above,

---

325 Proposed Section 23(1) and (2) in combination with Sections 18 and 19 of the Bill in its version of January 2014.

326 Sections 20 and 21 of the Bill in its version of January 2014. The Government special rapporteur on child protection considered the latter maximum age limit to amount to age discrimination. F. Gartland, 'Parental age limit in surrogacy law could be discrimination', *Irishtimes.com* 19 May 2014, www.irishtimes.com/news/crime-and-law/parental-age-limit-in-surrogacy-law-could-be-discrimination-1.1800599, visited 21 May 2014.

327 General Scheme of the Children and Family Relationship Bill (version January 2014), at p. 22.

328 *Idem*, at p. 31.

329 Art. 13(5) of the Children and Family Relationship Bill.

330 Art. 8(3) Children and Family Relationship Bill.

331 Art. 22(1) and (2) Children and Family Relationship Bill.

332 General Scheme of the Children and Family Relationship Bill (version January 2014), at p. 20.

the revised general scheme of the Children and Family Relationships Bill 2014, as published on 26 September 2014, no longer contained any provisions in relation to surrogacy. The following explanation was given in an accompanying summary of the Revised Bill:

> 'It was considered particularly problematic to finalise provisions on surrogacy in advance of the Supreme Court's ruling on the *MR & Ors – v- An tArd-Chláraitheoir* case given the uncertainty on the balance of constitutional rights between a birth mother and a genetic mother and because there are very critical issues needing to be resolved, relating for example to how the law deals with commercial surrogacies and to the rights of children born through surrogacies.'[333]

5.4. Statistics on cross-border movement

5.4.1. Statistics on cross-border abortions

Traditionally most women in Ireland who wish to have an abortion on medical or social grounds go to the United Kingdom. The UK Department of Health annually releases statistics on abortions carried out in England and Wales. These statistics also show how many women and girls gave addresses in Ireland to these abortion clinics.[334] On the basis of these statistics the Irish Family Planning Association (IFPA) has held that between January 1980 and December 2012, at least 156,076 women travelled from Ireland for abortion services in England and Wales.[335] The IFPA underlined that these numbers are an underestimation '[...] as not all women resident in the Republic of Ireland will provide their Irish addresses for reasons of confidentiality. Furthermore, some Irish women will give addresses in the UK at which they are not resident in order to obtain abortion care paid for by the [National Health Service].'[336]

The number of women giving Irish addresses to UK abortion clinics has been decreasing every year since 2001, from 6,673 to 3,982 in 2012.[337] Still, in 2013 it

333 General Scheme of the Children and Family Relationships Bill Summary of Provisions, online available at www.justice.ie/en/JELR/Note%20on%20the%20General%20Scheme%20of%20the%20Children%20and%20Family%20Relationships%20Bill.pdf/Files/Note%20on%20the%20General%20Scheme%20of%20the%20Children%20and%20Family%20Relationships%20Bill.pdf, visited October 2014.

334 These statistics are online available at the website of the UK Department of Health www.dh.gov.uk/en/Publicationsandstatistics/Publications/PublicationsStatistics/DH_099285, visited 22 March 2010.

335 Website of the Irish Family Planning Association (IFPA), www.ifpa.ie/eng/Hot-Topics/Abortion/Statistics, visited 26 May 2014.

336 *Idem*. See also Human Rights Watch, *A State of Isolation, Access to Abortion for Women in Ireland* (New York, Human Rights Watch 2010), www.hrw.org/node/87910, visited 3 June 2010, at p. 14.

337 'Number of Women Giving Irish Addresses at UK Abortion Clinics Decreases for Eleventh Year in a Row According to UK Department of Health', press release of the HSE Crisis Pregnancy Programme of 11 July 2013, www.crisispregnancy.ie/news/number-of-women-giving-irish-addresses-at-uk-abortion-clinics-decreases-for-eleventh-year-in-a-row-according-to-uk-department-of-health, visited 26 May 2014.

was held that at least 11 women left the Irish Republic every day for an abortion in Britain.[338] Also, in 2014, a steady rise was reported in the number of women from Ireland seeking abortion on medical grounds in UK hospitals.[339]

Women from Ireland have also been – and are – accessing safe and legal abortion services in other EU countries, principally the Netherlands,[340] allegedly due to the rise of low budget airline connections. These numbers have also been dropping every year. Statistics from the Dutch Expert Centre on Sexuality, *Rutgers Nisso Group* (now *Rutgers WPF*), for example, show that in 2007 the share of Irish women in the group of non-Dutch resident women obtaining abortions in Dutch clinics was 10 per cent (450 out of 4,469 abortions) in 2007, compared to 4 per cent (177 out of 4,436 abortions) in 2008.[341]

The so-called 'Abortion boat' of the Dutch NGO *Women on Waves* set sail to Ireland in 2001. Reportedly some 300 women from Ireland contacted the ship's hotline at the time, including '[...] women who had been raped, schoolgirls who could not find a feasible excuse to go to England for a couple of days, mothers who could not pay for childcare during their journeys to England, and political refugees who did not have the papers to travel'.[342]

5.4.2. (Insufficient) statistics on cross-border reproductive care

As far as the present author is aware, no governmental body in Ireland keeps any official statistics as regards CBRC. Various news reports and surveys, as well as statistics drawn up by private clinics may, however, give some picture of the actual scale of this phenomenon.

338 'Ireland: Government publishes draft legislation', *Reproductive Review* 3 May 2013, www.reproductivereview.org/index.php/rr/article/1404, visited 22 May 2014.

339 K. Holland, 'Concern voiced over UK hospital restrictions', *Irishtimes.com* 16 April 2014, www.irishtimes.com/news/social-affairs/concern-voiced-over-uk-hospital-restrictions-1.1764419, visited 26 May 2014.

340 *Supra* n. 337. *Human Rights Watch* also interviewed Irish women who had had abortions in Italy and France. Human Rights Watch 2010, *supra* n. 336, at p. 10.

341 L. van Lee and C. Wijsen, *Landelijke abortusregistratie 2007* [National abortion registration 2007] (Utrecht, Rutgers Nisso Groep 2008) pp. 47–48, online available at www.rng.nl/productenendiensten/onderzoekspublicaties/downloadbare-publicaties-in-pdf, visited 2 June 2010 and H. Kruijer et al., *Landelijke abortusregistratie 2008* [National abortion registration 2008] (Utrecht, Rutgers Nisso Groep 2010) p. 33, online available at www.rng.nl/productenendiensten/onderzoekspublicaties/downloadbare-publicaties-in-pdf, visited 2 June 2010. The Irish Crisis Pregnancy Agency has held that the number of women travelling from Ireland to clinics in the Netherlands was 461 in 2006, 451 in 2007, 351 in 2008, 134 in 2009, 31 in 2010 and 33 in 2011.'Number of Women Giving Irish Addresses at UK Abortion Clinics Decreases for Eleventh Year in a Row According to UK Department of Health', press release of the HSE Crisis Pregnancy Programme of 11 July 2013, www.crisispregnancy.ie/news/number-of-women-giving-irish-addresses-at-uk-abortion-clinics-decreases-for-eleventh-year-in-a-row-according-to-uk-department-of-health, visited 26 May 2014. The latter figures are, however, not verifiable as in the reports of the *Rutgers WPF* for those years, women from Ireland are covered by the more general category 'other' ('overig').

342 R. Gomperts, 'Women on Waves: Where Next for the Abortion Boat?', 19 *Reproductive Health Matters* (2002) p. 180 at p. 181. See also Ch. 6, section 6.4.1.3.

Many reports are made of Irish women and couples travelling to other jurisdictions for AHR treatment including gamete donation. Some news reports speak of 'many women' travelling to Spain and other European countries for ovum donation,[343] others speak of 'hundreds of Irish couples' heading to other European countries for that same purpose[344] and of 'hundreds of children born in Ireland every year' who are conceived using eggs or sperm sourced from Spain and other countries.[345] Certain individual clinics keep their own statistics. It was, for instance, reported that the *Instituto Marques* clinic in Barcelona, treated 50 Irish women in 2007 and had by August 2008 yet treated 70 that year.[346] *Reprofit*, a fertility clinic in the Czech city of Brno, was reported to have treated about six Irish couples a month and the Mediterranean Fertility Centre in Chania, Crete, claimed to have treated about 50 Irish women in 2008.[347]

The Irish private fertility clinic *Sims IVF Clinic* has, furthermore, set up the so-called 'European egg donation programme'. According to the clinic, the number of recipients of egg donation far exceeds the number of donors in Ireland. Because the converse allegedly applies in Eastern Europe, the Irish clinic has developed a partnership with a Ukrainian clinic. The Irish clinic transports frozen sperm to the Ukrainian clinic, where the *in vitro* fertilisation is carried out. The resulting fertilised eggs are then returned to Ireland for couples to proceed with embryo transfer.[348] A doctor of the *Sims* clinic estimated in 2005 that over half of the couples wishing to engage in AHR travelled to Spain and Eastern Europe.[349] In 2004, the clinic completed 120 treatments involving eggs donated from Middle or Eastern Europe, compared with 24 Irish donations.[350]

It has been submitted that particularly the existing non-commercial nature of the donation of gametes caused a shortage in available donor eggs in Ireland. With no financial incentive, Irish women have apparently been reluctant to donate their eggs out of altruism.[351] It has been reported that consequently '[...] hundreds of Irish

343 'We're having an IVF baby', *Sunday Business Post* 19 September 2004.

344 T. McTague, 'Costa del IVF', *Daily Mirror*, 11 August 2008 and G. Monaghan, 'Irish head to Europe for egg donation. More women are turning to fertility clinics abroad', *The Sunday Times* 10 August 2008.

345 C. O'Brien, 'The identity issue: how donated eggs and sperm are redefining parenthood', *Irishtimes.com* 21 November 2011, www.irishtimes.com/newspaper/features/2011/1121/1224307905627.html?via=rel, visited 15 May 2014.

346 T. McTague, 'Costa del IVF', *Daily Mirror*, 11 August 2008 and G. Monaghan, 'Irish head to Europe for egg donation. More women are turning to fertility clinics abroad', *The Sunday Times* 10 August 2008.

347 M. Tsouroupaki, embryologist and laboratory director of the Mediterranean Fertility Centre in Chania, Crete as quoted in G. Monaghan, 'Irish head to Europe for egg donation. More women are turning to fertility clinics abroad', *The Sunday Times* 10 August 2008.

348 Www.eggdonation.ie/Information_about_Donors/Information_about_Donors.710.html, visited 15 May 2014.

349 Dr Walsh of SIMS Clinic in Dublin as quoted in 'Reproduction becomes a (baby) booming industry', *The Irish Examiner* 28 July 2005. According to the news report, Irish women no longer travel to Britain as there is also a severe shortage in the UK after the lifting of anonymity for donors.

350 'Infertile women buy donor eggs abroad for €10k', *Irish Independent* 25 June 2007.

351 As submitted by Dr Aonghus Nolan of the Galway Fertility Clinic as quoted in G. Monaghan, 'Irish head to Europe for egg donation. More women are turning to fertility clinics abroad', *The Sunday Times* 10 August 2008.

women are travelling to clinics across the continent to receive IVF treatment using eggs donated from young European women.'[352] It has, furthermore, been reported that Irish clinics import sperm from a Danish sperm bank.[353]

Further, cross-border movement has been taking place for the purpose of having PGD. The Joint Research Centre of the European Commission held in a report of 2007 that all patients who requested PGD in Ireland were referred to clinics outside Irish jurisdiction, *inter alia*, Belgium and the UK.[354] While the total number of referrals made within Ireland was not known, the number of referrals for PGD made by the National Centre for Medical Genetics was known to be approximately 20 cases in the period 2005–2006, the report stated. Apart from formal referrals, patients could also inform themselves about PGD facilities abroad via the internet.

5.4.3. Statistics on cross-border surrogacy

While no official statistics are available, there is ample incidental evidence showing that individuals and couples in Ireland have entered into surrogacy agreements in other jurisdictions. Outside the EU these mainly concern the USA, Ukraine and India. Inside the EU, the UK has long been a preferred destination.

British surrogacy organisations like *Cots* (Childlessness Overcome Through Surrogacy)[355] have in the past helped various Irish couples in giving babies through surrogacy.[356] It was reported that a 2008 change in UK legislation regarding adoption prevented non-UK residents from adopting a child born in the UK through surrogacy.[357] Consequently, Irish couples had to set up permanent residency in the UK in order to qualify for a surrogacy treatment.[358] Perhaps partly due to this change in the UK law, Irish couples increasingly turned to the USA for surrogacy.[359] In 2006 the *Daily Mirror* reported that three US organisations had arranged babies for 30 Irish couples.[360]

352 *Idem.*

353 D. O'Donovan, 'UK trade in sperm and eggs', *The Sunday Mirror* 6 May 2007 and G. Pennings, 'The rough guide to insemination: cross-border travelling for donor semen due to different regulations', *Facts, Views and Vision in ObGyn, Monograph* (2010) p. 55, online available at www.fvvo.eu/assets/103/21-Pennings.pdf, visited 15 May 2014. Pennings referred to, *inter alia*, W. Pavia, 'How Danish sperm is conquering the world', *The Times* 27 November 2006.

354 Coverleyn et al. 2007, *supra* n. 275, at p. 41.

355 See www.surrogacy.org.uk/About_COTS.htm, visited 26 May 2014.

356 *Cots* has held to have helped on average five Irish couples a year. 'You'll have a baby in your arms within a year, NO questions asked.', *Daily Mirror* 16 January 2006 and C. O'Sullivan, 'More couples seeking British surrogate births', *The Irish Examiner* 9 August 2005. See also Sills and Healy 2008, *supra* n. 228.

357 See *inter alia* the submission by Dr Wingfield in *M. R. & Another* v. *An t Ard Chláraitheoir* [2013] IEHC 91, para. 28 and the UK Border Agency leaflet on inter-country surrogacy and the immigration rules, online available at www.gov.uk/government/uploads/system/uploads/attachment_data/file/261435/Intercountry-surrogacy-leaflet.pdf, visited 15 May 2014.

358 C. Palmer, 'Irish couples face an uphill struggle with surrogacy laws', *Independent.ie* 11 May 2009.

359 R. de Brun, 'I've had eight babies for other people', *Independent.ie* 4 February 2008.

360 'You'll have a baby in your arms within a year, NO questions asked.', *Daily Mirror* 16 January 2006.

5.5. Irish abortion and AHR legislation and cross-border movement

5.5.1. Criminal liability for abortions and AHR treatment abroad?

In 1980 Findlay held it inconceivable that Irish courts would punish arrangements for an abortion in another State that was lawful under the law of that State.[361] This observation seems confirmed by prosecution practice. There have, of course, in the past been cases where injunctions were sought and granted to prevent girls from travelling to another jurisdiction to have an abortion.[362] Other than that, the present author is not aware of any reports of any criminal prosecution in Ireland for abortions obtained abroad.

The present author is further not aware of any prosecutions in Ireland for involvement in prohibited treatment abroad. This may also have to do with the fact that AHR was for so long unregulated and thus also not expressly criminalised. There have, nonetheless, been reports of fear for prosecutions. For example, in 2007 it was reported that Irish doctors feared potential prosecution for referring patients to PGD clinics in other countries.[363]

5.5.2. Public funding for treatment obtained abroad

Most women who travel from Ireland to another State for an abortion, do so because the abortion is not legally available in Ireland. That implies that these women also have to cover the costs of their abortion themselves.[364]

In respect of AHR treatment, reimbursement depends on the terms of the private health insurer (see 5.5.9 above). The tax relief described in section 5.3.8 above, is also available if the treatment has been obtained abroad.

---

361 M.J. Findlay, 'Criminal Liability For Complicity In Abortions Committed Outside Ireland', 15 *The Irish Jurist* (1980) p. 88.

362 See section 5.5.2 above.

363 J. Lawford Davies as quoted in 'IVF test for deformities raises legal concerns', *The Irish Examiner* 10 December 2007.

364 Upon inquiry with the *Dublin Well Woman Centre* in 2006 it appeared that incidentally Irish authorities had reimbursed abortions for minors. The *Dublin Well Woman Centre* furthermore expected that abortions performed on women in state custody would also be paid for by the State, but it underlined that it did not have any statistics to that effect. Women in small communities could sometimes rely on private funding within that community. Other women had to finance their abortions themselves. Statement by Alison Begas, Chief Executive of *Dublin Well Woman* (Personal email correspondence 13 November 2006).

5.5.3. Information about treatment abroad and follow-up treatment

As explained in section 5.2.3 above, the right to information about foreign abortion facilities has been guaranteed under Irish law since 1992. It is laid down in various sources of law such as the Constitution, statutory law and the Guidelines of the Medical Council. In its judgment in the *A, B and C* case of 2010, the ECtHR implicitly approved of these regulations as sufficient to meet the ECHR standards.[365]

There have (in the past) been reports of Irish women who had difficulties in obtaining follow-up care in Ireland after they had abortions abroad.[366] The Guidelines on Crisis Pregnancy of 2004, as developed by the Crisis Pregnancy Agency in association with the Irish College of General Practitioners, have underlined that women are entitled to follow-up care.[367] As summarised in the *A, B and C* judgment, the guidelines note that:

> '[...] "[i]rrespective of what decision a woman makes in the crisis pregnancy situation, follow-up care will be important. This may include antenatal care, counselling, future contraception or medical care after abortion. The [...] response [of the General Practitioner (GP)] to the initial consultation will have a profound influence on her willingness to attend for further care." If a woman decides to proceed with an abortion, it is the GP's main concern to ensure that she does so safely, receives proper medical care, and returns for appropriate follow-up. GPs are advised to supplement verbal advice with a written handout. [...] A Patient Information Leaflet is attached to the Guidelines. It informs women that, should they choose an abortion, they should plan to visit their GP at least three weeks after the termination to allow the GP to carry out a full check-up and allow the woman to express any questions or concerns she may have.'[368]

Since 2009 the guidelines of the Medical Council recognise the medical profession's responsibility to provide aftercare for women who decide to leave the State for termination of pregnancy.[369] Also, the HSE Crisis Pregnancy Programme[370]

---

365 The Court considered in respect of the first and second applicants' submissions that there was a lack of information on the options available to them and that this added to the burden of the impugned restrictions on abortion in Ireland, 'general and unsubstantiated'. In this regard, the Court referred to 1995 Abortion Information Act; the establishment of the Crisis Pregnancy Agency (CPA) in 2001 and 'the Government's clarifications as regards care and counselling provided or facilitated by the CPA', as well as the adoption of the CPA Guidelines and Medical Council Guidelines. ECtHR [GC] 16 December 2010, *A, B and C* v. *Ireland*, no. 25579/05, para. 130.

366 See, for example, the submissions of the three applicants in ECtHR [GC] 16 December 2010, *A, B and C* v. *Ireland*, no. 25579/05.

367 Primary Care Guidelines for the Prevention and Management of Crisis Pregnancy ("CPA Guidelines"), online available at www.crisispregnancy.ie/wp-content/uploads/2012/05/primary-care-guidelines-preventing-crisis-pregnancy.pdf, visited 15 May 2014.

368 ECtHR [GC] 16 December 2010, *A, B and C* v. *Ireland*, no. 25579/05, para. 80.

369 See also A.A. Sheikh, 'The Latest Medical Council Guidelines: New and Improved', 16 *Medico-Legal Journal of Ireland* (2010) p. 62.

370 In 2010 the former functions of the Crisis Pregnancy Agency were transferred to Ireland's Health Service (HSE) under the Health (Miscellaneous Provisions) Act 2009 (Act Number 25 of 2009). See www.crisispregnancy.ie/about-us/overview, visited 15 May 2014.

launched a special campaign to raise awareness about these free services in 2008.[371] The programme since then, *inter alia*, funds '[...] free post-abortion counselling and medical checkups to any woman that is in need of these services'.[372]

Despite these regulations, the applicants in the *A, B and C* case complained about insufficient follow-up care in Ireland after they had had abortions abroad. *Doctors for Choice Ireland* and the British Pregnancy Advisory Service (BPAS), who intervened as third parties in this case, also '[...] suggested that vital post-abortion medical care and counselling in Ireland were randomly available and of poor quality due to a lack of training and the reluctance of women to seek care.'[373] The Irish government disputed these submissions and submitted, *inter alia*, that the Irish College of GPs had reported that 95 per cent of doctors provided medical care after abortion.[374] The ECtHR found no violation of the Convention in respect of follow-up care after an abortion abroad.[375]

In respect of AHR treatment no such provision in respect of information or follow-up care is made. Under the 2014 Bill advertisement for surrogacy was prohibited, however, such a prohibition does not necessarily exclude the provision of neutral information about foreign treatment options. In respect of follow-up treatment for AHR treatment equally no specific provision is made in Irish law, nor in guidelines by the medical profession.

5.5.4. Cross-border surrogacy under Irish law

Irish law does not provide for specific conflict-of-laws rules for cross-border surrogacy cases. Further, although there have been reports of such cases being initiated,[376] there have been very few published court judgments on the matter, as the Circuit Court, generally does not give written judgments. There are reportedly

371 See www.abortionaftercare.ie, visited 22 May 2014.

372 Www.crisispregnancy.ie/about-us/crisis-pregnancy-services, visited 23 May 2014. See also www.abortionaftercare.ie, visited 22 May 2014.

373 ECtHR [GC] 16 December 2010, *A, B and C* v. *Ireland*, no. 25579/05, paras. 121 and 207. *Human Rights Watch* (HRW) held in respect of the Irish situation in a 2010 report: '[...] many women struggle to access timely, accurate, and complete information about legal abortion services abroad. As a result, they experience delays in accessing care, which heightens the possibility of health complications from the intervention. The delays also contribute to the emotional distress that many women experience.' Human Rights Watch 2010, *supra* n. 336, at p. 22. The report refers to 'F. Gary Cunningham, Kenneth L Leveno, Williams Obstetrics (2005) Ch 9', where it is reportedly held that 'Abortion is generally a safe medical procedure if carried out under proper conditions. It is safest when provided within the first eight weeks of the pregnancy. As the pregnancy progresses, "[t]he relative risk of dying as the consequence of abortion approximately doubles for each 2 weeks after 8 weeks' gestation".'

374 ECtHR [GC] 16 December 2010, *A, B and C* v. *Ireland*, no. 25579/05, para. 122.

375 See more elaborately Ch. 2, section 2.2.3.

376 For example, it was reported in 2011 that High Court proceedings were brought by an Irishman and his wife, who was an EU citizen, in an effort to secure an Irish passport for their child who was born as a result of a surrogacy arrangement with a woman in Ukraine. Y. Daly, 'Surrogacy difficulties', *humanrights.ie* 1 March 2011, www.humanrights.ie/children-and-the-law/surrogacy-difficulties/#more-12454, visited 15 May 2014.

numerous Orders of Declaration of Parentage and Guardianship orders but these are not accessible to the public.

Since 2012, some guidance for international surrogacy cases can be found, in the guidance document on cross-border surrogacy cases that the Irish Department for Justice and Equality published in 2012 (see section 5.3.9 above).[377] This document was intended to provide guidance as to the principles that will be applied by the Irish authorities in examining applications for a travel document on behalf of children born outside Ireland as a result of surrogacy arrangements. It was made clear that Irish authorities take a child-centred approach to decision-making in this area. The view was expressed that '[...] best interests and welfare of children [could] most effectively be secured when they [were] in the care of a guardian who [had] legal authority to take decisions, including medical decisions, on their behalf.'

The rule that '[g]enerally speaking, only a parent or guardian of a child may apply for a passport on his or her behalf', can pose serious obstacles for intended parents who wish to acquire an Irish passport for their child if it was born to a foreign surrogate mother. As explained above (see section 5.3.9 above), under Irish law the birth mother – whether she is also the genetic mother or not – is considered the legal mother of the child. As explained in the guidance document:

> 'Under the Guardianship of Infants Act 1964, the mother of a child born outside marriage is the child's sole guardian. Under Irish law, family relationships and the rights and responsibilities that flow from them cannot be subjected to the ordinary law of contract and cannot, in particular, be transferred to another person, bought, or sold. This means that, under Irish law, the surrogate mother and the child will have a life-long legal relationship with one another.'[378]

If the surrogate mother is married, her husband is presumed, by law, to be the father of the child,[379] 'unless the contrary is proved on the balance of probabilities.'[380] The surrogate mother and the father will have joint guardianship over the child.

An intended father who is the genetic father of the child, can be recognised as the legal parent of the child, also if the surrogate mother is married. As explained in the guidance document:

> 'Under domestic Irish law, this requires an application for a declaration of parentage to be made to the Circuit Court under Part VI of the Status of Children Act 1987. The Attorney General must be put on notice of any such application if it is to be binding upon State authorities. Application should also be made by the commissioning father for a guardianship order. The commissioning father will need to provide evidence of paternity

377 Guidance document on cross-border surrogacy cases (version November 2014). The guidance document was published online at www.justice.ie/en/JELR/Pages/Surrogacy, visited 15 May 2014.

378 *Idem*, at p. 2.

379 Art. 46 of the Status of Children Act 1987.

380 Guidance document on cross-border surrogacy cases (version November 2014), p. 2.

> in support of this application. As a rule, the Irish authorities will require DNA evidence from a reliable source [...] to support a claim by a commissioning parent that he is a father of a child. Steps will have to be taken to serve any court proceedings issued on the surrogate mother and on her husband.'[381]

If the surrogate mother is unmarried the legal parenthood of the intended father who is also the genetic father of the child, can be recognised by the Irish authorities on the basis of DNA evidence.

The next step for intended parents, is the obtaining of travel documents for the child. In this regard it was noted in the Guidance document:

> 'In the best interests of the child and as a matter of best practice, a passport will be issued only where guardianship has been established but the Irish authorities may issue an Emergency Travel Certificate [...] to enable the child to enter the State.'[382]

An application for an Emergency Travel Certificate (ETC) must be made by a parent or guardian on the child's behalf. Only a genetic intended father can do so, after he has proven his genetic paternity on the basis of DNA evidence. The surrogate mother must consent to the granting of the travel document and if she is married, her husband's consent is also required.

The same principles apply to an application for an Irish passport for a child born outside Ireland, whereby, moreover, it must be established that one of the parents (the surrogate mother or the genetic intended father) has Irish nationality.[383] Hence, for non-Irish intended fathers resident in Ireland, it impossible to get an Irish passport for the child. Also, these rules render it impossible for same-sex couples consisting of two women, to obtain legal parenthood over a child born to a surrogate mother in another country, even if one of these women is the genetic mother of the child.

It was stressed in the guidance document that the Irish authorities could give no guarantees, before the birth of any particular child, that the child would be automatically regarded as an Irish citizen, that the intended parents would be regarded as parents or guardians of that child, and therefore that a passport or other travel document could be provided for that child. The document concluded with the strong advice that anybody considering becoming involved in an international surrogacy arrangement had to seek expert legal advice from a lawyer qualified in Ireland. Also, it was noted that the process could '[...] take some time and involve one or more applications to an Irish court.'

---

381 *Idem*, p. 3.

382 *Idem*, at p. 4.

383 As provided under the Irish Nationality and Citizenship Act 1956 as amended, and the Passports Act 2008.

The only written judgment in an international surrogacy case was issued by the High Court in March 2013.[384] In this case an Irish couple had concluded a surrogacy agreement in India. It concerned gestational surrogacy; an embryo had been created with the egg cell of an anonymous donor and the sperm of the intended father and had been implanted into the womb of the surrogate mother. Consequently a child was born in September 2010. It becomes clear from the judgment that an Emergency Travel Certificate had been issued in this case, but the subsequent application for an Irish passport for the child had been refused, because the intended father was not guardian over the child. The High Court was satisfied that the genetic paternity of the intended father had been established and that the child had been at all times in the care of both intended parents, who had occupied the role of holders of parental responsibility. The Court also considered it extremely unlikely that the surrogate mother would seek to play any role in relation to parental responsibility in the future. It was therefore 'a matter of considerable urgency and in the best interests of the child' that the child would obtain an Irish passport. The High Court appointed the intended father as guardian over the child and ordered that he be given the liberty to apply in the Circuit Court for a declaration of parentage.

After the family Relationships Bill had been published in January 2014, the Children's Ombudsman warned that by 'categorically ruling out the possibility of granting a declaration of parentage' where intended parents had illegally entered into a commercial surrogacy agreement, the children concerned risked being left stateless.[385] She held:

> 'With regard to non-commercial surrogacy, the proposed legislation does not address the recognition or otherwise of foreign surrogacy arrangements and/or court orders and the consequent parental status conferred on parties. Equally, the legislation does not address parental status under other types of assisted reproduction entered into abroad. These issues raise questions of European Union law and private international law which cannot be ignored. It may be that the legislature could enact regulations in a similar manner to statutory instruments that address the recognition of foreign same-sex relationships. There have been numerous statutory instruments which have recognised that certain classes of foreign relationships are entitled to be recognised in the State as a civil partnership.'[386]

The Children's Ombudsman accordingly recommended that a power was conferred on the Minister for Justice and Equality '[...] to recognise court orders relating to assisted reproduction or surrogacy from other jurisdictions that are compatible with

384 High Court 5 March 2013, 2011 No. 68 CAF, *unreported.*

385 R. Mac Cormaic, 'Ombudsman warns surrogacy law could leave children stateless', *theirishtimes.com* 24 June 2014, www.irishtimes.com/news/crime-and-law/ombudsman-warns-surrogacy-law-could-leave-children-stateless-1.1843869, visited 5 July 2014.

386 Advice of the Ombudsman for Children on the General Scheme of the Children and Family Relationships Bill 2014, May 2014, pp. 20–21, www.oco.ie/wp-content/uploads/2014/06/OCO AdviceonChildandFamilyRelBill2014.pdf, visited June 2014. In respect of the statutory instruments that address the recognition of foreign same-sex relationships, to which the Ombudsman refers, see ch. 11, section 11.4.4.

Irish law and public policy.'[387] Also, children should not be the victim of any decisions made by the parents in this regard, the Ombudsman held. She recommended:

> 'The General Scheme should retain a criminal sanction for those who engage in commercial surrogacy arrangements. The General Scheme should also provide for the legal consequences that arise for children born as a result of such arrangements; however, the Ombudsman for Children's Office does not believe that declarations of parentage should be denied where this would leave the child born as a result of a commercial surrogacy arrangement in a vulnerable legal position.'[388]

As noted above at various occasions, the Revised Family Relationships Bill of September 2014, no longer made any provision for (cross-border) surrogacy. As a result, couples and individuals who wish to engage in a surrogacy agreement in another country, have to resort to the guidance document referred to above, for any official guidance in this unregulated area.

5.6. Conclusions

While liberalising movements have taken place in most European States – including in the neighbouring UK – in recent decades, Ireland still firmly holds on to its restrictive abortion laws. The ban on abortion on medical and social grounds has not, however, remained unchallenged since its introduction. Pro-choice campaigners and individuals affected by the ban have tried to obtain a lifting or at least relaxation of the Irish abortion laws both at national and European levels. They have had some success, but the effects have been limited. The procedures that have taken place before the ECtHR have led to amendments to the Irish abortion laws to the effect that the necessary preconditions for obtaining an abortion abroad have been enshrined in national law. At the same time, the Irish government has sought further exclusion from the influence of European law on domestic policy decisions in this field, through the adoption of Protocols to various EU Treaties.

The ECtHR's judgment in the case of *A, B and C* v. *Ireland* (2010), prompted the adoption of legislation clarifying the existing restrictive abortion laws. Further action was taken after the tragic case of Mrs. Halappanavar, who died in a Galway hospital after having been refused an abortion. The Protection of Life During Pregnancy Act (2014) aimed to improve the procedural rights of women and has provided for more clarity for medical practitioners, but it has not brought about any material change. An abortion is still only allowed in Ireland if the life of the pregnant woman is endangered by the pregnancy. The ECtHR's finding in *the A, B and C* case that Ireland's ban on abortion for medical and social grounds did not violate the Convention, in combination with the awarding of a very wide margin of appreciation

[387] *Idem*, p. 21.
[388] *Idem*, p. 25.

to Ireland in this case, render it most likely that the Court would also hold the latest Irish abortion laws to be in conformity with the ECHR.

The Irish abortion laws have been subject to strong criticism. It has been held that the Irish government had regulated abortion services through 'delegation and doubt'.[389] Some observed that the Irish restrictive abortion laws 'merely exported the problem'[390] and that Ireland has taken a '"not in our own back yard" attitude to abortion'.[391] Wicks has spoken of 'the blatant hypocrisy of the Irish solution'. She wondered how the right to travel abroad for an abortion could be tolerated, if the views of the Irish people, and the Irish state, were so profound and fundamental to the continuation of its democratic society.[392] The Irish abortion policy has indeed often been referred to as an Irish solution to an Irish problem. This has annoyed others, who have pointed out that 'if it [was] to be called a problem [...] it [was] a world-wide problem'.[393] On the other hand, the Irish legislature has clearly proven itself not ready for any substantive liberalisation of the Irish abortion laws, and the pro-life movement is, next to the pro-choice movement, still very present in the public debate on the issue.[394]

The picture in respect of AHR treatment and surrogacy is somewhat different. Although AHR is a practical reality in Ireland – as is the case in many European States – it was long – and is mostly still – submerged in legal uncertainty. The Irish Courts unequivocally did not consider it the task of the judiciary to resolve this uncertainty (see section 5.3.1 above). It was therefore up to the Irish legislature to fill in the legal vacuum that continued to exist in Ireland as regards AHR and surrogacy. While the AHR Commission identified a need for such action as early as 2005, it was only in 2014 that first steps in this regard were taken.

In the meantime the demand for AHR treatment had not diminished – quite the contrary. AHR services are provided by private specialists and clinics only, and these services must be privately funded, apart from the fact that income tax relief applies. Because Irish fertility clinics and counsellors operated within a legal limbo and acted according to what they considered to be the boundaries of national law, they often referred patients to foreign clinics in jurisdictions where AHR was regulated more clearly, or where waiting lists were simply shorter, treatments were cheaper and/or more donors were available (see section 5.4).

The 2014 Children and Family Relations Bill provided for regulation of a number of AHR related issues. While initially not foreseen, its revised version provided

389 M. Fox and T. Murphy, 'Irish Abortion: Seeking Refuge in a Jurisprudence of Doubt and Delegation', 19 *Journal of Law and Society* (1992) p. 454. See also McGuinness 2011, *supra* n. 127, at p. 476.

390 Sherlock 1989, *supra* n. 10.

391 Schweppe 2001, *supra* n. 43, at p. 155.

392 E. Wicks, '*A, B, C v Ireland*: Abortion Law under the European Convention on Human Rights', 11 *HRLR* (2011) p. 556 at p. 563.

393 Fox and Murphy 1992, *supra* n. 389, at p. 456.

394 'Thousands turn out for Pro-Life vigil in Dublin', 8 June 2014, *thejournal.ie*, www.thejournal.ie/pro-life-vigil-for-life-dublin-942833-Jun2013, visited 24 June 2014.

for a right to know one's genetic origins in gametes donation cases. The proposed surrogacy legislation, on the contrary, was removed from the revised version of the Bill. Other matters, such as PGD, are still unregulated in the Irish jurisdiction.

Couples from Ireland that engage in cross-border surrogacy may encounter serious difficulties in establishing parental links with the child. Some guidance has been given by the Irish Department for Justice and Equality as to the principles that will be applied by the Irish authorities in examining applications for travel documents on behalf of children born outside Ireland as a result of surrogacy arrangements. It is however, uncertain as to how these principles apply if commercial surrogacy is concerned. Moreover, the policy is only helpful in cases where the intended father is the genetic father of the child (see section 5.5.4 above).

The importance that has been attached to genetic parenthood under Irish law has varied. It was because of his genetic parenthood, and the interests of the child in establishing contact with his genetic father, that a sperm donor was granted access to his child in *McD* v. *L & Anor.* In surrogacy cases the genetic parenthood of the intended father may be ground for recognising him as the legal father of the child. The genetic parenthood of an intended mother, on the other hand, does not have any effect in law.

All in all, an interesting picture has emerged from this chapter. While the protection of the unborn life under the Irish Constitution (which commences from the moment of implantation) has been the rationale behind very restrictive abortion laws, the rights of the child, on the other hand, have mainly been ground for regulating certain AHR practices and for the granting of travel documents in cross-border surrogacy cases. Generally, however, a legal limbo regarding AHR and surrogacy still exists.

Chapter 6
The Netherlands

6.1. Constitutional framework

At the outset it must be noted that the Dutch Constitution is not a very 'strong' Constitution[1] and as a result its prominence in respect of Dutch standard-setting in reproductive matters has been fairly modest. Hereafter first two Articles of the Constitution that are of relevance for reproductive matters are discussed, after which the rights of the (future) child; the status of the unborn under Dutch law and the right to know one's genetic parents are discussed.

6.1.1. The right to respect for private life (Article 10) and the right to inviolability of the person (Article 11)

Two Articles in the Dutch Constitution are particularly relevant for reproductive matters. Article 10(1) of the Dutch Constitution provides that everyone has a right to respect for his private life (*'eerbiediging van zijn persoonlijke levenssfeer'*), without prejudice to restrictions laid down by or pursuant to Act of Parliament. The Constitutional legislature explained that this right aimed to guarantee personal freedom, without interference by others.[2] The subsequent Article 11 (the right to inviolability of the person) is generally perceived as the *lex specialis* of Article 10.[3] Article 11 reads:

> 'Everyone shall have the right to inviolability of his person, without prejudice to restrictions laid down by or pursuant to Act of Parliament.'[4]

This right has been primarily perceived as a negative right. It grants two sub-rights: everyone has a right to be protected from interferences with his physical integrity and everyone has the right to freely decide upon his own body (the right to

---

1 See also ch. 1, section 1.4.

2 *Kamerstukken II* 1975/76, no. 13872, nos. 1–5, p. 41.

3 J. Gerards et al., 'Zelfbeschikking in de Nederlandse Grondwet' ['Personal autonomy in the Dutch Constitution'], in: *Achtergrondstudies Zelfbeschikking in de zorg* [Backgroundstudies on Personal autonomy in health care], Reeks evaluatie regelgeving: deel 35 (Den Haag, ZonMw 2013) p. 88, referring (in footnote 260) to B.C. van Beers, *Persoon en lichaam in het recht. Menselijke waardigheid en zelfbeschikking in het tijdperk van biotechnologie* [Person and body under the law. Human dignity and personal autonomy in the era of biotechnology] (Den Haag, Boom 2009) p. 126.

4 Translations of the Constitution by the Dutch Ministry of Foreign Affairs, online available at www.rijksoverheid.nl/documenten-en-publicaties/brochures/2008/10/20/the-constitution-of-the-kingdom-of-the-netherlands-2008.html, visited June 2014.

self-determination).[5] From this a requirement of informed consent follows, which has been very important in Dutch medical/ethical standard-setting.[6]

The Constitutional legislature expressly left it to the legislature and the courts to give (more) concrete interpretation to these rights.[7] These rights consequently do not play a very prominent role in Dutch debate and law on reproductive matters. This is reinforced by the fact that self-executing International Law standards have direct effect in the Dutch legal order,[8] while Courts cannot review the constitutionality of acts of parliaments.[9] In practice, Dutch courts tend to examine the compatibility of statutory law with International Treaty law, with the general effect that the ECHR has come to serve as a kind of shadow constitution.[10] Consequently, when in Dutch case law and academic literature the question is discussed whether a right to procreate exists, reference is generally made to Articles 8 and 12 ECHR and the nuanced jurisprudence of the ECtHR on this issue, as set out in Chapter 2.[11]

6.1.2. The rights of the (future) child

The Dutch Constitution does not contain a specific provision – comparable to Article 3 of the Convention on the Rights of the Child (CRC) – that establishes the principle of best interests of the child as a primary consideration in all actions and decisions affecting children.[12] However, as goes for many fundamental rights issues, the relevant international standards have played and continue to play a prominent role in the Dutch legal order. In 1997 a Dutch District Court ruled for the first time that Article 3 CRC has direct effect in the Dutch legal order and can thus be invoked in proceedings before the Dutch courts.[13] This means that Dutch authorities have to put the best interests of the child first in any law-making, policy decisions and judicial decisions. Children's rights have received increasingly more attention in Dutch politics and academia over the past decades, partly thanks to the lobby and

5 *Kamerstukken II* 1978/79, 15 463, nos. 1–2, p. 5.

6 Gerards et al. 2013, *supra* n. 3, at p. 86, referring to *Kamerstukken II* 1979/80, 16086, no. 3, p. 7.

7 *Idem*, at p. 93.

8 Art. 93 of the Dutch Constitution.

9 Art. 94 of the Dutch Constitution reads: 'Statutory regulations in force within the Kingdom shall not be applicable if such application is in conflict with provisions of treaties or of resolutions by international institutions that are binding on all persons.'

10 J.H. Gerards & M. Claes, 'National report – The Netherlands', in: J. Laffranque (ed.), The Protection of Fundamental Rights Post-Lisbon: The Interaction between the Charter of Fundamental Rights of the European Union, the European Convention on Human Rights and National Constitutions, Reports of the XXV FIDE Congress Tallinn, Vol. 1 (Tartu, Tartu University Press 2012) pp. 613–677.

11 See, for example, M. Eijkholt, 'Het recht op procreatie: voldragen of in statu nascendi?' ['The right to procreate: carried to term or in *statu nascendi*?'], 31 *Tijdschrift voor Gezondheidsrecht* (2007) p. 2 and A.C. Hendriks, 'Het recht op voortplanting en zijn grenzen. Redactioneel' ['The right to procreate and its limitations. Editorial'], 36 *Tijdschrift voor Gezondheidsrecht* (2012) p. 279.

12 This matter was also not discussed by the State Commission on the Constitution [*Staatscommissie Grondwet*] in its report of November 2010. Staatscommissie Grondwet, *Rapport Staatscommissie Grondwet*, Annex to *Kamerstukken II* 2010/11, 31570 no. 17.

13 Rb. Utrecht 26 March 1997 and 10 December 1997, *NJ* 1999 No. 462, ECLI:NL:RBUTR:1997:AC1768.

work of NGOs specialised in the area, such as *Defence for Children* and *Unicef Nederland*.[14]

6.1.3. The status of the unborn under Dutch law

Under Dutch law, the unborn does not individually bear rights; only as of birth is a child a bearer of rights. The Dutch Constitution does not contain any provision which explicitly sees at the unborn. In fact, it does not even contain a specific Article on the right to life.[15] This does not mean, however, that the unborn does not enjoy protection under Dutch law. The protection of human life is an important principle in medical-ethical decision-making.[16] It is considered to be always at stake if unborn life is concerned. From the moment of nidation,[17] the foetus enjoys a special status, the so-called '*status nascendi*'.[18] In medical-legal doctrine, the theory of '*groeiende beschermenswaardigheid*' – the idea that the more the unborn develops, the more worthy of protection it is – finds general support.[19] Article 1:2 Civil Code (*Burgerlijk Wetboek*, BW) provides that '[a] child of which a woman is pregnant, is regarded to have been born already as often as its interests require so.' This entails, *inter alia*, that an unborn child can be placed under guardianship ('*voogdij*')[20] or temporary supervision ('*voorlopige ondertoezichtstelling*'),[21] if the responsible authorities fear for the development and health of the unborn.[22]

---

14 Since 1995 these NGOs are united in the Kinderrechtencollectief [Children's rights Collective]. See www.kinderrechten.nl, visited 15 September 2014.

15 This right is protected by Arts. 2 ECHR, 2 CFR and 6 ICCPR, which have direct effect in the Dutch legal order. Further, Art. 114 of the Dutch Constitution provides that '[c]apital punishment may not be imposed.' Five out of ten members of the Dutch State Commission for the Review of the Constitution recommended that the right to life were included in the Dutch Constitution. This recommendation was, however, not followed-up by the legislature. State Commission for the Review of the Constitution 2010, *supra* n. 12, at p. 65.

16 *Kamerstukken II* 2006/07, 30 800 XVI, no. 183 and *Kamerstukken II* 2007/08, 29323, no. 46.

17 The status of conception before nidation (by Leenen referred to as 'status potentialis') is not regulated under Dutch law. See H.J.J. Leenen, 'De gezondheidsrechtelijke status van het embryo' ['The status of the embryo in medical law'], in J.K.M. Gevers and H.J.J. Leenen (eds.), *Rechtsvragen rond voortplanting en erfelijkheid* [Legal questions surrounding human reproduction and heredity] (Deventer, Kluwer 1986) p. 14.

18 *Idem*, at pp. 13–14.

19 *Inter alia* H.J.J. Leenen, *Handboek Gezondheidsrecht* [Handbook Medical Law], 2nd edn. (Alphen aan de Rijn, Samson 1988) p. 128; D.M. Fernhout, *Rechtsvragen rond in vitro fertilisatie en embryo-transfer* [Questions of law on *in vitro* fertilisation and embryo transfer] (Arnhem, Gouda Quint 1992) p. 5 and Th.A.M. te Braake, 'De juridische status van het embryo: een stevig aangemeerde leer' ['The legal status of the embryo, a firmly anchored doctrine'], 19 *Tijdschrift voor Gezondheidsrecht* (1995) p. 32. Critical was, however, W. van der Burg, 'De juridische 'status' van het embryo: een op drift geraakte fictie' ['The legal 'status' of the embryo: a drifting fiction'], 18 *Tijdschrift voor Gezondheidsrecht* (1994) p. 129. The theory of the '*groeiende beschermenswaardigheid*' of the unborn is clearly reflected in the Dutch abortion legislation, as set out in section 6.2 below.

20 E.g. Rb. Roermond 26 June 2009, ECLI:NL:RBROE:2009:BJ0644 and Rb. Rotterdam 9 May 2006, ECLI:NL:RBROT:2006:AX2185.

21 E.g. Rb. Groningen 27 April 2010, ECLI:NL:RBGRO:2010:BM3904; Rb. Dordrecht, 7 February 2012, ECLI:NL:RBDOR:2012:BV6246 and Rb. 's-Gravenhage 7 October 2008, ECLI:NL:RBSGR:2008:BG0849.

22 A still-born child is deemed to have never existed. Art. 1:2 (second sentence) BW.

Like in all medical-ethical issues the legislature's decision-making in respect of abortion and AHR treatment is furthermore guided by the principles of human dignity, personal autonomy of the patient and good health care (*'goede zorg'*).[23] Particularly in AHR cases, the best interests of the future child are, furthermore, an important guiding principle, as will be set out in section 6.3. Again, these principles are not included in the Dutch Constitution,[24] but are considered general medical ethical principles and general principles of law, which are furthermore (partly) codified in International Treaties, such as the ECHR and the United Nations Convention on the Rights of the Child.[25]

6.1.4. The right to know one's genetic parents

In 1994, in the *Valkenhorst* case,[26] the Dutch Supreme Court for the first time defined a right to know one's genetic parents (*'het recht om te weten van welke ouders men afstamt'*). The case concerned a woman who wished to know more about her genetic father, while her mother did not want to reveal his identity. The institution that had provided care to the mother right after she gave birth, did have more information about the father though, but refused to give the woman access to it as it relied on its duty of confidentiality towards its client, the mother. The Supreme Court ruled in this case that the plaintiff had a right to be informed by the institution about her genetic father, on the basis of the right to know one's genetic parents.

The Court derived the right to know one's genetic parents from the general personality right that was underlying the right to respect for private life; the right to freedom of thought, conscience and religion and the freedom of speech, which are all included in both the European Convention on Human Rights (ECHR) and the Dutch Constitution.[27] The Court thereby referred to both Article 7 of the International Convention for the Rights of the Child[28] and to case law of the ECtHR, namely the *Gaskin* case.[29]

---

23 *Kamerstukken II* 2006/07 30 800 XVI, no. 183; *Kamerstukken II* 2007/08, 29323 no. 46 and *Kamerstukken II* 2000/01, 27 423, no. 3, p. 5.

24 The State Commission for the Review of the Constitution [*'Staatscommissie Grondwet'*] recommended in 2010 to include a general clause in the Dutch Constitution, one paragraph of which would read: 'The State respects and guarantees human dignity, fundamental rights and fundamental principles'. Untill the day this research was concluded (31 July 2014), this recommendation had however not been followed up by the Dutch constitutional legislature. Staatscommissie Grondwet, *supra* n. 12, at p. 40.

25 Following Arts. 93 and 94 of the Constitution provisions of Internation Treaties which are binding on all persons by virtue of their contents have direct effect and take precedence over conflicting statutory regulations.

26 HR 15 April 1994, *NJ* 1994 No. 608, ECLI:NL:HR:1994:ZC1337 with case-note by W.C.E. Hammerstein-Schoonderwoerd.

27 *Idem*, para. 3.2.

28 Art. 7(1) CRC provides: 'The child shall be registered immediately after birth and shall have the right from birth to a name, the right to acquire a nationality and. as far as possible, the right to know and be cared for by his or her parents.'

29 ECtHR [GC] 7 July 1989, *Gaskin* v. *the United Kingdom*, no. 10454/83, as discussed in ch. 2 section 2.1.4.

The Court acknowledged that the right to know one's genetic parents was not absolute and had to be balanced with the rights and freedoms of others. The Court was also quite firm, however, that the right of the child had to prevail over the right of the mother to keep that information disclosed from her child, a right that was covered by the right to respect for private life. The Court stressed the 'vital importance' of this right for the child and held that its precedence was justified by the fact that the mother was partly responsible for the existence of the child. The Court remarked in this context that it was important to note that the case at hand did not concern donor insemination.

Since the year 2004 there is legislation in place that provides for protection of the right to know one's genetic parents in the context of gamete donation. The exact conditions under which this right can be effectuated are extensively discussed in section 6.3.2 below.

6.2. Dutch abortion legislation

The Dutch abortion legislation takes a primarily procedural approach. Under the Dutch law as currently in force, abortion is in principle lawful until the 24th week of pregnancy. The interests of the unborn child are in practice protected through a set of procedural requirements, which provide the decision-making procedure with the necessary guarantees.[30] The Dutch abortion legislation is aimed at ensuring that every decision to terminate a pregnancy is taken carefully and is only carried out if the emergency situation of the woman renders such termination inescapable.[31] Further, the treatment must be given by a medical practitioner in a hospital or clinic which is licensed to provide such treatment under the Termination of Pregnancy Act (*Wet afbreking zwangerschap*, Waz).[32] Abortion in a later stadium of pregnancy is criminalised,[33] but may exceptionally be exempted from punishment (see 6.2.2 below).

30 Commissie evaluatie regelgeving, *Evaluatie Wet afbreking zwangerschap* [Evaluation Termination of Pregnancy Act] (Enschede 2005) pp. 12 en 36, online available at www.ngva.net/downloads/WAZ_evaluatie_Definitieve_webversie_b.pdf, visited June 2014.

31 See *inter alia* Art. 5(1) Waz.

32 Act of 1 May 1981, *Stb.* 1981, 257, entry into force per 1 November 1984. Hence, this fifth paragraph functions as a statutory defence (ground for exemption from criminal liability). Paras. 2–4 of this Article provide for aggravating circumstances.

33 Art. 296(1) Sr provides: 'Any person who provides treatment which he knows, or could reasonably suspect, might terminate a pregnancy is liable to a term of imprisonment not exceeding four years and six months or a fourth category fine.'

6.2.1. Early legislative developments

The Criminal Code of 1881 penalised abortion.[34] Both the pregnant woman who carried out an abortion or who gave permission for having an abortion carried out, and the person carrying out an abortion (the abortionist) were liable to punishment. The maximum penalty to be imposed was dependent on whether the woman had given her consent to the termination, whether the abortionist was a medical practitioner and whether the termination resulted in the woman's death.[35] In a judgment of 1897 the Supreme Court had ruled that there was only criminal liability if the termination of a pregnancy concerned a foetus which was alive at the moment of termination.[36] Because this was practically impossible to prove, there were hardly any criminal convictions on the basis of these provisions.[37]

Following an amendment of the Criminal Code of 1911, it was no longer necessary to prove that the foetus was still alive at the time of the pregnancy termination.[38] This resulted in a certain increase in the number of prosecutions for abortions.[39] Nevertheless, a termination of pregnancy was permitted only in case a so-called 'medical indication' ('*medische indicatie*') was present.[40] According to the Explanatory Memorandum to the 1881 Penal Code, this requirement was met if the life of the woman was endangered by the pregnancy.[41]

From the mid-20th century onwards, fundamental societal changes took place, as a result of which abortion became the subject of public debate. During the 1950s and 1960s, opinions on issues like sexuality, marriage, pregnancy, preconception and family building changed.[42] In the words of the Dutch government:

> 'Abortion became the subject of public debate in the second half of the 1960s in the context of several far wider issues. The availability of oral contraceptives and sterilisation had

[34] Arts. 295 to 298 Sr (*old*), Act of 3 March 1881, entry into force 1 September 1886, *Stb.* 1886, 64. Before 1881 the *Code Pénal* contained provisions concerning abortion. See Commissie evaluatie regelgeving 2005, *supra* n. 30, at p. 23.

[35] Commissie evaluatie regelgeving 2005, *supra* n. 30, at pp. 23–24.

[36] HR 24 May 1897, W 6978, as referred to in P.F. van der Heijden, 'Juridisch voorspel tot de abortus ontwerpen' ['Legal prelude to the abortion plans'], 13 *Nederlands jurstenblad* (1976) p. 425 at p. 426.

[37] Heijden, van der 1976, *supra* n. 36, at p. 426 and Commissie evaluatie regelgeving 2005, *supra* n. 30, at p. 24.

[38] Art. 251*bis* Sr (*old*), *Stb.* 1911, 130.

[39] Before 1911 there were only a couple of prosecutions per year, whereas after 1911 the number of convictions on the ground of Art. 251 bis Sr (*old*) slowly increased (with some fluctuations), starting with 24 in the year 1912, to 79 in the year 1920. See J. Outshoorn, *De politieke strijd rondom de abortuswetgeving in Nederland 1964–1984* [The political fight surrounding abortion legislation in the Netherlands 1964–1984] ('s-Gravenhage, VUGA 1986), pp. 84 and 330. For more statistics, see section 6.2.4 below.

[40] See *inter alia* Ch.J. Enschedé, 'Abortus op medische indicatie en strafrecht' ['Abortion on the basis of a medical indication and criminal law'], 41 *Nederlands juristenblad, Njb* (1966) p. 1109 at p. 1114 and Heijden, van der 1976, *supra* n. 36, at p. 427 who refers to the Parliamentary discussions about abortion before the 1911 amendment.

[41] See Commissie evaluatie regelgeving 2005, *supra* n. 30, at p. 27.

[42] See *Kamerstukken II* 1978/79, 15 475, nos. 1–4, p. 11.

> paved the way for family planning, people's attitudes to sex were changing, the influence of the church had declined and abortion had been legalised in Great Britain. At the same time, economic growth in the Netherlands had raised the standard of living, and the population as a whole was more highly educated.'[43]

The possible harmful effects of an unintended pregnancy on the social well-being and personal development of the woman were recognised and the view that – within certain limits – abortion was a right of the woman, received increasing support.[44] Accordingly, from the beginning of the seventies, voices were raised to amend the existing restrictive abortion legislation.[45]

The call for a change of legislation was also produced by developments in the case law. The Dutch courts brought an increasing number of situations under the notion 'medical indication' and by doing so they gave a wider meaning to this notion than a danger to the woman's life only, as originally foreseen by the legislature. The first step in this direction was taken in 1942 when District Court Amsterdam ruled that a risk of suicide constituted a medical indication justifying an abortion.[46] Soon after, the physical and mental condition of the woman in a broader sense were accepted as medical indications.[47] It took until the 1970s, though, before also social factors were accepted as grounds for abortion.[48]

Because of these developments in the case law and the fact that medical profession was divided over the definition of the notion 'medical indication',[49] the monitoring and enforcement of the Dutch abortion legislation had become practically impossible.[50] Enforcement of the legislation was furthermore complicated by medical practitioners who refused to provide details on their professional activities to the health inspection

---

43 Communications Department, Corporate Communications and Public Diplomacy Division of the Dutch Ministry of Foreign Affairs, *Q&A Abortion in The Netherlands* (August 2011), online available at www.minbuza.nl/binaries/content/assets/minbuza/en/import/en/you_and_the_netherlands/about_the_netherlands/ethical_issues/qa-abortus-en-2011.pdf, visited April 2013.

44 J. de Bruijn, *Geschiedenis van de abortus in Nederland: een analyse van opvattingen en discussies 1600–1979* [History of abortion in the Netherlands; an analysis of views and debates 1600–1979] (Amsterdam, Van Gennep 1979) pp. 185–187, as referred to by Commissie evaluatie regelgeving 2005, *supra* n. 30, at p. 25 (footnote 15).

45 Outshoorn 1986, *supra* n. 39, at p. 13.

46 Rb. Amsterdam 5 February 1942, *NJ* 1942 No. 244.

47 Rb. Amsterdam 20 January 1949, *NJ* 1949 No. 586. See Commissie evaluatie regelgeving 2005, *supra* n. 30, at p. 27. See also the report of the so-called Commission 'Abortion question' (*'Commissie Abortusvraagstuk'*) *Kamerstukken II,* 1971, 11321, no. 2, p. 3, which explains that while the notion 'medical indication' was first considered to refer to a somatic indication only, later also psychological factors were accepted as medical indication.

48 Rb. Amsterdam 8 July 1976, *NJ* 1977 No. 477, ECLI:NL:RBAMS:1976:AC0431. See the report of the Commission 'Abortion question' 1971, *supra* n. 47, at p. 3. The Court ruled that it was for the medical practitioner to judge 'on good grounds'(*'op goede gronden'*) if a medical indication was present. In 1953 the Arrondissementsrechtbank Amsterdam rejected a social indication as justification for an abortion. Rb. Amsterdam 26 March 1953, *NJ* 1953 No. 377. See also Heijden, van der 1976, *supra* n. 36, at p. 427.

49 Outshoorn 1986, *supra* n. 39, at p. 292.

50 *Kamerstukken II* 1978/79, 15 475, nos. 1–4, p. 9 and Commissie evaluatie regelgeving 2005, *supra* n. 30, p. 27.

by referring to the legal duty of confidentiality.[51] The resulting mismatch between legislation and practice created legal uncertainty. Nevertheless, as a result of the enforcement difficulties, a rather large-scale abortion practice had developed in the Netherlands.[52] In the year 1970, the national *Stimezo* Foundation (the foundation for medically safe pregnancy terminations, *Stichting medisch verantwoorde zwangerschapsonderbreking*) established its first abortion clinic.[53] Many clinics were opened in the following years. The abortions provided by these clinics were, strictly speaking, illegal, but were tolerated by the authorities as long as certain quality standards were met. The Dutch abortion clinics treated a considerable number of women, amongst whom were many from neighbouring countries. For example, it was reported that in the year 1977 approximately 65,000 women were treated in Dutch abortion clinics, of whom about two thirds were women from the German Federal Republic (see also section 6.4.1.1 below).[54]

As a result of all these developments, revision of the abortion legislation was considered inevitable; it was held, even by governing parties, to be the only possible answer to the existing mismatch between legislation and practice and the resulting legal uncertainty and enforcement difficulties.[55] The first bills to the effect of an amendment of the existing abortion legislation were tabled in the early 1970s.[56] Serious controversy in Parliament, however, meant that it took another decade before any new abortion legislation was adopted. Abortion was considered 'extremely controversial', evoking 'deep emotions'.[57] There were confessional parties who held that human life was always to be protected, no matter its stage of development, while other parties felt that abortion was first of all a matter that fell within the woman's right to self-determination.[58] Not only was there serious controversy whether the abortion ban had to at all be levied, there was also no consensus on the content of any new abortion regulation. It was, for instance, debated whether legislation had to define the indications for abortion and there was debate about the role of doctors in abortion cases.[59] Because there were so many different approaches proposed, it was feared that none of the tabled bills would reach the required majority in Parliament,

51 *Kamerstukken II* 1978/79, 15 475, nos. 1–4, p. 9.

52 Outshoorn 1986, *supra* n. 39, at p. 14.

53 See www.mildred-rutgershuis.nl/historie.htm, visited April 2013. On this website it is explained that *Stimezo* was founded by a group of general practitioners who felt that it was not right that women had to go to England for the termination of a pregnancy. The clinic was financed with funds raised during a campaign on national television.

54 *Kamerstukken II* 1978/79, 15 475, nos. 1–4, p. 14, referring to 'E. Ketting and P. Schnabel, De abortus-hulpverlening in 1977'. For more statistics, reference is made to section 6.4.1.1 below.

55 *Kamerstukken II* 1978/79, 15 475, nos. 1–4, pp. 9 and 15.

56 *Kamerstukken II* 1969/70, 10719, no. 1; *Kamerstukken II* 1971/72, 11890, no. 1; *Kamerstukken II* 1974/75, 11890, no. 6; *Kamerstukken II* 1974/75, 13253, no. 1; *Kamerstukken II* 1974/75, 13302, no. 1 and *Kamerstukken II* 1975/76, 13 909, no. 1, as referred to in *Kamerstukken II* 1978/79, 15 475, nos. 1–4, pp. 11–12. See also the report of the so-called Commission 'Abortion question' (*supra* n. 47), which concluded yet in 1971 that the existing legislation had to be amended.

57 *Handelingen I* 1976/77, 14 December 1976, p. 136.

58 E.g. *Kamerstukken II* 1975/76, 13909, no. 5. For a profound study of the relevant Dutch debate, see Outshoorn 1986, *supra* n. 39. It must be noted, that there was also clear disagreement on the matter within (confessional) political parties. See *Handelingen I* 1976/77, 14 December 1976, p. 135.

59 E.g. *Kamerstukken II,* 1975/76, 13909, no. 5, pp. 3 and 11.

as a result of which the existing impasse would not be lifted.[60] After a 'compromise bill' was outvoted by the Senate in the year 1976,[61] a new government tabled a bill in the Parliamentary year 1978–1979. The initiating Ministers of Justice and Health held that abortion practice and abortion legislation had completely drifted apart and that the controversy around abortion formed a 'continuing burden for the Dutch political and mental climate'.[62] The Ministers considered that the changed views in society in respect to pregnancy termination rendered an amendment of the law inescapable.[63] In 1981 the Pregnancy Termination Act (*Wet afbreking Zwangerschap* (Waz))[64] was adopted with the smallest possible majority.[65] Under strong influence of the anti-abortion campaign, there was disagreement about the implementation of the Act, as a result of which it entered into force only more than three years later, in November 1984.[66] The Act was accompanied by an Implementing Order on Pregnancy Termination (*Besluit Afbreking Zwangerschap*).[67] The Pregnancy Termination Act was officially evaluated for the first time in the year 2005.[68] On the basis of that evaluation report, the at the time responsible Ministers saw no reason for amendment of the Act.[69]

6.2.2. The Pregnancy Termination Act (1981)

The 1981 Pregnancy Termination Act amended various existing laws, including the Criminal Code. The legislature attached value to maintaining *abortus provocatus* as separate criminal offence under the Criminal Code, as it gave expression to the protection offered to the unborn human life.[70] Since the entry into force of the Pregnancy Termination Act, paragraph 1 of Article 296 of the Dutch Criminal Code reads:

> 'A person who subjects a woman to treatment, where he knows or should reasonably suspect that by doing so pregnancy may be terminated, is liable to a term of imprisonment of not more than four years and six months or a fine of the fourth category.'[71]

---

60 *Kamerstukken II* 1975/76, 13 909, nos. 1–3, pp. 11–12.

61 *Handelingen I* 1976/77, 14 December 1976, p. 194.

62 *Kamerstukken II* 1978/79, 15 475, nos. 1–4, pp. 13 and 15.

63 *Kamerstukken II* 1978/79, 15 475, nos. 1–4, p. 24.

64 Act of 1 May 1981, *Stb.* 1981, 257, entry into force per 1 November 1984.

65 Parliament (Tweede Kamer) adopted the bill with 76 against 74 votes, the Senate (Eerste Kamer) with 38 to 37 votes. See *Handelingen II* 1980/81, p. 2316 and *Handelingen I* 1980/81, p. 82. See also Commissie evaluatie regelgeving 2005, *supra* n. 30, at p. 28 and Outshoorn 1986, *supra* n. 39, at pp. 13 and 272.

66 Outshoorn 1986, *supra* n. 39, at pp. 277–289.

67 Order of 17 May 1984, *Stb.* 1984, 356.

68 Commissie evaluatie regelgeving 2005, *supra* n. 30.

69 *Kamerstukken II* 2005/06, 30 371, no. 2, p. 4.

70 *Kamerstukken II* 1978/79, 15 475, nos. 1–4, p. 21.

71 Translation by L. Rayar and S. Wadsworth, *The Dutch Penal Code* (Colorado, Fred B. Rothman &Co Littleton 1997) p. 201. The Pregnancy Termination Act ended the criminal punishability of the woman, under the until that time existing Art. 295 Criminal Code. Since that time, the woman is only punishable if the child may reasonably be presumed capable of surviving independently of the mother.

Paragraph 5 of this Article provides that the act referred to in the first paragraph is not an offence if the treatment is given by a medical practitioner in a hospital or clinic which is licensed to provide such treatment under the Pregnancy Termination Act.[72] This statutory defence (*'strafuitsluitingsgrond'*) does not apply in situations where an aggravating circumstance applies[73] or in case the pregnancy has yet lasted more than 24 weeks.[74] The latter is so, because Article 82a of the Criminal Code clarifies that the killing of a foetus which may reasonably be presumed capable of surviving independently of the mother, amounts to the criminal offence of taking of the life of another person or of a child during or shortly after birth.[75] Hence, the killing of a viable foetus is qualified as homicide.[76] Expert opinion considers a foetus to be viable at 24 weeks and consequently 24 weeks is the absolute limit for the termination of a pregnancy.[77] Termination of pregnancy after 24 weeks of pregnancy (a so-called 'late abortion') is exempted from punishment only in cases of *force majeure* (*'overmacht'*). Such *force majeure* is considered to exist if there are reasons to believe that – despite the duration of the pregnancy – the foetus is not yet viable; in case the emergency situation of the woman has a medical cause; or in case the foetus has been diagnosed with abnormalities which would result in a life with serious and incurable suffering.[78]

This was established by the inclusion of a new Article (Art. 82 Sr) in the Criminal Code (See Art. II (A) and (D) of the Bill *Kamerstukken II* 1978/79, 15 475, nos. 1–4, pp. 22 and 32–34).

72 Any doctor who refers a pregnant woman to an illegal abortion clinic is accessory to the act criminalised in Art. 296 Sr. See C. van Oort, *Commentaar op Wetboek van Strafrecht, art. 296* [Commentary to the Criminal Code, Article 296] (OpMaat Sdu 2012).

73 Art. 296(2), (3) and (4) Sr.

74 See Van Oort 2012, *supra* n. 72.

75 Art. 82a Sr reads: "Taking a person's life or the life of an infant at birth or shortly afterwards' includes the destruction of a fetus which might be reasonably presumed to have a viable chance of existence independent of the mother's body.' Translation by Rayar and Wadsworth 1997, *supra* n. 71, at p. 107.

76 HR 29 May 1990, *NJ* 1991 No. 217, ECLI:NL:HR:1990:ZC8539 para. 5.3.2 and Commissie evaluatie regelgeving 2005, *supra* n. 30, p. 31.

77 Yet at the time of the drafting of the Pregnancy Termination Act, viability of the foetus was presumed from the 24th week of pregnancy. See *Kamerstukken II* 1978/79, 15 475, nos. 1–4, p. 33. See also HR 29 May 1990, *NJ* 1991 No. 217, ECLI:NL:HR:1990:ZC8539. In 2010 discussion arose in media and parliament on the question whether the time limit had to be brought back to, for example, 22 weeks of pregnancy. This debate arose after the *Nederlandse Vereniging voor Kindergeneeskunde (NVK)* [Dutch Association for Paediatrics] and the *Nederlandse Vereniging voor Obstetrie en Gynaecologie (NVOG)* [Dutch Association for Obstetrics and Gynaecology] published new professional guidelines to the effect that premature born between 24 and 25 weeks of pregnancy were actively kept alive and were treated. *Richtlijn Perinataal Beleid bij Extreme Vroeggeboorte* [Guideline perinatal policy in case of extreme premature birth], online available at www.nvk.nl/Nieuws/Dossiers/DossierRichtlijn24weken.aspx, visited June 2014. The NVK and the NVOG denounced the allegations that these guidelines implicated a lowering of the viability time limit of the foetus. See 'Reactie NVK op geluiden in de politiek om de abortusgrens te verlagen n.a.v. de richtlijn extreme vroeggeboorte' ['Reaction NVK to abortion discussion following the Guideline extreme premature birth'] of 21 February 2011, online available at www.nvk.nl/Nieuws/Dossiers/DossierRichtlijn24weken.aspx, visited May 2011. In 2011 the Minister of Health informed Parliament that following consultations with medical experts she saw no reason to amend the existing legislation and policy. *Kamerstukken II* 2010/11, 30 371, no. 21.

78 *Kamerstukken II* 1998/99, 26 717, no. 1 and Commissie evaluatie regelgeving 2005, *supra* n. 30, pp. 21–22. See also J.W. Wladimiroff and G.C.M.L. Christiaens, 'Het rapport 'Late zwangerschapsafbreking: zorgvuldigheid en toetsing' van de overleggroep Late Zwangerschapsafbreking' ['The Report 'Late pregnancy termination: care and examination' of the consultation group Late pregnancy termination'], 142 *Nederlands Tijdschrijft voor Geneeskunde* (1998) p. 2627.

The aim of the Pregnancy Termination Act is '[...] to balance two potentially conflicting interests: on the one hand protecting the life of the unborn child, and on the other helping women who are in a difficult position as a result of an unwanted pregnancy.'[79] Abortion is seen as a measure that can only be justified by an emergency situation for the woman.[80] Further, the decision to terminate a pregnancy must be taken with due regard for the individual circumstances of each case.[81] The legislature considered it impossible to set a general norm defining when abortion would be lawful or unlawful, as it considered the emergency and distress situations in which an abortion could be considered to be very diverse.[82] Instead, the legislature chose to set standards '[...] in the form of a set of requirements designed to guarantee that the decision to terminate is taken with all due care.'[83] The legislature considered it the State's responsibility to provide for such guarantees, while the woman and the medical practitioner involved in the procedure each have their own responsibility for the actual decision to terminate a pregnancy. According to the legislature the responsibility of the woman and the medical practitioner for such decision could only be done justice if the public authorities ensured that certain conditions were met. Therefore, abortions may only be carried out in licensed clinics and hospitals, a reflection period must be observed[84] and medical after care must be provided.[85] The various relevant conditions are explained in further detail in the subsections below. First, however, the scope of the Act is further clarified.

6.2.2.1. The scope of the Pregnancy Termination Act

The Termination of Pregnancy Act does not define any statutory time limit for pregnancy termination, but – as explained above – the absolute limit for the termination of a pregnancy is set at the point in time where the foetus may reasonably be presumed capable of surviving independently of the mother.[86] While expert opinion thus considers a foetus to be viable at 24 weeks,[87] in practice, '[...] most doctors will perform the procedure no later than 22 weeks into the pregnancy, because of the margin of error of ultrasound scans and to be sure they remain within the statutory time limit'.[88] Late abortions in situations in which the foetus is in principle viable,

---

79 *Kamerstukken II* 1978/79, 15 475, nos. 1–4, p. 17 and www.english.minvws.nl/en/themes/abortion/default.asp, visited April 2012. See also Commissie evaluatie regelgeving 2005, *supra* n. 30, at p. 11. This Commission concluded in 2005 that this aim was generally realised in practice.

80 *Kamerstukken II* 1978/79, 15 475, nos. 1–4, p. 15 and Art. 5(1) Waz.

81 Dutch Ministry of Foreign Affairs 2011, *supra* n. 43 and *Kamerstukken II* 1978/79, 15 475, no. 3, p. 15–16.

82 *Kamerstukken II* 1978/79, 15 475, nos. 1–4, pp. 10 and 15–16.

83 Dutch Ministry of Foreign Affairs 2011, *supra* n. 43.

84 Art. 3(1) Waz.

85 *Kamerstukken II* 1978/79, 15 475, nos. 1–4, p. 17. Art. 3(1) and Art. 5(2)(d) Waz. The after care includes a medical check-up and – if necessary – psychosocial care. If the woman consents, this care may be extended to her relatives. See Commissie evaluatie regelgeving 2005, *supra* n. 30, p. 39.

86 Art. 82a Sr.

87 *Kamerstukken II* 1978/79, 15 475, nos. 1–4, p. 33.

88 Dutch Ministry of Foreign Affairs 2011, *supra* n. 43. See also 'Verlagen abortusgrens ontneemt vrouwen kans op zorgvuldige afweging', press release of 12 November 2010 at the webiste of the KNMG www.knmg.artsennet.nl/Nieuws/Nieuwsarchief/Nieuwsbericht-1/

are excluded from the scope of the Pregnancy Termination Act. Such cases must be reported to a special expert committee, which examines if the medical practitioner in attendance has acted with due care.[89]

Pregnancy is assumed from the moment of nidation of the fertilised egg cell in the uterus. The admission of a drug to prevent nidation (e.g. the 'morning after pill') is excluded from the scope of the Termination of Pregnancy Act.[90] Initially this also held for so-called '*overtijdbehandeling*', i.e., pregnancy termination within 16 days of the expected menstruation failing to occur. At the time of the drafting of the Pregnancy Termination Act it was considered that within that 16-day period it could not be established with sufficient certainty whether the woman was pregnant or not.[91] Hence, the treatment – in practice often curettage – could not automatically be qualified as pregnancy termination.[92] In 2005 the Evaluation Commission recommended to bring the '*overtijdbehandeling*' within the scope of the Pregnancy Termination Act, as advanced medical techniques enabled to determine a pregnancy in a very early stage. The legislature agreed, but he also held that the existing practice had shown that no legislative amendment was necessary in this regard.[93] Hence, '*overtijdbehandeling*' is now considered to be covered by the Act.[94] As soon as a pregnancy is determined, any termination thereof must be in accordance with the criteria set in the Pregnancy Termination Act.[95] Administration of the 'abortion pill' – a combination of two medications (Mifepristone and Misoprostol (also

---

Verlagen-abortusgrens-ontneemt-vrouwen-kans-op-zorgvuldige-afweging.htm, visited April 2011 and www.english.minvws.nl/en/themes/abortion/default.asp, visited April 2012.

89 The *Centrale deskundigencommissie late zwangerschapsafbreking en levensbeëindiging bij pasgeborenen* [Central expert Commission late pregnancy termination and termination of life of neonates] was established in September 2006 to advise the Public Prosecutor. See www.lza-lp.nl, visited January 2010. See also the Protocol of the NVOG, as online available on www.nvog-documenten.nl/index.php?pagina=/richtlijn/item/pagina.php&richtlijn_id=756, visited 2 May 2010 and the instruction for the Public Prosecutor in cases concerning late pregnancy termination (*Aanwijzing vervolgingsbeslissing levensbeëindiging niet op verzoek en late zwangerschapsafbreking*), online available at www.om.nl/algemene_onderdelen/uitgebreid_zoeken/@151404/aanwijzing_0/, visited June 2010. See furthermore Commissie evaluatie regelgeving 2005, *supra* n. 30, pp. 32–33 G.G. Zeeman et al., 'Toetsing van late zwangerschapsafbreking, 2004–2007' ['Review of late pregnancy terminations, 2004–2007'], 152 *Nederlands Tijdschrift voor Geneeskunde* (2008) p. 2632.

90 Art. 1(2) Waz.

91 *Kamerstukken II* 1978/1979, 15 475, no. 6, pp. 42 and 61 and HR 29 May 1990, *NJ* 1991 No. 217, ECLI:NL:HR:1990:ZC8539, para. 3.10.

92 *Kamerstukken II* 2009/10, 32 123 XVI, no. 111, p. 3.

93 See *Kamerstukken II* 2005/06, 30 371, no. 8 and (later) *Kamerstukken II* 2009/10, 32 123 XVI, no. 111, pp. 1 and 3. In 2009 a proposal for an amendment to the Implementing Order was published, which would have the effect that licensed clinics and hospitals would be obliged to determine the duration of the pregnancy in every individual case (See *Staatsblad* 2009, 230). This amendment has, however, not (yet) entered into force. See also *Kamerstukken II* 2010/11, 30 371, no. 20, p. 5 (answer to question 19).

94 *Kamerstukken II*, 2005/06, 30 371, no. 3 and *Kamerstukken II*, 2006/07, 30 371, no. 8.

95 As Art. 296 Sr applies to the situation of '*overtijdbehandeling*', in any case the treatment must be performed by a medical practitioner in a licensed clinic or hospital. The requirement of a five-day reflection period is in practice often applied in a flexible way. The legislature considered it unnecessary and undesirable to make special provisions for the reflection period in cases of 'overtijdbehandeling'. See *Kamerstukken II* 2009/10, 32 123 XVI, no. 111, p. 3.

know as RU846)) that can cause an abortion until the 9th week of pregnancy – is unquestionably covered by the Pregnancy Termination Act.[96]

6.2.2.2. Emergency situation

The termination of a pregnancy may only be justified if the pregnant woman finds herself in an emergency situation.[97] The notion 'emergency situation' has not been defined by the legislature. Such definition was considered impossible as situations too diverse in nature could be covered by the notion (see also above).[98] The 2005 Commission evaluating the Act, did not see any reason to change this. The legislature also rejected a situation in which the medical practitioner in attendance would impose his or her judgment regarding the existence of an emergency situation on the woman.[99] As a result, it is actually the woman who decides if an emergency situation is present.[100] The medical practitioner has, however, the duty to inform the woman during the decision making process about alternative options and solutions.[101] At the same time, no-one can be obliged to carry out an abortion, or to participate in it.[102]

6.2.2.3. Five-day reflection period

To give a woman time for reflection, a five-day consideration period must be observed.[103] Article 3 of the Pregnancy Termination Act provides that an abortion cannot be carried out any sooner than on the 6th day after the woman has first consulted a doctor with whom she discussed her intention to have an abortion.[104] This reflection period – reportedly one of the most debated elements of the Pregnancy Termination Act[105] – is considered a means to protect the interests of the unborn and must

---

96 See *Aanhangsel Handelingen II* 1997/98, 1593 and *Aanhangsel Handelingen II* 1998/99, 1851.

97 See, *inter alia*, *Kamerstukken II* 1978/79, 15 475, nos. 1–4, p. 15.

98 *Kamerstukken II* 1978/79, 15 475, nos. 1–4.

99 Commissie evaluatie regelgeving 2005, *supra* n. 30, p. 37, under reference to *Kamerstukken II* 1979/80, 15 475, no. 6, pp. 9–10.

100 *Idem*, pp. 114 en 122.

101 Art. 5(2)(a) Waz.

102 Art. 20 Waz. If the doctor has (conscientious) objections against the abortion, he must inform the woman about it. If so requested and with the consent of the woman, the doctor has to give information to other doctors about the medical condition of the woman. The scope of this provision extends to non-medical staff members of clinics and hospitals, but the tax payer in general is not covered by it. *Kamerstukken II* 1978/79, 15 475, nos. 1–4, p. 22; HR 29 May 1990, *NJ* 1991 No. 217, ECLI:NL:HR:1990:ZC8539, para. 3.9 and Commissie evaluatie regelgeving 2005, *supra* n. 30, p. 39.

103 Art. 3(1) Waz. See also www.english.minvws.nl/en/themes/abortion/default.asp, visited April 2012 and Commissie evaluatie regelgeving 2005, *supra* n. 30, p. 41.

104 Under the Dutch health system it is usually the general practitioner with whom the woman first discusses her intention to have an abortion. The carrying out of an abortion before this reflection period has lapsed, is liable to punishment on the basis of Art. 16(1) Waz. The Act provides for a few exceptions to this rule, such as the situation where the health or the life of the woman is endangered by the pregnancy (Art. 16(2) Waz). See also *Kamerstukken II* 1979/80, 15 475, no. 6, pp. 40–41.

105 Commissie evaluatie regelgeving 2005, *supra* n. 30, p. 40. As the Evaluation Comission explains, it was initially debated whether the reflection period would commence at the moment the woman contacted a licensed abortion clinic or hospital or yet when she discussed her intention to have an abortion with her general practitioner. The latter was in the end decided.

therefore be strictly applied.[106] The medical practitioner in attendance must ascertain that the woman has maintained her intention for an abortion in full awareness of her responsibility for the unborn life and the consequences of the abortion for herself and others involved.[107] The legislature did not wish to formalise this issue any further.[108]

The 2005 Evaluation Committee recommended dropping the fixed term for the reflection period and instead to provide by law that in each individual case where a woman considered having an abortion, a reflection period was to be observed that would enable those involved to come to a well-considered decision.[109] This recommendation was not however followed-up by the legislature, as it held that observation of the minimum reflection period had not proven problematic in practice.[110]

6.2.2.4. Licensing and registration

The licensing system as introduced by the Pregnancy Termination Act aims to guarantee high quality of medical care.[111] In 2012 there were 16 licensed abortion clinics and 92 hospitals in the Netherlands who were licensed to carry out abortions.[112] The Health Inspectorate is responsible for monitoring their compliance with the Pregnancy Termination Act.[113] Licensed clinics and hospitals must submit quarterly reports to the Healthcare Inspectorate. These, *inter alia*, include information about the number of patients treated, their country of residence and age and the duration of the pregnancy at the time it was terminated.[114]

6.2.3. Reception of the Pregnancy Termination Act

The entry into force of the Pregnancy Termination Act did not take away all abortion controversy. From the moment of its adoption, the anti-abortion campaign continued its activities.[115] The legality of the Act has been (indirectly) challenged by lawyers' association *Pro Vita* who claimed that by financing the termination of pregnancies, the State and the National Medical Insurance Board (*Ziekenfondsraad*), *inter alia*, violated the rights of the unborn. In 1995 the Supreme Court dismissed their claims, ruling, amongst other things, that Article 2 ECHR did not preclude national legislation under which abortion was legalised under certain circumstances.[116] Since

106 *Kamerstukken II* 1978/79, 15 475, nos. 1–4, p. 18.
107 Art. 5(2) Waz.
108 Commissie evaluatie regelgeving 2005, *supra* n. 30, at p. 38.
109 *Idem*, at p. 13.
110 *Kamerstukken II* 2005/06, 30 371, no. 2, pp. 3–4.
111 *Kamerstukken II* 1978/79, 15 475, no. 6, p. 31 and Commissie evaluatie regelgeving 2005, *supra* n. 30, at pp. 28–29.
112 See www.rijksoverheid.nl/onderwerpen/abortus, visited 17 October 2012.
113 Art. 14a Waz.
114 Art. 11 Waz. See also the statistics as discussed in section 6.4.1 below.
115 See Outshoorn 1986, *supra* n. 39, at p. 282.
116 HR 16 June 1995, *NJ* 1997 No. 131, ECLI:NL:HR:1995:ZC1757.

that time, the anti-abortion campaign has become less prominent in Dutch society and politics.

6.2.4. Criminal prosecutions for abortions in the Netherlands

Before the 1911 amendment of the Criminal Code, there were hardly any criminal convictions on the basis of Article 295 et seq. Criminal Code (see 6.2.1 above).[117] After 1911, the number of convictions on the basis of the new Article 251*bis*, apart from some fluctuations from year to year, generally increased until the late 1940s.[118] From that time the number of convictions slowly decreased. In the 1960s the number of criminal convictions dropped considerably[119] and in the 1970s, there were even years without any convictions (see also section 6.2.1 above).[120] The present author is not aware of any specific prosecution statistics since the 1970s.[121]

6.2.5. Abortion and public funding

Since the entry into force of the Pregnancy Termination Act, women resident in the Netherlands who have their pregnancy terminated, do not have to pay for the abortion. The costs of a termination performed by a licensed clinic are covered by the Exceptional Medical Expenses Act (*Algemene Wet Bijzondere Ziektekosten* (AWBZ)), while abortions carried out in a licensed hospital are covered by the health

---

117 In 1911 a Member of Parliament maintained that there were no more than one to two criminal prosecutions or convictions per year. *Handelingen II* 1910/11, 2 March 1911, p. 1584. Enschedé 1966, *supra* n. 40, at p. 1111. See also Heijden, van der 1976, *supra* n. 36, at p. 426 Outshoorn 1986, *supra* n. 39, at p. 84.

118 The number of convictions on the basis of Art. 251 bis Sr (*old*) (following which treating a woman or subjecting a woman to treatment while indicating or arousing the expectation that the treatment could interrupt her pregnancy, was criminalised ('[...] *opzettelijk een vrouw in behandeling nemen of een behandeling doen ondergaan, te kennen geven of de verwachting opwekkende dat daardoor de zwangerschap kan worden verstoord.*')) during the years 1911–1978 were as follows: 1911: 3; 1912: 24; 1913: 34; 1914: 23; 1915:27; 1916: 44; 1917: 43; 1918:47; 1919: 32; 1920: 79: 1921: 69; 1922: 50; 1923: 55; 1924: 50; 1925: 72; 1926: 70; 1927: 98; 1928: 97; 1929: 53; 1930: 44; 1931: 75; 1932: 48; 1933: 97; 1934: 95; 1935:98; 1936: 112; 1937: 92; 1938: 119; 1939: 125; 1940: 74; 1941: 100; 1942: 96; 1943: 138; 1944: *no statistics available*; 1945: *no statistics available*; 1946: 235; 1947: 233; 1948: 237; 1949: 177; 1950: 201; 1951:183; 1952: 180; 1953: 136; 1954: 120; 1955: 120; 1956: 113: 1957: 95; 1958: 105; 1959: 81; 1960: 83; 1961: 82; 1962: 71; 1963: 48; 1964: 38; 1965: 38; 1966: 29; 1967: 33; 1968: 32; 1969: 23; 1970: 14; 1971: 6; 1972: 1; 1973: 3; 1974: 0; 1975: 0; 1976: 0; 1977: 0; 1978: 0. Bruijn, de 1979, *supra* n. 44, at p. 239. See Heijden, van der 1976, *supra* n. 36, at pp. 429–430 and Outshoorn 1986, *supra* n. 39, at p. 330.

119 The 2005 Evaluation Commission pointed out that in the 1960s, there was no systematic practice of prosecution of medical practitioners. Commissie evaluatie regelgeving 2005, *supra* n. 30, at pp. 25–26. When the Amsterdam District Court ruled in 1976 that social factors could justify an abortion, it took into account that in the preceding two decades the Public Prosecutor had only exceptionally initiated prosecution in abortion cases, whereas it was common knowledge that in hospitals and – since 1971 – abortion clinics ten thousands of women, had had an abortion. Rb. Amsterdam 8 July 1976, *NJ* 1977 No. 477, ECLI:NL:RBAMS:1976:AC0431.

120 See also *Kamerstukken II* 1974/75, 13 161, no. 1.

121 Only incidental and controversial cross-border cases have been reported in the media (see section 6.4 below).

insurer.[122] Women from abroad who have a pregnancy terminated in the Netherlands have to bear the expenses themselves.[123]

6.3. Dutch legislation on assisted human reproduction and surrogacy

While the first child was born through IVF treatment in the Netherlands in 1983,[124] the general legislative framework for assisted human reproduction (AHR) was set and is set by the Embryo Act of 2002.[125] This Act sets limits to the handling and use of human gametes and embryos[126] in fertility treatment and scientific research, 'by prohibiting what is deemed impermissible and attaching conditions to other procedures'.[127] The following section sketches the parliamentary history and the main features of the Embryo Act. The subsequent subsections discuss various elements of the Act and related acts thematically. It will become clear that the introduction and regulation of each new AHR technique was accompanied by elaborate public and political debate.

6.3.1. The Embryo Act (2002)

When the first *in vitro* fertilisation (IVF) treatments took place in the Netherlands in the 1980s, the debate on reproductive medicine and the use of embryos was triggered.[128] It was clear that very diverse views existed in society in respect of these sensitive issues[129] and that these views changed as medical science advanced continuously.[130] From the outset, the Dutch government developed a (provisional) policy in the field,[131] as it felt that certain interests at stake in matters of assisted

122 Dutch Ministry of Foreign Affairs 2011, *supra* n. 43.

123 *Idem.*

124 *Kamerstukken II* 2012/13, 33 400 XVI, no. 155.

125 *Wet van 20 juni 2002, houdende regels inzake handelingen met geslachtscellen en embryo's (Embryowet)* [Act of 20 June 2002, containing rules relating to the use of human gametes and embryos], *Stb.* 2002, 338.

126 Under this Act the term 'gametes' is defined as: 'human spermatozoa and oocytes' and 'embryo' is defined as: 'a cell or a complex of cells with the capacity to develop into a human being'. Art. 1(a) and (b) Embryowet.

127 E.T.M. Olsthoorn-Heim et al., *Evaluatie Embryowet* [Evaluation Embryo Act], Reeks evaluatie regelgeving deel 20, Den Haag: ZonMw 2006, Annex to *Kamerstukken II* 2005/06, 30486 no. 1, pp. 9 and 17. Those provisions that govern the use of embryos in research are not discussed in this chapter.

128 Artificial insemination has been applied in the Netherlands since the 1950's. *Kamerstukken II* 1987/88, 20 706, no. 2, p. 8 and 13.

129 *Kamerstukken II* 2000/01, 27 423, no. 3, p. 2.

130 *Idem*, p. 5.

131 The first step towards this policy was the government's request to the Health Council in July 1982 for an advice on the medical, ethical, financial and legal implications of *in vitro* fertilisation. This was followed by a *Besluit tijdelijke regeling ivf ex artikel 18 lid 3 van de WZV* [Decree temporary regulation of IVF under Article 18(3) WVZ]] of 18 July 1985. Further, IVF treatment was (provisionally) excluded from the national health insurance by means of the Besluit niet-klinische buitenlichamelijke bevruchting ziekenfondsverzekering (*Stcrt.* 1985, 113). See *Kamerstukken II* 1987/88, 20 706, no. 2, pp. 13–14.

human reproduction needed protection by the State. It held this to be the case in particular for the interests of the unborn and the child. Additionally, the quality and financing of health care were considered grounds for government intervention.[132] Since 1988 a licensing system has been in force, on the basis of which IVF treatment can only be carried out in a limited number of licensed hospitals.[133]

The drafting of a special legislative act on the matter took considerably longer;[134] it was only in 2002 that the *Act containing rules relating to the use of gametes and embryos* (Embryo Act) ('*Wet houdende regels inzake handelingen met geslachtscellen en embryo's*' ('*Embryowet*')) was adopted. This was partly due to the fact that the legislature felt that most groups in society had to agree with the decisions that were made in this field and that the choices were to retain some degree of validity in the face of advances in medicine.[135]

It has been held that the drafting of the Embryo Act must also be seen against the background of the Biomedicine Convention of the Council of Europe of 1997.[136] Until today, however, this Convention has been signed, but not ratified by the Netherlands.[137] Should the Netherlands proceed to ratification, a few reservations must be made in respect of points on which the Embryo Act conflicts with the Convention.[138]

Taking human dignity and respect for human life in general as basic point of departure,[139] the Embryo Act imposes conditions and limitations on the use of gametes

---

132 *Kamerstukken II* 1987/88, 20 706, no. 2, pp. 6 and 10.

133 Koninklijk besluit [Royal Decree] of 11 August 1988, *Stb.* 379. This was later replaced by the *Planningsbesluit in-vitrofertilisatie* [Planning decree on *in vitro* fertilisation], *Stcrt.* 1998, 95 in conjunction with Art. 1 (i) Besluit aanwijzing bijzondere medische verrichtingen [Exceptional Medical Expenses Order], *Stb.* 2007, 238 and Art. 2 Wet op de Bijzondere Medische Verrichtingen (WMBV) [Exceptional Medical Expenses Act], *Stb.* 1997, 515. See als *Kamerstukken II* 1987/88, 20 706, no. 2, pp. 14 and 16; *Kamerstukken II,* 2000/01, 27 423, no. 3, p. 3 and L.E. Kalkman-Bogerd, 'Het nieuwe Planningsbesluit in-vitrofertilisatie. Enkele kanttekeningen' ['The new planning decree *in vitro* fertilisation. Some comments'], 23 *Tijdschrift voor Gezondheidsrecht* (1999) p. 56.

134 See also T.A.M. te Braake, 'The Dutch 2002 Embryos Act and the Convention on Human Rights and Biomedicine: Some Issues', 11 *European Journal of Health Law* (2004) p. 139 at p. 148. The 2006 Evaluation Commission spoke of a 'carefull manoeuvring' legislature in the various periods of government, on a ethically and emotionally charged terrain, about which the views in society widely differed, and in respect of which medical science developed at a high pace. Olsthoorn-Heim et al. 2006, *supra* n. 127, at p. 35.

135 *Kamerstukken II* 2000/01, 27 423, no. 3, p. 6. For the English translation, see Olsthoorn-Heim et al. 2006, *supra* n. 127, at p. 17.

136 B. Winter et al., *Evaluatie Embryowet en Wet donorgegevens kunstmatige bevruchting* [Evaluation of the Embryo Act and the Donor Information Act on Artificial Insemination] (Den Haag, ZonMw 2012), Annex to *Kamerstukken II* 2012–2013, 30486 no. 4, at p. 256.

137 State of affairs on 31 July 2014.

138 According to the authors of 2012 Evaluation of the Embryo Act this would in any case concern Art. 13 (concerning interventions on the human genome) and Art. 18 (concerning research on embryos *in vitro*) of the Convention. Were the legal exceptions on the prohibition on gender selection to be broadened, possibly a reservation had to be made in resepct of Art. 14 of the Convention. Winter et al. 2012, *supra* n. 136, at p. 256.

139 *Kamerstukken II* 2000/01, 27 423, no. 3, p. 5. For the English translation, see Olsthoorn-Heim et al. 2006, *supra* n. 127, at p. 17.

and embryos and limits the purposes for which these may be used.[140] The legislature has strived to find a balance between the principles of respect for human dignity and human life, and various other interests and values such as the advancement of the quality and safety of reproductive medicine, the best interests of the future child, the cure of illnesses and the interests of infertile couples.[141]

The Embryo Act is based on a system of standard-setting, formulating rights and defining responsibilities, whilst also drafting protocols and providing for reporting obligations.[142] Certain practices – namely the creation of chimeras (human-animal hybrids); cloning and gender selection (see section 6.3.4 below) – are explicitly prohibited under the Act.

The Embryo Act entered into force on 1 September 2002. It has since been evaluated twice, in 2006 and 2012.[143] The Act is supplemented by the Model Regulations Embryo Act ('*Modelreglement Embryowet*').[144]

6.3.2. Access to AHR treatment

In the Netherlands, the standard applied in decision-making around reproduction is the reasonable well-being of the child ('*het redelijk welzijn van het kind*'): doctors must refrain from providing assistance in reproduction if they are of the opinion that the future child runs a real risk of serious psychosocial or physical harm.[145] Any decision must be made on the basis of an individual assessment of the case at hand; the categorical exclusion of certain groups in society is not allowed.[146]

140 *Idem*, at p. 6. The Preamble to the Act reads: 'We have considered that it is desirable out of respect for human life to prohibit certain uses of human gametes and embryos, to regulate the conditions under which other uses of human gametes and embryos with a view to improving medical care may be permitted, and to lay down rules regarding control over gametes and embryos [...].'

141 *Idem*, at pp. 3 and 5.

142 *Idem*, at p. 7.

143 Olsthoorn-Heim et al. 2006, *supra* n. 127 and Winter et al. 2012, *supra* n. 136. By Act of 10 July 2013 the Embryo Act was amended as a follow-up to the 2006 evaluation. Wet van 10 juli 2013 tot wijziging van de Embryowet in verband met de evaluatie van deze wet [Act of 10 July 2013 amending the Embryos Act with a view to the evaluation of this Act], *Stb.* 2013, 306. The amendment that is most relevant for the present research concerns counselling for egg cell donors.

144 Following Art. 2 Embryowet the establishments where embryos are created outside the human body, or other procedures involving embryos are carried out, must draw up a protocol regarding the use of gametes and embryos. The establishments draw up their protocol on the basis of the *Modelreglement Embryowet* [Model Regulations Embryo Act], which is online available at the website of the *Centrale Commissie Mensgebonden Onderzoek (CCMO)* [The Central Committee on Research Involving Human Subjects], www.ccmo-online.nl/hipe/uploads/downloads/Modelreglement-Embryowet(1).pdf, visited April 2013.

145 NVOG, *Modelprotocol Mogelijke morele contra-indicaties bij vruchtbaarheidsbehandelingen* [Model Protocol concerning possible moral counter-indications for fertility treatment] pp. 2–3, online available at www.nvog.nl/Sites/Files/0000000935_NVOG%20Modelprotocol%20Mogelijke%20Morele%20Contraindicaties%20Vruchtbaarheidsbehandelingen%202010.pdf, visited June 2014.

146 *Idem*, p. 3.

IVF treatment is only provided if there is a medical indication for the treatment.[147] Further, IVF clinics have a certain discretion when it comes to access to treatment.[148] For example, Dutch legislation does not oblige IVF clinics to offer treatment to single women.[149] The Dutch Equal Treatment Commission (now the Human Rights Institute) held in 2000 that a refusal to offer IVF treatment to singles could be justified on grounds of the best interests of the child.[150] IVF clinics are also in principle free to decide if they wish to cooperate with a sperm bank. This has as a result that the access to IVF treatment may be more limited for same-sex couples when compared to different-sex couples, but the Dutch government has held this to be acceptable.[151]

Different age limits apply for different kinds of AHR treatment. Generally the limits range between 40 and 45 years.[152] For example, in respect of egg cell donation, it has been specified in the Model Regulation Embryo Act that the donor must be between 18 and 40 years old, while the maximum age of the acceptor is 45 years.[153] Age is also a relevant factor for reimbursement of the costs of AHR treatment under the Health Insurance Act (see 6.3.7 below).

6.3.3. Donation of gametes and embryos

Insemination with donated sperm (semen) has been practice in the Netherlands for a long time and artificial insemination has been made possible through the establishment of sperm banks, in the late 1980s. Egg cell (oocyte or ovum) donation

147 The relevant principles are laid down in the *Richtlijn Indicaties voor ivf* [Guideline indications for IVF] as drafted by the the Dutch Association for Obstetrics and Gynaecology (*Nederlandse Vereniging voor Obstetrie en Gynaecologie* (*NVOG*)) in the year 1998, online available at www.nvog-documenten.nl/uploaded/docs/09_indicaties_ivf.pdf, visited February 2010. Medical practitioners can find further guidance in the NVOG's Model Protocol concerning possible moral counter-indications for fertility treatment, *supra* n. 145 and the Landelijke Netwerkrichtlijn Subfertiliteit [National guideline subfertility], online available at www.nhg.artsennet.nl/kenniscentrum/k_richtlijnen/k_nhgstandaarden.htm, visited April 2012.

148 See also Rb. 's-Gravenhage (pres.) 17 July 1990, ECLI:NL:RBSGR:1990:AD1197.

149 See on this question also T. Veerman and A. Hendriks, 'Recht op toegang tot IVF. IVF bij alleenstaande, lesbische en oudere vrouwen' ['A right to access to IVF treatment. IVF treatment for single, lesbian and women of age'], 12 *Nemesis* (1996) p. 136 and College voor zorgverzekeringen 27 April 2000, BZ-00-1103.

150 Dutch Equal Treatment Commission, Decision 2000-4, online available at www.mensenrechten.nl/publicaties/oordelen, visited June 2014.

151 *Kamerstukken II* 32 500 XVI, no. 112, p. 3. See also Dutch Equal Treatment Commission, Decision 2009-31 online available at www.mensenrechten.nl/publicaties/oordelen, visited June 2014.

152 J.T.M. Derksen and P.C. Staal, *Rapport Een leeftijdsgrens voor vruchtbaarheidsbehandelingen* [Report an age limit for fertility treatment] (Diemen, CVZ 2012) p. 8, Annex to *Kamerstukken II* 33000-XVI, no. 188. For an example see www.umcutrecht.nl/zorg/patienten/poliklinieken/V/vruchtbaarheid/Veel-gestelde-vragen.htm, visited January 2013.

153 Modelreglement Embryowet, paras. 3.2.2, 3.3.1 and 3.3.2, online available at www.ccmo-online.nl/hipe/uploads/downloads/Modelreglement-Embryowet(1).pdf, visited April 2013. The Model Regulation reccomends caution with donors under the age of 30 years (para. 3.3.2). In 2007 the government saw no reason to codify the age limit of 45 for acceptors of donor gametes in legislation, as they held that the age limit was widely supported in medical profession. *Kamerstukken II* 2007/08, *Aanhangsel* No. 113, p. 242.

became technically possible only much later. For many years egg cell donation was hardly practiced in the Netherlands, as the technique for vitrification of egg cells had not yet been developed.[154] This only changed in the last decade and in 2012 the first egg cell donation bank opened its doors in the Netherlands.[155] Perhaps for reasons of its limited practical relevance, egg cell donation has never been criminalised under Dutch law. This is different, however, for egg cell donation in combination with surrogacy (see section 6.3.8 below).[156]

The Embryo Act sets conditions for the donation of gametes and embryos.[157] It is based on two central principles namely: (1) consent for donation must be given freely; and (2) payment for gametes (as goes for organs and human tissue) is considered incommensurable with human dignity.[158]

Adults who are capable of making a reasonable assessment of their interests in this regard may make their gametes available in order to induce pregnancy in another person or for research purposes.[159] Donating 'surplus' embryos which have been created in the course of an IVF treatment, for the purpose of inducing a pregnancy in another person, is also permitted.[160]

Gametes and embryos may be made available only by means of a written donation and without consideration, and only after the donor has been informed by the person storing the gametes or embryos regarding the nature and the purpose thereof.[161] The donor may revoke his or her decision at any time before the gametes or embryos are used, without giving reasons.[162] If an invasive procedure is required in order to obtain gametes from the donor, the consent must be given in writing and the donor must be informed by the person who performs the procedure of the attendant risks and

154 *Kamerstukken II* 1993/94, 23 207, no. 6, p. 1.

155 'Eicelbank op zoek naar vrouwen die doneren', *Algemeen Dagblad* 2 April 2012, p. 4.

156 Annex to Planningsbesluit *in vitro* fertilisatie 1989, *Stcrt.* 31 July 1989 and *Handelingen II* 1998/99, 818.

157 Arts. 5, 6 and 8 Embryowet.

158 *Kamerstukken II* 2012/13, 33 400 XVI, no. 155, p. 2.

159 Art. 5(1) Embryowet. With the sperm of one donor a maximum of 25 children may be conceived. J.K. de Bruyn, *Advies medisch-technische aspecten van kunstmatige donorinseminatie* (Utrecht: Centraal Begeleiding Orgaan voor de intercollegiale toetsing 1992). The Guideline was drafted in consultation with the Dutch-Belgian Association for Artificial Insemination (Nederlands-Belgische Vereniging voor Kunstmatige Inseminatie), the Dutch Association for Obstetrics and Gynaecology (Nederlandse Vereniging voor Obstetrie en Gynaecologie (NVOG)) and the Dutch Association on Clinical genetics (de Vereniging voor Klinische Genetica Nederland).

160 Art. 8(1)(a) Embryowet provides that adults who are capable of making a reasonable assessment of their interests in this regard may make available embryos which have been created outside the body for their own pregnancy, but which will no longer be used for this purpose, to induce pregnancy in another person. Embryos may also be donated to culture embryonic cells for medical purposes, medical and biological research and medical and biological education or to carry out research that is permissible under the Embryo Act using those embryos. Art. 8(1)(b) and (c) Embryowet.

161 Arts. 5(2) and 8(2) Embryowet. By Act of 21 December 2006 (*Stb.* 2007, 58), two new paragraphs were included in Art. 5 Embryowet, in order to implement the rules of Directive 2004/23/EC in respect of the information that must be provided to the donor.

162 Arts. 5(2) and 8(2) Embryowet.

draw-backs.[163] The donor must be given sufficient time for reflection to allow him or her to make a carefully considered decision on the basis of the information provided about making his or her gametes available.[164] If gametes are made available in order to induce pregnancy in another person, the donor must be given the opportunity to stipulate that his or her consent is required for the use of embryos created using his or her gametes for any other purposes.[165]

By providing that the provision of gametes and embryos should not be remunerated, the legislature '[...] wanted to ensure that the pursuit of profit [did] not play a role in donation'.[166] The legislature felt that to value gametes and embryos in terms of money was in violation with human dignity and endangered the special protection the embryo enjoys.[167] Reimbursement of expenses directly incurred as a result of treatment in which the said gametes and embryos are used is, however, lawful.[168] Further, mediation in the demand and supply of egg cell and sperm donors is not prohibited under Dutch law, as long as no profit is pursued.[169]

Until the year 2004, when the Donor Information Act on Artificial Insemination (*Wet donorgegevens kunstmatige bevruchting*, hereafter 'Donor Information Act') entered into force, a gamete donor could remain anonymous permanently.[170] The first initiatives to change this date back to the late 1980s.[171] In 1992 a bill on donor

---

163 Arts. 5(3) and 6(1) Embryowet. See also *Kamerstukken II,* 2000/01, 27 423, no. 3, p. 17. In 2013 the Act was amended so as too rescind the mandatory assessment by the Medical-ethical examination Committee (*medisch-ethische toetsingscommissie* (METC)) in cases of egg-cell donation. Wet van 10 juli 2013 tot wijziging van de Embryowet in verband met de evaluatie van deze wet [Act of 10 July 2013 amending the Embryo Act with a view to its evaluation], *Stb.* 2013, 206.

164 Art. 6(2) Embryowet.

165 Art. 6(4) Embryowet.

166 Olsthoorn-Heim et al. 2006, *supra* n. 127, at p. 19.

167 *Kamerstukken II* 2000/01, 27 423, no. 3, p. 16.

168 Art. 27 Embryowet provides: 'It is prohibited to charge a fee for providing gametes and embryos made available pursuant to Sections 5, 8 and 9 of this Act to third parties if the said fee exceeds the costs directly incurred as a result of procedures carried out using the said gametes and embryos.' In the 2006 Evaluation Report it was noted that '[i]n practice reimbursement of expenses is evidently accepted.' Olsthoorn-Heim et al. 2006, *supra* n. 127, at pp. 11 and 19. In 2012 the Minister of Health informed Parliament that medical profession, even though it had not yet issued a formal opinion on the matter, considered an amount between 500 and 1,000 euros reasonable. *Aanhangsel Handelingen II* 2011/12, 1162, pp. 1–2. The authors of the 2012 Evaluation went even a bit further; it was held that it was acceptable if the reimbursement of expenses to some extent encouraged women to donate, as long as it did not lead to a financially motivated donation. The report invited the government to reconsider how the reimbursement for costs related to the prohibition to charge a fee. Winter et al. 2012, *supra* n. 136, at pp. 252–253.

169 *Aanhangsel Handelingen II* 2011/12, 792, pp. 1–2. Trade in gametes has always been prohibited under Dutch law. Annex to Planningsbesluit *in vitro* fertilisatie 1989, *Stcrt.* 31 July 1989 and *Handelingen II* 1998/99, 818.

170 Wet donorgegevens kunstmatige bevruchting [Donor Information Act on Artificial Insemination] Act of 25 April 2002, *Stb.* 2002, 240, entry into force per 1 January 2004. The Act is accompanied by an Implementing order (*Besluit donorgegevens kunstmatige bevruchting, Stb.* 2003, 320). The first Evaluation of this act was published in 2012. Winter et al. 2012, *supra* n. 136.

171 The 2012 Evaluation report noted that in 1988 there had yet been a bill tabled for the amendment of the parentage laws (*'herziening van het afstammingsrecht'*). Winter et al. 2012, *supra* n. 136, at p. 50. The bill was revoked five years later. The coalition agreement of 1989 provided that a survey would be

information in cases of artificial insemination was drafted and sent to various interest groups for feedback.[172] Its drafters considered knowledge about one's genetic origins a fundamental foundation for a deeper understanding of one's self.[173] Extensive political debate delayed the adoption of the Donor Information Act with another eight years. There was disagreement about the question of whether the long-term psychosocial effects for children conceived through anonymous donation had to be researched, before the law was amended. Furthermore, concerns were expressed that lifting of the anonymity would lead to a serious reduction of the number of donors and to a 'black market' in gametes and that people would have their recourse to other countries, where anonymous donation was legal.[174] The government, however, felt and maintained that these concerns were outweighed by the right of the child to know about its genetic origins.[175] In this reasoning the government was supported by a ruling of the Supreme Court of 1994, where it was held that the right to know one's genetic origins prevailed over the right to privacy of the (living) genetic parent.[176]

The Donor Information Act (2004) regulates the storing, administration and provision of the data of donors involved in artificial insemination.[177] Following its Article 2(1), all establishments that offer AHR treatment with the use of donated gametes have to provide data about these treatments and the donors involved to the Donor Information Registration Foundation (*Stichting Donorgegevens Kunstmatige Bevruchting*).[178] Apart from the personal data of the woman involved in the artificial insemination with the use of donor gametes, information about the donor must be registered.[179] In this regard a distinction is made between the donor's medical information; physical information (such as weight and colour of the hair and eyes); information about the donor's education; social information (such as the social situation and civil status) and personal (identifying) information (such as family name, name, date of birth and address) of the donor. While all these data are recorded by the Donor Information Registration Foundation and saved for at least 80 years,[180] the passing on of such information to third parties is subject to certain limitations.

---

conducted into the possible effects on children of not having access to information about their genetic links. *Kamerstukken II* 1989/90, 21 132 no. 8, p. 33.

172 *Kamerstukken II* 1992/93, 23 207, no. 3, p. 3. It was feared that an immediate lifting of the exisiting permanent donor anonymity would result in a strong decline in the number of donors and in an increase in what was called '*KID-toerisme*' (i.e. resorting to artificial insemination with the use of donated sperm in foreign countries).

173 *Kamerstukken II* 1992/93, 23 207, no. 3, p. 1.

174 See *Kamerstukken II* 2012/13, 30 486, no. 5, p. 17.

175 *Kamerstukken II* 1997/98, 23 207, no. 10, p. 8. For an adequate description of the legislative history of the Donor Information Act, see Winter et al. 2012, *supra* n. 136, at pp. 50–59. See also G.T. Oudhof, 'Het wetsvoorstel 'Wet donorgegevens kunstmatige inseminatie' en de (tegengestelde) belangen van het kind' [The Bill 'Act Donor Information Artificial Insemination' and the (conflicting) interests of the child'] *Tijdschrift voor Familie en Jeugdrecht* (2000) p. 229.

176 HR 15 April 1994, *NJ* 1994 No. 608, ECLI:NL:HR:1994:ZC1337.

177 Preamble to the Donor Information Act (*Wet donorgegevens kunstmatige bevruchting*), Act of 25 April 2002, *Stb.* 2002, 240 and *Stb.* 2003, 510.

178 Art. 2(1) Wet donorgegevens kunstmatige bevruchting.

179 Art. 3(2) Wet donorgegevens kunstmatige bevruchting. These personal data concern the woman's surname, given names, date of birth and address.

180 Art. 8 Wet donorgegevens kunstmatige bevruchting.

Medical information may be important for the health of the child conceived with gametes of a donor, and must therefore always be passed on to the child's general practitioner.[181] As of the age of 12, any child who reasonably suspects to have been conceived by artificial insemination with donated gametes can request information about his or her donor from the Donor Information Registration Foundation. The donor's medical, physical and social information, as well as information about the donor's education must be provided, if so requested by the child.[182] If the child has not yet reached the age of 12, any request of the child's parents for such information must be complied with.[183] Donors cannot object to and are not informed about the passing on of this information to the child or their parents by the Foundation.[184]

If the child has reached the age of 16, he or she may, furthermore, submit a request to obtain the donor's personal (identifying) information. This information is provided if the donor has given written permission for the passing on of this information to the child.[185] If the donor does not consent to the revelation of his personal data, only very weighty reasons may justify a refusal of the child's request for personal information.[186] In its assessment of the donor's refusal, the Donor Information Registration Foundation takes the interests of the child as a point of departure. Information about the donor may thus only be provided if the child (or exceptionally his or her parents or medical practitioner) so requests. The child must furthermore reasonably suspect to have been conceived by artificial insemination with donated gametes.[187] If no initiative is taken by the child, a gametes donor can remain anonymous.[188] Donors cannot themselves trace children conceived with their gametes.[189]

---

181 Art. 3(1)(a) Wet donorgegevens kunstmatige bevruchting. See also Art. 2 Besluit donorgegevens kunstmatige bevruchting [Donor Information Order] for a definition of the term 'medical information' in this context.

182 Art. 3(1)(b) Wet donorgegevens kunstmatige bevruchting. See also Art. 3 Besluit donorgegevens kunstmatige bevruchting for a specification of physical and social information of the donor.

183 Art. 3(1)(c) Wet donorgegevens kunstmatige bevruchting.

184 See www.donorgegevens.nl/informatievoordonoren, visited January 2013.

185 Art. 3(2) Wet donorgegevens kunstmatige bevruchting. If a child is conceived – whether before or after the entry into force of the Act – with the gametes of a donor who has declared in writing before June 2004 that he or she wishes to remain anonymous, no personal (identifying) information will be given to the child. If the donor has not made any such written statement, his or her consent will be sought by the Donor Information Registration Foundation. Only if the donor gives his or her permission, such personal data may be passed on to the child. See www.donorgegevens.nl/informatievoordonoren, visited January 2013.

186 Art. 3(2) Wet donorgegevens kunstmatige bevruchting. Boele-Woelki et al. give as an example of such a very weighty reason the situation in which the donor has founded his own family. K. Boele-Woelki et al., *Draagmoederschap en illegale opneming van kinderen* [Surrogacy and unlawful placement of children] (Utrecht, Utrecht Centre for European research into Family Law 2011) p. 54, Annex to *Kamerstukken II* 2010/11, 32500-VI. no. 83 and online available at www.wodc.nl/onderzoeksdatabase/draagmoederschap.aspx?cp=44&cs=6837, visited June 2014.

187 Some have held it to be a bottleneck that a child does not by definition know that its legal parents are not its genetic parents. Boele-Woelki et al. 2011, *supra* n. 186, at p. 54.

188 P.M.W. Janssens et al., 'Wet Donorgegevens Kunstmatige Bevruchting: inhoud en gevolgen' ['Act Donor Information Artificial Reproduction: content and consequences'], 149 *Nederlands Tijdschrift voor Geneeskunde* (2005) p. 1412 at p. 1416.

189 *Idem*, at p. 1412.

Donors of gametes or embryos do not, furthermore, establish any *de lege* family ties with a child born after donation.[190] The *mater semper certa est* principle implies that the woman who gave birth to a child after gamete or embryo donation is the legal mother of the child.[191] If she is married and her husband has consented to an act capable of resulting in conception – e.g. IVF treatment with the use of donated gametes – he is by law the legal father.[192] If the woman who gives birth is not married, her partner may acknowledge the child.[193] Hence, no adoption procedure is required for the acceptor parents to establish parental links.[194]

6.3.3.1. Post-mortem reproduction

Post-mortem reproduction was initially expressly rejected by the Dutch legislature.[195] As of the 1980s, however, the views in legal doctrine on this matter gradually changed, which development was reflected in the Embryo Act.[196] Its Article 7 provides that stored gametes are destroyed if the establishment responsible for their storage is informed that the donor has deceased, unless the donor has explicitly consented to the use of his gametes after his death.[197] In situations where such consent has been given and a request for use of the deceased's gametes has been made, the medical professionals involved in the AHR treatment must assess whether the interests of the future parent and child are sufficiently protected.[198] AHR establishments are under no obligation to assist in post-mortem reproduction[199] and some indeed refuse to do so.[200]

At the time when the Embryo Act was adopted, vitrification of egg cells was not yet common practice. When this method became lawful in the Netherlands in 2011, the legality of post-mortem reproduction through egg cell donation was debated by

---

190 Such family ties are established neither before nor after the birth of the child. *Aanhangsel Handelingen II* 2007/08, 1061, p. 2262.

191 Art. 1:198 BW.

192 Art. 1:200(3) BW. Paternity cannot be denied in this situation. See also *Kamerstukken II* 1995/96, 24 649, n. 3, p. 7.

193 Art. 1:199(c) BW.

194 *Aanhangsel Handelingen II* 2007/08, 1061, p. 2262.

195 Regeringsnota (Notitie) "Kunstmatige bevruchting en draagmoederschap" [Memorandum of the Dutch government on artificial insemination and surrogacy], *Kamerstukken II* 1987/88, 20706, no. 2, pp. 27 and 30.

196 For an overview of the relevant literature, see para. 3.4 of Hof Arnhem 16 April 2002, ECLI:NL:GHARN:2002:AE1479. See also Rb. 's-Gravenhage (pres.) 9 March 1989, ECLI:NL:RBSGR:1989:AH2615.

197 See also Hof Arnhem 16 April 2002, ECLI:NL:GHARN:2002:AE1479.

198 *Kamerstukken II* 2001/01, 27 423, no. 3, p. 19. See also T. Oudhof, 'Het belang van het kind bij kunstmatige voortplanting na overlijden: What's in the name', *Tijdschrift voor Familie- en Jeugdrecht* (2002) p. 288.

199 Modelreglement Embryowet [Model Regulations Embryo Act], pp. 25 and 39–44, online available at www.ccmo-online.nl/hipe/uploads/downloads/Modelreglement-Embryowet(1).pdf, visited April 2013.

200 W.J. Dondorp and G.M.W.R. de Wert, 'Postmortale eiceldonatie: wat is er tegen?' ['Postmortal egg-cell donation; what to object against it?'], 156 *Nederlands Tijdschrift voor Geneeskunde* (2012) p. 564 at p. 565.

some, but the relevant laws do not make a distinction between different types of gametes.[201]

6.3.4. Gender selection

In the mid-1990s, an initiative to open a so-called 'gender clinic' in the city of Utrecht where gender selection would be practised, attracted wide attention in media and politics.[202] Even though the Minister of Health denounced the clinic's practice immediately, it took until 1 October 1998 before a Ministerial Order prohibiting gender selection entered into force.[203] The clinic was ordered to close its doors as of the same date.[204]

The legislature considered gender selection to reduce children to the mere object of the wishes and desires of their parents and to give reproduction a purely instrumental character.[205] For that reason, a prohibition on gender selection was included in the Embryo Act. Its Article 26(1) prohibits gender selection in the course of the handling and use of gametes and embryos,[206] subject to a maximum penalty of one year imprisonment or a fine of the fourth category.[207] So-called 'additional' gender selection in the course of preimplantation genetic diagnosis (see 6.3.5 hereafter), is also prohibited.[208] The gender of the unborn in itself can never constitute a lawful

201 *Idem.* The authors of the 2012 Evaluation of the Embryo Act held, however, that from an ethical point of view, there was no fundamental difference between post-mortem reproduction with donated sperm and post-mortem reproduction with donated egg cells. They therefore held that the latter also had to be considered lawful and ethically acceptable. Winter et al 2012, *supra* n. 136, at p. 231. The Minster of Health, Welfare and Sports seemed to endorse this approach, as she did not make any distinction between the two types of gametes in her official reaction to the Evaulation. *Kamerstukken II* 2012/13, 30 486, no. 5.

202 *Kamerstukken II* 1994/95, 24 238, nos. 1 and 2. See also 'Er is ook veel te zeggen voor sekse-selectie', *de Volkskrant* 17 June 1995.

203 Besluit verbod geslachtskeuze om niet-medische redenen [Ministerial Order gender selection on non-medical grounds] of 16 June 1998, *Stb.* 1998, 336 and *Stb.* 1998, 567.

204 *Kamerstukken II* 1997/98, 26 083, nos. 362 and 1. Criminal charges were brought, but later dropped against the founder of the clinic. See *Aanhangsel Handelingen II* 2004/05, 825 and 1797. The founder unsuccesfully tried to re-open his clinic in 2002. *Kamerstukken II* 2002/03, 28 600 XVI, no. 4. In 2010 new controversy arose when it was – inaccurately – reported that the genderclinic had re-opened its doors. *Inter alia*, *Aanhangsel Handelingen II* 2009/10, 2408 and 2409.

205 *Kamerstukken II* 2000/01, 27 423, no. 3, p. 48.

206 With the entry into force of the Embryo Act in September 2002, the existing Ministerial Order of 1998 (*supra* n. 203) was repealed.

207 Art. 28 Embryowet.

208 'Additional selection' may occur '[...] when the sex is known as a result of the PGD or PGS procedure (which was carried out for a medical reason) and a choice is possible without further interventions being required.' The Health Council of the Netherlands held for the first time in 1995 that there was little objection in that situation to respecting the parents' wishes, provided that indeed no further interventions were carried out. It reiterated its opinion of 2006. See Gezondheidsraad, *Advies Preïmplantatie genetische diagnostiek en screening* [Advice preimplantation genetic diagnosis and screening], Advice no. 2006/1, pp. 19 and 22, online available at www.gezondheidsraad.nl/sites/default/files/06@01N3.pdf, visited June 2014. The legislature, however, disagreed and considered that also in this situation reproduction would have a purely instrumental character. Additional sex selection is therefore prohibited in Annex 2 to *Regeling preïmplantatie genetische diagnostiek* [Regulation

ground for abortion.[209] However, the second paragraph of Article 26 provides for an exception to this prohibition if there is a risk that the child suffers from a serious gender-linked hereditary disorder, such as Duchenne muscular dystrophy.[210] Recommendations by the relevant Evaluation Committees in 2006 and 2012 to reconsider this strict prohibition on gender selection, were only partly followed up by the legislature.[211]

6.3.5. Preimplantation genetic diagnosis (PGD)

Prenatal screening – blood tests, echoes and/or (non-)invasive diagnoses – forms part of the medical screening of the population and is therefore covered from public funds.[212] Such screening is not obligatory, but available to pregnant women in the Netherlands if they so desire.[213]

Preimplantation genetic diagnosis (PGD) has been subject to much debate since it was first practiced in the Netherlands in 1995.[214] The Dutch government's decision-making in medical-ethical matters, including PGD, is based on the principles of personal autonomy, protection of human life and good care.[215] While

---

preimplantation genetic diagnosis] *Stcrt.* 2009, 42. See also *Kamerstukken II* 2005/06, 30 300 XVI, no. 136, pp. 8–9.

209 *Aanhangsel Handelingen II* 2003/04,1914, p. 4049 and *Aanhangsel Handelingen II* 2006/07, 2267, p. 4804.

210 See also www.pgdnederland.nl/wat-is-pgd/wat-wordt-onderzocht/geslachtsgebonden-aan doeningen, visited March 2013.

211 The 2006 Evaluation Commission suggested that the prohibition of Art. 26 Embryowet was (possibily) too strictly formulated, as selection could also be desired in cases where the child risked to be the carrier of a serious gender-linked hereditary disease. The legislature disagreed and saw no ground for amendment of the law on this point. *Kamerstukken II,* 2006/07, 30 486, no. 3, p. 12. See earlier yet *Kamerstukken II* 2005/06, 30 300 XVI, no. 136, p. 10. The 2012 Evaluation Report recommended to reconsider the prohibition on gender-selection on non-medical grounds (Recommendation 4); to clarify whether the prohibition in Art. 26(1) Embryowet also saw at additional gender-slection in the course of genetic tests on medical grounds (Recommendation 5); to allow for gender-selection on grounds of a risk for 'non-Mendelian' hereditary disorders with unequal gender incidence (Recommendation 6) and to allow for gender selection in cases where the child risked to be the carrier of a serious gender-linked hereditary disease (Recommendation 7). Winter et al. 2012, *supra* n. 136, at p. 238. In respect of Recommendation 6, the Minister of Health considered that this matter required further scientific research and therefore considered it not (yet) correct to amend the law. The seventh recommendation was followed up though. *Kamerstukken II* 2012/13, 30 486, no. 5, pp. 5–6.

212 The costs of non-invasive prenatal testing are reimbursed from Public Health Insurance to women up to 36 years old. See *Kamerstukken II* 2013/14, 29 323, no. 90.

213 See the website of the *Rijksinstituut voor Volksgezondhied en Milieu* (RIVM) [National Institute for Public Health and the Environment] www.rivm.nl/Onderwerpen/B/Bevolkings onderzoeken_en_screeningen/Juridische_informatie_Screeningen_bij_zwangeren_en_ pasgeborenen, visited 9 September 2014.

214 *Kamerstukken II* 2011/12, 25424 no. 135, p. 1. In the year 1997 the first child was born after PGD in the Netherlands. PGD Nederland, *Jaarverslag PGD Nederland 2008 en cumulatief overzicht 1995–2008* [Annual Report PGD the Netherlands and cumulative overview 1995–2008] p. 3, Annex to *Kamerstukken II* 2009/10, 29323, no. 76.

215 *Kamerstukken II* 2007/08, 29323 no. 46, pp. 5–6. These principles were first set out in the Government Position on Medical-Etchical Policymaking, as laid down in *Kamerstukken II* 2007/08, 30 800 XVI, no. 183.

often these principles complement and strengthen one another, in the case of PGD, the legislature considered that personal autonomy of the patient had to be balanced against the protection of the (unborn and future) life.[216]

Under the present state of the law couples only qualify for PGD if they run a high individual risk of conceiving a child with a serious, hereditary illness or disorder that presents in most cases and which can be detected with PGD.[217] Further criteria to assess if an individual case qualifies for PGD are: the gravity and nature of the illness concerned; the treatment options; complementing medical criteria; and physical and moral factors.[218] PGD on non-medical grounds is prohibited.[219] Preimplantation genetic screening (PGS) – automatic screening in the course of every IVF treatment – is not regular practice in the Netherlands, but it has been on trial.[220] Selection on the basis of a child's human leukocyte antigen system (HLA system) with a view to future donorship for the child's sibling[221] is permitted only in case the future child itself runs a serious and individual risk of contracting the hereditary disease.[222]

The first initiative of State regulation in respect of PGD was taken in 2003, when a planning decree on clinical genetic research and heredity counselling (*Planningsbesluit klinisch genetisch onderzoek en erfelijkheidsadvisering*) was issued. Since then it has been provided that PGD may only be carried out in a licensed establishment.[223] To date, the government has considered one establishment sufficient to meet the demand for PGD in the Netherlands and consequently the

---

216 *Kamerstukken II* 2007/08, 29323 no. 46, p. 6. On relevant ethical principles in respect to PGD see also Th.A.M. te Braake, 'Preïmplantatie genetische diagnostiek: een stand van zaken' ['Preimplantation genetic diagnosis: a state of affairs'], 32 *Tijdschrift voor Gezondheidsrecht* (2008) p. 174.

217 Annex 2 to Regeling preïmplantatie genetische diagnostiek [Regulation preimplantation genetic diagnosis], *Stcrt.* 2009, 42.

218 *Idem.*

219 *Idem.*

220 As the Health Council of the Netherlands explained in its 2006 report on PGD: 'Pre-implantation genetic screening (PGS) involves *in vitro* investigation of embryos to detect numerical chromosomal abnormalities (aneuploidies).' The Council, furthermore, explained that the CCMO [Central Committee on Research involving Human Subjects] had 'issued permits for PGS trial protocols to four centres.' Gezondheidsraad 2006, *supra* n. 208. See also *Kamerstukken II* 2005/06, 30 300 XVI, no. 136 10.

221 As the Health Council of the Netherlands explained in its 2006 report on PGD: 'The question of selecting a future child on the basis of its HLA system can arise if a child already born to the couple has a life-threatening condition that needs stem cell therapy, but no suitable donor is available. Stem cells are rejected if the HLA systems of the donor and recipient are too different from one another. The required stem cells can be obtained from the navel cord blood of a brother or sister with a matching HLA system. The conditions for which this treatment is carried out include certain forms of leukemia and hereditary anemia that are associated with a severely diminished life expectancy if a transplant is not performed.' Gezondheidsraad 2006, *supra* n. 208, at, p. 20.

222 *Kamerstukken II* 2005/06, 30 300 XVI, no. 136, p. 10.

223 Art. 1 Planningsbesluit klinisch genetisch onderzoek en erfelijkheidsadvisering [Planning decree clinical genetic research and heridity counselling], *Stcrt.* 2003, 16 and Art. 1 (h)(fifth dash) Besluit aanwijzing bijzondere medische verrichtingen [Order instructions medical performances], *Stb.* 2007, 238.

University Hospital, Maastricht[224] presently has the monopoly on PGD.[225] The Centre has concluded partnership agreements with other Academic Medical Centres in respect of so-called 'transport PGD'.[226]

After the entry into force of the aforementioned 2003 planning decree, the Minister of Health requested the Health Council of the Netherlands (*Gezondheidsraad*) to deliver its opinion on PGD.[227] Following this opinion, the Secretary of State for Health announced in 2008 that PGD would also be made possible in respect of hereditary cancers, such as breast cancer and some forms of intestinal cancer.[228] These types of cancer are diseases that do not present themselves in all cases, which means that '[...] not all individuals with the mutation contract the disease'.[229] The letter by the Secretary of State caused political controversy about – what was called – 'embryo selection'.[230] Despite the strong opposition of certain confessional political parties, the government maintained its position on this point. This position was codified in a new Regulation on PGD (*Regeling preïmplantatie genetische diagnostiek*) which entered into force in 1999.[231] In the same year a national Committee on PGD indications (*Landelijke Indicatiecommissie PGD*) was established, which had the task of drafting guidelines and assessing new indications for PGD.[232]

The new Regulation did not end the debate. Particularly as medical science advanced, the debate about possible new indications and grounds for PGD continued.[233] In the 2010, political controversy emerged with regard to PGD for Huntington's disease (HD).[234] HD is a 'dominant genetic neurodegenerative disease, which causes physical

224 Www.english.azm.nl, visited June 2014.

225 Art. 1 and Annex 1 to Regeling preïmplantatie genetische diagnostiek [Regulation preimplantation genetic diagnosis], *Stcrt.* 2009, 42 (earlier Art. 2.3 of Annex to Planningsbesluit klinisch genetisch onderzoek en erfelijkheidsadvisering [Planning decree clinical genetic research and heridity counselling], *Stcrt.* 2003, 16). The option is left open that in the future the capacity will be extended to two establishments (see Annex 1).

226 The term 'transport PGD' sees at the situation where in the course of IVF treatment carried out in a partner Medical Centre, certain cells from the embryo created in the course of that IVF treatment are transported to the licensed Academic Hospital Maastricht for the actual PGD. Annex 1 to Regeling preïmplantatie genetische diagnostiek, *Stcrt.* 2009, 42.

227 Gezondheidsraad 2006, *supra* n. 208. For the government's reaction to the Advice, see *Kamerstukken II* 2005/2006, 30 300 XVI, no. 136.

228 *Kamerstukken II* 2007/08, 31 200 XVI, no. 147. For earlier opinions on the matter see *Kamerstukken II* 2005/06 30 300 XVI, no. 136 and *Kamerstukken II* 2007/08, 31 200 XVI, no. 10.

229 Gezondheidsraad 2006, *supra* n. 208, at, p. 18.

230 See, *inter alia*, *Kamerstukken II* 2007/08, 29 323, nos. 41, 43, 46 and 47 and *Aanhangsel Handelingen II* 2007/08, 6593 no. 93. See also PGD Nederland, *Annual Report PGD the Netherlands and cumulative overview 1995–2008* (Jaarverslag PGD Nederland 2008 en cumulatief overzicht 1995–2008), p. 4, Annex to *Kamerstukken II* 2009/10, 29323, no. 76.

231 *Stcrt.* 2009, 42.

232 See www.pgdnederland.nl/pgd-en-de-samenleving/landelijke-indicatiecommissie, visited January 2012. The Committee was established at the request of the Secretary of State of Health and consists of prominent medical experts, ethicists and a representative of patient interest groups.

233 See, for example, G. de Wert and I. De Beaufort, 'Sta nú ook andere varianten van PGD toe', *NRC* 1 July 2008, online available at www.nrc.nl/article1933210, visited August 2010.

234 *Kamerstukken II*, 2010/11, 25 424, no. 117.

and cognitive deterioration.'[235] All carriers of the HD gene contract the disease at some point in life, usually between the ages of 35 and 45. Each child of a parent with HD carries a 50 per cent risk of inheriting the HD gene. Persons with a family history of HD may prefer not to know their carrier status. They may, however, still wish to prevent the birth of a carrier child. With the combination of IVF treatment and PGD it is possible to select embryos without the HD gene. This is can be done without informing the person at risk and his or her partner whether any embryos were found to have the HD gene. This so-called 'non-disclosing PGD', where the person at risk is thus not informed if he or she carries the HD gene was explicitly ruled out in the Netherlands, as the 2009 PGD Regulation provided that in order to qualify for preimplantation genetic diagnosis (PGD), prospective parents had to be willing to find out their own genetic status.[236]

An alternative method is 'exclusion PGD'. Because in this method DNA linkage testing is utilised, the screening does not reveal if the person at risk in fact carries the HD gene.[237] For a long time this method was prohibited under Dutch law and as a consequence various couples in which one partner was at 50 per cent risk, went to Belgium for exclusion PGD.[238] In January 2011 the Committee on PGD indications recommended lifting the prohibition on exclusion PGD.[239] The Secretary of State for Health agreed with the Committee that the parent's right not to know had not been taken into consideration sufficiently in the debate on exclusion PGD.[240] He therefore announced that an amendment of the PGD-regulation would legalise exclusion PGD for HD and similar diseases.[241]

The PGD regulation was evaluated in 2012.[242] The authors of the report, *inter alia*, identified a couple of moral matters involved in PGD which needed further research,

---

235 E. Asscher and B.-J. Koops, 'The right not to know and preimplantation genetic diagnosis for Huntington's disease', 36 *J Med Ethics* (2010) p. 30.

236 See *Kamerstukken II* 2005/06, 30 300 XVI, no. 136, p. 10.

237 As explained in an article by Van Rij et al.: 'The exclusion test is based on identifying the grandparental origin of the two HTT alleles. If one of the two alleles from the affected grandparent is found in the fetus after exclusion PND, a termination of pregnancy [...] is offered, although the fetus only has a 50 per cent risk of being a carrier of the CAG expansion. In exclusion PGD, only embryos with one of the two HTT alleles from the non-affected grandparent are transferred. Both the availability and cooperation of family members in providing a sample for PGD workup is necessary for exclusion testing.' M.C. Van Rij et al., 'Preimplantation genetic diagnosis (PGD) for Huntington's disease: the experience of three European centres', 20 *European Journal of Human Genetics* (2012) p. 368. For another explanation of the method, see www.pgd.org.uk/resources/tests/huntingdon_exclusion.pdf, visited November 2012.

238 *Kamerstukken II* 2011/12, 25 424, no. 135, p. 3.

239 Www.pgdnederland.nl/pgd-en-de-samenleving/standpunt-werkgroep-PGD-HD, visited July 2011.

240 *Kamerstukken II* 2011/12, 25 424, no. 135, p. 4. On 'the right not to know', see also Asscher and Koops 2010, *supra* n. 235.

241 *Idem.*

242 N. Steinkamp et al., *Evaluatie Regeling Preïmplantatie Genetische Diagnostiek (PGD). Besliskader – behoefteraming – ethisch debat* [Evaluation of the Regulation preimplantation genetic diagnosis (PGD). Framework for decision-making – assessment of needs – ethical debate] (Nijmegen, IQ healthcare 2012), online available at www.zonmw.nl/nl/projecten/project-detail/evaluatie-van-het-beslissingskader-pgd-ervaringen-van-professionals-en-paren-met-kinderwens/rapport, visited June 2014.

such as a further broadening of the indications for PGD (e.g. hereditary cancers) and the concept of 'desire health care' ('*wensgeneeskunde*') which could lead to 'designer babies'.

6.3.6. Vitrification of egg cells

Vitrification of egg cells (oocyte vitrification or freezing) and subsequent cryopreservation have been lawful in the Netherlands since 2011. When the Medical Centre of the Free University of Amsterdam announced in 2009 that it intended to start offering this treatment, including on non-medical grounds, this attracted media attention[243] and various parliamentary questions were asked.[244] These prompted the Minister of Health, Welfare and Sports to ask the Amsterdam Medical Centre to postpone the actual carrying out of the treatment until political agreement upon the matter was reached.[245] The most controversial was cryopreservation of egg cells on non-medical grounds.[246] Some (confessional) political parties claimed, *inter alia*, that vitrification of egg cells was a form of 'desire health care', that it encouraged the postponement of family planning and that the method unacceptably stretched the moratorium on embryo research, as in force at the time.[247] Various other parties did not object to the method as such, but felt that vitrification was not to be covered by the Health Insurance Act, as they considered it 'a luxurious type of care'.[248] In 2011 a majority in Parliament agreed that vitrification of egg cells, both on medical and non-medical grounds, was lawful under the existing Dutch legislation, provided some conditions were met.[249] The reimbursement question was postponed. In 2012 the Health Care Insurance Board (*College voor zorgverzekeringen* (CVZ)

---

243 *Inter alia*, J. Koelewijn, 'AMC vriest eicellen in voor de 35-plus wensmoeder', *NRC Handelsblad* 3 October 2009 and p. 1; 'AMC biedt eicelbewaarservice', *De Telegraaf* 5 October 2009, p. 5.

244 *Aanhangsel Handelingen II* 2009/10, 255–257. See also W. Dondorp and G. de Wert, *Reageerbuisdebat. Over de maakbaarheid van de voortplanting* [Test tube debate. On the manipulability of human reproduction] (Den Haag, ZonMw 2012) pp. 15–16, online available at www.zonmw.nl/uploads/tx_vipublicaties/ZonMw_E_G_Reageerbuisdebat170x240.pdf, visited June 2014.

245 'Kamer staat vitrificatie toe', *Trouw* 15 April 2011, p. 10 and P. Herderscheê, 'AMC zet gezinspolitiek op de agenda; Eicellen invriezen om zwangerschap tot het 50ste jaar mogelijk te maken is volgens CU en CDA een brug te ver', *de Volkskrant* 16 July 2009, p. 3.

246 Winter et al. 2012, *supra* n. 136, at pp. 177–178. See also J. Nekkebroeck et al., 'A preliminary profile of women opting for oocyte cryopreservation for non-medical reasons', 25 *Human Reproduction* (2010) p. i15. See furthermore W. Dondorp et al., 'Oocyte cryopreservation for age-related fertility loss', 27 *Human Reproduction* (2012) p. 1231 and H. Mertes et al., 'Implications of oocyte cryostorage for the practice of oocyte donation', 27 *Human Reproduction* (2012) pp. 2886–2893.

247 P. Herderscheê, 'AMC zet gezinspolitiek op de agenda; Eicellen invriezen om zwangerschap tot het 50ste jaar mogelijk te maken is volgens CU en CDA een brug te ver', *de Volkskrant* 16 July 2009, p. 3.

248 A. Reerink, 'Alleen rijke vrouwen zullen zwangerschap kunnen uitstellen; Politieke partijen voelen in periode van bezuinigen weinig voor vergoeden van invriezen eicellen via verzekering', *NRC Handelsblad* 31 August 2010, p. 3; A. Reerink, 'Alleen voor rijke vrouwen; Politiek: invriezen eicellen voor later gebruik is luxezorg', *NRC Next* 1 September 2010 and 'Eicellen invriezen mag, maar wel op eigen kosten', *Nederlands Dagblad* 7 April 2011.

249 *Kamerstukken II* 2010/11, 32 500 XVI, no. 141 and 'Kamer staat vitrificatie toe', *Trouw* 15 April 2011, p. 10. The conditions are, *inter alia*, that women are well informed about the chances of reproduction after vitrification and that they are informed that little is as yet known regarding the long-term effects for children born through this technique. Another condition is that the women who make use of

now *Zorginstituut Nederland* (the National Health Care Institute)) recommended reimbursing vitrification only in cases where certain medical indications were present,[250] advice which the Minister for Health, Welfare and Sports followed on.[251]

6.3.7. AHR treatment and public funding

Reimbursement for AHR treatment under the Health Insurance Scheme, which is based on the principle of solidarity, has always been a much debated issue in the Netherlands. Debates have focused on the ethical acceptability and the medical necessity of (certain types of) AHR treatment, as well as on questions of cost efficiency.

In 1985 the Central Appeals Court for Public Service and Social Security Matters ('*Centrale Raad van Beroep*') ruled that IVF treatment had belonged to standard medical practice in the Netherlands since the year 1983.[252] This ruling was, however, no ground for the legislature to include IVF treatment in the cover under the Health Insurance Act ('*Ziekenfondswet*').[253] Instead, the Health Care Insurance Board (at that time named the '*Ziekenfondsraad*')[254] decided to include IVF treatment in its subsidy scheme ('*subsidieregeling*') on the basis of which experimental care was financed.[255] At maximum three cycles were reimbursed.[256] This situation lasted for many years.[257]

---

cryopreserved egg cells, may not be older than 45 years old. See Winter et al. 2012, *supra* n. 136, at p. 178.

250 CVZ, 'Vitrificatie van eigen eicellen', report of 3 April 2012, Annex to *Kamerstukken II* 2011/12, 33 000 XVI, no. 190, online available at www.cvz.nl, visited June 2014. See also Dondorp and De Wert 2012B, *supra* n. 200, at p. 62.

251 *Kamerstukken II* 2011/12, 33 000 XVI, no. 190.

252 CRvB 19 November 1985, ECLI:NL:CRVB:1985:AK2681.

253 See also. G. van Malestein, 'In vitro fertilisatie in het ziekenfondspakket! Afwijzend besluit Van der Reijden juridisch niet meer houdbaar' ['In vitro fertilisation in the National Health Scheme! Refusal Van der Reijden no longer legally tenable'], 41 *Medisch Contact* (1986) p. 722. Van Malenstein notes, however, that many private insurers nevertheless provided for reimbursement for IVF treatment.

254 Until 1999 the relevant body was called *Ziekenfondsraad*. From 1999 to 2014 it was named *College voor zorgverzekeringen* (CVZ) and since 1 April 2014 it carries the name *Zorginstituut Nederland* [National Health Care Institute]. See www.zorginstituutnederland.nl/organisatie/historie, visited June 2014.

255 This decision had retrospective effect untill the year 1983. Van Malestein 1986, *supra* n. 253, at p. 41.

256 Yet in 1993 critique was issued by medical profession on this limitation to three cycles. It was held that because of this limitation doctors felt under pressure to make the IVF treatment successful and therefore often implanted too many embryos in one cycle, thereby increasing the chances of multiply births (and accompanying costs). "IVF vaker vergoeden' Grens dwingt artsen tot verhoging', *Trouw* 9 August 1993.

257 See 'Simons wil subsidie IVF voorlopig handhaven', *Trouw* 5 November 1993, p. 5. As of 1998 de *Ziekenfondsraad* even reimbursed IVF treatment carried out in a private (initially non-licensed) clinic. 'Ziekenfonds gaat IVF vergoeden in prive-kliniek', *de Volkskrant* 25 March 1998, p. 7 and 'Ook vergoeding IVF-behandeling in kliniek Leiden', *NRC Handelsblad* 25 March 1998, p. 3. The Regeling subsidiëring ziekenfondsraad IVF [Regulation public financing IVF] of 23 November 1989, *Stcrt.* 1990, 20 expired per 1 January 2001.

In 2002 the Health Care Insurance Board held that IVF treatment could no longer be considered 'experimental' and proposed including it amongst the benefits under the Health Insurance Act.[258] This recommendation was not fully followed up by the legislature; as of 2004 only the second and third IVF cycles were reimbursed under the Health Insurance Act.[259] The first IVF cycle (including all medicine involved) was at the patient's own cost.[260] From the beginning this measure was criticised in politics[261] and in medical professional circles[262] as well by patient interest groups.[263] *Inter alia*, the argument was made that infertility was an illness and that this plan involved serious medical risks, for instance because patients would seek less expensive, but risky alternatives. The Netherlands Organisation for Health Research and Development furthermore endorsed the widely supported finding that it was possible to organise fertility treatment in a more efficient manner (*'doelmatiger zorg'*), for instance by setting a limit on the number of embryos that could be implanted in one IVF cycle.[264] At the same time there were (confessional) political parties who felt that imposed solidarity by means of the Health Insurance Act was undesirable for 'ideologically highly controversial' types of treatment like IVF treatment, abortion and euthanasia.[265] After lengthy discussions,[266] the government decided to reverse the measure from 2007; the first three IVF/ICSI cycles – including necessary medicine and including situations where gametes were donated – were reimbursed under the Health Insurance Act. The treatment had to be carried out in a licensed establishment; a female insured was entitled to reimbursement up the age of 40 only and patients had to pay a fixed amount of 500 euros per IVF cycle.[267]

This legislation soon again came under pressure as part of the government's general austerity policy. The coalition agreement of 2010 provided that as of January 2013

---

258 CVZ, *IVF/ICSI: aanbevelingen voor wijziging van de regeling op basis van de resultaten van effect- en evaluatieonderzoek* [IVF/ICSI: recommendations for amendment of the regulation on the basis of the results of effects and evaluation research] (Diemen, CVZ 2002).

259 See *Kamerstukken II* 2005/06, 30 300 XVI, no. 9.

260 This austerity measure was expected to bring in 25 million euros, but in fact brought in 20 million. Stichting Farmaceutische Kengetallen, 'IVF-maatregel bespaarde € 20 miljoen', *Pharmaceutisch Weekblad* (2007) p. 13.

261 *Kamerstukken II* 2003/04, 29 200 XVI, no. 143.

262 F. Santing, 'Meer meerlingen als patient betaalt; Deskundigen vrezen onbedoeld effect van schrappen IVF-vergoeding', *NRC Handelsblad* 28 August 2003, p. 2. The *Nederlandse Vereniging voor Obstetrie en Gynaecologie (NVOG)* [Dutch Association for Obstetrics and Gynaecology] even called the austerity measures 'inhuman'. 'Bezuinigingen op ivf zijn onmenselijk', *de Volkskrant* 13 November 2003, p. 3.

263 E. Bor, 'Harde streep door kinderwens', *Algemeen Dagblad* 2 December 2003, p. 9.

264 ZonMw [The Netherlands Organisation for Health Research and Development], *Vruchtbaarheidsstoornissen. Kansen voor doelmatiger zorg* [Fertility problems. Opportunities for more efficient care], report of June 2005, p. 12, Annex to *Kamerstukken II* 2004/05, 29800 XVI, no. 191. See also 'IVF kan twaalf miljoen euro goedkoper; Onderzoek voor ministerie', *NRC Handelsblad* 28 June 2005, p. 3.

265 *Kamerstukken II* 2004/05, 29 763, nos. 23 and 57.

266 *Inter alia* 'Kamer wil IVF in basisverzekering', *Algemeen Dagblad* 6 October 2005, p. 5; 'Politiek kibbelt nog over vergoeding ivf', *Het Financieele Dagblad* 19 October 2005, p. 5; 'Hoogervorst en Kamer botsen over vergoeding ivf', *Trouw* 14 October 2005, p. 218.

267 *Kamerstukken II* 2005/06, 30 300 XVI, no. 142, p. 3 and Art. 2.5(1)(3) in conjunction with Art. 1(e) Besluit Zorgverzekering [Health Insurance Order], *Stb.* 2005, 389.

only the first IVF cycle would be reimbursed.[268] This plan met with criticism from Members of Parliament[269] and medical professionals[270] and discussions arose which were similar to those held in 2004. Once again, more efficient and more patient-friendly alternatives were sought.[271] Following a report of the Health Care Insurance Board on the matter of 2012,[272] a more diversified approach was taken, whereby the entitlement to reimbursement was, *inter alia*, made dependent on the woman's age.[273]

Since 2013, reimbursement under the Health Insurance Act is provided for the first two IVF cycles for female insured patients until the age of 38, provided only one embryo is implanted in the woman's body.[274] If the woman is between 38 and 43 years old, the first three cycles are reimbursed, provided no more than two embryos are implanted during the treatment. If the woman has reached the age of 43, IVF treatment and other fertility treatment is reimbursed under the Health Insurance Act in exceptional circumstances only.[275] Preimplantation genetic diagnosis (PGD) – if carried out in conformity with the relevant regulations (see 6.3.5 above) – is also covered by the Health Insurance Act.[276] Treatment to obtain gametes from a

---

[268] 'Vrijheid en verantwoordelijkheid' ['Freedom and Responsibility'], Regeerakkoord [Coaltion Agreement] VVD-CDA, 30 September 2010, p. 18, online available at www.rijksoverheid.nl/documenten-en-publicaties/rapporten/2010/09/30/regeerakkoord-vvd-cda.html, visited February 2011. See also *Kamerstukken II* 2011/12, 33 000 XVI, no. 24. This austerity measure brought in 30 million euros. *Kamerstukken II* 2005/06, 30 300 XVI, no. 142, p. 1.

[269] *Kamerstukken II* 2010/11, 32 500 XVI, no. 46. See also F. Weeda, 'Ivf bij 41-plus, dat zijn meestal hoger opgeleiden; Vier vragen over bezuinigingen op ivf-behandelingen', *NRC Handelsblad* 15 May 2012.

[270] See C. Vos, 'Bezuinigen op ivf jaagt de kosten op', *de Volkskrant* 6 November 2010.

[271] *Kamerstukken II* 2011/12, 33 000 XVI, no. 24.

[272] CVZ, *Rapport Uitvoeringstoets alternatieven IVF-pakketmaatregel* [Report examining alternatives to the regulation in relation to reimbursement for IVF treatment under the Health Insurance], June 2012, Annex to *Kamerstukken II* 33000 XVI, no. 188, online available at www.cvz.nl/binaries/live/cvzinternet/hst_content/nl/documenten/rapporten/2012/rpt1206-uitvoeringstoets-alt.-ivf-maatregel.pdf, visited October 2012.

[273] See *Kamerstukken II* 2011/12, 33 000 XVI, no. 188 and CVZ, *Een leeftijdsgrens voor vruchtbaarheidsbehandelingen* [An age limit for fertility treatment], Annex to *Kamerstukken II* 2011/12, 33000-XVI no. 188.

[274] Exceptionally the implantation of two embryos is reimbursed under the Health Insurance Act.

[275] *Kamerstukken II* 2011/12, 33 000 XVI, no. 188, p. 2. See also www.rijksoverheid.nl/onderwerpen/zorgverzekering/basisverzekering, visited January 2013.

[276] See CVZ, *Preïmplantatie genetische diagnostiek (PGD) bij erfelijke borst/ovariumkanker is een te verzekeren prestatie* [Preimplantation genetic diagnosis (PGD) in case of hereditary breast or ovary cancer is a performance that qualifies for insurance under the Health Insurance Act], standpunt Zvw [Opinion Health Insurance Act] of 30 June 2008, online available at www.cvz.nl/binaries/live/cvzinternet/hst_content/nl/documenten/standpunten/2008/sp0806+pgd+bij+borst-ovariumkanker.pdf, visited June 2011 and CVZ, *Preïmplantatie genetische diagnostiek (PGD) in combinatie met HLA-typering van IVF-embryo's ten behoeve van eventuele stamceltransplantatie is verzekerde prestatie* [Preimplantation genetic diagnosis (PGD) in combination with HLA typification of IVF embryos with a view to a possible stem cell transplantation is a performance that qualifies for insurance under the Health Insurance Act], adviesaanvraag Zvw [request for advice under the Health Insurance Act] of 24 September 2007, online available at www.cvz.nl/binaries/live/cvzinternet/hst_content/nl/documenten/standpunten/2007/sp0709+typering+ivf-embryo-s.pdf, visited June 2011. It is noteworhty that the CVZ had held yet in 2010 (thus before the treatment was legally available in the Netherlands) that exclusion-PGD for HD was covered by the Health Insurance Act. CVZ, *Preïmplantatie genetische diagnostiek (PGD) met exclusietest bij de ziekte van Huntington* [Preimplantation genetic diagnosis

donor,[277] high-technological surrogacy[278] and egg cell vitrification on other grounds than medical grounds (see above) are not covered.

Certain costs made in the course of AHR treatment may furthermore qualify for tax deductions, so long as these costs are directly related to illness, invalidity or child delivery.[279]

6.3.8. Surrogacy

Dutch legislation and policy takes the discouragement of commercial surrogacy as a starting point. With a view to protecting both the interests of the child and the interests of the surrogate mother, the relevant legislation has since the late 1980s aimed to prevent commercial surrogacy from developing as a phenomenon in society.[280] The legislature at the time pointed at the risk of emotional problems for the surrogate mother in the long run; increased identity problems for any child born through surrogacy; the possibility that the natural process of bonding between mother and child after birth would be distorted; and the risk that the expectations of the intended parents (also referred to as commissioning parents) would not be met, even risking their rejection of the child.[281] Further grounds for this approach of discouragement that have been put forward also more recently are the complex ethical and legal questions involved in surrogacy; the view that this practice degrades a surrogate mother to a mere 'means of reproduction'; risks of exploitation of generally less wealthy and less educated surrogate mothers; and risks of trade in babies.[282]

With the inclusion of Articles 151b and 151c in the Criminal Code in the 1993,[283] all conduct that may advance the supply and demand of surrogacy – such as mediation by means of a professional practice or company and advertisements for surrogacy – is

(PGD) with exclusion test for Huntington's disease], Standpunt Zvw [Opinion Health Insurance Act] of 30 August 2010, online available at www.cvz.nl/binaries/live/cvzinternet/hst_content/nl/documenten/standpunten/2010/sp1008+pgd+bij+ziekte+van+huntington.pdf, visited July 2011. See also *Kamerstukken II* 2011/12, 25 424, no. 135, p. 5.

277 College voor zorgverzekeringen [Health Care Insurance Board] Opinion of 24 October 2006, no. 26084415.

278 College voor zorgverzekeringen [Health Care Insurance Board] Opinion of 20 November 2006, no. 26080732.

279 Art. 6.17 Wet Inkomstenbelasting 2001 [Income Tax Act 2001]. Rb. 's-Gravenhage 8 January 2013, ECLI:NL:RBDHA:2013:18948, referring (in para. 11) to HR 22 April 2005, ECLI:NL:HR:2005:AT4486.

280 *Kamerstukken II* 1987/88, 20 706, no. 2, p. 30 et seq; *Kamerstukken II* 1990/91, 21 968, no. 3, p. 3 and *Kamerstukken II* 2011/12, 33 000 VI, no. 69, p. 2.

281 *Kamerstukken II* 1990/91, 21 968, no. 3, pp. 1–2.

282 *Kamerstukken II* 2009/10, 32 123 XVI, no. 30, p. 2.

283 Act of 16 September 1993, *Stb.* 1993, 486. The Act entered into force on 1 November 1993. Its Art. 151b Sr reads:
'1. A person, who, in the practice of a profession or in carrying on a business, intentionally brings about or encourages either direct or indirect negotiations between a surrogate mother or a woman who wishes to be a surrogate mother and another person or arranges an appointment in order to carry out the intention specified in section 3, is liable to a term of imprisonment of not more than one year or a fine of the fourth category.

punishable.[284] In practice hardly any prosecutions have been brought on the basis of these provisions.[285] This has been held to be due to a lack of clarity of the rules and difficulties in meeting the burden of proof.[286]

Altruistic surrogate motherhood or the conclusion of a surrogacy contract as such are not punishable, but any such contract cannot be legally enforced in practice.[287] It is not lawful for Dutch clinics to assist in low-technological surrogacy, but people can establish this without medical assistance. As further explained hereafter, the

---

2. The punishment in section 1 is also applicable to a person who:
   a. publicly offers services consisting of bringing about or promoting negotiations or an appointment as specified in setion 1;
   b. discloses that a woman wishes to be surrogate mother or is available as such, or thath a woman is being sought who wishes to be a surrogate mother or is available as such.
3. The term 'surrogate mother' is to be taken to mean a woman who has become pregnant with the intention of bearing a child for another who wishes to acquire parental authority over the child or otherwise wishes on a permanent basis to care for the child and bring it up.

Art. 151c Sr reads:

'1. A person, who, in the practice of a profession or in carrying on a business, intentionally brings about or encourages either direct or indirect negotiations between a woman and another person or arranges an appointment with respect to her wish on a permanent basis to leave the care for and the upbringing of her child to another person, is liable to a term of imprisonment of not more than six months or a fine of the third category.
2. Without prejudice to the provisions in Art. 151b, section 1, section 1 of this Article is not applicable:
   a. where the bringing about or promotion specified in that section is by the Child Care and Protection Board or by a juristic person so designated by this Board;
   b. where the bringing about or promoting specified in that section consists in a referaal to an organization as specified under *a*.'

Translations by Rayar and Wadsworth 1997, *supra* n. 71, at pp. 142–143. Other relevant provisions of the Criminal Code are Art. 225 Sr (forgery); Art. 236 Sr (embezzlement of civil status); Art. 442a Sr (placement of a child younger than six months old, without permission of the Dutch Children Protection Board). Another relevant provision concerns the penalisation of placement of a foreign child for adoption without permission of the Central Authority for International Adoption under Art. 28 Wet opneming buitenlandse kinderen ter adoptie (Wobka) [Act on the fostering of children from foreign countries with the purpose of adoption]. See also *Kamerstukken II* 2011/12, 33 000 VI, no. 69, p. 3.

284 *Kamerstukken II* 2011/12, 33 000 VI, no. 69, p. 2. For an overview of the legal situation in respect of surrogacy until the 1993 legislation, see *inter alia* A.M.L. Broekhuijsen-Molenaar, *Civielrechtelijke aspecten van kunstmatige inseminatie en draagmoederschap* [Civil law aspects of artificial insemination and surrogacy] (Deventer, Kluwer 1991) pp. 151–177.

285 Boele Woelki et al. point out: 'An analysis of the legal databases in the field does [...] indicate that there are very few actual prosecutions. However, it is extremely difficult to obtain a clear impression of why few of the cases reported ultimately lead to charges being brought or penalties levied. Nevertheless, no real conclusion can be attached to this factual situation, as the causes for the low number of prosecutions are diverse and have not been able to be identified.' Boele-Woelki et al. 2011, *supra* n. 186, at p. 305. For cases brought on the basis of related provisions of the Criminal Code, see also pp. 44–48 of the report. In 1997 report was made of two criminal convictions for mediation in commercial surrogcay by the District Court Zutphen. See 'Vrouw veroordeeld voor advertentie draagmoeder', *de Volkskrant* 3 April 1997. For a published case in which the Dutch State put forward that an international commercial surrogacy agreement was against Art. 151b (2)(b) Sr, see Rb. 's-Gravenhage (vrzr.) 9 November 2010, ECLI:NL:RBSGR:2010:BP3764.

286 *Kamerstukken II* 2011/12, 33 000 VI, no. 69, p. 3.

287 *Idem*, p. 2 and Boele-Woelki et al. 2011, *supra* n. 186, at pp. 36 and 59. The authors conclude (on p. 61 of the report) that on the one hand a surrogacy agreement has limited effects, but on the other hand, it is not entirely without importance. For instance, a contractual agreement is a prerequisite for acces to supervised high-technological surrogacy in the VU Medical Centre (see below).

establishment of parental links between the intended parents and the child may, however, be difficult. The Dutch medical profession may only lawfully assist in so-called high-technological surrogacy and this is subject to strict conditions.[288] In 1998 the Dutch Association for Obstetrics and Gynaecology (*Nederlandse Vereniging voor Obstetrie en Gynaecologie* (NVOG)) drafted a guideline on high-technological surrogacy (*Richtlijn Hoogtechnologisch draagmoederschap*)[289] which, *inter alia*, set medical indications for access to this treatment and conditions for the intended parents and the surrogate mother. Also, it provided that counselling must always be provided in surrogacy situations. In the Dutch context only the gametes of the intended parents may be used in high-technological surrogacy,[290] which implies that same-sex couples are excluded from this treatment. Since 2006 the Medical Centre of the Free University of Amsterdam has been exclusively licensed to carry out this kind of treatment[291] and access to it is subject to strict conditions.[292] For instance, there must be a medical reason for the surrogacy and the surrogate mother must have at least one child of her own. Further, the surrogacy must be altruistic in character, although the reimbursement of certain expenses is accepted.[293] The Medical Centre of the Free University of Amsterdam itself has furthermore set the conditions that both the intended parents and the surrogate mother must have Dutch nationality, must speak the Dutch language and must be resident in the Netherlands.[294] The Minister of Health, Welfare and Sports announced in 2012 that she intended to critically review the conditions set by the medical profession,[295] but, as far as the present

---

288 High-technological surrogacy was introduced in the Netherlands in 1997. See also M.F.M. van den Berg and C. Buijssen, 'Hoogtechnologisch draagmoederschap' ['High-technological surrogacy'], 79 *Nederlands Juristenblad* (2004) p. 724 and S.M. Dermout, *De eerste logeerpartij, hoogtechnologisch draagmoederschap in Nederland* [The first time staying over, hightechnological surrogacy in the Netherlands] (Groningen, s.n. 2001).

289 Nederlandse Vereniging voor Obstetrie en Gynaecologie (NVOG) [Dutch Association for Obstetrics and Gynaecology], *Richtlijn Hoogtechnologisch draagmoederschap*]Guideline on high-technological surrogcay] (Utrecht 1999), online available at www.nvog-documenten.nl/uploaded/docs/richtlijnen_pdf/18_hoog_draagmoeder.pdf, visited June 2010.

290 Other forms of high-technological surrogacy – e.g. with the use of donated gametes – are not lawful in the Netherlands. See, however, Rb. 's-Hertogenbosch 18 August 2011, ECLI:NL:RBSHE:2011:BR5334. In this surrogacy case the Court entrusted the guardianship to the commissioning parents, while the child had been conceived during an IVF treatment, whereby use had been made of an egg cell donated by a third party (neither the commissioning mother, nor the surrogate mother).

291 *Kamerstukken II* 2011/12, 33 000 VI, no. 69, p. 2. From 1997 to 2004 high-technological surrogacy was provided in the Dutch Centre for non-commercial IVF Surrogacy in Zaandam. Due to financial problems, this centre closed its doors in 2004. In 2006, the Medical Centre of the Free University of Amsterdam initiated the second Dutch centre. See S. Dermout et al., 'Non-commercial surrogacy: an account of patient management in the first Dutch Centre for IVF Surrogacy, from 1997 to 2004', 25 *Human Reproduction* (2010) p. 449. The Amsterdam centre '[...] receives on average 20 requests annually from those wishing to conceive a child using a surrogate', of which 'approximately 10 cases annually actually lead to a course of treatment.' Boele-Woelki et al. 2011, *supra* n. 186, at p. 305.

292 Art. 2(4) of Annex to Planningsbesluit in-vitrofertilisatie, *Stcrt.* 1998, 95 and the (outdated) guideline on high-technological surrogcay by the Dutch Association for Obstetrics and Gynaecology of 1999, *supra* n. 289.

293 E.g. Rb. 's-Gravenhage 11 December 2007, ECLI:NL:RBSGR:2007:BB9844.

294 See www.vumc.nl/afdelingen/patientenfolders-brochures/zoeken-alfabet/D/hoog_technologisch_draagmoe1.pdf, visited October 2012.

295 As indicated by the Secretary of State of Justice in his letter to Parliament on surrogate motherhood of 16 December 2011, *Kamerstukken* II 2011/12, 33 000 VI, no. 69.

author is aware, this has as yet not resulted in any changes. Also, the aforementioned guidelines on high-technological surrogacy from 1998 have been outdated since 2003,[296] but have not yet been renewed.[297]

Dutch civil law does not contain any specific provision on surrogacy.[298] Hence, 'the regular rules in the field of parentage, parental responsibility and child protection' apply in surrogacy situations.[299] A 2011 research report on surrogacy and unlawful placement of children in the Netherlands, concluded that '[…] the position of a child born by means of surrogacy [was] legally unclear, and uncertainty exist[ed] with respect to the legal position of the commissioning parents and the surrogate parents.'[300] The fact that it is so difficult to establish parental links in surrogacy cases, fits in with the policy of discouragement of this phenomenon.[301]

Following the *mater semper certa est* rule, the surrogate mother is automatically regarded as the legal mother of the child, even if the intended mother is in fact genetically related to the child.[302] In the case that the surrogate mother is married or has a registered partner, her spouse or registered partner is, by operation of the law, the second legal parent.[303] The establishment of parental links between the intended parents and the child requires a (court) procedure.[304] While surrogacy agreements are non-enforceable under Dutch law, parties are nonetheless advised to draft an agreement, because the Child Welfare Council and the courts may take this into account in their assessments related to the establishment of parental links.[305]

296 *Supra* n. 286. At p. 6 of the Guideline it is indicated that it ceases to be valid five years after their publication.

297 See also *Kamerstukken II* 2012/13, 33 400 XVI, no. 155, p. 7.

298 See Boele-Woelki et al. 2011, *supra* n. 186, at p. 310.

299 *Idem*, at pp. 306–307.

300 *Idem*, at p. 310. At pp. 306–307 of the report, the authors explain in more detail: 'Dutch law does not specifically regulate the consequences of surrogacy in the field of parentage. Accordingly, the regular rules in the field of parentage, parental responsibility and child protection apply in these cases. The legal position of a child born as a result of surrogacy is uncertain and dependent upon a significant number of factors that in and of themselves have little relevance to the surrogacy arrangement. The surrogate is always regarded as the legal mother of the child, regardless of whether she has also provided the genetic material for the birth. If the surrogate is married, then her husband is also automatically the child's legal father. The transfer of parental rights to the commissioning parents is difficult and the result dependent upon a variety of different circumstances. Adoption by at least one of the commissioning parents will also be necessary prior to the final transfer of parental rights to both commissioning parents. […] The law with respect to the legal transfer of parental rights from the surrogate family to the commissioning family is also not catered specifically, meaning that the normal rules of parentage law will apply in these cases too.'

301 *Idem*, at p. 52.

302 Art. 1:198 BW. See also *Kamerstukken II* 2011/12, 33 000 VI, no. 69, p. 2.

303 Arts. 1:199(a) and 1:198(2) BW. When the surrogate mother is not married, the intended father may legally recognise the child before it is born (Art. 1:230 BW).

304 Boele-Woelki et al. noted in 2011 that in case of supervised high-technological surrogacy, the procedure may be accelerated. In that case the intended parents may be awarded parental rights within one year after the child's birth. Boele-Woelki et al. 2011, *supra* n. 186, at p. 52.

305 See www.rijksoverheid.nl/onderwerpen/erkenning-kind/vraag-en-antwoord/wat-is-een-draagmoeder.html, visited September 2012.

To establish parental links, first the parental rights of the surrogate mother (and her spouse or registered partner) must be removed. This is a child protection measure, which requires the involvement of the Child Welfare Council.[306] While the intended father can recognise the child before birth, joint parental authority with the surrogate mother thus must be removed, and the father must be exclusively entrusted with parental authority over the child.[307]

The intended mother – even if she is the genetic mother of the child – or the same-sex partner of the intended father, must subsequently start an adoption procedure.[308] The couple can ask the Child Welfare Council in advance for permission to foster the child (be guardian of the child, '*voogdij*') until the other intended parent adopts it.[309] Initially it was provided that the other intended parent could request from the Court the authorisation of such adoption only if (s)he and the intended father had lived together uninterruptedly for a period of at least three years and had jointly cared for the child for a period of at least one uninterrupted year immediately preceding the adoption request.[310] The latter requirement was, however, successfully challenged in 2013. On 11 September 2013, the District Court of Northern Netherlands ruled that the requirement of Article 1:228(1)(f) that intended parents could adopt a child in surrogacy cases only after foster care of one year, constituted an unjustified difference in treatment under Article 8 and 14 ECHR.[311] Since the year 2009, Article 1:228(3) provides for an exception to this rule where a child was born 'within the relationship' of the birth mother and her same-sex life partner (the so-called social mother; see Chapter 12, section 12.3.6.4). The Court ruled that in the case at hand, the child was not born within the relationship of the intended parents, since a third person (the surrogate mother) was involved. Still, the Court compared the situation of the intended mother with that of a social mother and concluded that the possibilities to establish legally recognised parental links with the child were more limited for the intended mother when compared to a social mother. The Court found this difference in legal position incompatible with Article 8 (the right to respect for family life) in conjunction with Article 14 (prohibition on discrimination) ECHR. It held the relevant Article 1:228(1) Civil Code not applicable in this case[312] and granted the adoption order.[313]

---

306 *Kamerstukken II* 2011/12, 33 000 VI, no. 69, p. 2.

307 Art. 1:253c (1) and (3) BW.

308 See, *inter alia*, Hof 's-Gravenhage 21 August 1998, ECLI:NL:GHSGR:1998:AD2927; Rb. Arnhem 20 February 2008, ECLI:NL:RBARN:2008:BC8012; Hof 's-Gravenhage 10 February 2010, ECLI:NL:GHSGR:2010:BL8563 and Hof 's-Gravenhage 1 December 2010, ECLI:NL:GHSGR:2010:BO7387. See also Rb. Noord-Holland 20 November 2013, ECLI:NL:RBNHO:2013:11109, where in a case concerning low-technological surrogacy, an adoption order was granted to the unmarried, cohabiting intended mother of the intended (and genetic) father.

309 Art. 1:241(3) BW.

310 Art. 1:227(3) and Art. 1:228(1)(f) BW.

311 Rb. Noord-Nederland 11 September 2013, ECLI:NL:RBNNE:2013:5503.

312 Following Art. 94 of the Dutch Constitution, statutory regulations in force within the Kingdom are not applicable if such application is in conflict with provisions of treaties or of resolutions by international institutions that are binding on all person.

313 The Court found it established in this case that the surrogate mother had, after the birth of the child, confirmed her decision to give up the child and that she had not developed any emotional parental

The scale on which surrogacy takes place in the Netherlands seems to be fairly limited, although exhaustive statistics are lacking. In 2012 the Secretary of State for Security and Justice informed Parliament that 'over the past years' 10 children had been born following high-technological surrogacy in the Amsterdam VU Medical Centre.[314] He also mentioned that the Child Welfare Council had come across about ten cases of unlawful placement of children (following surrogacy).[315] The need for a better insight in the scale of the phenomenon has been recognised at government level.[316]

The Dutch government has put an effort in providing clear and accessible information about the legal situation concerning surrogacy in the Netherlands, for instance, through the websites of the Dutch Ministries of Justice and Security and of Foreign Affairs.[317] In 2014 it was decided to establish a State Commission on Parenthood (*'Staatscommissie Herijking Ouderschap'*), which, *inter alia*, was given the task to examine whether there is a need for providing for particular regulation of surrogacy in the Dutch Civil Code.[318] The Commission will have to issue a report before May 2016.

6.4. Statistics on cross-border movement

6.4.1. Statistics on cross-border abortions

6.4.1.1. Cross-border movement towards the Netherlands

The Netherlands has been a 'destination' country in respect of abortion since the first moment abortion practice was liberalised in the 1970s. Cross-border movement took place on a great scale, even though at the time abortions were, strictly speaking, illegal (see 6.2.1 above). Because the Pregnancy Termination Act does not set any domicile requirement, women from abroad can legally have an abortion in the Netherlands.[319] Non-resident women remain anonymous. They have to bear their own costs (see 6.2.5 above) and are responsible for obtaining medical aftercare upon return to the country of origin.[320]

---

relationship with the child. This constituted a sufficient ground for removing her parental authority. Also, the best interests of the child did not stand in the way of such removing of her parental authority, now that it had been established that the intended parents were the genetic parents of the child.

314 *Aanhangsel Handelingen II* 2012/13, 646.

315 *Idem*, under reference to *Kamerstukken II* 2010/11, 32 500 VI, no.83.

316 *Kamerstukken II* 2011/12, 33 000 VI, no. 69, pp. 4–5.

317 E.g. www.rijksoverheid.nl/onderwerpen/erkenning-kind/vraag-en-antwoord/wat-is-een-draagmoeder.html, visited July 2013. See also *Kamerstukken II* 2011/12, 33 000 VI, no. 69, pp. 4–5.

318 Regeling van 28 april 2014, no. 512296, houdende instelling van een Staatscommissie Herijking Ouderschap *[Regulation of 28 April 2014, no. 512296, concerning the installation of a State Commission on Parenthood]*, *Stcrt.* 2014, 12556.

319 *Kamerstukken II* 2010/11, 30 371, no. 20, p. 8.

320 *Idem*, at p. 3.

The Healthcare Inspectorate has been reporting on recorded abortion data since 1985. Earlier statistics are based on estimates. For a long time registration on the basis of the Pregnancy Termination Act provided a specification for four countries only: Germany, Belgium, Luxembourg and Spain. In 1984, when the relevant registration forms were drafted, most foreign women who had an abortion in the Netherlands came from these four countries.[321] Other countries of origin were not explicitly specified in the registration. Since 1 January 2011 a new registration form has been in use, in which Belgium, Germany, France, Ireland and Poland are included. The duration of the pregnancy of women who are not resident in the Netherlands is not separately registered.[322]

It was estimated that in 1975 approximately 80,000 non-resident women were treated in Dutch abortion clinics,[323] compared to 15,000 women resident in the Netherlands. Most of the foreign women were resident in the Federal Republic of Germany, Belgium and Luxembourg.[324] For the 1977 it was reported that approximately 65,000 women were treated in Dutch abortion clinics, of whom about two thirds were women from the Federal Republic of Germany.[325] Only since 1986 has the number of women residing in the Netherlands, outweighed the number of non-resident women.[326] Since that time the number of non-resident women who had their pregnancies terminated in the Netherlands has gradually declined.[327] In 2010 approximately one out of eight abortions involved a woman who was resident outside the Netherlands.[328]

---

321 *Jaarrapportage 2010 van de Wet afbreking zwangerschap* [Annual Report under the Pregnancy Termination Act 2010] Utrecht, December 2011, Annex 2, table A, online available at www.rijksoverheid.nl/onderwerpen/abortus/documenten-en-publicaties/rapporten/2011/12/14/igz-jaarrapportage-2010-wet-afbreking-zwangerschap.html, visited March 2012.

322 *Kamerstukken II* 2010/11, 30 371, no. 20, pp. 7–8. See also Appendix B to Besluit vaststelling model formulieren Besluit afbreking zwangerschap [Decree on model forms for Decree termination pregnancy], *Stcrt.* 2010, no. 20555.

323 *Kamerstukken II* 1978/79, 15 475, nos. 1–4, p. 14.

324 J. Rademakers, *Abortus in Nederland 1993–2000. Jaarverslag van de landelijke abortusregistratie* [Abortion in the Netherlands 1993–2000. Annual report of the national abortion registration] (Heemstede, StiSAN 2002) p. 37.

325 *Kamerstukken II* 1978/79, 15 475, nos. 1–4, p. 14, referring to 'E. Ketting and P. Schnabel, De abortus-hulpverlening in 1977'. See also Rademakers 2002, *supra* n. 324, at p. 37.

326 Rademakers 2002, *supra* n. 324, at p. 37.

327 The exact numbers of pregnancy termination with non-resident women, when compared to the total number of pregnancy terminations in the Netherlands are as follows: 1980: 36,700 out of 56,400 (65.07 per cent); 1985: 20,721 of 37,900 (54.57 per cent); 1995: 7,753 of 28,685 (27.02 per cent); 2000: 6,130 of 33,335 (18.39 per cent); 2005: 4,244 of 28,738 (14.77 per cent); 2006: 5,251 of 32,992 (15.92 per cent); 2007: 4,818 of 33,148 (14.53 per cent); 2008: 4,513 of 32,983 (13.38 per cent); 2009: 4,108 of 32,427 (12.67 per cent); 2010: 4,260 of 30,984 (13.75 per cent). The figures in respect of the year 2010 were estimated. *Jaarrapportage 2010 van de Wet afbreking zwangerschap*, December 2011, p. 14, online available at www.rijksoverheid.nl/onderwerpen/abortus/documenten-en-publicaties/rapporten/2011/12/14/igz-jaarrapportage-2010-wet-afbreking-zwangerschap.html, visited March 2012.

328 *Jaarrapportage 2010 van de Wet afbreking zwangerschap*, December 2011, p. 7, online available at www.rijksoverheid.nl/onderwerpen/abortus/documenten-en-publicaties/rapporten/2011/12/14/igz-jaarrapportage-2010-wet-afbreking-zwangerschap.html, visited 30 March 2012.

6.4.1.2. Cross-border movement from the Netherlands

Halfway through the first decade of the new millennium, some media reports were made of women having abortions in countries where the statutory limit for a lawful abortion was set later than the 24-week limit of the Netherlands. Consequently parliamentary questions were asked.[329] The Dutch Secretary of State for Health, Welfare and Sports responded that this occurred only incidentally and that a Dutch doctor who referred a woman to a foreign clinic was not liable to punishment.[330] Soon, a new controversy arose in respect of a particular abortion clinic in Barcelona (Spain), where – so it was reported – women who were seven months pregnant could have their pregnancies terminated.[331] In one case charges were brought against a Dutch woman who had an abortion in the Spanish clinic after 28 weeks of pregnancy, but later these were dropped, on grounds of the special circumstances of the case.

6.4.1.3. Women on Waves

The Dutch NGO *Women on Waves* (WoW) has played its own particular role in respect of cross-border abortions. WoW 'aims to prevent unsafe abortions and empower women to exercise their human rights to physical and mental autonomy.'[332] With its ship that sails under the Dutch flag, WoW regularly sets sail to countries with restrictive abortion regimes. Just outside the territorial waters – where the local laws do not apply – the organisation provides 'contraceptives, information, training, workshops, and safe and legal abortion services'.[333] Since 2008, the organisation has been licensed to carry out first trimester abortions in a mobile clinic aboard the ship.[334] Various court proceedings preceded the award of this license, as the Minister of Health, Welfare and Sports first refused to award any license and later subjected the license to the condition that pregnancy termination could only be carried out within a radius of 25 kilometres from the Slotervaart hospital in Amsterdam, with which WoW had concluded a cooperation-agreement.[335] This requirement was, however, nullified by the highest administrative court, after which the Minister awarded the license without the radius condition.[336] Before the license was awarded, *Women on Waves* was active in respect of the so-called '*overtijdbehandeling*', as this treatment was, at the time, held to fall outside the scope of the Pregnancy Termination Act (see

---

329 *Handelingen II* 2004/05, 71, pp. 4362–4364.

330 *Kamerstukken II* 2004/05, 29 800 XVI, no. 211, pp. 1–2.

331 See 'Spaanse kliniek aborteert foetussen van zeven maanden', *de Volkskrant* 31 October 2006, online available at www.volkskrant.nl/vk/nl/2668/Buitenland/article/detail/788533/2006/10/31/Spaanse-kliniek-aborteert-foetussen-van-zeven-maanden.dhtml, visited June 2010. See also www.eenvandaag.nl/buitenland/31272/abortus_na_zwangerschap_van_7_maanden, visited June 2010; www.netwerk.tv/node/1696, visited June 2010 and www.nos.nl/artikel/58692-abortusklinie k-spanje-opnieuw-in-opspraak.html, visited June 2010. See also *Aanhangsel Handelingen II* 2006/07, 987.

332 Www.womenonwaves.org/en/page/650/who-are-we, visited June 2014.

333 *Idem.*

334 The license has been awared on the basis of Art. 2 Waz.

335 Rb. Amsterdam 1 June 2004, ECLI:NL:RBAMS:2004:AP1251 and Rb. Amsterdam 28 February 2005, AWB 04/3469, *unpublished.* See also *Aanhangsel Handelingen II* 2003/04, 1895.

336 ABRvS 3 May 2006, ECLI:NL:RVS:2006:AW7365.

6.2.2.1 above).[337] Within Europe WoW has visited Ireland (2001),[338] Poland (2003), Portugal (2004) and Spain (2008)[339] and by doing so it has facilitated cross-border movement for abortions in its own and unique way.

6.4.2. Statistics on cross-border reproductive care

Cross-border reproductive care (CBRC) is a hot topic in Dutch media, academia and politics.[340] The incidence of CBRC is generally acknowledged by the Dutch government, and has in some cases formed part of the grounds on which policy choices were based. As is the case for many more countries, the Dutch authorities do not keep statistics on CBRC on a structural basis. For example, unlike abortion clinics, AHR clinics are not under a legal obligation to register the country of residence of their patients, the services recipients. This is different, however, when it comes to donation of gametes, as the Donor Information Act requires clinics to register all personal information of the donor, as well as of the woman receiving the donor material (see 6.3.3 above).

In general it is estimated that annually 9,000 IVF treatments are carried out in the Netherlands. In addition, on an annual basis approximately 1,000 women from the Netherlands have IVF treatment in a foreign country.[341] The Dutch authorities are not aware how many of them are reimbursed for the costs under the Health Insurance Act.[342] The estimates for the wider Europe are between 10,000 and 15,000 patients involved in CBRC every year.[343]

The following subsections discuss statistics (to the extent that these are available) as well as estimates of the scale on which cross-border movement takes place in respect of particular kinds of treatment. Discussed are, *inter alia*, cross-border donation of gametes and the import of gametes, PGD and surrogacy.

---

337 Www.womenonwaves.org/en/page/611/legal-position-of-women-on-waves, visited June 2014. See also 'Abortusboot mag de overtijdpil geven', *Het Parool* 1 July 2002, p. 6.

338 According to CNN about 80 Irish women had contacted *Women on Waves*. 'Crossing the sea for an abortion', *cnn.com* 4 March 2002. *The Lancet* even spoke of more than 300 women. K. Birchard, 'Abortion boat faces legal complications', *The Lancet* 23 June 2001. See also 'Irish should not have to travel for abortion – poll', *The Irish Times* 1 June 2001, p. 5 and 'Abortusboot vaart volgende week uit; Women on Waves verwacht geen juridische problemen in Ierland', *de Volkskrant* 7 June 2001, p. 38.

339 See www.womenonwaves.org/en/page/2582/ship-campaigns, visited June 2014. On its visit to Portugal, see also ch. 2, section 2.4.1.

340 E.g. '600 paren jaarlijks naar België voor ivf', *Algemeen Dagblad* 30 June 2009, p. 11; 'Vergoeding Ivf-behandeling leent zich niet voor 'u vraagt, wij draaien' Nadya wilde groot gezin', *Nederlands Dagblad* 11 February 2009, p. 12.; J. Kremer et al., 'Zorg over de grens. Geen grip op kwaliteit van buitenlandse fertiliteitsbehandelingen' ['Care across the border. No grip on the quality of foreign fertily treatment'], 62 *Medisch Contact* (2007) p. 1343 and *Aanhangsel Handelingen II* 2010/11, 238.

341 Derksen and Staal 2012, *supra* n. 152, at p. 19 and 'Uw lichaam is geld waard', *Trouw* 4 March 2011.

342 Derksen and Staal 2012, *supra* n. 152, at p. 19.

343 *Idem*, at p. 6.

6.4.2.1. *Cross-border donation of gametes and import of gametes*

Dutch media regularly report on Dutch women and couples going abroad – many to Belgium or Spain – for IVF treatment with the use of (anonymously and/or commercially) donated gametes.[344] The strict Dutch legislation in respect of the donation of gametes and embryos is often held to be a cause for the shortage of gametes in the Netherlands and therefore a ground for going abroad. Some Dutch couples find donor identifiability simply not desirable.[345] The Dutch age limits for access to IVF treatment are another often reported reason.[346] It has been reported that in addition to the 100 to 150 women who have IVF treatment with the use of donated gametes in the Netherlands, every year another 1,000 women go to Spain and Belgium for such treatment.[347] According to Pennings, the entry into force of the Donor Information Act in 2004 led to a 'steep increase in patients going to Belgium where anonymity [was] maintained'. He reported that '[...] between 2004 and 2005, the number of Dutch patients going to Belgium for donor insemination almost doubled from 57 to 99 patients'.[348]

In 2010 a team of researchers from various Dutch universities carried out a survey on egg cell donation amongst gynaecologists registered with the Dutch Society of Obstetrics and Gynaecology (NVOG). The following results were reported:

> 'Of 94 out 101 Dutch fertility units at least one gynaecologist answered the questionnaire (response 93.1%). Gynaecologists in 47 hospitals supported patients who participated in commercial egg donation programmes in a foreign country. The same number provided no support for these patients. Compared to the interval 2000–2004 in the interval 2005–2008 requests for participation increased from 62 to 179 (increase 288%). We also found a three fold increase of patients who actually went abroad to participate in a commercial egg donation program (45 versus 149, increase 331%) and a similar increase in care for pregnancies originating from commercial egg donation (32 versus 98, increase 306%).

344 E.g. E. van Zalinge, 'In Nederland bijna geen eiceldonor beschikbaar Buitenland kan oudere vrouw uitkomst bieden', *Het Parool* 25 August 1994, p. 5; 'Uw lichaam is geld waard', *Trouw* 4 March 2011; C. Houtekamer, 'Het lichaam is geld waard, maar niet bij ons; Daarom wijken sommige kopers voor een nier, bot of een eicel uit naar het buitenland', *NRC Handelsblad* 4 March 2011, p. 5. The CVZ reported that many Dutch women go to Spain and Russia, where young women donate egg-cells in return for high sums of money. CVZ, *In-vitrofertilisatiebehandelingen. Een verkenning* [IVF treatment. An exploration] Report of 10 April 2010, pp. 11–12, online available at www.cvz.nl/binaries/live/cvzinternet/hst_content/nl/documenten/rapporten/2010/rpt1004+pakketadvies+2010+-+ivf.pdf, visited October 2010. See also *Aanhangsel Handelingen II* 2010/11, 238 and I. Geesink and C. Steegers, *Nier te koop, baarmoeder te huur: wereldwijde handel in lichaamsmateriaal* [Kidney for sale, uterus to let: worldwide trade in human body material] (Amsterdam, Bakker 2011).

345 G. Pennings, 'The rough guide to insemination: cross-border travelling for donor semen due to different regulations', *Facts, Views and Vision in ObGyn, Monograph* (2010) pp. 56–57, online available at www.fvvo.eu/assets/103/21-Pennings.pdf, visited May 2014. See also *Kamerstukken II* 2012/13, 30 486, no. 5, p. 18.

346 'Uw lichaam is geld waard', *Trouw* 4 March 2011.

347 C. Houtekamer, 'Het lichaam is geld waard, maar niet bij ons; Daarom wijken sommige kopers voor een nier, bot of een eicel uit naar het buitenland', *NRC Handelsblad* 4 March 2011, p. 5.

348 Pennings 2010, *supra* n. 345, at pp. 56–57, referring to G. Pennings et al., 'Cross-border reproductive care in Belgium', 24 *Human Reproduction* (2009) p. 3108.

> The large majority of patients took their own initiative to find an institution to help them with their aim to achieve a pregnancy. [...] Only in about 10% gynaecologists referred patients to an acquainted clinic abroad or recommended such a clinic. Most Dutch couples visit Spain (n=109) for commercial-egg donation, followed by Belgium (n=32), Eastern Europe (15) and the United States of America (11). Most women who travel abroad for a commercial egg donation program are 41 years or older. [...] The estimated price per treatment cycle lies between 3,000 and 10,000 euro's. Especially in the United States couples paid up till more than 30,000 euro's per treatment.'[349]

The Dutch Minister of Health, when referring to this research, underlined that these only concerned cases in which Dutch gynaecologists were involved. The Minister therefore assumed that the actual numbers were higher. Still, the Minister considered this to be a small portion of the 9,000 IVF treatments carried out in the Netherlands annually. She maintained that a (possible) shortage in donated egg cells was not an automatic consequence of the Dutch prohibitions on anonymous and commercial egg cell donation.[350]

The aforementioned researchers furthermore concluded that 34 per cent of the Dutch gynaecologists who participated in their research, considered commercial egg donation unethical, while 56 per cent were willing to provide support for those who seek help for commercial egg donation abroad. It was reported that 36 per cent of the responding Dutch gynaecologists were of the opinion that commercial egg donation should be legalised in the Netherlands.[351]

Cross-border movement may also take more implicit forms, for instance when gametes originating of foreign donors are used in the course of IVF treatment in Dutch clinics. Statistics of the Dutch Donor Information Registration Foundation (*Stichting Donorgegevens Kunstmatige Bevruchting*)[352] paint the following picture.[353] In the period May 2006 – the date when the central digital registration system of the Foundation came into operation – up until 2012, 320 egg cell donors

349 M.H. Van Hooff et al., 'O-199 Cross-border reproductive care for egg-donation in Dutch women', 25 *Human Reproduction* (2010) p. i79, online available at www.humrep.oxfordjournals.org/content/25/suppl_1/i77.abstract3, visited May 2014. The authors explicitly stated that '[t]he incidence of cross border reproductive care for commercial egg-donation between 2000–2008 was estimated.' See also *Aanhangsel Handelingen II* 2010/11, 2303, p. 2, where reference to this research is made. The same research was also discussed in I. van der Meer-Noort et al., 'Cross border reproductive care; gebruik van eiceldonatie in het buitenland door Nederlandse vrouwen' ['Cross-border reproductive care; use of egg cell donation by Dutch women in foreign countries'], 128 *Nederlands Tijdschrift voor Obstetrie & Gynaecologie* (2011) p. 98.

350 *Aanhangsel Handelingen II* 2010/11, 2303, p. 2. See also Derksen and Staal 2012, *supra* n. 152, at p. 6, where – so it seems- reference is made to the same survey.

351 Van Hooff et al. 2010, *supra* n. 349, at p. i79.

352 Following Art. 2(1) Wet donorgegevens kunstmatige bevruchting, all establishments who offer AHR treatment with the use of donated gametes have to provide data about these treatments and donors involved to the *Stichting Donorgegevens Kunstmatige Bevruchting* [Donor Information Registration Foundation].

353 Stichting Donorgegevens Kunstmatige Bevruchting, *Jaarverslag 2012* [Annual report 2012], Annex to *Kamerstukken II* 2012/13, 33750-XVI-76.

where registered, of which 4 donors were resident abroad.[354] This resulted in 289 successful treatments including donated egg cells, 4 of which involved acceptors resident abroad.[355] The Foundation registered 1,224 sperm donors, of whom 157 were resident abroad.[356] A total number of 4,381 successful treatments with donated sperm were registered, of which 146 concerned situations were the acceptors (the women) were resident abroad.[357] Particularly since the 2010 a clear increase in cross-border cases is visible.[358]

6.4.2.2. Cross-border movement for PGD

When it comes to PGD, little is known in respect of cross-border movement to and from the Netherlands. There are no official statistics kept in this respect. The Maastricht Medical Centre only registers the number of official references to their Brussels based partner clinic.[359] For example, in the period 1995–2010 – before exclusion PGD for HD was lawful in the Netherlands (see 6.3.5 above) – the Maastricht Medical Centre referred 22 couples to the Brussels clinic.[360]

6.4.2.3. Miscellaneous

In addition to cross-border movement related to IVF, gamete donation and PGD, other types of CBRC involves movement from (and possibly to) the Netherlands. In the past, there have been various reports of cross-border movement in respect of treatment which at the time was still considered 'experimental' and thus not offered in the Netherlands, such as ICSI,[361] TESA and MESA.[362] Further, there have been

---

[354] One egg cell donor was resident in Belgium, one in France and two others in Germany.

[355] One acceptor was resident in France, the other three in Germany.

[356] The breakdown of these numbers is as follows: 1 in Australia; 4 in Belgium; 101 in Germany; 2 in Canada; 1 in Costa Rica; 32 in Denmark; 1 in France; 1 in Greece; 1 in Indonesia; 1 in Latvia; 1 in New Zealand; 1 in Portugal; 1 in Surinam and 2 in Switzerland; and 7 in the United States of America.

[357] The breakdown of these numbers is as follows: 1 in Australia; three in Belgium; 92 in Germany; 38 in France; 7 in Italy; 1 in Luxembourg; 1 in Austria; 1 in Spain; and 1 in Switzerland.

[358] In the period May 2006 up until 2010, 152 egg cell donors were registered, of which three were resident abroad. This resulted in 152 successful treatments including donated egg cells, two of which involved acceptors resident abroad. The Foundation registered 696 sperm donors, of whom 54 were resident abroad. A total number of 2,798 successful treatments with donated sperm were registered, of which 79 concerned situations were the acceptors (the women) were resident abroad. Stichting Donorgegevens Kunstmatige Bevruchting, *Jaarverslag 2010* [Annual report 2010], Annex to *Kamerstukken II* 32500-XVI, no. 154, pp. 8–9.

[359] See www.brusselsivf.be/default.aspx?lang=EN, visited July 2013 and *Kamerstukken II* 2011/12, 32279, no. 24, p. 7.

[360] *Kamerstukken II* 2011/12, 25 424, no. 135, p. 4, specifiying (in footnote 9) the following numbers for the following years: 2010: 3 referrals; 2009: 7 referrals; 1995–2008: 12 referrals.

[361] *Inter alia*, V. Cotterell, 'Supermethode in buurlanden', *Het Parool* 24 March 1997, p. 1 and Ziekenfondsraad (Commissie beroepszaken) [Health Care Insurance Board (Appeals Commission)] 24 November 1994, case 260-4451.

[362] See 'Zorgverzekeraars: reageerbuisbaby hoort thuis in ziekenfondspakket', *de Volkskrant* 27 March 2002, p. 1, where it was reported that annually 'hundreds of Dutch people' went to Belgian and German hospitals for PESA, MESA and TESE techniques. See also Health Care Insurance Board (CVZ) 19 December 2006, case GS/26100379.

reports of couples or women going abroad for so-called 'assisted hatching'[363] and for egg cell vitrification on social grounds at a time when it was not yet practiced in the Netherlands.[364] Also, in early 2011, it was reported that a Dutch IVF clinic referred clients to a clinic in Belgium, where – allegedly – gender selection was carried out.[365] Indirect forms of cross-border movement concern situations in which certain aspects of AHR treatment are outsourced to foreign clinics.[366]

6.4.3. Cross-border surrogacy

There are no official or exhaustive statistics in respect of the number of Dutch couples and individuals who conclude surrogacy agreements in foreign countries. There is only incidental evidence from case law or cases that are reported to authorities in any other way. As Boele-Woelki et al. explain:

> '[...], it is [...] difficult to determine the scope of occurrence of surrogacy and any connected unlawful placements of children in The Netherlands. The Child Protection Board and the Central Authority for Adoption probably only receive a section of the surrogacy cases that occur in The Netherlands or abroad.'[367]

That some cross-border movement takes place, is not, however, in question.[368] Particularly in the past decade, various cross-border surrogacy cases have come before the Dutch courts, some of which attracted wide media coverage and political attention.[369] Greece is the most often mentioned destination country within the EU,

363 The American Society for Reproductive Medicine defines assisted hatching as 'a procedure in which the zona pellucida (outer covering) of the embryo is partially opened, usually by application of an acid or laser, to facilitate embryo implantation and pregnancy.' See www.asrm.org/topics/detail.aspx?id=374, visited June 2014.

364 Van der Meer-Noort et al. 2011, *supra* n. 349, at p. 100.

365 The report was made in the TV programme *Uitgesproken EO* (broadcast of 27 January 2011), online available at www.eo.nl/tv/devijfdedag/aflevering-detail/uitgesproken-94, visited April 2011. As is the case under Dutch law, gender selection is prohibited under Belgian law. The Minister of Health, Welfare and Sports informed Parliament that the Belgian Health Inspectorate had referred the case to the police and that the Dutch Public Prosecutor saw no reason to prosecute the case. Possible grounds for criminal liability were Art. 26(2) Embryowet; Wet op de beroepen in de individuele gezondheidszorg (Wet BIG) [Act on professions in individual health care] and Art. 326 Sr (the relevant provision of the Criminal Code on fraud). *Aanhangsel Handelingen II* 2010/11, 2019–2020.

366 For example the Dutch Geertgen clinic, a non-licensed IVF clinic which operates the only egg cell donation programme in the Netherlands, outsources the actual *in vitro* fertilisation of embryos to an IVF-clinic in Düsseldorf (Germany). The Dutch Minister of Health, Welfare and Sports held this to be not against the relevant Dutch legislation, such as the WMBV and the IVF planningsbesluit. *Aanhangsel Handelingen II* 2011/12, 761, p. 3 and *Aanhangsel Handelingen II* 2011/12, 819, p. 2.

367 Boele-Woelki et al. 2011, *supra* n. 186, at p. 310.

368 *Idem*, at p. 303.

369 A case which attracted an extraordinary amount of media and political attention concerned the case of 'baby Donna', concerning a Belgian woman who had concluded a surrogacy agreement with a Belgian couple. She became pregnant after insemination with the sperm of the intended father. Halfway the pregnancy she falsely informed the intended parents that she had had a miscarriage. After the child was born, a Dutch couple adopted the child, paying the surrogate mother an amount of – so it was reported – 12,000 euro. When the Belgian couple found out about the deceit, they intiated

but there have also been reports from couples who went to Belgium,[370] the United Kingdom[371] and France[372] for surrogacy purposes. Most other reported cases concern countries outside the EU, such as Ukraine, India and the United States of America.[373]

Given the strict Dutch legislation in respect of surrogacy, it is not very likely that the Netherlands functions as a destination country in respect of surrogacy. In fact, the (debatable) rules set by the Medical Centre of the Free University of Amsterdam (see 6.3.8 above) – the only licensed centre in the Netherlands for high-technology surrogacy – explicitly exclude foreigners, whether intended parents, or surrogate mothers.

6.5. Dutch abortion and AHR legislation and cross-border movement

6.5.1. Criminal liability for abortions and AHR treatment carried out abroad

The Dutch Criminal Code applies to anyone who commits a crime on Dutch territory.[374] The Dutch Criminal Code may also apply to certain crimes committed outside Dutch territory, but its provisions on abortion and surrogacy are not amongst the provisions of the Criminal Code in respect of which this is made possible.[375] The same holds for the penal provisions of the Embryo Act.

court proceedings against the surrogate mother and the Dutch adoptive parents. The Dutch Court of Appeal ruled in 2008 that it was in the child's best interests if she stayed with the Dutch couple who had adopted her. In 2012, the Belgian judge imposed (modest) fines on all persons involved in the illegal adoption of the child. See, *inter alia*, J. van Poppel, 'Draagmoederdrama verscheurt Vlaams gezin; Baby Donna', *Algemeen Dagblad* 24 May 2005, p. 3; D. de Gruijl, 'Kinderdroom gezin uit Leusden loopt uit op nachtmerrie, draagmoeder van Donna opgepakt; Jansen: 'het is mijn kind. we zijn een gelukkig gezin'', *Het Parool* 25 May 2005, p. 99; 'Baby Donna blijft na kort geding voorlopig in Nederland', *Trouw* 6 July 2005, p. 6 and 'Rechter geeft boetes voor babyverkoop', *AD/ Algemeen Dagblad* 13 October 2012, p. 10. For the Dutch court judgments in this case, see Rb. Utrecht 24 October 2007, ECLI:NL:RBUTR:2007:BB6360 and Hof Amsterdam 25 November 2008, ECLI:NL:GHAMS:2008:BG5157. For other examples see *Kamerstukken II* 2007/08, 31 200 XVI, no. 154 and *Kamerstukken II* 2008/09, Aanhangsel, nos. 1225, 1226 and 1227.

370 Although from the Dutch perspective it was strictly speaking an interstate adoption case, the *Baby Donna* case (see above), was an example of cross-border movement from the Netherlands to Belgium in which surrogacy was involved. Rb. Utrecht 24 October 2007, ECLI:NL:RBUTR:2007:BB6360 and Hof Amsterdam 25 November 2008, ECLI:NL: GHAMS:2008:BG5157. Another Belgian surrogacy case was reported in E. Winkel et al., 'Draagmoederschap na ivf in het buitenland. Dilemma's bij de begeleiding', 154 *Nederlands Tijdschrijft voor Geneeskunde* (2010) p. A1777.

371 Rb. 's-Gravenhage 11 December 2007, ECLI:NL:RBSGR:2007:BB9844.

372 Rb. 's-Gravenhage 14 September 2009, ECLI:NL:RBSGR:2009:BK1197.

373 E.g. Rb. 's-Gravenhage (vrzr.) 9 November 2010, ECLI:NL:RBSGR:2010:BP3764; Rb.'s-Gravenhage 24 October 2011, ECLI:NL:RBSGR:2011:BU3627 and Rb. 's-Gravenhage 18 January 2012, ECLI:NL:RBSGR:2012:BV2597.

374 Art. 2 Sr.

375 Art. 4 Sr.

Article 5(1) of the Criminal Code provides that the Criminal Code may also be applicable in situations where a Dutchman has committed a crime in another country, but a requirement of double criminality applies in these cases.[376] This condition renders criminal prosecution for abortions, AHR treatment or surrogacy on the basis of this Article uncommon. A rare example where criminal investigations were initiated (but later dropped) against a Dutch woman who had had an abortion in Spain, has been referred to above (section 6.2.4).

6.5.2. Public funding for treatment obtained abroad

Dutch legislation does not make special provision for the reimbursement for abortions obtained abroad under the statutory health scheme, but there is no reason to assume that this would not be remunerated if the general conditions for reimbursement for medical treatment obtained abroad have been met.[377]

Reimbursement for AHR treatment obtained abroad, however, has been and is much debated and has resulted in various legal disputes.[378] The CJEU's case law in respect of cross-border health care (see chapter 3) has had a clear impact on the relevant rulings of the Dutch Courts.

Until 2004, AHR treatment, including IVF treatment, was not covered by the Dutch Health Insurance Act (*Ziekenfondswet*), but only financed on the basis of the subsidy scheme (*Subsidieregeling*; see 6.3.7 above). This had as a consequence that in cross-border situations, Dutch courts initially ruled that the reciprocity rule did not apply and hence that a refusal to reimburse AHR treatment obtained in another EU Member State constituted no violation of free movement rules.[379] Later, various courts accepted that a refusal to reimburse IVF treatment obtained in another EU Member State under the subsidy scheme constituted a restriction of free movement, but held that this restriction could be justified, for instance, as some Dutch courts held, for reasons of complexity of the treatment and quality of the care as well as on ethical grounds.[380]

376 See Boele-Woelki et al. 2011, *supra* n. 186, at pp. 40–41, under reference (in footnote 49) to: 'Noyon Langemeyer Remmelink, *Het wetboek van strafrecht, Artikel 5*, J.W. Fokkens, aantek. 9.'

377 See Ch. 3, section 3.5 for the relevant standards in the EU context. As noted above in section 6.2.5 women from abroad who have a pregnancy terminated in the Netherlands have to bear the expenses themselves.

378 Derksen and Staal 2012, *supra* n. 152, at p. 6. See also *inter alia* Rb. Utrecht 24 May 2002, ECLI:NL:RBUTR:2002:AE3518; and CRvB 31 January 2007, ECLI:NL:CRVB:2007:AZ8510.

379 In the year 2000 – when IVF treatment was not yet covered by the Health Insurance Act – the Central Appeals Court for Public Service and Social Security Matters ruled that an insured was not entitled to reimbursement for IVF treatment obtained in a Belgian clinic. CRvB 11 July 2000, ECLI:NL:CRVB:2000:ZB8921.

380 For example, in 2002 the District Court of Utrecht ruled that a refusal by a health insurer to reimburse the costs of treatment carried out in a Belgian IVF clinic constituted a restriction of the freedom to receive services, which could be justified on grounds of the CJEU judgments in the cases *Decker and Kohll* and *Smits and Peerbooms* (see Ch. 3). Rb. Utrecht 24 May 2002, ECLI:NL:RBUTR:2002:AE3518. See also Rb. Almelo 13 November 2003, ECLI:NL:RBALM:2003:BM5834. The Court ruled first of all

As the case law of the CJEU on cross-border health care evolved,[381] Dutch courts increasingly often ruled that a refusal to reimburse IVF treatment obtained in a clinic in another EU Member State on the ground that this clinic was not licensed under Dutch law, constituted an unjustified restriction of free movement.[382] Of particular importance was a ruling of the Central Appeals Court for Public Service and Social Security Matters of 2007.[383] This Court accepted that the Dutch rule that treatment was only reimbursed if obtained in a licensed establishment, constituted a restriction of the freedom to receive services. In its assessment of the possible justifications for this restriction, the Court held that purely financial reasons were insufficient. It was not convinced that without the licensing requirement, it would be impossible to control expenditure without adversely affecting the overall level of public health protection. The Court furthermore rejected the argument put forward by the health insurer that an efficient organisation of the supervision of the quality of care could only be guaranteed if AHR treatment was only reimbursed when obtained in a clinic licensed under Dutch law. The Central Appeals Court did not exclude that ethical reasons could constitute an imperative requirement under *rule of reason* exception, but held that these ethical objectives could be attained by a less restrictive measure, namely by the relevant Planning Order for *in vitro* fertilisation (*Planningsbesluit in vitro fertilisatie*).[384] With this ruling, many of the previously accepted justifications were no longer valid.

In line with the case law of the CJEU, it is now well-established case law that all medical care – including AHR treatment – that is covered by the Dutch Health Insurance Act, is also reimbursed if obtained in another EU Member State.[385] Further, also in line with CJEU case law, various Dutch Health Insurers require a referral from the general practitioner and set a prior authorisation requirement for IVF treatment in a foreign country.[386] More controversial are those situations where the treatment

ruled that IVF treatment was not amongst the benefits provided for under the Health Insurance Act, and that therefore Art. 22 of Regulation 1408/71 did not apply to a case where IVF treatment was obtained in a German clinic. It furthermore ruled that the *Subsidieregeling* did not apply to the case at hand as the German clinic was no licensed establishment within the meaning of the *Subsidieregeling*. See also Rb. Maastricht 28 June 2004, ECLI:NL:RBMAA:2004:AP8808.

381 Most importantly Case C-385/99 *Müller-Fauré and van Riet* [2003] ECR I-4509, ECLI:EU:C:2003:270. See ch. 3 section 3.5.2.1.

382 E.g. Rb. Amsterdam 7 October 2003, ECLI:NL:RBAMS:2003:AN9606 and Rb. Utrecht 13 July 2004, case no. SBR03/1073, unpublished. For a ruling to a contrary effect, see Rb. Maastricht 28 June 2004, ECLI:NL:RBMAA:2004:AP8808.

383 CRvB 31 January 2007, ECLI:NL:CRVB:2007:AZ8510.

384 *Idem.*

385 See Ch. 3, section 3.5.2.4. In some cases, the Dutch Courts found no violation of the free movement rules, because a particular type of AHR treatment that was available abroad, was (still) considered experimental in the Netherlands, and therefore excluded from cover under the Health Insurance Act. For example, in 2007 the Central Appeals Court ruled that the at the time of treatment still experimental ICSI MESA treatment, was not covered under the Dutch Health Insurance Act, and that there was accordingly no entitlement to reimbursement for such treatment obtained abroad. CRvB 14 February 2007, ECLI:NL:CRVB:2007:AZ9694. This ruling confirmed the judgment of Rb. 's-Gravenhage 12 February 2004, ECLI:NL:RBSGR:2004:AO3791. See also College voor zorgverzekeringen 27 April 2000, case no. BZ-00-1156 and CRvB 13 July 2005, ECLI:NL:CRVB:2005:AT9545.

386 See *inter alia* www.zilverenkruis.nl/consumenten/vergoedingen/Pages/ivf.aspx, visited June 2013; www.menzis.nl/web/Consumenten/VergoedingZorgverzekering/VergoedingenAZ/Invitrofertili

is carried out in a manner that is not in compliance with Dutch medical and ethical standards, for instance if gametes have been used which were donated anonymously and/or on a commercial basis, or if more than two embryos have been implanted in the course of one IVF cycle.[387] The Health Care Insurance Board ('CVZ', now the National Health Care Institute[388]) and the Dutch government have taken the position that it is irrelevant for the entitlement to reimbursement of the costs whether AHR treatment is obtained within the Netherlands or abroad, as long as the conditions of the Health Insurance Act and the Health Insurance Order are met.[389] Accordingly, age limits apply also in respect of foreign treatment.[390] Medical and ethical standards in Dutch legislation concerning the carrying out of AHR treatment, such as those laid down in the Embryo Act, are directed to health care providers within the Dutch jurisdiction, not to the persons insured under the Health Insurance Act.[391] These conditions therefore do not have automatic effect in respect of the Health Insurance Act and thus, do not affect the insurance coverage.[392] This also holds for the licensing obligation under the Dutch Exceptional Medical Expenses Act (*Wet bijzondere medische verrichtingen* (WBMV))[393] and the Dutch rules concerning donation of gametes and embryos, as provided for in the Donor Information Act.[394] This means that, for example, where anonymously donated gametes are used in the course of IVF treatment, this treatment nevertheless belongs to the entitlements under the

satieIVFInHetBuitenland.htm, visited June 2013; www.cz.nl/ivf-icsi-fertiliteitsbehandeling-buitenland.pdf, visited June 2013 and www.anderzorg.nl/web/Vergoedingen/Vergoeding/IVFBehandelingInHetBuitenland.htm, visited June 2013.

387 *Aanhangsel Handelingen II* 2010/11, 238.

388 See *supra* n. 354.

389 *Aanhangsel Handelingen II* 2010/11, 238, pp. 1–2. See also CVZ, *IVF behandelingen uit 2005 tellen mee voor de zorgverzekeringswet* [IVF treatment obtained in 2005 counts for the Health Insurance Act], adviesaanvraag Zvw [Request for advice under the Health Insurance Act] of 23 May 2006, online available at www.cvz.nl/binaries/live/cvzinternet/hst_content/nl/documenten/standpunten/2006/sp0606+ivf-behandelingen+2005.pdf, visited June 2013.

390 CVZ Report *Een leeftijdsgrens voor vruchtbaarheidsbehandelingen* [An age limit for fertility treatment], Annex to *Kamerstukken II* 2011/12, 33000-XVI no. 188, p. 17. This is in line with a judgment by the District Court Amsterdam of 2003. Under reference to Case C-157/99 *Geraets-Smits and Peerbooms* [2001] ECR I-5473, ECLI:EU:C:2001:404 and Case C-385/99 *Müller-Fauré and van Riet* [2003] ECR I-4509, ECLI:EU:C:2003:270, this Court ruled that a refusal to reimburse IVF treatment obtained by a woman over 45 years of age in a Belgian clinic, constituted no violation of the free movement rules, as this treatment was not amongst the benefits provided for under Dutch law, given that under Dutch law a age limit of 40 was set (while one licensed hospital by way of experiment treated women until the age of 45). Rb. Amsterdam 7 October 2003, ECLI:NL:RBAMS:2003:AN9605. See also College voor zorgverzekeringen, Opinion of 25 May 2010, *LJN* BN1229.

391 *Aanhangsel Handelingen II* 2010/11, 238, pp. 1–2.

392 Derksen and Staal 2012, *supra* n. 152, at p. 5.

393 *Inter alia*, Geschillencommissie Zorgverzekeringen [Conciliation Board Health Insurance], Opinion of 8 August 2007, case no. ANO07.155 and the following Opinions of the College voor zorgverzekeringen [Health Care Insurance Board]: no. 26026338 of 23 May 2005; no. 26035826 of 19 June 2006 and no. 27028502 of 24 September 2007.

394 CVZ, *IVF met gebruik van anonieme eiceldonatie (in het buitenland) in beginsel een te verzekeren prestatie* [IVF with the use of anonymous egg-cell donation (in a foreign country) is in principle a performance within the meaning of the Health Insurance Act], adviesaanvraag Zvw Zvw [Request for advice under the Health Insurance Act] of 24 October 2006, online available at: www.cvz.nl/binaries/live/cvzinternet/hst_content/nl/documenten/standpunten/2006/sp0606+ivf+met+eiceldonatie.pdf, visited June 2013.

Health Insurance Act.[395] Under the Health Insurance Act only high-quality health care is reimbursed, however, as the Dutch government is aware – on the basis of CJEU case law (*inter alia, Decker and Kohl* and *Smits-Peerbooms*) – the relevant standard is whether the care has been sufficiently tried and tested by *international* medical science. In other words, States must trust each other's health care standards. In the words of the Minister of Health, Welfare and Sports: no matter how important the Dutch society may find it that a child can learn about his or her genetic origins, the fact that use is made of an anonymous donor, does not affect the quality of the care provided.[396]

The Central Appeals Court for Public Service and Social Security Matters has taken a different approach. This Court ruled in 2007 that IVF treatment with the use of anonymously donated egg cells was not amongst the benefits provided for under the Dutch Health Insurance Act and that therefore the refusal to reimburse for such treatment obtained abroad, constituted no obstacle of the freedom to receive services.[397]

Although not uncontroversial, it is generally accepted that the Dutch Health Insurance bears the costs that occur when insured persons return to the Netherlands after having obtained treatment abroad, even if that treatment itself would not be reimbursed under the Health Insurance Act. For example, the implantation of two or more embryos in the course of one IVF cycle frequently results in multiple births, which often involve premature births and an increased risk of complications during the pregnancy and thus extra costs.[398]

Tax deductions have generally been held to apply also in cross-border cases, so long as the relevant criteria are met that would apply if the costs had been made in the Netherlands.[399]

6.5.3. Information about treatment abroad and follow-up treatment

Dutch legislation or policy does not provide anything particular in respect of access to information about foreign abortion services or AHR treatment. The Dutch government has, however, considered it its task to inform the Dutch public about the legal complexities that may be involved when entering into surrogacy agreements

395 Derksen and Staal 2012, *supra* n. 152, at p. 6, *Aanhangsel Handelingen II* 2010/11, 238, pp. 1–2 and College voor zorgverzekeringen [Health Care Insurance Board] Opinion no. 26084415 of 24 October 2006.

396 *Aanhangsel Handelingen II* 2010/11, 238, pp. 1–2.

397 CRvB 31 January 2007, ECLI:NL:CRVB:2007:AZ8510. See also CRvB 14 February 2007, ECLI:NL:CRVB:2007:AZ9700.

398 CVZ 2010, *supra* n. 344, at pp. 11–12.

399 See Rb. 's-Gravenhage 8 January 2013, ECLI:NL:RBDHA:2013:18948, where various non-medical costst in the course of an international surrogacy agreement (such as hotel costs, the reimbursement of the surrogate mother and the egg-cell donor and the costs of counselling) were not held to qualify for tax deduction.

abroad.[400] In particular, the government has provided information about the legal situation upon return to the Netherlands on relevant Ministerial websites (see 6.3.8 above).

As goes for any other medical treatment legally obtained abroad, people who had an abortion or AHR treatment abroad, are entitled to medical follow-up treatment upon return to the Netherlands. In practice, they may, however, encounter objections of medical practitioners. For example, in 2010 it was reported that 50 per cent of the Dutch gynaecologists refused to provide treatment to women who had AHR treatment with the use of commercially and anonymously donated egg cells in Spain.[401] Apart from such incidental reports, is the present author not aware of any established practice of refusing follow-up treatment, safe of any official policy in this respect.

6.5.4. Access to abortion for foreign women

In the Explanatory Memorandum to the Pregnancy Termination Act (1981) it was acknowledged that the requirement of a five-day reflection period (see 6.2.2.3 above) could imply for non-resident women that they had to extend their stay in the Netherlands before they could have an abortion. This could be held to constitute an obstacle to the free movement of these women. The legislature submitted, however, that this was the inescapable consequence of the fact that the abortion legislation of the (then) EEC Member States varied considerably. It held that the requirement aimed to guarantee that any decision to terminate a pregnancy was taken carefully and well-considered, so it was justified and proportionate and therefore raised no issue under EEC free movement law.[402]

6.5.5. (Non-)applicability of the Dutch Donor Information Act in cross-border situations

It has been reported that '[d]uring the period preceding and immediately following the enactment of the Donor Information Act law, the number of semen (sperm) donors

---

400 In 2012 the Dutch National Rapporteur on Trafficking in Human Beings also advised the government to inform the public that surrogacy in foreign countries may involve human trafficking. National Rapporteur on Trafficking in Human Beings, *Human trafficking for the purpose of the removal of organs and forced commercial surrogacy* (The Hague, BNRM 2012), online available at www.bnrm.nl/publicaties/orgaanverwijdering-draagmoederschap/index.aspx, visited June 2014.

401 As stated by the spokesman of the Dutch Association for Gynaeclogists during an interview for the Dutch tv programme *Nieuwsuur*, broadcasted on Dutch television on 9 September 2010, www.nieuwsuur.nl/onderwerp/183384-spanje-is-hoop-voor-onvruchtbare-vrouwen.html, visited March 2014. The spokesman held that 50 per cent of the genealogists in the Netherlands refused to provide treatment to women who had AHR treatment with the use of commercially and anonymously donated egg cells in Spain. Their reasons to refuse treatment were twofold: (1) because commercial and anonymous egg cell donation was illegal under Dutch law and (2) because they were concerned about quality and safety of the treatment in Spain.

402 *Kamerstukken II* 1978/79, 15 475, no. 3, pp. 25–26.

and semen banks dropped drastically and there was a change in the type of donor.'[403] Waiting lists were the result.[404] In addition, there was a clear deficit in donated egg cells in the Netherlands.[405] Presumably as a consequence, there have been reports of women and couples resident in the Netherlands who resorted to foreign donation options (see also 6.4.2.1 above).[406] Although the reasons for going abroad were often not made explicit, these women and couples regularly travelled to countries which provided for permanent anonymity of gamete donors.[407]

When a child is born or raised in the Netherlands that was conceived in another country with the use of (anonymously) donated gametes, the Dutch Donor Information Act does not apply. It only imposes an obligation on AHR clinics established under Dutch law to register the details of gamete donors. In cross-border situations, children depend on their parents if they wish to be informed about their genetic origins.[408] The Dutch government has called this an 'undesirable' situation but felt that it could, nonetheless, not be prevented from occurring.[409] Nevertheless, concerns have been expressed that this involved medical risks for children conceived through IVF treatment with the use of anonymously donated gametes in a foreign country, as the hereditary family history may be unknown.[410]

Gametes which have been donated in a foreign country may only be used in IVF treatment in a Dutch establishment if all requirements of the Donor Information Act – including those regarding the information about the donor – have been met.[411]

---

403 Janssens et al. 2005, *supra* n. 188, at p. 1416. See also Pennings 2010, *supra* n. 345, at pp. 56–57; 'Dutch sperm laws threaten donations', *BBC* 12 August 2004, www.news.bbc.co.uk/2/hi/europe/3555202.stml, visited 30 March 2014 and Winter et al. 2012, *supra* n. 136, at p. 248.

404 Winter et al. 2012, *supra* n. 136, at p. 114.

405 As the 2012 Evaluation Report explains, this has to do with the burdens involved in the procedure of egg cell donation and with the fact that donation has to be altruistic under Dutch Law. Apart from women who donate in the course of the (much debated) 'cooperative reciprocity' ('coöperatieve wederkerigheid') programme of one Dutch AHR-clinic (the Geertgen clinic, see www.geertgen.nl/onze-werkwijze/coorperatieve-wederkerigheid, visited July 2013), there are hardly any egg cell donors in the Netherlands. This cooperative reciprocity programme (also referred to as 'mirror-donation' ('*spiegeldonatie*')) implies that people who receive donated gametes, also (indirectly) provide gametes for donation. Winter et al. 2012, *supra* n. 136, at pp. 223 and 252. See also *Aanhangsel Handelingen II* 2011/12, 761 and Nederlandse Vereniging voor Obstetrie en Gynaecologie (NVOG) [Dutch Association for Obstetrics and Gynaecology], *Standpunt Gameetdonatie in een systeem van faire wederkerigheid* [Opinion on gamete donation in a system of fair reciprocity], online available at www.nvog-documenten.nl/richtlijn/item/pagina.php?richtlijn_id=900, visited July 2013.

406 *Aanhangsel Handelingen II* 2010/11, 238, p. 1.

407 *Idem*.

408 *Kamerstukken II* 2012/13, 30 486, no. 5, p. 18.

409 *Aanhangsel Handelingen II* 2007/08, 113, p. 242 and *Aanhangsel Handelingen II* 2013/14, 702.

410 CVZ 2010, *supra* n. 344, at pp. 11–12.

411 *Aanhangsel Handelingen II* 2007/08, 113, p. 242.

6.5.6. Cross-border surrogacy under Dutch law

The strict conditions for surrogacy in the Netherlands, and the legal uncertainty surrounding it, have been reason for some Dutch couples to engage in surrogacy agreements abroad.[412] Couples or individuals from the Netherlands who entered into surrogacy agreements abroad may encounter problems in establishing parental links with the child upon return to the Netherlands. Different situations are conceivable, and accordingly, different rules of Dutch Private International Law may apply.

As Boele-Woelki et al. have made clear, the intended parents may rely on different grounds for their claim that parentage has been created; they may refer to a decision of a foreign judge; or they may rely on legal fact or act.[413] Consequently, different regimes may apply.

Article 9 of the Parentage (Conflicts of Laws) Act (*Wet conflictenrecht afstamming* (Wca))[414] provides for the recognition of foreign judgments in which family ties (*'familierechtelijke betrekkingen'*) are established. Although this provision foresees in a public policy exception, reportedly '[...] few problems have arisen thus far concerning surrogacy arrangements [...]' in cases where recognition of a foreign judgment was sought.[415]

The intended parent(s) may also rely on a foreign birth certificate on which he/she/they is or are stated as legal parent(s).[416] Under Dutch law this is, however, considered to be contrary to public policy.[417] Apart from the fact that surrogacy is considered to be in violation of the *mater semper certa est* rule,[418] generally the view is taken that the rationale lays in the right of the child to know his or her genetic origins (Article 7 of the United Nations Convention on the Rights of the Child).[419] Where intended parents rely on a foreign birth certificate, it may therefore first of all be difficult to enter the Netherlands with the child, as Dutch authorities may refuse a Dutch passport

---

412 S.C.A. van Vlijmen and J.H. van der Tol, 'Draagmoederschap in opkomst: specifieke wet- en regelgeving noodzakelijk?' ['Surrogacy booming: specific regulation necessary?'], *Tijdschrift voor Familie- en Jeugdrecht* (2012) p. 160. In 2012 the Dutch National Rapporteur on Human trafficking concluded that a liberalisation of the strict conditions for supervised high-technological surrogacy could reduce the demand for foreign surrogate mothers, who may be vulnerable to exploitation. See National Rapporteur on Trafficking in Human Beings 2012, *supra* n. 400.

413 Boele-Woelki et al. 2011, *supra* n. 186, at p. 308.

414 Act of 14 March 2002, *Stb.* 2002, 153. The Act entered into force per 11 April 2003.

415 Boele-Woelki et al. 2011, *supra* n. 186, at p. 308.

416 This is for example the case in Ukraine.

417 E.g. Rb. 's-Gravenhage 24 October 2011, ECLI:NL:RBSGR:2011:BU3627.

418 *Kamerstukken II* 2001/02, 26 675, no. 6, p. 19.

419 Van Vlijmen and Van der Tol 2012, *supra* n. 412. This approach was also taken by Rb. 's-Gravenhage 14 September 2009, ECLI:NL:RBSGR:2009:BK1197. The case concerned a Dutch married same-sex couple, who entered into a surrogacy agreement with a Dutch woman. The woman gave birth to the child – to whom she and one of the spouses were genetically related – in France, so that she could give the child up for adoption anonymously. The genetic father recognised the child and was stated as being the father on the French birth certificate. The certificate did not mention the mother. The Court refused to recognise the French birth certificate, because it held it to be contrary to Dutch public policy that the child would not be able to know who his genetic mother was.

to the child on public order grounds. This implies that the child – who has no other passport – cannot leave the country where it was born. In two such cases the Dutch judge ordered the Ministry of Foreign Affairs to issue emergency travel documents, as the judge considered this in the best interests of the child.[420] The issuance of such travel documents neither automatically implies the establishment of parental rights for the intended parents, however, nor the awarding of Dutch nationality or residence rights to the child.[421]

If the intended parents subsequently try to establish their parental links by means of a court procedure, the foreign birth certificate on which they are stated as legal parents, may not – again on public policy grounds – be recognised under Dutch law. In that situation, the Dutch court has to establish the necessary data for the drawing up of a birth certificate.[422] It can only do so if the child has Dutch nationality; which may require, first of all, that the paternity of the intended and genetic father is determined by the court.[423]

In all cases the Dutch Courts put the interest of the child first, which may – as time elapses – lead to the awarding of parental rights to (at least one of) the intended parents.[424] As Boele-Woelki et al. explain:

> 'Although up until now it is clear that a birth certificate upon which no mother is recorded will be regarded as contrary to Dutch public policy, other cases are far from clear. This uncertainty exists with respect to original birth certificates in which the genetic mother is recorded instead of the birthmother, or where the non-genetic commissioning parents are recorded on the birth certificate. Nevertheless, children do arrive in The Netherlands with such birth certificates. Once these children have remained in The Netherlands for some time, it is very difficult for the State to remove the child from the commissioning parents, due to the weight given to the best interests of the child and the protection of the family life created between the child and the commissioning parents.'[425]

The Dutch Secretary of State for Security and Justice concluded in 2011 that as a result of the approach of the Dutch courts, standing policy was overtaken by practice and its enforcement was rendered more difficult.[426] He therefore proposed that foreign surrogacy agreements would be given legal effect in the Netherlands if at least one of the intended parents was genetically related to the child and the other genetic parent

420 Rb. 's-Gravenhage (vrzr.) 9 November 2010, ECLI:NL:RBSGR:2010:BP3764 and Rb. Haarlem (vrzr.) 10 January 2011, ECLI:NL:RBHAA:2011:BP0426.

421 *Kamerstukken II* 2011/12, 33 000 VI, no. 69, p. 3.

422 Art. 1:25c BW. See also Rb. 's-Gravenhage 24 October 2011, ECLI:NL:RBSGR:2011:BU3627 and Van Vlijmen and Van der Tol 2012, *supra* n. 412.

423 E.g. Rb. 's-Gravenhage 24 October 2011, ECLI:NL:RBSGR:2011:BU3627.

424 E.g. Rb. 's-Gravenhage 11 December 2007, ECLI:NL:RBSGR:2007:BB9844 and Rb. 's-Gravenhage 18 January 2012, ECLI:NL:RBSGR:2012:BV2597. For a critical note, see the case note (in Dutch) of P. Vlaardingerbroek to the 2007 judgment in *JPF* 2008/72.

425 Boele-Woelki et al. 2011, *supra* n. 186, at p. 308.

426 *Kamerstukken II* 2011/12, 33 000 VI, no. 69, p. 4.

was known.[427] In line therewith he proposed that the reimbursement of expenses for foreign surrogate mothers would not be taken into account in the examination of the public policy exceptions in international surrogacy cases, as – so he alleged – 'profit' could not be defined unequivocally in the international context. The Secretary of State furthermore submitted that on the basis of Article 7 of the United Nations Convention on the Rights of the Child, any child born through surrogacy – be it with the use of donor gametes or not – had the right to know who his or her genetic parents were.[428] Still, this has proven difficult to enforce in cross-border situations (see 6.6.4 above). The proposed policy for cross-border surrogacy cases has been endorsed by the authorities,[429] but the present author is not aware of any published policy documents in which the policy has been laid down.

The Dutch government at the same time saw no need to amend Dutch law fundamentally so as to ensure that people would no longer feel a need to go abroad for surrogacy. They acknowledged that the Netherlands could not take an isolated position on this matter, but they also held it to be impossible to rule out any cross-border movement for this purpose.[430] The Dutch government has furthermore seemed somewhat sceptical about the feasibility of the adoption of international instruments in respect of surrogacy. For example, they felt that the development of an International Treaty on surrogacy by the Hague Conference for Private International Law could not be awaited, as the occurring questions were too pressing.[431]

The courts have, since then, continued to decide international surrogacy cases on the basis of the best interests of the child. In most – if not all – cases, the genetic parenthood of the intended father played an important role.[432] A case of 2013

---

427 This has been charactarised as a 'defeatist and pragmatic' stance. B. van Beers, Case-note to ECtHR [GC] 3 November 2011, *S.H. a.o* v. *Austria*, no. 57813/00, 13 *European Human Rights Cases* 2012/38 (in Dutch).

428 *Kamerstukken II* 2011/12, 33 000 VI, no. 69, p. 4.

429 *Kamerstukken II* 2011/12, 31 265, no. 42.

430 *Kamerstukken II* 2012/13, 33 400 XVI, no. 155, pp. 7–8.

431 *Kamerstukken II* 2011/12, 33 000 VI, no. 69, p. 4. See also Hague Conference of Private international law, Council on General Affairs and Policy of the Conference (17–20 April 2012), *Conclusions and Recommendations adopted by the Council*, 2012, www.hcch.net/upload/wop/gap2012concl_en.pdf, visited June 2014.

432 For example, in a case of 2012, the District Court of Haarlem entrusted an intended father exclusive parental authority over his genetic child that was born to an Indian surrogate mother who was married. The intended father, who had recognised the child before the Dutch Registry and was subsequently appointed as the child's guardian, requested the Court to entrust him with parental authority under Art. 1:253 c (1) BW. The man had concluded a surrogacy agreement in India with a surrogate mother who was married. From the judgment it does not become clear whether she was also the genetic mother of the child, but the court found it established that the intended father was the genetic father of the child. The judgment also gives no information about the birth certificate. However, the surrogate mother had waived all her rights and obligations towards the child, by means of an affidavit. The Court ruled that the it was in the interests of the child concerned, that the intended father, who had cared for the child from the moment of its birth, could make parental decisions, without needing to acquire the consent of the Indian surrogate mother, who was difficult to reach as she lived in India and who had never intended to care for the child. The Court accordingly entrusted the intended father (exclusively) with authority over the child. It is stated in the case that the intended father had a partner, but the case did not deal with the question of the legal recognition of her or his relationship to the child. Rb. Haarlem 6 November

concerned a same-sex couple.[433] The child in this case had been born to an Indian surrogate mother who was married, with the use of an anonymously donated egg cell and sperm of the Dutch intended father who was in a same-sex relationship.[434] The District Court of Haarlem held that by way of recognition before the Dutch Registry, the legal paternity of the intended father of his genetic child had been established. The Court subsequently granted an adoption order for the same-sex partner of the intended father, because such adoption was in the best interest of the child, and because the child could not – as could be reasonably foreseen – expect anything from the surrogate mother in her capacity as mother.[435]

6.6. Conclusions

Both abortion and AHR treatment have been the subject of heated discussions in Dutch society and politics. In respect of both these sensitive issues it took the legislature considerable time to draft and adopt legislation and in most cases this regulation followed an already existing practice. For instance, the Pregnancy Termination Act was only adopted after abortion clinics had been in operation for almost a decade, and until the entry into of the Embryo Act in 2002, assisted human reproduction (AHR) was only marginally regulated. Further, in both areas of law, criminal law sets the very boundaries of what is (ethically) acceptable. In practice, criminal law is, however, enforced to a very limited extent only. The relevant legislation primarily aims to provide for the necessary safeguards in respect of quality and safety of the treatment. Particularly in respect of abortion a rather procedural approach has been taken by the legislature; the Pregnancy Termination Act serves to guarantee a careful decision-making around abortion.

In a way the abortion debate paved the way for the introduction of AHR, as some form of human interference with the natural process of procreation was thereby accepted. Nevertheless, each new technological development in the field of AHR has stirred

2012, ECLI:NL:RBHAA:2012:5285. In another case, concerning the Philippenes, the judgment did not state explicitly who the genetic parents of the child were, but the impression is conveyed that these were the surrogate mother and the intended father, because they were stated as the parents of the child on the Philippene birth certificate. The Court determined that the intended father had established his legal paternity under Philippene law, by means of signing an affidavit of acknowledgment – admission of paternity. Because a close personal relationship existed between the intended father and child, this recognition of paternity was recognised under Dutch law on the basis of Art. 10:101 BW. The Court accordingly ordered the entry of the birth certificate in the Dutch Register. Rb. 's-Gravenhage 13 August 2013, ECLI:NL:RBDHA:2013:12313.

433 Rb. Noord-Holland 18 December 2013, ECLI:NL:RBNHO:2013:12578.

434 The Indian birth certificate – which had stated that the surrogate mother was the mother and the intended father was the father of the child – could not be entered in the Dutch registry on public order grounds, because this was a surrogacy case. As the husband of the Indian surrogate mother (whom under Dutch law would be presumed the father of the child, due to the fact that the child was born within his marriage to the surrogate mother) had expressly denied paternity of the child, the Court established that the child would have no legal father under Dutch law, had the intended (and genetic) father not recognised the child. The Court declared for law that with this recognition the legal parenthood of the father had been established.

435 Art. 1:227(2) and (3) and Art. 1:227(3) BW.

a new and often heated debate about the acceptability of the new technique from an ethical viewpoint. Dondorp and De Wert have characterised the structure of the Dutch debate on AHR as a 'repeating break' ('*de repeterende breuk*').[436] According to the authors the debate repeatedly follows the same pattern: each time there is a new medical technological development, the argument is put forward that this new development crosses the line of ethical acceptability. However, these objections of principle soon prove to enjoy too little support to stop the development. No matter how heated the debate has been, the outcome is the same each and every time: subject to certain conditions, the new medical technology can be employed.[437] This chapter has shown that in this regard the argument that people will otherwise resort to foreign treatment options, is frequently heard.

Through licensing systems and by requesting the medical profession to draft guidelines, the legislature has aimed to regulate these sensitive areas of laws. Prominent guiding principles for the legislature's decision-making in respect of abortion and AHR are the protection of human life, the personal autonomy of the patient, the principle of good medical care and the best interests of the (future) child (see section 6.1.2). These principles are not embedded in the Dutch Constitution but follow from general principles of medical ethics and from International Treaty instruments. In all situations the legislature has aimed to strike a balance between these (competing) interests. In some cases greater weight has been attached to one of these interests. While the personal autonomy of the woman was in the end the most dominant principle on which the abortion legislation was based, the right of the child to know ones genetic origin was a decisive consideration for the legislature to set limits to the donation of gametes.

Cross-border movement has been taking place in respect of both abortion and AHR treatment. In respect of abortion, movement to the Netherlands was particularly large in scale in the 1970s and 1980s. Nonetheless, the number of abortions carried out in Dutch clinics involving non-resident women still makes up a non-negligible percentage of the total number of abortions carried out in the Netherlands. There have been only incidental reports of Dutch women going to other EU Member States for abortions. In respect of AHR treatment, most reports of cross-border movement concern couples and individuals from the Netherlands who go abroad for AHR treatment, for instance for IVF treatment with the use of anonymously donated egg cells. Cross-border movement to the Netherlands for reproductive care has also been reported, but no official statistics are available.

The existence of CBRC is expressly acknowledged by the Dutch authorities. Although (medical) risks may be involved, it is felt that such cross-border movement cannot be prevented from occurring. In fact, a certain form of resignation on the side of the government can be noticed. For example, in response to parliamentary questions, the

---

436 Dondorp and De Wert 2012B, *supra* n. 200, at pp. 7–12.

437 *Idem*, at pp. 5–6. The present chapter has shown that the only exception to this 'ritual dance' is the case of gender selection, which has been probihited soon after it was introduced and still is prohibited under Dutch law.

Minister of Health held in 2011 that she had no means to stop women from turning to foreign clinics for anonymous egg cell donation. According to the Minister this very fact rendered the question of whether this development was desirable or not, out of order.[438] It is furthermore generally accepted that the Dutch Health Insurance system has to carry the costs of foreign treatments, even if they are not in conformity with the Dutch professional standards or laws.[439] Some difference of opinion on this issue between the government and the Health Care Insurance Board on the one side, and the Central Appeals Court for Public Service and Social Security Matters on the other, has been, however, visible (see section 6.5.2 above).

Cross-border movement and related quality and safety concerns have in some cases been an express ground for the Dutch legislature to regulate certain issues. The fact that couples from the Netherlands went abroad for PGD, for instance, was one of the reasons for the Dutch legislature to legalise and regulate this diagnosis and surrogacy agreements concluded in other countries, made the Dutch government feel that the Private International Law rules on the establishment of parental links had to be amended (see sections 6.4.3 and 6.5.6 above).

---

438 *Aanhangsel Handelingen II* 2010/11, 2303, p. 2.

439 CVZ 2010, *supra* n. 344, at pp. 11–12.

Chapter 7
Conclusions Case Study I

7.1. The internal picture – How are reproductive matters dealt with in the various jurisdictions?

7.1.1. Balancing; the same interests but different weights

The present case study has confirmed that the regulation of reproductive matters involves a careful balancing of various individual and general interests. As such, there is not much difference between the kind of interests and considerations that have been addressed in legislative debates and included in decision-making in the various jurisdictions studied. It is the weight that has been accorded to these interests and correspondingly the balancing of the various interests involved that has differed. Some States accord particularly strong protection to a specific interest. The Irish protection of the unborn and the German protection of human dignity, which are included in the Constitutions of these countries, are two examples that stand out in this regard. This is not to say that the other States studied do not protect these interests at all, but they do so less prominently, have interpreted these notions differently and/or have accepted that in certain circumstances counter-values may outbalance these interests.

At the European level, States are left ample room to undertake balancing exercises in reproductive matters, and consequently, to make principled choices in this area. Chapter 3 has shown that EU law basically does not reduce this national freedom, apart from by setting certain safety and quality requirements for the placing in the market of *in vitro* diagnostic medical devices. The ECtHR also generally leaves States a wide margin of appreciation in the area, which extends both to the States' decision to intervene in the area and, once they have intervened, to the detailed rules they set down in order to achieve a balance between the competing public and private interests. As explained in Chapter 2, the margin is wide because morally and ethically sensitive issues are concerned, which involve a complex balancing of various individual interests and upon which generally no European consensus exists. Another reason is that the Strasbourg Court respects the democratic processes at the national level. Especially where a certain national 'choice' emerged from a 'lengthy, complex and sensitive debate' at the domestic level,[1] or where it was the 'culmination of an exceptionally detailed examination of the social, ethical and legal implications of developments in the field [...] and the fruit of much reflection, consultation and

[1] ECtHR [GC] 16 December 2010, *A, B and C* v. *Ireland*, no. 25579/05.

debate',[2] has the ECtHR granted the States much leeway to make their own decisions and set their own rules and procedures. The Strasbourg Court has at the same time stressed that the margin of appreciation is not unlimited and that national 'solutions' are not beyond the scrutiny of this Court.[3] The ECtHR supervises whether interferences constitute a proportionate balancing of the competing interests involved.[4] At times such examination has resulted in the finding of a violation. Further, the margin of appreciation has not been wide in all situations covered by this case study.[5]

So what are the various individual and general interests that have been included in balancing exercises at the national level and (approved of at) European level? In all three States, it appears that values like human dignity and non-commercialisation of (parts of) the human body have played a prominent role in (legislative) debates on and standard-setting in reproductive matters.[6] Another such value is personal autonomy, in respect of which it can be noted – in any case in the abortion context that – that it has generally been granted more protection in Germany and the Netherlands, when compared to Ireland. All three States have furthermore protected interests of individuals who cannot easily claim protection of their own rights. These concern the (unborn or future) child and vulnerable parties (indirectly) involved in reproductive matters, such as gamete donors and surrogate mothers.

The unborn is protected to some extent in all three States studied in this research, as well as by the ECtHR, but to differing degrees. The ECtHR has not taken a strong stance on the status of the unborn life, but, leaving a wide margin of appreciation in this particularly sensitive area, it has upheld systems like the Irish that grant the unborn almost absolute protection against abortion. Also in Germany and the Netherlands the principled choice has been made to criminalise abortion in order to give expression to the protection of the unborn life, but both regimes provide for important exceptions to this rule. The Dutch legislature chose to protect the interests of the unborn child through a set of procedural requirements which provide the decision-making procedure with the necessary guarantees (see also section 7.4

---

2 ECtHR [GC] 10 April 2007, *Evans* v. *the United Kingdom*, no. 6339/05, para. 86.

3 ECtHR 28 August 2012, *Costa and Pavan* v. *Italy*, no. 54270/10 and ECtHR [GC] 3 November 2011, *S.H. a.o.* v. *Austria*, no. 57813/00.

4 ECtHR [GC] 16 December 2010, *A, B and C* v. *Ireland*, no. 25579/05, para. 238 under reference to ECtHR 29 October 1992, *Open Door and Dublin Well Woman* v. *Ireland*, nos. 14234/88 and 14235/88, para. 68. In *S.H. and Others* – a case on gamete donation – the Court held that it fell to it to carefully examine the arguments which had been taken into consideration during the legislative process and which had led to the choices that had been made by the legislature and to determine whether a fair balance had been struck between the competing interests of the State and those directly affected by those legislative choices. While the Court held expressly that a wide margin of appreciation applied in that case, this formulation in fact directs at a stricter scrutiny. ECtHR [GC] 3 November 2011, *S.H. a.o.* v. *Austria*, no. 57813/00, para. 97.

5 One concrete issue in respect of which the margin of appreciation has narrowed over the years, concerns the right to know one's genetic origins. See Ch. 2, section 2.1.4.

6 Non-commercialisation of (parts of the) human body, is in fact one of the few principled standpoints that the EU legislature has taken in this area, as confirmed in Case C-34/10 *Oliver Brüstle* v. *Greenpeace eV* [2011] ECR I-9821, ECLI:EU:C:2011:669. See ch. 3, section 3.1.1.

below).[7] In Germany a similar approach was chosen, albeit that the State's duty to protect unborn life has resulted in stricter time limits and more instructive positive obligations for the authorities in abortion procedures.[8]

Both in the States studied in this research and under the ECHR as well as the EU Charter of Fundamental Rights, it is provided that the best interests of the child must be an important, if not the primordial consideration in any law-making, policy decisions and judicial decisions concerning children. This 'best interests of the child' principle both sees at protection of the child in a more abstract sense, including before it has actually come into being, and at concrete rights that any child bears once it is born and that may extend into adulthood.

It the context of the present case study, protection of the future child, or 'the child' in general, has at times in fact been an argument for not letting a child come into existence in the first place.[9] It has, for example, been put forward – and at times accepted – as (one of the) argument(s) against surrogacy or against certain forms of AHR treatment, such as post-mortem fertilisation or preimplantation genetic diagnosis (PGD). Arguments against surrogacy have been that it was considered unethical to make a child the object of a legal act and that this affected the human dignity of children. Also, divided motherhood has been held not to be in the child's interest.[10] Other concerns have been identity problems for any child born through surrogacy; the possibility that the natural process of bonding between mother and child after birth would be distorted and the risk that the child could be rejected if the expectations of the intended parents were not met. When it comes to PGD, a fear for eugenics and 'designer babies' has been a concern in all three States. On the other hand, there has been the desire to protect the future child's physical integrity, by protecting it against suffering from a serious genetic disorder.

The rights of the child have, furthermore, been put forward by various AHR clinics as an argument for excluding single women as well as same-sex couples from access to AHR. Reimbursement for AHR treatment has in some States been confined to certain groups on similar grounds has. For example, in Germany the fact that only married couples qualify for such reimbursement under the public health insurance, was held to serve best interests of the child and approved of by the German Constitutional Court.[11] Clear bottom lines that have emerged from the present case study are reproduction for profit and gender selection. It has been

---

7 A reflection period, as in place in the Netherlands, is a clear example of such a procedural guarantee. See Ch. 6, section 6.2.2.3.

8 For example, because the goal of counselling in pregnancy conflict situations must be the protection of the unborn child, counsellors must to try to encourage the woman to continue her pregnancy and show her opportunities for a life with the child.

9 In the Netherlands, for example, doctors must refrain from providing assistance to reproduction if they are of the opinion that the future child runs a real risk of serious psychosocial or physical harm. See Ch. 6, section 6.3.2.

10 In the case of Germany this consideration has also been one of the grounds for the German prohibition on egg cell donation. See Ch. 4, section 4.3.4.1.

11 See Ch. 4, section 4.3.8.

considered incommensurable with human dignity to value children, human embryos and gametes in terms of money and thus as objects or trade, or to give reproduction a purely instrumental character.

When it comes to more concrete rights children have once they are born, the right to personal identity and development of the child has proven to be particularly relevant in the present case study. It has been on the basis of this right that a right to know one's genetic origins has been recognised in the States studied for this research, as well as under the ECHR.[12] The level of its protection has varied, however. In the Netherlands, the right of the child to know about its genetic origins has enjoyed protection since 1994 and has been strongly protected through detailed legislation since 2004. In Germany this right has been recognised in case law and in Ireland legislation preserving a child's right to know its identity in the context of gamete donation is in the making. Further, as explained in Chapter 2, under the ECHR a development towards stronger protection of this right has been visible.

Related thereto is the importance that has been attached to genetic lineage in all jurisdictions studied. This is illustrated, for example, by the fact that in the Netherlands only high-technological surrogacy is legalised under certain strict conditions. Another example is the Irish *McD* v. *L & Anor* case (2010), where a sperm donor was granted access to his child, because it was held to be in the interests of the child to establish contact with its genetic father. At the same time, the *mater semper certa est* principle – following which the birth mother is the legal mother of a child whether she is also the genetic mother or not – is adhered to by all three States studied in this research. This principle is closely related to the general principle of legal certainty, which has been another motive for standard-setting in the area.

The present case study has furthermore made clear that States have wished to protect other vulnerable parties involved in abortion, AHR treatment and surrogacy. For example, Germany and the Netherlands have regulated for abortions, *inter alia*, in order to protect women against the health risks involved in illegal abortions.[13] The need has also been felt to protect gamete donors and surrogate mothers against health risks, commodification and commercial exploitation and against psychological or emotional problems in the long run. Further, a prohibition on post-mortem fertilisation without explicit consent, as in place in Germany and the Netherlands, aims to protect the deceased's personal autonomy.

Lastly, quality and safety concerns have been ground for regulating in this area. This certainly also holds for the relevant standard-setting in the area as adopted at EU level, albeit that such requirements also – or primarily – aim to serve the internal market. At national level, quality and safety concerns have been grounds for setting

12 Protection of the child's personal identity was also the primordial consideration of the ECtHR in the cross-border surrogacy cases *Mennesson* and *Labassee* (see ch. 2, section 2.4.2). Because these rulings related to cross-border situations only, they are left out of the equation in the present section that is concerned with the internal picture. See, however, section 7.2 below.

13 Ch. 4, section 4.2.2 and Ch. 6, section 6.2.2.

up licensing systems and for requesting that the medical profession draft guidelines, as has been, for example, the case in the Netherlands.

Thus, there is a wide spectrum of individual and general interests included in the balancing exercises in reproductive matters in the various jurisdictions. As noted above, European regulation and case law leaves the States much room to balance those interests, so long as they ensure that the general legal framework allows the different legitimate interests involved to be adequately taken into account.

7.1.2. Room for bright line rules

Because of the complex balancing exercises involved in reproductive matters, States have at times adopted 'bright line rules', which by nature exclude detailed examinations of individual cases. Examples are complete prohibitions on certain practices, such as the German prohibition on egg cell donation, or principles like the *mater semper certa est* rule – entailing that when a child is born its mother is the woman who gave birth to it – that is upheld in all three States studied.

From the ECtHR's case law it follows that bright line rules in the area of reproductive matters may be acceptable under the Convention. As explained in Chapter 2, this Court has made clear that it is not necessary that legislation governing important aspects of private life provides for the weighing of competing interests in the circumstances of each individual case. Where such important aspects are at stake, so the Court has held, it is not inconsistent with Article 8 ECHR that the legislature adopts rules of an absolute nature which serve to promote legal certainty.[14] It has thereby underlined that concerns based on moral considerations or on social acceptability were not in themselves sufficient reasons for a complete ban on a specific AHR technique.[15] At the same time, the Court has held that the Irish ban on abortion on health and social grounds, could indeed be justified on moral grounds. It accepted that the Irish prohibition of abortion for reasons of health and/or well-being served the legitimate aim of protection of morals, of which the protection in Ireland of the right to life of the unborn was 'one aspect'.[16]

Initially a similar approach was taken by the Strasbourg Court in respect of the question of knowledge about one's genetic origins, as domestic legislation that protected the parent's right to remain anonymous in all situations was upheld by the ECtHR. Over time such bright line rules have become more problematic as increasingly more weight has been attached to the rights of the child in the relevant case law.[17] A similar development has taken place at the national level in the States studied in this research. For example, in the Netherlands initially sperm donors could

---

14 ECtHR [GC] 10 April 2007, *Evans* v. *the United Kingdom*, no. 6339/05, para. 74 and ECtHR [GC] 3 November 2011, *S.H. a.o.* v. *Austria*, no. 57813/00, para. 110.

15 ECtHR [GC] 3 November 2011, *S.H. a.o.* v. *Austria*, no. 57813/00, para. 100.

16 ECtHR [GC] 16 December 2010, *A, B and C* v. *Ireland*, no. 25579/05, para. 222. See Ch. 2, section 2.2.3.

17 See Ch. 2, section 2.1.4.

remain anonymous indefinitely, but this rule was lifted in 2004 and replaced by a system that provided for rules that differentiate between types of donor information and the age of the child concerned. These developments in respect of the question of knowledge about one's genetic origins fit in with a broader development that once an actual child is concerned, it is important to carry out a concrete examination of each case.[18]

The foregoing confirms that it is thus well possible that the more (regulation in respect of) a certain reproductive matter becomes 'commonplace', the more a desire emerges to provide for differentiation in regulation and for possibilities to pay due regard to the individual circumstances of each case.

7.1.3. Consistency of laws required

Another comparable feature that has come to light as a result of the present case study, is that at times a 'consistency of laws' reasoning has come up in some of the jurisdictions studied in this case study. (Parts of) proposed AHR regulation have been considered inconsistent with existing laws, such as abortion laws. Where existing regulation witnessed that a certain principled choice had been made in the respective jurisdiction, it undermined arguments against the introduction of a new type of treatment which raised similar concerns. For example, in Germany, such a consistency of laws argument has been put forward both in respect to the Embryo Protection Act in general, and in respect to PGD in particular, and it has been one of the grounds for lifting the prohibition on PGD. The ECtHR has employed similar reasoning, and on that basis held Italian legislation prohibiting PGD on grounds for which abortion was allowed for, to be in violation of Article 8 ECHR.[19] Hence, under the ECHR, it can be seen that if States regulate in the area of reproductive matters, they must guarantee that the relevant legislative framework is coherent and consistent. This may be particularly challenging now that the relevant legislative framework is generally fragmented (see below).

7.1.4. Importance of procedures allowing for careful decision-making

What furthermore comes to the fore if one compares how reproductive matters have been dealt with in the various jurisdictions studied, is the importance that has been attached – particularly in the context of abortion – to procedures that allow for careful decision-making. This can of course be explained by the fact that, as discussed above, these matters involve a balancing of various interests and such procedures are aimed to enable balancing exercises with due regard for the individual circumstances of each case.

[18] As also stressed in the cross-border surrogacy cases decided by the ECtHR (see Ch. 2, section 2.4.2, as well as section 7.2 below).

[19] See Ch. 2, section 2.3.4.

This attention to procedural guarantees allowing for careful decision-making has been particularly visible in respect of abortion. The Dutch Pregnancy Termination Act, for example, serves first and foremost to guarantee a careful decision-making around abortion. As explained in Chapter 6, the Dutch legislature considered it impossible to set a general norm defining when abortion would be lawful or unlawful, as it considered the emergency and distress situations in which an abortion could be considered to be very diverse.

As discussed in Chapter 2, an obligation to provide for certain procedural rights in respect of abortion also follows from the ECHR, where the Court has based this obligation on the doctrine that Convention rights must be safeguarded in a practical and effective manner. In other words, once the legislature decides to allow abortion, it must structure its legal framework in a way which allows for real possibilities to obtain it. Hence, while the ECtHR does not rule on the substantive choices of principle made by States with regard to abortion, it does require that when there is a legal option to have an abortion at the domestic level, the pregnant woman at least has a possibility to be heard in person and to have her views considered; that the competent body or person issues written grounds for its decision and that the pregnant woman has effective access to relevant information on her and the foetus' health. The latter requirement includes access to diagnostic services, decisive for the possibility for the pregnant woman of exercising her right to take an informed decision as to whether to seek an abortion or not.[20]

This line of ECtHR case law has had very concrete impact at national level, as is particularly visible in respect of Ireland. The Irish abortion procedures were for long unclear, but following the ECtHR judgment in the case of *A, B and C*, the Protection of Life During Pregnancy Act (2014) was adopted. This Act improved the procedural rights of women and has provided for more clarity for medical practitioners, without bringing about any material change.

7.1.5. Fragmented regulation

Apart from differences in the balancing exercises in the various national jurisdictions, the 'level' at which reproductive matters have been regulated in the States – if there is any regulation at all – also appears to differ. In Ireland Article 40.3.3° of the Constitution plays a dominant role in the abortion legislation, while in Germany and the Netherlands those Constitutional provisions applicable are also important guiding principles for standard-setting in the area – in Germany even more prominently than in the Netherlands – but they are less directive in their wording. In Germany and the Netherlands the legislature has generally set the relevant legal framework, while certain matters are left to the medical profession to regulate. In the Netherlands the medical profession is generally given quite substantial leeway, while in Germany the legislature has generally laid down more detailed rules in statutory legislation.

[20] See Ch. 2, section.

While both these States have an Embryo Act that deals with various issues related to AHR and – in the case of Germany – surrogacy, in Ireland, no such legislative framework is in place for AHR treatment and surrogacy.[21] Also, until as recently as January 2014 there was hardly any legislation on abortion.

The present case study has furthermore made clear that various realms of the law may be involved in the relevant legal framework on reproductive matters. In all three States criminal law applies in the area, in any case in abortion regulation. The maximum penalties for illegal abortions have been most severe in Ireland, with life imprisonment until 2014, and imprisonment for a term of 14 years, maximum, since that time. In the Netherlands and Germany the maximum terms of imprisonment are much lower and many more exemption grounds apply. The latter States have also employed criminal law in their regulation in the area of AHR and surrogacy. In both the Netherlands and Germany surrogacy mediation and gender selection are criminalised, while in Germany by means of the Embryo Protection Act, criminal law applies also in respect of matters like post-mortem fertilisation and PGD. Such criminal law provisions were often deliberately chosen to reflect very principled approaches (such as protection of the unborn life; see 7.1.1 above), and to set the very boundaries of what is (ethically and morally) acceptable. Their actual employment has been much more limited; prosecution practice for abortions has decreased considerably over the decades in all three States, while prosecutions for surrogacy and AHR related matters have been only very incidentally reported.[22]

Other areas of law that are covered by the relevant legal frameworks of the States studied concern social security law for public funding issues and civil law in respect of questions of parenthood. Furthermore, in all three States medical profession sets certain ethical and quality standards, while access to AHR treatment is often regulated by clinics themselves and may thus differ from clinic to clinic.

The various national regimes thus differ not only in respect of substance, but also in respect of form and the level at which reproductive matters are regulated for.

7.1.6. How was change brought about? A typification of (legislative and judicial) processes

Not only do the balancing exercises in reproductive matters and the level at which these matters were regulated differ between the various jurisdictions, but also the way in which change has been brought about. For instance, sometimes the legislature has proven to be the driving force behind change, while in other situations it has been the judiciary. Also, the extent to which European law has been influential in these (legislative and judicial) processes differs between the States studied.

---

21 It is reminded that this research was concluded on 31 July 2014.

22 See Ch. 4, section 4.2; Ch. 5, section 5.2.9 and Ch. 6, section 6.2.4 respectively. See also section 7.2.1.1 below.

What the processes in the various jurisdictions have in common is that change has never been brought about quickly. In all three States, there has been generally a certain or even considerable reluctance on the side of the legislature to regulate this area. This can be explained by the sensitivity of the subject-matter and the diversity of interests that need to be balanced in this area, as set out above in section 7.1.1 Also, the area concerned is one in respect of which medical and scientific developments are moving fast. Legislatures and courts – including those at European level – have been uncertain about (the effects of) such developments and have therefore acted with caution. In all three States there have been fairly lengthy debates and considerable lapses in time before regulation has been introduced, if at all. For example, in Germany, adoption of the German Pregnancy and Family Assistance Act of 1992 was preceded by two years of heated and emotive debates that had even jeopardised the signing of the Reunification Treaty. Not uncommonly, practice has outpaced regulation. For instance, the Dutch Pregnancy Termination Act was only adopted after abortion clinics had been in operation for almost a decade, and the introduction of the Embryo Act took until 2002, while IVF treatments had been carried out in the Netherlands since the 1980s. The ECtHR, while at times urging the States to keep the area under review, has not reproached States for such delays in the adoption of legislation on reproductive matters.[23]

As observed in Chapter 6, the Dutch process in respect of AHR legislation can been described as a ritual dance with a 'repeating break', entailing that each new medical technological development has been met with concerns about its ethical acceptability, but has nonetheless been regulated for, by subjecting it to certain limitations.[24] The German legislature has also taken a careful piecemeal approach in the area, but followed a different pattern. From early on it covered many issues in the Embryo Protection Act of 1991 and outlawed a considerable number of practices such as surrogacy, egg cell donation and PGD. Over time some of these rules have been amended and relaxed, for example those in respect of PGD. Also, in Germany the Courts have played a more prominent role in this process. At times, they have given an extra push for change. The lifting of the absolute prohibition on PGD in 2011, for instance, has been the result of a judgment of the Constitutional Court. In other cases, German courts have shown more deference to political and societal sensitivities and have given the legislature discretion to regulate matters, for instance in respect of reimbursement for AHR treatment.

In the case of Ireland, the process has been different. The pattern that can be discerned is that individual cases have frequently caused considerable public outcry, while basically all change – albeit limited in any case – has been triggered or even forced upon the legislature by (European) case law. The legislature has often resisted giving a follow-up to these judgments, or has in any case been hesitant to do so. For

23 Only in the Irish abortion case *A, B and C* did the ECtHR note that Ireland had failed to implement Art. 40.3.3° of the Irish Constitution, and the lack of a regulations on the abortion procedures was a ground for the finding of a violation of Art. 8 ECHR in respect of the third applicant. See Ch. 2, section 2.2.3.

24 Ch. 6, section 6.6.

instance, it was only in 2014, after the ECtHR's *A, B and C* ruling and the public debate sparked by the tragic death of a woman who had been refused an abortion in a hospital in Galway, that a law was adopted that implemented the *X Case* of 1992, and has regulated access to lawful termination of pregnancy in Ireland. AHR and surrogacy have long been, and are mostly still, submerged in legal uncertainty in Ireland. The AHR Commission identified a need for action in 2005, but for years the Irish legislature did not take any action. After the Irish courts unequivocally stated that they did not consider it the task of the judiciary to resolve the existing uncertainty, it has been evidently up to the Irish legislature to fill in the legal vacuum that has continued to exist in Ireland as regards AHR and surrogacy. It was (again) only in 2014 that first steps in this regard were taken, although some initiatives – most prominently the proposed surrogacy legislation – were withdrawn before they were even debated in Parliament.

To remain in the metaphor of dance, other processes can be best described as two steps forward, one step back, resembling the dancing procession of Echternach.[25] Sometimes courts have blown the whistle on excessively proactive legislatures, as was, for example, the case in the German abortion judgment of 1975, in which the Constitutional Court ruled that the Abortion Reform Act as passed by the German legislature insufficiently protected the unborn.[26] On other occasions higher Courts have overruled judgments of lower Courts for being overly progressive. For example, the Irish Supreme Court blew the whistle on the High Court which had, in the of *McD* v. *L & Anor* case, recognised *de facto* family life of a same-sex couple and had accordingly denied a sperm donor access to his biological child.[27] Another such example concerns the ECtHR, where the Grand Chamber of the ECtHR overruled the Chamber in the *S.H. and Others* case, and so upheld the Austrian prohibition on ovum donation, that the Chamber had previously found discriminatory.[28]

7.1.7. Resumé and outlook

In sum, it can be derived from this case study that the balancing of interests related to reproductive matters has resulted different outcomes in the three States studied and the legislative and judicial processes in the States have taken different shapes. European law explicitly allows for such diversity between legal regimes on reproductive matters. States are left room to make their own principled choices in these moral and ethical issues and they are free to prohibit practices, as long as the relevant interests have been balanced in the decision-making and as long as their principled choices are consistent. However, once they decide to regulate in the area, they must also provide for the effective enjoyment of rights and entitlements, which entails that they must ensure that the applicable procedures enable careful decision-making.

---

25 The original dancing procession of Eternach consisted of three steps forward, two steps back.

26 See Ch. 4, section 4.2.2.

27 See Ch. 5, section 5.3.4.

28 See Ch. 2, section 2.3.3.

The present case study has furthermore shown that there are not only differences, but also similarities in the ways in which reproductive matters have been dealt with in the various jurisdictions. Generally, over time more reproductive practices have been legalised and regulated for, or at least initiatives to that effect have been taken. Also, a gradual development towards a central role for the best interests of the child is clearly visible, although the views on what these require exactly have in some cases changed over time. Furthermore, blanket rules have been adopted and approved of at the European level, while at the same time a development towards the assessment of reproductive matters with due regard to the individual circumstances of the case has been visible. Both at European and national levels, there has been increased attention focused on the introduction of procedures allowing for careful decision-making in reproductive matters.

Given that AHR is an area with particularly fast-moving medical and scientific developments, it is in this area that there is most potential for new questions being raised by new medical possibilities. It is also possible that the case law of the ECtHR will in the future have a more substantive impact on standard-setting in the area of reproductive matters, particularly if more European consensus would develop on certain issues.

7.2. The cross-border picture – Legal responses to cross-border movement

As set out in the various chapters of this case study, cross-border movement in reproductive matters has taken and is taking place from and to the three States studied in this research and within the European Union as such, and in some cases the scale of this mobility has been considerable. The present case study has shown that the three States studied – functioning as countries of origin or countries of destination or both – have dealt in different manners with such cross-border movement. Firstly, forms of resignation have been identified. For example, as discussed in Chapter 6, Dutch authorities acknowledged that there were no means to stop cross-border reproductive care (CBRC) and concluded that this very fact rendered the question of whether this development was desirable or not, out of order. Secondly, there have been more (pro)active responses to (the effects of) cross-border movement in reproductive matters. This section identifies and categorises various such legal responses on the basis of the present case study. The extent to which European law (both EU law and the ECHR) leaves room for these legal responses at national level, or in fact even encourages or dictates them, is thereby examined.

A first category of legal responses to cross-border movement in reproductive matters that can be distinguished based on the findings of this case study consists of warding off such cross-border movement: States may try to deter people from going to other States or from coming to their State for reproductive matters. As further explained in section 7.2.1, such warding off may take different shapes, ranging from travel bans to non-recognition of legal parenthood established in another State. Secondly, as a mirror to the 'warding off' approach, States may choose to accommodate (the effects of) cross-border movement in reproductive matters, as is discussed in section 7.2.2. A third type of response is adaptation, which means the adjustment of national standard-setting in the area to that of another State or other States to which cross-border movement takes place (section 7.2.3). Lastly, cross-border movement has in some situations enabled States to outsource the protection of certain interests in these sensitive matters to other States (section 7. 2.4).

Importantly, these responses are generally not mutually exclusive; it has turned out that States often combine various categories of responses in their dealing with cross-border movement in reproductive matters. Nevertheless, for each of these four categories what interests, considerations, perspectives or values have inspired or dictated these legal responses can be examined. Of course, one thereby needs to take care not to ascribe more intentions or underlying motives to the various State measures discussed than can be derived from the type of legal research conducted in this case study. What can be assessed here, however, is what the implications of each respective category of legal responses are, or may be, for the States concerned, as well as for the individuals involved in the cross-border movement. Each subsection therefore finishes with observations about such implications for these actors, whereby reference is also made – where relevant – to sociological research in the area. In the final subsection (section 7.2.5) it is assessed how the various legal responses to cross-border movement relate to one another.

7.2.1. Warding off

Legal responses that ward off (the effects of) cross-border movement in reproductive matters may take different shapes. The most far-reaching response consists in trying to prevent cross-border movement in reproductive matters from taking place in the first place, for instance by imposing a travel ban or by criminally prosecuting people for obtaining treatment abroad (section 7.2.1.1).[29] Other – less drastic – forms of deterring people from crossing borders for reproductive reasons that can be identified on the basis of the present case study are bans on information about such foreign options (section 7.2.1.2), refusals to provide follow-up care (section 7.2.1.3) and refusals to reimburse treatment obtained abroad (section 7.2.1.4). Furthermore, in cross-border surrogacy cases, recognition of legal parenthood established in another State has been refused (section 7.2.1.5). While these measures all concern States that function as countries of origin in cross-border situations, also States that function as countries of destination – States to which cross-border movement takes place – may ward off cross-border movement (section 7.2.1.6).

[29] See also R.F. Storrow, 'Assisted Reproduction on treacherous terrain: the legal hazards of cross-border reproductive travel', 23 *Reproductive BioMedicine Online* (2011) pp. 538–545 and W. van Hoof and G. Pennings, 'Extraterritoriality for cross-border reproductive care; should states act against citizens travelling abroad for illegal infertility treatment?', 23 *Reproductive BioMedicine Online* (2011) pp. 546–554.

7.2.1.1. Travel bans and criminal prosecution upon return

Incidentally, there have been reports of such drastic measures as travel bans being taken by one of the States studied in this research. The Irish *X* and *C* cases of the early 1990s stand out in this regard. As discussed in Chapter 5, these cases where solved at the national level, as the Supreme Court held that there was in the particular circumstance of the cases at hand, where there was a real and substantial risk of loss of the woman's life by way of suicide, a right to an abortion *within* Ireland. This approach could in fact be perceived as a certain form of adaptation (see 7.2.3 below) as it rendered any cross-border movement redundant in such exceptional situations. The *X Case* was, however, also the trigger for the 1992 amendment of Article 40.3.3° of the Irish Constitution, which expressly provides that the freedom to travel between Ireland and other States for the purpose of an abortion will not be limited. The initial warding off that was at stake in the *X Case* and *C Case* thus consequently resulted in an express form of accommodation of cross-border movement for abortions (see also 7.2.2.2 below).[30]

Criminal prosecutions for having obtained reproductive treatment abroad have not been identified in the present case study.[31] They are, however, not illusory. German law, for example, provides expressly for a possibility to criminally prosecute for abortions obtained abroad. At the same time, as noted in Chapter 3, such criminal prosecutions – as for travel bans – seem hard to justify under EU free movement law. Moreover, there may be difficulties in enforcing such prosecutions in cross-border cases.[32]

7.2.1.2. Bans on information about foreign services

Cross-border movement in reproductive matters may also be warded off by means of bans or limitations on information provision about foreign treatment options. As explained in Chapters 2 and 5, Ireland adopted such a policy in respect of information about foreign abortion services in the 1990s, which subsequently proved problematic under the ECHR.[33] The ECtHR's ruling in *Open Door* prompted the adoption of the Abortion Information Act in Ireland, as a result of which, again, the challenge in court of a warding off measure resulted in an accommodation obligation for the

30 This was confirmed by the 2007 ruling of the Irish High Court in the case of Miss *D.*, where the Court ruled that the Health Service Executive could not prevent a 17-year-old pregnant girl from travelling to the UK to obtain an abortion, as there was no stay or constitutional impediment which served to prevent her from travelling to the UK to terminate her pregnancy if she so wished. See Ch. 5, section 5.2.5.

31 As discussed in Ch. 6, in the Netherlands in one case prosecution was initiated for late abortion in Spain, but the charges were later dropped.

32 Van Hoof and Pennings 2011, *supra* n. 29, at p. 551. As also discussed in Ch. 3, section 3.6.4, there are still various open questions as to the application of the European Arrest Warrant in this context.

33 As discussed in Ch. 2, section 2.4.1, in ECtHR 29 October 1992, *Open Door and Dublin Well Woman* v. *Ireland*, nos. 14234/88 and 14235/88, the ECtHR held an injunction restraining Irish counselling agencies from assisting pregnant women in seeking legal abortion services abroad, to violate the freedom to impart and receive information (Art. 10 ECHR).

State.[34] The ECtHR later held the new abortion information legislation acceptable, and considered it one of the elements that justified the restrictive Irish abortion laws (see more elaborately section 7.2.4 below).[35] Given the specific context of the Irish abortion cases, one may need to be careful in applying the ECtHR's findings analogously to situations concerning AHR or surrogacy, but the ECtHR's reasoning concerning effectiveness[36] and the implications of the Irish abortion information ban on the individuals concerned,[37] may very well apply also in such cases.

Moreover, the EU Patient Mobility Directive has introduced considerable rights to information for patients involved in cross-border care (see also section 7.2.2.3 below), rendering bans on information about abortion and AHR treatment options in other EU Member States unacceptable under EU law.

7.2.1.3. Refusals to provide follow-up care

At a more practical level warding off may consist of refusals to providing aftercare. Not many such examples have been found in the present case study.[38] There have been incidental reports from the Netherlands of gynaecologists refusing to treat women who had been to Spain for AHR treatment with the use of commercially and anonymously donated egg cells.[39] Refusals to provide follow-up care have, furthermore, been claimed to have occurred in Ireland in respect of abortion, but in 2010 the ECtHR found the provision of medical care in Ireland for women who had had abortions in other countries to be sufficient.[40]

As discussed in Chapter 3, it remains an open question whether European law leaves room for refusals to provide aftercare.[41] A refusal to provide follow-up care after abortion may furthermore contribute to a violation of the ECHR, as follows from the *A, B and C* case, where the Court considered access to medical care in Ireland after an abortion abroad a precondition for the justification of the very restrictive Irish

---

34 The first two applicants in the *A, B and C* case (2010), who sought an abortion for reasons of health and/or well-being, maintained that there was a lack of information on the options available to them and that this added to the burden of the impugned restrictions on abortion in Ireland, but the ECtHR found these submissions to be overly general and unsubstantiated. ECtHR [GC] 16 December 2010, *A, B and C* v. *Ireland*, no. 25579/05, para. 130.

35 *Idem*, para. 241.

36 The Court noted that the an injunction restraining Irish counselling agencies from assisting pregnant women in seeking legal abortion services abroad was ineffective, as it did not prevent large numbers of Irish women from continuing to obtain abortions in the UK.

37 The Court noted that the injunction created a risk to the health of women seeking abortions at a later stage in their pregnancies due to the lack of proper counselling, and it had adverse effects on women who were not sufficiently resourceful or did not have the necessary level of education to have access to alternative sources of information. *Idem*, paras. 73–77.

38 It must be noted that the present research is confined to legal research, while a complete picture of whether such refusals occur and if so at what extent, requires sociological research.

39 Ch. 6, section 6.5.3.

40 See Ch. 2, section 2.4.1.

41 Ch. 3, section 3.6.2.3.

abortion laws (see also 7.2.4 below).[42] Again, while there is no case law on this point yet, it is well possible that such reasoning would also apply in CBRC cases.

7.2.1.4. Refusals to reimburse treatment and prior authorisation requirements

Another way in which countries of origin may ward off cross-border movement in the context of the present case study, is through refusing reimbursement to individuals or couples who availed themselves of foreign treatment options, or by setting prior authorisation requirements.

The present case study has shown several examples where courts in Germany and the Netherlands rejected claims for reimbursement for treatment obtained abroad. As discussed in Chapter 3, the basic rule under EU free movement law is that States do not have to reimburse treatment obtained abroad, if such treatment is prohibited under the domestic law, or if its national scheme does not provide for reimbursement for that kind of treatment.[43] Hence, if a State prohibits certain reproductive treatment, it may also refuse to reimburse the costs if such treatment is obtained abroad. However, as also discussed in Chapter 3, in practice, this rule may prove problematic in the context of reproductive treatment, as it may be debated if medical and ethical standards may be taken into account in this assessment. Also, there are various questions as to whether EU law allows for the setting of prior authorisation requirements for pregnancy terminations and AHR treatment (either or not involving surrogacy).

7.2.1.5. Non-recognition of legal effects

Cross-border movement in reproductive matters may also be warded off by way of refusing to give recognition to the legal effects of such cross-border movement. In the present case study this has been particularly visible in the context of cross-border surrogacy cases. In various such cases States have refused to recognise the legal parenthood of intended parents as established abroad. Intended parents have in some cases met with refusals by authorities in their home country to issue a passport to a child that was born to a surrogate mother in a foreign country. And even if the intended parents were able to enter their State with the child, they often still encountered problems in establishing parental links with the child. Various national courts have, on public policy grounds, refused recognition of foreign birth certificates on which intended parents were stated as legal parents, or refused to enforce a foreign judgment declaring the intended parents the legal parents of the child. There have even been examples where the child was subsequently put up for adoption[44] and the concern has been expressed that children risked being left stateless.[45]

---

42 ECtHR [GC] 16 December 2010, *A, B and C* v. *Ireland*, no. 25579/05, para. 241.

43 Ch. 3, section 3.6.2.1.

44 E.g. Paradiso and Campanelli, *Paradiso and Campanelli* v. *Italy*, no. 25358/12, which case was pending before the ECtHR at the time this research was concluded.

45 See Ch. 5, section 5.5.4; and Ch. 6, section 6.5.6.

The public policy grounds relied on in these cross-border surrogacy cases reflect national standard-setting in the area and are consequently often grounded in the same interests, such as human dignity, the interests of the child and protection of the surrogate mother (see 7.1.1 above). For example, as discussed in Chapter 4, in a German case of 2007, a court held a Turkish judgment awarding adoption rights of a child to a German couple who had arranged a surrogacy agreement with a Turkish family, to be against the child's best interests, as the child had only been given birth with the aim of being handed over to the German intended parents.[46]

The ECtHR has shown understanding for States' wishes to deter their nationals from having recourse to methods of assisted reproduction outside the national territory that are prohibited on their own territory. It has accepted that this may, in accordance with their perception of the issue, aim to protect children and surrogate mothers. The Court has furthermore acknowledged that the community has an interest '[...] in ensuring that its members conform to the choice made democratically within that community.'[47] Still, the Strasbourg Court has also found that in cross-border surrogacy cases a fair balance has to be struck between these interests and the interests of the individuals concerned, the children's best interests being paramount.[48] As further explained in section 7.2.2.1 below, the interests of the child have consequently led to exactly opposite conclusions in other – generally more recent – cross-border surrogacy cases.

7.2.1.6. *Warding off by countries of destination*

The present case study has made clear that States may also wish to ward off cross-border movement to their countries in reproductive matters. The readiest, but also most far-reaching way of doing so is by imposing restrictions on access to services for people from abroad. A unique explicit example of such a measure is the restrictions on access to high-technological surrogacy as they apply in the Netherlands. As explained in Chapter 3, the hospital that is exclusively licensed to carry out high-technological surrogacy has set the conditions that both the intended parents and the surrogate mother must have Dutch nationality, must speak the Dutch language and must be resident in the Netherlands. These requirements render it absolutely impossible for intended parents from abroad to engage in surrogacy in the Netherlands. While the rationale of these rules has not been made explicit, the commensurability of these rules with EU free movement law may be seriously questioned.

7.2.1.7. *Observations*

The warding off of cross-border movement to other States may enable States to uphold and protect – as much as possible – certain national standards in respect of

46 AG Hamm 19 March 2007 (dec.), Az. XVI 23/06. See also LG Dortmund 13 August 2007 (dec.), Az. 15 T 87/07.

47 ECtHR 26 June 2014, *Mennesson* v. *France*, no. 65192/11, para. 84.

48 *Idem.*

their citizens and residents. For example, unborn life may be protected from being terminated on social grounds and the coming into being of a human being by means that are considered to violate human dignity may be prevented. Warding off can thus be seen as a principled and 'protectionist' response of States. Where warding off may aim to protect the interests of legal subjects outside the States' jurisdiction, such as surrogate mothers in other countries, it can also be perceived as an effort to have such national standards apply extra-territorially.[49] Concerns of a less principled nature may further be grounds for States to ward off cross-border movement in reproductive matters. For instance, although not identified as such in the present case study, it is conceivable that States that function as a country of destination wish to ward off cross-border movement to prevent the overburdening of their health systems.

The present case study has shown that it is very difficult, nigh impossible, for States to literally withhold people from actually going to another State for reproductive purposes. In other words, cross-border movement in reproductive matters cannot be ruled out; bans on access to medical services in other Member States, including abortion and AHR treatment, that are not available or even prohibited in their home country, are not easily justified under EU free movement law. Still the warding off measures as described in sections 7.2.1.2 to 7.2.1.5 may deter people from going abroad and States may thus employ these to minimise cross-border movement to the greatest extent possible.

Where warding off measures indeed successfully deter individuals from going to another country for an abortion, AHR treatment or surrogacy, this implies for these individuals that their treatment options are restricted. This can be said to affect their reproductive autonomy. Also, there is a risk that these individuals will instead resort to illegal treatment options within their country, which inevitably carries health risks. This concern has been expressed particularly in respect of illegal abortions.[50]

Where individuals are not deterred from going abroad for reproductive services, they have a broader range of choices when it comes to reproductive treatment. They can access treatment that is not available in the home country.[51] At the same time, these individuals may bear burdens that occur particularly, or may gain particular weight, in cross-border cases and that may consist of physical burdens and health risks, financial burdens, legal uncertainty, legal complications and emotional

[49] According to Storrow '[...] cross-border reproductive care has been shown to have deleterious extraterritorial effects that violate the spirit behind restrictive reproductive laws.' With warding off, such spill-over effects can be reduced or prevented. R. Storrow, 'The pluralism problem in cross-border reproductive care', 25 *Human Reproduction* (2010) p. 2939.

[50] E.g. Human Rights Watch, *A State of Isolation, Access to Abortion for Women in Ireland* (New York, Human Rights Watch 2010), online available at www.hrw.org/node/87910, visited June 2010.

[51] Sociological research has shown that there are various reasons why people engage in cross-border reproductive care, namely, treatment costs, treatment quality and treatment availability. See G. Pennings and M. Heidi, 'The state and the infertile patient looking for treatment abroad: a difficult relationship', in: A. Tupasela (ed.), *Consumer Medicine* (TemaNord 2010, no. 530) p. 99 at p. 100.

burdens.[52] Treatment is in many instances only available to those with the financial means of travelling[53] and there may be medical risks involved, particularly if there is insufficient information about foreign treatment options. Also, families that were formed in the course of cross-border surrogacy may meet serious difficulties in being legally recognised as families in their home countries.[54] Warding off measures like the ones described in this section may aggravate or even cause such individual burdens. Accommodation measures may, on the other hand, (partly) alleviate them. The discussion of such measures in the following section will make clear, however, that they cannot take away all individual burdens involved in cross-border movement in reproductive matters.

7.2.2. Accommodation

Instead of warding them off, States may also opt for an entirely different approach towards (the effects of) cross-border movement, which is to accommodate them. Because the accommodating responses discussed below form a mirror image to the warding off responses extensively discussed in the previous section, their discussion in the present section is more concise and, in some cases, clustered.

7.2.2.1. Recognition of legal parenthood in cross-border surrogacy cases

A highly visible and concrete way of accommodating the effects of cross-border movement reproductive matters is by recognising the legal effects of foreign treatment options. Such recognition may be inspired or even dictated by overriding interests, such as the rights of the child.

As discussed in Chapter 3, it remains an open question whether EU (free movement) law actually obliges the Member States to adopt such an accommodation approach in cross-border surrogacy situations. In most situations where EU Member States refused recognition in cross-border surrogacy cases, the reproductive treatment

[52] In a 2010 survey into experiences of past services recipients of cross-border reproductive care, the following 'negative experiences' were reported: 'difficulty in finding a clinic in the home country to undertake tests and scans'; 'travel difficulties'; 'higher costs than expected'; 'language problems'; 'lack of regulation in destination country' and 'legal/liability issues'. E. Blyth, 'Fertility patients' experiences of cross-border reproductive care', 94 *Fertility and Sterility* (2010) p. e11 at p. e13.

[53] ESHRE, *Comparative Analysis of Medically Assisted Reproduction in the EU: Regulation and Technologies* (SANCO/2008/C6/051), p. 86, online available at www.ec.europa.eu/health/blood_tissues_organs/docs/study_eshre_en.pdf, visited June 2014. Ferraretti et al. have observed that his may promote 'economically based discrimination [...] since only services recipients with adequate financial resources can afford treatments abroad.' A.P. Ferraretti et al., 'Cross-border reproductive care: a phenomenon expressing the controversial aspects of reproductive technologies', 20 *Reproductive BioMedicine Online* (2010) pp. 261–266 at p. 264. See also T.K. Hervey and J. V. McHale, *Health Law and the European Union* (Cambridge, Cambridge University Press 2004) p. 142. The authors have furthermore pointed out that even if a service recipient is entitled to reimbursement, the practical reality may still be that only services-recipients with sufficient independent means to pay up-front may have access to cross-border health care services.

[54] Individual burdens that may be involved in cross-border movement in reproductive matters are set out more extensively in section 7. 2.4.1 below.

involving the surrogacy agreement had taken place in a third country.[55] Such situations fall outside the scope of EU law and there is thus no obligation under EU law on Member States to recognise court judgments or birth certificates from these countries. This could be different, however, if another EU Member State is involved, but as discussed in Chapter 3, the present state of EU law gives little guidance in this regard.

The ECtHR, for its part, however, has ruled that in cross-border surrogacy cases States must recognise legal parenthood established in another country, regardless of whether the case concerns two EU Member States or at least one non-EU State. Decisive in the relevant *Mennesson* and *Labassee* rulings was the right to personal identity of the child concerned. Nevertheless, it must be noted that the accommodation obligations imposed on States under the ECHR in this context have been thus far restricted to the situation where the intended father is the genetic father of the child. Future case law will have to show whether this obligation also applies in cases where neither of the intended parents is the genetic parent of the child concerned. The ECtHR has furthermore made clear that States may subject accommodation to certain (procedural) conditions. In *D. and Others* (2014) the Court held that States were under no obligation under the Convention to authorise the entry of a child born to a foreign surrogate mother, without first subjecting the case to some form of legal examination.[56]

In various cross-border surrogacy cases national courts have indeed taken such an accommodating approach. Even before the ECtHR issued its important *Mennesson* and *Labassee* rulings, in all three States in recent years a trend has emerged in favour of recognising parental links established in another country or of enabling intended parents to establish parental links with the child under domestic law, because the best interests of the child were held to require this.[57] In the various national jurisdictions, the precondition that at least one of the intended parents is the genetic parent of the child concerned has been set as well.[58]

7.2.2.2. Information, reimbursement and follow-up care

States may also accommodate cross-border movement by providing independent information about foreign treatment options, by reimbursing treatment obtained abroad or by providing follow-up care.

As noted above (in section 7.2.1.2), bans on information about foreign abortion services have proven incommensurable with the ECHR. In fact, from *A, B and C* it can be inferred that States have an obligation under the Convention to provide

55 This, for instance, holds for all relevant surrogacy cases decided by the ECtHR and those currently pending before this Court. See Ch. 2, sections 2.3.5 and 2.4.2.

56 ECtHR 8 July 2014 (dec.), *D. a.o.* v. *Belgium*, no. 29176/13, para. 59.

57 See Ch. 4, section 4.5.3, Ch. 5, section 5.5.4 and Ch. 6, section 6.5.6.

58 *Idem.*

for access to 'appropriate' information about abortion services in other countries.[59] Further, as discussed in Chapter 3, by introducing considerable rights to information for patients involved in cross-border care, the EU Patient Mobility Directive of 2011 has imposed certain accommodation obligations on the Member States. National contact points in each Member State – both States of affiliation and States where the treatment takes place – must deliver information (in their official languages) to patients involved in cross-border care on matters like the applicable standards and guidelines, healthcare providers and patients' rights.

As surrogacy does not qualify as health care under the Patient Mobility Directive, such accommodation obligations by means of information provision do not hold for surrogacy.[60] Some State authorities, like the Irish and the Dutch, have, however, considered it their task to provide clear guidance on the principles they apply in examining applications for a travel document on behalf of children born outside the State as a result of surrogacy arrangements, as well as about the (im)possibilities under their national law to have legal parenthood recognised or established in such surrogacy cases. Here, too, a trend towards accommodation therefore can be discerned.

States may also accommodate cross-border movement in reproductive matters by providing for reimbursement for treatment obtained abroad, even if the treatment is not available domestically. For example, in the Netherlands it is generally accepted that the Dutch Health Insurance bears the costs that occur when insured persons return to the Netherlands after having obtained treatment abroad, even if that treatment itself would not be reimbursed under the Health Insurance Act.[61] As explained in Chapter 3, under EU law states are free to offer such reimbursement, although as yet there is no conclusive decision as to the matter of whether they may, in certain circumstances, also be under an obligation to accommodate cross-border movement in reproductive matters in this way.[62] There are in any case presently no indications in the ECtHR case law that hint at any such accommodation obligation.

Another way of accommodating cross-border movement is by means of the provision of follow-up care upon return to the home country. As discussed in Chapter 3 it is insufficiently clear whether under EU law States are under an obligation to provide such aftercare. Under the ECHR access to appropriate follow-up care has in any case been set as a minimum accommodation obligation in cross-border abortion cases.[63] It is very possible that in future case law the Court will define a similar obligation in situations involving CBRC.

59 ECtHR [GC] 16 December 2010, *A, B and C* v. *Ireland*, no. 25579/05, para. 241.
60 See Ch. 3, section 3.6.2.
61 See Ch. 6, section 6.5.2.
62 See Ch. 3, section 3.6.2.1.
63 ECtHR [GC] 16 December 2010, *A, B and C* v. *Ireland*, no. 25579/05, para. 241.

7.2.2.3. Observations

The discussion above has shown that accommodation may be required by interests and perspectives that must be taken into account in all reproductive matters, but which may gain particular importance in cross-border situations. Clear examples are the rights of the child and the possibility of making an informed decision on the basis of appropriate information. In respect of the rights of the child, views have changed over time as to what the best interests of the child require exactly.

States may perceive accommodation, if imposed on them by means of EU legislation or ECtHR judgments, as a thwarting of their national standards, even if accommodation does not require them to amend their internal standard-setting in the area and they remain free to decide what treatment they wish to regulate or to prohibit within their own jurisdictions. Indeed, it cannot be ruled out that certain accommodation measures, like recognition of legal parenthood established abroad, put pressure on States to change their national standards, and may thus force them to adaptation (see below). However, the opposite is also possible. Accommodation may in some cases in effect be seen as another means of protecting national standards, albeit in a more pragmatic way. For example, where States provide information about the legal implications of cross-border surrogacy, they may do so in order to protect the interests of the child. They may want to discourage people from engaging in international surrogacy agreements and minimise or reduce possible harm involved if such movement is taking place after all. Consequently, as further explained below (section 7.2.2.3), accommodation of cross-border movement may sometimes contribute to the maintaining of less permissive national standards.

Accommodation measures as here discussed may alleviate individual burdens, for instance by providing for recognition of legal parenthood established abroad, but they may not take away all burdens. Even if cross-border movement is fully accommodated, there are still – physical, emotional and financial – burdens involved in the travelling itself, as set out more extensively in section 7.2.4 below. The only way to fully take those burdens away as well is by means of adaptation, which, however, may raise other objections.

7.2.3. Adaptation

States may also respond to cross-border movement by removing the need for it, which they can do by adapting their national standards to equalise them to those of the States to which cross-border movement is taking place. In the three jurisdictions studied, the existence of foreign options has never been put forward as the only reason for amending national laws, or for interpreting existing standards differently, but certainly some hints can be found in the present case study that foreign treatment options have played a role in national standard-setting in reproductive matters. For example, as noted above, the judgment of the Irish Supreme Court in the *X Case* could be perceived as such. Further, as observed in Chapter 4, the German debates about cross-border movement for abortion and PGD have contributed to the relaxation of the relevant national law. The fact that couples from the Netherlands went abroad for PGD, was also for the Dutch legislature one of the reasons to legalise and regulate this method, *inter alia*, because of quality and safety concerns involved in the cross-border movement. Cross-border movement for surrogacy to other States further was one of the reasons for the Dutch government to install a State Commission on Parenthood in 2014, that was, *inter alia*, given the task to reconsider the national surrogacy legislation.

Depending on how one approaches the matter, adaptation either can be regarded as the ultimate form of accommodation, since it can be perceived as 'giving in', or it can be looked at as a variant of warding off, since it makes cross-border movement redundant. Evidently, for individuals who wish to have access to treatment provided abroad, adaptation can be perceived as the most beneficial response of States to cross-border movement. Particularly where it is combined with accommodation of cross-border movement they can be said to have the best of two worlds.

7.2.4. Outsourcing

The last category of legal responses is best described by the term 'outsourcing'. It is not so much expressly voiced at national level, but it is an implication of an approach taken by the ECtHR in certain cross-border cases concerning reproductive matters. The discussion of the ECtHR's case law in Chapter 2 has made clear that in some of those cases the Court accepted the existence of foreign treatment options as an element relevant to the justification of prohibitive domestic laws in reproductive matters. This was especially held in the Irish abortion case of *A, B and C* v. *Ireland* (2010), where the Court concluded that '[...] having regard to the right to lawfully travel abroad for an abortion with access to appropriate information and medical care in Ireland', the prohibition in Ireland of abortion for health and well-being reasons did not exceed the margin of appreciation accorded in that respect to Ireland. The fact that women from Ireland could lawfully travel abroad for an abortion with access to appropriate information and medical care in Ireland, was thus considered sufficient by the ECtHR as minimum level of protection under the Convention.[64]

With this line of reasoning, the Strasbourg Court has thus authorised, if not encouraged, States to outsource their accountability under the ECHR by referring to other States' legal regimes. This approach raises a number of questions that have yet to be addressed by the Court. For example, it is unclear whether distance or the

---

64 Another example is *S. H. and Others* (2011) – the Austrian case on gamete donation – where the Court noted that there was '[...] no prohibition under Austrian law on going abroad to seek treatment of infertility that use[d] artificial procreation techniques not allowed in Austria and that in the event of a successful treatment the Civil Code [contained] clear rules on paternity and maternity that respect[ed] the wishes of the parents.' ECtHR [GC] 3 November 2011, *S.H. a.o.* v. *Austria*, no. 57813/00, para. 114.

costs of travelling to the foreign country make a difference in this regard.[65] Also, the question has been raised whether the State is under an obligation to guarantee that the foreign treatment option is actually an option that can be used effectively. For example, it has been questioned whether States must also support the costs of the travelling for such foreign services or allow individuals who are in (aliens') detention to go abroad for an abortion or reproductive treatment if they so desire.[66] In other words, it is as yet unclear to what extent outsourcing must be combined with accommodation. In *A, B and C*, certain accommodation obligations were indeed set as preconditions for outsourcing in the Court's reasoning, as the Court took into account that there was access to abortion information and follow-up care in Ireland. In this case the Court simply took into account what was already provided for under the national law of Ireland. Future case law will therefore have to make clear whether any further such accommodation obligations will be defined as preconditions for outsourcing.

So far, the outsourcing approach has not always been applied by the ECtHR, not even in cases before it where it easily could have done so, such as the *Costa and Pavan* case, concerning PGD. It remains to be seen whether it will also be applied in potential future complaints about restrictive domestic laws on surrogacy. If the Court would indeed hold such a situation to come within the scope of the right to private life under Article 8 ECHR, it cannot be ruled out that in its assessment of the justification for the interference with this right, the Court would take account of the fact that there is a realistic option to engage in a surrogacy agreement in another country. Especially now that the Court, in *Mennesson* and *Labassee*, has formulated certain accommodation obligations for such cross-border surrogacy cases, it is not wholly illusory that such a minimum guarantee contributes to the justification of, or even constitutes the justification of, a restrictive regime at the national level.

Outsourcing allows States to refer people within their jurisdictions to other States for the protection of rights that come within the scope of the ECHR. This way cross-border movement in reproductive matters becomes a 'safety valve',[67] a means to 'hide behind' the more permissive regimes of other States. The existence of foreign options may thus enable States to maintain their own deviating (and generally less permissive) standards. The choice for outsourcing is understandable mainly from a more 'political' perspective. It is a pragmatic approach of the Strasbourg Court,

---

65 A.C. Hendriks 'Case note to ECtHR [GC] 16 December 2010, *A, B and C* v. *Ireland*, no. 25579/05', 12 *European Human Rights Cases* 2011/40 (in Dutch) and N.R. Koffeman, 'Het Ierse abortusverbod en het EVRM; is uitbesteding de nieuwe norm?' ['The Irish abortion ban and the ECHR: is outsourcing the new standard?'], 36 *NTM/NJCM-Bulletin* (2011) p. 372. As noted by these authors, the bigger the distance, the bigger certain individual burdens may be (see 7.2.4.1 below).

66 Koffeman 2011B, *supra* n. 65, at p. 372.

67 For the use of this term in the context of CBRC, see *inter alia* Hervey and McHale 2004, *supra* n. 53, at p. 157; G. Pennings et al., 'Cross-border reproductive care', 23 *Human Reproduction* (2008) p. 2183 and Ferraretti et al. 2010, *supra* n. 53, at p. 264.

that underlines the subsidiary role of this Court in these morally sensitive cases.[68] Nevertheless, this approach generally can be assessed negatively. First of all, it may take away internal pressure for change and may in fact result in inactivity by the legislature.[69] Gilmartin and White have opined in this regard in 2011, for example, that because women in Ireland have '[...] "won" the right to travel, the Irish state has been excused from any responsibility to provide safe, legal, and affordable abortion services in the years since 1992.'[70]

Moreover, as also noted by the dissenters in *S.H. and Others*, it really is a pragmatic, rather than a principled, approach. Indeed, it is difficult to understand why certain interests that were grounds for restrictive laws on reproductive matters at domestic level – such as the protection of human dignity or the unborn – would no longer hold in cross-border situations.[71] In fact, precisely in cross-border situations may such interests require even more protection. It has been observed in respect of the *A, B and C* case that 'hypocrisy' at national level '[...] should not have been so keenly approved by a Court whose task is to uphold human rights across a region in which it recognised a consensus to prioritise the rights of pregnant women over those of the foetus.'[72]

Outsourcing does not, furthermore, fit in well with the foundations and objectives of the ECHR, following which each State is responsible for securing the Convention rights to everyone within their jurisdiction (the principle of State accountability as laid down in Article 1 ECHR).[73] The Court's reasoning in the relevant cases gives the impression that it is sufficient if the High Contracting Parties at least jointly (rather than separately) provide for a certain minimum level of protection.

The implications for individuals of this outsourcing approach, particularly if not sufficiently combined with accommodation obligations, cannot be overlooked either. In particular, much has been reported in respect of women from Ireland who need to go abroad if they wish to have an abortion on medical and social grounds. It has been claimed that these women bear unduly harsh emotional, medical and financial burdens.[74] The abortion procedures of these women are alleged to be expensive,

---

68 The approach is pragmatic particularly in respect of abortion, as that is legalised in almost all Council of Europe Member States. See ECtHR [GC] 16 December 2010, *A, B and C* v. *Ireland*, no. 25579/05, as discussed in ch. 2, sections 2.2.3 and 2.4.1.

69 In fact, resignation (see 7.2 above) can be a hidden form of outsourcing.

70 M. Gilmartin and A. White, 'Comparative Perspectives Symposium: Gender and Medical Tourism. Interrogating Medical Tourism: Ireland, Abortion, and Mobility Rights', 36 *Signs* (2011) p. 275 at p. 277.

71 See the Joint dissenting opinion of Judges Tulkens, Hirvelä, Lazarova Trajkovska and Tsotsoria to ECtHR [GC] 3 November 2011, *S.H. a.o.* v. *Austria*, no. 57813/00. See also R.F. Storrow, 'Judicial review of restrictions on gamete donation in Europe', 25 *Reproductive BioMedicine Online* (2012) p. 655 at p. 657 and I.G. Cohen, 'S.H. and Others v. Austria and circumvention tourism', 25 *Reproductive BioMedicine Online* (2012) p. 660 at p. 662.

72 E. Wicks, '*A, B, C v Ireland*: Abortion Law under the European Convention on Human Rights', 11 *HRLR* (2011) p. 556 at p. 563.

73 See Art. 1 ECHR.

74 See, for instance, ECtHR 27 June 2006 (dec.), *D.* v. *Ireland*, no. 26499/02.

complicated and traumatic.[75] Although perhaps difficult to establish and measure in an objective manner,[76] their emotional burdens may consist of great distress and anguish and the feeling of being stigmatised.[77] Even medical risks may be entailed in cross-border abortions. Such risks may be either directly caused by the travelling itself, or by the inherent delay in the carrying out of an abortion that is to take place abroad.[78] A related difficulty is that not all women can stay in the destination country as long as would be desirable with regard to the necessary post-abortion counselling and care.[79] Language barriers that may occur when women go to other countries, may also have health implications.[80] The costs of travelling abroad for an abortion may furthermore constitute 'a significant financial burden' for the women concerned.[81] The financial burden of having an abortion abroad, may also be the cause of delays in the carrying out of the abortion, which – as yet clarified above – may have

[75] See the complaints of the applicants in ECtHR [GC] 16 December 2010, *A, B and C* v. *Ireland*, no. 25579/05, para. 173.

[76] Understandably, the ECtHR held in the case of *A, B and C* v. *Ireland* (in para. 126) that the psychological impact of such travelling on the applicants, was '[...] by its nature subjective, personal and not susceptible to clear documentary or objective proof.' The Court nonetheless considered it reasonable to find that '[...] each applicant felt the weight of a considerable stigma prior to, during and after their abortions: they travelled abroad to do something which, on the Government's own submissions, went against the profound moral values of the majority of the Irish people [...] and which was, or (in the case of the third applicant) could have been, a serious criminal offence in their own country punishable by penal servitude for life [...]. Moreover, obtaining an abortion abroad, rather than in the security of their own country and medical system, undoubtedly constituted a significant source of added anxiety.'

[77] Compare the complaints of all three applicants in ECtHR [GC] 16 December 2010, *A, B and C* v. *Ireland*, no. 25579/05, para. 119 ('All felt stigmatised as they were going abroad to do something that was a criminal offence in their own country') and the assessment of their complaints by the Court in para. 127. *Human Rights Watch* (HRW) has observed that '[...] having to travel abroad for a procedure at a time when many women are already in distress because of an unwanted or unhealthy pregnancy' may constitute 'a major source of anxiety'. Human Rights Watch 2010, *supra* n. 50, p. 35, online available at www.hrw.org/node/87910, visited 3 June 2010. Wicks has held: 'Having already recognised the "significant psychological burden" faced by the applicants in being required to leave their home country to seek medical treatment prohibited there, the Court should have been more reluctant to present that psychological burden as the very guarantee of respect for the women's private life.' Wicks 2011, *supra* n. 72, at p. 563.

[78] In general it goes that the later an abortion is carried out, the more physically arduous the procedure is, as a late abortion often means a surgical abortion, instead of a medical one. Compare the complaints of the applicants in ECtHR [GC] 16 December 2010, *A, B and C* v. *Ireland*, no. 25579/05, para. 173.

[79] The applicant in ECtHR 27 June 2006 (dec.), *D* v. *Ireland*, no. 26499/02, for example, claimed that with two children in Ireland, she could not remain in the UK for counselling after her abortion.

[80] Hendriks has also pointed at the risk of such language barriers occurring. Hendriks 2011, *supra* n. 65 .

[81] ECtHR [GC] 16 December 2010, *A, B and C* v. *Ireland*, no. 25579/05, para. 128. In its report *A State of Isolation, Access to Abortion for Women in Ireland* of 2010, Human Rights Watch (HRW) concluded that '[...] for someone living under the poverty line, the cost of an abortion could easily represent more than a monthly salary'. HRW referred to Irish service providers estimating the total costs to be between € 800 and € 1,000. By comparison, HRW noted that the average salary in Ireland fluctuated around € 30,000 per year. HRW furthermore claimed that for women who were in the asylum seeking process in Ireland, the travelling abroad to obtain an abortion was 'plainly out of reach' from a financial perspective. The HRW report furthermore outlined that 'service providers interviewed by *Human Rights Watch* confirmed how difficult it is for many women to raise the money to travel and the lengths that some must go to to ensure their access to safe and legal abortions'. Human Rights Watch 2010, *supra* n. 50, at pp. 31–32.

implications for the woman's health.[82] Moreover, in certain cases it is practically impossible for women to travel to another state for an abortion.[83] Particular concerns have been expressed about the vulnerable status of asylum seekers in this regard.[84]

Many of the above described individual burdens may, *mutatus mutandis* also hold in CBRC cases and cross-border surrogacy. Individuals and couples that go abroad for AHR treatment or surrogacy may also carry physical, emotional, financial and medical burdens,[85] or may not be practically in the position to travel abroad. AHR treatment may involve various appointments at different points in time, which may be particularly burdensome if the travel distance to the foreign clinic is considerable.[86] CBRC services recipients returning home without adequate information about their prior treatment, may also run substantial health risks.[87] If services recipients have been self-referred, their prior treatment may go unnoticed. In particular in cases where the foreign treatment is prohibited in their home country, proper monitoring and follow-up may be hindered.[88] This may also be the case if the relevant treatment is not prohibited as such, but still not common practice amongst medical practitioners in the home country. In cross-border surrogacy cases, intended parents may come across legal obstacles with potentially serious implications for their chances of building and enjoying family life with the child concerned. While

---

82 There are even reports that '[...] many women see through crisis pregnancies "because they can't afford the abortion"'. Human Rights Watch 2010, *supra* n. 50, at p. 36, referring to an interview with Juliet Bressan, *Doctors for Choice*, Dublin, 25 August 2008.

83 Some cannot travel because of their immigration status, because they are in state custody, because they are in mandatory daily treatment for drugs addiction or because of an illness or disability. Human Rights Watch 2010, *supra* n. 50, at pp. 16 and 36–37. See also K.J. Johnson, '"New thinking about an old issue;" the abortion controversy continues in Russia and Ireland – *Could Roe* v. *Wade* have been the better solution?', 15 *Indiana International and Comparative Law Review* (2004) p. 183 at p. 201 and J. Burns, 'Laying down the law' *Sunday Times* 31 October 2004, p. 14. See also C. Staunton, 'As Easy as A, B and C: Will A, B and C v. Ireland Be Ireland's Wake-up Call for Abortion Rights?', 18 *European Journal of Health Law* (2011) p. 205 at p. 218. Gilmartin and White 2011, *supra* n. 70, at p. 278.

84 UN Committee on the Elimination of Discrimination Against Women on the second and third periodic reports of Ireland (CEDAW/C/IRL/2-3) at its 440th and 441st meetings on 21 June 1999 (see CEDAW/C/SR.440 and 441), para 185, online available at www2.ohchr.org/english/bodies/cedaw/docs/IrelandCO21st_en.pdf, visited 15 February 2015. Human Rights Watch 2010, *supra* n. 50, at pp. 5 and 32–33. In August 2003, the Irish newspaper *The Times* reported that 20 asylum seekers in Ireland were granted a temporary permit and visa to leave Ireland to travel to the UK for an abortion and to return to Ireland afterwards. While granting the visa, the authorities had stressed that these concerned highly exceptional measures. Many others had to resort to illegal means. K. Holland, 'Asylum-seekers granted visas for UK abortions' *The Irish Times* 30 August 2003, p. 4.

85 See *supra* n. 52. Ferraretti et. al have furthermore observed that CBRC '[...] is often associated with a high risk of health dangers, frustration and disparities.' Ferraretti et al.2010, *supra* n. 53, at p. 261.

86 The Californian Centre for Surrogate Parenting Inc. for instance indicates that intended parents will need to come to the USA for a minimum of two or three trips. No doubt these overseas trips have financial implications as well. See www.creatingfamilies.com/IP/IP_Info.aspx?Type=18, visited January 2011.

87 B. Dickens, 'Cross-border reproductive services', 111 *International Journal of Gynecology and Obstetrics* (2010) p. 190 at p. 190.

88 The authors of the report *Pre-implantation Genetic Diagnosis in Europe* observe that evidence gathered painted 'a contrasting picture' on this point. While some clinics were clearly not deterred, others did not see it is as their responsibility. A. Coverleyn et al., *Pre-implantation Genetic Diagnosis in Europe'* (Joint Research Centre of the European Commission, January 2007) p. 80, online available at www.ftp.jrc.es/EURdoc/eur22764en.pdf, visited July 2014.

the relevant ECtHR case law has ruled out various such obstacles, the occurrence of such obstacles is still not wholly illusory, for example if the intended parents are not the genetic parents of the child.

7.2.5. Resumé and outlook

In the present case study four types of legal responses to cross-border movement for reproductive matters have been identified: warding off, accommodation, adaptation and outsourcing. For most of these – warding off, adaptation, and at times also accommodation – the initiative was taken at national level, while in respect of some others – accommodation and outsourcing – the European level has also been influential. The States studied in this research have combined various categories of the here described legal responses to cross-border movement and different responses may apply in the same area. Ireland – in any case initially and mainly in the context of cross-border abortions – has resorted more to warding off responses than Germany and the Netherlands. But in all three States such measures have – again in any case initially – been employed in respect of cross-border surrogacy.

Warding off (the effects of) cross-border movement in respect of reproductive services by means of non-recognition of legal effects of foreign options or by means of bans on information on foreign treatment options has, however, generally proven not easily justified under European law. Refusing follow-up care may also be problematic. While a refusal to reimburse the costs of treatment obtained abroad may be acceptable, it is questionable whether prior authorisation requirements can be set.

Various warding off responses have, over time, often been converted into accommodation. In some cases, this was the direct consequence of European law, in others national authorities had decided of their own accord to adopt an accommodating approach. Accommodation – for example providing for information and follow-up care in case of abortion and recognising parental links established abroad in surrogacy cases – may alleviate the individual burdens involved in outsourcing, though the burdens of the actual travelling remain. There is potential for the easing of even more of these burdens, for instance by providing for financial support for those for whom the costs of travelling are insurmountable.[89] The more such accommodating measures are taken, the less there seems to be a need for actual adaptation. This is all the more true since the 'outsourcing' approach of the ECtHR clearly allows for the States' accommodation response and thus does not provide a direct incentive for changing the national standards as such.

---

89 There may be limits to the accommodating role of States, however, and perhaps certain burdens involved in travelling abroad will remain the individuals' own responsibility. For example, in the international surrogacy case *D. and Others*, the ECtHR held that the Belgian State could not be held responsible for the fact that the couple had not been granted a visa in the Ukraine for an extended period and thus could not have spent more time with their child in that country.

Whether the legal responses identified on the basis of the present case study are accommodating, adapting or rather warding off, they are all characterised by being mainly unilateral legal responses, even if some responses are imposed or inspired by European law. Nevertheless, there is room and potential for bilateral or coordinated legal responses to develop. This may be done, for example, by means of the harmonisation of Private International Law.[90] In addition, States could bilaterally regulate certain matters. For example, it has been suggested in respect of AHR treatment involving surrogacy arrangements, that countries of origin and countries of destination agree that the latter country will not carry out treatment if the individual or couple concerned do not meet the conditions for access to treatment in the home country.[91] Such changes would basically come down to adaptation in individual cases by the destination country to the standards of the home country. In other words, the standards of the home country are given an extra-territorial effect in individual cases. Such approach could possibly also be taken where people from a State where gamete donors must be known have AHR treatment in a country where use is made of anonymously donated gametes. In this situation even more would be required from the destination country, however, as this State may not even have an infrastructure in place to trace the donor. Such coordinated approaches could be initiated by (a group of) States or imposed on them at European level, either by the EU legislature or judiciary, or by the ECtHR.

---

90 See, for example, K. Saarloos, *European private international law on legal parentage? Thoughts on a European instrument implementing the principle of mutual recognition in legal parentage* (Maastricht, s.n. 2010).

91 E. Winkel et al., 'Draagmoederschap na ivf in het buitenland. Dilemma's bij de begeleiding' ['Surrogacy after IVF treatment in a foreign country. Dillemas in the counselling'], 154 *Nederlands Tijdschrijft voor Geneeskunde* (2010) p. A1777.

Case Study II – Legal Recognition of Same-Sex Relationships

CHAPTER 8
ECHR

8.1. FRAMEWORK OF ECHR RIGHTS

This first section provides for a brief introduction to a number of ECHR rights that have been most important in the case law of the ECtHR on legal recognition of same-sex relationships. The first is the right to respect for private life (Article 8 ECHR). It has been on the basis of this Article that the Court has ruled that criminalisation of homosexual acts was in violation of the Convention (section 8.1.1). The second subsection discusses the right to respect for private and family life (Article 8 ECHR), while sections 8.1.3 and 8.1.4 discuss the right to marry (Article 12) and the prohibition on discrimination (Article 14 ECHR), which includes a prohibition on grounds of sexual orientation. For a discussion of the rights of the child under the Convention, reference is made to Chapter 2, section 2.1.3.

8.1.1. Sexual orientation as most intimate aspect of private life (Article 8 ECHR)

The first line of ECtHR judgments which have improved the legal position of persons with a homosexual orientation date back to the 1980s and concerned national legislation criminalising homosexual conduct or acts. The Court examined these complaints on the basis of the right to respect for private life (Article 8 ECHR).

In *Dudgeon* (1981),[1] the applicant complained about the fact that homosexual acts, even if committed in private by consenting males over the age of 21, were criminal offences under the law of Northern Ireland. The then existing European Commission of Human Rights (ECmHR) observed that the applicant's complaint related only to the prohibition of private, consensual acts, and found that the complaint therefore fell within the scope of Article 8 ECHR.[2] The Court subsequently saw no reason to differ from these views and held that the maintenance in force of the impugned legislation constituted a continuing interference with the applicant's right to respect for his private life – including his sexual life – within the meaning of Article 8(1).[3] In the personal circumstances of the applicant, the very existence of this legislation continuously and directly affected his private life.[4]

---

1 ECtHR [GC] 22 October 1981, *Dudgeon* v. *the United Kingdom*, no. 7525/76.

2 ECmHR 13 March 1980 (report), *Dudgeon* v. *the United Kingdom*, no. 7525/76.

3 ECtHR [GC] 22 October 1981, *Dudgeon* v. *the United Kingdom*, no. 7525/76, para. 41.

4 *Idem*, para. 41.

In its examination of whether this interference could be justified, the Court accepted that the general aim pursued by the legislation was the protection of morals.[5] The Court furthermore acknowledged that some degree of regulation of male homosexual conduct, as indeed of other forms of sexual conduct, by means of the criminal law could be justified as 'necessary in a democratic society', as the overall function served by the criminal law in this field was to preserve public order and decency and to protect the citizen from what is offensive or injurious. The Court stressed the fact that the case at hand concerned a most intimate aspect of private life,[6] and that the right affected by the impugned legislation 'protects an essentially private manifestation of the human personality.'[7] Accordingly there had to be particularly serious reasons before interferences on the part of the public authorities could be justified.

The Court found that it could not be maintained that there was a pressing social need to make such acts criminal offences, as there was no sufficient justification provided by the risk of harm to vulnerable sections of society requiring protection or by the effects on the public.[8] On the issue of proportionality, the Court considered that such justifications as there were for retaining the law in force unamended were outweighed by the detrimental effects which the very existence of the legislative provisions in question could have on the life of a person of homosexual orientation like the applicant.[9] The Court concluded that the restriction imposed on the applicant under Northern Ireland law was disproportionate by reason of its breadth and absolute character.[10] As regards the prohibition on conducting homosexual acts for males under the age of 21, the Court ruled that it fell in the first instance to the national authorities to decide upon the question.[11] The ECtHR did not find a violation in this respect.

The Court repeated this line of reasoning in two later cases concerning the criminalisation of male homosexual conduct by adults.[12] It took the Court remarkably longer to apply this reasoning also in regard of homosexuality in the military. In 1983 the Commission was of the opinion that a ban on homosexuality in the military could be justified for the protection of morals and for the prevention of disorder, as it found that homosexual conduct by members of the armed forces could pose a particular risk to order within the forces which would not arise in civilian life. In 1999 however, the Court ruled in *Smith and Grady* that there were no convincing and weighty reasons that could justify discharging homosexuals from the military

5 *Idem*, para. 46.
6 *Idem*, para. 52.
7 *Idem*, para. 60.
8 See also ECtHR 19 February 1997, *Laskey, Jaggard and Brown* v. *the United Kingdom*, nos. 21627/93 a.o.
9 ECtHR [GC] 22 October 1981, *Dudgeon* v. *the United Kingdom*, no. 7525/76, para. 60.
10 *Idem*, para. 61.
11 *Idem*, para. 62.
12 ECtHR 26 October 1986, *Norris* v. *Ireland*, no. 10581/83 and ECtHR 22 April 1993, *Modinos* v. *Cyprus*, no. 15070/89. For a pending case on this matter see *H.Ç.* v.*Turkey*, no. 6428/12, lodged on 30 January 2012.

because of their homosexuality.[13] The Court has furthermore held differing ages of consent under criminal law for homosexual relations to be in violation of Article 8 the Convention.[14]

By qualifying sexual orientation as a most intimate aspect of private life, and as an essentially private manifestation of the human personality, the Court has placed sexual orientation at the centre of the right to private life as protected by Article 8. This finding has been an important ground for the formulation and application of a strict test in cases where a difference in treatment was based on sexual orientation (see section 8.1.4 below).

8.1.2. Same-sex relationships and the right to respect for private and family life (Article 8 ECHR)

After the Court had accepted in *Dudgeon* that sexual orientation forms part of private life and enjoys protection under Article 8 ECHR, the Commission and the Court soon thereafter also accepted that relationships between persons of the same sex fell within the notion of 'private life' under Article 8.[15] However, for a long time, the Commission – and later the Court – held that stable homosexual relationships did not fall within the scope of the right to respect for family life within the meaning of that provision.[16] This was so despite the fact that the Court had ruled yet in the late 1970s that also *de facto* family relations enjoyed protection under Article 8.[17] Relevant factors to decide whether a relationship [could] be said to amount to 'family life', included whether the couple lived together, the length of their relationship and whether they had demonstrated their commitment to each other by having children together or by any other means.[18]

---

13 Accordingly, the Court considered that the applicants' complaints under Art. 14 in conjunction with Art. 8 did not give rise to any separate issue. ECtHR 27 September 1999, *Smith and Grady* v. *the United Kingdom*, nos. 33985/96 and 33986/96.

14 ECtHR 9 January 2003, *L. and V.* v. *Austria*, nos. 39392/98 and 39829/98.

15 E.g. ECmHR 3 May 1983 (dec.), *X. and Y* v. *the United Kingdom*, no. 9369/81 and ECmHR 9 October 1989 (dec.), *C. and L.M.* v. *the United Kingdom*, no. 14753/89. See also *Mata Estevez*, where the Court acknowledged 'that the applicant's emotional and sexual relationship [with a same-sex partner] related to his private life within the meaning of Art. 8 para. 1 of the Convention'. ECtHR 10 May 2001 (dec.), *Mata Estevez* v. *Spain*, no. 56501/00.

16 ECmHR 3 May 1983 (dec.), *X. and Y* v. *the United Kingdom*, no. 9369/81; ECmHR 14 May 1986 (dec.), *S.* v. *the United Kingdom*, no. 11718/85 and ECmHR 19 May 1992 (dec.), *Kerkhoven and Hinke* v. *the Netherlands*, no. 15666/89. In *Mata Estevez* (2001), the Court referred to these decisions, while reiterating that '[...] long-term homosexual relationships between two men [did] not fall within the scope of the right to respect for family life protected by Article 8 of the Convention.' ECtHR 10 May 2001 (dec.), *Mata Estevez* v. *Spain*, no. 56501/00. Hodson observed that the *X. and Y* decision 'set a precedent that proved fatal to the family rights claims of all same-sex couples before the Commission, even where they were raising a child together.' L. Hodson, 'A Marriage by any other Name? Schalk and Kopf v. Austria,' 11 *Human Rights Law Review* (2011) p. 170 at p. 174.

17 ECtHR 13 June 1979, *Marckx* v. *Belgium*, no. 6833/74, para. 31. See also ch. 2, section 2.1.3.

18 ECtHR 27 October 1994, *Kroon a.o.* v. *the Netherlands*, no. 18535/91, para. 30.

The Court held on to this line of reasoning for many years, considering that there was too little common ground within the Council of Europe to hold that same-sex relationships constituted 'family life'.[19] Later, the Court explicitly left the issue to the Contracting Parties,[20] or it left the question open.[21] Only in 2010, in the landmark case *Schalk and Kopf* – a judgment that will be discussed in more detail below – the Court for the first time ruled that the relationship of a same-sex couple enjoyed protection under the notion of 'family life' within the meaning of Article 8 ECHR. The Court reiterated that the notion of 'family' under Article 8 was not confined to marriage-based relationships and could encompass other *de facto* family ties where the parties were living together.[22] The Court noted 'a rapid evolution of social attitudes towards same-sex couples' since 2001, resulting in a considerable number of States having afforded these couples legal recognition. It continued:

> 'In view of this evolution the Court considers it artificial to maintain the view that, in contrast to a different-sex couple, a same-sex couple cannot enjoy "family life" for the purposes of Article 8. Consequently the relationship of the applicants, a cohabiting same-sex couple living in a stable de facto partnership, falls within the notion of "family life", just as the relationship of a different-sex couple in the same situation would.'[23]

This ruling has been confirmed in subsequent case law.[24] In *Vallianatos and Others* (2013) the Court once again stressed that '[...] same-sex couples sharing their lives have the same needs in terms of mutual support and assistance as different-sex couples'.[25] The Court held that it was immaterial if the couple was living together, since – in any case in the case before it – the fact of not cohabiting did not deprive the couples concerned of the stability which brought them within the scope of family life within the meaning of Article 8.[26]

---

19 ECtHR 10 May 2001 (dec.), *Mata Estevez* v. *Spain*, no. 56501/00.

20 *Idem.* The Court considered 'that [...] despite the growing tendency in a number of European States towards the legal and judicial recognition of stable *de facto* partnerships between homosexuals, this is, given the existence of little common ground between the Contracting States, an area in which they still enjoy a wide margin of appreciation.'

21 E. g. ECtHR 24 July 2003, *Karner* v. *Austria*, no. 40016/98, para. 33 and ECtHR 28 September 2010, *J.M.* v. *the United Kingdom*, no. 37060/06, para. 50.

22 ECtHR 24 June 2010, *Schalk and Kopf* v. *Austria*, no. 30141/04, para. 91.

23 *Idem*, para. 94.

24 The first case after *Schalk and Kopf* in which the Court repeated this finding was ECtHR 22 July 2010, *P.B. and J.S.* v. *Austria*, no. 18984/02. Remarkably, in some other rulings delivered soon after *Schalk and Kopf*, such as ECtHR 21 September 2010 (dec.), *Manenc* v. *France*, no. 66686/09 and ECtHR 28 September 2010, *J.M.* v. *the United Kingdom*, no. 37060/06, the Court did not repeat this finding. In later cases, it was confirmed, however.

25 ECtHR [GC] 7 November 2013, *Vallianatos a.o.* v. *Greece*, nos. 29381/09 and 32684/09, para. 81.

26 *Idem*, para.73.

8.1.3. The right to marry (Article 12 ECHR)

Article 12 ECHR protects the right to marry and to found a family.[27] The connection between these two rights laid down in Article 12 has yet been discussed in Chapter 2.[28] The discussion here accordingly focuses on the first limb of the Article, containing the right to marry.

The Court has repeatedly confirmed that 'notwithstanding social changes',[29] '[...] marriage remains an institution which is widely accepted as conferring a particular status on those who enter it'.[30] It has been held to be 'singled out for special treatment under Article 12 of the Convention'.[31] States are accordingly free to promote marriage, for instance by granting limited benefits to surviving spouses,[32] and to strengthen the institution of marriage within society.[33]

The wording of Article 12 makes clear that the exercise of the right to marry is governed by the national laws of the Contracting Parties to the ECHR. Even though the Article does not contain a justification clause like Articles 8 to 11 do, it is thus clear that the right to marry is not absolute, but may be restricted.[34] It is the States that may introduce limitations since matrimony is '[...] closely bound up with the cultural and historical traditions of each society and its deep-rooted ideas about the family unit'.[35]

States may introduce limitations on this right by way of 'formal rules concerning such matters as publicity and the solemnisation of marriage', as well by '[...] substantive provisions based on generally recognised considerations of public interest, in particular concerning capacity, consent, prohibited degrees of affinity or the prevention of bigamy.'[36] Any limitation of the right to marry must, however, be accessible and foreseeable[37] and moreover '[...] must not restrict or reduce the right

---

27 Art. 12 ECHR reads: 'Men and women of marriageable age have the right to marry and to found a family, according to the national laws governing the exercise of this right.'

28 Section 2.1.1.

29 ECtHR 4 November 2008 (dec.), *Courten* v. *the United Kingdom*, no. 4479/06.

30 ECtHR 27 April 2000 (dec.), *Shackell* v. *the United Kingdom*, no. 45851/99. Confirmed in ECtHR [GC] 29 April 2008, *Burden* v. *the United Kingdom*, no. 13378/05, para. 63. See also section 8.2.3.1 below.

31 E.g. ECtHR 22 May 2008, *Petrov* v. *Bulgaria*, no. 15197/02, para. 53.

32 ECtHR 27 April 2000 (dec.), *Shackell* v. *the United Kingdom*, no. 45851/99.

33 ECtHR [GC] 7 November 2013, *Vallianatos a.o.* v. *Greece*, nos. 29381/09 and 32684/09, para. 83.

34 See P. van Dijk et al. (eds.), *Theory and Practice of the European Convention on Human Rights* (Antwerpen, Intersentia 2006) p. 842 and Harris et al., *Law of the European Convention on Human Rights* (Oxford, Oxford University Press 2009) p. 550.

35 ECtHR 18 December 1987, *F.* v. *Switzerland*, no. 11329/85, para. 33.

36 ECtHR 5 January 2010, *Frasik* v. *Poland*, no. 22933/02, para. 89. In the context of immigration laws and for justified reasons, the States may be entitled to prevent marriages of convenience, entered solely for the purpose of securing an immigration advantage.

37 *Idem*, para. 89, under reference to ECmHR 13 December 1979 (report), *Hamer* v. *the United Kingdom*, no. 7114/75, para. 55 et seq.; ECmHR 10 July 1980 (report), *Draper* v. *the United Kingdom*, no. 8186/78, para. 49; ECmHR 16 October 1996 (dec.), *Sanders* v. *France*, no. 31401/96; ECtHR 18 December 1987, *F.* v. *Switzerland*, no. 11329/85 and ECtHR 13 September 2005, *B. and L.* v. *the United Kingdom*, no. 36536/02, para. 36 et seq.

in such a way or to such an extent that the very essence of the right is impaired'.[38] Hence,

> '[...] the matter of conditions for marriage in the national laws is not left entirely to Contracting States as being within their margin of appreciation. This would be tantamount to finding that the range of options open to a Contracting State included an effective bar on any exercise of the right to marry. The margin of appreciation cannot extend so far [...]'.[39]

In *Frasik* (2010) the Court clarified that national legislation may not deprive a person or a category of persons of full legal capacity of the right to marry with the partners of their choice. The Court explained the relevant test under Article 12 as follows:

> 'In contrast to Article 8 of the Convention, which sets forth the right to respect for private and family life, and with which the right "to marry and to found a family" has a close affinity, Article 12 does not include any permissible grounds for an interference by the State that can be imposed under paragraph 2 of Article 8 "in accordance with the law" and as being "necessary in a democratic society", for such purposes as, for instance, "the protection of health or morals" or "the protection of the rights and freedoms of others". Accordingly, in examining a case under Article 12 the Court would not apply the tests of "necessity" or "pressing social need" which are used in the context of Article 8 but would have to determine whether, regard being had to the State's margin of appreciation, the impugned interference was arbitrary or disproportionate [...].'[40]

The *Frasik* case concerned a prisoner who was not allowed to marry. The Court stressed that there was no place under the Convention for an automatic interference with his right to establish a marital relationship with the person of his choice, '[...] based purely on such arguments as what – in the authorities' view – might be acceptable to or what might offend public opinion.'[41] The Court thereby noted that tolerance and broadmindedness were the acknowledged hallmarks of a democratic society under the Convention system.

The Court has furthermore defined 'marriage' under Article 12 ECHR, as 'traditional marriage', that is as between man and woman only. This line of case law is extensively discussed in section 8.2 below.

---

38 *Idem*, para. 88, under reference to ECtHR 18 December 1987, *F.* v. *Switzerland*, no. 11329/85, para. 32 and ECtHR [GC] 11 July 2002, *Christine Goodwin* v. *the United Kingdom*, no. 28957/95, para. 29.

39 ECtHR 5 January 2010, *Jaremowicz* v. *Poland*, no. 24023/03, para. 48, referring to ECtHR 28 November 2006 (dec.), *R. and F.* v. *the United Kingdom*, no. 35748/05.

40 ECtHR 5 January 2010, *Frasik* v. *Poland*, no. 22933/02, para. 89.

41 *Idem*, para. 93, referring to: *mutatis mutandis*, ECtHR [GC] 6 October 2005, *Hirst (no. 2)* v. *the United Kingdom*, no. 74025/01, para. 70; ECtHR [GC] 4 December 2007, *Dickson* v. *the United Kingdom*, no. 44362/04, paras. 67–68; ECmHR 13 December 1979 (report), *Hamer* v. *the United Kingdom*, no. 7114/75, para. 67; ECmHR 10 July 1980 (report), *Draper* v. *the United Kingdom*, no. 8186/78, para. 54; and ECtHR 18 December 1987, *F.* v. *Switzerland*, no. 11329/85 43 et seq.

8.1.4. Discrimination on grounds of sexual orientation

The prohibition on discrimination of Article 14 ECHR has played an important role in the Court's case law on homosexuals' rights. Article 14 may apply as soon as a case comes within the scope of one or more of the substantive Convention rights. In cases concerning homosexuals or same-sex relationships, Article 14 has often been invoked and applied in combination with the right to respect for private and family life (Article 8 ECHR), the right to property (Article 1 First Protocol to the ECHR) and – less relevant for the present research – the right to freedom of association (Article 11 ECHR).[42] There have also been various cases where the Court considered examination of a complaint under Article 14 no longer necessary, as it had already found a violation of a material Convention Article.[43]

When examining discrimination complaints under Article 14, the first matter to be assessed is whether there is a difference in treatment of persons in relevantly similar situations.[44] This entails that the comparability of situations has to be examined in relation to a certain matter, for example in relation to a certain entitlement, such as a survivor's pension. As further explained in section 8.2.3 below, in cases involving civil status, the Court has taken a rather formalistic approach in respect of this part of the Article 14 test.

For a difference in treatment of persons in relevantly similar situations not to constitute discrimination under Article 14 ECHR, it must have an objective and reasonable justification. This means that the difference in treatment must pursue a legitimate aim and that there must be a reasonable relationship of proportionality between the means employed and the aim sought to be realised. States enjoy a margin of appreciation in assessing whether and to what extent differences in otherwise similar situations justify a difference in treatment.[45] However, where a difference of treatment is based on sexual orientation, the State's margin of appreciation is narrow.[46] It has become standing case law that differences in treatment on the basis of sexual orientation require 'convincing and weighty reasons'[47] or, 'particularly serious reasons by way of justification',[48] while differences based solely on

---

42 *Inter alia*, ECtHR 3 May 2007, *Baczkowski a.o.* v. *Poland*, no. 1543/06; ECtHR 21 October 2010, *Alekseyev* v. *Russia*, nos. 4916/07 a.o. and ECtHR 12 June 2012, *Genderdoc-M* v. *Moldova*, no. 9106/06.

43 This was, for instance, the case in ECtHR 22 October 1981, *Dudgeon* v. *the United Kingdom*, no. 7525/76.

44 E.g. ECtHR [GC] 29 April 2008, *Burden* v. *the United Kingdom*, no. 13378/05, para. 60 and ECtHR [GC] 16 July 2014, *Hämäläinen* v. *Finland*, no. 37359/09, para. 108.

45 *Inter alia* ECtHR [GC] 29 April 2008, *Burden* v. *the United Kingdom*, no. 13378/05, para. 60.

46 The Court referred to ECtHR 2 March 2010, *Kozak* v. *Poland*, no. 13102/02, para. 92 and ECtHR 24 July 2003, *Karner* v. *Austria*, no. 40016/98, para. 41.

47 ECtHR 24 July 2003, *Karner* v. *Austria*, no. 40016/98. See also ECtHR 2 March 2010, *Kozak* v. *Poland*, no. 13102/02.

48 ECtHR 24 July 2003, *Karner* v. *Austria*, no. 40016/98, para. 37, referring to ECtHR 27 September 1999, *Smith and Grady* v. *the United Kingdom*, nos. 33985/96 and 33986/96, para. 90 and ECtHR 9 January 2003, *S.L.* v. *Austria*, no. 45330/99, para. 37.

considerations of sexual orientation are unacceptable under the Convention.[49] The Court explained this strict scrutiny test in *Karner* (2003). In that case the Court did not accept that a blanket exclusion of persons living in same-sex relationships from succession to a tenancy was necessary for the protection of the family. In respect of the proportionality of the measure, the Court considered:

> 'In cases in which the margin of appreciation afforded to States is narrow, as is the position where there is a difference in treatment based on sex or sexual orientation, the principle of proportionality does not merely require that the measure chosen is in principle suited for realising the aim sought. It must also be shown that it was necessary in order to achieve that aim to exclude certain categories of people – in this instance persons living in a homosexual relationship – from the scope of application of [the relevant provision of national law].'[50]

In *Karner*, the Court found a violation of Article 14 (prohibition of discrimination) taken in conjunction with Article 8 (right to respect for home).[51] Most other cases in which application of this 'very weighty reasons test' resulted in the finding of a violation, concerned matters in the social policy sphere, such as the extension of a sickness insurance.[52] The Court has furthermore found violations of Article 14 in conjunction with Article 8 in cases concerning parental issues, as discussed in section 8.2.4 below. Section 8.2.3 explains how the Court has dealt with discrimination complaints where civil status also played a role.

8.2. Legal recognition of same-sex relationships and the ECHR

This section discusses the ECtHR case law on legal recognition of same-sex relationships. First, the Court's case law on the implications of Article 12 ECHR in cases involving same-sex couples is examined. Thereafter, in section 8.2.3, a detailed overview is given of the Court's approach in cases where same-sex couples complained that they did not enjoy the same rights and entitlements as different-sex couples. As will become clear, it has proven decisive what civil status was involved in such cases. This has been (partly) confirmed by the Court's case law on parental rights, as discussed in subsection 8.2.4. The availability of alternative forms of registration has also played a role in the Court's case law in respect of legal recognition of same-sex relationships (see subsection 8.2.5). All in all, the question has come to the fore whether the Convention provides for a right to some form of legal recognition of (same-sex) relationships, as set out in subsection 8.2.6.

---

49 *Inter alia* ECtHR [GC] 19 February 2013, *X. a.o.* v. *Austria*, no. 19010/07, para. 99, under reference to: ECtHR [GC] 22 January 2008, *E.B.* v. *France*, no. 43546/02, paras. 93 and 96 and ECtHR 21 December 1999, *Salgueiro da Silva Mouta* v. *Portugal*, no. 33290/96, para. 36.

50 ECtHR 24 July 2003, *Karner* v. *Austria*, no. 40016/98, para. 41.

51 See also ECtHR 2 March 2010, *Kozak* v. *Poland*, no. 13102/02.

52 ECtHR 22 July 2010, *P.B. and J.S.* v. *Austria*, no. 18984/02. The Court also found a violation in cases concerning differing ages of consent under criminal law for homosexual relations. See ECtHR 9 January 2003, *L. and V.* v. *Austria*, nos. 39392/98 and 39829/98.

The first cases where the Court expressly dealt with the question as to the sex of the two persons claiming a right to marry, concerned transsexuals. This case law formed a prelude to the landmark case of *Schalk and Kopf* (2010), as discussed in detail in subsection 8.2.2 below. As will become clear, the Court has repeatedly held that the right to marry of Article 12 ECHR referred to the traditional marriage between persons of different biological sex.

8.2.1. Early case law on transsexuals' right to marry

In its case law on the recognition of the post-operative sex of transsexuals, the Court also made clear statements about the right to marry of post-operative transsexuals. The legal recognition of the post-operative sex of transsexuals has for a long time been a delicate issue in the Council of Europe Member States. For decades the ECtHR was reluctant to find a refusal of state authorities to change the sex of a person in the birth register after a change sex operation in violation of the Convention.[53]

Rees (1986)[54] was the first case concerning the legal recognition of the post-operative sex of transsexuals where a complaint under Article 12 ECHR (the right to marry) was also assessed. The question arose as to whether a refusal to allow a post-operative transsexual to marry a person of the post-operative different sex violated this Convention Article. The Court was of the opinion that the right to marry, as guaranteed by Article 12, referred to the traditional marriage between persons of a different biological sex. According to the ECtHR this appeared also from the wording of the Article which made it clear that Article 12 was 'mainly concerned to protect marriage as the basis of the family.'[55] The Court held that the legal impediment in the United Kingdom on the marriage of persons who were of the same biological sex could not be said to restrict or reduce the right marry in such a way or to such an extent that the very essence of the right was impaired.[56] Accordingly the Court unanimously held that Article 12 ECHR was not violated.[57]

---

53 ECmHR 1 March 1979 (report), *Van Oosterwijck* v. *Belgium*, no. 7654/76; ECtHR [GC] 6 November 1980, *Van Oosterwijck* v. *Belgium*, no. 7654/76; ECtHR [GC] 17 October 1986, *Rees* v. *the United Kingdom*, no. 9532/81 and ECmHR 15 December 1988 (dec.), *Paula James* v. *the United Kingdom*, no. 10622/83. To make an such alteration in the birth register possible would require detailed legislation from those States where for purposes of social security, national insurance and employment, a transsexual was recorded as being of the sex recorded at birth, the Court noted. Having regard to the wide margin of appreciation to be afforded to the State in this area and to the relevance of protecting the interests of others in striking the requisite balance, the Court ruled that the positive obligations arising from Article 8 ECHR could not be held to extend that far. E.g. ECtHR [GC] 17 October 1986, *Rees* v. *the United Kingdom*, no. 9532/81, paras. 42–47.

54 ECtHR [GC] 17 October 1986, *Rees* v. *the United Kingdom*, no. 9532/81.

55 *Idem*, para. 49.

56 *Idem*, para. 50.

57 *Idem*, para. 51.

In the subsequent and comparable *W* v. *the UK* (1989),[58] *Cossey* (1990),[59] and *Sheffield and Horsham* (1998)[60] cases, neither the ECmHR nor the Court found any violation of the Convention. It must be noted however that these decisions were no longer adopted by unanimity.[61] In *Cossey*, the Court held in favour of the traditional concept of marriage and did not see any evidence of 'any general abandonment' of that traditional concept. It therefore did not consider it '[...] open to it to take a new approach to the interpretation of Article 12'.[62] In the Court's view, attachment to the traditional concept of marriage provided '[...] sufficient reason for the continued adoption of biological criteria for determining a person's sex for the purposes of marriage, this being a matter encompassed within the power of the Contracting States to regulate by national law the exercise of the right to marry.'[63]

Judge Schermers was the only judge at the time who was of the opinion that '[...] the fundamental human right underlying Article 12 should also be granted to homosexual and lesbian couples'. In his dissent to *W* v. *the United Kingdom* (1989), he held that denial of this right meant 'condemnation to solitude and loneliness' and he therefore found that good reasons had to be given for denying these couples the right to found a family.[64] As Schermers also acknowledged, this question was not, however, at stake in the cases of post-operative transsexuals, as all cases concerned applicants who wished to marry a person of a *different* sex. None of the other dissenting judges to the three abovementioned decisions or judgments made a comparable plea. On the contrary, some judges explicitly stressed that by speaking of 'men and women', Article 12 'clearly' indicated that marriage was the union of two persons of different sex.[65]

In *Christine Goodwin* (2002)[66] the Grand Chamber of the ECtHR departed from the previously followed line of case law and found a violation of both Articles 8 and 12 ECHR. For 16 years the Court had held that there was no violation of the right to respect for private life if a post-operative transsexual was refused an alteration of his or her sex in the birth register. In this case the Court for the first time found that the respondent government could no longer claim that the matter fell within their margin of appreciation. The Court thereby had regard to the applicants' personal

---

58 ECmHR 17 March 1989 (report), *W.* v. *the United Kingdom*, no. 11095/84.

59 ECtHR [GC] 27 September 1990, *Cossey* v. *the United Kingdom*, no. 10843/84.

60 ECtHR [GC] 30 July 2007, *Sheffield and Horsham* v. *the United Kingdom*, nos. 22985/93 and 23390/94, para. 66.

61 In *Cossey* the Grand Chamber of the ECtHR held by 10 votes to 8 that there was no violation of Art. 8 ECHR and by 14 votes to 4, the Court also did not find a violation of Art. 12 ECHR. In *Sheffield and Horsham* 11 judges voted against a violation of Art. 8 ECHR against 9 who did find the situation to be in violation of Art. 8; as for Art. 12 ECHR the vote was 18 to 2.

62 ECtHR [GC] 27 September 1990, *Cossey* v. *the United Kingdom*, no. 10843/84, para. 46.

63 *Idem.*

64 Partly dissenting opinion of Judge Schermers to ECmHR 17 March 1989 (report), *W.* v. *the United Kingdom*, no. 11095/84.

65 Dissenting opinion of Judge Martens to ECtHR [GC] 27 September 1990, *Cossey* v. *the United Kingdom*, no. 10843/84, para. 4.5.1. See also para. 5 of the the joint dissenting opinion of Judges Palm, Foighel and Pekkanen to this judgment.

66 ECtHR [GC] 11 July 2002, *Christine Goodwin* v. *the United Kingdom*, no. 28957/95.

circumstances as a transsexual, to the prevailing medical and scientific considerations at the time, to the state of European and international consensus, and to the impact on the birth register and social and domestic law developments. As there were no significant factors of public interest to weigh against the interests of the individual applicant in obtaining legal recognition of her gender re-assignment, the Court reached the conclusion that the fair balance that was inherent in the Convention now tilted decisively in favour of the applicant. The Court accordingly found a violation of Article 8.

In its examination of the complaint under Article 12 ECHR, the Court considered that the fact that fewer countries permitted the marriage of transsexuals in their assigned gender than recognised the change of gender itself, could not support an argument for leaving the matter entirely to the Contracting States as being within their margin of appreciation. The Court held that the margin of appreciation could not be extended so far as that '[...] would be tantamount to finding that the range of options open to a Contracting State included an effective bar on any exercise of the right to marry.'[67] The ECtHR concluded that the very essence of the applicant's right to marry had been infringed by the allocation of sex in national law to that registered at birth, and unanimously found a violation of Article 12 ECHR.

The Court's finding of a violation of Article 12 in this case in itself had no direct implications for the same-sex marriage discussion, as the applicant wished to marry a person of post-operative *different* sex, and thus claimed a right that encompassed the traditional definition of marriage as between man and woman. The considerations of the Court are nevertheless of a certain relevance. The Court held, for instance, that '[...] the inability of any couple to conceive or parent a child [could not] be regarded as *per se* removing their right to enjoy the first limb of this provision.'[68] It also observed 'major social changes in the institution of marriage since the adoption of the Convention'.[69] The Court furthermore noted that Article 9 of the Charter of Fundamental Rights of the European Union departed, 'no doubt deliberately', from the wording of Article 12 of the Convention in removing the reference to men and women.[70]

Later cases on transsexuals' right to marry concerned the effects of the change of sex on pre-existing marriages.[71] Married couples from the UK, consisting of a woman and a male-to-female post-operative transsexual, unsuccessfully complained before the ECtHR that they were required to end their marriage if the transsexual partner wished to obtain full legal recognition of her change of sex, because the domestic law did not permit same-sex marriages. Under reference to *Rees* the ECtHR held

67 *Idem*, para. 103.
68 *Idem*, para. 98.
69 *Idem*, para. 100.
70 *Idem*.
71 ECtHR 28 November 2006 (dec.), *Parry* v. *the United Kingdom*, no. 42971/05 and ECtHR 28 November 2006 (dec.), *R. and F.* v. *the United Kingdom*, no. 25748/05.

in *Parry* that '[...] Article 12 of the Convention similarly enshrines the traditional concept of marriage as being between a man and a woman.' The Court continued:

> 'While it is true that there are a number of Contracting States which have extended marriage to same-sex partners, this reflects their own vision of the role of marriage in their societies and does not, perhaps regrettably to many, flow from an interpretation of the fundamental right as laid down by the Contracting States in the Convention in 1950.'[72]

Accordingly the Court held that the regulation of the effects of the change of sex in the context of marriage fell within the appreciation of the Contracting State. States could not be required to make allowances for the small number of marriages where both partners wished to continue that marriage notwithstanding the change of sex of one of them. Interesting to note is that the Court considered it '[...] of some relevance to the proportionality of the effects of the gender recognition regime that the civil partnership provisions allow[ed] such couples to achieve many of the protections and benefits of married status'.[73] The Court furthermore noted that the applicants had referred 'forcefully' to the historical and social value of the institution of marriage which gave it such emotional importance to them, but also noted, however, that it was that value, as at the time recognised in national law which excluded them. In conclusion, the ECtHR dismissed the complaints as being manifestly ill-founded. Even more recently, in a judgment of 2014 the Grand Chamber of the Court found no violation of Article 8 ECHR in a Finnish case where the full recognition of the new sex of a post-operative was made conditional on the transformation of her marriage into a civil partnership.[74] This case is discussed in greater detail in section 8.2.5 below.

In the discussed case law concerning transsexuals as well as in subsequent cases in a different context,[75] the Court repeatedly held that the right to marry of Article 12 enshrines 'the traditional concept of marriage' as being between a man and a woman. It has held the formation of a legal union of a man and a woman to be the essence of the right to marry.[76] The fact that 'major social changes in the institution of marriage since the adoption of the Convention'[77] have taken place, has not to date altered this conclusion.[78] These rulings laid a basis for case law to follow on the issue of access to marriage for same-sex couples. The complaint of the Austrian same-sex couple Schalk and Kopf, lodged in 2004, was the first to provide the ECtHR with '[...] an opportunity to examine whether two persons who are of the same sex can claim to have a right to marry.'[79]

---

72 ECtHR 28 November 2006 (dec.), *Parry* v. *the United Kingdom*, no. 42971/05.

73 On this point, see more extensively section 8.2.5 below.

74 ECtHR [GC] 16 July 2014, *Hämäläinen* v. *Finland*, no. 37359/09.

75 E.g. ECtHR [GC] 29 April 2008, *Burden* v. *the United Kingdom*, no. 13378/05, para. 63.

76 ECtHR 5 January 2010, *Jaremowicz* v. *Poland*, no. 24023/03, para. 60.

77 ECtHR [GC] 11 July 2002, *Christine Goodwin* v. *the United Kingdom*, no. 28957/95, para. 100.

78 This research was concluded on 31 July 2014.

79 ECtHR 24 June 2010, *Schalk and Kopf* v. *Austria*, no. 30141/04, para. 50.

8.2.2. The case of *Schalk and Kopf* v. *Austria* (2010)

In 2002 the Austrian cohabiting same-sex couple Mr. Schalk and Mr. Kopf asked the competent authorities to allow them to marry. Their request was refused on the grounds that under Austrian law marriage could only be contracted between two persons of different sex. The couple subsequently brought their case before the Austrian Constitutional Court, but to no avail. In 2004 Schalk and Kopf lodged a complaint with the ECtHR. While their application was pending, on 1 January 2010, the Austrian Registered Partnership Act entered into force, which provided for a registered partnership for same-sex couples. The main differences in rights and obligations for spouses and those for registered partners concerned rules on the choice of name and parental rights.

Before the ECtHR the couple primarily argued that the authorities' refusal to allow them to marry violated Article 12 ECHR (the right to marry). The applicants furthermore invoked Article 14 in conjunction with Article 8 complaining that they were discriminated against on account of their sexual orientation since they were denied the right to marry and did not have any other possibility to have their relationship recognised by law before the entry into force of the Registered Partnership Act.

8.2.2.1. The Court's examination of the complaint under Article 12 ECHR

The ECtHR first examined whether the right to marry granted to 'men and women' in Article 12 could be applied to the applicants' situation. In that respect the Court noted that from its case law relating to transsexuals certain principles could be derived. The Court did not spell out what those principles were exactly, but one of the findings the Court referred to came from *Christine Goodwin*, where the Court had held, as noted above, that '[...] the inability of any couple to conceive or parent a child [could not] be regarded as *per se* removing the right to marry'.[80] In *Schalk and Kopf* the Court held – without any further motivation – that '[...] this finding [did] not allow any conclusion regarding the issue of same-sex marriage.'[81]

In order to answer the question of whether the right to marry granted to 'men and women' in Article 12 of the Convention could be applied to the situation of the applicants, the Court next resorted to textual, contextual and historical interpretation methods. In principle, the reference to 'men and women' in the English version could be interpreted as including couples consisting of two 'men' and two 'women'. The French version of the Article – to which the Court also referred – was, however, phrased in the singular: '*l'homme et la femme ont le droit de se marier*'. The Court held that '[...] looked at in isolation, the wording of Article 12 might be interpreted

---

80 ECtHR [GC] 11 July 2002, *Christine Goodwin* v. *the United Kingdom*, no. 28957/95, para. 98 (see above).

81 ECtHR 24 June 2010, *Schalk and Kopf* v. *Austria*, no. 30141/04, para. 56.

so as not to exclude the marriage between two men or two women.'[82] However, when contrasting the wording of Article 12 ECHR to the other substantive Articles of the Convention, the Court observed that the latter all '[granted] rights and freedoms to "everyone" or [stated] that "no one" [was] to be subjected to certain types of prohibited treatment.'[83] In the Court's view this showed that the choice of wording in Article 12 had to be regarded as 'deliberate'. Thirdly, the Court held that regard had to be had to the historical context in which the Convention was adopted. As the Court noted, '[...] in the 1950s marriage was clearly understood in the traditional sense of being a union between partners of different sex.'[84]

On the basis of the 'living instrument' doctrine, the Convention is usually interpreted in the light of present day conditions.[85] In particular the textual and historical interpretation methods have often been overruled by this evolutive interpretation method. It was therefore not surprising that the applicants in this case relied primarily on this doctrine of the Court. They contended that in present day conditions Article 12 had to be read as granting same-sex couples access to marriage or, in other words, as obliging Member States to provide for such access in their national laws. The Court was not, however, persuaded by this argument. It repeated its previous acknowledgement that the institution of marriage had undergone 'major social changes since the adoption of the Convention',[86] but attached decisive value to the lack of European consensus on this point. As the Court noted, at that time only 6 out of 47 Convention States allowed same-sex marriage.

The Court furthermore referred to the right to marry as provided for in Article 9 of the EU Charter of Fundamental Rights, which contains no reference to 'men and women', and which leaves the decision whether or not to allow same-sex marriage to regulation by Member States' national law.[87] The Court therefore 'no longer' considered '[...] that the right to marry enshrined in Article 12 [had to] in all circumstances be limited to marriage between two persons of the opposite sex' and held that it could not be said that Article 12 was inapplicable to the applicants' complaint.[88] The applicant's case did not benefit from this cautiously worded finding however, for the Court continued that because marriage had 'deep-rooted social and cultural connotations differing largely from one society to another', national

82 *Idem*, para. 55. Judges Maliverni and Kovler were unable to share that view. In their concurring opinion they held that, '"the ordinary meaning to be given to the terms of the treaty" in the case of Art. 12 [could not] be anything other than that of recognising that a man and a woman, that is, persons of opposite sex, have the right to marry.'

83 *Idem*.

84 *Idem*.

85 *Inter alia*, ECtHR 25 April 1978, *Tyrer* v. *the United Kingdom*, no. 5856/72, para. 31; ECtHR [GC] 8 July 2004, *Vo* v. *France*, no. 53924/00, para. 82 and ECtHR [GC] 4 February 2005, *Mamatkulov and Askarov* v. *Turkey*, nos. 46827/99 and 46951/99, para. 121.

86 ECtHR 24 June 2010, *Schalk and Kopf* v. *Austria*, no. 30141/04, paras. 52 and 58 under reference to *Christine Goodwin*.

87 *Idem*, para. 61.

88 ECtHR 24 June 2010, *Schalk and Kopf* v. *Austria*, no. 30141/04, para. 61. Two concurring judges did not subscribe to this finding. Concurring opinion of Judge Malinverni joined by Judge Kovler to ECtHR 24 June 2010, *Schalk and Kopf* v. *Austria*, no. 30141/04, para. 2.

authorities were best placed to assess and respond to the needs of society in this field.[89] The Court accordingly concluded that Article 12 ECHR does not impose an obligation on States to grant same-sex couples access to marriage. The Chamber was unanimous in its conclusion that there had been no violation of this provision.

Now that the Court declared Article 12 applicable in the present case, some wondered if an absolute prohibition on the right to marry for same-sex couples impaired the essence of that right (see 8.1.3 above).[90] The Court, however, did not assess this question.

8.2.2.2. The Court's examination of the complaints under Articles 8 and 14 ECHR

As discussed in section 8.1.2 above, in *Schalk and Kopf* the Court held for the first time that the relationship of cohabiting same-sex couples living in a stable partnership, fell within the notion of 'family life', within the meaning of Article 8. While a lack of consensus was reason for the Court not to find a violation of Article 12, here the Court considered there to be sufficient consensus to interpret the notion 'family life' of Article 8 in the light of present day conditions. Just like the applicability of Article 12 did not benefit the applicants' case under Article 12, also this finding did not result in any material consequences to the applicants' benefit.[91]

Having found that the case fell within the ambit of Article 8, the Court next examined whether a violation had occurred of this Article in conjunction with Article 14 (the prohibition of discrimination). The Court held that because 'same-sex couples are just as capable as different-sex couples of entering into stable committed relationships', the applicants were in a relevantly similar situation to different-sex couples as regards their need for legal recognition of their relationship.[92] The ECtHR made a distinction between three limbs of the applicants' complaint: (1) that they still did not have access to marriage; (2) that no alternative means of legal recognition was available to them until the entry into force of the Registered Partnership Act; and (3) that certain differences existed in rights and obligations for spouses and those for registered partners under Austrian law.

As regards the first limb, the Court was brief: now that the Court had concluded that Article 12 did not impose an obligation on Contracting States to grant same-sex couples access to marriage, Article 14 taken in conjunction with Article 8 – a provision of more general purpose and scope – could not be interpreted as imposing such an obligation either. As regards the second limb, the Court considered it not its task to

89 *Idem*, para. 62.

90 N.R. Koffeman, 'Case note to ECtHR 24 June 2010, *Schalk and Kopf* v. *Austria*, no. 30141/04', 11 *European Human Rights Cases* 2010/92 (in Dutch).

91 In this regard Cooper noted that in *Schalk and Kopf* the Court made 'a number of major, but seemingly contradictory rulings.' S.L. Cooper, 'Marriage, Family, Discrimination & Contradiction: An Evaluation of the Legacy and Future of the European Court of Human Rights' Jurisprudence on LGBT Rights', 12 *German Law Journal* (2011) p. 1743 at pp. 1746–1747, online available at: www.germanlawjournal.com/pdfs/Vol12-No10/PDF_Vol_12_No_10_1746-1763_Articles_Cooper.pdf, visited June 2014.

92 ECtHR 24 June 2010, *Schalk and Kopf* v. *Austria*, no. 30141/04, para. 99.

establish whether the lack of any means of legal recognition for same-sex couples would have constituted a violation of Article 14 taken in conjunction with Article 8 if this situation had still persisted at the time, now that the Registered Partnership Act had entered into force in Austria. The Court next examined whether Austria should have provided the applicants with an alternative means of legal recognition of their partnership any earlier than it did. The Court noted an emerging European consensus towards legal recognition of same-sex couples, but concluded that there was not yet a majority of States providing for it:

> 'The Court cannot but note that there is an emerging European consensus towards legal recognition of same-sex couples. Moreover, this tendency has developed rapidly over the past decade. Nevertheless, there is not yet a majority of States providing for legal recognition of same-sex couples. The area in question must therefore still be regarded as one of evolving rights with no established consensus, where States must also enjoy a margin of appreciation in the timing of the introduction of legislative changes [...].'[93]

The Court concluded that 'though not in the vanguard', the Austrian legislature could not be reproached 'for not having introduced the Registered Partnership Act any earlier.' Whether this reasoning implies that States are under an obligation to give some form of legal recognition to same-sex relationships cannot be said with certainty (on this point, see more extensively 8.2.6 below). The Court in any case avoided the difficult question of the moment from which sufficient consensus existed to come to any such conclusion.[94]

Finally, in its examination of the third limb of the complaint, the Court found that it did not have to examine every one of the differences in rights and obligations for spouses and those for registered partners in detail, as the applicants had not claimed that they were directly affected by any of these differences. The Court observed that, following a trend in other Member States, the Austrian Registered Partnership, was equal or similar to marriage in many respects, while some substantial differences remained in respect of parental rights. The Court was not convinced by the applicants' argument that if a State chooses to provide same-sex couples with an alternative means of recognition, it is obliged to confer a status on them which – though carrying a different name – corresponds to marriage in each and every respect. On the contrary, it considered that 'States enjoy a certain margin of appreciation as regards the exact status conferred by alternative means of recognition.'[95] The Court repeated its standing case law that different treatment based on sexual orientation

[93] ECtHR 24 June 2010, *Schalk and Kopf* v. *Austria*, no. 30141/04, para. 105, referring to ECtHR 4 November 2008 (dec.), *Courten* v. *the United Kingdom*, no. 4479/06. See also ECtHR 23 June 2009 (dec.), *M.W.* v. *the United Kingdom*, no. 11313/02.

[94] The difficulty of this question is well illustrated by the case *P.B and J.S.* v. *the United Kingdom*. The dissenters to this judgment criticised the fact that the majority decided the case on the basis of a then existing consensus, which had not yet been visible in 1997 from when the case originated. Joint partly dissenting opinion of Judges Vajic and Malinverni to ECtHR 22 July 2010, *P.B. and J.S.* v. *Austria*, no. 18984/02.

[95] ECtHR 24 June 2010, *Schalk and Kopf* v. *Austria*, no. 30141/04, para. 108.

requires 'particularly serious reasons' by way of justification,[96] but did not assess if there was any justification at all for the difference in treatment here complained of.[97] Instead, it dealt with the case on the basis of the margin of appreciation to be accorded to States in issues where there is no consensus amongst the Contracting Parties.[98] In this regard it also noted that the margin is usually wide in respect of general measures of economic or social strategy.[99] 'On the whole', the Court did not see 'any indication' that Austria had exceeded its margin of appreciation in its choice of rights and obligations conferred by registered partnership. In conclusion, the Court found, by four votes to three, that there had been no violation of Article 14 in conjunction with Article 8 in this case.

Hence, while on the one hand, the Court was very clear that the Convention did not impose any obligation on States to open up marriage to same-sex couples, on the other hand, the Court left clear openings for further development of its case law to at least some form of legal recognition of same-sex relationships.[100] The Court stressed that there was *not yet* a majority of States providing for legal recognition of same-sex couples[101] and that States were *still* free to restrict access to marriage to different-sex couples.[102] The Court furthermore held that States enjoyed a margin of appreciation in the *timing* of the introduction of legislative changes[103] and that they enjoyed 'a certain margin of appreciation as regards the exact status conferred by alternative means of recognition'.[104] This point is further developed below in subsection 8.2.6 below.

All in all, in its assessment of the complaint under Article 8 in combination with Article 14, the Court attached considerable weight to the lack of common ground among the Contracting Parties.[105] Consequently the Court did not assess the discrimination complaint in substance. This can be held to be somewhat difficult to

---

96 *Idem*, para. 97, referring to ECtHR 24 July 2003, *Karner* v. *Austria*, no. 40016/98, para. 37; ECtHR 9 January 2003, *L. and V.* v. *Austria*, nos. 39392/98 and 39829/98, para. 45 and ECtHR 27 September 1999, *Smith and Grady* v. *the United Kingdom*, nos. 33985/96 and 33986/96, para. 90. See also section 8.1.4 above.

97 In *Karner* and *Mata Estevez* the Court had accepted that 'protection of the family in the traditional sense [was], in principle, a weighty and legitimate reason which might justify a difference in treatment.' In *Schalk and Kopf* (in para. 108), the Court merely considered that States were '[...] still free, under Article 12 of the Convention as well as under Article 14 taken in conjunction with Article 8, to restrict access to marriage to different-sex couples.' ECtHR 24 July 2003, *Karner* v. *Austria*, no. 40016/98, para. 40 and ECtHR 10 May 2001 (dec.), *Antonio Mata Estevez* v. *Spain*, no. 56501/00.

98 ECtHR 24 June 2010, *Schalk and Kopf* v. *Austria*, no. 30141/04, para. 98. The Court referred to ECtHR 27 March 1998, *Petrovic* v. *Austria*, no. 20458/92, para. 38.

99 *Idem*, para. 97. The Court referred to ECtHR [GC] 12 April 2006, *Stec a.o.* v. *the United Kingdom*, no. 65731/01, para. 52.

100 See also M. Melcher, 'Private international law and registered relationships: an EU perspective', 20 *European Review of Private Law* (2012) p. 1075 at pp. 1080–1081.

101 ECtHR 24 June 2010, *Schalk and Kopf* v. *Austria*, no. 30141/04, para. 105.

102 *Idem*, para. 108.

103 *Idem*, para. 105.

104 *Idem*, para. 108.

105 See also F. Hamilton, 'Why the margin of appreciation is not the answer to the gay marriage debate', 13 *European Human Rights Law Review* (2013) p. 47.

reconcile with the earlier finding of the Court in this very same judgment that there was – by 2010 – a sufficient consensus for extending the protection of the right to respect for family life to same-sex couples.

The three dissenting judges were critical of the fact that the majority did not draw inferences from its finding that same-sex relationships enjoyed a right to respect for family life. They claimed:

> 'Having decided [...] that "the relationship of the applicants falls within the notion of 'family life'", the Court should have drawn inferences from this finding. However, by deciding that there has been no violation, the Court at the same time endorses the legal vacuum at stake, without imposing on the respondent State any positive obligation to provide a satisfactory framework, offering the applicants, at least to a certain extent, the protection any family should enjoy.'[106]

These judges were of the opinion that '[a]ny absence of a legal framework offering [same-sex couples in stable relationships], at least to a certain extent, the same rights or benefits attached to marriage would need robust justification, especially taking into account the growing trend in Europe to offer some means of qualifying for such rights or benefits.'[107] They concluded that the Court should have found a violation of Article 14 taken in conjunction with Article 8 of the Convention in this case, because the Austrian government had not put forward any cogent reason to justify the difference of treatment between same-sex and different-sex couples in stable committed relationships, as regards legal recognition and protection of their relationship.

The four-to-three Chamber judgment in *Schalk and Kopf* became final in November 2010 after the applicants' request for referral of the case to the Grand Chamber had been rejected.[108]

8.2.2.3. *Affirmation of the special status of traditional marriage in subsequent case law*

After the landmark *Schalk and Kopf* judgment, the Court has on various occasions repeated that the right to marry ex Article 12 ECHR sees at marriage between man and woman only. In *Hämäläinen* (2014), the Grand Chamber held:

> 'While it is true that some Contracting States have extended marriage to same-sex partners, Article 12 cannot be construed as imposing an obligation on the Contracting States to grant access to marriage to same-sex couples [...]'[109]

---

106 Joint Dissenting Opinion of Judges Rozakis, Spielmann and Jebens to ECtHR 24 June 2010, *Schalk and Kopf* v. *Austria*, no. 30141/04, para. 8.

107 *Idem*, para. 9.

108 ECtHR press release no. 906 of 29 November 2010. Hodson called this 'surprising and disappointing'. Hodson 2011, *supra* n. 16, at p. 170.

109 ECtHR [GC] 16 July 2014, *Hämäläinen* v. *Finland*, no. 37359/09, para. 96. See section 8.2.5 below.

The Court has furthermore – including in cases outside the context of same-sex relationships – reiterated that marriage confers a special status on those who enter into it.[110] As explained in the following section, the Court has repeatedly accepted this special status as justification for a difference in treatment between married and unmarried couples, and possibly also between spouses and registered partners.

8.2.3. Spouses, registered partners and stable partners compared under Article 14 ECHR

As explained in section 8.1.4 above, for any exanimation of a discrimination complaint it must be assessed whether there is a difference in treatment of persons in relevantly similar situations, and if so, whether this difference in treatment can be justified. The following subsections analyse these questions for four comparative groups that have been compared in the relevant Strasbourg case law, namely: (1) spouses and unmarried partners, (2) spouses and registered partners, (3) registered partners and unmarried partners, and (4) same-sex unmarried partners compared to different-sex unmarried partners. While this is already apparent from the definition of the latter comparative group, in respect of all four groups there have been cases where not only the civil status of the partners was at issue, but also their sexual orientation. To date there have[111] been no cases decided where complaints were brought in respect of differences in treatment between different-sex spouses and same-sex spouses, or different-sex registered partners and same-sex registered partners.[112]

8.2.3.1. Spouses compared to unmarried partners

The Court has held on several occasions that unmarried couples and married couples were not in relevantly similar situations. While 'unmarried' is, of course, a broad term, the focus in this subsection lies on stable partners; the comparability of spouses and partners who concluded (some form of) registered partnership is assessed in the next subsection. It is understandable that the Court has used the broader term 'unmarried', because at the time it first decided upon such matters, none of the High Contracting Parties had introduced any alternative form of legal recognition of relationships.

In *Lindsay* (1986) the ECmHR found that different-sex married couples could not claim to be in an analogous situation with different-sex unmarried couples where tax allowances were concerned.[113] The Commission held that marriage was characterised by 'a corpus of rights and obligations' which differentiated it 'markedly' from the

110 E.g. ECtHR [GC] 11 November 2010, *Şerife Yiğit* v. *Turkey*, no. 3976/05, para. 72 and ECtHR 3 April 2012, *Van der Heijden* v. *The Netherlands*, no. 42857/05, para. 69.

111 This research was concluded on 31 July 2014.

112 See T. Loenen, 'Gelijk recht op tweede-ouderadoptie voor ongehuwde homoseksuele en heteroseksuele paren. X e.a. tegen Oostenrijk' ['Equal right to joint adoption for unmarried homosexual and heterosexual couples. X. a.o. v. Austria'], 38 *NJCM-Bull/NTM* (2013) p. 627 at p. 643.

113 ECmHR 11 November 1986 (dec.), *Lindsay* v. *the United Kingdom*, no. 11089/84.

situation of a man and woman who cohabited. This conclusion was confirmed by the Court in various cases where same-sex stable partners claimed to be in a comparable situation to different-sex married couples. In *Courten* (2008), upon the death of his same-sex partner with whom he had been cohabiting for over 25 years, a man applied for extra-statutory tax concession equivalent to the exemption from inheritance tax which a spouse would have received under the law in force at the time. The Court ruled that the applicant could not claim that his situation was analogous to that of married couples.[114] It reiterated that 'notwithstanding social changes', marriage remained an institution that was widely accepted as conferring 'a particular status' on those who entered it and that it was 'singled out for special treatment' under Article 12 ECHR. The applicant in *Courten* submitted that the Court had to take into consideration that he was unable at the relevant time 'to enter into a legally-binding arrangement akin to marriage', because at the time that he applied for the tax exemption UK law did not allow same-sex partners to conclude a civil union, or to marry. The Court did not let this fact have a bearing on the finding of a lack of comparability of the situation of the applicant and that of spouses. It merely noted in respect of this claim that '[...] in the area of evolving social rights where there [was] no established consensus', States enjoyed a margin of appreciation in the timing of the introduction of legislative changes. The government could therefore not be criticised for not having introduced the 2004 registered partnership legislation at an earlier date.[115]

This finding of non-comparability has been upheld in cases concerning parental matters. In *X. and Others* v. *Austria* (2013), the Grand Chamber of the Court held that same-sex stable partners were not in a relevantly similar situation to different-sex married couples in respect of second-parent adoption.[116] By way of justification, the Court, *inter alia*, reiterated that neither Article 12 ECHR nor Article 8 in conjunction with Article 14 ECHR imposed an obligation on the Contracting States to grant same-sex couples access to marriage, that marriage conferred a special status on those who enter into it, and that the exercise of the right to marry as protected by Article 12 of the Convention gave rise to social, personal and legal consequences.[117]

In other cases where unmarried couples complained about a difference in treatment when compared to married couples, the Court did not explicitly assess whether there were relevantly similar situations, but implicitly accepted that this was the case and

114 ECtHR 4 November 2008 (dec.), *Courten* v. *the United Kingdom*, no. 4479/06. See also ECtHR 23 June 2009 (dec.), *M.W.* v. *the United Kingdom*, no. 11313/02.

115 See again also ECtHR 23 June 2009 (dec.), *M. W.* v. *the United Kingdom*, no. 11313/02.

116 ECtHR [GC] 19 February 2013, *X. a.o.* v. *Austria*, no. 19010/07, paras. 105–110. The Court, however, found the applicants to be in a similar situation with different-sex unmarried couples (see section 8.2.4.1.2 below).

117 Concurring Judge Spielmann was the only judge in the Grand Chamber to believe that the situation of the applicants was comparable to that of a married different-sex couple in which one partner wished to adopt the other partner's child. He held that the fact that the Convention does not require Contracting States to make marriage available to same-sex couples and that marriage confers a special status on those who enter into it had no bearing on that finding. Still, he did not vote in favour of finding a violation of Art. 14 ECHR taken in conjunction with Article 8 because he believed that it was not necessary to examine this issue. Concurring opinion Judge Spielmann to ECtHR [GC] 19 February 2013, *X. a.o.* v. *Austria*, no. 19010/07, para. 2.

held that the difference in treatment could in any case be justified on the basis of the protection of marriage. In *Şerife Yiğit* (2010), the Grand Chamber noted in this regard:

> 'The protection of marriage constitutes, in principle, an important and legitimate reason which may justify a difference in treatment between married and unmarried couples [...]. Marriage is characterised by a corpus of rights and obligations that differentiate it markedly from the situation of a man and woman who cohabit [...]. Thus, States have a certain margin of appreciation to treat differently married and unmarried couples, particularly in matters falling within the realm of social and fiscal policy such as taxation, pensions and social security [...].'[118]

As noted above, and as confirmed in this ruling, the matter at stake is relevant for determining comparability and for the question of whether a difference in treatment can be justified. The Court here stressed that '[...] particularly in matters falling within the realm of social and fiscal policy such as taxation, pensions and social security', States could treat married and unmarried couples differently. These policy areas cover many issues, of course, and it has consequently only exceptionally been that the Court held a difference in treatment between married and unmarried couples not to be justified.[119] Such a finding has, moreover, only occurred in cases involving different-sex couples.

Differences in treatment between unmarried and married couples have also been upheld in situations where same-sex couples had no access to marriage. An example is *Mata Estevez* (2001).[120] The applicant, who had been in a stable same-sex relationship for more than ten years when his partner deceased, was refused a right to a survivor's pension. Under Spanish law marriage constituted an essential precondition for eligibility for such a pension at the time, while same-sex couples were barred from access to marriage. The Court, 'even supposing' that this refusal constituted an interference with respect for his private life, held that this interference was justified under Article 8(2) and that there was no violation of this Article in conjunction with Article 14. It accepted that the relevant Spanish legislation pursued the legitimate aim of 'the protection of the family based on marriage bonds'.[121] The Court considered the difference in treatment to fall within the State's margin of appreciation and ruled that the refusal did not constitute a discriminatory interference with the applicant's right to respect private life contrary to Article 8, taken in conjunction with Article 14

---

118 ECtHR [GC] 11 November 2010, *Şerife Yiğit* v. *Turkey*, no. 3976/05, para. 72. In the Chamber judgment preceding this Grand Chamber judgment, the Court had accepted 'the protection of the traditional family based on the bonds of marriage' as legitimate aim and objective and reasonable ground. ECtHR 20 January 2009, *Şerife Yiğit* v. *Turkey*, no. 3976/05, para. 30.

119 In *Petrov* the Court held it 'not readily apparent', why different-sex married and different-sex unmarried partners who have an established family life were to be given disparate treatment as regards the possibility to maintain contact by telephone while one of them is in custody. ECtHR 22 May 2008, *Petrov* v. *Bulgaria*, no. 15197/02, para. 55.

120 ECtHR 10 May 2001 (dec.), *Antonio Mata Estevez* v. *Spain*, no. 56501/00.

121 The Court referred to *mutatis mutandis*, ECtHR 13 June 1979, *Marckx* v. *Belgium*, no. 6833/74, para. 40.

ECHR. The Court accordingly declared the application manifestly ill-founded and thus inadmissible.

The discussed case law thus shows that the special status of marriage has been a ground for the Court both for not finding comparability of married and unmarried couples, and, in those cases where it did (implicitly) find such comparability, for justifying the difference in treatment between these groups. In cases involving same-sex couples, the fact that these couples did not at all have access to marriage, was considered to have no bearing on these findings.[122]

8.2.3.2. Spouses compared to registered partners

The Court's findings in respect of the question of whether (same-sex) couples in a registered partnership or civil union were in a relevantly comparable situation to spouses have differed from case to case. In a 2008 ruling, the Grand Chamber of the Court implicitly accepted comparability of the situation of different-sex spouses and same-sex partners in a civil union under UK law. In *Burden* the Grand Chamber of the Court held:

> 'As with marriage, the Grand Chamber considers that the legal consequences of civil partnership under the 2004 Act, which couples expressly and deliberately decide to incur, set these types of relationship apart from other forms of co-habitation. Rather than the length or the supportive nature of the relationship, what is determinative is the existence of a public undertaking, carrying with it a body of rights and obligations of a contractual nature. Just as there can be no analogy between married and Civil Partnership Act couples, on one hand, and heterosexual or homosexual couples who choose to live together but not to become husband and wife or civil partners, on the other hand [...], the absence of such a legally binding agreement between the applicants renders their relationship of co-habitation, despite its long duration, fundamentally different to that of a married or civil partnership couple.'[123]

At first sight, this phrasing still seems to leave some room for doubt as to whether the Court indeed considered spouses and civil partners to be in relevantly similar situations, as it can be held that the quoted paragraphs only contrasted these two groups with stable partners (on this point, see the next subsection), and does not say much about the interrelationship between marriage and civil partnership. The Court itself has nonetheless made clear how the above quoted paragraph must be read, as in *Courten* (2008) it held that in *Burden* it had '[...] equated civil partnerships between homosexual couples with marriage'.[124]

---

122 See also section 8.2.3.4 below.

123 ECtHR [GC] 29 April 2008, *Burden* v. *the United Kingdom*, no. 13378/05, para. 65, under reference to ECtHR 27 April 2000 (dec.), *Shackell* v. *the United Kingdom*, no. 45851/99.

124 ECtHR 4 November 2008 (dec.), *Courten* v. *the United Kingdom*, no. 4479/06. See also Cooper 2011, *supra* n. 91, at p. 1759.

The finding of this comparability is all the more interesting now that in subsequent French cases, the Court by contrast held that partners who had concluded a civil partnership agreement under French law (*pacte civil de solidarité* (PACS)) were not in a comparable situation with married partners.

In *Manenc* (2010),[125] the Court held that the applicant's situation, a surviving partner who had concluded a PACS with his same-sex partner, was not comparable to that of a surviving spouse. While the French PACS created certain rights and obligations for the partners in respect of taxes, property and social benefits, it was only spouses in a civil marriage who were under an obligation to maintain financial solidarity, the Court observed. It found the fact that civil marriage was not open to same-sex couples under French law in itself not sufficient to hold that the applicant was in a relevantly similar situation to surviving spouses. It considered that the applicant's sexual orientation played no role in the refusal of his request for the award of a survivor's pension, as different-sex PACS partners were also refused such pensions. In this regard the Court noted that the vast majority of PACS partnerships concerned different-sex partners. The Court accepted that the relevant French legislation pursued the legitimate aim of the protection of the marriage-based family ('*protection de la famille fondée sur les liens du mariage*') and that it fell within the wide margin of appreciation that States enjoyed in this area.[126] The Court did not make explicit why the margin was wide.[127] Without any examination of the proportionality of the refusal, the Court declared the complaint manifestly ill-founded.

The Court applied the same line of reasoning in *Gas and Dubois* (2012),[128] concerning second-parent adoption by same-sex partners. In the year 2000 Ms. Dubois had given birth to a daughter, conceived by means of anonymous donor insemination, and had formally recognised her. Her partner, Ms. Gas, had subsequently applied to adopt the child, with Dubois' express consent. They wished to obtain a simple adoption order under French law in order to create a parent-child relationship between the child and Ms. Gas with the possibility of sharing parental responsibility. The domestic courts had refused the adoption request on the ground that it would transfer parental rights from the child's biological and legal mother, Ms. Dubois, to Ms. Gas, which was

---

125 ECtHR 21 September 2010 (dec.), *Manenc* v. *France*, no. 66686/09.

126 In legal scholarship it was noted that other case law of the ECtHR gave the impression that civil status was in itself a suspect ground, that narrowed the margin of appreciation to be accorded to States in these matters. N.R. Koffeman, 'Case note to ECtHR 21 September 2010 (dec.), *Manenc* v. *France*, no. 66686/09', 12 *European Human Rights Cases* 2011/28 (in Dutch), referring to ECtHR 4 June 2002, *Wessels-Bergervoet* v. *the Netherlands*, no. 34462/97, para. 49.

127 In legal scholarship it has been noted that this was presumbably so because a measure of economic or social strategy was concerned. Koffeman 2011A, *supra* n. 126, referring to ECtHR [GC] 16 March 2010, *Carson a.o.* v. *the United Kingdom*, no. 42184/05, para. 61. Koffeman has furthermore noted that in *Şerife Yiğit* v. *Turkey* (ECtHR [GC] 11 November 2010, no. 3976/05, para. 72) the Court ruled that '[...] States have a certain margin of appreciation to treat differently married and unmarried couples, particularly in matters falling within the realm of social and fiscal policy such as taxation, pensions and social security.' On the other hand, so Koffeman has observed, other case law has given the impression that in cases concerning civil status, the margin of appreciation must be narrowed. See also ECtHR 4 June 2002, *Wessels-Bergervoet* v. *the Netherlands*, no. 34462/97.

128 ECtHR 15 March 2012, *Gas and Dubois* v. *France*, no. 25951/07.

not in the child's interests. The national law provided for only one exception to this rule, namely where the adoptive parent was the spouse of the biological parent. At the time same-sex couples were not allowed to marry under French law, rendering it impossible for the applicant couple to qualify for this exception.

Before the ECtHR the applicants complained under Article 14 taken in conjunction with Article 8 ECHR about the fact that Ms. Gas could not adopt Ms. Dubois' child. The Court held that for the purposes of second-parent adoption, the applicants' legal situation could not be said to be comparable to that of a married couple.[129] The Court reiterated in this regard that no right to same-sex marriage could be derived from the Convention, that marriage conferred a special status on those who enter into it and that the exercise of the right to marry was protected by Article 12 of the Convention and gave rise to social, personal and legal consequences. The applicants had also alleged indirect discrimination because it was impossible for them to marry, but the Court's only answer to this argument was that 'in that connection' it could only refer to its earlier findings regarding, *inter alia*, the special status of marriage.[130] The Court subsequently compared the situation of the applicants with unmarried different-sex couples and concluded that '[...] any couple in a comparable legal situation by virtue of having entered into a civil partnership would likewise have [had] their application for a simple-adoption order refused'.[131] The Court therefore did not observe any difference in treatment based on the applicants' sexual orientation and concluded that there had been no violation of Article 14 taken in conjunction with Article 8 ECHR.

Concurring, Judge Costa underlined that the national legislature was better placed than the Strasbourg Court '[...] to bring about change in institutions concerning the family, relations between adults and children, and the concept of marriage'.[132] His call for the legislature to revisit the issue by bringing the relevant French law into line with contemporary social reality, was echoed by concurring Judge Spielmann, who was in turn joined by Judge Berro-Lefèvre. The latter Judges were, furthermore, of the opinion that for the purposes of second-parent adoption the applicants' legal situation was comparable to that of a married couple. They did not find this difference in treatment to be contrary to the Convention, however, as it did not appear to them to stand in the way of 'a normal family life'.[133]

Dissenting Judge Villiger adopted a reasoning that was fundamentally different from that of the majority. He argued that in this case it had to be assessed if the child concerned was suffering from a difference in treatment. The Judge held:

---

129 *Idem*, para. 68.

130 *Idem*, paras. 70–71.

131 *Idem*.

132 Concurring opinion of Judge Costa, joined by Judge Spielmann to ECtHR 15 March 2012, *Gas and Dubois* v. *France*, no. 25951/07.

133 Concurring opinion of Judge Spielmann, joined by Judge Berro-Lefèvre to ECtHR 15 March 2012, *Gas and Dubois* v. *France*, no. 25951/07.

> 'My difficulty lies with the position of the children of the various relationships. The children of a heterosexual couple benefit from joint parental responsibility if the couple are married; those of a same-sex couple do not as, in such a case, adoption is excluded. Therein lies for me the difference of treatment viewed under Article 14 of the Convention taken together with Article 8. At this stage I should add that I firmly believe – and I consider this undisputed – that joint parental custody is in the best interests of the child. I fail to see a justification for this difference in treatment. In my view, all children should be afforded the same treatment. I cannot see why some children, but not others, should be deprived of their best interests, namely of joint parental custody. Indeed, how can children help it that they were born of a parent of a same-sex couple rather than of a parent of a heterosexual couple? Why should the child have to suffer for the parents' situation? [...] To say in the present case that this difference in treatment is justified because marriage has a special status in society does not convince me. This reasoning may, possibly, be justified from the point of view of the legislator when distinguishing marriage from other forms of cohabitation. But this is not the only point of view as regards the balancing of the various interests under Articles 14 and 8. Indeed, society's views should not even be the main point of view (let alone, as in the present judgment, the only one). Should not the child's position be equally important? Justifying discrimination in respect of the children by pointing out that marriage enjoys a particular status for those adults who engage in it is, in my view, insufficient in this balancing exercise.'[134]

As also discussed below in section 8.2.4 below, the approach as suggested by Judge Villiger has – so far – not been adopted by the Court, although the best interests of the child have been given increasingly more weight in cases concerning parental rights of same-sex couples.

In *Manenc* and *Gas and Dubois* the Court thus found the situations of PACS partners and spouses to be not relevantly similar. This stands in clear contrast with the above quoted finding of comparability between civil partners and spouses in *Burden*. It must be noted that the French PACS is open to both different-sex and same-sex couples, and that the rights and obligations that it confers upon the partners are more limited than those involved in marriage.[135] The UK civil partnership as referred to in *Burden*, on the other hand, was introduced exclusively for same-sex couples and as alternative to marriage, and was thus (generally) equivalent to marriage. Therefore it may be presumed that the Court found no comparability in the discussed French cases, because of the nature of the French PACS. This reading is furthermore confirmed by the fact that the Court itself has in *X. and Others* (2013) referred to *Gas and Dubois* as a case concerning two women who were 'living together as a same-sex couple', without mentioning the fact that the applicants in *Gas and Dubois* had concluded a PACS.[136]

---

134 Dissenting opinion of Judge Villiger to ECtHR 15 March 2012, *Gas and Dubois* v. *France*, no. 25951/07.

135 See the discussion of the *Hay* case in Ch. 9, section 9.3.3.3.

136 ECtHR [GC] 19 February 2013, *X. a.o.* v. *Austria*, no. 19010/07, paras. 105–106.

There is on the other hand a German case of a later date, which seems to refute this reading of the Court's case law. In *Boeckel and Gessner-Boeckel* (2013)[137] the Court found two women in a registered civil partnership under German law to be not in a relevantly similar situation to a married different-sex couple when it came to the issue of the entries to be made on a child's birth certificate (see also 8.2.4.2 below). As extensively discussed in Chapter 10, the German registered partnership is almost equivalent to marriage, except for certain parental matters. Also, it is open to same-sex couples only.

The conclusion must therefore be that the Court has thus far only implicitly accepted the comparability of the situation of spouses and registered partners. In concrete cases it has held that these situations are not comparable and has declared the application manifestly ill-founded or has found no violation of the Convention. In these cases, as was the case in *Mata Estevez* (see above), the Court again did not find indirect discrimination, nor did it otherwise take into account that, other than different-sex couples, same-sex couples had (at the time) no access to marriage under domestic law.[138] As further explained in section 8.2.5 below, in 2014 the Court found existing (small) differences between marriage and registered partnerships not in themselves to be sufficient to find a violation of the Convention in a Finnish case where the marriage of a post-operative transsexual had to be converted into a registered partnership in order to gain legal recognition as being of the post-operative sex.

8.2.3.3. Registered partners compared to unmarried partners

In *Burden* the Court thus made very clear that registered partners and stable partners were not in similar situations, as in the latter situation the parties had not undertaken public and binding obligations towards each other.[139] As noted above, the Court held:

> 'Rather than the length or the supportive nature of the relationship, what is determinative is the existence of a public undertaking, carrying with it a body of rights and obligations of a contractual nature.'[140]

Because the *Burden* case concerned two cohabiting sisters who wished to have tenancy succession rights on an equal footing with spouses and civil partners, the 'purely platonic' nature of their relationship – 'a relationship of economic dependency

137 ECtHR 7 May 2013 (dec.), *Boeckel and Gessner-Boeckel* v. *Germany*, no. 8017/11.

138 See also N.R. Koffeman, 'Case-note to ECtHR 15 March 2012, *Gas and Dubois* v. *France*, no. 25951/07', 13 *European Human Rights Cases* 2012/114.

139 ECtHR [GC] 29 April 2008, *Burden* v. *the United Kingdom*, no. 13378/05, para. 65. See also ECtHR 4 November 2008 (dec.), *Courten* v. *the United Kingdom*, no. 4479/06.

140 ECtHR [GC] 29 April 2008, *Burden* v. *the United Kingdom*, no. 13378/05, para. 63. This finding was later confirmed in ECtHR [GC] 11 November 2010, *Şerife Yiğit* v. *Turkey*, no. 3976/05, para. 72, and ECtHR [GC] 3 April 2012, *Van der Heijden* v. *the Netherlands*, no. 42857/05, para. 69.

rather than a long-lasting life community'[141] – also contributed to the Court's finding of no comparability.[142]

The Court has in subsequent case law confirmed that it is particularly the legal consequences of civil partnerships 'which couples expressly and deliberately decide to incur'[143] which set these types of relationship apart 'from informal personal relationships, however permanent and supportive.'[144] In a 2012 judgment, the Court even spoke of a 'special status' that States may confer not only on marriage but also on registered partnerships. The Court held that the relationship of cohabiting partners differed 'fundamentally' from that of married couples or couples in a registered partnership. On a more practical note, the Court observed:

> 'The Court would add that, were it to hold otherwise, it would create a need either to assess the nature of unregistered non-marital relationships in a multitude of individual cases or to define the conditions for assimilating to a formalised union a relationship characterised precisely by the absence of formality.'[145]

A partnership status has thus proven a clear factor for holding situations as being dissimilar.

8.2.3.4. Same-sex unmarried partners compared to different-sex unmarried partners

In cases where no legally recognised relationships were involved, the Court has had less difficulty in establishing relevantly similar situations. In other words, if there is no 'special legal status' involved, there is no ground for holding same-sex couples and different-sex couples not to be in a similar situation, as confirmed by the Court in *X. and Others* v. *Austria* (2013):

> 'The Court observes that, in contrast to the comparison with a married couple, it has not been argued that a special legal status exists which would distinguish an unmarried heterosexual couple from a same-sex couple.'[146]

Consequently the Court has also often found differences in treatment between same-sex unmarried partners and different-sex unmarried partners not to be justified. This has not, however, always been the case. During the 1980s and 1990s the European Commission of Human Rights accepted in various decisions that a difference in treatment between same-sex couples in stable relationships and

---

141 The Court chose this wording in ECtHR 12 May 2009, *Korelc* v. *Slovenia*, no. 28456/03, when referring to ECtHR [GC] 29 April 2008, *Burden* v. *the United Kingdom*, no. 13378/05, para. 65.

142 Cooper rightly observed that '[...] by holding that the relationship shared by cohabiting same-sex siblings was not qualitatively the same as that shared by civil partners, the ECtHR [had] not dilute[d] the significance of same-sex relationships in general'. Cooper 2011, *supra* n. 91, at p. 1759.

143 ECtHR 12 May 2009, *Korelc* v. *Slovenia*, no. 28456/03, para. 90, referring to ECtHR [GC] 29 April 2008, *Burden* v. *the United Kingdom*, no. 13378/05, para. 65.

144 ECtHR 23 June 2009 (dec.), *M.W.* v. *the United Kingdom*, no. 11313/02.

145 ECtHR [GC] 3 April 2012, *Van der Heijden* v. *the Netherlands*, no. 42857/05, para. 69.

146 ECtHR [GC] 19 February 2013, *X. a.o.* v. *Austria*, no. 19010/07, para. 112.

different-sex stable partners could be justified on grounds of the protection of the family. For instance, in a case concerning succession to the tenancy of a home by the cohabiting same-sex partner of the tenant, the Commission held:

> 'The Commission considers that the family (to which the relationship of heterosexual unmarried couples living together as husband and wife can be assimilated) merits special protection in society and it sees no reason why a High Contracting Party should not afford particular assistance to families. The Commission therefore accepts that the difference in treatment between the applicant and somebody in the same position whose partner had been of the opposite sex can be objectively and reasonably justified.'[147]

In subsequent cases where a complaint was lodged that the domestic immigration policy gave better protection to heterosexual couples than to homosexual couples, the Commission adopted the same reasoning. It held that no discrimination existed contrary to the Convention where the Immigration Rules gave priority and better guarantees 'to established couples living in a family relationship as opposed to other established relationships such as lesbian or homosexual relationships'.[148] The Commission found that the difference in treatment pursued the legitimate aim of '[...] protecting family based relationships (including relationships existing outside marriage) in a manner proportionate to the achievement of that aim.'[149]

Later – once the Court had established that same-sex relationships came within the scope of the right to respect for private life and particularly once it had held that they also enjoyed the right to respect for their family life (see 8.1.2 above) – the Court applied its strict scrutiny test in cases where a difference in treatment between unmarried partners was based on sexual orientation. It no longer accepted such differences in treatment on the ground of protection of the family, or any other ground.[150] As a result, differences in treatment of unmarried same-sex couples and unmarried different-sex couples in respect of matters like tenancy,[151] the extension of insurance cover,[152] and also certain parental matters (see 8.3.7 below), have been held to constitute discrimination on grounds of sexual orientation in violation of Article 14 ECHR.

Moreover, in 2013 the Grand Chamber of the Court found in *Vallianatos and Others*[153] that States which have introduced a registered partnership in their national

---

147 ECmHR 14 May 1986 (dec.), *S.* v. *the United Kingdom*, no. 11716/85, para. 7. See also ECmHR 9 October 1989 (dec.), *C. and L.M.* v. *the United Kingdom*, no. 14753/89, para. 2 and ECmHR 10 February 1990 (dec.), *B.* v. *the United Kingdom*, no. 16106/90, para. 2.

148 ECmHR 9 October 1989 (dec.), *C. and L.M.* v. *the United Kingdom*, no. 14753/89, para. 2.

149 ECmHR 10 February 1990 (dec.), *B.* v. *the United Kingdom*, no. 16106/90, para. 2.

150 ECtHR 22 July 2010, *P.B. and J.S.* v. *Austria*, no. 18984/02. In some cases (such as *Gas and Dubois* as discussed above), the Court found no difference in treatment as unmarried different-sex couples and unmarried same-sex couples were treated alike in respect of a certain matter (in *Gas and Dubois* in respect of second-parent adoption).

151 ECtHR 24 July 2003, *Karner* v. *Austria*, no. 40016/98. See 8.1.4 above.

152 ECtHR 22 July 2010, *P.B. and J.S.* v. *Austria*, no. 18984/02.

153 ECtHR [GC] 7 November 2013, *Vallianatos a.o.* v. *Greece*, nos. 29381/09 and 32684/09.

laws may not limit access to that civil status to different-sex couples only. Greece was one of the two Council of Europe Member States that had introduced a civil union that was open to different-sex couples only. The applicants in this case were four same-sex couples and a LGBT interest group, who complained that this law was discriminatory. The Chamber relinquished jurisdiction in this case to the Grand Chamber.

The Court delimited the scope of the case and explicitly held that the applicants' complaint did not relate '[...] in the abstract to a general obligation on the Greek State to provide for a form of legal recognition in domestic law for same-sex relationships.' Their complaint was not '[...] that the Greek State failed to comply with any positive obligation which might be imposed on it by the Convention'.[154] The issue to be examined was therefore

> '[...] whether the Greek State was entitled, from the standpoint of Articles 14 and 8 of the Convention, to enact a law introducing alongside the institution of marriage a new registered partnership scheme for unmarried couples that was limited to different-sex couples and thus excluded same-sex couples'.[155]

Under reference to *Schalk and Kopf*, the Court held that the applicants were in a comparable situation to different-sex couples as regards their need for legal recognition and protection of their relationship.[156] It also had no difficulty in establishing that the relevant Greek law had introduced a difference in treatment based on sexual orientation.[157] The government had put forward two sets of arguments to justify this difference. The first was readily dismissed by the Court. It found the argument that the applicants could already provide for the rights and obligations involved in civil unions on a contractual basis unconvincing because this argument disregarded that the Greek civil partnership '[...] as an officially recognised alternative to marriage [had] an intrinsic value for the applicants irrespective of the legal effects, however narrow or extensive, that they would produce'.[158] Also, the option of entering into a civil partnership would have been the only opportunity available to same-sex partners under Greek law '[...] of formalising their relationship by conferring on it a legal status recognised by the State', which would allow them '[...] to regulate issues concerning property, maintenance and inheritance not as private individuals entering into contracts under the ordinary law but on the basis of the legal rules governing civil unions, thus having their relationship officially recognised by the State.'[159]

The government had further alleged that the relevant legislation aimed to protect children born out of wedlock, to protect single-parent families, to respond to the

154 *Idem*, para. 75.
155 *Idem*, para. 75.
156 *Idem*, para. 78.
157 *Idem*, para. 79.
158 *Idem*, para. 81.
159 *Idem*, para. 81.

wishes of parents to raise their children without being obliged to marry, and, ultimately, to strengthen the institutions of marriage and the family in the traditional sense.[160] In respect of these aims the Court considered the following:

> 'The Court considers it legitimate from the standpoint of Article 8 of the Convention for the legislature to enact legislation to regulate the situation of children born outside marriage and also indirectly strengthen the institution of marriage within Greek society by promoting the notion, as explained by the Government, that the decision to marry would be taken purely on the basis of a mutual commitment entered into by two individuals, independently of outside constraints or of the prospect of having children [...]. The Court accepts that protection of the family in the traditional sense is, in principle, a weighty and legitimate reason which might justify a difference in treatment [...]. It goes without saying that the protection of the interests of the child is also a legitimate aim [...].'[161]

The Court was not, however, convinced that it was necessary, in pursuit of the legitimate aims which the Greek government invoked, to bar same-sex couples from entering into the civil unions. It noted that the Greek civil union had been designed 'first and foremost' to afford legal recognition to a new form of non-marital partnership, which allowed different-sex couples, whether or not they had children, 'to regulate numerous aspects of their relationship'.[162] The Greek government had not justified why same-sex couples without children were treated differently from different-sex couples without children.[163] While different-sex couples had no less than three ways to have their relationship legally recognised (marriage, civil union or *de facto* partnerships), same-sex couples had none. The Court held that:

> '[c]onsequently, same-sex couples would have a particular interest in entering into a civil union since it would afford them, unlike different-sex couples, the sole basis in Greek law on which to have their relationship legally recognised.'[164]

The Court considered it possible for the legislature '[...] to include some provisions dealing specifically with children born outside marriage, while at the same time extending to same-sex couples the general possibility of entering into a civil union.'[165] It noted 'in addition' that a trend was emerging with regard to the introduction of forms of legal recognition of same-sex relationships. Out of the nineteen who opted to enact some form of partnership other than marriage, only two States, Lithuania and Greece, reserved it exclusively to different-sex couples.[166] The Court concluded that the government had not given convincing and weighty reasons capable of justifying the exclusion of same-sex couples from the Greek civil union and found a violation of Article 14 taken in conjunction with Article 8 ECHR.

---

160 *Idem*, para. 80.
161 ECtHR [GC] 7 November 2013, *Vallianatos a.o.* v. *Greece*, nos. 29381/09 and 32684/09, para. 83.
162 *Idem*, para. 88.
163 *Idem*, para. 89.
164 *Idem*, para. 90.
165 *Idem*, para. 89. The implications of this finding are further discussed below in section 8.2.6.
166 *Idem*, para. 91.

The judgment gives the impression that there is no room for any conclusion other than that also different-sex couples who wish to have access to a registered partnership that is available in their country for same-sex couples only, can take a successful case before the ECtHR.[167] Still, it is not entirely ruled out that the Court would in those cases accept that the difference in treatment could be justified because different-sex couples have the alternative and 'real option'[168] of concluding a marriage. This point is further developed in subsection 8.2.5 below, where the role of existing alternative forms of registration in the ECtHR's case law is discussed.

8.2.4. Parental rights for same-sex couples

As discussed above in section 8.1.2 above, for a long time the Commission and the Court ruled that same-sex relationships did not enjoy protection of the right to respect for family life under Article 8 ECHR. This also had implications for the parental rights of persons in same-sex relationships. For instance, in a case of 1992, where a woman wished to get parental rights over the child of her female partner, the Commission was of the opinion

> '[...] that the [...] positive obligations of a State under Article 8 do not go so far as to require that a woman such as the first applicant, living together with the mother of a child and the child itself, should be entitled to get parental rights over the child. The Commission therefore considers that there has been no interference with the applicants' right to respect for their family life. [...] the relationship of a homosexual couple constitutes a matter affecting their private life. However, the Commission considers that the statutory impossibility for the first applicant to be vested with the parental authority over the third applicant does not entail any restriction in the applicants' enjoyment of their private life.'[169]

Later, the Court made clear that sexual orientation may not be the decisive factor in decisions on parental rights. The applicant in *Salgueiro da Silva Mouta* (1999)[170] was a homosexual who lived with another man. The national judge had awarded parental responsibility for the applicant's daughter to his ex-wife rather than to himself. In granting the custody to the child's mother, the national court had stated that the child had to live in 'a traditional Portuguese family', that homosexuality was an abnormality and that children were not to grow up 'in the shadow of abnormal situations'. The ECtHR considered that the judgment of the domestic court

[167] N.R. Koffeman, 'Case note to ECtHR [GC] 19 February 2013, *X. a.o.* v. *Austria*, no. 19010/07', 14 *European Human Rights Cases* 2013/104 (in Dutch).

[168] See the *Hämäläinen* judgment as discussed in section 8.2.5 below.

[169] ECmHR 19 May 1992 (dec.), *Kerkhoven and Hinke* v. *the Netherlands*, no. 15666/89. See also ECtHR [GC] 22 April 1997, *X, Y and Z* v. *the United Kingdom*, no. 21830/93. The latter case concerned *X*, a female-to-male transsexual who was living in a stable relationship with a woman, *Y*, and their child, *Z*, born after artificial insemination with donated sperm. The applicants complained that *X*'s role as *Z*'s father was not recognised and that their situation amounted to discrimination. Noting that transsexuality raised complex issues in respect of which there was no generally shared approach in Europe, the Court found no violation of the right to respect for family life (Art. 8 ECHR).

[170] ECtHR 21 December 1999, *Salgueiro da Silva Mouta* v. *Portugal*, no. 33290/96.

constituted an interference with the applicant's right to respect for his family life as protected under Article 8 ECHR. It found that the applicant's homosexuality had been a decisive factor in the final decision and ruled that the distinction based on considerations regarding the applicant's sexual orientation constituted a violation of Article 8 taken in conjunction with Article 14.[171] In view of that conclusion the Court did not consider it necessary to rule on the allegation of a violation of Article 8 taken alone.

Yet later the Court brought same-sex relationships within the scope of the right to respect for family life.[172] This holds not only for the relationship between the partners but also for their relationships with children born and/or raised within those relationships.[173] The right to respect for family life presupposes the existence of a family and does not safeguard the mere desire to found a family.[174] Where family life has not yet been established, for example in joint adoption cases, the right to respect for private life generally applies.

Most complaints lodged with the ECtHR in respect of parental rights of same-sex couples have been phrased as discrimination complaints. Same-sex couples or individuals with a homosexual orientation have claimed entitlement to the same rights as different-sex couples or heterosexual individuals. Parental matters further often concern issues which in themselves do not constitute rights under the Convention, for example adoption, but which nonetheless come within its scope. As will become clear from the discussion below, in those situations where a State has voluntarily created a particular right or entitlement at the national level, it is not allowed to take discriminatory measures when it comes to applying it.[175]

The following subsections discuss the Court's case law on parental rights for same-sex couples and lesbians and gays thematically, addressing matters like adoption (subsection 8.2.4.1), legal parenthood by operation of the law (subsection 8.2.4.2) and access to AHR treatment (subsection 8.2.4.3). Some of the relevant cases, or aspects thereof, have yet been referred to or briefly discussed in section 8.2.3 above. Here, the focus lies not so much on the comparability question, but on the material findings of the Court.

It is noted that at the time this research was concluded (i.e., 31 July 2014), there were two more French cases pending before the ECtHR which related to parental matters. The one application concerned two female PACS partners, who both had a child using medically assisted procreation. They complained about the authorities' refusal to grant them parental authority each in respect of the other's child (see also

171 *Idem*, paras. 35–36.

172 ECtHR 24 June 2010, *Schalk and Kopf* v. *Austria*, no. 30141/04, paras. 91 and 94.

173 *Inter alia*, ECtHR [GC] 16 July 2014, *Hämäläinen* v. *Finland*, no. 37359/09, para. 85 (under reference to ECtHR 24 June 2010, *Schalk and Kopf* v. *Austria*, no. 30141/04, paras. 91 and 94) and ECtHR 15 March 2012, *Gas and Dubois* v. *France*, no. 25951/07. See also ECtHR [GC] 19 February 2013, *X. a.o.* v. *Austria*, no. 19010/07.

174 ECtHR 13 June 1979, *Marckx* v. *Belgium*, no. 6833/74, para. 31 See also ch. 2, section 2.1.3.

175 ECtHR [GC] 22 January 2008, *E.B.* v. *France*, no. 43546/02.

Chapter 2, section 2.3.6).[176] In the other case two female PACS partners complained about the refusal to grant one of them paternity leave on the occasion of the birth of her partner's child.[177]

8.2.4.1. Adoption by same-sex partners or couples

The ECtHR has repeatedly held that '[a]doption means "providing a child with a family, not a family with a child"'.[178] Accordingly, where a family tie is established between a parent and a child, '[...] particular importance must be attached to the best interests of the child, which, depending on their nature and seriousness, may override those of the parent'.[179] While the ECtHR has only ruled in cases concerning single-parent adoption and second-parent adoption, the implications of this case law for successive adoption and joint adoption are also discussed.

8.2.4.1.1. Single-parent adoption

The ECtHR's case law in respect of single-parent adoption by homosexuals, has evolved over the years. Two French cases are the main authorities in this regard. In *Fretté* (2002),[180] a homosexual man complained under Article 14 in combination with Article 8 ECHR about the refusal by the French authorities of his request for authorisation to adopt a child, on the ground that owing to his 'choice of lifestyle' the applicant did not provide the requisite safeguards for adopting a child. The Court concluded on the basis of the case file that this criterion 'implicitly yet undeniably made the applicant's homosexuality the decisive factor' and that the refusal for authorisation was thus based on the applicant's sexual orientation.[181] This was ground for the Court to hold Article 14 taken in conjunction with Article 8 applicable in the case.[182]

According to the Court there was 'no doubt' that this refusal pursued a legitimate aim, namely to protect the health and rights of children who could be involved in an adoption procedure.[183] The Court considered it impossible 'to find in the legal and

176 *Francine Bonnaud and Patricia Lecoq* v. *France* (no. 6190/11), communicated on 3 February 2012. In May 2013 the Court invited the government to submit observations 'in the light of the judgments in *Gas and Dubois* v. *France* and *X a.o.* v. *Austria*, and the adoption in France of the law of 17 May 2013 opening marriage to same sex couples.' See also ch. 2, section 2.3.6.

177 *Hallier and Lucas* v. *France*, no. 46386/10, application communicated to the French Government on 6 April 2011.

178 *Inter alia*, ECtHR 26 February 2002, *Fretté* v. *France*, no. 36515/97, para. 42.

179 ECtHR 26 February 2002, *Fretté* v. *France*, no. 36515/97, para. 42, under reference to ECtHR 16 November 1999, *E.P.* v. *Italy*, no. 31127/96, para 62 and ECtHR 7 August 1996, *Johansen* v. *Norway*, no. 17383/90, para. 78.

180 ECtHR 26 February 2002, *Fretté* v. *France*, no. 36515/97.

181 *Idem*, para. 32.

182 *Idem*, paras. 32–33. Judge Costa, joined by Judges Jungwiert and Traja, was very critical of this finding in his partly concurring opinion to the judgment. He called the majority's reasoning on this point circular. Partly concurring opinion by Judge Costa, joined by Judges Jungwiert and Traja to ECtHR 26 February 2002, *Fretté* v. *France*, no. 36515/97.

183 *Idem*, para. 38. The respondent government had asserted that the difference in treatment stemmed from the doubts that prevailed, in view of what was at the time known about the subject, about the

social orders of the Contracting States uniform principles on these social issues' and it observed that 'generally speaking', the law appeared to be in a transitional stage. For these reasons, the Court left States a wide margin of appreciation to make rulings on such matters.[184] In respect of the competing interests of the applicant and children eligible for adoption, the Court noted that the scientific community was divided over the possible consequences of a child being adopted by one or more homosexual parents. Also, until that time only a limited number of scientific studies had been conducted on the subject and there were wide differences in national and international opinion.[185] The Court concluded that the refusal to authorise adoption had not infringed the principle of proportionality and that, accordingly, the justification given by the government appeared objective and reasonable and the difference in treatment complained of was not discriminatory within the meaning of Article 14 ECHR.[186] Three dissenting Judges noted that the refusal had been based '[...] on the view that to be brought up by homosexual parents would be harmful to the child at all events and under any circumstances'. They pointed out that the domestic authorities and courts had failed to explain why and how the child's interests militated in the instant case against the authorisation of the applicant's adoption request.[187]

Six years later, in the case of *E.B.* v. *France* (2008),[188] the Grand Chamber reversed this position.[189] This time a woman who was living with another woman in a stable same-sex relationship, was refused authorisation to adopt a child. The Court explained the subject-matter of the case and its approach in the case as follows:

> 'The present case does not concern adoption by a couple or by the same-sex partner of a biological parent, but solely adoption by a single person. Whilst Article 8 of the Convention is silent as to this question, the Court notes that French legislation expressly grants single persons the right to apply for authorisation to adopt and establishes a procedure to that end. Accordingly, the Court considers that the facts of this case undoubtedly fall within the ambit of Article 8 of the Convention. Consequently, the State, which has gone beyond its obligations under Article 8 in creating such a right – a possibility open to it under Article 53 of the Convention – cannot, in the application of that right, take discriminatory measures within the meaning of Article 14 [...].'[190]

development of a child brought up by a homosexual and deprived of a dual maternal and paternal role model. It held (as quoted in para. 36 of the judgment) that '[t]here was no consensus about the potential impact of being adopted by an adult who openly affirmed his homosexuality on a child's psychological development and, more generally, his or her future life, and the question divided both experts on childhood and democratic societies as a whole.'

184 *Idem*, para. 41. The Court considered it 'quite natural' to leave such a wide margin.

185 ECtHR 26 February 2002, *Fretté* v. *France*, no. 36515/97, para. 42.

186 *Idem*, paras. 42–43.

187 Joint partly dissenting opinion of Judge Sir Nicolas Bratza and Judges Fuhrmann and Tulkens to ECtHR 26 February 2002, *Fretté* v. *France*, no. 36515/97.

188 ECtHR [GC] 22 January 2008, *E.B.* v. *France*, no. 43546/02.

189 See also K.A. Doty, 'From *Fretté* to *E.B.*: The European Court of Human Rights on Gay and Lesbian Adoption', 18 *Law and Sexuality Rev. Lesbian Gay Bisexual & Legal Issues* (2009) p. 121.

190 ECtHR [GC] 22 January 2008, *E.B.* v. *France*, no. 43546/02, para. 49.

The Court held that although the authorities had based their decision on an overall assessment of the applicant's situation, two grounds played a primordial role in the decision-making, namely the lack of a 'paternal referent' in the applicant's household or immediate circle of family and friends and the lack of commitment on the part of her declared partner. According to the Court these grounds had to be assessed concurrently, implying that the illegitimacy of one ground contaminated the entire decision.[191] While the second main ground was reasonable and had nothing to do with any consideration relating to the applicant's sexual orientation, the first ground could have served as a pretext for rejecting the applicant's application on grounds of her homosexuality.[192] The illegitimacy of this ground had 'the effect of contaminating the entire decision'.[193] After a detailed examination of the domestic authorities' reasoning, the Court concluded that the applicant's avowed homosexuality had indeed influenced the assessment of her application and had been a determining factor in refusing her authorisation to adopt.[194] The applicant had therefore suffered a difference in treatment, the Grand Chamber held.[195]

The Court reiterated that a difference in treatment based on sexual orientation could only be justified if 'particularly convincing and weighty reasons' were present[196] and that differences in treatment based solely on considerations regarding the applicant's sexual orientation amounted to discrimination in violation of the Convention.[197] The Grand Chamber pointed out that under French law any unmarried person, man or woman, was allowed to adopt and that it was not disputed that this opened up the possibility of adoption by a single person with a homosexual orientation. The Court considered the reasons put forward by the government[198] not particularly convincing and weighty such as to justify refusing to grant the applicant authorisation. The authorities had made a distinction on the basis of the applicant's sexual orientation which was therefore not acceptable under the Convention.[199] With ten votes to seven, the Court found a violation of Article 14 taken in conjunction with Article 8 ECHR. The dissenting Judges all had difficulties with the 'contamination theory' propounded by the majority, following which also the second ground for the refusal – the lack of commitment on the part of the applicant's partner – could not in itself justify the adoption refusal.[200]

---

191 *Idem*, para. 80.
192 *Idem*, para. 71.
193 *Idem*, para. 80.
194 *Idem*, para. 89.
195 *Idem*, para. 90.
196 *Idem*, para. 91.
197 *Idem*, para. 93.
198 Para. 37 of the judgment reads: 'The reason for refusing [the adoption] authorisation had been dictated by the child's interests alone and had been based on two grounds: lack of a paternal referent and the ambivalence of the applicant's partner's commitment to her adoption plans.'
199 ECtHR [GC] 22 January 2008, *E.B.* v. *France*, no. 43546/02, para. 96.
200 Dissenting opinion of Judge Costa joined by Judges Türmen, Ugrekhelidze and Jočienė; dissenting opinion of Judge Zupančič, dissenting opinion of Judge Loucaides and dissenting opinion of Judge Mularoni to ECtHR [GC] 22 January 2008, *E.B.* v. *France*, no. 43546/02. See also the Concurring Opinion of Judges Lorenzen and Jebens to this judgment.

It is important to note that in these single-parent adoption cases no 'special' civil status was involved which could be held to (indirectly) set registered or married (different-sex) partners apart from (same-sex) stable partners (see 8.2.3.1 above). This was different in some cases concerning second-parent adoption.

8.2.4.1.2. Second-parent and successive adoption

The ECtHR has decided two cases concerning adoption of a child by the same-sex partner of the child's legal and genetic parent (second-parent adoption). In *Gas and Dubois* – as discussed in section 8.2.3.2 above – the Court held that the applicants, who were in a stable same-sex relationship, were not treated differently from different-sex unmarried partners in respect of second-parent adoption and therefore it found no violation of Article 14 ECHR in combination with Article 8. In *X. and Others* v. *Austria* (2013)[201] such a difference in treatment was instead established and the Court's reasoning for holding this treatment unjustified warrants a more extensive discussion at this place.

The *X. and Others* case concerned two women who were living together in a stable homosexual relationship. One of them had a son. She had sole custody of the child while his father had recognised paternity. The women had been living in a common household since the son was about five years old and cared for him jointly. In 2005 the women, wishing to obtain legal recognition of their *de facto* family unit, concluded an adoption agreement. The father of the child did not consent to the adoption, but the women submitted that it was in the best interests of the child and asked the competent district court to override his refusal to consent. The district court refused to approve the adoption agreement, because under the applicable provisions of the Austrian Civil Code, the child's adoption by the female partner of the mother would sever his relationship with his mother. The appeals court upheld this ruling, taking the view that the relevant Austrian law was clearly based on the premise that the term 'parents' necessarily referred to two persons of different sex. It noted furthermore that the child had two parents (his mother and father) and held that there was no need to replace one of them by an adoptive parent. The applicants appealed on points of law to the Supreme Court, holding that the relevant provisions of the Civil Code were unconstitutional, but in September 2006, this Court dismissed their appeal. The Supreme Court held that:

> '[n]ot least in view of the wide differences in national and international opinion concerning the possible consequences of a child being adopted by one or more homosexual parents, and bearing in mind the fact that there were not enough children to adopt to satisfy demand, States had to be allowed a broad margin of appreciation in this sphere'.[202]

The applicants had not demonstrated, nor was there any other evidence to suggest, that the relevant provisions of the Austrian Civil Code overstepped the margin

201 ECtHR [GC] 19 February 2013, *X. a.o.* v. *Austria*, no. 19010/07.
202 As quoted in ECtHR [GC] 19 February 2013, *X. a.o.* v. *Austria*, no. 19010/07, para. 20.

of appreciation accorded by the European Court, or that they infringed the proportionality principle. In 2010 the Austrian Registered Partnership entered into force, which explicitly outlawed second-parent adoption by same-sex registered partners.

Before the ECtHR the applicants complained that they had been discriminated against on grounds of sexual orientation because so-called second-parent adoption was possible for married or unmarried heterosexual couples but not for same-sex couples. Presumably having studied the ECtHR case law carefully, they focused on the unequal treatment between unmarried different-sex couples and unmarried same-sex couples and held that the gist of their complaint was that they were automatically excluded from any chance of adoption.[203] The respondent government on the other hand submitted that Austrian law gave priority to the biological parents when it came to the care of their child. Second-parent adoption was only to be authorised if it was clearly in the child's interests and if the replaced parent consented. In the case at hand there was no difference in treatment on grounds of sexual orientation, because decisive for the refusal of the adoption agreement had been that the father of the child did not consent to it. They furthermore argued that if the Court was to find a difference in treatment, 'recreating the biological family and securing the child's well-being' were legitimate aims.[204] The relevant law did not aim to exclude same-sex couples but sought, as a general rule, to avoid situations where a child had two mothers or two fathers for legal purposes. The government furthermore put forward that States enjoyed a wide margin of appreciation in the area of adoption law, in particular on the issue of second-parent adoption by same-sex couples.

The Chamber relinquished jurisdiction in favour of the Grand Chamber in this case. As set out in section 8.2.3.4 above, the Court found that the applicants were not in a similar situation to spouses in respect of second-parent adoption. It did accept, however, that their situation was comparable to that of unmarried different-sex couples.

The Court expressly delineated the scope of the case; it was not about the general question of same-sex couples' access to second-parent adoption, 'let alone [...] the question of adoption by same-sex couples in general', but only about the difference in treatment between unmarried different-sex couples and unmarried same-sex couples in respect of this type of adoption.[205] Also, it was not about the question of whether the adoption request of the applicants had to be granted in this particular case.[206] There was no obligation under Article 8 ECHR to extend the right to second-parent adoption to unmarried couples. Because the Austrian legislature had chosen to allow second-parent adoption by unmarried different-sex couples, however, the Court had to examine whether refusing that right to (unmarried) same-sex couples served a

[203] *Idem*, para. 66.
[204] *Idem*, para. 76.
[205] *Idem*, paras. 134 and 149.
[206] *Idem*, para. 152.

legitimate aim and was proportionate to that aim.[207] The central question was '[...] whether the applicants [had been] discriminated against on account of the fact that the courts had [had] no opportunity to examine in any meaningful manner whether the requested adoption was in the second applicant's interests, given that it [had] in any case [been] legally impossible.'[208]

The Austrian government had thus argued that the law was aimed at 'recreating the circumstances of a biological family'.[209] As the Court noted they '[...] relied on the protection of the traditional family, based on the tacit assumption that only a family with parents of different sex could adequately provide for a child's needs.' The Court reiterated that 'the protection of the family in the traditional sense' was, in principle, a weighty and legitimate reason which could potentially justify a difference in treatment on grounds of sexual orientation. It added that the protection of the interests of the child was indisputably a legitimate aim.[210]

As the Court thus quite readily accepted that the Austrian adoption law pursued a legitimate aim, the proportionality test proved crucial in the *X. and Others* case. The Court first reiterated the following principles:

> 'The aim of protecting the family in the traditional sense is rather abstract and a broad variety of concrete measures may be used to implement it [...]. Also, given that the Convention is a living instrument, to be interpreted in present-day conditions, the State, in its choice of means designed to protect the family and secure respect for family life as required by Article 8, must necessarily take into account developments in society and changes in the perception of social, civil-status and relational issues, including the fact that there is not just one way or one choice when it comes to leading one's family or private life [...].'[211]

The Court noted that where a difference in treatment on grounds of sexual orientation was concerned, a strict scrutiny test applied. The government had not adduced any evidence showing that it was not in the child's best interests to be raised by two parents of the same sex.[212] Quite the contrary, they had conceded that '[...] same-sex couples could be as suitable or unsuitable as different-sex couples when it came to adopting children'.[213] Also, single-parent adoption by persons in a same-sex relationship was possible under Austrian law. The Court found the domestic law incoherent; on the one hand it accepted that a child grew up with same-sex parents, 'thus accepting that this [was] not detrimental to the child', on the other hand it insisted that a child was not have two mothers or two fathers. The Court also stressed the importance of granting legal recognition to *de facto* family life and noted that second-parent

207 *Idem*, para. 136.
208 *Idem*, para. 152.
209 *Idem*, para. 137.
210 *Idem*, para. 138.
211 *Idem*, para. 139.
212 *Idem*, para. 142.
213 *Idem*, para. 142.

adoption was aimed at doing exactly that, as it served to confer rights *vis-à-vis* the child on the partner of one of the child's parents.[214] All in all, there was considerable doubt about the proportionality of the relevant Austrian law. The Court held:

> 'Unless any other particularly convincing and weighty reasons militate in favour of such an absolute prohibition, the considerations adduced so far would seem rather to weigh in favour of allowing the courts to carry out an examination of each individual case. This would also appear to be more in keeping with the best interests of the child, which is a key notion in the relevant international instruments […].'[215]

While yet the Court had earlier – albeit implicitly – noted that a narrow margin applied in this case, and had therefore applied a strict scrutiny test, it nonetheless next addressed the argument raised by the government that a wider margin of appreciation had to be accorded in the sphere of adoption law, as it involved the balancing of different interests, and as there was no European consensus on the issue of second-parent adoption by same-sex couples. The Court thereby implied that this would have been an argument that could justify the difference in treatment complained of.[216] Still, it was not accepted by the Strasbourg Court. The ECtHR reaffirmed that in situations involving a difference in treatment on the basis of sexual orientation, a narrow margin applied. In respect of the alleged absence of consensus, the Court took an unprecedented approach, which linked in with the way in which it had earlier delineated the scope of the case before it (see above). Because the case was only about the question of whether a State, once it decided to introduce second-parent adoption for unmarried couples, was allowed to differentiate between different-sex couples and same-sex couples,[217] only those States which allowed for second-parent adoption in unmarried couples could be used for comparison. This concerned a group of ten States, of which six allowed both same-sex and different-sex partners to adopt the child of their partners, while four had excluded same-sex couples from second-parent adoption. The Court held this sample to be too narrow to draw a conclusion as to the existence of a possible European consensus on this issue.[218]

The Court acknowledged that '[…] striking a balance between the protection of the family in the traditional sense and the Convention rights of sexual minorities [was] in the nature of things a difficult and delicate exercise, which [could] require the State to reconcile conflicting views and interests perceived by the parties concerned as

---

214 *Idem*, para. 145, referring to ECtHR 28 June 2007, *Wagner and J.M.W.L.* v. *Luxembourg*, no. 76240/01, para. 119; ECtHR 25 January 2007, *Eski* v. *Austria*, no. 21949/03, para. 39 and ECtHR 13 December 2007, *Emonet a.o. v. Switzerland*, no. 39051/03, paras. 63–64.

215 ECtHR [GC] 19 February 2013, *X. a.o.* v. *Austria*, no. 19010/07, para. 147, referring to ECtHR [GC] 22 January 2008, *E.B.* v. *France*, no. 43546/02, para. 95.

216 The Court held: 'The Government advanced another argument to justify the difference in treatment complained of. Relying on Art. 8 of the Convention, they asserted that the margin of appreciation was a wide one in the sphere of adoption law, which had to strike a careful balance between the interests of all the persons involved. In the present context it was even wider, as there was no European consensus on the issue of second-parent adoption by same-sex couples.' ECtHR [GC] 19 February 2013, *X. a.o.* v. *Austria*, no. 19010/07, para. 147.

217 ECtHR [GC] 19 February 2013, *X. a.o.* v. *Austria*, no. 19010/07, para. 149.

218 *Idem*, para. 149.

being in fundamental opposition [...]'.[219] It nonetheless found that the government had failed to adduce particularly weighty and convincing reasons to show that excluding second-parent adoption in a same-sex couple, while allowing that possibility in an unmarried different-sex couple, was necessary for the protection of the family in the traditional sense or for the protection of the interests of the child. The Court accordingly – by ten votes to seven – found a violation of Article 14 in conjunction with Article 8 of the Convention.

The seven Judges who wrote a dissenting opinion to this judgment held that the majority had gone 'beyond the usual limits of the evolutive method of interpretation'.[220] They were particularly critical of the Court's methodology in determining the relevant consensus, which resulted in an 'unduly technical – and hence reductive – view of the situation Europe-wide'. In their view 'a clear trend' was discernible whereby the great majority of the States Parties did 'not authorise second-parent adoption for unmarried couples in general, still less for unmarried same-sex couples' and held that this trend was reflected in international instruments.[221] The dissenters furthermore found that the Court should have paid more attention to the particular facts of the case, such as the fact that the father of the child objected to the adoption by his mother's female partner. It should also have considered what the best interests of the child required in this particular situation.

Both *Gas and Dubois* and *X. and Others* concerned second-parent adoption, whereby the legal mother whose same-sex partner wished to adopt her child, was also the biological and genetic mother of the child. The Court has not yet dealt with a case involving successive adoption, where a partner adopts the child of an adoptive parent. While this matter may be more sensitive for some States,[222] the emphasis the Court placed on legal recognition of *de facto* family life in the *X. and Others* judgment may equally apply in a case concerning successive adoption. It is, by contrast, exactly for the reason that no family life has yet been established that joint adoption may be distinguished from this situation.

8.2.4.1.3. Joint adoption

The Court has so far not dealt with any complaint of same-sex couples who were not allowed to jointly adopt a child.[223] The *X. and Others* case gives ground for concluding that where the legislation of a State allows different-sex unmarried, but not same-sex unmarried couples to jointly adopt, this would constitute discrimination contrary to Article 14 ECHR. As noted above, it may also be, however, that the Court would attach (decisive) weight to the fact that in that situation no family life has been established. Further, if the national law allows only spouses to jointly adopt a child,

---

219 *Idem*, para. 151, under reference to ECtHR 2 March 2010, *Kozak* v. *Poland*, no. 13102/02, para. 99.

220 Joint partly dissenting opinion of Judges Casadevall, Ziemele, Kovler, Jočienė, Šikuta, De Gaetano and Sicilianos to ECtHR [GC] 19 February 2013, *X. a.o.* v. *Austria*, no. 19010/07, para. 23.

221 *Idem*, para. 15.

222 See as an illustration Ch. 10, section 10.3.5.3.

223 It is recalled that this research was concluded on 31 July 2014.

while marriage is open to different-sex couples only under the relevant jurisdiction, the Court may rule that, because of the special status of marriage, same-sex couples are not in a relevantly similar situation to spouses in respect of the joint adoption of a child.

8.2.4.2. Legal parenthood by operation of the law

So far the Court has ruled in only one case concerning legal parenthood for same-sex partners in situations other than adoption. The applicants in *Boeckel and Gessner-Boeckel* (2013)[224] were two German women, Ms. Sabine Boeckel and Ms. Anja Gessner-Boeckel who had entered into a civil partnership (*Eingetragenes Lebenspartnershaft*) in 2001. In 2008 Ms. Anja Gessner-Boeckel gave birth to a son. The birth certificate issued named her as the child's mother, but left the space provided in the form for the father's name blank. The competent Court subsequently granted an adoption order, allowing for the adoption of the child by Ms. Sabine Boeckel. The child thereby was legally recognised as a child of both applicants. In the meantime the applicants requested the competent District Court to rectify the child's birth certificate, by inserting Ms. Sabine Boeckel as the child's second parent. They put forward that under German law the father was the man who was married to the mother of the child at the time of birth, whether he was also the biological father of the child or not, and claimed that this presumption had to be applied analogously to their situation.

As discussed above in section 8.2.3.2, the Court ruled that the applicants were not in a relevantly similar situation to that of a married different-sex couple in which the wife gave birth to a child. The Court accepted that biological differences between different-sex couples and same-sex couples, which had also been grounds for the relevant domestic law, decisively distinguished these groups in this respect. It held:

> 'The Court takes note of the domestic courts' reasoning according to which section 1592 § 1 of the Civil Code contained the – rebuttable – presumption that the man who was married to the child's mother at the time of birth was indeed the child's biological father. This principle is not called into question by the fact that this legal presumption might not always reflect the true descent. The Court also notes that it is not confronted with a case concerning transgender or surrogate parenthood. Accordingly, in case one partner of a same-sex partnership gives birth to a child, it can be ruled out on biological grounds that the child descended from the other partner. The Court accepts that, under these circumstances, there is no factual foundation for a legal presumption that the child descended from the second partner.'[225]

Because there was thus no appearance of a violation of the Convention, the Court declared this complaint manifestly ill-founded. This decision leaves unanswered the question of whether the Court would have come to a different conclusion if same-sex

---

[224] ECtHR 7 May 2013 (dec.), *Boeckel and Gessner-Boeckel* v. *Germany*, no. 8017/11.
[225] *Idem*, para. 30.

couples and different-sex couples who had acquired the same civil status (e.g. both spouses), would have been treated differently in this regard.[226]

8.2.4.3. Access to AHR treatment

As discussed in Chapter 2, in the case *S.H. and Others* v. *Austria* (2011),[227] the Court ruled that '[...] the right of a couple to conceive a child and to make use of medically assisted procreation for that purpose is also protected by Article 8, as such a choice is an expression of private and family life'.[228] The Court has not made explicit whether the term 'couple' in this context includes same-sex couples.

The question of whether in respect of access to AHR treatment same-sex couples are in a comparable situation to different-sex couples, was shortly addressed in *Gas and Dubois* (see 8.2.3.2 above).[229] In this case, the Court dismissed the applicants' complaint that they were discriminated against on the ground of their sexual orientation because under French law IVF treatment with the use of anonymously donated gametes was available only to married and cohabiting different-sex couples of reproductive age, and for therapeutic purposes only. The applicants had not brought this complaint before the national courts, which in itself was a ground for declaring this part of the complaint inadmissible for non-exhaustion of domestic remedies. The ECtHR, however, in addition noted that such treatment was available in France only for different-sex couples and '[...] for therapeutic purposes only, with a view in particular to remedying clinically diagnosed infertility or preventing the transmission of a particularly serious disease'. Without explaining this further, the Court considered that this situation was not comparable to that of the applicants and held that they were therefore no victim of a difference in treatment.[230]

In the *Gas and Dubois* case,[231] civil status was not the decisive distinguishing factor as under French law cohabiting different-sex couples could also acquire access to AHR treatment. The fact that AHR treatment was furthermore only available for specific therapeutic reasons, may thus have been even more important for the Court to find that the situations were not comparable. This may prove indicative for future cases. On the other hand, as the Court did not explain its finding any further, not too many conclusions can be drawn from this case. It is, for instance, insufficiently clear if States are allowed to generally limit access to AHR treatment to different-sex couples only.[232] The area of AHR treatment is in any case one in which the Court is generally reluctant to intervene with State practices. It has left States a wide margin of appreciation both in respect of their decision to intervene in the area and, '[...]

---

226 See Loenen 2013, *supra* n. 112, at p. 643.

227 ECtHR [GC] 3 November 2011, *S.H. a.o.* v. *Austria*, no. 57813/00. See ch. 2, section 2.3.3.

228 *Idem*, para. 82.

229 ECtHR 15 March 2012, *Gas and Dubois* v. *France*, no. 25951/07.

230 *Idem*, para. 63.

231 See section 8.2.3.2 above.

232 Koffeman 2012A, *supra* n. 138.

once having intervened, to the detailed rules it lays down in order to achieve a balance between the competing public and private interests' (see also Chapter 2).[233]

8.2.5. The role of existing alternative forms of registration in the Court's case law

The ECtHR case law paints a mixed picture when it comes to how alternative forms of recognition of relationships are weighed in the Court's assessment of a complaint. In a judgment of 2007 the Court had held that it was not for the national authorities to take the place of those concerned in reaching a decision regarding the form of communal life they wished to adopt. The case concerned a man who wished to adopt the child of his partner, but under the relevant domestic law this was only possible if the parental links between the mother and her daughter were severed. The government had asserted that the links would not be severed if the couple married, but the Court thus refuted that it was not for the authorities to take the applicants' place in deciding on their 'form of communal life'.[234]

In *Van der Heijden* (2012) a different view was expressed. The applicant had been cohabiting with her partner for more than 18 years and wished to be exempted from testifying against him in a criminal case, just like spouses and registered partners who were entitled to immunity from testifying against their spouses or registered partners respectively under Dutch law. The Court held that the applicant had had realistic options to have her relationship formally registered and that she therefore had to accept the legal consequences of having chosen not take up such options:

> 'The applicant has chosen not to register, formally, her union and no criticism can be made of her in this regard. However, having made that choice she must accept the legal consequence that flows therefrom, namely that she has maintained herself outside the scope of the "protected" family relationship to which the "testimonial privilege" exception attaches. That being so, the Court does not consider that the alleged interference with her family life was so burdensome or disproportionate as to imperil her interests unjustifiably.'[235]

The Court in this case thus held that authorities may legitimately ask from a couple to have their relationship formally registered in order to enjoy certain rights.

The argument that an alternative registration option was available has also played a role in the ECtHR's case law on the effects of gender reassignments on pre-existing marriages. As discussed above (see section 8.2.1), in cases pre-dating *Schalk and Kopf* the Court held the fact that such couples could conclude a civil partnership under which they enjoyed 'many of the protections and benefits of married status' to be of 'of some relevance to the proportionality of the effects of the gender

---

233 ECtHR [GC] 3 November 2011, *S.H. a.o.* v. *Austria*, no. 57813/00, para. 97.

234 ECtHR 13 December 2007, *Emonet a.o.* v. *Switzerland*, no. 39051/03, para. 82.

235 ECtHR [GC] 3 April 2012, *Van der Heijden* v. *the Netherlands*, no. 42857/05, para. 76.

recognition regime'.[236] A similar issue arose in the more recent case of *Hämäläinen* (2014),[237] where a male-to-female transsexual complained that the full recognition of her post-operative sex was made conditional on the transformation of her marriage into a civil partnership.

In the *Hämäläinen* case the Chamber in 2012 had found no violation of the Convention.[238] In its assessment of the complaint under Article 8 ECHR (the right to respect for private life) the Chamber had considered that there were two competing rights which needed to be balanced against each other, '[...] namely the applicant's right to respect for her private life by obtaining a new female identity number and the State's interest to maintain the traditional institution of marriage intact.' The Chamber noted that the applicant had two options: to have her marriage converted into a civil partnership, or to divorce.[239] It found that civil partnership, which provided legal protection for same-sex couples and which was almost identical to that of marriage, was a 'real option' for the applicant.[240] The Court furthermore noted that the applicant's child, would not be adversely affected if her marriage were turned into a civil partnership, as the applicant's rights and obligations arising either from paternity or parenthood would not be altered in such circumstances.[241] The Chamber concluded that a fair balance had been struck between the competing interests in the case before it and that there was therefore no violation of Article 8 ECHR.[242] In view of those findings, the Chamber found it unnecessary to examine the facts of the case separately under Article 12 of the Convention.

At the request of the applicant, the case was referred to the Grand Chamber, which in July 2014 confirmed the Chamber's finding that the Convention had not been violated in this case.[243] The Grand Chamber, however, chose a different approach in assessing the complaint under Article 8 ECHR, which it found to be applicable under both its private-life and family-life aspects.[244] Instead of examining it as a case in which the applicant's Article 8 rights had been interfered with, the Grand Chamber considered it more appropriate to analyse the applicant's complaint with regard to the positive aspect of that Article. It accordingly held that the question to be determined by the Court was:

---

236 In *Schalk and Kopf* the Court itself explained that in *Parry* and *R.F.* it had '[...] considered that, should they chose to divorce in order to allow the transsexual partner to obtain full gender recognition, the fact that the applicants had the possibility to enter into a civil partnership contributed to the proportionality of the gender recognition regime complained of.' ECtHR 24 June 2010, *Schalk and Kopf* v. *Austria*, no. 30141/04, para. 53.

237 ECtHR [GC] 16 July 2014, *Hämäläinen* v. *Finland*, no. 37359/09.

238 ECtHR 12 November 2012, *H.* v. *Finland*, no. 37359/09.

239 *Idem*, para. 50.

240 *Idem*, para. 50.

241 *Idem*, para. 51.

242 *Idem*, para. 52.

243 ECtHR [GC] 16 July 2014, *Hämäläinen* v. *Finland*, no. 37359/09. While the name of the applicant had been anonymised in the Chamber judgment, it was revealed in the Grand Chamber ruling.

244 *Idem*, para. 61.

'[...] whether respect for the applicant's private and family life entail[ed] a positive obligation on the State to provide an effective and accessible procedure allowing the applicant to have her new gender legally recognised while remaining married.'[245]

The three Judges who wrote a joint dissenting opinion to this judgment disagreed in doctrinal terms with this approach and held that the granting of a new identity card neither required any major steps by the authorities, nor entailed important social or economic implications.[246]

The Court was mindful of the fact that the applicant was not advocating same-sex marriage in general but merely wanted to preserve her own marriage.[247] However, according to the Court accepting the applicant's claim 'would in practice lead to a situation in which two persons of the same sex could be married to each other', and such was outlawed under Finnish law. The Court therefore held that it first had to examine whether the recognition of such a right was required in the circumstances by Article 8 of the Convention.[248]

The Court reiterated that Article 8 ECHR could not be interpreted as imposing an obligation on Contracting States to grant same-sex couples access to marriage. It noted that there was no European consensus on allowing same-sex marriages, nor was there any consensus in those States which did not allow same-sex marriages as to how to deal with gender recognition in the case of a pre-existing marriage. Because of this absence of a European consensus and because the case at stake 'undoubtedly' raised 'sensitive moral or ethical issues', the Court considered that the margin of appreciation to be afforded to the respondent State 'still' had to be a wide one.[249] The dissenters disagreed also on this point, pointing out that the margin was to be narrow, where a particularly important facet of an individual's existence or identity was at stake. Also, they adduced that proof of the existence of a consensus was not to depend 'on the existence of a common approach in a super-majority of States' and that the Court had some discretion regarding its acknowledgment of trends.[250]

The majority of the Court found that the applicant had several options under Finnish law, including maintaining the status quo, converting her marriage into a registered partnership or divorce. In respect of the second option, around which the complaint revolved, the Court held that the differences between a marriage and a registered partnership were 'not such as to involve an essential change in the applicant's legal situation' and that the applicant would be able 'to continue enjoying in essence, and in practice, the same legal protection under a registered partnership as afforded by

245 *Idem*, para. 64.
246 Joint dissenting opinion of Judges Sajó, Keller and Lemmens, to ECtHR [GC] 16 July 2014, *Hämäläinen* v. *Finland*, no. 37359/09, para. 4.
247 ECtHR [GC] 16 July 2014, *Hämäläinen* v. *Finland*, no. 37359/09, para. 70.
248 Critical on this point was Judge Ziemele in her concurring opinion to the *Hämäläinen* judgment.
249 ECtHR [GC] 16 July 2014, *Hämäläinen* v. *Finland*, no. 37359/09, para. 75.
250 Joint dissenting opinion of Judges Sajó, Keller and Lemmens to ECtHR [GC] 16 July 2014, *Hämäläinen* v. *Finland*, no. 37359/09, para. 5, under reference to ECtHR [GC] 7 November 2013, *Vallianatos a.o.* v. *Greece*, nos. 29381/09 and 32684/09, para. 91.

marriage'.[251] This was the third assumption underlying the majority's reasoning with which the dissenters disagreed. They felt that the majority had overlooked the fact that the applicant and her wife felt united by a religious conviction which did not allow the transformation of their relationship into a partnership.[252]

What was furthermore specific to the *Hämäläinen* case was that in the case of the conversion of her marriage into a registered partnership, the applicant and her family would not lose any of the rights which they had earlier established by marrying, and it would not affect the paternity of the applicant's child, nor the responsibility for the care, custody or maintenance of the child. The effect of the conversion of the marriage into a registered partnership on the applicant's family life would thus be 'minimal or non-existent'.[253] The Court concluded that the Convention had not been violated, noting the following:

> 'While it is regrettable that the applicant faces daily situations in which the incorrect identity number creates inconvenience for her, the Court considers that the applicant has a genuine possibility of changing that state of affairs: her marriage can be converted at any time, *ex lege*, into a registered partnership with the consent of her spouse. If no such consent is obtained, the possibility of divorce, as in any marriage, is always open to her. In the Court's view, it is not disproportionate to require, as a precondition to legal recognition of an acquired gender, that the applicant's marriage be converted into a registered partnership as that is a genuine option which provides legal protection for same-sex couples that is almost identical to that of marriage [...]. The minor differences between these two legal concepts are not capable of rendering the current Finnish system deficient from the point of view of the State's positive obligation.'[254]

The applicant had further submitted before the Grand Chamber that the Court had to assess under Article 12 whether the compulsory termination of marriage affected 'the substance of the right to marry' in line with the Court's case law. The Grand Chamber, however, found as the Chamber had done, that this question had already been examined under Article 8 and had resulted in the finding of no violation of that Convention right. In these circumstances, the Court considered that no separate issue arose under Article 12, and accordingly made no separate finding under that Article.[255]

As noted above, the three dissenters in this case felt that the case had to be examined from the perspective of negative instead of positive obligations under the Convention. They concluded that the applicant had suffered an interference with her Article 8 rights and noted that the only two legitimate aims that could possibly be claimed

---

251 ECtHR [GC] 16 July 2014, *Hämäläinen* v. *Finland*, no. 37359/09, para. 83, referring *mutatis mutandis* to ECtHR 24 June 2010, *Schalk and Kopf* v. *Austria*, no. 30141/04, para. 109.

252 Joint dissenting opinion of Judges Sajó, Keller and Lemmens, to ECtHR [GC] 16 July 2014, *Hämäläinen* v. *Finland*, no. 37359/09, para.8.

253 ECtHR [GC] 16 July 2014, *Hämäläinen* v. *Finland*, no. 37359/09, paras. 84–86.

254 *Idem*, para. 87.

255 *Idem*, para. 97.

to be pursued by this interference were the protection of the rights and freedoms of others or morals. They were brief in rejecting the first aim, as they believed that the continuation of the applicant's marriage would have no detrimental effects for the rights and freedoms of others. Also, while acknowledging that the protection of the traditional family could be justified 'by certain moral concerns', they felt that the protection of morals did not provide sufficient justification for the interference in this case, as the government had not shown that the danger to morals was substantial enough to warrant the interference in issue. The dissenters held:

> 'The only interest in issue is, in plain terms, the public interest in keeping the institution of marriage free of same-sex couples. While we do not purport to deny the legitimacy of the State's interest in protecting the institution of marriage, we do consider that the weight to be afforded to this argument is a different question and one that must be considered separately. In our view, the institution of marriage would not be endangered by a small number of couples who may wish to remain married in a situation such as that of the applicant. In the light of the above, we are not able to conclude that the respondent State can invoke a pressing social need to refuse the applicant the right to remain married after the legal recognition of her acquired gender.'[256]

The dissenting Judges accordingly found a violation of Article 8 in this case. Given that finding, they felt that no separate issue under Article 12 arose. However, given the approach that the majority had taken, they believed that the majority should have assessed under Article 12 whether this Article also guaranteed '[...] a right to remain married unless compelling reasons justify an interference with the civil status of the spouses.'[257]

8.2.6. (Towards) a right to some form of legal recognition of (same-sex) relationships?

So far the Court has never directly addressed the question of whether the Convention imposes a positive obligation on States to introduce some form of legal recognition of same-sex relationships.[258] Although there have been cases were this issue has been (indirectly) put before it, the Court has held the answering of this question as not or no longer necessary, or 'not its task', in the respective cases. For instance, in *Schalk and Kopf*, the Court referred to the fact that the respondent State had introduced legislation on registered partnerships in the meantime (see above)[259] and

256 Joint dissenting opinion of Judges Sajó, Keller and Lemmens to ECtHR [GC] 16 July 2014, *Hämäläinen v. Finland*, no. 37359/09, para.12.

257 *Idem*, para.16.

258 State of affairs on 31 July 2014.

259 The three dissenters to this judgment were also critical in this regard. They held: 'We do not want to dwell on the impact of the Act, which came into force only in 2010, and in particular on the question whether the particular features of this Act, as identified by the Court in paragraphs 18 to 23 of the judgment, comply with Art. 14 of the Convention taken in conjunction with Art. 8, since in our view the violation of the combination of these provisions occurred in any event prior to the entry into force

in *Vallianatos* the Court explicitly stressed that the case before it was not about that general question in the abstract (see 8.2.3.4 above).

Still, in the more recent case law of the Court some hints may be found of a development towards the formulation of such an obligation.[260] The first is the fact that the Court has stressed at a number of times that practice in this area is evolving in Europe. It expressly kept the option open that at some point there would be a consensus, which could constitute a ground for the Court to apply an evolutive interpretation of the Convention on this matter. The employment by the Court of terms like 'not yet' and 'still' in the relevant case law (see 8.2.2 above)[261] may be telling in this regard.[262] Accordingly, the Court may in the future come to formulate of a (minimum) positive obligation for States to recognise same-sex relationships in some form.[263]

The Court has at the same time made clear that European consensus does not necessarily imply that a State holding on to a different position is in violation of the Convention. In *Vallianatos* the Court reiterated its older case law, where it had held that:

> 'The fact that, at the end of a gradual evolution, a country finds itself in an isolated position as regards one aspect of its legislation does not necessarily imply that that aspect offends the Convention, particularly in a field – matrimony – which is so closely bound up with the cultural and historical traditions of each society and its deep-rooted ideas about the family unit.'[264]

Still, in that case, Greece was obliged to change its civil union legislation in order to open it up to same-sex couples. Hence, the relevant cultural and historical traditions of the Greek society and its deep-rooted ideas about the family unit were outweighed by the individual interests of same-sex couples. It must be noted, however, that in this case the State had made the first step itself by introducing partnership legislation, and that the case was about the question of whether it could be justified that this newly introduced institute was available to different-sex couples only.

The Court has in any case expressly left States a margin of appreciation as regards the *timing* of the introduction of legislative changes in the '[...] area of evolving

of the Act.' Joint Dissenting Opinion of Judges Rozakis, Spielmann and Jebens to ECtHR 24 June 2010, *Schalk and Kopf* v. *Austria*, no. 30141/04, para. 7.

260 N.R. Koffeman, 'Case-note to ECtHR [GC] 7 November 2013, *Vallianatos a.o.* v. *Greece*, nos. 29381/09 and 32684/09', 15 *European Human Rights Cases* 2014/34 (in Dutch).

261 ECtHR 24 June 2010, *Schalk and Kopf* v. *Austria*, no. 30141/04, para. 105 and ECtHR 15 January 2013, *Eweida a.o.* v. *the United Kingdom*, nos. 48420/10 a.o., para. 105.

262 Koffeman 2014A, *supra* n. 138. See also N. Bamforth, 'Families But Not (Yet) Marriages? Same-Sex Partners and the Developing European Convention 'Margin of Appreciation', 23 *Child and Family Law Quarterly* (2011) p. 128.

263 See Cooper 2011, *supra* n. 91, at p. 1763 and Hodson 2011, *supra* n. 16, at p. 176.

264 ECtHR 18 December 1987, *F.* v. *Switzerland*, no. 11329/85, para. 33, as referred to by the Court in ECtHR [GC] 7 November 2013, *Vallianatos a.o.* v. *Greece*, nos. 29381/09 and 32684/09, para. 92.

social rights where there is no established consensus'.[265] It held that it was not to '[...] rush to substitute the legal provisions of national authorities, who [were] best placed to assess and respond to the needs of society'.[266] Accordingly, it has held that States 'not in the vanguard',[267] could not be 'criticised'[268] or 'reproached'[269] for not having introduced their civil partnership legislation any earlier. This phrasing makes one wonder if these States could have been reproached if they had introduced such legislation much later, and even more if States who have not introduced any partnership legislation could be reproached for not having introduced it at all. The answer may, again, depend on whether a European consensus can be held to exist. As the Court explained in *M.W.* v. *the UK* (2009) the UK could not be criticised because there existed at the material time no sufficient consensus:

> 'The comparative material before the Court is not such as to suggest that at the relevant point in time (10 April 2001) there was sufficient consensus among the Contracting Parties to the Convention on the formal recognition of same-sex relationships that would have significantly narrowed the United Kingdom's margin of appreciation in this respect. Nor can the enactment of the Civil Partnership Act be taken as an admission by the domestic authorities that the non-recognition of same-sex couples, and their consequent exclusion from many rights and benefits available to married couples, was incompatible with the Convention. Instead, by acting as they did and when they did, the United Kingdom authorities remained within their margin of appreciation. Moreover, the comprehensive manner in which the Act ensures equal entitlements for same-sex couples who enter into a civil partnership means that, although it was not in the vanguard, the United Kingdom is certainly part of the emerging European consensus described by the third party interveners.'[270]

This approach is understandable from the perspective that it may be very complex for the Court to decide at what point in the past consensus has come into being.[271] It may be easier for the Court to decide at some point that a consensus on legal recognition of same-sex relationships exists and to set a new standard from then on.[272]

---

265 Under reference to ECtHR 27 March 1998, *Petrovic* v. *Austria*, no. 20458/92, paras. 36–43 and ECtHR [GC] 12 April 2006, *Stec a.o.* v. *the United Kingdom*, no. 65731/01, paras. 63–65.

266 ECtHR 24 June 2010, *Schalk and Kopf* v. *Austria*, no. 30141/04, para. 62.

267 ECtHR 23 June 2009 (dec.), *M.W.* v. *the United Kingdom*, no. 11313/02 and ECtHR 24 June 2010, *Schalk and Kopf* v. *Austria*, no. 30141/04, para. 106.

268 ECtHR 4 November 2008 (dec.), *Courten* v. *the United Kingdom*, no. 4479/06 and ECtHR 23 June 2009 (dec.), *M.W.* v. *the United Kingdom*, no. 11313/02.

269 ECtHR 24 June 2010, *Schalk and Kopf* v. *Austria*, no. 30141/04, para. 106.

270 ECtHR 23 June 2009 (dec.), *M. W.* v. *the United Kingdom*, no. 11313/02.

271 Koffeman 2010, *supra* n. 90. On this time aspect, see also the Joint partly dissenting opinion of Judges Vajic and Malinverni to ECtHR 22 July 2020, *P.B. and J.S.* v. *Austria*, no. 18984/02.

272 In *J. M.* v. *the United Kingdom* where the relevant facts equally dated back to 2001, the Court had less difficulty in finding discrimination on grounds of sexual orientation. This case may be distinguished however, in that it concerned not the question of legal recognition of same-sex relationships as such, but a difference in treatment between unmarried same-sex couples and unmarried different-sex couples in respect of child support (see section 8.2.3.4 above). ECtHR 28 September 2010, *J. M.* v. *the United Kingdom*, no. 37060/06.

Hence, since the Court has so far noted at several occasions that a consensus in the area of legal recognition of same-sex relationships is emerging, it is conceivable, although not inescapable, that at some point it will hold this to have developed sufficiently so as to find that a lack of any such recognition is incommensurable with the Convention. The formulation of a positive obligation to provide for some form of legal recognition of same-sex relationships has also been held to be a logical consequence of the importance the Court attaches to legal recognition of *de facto* family life and the Court's finding that same-sex relationships fall within the scope of the right to respect for family life. Indeed, as Hodson has observed, it may be '[...] hard to see how family life can be fully enjoyed without some form of legal recognition being offered to those in same-sex relationships.'[273]

The exact shape that such legal recognition would have to take, remains an open question. In *Schalk and Kopf* the Court underlined that where a State chose to provide same-sex couples with an alternative means of legal recognition, it enjoyed a certain margin of appreciation as regards the exact status conferred.[274] It was thus not required that registered partnership had the same legal consequences as marriage.[275] Also, *Vallianatos* implied that such an institution would not have to exhaustively regulate for parental matters.[276]

The Court has also noted an 'evolving consensus on same-sex marriages in the European context'.[277] Nevertheless, the Grand Chamber as recent as in 2014 emphasised that 'it [could not] be said that there [existed] any European consensus on allowing same-sex marriages'.[278] Here, it seems less likely that the Court will in the near future rule differently on this point. On the other hand, the fact that it has declared Article 12 applicable to the complaint in *Schalk and Kopf*, is an important step that leaves further development of the case law in this area open.[279]

The questions raised here may be addressed in two cases that were pending before the Court at the time of conclusion of this research (i.e., 31 July 2014). The first is *Chapin and Charpentier*,[280] in which two men complained that their marriage as conducted by the Mayor of the French commune, Bègles, was subsequently declared

273 Hodson 2011, *supra* n. 16, at p. 176.

274 ECtHR 24 June 2010, *Schalk and Kopf* v. *Austria*, no. 30141/04, para. 108, ECtHR 15 March 2012, *Gas and Dubois* v. *France*, no. 25951/07, para. 66 and ECtHR [GC] 19 February 2013, *X. a.o.* v. *Austria*, no. 19010/07, para. 106.

275 Hodson considered it likely that the Court would '[...] tolerate a degree of differentiation between marriage and registered partnership for some time to come.' Hodson 2011, *supra* n. 16, at p. 177.

276 The Court considered it 'possible for the legislature to include some provisions dealing specifically with children born outside marriage, while at the same time extending to same-sex couples the general possibility of entering into a civil union.' ECtHR [GC] 7 November 2013, *Vallianatos a.o.* v. *Greece*, nos. 29381/09 and 32684/09, para. 89.

277 ECtHR 12 November 2012, *H.* v. *Finland*, no. 37359/09, para. 49.

278 ECtHR [GC] 16 July 2014, *Hämäläinen* v. *Finland*, no. 37359/09, para. 74.

279 *Idem*, para. 61. Hodson also observed that '[...] the Court's decision on Article 12 [contained] progressive elements and hints at a future in which the right to marry is extended to same-sex couples [...]. Hodson 2011, *supra* n. 16, at p. 173.

280 *Chapin and Charpentier* v. *France*, no. 40183/07, application lodged 6 September 2007.

null and void by the courts.[281] The other set of pending cases is potentially even more interesting. These concern complaints originating from Italy about refusals of the Italian authorities to register same-sex marriages contracted abroad. Apart from this cross-border aspect – which is of course highly relevant to the present research (see also 8.3.1 and 8.3.2 below) – the complaints also concern the fact that in Italy it is impossible for same-sex couples to obtain any legal recognition of their relationship.[282] Because there is no national partnership legislation to refer to, it seems inescapable that the Court will have to examine whether a sufficient consensus has evolved for the Court to rule that the right to respect for private and family life requires States to provide for some form of legal recognition of same-sex couples. If it indeed rules accordingly, another question – which is most likely to be answered in the affirmative – is whether that alternative registration form must then be available to different-sex couples (see 8.2.3.4 above).

8.3. Cross-border cases

As yet there have not been any cross-border cases decided by the Court in matters directly pertaining to this case study.[283] There are, however, very interesting (mostly Italian) cases pending. Further, inspiration for deciding these cases may be drawn from a handful of other cross-border cases. For example, an often quoted judgment in this context has been *Wagner* (2007),[284] in which the Court held that a Peruvian single-parent adoption decision had to be recognised in Luxembourg. As also discussed in Chapter 2, section 2.4.2, the Court noted that there was a consensus in Europe on single-parent adoption and stressed that the child's best interests were paramount in such a case. It concluded that the right to respect for family life as protected by Article 8 ECHR had been violated as the Luxembourg courts could not reasonably have refused to recognise the family ties that pre-existed *de facto* between the child and its adoptive mother.[285] The case has been held to be a possible authority for the claim that respect for family life requires States to recognise civil statuses legally established elsewhere.[286] The subsequent cross-border surrogacy cases *Mennesson* and *Labasssee* (2014) – that were decided on the basis of the right

---

[281] The Court communicated the application to the French Government on 7 April 2009 and put questions to the parties under Art. 14 (prohibition of discrimination) in conjunction with Art. 12 (right to marriage) and in conjunction with Art. 8 (right to respect for private and family life) of the Convention.

[282] *Orlandi and Others* v. *Italy*, no. 26431/12 a.o., applications lodged on 20 April 2012 and subsequent dates. The Court communicated the applications to the Italian Government on 3 December 2013 and put questions to the parties under Art. 8 (right to respect for private and family life) and under Art. 14 (prohibition of discrimination) read in conjunction with Art. 8 and/or Art. 12 (right to marry) of the Convention. See also *Enrico Oliari and A.* v. *Italy and Gian Mario Felicetti a.o.* v. *Italy*, nos. 18766/11 and 36030/11, lodged on 21 March 2011 and 10 June 2011 respectively.

[283] It is recalled that this research was concluded on 31 July 2014.

[284] ECtHR 28 June 2007, *Wagner and J.M.W.L.* v. *Luxembourg*, no. 76240/01.

[285] See also ECtHR 3 May 2011, *Negrepontis-Giannisis* v. *Greece*, no. 56759/08.

[286] J. Rijpma and N. Koffeman, 'Free Movement Rights for Same-Sex Couples Under EU Law; What role to Play for the CJEU?', in: D. Gallo et al. (eds.), *Same-Sex Couples before National, Supranational and International Jurisdictions* (Berlin, Springer 2014) p. 455 at pp. 462–463.

to personal identity of the child (see Chapter 2, section 2.4.2) – may also prove relevant in this regard.

8.3.1. Recognition of foreign same-sex marriages and partnerships

In 2010 a complaint was lodged with the Court by two Russian women, Irina Fedotova-Fet and Irina Shipitko, who had married in Canada in 2009.[287] They complained about the refusal of the Russian authorities to register their marriage in the Russian register on the ground that under the Russian Family Code a marriage could only be registered between a man and a woman. Before this case was given an application number, it disappeared from the Court's docket and could no longer be traced in the search engine *HUDOC* on the Court's website, for reasons unknown to the present author.[288] Yet earlier, however, another set of cases concerning the recognition of foreign same-sex marriages, this time originating from Italy, had been brought before the Court.[289] These cases were still pending at the time this research was concluded (i.e., 31 July 2014).

8.3.2. Refusal of a residence permit to a same-sex partner

In September 2009 a same-sex couple, one of whom is an Italian and the other a New Zealand national, made an application to the ECtHR against Italy (see also 8.2.6 above).[290] They complained that the Italian authorities had refused to issue the second applicant with a residence permit because the national immigration legislation did not allow unmarried partners to obtain a family member's residence permit. The applicants claimed that they had no other means of living together as a couple in Italy. At the time of writing, these cases are still pending for the Court.

8.3.3. Cross-border cases involving children

So far the ECtHR has not decided any cross-border cases involving a same-sex couple with children and the present author is not aware of any such cases pending. As discussed extensively in Chapter 2, the Court has, however, decided cross-border surrogacy cases. The judgments in *Mennesson* and *Labassee* are also relevant for same-sex couples who engage in international surrogacy, in any case as long as one of them is genetically related to the child. In these cases the Court ruled that a refusal to recognise the legal parenthood of a father whose genetic children were born

[287] According to an earlier version of the ECtHR's factsheet on 'Sexual orientation issues' the complaint by Fedotova-Fet and Shipitko v. Russia, was lodged on 21 July 2010.

[288] See also www.archive.gayrussia.eu/en/inf/detail.php?ID=16197, visited October 2010.

[289] *Orlandi and Others* v. *Italy*, no. 26431/12 a.o., applications lodged on 20 April 2012 and subsequent dates.

[290] *Taddeucci and McCall* v. *Italy*, no. 51362/09, application lodged in September 2009 and communicated to the Italian Government on 10 January 2012.

following surrogacy arrangements abroad, violated the right to respect for private life of the children concerned, in particular their right to personal identity. There is no indication in the judgments that this reasoning would not apply if the intended parents had been a same-sex couple. This is even more so, now that the reasoning adopted by the Court in *Mennesson* and *Labassee* did not focus on the (non-genetic) intended mother, while no importance was attached to the civil status of the intended parents (in those cases spouses).[291]

8.4. Conclusions

A number of findings of the ECtHR have been important for the advancement of the rights of persons with a homosexual orientation and (consequently) for same-sex couples. The first is the finding that a person's sexual orientation forms part of the most intimate aspects of private life and that consequently discrimination on grounds of sexual orientation requires particularly serious reasons by way of justification. The other is the finding that same-sex relationships come within scope of right to respect for private *and* family life under Article 8 ECHR.

When it comes to legal recognition of same-sex relationships, however, no enforceable rights have followed from the ECtHR's case law. The Court has acknowledged that same-sex couples have, just as much as different-sex couples, a 'need for legal recognition of their relationship',[292] and has even ruled that they come within the scope of the right to marry (Article 12 ECHR). Still it has not (yet) ruled that they therefore have a right to (some form of) legal recognition of their relationship. For one thing, they do not have a right under the Convention to marry. The Court has repeatedly held that 'marriage' under Article 12 ECHR concerns traditional marriage between a man and a woman only. While it has noted that the institution of marriage has undergone 'major social changes since the adoption of the Convention', it has attached decisive value to the lack of European consensus on this point. It has been noted that by holding on to this traditional concept of marriage, '[t]he Court is in danger of treating marriage as an untouchable, almost sacred, category.'[293]

In cases where same-sex couples claimed that they were treated unequally from different-sex couples, the special status of marriage has often been a ground for not even finding comparability in the situations of same-sex couples and those of different-sex couples, or in any case for justifying a difference in treatment between these groups. The fact that same-sex couples did not at all have access to marriage, was not considered to have a bearing on these findings.

---

291 Compare N.R. Koffeman, 'Case-note to ECtHR 26 June 2014, *Mennesson* v. *France*, no. 65192/11 and ECtHR 26 June 2014, *Labassee* v. *France*, no. 65941/11', 15 *European Human Rights Cases* 2014/222 (in Dutch).

292 ECtHR 24 June 2010, *Schalk and Kopf* v. *Austria*, no. 30141/04, para. 99.

293 Hodson 2011, *supra* n. 16, at p. 177.

Generally, in discrimination cases, the Court has held it determinative whether 'a special legal status' was involved – in other words 'a public undertaking, carrying with it a body of rights and obligations of a contractual nature'. Only where no such status was involved, has the Court applied its strict scrutiny test for cases involving a difference in treatment on grounds of sexual orientation. In those cases the Court has furthermore tested if the relevant national law was coherent (*X. and Others* v. *Austria* (2013)). In this context it has been submitted that there is also Strasbourg case law that implies that civil status in itself is a suspect ground, that attracts a weighty reasons test,[294] but such a finding has clearly not been upheld in cases involving same-sex couples. Further, the critique has been issued that by taking this formalistic approach, the Court has overlooked the indirect discrimination involved in cases where same-sex couples simply had no access to a particular civil status.[295] The Court's approach in these cases has also been held as being more difficult to reconcile with those cases in which it held that the applicants could and should have resorted to alternative forms of registration.[296]

In cases concerning parental matters, the Court has accepted protection of the family in the traditional sense, as well as the best interests of the child, as legitimate aims for a difference in treatment, but it has been increasingly stricter in its examination of the proportionality of the measure in these cases. In choosing means to protect the family, States must take into account developments in society and changes in the perception of social and civil status and relationship issues. An examination of each individual case must also be made possible, as that is most in keeping with the best interests of the child. In *X. and Others* v. *Austria*, the Court even concluded that it was in fact in the interest of the child that no difference in treatment was made between same-sex couples and different-sex couples in respect of second-parent adoption. While the Court has not adopted reasoning purely from the perspective of the child, as advocated by some of its Judges,[297] it has increasingly taken the bests interests of the child into account in its reasoning. It has at the same time accepted that biological differences between different-sex couples and same-sex couples, decisively distinguish these groups in respect of parental matters.

The Court has accepted that a consensus in respect of alternative forms of registration for same-sex couples is evolving in Europe and in its case law some hints can be found that the Court may go in the direction of the definition of a positive obligation for the States to provide for some form of legal recognition of same-sex relationships. This precise question has to date only come indirectly before the Court, and in those cases the Court – for different reasons – has not addressed the matter. It therefore remains to be seen what the future case law may bring in this regard. What is clear, is that, *when* States choose to provide for some alternative form of registration, they must guarantee that this alternative registration option is also accessible for

294 Koffeman 2011A, *supra* n. 126.

295 *Idem.*

296 Koffeman 2014A, *supra* n. 138.

297 Dissenting opinion of Judge Villiger to ECtHR 15 March 2012, *Gas and Dubois* v. *France*, no. 25951/07. See section 8.2.3.2 above.

same-sex couples. States enjoy a certain margin of appreciation as regards the exact status conferred by alternative means of recognition, and the Court has indicated that differences between same-sex partners and different-sex partners in respect of parental matters could potentially be justified.

All in all, from the case law as discussed in this chapter it becomes clear that States are generally given a lot of room in this area of law. Because marriage has 'deep-rooted social and cultural connotations differing largely from one society to another', States may each decide for themselves whether or not they want to open up marriage to same-sex couples. They are furthermore free to grant certain rights or entitlements only to couples with a specific civil status, even when that status is not accessible for same-sex couples. Where no such special status is involved, however, the Court has been much stricter, and in cases concerning parental matters it has increasingly ruled out discrimination on grounds of sexual orientation on the basis of the best interests of the child.

Chapter 9
EU

9.1. Constitutional framework[1]

9.1.1. Relevant Charter rights

Several Charter rights are relevant in the context of the present case study. Many of them have been briefly introduced in Chapter 3, namely the right to private and family life (Article 7 CFR); the right to found a family (Article 9 CFR); the prohibition of discrimination (Article 21 CFR); the rights of the child (Article 24 CFR); the legal economic and social protection of the family (Article 33 CFR) and the right to free movement (Article 45 CFR).

Article 9 of the Charter is of particular relevance for the present case study, because it provides also for a right to marry.[2] The Article reads:

> 'The right to marry and to found a family shall be guaranteed in accordance with the national laws governing the exercise of these rights.'

This Article greatly resembles Article 12 ECHR, and equally refers to national laws. The reference to 'men and women' has been taken out, however, rendering the provision gender-neutral.[3] As a result Article 9 CFR does not seem to stand in the way of granting same-sex couples access to marriage, but the wording of the Article does not require so either.[4] The scope of this Article is also broader in the sense that it does not focus on marriage exclusively, but also covers other forms of legal recognition of relationships. The Explanations to the Charter explain in this regard:

> 'This Article is based on Article 12 of the ECHR [...]. The wording of the Article has been modernised to cover cases in which national legislation recognises arrangements other than marriage for founding a family. This Article neither prohibits nor imposes the granting of the status of marriage to unions between people of the same sex. This right

---

1 The present chapter – particularly its section 9.6 – is based on J. Rijpma and N. Koffeman,'Free Movement Rights for Same-Sex Couples Under EU Law; What role to Play for the CJEU? in: D. Gallo et al. (eds.), *Same-Sex Couples before National, Supranational and International Jurisdictions* (Berlin, Springer 2014) pp. 455–491.

2 On the connection between the right to marry and the right to found a family in this Article, see ch. 3, section 3.1.

3 EU Network of Independent Experts on Fundamental Rights, *Commentary of the Charter of Fundamental Rights of the European Union*, June 2006, p. 98, www.ec.europa.eu/justice/fundamental-rights/files/networkcommentaryfinal_en.pdf, visited June 2014.

4 *Idem*, p. 102.

is thus similar to that afforded by the ECHR, but its scope may be wider when national legislation so provides.'[5]

There has not to date been any CJEU judgment in which this Charter Article has been referred to, safe interpreted.[6]

9.1.2. Relevant EU competences

The EU has no competence in the field of civil status or any related family law matters as such. For instance, there is no EU marriage institute and there are no EU rules on parental rights for same-sex couples. These concern matters where the Member States have deliberately refrained from attributing any competences to the Union.[7] Hence, in respect of legal recognition of same-sex couples, the EU cannot set, and therefore has never set, any binding Union standards, and this is not likely to change in the near future. Civil status is nonetheless relevant in some areas of EU law, where obviously the EU does have competence. For instance, references to civil status have been made in the EU Staff Regulations as well as under various EU non-discrimination instruments in the field of employment. Particularly in situations where same-sex couples have been concerned, such references have raised questions as to their interpretation (see sections 9.2 and 9.3 respectively).

Several of the EU's existing competences pertain to the present case study. The EU's competence to adopt equal treatment law and its application in respect of LGBT rights is discussed in more detail in section 9.3 below. Another important competence concerns the free movement of persons. The application of this freedom in the context of the present case study is extensively set out in section 9.6. The EU's competence to adopt measures relating to family law having cross-border implications (Article 81(3) TFEU), has been set out in Case Study I (see Chapter 3, section 3.1.3.3), and will therefore not be discussed separately here. Private International Law instruments that have been adopted on this legal basis, or that may potentially be adopted in the future, and that are relevant or may prove to be so for the present case study are discussed in section 9.7 below.

---

5 Explanations relating to the Charter of Fundamental Rights [2007] OJ C303/17.

6 This research was concluded on 31 July 2014. The provision has only been referred to by a few Advocate Generals in Opinions, for instance: Joined Cases C-122/99 P and C-125/99 P *D and Kingdom of Sweden* v. *Council* [2001] ECR I-4319, ECLI:EU:C:2001:113, Opinion of AG Mischo and Case C-147/08 *Römer* [2011] ECR I-3591, ECLI:EU:C:2010:425, Opinion of AG Jääskinen.

7 In the words of Lenaerts '[...] Member States enjoy absolute discretion over the definition and legal effects of marriage, registered partnership, divorce, and other domestic issues [...]'. K. Lenaerts, 'Federalism and the rule of law: perspectives from the European Court of Justice', 33 *Fordham International Law Journal* 2009–2010, p. 1338 at p. 1359.

9.2. The EU Staff Regulations and same-sex relationships

Under the present EU Staff Regulations the rights of staff members in same-sex relationships are fully equal to those of staff members in different-sex relationships. This has not, however, always been the case. As will be discussed hereafter, the CJEU exercised considerable judicial restraint when it was asked if certain terms in the Regulations, such as 'marriage', included 'non-traditional' unions, such as same-sex registered partnerships. As further explained in section 9.6.2.1 below, this line of case law has often been referred to in academia when discussing the definition of the term 'spouse' under the Free Movement Directive.

The *Dumay* case (1993) concerned an application for a widow's pension by the widow of Mr. Dumay, a Community Official who died in 1991.[8] While Mr. and Mrs. Dumay had cohabited for many years, they married in 1989 only. The European Commissions' Directorate General for Personnel and Administration rejected Mrs. Dumay's application, informing her that because they were married for less than five years, she did not qualify for a widow's pension. The CJEU, 'while aware of the social context' in which the action had been brought, did not consider that it was competent '[...] to widen the judicial interpretation of the specific terms used in the Staff Regulations in order to bring cohabitation' – *in casu* by a different-sex couple – 'within the definition of "marriage", or "cohabitee" within that of "husband" or "wife".'[9] The Court took account of the fact that any extension of those concepts would have 'serious legal and financial consequences' for the then Communities and for third parties.[10] It ruled that 'a change on that scale' could only be made by the Community legislature if it considered such a change to be necessary.[11] The Court did not consider it 'appropriate' in the case at hand to refer to provisions of national law for the purpose of interpreting the Community provisions in question.[12]

The subsequent case of *D. and Sweden* v. *Council* (2001),[13] concerned a same-sex couple and *de facto* had the same outcome as *Dumay*. A Swedish national, referred to as '*D.*', was working for the Council, and had concluded a registered partnership with another Swedish national of the same sex under Swedish law. *D.* applied to the Council for his status as a registered partner to be treated as being equivalent to marriage for the purpose of obtaining the household allowance provided for in the Staff Regulations for EC Officials. The Council rejected his application on

---

8 Case T-65/92 *Dumay* [1993] ECR II-597, ECLI:EU:T:1993:47.

9 *Idem*, para. 30. The Court referred to its preceding *Reed* judgment. Case 59/85 *Netherlands* v. *Reed* [1986] ECR 1283, ECLI:EU:C:1986:157.

10 Such financial considerations do not come back explicitly in later case law on the matter, although Reid and Caracciolo suggested it as a plausible explanation for the restrictive approach of the CJEU in Joined Cases C-122/99 P and C-125/99 P *D and Kingdom of Sweden* v. *Council* [2001] ECR I-4319, ECLI:EU:C:2001:304 (see below). E. Reid and E. Caracciolo Di Torella, 'The changing shape of the "European family" and fundamental rights', 27 *European Law Review* (2002) p. 80 at p. 86.

11 Case T-65/92 *Dumay* [1993] ECR II-597, ECLI:EU:T:1993:47, para. 30.

12 *Idem*, para. 31.

13 Joined Cases C-122/99 P & C-125/99 P *D. and Sweden* v. *Council* [2001] ECR I-4319, ECLI:EU:C:2001:304.

the ground that the provisions of the Staff Regulations could not be construed as allowing a registered partnership to be treated as being equivalent to marriage.[14] *D.* subsequently applied to the Court of First Instance (now General Court).[15] This Court dismissed his appeal, observing, *inter alia,* that for the purposes of the Staff Regulations the concept of marriage was to be understood as meaning '[...] a relationship based on civil marriage within the traditional meaning of the term'.[16]

In the subsequent appeal proceedings before the CJEU, *D.* and the Kingdom of Sweden, supported by Denmark and the Netherlands,[17] asserted that, since civil status was a matter which came within the exclusive competence of the Member States, terms such as 'married official' or 'spouse' in the Staff Regulations were to be interpreted by reference to the law of the Member States and not to be given an independent definition. The parties argued that where a Member State had legislated to give legal status to an arrangement such as a registered partnership, which was to be treated in respect of the rights and duties it comprised as being equivalent to marriage, the same treatment was to be accorded in the application of the Staff Regulations.[18] The Council, on the other hand, claimed that the wording of the Staff Regulations was unambiguous. To treat a registered partnership as being equivalent to marriage for the purposes of applying the Staff Regulations was to extend the scope of the benefits concerned, which, the Council alleged, required a prior assessment of its legal and budgetary consequences and 'a decision on the part of the Community legislature rather than a judicial interpretation of the existing rules.'[19] In the words of Bogdan '[...] the issue boiled down to the question whether under the Staff Regulations D. was to be considered married or not'.[20]

Basing himself on *Reed* (as discussed in section 9.6.1 below), Advocate General Mischo submitted that where the term 'spouse', or analogous terms such as 'marriage' or 'married person', were used in an EU Regulation, they were to be given an independent interpretation.[21] He held there to be no indication in the case

14 *Idem*, para. 5.

15 By the Treaty of Lisbon (2009) the Court of First Instance (CFI) was renamed to 'the General Court'.

16 Case T-264/97 *D.* v. *Council* [1999] ECR FP-I-A-00001, ECLI:EU:T:1999:13, para. 26–27, as paraphrased in para. 11 of the CJEU judgment. For a critical discussion of the judgment of the Court of First Instance, see C. Denys, 'Homosexuality: a non-issue in Community law?', 24 *European Law Review* (1999) p. 419.

17 As Tridimas put it: '[...] this was not a one-man legal struggle.' He noted that by contrast, no government intervened in support of the Council. T. Tridimas, *The General Principles of EU law*, 2nd edn. (Oxford, Oxford University Press 2006) p. 108.

18 See Joined Cases C-122/99 P & C-125/99 P *D. and Sweden* v. *Council* [2001] ECR I-4319, ECLI:EU:C:2001:304, para. 29.

19 *Idem*, para. 31. In this connection, the Council furthermore pointed out that at the time when Regulation 781/98 was adopted a request by the Kingdom of Sweden for registered partnership to be treated as being equivalent to marriage had been rejected.

20 M. Bogdan, 'Registered Partnerships and EC law', in: K. Boele-Woelki and A. Fuchs (eds.), *Legal recognition of same-sex couples in Europe* (Antwerp, Intersentia 2003) p. 171 at p. 172.

21 'An independent interpretation' was defined by AG Mischo as '[...] an interpretation which takes into account the situation in the whole Community, and not merely in one Member State.' Joined Cases C-122/99 P and C-125/99 P *D and Kingdom of Sweden* v. *Council of the European Union* [2001] ECR I-4319, ECLI:EU:C:2001:113, Opinion of AG Mischo, para. 43.

at hand of a general social development allowing a registered partnership between two people of the same sex to be included within the term 'marriage'. He therefore concluded that the definition of 'marriage' included only 'traditional' marriage between two people of a different sex.[22] On the basis of the CJEU's case law, Mischo furthermore found that an official who had entered into a registered partnership was not in a situation comparable to that of a married official. He therefore concluded that the general principle of equal treatment did not require that the former was treated in the same way as the latter.[23]

In line with the Advocate General's Opinion,[24] the CJEU dismissed the appeals in their entirety. It ruled that 'married official' within the meaning of the Staff Regulations could not be interpreted as covering an official who had contracted a registered partnership.[25] It held it to be 'not in question' that, according to the definition generally accepted by the Member States, the term 'marriage' meant a union between two persons of a different sex.[26] The CJEU observed that in the preceding decade 'an increasing number of Member States' had introduced, '[...] alongside marriage, statutory arrangements granting legal recognition to various forms of union between partners of the same sex or of the opposite sex and conferring on such unions certain effects which, both between the partners and as regards third parties', were 'the same as or comparable to those of marriage'.[27] The Court also noted, however, that such arrangements were regarded in the Member States concerned as being distinct from marriage.[28] The CJEU therefore found that as 'Community judicature' it could not interpret the Staff Regulations in such a way that 'legal situations distinct from marriage' were treated in the same way as marriage.[29] The Court held it to be for the legislature instead to adopt measures in this matter. It noted, however, that the legislature had at that stage ruled out '[...] any idea of other forms of partnership being assimilated to marriage for the purposes of granting the benefits reserved under the Staff Regulations for married officials'.[30]

---

22 Joined Cases C-122/99 P and C-125/99 P *D and Kingdom of Sweden* v. *Council of the European Union* [2001] ECR I-4319, ECLI:EU:C:2001:113, Opinion of AG Mischo, para. 48.

23 *Idem,* para. 89.

24 See E. Ellis, 'Case note to Joined Cases C-122 & 125/99P, *D. and Sweden* v. *Council.* Judgment of the European Court of Justice of 31 May 2001, Full Court,' 39 *CMLRev* (2002) p. 151 at p. 152.

25 See R. Wintemute, 'Conclusion', in: R. Wintemute and M. Andenæs (eds.), *Legal Recognition of Same-Sex Partnerships, A Study of National, European and International Law* (Oxford, Hart Publishing 2001) p. 759, at p. 767.

26 Joined Cases C-122/99 P and C-125/99 P *D and Kingdom of Sweden* v. *Council* [2001] ECR I-4319, ECLI:EU:C:2001:304, para. 34.

27 *Idem*, para. 35.

28 *Idem*, para. 36.

29 In the words of Bonini-Baraldi the *ratio decidendi* of the judgment lied in the assessment of the (dis)similiarity between registered partnership and marriage. M. Bonini-Baraldi, 'The Employment Equality Directive and other aspects of European Law', in: C. Waaldijk and M. Bonini-Baraldi, *Sexual orientation discrimination in the European Union, National laws and the Employment Equality Directive* (The Hague, TMC Asser Press 2006) p. 5 at p. 22.

30 Joined Cases C-122/99 P and C-125/99 P *D and Kingdom of Sweden* v. *Council* [2001] ECR I-4319, ECLI:EU:C:2001:304, para. 38.

This part of the judgment received much attention in legal academia. Ellis criticised that the Court had '[...] strayed into the dangerous territory of setting out what it regarded as the essential component of a "marriage" for the purposes of EU law, that is to say partners of opposite sex.'[31] According to Bogdan the reasoning of the Court amounted '[...] in fact, to an autonomous interpretation of the concept of marriage'. He also noted however, that such interpretation was 'not really independent' as it was 'based on the legal systems of the totality of Member States'.[32] The author also warned that one had to understand that the Court '[...] did not feel free to experiment by going beyond the views prevailing in the totality of Member States at that time'.[33] Others were less understanding in this respect.[34] Reid and Caracciolo Di Torella held that the Court's ruling did not reflect the social reality that existed at the time.[35] They furthermore pointed out that in *D. and Sweden* v. *Council*, a European notion was used to remove protection offered by the Member State,[36] and argued that the Court should have recognised the '[...] principle of respect throughout the Community for the civil status enjoyed by a national in their own Member State', as was also claimed by *D.*[37] The authors acknowledged that this would have resulted in 'some discrimination between the different Member States', but they held such disparity in treatment '[...] (unfortunately) a necessary consequence of the need to respect national choices.'[38]

Tridimas observed that the judgment implied that the Court would be '[...] prepared to equate same sex relations with marriage if there was a sufficient degree of political and social consensus at the national level and this had crystallised in the laws of the Member States'. The author posed the question of what precise degree of support from the laws of the Member States would be required for the Court to take that step of equation.[39] Lenaerts underlined that *D. and Sweden* v. *Council* '[...] dealt with a

31 Ellis 2002, *supra* n. 24, at p. 155.

32 Bogdan 2003, *supra* n. 20, at p. 173.

33 *Idem*. Ellis also found it '[...] wholly understandable that the Court concluded that the extension of the law to protect homosexuals was a step for the legislature rather than the judiciary.' She added '[i] ndeed' one has only to think of the criticism which the Court has attracted for its "activism" in far less controversial fields in the past to realize that this was a prudent course to take.' Ellis 2002, *supra* n. 24, at p. 156.

34 Reid and Caracciolo Di Torella held that the CJEU's approach in this case was '[...] in sharp contrast with the activist stand that the Court has taken on many occasions.' They gave the example of the CJEU's definitions of the concepts of indirect effect or state liability. Reid and Caracciolo Di Torella 2002, *supra* n. 10, at p. 86 and footnote 37.

35 *Idem*, p. 89.

36 *Idem*, p. 82.

37 *D.* had also claimed that because the decision treated his situation as being equivalent to that of an unmarried official, his right as a national of a Member State to have his civil status respected throughout the Community (also referred to by the applicant as 'the principle of the "integrity of a person's status"') had been infringed (see para. 42 of the judgment). As Reid and Caracciolo Di Torella observed, the CJEU did not challenge the existence of this principle, but side-stepped it, by holding (in para. 43) that '[...] in applying to the appellant a provision of the Staff Regulations concerning an allowance, the competent institution was not taking a decision affecting his situation with regard to his civil status.' Reid and Caracciolo Di Torella 2002, *supra* n. 10, at p. 85. Later on (at p. 90) the authors speak of 'the principle of the unicity of legal status'.

38 Reid and Caracciolo Di Torella 2002, *supra* n. 10, at p. 87.

39 Tridimas 2006, *supra* n. 17, at p. 108.

common definition of marriage in a field of exclusive competence of the EU' and that 'the case involved questions of statutory interpretation alone'.[40] The author warned that the ruling of the CJEU in *D. and Sweden* v. *Council* could not be extended without reservation 'to the mobility of same-sex married couples', as this judgment '[...] did not examine the alterations in the civil status of same-sex couples resulting from free movement' (on this point see also section 9.6.2 below).[41]

As regards *D.*'s claim that the principle of equal treatment of officials irrespective of their sexual orientation had been infringed, the CJEU held it to be 'clear' that it was not the sex of the partner which determined whether the household allowance was granted, 'but the legal nature of the ties between the official and the partner.'[42] This finding – by some referred to as a 'faulty reasoning'[43] – has been criticised for not addressing the claim that the requirement of marriage was indirectly discriminatory on grounds of sexual orientation, insofar as same-sex couples had no access to marriage.[44] The Court held, however, that the general principle of equal treatment was not violated, as – given the great diversity of laws and the absence of any general assimilation of marriage and other forms of statutory union in the 'Community as a whole' – the situation of an official who had registered a partnership between persons of the same sex could not be considered to be comparable to that of a married official.[45]

The CJEU held, furthermore, that the contested decision was 'not [...] on any view, capable of constituting interference' in private and family life within the meaning of Article 8 ECHR.[46] While AG Mischo had also examined the case under Article 9 of the EU Charter of Fundamental Rights – which at that time was recently adopted, but still legally non-binding – the CJEU remained silent on this point.[47] *D.*'s sixth argument – that by depriving partners registered under the legislation in force in some Member States of the rights associated with their status under national law, a decision such as the contested decision constituted discrimination on grounds of nationality and at the same time an obstacle to the freedom of movement for

---

40 Lenaerts 2009–2010, *supra* n. 7, at p. 1358.

41 *Idem*, p. 1358, referring (in footnote 96) to H. Toner, *Partnership Rights, Free Movement and EU Law*, Hart Publishing: Oxford 2004, p. 187.

42 Joined Cases C-122/99 P and C-125/99 P *D and Kingdom of Sweden* v. *Council* [2001] ECR I-4319, ECLI:EU:C:2001:304, para. 47.

43 Wintemute 2001, *supra* n. 25, at pp. 767–769.

44 Tridimas 2006, *supra* n. 17, at p. 108. Bogdan called this line of reasoning 'hard to follow'. Bogdan 2003, *supra* n. 20, at p. 173.

45 Joined Cases C-122/99 P and C-125/99 P *D and Kingdom of Sweden* v. *Council* [2001] ECR I-4319, ECLI:EU:C:2001:304, paras. 50–51.

46 *Idem*, paras. 59–60. The Court considered: '[...] refusal by the Community administration to grant a household allowance to one of its officials does not affect the situation of the official in question as regards his civil status and, since it only concerns the relationship between the official and his employer, does not of itself give rise to the transmission of any personal information to persons outside the Community administration.' See also Wintemute 2001, *supra* n. 25, at pp. 767–769.

47 See Reid and Caracciolo Di Torella 2002, *supra* n. 10, at p. 80. The authors criticised (on p. 83) the fact that the Advocate General omitted to refer to the prohibition of discrimination in Art. 21 of the Charter. They furthermore (on p. 89) suggested several possible explanations for the silence of the Court on this point, all reflecting 'the political sensitivity of the Court'.

workers – was declared inadmissible as this plea was introduced for the first time at the appeal stage. Bogdan considered it 'regrettable' that this argument was not examined on the content, as he claimed there to be 'an obvious risk' that registered partners would refrain from moving from one Member State to another if their status would not be accepted there (on this issue, see also section 9.6.3 below).[48]

A couple of years after the *D.* v. *Council* judgment, the EU Staff Regulations were amended to the extent that from then on the term 'spouse' was interpreted as including same-sex spouses.[49] The amendment further provided for an extension of entitlement to the household allowance to officials registered as stable non-marital partners, including those of the same sex.[50] To qualify as stable non-marital partners, the couple must produce a legal document recognised as such by a Member State, or any competent authority of a Member State, acknowledging their status as non-marital partners.[51] Given that, for example, the German registered partnership is also open to couples with no link to the German jurisdiction, it is submitted that in theory all EU officials and their same-sex partners – including those from countries which do not provide for any form of legal recognition of their relationship – can qualify as 'non-marital partners' and are thus entitled to the household allowance on the same footing as different-sex married officials. If the partners have practical and effective access to legal marriage in an EU Member State, they cannot qualify as non-marital partners for the purposes of the Staff Regulations.[52] This presumably holds for most – if not all – different-sex couples. For same-sex couples, however, often no marriage alternative is open.[53]

In *Roodhuijzen* (2009) the General Court gave an autonomous interpretation of the term 'non-marital partnership' within the meaning of the revised Staff Regulations, holding that it implied on the one hand, a union between two persons

48 Bogdan 2003, *supra* n. 20, at p. 173.

49 Accordingly a case similar to *D*, was dismissed. Order of the Court of First Instance of 3 April 2003, Case T-258/02 *Hendrikus Boukes* v. *European Parliament* [2003] OJ C171/27.

50 Council Regulation 723/2004/EC, Euratom of 22 March 2004 amending the Staff Regulations of officials of the European Communities and the Conditions of Employment of other servants of the European Communities [2004] OJ L124/1, p. 37, annex I, para. 97. The present Staff Regulations can be found on www.ec.europa.eu/civil_service/docs/toc100_en.pdf, visited June 2014.

51 Art. 1d (77)(96)(1) of the Staff Regulations juncto Art. 1(2)(c)(i) of Annex VII to the Staff Regulations.

52 Art. 1d (77)(96)(1) of the Staff Regulations juncto Art. 1(2)(c)(iv) of Annex VII to the Staff Regulations. A 2010 staff case concerned an EU official with both Belgian and Moroccan nationality who was cohabiting in Belgium with a same-sex partner. The couple was refused the household allowance on the ground, that they did not satisfy the condition laid down in Art. 1(2)(c)(iv) of Annex VII to the Staff Regulations, since they had access to legal marriage in Belgium. The Civil Service Tribunal annulled the contested decisions, holding that the applicant's access to marriage in Belgium was not 'practical and effective', as he risked persecution on grounds of his homosexuality in Morocco. Case F-86/09 *W* v. *Commission* [2010] ECR 0000, ECLI:EU:F:2010:125.

53 If any of the EU Member States would give same-sex couples access to marriage, irrespective of their nationality or their habitual residence, all EU officials in a same-sex relationship would have access to marriage in a Member State and consequently none could qualify as 'non-marital partners'. However, since all States have made access to marriage dependent upon nationality and/or habitual residence, this does not hold.

and, on the other hand, certain formal aspects.[54] The Court noted that the concept of 'non-marital partnership' in the Staff Regulations had 'a certain resemblance to that of marriage',[55] but held that it could not be interpreted '[...] as covering solely partnerships exclusively designed, under national law, to have effects similar to those of a marriage.'[56] Evidence of cohabitation characterised by a certain stability was required by the Staff Regulations, but the partners were not required to be bound by specific reciprocal rights and obligations. The General Court rejected the Commission's submission that earlier case law confirmed that a term like 'non-marital partnership' could not be given an autonomous interpretation, as the civil status of persons fell within the exclusive competence of the Member States.[57] It called to mind that in *D.* v. *Council*, the CJEU had interpreted the concept of marriage 'as being in principle a Community concept'[58] and held that any such autonomous interpretation did not affect the exclusive competence of Member States with regard to the civil status of persons and the determination of the benefits deriving therefrom.[59]

9.3. EU NON-DISCRIMINATION LAW AND SAME-SEX RELATIONSHIPS

Over the years, in accordance with social developments, sexual orientation has gradually gained a more prominent position in EU non-discrimination law. This section sets out this development, both in legislation and case law. It also provides an outlook on relevant possible future developments in this realm of EU law.

Particularly at the time when sexual orientation was not yet included as a prohibited ground in the Treaties, complaints concerning same-sex relationships were often construed as gender (or sex)[60] equality cases, for instance based on the so-called

---

54 Case T-58/08 P *Roodhuijzen* [2009] ECR II-3797, ECLI:EU:T:2009:385.

55 *Idem*, para. 93.

56 *Idem*, para. 89.

57 *Idem*, para. 58. The Commission referred to Joined Cases C-122/99 P and C-125/99 P *D and Kingdom of Sweden* v. *Council* [2001] ECR I-4319, ECLI:EU:C:2001:304, paras. 34 and 35 and Case C-267/06 *Tadao Maruko* v. *Versorgungsanstalt der deutschen Bühnen* [2008] ECR I-1757, ECLI:EU:C:2008:179, paras. 59, 67 to 69 and 72.

58 *Idem*, para. 79.

59 *Idem*, para. 87.

60 As Gerards has explained: 'In legal discourse, the term "sex" is used to refer to biological, genetically determined differences between women and men, such as differences related to pregnancy and lactation or average differences in physical strength. Other differences between men and women appear to be more social than biological in nature, such as (perceived) differences in the relation between parent and child. To describe these "social" differences between the sexes, the term "gender" is usually employed. Thus, "sex" refers to a biological reality, whereas "gender" refers to a social reality. [...] In practice, it is sometimes hard to separate the two notions, as it is not always easy to classify a difference between men and women as either socially constructed or biological in nature. The result is that academic writers, courts and legislators do not always carefully distinguish between the terms, rendering the difference rather fuzzy. Indeed, although the term "gender" is now used more often than "sex", many legal texts still primarily contain the ground "sex". Further, it is important to remember that not all states distinguish between the two notions in their own languages; often, "sex" and "gender" are covered by a single term.' J. Gerards, 'Discrimination grounds', in: D. Schiek et al. (eds), *Cases, materials and text on national, supranational and international non-discrimination law* (Oxford, Hart Publishing 2007) pp. 70–71.

Gender Equality Directives.[61] This was also the case in the much debated *Grant* case (1998), the first case in the field of EU non-discrimination law involving a same-sex couple.[62]

9.3.1. The *Grant* case (1998)

In 1995, Ms. Grant applied to her employer South-West Trains (SWT) for travel concessions for her female partner, with whom she claimed to be in a stable relationship for over two years. SWT refused to allow the benefit sought, on the ground that for unmarried persons such concessions could be granted only for a partner of the opposite sex.[63] Ms. Grant argued that this refusal constituted discrimination based on sex, prohibited by Article 119 EC Treaty (the present Article 157 TFEU) and Directive 75/117[64] (later repealed by Directive 2006/54/EC[65]). She pointed out that '[…] her predecessor in the post, a man who had declared that he had had a meaningful relationship with a woman for over two years, had enjoyed the benefit which had been refused her.'[66] Ms. Grant contended, next, that such a refusal constituted discrimination based on sexual orientation.[67]

Advocate General Elmer concluded that the refusal by Ms. Grant's employer constituted direct discrimination on the basis of gender, which could not be justified.[68] He disagreed with the argument put forward by the Commission that the case concerned the definition of a 'common law spouse' and was thus a family law issue which did not fall under the (then) EC Treaty.[69] He answered the question if the discrimination could be justified by reference to the employer's conception of morality, in the negative:

> 'South-West Train's justification amounts, in reality, to nothing more than saying that on the basis of its own private conceptions of morality that employer wishes to set aside a fundamental principle of Community law in relation to some people because it does

---

61 Council Directive 75/117/EEC of 10 February 1975 on the approximation of the laws of the Member States relating to the application of the principle of equal pay for men and women [1975] OJ L45/19 and Council Directive 76/207/EEC of 9 February 1976 on the implementation of the principle of equal treatment for men and women as regards access to employment, vocational training and promotion, and working conditions [1976] OJ L39/40.

62 Case C-249/96 *Grant* v. *South-West Trains Ltd* [1998] ECR I-621, ECLI:EU:C:1998:63.

63 Case C-249/96 *Grant* v. *South-West Trains Ltd* [1998] ECR I-621, ECLI:EU:C:1998:63, para. 8.

64 Council Directive 75/117/EEC of 10 February 1975 on the approximation of the laws of the Member States relating to the application of the principle of equal pay for men and women [1975] OJ L45/19.

65 Directive 2006/54/EC of the European Parliament and of the Council of 5 July 2006 on the implementation of the principle of equal opportunities and equal treatment of men and women in matters of employment and occupation (recast) [2006] OJ L204/23.

66 Case C-249/96 *Grant* v. *South-West Trains Ltd* [1998] ECR I-621, ECLI:EU:C:1998:63, para. 9.

67 *Idem*, para. 18.

68 Case C-249/96 *Grant* v. *South-West Trains Ltd* [1998] ECR I-621, ECLI:EU:C:1997:449, Opinion of AG Elmer, paras. 26, 38 and 43.

69 *Idem*, para. 27. In para. 34 of his Opinion Elmer concluded: 'Gender discrimination is […], in this case, not the result of family law legislation in the Member State in question and for that reason outside the scope of Community law.'

> not care for their life style. Whether the private conceptions of morality held by the employer in question correspond to those prevalent in the United Kingdom or not must be irrelevant in this connection. Under the Treaty it is the rule of law in the Community that the Court must safeguard; it is not its task to watch over questions of morality either in the individual Member States or in the Community, nor does it have any practical possibility of or political mandate for doing so. If a choice should have to be made in the Community between various views of morality that must be a task for the Community's political institutions, and hence it is for the legislature to make such choices by way of treaty or Community legislation.'[70]

The CJEU took a somewhat different approach in this case. It ruled that the refusal by Ms. Grant's employer to allow travel concessions to her same-sex partner, did not constitute prohibited discrimination.[71] The Court held, firstly, that the condition imposed by the employer's regulations applied 'in the same way to female and male workers' and could therefore not be regarded as constituting discrimination directly based on sex.[72] The Court next considered whether, with respect to the application of a condition such as that imposed by Ms. Grant's employer, persons who had a stable relationship with a partner of the same sex were in the same situation as those who were married or had a stable relationship outside marriage with a different-sex partner. It took note of the fact that the European Parliament had declared that it deplored all forms of discrimination based on an individual's sexual orientation,[73] but also noted that the Community had, at the time, not adopted 'rules providing for such equivalence'.[74] The CJEU furthermore took into account that most Member States either treated cohabitation by two persons of the same sex as equivalent to a stable same-sex relationship outside marriage only with respect to a limited number of rights, or did not recognise such cohabitation in any particular way.[75] Lastly, the CJEU referred to the case law of the ECtHR and the ECmHR, which at the time had not (yet) ruled that stable homosexual relationships fell within the scope of the right to respect for family life under Article 8 ECHR and who had interpreted the right to

---

70 *Idem*, paras. 40–41.

71 Following *Grant* the English High Court withdrew its reference in the Perkins case (Case C-168/97, *R.* v. *Secretary of State for Defence, ex parte Perkins*), concerning the discharge of persons from the armed forces of a Member State on account of their sexual orientation. See M. Bell, 'Sexual Orientation Discrimination in Employment; An Evolving Role for the European Union', in: R. Wintemute and M. Andenæs (ed.), *Legal Recognition of Same-Sex Partnerships, A Study of National, European and International Law* (Oxford, Hart Publishing 2001) p. 653 at p. 653.

72 Case C-249/96, *Grant* v. *South-West Trains Ltd* [1998] ECR I-621, ECLI:EU:C:1998:63, para. 28. McInnes called this argument flawed, for failing to recognise 'that the terms "opposite-sex" and "same-sex" are in themselves sex-base criteria'. J. McInnes, 'Case note to Case C249/ 96, Lisa Jacqueline Grant v. South West Trains Ltd, Judgment of the Full Court of 17 February 1998, [1998] ECR I636', 36 *CMLRev* (1999) p. 1043 at p. 1049. See pp. 1050–1053 on the discussion whether discrimination on grounds of sexual orientation is a species of sex discrimination.

73 Case C-249/96 *Grant* v. *South-West Trains Ltd* [1998] ECR I-621, ECLI:EU:C:1998:63, para. 31.The CJEU did not refer to any specific EP Resolution or document.

74 *Idem*, para. 31.

75 *Idem*, para. 32.

marry of Article 12 ECHR as applying only to the traditional marriage between two persons of different biological sex.[76]

On these grounds, the CJEU concluded that in the state of the law within the Community at the time, stable relationships between two persons of the same sex were not regarded as equivalent to marriages or stable relationships outside marriage between persons of different sex.[77] The Court held it to be '[...] for the legislature alone to adopt, if appropriate, measures which may affect that position.'[78] The Court further rejected Ms. Grant's submission that differences of treatment based on sexual orientation were included in the 'discrimination based on sex' as prohibited by Article 119 EC Treaty (now 157 TFEU).[79] It ruled that Community law as it stood at the time did not cover discrimination based on sexual orientation. In this respect the Court noted, however, that the Treaty of Amsterdam (1999)[80] – which had not yet entered into force at the time[81] – provided for a Union competence in this respect.[82]

9.3.2. The inclusion of sexual orientation in the Treaties in 1999

Since the Treaty of Amsterdam, the Council is competent – on a proposal from the Commission and after consulting the European Parliament – to '[...] take appropriate action to combat discrimination based on sex, racial or ethnic origin, religion or belief, disability, age or sexual orientation.' The inclusion of this 'enabling clause'[83] – at the time Article 13 EC Treaty and presently Article 19 TFEU – was preceded by various discussions.[84] It has, for example, been reported that the Dutch Presidency at a certain moment suggested dropping the reference to, *inter alia*, sexual orientation, as it was

---

76 *Idem*, paras. 33–34. The ECtHR later ruled in the case of *Schalk and Kopf* v. *Austria* (2010) that same-sex couples enjoy a right to respect for family life (see ch. 8 section 8.2.2.2).

77 *Idem*, para. 35. McInnes argued that the CJEU's discussion of the equivalence of same-sex and opposite-sex relationship could, implicitly be seen as 'one centred on morality'. McInnes 1999, *supra* n. 72, at p. 1053.

78 Case C-249/96 *Grant* v. *South-West Trains Ltd* [1998] ECR I-621, ECLI:EU:C:1998:63, para. 36.

79 This position was also taken by the European Commission. The Commission submitted, however, that the discrimination of which Ms. Grant complained was based not on her sexual orientation but on the fact that she was not living as a couple or with a spouse, and that therefore the difference of treatment applied by the regulations of her employer was not contrary to Article 119 ECT Treaty. Case C-249/96 *Grant* v. *South-West Trains Ltd* [1998] ECR I-621, ECLI:EU:C:1998:63, para. 23.

80 Treaty of Amsterdam amending the Treaty on European Union, the Treaties establishing the European Communities and certain related acts [1997] OJ C340/1.

81 The Treaty of Amsterdam was signed on 2 October 1997 and entered into force on 1 May 1999.

82 Case C-249/96 *Grant* v. *South-West Trains Ltd* [1998] ECR I-621, ECLI:EU:C:1998:63, para. 48. By some this was perceived as 'a sign of judicial deference to the Member States'. McInnes 1999, *supra* n. 72, at p. 1055. The author explains that '[i]n choosing to keep Article 13 as an enabling provision, as opposed to a judicially enforceable right to non-discrimination, the Member States have made it clear that they do not wish to relinquish their sovereignty. If, and only if, all the Member States agree will action be taken. Consequently, had the Court in *Grant* interpreted the existing law in such a way as to include sexual orientation discrimination, it would have been acting in defiance of the Member States.'

83 McInnes 1999, *supra* n. 72, at p. 1056.

84 According to McInnes, '[t]he disagreements during the IGC as to the actual grounds of protection in Article 13 are indicative of how controversial this area is and how difficult it is going to be to achieve the support of all the Member States.' McInnes 1999, *supra* n. 72, at p. 1056, referring (in footnote 58),

feared that its inclusion would prevent the clause from being accepted at all.[85] This suggestion was not, in the end, accepted by the Intergovernmental Conference.[86] Bell concluded that '[o]ne of the important lessons from the negotiation of Article 13 EC [was] the possibility of advancing sexual orientation issues when placed in the context of wider anti-discrimination law reform.'[87]

The adoption of the new Article 13 EC Treaty was at the time perceived as '[a]n important, but largely symbolic step'.[88] This is because the Council can only act unanimously,[89] and because the provision has no direct effect.[90] Nevertheless, soon after its creation, the new competence was employed. As Bell has explained, the European Commission '[k]een to build upon the existing momentum [...] swiftly committed itself to proposing anti-discrimination legislation founded on the new competence.'[91] The two most prominent instruments adopted since Article 13 was included in the EC Treaty, are the Employment Equality Directive (2000/78/EC)[92] and the Race Equality Directive (2000/43/EC).[93] While the latter has no significant relevance for the present case study on same-sex relationships, interesting cases on the application of the Employment Equality Directive in situations concerning same-sex relationships have come before the CJEU.

---

to: 'NonPaper No. 6, Fundamental Rights and Non Discrimination, Conference of the Representatives of the Governments of the Member States, Secretariat, Brussels, 26 Feb. 1997, Conf/3827/97.'

85 See McInnes 1999, *supra* n. 72, at p. 1056.

86 L. Flynn, 'The implications of article 13 EC – after Amsterdam, will some forms of discrimination be more equal than others?', 36 *CMLRev* (1999) p. 117 at p. 132, referring (in footnote 18) to 'Kingston, "Fundamental rights and non-discrimination in the Treaty of Amsterdam", in Tonra (ed.), *Legal and Constitutional Implications of the Amsterdam Treaty* (Institute of European Affairs, 1997), p. 49, 53.'

87 Bell 2001, *supra* n. 71, at p. 676.

88 K. Waaldijk, 'Towards the Recognition of Same-Sex Partners in EU law', in: R. Wintemute and M. Andenæs (ed.), *Legal Recognition of Same-Sex Partnerships, A Study of National, European and International Law* (Oxford, Hart Publishing 2001) p. 635 at p. 648. Also McInnes expected in 1999 that Art. 13 EC Treaty would 'prove to be of greater symbolic that practical value.' McInnes 1999, *supra* n. 72, at p. 1057.

89 The present Art. 19(1) TFEU reads: 'Without prejudice to the other provisions of the Treaties and within the limits of the powers conferred by them upon the Union, the Council, acting unanimously in accordance with a special legislative procedure and after obtaining the consent of the European Parliament, may take appropriate action to combat discrimination based on sex, racial or ethnic origin, religion or belief, disability, age or sexual orientation.'

90 As Guild has explained, the provision 'clearly lacks sufficient clarity, precision and unconditionality'. E. Guild, 'Free Movement and Same-Sex Relationships', in: R. Wintemute and M. Andenæs (ed.), *Legal Recognition of Same-Sex Partnerships, A Study of National, European and International Law* (Oxford, Hart Publishing 2001) p. 677 at p. 687. See also P. Craig and G. De Búrca, *EU law, Text, cases and materials*, 5th edn. (Oxford, Oxford University Press 2011) p. 868.

91 Bell 2001, *supra* n. 71, at p. 655, referring to 'Commission, "An action plan against racism", COM (1998) 183 (25 April 1998), at para. 2.2.2'.

92 Council Directive 2000/78/EC of 27 November 2000 establishing a general framework for equal treatment in employment and occupation [2000] OJ L303/16.

93 Council Directive 2000/43/EC of 29 June 2000 implementing the principle of equal treatment between persons irrespective of racial or ethnic origin [2000] OJ L180/22. In 2008 the Commission furthermore made a proposal for a Council Directive which aims to implement the principle of equal treatment between persons irrespective of religion or belief, disability, age or sexual orientation outside the labour market. This proposal and its implications for the present case study are discussed in section 9.3.4.1 below.

9.3.3. The Employment Equality Directive and relevant case law

The Employment Equality Directive put in place a general framework to ensure the equal treatment of individuals in the European Union, regardless of their religion or belief, disability, age or sexual orientation, as regards access to employment or occupation and membership of certain organisations.[94] It was held that discrimination on the aforementioned grounds could undermine the achievement of the EU's objectives, '[...] in particular the attainment of a high level of employment and social protection, raising the standard of living and the quality of life, economic and social cohesion and solidarity, and the free movement of persons.'[95] The Directive covers matters like harassment[96] and indirect discrimination,[97] and has been received as '[...] a significant advantage for lesbian and gay rights within European Union law'.[98]

Of particular interest for the present research is Recital No. 22 in the Preamble to the Directive, which reads:

> 'This Directive is without prejudice to national laws on marital status and the benefits dependent thereon.'

The interpretation and legal status of this text was at stake in three prominent CJEU judgments concerning same-sex couples, namely *Maruko* (2008),[99] *Römer* (2011) and *Hay* (2013).[100] The discussion of these three judgments hereafter will make clear that neither Directive 2000/78, nor the Court's case law, require Member States to introduce a form of registered partnership.[101] As Tobler and Waaldijk have made clear, '[u]nder the constitutional framework set up by the [...] Treaty the Member States retain the competence to decide on the forms of civil status that are available under their national legal system.'[102] However, once they introduce an alternative form of registration, States must observe the principle of equal treatment, so the case law shows.

---

94 See www.europa.eu/legislation_summaries/employment_and_social_policy/employment_rights_and_work_organisation/c10823_en.htm, visited July 2013.

95 Recital 11 of Council Directive 2000/78/EC.

96 Art. 2(3) Council Directive 2000/78/EC.

97 Art. 2(2)(b) Council Directive 2000/78/EC describes indirect discrimination on grounds of sexual orientation as the situation '[...] where an apparently neutral provision, criterion or practice would put persons having [...] a particular sexual orientation at a particular disadvantage compared with other persons unless: [...] that provision, criterion or practice is objectively justified by a legitimate aim and the means of achieving that aim are appropriate and necessary [...].'

98 Bell 2001, *supra* n. 71, at p. 675.

99 Case C-267/06 *Tadao Maruko* v. *Versorgungsanstalt der deutschen Bühnen* [2008] ECR I-1757, ECLI:EU:C:2008:179.

100 Case C-147/08 *Jürgen Römer* v. *Freie und Hansestadt Hamburg* [2011] ECR I-3591, ECLI:EU:C:2011:286. Since both *Maruko* and *Römer* concerned a preliminary reference by a German Court, reference is also made to discussion of these cases and their follow-up in the German legal order in ch.10, section 10.3.4.

101 C. Tobler and K. Waaldijk, 'Case note to Case C-267/06, *Tadao Maruko* v. *Versorgungsanstalt der deutschen Bühnen*, Judgment of the Grand Chamber of the Court of Justice of 1 April 2008', 46 *CMLRev* (2009) p. 743.

102 *Idem.*

9.3.3.1. *The Maruko judgment (2008)*

The principal question in *Maruko* was whether Directive 2000/78/EC precluded regulations governing a supplementary pension scheme under which, after the death of his registered partner, the surviving partner did not receive a survivor's benefit equivalent to that granted to a surviving spouse, even though he had lived in a union of mutual support and assistance which had been formally constituted for life.[103] In its judgment of 1 April 2008 the Grand Chamber of the CJEU ruled that an occupational pension scheme as the one at issue in the *Maruko* case, was indeed precluded if, under national law, civil partnership placed persons of the same sex in a situation comparable to that of spouses so far as that survivor's benefit was concerned.[104] The CJEU left it up to the referring court to determine in a concrete case whether such comparability of situations could be found.[105]

Mr. Maruko and the Commission had qualified the refusal to grant a widower's pension to Mr. Maruko as indirect discrimination on grounds of sexual orientation, because two persons of the same sex could not marry in Germany and, consequently, could not qualify for the widower's pension, a benefit that was reserved to surviving spouses.[106] In their opinion, surviving civil partners had to be granted the widower's pension, because spouses and civil partners were in a comparable legal situation.[107] Advocate General Ruiz-Jarabo Colomer adopted a similar line of reasoning[108] and held in this respect:

---

[103] The discussion here will focus on the third and fourth questions as posed by the referring court. The third question focussed in particular at compatibility of the pension scheme with Art. 1 in conjunction with Art. 2(2)(a) of 2000/78/EC. The preliminary questions as to (other elements of) the scope of the Directive and the temporal aspect of the matter, will not be discussed here.

[104] Case C-267/06 *Tadao Maruko* v. *Versorgungsanstalt der deutschen Bühnen* [2008] ECR I-1757, ECLI:EU:C:2008:179.

[105] As further explained in Ch. 10, the CJEU noted in its judgment that the referring court itself had acknowledged that in Germany a 'harmonisation between marriage and life partnership' took place, which could be regarded as 'a gradual movement towards recognising equivalence' and that therefore registered civil partnership, while not identical to marriage, placed persons of the same sex in a situation comparable to that of spouses as far as the survivor's benefit was concerned. *Idem*, para. 69.

[106] Case C-267/06 *Tadao Maruko* v. *Versorgungsanstalt der deutschen Bühnen* [2008] ECR I-1757, ECLI:EU:C:2008:179, para. 63.

[107] H. Graupner, 'Comparing people or institutions? Sexual Orientation Discrimination and the Court of Justice of the European Union', in: K. Boele-Woelki and A. Fuchs (eds.), *Legal recognition of same-sex Relationships in Europe, National, cross-border and European perspectives*, 2nd edn. (Cambridge, Intersentia 2012) p. 271 at p. 275. As Graupner explains (on pp. 275–276) '[t]his conclusion was [...] made under the assumption that, under national law, a registered partnership is equivalent to a marriage [...]. Accepting such an assumption would lead to the strange, and perhaps even somewhat absurd, result that the lesser discrimination exhibited in Member States with a marriage-equivalent registered partnership would be outlawed, whereas the (arguably) more serious discrimination (prevalent in Member States without registered partnership or with a form of registered partnership inferior to marriage) would remain admissible. This would be the result notwithstanding that in both cases the parties involved were subjected to the same kind of unequal treatment.'

[108] According to the AG, Mr. Maruko had been refused a survivor's pension '[...] because he was not married to his partner and [was] not a 'widower', a status which [was] restricted by law to the spouse of the deceased, and because there [was] no evidence that such a pension [had] been granted to other individuals in identical or analogous situations.' Case C-267/06 *Tadao Maruko* v. *Versorgungsanstalt*

'[...] it is not for the Court to define emotional relationships between persons of the same sex, a matter which is the subject of fierce debate, [...] or to rule on the effects which the legislation of each Member State attributes to the registration of such partnerships. [...] [It] is not a question of developing "European matrimonial law" but of ensuring that the principle that there should be no discrimination [...] is fully effective [...].'[109]

In legal scholarship it had been likewise anticipated that the CJEU would find indirect discrimination on grounds of sexual orientation in a *Maruko* type of case.[110] It therefore came as a surprise to many that the CJEU established direct discrimination on this ground, instead.[111] The CJEU's approach has been welcomed by some, although it was regretted that the Court gave little explanation for its approach.[112] The CJEU was indeed brief on this point: it reiterated the definitions of direct and indirect discrimination as laid down in Article 2 of the Directive[113] and proceeded by examining the relevant German national law. It observed a gradual harmonisation between marriage and life partnership under German law and it concluded as follows:

'If the referring court decides that surviving spouses and surviving life partners are in a comparable situation so far as concerns that survivor's benefit, legislation such as that at issue in the main proceedings must, as a consequence, be considered to constitute direct discrimination on grounds of sexual orientation, within the meaning of Articles 1 and 2(2)(a) of Directive 2000/78.'[114]

der deutschen Bühnen [2008] ECR I-1757, ECLI:EU:C:2007:486, Opinion of AG Ruiz-Jarabo Colomer, para. 96.

109 *Idem*, para. 98, referring (in footnote 96) to *D. and Sweden* v. *Council* and Moliner Navarro, R.M., 'El matrimonio de personas del mismo sexo en el Derecho comparado', Matrimonio y adopción por personas del mismo sexo, Cuadernos de Derecho Judicial, no XXVI/2005, Consejo General del Poder Judicial, Madrid, 2006, p. 221 et seq.; (in footnote 97) to 'Alonso Herreros, D., 'Funcionamiento y eficacia de los Registros de uniones civiles de hecho en España y en otros países europeos', Cuadernos de derecho público, no 15, January-April 2002, p. 103 et seq.' and to Case C-117/01 *K.B* [2004] ECR I-541, ECLI:EU:C:2007:486, Opinion of AG Ruiz-Jarabo Colomer.

110 K. Waaldijk, 'Case note to ECJ (GC) judgment of 1 April 2008 in Case C-267/06 Tadao Maruko/ Versorgungsanstalt der deutschen Bühnen' (in Dutch), 9 *European Human Rights Cases* 2008/65, who explains that most scholars anticipated indirect discrimination (Waaldijk referred to Bell 2001, *supra* n. 71, at p. 668 and 'K. Waaldijk & M. Bonini-Baraldi, *Sexual Orientation Discrimination in the European Union*, Den Haag: Asser 2006, p. 42 en 115–117'), while some saw legal ground for finding direct discrimination (Waaldijk referred to Bell 2001, *supra* n. 71, at p. 668; Waaldijk 2001B, *supra* n. 88, at p. 645; H. Ytterberg, 'Sweden', in: K. Waaldijk & M. Bonini-Baraldi, *Combating sexual orientation discrimination in employment* (Leiden, Universiteit Leiden 2004) pp. 459–460 and R. Wintemute, 'United Kingdom', in: Waaldijk & Bonini-Baraldi 2004, p. 495).

111 Direct discrimination on grounds of sexual orientation is described in Art. 2(a) Directive 2000/78/EC as a situation '[...] where one person is treated less favourably than another is, has been or would be treated in a comparable situation, on [...] grounds [of sexual orientation]'.

112 Tobler and Waaldijk 2009, *supra* n. 101, at pp. 736–737.

113 Case C-267/06 *Tadao Maruko* v. *Versorgungsanstalt der deutschen Bühnen* [2008] ECR I-1757, ECLI:EU:C:2008:179, para. 66.

114 *Idem*, para. 72.

Others considered the CJEU's decision to treat the case as a case of direct discrimination problematic.[115] There has been criticism of the fact that the logic was only applicable in States that had introduced a form of legal recognition of same-sex relationships comparable to marriage.[116] This involved a risk of 'differing approaches to comparability'[117] and some even called this a 'circular' reasoning.[118] Others noted that with this reasoning the CJEU strengthened citizens' rights, while displaying '[...] some respect for the constitutional differences between the Member States regarding same-sex relations.'[119] It has furthermore been observed that the Court opted for a finding of direct discrimination in *Maruko* '[...] in order to exclude the objective justification argument of fostering marriage, that had been accepted by the German courts on the basis of Article 6 of the German Constitution.'[120]

The referring court had also asked if – in the case that discrimination on grounds of sexual orientation was found – such discrimination was permissible by virtue of Recital 22 to the Directive, following which the Directive, as noted above, was held to be '[...] without prejudice to national laws on marital status and the benefits dependent thereon'. Both Mr. Maruko and the Commission asserted that the content of this Recital was not reflected in any of the enacting terms of the Directive.[121] According to the Commission, the Recital did '[...] no more than state that the European Union lack[ed] competence in matters regarding civil status.'[122] AG Ruiz-Jarabo Colomer concurred that the Recital had no binding force and 'merely' assisted 'with the interpretation of the provisions of the Directive'. He held that its significance was not to be overstated.[123] The employer of Mr. Maruko's deceased partner and the

115 M. Moschel, 'Germany's Life Partnerships: Separate and Unequal', 16 *Colum. J. Eur. L.* (2009–2010) p. 37 at p. 44 and J. Mulder, 'Some More Equal than Others? Matrimonial Benefits and the CJEU's Case Law on Discrimination on the Grounds of Sexual Orientation', 19 *Maastricht Journal of European and Comparative Law* (2012) p. 505.

116 Moschel observed that the case brought '[...] no relief for nationals of Member States where the Member State [had] not provided for any legal recognition for same-sex relationships, as in those cases no comparison between similar situations [was] possible since no institution similar or parallel to marriage exist[ed].' *Idem*, at p. 44.

117 *Idem*, at p. 44.

118 J. Cornides, 'Three Case Studies on Anti-Discrimination', 23 *European Journal of International Law* (2012) p. 517 at p. 523.

119 H. de Waele and A. van der Vleuten, 'Judicial Activism in the European Court of Justice – The Case of LGBT Rights', 19 *Mich. St. U. Coll. L. J. Int'l L.* (2010–2011) p. 639 at p. 662. Compare A. Eriksson, 'European Court of Justice: Broadening the Scope of European Nondiscrimination Law [notes]', 7 *International Journal of Constitutional Law* (2009) p. 731 at p. 744.

120 Tobler and Waaldijk 2009, *supra* n. 101, at p. 736, referring (in footnote 23) to 'Lembke, 'Sind an die Ehe geknüpfte Leistungen des Arbeitgebers auch an Lebenspartner zu gewähren? ', (2008) *NJW* p. 1631 at p. 1633'.

121 Case C-267/06 *Tadao Maruko* v. *Versorgungsanstalt der deutschen Bühnen* [2008] ECR I-1757, ECLI:EU:C:2008:179, para. 38. See also Tobler and Waaldijk 2009, *supra* n. 101, at p. 731.

122 Mr. Maruko asserted that '[...] if the Community legislature had wanted to exclude all benefits bound up with civil status from the scope of Directive 2000/78, the content of that recital would have been the subject of a particular provision among the enacting terms of the Directive.' Case C-267/06 *Tadao Maruko* v. *Versorgungsanstalt der deutschen Bühnen* [2008] ECR I-1757, ECLI:EU:C:2008:179, para. 38.

123 Case C-267/06 *Tadao Maruko* v. *Versorgungsanstalt der deutschen Bühnen* [2008] ECR I-1757, ECLI:EU:C:2007:486, Opinion of AG Ruiz-Jarabo Colomer, para. 76.

intervening United Kingdom government argued instead that on the basis of Recital 22, provisions of national law relating to civil status or to benefits dependent on that status, were excluded from the scope of the Directive.[124] The CJEU did not adopt this reasoning and ruled that Recital 22 could not affect the application of the Directive.[125] It acknowledged that civil status and the benefits flowing therefrom were '[...] matters which [fell] within the competence of the Member States and Community law [did] not detract from that competence'. It also recalled, however, that '[...] in the exercise of that competence the Member States [had to] comply with Community law and, in particular, with the provisions relating to the principle of non-discrimination'.[126] On this ground, Tobler and Waaldijk called this an important case in the context of division of competences between the EU (at the time the EC) and the Member States, in particular in relation to civil status.[127] They argued that

> '[...] the fact that the Treaty does not give the EC an explicit competence in a given field, thereby leaving it with the Member States, does not mean that EC law from other areas – either on the level of Treaty provisions or that of secondary law – cannot apply in this field. Put differently, the Member States' competences are not "exclusive" in the sense that national legislation is immune from EC law. For the Member States, this may be difficult to accept, in particular where EC law touches upon fields that have traditionally been considered as Member State reserves, such as [...] marriage.'[128]

Various other authors pointed out that the CJEU's finding in respect of Recital 22 was particularly important because the Recital had at the time been welcomed by Member States as providing strong protection for favourable treatment of spouses.[129] Bruns noted that States were still free to introduce an alternative registration form and to equalise this with marriage or not. However, once they decided to introduce such a registration or once they took the opportunity to equalise treatment, they were bound to observe the principle of equal treatment.[130]

---

124 Case C-267/06 *Tadao Maruko* v. *Versorgungsanstalt der deutschen Bühnen* [2008] ECR I-1757, ECLI:EU:C:2008:179, para. 39. As Tobler and Waaldijk explain, '[...] when implementing this Directive, at least three Member States (Ireland, Italy and the United Kingdom) interpreted this recital as a basis allowing for more beneficial treatment of married partners.' Tobler and Waaldijk 2009, *supra* n. 101, at p. 732, referring (in footnote 22) to C. Waaldijk and M. Bonini-Baraldi, *Sexual orientation discrimination in the European Union, National laws and the Employment Equality Directive* (The Hague, TMC Asser Press 2006) p. 115.

125 Case C-267/06 *Tadao Maruko* v. *Versorgungsanstalt der deutschen Bühnen* [2008] ECR I-1757, ECLI:EU:C:2008:179, para. 60.

126 *Idem*, para. 59, under reference to Case C-372/04 *Watts* [2006] ECR I-4325, ECLI:EU:C:2006:325, para. 92 and Case C-444/05 *Stamatelaki* [2007] ECR I-3185, ECLI:EU:C:2007:231, para. 23.

127 Tobler and Waaldijk 2009, *supra* n. 101, at p. 723.

128 *Idem*, p. 735. In footnote 31 the authors explain: 'Apart from the issue of competences, family law is a prime example of an area where EC law has an influence simply because of the frequent reference in EC law to concepts coming from this area; see e.g. Tobler, "Der Begriff der Ehe im EG-Recht", (2001) *Die Praxis des Familienrechts*, p. 479–499. More recently, see e.g. Art. 2 of Directive 2004/38/EC [...].'

129 Moschel 2009, *supra* n. 116, at p. 42. See also Waele, de and Vleuten, van der 2011, *supra* n. 119, at p. 662.

130 M. Bruns, 'Die Maruko-Entscheidung im Spannungsfeld zwischen europäischer und nationaler Auslegung', *NJW* (2008) p. 1929. Along similar lines, Eriksson observed that the finding of the Court meant that '[i]f the member states decide[d] to introduce a special civil status for homosexual couples,

The subsequent *Römer* case (2011)[131] '[…] provided the CJEU with the opportunity […] to specify or even extend the scope of the Maruko-judgment (and rule beyond comparability, on indirect discrimination).'[132]

9.3.3.2. The Römer judgment (2011)

The Grand Chamber of the CJEU ruled in *Römer* that a provision of national law under which a pensioner who had entered into a registered partnership received a supplementary retirement pension lower than that granted to a married pensioner could constitute discrimination on grounds of sexual orientation, prohibited by Directive 2000/78.[133] The Court held this to be the case if: (1) in the Member State concerned, marriage is reserved to persons of different sex and exists alongside a registered partnership which is reserved to persons of the same sex; and (2) there is direct discrimination on the ground of sexual orientation because, under national law, that registered partner is in a legal and factual situation comparable to that of a married person as regards that pension. The Court, like it had done in *Maruko*, left it to the referring court to assess the comparability of situations.[134] This time it gave more guidelines, however, and made clear that this assessment should focus '[…] on the respective rights and obligations of spouses and persons in a registered partnership, as governed within the corresponding institutions, which are relevant taking account of the purpose of and the conditions for the grant of the benefit in question'.[135]

Other than Advocate General Jääskinen, the CJEU did not address the referring court's question of whether, and under what conditions, an objective pursued by a Member State on the basis of a national constitutional norm, such as the protection of marriage, contained in Article 6(1) of the German Basic Law, could justify direct discrimination on ground of sexual orientation.[136] In this respect, the CJEU merely noted, in line with its previous *Maruko* judgment that as European Union law stood at that point in time, legislation on the marital status of persons fell within the competence of the Member States.[137]

they [had to] do so in conformity with the principle of non discrimination as contained in Directive 2000/78/EC and ensure that they [were] not discriminated against in the field of employment.' A. Eriksson, 'European Court of Justice: Broadening the Scope of European Nondiscrimination Law [notes]', 7 *International Journal of Constitutional Law* (2009) p. 731 at pp. 745–746.

131 Case C-147/08 *Jürgen Römer* v. *Freie und Hansestadt Hamburg* [2011] ECR I-3591, ECLI:EU:C:2011:286.

132 Graupner 2012, *supra* n. 107, at p. 279. As Tobler and Waaldijk explained, it was, for example, 'unclear whether, in countries without registered partnership, […] unregistered same-sex partners challenging their exclusion from a marital benefit, should invoke the prohibition of direct sexual orientation discrimination or that of indirect sexual orientation discrimination.' Tobler and Waaldijk 2009, *supra* n. 101, at p. 744.

133 In particular Art. 1 in conjunction with Arts. 2 and 3(1)(c).

134 Case C-147/08 *Jürgen Römer* v. *Freie und Hansestadt Hamburg* [2011] ECR I-3591, ECLI:EU:C:2011:286, para. 52.

135 *Idem*, para. 52.

136 As rephrased by the CJEU in *idem*, para. 37.

137 *Idem*, para. 38.

Advocate General Jääskinen had underlined that it was exclusively for States to decide if they provided in their national legal order for a legal union between partners of the same sex. The AG had been of the opinion that it constituted discrimination on grounds of sexual orientation if a State did not provide for any form of legal recognition of same-sex relationships. He had held that, on grounds of the principle of equal treatment in combination with the obligation to respect the human dignity of homosexuals, States had an obligation to provide for some form of legal recognition for same-sex couples. Jääskinen had acknowledged, however, that this matter of civil law fell outside the scope of EU law.[138] With respect to matters that fell within the scope of EU law, on the contrary, such as matters within the scope of the free movement rules or within the scope of the Employment Equality Directive, the AG had held a reference to national law concerning civil status to be insufficient as justification for an infringement of these rights.[139] Jääskinen had questioned whether protection of the family and marriage could form a valid objective justification for indirect discrimination.[140] In any case, he had not seen how the disputed rule could be necessary and proportionate to attain this interest, as there was no causal relationship between this type of discrimination as a means and the protection of marriage as possible beneficial effect of this discrimination.[141] He had furthermore made a plea for the recognition of a general principle of EU law of non-discrimination on grounds of sexual orientation (see section 9.3.4.2 below). On this point also Jääskinen was not followed by the CJEU.

Graupner observed that the *Maruko* and the *Römer* cases ultimately boiled down to the issue of deciding upon the comparative parameters.[142] The author concluded that the Court's case law made clear that '[p]eople (couples) [were] to be compared, not abstract legal institutions'.[143] According to Graupner, the CJEU established an 'individual-specific comparison', whereby comparability has to be established in the light of the benefit concerned.[144] This line of reasoning was continued and even taken one step further in *Hay* (2013).[145]

9.3.3.3. The Hay judgment (2013)

The *Hay* case was not – unlike *Maruko* and *Römer* – decided by a Grand Chamber, and no Advocate General delivered an Opinion in this case. The CJEU held in this

---

138 Case C-147/08 *Jürgen Römer* v. *Freie und Hansestadt Hamburg* [2011] ECR I-3591, ECLI:EU:C:2010:425, Opinion of AG Jääskinen, para. 76.

139 *Idem*, para. 77.

140 *Idem*, paras. 109–110. In para. 175 of his Opinion, the AG was even firmer in holding that it went without saying '[…] that the aim of protecting marriage or the family [could not] legitimise discrimination on grounds of sexual orientation.' The AG found it '[…] difficult to imagine what causal relationship could unite that type of discrimination, as grounds, and the protection of marriage, as a positive effect that could derive from it.'

141 *Idem*, paras. 109–111.

142 Graupner 2012, *supra* n. 107, at p. 276.

143 *Idem*, at p. 281.

144 *Idem*, at pp. 276 and 280.

145 Case C-267/12 *Frédéric Hay* v. *Crédit agricole mutuel de Charente-Maritime et des Deux-Sèvres* [2013] ECR 0000, ECLI:EU:C:2013:823.

case that partners who had concluded a civil solidarity pact under French law (*Pacte civil de solidarité* (PACS)) were in a comparable situation with spouses in respect of benefits that were granted under a national collective agreement to employees on the occasion of their marriage, such as days of special leave and a salary bonus.[146] Not granting an employee such benefits upon the occasion of the conclusion of a civil solidarity pact, constituted direct discrimination on grounds of sexual orientation in breach of Directive 2000/78, the Court held. Thereby it was relevant that under French law at the time same-sex couples had no access to marriage, rendering the PACS '[...] the only possibility under French law for same-sex couples to procure legal status for their relationship which could be certain and effective against third parties.'[147] Because marriage was not open to same-sex couples, it was impossible for homosexual employees to meet the condition required for obtaining the benefit claimed, and they were thus directly discriminated against on grounds of sexual orientation.[148] The fact that the French PACS was open to both different-sex and same-sex partners and the fact that there were general differences between the systems governing marriage and the PACS arrangement – for example with respect to the reciprocal obligations under property law, succession law and law relating to parenthood – did not alter that conclusion. The Court summarised its position in this regard as follows:

> '[...] as regards benefits in terms of pay or working conditions, such as days of special leave and a bonus like those at issue in the main proceedings, granted at the time of an employee's marriage – which is a form of civil union – persons of the same sex who cannot enter into marriage and therefore conclude a PACS are in a situation which is comparable to that of couples who marry.'[149]

The CJEU thus by itself examined the question of comparability, instead of leaving this matter to the referring court, as it had done in both *Maruko* and *Römer*. Moreover, for the first time the Court also addressed the question of justification. As it had found that there was direct discrimination, this could only be upheld if one of the justification grounds of Article 2(5) of Directive 2000/78 applied, namely public security, the maintenance of public order and the prevention of criminal offences, the protection of health and the protection of the rights and freedoms of others. By finding that none of these grounds had been relied upon in the main proceedings and stressing that Article 2(5) had to be interpreted strictly, the Court implied that the discrimination could not be justified.[150]

---

146 The Court reiterated that such an assessment of comparability had to be carried out 'not in a global and abstract manner, but in a specific and concrete manner in the light of the benefit concerned'. *Idem*, para. 33.

147 *Idem*, para. 36.

148 *Idem*, para. 44.

149 *Idem*, para. 37.

150 *Idem*, para. 46.

9.3.4. Possible future developments in EU non-discrimination law

9.3.4.1. Proposed horizontal Equal Treatment Directive

Under the present EU legal framework, discrimination based on sexual orientation is prohibited only in employment, occupation and vocational training (see above). In 2008 the Commission proposed a new Council Directive based on Article 19 TFEU, which would apply outside the field of employment.[151] The proposed Directive was aimed to combat discrimination based on religion or belief, disability, age or sexual orientation[152] in respect of social protection (including social security and health care), social advantages, education and access to and supply of goods and services which are available to the public, including housing.[153] Because of this 'broad-brush'[154] approach many doubted whether the proposal would receive the required unanimity in the Council.[155]

It has been submitted that in respect of legal recognition of same-sex relationships, the proposed Directive could imply 'a setback'.[156] The original proposal clearly held that the Directive was to be without prejudice to national laws on marital or family status, adoption and reproductive rights.[157] The Explanatory Memorandum explained in this respect:

> 'The diversity of European societies is one of Europe's strengths, and is to be respected in line with the principle of subsidiarity. Issues such as the organisation and content of education, recognition of marital or family status, adoption, reproductive rights and other similar questions are best decided at national level. The Directive does not therefore require any Member State to amend its present laws and practices in relation to these issues.'[158]

---

151 Commission, 'Proposal for a Council Directive on implementing the principle of equal treatment between persons irrespective of religion or belief, disability, age or sexual orientation', COM (2008) 426 final, 2008/0140 (CNS). See also L.B. Waddington, 'Future Prospects for EU Equality Law. Lessons to be Learnt from the Proposed Equal Treatment Directive', 17 *European Law Review* (2011) p. 163.

152 Art. 1 of the Proposed Directive.

153 Art. 3 of the Proposed Directive.

154 M. Bell, 'The Principle of Equal Treatment; widening and deepening', in: P. Craig and G. De Búrca, *The evolution of EU Law*, 2nd edn. (Oxford, Oxford University Press 2011) p. 611 at p. 620.

155 Waddington 2011, *supra* n. 151, at pp. 163–164 and Bell 2011, *supra* n. 154, at p. 620.

156 B. Verschraegen, 'The Right to Private and Family Life, the Right to Marry and to Found a Family, and the Prohibition of Discrimination', in: K. Boele-Woelki and A. Fuchs (eds.), *Legal recognition of same-sex Relationships in Europe, National, cross-border and European perspectives*, 2nd edn. (Cambridge, Intersentia 2012) p. 255 at p. 268.

157 Art. 3(2) of the Proposed Directive. See also Recital No. 17 of the Preamble to the Proposed Directive which reads: 'While prohibiting discrimination, it is important to respect other fundamental rights and freedoms, including the protection of private and family life and transactions carried out in that context, the freedom of religion, and the freedom of association. This Directive is without prejudice to national laws on marital or family status, including on reproductive rights. [...]'. 'Family status' was held to include adoption. COM (2008) 426 final, p. 8.

158 COM (2008) 426 final, p. 6.

An amendment by the European Parliament provided more neutrally that the Directive would not '[...] alter the division of competences between the European Union and its Member States.'[159] It was furthermore explicitly held in the Memorandum that Member States remained '[...] free to decide whether or not to institute and recognise *legally* registered partnerships.'[160] The Explanatory Memorandum also underlined however that once national law recognised such relationships as comparable to that of spouses, then the principle of equal treatment applied.[161] The European Economic and Social Committee (EESC) was very critical on this point.[162] It acknowledged that marital status, family status and reproductive rights were matters on which Member States had competence to legislate, but did not accept that such competence was to '[...] wholly negate EU-wide legal protections against discrimination.'[163] The EESC believed that Article 3(2) as a whole had to be reconsidered, whereby 'any final formulation' had to state that '[...] national laws relating to marital status, family status or reproductive rights [had to] be implemented without discrimination against any persons on any of the grounds within the Directive.'[164] The Directive was debated for a number of years and in 2011 the legislative process stagnated.[165] The division of competences, the overall scope of the Directive and subsidiarity were deemed

159 The accompanying Recital 17 was changed into: 'While prohibiting discrimination, it is important to respect other fundamental rights and freedoms, including the freedom of religion, the freedom of association, freedom of expression and freedom of the press. This Directive is without prejudice to the secular nature of the State, state institutions or bodies, or education. This Directive does not alter the division of competences between the European Union and its Member States, including in the area of marital and family law and health law.' European Parliament legislative resolution of 2 April 2009 on the proposal for a Council directive on implementing the principle of equal treatment between persons irrespective of religion or belief, disability, age or sexual orientation (COM(2008)0426 – C6-0291/2008 – 2008/0140(CNS)) [2010] OJ C 137E/68, Amendments 28 and 50.

160 COM (2008) 426 final, p. 8. See also the Commission, 'Staff working document accompanying the proposal for a Council directive on implementing the principle of equal treatment between persons irrespective of religion or belief, disability, age or sexual orientation – Impact assessment (COM(2008) 426 final)', SEC (2011) 328 final where it was held (at p. 6) that the new Directive '[...] would only prohibit discrimination in the areas that fall within EC competence, so would not affect [...] questions of marital status (e.g. same sex partnerships/marriages) or family law (e.g. adoption) [...]'.

161 COM (2008) 426 final, p. 8, referring (in footnote 21) to Case C-267/06 *Tadao Maruko* v. *Versorgungsanstalt der deutschen Bühnen* [2008] ECR I-1757, ECLI:EU:C:2008:179.

162 European Economic and Social Committee, 'Opinion on the 'Proposal for a Council directive on implementing the principle of equal treatment between persons irrespective of religion or belief, disability, age or sexual orientation'', COM (2008) 426 final (Additional opinion) [2009] OJ C182/19.

163 *Idem*, para. 3.2.2.1. In para. 3.2.2.2, the EESC referred (in footnote 9) to Case C-267/06 *Tadao Maruko* v. *Versorgungsanstalt der deutschen Bühnen* [2008] ECR I-1757, ECLI:EU:C:2008:179, para. 59.

164 *Idem*, para. 3.2.2.5.

165 The European Parliament declared in a 2012 Resolution to remain committed to the adoption of the Directive, which, so it was noted, had been blocked 'due to the objections of some Member States'. European Parliament resolution of 24 May 2012 on the fight against homophobia in Europe (2012/2657(RSP)) P7_TA(2012)0222). The EU Fundamental Rights Agency has also held that '[e]qual protection against discrimination on the grounds of sexual orientation across all EU Member States would significantly improve if the EU-wide prohibition of such discrimination extended beyond the field of employment and occupation'. European Union Agency for Fundamental Rights, *EU LGBT survey, European Union lesbian, gay, bisexual and transgender survey, Results at a glance* (Luxembourg, Publications Office of the European Union 2013) p. 12, online available at www.fra.europa.eu/sites/default/files/eu-lgbt-survey-results-at-a-glance_en.pdf, visited June 2014.

amongst the pressing issues around which further discussion was considered to be needed.[166]

9.3.4.2. Non-discrimination on grounds of sexual orientation as a general principle of EU law?

As discussed above, Advocate General Jääskinen held in his Opinion to the *Römer* case (2011) that non-discrimination on grounds of sexual orientation was a general principle of EU law, on the same footing as non-discrimination on grounds of age.[167] From a pure legal viewpoint the AG held there to be no justification for a weaker protection of the principle of equal treatment in situations of discrimination on grounds of sexual orientation, when compared to the other prohibited grounds in Article 19 TFEU. Jääskinen held that if the CJEU recognised the existing sensitivities in this regard, it would attach value to unjustified prejudices, irrespective of their origin, and it would withhold members of a minority equal legal protection.[168] While the CJEU did not follow up this point, Graupner concluded that it was implicit in the CJEU judgment in *Römer*, that the prohibition of discrimination on the basis of sexual orientation was a general principle of Union law.[169] It is questionable, however, if this conclusion really can be drawn from the Court's ruling in that case.

9.4. LGBT rights in the EU's fundamental rights agenda

LGBT rights take a prominent place on the EU's fundamental rights agenda. The reach of Union action in respect of fundamental rights is, however, limited to those areas in which the EU has competences under the Treaties. For the present case study the EU's competences in respect of the internal market (Articles 26 and 115(1) TFEU) and equal treatment (Article 19 TFEU) as discussed above, are most relevant.

Since 2010, the Commission has monitored the implementation of the EU Fundamental Rights Charter.[170] It, *inter alia*, sees to it that the prohibition on

---

166 Press release 3131st Council meeting Employment, Social Policy, Health and Consumer Affairs, Brussels, 1 and 2 December 2011, 17943/1/11 REV 1, PRESSE 471, PR CO 75. The Dutch Government, for example, took the position that States had to be left as much room for making their own policy decisions in these matters. It held that access to social protection and education were matters to be regulated at national level. *Inventarisatie EU-regelgeving op subsidiariteit en proportionaliteit – Nederlandse lijst van actiepunten* [Inventory of EU regulation with a view to subsidiarity and proportionality – Netherlands list of action points], p. 14, point 50.

167 Case C-147/08 *Jürgen Römer* v. *Freie und Hansestadt Hamburg* [2011] ECR I-3591, ECLI:EU:C:2010:425, Opinion of AG Jääskinen, para. 131.

168 *Idem*, para. 129.

169 Graupner 2012, *supra* n. 107, at p. 281, referring (in footnote 52), to para. 59 of the judgment, where the Court held that Directive 2000/78 '[...] does not itself lay down the principle of equal treatment in the field of employment and occupation, which derives from various international instruments and from the constitutional traditions common to the Member States, but has the sole purpose of laying down, in that field, a general framework for combating discrimination on various grounds '[...], including sexual orientation.'

170 Commission, 'Strategy for the effective implementation of the Charter of Fundamental Rights by the European Union (Communication)', COM (2010) 573 final.

discrimination on grounds of sexual orientation under Article 21 of the Charter is applied systematically in the preparation, adoption and implementation of EU law.[171] In the 2010 annual report on the implementation of the Charter, the Commission reiterated its position that '[t]he benefits of EU rules guaranteeing free movement and residence apply also to same-sex couples.'[172] In the report of the following year, the Commission qualified homophobia as 'incompatible with the founding values of the EU' and held that it was using all the powers at its disposal to fight against this phenomenon. It explained that it '[...] followed-up petitions and parliamentary questions on discriminatory practices on grounds of sexual orientation, when they concerned matters falling within EU competence.'[173] One such case concerned the refusal of Polish authorities to issue certificates on civil status to citizens who wished to marry or conclude a registered partnership with a person of the same sex in a Member State where this was possible (see also section 9.6.3 below). The Commission furthermore implements 'a comprehensive anti-discrimination policy' which includes the 'funding of a communication campaign to inform citizens about their rights; funding of NGO networks fighting against discrimination faced by LGBT people in the EU; conducting studies and exchanging good practices related to these issues.'[174]

The Commission is not the only EU institution actively advocating for LGBT rights. Indeed, the European Parliament (EP) has been '[...] a principal driving force in bringing LGB rights onto the European political agenda.'[175] From early on it has strongly condemned discrimination on the basis of sexual orientation and in its non-binding Resolutions and Recommendations on the issue, the Parliament did not limit itself to those areas of law in which the EU has competences. For example, as early as 1994 the EP passed a resolution on equal rights for homosexuals and lesbians in the EC, in which it also appealed to the Commission to present a draft Recommendation, that as a minimum would seek to end, *inter alia*, the exclusion of same-sex couples from access to marriage or from 'an equivalent legal framework', as well as 'any restrictions on the rights of lesbians and homosexuals to be parents or to adopt or foster children'.[176] More recently, in 2012, the Parliament explicitly called on Member States to provide same-sex couples access to legal institutions such as cohabitation, registered partnership or marriage, as it considered that as a result their fundamental rights were 'more likely to be safeguarded'.[177] The freedom

---

171 European Commission, *2010 Report on the Application of the EU Charter of Fundamental Rights*, p. 44, www.ec.europa.eu/justice/fundamental-rights/files/annual_report_2010_en.pdf, visited June 2014.

172 *Idem*, p. 44.

173 *Idem*, p. 52.

174 Www.ec.europa.eu/justice/fundamental-rights/homophobia/index_en.htm, visited June 2014.

175 Www.ilga-europe.org/home/guide_europe/eu/lgbt_rights/european_parliament, visited June 2014.

176 European Parliament Resolution on equal rights for homosexuals and lesbians in the EC, [1994] OJ C61/20, pp. 40–43.

177 European Parliament Resolution of 24 May 2012 on the fight against homophobia in Europe (2012/2657(RSP)) P7_TA(2012)0222, para. 9 and European Parliament resolution of 12 December 2012 on the situation of fundamental rights in the European Union (2010–2011)(2011/2069(INI)), P7_TA(2012)0500, para. 103.

of movement for same-sex couples is further amongst the priorities of the European Parliament's Intergroup on LGBT rights.[178]

It was also the European Parliament that requested that the EU Fundamental Rights Agency (FRA) investigated LGBT discrimination and homophobia in the EU.[179] Since its foundation in 2007, discrimination on grounds of sexual orientation has been one of the thematic areas in which the FRA carries out its tasks.[180] The FRA has frequently reported on legislative and policy developments in the Member States on issues concerning LGBT rights that strictly speaking do not come within the EU's competences, such as hate crimes and legal recognition of same-sex couples.[181] In the FRA's annual report on 2012 it was explained in respect of the latter, that some EU citizens had claimed that there were obstacles to the right of free movement 'as a result of either the absence of provisions on legal recognition of same-sex couples or the lack of harmonisation throughout the EU.' The agency held that '[d]espite the lack of direct EU competence in the area of family and private life, observing developments in this field help[ed] in understanding the application of the EU right to free movement for all, including same-sex couples wishing to move between Member States.'[182] The FRA has, *inter alia*, pled for the incorporation of same-sex partners 'whether married, registered, or in a *de facto* union', within the definitions of 'family member' in relevant areas of EU law, '[...] in particular employment related partner benefits, free movement of EU citizens, and family reunification of refugees and third-country nationals'.[183] The European Parliament subsequently called on the

178 See www.lgbt-ep.eu/work, visited June 2014. According to its website, the Intergroup is '[...] an informal forum for Members of the European Parliament who are committed to upholding the fundamental rights of lesbian, gay, bisexual and transgender (LGBT) people.' In August 2013 the Intergroup had 153 Members.

179 European Parliament press release of 17 May 2013, REF 20130513IPR08207, www.europarl.europa.eu/news/en/pressroom/content/20130513IPR08207/html/International-Day-against-Homophobia-MEPs-react-to-LGBT-survey-findings, visited June 2014.

180 Council Decision of 28 February 2008 implementing Regulation (EC) No 168/2007 as regards the adoption of a Multi-annual Framework for the European Union Agency for Fundamental Rights for 2007–2012 (2008/203/EC) [2008] OJ L 63/14 and Council Decision No 252/2013/EU of 11 March 2013 establishing a Multiannual Framework for 2013–2017 for the European Union Agency for Fundamental Rights (252/2013/EU) [2013]OJ L 79/1.

181 See European Union Agency for Fundamental Rights, *Homophobia, transphobia and discrimination on grounds of sexual orientation and gender identity. Comparative legal analysis* (Luxembourg, Publications Office of the European Union 2008) online available at www.fra.europa.eu/en/publication/2010/homophobia-and-discrimination-grounds-sexual-orientation-eu-member-states-part-i, visited June 2014 and European Union Agency for Fundamental Rights, *Homophobia, transphobia and discrimination on grounds of sexual orientation and gender identity. Comparative legal analysis. 2010 update* (Luxembourg, Publications Office of the European Union 2010), online available at www.fra.europa.eu/en/publication/2012/homophobia-transphobia-and-discrimination-grounds-sexual-orientation-and-gender, visited June 2014.

182 European Union Agency for Fundamental Rights, *Fundamental rights: challenges and achievements in 2012, Annual report 2012* (Luxembourg, Publications Office of the European Union 2013) p. 155, online available at www.fra.europa.eu/sites/default/files/annual-report-2012_en.pdf, visited June 2014.

183 European Union Agency for Fundamental Rights 2010, *supra* n. 181, at p. 9.

Commission and Member States to implement the relevant FRA opinions to the greatest possible extent.[184]

In 2013 the FRA conducted an online EU-wide LGBT survey.[185] On the basis of its results the FRA, *inter alia*, took the position that '[e]qual protection against discrimination on the grounds of sexual orientation across all EU Member States would significantly improve if the EU-wide prohibition of such discrimination extended beyond the field of employment and occupation', as proposed by the European Commission in its Proposal for an Equal Treatment Directive (see 9.3.4.1 above). The Parliament called on the Commission to carefully examine the results of this survey, and to take 'appropriate action'.[186] The Parliament has also called on the Commission, Member States and relevant agencies 'to work jointly on 'a comprehensive multiannual policy' to protect the fundamental rights of LGBT people, by means of 'a roadmap, a strategy or an action plan'.[187]

9.5. Cross-border movement of rainbow families in the EU; some statistics

There are no exact and exhaustive EU-wide statistics on the cross-border movement of same-sex couples within the EU. For example, there are no statistics available in respect of the number of same-sex couples who go from one EU Member State to another to have their relationship legally recognised by means of a registered partnership or marriage. Nor are there any statistics available concerning the number of same-sex couples, or individuals with a homosexual orientation, who are deterred from making use of their free movement rights, because of restrictive legislation in the host Member State. There are not even exhaustive and reliable numbers available regarding the number of same-sex partners of EU citizens who were given entry and residence as a 'family member' under the Free Movement Directive when moving to another EU Member State (see section 9.6.2 below). Nevertheless, there are some statistics available that may give some context to the present case study.

According to Eurostat, 12.8 million EU citizens – accounting for 2.5 per cent of the total EU population – were living in another Member State in the year 2011.[188] In 2014 that number was held to have risen to nearly 14 million.[189] Further, in 2011

184 European Parliament Resolution of 24 May 2012 on the fight against homophobia in Europe (2012/2657(RSP)) P7_TA(2012)0222, para. 5.

185 European Union Agency for Fundamental Rights 2013B, *supra* n. 165.

186 *Supra* n. 184, para. 6.

187 European Parliament Resolution of 4 February 2014 on the EU Roadmap against homophobia and discrimination on grounds of sexual orientation and gender identity (2013/2183(INI)).

188 Eurostat press release of 11 July 2012, STAT/12/105, online available at www.europa.eu/rapid/pressReleasesAction.do?reference=STAT/12/105&format=HTML&aged=0&language=EN&guiLanguage=en, visited June 2014.

189 The European Commission held in 2014 that nearly 14 million EU citizens were residing in a Member State of which they were not a national. See European Commission, *The Future EU Justice and Home Affairs Agendas: Questions and Answers*, Memo of 11 March 2014, Strasbourg, online available at www.europa.eu/rapid/press-release_MEMO-14-174_nl.htm,

the Commission held that '[o]f the approximately 122 million marriages in the EU, around 16 million (13%) ha[d] [...] a cross-border dimension.'[190] In respect of registered partnerships, the latest figures stem from 2007. In that year there were reportedly approximately 211,000 registered partnerships in the EU, of which over 41,000 had an 'international dimension'.[191]

These European figures are not broken down into same-sex and different-sex couples. One may, however, assume that the statistics on the number of marriages include at least some same-sex marriages, as there are (increasingly more) EU Member States in which same-sex couples have access to marriage. The registered partnership statistics presumably include an even higher number of same-sex couples, as considerably more States provide for a registered partnership, where in most cases such a partnership is not open to different-sex couples, but to same-sex couples only. One would need statistics on the number of same-sex couples in the EU to make an estimate of the potential number of people that are involved. Such statistics are not, however, available. Some have tried to estimate the number of rainbow families in the EU. *ILGA-Europe*, for example, has estimated that within the EU at least 43,000 children were growing in same-sex families.[192]

In any case, even though no complete or exhaustive statistics are available, there is considerable anecdotal evidence which shows that cross-border movement of same-sex couples and their families is taking place within the EU.[193]

---

visited June 2014. In 2013, at the website of the European Commission (last updated 16 July 2013), it was held that there were 'around 16 million international couples in the EU including a certain number of same-sex couples.' See www.ec.europa.eu/justice/discrimination/orientation/legal-aspects/index_en.htm, visited July 2014.

190 In a 2014 Commission Communication it was held: 'Of 2.4 million marriages celebrated in the EU in 2007, about 300,000 fell into this category. So did 140,000 (13 per cent) of the 1,040,000 divorces that took place in the EU in the same year. In addition, 8,500 international couples in registered partnerships were dissolved by separation and 1 266 were ended by the death of one of the partners.' Commission, 'Bringing Legal Clarity To Property Rights For International Couples' (Communication), COM (2011) 125 final, p. 2. See also Commission, 'EU Citizenship Report 2010, Dismantling the obstacles to EU citizens' rights', COM (2010) 603 final, p. 5.

191 This international dimension included international registered partnerships and couples in a registered partnership who were living abroad or who were having property abroad. SEC (2011) 328 final. See also European Economic and Social Committee, 'Opinion on COM (2011) 126 final and COM (2011) 127 final' [2011] OJ C376/87.

192 ILGA-Europe, *ILGA-Europe's contribution to the Green Paper* (ILGA-Europe 2011) p. 19, online available at www.ilga-europe.org/home/publications/policy_papers/green_paper_april_2011, visited June 2014. *ILGA-Europe* refers (in footnotes 37 and 38 respectively) to: 'E. Jansen, *Gay and lesbian family planning in Germany: Options and constraints* (2009)' and 'L. Hodson, *The Rights of Children Raised in Lesbian, Gay, Bisexual or Transgender Families: A European Perspective* (2008)'.

193 For such anecdotal evidence reference is also made to Ch. 10, section 10.4.1; Ch. 11, section 11.4.1 and Ch. 12, section 12.4.1 respectively.

9.6. Free movement law and rainbow families – open questions

While free movement of persons under the original EEC Treaty was limited to the economically active, i.e., the workers (Article 3(1)(c) EEC Treaty, now Article 45 TFEU), this gradually has been extended to economically inactive EU citizens. Under the present Article 21 TFEU every citizen of the Union has the right 'to move and reside freely within the territory of the Member States'.

Already at an early stage it was clear to the Union legislature that if an EU citizen's (a worker's) right to move were to be effective, he had to be allowed to be joined by his relatives. Since this right was not written expressly in the Treaty, it was laid down in secondary legislation (first Regulation 1612/68[194] and later Directive 2004/38[195]). Once exercised, this right remains effective also upon return to the home State.[196] Although more recently, in line with a less economic-oriented approach to citizenship, the rights of family members have increasingly been placed in the light of the right to respect for family life,[197] these rights remain first and foremost instrumental to the right of free movement of the EU citizen. They are derived rights, which exist only by virtue of the EU citizen's right of free movement and the family tie between him and his relative. Since the free movement rights are really rights of the EU citizen, the nationality of the family member is irrelevant. Further, the right of an EU citizen to be joined by his close relatives does not depend on a prior right of residence of these family members in the home Member State.[198] Being one of the fundamental Treaty freedoms, the CJEU has always interpreted the freedom of movement of persons broadly and the exceptions to it narrowly.[199] This is particularly true also for the provisions of Directive 2004/38 the Free Movement Directive, which aims to facilitate the exercise of the fundamental right to free movement of EU citizens.[200]

---

194 Council Regulation (EEC) 1612/68 of 15 October 1968 on freedom of movement for workers within the Community [1968] OJ L257/2. Regulation 1612/68 was for the greater part repealed by the later Directive 2004/38 (see section 9.6.2 below).

195 European Parliament and Council Directive 2004/38/EC of 29 April 2004 on the right of citizens of the Union and their family members to move and reside freely within the territory of the Member States [2004] OJ L158/77.

196 Case C-370/90 *Surinder Singh* [1992] ECR I-4265, ECLI:EU:C:1992:296, para. 21. In addition, the Court has held that the possibility for an EU worker to be joined by his long-term stable partner who does not fall within the definition of 'family' as laid down in secondary legislation, may constitute a social advantage to the worker, requiring at least equal treatment as regards the right of entry and residence of long-term partners of nationals of the host Member State. Case 59/85 *Netherlands* v. *Reed* [1986] ECR 1283, ECLI:EU:C:1986:157, para. 28.

197 Commission, 'Proposal for a European Parliament and Council Directive on the right of citizens of the Union and their family members to move and reside freely within the territory of the Member States', COM (2001) 257 final, p. 5. See Case C-540/03 *Parliament* v. *Council* [2006] ECR I-5769, ECLI:EU:C:2006:429, para. 53 and the references to the case-law of the ECtHR therein.

198 Case C-127/08 *Metock* [2008] ECR I-6241, ECLI:EU:C:2008:449, para. 58.

199 Joined Cases C-482/01 and C-493/01 *Orfanopoulos and Oliveri* [2004] ECR I-5257, ECLI:EU:C:2004:262, paras. 64–65.

200 Case C-127/08 *Metock* [2008] ECR I-6241, ECLI:EU:C:2008:449, para. 89.

There has never been a free movement case before CJEU involving an EU citizen with a same-sex partner, safe a same-sex couple with children.[201] There are consequently many open questions as to the free movement rights of rainbow families. Some guidance may be found in preparatory documents and in the CJEU's free movement case law. In legal scholarship, where the issue has been discussed quite extensively,[202] reference has often also been made to the CJEU's case law in employment cases, as discussed in section 9.3 above. Hereafter the matter is first assessed under Regulation 1612/68 (section 9.6.1) and the Free Movement Directive (section 9.6.2 below) as where a secondary law instrument is available, this must be applied first.[203] However, as primary law has precedence over secondary law, any such application must still be assessed in light of the latter. When the application of secondary law results in an unjustified restriction of the fundamental Treaty freedom found in primary law, the conflict must be resolved either through a harmonious interpretation of secondary law or by applying directly the Treaty freedom.[204] Section 9.6.3 therefore provides for an assessment of the free movement rights of rainbow families under primary law. Although other free movement issues are conceivable in relation to the present case study,[205] the focus here lies on the primordial free movement of persons.

Third-country nationals (TCNs) do not fall under the free movement regimes as laid down in the Treaties and the Free Movement Directive, as these exclusively apply to EU citizens. Third-country nationals and their families fall under a distinct and less favourable regime that has been developed in the Area of Freedom, Security and Justice (AFJS),[206] and of which the Family Reunification Directive[207] forms a prominent part. This Directive and the rights of entry and residence that it grants to limited categories of third-country nationals are discussed in section 9.6.4 below.

---

201 Lenaerts has called the mobility of same-sex married couples '[a]nother aspect of family law that [was] likely one day to find its way to Luxembourg'. Lenaerts 2009–2010, *supra* n. 7, at p. 1355. See also Rijpma and Koffeman 2014, *supra* n. 1, at p. 489.

202 E.g. C. Karakosta, 'Portability of same-sex marriages and registered partnerships within the EU', 2 *Cyprus Human Rights Law Review* (2013) p. 53 and M. Župan, 'Registered partnership in cross-border situations – where invisibility to law lies?', in: N. Bodigora-Vukubrat et al. (eds.), *Invisible Minorities in Law* (Hamburg, Verlag Dr. Kovac 2013) p. 95.

203 Following the 'Tedeschi principle', substantive Treaty rules are applied only in the absence of secondary legislation. Case 5/77 *Tedeschi* [1977] ECR 1555, ECLI:EU:C:1977:144.

204 K. Ensig Sørensen, 'Reconciling secondary legislation and the treaty rights of free movement', 17 *European Law Review* (2011) p. 339.

205 The interesting question of whether the conclusion of marriage and the registration of a partnership can be qualified as the provision of services and therefore whether nationality and residency requirements to enter into marriage or registered partnership constitute obstacles to the freedom to receive services, is not examined in detail here. It is only noted that if marriage and registered partnership can be regarded as services under the Treaty, the argument could be made that the nationality and residency requirements that Member States like the Netherlands set for the conclusion of a marriage or the registration of a partnership under their national laws, form an obstacle to the freedom to receive services. Such a restriction on the free movement of services recipients is, however, probably quite easily to justify on public policy grounds.

206 Art. 79 TFEU.

207 European Council Directive 2003/86/EC of 22 September 2003, on the right to family reunification, [2003] OJ L251/12.

9.6.1. Regulation 1612/68 and workers with rainbow families

Regulation 1612/68 provided for the free movement of workers and their families. When the Regulation was drafted, a proposal was made to include a Recital holding that discrimination on grounds of sexual orientation represented an obstacle to the free movement of workers and their families, which could seriously impair the integration of migrant workers exercising their right to freedom of movement, and that of their families, into the host country.[208] No such Recital was, however, included in the final version of the Regulation, although it was provided that freedom of movement constituted 'a fundamental right of workers and their families' which required 'equality of treatment'. It was also held in the Preamble that '[...] obstacles to the mobility of workers [had to] be eliminated, in particular as regards the worker's right to be joined by his family and the conditions for the integration of that family into the host country'. Article 10(1) of the Regulation accordingly provided that 'irrespective of their nationality' certain family members had the right to install themselves with a worker who was a national of one Member State and who was employed in the territory of another Member State. These concerned the worker's spouse and their descendants who were under the age of 21 years or were dependants and dependent relatives in the ascending line of the worker and his spouse.[209]

In the *Reed* case (1986),[210] the question was raised if Article 10(1) was to be interpreted as meaning that in certain circumstances a person who had a stable relationship with a worker within the meaning of that provision was to be treated as his 'spouse'.[211] Ms. Reed was a British national who unsuccessfully applied for a residence permit in the Netherlands on the ground that she was living with Mr. *W.* in a stable non-marital relationship. *W.* was also a British national and he legally resided in the Netherlands as a worker within the meaning of the Treaty. The Netherlands government argued that a dynamic interpretation of the term spouse was only acceptable if it were based on developments in social and legal conceptions that were visible in the whole of the Community.[212] The Commission concurred that in the Community as it stood at that time it was 'impossible to speak of any consensus' that unmarried companions were

[208] The proposed Recital No. 5 read: 'Whereas discrimination on grounds of sex, race or ethnic origin, religion or convictions, disability, age or sexual orientation represents an obstacle to the free movement of workers and their families; whereas the integration of migrant workers exercising their right to freedom of movement, and that of their families, into the host country can be seriously impaired by discrimination of this kind; whereas it is therefore essential to prohibit such discrimination within the scope of Regulation (EEC) No 1612/68 [...].' Proposal for a European Parliament and Council Regulation amending Council Regulation 1612/68/EEC on free movement for workers within the Community [1998] OJ C344/9. See Guild 2001, *supra* n. 90, at p. 687.

[209] Art. 10(2) Regulation 1612/68 provided that Member States had to facilitate the admission of any member of the family not coming within the provisions of paragraph 1, if they were dependent on the worker or living under his roof in the country whence he came.

[210] Case 59/85 *Netherlands* v. *Reed* [1986] ECR 1283, ECLI:EU:C:1986:157.

[211] This concerned the third question as posed by the referring court.

[212] According to the Netherlands government there was no reason to give the term 'spouse' an interpretation which would go beyond the legal implications of that term, which embraced rights and obligations which did not exist between unmarried companions.' Case 59/85 *Netherlands* v. *Reed* [1986] ECR 1283, ECLI:EU:C:1986:157, para. 10.

to be treated as spouses.[213] The Court proved sensitive to this line of argumentation. It ruled that because Regulation 1612/68 had general application, was binding in its entirety and was directly applicable in all Member States, 'any interpretation of a legal term on the basis of social developments' had to 'take into account the situation in the whole Community, not merely in one Member State.'[214] It ruled that '[i]n the absence of any indication of a general social development which would justify a broad construction, and in the absence of any indication to the contrary in the regulation,' it was to be held that the term 'spouse' in Article 10 of the Regulation referred to a marital relationship only.[215] The Court concluded:

> '[...] Article 10(1) of Regulation No 1612/68 cannot be interpreted as meaning that the companion, in a stable relationship, of a worker who is a national of a Member State and is employed in the territory of another Member State must in certain circumstances be treated as his 'spouse' for the purposes of that provision.'[216]

The Court redressed the issue, however, by application of the 'social advantage' concept ex Article 7(2) of Regulation 1612/68.[217] It held that '[...] the possibility for a migrant worker of obtaining permission for his unmarried companion to reside with him, where that companion [was] not a national of the host Member State, [could] assist his integration in the host State and thus contribute to the achievement of freedom of movement for workers'.[218] It made clear that if a Member State permitted the unmarried companions of its nationals, who were not themselves nationals of that Member State, to reside in its territory, it could not refuse to grant the same advantage to migrant workers who were nationals of other Member States.[219]

The CJEU thus ruled in *Reed* that non-marital partners were not 'spouses' within the meaning of Regulation 1612/68. In 2004, this Regulation was, for the greater part, repealed and replaced by Directive 2004/38. Because by that time some States had introduced alternative forms of registration of (same-sex) relationships, the question was raised when the latter Directive was drafted, of whether explicit provision had to be made for these registration forms.

---

213 According to the Commission the problem could not be resolved by means of a broad construction of Art. 10 of Regulation 1612/68. *Idem*, para. 11.

214 *Idem*, paras. 12–13.

215 *Idem*, para. 15.

216 *Idem*, para. 16.

217 *Idem*, para. 28. See also M. Fallon, 'Constraints of internal market law on family law', in: J. Meeusen et al. (eds.), *International family law for the European Union* (Antwerpen, Intersentia 2007) p. 149 at p. 174.

218 *Idem*, para. 28.

219 *Idem*, para. 29.

9.6.2. The Free Movement Directive and EU citizens with rainbow families

The Free Movement Directive (Directive 2004/38, also often referred to as 'Citizens' Directive') grants EU citizens a general right of entry and stay of three months.[220] After three months the residence right is maintained if the EU citizen can prove themselves to be economically active or either a student or a person of independent means.[221] Importantly, as noted above, the Directive lays down the rights of family members of the EU citizen to join him in the host Member State. Once these family members have been granted entry and residence in the host Member State, they are also entitled to take up employment or self-employment there,[222] and they must be treated equally to the nationals of that Member State within the scope of the Treaty.[223]

During the deliberations in the preparation of the Free Movement Directive, the European Parliament made a plea for the inclusion of same-sex partners in the scope of the Free Movement Directive.[224] It proposed recognising as family members the spouse and registered partner, irrespective of sex, on the basis of the relevant national legislation, and the unmarried partner, irrespective of sex, with whom the Union citizen had a durable relationship, if the legislation or practice of the host and/or home Member States treated unmarried couples and married couples in a corresponding manner and in accordance with the conditions laid down in any such legislation.[225] The Council, however, was reluctant to opt for a definition of the term 'spouse' which made a specific reference to spouses of the same sex.[226] It noted that at the time, only two Member States provided for same-sex marriages and referred to CJEU's definition of marriage in *D. and Sweden* v. *Council* (see section 9.2 above).[227] The Council furthermore held that recognition of registered partners or unmarried partners had to be based exclusively on the legislation of the host Member State. It noted in this respect that '[r]ecognition for purposes of residence of non

---

220 Art. 5 and 6(1) Directive 2004/38.

221 Art. 7 Directive 2004/38.

222 Art. 23 Directive 2004/38.

223 Art. 25(1) Directive 2004/38.

224 The original Commission proposal was laid down in COM (2001) 257 final.

225 See the paraphrasing in Commission, 'Amended proposal for a Directive of the European Parliament and of the Council on the right of citizens of the Union and their family members to move and reside freely within the territory of the Member States', COM (2003) 199, pp. 10–11. The original Amendments 14, 15 and 16 read:
'(a) the spouse, irrespective of sex, according to the relevant national legislation;
(b) the registered partner, irrespective of sex, according to the relevant national legislation;
(c) the unmarried partner, irrespective of sex, with whom the Union citizen has a durable relationship, if the legislation or practice of the host and/or home Member State treats unmarried couples and married couples in a corresponding manner and in accordance with the conditions laid down in any such legislation [...].'

226 Common Position (EC) No 6/2004 adopted by the Council on 5 December 2003 with a view to adopting Directive 2004/.../EC of the European Parliament and of the Council of... on the right of citizens of the Union and their family members to move and reside freely within the territory of the Member States amending Regulation (EEC) No 1612/68 and repealing Directives 64/221/EEC, 68/360/EEC, 72/194/EEC, 73/148/EEC, 75/34/EEC, 75/35/EEC, 90/364/EEC, 90/365/EEC and 93/96/EEC (2004/C 54 E/02), p. 28.

227 See also M. Bell, 'Holding Back the Tide? Cross-Border Recognition of Same-Sex Partnerships within the European Union', 12 *European Review of Private Law* (2004) p. 613 at p. 621.

married couples in accordance with the legislation of other Member States could pose problems for the host Member State if its family law [did] not recognise this possibility.' The Council added that '[t]o confer rights which [were] not recognised for its own nationals on couples from other Member States could in fact create reverse discrimination' and this had to be avoided according to the Council.[228] It was observed that the Council discussions revealed that several Member States stuck 'to a very traditional definition of the family'.[229]

The European Commission subsequently amended its proposal in line with the Council's Position. It reportedly felt that '[...] harmonisation of the conditions of residence for Union citizens in Member States of which they [were] not nationals' was not supposed to 'result in the imposition on certain Member States of amendments to family law legislation, an area which [did] not fall within the Community's legislative jurisdiction.'[230] The Commission preferred to restrict the proposal to the concept of spouse as meaning 'in principle' spouse of the opposite sex. Under reference to *Reed*, it indicated that this could be different if there would be 'subsequent developments'.[231]

According to the Commission its amended proposal presented 'an equitable solution' to the issues as identified during the deliberations in Parliament and Council.[232] Others qualified the final text as '[...] a compromise which did not deliver as much for same-sex couples as many had hoped.'[233] According to Toner the Directive clearly showed the existence of '[...] a considerable reluctance to use EU law to push skeptical and reluctant Member States too far along the road of recognition of [non-traditional] relationships until they are ready and willing to adopt such measures in national law.'[234] Lenaerts observed that the EU legislature opted for a 'hands-off approach', leaving the sensitive decision as to the definition of the term 'spouse' to judicial interpretation.[235] Bell held that the overall picture painted by the Free Movement Directive was that of a legislature '[...] caught between acknowledging the pace of social and legal change within the Member States whilst respecting those states unwilling to see these changes crystallised in EU law.'[236] The author held that '[...] the ambiguity on same-sex marriage, the partial free movement rights for

228 Common Position (EC) No 6/2004, *supra* n. 226, at p. 28.

229 H. Toner, 'Immigration Rights of Same-Sex Couples in EC Law', in: K. Boele-Woelki and A. Fuchs (eds.), *Legal recognition of same-sex couples in Europe* (Antwerp, Intersentia 2003) p. 178 at p. 181.

230 COM (2003) 199, at p. 3.

231 *Idem*, at pp. 10–11.

232 *Idem*, at p. 3.

233 H. Toner, 'Migration rights and same-sex couples in EU law: a case study', in: K. Boele-Woelki and A. Fuchs (eds.), *Legal recognition of same-sex Relationships in Europe, National, cross-border and European perspectives*, 2nd edn. (Cambridge, Intersentia 2012) p. 285 at p. 287.

234 *Idem*, at p. 289.

235 Lenaerts held that '[...] if a national court asks for guidance in the interpretation of this concept, the [CJEU] would have no choice but to provide a definition through the medium of common-lawmaking.' Lenaerts 2009–2010, *supra* n. 7, at pp. 1355–1356. In footnote 83 Lenaerts referred to: 'H. Toner, *Partnership Rights, Free Movement and EU Law*, 2004, p. 60–68', who reportedly explained '[...] that the regime laid down in the directive was the result of a political compromise among conservative and liberal Member States.' For further discussion of this question, see section 9.6.2.1 below.

236 Bell 2004, *supra* n. 227, at p. 626.

registered partners and the non-rights for unmarried partners [left] the Directive rather fork-tongued in the signals it [was] sending.'[237]

The present Article 2 of Directive 2004/38 provides that the term 'family member' covers both the 'spouse' and '[...] the partner with whom the Union citizen has contracted a registered partnership, on the basis of the legislation of a Member State, if the legislation of the host Member State treats registered partnerships as equivalent to marriage in accordance with the conditions laid down in the relevant legislation of the host Member State'.[238] Provision has also been made for unmarried and unregistered partners: on the basis of Article 3(2)(b) the host state has an obligation 'to facilitate entrance' of 'the partner with whom the Union citizen has a durable relationship, duly attested'. Article 24 provides that '[...] all Union citizens residing on the basis of this Directive in the territory of the host Member State [...] enjoy equal treatment with the nationals of that Member State within the scope of the Treaty.' The benefit of this right is extended to third-country national family members who have the right of residence or permanent residence.[239] Further, Recital No. 31 of the Preamble to the Free Movement Directive, holds that

> '[i]n accordance with the prohibition of discrimination contained in the Charter, Member States should implement this Directive without discrimination between the beneficiaries of this Directive on grounds such as [...] sexual orientation.'[240]

Following Article 27(1) of the Free Movement Directive, Member States may restrict the freedom of movement and residence of Union citizens and their family members on grounds of public policy, public security or public health. Any measure taken on ground of public policy must comply with the principle of proportionality and must be based exclusively on the personal conduct of the individual concerned, which conduct must represent 'a genuine, present and sufficiently serious threat affecting one of the fundamental interests of society'.[241]

As the CJEU has never ruled upon this issue, it remains an open question if or when same-sex partners of EU citizens can be regarded as 'family members' within the meaning of the Free Movement Directive.[242] This question becomes vital if the

237 *Idem*, at p. 626.

238 Art. 2(a) and (b) Directive 2004/38 respectively. The term 'family member' furthermore covers the direct descendants who are under the age of 21 or are dependants and those of the spouse or partner and the dependent direct relative in the ascending line and those of the spouse or partner. Art. 2 (c and d) Directive 2004/38. As noted by Fallon this excludes registration following the law of a third State. Fallon 2007, *supra* n. 217, at p. 175.

239 Art. 25(1) Directive 2004/38.

240 As Lenaerts explains: 'This would mean, for example, that once a person is qualified as "a family member," the host Member State cannot deprive him or her from receiving the benefits to which he or she is entitled under Directive 2004/38/EC just because of his or her sexual orientation [...].' Lenaerts 2009–2010, *supra* n. 7, at p. 1360, footnote 108.

241 Art. 27(2) Directive 2004/38.

242 Lenaerts has noted that in any case the definition of 'family member' was considered to be a 'broad' one. Lenaerts 2009–2010, *supra* n. 7, at p. 1355.

relative of an EU citizen cannot himself claim free movement rights.[243] Should a preliminary reference on this issue be made to the CJEU,[244] there would be various possible avenues the Court could take.

In exploring these avenues, a distinction must be drawn between same-sex spouses, same-sex registered partners and same-sex stable (or '*de facto*') partners, respectively. The following subsections discuss different views on how the relevant Directive provisions must be read for each of these respective civil statuses and types of relationships. A recurring question in the academic debate on the matter has been – and still is – whether and if so, the extent to which the CJEU's case law in other realms of EU law, such as in staff cases or in non-discrimination cases, applies in this context. The following subsections intend to unravel these different arguments and try to analyse what the (minimum) requirements of EU law are in this respect.

9.6.2.1. Same-sex spouses

The term 'spouse' under Article 2(2)(a) of Directive 2004/38 is not defined. In fact, the EU legislature deliberately left definition of this term to the judiciary.[245] Because it concerns a term of EU law, the CJEU is indeed competent to interpret and define the term 'spouse'.[246] So far, there has not been a case before the CJEU in which it has been asked if the term 'spouse' in the Free Movement Directive also covers same-sex spouses. The only relevant free movement case concerning the definition of 'spouse' is the above discussed *Reed* ruling, in which the Court ruled that unmarried partners were not covered by the term 'spouse' as at the time provided for in Regulation 1612/68.

Various claims can and have been made in respect of what the CJEU could and should rule if the question is referred to it whether 'spouse' in Article 2(2)(a) of Directive 2004/38 includes same-sex spouses. In the first place, the view can be defended that

---

243 In fact, most free movement cases that have been brought before the Court regarding the rights of family members of EU citizens have concerned third-country national relatives.

244 Art. 267 TFEU. 'In theory, the Court could be seized of a question concerning the compatibility of national rules on the recognition of same-sex relationships with EU law through infringement proceedings. These could be initiated either by the Commission or a Member State, if they were to believe that (non-)recognition would amount to a violation of EU law. However, infringement proceedings initiated by Member States are extremely rare for their political implications. Likewise, the Commission has discretion to initiate infringement proceedings and is unlikely to do in such a sensitive area. It is therefore more probable that a case would reach Luxembourg by way of a preliminary reference from a national judge, who in domestic proceedings is confronted with a case in which a same-sex couple challenges the non-recognition of their relationship on the basis of EU law.' Rijpma and Koffeman 2014, *supra* n. 1 at p. 460.

245 Lenaerts 2009–2010, *supra* n. 7, at pp. 1355 and 1360.

246 As Bogdan has rightly observed, the concept of marriage in EU law is 'in principle an autonomous concept, independent of the definitions of marriage in national legal systems'. M. Bogdan, 'Private International Law Aspects of the Introduction of Same-Sex Marriages in Sweden', 78 *Nordic Journal of International Law* (2009) p. 253 at pp. 255–256, referring (in footnote 8) to the *Reed* judgment. In the words of Lenaerts '[...] if a national court asks for guidance in the interpretation of this concept, the ECJ would have no choice but to provide a definition through the medium of common-lawmaking.' Lenaerts 2009–2010, *supra* n. 7, at pp. 1355–1356.

because Article 2(2)(a) Directive 2004/38 makes no reference to national laws, an independent and uniform interpretation of this term of EU law is in place. Others have questioned whether Article 2(2)(a) lends itself to autonomous interpretation.[247] An alternative approach therefore claims that the Court should defer to national law, either the law of the host Member State or that of the home Member State. These different options are now explored in more detail.

It is settled CJEU case law that '[...] the need for a uniform application of European Union law and the principle of equality require that the terms of a provision of European Union law which makes no express reference to the law of the Member States for the purpose of determining its meaning and scope must normally be given an independent and uniform interpretation throughout the European Union.'[248] Because Article 2(2)(a) of Directive 2004/38 does indeed not make any express reference to national law, the question arises as to what independent and uniform meaning could be given to the term 'spouse' in this provision.

For the interpretation of a provision of European Union law its wording, the context in which it occurs and the objectives pursued by the rules of which it is part must be considered.[249] In the present case, a textual interpretation of Article 2(2)(a) has been held to provide limited guidance, since the wording of Article does not make any reference to the (combined) gender of the spouses.[250] When applying a contextual and a teleological interpretation, it has been noted that the legislature deliberately chose not to provide for same-sex couples explicitly (see above).[251] It furthermore made separate provision for registered partnerships – at the time the most common alternative to marriage for same-sex couples – and made recognition of such partnerships subject to the legislation of the host Member State. These considerations support the conclusion that the EU legislature did not intend to oblige the Member States to recognise same-sex spouses as spouses for the purposes of the Free Movement Directive.

---

[247] Rijpma and Koffeman 2014, *supra* n. 1, at p. 468.

[248] Case C-34/10 *Oliver Brüstle* v. *Greenpeace eV* [2011] ECR I-9821, ECLI:EU:C:2011:669, para. 25, under reference to Case 327/82 *Ekro* [1984] ECR 107, ECLI:EU:C:1984:11, para. 11; Case C-287/98 *Linster* [2000] ECR I-6917, ECLI:EU:C:2000:468, para. 43; Case C-5/08 *Infopaq International* [2009] ECR I-6569, ECLI:EU:C:2009:465, para. 27 and Case C-467/08 *Padawan* [2010] ECR I-10055, ECLI:EU:C:2010:620, para. 32.

[249] Case C-648/11, *MA a.o.* [2013] ECR 0000, ECLI:EU:C:2013:367, para. 50; Case C-19/08 *Petrosian* [2009] ECR I-495, ECLI:EU:C:2009:41, para. 34 and Case C-403/09 *Detiček* [2009] ECR I-12193, ECLI:EU:C:2009:810, para. 33 and Case C-287/98 *Linster* [2000] ECR I-6917, ECLI:EU:C:2000:468, para. 43, under reference to Case 327/82 *Ekro* [1984] ECR 107, ECLI:EU:C:1984:11, para. 11. See also P. Rott, 'What is the Role of the ECJ in EC Private Law? – A Comment on the ECJ judgments in Océano Grupo, Freiburger Kommunalbauten, Leitner and Veedfald', 1 *Hanse Law Review* (2005) pp. 7–9.

[250] Rijpma and Koffeman 2014, *supra* n. 1, at p. 468.

[251] A 2008 report of the for Fundamental Rights (FRA) was very critical in this respect, deeming it a problem that the EU legislature '[...] failed to impose a clear obligation on the host Member State to recognise as 'spouse' a person of the same-sex validly married under the laws of the Member State of origin.' This was considered an 'omission in the wording of the Directive.' European Union Agency for Fundamental Rights 2008, *supra* n. 181, at p. 63.

In interpreting the term 'spouse', the CJEU could also – as it did in *Grant* and *D* v. *Council* – refer to the national laws of the various EU Member States.[252] These indicate certain social and legal developments,[253] which the CJEU may be inclined to follow, even though it is under no Treaty obligation to do so and even though it would be somewhat circular to base the definition of an EU law term on the implementation of that same EU provision at national level. The Court could thereby take into account the number of Member States that have opened up marriage to same-sex couples[254] as well as the number of Member States that authorise the entry and residence of same-sex spouses as 'spouse' for the purposes of the Free Movement Directive.[255] The primordial question will then be whether those numbers are enough to prompt the CJEU to rule that 'spouse' within the meaning of Article 2(2) Directive 2004/38 includes same-sex spouses. While some have held that new social and legal developments in only a few Member States could not justify an autonomous interpretation of the term 'spouse',[256] others have not outright rejected this idea. Lenaerts and Gutierrez-Fons have held that *Grant* illustrated that '[...] the existence of divergences among national legal systems may not *automatically* rule out the incorporation, into the EU legal order, of a legal principle which is recognized in only a minority of Member States'. The authors explained this as follows:

> '[...] since the [CJEU] follows an evaluative approach in the discovery of general principles, incorporation may take place where "such a legal principle is of particular significance [for the project of European integration], or where it constitutes a growing trend".'[257]

If applied in the present context, it must be assessed whether the increased legal recognition of same-sex relationships throughout the EU Member States can

252 In 1998, in *Grant*, the Court held that in the state of the law within the Community at that time, stable relationships between two persons of the same sex were not regarded as equivalent to marriages or stable relationships outside marriage between persons of opposite sex. The Court came to a similar conclusion in Joined Cases C-122/99 P & C-125/99 P *D. and Sweden* v. *Council* [2001] ECR I-4319, ECLI:EU:C:2001:30.

253 Compare Waaldijk 2001B, *supra* n. 88, at p. 648, who held it to be likely that the EU would follow 'the standard sequence followed by the member states' in resect of recognition of same-sex partners in fields other than employment.

254 In 2014 eight Member States had opened up marriage to same-sex couples, namely the Netherlands, Belgium, Portugal, Spain, Denmark, Sweden, France and the United Kingdom, while it was anticipated that Luxembourg would do so as of 1 January 2015.

255 This concerns at least nine Member States (Belgium, Denmark, Finland, Italy, the Netherlands, Portugal, Spain, Sweden, and the UK). See Rijpma and Koffeman 2014, *supra* n. 1, at p. 470, referring (in footnote 90) to: European Union Agency for Fundamental Rights 2010, *supra* n. 181, at p. 46 and Ministry of the Interior of Italy, Administrative Guideline n. 8996 of 26 October 2012.

256 Bogdan 2009, *supra* n. 246, at pp. 255–256, referring (in footnote 8) to *Reed.* In this respect Bogdan had previously noted that in *D. and Sweden* v. *Council* (2001) the interpretation of 'marriage' had 'not [been] really independent' as in it had been 'based on the legal systems of the totality of Member States'. Bogdan 2003, *supra* n. 20, at p. 173. Referring to *Grant*, Lenaerts and Gutiérrez-Fons observed that the CJEU would be 'careful before adopting an "EU" solution', where there were important divergences among national legal systems. The authors pointed out that for EU law to develop in this field, legislative action was said to be needed. K. Lenaerts, J.A. Gutiérrez-Fons, 'The constitutional allocation of powers and general principles of EU law', 46 *CMLRev* (2010) p. 1629 at p. 1634.

257 *Idem*, at p. 1635.

constitute a growing trend, as well as whether an interpretation of 'spouse' as covering same-sex spouses is of particular significance for European integration.

Altogether, it cannot be ruled out that if the CJEU were to interpret the term 'spouse' under Article 2(2)(a) autonomously, it would conclude that it sees at different-sex spouses only. In this regard it must be noted that the Directive sets a minimum norm only; States are free to offer more protection and thus to recognise also same-sex spouses as 'spouse' for the purposes of the Directive. On the basis of the equal treatment provision (Article 24 of the Directive) there is even an obligation to do so for States who authorise the entry and residence of same-sex spouses of their own nationals as 'spouse' for the purposes of the Directive. They must apply the same rules to the same-sex spouses of migrating nationals of other EU Member States.[258] States who do not provide for same-sex marriages under their national laws, are free, nevertheless, to recognise migrating same-sex spouses as 'spouse' for the purpose of the Free Movement Directive. States may also decide to authorise the entry and residence of a foreign same-sex spouse under Article 2(2)(b) or Article 3(2) (see sections 9.6.2.2 and 9.6.2.3 below).

If the CJEU, on the other hand, were to adopt a uniform definition of 'spouse' as including same-sex spouses, reverse discrimination – whereby nationals of the host Member States would be treated less favourably when compared to EU citizens migrating to that Member State – would be the result in those States that do not foresee in same-sex marriages. While the Council held this to be undesirable (see 9.6.2 above), the practice of reverse discrimination is in itself not at variance with EU law.

As explained by Lenaerts, the fact that the CJEU is competent to define the concept 'spouse' does not necessarily imply that the Court has to adopt an independent definition of 'spouse', if ever asked to interpret it.[259] According to the author this would '[...] foster uniformity and legal certainty, but it would disregard the sensitivities of some Member States to the benefit of others.'[260] Others have submitted that '[...] in view of the legislative developments in the Member States since *D.* v. *Council*, the CJEU [was] no longer in the position to identify in EU law or in the general principles of Union law criteria enabling it to define the meaning and scope of marriage by way of independent interpretation'.[261] As an alternative it has therefore been claimed that the CJEU should defer to national law as interpreted by national courts.

---

258 See Case 59/85 *Netherlands* v. *Reed* [1986] ECR 1283, ECLI:EU:C:1986:157.

259 Lenaerts 2009–2010, *supra* n. 7, at p. 1356. This conclusion is supported by the finding of the CJEU that '[...] the terms of a provision of European Union law which makes no express reference to the law of the Member States for the purpose of determining its meaning and scope must *normally* [emphasis added] be given an independent and uniform interpretation throughout the European Union.' See *supra* n. 248.

260 *Idem*, at pp. 1356–1357.

261 Rijpma and Koffeman 2014, *supra* n. 1, at pp. 470–471, referring (in footnote 95) to Case T-43/90 *Díaz García* [1992] ECR II-2619, ECLI:EU:T:1992:120, para. 36 and Case T-85/91 *Khouri* [1992] ECR II-2637, ECLI:EU:T:1992:121, para. 32.

In interpreting Article 2(2)(a) of the Directive, the CJEU may defer to either the law of the host State or to that of the home State. The home State principle is strongly embedded in EU free movement law and has its basis in the principle of mutual recognition. Application of the latter principle in this context has been held to be consistent with the Directive's objective to promote free movement,[262] as well as to serve legal certainty.[263] Taking the principle of mutual recognition as a starting point, it has been claimed, recently, even by EU institutions, that 'a spouse is a spouse'.[264] In its 2009 *Guidance for better transposition and application of the Free Movement Directive*, for example, the Commission held that '[m]arriages validly contracted anywhere in the world must be in principle recognized for the purpose of the application of the Directive.'[265] While the wording 'in principle' leaves room for exceptions, former Justice Commissioner Reding, while addressing the European Parliament in 2010, was considerably firmer. She held:

> 'If you live in a legally-recognised same-sex partnership, or marriage, in country A, you have the right – and this is a fundamental right – to take this status and that of your partner to country B. If not, it is a violation of EU law, so there is no discussion about this. This is absolutely clear, and we do not have to hesitate on this. The Free Movement Directive does not give the Member States discretion to discriminate – no EU directive does. We should not allow a mythology to be developed saying that, actually, it is possible to discriminate. We have to be very firm on the principles.'[266]

In fact, the Commissioner thus made an argument for the portability of civil statuses within the European Union. She argued that once an EU citizen and his or her same-sex partner have married under the law of one Member State, all other Member States, regardless of their own national laws, *must* recognise this partner as 'spouse' within the meaning of the Free Movement Directive. The Commissioner stressed, in this regard, that in applying the Directive, Member States have to respect fundamental rights, including the prohibition of discrimination on the grounds of sexual orientation (Article 21 Charter).

262 *Idem*, at p. 471.

263 *Idem*.

264 Compare Barnard who has held that a 'spouse' in the meaning of the Free Movement Directive is '[...] the person to whom the EU citizen is married under the laws of the state where the marriage was entered into.' C. Barnard, *The substantive law of the EU. The four freedoms*, 2nd ed (Oxford, Oxford University Press 2007) p. 418. Bogdan observed in 2003 that it was at that time 'very doubtful' whether (then existing) EC law contained any 'country-of-origin principle' with regard to civil status. Bogdan 2003, *supra* n. 20, at p. 173.

265 It must be noted that the Commission 'in principle' extended the mutual recognition principle to outside the EU context, by holding that marriages 'validly contracted anywhere in the world' have to be recognised. Commission, 'Communication to the European Parliament and the Council on guidance for better transposition and application of Directive 2004/38/EC on the right of citizens of the Union and their family members to move and reside freely within the territory of the Member States', COM (2009) 313 final, p. 4, para. 2.1.1. See critically Toner 2012, *supra* n. 233, at p. 290.

266 Tuesday, 7 September 2010 – Strasbourg, PV 07/09/2010 – 17 CRE 07/09/2010 – 17, online available at www.europarl.europa.eu/sides/getDoc.do?pubRef=-//EP//TEXT+CRE+20100907+ITEM-017+DOC+XML+V0//EN&language=EN, visited 24 June 2014.

This approach has also been taken in various reports of the EU Fundamental Rights Agency (FRA). Its 2008 Legal study on homophobia and discrimination on grounds of sexual orientation concluded that any refusal to grant a same-sex spouse, who entered into marriage under the laws of an EU Member State, an automatic and unconditional right of entry and residence, would constitute '[...] a form of direct discrimination on grounds of sexual orientation, in violation of Article 26 of the International Covenant on Civil and Political Rights, the general principle of equality, and of the prohibition on discrimination as reiterated in Article 21 of the Charter of Fundamental Rights.'[267] This view was later repeated in other FRA publications on the subject matter.[268]

Apart from the non-discrimination argument, other grounds have been put forward to support the view that a spouse is a spouse. Costello, for example, based an argument on the CJEU judgment in the *Metock* case (2008).[269] The author held that this judgment's '[...] insistence that the time and place of the marriage [were] irrelevant to the enjoyment of the EC residence rights could lend some support to the assertion that a spouse [was] a spouse, in that it seem[ed] to remove marriages from the normal realms of private international law on recognition of legal relationships contracted elsewhere.'[270]

While the former Justice Commissioner has thus advocated application of the host State principle in all situations, Lenaerts has made a plea for leaving room for States to justify refusals to authorise entry and residence of same-sex spouses on the basis of overriding requirements. In principle, the author and CJEU Judge considered application of the home State principle to be 'most consistent with the fundamental freedoms' and held that the term 'spouse' under Article 2(2)(a) of the Free Movement Directive had to be interpreted 'in light of the principle of mutual recognition'.[271] However, because the EU legislature deferred to the judiciary on this point, the CJEU would have to proceed on the basis of a case-by-case analysis, 'while embarking on an analogous legal reasoning to *Maruko*'.[272] According to Lenaerts, Member States should be entitled to invoke overriding reasons of general interest to justify a refusal to recognise a same-sex spouse as spouse under the Free Movement Directive. Any justification advanced by a Member State '[...] would have to be applied in compliance with fundamental rights, particularly the protection of family life.'[273] In the words of Lenaerts, the Court would thus engage '[...] in a balancing exercise, scrutinizing whether the reasons put forward by the host Member State pass muster under free movement law.'[274]

---

267 European Union Agency for Fundamental Rights 2008, *supra* n. 181, at p. 70.

268 E.g. European Union Agency for Fundamental Rights 2010, *supra* n. 181, at p. 46.

269 Case C-127/08 *Metock* [2008] ECR I-6241, ECLI:EU:C:2008:449.

270 C. Costello, 'Metock: free movement and "normal family life" in the Union', 46 *CMLRev* (2009) p. 587 at pp. 615–616.

271 Lenaerts 2009–2010, *supra* n. 7, at pp. 1360–1361.

272 *Idem*, at p. 1359.

273 *Idem*, at p. 1360.

274 *Idem*, at pp. 1360–1361.

Lenaerts' alternative proposal to assess each case individually has been held to carry the risk of leading to 'conceptual confusion, legal uncertainty and unnecessary litigation'.[275] Also, various questions are left unanswered; it is not explained what is meant by an interpretation 'in light of the principle of mutual recognition', nor which overriding reasons of general interest are considered suitable 'to pass muster under free movement law'. As noted above, Article 27(1) of the Directive provides for a limited number of grounds, of which only public policy has been held to be possibly applicable in the situation where a host State imposes restrictions on the free movement of an EU citizen and his or her same-sex partner. It has been submitted that the mere fact that the spouse (or more generally the partner) of a migrating EU citizen is of the same sex cannot be said to constitute the required personal conduct which represents '[...] a genuine, present and sufficiently serious threat affecting one of the fundamental interests of society'.[276]

In fact, Lenaerts' proposal for the interpretation of this secondary law provision is based on a primary law reasoning. The application of primary law in this areas is discussed in section 9.6.3 below. First, however, the rights of same-sex registered partners and same-sex stable partners under the Free Movement Directive, are discussed.

9.6.2.2. Same-sex registered partners

Article 2(2)(b) of Directive 2004/38 expressly refers to the laws of the Member States. It defines the term 'registered partner' as '[...] the partner with whom the Union citizen has contracted a registered partnership, on the basis of the legislation of a Member State, if the legislation of the host Member State treats registered partnerships as equivalent to marriage in accordance with the conditions laid down in the relevant legislation of the host Member State'. Because of the explicit choice for the host State principle in Article 2(2)(b), the dominant view is that the obligations of States, and the corresponding rights of migrating same-sex couples, are dependent upon the laws of the host State.

It is not entirely clear, however, how the phrase 'equivalent to marriage' should be interpreted. It can be debated, for example, if the French PACS meets this standard. The CJEU judgment in the *Hay* case may be held to support a conclusion in the affirmative, but one must be aware that the Court in that case only found comparability in respect of certain benefits that were granted on the occasion of marriage. Hence

---

275 Rijpma and Koffeman 2014, *supra* n. 1, at p. 472.

276 Art. 27(2) Directive 2004/38. Rijpma and Koffeman 2014, *supra* n. 1, at p. 479. Papadopoulou has held in this regard: 'Allowing for wide and open-ended grounds for restrictions on free movement within the EU based on the ambiguous notion of 'public order' would severely undermine the supremacy and autonomy of EC law and underestimate the depth and force of European integration. It can therefore safely be concluded that even Member States whose national laws do not recognize same-sex partnerships will still be obliged to grant access to same-sex married spouses of EU citizens or third-country nationals legally residing in their territory.' L. Papadopoulou, 'In(di)visible Citizens(hip): Same-sex Partners in European Immigration Law', 21 *Yearbook of European Law* (2002) p. 229 at pp. 235–236.

such comparability does not necessarily imply the finding of equivalence to marriage as required in the context of the Free Movement Directive. A related question is who is to decide if a national registered partnership regime is equivalent to marriage.[277] A further question is whether a couple that has concluded a partnership under a relatively weak regime, such as a French PACS, is able to 'boost' its PACS by moving to a Member State that provides for a stronger registered partnership, and if so, whether they could subsequently retain stronger partnership rights upon return to their home Member State.[278]

Host States that do not provide for any registered partnership equivalent to marriage in their national laws, are under no obligation to recognise the registered partner of a migrant EU citizen as 'family member' within the meaning of the Free Movement Directive, although they are of course free to do so.[279] In this situation the couple presumably falls under the rules on stable partners in a 'durable relationship' (Article 3(2), as discussed below). If the host State, however, provides for a partnership for same-sex couples that is equivalent to marriage, it must authorise the entry and residence of same-sex registered partners from other Member States as 'family member' within the meaning of Directive 2004/38.[280] This has made some conclude that there were '[...] two zones of migration for registered partners within the Union'.[281]

Former Justice Commissioner Reding has instead argued that host States have to recognise the registered partners from migrating EU citizens, regardless of their own national laws (see the quote in section 9.6.2.1 above). Thus, in her opinion, even host States who do not provide for any form of legal recognition of same-sex relationships under their national laws, would have to authorise entry and residence of same-sex registered partners from other Member States under the Free Movement Directive. This view seems rather difficult to reconcile with the wording of Article 2(2)(b), which clearly reflects the host State principle. It is furthermore provided that only host States which in their national laws provide for a partnership 'equivalent to marriage', have to authorise entry and residence of the (same-sex) registered partners of nationals of other EU Member States. To claim that *any* host State, including those which in their national laws do not provide for any legal recognition of same-sex relationships, has to recognise same-sex registered partners as 'family member' within the meaning of Article 2(2)(b) may be stretching the interpretation limits of this text too far. The Commissioner's position furthermore raises the question

277 In the employment cases *Maruko* (2008) and *Römer* (2011), the CJEU left this to the national courts to assess, while in *Hay* (2013) the CJEU was prepared to examine this itself. See section 9.4 above.

278 Rijpma and Koffeman 2014, *supra* n. 1, at p. 473, referring (in footnote 109) to Toner 2012, *supra* n. 233, at pp. 288–289.

279 *Idem*, at p. 473, explaining in footnote 105 that Portugal, Belgium, Sweden and Denmark indeed do so.

280 As Fallon has pointed out, the wording of the Directive seems to exclude recognition of a registered partnership concluded outside the EU. Fallon 2007, *supra* n. 217, at p 175.

281 Bell 2004, *supra* n. 227, at p. 624. The author explained that '[i]n an inner zone of states that include registered partnership in their domestic legislation, there is unrestricted free movement. In the outer zone of states without registered partnership legislation, admission of the couple will be at the discretion of the national authorities.'

of how Member States who do not provide for any other form of legal recognition of relationships but marriage, should implement this in practice, namely whether they should treat such foreign registered partnerships as marriages, or create a new institution in their national laws.

The statements by former Commissioner Reding have not been supported by the Commission on all occasions. In 2010 a Luxembourg national petitioned to the European Parliament to have the Commission investigate the non-recognition by Luxembourg of the British civil partnership that he and his partner had concluded in the UK.[282] The petitioner held that this non-recognition constituted a restriction on his and his partner's right to freedom of movement within EU.[283] In its response of May 2011, the Commission commented:

> 'There is currently no EU legislation providing for the mutual recognition of registered partnerships in the European Union. The European Union, although committed to providing its citizens with a wide spectrum of civil rights, has no role to play in relation to Member States' decisions to recognise registered partnerships. It is up to each Member State to resolve this issue and decide whether or not to recognize partnerships registered in other Member States. The issue raised by the petitioner is of exclusive competence of the Member States. However, the Commission is aware of the possible difficulties faced by EU citizens and has therefore published a Green Paper in order to obtain views on ways to reduce these problems.'[284]

The Commission thus held otherwise than Commissioner Reding had done earlier. In fact, it did not even explicitly qualify the matter as a free movement issue, although it did acknowledge, that the situation was problematic for EU citizens in the situation of the petitioner. The Green Paper to which it referred is discussed in section 9.7.3 below.

---

282 The petitioner, who entered into a civil partnership in United Kingdom, and, therefore, could not engage in a Luxembourg civil union, considered that the two forms of partnership had to be regarded as equivalent.

283 This petition was similar to an earlier petition of 2009, namely Petition 1052/2008 by Aldwyn Llewelyn (British) on legal rights in connection with cohabitation agreements in France (PACS) and Britain (civil partnerships). In response to that petition the Commission had also underlined that there was at the time no Community legislation providing for recognition of civil partnerships in the European Union. It also acknowledged, however, that the situation in which the petitioner found himself '[...] could raise issues relating to Community law, in particular the principle of the ban on discrimination on grounds of nationality and the right of Union citizens to reside freely in the territory of another Member State.' In this case the Commission had written a letter to the French Minister of Justice on the issue, although the comment to the petition does not make clear what the content or tenor of that letter was. The Commission did in any case welcome the final adoption by the National Assembly of a proposal for a law designed to recognise foreign partnerships in France.

284 European Parliament, Committee on Petitions (2011), Petition 0178/2010 by Oliver Hepworth (British), on the non-recognition of the British civil partnership by Luxembourg, 6 May 2011, PETI_CM(2011)464844, online available at: www.europarl.europa.eu/meetdocs/2009_2014/documents/peti/cm/866/866779/866779en.pdf, visited June 2014.

9.6.2.3. Same-sex stable partners

Same-sex stable partners of EU citizens who do not enjoy an automatic right of entry and residence in the host Member State as 'family members' within the meaning of Article 2(2) of the Free Movement Directive may, nevertheless, fall within the scope of Article 3(2) of this Directive. Following the latter provision the host State has an obligation 'to facilitate entrance' of 'other family members' who are members of the household of the Union citizen in the State of origin and of 'the partner with whom the Union citizen has a durable relationship, duly attested'. The host Member State must undertake an extensive examination of the personal circumstances and must justify any denial of entry or residence to these partners.[285] In examining their situation on the basis of its own national legislation, the host State must take into consideration their relationship with the EU citizen or any other circumstances, such as their financial or physical dependence on the EU citizen.[286]

The general prohibition of discrimination on grounds of nationality ex Article 24 of the Directive must be observed when applying this Article. Thus, a State may not authorise the entry and residence of all unmarried stable same-sex partners of its own nationals, while refusing to do so for migrating EU citizens. Further, following Recital No. 31 of the Preamble to the Directive, States may not discriminate on grounds of sexual orientation when applying the Directive. They may not thus, for example, systematically refuse same-sex partners when applying this provision.[287] It has furthermore been observed that States cannot adopt a blanket policy of not admitting unmarried partners under any circumstances, as they have to assess each case individually.[288]

The obligations of the host State under Article 3(2) are defined in considerable looser terms than under Article 2(2).[289] The language of facilitation has been called 'hazy and unclear'.[290] A 2010 FRA report qualified the 'duty to facilitate' as '[...] a vague expression which does not necessarily translate into practical consequences in the absence of specific and inclusive yardsticks.'[291] The CJEU's has case law given only limited guidance since.[292] In *Rahman* (2012), the CJEU ruled that Article 3(2) imposes '[...] an obligation on the Member States to confer a certain advantage, compared with applications for entry and residence of other nationals of third

285 Art. 3(2) Directive 2004/38. See also COM (2009) 313 final, p. 4.

286 Recital 6 and Art. 3(2) Directive 2004/38.

287 This also follows from the obligation to respect fundamental rights – including the right to family life – in applying the Directive ex Art. 6(3) TEU. In 2011 Malta amended its law implementing Art. 3(2) Directive 2004/38 under which same-sex partners could not qualify as durable, duly attested partners. It did so in response to an inquiry and negotiations by the Commission. European Union Nationals and their Family Members (Amendment) Order, 2011 (L.N. 329 of 2011).

288 Bell 2004, *supra* n. 227, at p. 625.

289 European Union Agency for Fundamental Rights 2008, *supra* n. 181, at p. 63.

290 Toner 2012, *supra* n. 233, at p. 289.

291 European Union Agency for Fundamental Rights 2010, *supra* n. 181, at p. 50.

292 The CJEU further ruled that because of its imprecise formulation the provision could not be relied on directly against a Member State. Case C-83/11 *Rahman* [2012] ECR 0000, ECLI:EU:C:2012:519, para. 21 and 24.

States, on applications submitted by persons who have a relationship of particular dependence with a Union citizen.' States are left a wide discretion as regards the selection of the factors that could be relevant for the examination of the applicant's personal circumstances. As a minimum they had to guarantee that they employed criteria that are consistent with the normal meaning of the term 'facilitate' and of the words relating to 'dependence' used in Article 3(2), and which do not deprive the provision of its effectiveness.

It is furthermore unclear how the terms 'partner' and 'durable relationship, duly attested' in this context should be interpreted. Following guidelines of the Commission on the Directive national rules on durability of the partnership can refer to a minimum amount of time as a criterion for whether a partnership can be considered as durable. However, other relevant aspects, such as a joint mortgage or children, should also be taken into account.[293] The guidelines do not mention legal recognition of the relationship in another Member State as relevant criterion in this regard.

Generally, the application of this discretionary provision is unlikely to be problematic in States which provide in their national laws for some form of legal recognition of same-sex relationships. In the words of Toner, it is '[...] unlikely that we would find any State treating registered partnership as equivalent to marriage without granting residence rights for a non-national partner in some form or other.'[294] It has been submitted, particularly in view of the wide discretion left to States in *Rahman*, that '[...] a host Member State that does not provide for any form of legal recognition of same-sex relationships, must accept that the condition that the relationship is duly attested is fulfilled in case the partners have entered into a registered partnership or marriage in another state.'[295]

9.6.2.4. Children of same-sex couples

Following Article 2(2)(c) of the Free Movement Directive, the children ('direct descendants') of an EU citizen qualify for entry and residence as family members of the EU citizen. This only holds for children under the age of 21 or who are dependants. These rights extend to the children of the spouse or registered partner[296] of the EU citizen. Even though the Directive does not specify this, it may be presumed that the EU citizen and/or his spouse or registered partner do not have to be the biological and genetic parents of the child, so it as long they are its legal parent(s). Hence, also adopted children qualify as family members under the Free Movement Directive and may consequently join their parent(s) when they move within the EU.

Complications could arise where the partner of a migrating EU citizen is not recognised by the host State as a family member under the Directive. For example,

293 COM (2009) 313 final, at p. 4.
294 Toner 2012, *supra* n. 233, p. 287.
295 Rijpma and Koffeman 2014, *supra* n. 1, at p. 475.
296 As defined in Art. 2(2)(b), see above.

a situation could arise in which a third-country national same-sex registered partner of an EU citizen has a child with whom the EU citizen has not (yet) established parental links. When the partner is not recognised as a family member under the Directive, neither is the child. Matters may become even more complicated when the relationship of the partners has not at all been legally recognised in the home State. Where the child is a member of the household of the EU citizen, its entry and residence must be facilitated.[297] Borg-Barthet has observed that the child could thus '[...] be granted free movement rights by virtue of the vertical relationship with one parent, while the horizontal relationship between the parents does not benefit similarly.' The author held that '[i]n theory, the child could be denied the right to reside with one of its parents', but found it more likely that in practice the right to free movement would be denied '[...] to the entire family, including any EU citizens in the family'.[298] As Borg-Barthet also noted, there have indeed been reports of rainbow families being denied free movement rights.[299]

9.6.3. The free movement of rainbow families under primary law

The foregoing discussion of the rights of migrating EU citizens and their family members under Directive 2004/38 has shown that there are various situations conceivable where application of the Directive does not preclude host States from refusing entry and residence to same-sex spouses and registered partners of EU citizens as family members under Article 2 of the Directive. This may leave these same-sex partners with a mere right to have their entry and residence 'facilitated' under Article 3 of the Directive. What is more, even if entry and residence are indeed facilitated by a host Member State, the same-sex couple (and their family) may experience the consequences of the different regime in the host State in everyday life. When their civil status is downgraded or when their relationship is not at all legally recognised in the host State, the couple (or family) may experience difficulties, for instance in making their property rights effective, in obtaining social and fiscal benefits or in founding a family.[300] Where they have children, this may also affect them, particularly when their parental links are not legally recognised in the host State.

---

297 Art. 3(2)(a) provides that host States must facilitate the entry and residence of 'any other family members, irrespective of their nationality' who, in the home State are dependants or members of the household of the EU citizen having the primary right of residence. This also applies where serious health grounds strictly require the personal care of the family member by the Union citizen.

298 J. Borg-Barthet, 'The principled imperative to recognise same-sex unions in the EU', 8 *Journal of Private International Law* (2012) p. 359 at p. 364.

299 Borg-Barthet referred (at pp. 364–365) to cases reported by *ILGA-Europe* in its contribution to the Green Paper of 2011. ILGA-Europe 2011, *supra* n. 192. This Green Paper is further discussed in section 9.7.3 below.

300 For instance when same-sex couples have no access to AHR treatment, or where they may not jointly adopt a child.

Because any application of secondary law must be commensurable with primary law,[301] these situations require an examination under the Treaty rules. Space does not allow a detailed examination of each possible individual case at this place, but a couple of observations about the relevant legal examination can be made.

Where an EU citizen and his or her same-sex partner (and their children) move to another Member State, this situation comes within the scope of the free movement of persons as provided for under Articles 21 and 45 TFEU (see above). It must next be examined whether there is a restriction of these rights. Not only rules that discriminate on the basis of nationality, but also national rules which hinder free movement or make the use of free movement rights less attractive are incompatible with the Treaties.[302] A refusal to grant entry and residence to the same-sex partner of a migrating EU citizen may indeed constitute such a restriction. The CJEU has on various occasions stressed that the possibility for an EU citizen to be joined by his or her partner, whatever the legal status of their relationship, is instrumental to the free movement of persons.[303] Therefore, when the EU citizen is not allowed so, particularly when he or she is economically active, this may constitute a restriction of his right to free movement.[304] The view has furthermore been taken that an EU citizen who wishes to use his or her free movement rights, but is effectively confined to the territory of those Member States that recognise his or her same-sex marriage or registered partnership, is effectively deprived of the 'genuine enjoyment' of his or her citizenship rights in part of the EU territory.[305]

While in practice entry and residence may in many cases be facilitated under Article 3(2) of the Free Movement Directive, the couple or family may, as noted above, still come across difficulties once resident in the host Member State. The effects of the non-recognition or downgrading of their civil status may have a (great) impact on their daily life in that State. While the CJEU has never pronounced itself on this particular issue, it has been submitted that a change in the civil status of incoming same-sex couples may be seen as an obstacle to free movement.[306] The Court has in any case held that changes in a person's surname constitute such obstacles, as they have been held liable to cause serious inconvenience for those concerned at both

---

[301] In case of conflict, the conflict should be resolved either through a harmonious interpretation of secondary law or by applying directly the Treaty freedom. See Ensig Sørensen 2011, *supra* n. 204.

[302] Case C-415/93 *Bosman* [1995] ECR I-4921, ECLI:EU:C:1995:463. In the words of Toner: 'Choice, and effective freedom to exercise that choice (not just legal rights subjected to conditions making them unattractive and unreasonable to exercise in practice), is the cornerstone of Community law on free movement, whether of goods, persons, establishment or service. [...] The entire structure of free movement law is built around the concept that borders should be eliminated as far as possible.' Toner 2003, *supra* n. 229, at p. 186.

[303] Rijpma and Koffeman 2014, *supra* n. 1, at p. 476, referring (in footnotes 120 and 121) to Case 59/85 *Netherlands* v. *Reed* [1986] ECR 1283, ECLI:EU:C:1986:157, para. 28 and Case 249/86 *Commission* v. *Germany* [1989] ECR 1263, ECLI:EU:C:1989:204, para. 11.

[304] *Idem*, at p. 476.

[305] *Idem*, at p. 478.

[306] Lenaerts 2009–2010, *supra* n. 7, at p. 1359. See also Karakosta 2013, *supra* n. 202, at pp. 66–68.

professional and private levels.[307] The Court has furthermore acknowledged that civil status documents are of great importance to the free movement of persons.[308] Further, in relation to legal persons, the Court has held in cases such as *Centros* and *Überseering*, that the failure to recognise the legal personality of a company set up under the laws of another Member State could amount to a violation of the freedom of companies to move their business elsewhere within the EU.[309] It has been submitted that legal personality is, like marriage, a construct of national law, and that by analogy the non-recognition of a marriage could also be considered to constitute a restriction of the free movement of persons.[310]

The next question is which grounds may be invoked in order to justify such restrictions to the free movement rights. The Treaty itself provides for three grounds, namely public policy, public security and public health. Since the non-recognition of same-sex marriages or registered partnerships would amount to a restriction that does not differentiate on the basis of nationality, additional overriding reasons of public interest could also be invoked.[311] The public policy argument is the broadest ground for justification, and possibly a public moral argument could be brought under this heading.[312] The Court has at the same time consistently underlined that the concept of public policy as justification for a derogation from a fundamental freedom must be interpreted strictly, so that its scope cannot be determined unilaterally by each Member State without any control by the European Union institutions.[313]

Further, even if a justification ground has been accepted by the CJEU, the measure must still pass the proportionality test. It must be examined whether the measure is suitable for securing the objective which it pursues and whether it does not go beyond what is necessary in order to meet the pursued objective. Whether these criteria would be satisfied in cases where same-sex relationships are refused recognition or where the civil status of same-sex couple is downgraded, has been questioned.[314] It has thereby been noted that once a same-sex marriage or registered partnership has been recognised for the purpose of entry and residence, the couple is 'firmly drawn within the scope of EU law', at which point general principles and

---

307 Case C-148/02 *Garcia Avello* [2003] ECR I-11613, ECLI:EU:C:2003:539 and Case C-353/06 *Grunkin* [2008] ECR I-7639, ECLI:EU:C:2008:559. In *Konstantinidis* the Court had held that the misspelling of an EU citizen's name could create an inconvenience to such a degree that it would interfere with his freedom to exercise the right of establishment. Case C-168/91 *Konstantinidis* [1993] ECR I-1191, ECLI:EU:C:1993:115.

308 Case C-336/94 *Dafeki* [1997] ECR I-6761, ECLI:EU:C:1997:579, para. 19.

309 Case C-212/97 *Centros* [1999] ECR I-1459, ECLI:EU:C:1999:126, para. 22 and Case C-208/00 *Überseering* [2002] ECR I-9919, ECLI:EU:C:2002:632, para. 82.

310 Rijpma and Koffeman 2014, *supra* n. 1, at p. 477, referring (in footnote 128) to M. Melcher, 'Private international law and registered relationships: an EU perspective', 20 *European Review of Private Law* (2012) p. 1075 at p. 1081.

311 Case C-55/94 *Gebhard* [1995] ECR I-4165, ECLI:EU:C:1995:411, para. 35.

312 Rijpma and Koffeman 2014, *supra* n. 1, at pp. 478–479. For a contrary viewe see D. Kochenov, 'On options of citizens and moral choices of states: gays and European federalism', 33 *Fordham International Law Journal* (2009) p. 156 at p. 203.

313 Case C-36/02 *Omega* [2004] ECR I-9609, ECLI:EU:C:2004:614, para. 30 and Case C-33/07 *Jipa* [2008] ECR I-5157, ECLI:EU:C:2008:396, para. 23.

314 Rijpma and Koffeman 2014, *supra* n. 1, at p. 480.

fundamental rights – including the prohibition on discrimination on grounds of sexual orientation – apply as a matter of EU law.[315]

Another open question is what value the CJEU would attribute to an argument against the recognition of same-sex relationships based on a Member State's national identity under Article 4(2) TEU. In its case law the Court has given only limited guidance on the definition of this concept, and there have only been a handful of cases where this was accepted as a justification for an obstacle to free movement.[316] It has often been held to be a limited concept, which should be defined as national constitutional identity,[317] while not every rule of a constitutional nature would qualify for protection under Article 4(2) TEU.[318] In *Sayn-Witgenstein* (2010) and *Runevič-Vardyn* (2011) the CJEU held that rules regarding the composition and spelling of surnames constituted justified restrictions on the basis of national identity.[319] Also, in *Sayn-Wittgenstein* the constitutional rule was held to protect not only constitutional identity, but also pursued the principle of equality, which has been recognised as a general principle of EU law as well. In *Toressi* (2013), by referring, *inter alia*, to national identity under Article 4(2) TEU,[320] the Court accepted that the objective of promoting and encouraging the use of one of the official languages of the host State constituted a legitimate interest which, in principle, justified a restriction to the free movement of workers under Article 45 TFEU. When applied in the context of the present case study, the question must, for instance, be answered of whether the definition of marriage as a union between two people of a different-sex in a Member State's constitution would qualify as part of that State's national identity. If it were, the next issue to be examined would, again, be whether the restrictive measure complied with the principle of proportionality.[321] Here, weight could be attributed to the question of

---

315 *Idem*, at p. 484.

316 Case C-208/09 *Sayn-Wittgenstein* [2010] ECR I-13693, ECLI:EU:C:2010:806 and Case C-391/09 *Runevič-Vardyn* [2011] ECR I-3787, ECLI:EU:C:2011:291.

317 G. van der Schyff, 'The constitutional relationship between the European Union and its member states: the role of national identity in article 4(2) TEU', 37 *European Law Review* (2012) p. 563, at pp. 567–568. In a judgment of 2014, the Court confirmed that national identity within the meaning of Art. 4(2) TEU saw at the fundamental political and constitutional structures or the essential functions of the Member State. Joined Cases C-58/13 and C-59/13 *Torresi, nyr,* ECLI:EU:C:2014:2088.

318 Case C-213/07 *Michaniki* [2008] ECR I-9999, ECLI:EU:C:2008:544, Opinion of AG Maduro, para. 33. See Case C-393/10 *O'Brien* [2012] ECR 0000, ECLI:EU:C:2012:110, para. 49 as regards the status of a Member State's judiciary Case C-399/11 *Melloni* [2013] ECR 0000 ECLI:EU:C:2012:600, Opinion of AG Bot, para. 142 as regards fundamental rights included in national constitutions.

319 In *Sayn-Wittgenstein* the Court ruled that the Austrian prohibition to use titles of nobility as part of the surname could be saved on the basis of the public policy exception. The rule formed part of the country's constitutional identity as a Republic and implemented the fundamental constitutional objective of equality before the law. In *Runevič-Vardyn,* the Court allowed a Lithuanian rule under which the spelling of names in official documents would have to comply with the rules governing the spelling of the official national language. See *supra* n. 316.

320 The Court furthermore referred to the fourth subparagraph of Art. 3(3) TEU and Art. 22 CFR, following which the Union must respect its rich cultural and linguistic diversity.

321 As noted by Rijpma and Koffeman '[i]n *Sayn-Witgenstein* the Court exercised a – very light – proportionality test itself, while in *Runevič-Vardyn* it referred back to the national court, hinting at the disproportionality of at least part of the measure'. Rijpma and Koffeman 2014, *supra* n. 1, at p. 482, referring (in footnote 156) to L. Besselink, 'Case C-208/09, Ilonka Sayn-Wittgenstein

whether the objective pursued by the restrictive measures had an equivalent at EU level.[322]

There are other situations conceivable in which the free movement rights of EU citizens in same-sex relationships may be obstructed. For example, an obstacle to free movement may be formed by refusals by Member State authorities to issue civil status records to same-sex couples who request such documents for the purpose of marrying or registering their partnership in another Member State. This was the case for Poland, until the Commission intervened in the matter,[323] and has been reported to be the case in Estonia.[324] Further, it has been pointed out that for same-sex third-country national partners of EU citizens it may be harder to obtain EU citizenship through marriage.[325]

9.6.4. The Family Reunification Directive and third-country nationals with rainbow families

The Family Reunification Directive (2003/86) – which applies to third-country nationals – provides for more discretion for States than the Free Movement Directive.[326] When a third-country national resides lawfully in a Member State he or she or his or her family members may apply for family reunification to be joined with him/her. While spouses are amongst the family members whose entry and residence States must authorise,[327] the authorisation of entry and residence of the third-country national registered partner or the third-country national unmarried partner, with whom 'the sponsor' is in a 'duly attested stable long-term relationship', is left to the

v. Landeshauptmann von Wien, judgment of the Court (second chamber) of 22 December 2010', 49 *CMLRev* (2012) p. 671 at p. 692.

322 See Rijpma and Koffeman 2014, *supra* n. 1, at p. 483.

323 European Commission – Directorate-General for Justice, *2011 Report on the Application of the EU Charter of Fundamental Rights* (Luxembourg, Publications Office of the European Union 2012) p. 52, online available www.ec.europa.eu/justice/fundamental-rights/files/charter_report_en.pdf, visited June 2014. See also www.equal-jus.eu/node/229 and www.equal-jus.eu/node/237 visited June 2014.

324 ILGA-Europe 2011, *supra* n. 192.

325 A. Tanca, 'European Citizenship and the Rights of Lesbians and Gay Men', in: K. Waaldijk and A. Clapham, *Homosexuality: a European Community issue, Essays on Lesbian and gay rights in European Law and Policy* (Dordrecht, Martinus Nijhoff Publishers 1993) p. 271 at p. 280.

326 European Council Directive 2003/86/EC of 22 September 2003, on the right to family reunification, deals with the conditions for the exercise of the right to family reunification by third-country nationals residing lawfully in the territory of the Member States [2003] OJ L 251/12. The Family Reunification Directive determines the conditions under which third-country nationals residing lawfully on the territory of the Member States may exercise the right to family reunification. The separate and less favourable regime for third-country nationals has been held to appear '[...] difficult to reconcile with the EU's commitment to a "fair" policy towards third-country nationals who reside legally on the territory of its Member States, the aim of which should be to grant them rights and obligations comparable to those of EU citizens'. Rijpma and Koffeman 2014, *supra* n. 1, at p. 486, referring (in footnote 171) to Art. 67(2) TFEU and the Stockholm Programme [2010] OJ C115/1, para. 6.1.4.

327 Art. 5(1)(a) Directive 2003/86.

discretion of the Member States.[328] They may decide that registered partners are to be treated equally as spouses with respect to family reunification.[329]

In respect of spouses, similar questions arise as under the Free Movement Directive (see 9.6.2 above), however if it were accepted that the term does not cover same-sex spouses, the consequences would be much graver. This is so because of the Member States' discretion in respect of unmarried partners under the Family Reunification Directive and the absence of a corresponding duty to facilitate the entry of long-term stable partners.

When implementing and applying the provisions of the Directive, Member States are bound to observe fundamental rights.[330] Recital No. 5 of the Preamble to the Family Reunification Directive furthermore provides that Member States must give effect to the provisions of the Directive without discrimination on the basis of, *inter alia*, sexual orientation. According to the Commission, it flows from this Recital that 'Member States that recognise same-sex marriages within their national family law should also do so in application of the Directive.'[331] Conversely, it can be held that host States that do not recognise same-sex marriages under their national law, are under no obligation to recognise same-sex marriages legally concluded in other Member States. The Commission has furthermore held Recital No. 5 to imply that '[...] whenever same sex registered partners are recognised under national family law and Member States apply the "may" clause of the Directive for registered partners, they should also do so for same sex partners.'[332] This 'may clause' only binds the host State which applies it. If the same-sex couple subsequently moves to another Member State, it is for this new host State to decide if the relationship is recognised for family reunification purposes.

A 2010 FRA report argued in even broader terms that '[...] the same-sex spouse of the sponsor [had to] be granted the same rights as would be granted to an opposite-sex spouse.'[333] On the basis of the States' obligation to implement the Directive without discrimination on grounds of sexual orientation, while observing fundamental rights such as the right to respect for family life, this report supported the view that a spouse is a spouse.[334] It was furthermore submitted that the fact that the Family

328 Art. 4(3) Directive 2003/86.

329 *Idem.*

330 Case C-540/03 *Parliament* v. *Council* [2006] ECR I-5769, ECLI:EU:C:2006:429, paras. 62–64.

331 Commission, 'Green paper on the right to family reunification of third-country nationals living in the European Union (Directive 2003/86/EC)', COM (2011) 735 final, p. 4.

332 *Idem.* See also European Union Agency for Fundamental Rights 2008, *supra* n. 181, p. 151.

333 European Union Agency for Fundamental Rights 2010, *supra* n. 181, at p. 50.

334 *Idem.* The relevant para. reads: 'The Directive does not define the meaning of 'spouse' in Article 4. However, the Member States should take into account their obligations under Art. 6(1) and 6(3) of the Treaty on European Union (TEU), to comply with the EU Charter of Fundamental Rights and with fundamental rights as general principles of EU Law. [...] Where, by denying the possibility for the same-sex spouse to join the sponsor, a Member State does not allow a durable partnership to continue, this would result in a disruption of private and family life and could constitute a violation of Article 8 ECHR where the relationship could not develop elsewhere, for instance due to harassment against LGBT people in the countries of which the individuals concerned are nationals or where they could

Reunification Directive granted more rights to the spouse of the sponsor, than to the unmarried partner of the sponsor, could 'generate a form of indirect discrimination', as the option of marrying was often not open to same-sex couples.[335]

States must furthermore authorise the entry and residence of the joint minor children of the sponsor (the third-country national who is residing lawfully in a Member State) and his or her spouse.[336] This also holds for the children of either of them, where the sponsor or his or her spouse has custody and the children are dependent on him or her.[337] The authorisation of entry and residence for children of third-country national same-sex couples who are in a registered partnership or who are unmarried, is left to the discretion of the Member States.[338]

The definition of 'family' under the Family Reunification Directive is also employed under the Long-term Resident Directive, which grants third-country nationals who have been legally present in EU territory a more permanent residence right, as well as a (limited) right to move to a second Member State.[339] This implies that if a long-term resident has entered into a (same-sex) registered partnership in one of the Member States[340] and wishes to move to another Member State, it is up to the discretion of the second Member State to allow him or her to bring his or her registered partner.

9.7. European Private International Law and rainbow families

As illustrated by Chapters 10 and 12 on German, Dutch and Irish legislation, all EU Member States have their own set of conflict-of-laws rules. Over the years, a couple of EU instruments have entered into force, or have been proposed, that approximate certain elements of these national Private International Law regimes in respect of family law. These instruments have as their legal basis Article 81(3) TFEU (or any of its predecessors), according to which the Union is competent to take measures for the approximation of the laws and Regulations of the Member States in 'family law with cross-border implications'. For many of these instruments it is debated if they apply to same-sex relationships.

Since 2007, the EU has been a Member of the Hague Conference on Private International Law.[341] It has ratified the Protocol of 23 November 2007 on the Law

establish themselves. In addition, the Directive should be implemented without discrimination on grounds of sexual orientation. The implication is that the same-sex spouse of the sponsor should be granted the same rights as would be granted to an opposite-sex spouse.'

335 *Idem*. Such reasoning could be analogously applied to the Free Movement Directive, although there in more cases same-sex couples may have the alternative option of registered partnership.

336 Art. 5(1)(b) Directive 2003/86.

337 Art. 5(1)(c) and (d) Directive 2003/86.

338 Art. 4(3) Directive 2003/86.

339 Art. 2(e) Directive 2003/109.

340 Art. 16(1) Directive 2003/109.

341 Council Decision of 5 October 2006 on the accession of the Community to the Hague Conference on Private International Law (2006/719/EC) [2006] OJ L297/1. The European Community became a Member of the Hague Conference on 3 April 2007. With the entry into force of the Treaty of Lisbon on

Applicable to Maintenance Obligations,[342] and it is debated whether this instrument applies to same-sex relationships.[343] The EU is no party to the 1978 Hague Convention on Celebration and Recognition of the Validity of Marriages, and it is equally widely discussed if this could be interpreted as extending to same-sex marriages.[344] The same holds for the Hague Adoption Convention (1993),[345] which 'does not deal specifically with adoption by homosexual couples.'[346]

9.7.1. The *Brussels I* and *Brussels II bis* Regulations and subsequent EU PIL instruments

The *Brussels I* Regulation of 2000 provides for rules governing the jurisdiction of courts and the recognition and enforcement of judgments in civil and commercial matters in EU Member States.[347] Because the Regulation does not apply to matrimonial matters,[348] *Brussels II*[349] was subsequently adopted, which was soon replaced by the present *Brussels II bis*.[350] The latter Regulation applies in civil matters relating to

---

1 December 2009, the European Union replaced and succeeded the European Community as from that date. The Hague Conference on Private International Law is 'a global inter-governmental organisation', which aims at the 'progressive unification' of private international law rules. See the website of the Hague Conference, www.hcch.net/index_en.php?act=text.display&tid=26, visited June 2014.

342 Protocol of 23 November 2007 on the Law Applicable to Maintenance Obligations, online available at www.hcch.net/index_en.php?act=conventions.text&cid=133, visited June 2014. See also Council Decision of 30 November 2009 on the conclusion by the European Community of the Hague Protocol of 23 November 2007 on the Law Applicable to Maintenance Obligations (2009/941/EC) [2009] OJ L 331/17.

343 Following its Art. 1(1), the Protocol applies to maintenance obligations '[...] arising from a family relationship, parentage, marriage or affinity'. See also D. Martiny, 'Workshop: cross-border recognition (and refusal of recognition) of registered partnerships and marriages with a focus on their financial aspects and the consequences for divorce, maintenance and succession', in: K. Boele-Woelki and A. Fuchs (eds.), *Legal recognition of same-sex Relationships in Europe, National, cross-border and European perspectives*, 2nd edn. (Cambridge, Intersentia 2012) p. 225 at p. 246.

344 E.g. Bell 2004, *supra* n. 227, at p. 627, referring (in footnote 70) to H.U. Jessurun d'Oliveira, 'Freedom of movement of spouses and registered partners in the European Union', in: J. Basedow et al. (eds), *Private Law in the international arena – From national conflict rules towards harmonization and unification, Liber amicorum Kurt Siehr* (The Hague, TCM Asser Press 2000) p. 527 at p. 534 and K. Siehr, 'Family unions in private international law', 50 *Netherlands International Law Review* (2003) p. 419 at p. 426. See also Martiny 2012B, *supra* n. 343, at p. 233.

345 Convention of 29 May 1993 on Protection of Children and Co-operation in Respect of Intercountry Adoption, entry into force on 1 May 1995.

346 D. Martiny, 'Private International Law Aspects of Same-Sex couples under German Law', in: K. Boele-Woelki and A. Fuchs (eds.), *Legal recognition of same-sex Relationships in Europe, National, cross-border and European perspectives*, 2nd edn. (Cambridge, Intersentia 2012) p. 189 at p. 219.

347 Council Regulation (EC) No 44/2001 of 22 December 2000 on jurisdiction and the recognition and enforcement of judgments in civil and commercial matters [2010] OJ L 12/1. The regulation supersedes the Brussels Convention of 1968, which was applicable between the EU countries before the regulation entered into force. See also Ch. 3, section 3.6.3.

348 *Idem.*

349 Council Regulation 1347/2000/EC of 29 May 2000 on jurisdiction and the recognition and enforcement of judgments in matrimonial matters and in matters of parental responsibility for children of both spouses [2000] OJ L160/19.

350 Council Regulation 2201/2003/EC of 27 November 2003 concerning jurisdiction and the recognition and enforcement of judgments in matrimonial matters and the matters of parental responsibility,

divorce, legal separation and the annulment of marriage, as well as to all aspects of parental responsibility. The latter excludes decisions on adoption.[351] It provides for automatic recognition of all judgments without any intermediary procedure being required. Recognition of judgments relating to matrimonial matters and matters of parental responsibility may be refused if such recognition is manifestly contrary to public policy.[352] In cases concerning parental responsibility, this exception may only be applied if it is in the best interests of the child. Generally any such application of the public policy exception must be in conformity with the Charter of Fundamental Rights, of which also the prohibition of discrimination (Article 21) is particularly relevant in the present case study.[353]

The *Brussels I* and *Brussels II bis* Regulations function as a backbone for Union action in the field of cross-border civil matters. In fact, *Brussels II* has been perceived as marking 'the beginning of the 'Europeanisation' of family law', '[...] with Member States ceding competence in core areas of social policy', as it was '[...] the first EU measure to deal exclusively and directly with core family law matters'.[354]

It has been much debated if same-sex marriages and registered partnerships fall within the scope of *Brussels II bis*.[355] As Martiny explained, at the time of the drafting of the Regulation a same-sex marriage was not a familiar element of the Member States' family law, '[...] so that only a change of the concept based on systematic and teleological arguments could justify including same-sex marriages in the Regulation's scope.'[356] So far none of the EU institutions have provided guidance on the matter.[357] Wautelet has argued that '[...] the principle of autonomous interpretation probably means that there is today no room for application of the *Brussels II bis* Regulation when the court is seized of a petition concerning a same-sex marriage.'[358]

---

repealing Regulation 1347/2000/EC [2003] OJ L338/1. Somewhat confusing, this Regulation is referred to as *Brussels II Bis* or *Brussels II A*, or sometimes as 'the new Brussels II'.

351 Art. 3(b) Regulation 2201/2003.

352 Arts. 22 and 23 Regulation 2201/2003.

353 Compare Recital No. 58 of the Preamble to European Parliament and Council Regulation 650/2012/EU of 4 July 2012 on jurisdiction, applicable law, recognition and enforcement of decisions and acceptance and enforcement of authentic instruments in matters of succession and on the creation of a European Certificate of Succession [2012] OJ L201/107.

354 M. Ní Shúilleabháin, 'Ten years of European family law: Retrospective reflections from a common law perspective', 59 *International and Comparative Law Quarterly* (2010) p. 1021 at pp. 1021-1023.

355 Wautelet has called looking for the answer to this question 'a frustrating experience, as there is very limited practice on the subject.' P. Wautelet, 'Private International Law aspects of same-sex marriages and partnerships in Europe – Divided we stand?', in: K. Boele-Woelki and A. Fuchs (eds.), *Legal recognition of same-sex Relationships in Europe, National, cross-border and European perspectives*, 2nd edn. (Cambridge, Intersentia 2012) p. 143 at pp. 158–159. Verschraegen has opined that the Regulation does not apply to same-sex relationships. Verschraegen 2012, *supra* n. 156, at p. 267.

356 Martiny 2012B, *supra* n. 343, at p. 236.

357 There is, for instance, no mention of same-sex couples in: Commission, 'Report from the Commission to the European Parliament, the Council and the European Economic and Social Committee on the application of Council Regulation (EC) No. 2201/2003 concerning jurisdiction and the recognition and enforcement of judgments in matrimonial matters and the matters of parental responsibility, repealing Regulation (EC) No 1347/2000', COM (2014) 225 final.

358 Wautelet 2012, *supra* n. 355, at p. 160, referring (in footnote 82) to M. Ní Shuilleabhan, *Cross-Border Divorce Law. Brussels II bis* (Oxford, Oxford University Press 2010) pp. 110–111 and 114–116.

The dominant view is, further, that the Regulation is not applicable to registered partnerships.[359] ILGA-Europe has urged the European Commission to 'clarify' that the *Brussels II* Regulation '[...] applies to marriages of same-sex partners, and that the validity of marriages and the conditions for marriage are determined by the law of the place where the marriage was celebrated'.[360] ILGA-Europe furthermore has recommended extending the application of this Regulation '[...] to registered partnerships and possibly to other forms of legal cohabitation (where they are treated in a way comparable to married couples), and expressly exclude that any public policy claim can be made solely on the grounds that the decision concerns one of such schemes.'[361]

There is, furthermore, uncertainty in respect of the application of other EU PIL instruments to same-sex relationships, such as the EU Regulation on maintenance of 2008[362] and the 2012 Regulation on succession.[363] In respect of divorce and legal separation, only few Member States could reach agreement through enhanced cooperation.[364] Following Article 13 of the relevant Regulation 1259/2010, the courts of a participating Member State whose laws do not provide for divorce or do not deem the marriage in question valid for the purposes of divorce proceedings, are not obliged to pronounce a divorce by virtue of the application of this Regulation. According to Wautelet this '[...] seem[ed] to open up the possibility for States to refuse to entertain a petition for divorce filed by same-sex partners.'[365]

All in all, the existing EU PIL instruments provide very little guidance in respect of cross-border cases involving same-sex couples and rainbow families. While,

359 Martiny 2012A, *supra* n. 346, at p. 221, referring (in footnote 190) *inter alia* to R. Wagner, 'Das neue Internationale Privat- und Verfahrens- recht zur eingetragenen Lebenspartnerschaft' ['The new international private and procedural law on civil partnerships'], 21 *IPRax* (2001) p. 281 at p. 282 and Martiny 2012B, *supra* n. 343, at p. 236.

360 ILGA-Europe 2011, *supra* n. 192, at p. 5.

361 *Idem.*

362 Council Regulation 4/2009/EC of 18 December 2008 on jurisdiction, applicable law, recognition and enforcement of decisions and cooperation in matters relating to maintenance obligations [2009] OJ L7/1. As Storskrubb explains, the Regulation is closely linked to the 2007 Hague Protocol on the Law Applicable to Maintenance Obligations and the Hague Convention on the International Recovery of Child Support and other forms of Family Maintenance. E. Storskrubb, 'Civil Jusitice – A newcomer and an unstoppable wave?', in: P. Craig and G. De Búrca, *The evolution of EU Law*, 2nd edn. (Oxford, Oxford University Press 2011) p. 313.

363 European Parliament and Council Regulation 650/2012/EU of 4 July 2012 on jurisdiction, applicable law, recognition and enforcement of decisions and acceptance and enforcement of authentic instruments in matters of succession and on the creation of a European Certificate of Succession [2012] OJ L201/107. Following its Art. 1(3)(a) this Regulation does not apply to '[...] the status of natural persons, as well as family relationships and relationships deemed by the law applicable to such relationships to have comparable effects'. Martiny has argued that the Regulation applies to same-sex registered partners. See Martiny 2012B, *supra* n. 343, at pp. 247 and 249.

364 Council Regulation 1259/2010/EU of 20 December 2010 implementing enhanced cooperation in the area of the law applicable to divorce and legal separation [2010] OJ L343/10. On enhanced cooperation, see Art. 20 TEU.

365 Wautelet 2012, *supra* n. 355, at p. 182. Martiny considered this Regulation to apply to situations involving two nationals from Member States with same-sex marriages. Martiny 2012B, *supra* n. 343, at pp. 238–239.

as hereafter discussed, initiatives have been taken for new PIL instruments that may prove very relevant to the present case study, none of them expressly refers to same-sex couples.

9.7.2. Proposals for Regulations on property regimes (2010)

In 2006 the Commission launched '[...] a wide-ranging consultation exercise on the legal questions which arise in an international context as regards matrimonial property regimes and the property consequences of other forms of union.'[366] The consultation addressed questions that arise in connection with determination of the law applicable to property and the ways in which the recognition and enforcement of court decisions can be facilitated. In 2010, this exercise resulted in two separate proposals for Council Regulations, one on matrimonial property regimes and the other on the property consequences of registered partnerships.[367]

The proposals aimed to establish 'a comprehensive set of rules of international private law' applicable to matrimonial property regimes as well as to the property consequences of registered partnerships, and to facilitate 'the movement of decisions and instruments among the Member States.'[368] It was held that '[g]iven the nature and the scale of the problems experienced by European citizens', these objectives could be achieved only at Union level.[369] At the same time, the Commission stressed

366 Commission, 'Green Paper on conflict of laws in matters concerning matrimonial property regimes, including the question of jurisdiction and mutual recognition', COM (2006) 400. As the Green Paper explains at p. 3: '[T]he adoption of a European instrument relating to matrimonial property regimes was among the priorities identified in the 1998 Vienna Action Plan [...]. The programme of measures for implementation of the principle of mutual recognition of decisions in civil and commercial matters, adopted by the Council and the Commission at the end of 20003, provided for the development of an instrument on jurisdiction and the recognition and enforcement of decisions as regards matrimonial property regimes and property consequences of the separation of unmarried couples. The Hague programme, which was adopted by the European Council on 4 and 5 November 2004 and established the implementation of the mutual recognition programme as a first priority, and the Council and Commission Action Plan implementing it called on the Commission to submit a Green Paper on "the conflict of laws in matters concerning matrimonial property regimes, including the question of jurisdiction and mutual recognition".' See Hague Programme, "Strengthening freedom, security and justice in the European Union", included in the conclusions of the Presidency of the European Council of 4 November 2004 and Council and Commission Action Plan implementing the Hague Programme on strengthening freedom, security and justice in the European Union [2005] OJ C198/1.

367 Commission, 'Proposal for a Council Regulation on jurisdiction, applicable law and the recognition and enforcement of decisions in matters of matrimonial property regimes', COM (2011) 126 final and Commission, 'Proposal for a Council Regulation on jurisdiction, applicable law and the recognition and enforcement of decisions regarding the property consequences of registered partnerships', COM (2011) 127 final.

368 COM (2011) 126 final, p. 3 and COM (2011) 127 final, p. 3. Coester furthermore observed that non-discrimination was an important motive ('Leitgedanke') of the proposed Regulations. M. Coester, 'Art. 17b EGBGB unter dem Einfluss des Europäischen Kollisionsrechts', 22 *IPRax* (2013) p. 114 at p. 116.

369 COM (2011) 126 final, p. 4 and COM (2011) 127 final, p. 4.

that it was not trying to harmonise the Member States' laws concerning matrimonial property regimes and the property aspects of registered partnerships.[370]

The text of both proposals is gender neutral; there is no mention of terms like 'husband' or 'wife'.[371] Furthermore, neither of the Proposals refers explicitly to same-sex couples, not even in the Explanatory Memorandum.[372] Initially it was held in both proposals that the terms 'marriage' and 'registered partnership' were defined by the national laws of the Member States. The European Parliament later subtly nuanced this. In respect of marriage, the new Recital No. 10 reads:

> 'This Regulation covers issues in connection with matrimonial property regimes. It does not define "marriage", which is defined by the national laws of the Member States. Rather, it adopts a neutral attitude towards that concept. This Regulation does not affect the definition of the concept of marriage in the national law of the Member States.'[373]

In respect of registered partnerships it is provided as follows:

> 'This Regulation covers matters arising from the property consequences of registered partnerships. "Registered partnership" is defined here solely for the purposes of this Regulation. For the purposes of this Regulation, a registered partnership is a form of union other than marriage. The actual substance of the concept of a registered partnership is defined in the national laws of the Member States.'[374]

In respect of the applicable law, married couples had a choice of law under the Commission proposals,[375] while the property consequences of registered partnerships were governed by the law of the State of registration.[376] The Explanatory Memorandum made clear that this principle was adopted '[...] in view of the differences between the national laws of those Member States that make provision for registered partnerships'. The principle was furthermore held to be '[...] in line with the Member States' laws on registered partnerships, which usually provide for application of the law of the State of registration, and do not offer partners the option

---

370 *Idem.*

371 Martiny observed that this 'gender-neutral approach', showed 'that there [was] an intention that same-sex marriages [were] not [to] be treated differently from opposite-sex marriage under matrimonial law.' The author suggested that under the influence of changes in substantive family law within the Member States, the Court could also change its position. Martiny 2012B, *supra* n. 343, at p. 237, referring (in footnote 26) to Bogdan 2009, *supra* n. 246, at p. 255.

372 Wautelet found it 'striking' that the text was 'very timid'. Wautelet 2012, *supra* n. 355, at p. 182.

373 European Parliament legislative resolution of 10 September 2013 on the proposal for a Council regulation on jurisdiction, applicable law and the recognition and enforcement of decisions in matters of matrimonial property regimes (COM (2011)0126 – C7-0093/2011 – 2011/0059(CNS)), P7_TA(2013)0338, Amendment 1.

374 European Parliament legislative resolution of 10 September 2013 on the proposal for a Council regulation on jurisdiction, applicable law and the recognition and enforcement of decisions regarding the property consequences of registered partnerships (COM (2011)0127 – C7-0094/2011 – 2011/0060(CNS)), P7_TA(2013)0337, Amendment 3.

375 Proposed Arts. 16 and 17 COM (2011)126 final.

376 Proposed Art. 15 COM (2011) 127 final.

of choosing any law other than the State of registration, even though they may be entitled to conclude agreements between themselves.' Lastly, it was held to ensure '[...] the unity of the law applicable to all properties owned by the couple that [were] subject to the property consequences of registered partnerships, whatever their form or location.'[377] While the Commission claimed to have verified that the proposal complied with the prohibition of discrimination ex Article 21 CFR, the Fundamental Rights Agency (FRA) issued harsh criticism, holding that this distinction between married couples and registered partners in respect of the choice of law constituted indirect discrimination on grounds of sexual orientation.[378] The amended version of the Regulation on the property consequences of registered partnerships, as adopted by the European Parliament in September 2013, subsequently also provided for a choice of law for registered partners.[379]

Both proposals provide for public policy exceptions,[380] however, it has been explicitly held that these may not be discriminatory.[381] The application of a rule of the law determined by the Regulation can be refused only if such application is 'manifestly incompatible' with the public policy of the forum or the Member State concerned.[382] The accompanying Memorandum of the Proposal in respect of matrimonial property regimes explained:

> 'Considerations of public interest dictate that courts in the Member States be given the possibility in exceptional circumstances of setting aside the foreign law in a given case where its application would be manifestly contrary to the public policy of the forum. However, the courts should not be able to apply the public policy exception in order to set aside the law of another Member State or to refuse to recognise or enforce a decision, authentic instrument or legal transaction drawn up in another State if the application of the public policy exception would be contrary to the Charter of Fundamental Rights of the European Union, and in particular Article 21, which prohibits all forms of discrimination.'[383]

For registered partnerships it is explicitly provided that the application of a rule of the law determined by the proposed Regulation can '[...] not be regarded as contrary to the public policy of the forum merely on the grounds that the law of the forum does not recognise registered partnerships.'[384] The forum of habitual residence may however decline jurisdiction on this ground. Proposed Article 5(2) provides that in

377 COM (2011) 126 final, p. 8.

378 European Union Agency for Fundamental Rights, *Opinion on the Proposal for a regulation on jurisdiction, applicable law and the recognition and enforcement of decisions regarding the property consequences of registered partnerships*, Opinion No. 1/2012 (FRA, Vienna 2012), online available at www.fra.europa.eu/fraWebsite/research/opinions/opinions_en.htm, visited June 2014.

379 European Parliament, *supra* n. 373, Amendment 3.

380 Proposed Art. 23 COM (2011) 126 final and Proposed Art. 18 COM (2011) 127 final.

381 Consideration 25 of COM (2011) 126 final and Considerations 20–21 of COM (2011) 127 final. In both proposals reference is made to Art. 21 CFR. See also Art. 17 of the version of the Registered Partnership Regulations adopted by the European Parliament in September 2013. European Parliament, *supra* n. 373.

382 Proposed Art. 23 COM (2011) 126 final and European Parliament, *supra* n. 373, Amendment 70.

383 Consideration 25 of COM (2011) 126 final.

384 Proposed Art. 18(2) COM (2011) 127 final.

situations other than the death of one of the partners or the separation of the partners the forum of habitual residence may decline jurisdiction '[...] if their law does not recognise the institution of registered partnership'.

9.7.3. Green Paper on recognition of civil status records (2010)

In 2010 the Commission published a Green Paper on the recognition of civil status records,[385] which has been discussed in Chapter 3, section 3.6.3.1. The Green Paper is also important for cross-border cases involving same-sex couples, even though this matter was not explicitly addressed in the Green Paper, a fact of which Toner was very critical:

> '[...] as before, the Commission does not seem to address head-on the issues involved here. For example, there is no explicit mention at all of the cross-border recognition of the validity [of] same-sex marital relationships, and the only mention of registered partnership appears to be the possibility of a change of surname involved after such a partnership is entered into! [...] there are far wider and more problematic issues than this involved.'[386]

The Green Paper is also relevant for migrating rainbow families, as civil status records were defined in the Green Paper as including records recording birth, filiation, adoption and recognition of paternity.[387]

As explained in Chapter 3, three policy options were proposed by the Commission in the Green Paper: (1) assisting national authorities to cooperate more effectively '[...] until there [was] greater convergence of MS' substantive family law'; (2) automatic recognition of civil status situations established in other Member States; or (3) harmonisation of conflict-of-law rules.[388]

The Commission explained that automatic recognition (the second option) would be '[...] simple and transparent [...] with respect to all citizens exercising their right of freedom of movement throughout the European Union', and that it would provide the citizen with 'legal certainty'. It was also maintained that the host Member State '[...] would not have to change its substantive law or modify its legal system.' Some disagreed with this observation. The UK House of Lords, for example, held:

> 'Contrary to the Commission's assertion, that would involve a significant change to the law of a Member State, for example if a same sex marriage legally contracted and registered in

---

385 Commission, 'Green Paper 'Less bureaucracy for citizens: promoting free movement of public documents and recognition of the effects of civil status records'', COM (2010) 747 final.

386 Toner 2012, *supra* n. 233, at pp. 290–291.

387 According to the Green paper, civil status records are '[...] records executed by an authority in order to record the life events of each citizen such as birth, filiation, adoption, marriage, recognition of paternity, death and also a surname change following marriage, divorce, a registered partnership, recognition, change of sex or adoption.' See COM (2010) 747 final, para. 4.1.

388 The Green Paper made clear that the Commission had 'neither the power nor the intention [...] to modify the national definition of marriage.' COM (2010) 747 final, para. 4.3.

Member State A had to be given effect in Member State B which did not otherwise permit or recognise same-sex marriages.'[389]

In respect of registered partnerships, this question may be even more important, as it has not been made clear what 'automatic recognition' entails if the host State does not provide for any form of registered partnership under its national law. Must this State then treat the foreign partnership as 'marriage' under its national law? The latter option would indeed not require any change of substantive domestic law, but it may also be politically sensitive. The Commission acknowledged automatic recognition could '[…] prove to be […] complicated in [...] civil status situations such as marriage' and noted that in any case, this possibility had to take 'due account of the public order rules of the Member States.'[390]

In respect of the harmonisation of conflict-of-law rules the Commission held that this

> '[…] might be another possible way of allowing citizens to exercise fully their right to freedom of movement while providing them with greater legal certainty in relation to civil status situations created in another Member State. A body of common rules developed in the European Union would enshrine the right which would be applicable to a cross-border situation when a civil status event takes place. This right would be defined on the basis of one or more connecting factors taking into account citizen mobility.'[391]

The Green Paper also stressed that the Commission had '[…] neither the power nor the intention to propose the drafting of substantive European rules on, for instance, […] marriage or to modify the national definition of marriage.'[392]

Some of the State authorities and interested parties that had an input in the Consultation process[393] explicitly addressed issues concerning same-sex relationships. The Dutch Ministry of Justice, for example, held subsidiarity to be 'the key principle' in this context. Accordingly, it welcomed the Commission's observation that the EU had no competence to intervene in the substantive family law of Member States. 'However', it was added, '[…] this [did] not alter the fact that the Netherlands [would] continue to push for the multilateral recognition of same-sex marriages and registered partnerships in the EU.'[394] The Federal Government of Germany was very critical in respect of the recognition option as proposed by the Commission. It believed that this was

---

389 House of Lords, European Union Committee, p. 5, online available at www.ec.europa.eu/justice/newsroom/civil/opinion/files/110510/organisations/uk_house_lords_en.pdf, visited June 2014.

390 COM (2010) 747 final, para. 4.3.

391 *Idem.*

392 *Idem.*

393 See the official Commission website on the public consultation www.ec.europa.eu/justice/newsroom/civil/opinion/110510_en.htm, visited June 2014. No contributions by the Irish authorities were published on this website.

394 The Netherlands asserted that '[…] any issue that can be regulated more effectively by the member states [was] not [to] be decided in Brussels.' Dutch response to COM (2010) 747 final, p. 2, online available at ec.europa.eu/justice/newsroom/civil/opinion/files/110510/public_authorities/netherlands_minjust_en.pdf, visited May 2012.

'[...] an unbalanced, systematically incorrect and incoherent makeshift solution.'[395] The German government considered the harmonisation of conflict-of-laws rules the only appropriate solution. The German *Bundesrat* for its part acknowledged that automatic recognition probably came 'closest to a Community ideal' and could for that reason be a desirable goal, but held that this could only be achieved if the applicable conflict-of-laws rules were first harmonised.[396] ILGA-Europe made a strong plea for the portability of rights of same-sex partners in its response to the Green Paper.[397] The NGO umbrella organisation held that all EU citizens had to be able to

> '[...] validly acquire a personal status of their choice elsewhere in the Union (especially if it is not possible in their own state); have a portable status wherever they go (including returning to the State); and circulate freely with an unmarried or unregistered partner.'[398]

ILGA-Europe furthermore held that there were specific legal difficulties for the children of same-sex parents in cross-border situations as '[...] the varying degrees of non-recognition of same-sex partners' had 'an automatic negative impact on the rights of children of gay and lesbian parents.'[399] The LGBT interest organisation stressed that in a majority of EU Member States children could not establish full parental links with both their same-sex parents.[400] Also, it was noted that there was a risk of parental links being stripped away from children upon movement to another Member State (see also 9.6.2.4 above).

As noted in Chapter 3 section 3.6.3.1, no further legislative initiative has been taken in respect of recognition of civil status documents, although in 2014 the Parliament called on the Commission to '[...] make proposals for the mutual recognition of the effects of all civil status documents across the EU, in order to reduce discriminatory legal and administrative barriers for citizens and their families who exercise their right to free movement'.[401]

---

395 Federal Government observations on COM (2010) 747 final, p. 14, online available at www.ec.europa.eu/justice/newsroom/civil/opinion/files/110510/public_authorities/germany_minjust_en.pdf, visited June 2014.

396 *Idem*, pp. 12–13 and Bundesrat Resolution of 15 April 2011, Document 831/10, point 12, online available at www.ec.europa.eu/justice/newsroom/civil/opinion/files/110510/public_authorities/germany_parliament_en.pdf, visited June 2014.

397 ILGA-Europe 2011, *supra* n. 192.

398 *Idem*, at p. 20.

399 *Idem*.

400 It was claimed that this was so, as there was no second-parent adoption for same-sex partners in those countries. This may have been partly redressed as a result of ECtHR [GC] 19 February 2013, *X. a.o.* v. *Austria*, no. 19010/07 (see ch. 8, section 8.2.4.1.2).

401 European Parliament Resolution of 4 February 2014 on the EU Roadmap against homophobia and discrimination on grounds of sexual orientation and gender identity (2013/2183(INI)).

9.8. Conclusions

While LGBT rights form a prominent part of the EU's fundamental rights agenda (section 9.4) and while EU institutions have undoubtedly played a stimulating role in respect of the promotion of LGBT rights in the Member States, the actual protection that EU law offers in this regard has its limitations. Limitations, first of all, exist in the fact that the EU does not have competences in all areas of law, for instance, not in substantive family law. In addition, in some areas where the EU does have competence, for example in respect of free movement, there remain open questions as to the application of the relevant rules in cases concerning same-sex couples and rainbow families.

Full equal rights for same-sex couples have been guaranteed by the EU legislature under the EU Staff Regulations since 2004. Staff cases are of EU law *pur sang* in the sense that the Member States' national legislation is not affected by them. On the other hand, as certain entitlements depend on the civil status of the staff member, national legislation still plays an important role in the obtainment of equal rights under EU law. That also holds for EU non-discrimination law (section 9.3). Importantly, the CJEU has held that there is direct discrimination on grounds of sexual orientation where at national level certain employment benefits are reserved to spouses, while marriage is reserved to different-sex couples only and while under national law, a same-sex registered partner is in a legal and factual situation comparable to that of a spouse as regards that benefit. The existence of some form of civil status under national law has thus been decisive in the *Maruko, Römer* and *Hay* judgments, and it has therefore been held 'arguable' that the Union's approach in this realm of EU law has perpetuated 'the individuality of each Member State's family law traditions.'[402] It remains to be seen what the Court would rule in a case where there is no alternative form of recognition at national level. In *Grant* (1998) the Court expressly held that in respect of a certain employment benefit the situation of a same-sex couple in a non-marital relationship was not comparable to that of a married couple, but whether this would still be upheld today, particularly after the *Hay* judgment, remains to be seen.

The rights that are granted to same-sex couples under EU free movement law are equally dependent on national legislation on civil status. Both the Free Movement Directive and the Family Reunification Directive leave room for host States to apply their own national standards to migrating same-sex couples. While in respect of registered partners, the host State principle is clearly adopted by the EU legislature under the Free Movement Directive, this is less clear in respect of the term 'spouse'. It has been observed that '[...] an uneven landscape with respect to freedom of movement and family reunification for same-sex couples' exists.[403] Both

---

402 Borg-Barthet 2012, *supra* n. 298, at p. 359.

403 European Union Agency for Fundamental Rights, *Homophobia, transphobia and discrimination on grounds of sexual orientation and gender identity in the EU Member States. Summary of findings, trends, challenges and promising practices* (Luxembourg, Publications Office of the European Union 2011) p. 28, online available at www.fra.europa.eu/en/publication/2011/

up and downgrading of foreign same-sex marriages and registered partnerships takes place.[404] While various Member States changed their definition of 'family member' to include same-sex partners for the purposes of free movement and family reunification,[405] in some Member States, contrary developments have taken place.[406] The diverse practice has been heavily criticised, since as a consequence '[...] the freedom of movement of LGBT persons is restricted and not uniformly recognised throughout the European Union'.[407] While the Parliament has repeatedly called on the Member States and the Commission to guarantee the free movement of rainbow families,[408] no legislative change has yet been implemented in this regard, rendering it even more probable that the matter will one day be decided by the CJEU. When confronted with a preliminary reference concerning the interpretation of the term 'spouse', it has been explained that the CJEU has different options; it may interpret this term independently or apply a host State or a home state principle. The home State principle would provide the strongest protection of the free movement rights of both the EU citizen and his or her same-sex spouse. In most situations the entry and residence of a same-sex spouse will presumably be facilitated on the basis of Article 3(2) of the Directive.

This is different for same-sex spouses of third-country nationals, as the Family Reunification Directive does not provide for such a fall back option like Article 3(2) of the Free Movement Directive. The entry and residence of same-sex registered

homophobia-transphobia-and-discrimination-grounds-sexual-orientation-and-gender, visited June 2014.

404 Costello 2009, *supra* n. 270, at pp. 615–616. See ch. 10, section 10.4.6 and ch. 11, section 11.4.4, which shows that under German and Irish Private international law, foreign same-sex marriages are 'downgraded' to the German and Irish civil partnership.

405 European Union Agency for Fundamental Rights, *Annual Report 2011; Fundamental rights: challenges and achievements in 2011* (Luxembourg, Publications Office of the European Union 2012). The report refers (on p. 134) to Austria, Estonia, Greece, Latvia, Malta, Romania, Slovakia, Slovenia as well as Lithuania. In 2008, the Commission concluded in its report on compliance with the Free Movement Directive that '[s]ame-sex couples enjoy[ed] full rights of free movement and residence in thirteen Member States which consider[ed] registered partners as family members.' COM (2008) 840, para. 3.1. at p. 4. The Commission indicated that these thirteen states were: BE, BG, CZ, DK, FI, IT, LT, LU, PT, NL, ES, SE and the UK. Toner has called this a '[...] laconic and quite possibly dubiously accurate assessment'. Toner 2012, *supra* n. 233, at p. 290.

406 The 2011 annual report of the European Union Agency for Fundamental Rights pointed out: '[...] [N] ew legislation in Romania prohibits the transcription/registration of civil status certificates or extracts issued by foreign authorities for same-sex marriages or same-sex civil partnerships concluded abroad. This transcription is a requirement for obtaining entry and residence into Romania for spouses or partners, which necessarily only recognise partnerships between men and women.' European Union Agency for Fundamental Rights 2011A, *supra* n. 405, at p. 135.

407 European Union Agency for Fundamental Rights 2008, *supra* n. 181, at p. 64.

408 The Parliament has repeatedly called on the Commission and the Member States to ensure that the Free Movement Directive was implemented without any discrimination based on sexual orientation. European Parliament Resolution of 26 April 2007 on homophobia in Europe, P6_TA(2007)0167 and European Parliament resolution of 24 May 2012 on the fight against homophobia in Europe (2012/2657(RSP)) P7_TA(2012)0222, para. 4. In 2014, the Parliament asked the Commission to produce '[...] guidelines to ensure the Free Movement Directive and the family reunification Directive were '[...] implemented so as to ensure respect for all forms of families legally recognised under Member States' national laws.' European Parliament Resolution of 4 February 2014 on the EU Roadmap against homophobia and discrimination on grounds of sexual orientation and gender identity (2013/2183(INI)).

partners and same-sex stable partners of third-country nationals is, moreover, within the discretion of the Member States, although they may not discriminate on the basis of sexual orientation when implementing this Directive.

What has furthermore become clear is that while the authorisation of the entry and residence of same-sex partners of EU citizens or third-country nationals is an essential step, the story does not end there. Same-sex couples may still encounter difficulties in their daily lives if their relationships are not legally recognised in the host Member State. In cases involving EU citizens such difficulties can possibly be challenged on the basis of the primary free movement rules, as set out in section 9.6.3. The EU legislature may also redress these issues by adopting instruments on the basis of Article 81(3) TFEU, the legal basis for the approximation of conflict-of-laws rules concerning family law. The proposed Regulations on Property regimes (section 9.7.2) are a clear step in that direction and possibly further EU PIL instruments on the basis of the Green Paper on recognition of civil status records may follow. That is still in the future, however, and for the time being the automatic recognition of civil status records is not in sight.

Chapter 10
Germany

10.1. Constitutional framework

This first section discusses two Articles of the German Basic Law that are fundamental to the present case study, namely Article 3 (equality before the law) and Article 6 (protection of marriage and the family). The right to free development of the personality (including personal autonomy and private sphere) of Article 2 German Basic Law was introduced Chapter 4.[1] Reference is also made to that Chapter for a discussion of how the principle of the best interests of the child is consolidated in German law.[2]

10.1.1. Article 3 Basic Law: equality before the law

Article 3 of the German Basic Law lays down a guarantee for equality before the law. Its third paragraph lists a number of prohibited discrimination grounds, such as race and sex. Sexual orientation – in some German legislation and case law also referred to as sexual identity[3] – is not amongst these grounds.[4] By amendment of 1994 disability was included as a suspect ground,[5] but the proposal to also include sexual orientation did not receive the required two thirds majority in Parliament. Inclusion of this ground was considered to be unnecessary as Article 2(1) (the right to free development of the personality) and Article 1 Basic Law (protection of human dignity), as well as the case law of the German Federal Constitutional Court (*Bundesverfassungsgericht*, BVerfG), were considered to offer sufficient protection to homosexuals. Further – it was held – remaining deficits in the protection could best be remedied by the legislature and not by amendment of the Constitution.[6]

LGBT people nevertheless enjoy protection against discrimination by the general principle of equality of Article 3(1) Basic Law. This provision demands that all

---

1 Ch. 4, section 4.1.2.

2 Ch. 4, section 4.1.5.

3 See for instance Art. 1 Allgemeines Gleichbehandlungsgesetz (AGG) [Equal Treatment Act] and BVerfG 7 July 2009 (dec.), Az. 1 BvR 1164/07, *NJW* 2010 p. 1439, para. 55.

4 Art. 3(3) Basic Law reads: 'No person shall be favoured or disfavoured because of sex, parentage, race, language, homeland and origin, faith, or religious or political opinions. No person shall be disfavoured because of disability.' Translation taken from www.gesetze-im-internet.de/englisch_gg/englisch_gg.html#p0034, visited June 2014.

5 Gesetz zur Änderung des GG [Act on the Amendment of the Constitution] Act of 27 October 1994, *BGBl.* p. 4216.

6 *BT-Drs.* 12/6000, p. 54.

persons be treated equally before the law. It does not necessarily stand in the way of the granting of favourable treatment to one group of persons while it is denied to another group of persons.[7] Following established case law of the BVerfG, the general principle of equality results in differing limits for the legislature or rulemaker, varying from the mere prohibition of arbitrariness to a strict subjection to proportionality requirements. The subject involved and the 'differentiating elements' (grounds of discrimination), are relevant factors to be taken into account in setting this limit.[8] If unequal treatment is linked to sexual orientation, a strict standard of review is applied. As the Constitutional Court explained in 2009, while referring to European law standards:

> 'If a legal provision treats a group of persons to whom a specific statute applies differently from other persons to whom the statute applies, although there are no differences between the two groups of such a nature and such weight that they could justify the unequal treatment, it violates the general principle of equality of Article 3.1 of the Basic Law [...]. Article 3.1 of the Basic Law requires that the unequal treatment must be linked to a factually justified distinguishing element. It is not sufficient to justify unequal treatment of groups of persons that the legislator or rulemaker took account of a distinguishing element that was suitable by its nature. Instead, there must also be an inner connection between the differences found and the differentiating provision to justify the degree of differentiation, a connection which can be adduced as an objectively justifiable differentiating factor of sufficient weight [...]. [...] The requirements in the case of unequal treatment of groups of persons are all the stricter the greater the danger is that a link to personal characteristics that are comparable to those of Article 3.3 of the Basic Law will lead to the discrimination of a minority [...]. This is so in the case of sexual orientation.'[9]

For justification of a difference in treatment based on sexual orientation serious grounds ('*ernstlichte Gründe*') are thus required.[10]

'Sexual identity' is furthermore included as a prohibited ground of discrimination in Article 1 of the Equal Treatment Act (*Allgemeines Gleichbehandlungsgesetz* (AGG)),[11] by which Germany implemented Directive 2000/78/EC.[12] The scope of this Act encompasses labour law, social security and public health matters, education and access to public goods and services.[13] Further, a handful of other provisions concerning the legal position of employees and civil servants, explicitly prohibit

---

7 BVerfG 7 July 2009 (dec.), Az. 1 BvR 1164/07, *NJW* 2010 p. 1439, para. 85.

8 *Idem*.

9 *Idem*, para. 86–87.

10 E.g. OLG Hamburg 22 December 2010 (dec.), Az. 2 Wx 23/09, *NJW* 2011 p. 1104, para. 16.

11 Act of 14 August 2006, *BGBl.* I 2006, p. 1897. This Act entered into force on 18 August 2006.

12 Council Directive 2000/78/EC of 27 November 2000 establishing a general framework for equal treatment in employment and occupation [2000] OJ L303/16. The Member States were required to have transposed the Directive into national law no later than 2 December 2003.

13 Art. 2 AGG.

discrimination on ground of sexual identity.[14] Lastly, the constitutions of several German States ('*Länder*') also contain a prohibition of unequal treatment on grounds of sexual identity[15] or sexual orientation.[16]

In more recent years, bills were tabled which saw at the inclusion of 'sexual orientation' as a prohibited ground in Article 3(3) Basic Law,[17] but at the time this research was concluded (i.e., 31 July 2014), none of them had yet made it into law. The *Bundesrat* held in 2009 that such inclusion would only be 'symbol politics', as the Constitutional Court had in the meantime granted strong protection against discrimination on grounds of sexual orientation (see 10.4 below).[18] Other objections voiced in the debates have been the suggestion that including sexual orientation would also mean including and protecting a particular sexual orientation towards children (paedophilia) and that it would do away with the special protection of marriage.

10.1.2. Article 6(1) Basic Law: special protection of marriage and the family

According to Article 6(1) of the German Basic Law, 'Marriage and the family shall enjoy the special protection of the state.' The second paragraph of Article 6 Basic Law provides that parents have a natural right to as well as a duty for the care and the upbringing of children, while the State watches over them in the performance of this duty. While the third and the fifth paragraphs provide for special protection for children,[19] the fourth paragraph concentrates on the mother and provides that 'every mother shall be entitled to the care and protection of the community.' The '*Mutterkult*', of which this provision is an expression, can be considered unique to the German legal culture.

Article 6(1) finds its origin in Article 119 of the Weimar Constitution of 1919, which provided that marriage, 'as the foundation of the family and the preservation and expansion of the nation', enjoyed the special protection of the Constitution. The Weimar Article furthermore stated that it was task of both the State and the

---

14 Art. 75(1) Betriebsverfassungsgesetz [Works Constitution Act]; Art. 9 Bundesbeamtengesetz [Federal Civil Service Act]; Art. 9 Beamtenstatusgesetz [Act on the status of members of the State civil service] and Art. 19a Vierten Buches Sozialgesetzbuch [Social Code, Fourth Volume].

15 Art. 10(2) Constitution of Berlin; Art. 12(2) Constitution of the State of Brandenburg and Art. 2 Constitution of the Free Hansa town of Bremen.

16 Art. 2(3) Constitution of the Free State of Thüringen.

17 For example, *BR-Drs.* 741/09, *BT-Drs.* 16/13596, p. 3; *BT-Drs.* 17/88 p. 1 and *BT-Drs.* 17/254.

18 The Bundesrat decided on 27 November 2009 not to put the Bill before the German Bundestag. See U. Kischel, 'BeckOK GG Art. 3–2. Sexuelle Orienterung' ['BeckOK GG Art. 3–2. Sexual Orientation'], in: V. Epping and C. Hillgruber (eds.), *Beck'scher Online-Kommentar GG* [Beck Online Commentary to the German Basic Law], 21st edn. (München, Verlag Beck 2014) Rn. 130.

19 Art. 6(3) Basic Law reads: 'Children may be separated from their families against the will of their parents or guardians only pursuant to a law, and only if the parents or guardians fail in their duties or the children are otherwise in danger of serious neglect.' and Art. 6(5) reads: 'Children born outside of marriage shall be provided by legislation with the same opportunities for physical and mental development and for their position in society as are enjoyed by those born within marriage.' Translations taken from www.gesetze-im-internet.de/englisch_gg/englisch_gg.html#p0034, visited June 2014.

communities to strengthen and socially promote the family.[20] While the reference to the expansion of the nation was removed in the Basic Law of 1949, the special protection of 'marriage and the family' was included in Article 6, expressly and deliberately mentioning marriage and the family in one and the same sentence. Legal opinion differs strongly, however, as to the question of whether this also means that these two institutions are inseparably – or at least closely – interconnected. There is wide agreement that the Basic Law is more subjective and individualistic oriented than the Weimar Constitution was.[21] In respect of Article 6 in particular, a clear freedom-oriented trend ('*freiheitliche Tendenz*') since the Weimar Constitution, has been observed.[22] Hofmann nevertheless argued that also the drafters of the Basic Law had population policy considerations in mind when awarding marriage a privileged status in the Basic Law.[23] Robbers, for his part, claimed that from the systematics and wording of the Basic Law it follows that marriage and the family are 'socially and legally' connected with one another – together with the care and upbringing of children, the protection of the mother and the protection of children born outside of marriage, as protected in paragraphs 2 to 5 of Article 6.[24] The author has held that the Basic Law protects an ideal of the free development of the personality as well as an 'in life positively perceived normality'. Marriage is the principled foundation of the family, he argues, and Article 6 protects and structures with the help of legal institutions, social relations. Others have disagreed with this interpretation of Article 6(1). Grösschner, for example, has held the word 'and' between 'marriage' and 'the family' in Article 6(1) to be 'dogmatically meaningless'.[25] He holds that Article 6 represents the difficult dilemma of 'dualism' ('*Dualismus*'), whereby the provision is intended to have both personal meaning for the individual, as well as 'transpersonal' meaning for the society and the State (see also 10.1.2.2 below, concerning the three functions of Article 6).[26]

---

20 Art. 119(1) and (2) *Die Verfassung des Deutschen Reichs* ('*Weimarer Reichsverfassung*') [Weimar Constitution of 11 August 1919], *Reichsgesetzblatt* 1919, No. 152, pp. 1383–1418. Other than the subsequent Basis Law of 1949, did the Weimar Constitution not foresee in the possibility for individuals to enforce their rights before a Constitutional Court. H. Dreier (ed.), *Grundgesetz-Kommentar, Band 1, Präambel, Artikel 1–19* [Commentary to the Basic Law, Volume 2, Preamble, Articles 1–19], 2nd edn. (Tübingen, Mohr Siebeck 2004) p. 55. On the history of Art. 6 Basic Law, see also A. Saunders, 'Marriage, Same-Sex Partnership, and the German Constitution', 13 *German Law Journal* (2012) p. 911 online available at www.germanlawjournal.com/index.php?pageID=11&artID=1448, visited June 2014.

21 H. Hofmann, 'Art 6', in: B. Smidt-Bleibtreu et al., *GG Kommentar*, 11th edn. (Berlin, Carl Heymanns Verlag 2011) at pp. 269–270 and G. Robbers, 'Artikel 6' ['Article 6'], in: C. Starck et al., *Kommentar zum Grundgesetz* [Commentary to the Basic Law] (München, Verlag Franz Vahlen 2010) p. 683 at p. 687, Rn. 5.

22 R. Grösschner, 'Art. 6' ['Art. 6'], in H. Dreier (ed.), *Grundgesetz-Kommentar, Band 1, Präambel, Artikel 1–19* [German Basic Law Commentary, Volume 1, Preamble, Articles 1–19], 2nd edn. (Tübingen, Mohr Siebeck 2004) p. 748 at p. 755, Rn. 4.

23 Hofmann 2011, *supra* n. 21, at pp. 269–270.

24 Robbers 2010, *supra* n. 21, at p. 691, Rn. 17.

25 Grösschner 2004, *supra* n. 22, at p. 755, Rn. 4.

26 *Idem*, at p. 755, Rn. 5.

10.1.2.1. Definition of 'marriage' and 'family' in Article 6(1) Basic Law

The Basic Law itself contains no definition of the terms 'marriage' and 'the family'. The German Constitutional Court has repeatedly defined marriage as the union of one man with one woman to form a permanent partnership, based on a freely made decision and with the support of the State,[27] in which man and woman are in an equal partnership[28] and may decide freely on the organisation of their cohabitation.[29] The fact that the spouses are of a different sex is considered one of the constitutive characteristics of marriage.[30] Therefore, no right to marry for same-sex couples can be derived from Article 6(1), as the BVerfG has on several occasions explicitly held.[31] This case law is discussed in further detail in section 10.3 below.

The 'family' within the meaning of this Article has been defined by the BVerfG as *'die umfassende Gemeinschaft von Eltern und Kindern'*,[32] thus limiting the protection to the first bloodline. Müller-Terpitz argues that the notions of 'family' and 'marriage' ex Article 6(1) are dogmatically separated from one another and that family exists, 'where there are children'. Accordingly, the author claims, the notion should be broadly interpreted, encompassing, *inter alia*, a right to found a family for same-sex oriented persons, for instance through heterologous insemination.[33]

10.1.2.2. The meaning of 'special protection' in Article 6(1) Basic Law

Under Article 6(1) marriage and the family enjoy the 'special protection' of the State. This entails a positive obligation on the State to protect marriage and the family from third party interference (*'Drittbeeinträchtigungen'*), as well a negative obligation for the State not to interfere with marriage and family matters.[34] In legal scholarship, three – closely related – functions (*'Regelungsinhalte'*) of Article 6(1) are identified: it contains an individual fundamental right (*'Grundrecht'*); it functions as an institutional guarantee (*'Institutsgarantie'*); and it constitutes a general principle of law (*'Grundsatznorm'*) that influences all areas of law that relate to marriage and the

27 BVerfG 17 July 2002, Az. 1 BvF 1/01, *NJW* 2002 p. 2543.

28 *Idem.*

29 *Idem.*

30 *Cf.* BVerfG 27 May 2008 (dec.), Az. 1 BvL 10/05, *NJW* 2008 p. 3117 and BVerfG 27 May 2008 (dec.), Az. 1 BvL 10/05, *NJW* 2008 p. 3117, para. 50.

31 See K.S. Gerhard, *Die eingetragene Lebensparterschaft – Eine historisch-dogmatische Bestandsaufnahme zur Frage nach einem neuen familienrechtlichen Institut* [The German Civil partnership – a historic-dogmatic inventory of the question for a new family law institute] (Göttingen, Sierke Verlag 2009), p. 25, and BVerfG 4 October 1993 (dec.), Az. 1 BvR 640/93, *NJW* 1993 p. 3058.

32 BVerfG 29 July 1959, Az. 1 BvR 205/58 a.o., *NJW* 1959 p. 1483.

33 R. Müller-Terpitz, 'Das Recht auf Fortpflanzung – Vorgaben der Verfassung und der EMRK' ['The right to procreate – guidelines of the German Constitution and the ECHR'], in: H. Frister and D. Olzen (eds.), *Reproduktionsmedizin, Rechtliche Fragestellungen. Dokumentation der Tagung zum 10-jahrigen Bestehen des Instituts fur Rechtsfragen der Medizin Dusseldorf* [Reproduction medicine, legal questions. Proceedings of the Conference for the 10 year anniversary of the Düsseldorf institute for medical legal issues] (Düsseldorf, Düsseldorf University Press 2010) p. 9 at. p. 14.'

34 *Cf.* BVerfG 17 January 1957, Az. 1 BvL 4/54, *NJW* 1957 p. 417 and BVerfG 17 July 2002, Az. 1 BvF 1/01, *NJW* 2002 p. 2543.

family.[35] As a fundamental right, it has been held to be first of all a negative right ('*Abwehrrecht*'), entailing, *inter alia*, the right to unhindered access to marriage with a freely chosen partner[36] and the right to decide upon the marriage settlement.[37] As institutional guarantee Article 6(1) provides spouses with a normative framework which provides legal clarity and certainty for third parties.[38] Article 6(1) protects an '*Ordnungskern*' that the legislature must take into account when legislating on the institute of marriage,[39] whereby the legislature enjoys considerable discretion.[40] The role of Article 6(1) as institutional guarantee finds its expression in, *inter alia*, the matrimonial property rights and the role of registrars ('*Standesbeamten*'). As a general principle, Article 6(1) implies a binding value judgment ('*eine verbindliche Wertentscheidung*') for all areas of law concerning marriage and the family.[41] According to Schmitt-Kammler and Von Coelln, from this a (positive) State obligation to protect and to give preferential treatment to marriage follows. The latter obligation to give preferential treatment means that marriage can not be put at a disadvantage *vis-à-vis* other partnerships, or ways of living.[42] This reading has had a particular effect in economic areas of law, such as social insurance law.[43] It has been widely discussed in legal commentaries as well as in case law whether this obligation to give preferential treatment also means that other partnerships cannot be treated as favourably as marriage. In other words, the question is whether Article 6(1) of the Basic Law contains a so-called 'requirement of distance' ('*Abstandsgebot*'), an obligation to differentiate between marriage and other partnerships, to the disadvantage of the latter. This discussion will recur throughout the various sections of this chapter. As will be set out in more detail, the BVerfG has held there not to be any such requirement of distance or disadvantage to other partnerships, because

35 A. Schmitt-Kammler and C. von Coelln, 'Art. 6 [Ehe und Familie]' ['Art 6 [Marriage and Family'], in M. Sachs, *Grundgesetz Kommentar* [Basic Law Commentary], 5th edn. (München Verlag C.H. Beck 2009 p. 348 at p. 357 and Hofmann 2011, *supra* n. 21, at pp. 270–271.

36 *Cf.* BVerfG 4 May 1971, Az 1 BvR 636/68, *NJW* 1971 p. 1509; BVerfG 14 November 1973 (dec.), Az. 1 BvR 719/69, *NJW* 1974 p. 545; BVerfG 17 July 2002, Az. 1 BvF 1/01, *NJW* 2002 p. 2543 and BVerfG 9 November 2004, Az. 1 BvR 684/98, *NJW* 2005 p. 1413. See Schmitt-Kammler and von Coelln 2009, *supra* n. 35, at p. 359 and M. Antoni, 'Art 6 [Schutz von Ehe und Familie, nichteheliche Kinder]' ['Art. 6 [Protection of marriage and family, children born out of wedlock]'], in D. Hömig (ed.) *Grundgesetz für die Bundesrepublik Deutschland* [Constitution for the Federal Republic of Germany], 9th edn. (Baden-Baden, Nomos Verlagsgesellschaft 2010) p. 110 at p. 112.

37 Schmitt-Kammler and von Coelln 2009, *supra* n. 35, at p. 360 under reference to, *inter alia*, BVerfG 14 November 1984 (dec.), Az. 1 BvR 14/82 and 1642/82 and BVerfG 5 February 2002 (dec.), Az. 1 BvR 105/95 a.o., *NJW* 2002 p. 1185.

38 *Idem*, at pp. 361–362.

39 *Idem*.

40 *Cf.* BVerfG 28 February 1980, Az. 1 BvL 136/78 and BVerfG 17 July 2002, Az. 1 BvF 1/01, *NJW* 2002 p. 2543.

41 BVerfG 17 July 2002, Az. 1 BvF 1/01, *NJW* 2002 p. 2543, para. 90. Schmitt-Kammler and von Coelln 2009, *supra* n. 35, at p. 363 and Antoni 2010, *supra* n. 36, at p. 110. Saunders speaks of an 'objective value'. Saunders 2012, *supra* n. 20, at p. 917.

42 *Cf.* Schmitt-Kammler and von Coelln 2009, *supra* n. 35, at p. 363 and M. Forkert, *Eingetragene Lebenspartnerschaften im deutschen IPR: Art. 17b EGBGB* [Civil partnerships in German Private international law: Art. 17b EGBGB] (Tübingen, Mohr Siebeck 2003) p. 32.

43 Antoni 2010, *supra* n. 36, at p. 115.

it considers marriage not be endangered by such other partnerships.[44] In literature however, this ruling has met with strong criticism.[45]

10.1.2.3. The relationship of Article 6(1) to other provisions of the Basic Law

Article 6(1) is considered to strengthen the right to free development of one's personality of Article 2(1).[46] As discussed in section 10.3 below, it was the desire to give further protection to homosexuals' right to free development of the personality that was a basis for the introduction of the registered civil partnership in Germany. From the latter right, however, no right to contract a marriage follows.[47]

For a long time Article 6(1) was considered to be a *lex specialis* of Article 3(1) and (3) Basic Law (the principle of equality) and thus to have precedence over this provision.[48] As will become clear from section 10.3, the relationship between these two provisions has over time been reversed. Henkel has spoken of a change of perspective in respect of the relationship between Article 3 and Article 6 of the Basic Law, which according to the author found its cause in European law impulses in particular.[49]

10.1.2.4. Article 6(1) Basic Law as expression of a cultural identity

Hofmann has argued that, next to the 'identity essence' of Articles 1 (human dignity) and 20 (basic institutional principles; defence of the constitutional order), the German Basic Law contains various cultural identity elements. The author holds that the institutional guarantee of marriage – together with the right to equal treatment, the protection of Sundays and holidays and the prohibition of a State Church – belongs to these cultural identity elements.[50] Hofmann distinguishes between the culturally infused constitutional order in its totality and the exceptional cultural infusion ('*Prägung*') of certain fundamental rights in the Basic Law. Following this distinction, the constitutional protection of freedoms ('*verfassungsrechtliche Freiheitsverbürgung*') is allegedly dependent upon the fulfilment of culturally

---

44 BVerfG 17 July 2002, Az. 1 BvF 1/01, *NJW* 2002 p. 2543 and BVerfG 7 July 2009 (dec.), Az. 1 BvR 1164/07, *NJW* 2010 p. 1439.

45 *Inter alia*, Hofmann 2011, *supra* n. 21.

46 *Cf.* Antoni 2010, *supra* n. 36, at p 110. See also P. Badura 'GG Art 6' ['Art. 6 Basic Law'] in: R. Herzorg et al. (eds.), *Maunz und Dürig Grundgesetz-Kommentar* [Maunz and Dürig Commentary to the Basic Law], 71st edn. (München, Verlag Beck 2014).

47 Schmitt-Kammler and von Coelln 2009, *supra* n. 35, at p. 352.

48 *Idem*, at pp. 353 and 356, under reference to BVerfG 17 January 1957 (dec.), Az. 1 BvL 4/54, *NJW* 1957 p. 417. See also W. Pauly, 'Sperrwirkungen des verfassungsrechtlichen Ehebegriffs' ['Barrier effects of the constitutional concept of marriage'], *NJW* (1997) p. 1955.

49 Henkel refers primarily to Case C-267/06 *Tadao Maruko* v. *Versorgungsanstalt der deutschen Bühnen* [2008] ECR I-1757, ECLI:EU:C:2008:179. J. Henkel, `Fällt nun auch das "Fremdkindadoptionsverbot"?' ['Is the 'ban on international abortion' now also being dropped?'], *NJW* (2011) p. 259 at p. 262. See R. Wiemann, `Rosige Aussichten für die Gleichstellung gleichgeschlechtlicher Lebenspartner mit Ehegatten?' ['A rosy future for the equal treatment of registered partners and spouses?'] *NJW* (2010) p. 1427 at p. 1428.

50 Hofmann 2011, *supra* n. 21, at p. 271. The author refers to A. Uhle, *Freiheitlicher Verfassungsstaat und 'kulturelle Indentität*, (Tübingen, Mohr Siebeck 2004) p. 505.

infused preconditions, of which the constitutional protection of marriage is illustrative. From a cultural perspective, so Hofmann argues, the institute of marriage is open to one man and one woman only. The Constitutional State with a Basic Law based on freedom is bound to guarantee and protect its 'cultural identity' through the totality of the cultural State's power to act ('*die Gesamtheit kulturstaatlicher Handlungsoptionen*'). The Constitutional State is thus obliged to found a legal order based on human dignity, respect for freedom and equality, the rule of law and democracy, the institutional protection of the constitutive characteristics of marriage, the protection of Sundays and on the prohibition of a State Church. In other words, the State is bound to found an institutional order that is infused by identity ('*einer identitätsgeprägten institutionellen Ordnung*'), which, so Hofmann argues, excludes constitutional neutrality.

The view of this author has not been widely endorsed in German legal academia and so far no German Court has adopted such reasoning in respect of Article 6(1) Basic Law. On the other hand, it is noted that in its important so-called 'Lisbon judgment' of June 2009 the Constitutional Court qualified decisions on family law as 'of particular cultural importance' and therefore as '[...] particularly sensitive for the ability of a constitutional state to democratically shape itself [...].'[51] The BVerfG explained this by the fact that 'the law on family relations' particularly affected '[...] established rules and values rooted in specific historical traditions and experience.'[52]

10.2. (De-)criminalisation of homosexual activities

Articles 175ff of the Prussian Criminal Code of 1871 criminalised sexual acts between men. In 1949, when the German Basic law was adopted, this provision was still in force. During World War II and also during the decades after the war, in the FRG, Article 175 Criminal Code was far from obsolete: on the basis of this provision homosexuals were persecuted in the name of the State with considerable numbers of convictions as a result. Between 1950 and 1965, nearly 2,800 homosexuals were convicted annually.[53] Under reference to the principle of morality, the BVerfG ruled in 1957 that Article 175 of the Criminal Code was compatible with the Basic Law.[54] The Court, *inter alia*, held the prohibition not to be incompatible with the right to

51 BVerfG 30 June 2009, Az. 2 BvE 2/08 a.o., *NJW* 2009 p. 2267, para. 253.

52 *Idem*, para. 260.

53 EU Fundamental Rights Agency, *Legal Study on Homophobia and Discrimination on Grounds of Sexual Orientation – Germany*, February 2008, p. 3, online available at www.fra.europa.eu/fraWebsite/attachments/FRA-hdgso-NR_DE.pdf, visited June 2014. The report refers to J. Müller, *Ausgrenzung der Homosexuellen aus der 'Volksgemeinschaft': die Verfolgung von Homosexuellen in Köln 1933–1945* (Cologne, Emons 2003) p. 218. From this reference it is not clear if this goes for the former FRG only or whether the former GDR is included in these calculations. See also Gerhard 2009, *supra* n. 31, at pp. 17–19 who refers, *inter alia*, to H.-G. Stümke, *Homosexuelle in Deutschland, Eine politische Geschichte* (München, Beck 1989) p. 127 and 132 and to F.J Wetz, *Homosexualität, Ein rechtlicher Vorstoß als moralischer Anstoß*, 88 ARSP (2002) pp. 102–113.

54 BVerfG 10 May 1957, Az. 1 BvR 550/52, *NJW* 1957 p. 865.

free development of the personality (Article 2(1) Basic Law),[55] because homosexual conduct was considered to be in violation of the moral law, a factor which constituted a justification for interferences with this right. Under influence of the emancipation movement of the end of the 1960s, at beginning of the 1970s this criminal law provision was amended for the first time. In 1969 the complete prohibition on sexual acts between men was lifted and an age limit was set: from then on, only sexual acts between an adult man and a man under 21 years old were punishable with imprisonment.[56] In 1973 this age limit was further lowered to the age of 18 years.[57] It was only in 1994 that Article 175 of the Criminal Code was repealed in its entirety, thus paving the way for further equalisation of the legal position of homosexuals and heterosexuals through the introduction of a registered civil partnership for same-sex couples.[58]

10.3. Legal recognition of same-sex relationships under German law

10.3.1. Early (legislative) developments

The first parliamentary initiatives to introduce legislation opening up marriage to same-sex couples in the Federal Republic of Germany were taken in 1990 by the Greens (*'die Grünen'*), a political party holding a small number of seats in the federal parliament (*Bundestag*).[59] Although this proposal did not lead to any concrete legislative change, the (academic and public) discussion on the topic was initiated.[60] In August 1992, during the so-called *'Sturm of die Standesämter'* (Siege of the Registry Offices) on the initiative of the *Schwulenverbands in Deutschland* (the Gay Federation in Germany), approximately 250 lesbian and gay couples 'besieged' Registry Offices throughout the country, to apply for the issuances of notices of their intended marriage.[61] Having met with refusals by the Registry Offices, several couples initiated judicial proceedings, but to no avail.[62] Only one couple was successful in

55 Art. 2(1) Basic Law reads: 'Every person shall have the right to free development of his personality insofar as he does not violate the rights of others or offend against the constitutional order or the moral law.' Translation taken from www.gesetze-im-internet.de/englisch_gg/englisch_gg.html#p0034, visited June 2014.

56 Erste Gesetz zur Reform des Strafrechts (1. StrRG) [First Act on the Reform of the Criminal Law] Act of 25 June 1969, *BGBl. I* p. 645.

57 The Constitutional Court confirmed in 1973 that this provision was compatible with the Basic Law. BVerfG 2 October 1973, Az. 1 BvL 7/72, *NJW* 1973 p. 2195.

58 Act of 31 May 1994, *BGBl.* I, p. 1168. Reportedly in the year 1987 there had still been over 100 convictions on the basis of Art. 175 Criminal Code. See C. von der Tann, 'Entwicklungen in der Rechtsstellung eingetragener Lebenspartnerschaften' ['Developments in the legal position of civil partnerships'], *FamFR* (2012) p. 195 at p. 196.

59 *BT-Drs.* 11/7197.

60 Gerhard 2009, *supra* n. 31, at p. 24, footnote 167.

61 See the website of the present *Lesben- und Schwulenverbands in Deutschland* (LSVB) www.lsvd.de/1399.0.html, visited June 2014.

62 See Gerhard 2009, *supra* n. 31, at p. 25, footnotes 170 and 171.

first instance: in December 1992, the district court (*Amtsgericht*) of Frankfurt am Main held non-recognition of same-sex marriage to be against the Basic Law.[63] This judgment was however shortly overturned by the State Court (*Landesgericht*) of Frankfurt.[64]

Another couple filed a constitutional complaint with the Federal Constitutional Court, but the BVerfG did not take that complaint into consideration, as it considered it to contain no fundamental constitutional interest.[65] In its decision of 1993, the Court held that the complaint did not raise any new points: the BVerfG's case law was clear on the point that marriage within the meaning of Article 6(1) of the Basic Law was defined as a union between one man and one woman.[66] Furthermore, it held that no right to access to marriage for same-sex couples could follow from the right to free development of the personality nor the right to equal treatment (Articles 2(1) and 3 Basic Law respectively), as Article 6(1) as their *lex specialis* had precedence over these provisions. The Court added that the question of whether the legislature was under an obligation to provide same-sex couples with some form of legal recognition of their relationship would be one of fundamental constitutional interest.[67] As that question was however not raised by the complaint at hand, the Court did not examine the matter.

A Resolution of the European Parliament of 1994[68] triggered the discussion anew.[69] In this Resolution the European Parliament called on the EU Member States to avoid unequal treatment of persons of same-sex orientation in their individual legal and administrative provisions, and appealed to the European Commission to grant same-sex couples access to marriage or to corresponding legal institutions. In the years following the Resolution, several new proposals entailing the opening up of marriage[70] or the introduction of a registered civil partnership for same-sex couples were tabled in German Parliament, but none of them was followed up.[71] In the meantime, however, the State of Hamburg introduced the possibility for same-sex couples to have their partnerships registered in a designated register

---

63 AG Frankfurt a.M. 21 December 1992 (dec.), Az. 40 UR III E 166/92, *NJW* 1993 p. 940.

64 LG Frankfurt 22 March 1993 (dec.), Az. 2/9 T 17/93, *NJW* 1993 p. 1998.

65 Fundamental constitutional interest ('*grundsätzliche verfassungsrechtliche Bedeutung*') is one of the admissibility criteria ex Art. 93a (2) BVerfGG. BVerfG 4 October 1993 (dec.), Az. 1 BvR 640/93, *NJW* 1993 p. 3058.

66 The Court referred to, *inter alia*, BVerfG 29 July 1959, Az. 1 BvR 205/58 a.o, *NJW* 1959 p. 1483; BVerfG 11 October 1978, Az. 1 BvR 16/72, *NJW* 1979 p. 595 and BVerfG 17 November 1992, Az. 1 BvL 8/87, *NJW* 1993 p. 643.

67 See also Pauly 1997, *supra* n. 48.

68 European Parliament Resolution on equal rights for homosexuals and lesbians in the EC [1994] OJ C61/20, pp. 40–41.

69 As referred to in BVerfG 17 July 2002, Az. 1 BvF 1/01, *NJW* 2002 p. 2543, para. 2. See also K. Strick, 'Gleichgeschlechtliche Partnerschaft – Vom Straftatbestand zum Status?' ['Same-sex partnership – from criminal offence to legal status?'], *Deutsches und Europaisches FamilenRecht, DEuFamR* (2002) p. 82 at p. 86.

70 *BT-Drs.* 13/2728.

71 See *BT-Drs.* 13/7228; *BT-Drs.* 13/10081 and *BT-Drs.* 544/98.

('*Partnerschaftsbuch*') at the Civil Registry.[72] This so-called '*Hamburger Ehe*' ('Hamburger Marriage') had no legal effect,[73] and has therefore often been referred to as 'symbol politics'.[74]

After the parliamentary elections of 1998, the introduction of a registered partnership for same-sex couples was included in the coalition agreement of the new governing parties, the Social Democrats and the Greens.[75] While the Liberals were the first to draw up a bill to this effect,[76] it was the bill of the coalition, as tabled in July 2000,[77] that resulted in the adoption of the Civil Partnerships Act in 2001.[78]

Given the division of seats amongst the political parties at the time and the anticipated opposition of the *Bundesrat* to the introduction of a civil partnership for same-sex couples, the governing parliamentary parties intended to divide the original civil partnership bill into two statutes: one requiring the approval of the *Bundesrat* and the other requiring no such approval. After the Committee on Legal Affairs of the *Bundestag* also advised to that effect,[79] the bill was indeed divided into two statutes: firstly, the Civil Partnerships Act (Act on the Termination of the Discrimination of Same-Sex Couples: Civil Partnerships (*Gesetz zur Beendigung der Diskriminierung gleichgeschlechtlicher Gemeinschaften: Lebenspartnerschaften,* LPartEDiskrG))[80] which concerned the civil partnership itself and its essential legal consequences; and secondly, the Civil Partnerships Act Supplementary Act (Act to Supplement the Civil Partnerships Act and other Acts (*Gesetz zur Ergänzung des Lebenspartnerschaftsgesetzes und anderer Gesetze, Lebenspartnerschaftsgesetzergänzungsgesetz,* LPartGErgG)), which concerned primarily procedural law implementing regulations.[81]

---

72 *BT-Drs.* 16/1288. See also I. von Münch, 'Antidiskriminierungsgesetz – notwendig oder überflüssig?' ['Anti-discrimination Act – necessary or superfluous?'] *NJW* (1999) p. 260 at p. 261.

73 As Gerhard explains, the Hamburger Senate held that such an issue could only be regulated at State level. On the basis of Art. 74 Basic Law, does the registration of marriages belong to the list of subjects where the Federation and the States have concurrent legislative power. Gerhard 2009, *supra* n. 31, at p. 30.

74 On the symbolic character of the '*Hamburger Ehe*', see also M. Schüffner, *Eheschutz und Lebenspartnerschaft, Eine verfassungsrechtliche Untersuchung des Lebenspartnerschaftsrechts im Lichte des Art. 6 GG* [Marriage protection and civil partnership, a constitutional examination of the law on civil partnership in light of Art. 6 of the German Basic Law] (Berlin, Duncker & Humblot 2007) p. 101.

75 Coalition agreement of 20 October 1998, *ZRP* 1998, 485 ff.

76 *BT-Drs.* 14/1259.

77 *BT-Drs.* 14/3751.

78 Gesetz zur Beendigung der Diskriminierung gleichgeschlechtlicher Gemeinschaften: Lebenspartnerschaften [Act on the Termination of the Discrimination of Same-Sex Couples: Civil Partnerships] Act of 16 February 2001, *BGBl. I*, p. 266. Henkel 2011, *supra* n. 49, at p. 260, points at various constitutional concerns that were expressed at the time, *inter alia*, U. Diederichsen, 'Homosexuelle – von Gesetzes wegen?' ['Homosexual – by law?'], *NJW* (2000) p. 1841; P. Kirchhof, 'Lebenspartnerschaftsgesetze und Grundgesetz' ['Law on civil partnerships and the Constitution'], *FPR* (2001) p. 436 and R. Scholz and A. Uhle, ''Eingetragene Lebenspartnerschaft' und Grundgesetz' [''Civil partnership' and Basic Law'], *NJW* (2001) p. 393 at p. 398.

79 *BT-Drs.* 14/4545 with annexes.

80 Act of 16 February 2001, *BGBl. I* p. 266.

81 See also BVerfG 17 July 2002, Az. 1 BvF 1/01, *NJW* 2002 p. 2543, para. 5.

In November 2000, the Committee on Legal Affairs of the Bundestag advised adopting the bill. It explained that the intimate personal sphere was constitutionally protected by Article 2(1) in conjunction with Article 1(1) of the German Basic Law, and encompassed – as an element of the right to free development of the personality – the freedom to live in a same-sex partnership.[82] It acknowledged that such partnerships between same-sex partners did not enjoy the special protection of Article 6(1) of the Basic Law, but stressed that the different treatment of certain groups in society required special justification on the basis of Article 3 of the Basic Law. Reference was made to judgments of the Constitutional Court (BVerfG) and the Federal Administrative Court (BVerwG) of 1993 and 1996 respectively (see above),[83] from which it followed – as the Committee observed – that the legislature could protect the personality rights of same-sex partners and their rights to equal treatment without opening up the institution of marriage. While the Courts had held that the legislative measures taken in various European states strengthening the legal position of same-sex partnerships, had at that time not yet resulted in a European consensus that same-sex partnerships fell within the scope of the right to respect for family life ex Article 8 ECHR,[84] the Committee stressed that they had accepted that such partnerships enjoyed the protection of the right to private life.[85]

The Civil Partnerships Act (LPartG) was adopted in February 2001 and was passed by the *Bundesrat* unaltered.[86] The Civil Partnerships Act Supplementary Act, on the other hand, was approved by the *Bundestag*, but it encountered the opposition of the State of Bavaria in the *Bundesrat*. As a consequence, it was not approved by the *Bundesrat* and therefore did not make it into law.[87] As a result, certain matters, such as the position of civil servants, were not covered (see 10.4.4.2 below).

10.3.2. The Civil Partnerships Act (2001)

The Civil Partnerships Act introduced a registered civil partnership for same-sex partners – and for same-sex couples only – as of 1 August 2001.[88] The Explanatory Memorandum to the draft Act[89] explained that the Act intended to reduce the discrimination of same-sex couples *vis-à-vis* different-sex-couples. It aimed to give shape to the constitutional protection of relationships between persons of the same sex on the basis of Article 2(1) Basic Law, through the creation of a new

82 *BT-Drs.* 14/4550, pp. 4–5.

83 BVerfG 4 October 1993 (dec.), Az. 1 BvR 640/93, *NJW* 1993 p. 3058 and BVerwG 27 February 1996, Az. 1 C 41/93, *NJW* 1997 p. 956.

84 The Committee on Legal Affairs refers to BVerwG 27 February 1996, Az. 1 C 41/93, *NJW* 1997 p. 956.

85 *BT-Drs.* 14/4550, pp. 4–5.

86 *BT-Prot.*14/131, p. 12629 D *BR-Prot.* 757, p. 551 (C, D).

87 *BT-Drs.* 14/4875 and *BR-Prot.* 757, p. 551 (D).

88 This partnership has also been referred to as a 'life partnership'. See, *inter alia*, Case C-267/06 *Tadao Maruko* v. *Versorgungsanstalt der deutschen Bühnen* [2008] ECR I-1757, ECLI:EU:C:2008:179. Here the English term 'civil partnership' or 'registered civil partnership' as used in the official English translations of BVerfG judgments (that can be found on www.bverfg.de/en/index.html, visited June 2014) will be used.

89 *BT-Drs.* 14/3751, p. 33 ff.

legal institution.[90] It was stressed that the Civil Partnerships Act aimed to adopt and transpose two documents of European origin in which States were called upon to create legal options for the registration of same-sex unions, namely the aforementioned EP Resolution on equal rights for homosexuals and lesbians in the EC of 1994[91] as well as a draft Recommendation of the Parliamentary Assembly of the Council of Europe of 6 June 2000.[92]

A civil partnership is created by a contract between two persons of the same sex that is registered with the public office responsible for marriage ceremonies ('*Standesamt*').[93] A civil partnership is terminated by a decree of annulment by a Court, on the application of one or both partners.[94]

While the responsibilities of partners engaging in a partnership are the same as for married couples, the set of rights awarded to registered partners was more limited in the first version of the Act. In 2002 the BVerfG summarised the main features of the civil partnership as follows:

> 'The partners are bound to each other in care and support and committed to plan their lives together. They are responsible for each other (Article 1 § 2). The statute does not require sexual intercourse. The legal consequences of the registered partnership are in part based on the legal consequences of marriage, but they also diverge from the latter. Thus, the partners owe each other support. This applies to a modified extent also to persons living apart and after the termination of the partnership (Article 1 §§ 5, 12 and 16). The partners must make a statement on their financial status; they may choose between a property regime of equalisation of surplus and a contract governing their financial relations (Article 1 §§ 6 und 7). They may choose a joint name (Article 1 § 3). The civil partner or former partner of a parent who has lived for a long period in a domestic community with the child has a right of access (Article 2 number 12, § 1685.2 of the German Civil Code). A partner is deemed to be a member of the other's family (Article 1 § 11). A right of intestate succession of the civil partner corresponding to that of the spouse has been introduced (Article 1 § 10). In social security law too, entering into the civil partnership has legal consequences (Article 3 §§ 52, 54 und 56). Thus, for example, in the statutory health insurance scheme civil partners are covered by the family insurance (Article 3 § 52 number 4). In the law concerning foreign nationals, the provisions relating to the right of entry of foreign families that apply to marital relationships are correspondingly extended to same-sex partnerships (Article 3 § 11). In addition the Civil Partnerships Act grants the partner of a parent with sole custody, with the consent of the latter, the authority to

---

90 *Idem*, p. 33.

91 *Idem*. For the Resolution, see *supra* n. 68. The Resolution was also printed in *BT-Drs.* 12/7069.

92 *BT-Drs.* 14/4550, pp. 4–5 and Parliamentary Assembly to the Council of Europe Doc. 8755 (6 June 2000), *Situation of lesbians and gays in Council of Europe member states.*

93 Art. 1(1)(1) LPartG. As Saunders explained, originally the States were free to choose whether they assigned the partnership ceremony '[...] to private notaries or to the public office responsible for marriage ceremonies ('*Standesamt*'). Since 1 January 2012, however, partnership ceremonies are performed in all German Federal states at the Standesamt.' Saunders 2012, *supra* n. 20, at p. 926.

94 Art. 15 LPartG.

make joint decisions in matters of the child's everyday life, known as "limited custody" (Article 1 § 9).'[95]

Hence, while the legal consequences of the registered partnership were in part based on the legal consequences of marriage and while they show considerable resemblance, some differences in rights and entitlements between civil partners and married partners remained. These concerned, first of all, certain taxes, social benefits and social insurances. The Act did not, for instance, provide for adjustment of old-age pension rights between the civil partners if their partnership was annulled, and contained no rules on pensions in case of death.[96] Further differences remained in respect of asylum applications,[97] the legal position of civil servants and parental rights (see 10.4.5 below).

Most issues regarding the legal position of members of the public service were excluded from the scope of the Civil Partnerships Act. Because the legal position of civil servants at State level is a matter of so-called concurrent legislative power,[98] the German federal legislature may only enact so-called framework legislation; more detailed legislation requires the approval of the *Bundesrat*.[99] The original bill for the Civil Partnerships Act was – as explained in section 10.3.1 above – divided over two statutes. The bill for the Act to Supplement the Civil Partnerships Act and other Acts, provided for the equalisation of civil servants in a civil partnership and married civil servants, but this bill was rejected by the *Bundesrat*. Only the bill for the Civil Partnerships Act, which did not require the approval of the *Bundesrat*, made it into law. This Act – and its 2004 Revision – necessarily applied only marginally to federal civil servants.[100] The division of competences between the *Bundestag* and the *Bundesrat* and the political make up of both bodies at the time of the introduction of the Civil Partnerships Act, thus resulted in the exclusion of federal civil servants from the scope of this Act.

95 BVerfG 17 July 2002, Az. 1 BvF 1/01, *NJW* 2002 p. 2543.

96 Description of the law in BVerfG 17 July 2002, Az. 1 BvF 1/01, *NJW* 2002 p. 2543.

97 See *BT-Drs.* 16/13596, p. 3.

98 Art. 75(1)(27) Basic Law, which reads: 'Concurrent legislative power shall extend to the following matters: [...] the statutory rights and duties of civil servants of the Länder, the municipalities and other corporations of public law as well as of the judges in the Länder, except for their career regulations, remuneration and pensions [...].' In 2006 the powers of the States were widened. C.D. Classen, 'Die Lebenspartnerschaft im Beamtenrecht' ['The registered partnership in civil servants law'], *FPR* (2010) p. 200.

99 Arts. 75, 74a and 73(8) Basic Law.

100 Originally full equalisation was foreseen (Art. 3 (10) of the LPartG Bill (*BT-Drs.* 14/3751)), however those regulations were taken up in the Statute that required, but did not obtain Bundesrat approval. The 2001 Act nevertheless provided for equalisation in respect of certain matters of secondary importance, namely in respect of special leave (Art. 12 III SUV); career regulations (Art. 10 IV BundeslaufbahnVO), travel expenses (Art. 6 IV BundesreisekostenG), costs for moving and in respect of allowances in case of divorce (Art. 1 II BundesumzugskostenG). Differences remained in respect of essential partner-related allowances (Art. 40 I Nr. 1 BBesG and Art. 4 BeihVO) and survivors pensions (Art. 18 and Art. 27 BeamtVG). The 2004 Revision Act provided for full equalisation in respect of maintenaince and in respect of the legal situation of civil servants. See also Classen 2010 *supra* n. 98, at p. 200.

In the years following the entry into force of the Civil Partnerships Act, the existing differences in rights between civil partners and spouses were gradually removed through successive legislative amendments and court decisions. Below, in section 10.3.4, these gradual changes are discussed in greater detail. The following section, however, first discusses the 2002 BVerfG judgment upholding the constitutionality of the Act in its original form.

10.3.3. The 2002 BVerfG judgment upholding the Civil Partnerships Act

The constitutionality of the Civil Partnerships Act was challenged by the governments of the States (*Länder*) of Bavaria and Saxony. They initially applied for an interim injunction against the entry into force of the Act before the Federal Constitutional Court, but were unsuccessful in their action.[101] The applicant States held the Act to be unconstitutional on both procedural and substantive grounds.[102] They, *inter alia*, argued that the requirement of differentiation and distance of Article 6 Basic Law (special protection of marriage) was violated, because civil partnership imitated marriage.[103] The Court considered there to be no urgent need justifying an interim injunction, as the entering into force of the Act was not to be expected to cause irreparable harm to the institute of marriage and because no serious detriment to the common weal[104] was identifiable.[105]

After the entry into force of the Civil Partnerships Act, these same States, together with the Free State of Thuringia, again applied to the Federal Constitutional Court to have the compatibility of the Act with the Federal Basic Law examined. The applicant States again put forward both procedural and substantive grounds for their claim that the Act was unconstitutional. Here, only the substantive arguments as put forward by the States and the assessment thereof by the Court in its judgment of 17 July 2002 are discussed.[106]

---

101 BVerfG 18 July 2001 (dec.), Az. 1 BvQ 23/01, *NJW* 2001 p. 2457. Such an action is possible on the basis of Art. 32 BVerfGG. See also A. Maurer, 'Federal Constitutional Court Does Not Issue Temporary Injunction to Block the Entry Into Force of the Lifetime Partnership Law', 2 *German Law Journal* (2001), available at www.germanlawjournal.com/index.php?pageID=11&artID=73.

102 The procedural grounds concerned the fact that the *Bundestag* had divided the subject-matter between two statutes in order to prevent the *Bundesrat* from preventing provisions that in themselves were not subject to its consent. The BVerfG held this to be constitutionally unobjectionable.

103 The applicant States further held the Act to be in violation of Art. 3(1), Art. 2(1) and Art. 15(1) Basic Law, because they held it to interfere unjustifiably with civil partners' parental rights, their maintenance and care rights and their right to and testamentary freedom respectively.

104 Art. 93(2) Basic Law and Art. 32(1) Gesetz über das Bundesverfassungsgericht, BVerfGG [Law on the Federal Constitutional Court]. Art. 32(1) BVerfGG reads: 'In a dispute the Federal Constitutional Court may deal with a matter provisionally by means of a temporary injunction if this is urgently needed to avert serious detriment, ward off imminent force or for any other important reason for the common weal.' English translation taken from: www.iuscomp.org/gla/statutes/BVerfGG.htm#32, visited June 2014.

105 The judgment was based on a two to one vote.

106 BVerfG 17 July 2002, Az. 1 BvF 1/01, *NJW* 2002 p. 2543. For the English translation of the judgment, see www.bverfg.de/en/decisions/fs20020717_1bvf000101en.html, visited June 2014. The BVerfG held the fact that the *Bundestag* had divided the subject-matter between two statutes in order to prevent

The applicant States held that marriage enjoyed special protection as an essential element of State order to guarantee the conditions for the care and upbringing of children in the interest of parents and children, but also of the State community. They alleged that if parallel institutions were created for other forms of partnership that would be equal to marriage, marriage would be robbed of its special protection.[107] According to the applicant States, Article 6(1) of the Basic Law prohibited not only that marriage was made available to same-sex partnerships, but also that, besides marriage, an institution was created incorporating structural elements of marriage, without there being any objective necessity to do so. They held that the Basic Law required a differentiation to be made between the legal form of marriage and that of a civil partnership and a prohibition on the reproduction of the legal structure of marriage by other partnerships. The applicant States argued that the partnership created by the Act was to a large extent brought into line with marriage, and therefore constituted an infringement of this prohibition and the 'requirement to differentiate'.[108]

The Federal Government asserted that the Act did not violate Article 6(1) of the Basic Law, as this provision did not outlaw other institutions than marriage and contained no requirement to discriminate against persons who did not have access to marriage by reason of their sexual orientation. According to the government, the civil partnership in the statute was essentially different from that of marriage:

> 'The Act contains no provisions on the housekeeping of civil partners and does not impose on them an obligation to show consideration for each other when they choose and exercise a gainful occupation. Civil partners are merely permitted to decide on a common name. Civil partners are not permitted to make a joint adoption or to adopt a stepchild. Under maintenance law, each partner is in principle referred to his or her own gainful employment. This and other differences show that the registered civil partnership is not a duplication of marriage.'[109]

The BVerfG held that the institution of marriage as guaranteed by the Basic Law had to be interpreted in correspondence with prevailing opinions,[110] while taking into account '[...] the essential structural principles that follow from the application of Article 6.1 of the Basic Law to marriage as it is actually encountered in connection with the nature of the fundamental right guaranteed as a freedom and in connection with other constitutional norms'.[111] On that basis, the Court provided the following definition of marriage:

---

the *Bundesrat* from preventing provisions that in themselves were not subject to its consent, to be constitutionally unobjectionable.

107 *Idem*, para. 20.

108 *Idem*.

109 *Idem*, para. 31.

110 *Idem*. The Court referred to BVerfG 4 May 1971, Az 1 BvR 636/68, *NJW* 1971 p. 1509.

111 *Idem*.

> 'Part of the content of marriage, as it has stood the test of time despite social change and the concomitant changes of its legal structure and been shaped by the Basic Law, is that it is the union of one man with one woman to form a permanent partnership, based on a free decision and with the support of the state [...], in which man and woman are in an equal partnership with one another [...] and may decide freely on the organisation of their cohabitation [...].'[112]

With five votes to three,[113] the Federal Constitutional Court agreed with the government that the registered civil partnership was not interchangeable with marriage and could not enter into competition with marriage, '[...] if for no other reason than that the group of persons for whom the institution is intended does not overlap with the group of married persons'.[114] According to the majority of the Court the introduction of the legal institution of the registered civil partnership for same-sex couples did not infringe Article 6(1) of the Basic Law: it infringed neither the right to unhindered access to marriage guaranteed by this provision nor the institutional guarantee laid down in it.[115] The Court furthermore held the registered civil partnership to be compatible with Article 6(1) in its character as a fundamental principle on which values are based. The Court considered that the special protection accorded to marriage by Article 6(1) Basic Law did not cover the institution of the registered civil partnership:

> 'The fact that the partners are of the same sex distinguishes it from marriage and at the same time constitutes it. The registered civil partnership is not marriage within the meaning of Article 6.1 of the Basic Law. It grants rights to same-sex couples. In this way, the legislature takes account of Article 2.1 and Article 3.1 and 3.3 of the Basic Law, by helping these persons to better develop their personalities and by reducing discrimination.'[116]

According to the Court the particular protection of marriage in that provision did not prevent the legislature from offering legal forms for permanent cohabitation other than the union of man and woman to different groups. Thus, the Court held, the special protection accorded to marriage by Article 6(1) did not prohibit the legislature from providing rights and duties for the same-sex civil partnership that are equal or similar to those of marriage, precisely because it relates only to marriage.[117] The Court considered the institution of marriage could not actually be at risk as a result of the introduction of an institution that is directed at persons who cannot be married to each other. In introducing the new institution of the registered civil partnership, the legislature did not violate the requirement of promoting marriage as a way of life.

---

112 BVerfG 17 July 2002, Az 1 BvF 1/01, *NJW* 2002 p. 2543, para. 87.

113 On the basis of Art. 30(2) BVerfGG a judge holding a dissenting opinion on the decision or the reasons during deliberations may have it recorded in a separate vote (or dissenting opinion) which shall be annexed to the decision. In their decisions the Senates of the Court may state the number of votes for and against. In the here discussed case, two of the three dissenting judges, Papier and Haas, wrote dissenting opinions which were annexed to the judgment. These opinions will be discussed below.

114 BVerfG 17 July 2002, Az. 1 BvF 1/01, *NJW* 2002 p. 2543, para. 103.

115 *Idem*, para. 70.

116 *Idem*, para. 88.

117 *Idem*, para. 89.

A second substantive argument put forward by the applicant States, was that the Act infringed the principle of equality of Article 3(1) of the Basic Law because persons of a different sex cohabiting with each other and groups of people related to each other and living together had no possibility of becoming registered civil partners. The Federal Government rebutted that the fact that the registered civil partnership was reserved to persons of the same sex was not in violation of Article 3(3) (prohibition of discrimination on suspect grounds) of the Basic Law, since it was based not on gender, but on the choice of partner, which is not included in the list of suspect grounds of Article 3(3) Basic Law. The Constitutional Court (with a seven to one vote) followed the reasoning of the Federal Government on this point and held:

> 'Men and women are always treated equally. They may enter into marriage with a person of the opposite sex, but not with one of their own sex. They may enter into a civil partnership with a person of their own sex, but not with one of the other sex.'[118]

The Court left open the option of the introduction of a civil partnership for different-sex couples, but held there to be no constitutional requirement to create such a possibility.[119] It held that the Civil Partnerships Act violated neither the prohibition of discrimination of Article 3(3) of the Basic Law nor the general principle of equality in Article 3(1) of the Basic Law. As the Court explained, this Article prohibited treating a group of persons who are addressed by a statute differently from other persons addressed by the statute while there were no differences between the two groups of such a nature and such weight that they could justify the unequal treatment. The Court held such differences to exist, however, 'between same-sex couples and the other social communities of persons'.[120] The Court emphasised that civil partnership was open to same-sex couples only, while marriage was only open to couples of a different sex. The fact that children of both spouses could be born to a permanent two-person relationship between man and woman, but not to a same-sex partnership, justified directing heterosexual couples to marriage if they wished to give their relationship a permanent legally binding form.[121] Further, the Court held that there were differences in the relationship of the same-sex partnerships to the communities of mutual support between siblings or other relatives, and that these differences justified different treatment.[122] Lastly, the Court held the legislature to be free, but not constitutionally required, to create new possibilities for different-sex couples or for other communities of mutual support to acquire legal recognition

118 *Idem*, para. 106.
119 *Idem*, para. 111.
120 *Idem*, para. 108.
121 *Idem*, para. 109.
122 *Idem*, para. 110. The Court held: 'This relates even to the exclusivity of the registered civil partnership, which admits no further relationship of the same kind beside itself, whereas communities of mutual support between siblings and other relations are often part of further comparable relationships and also exist side-by-side with another relationship by marriage or partnership. Communities of mutual support between relations, in addition, are given a certain support even under existing law, a support that was first granted to same-sex couples in the form of the civil partnership. Thus, in connection with relations, there are rights to refuse to give evidence, rights of succession and in part also rights to a compulsory portion and for it to be given favourable tax treatment.'

of their relationships if this could be done without the given institute being interchangeable with marriage.[123] The arguments put forward by the applicant States that the provisions in the Act on the rights to custody and succession of civil partners and on maintenance law were objectionable from a constitutional point of view, were unanimously rejected by the Constitutional Court.

Judges Papier and Haas dissented. They both held that the principle that marriage was the union of one man and one woman in a comprehensive, essentially indissoluble partnership,[124] was an essential fundamental principle defining the institution of marriage[125] that enjoyed special protection under Article 6(1) of the Basic Law. With the creation of a civil partnership between persons of the same sex, with rights and duties corresponding to those of marriage, the legislature disregarded this essential structural principle, laid down by Article 6(1) of the Basic Law. The judges considered it '[...] a false conclusion to assume that precisely because of deviation from an essential structural principle the constitutional institutional guarantee cease[d] to apply as a standard.' Judge Haas opined that the Constitutional Court should have examined more closely whether the civil partnership was comparable to that of the institution of marriage. Judge Papier was convinced that this was the case; the Judge held that the civil partnership as created by the disputed Act resembled marriage in basically all respects but its name.

Following the judgment, an intense debate was initiated in German academic literature about the compatibility of the Act with the German Basic Law.[126] One of the issues widely debated was whether the Act was in violation of fundamental rights as enshrined in Article 3 (principle of equal treatment) and Article 6(1) (special protection of the marriage and the family) of the Basic Law.[127] Hofmann was very critical to the 'obvious' watering down ('*Relativierung*') of the wording of Article 6(1) by the Court. According to the author, the Court did not satisfactorily take into account the legislative history of the Article and its predecessor, Article 119 of the Weimar Constitution (see 10.1.2 above).[128]

---

123 *Idem*, para. 111.

124 Judge Papier referred to BVerfG 30 November 1982, Az. 1 BvR 818/81, *NJW* 1983 p. 511.

125 Judge Papier referred to BVerfG 4 May 1971, Az 1 BvR 636/68, *NJW* 1971 p. 1509.

126 See Forkert 2003, *supra* n. 42, at p. 12; J. Braun, 'Das Lebenspartnerschaftsgesetz auf dem Prüfstand' ['The Civil Partnership Act in trial phase'], *Juristische Schulung, JuS* (2002) p. 21; R. Kemper, `Die Lebenspartnerschaft in der Entwicklung – Perspektiven für die Weiterentwicklung des Lebenspartnerschaftsrechts nach dem Urteil des BVerfG vom 17. 7. 2002' ['The civil partnership in development – Prospects for the further development of the law on civil partnership after the judgment of the German Constitutional Court of 17 July 2002'], *FPR* (2003) p. 1; A. Maurer, 'Federal Constitutional Court To Decide Whether to Issue a Temporary Injunction Against Germany's New Lifetime Partnerships Law for Homosexual Couples', 2 *German Law Journal* (2001), available at www.germanlawjournal.com/index.php?pageID=11&artID=42, visited June 2014; Maurer 2001B, *supra* n. 101 and S. Stüber, `Lebenspartnerschaft – viele offene Fragen' ['Civil partnership – many open questions'], *NJW* (2003)p. 2721.

127 E.g. Forkert 2003, *supra* n. 42, at p. 16, footnotes 29 and 33. The procedural elements of the case, that have not been discussed here, were also a great cause for discussion. This critique will not be discussed here.

128 Hofmann 2011, *supra* n. 21, at p. 270, para. 50.

In 2008, in a judgment concerning the German Transsexuals Act,[129] the Federal Constitutional Court once again stressed that the institute of marriage was exclusively reserved for partners of different sex.[130] However, because post-operative transsexuals also have a right under Article 2(1) in combination with Article 1(1) Basic Law to choose their own sexual identity, the Court held that marriages concluded before one of the spouses had a change-sex operation, deserved legal protection after the sex change.[131] The Court left it up to the legislature to decide in such situation how a yet existing marriage was to be registered: as marriage ('*Ehe*'), as civil partnership ('*Lebenspartnerschaft*') or as civil union sui generis ('*Lebensgemeinschaft sui generis*').[132] Following this judgment the German legislature struck out the impugned provision (Article 8(1)(2))[133] of the Transsexuals Act.[134] The Administrative Court of Berlin ruled in 2010 that from the fact that the legislature had thus allowed for a same-sex marriage in the exceptional circumstance that one of the spouses had changed sex during marriage, it did not follow that in general same-sex marriage was permitted in Germany.[135]

As the following sections show, in the years after its entry into force, the German civil partnership was made increasingly more equivalent to marriage. On the one hand, this mitigated the debate on the constitutionality of the partnership in itself, yet on the other hand, it made the question as to the meaning of Article 6(1) Basic Law even more pressing.

10.3.4. Further equalisation of the Civil Partnership with marriage

In the years after the entry into force of the Civil Partnerships Act, the civil partnership was 'gradually made equivalent to [...] marriage.'[136] The first amendment

---

129 Gesetz über die Änderung der Vornamen und die Feststellung der Geschlechtszugehörigkeit in besonderen Fällen (Transsexuellengesetz – TSG) [Act on changing the first name and on determination of one's sex in special circumstances (Act on Transsexuals)], Act of 10 September 1980 (BGBl. I p. 1654).

130 BVerfG 27 May 2008 (dec.), Az. 1 BvL 10/05, *NJW* 2008 p. 3117, para. 50.

131 *Idem*, para. 36 ff.

132 *Idem*, paras. 67- 71.

133 Art. 8(1)(2) TSG provided: ‚Auf Antrag einer Person, die sich auf Grund ihrer transsexuellen Prägung nicht mehr dem in ihrem Geburtseintrag angegebenen, sondern dem anderen Geschlecht als zugehörig empfindet und die seit mindestens drei Jahren unter dem Zwang steht, ihren Vorstellungen entsprechend zu leben, ist vom Gericht festzustellen, dass sie als dem anderen Geschlecht zugehörig anzusehen ist, wenn sie [...] nicht verheiratet ist [...]'.

134 Art. 1 Act of 17 July 2009, *BGBl. I* p. 1978.

135 VG Berlin 15 June 2010, Az. 23 A 242/08, para. 13. For discussion of other elements of this judgment see section 10.4 below.

136 As observed by the CJEU in Case C-267/06 *Tadao Maruko* v. *Versorgungsanstalt der deutschen Bühnen* [2008] ECR I-1757, ECLI:EU:C:2008:179, para. 67. On this equalisation, see for example, F. Brosius-Gersdorf, 'Gleichstellung von Ehe und Lebenspartnerschaft' ['Equalisation of marriage and civil partnership'], *FamFR* (2013) p. 169 and G.D. Gade and C. Thiele, 'Ehe und eingetragene Lebenspartnerschaft: Zwei namensverschiedene Rechtsinstitute gleichen Inhalts?' ['Marriage and civil partnership: Two legal institutions with a different name but the same content?'], *DÖV* (2013) p. 142.

of the Act dates from 2005.[137] The drafters of this Civil Partnership Law (Revision) Act ('*Gesetz zur Überarbeitung des Lebenspartnerschaftsrechts*') held that the 2002 BVerfG judgment, upholding the constitutionality of the Civil Partnerships Act, had paved the way for a far-reaching equalisation of the civil partnership with marriage.[138] The 2004 Revision Act – which entered into force on 1 January 2005 – has indeed been held to contribute to 'the gradual harmonisation of the regime put in place for the life partnership with that applicable to marriage.'[139] It governed the adoption of matrimonial property law; a more extensive harmonisation of maintenance law; the assimilation of the requirements for dissolution of a registered partnership to those of divorce law; the introduction of second-parent adoption;[140] the introduction of pension rights adjustment; and the extension of the statutory old-age pension scheme to civil partners. Certain areas, such as taxes and the legal position of civil servants, were not covered by this Act. Consequently, various differences remained between civil partners and spouses.

After the 2004 revision of the Civil Partnership Act, several other bills envisaging (further or full) equalisation of the civil partnership with marriage were drafted and tabled, both at federal[141] and state level.[142] None of these, however, resulted in legislative amendments.[143] Instead, it proved to be judicial decisions – both at the national and the European levels – in cases concerning issues like taxes, social benefits for civil servants and adoption rights that prompted the legislature to adopt further amendments to civil partnership law. The latest change to the Civil Partnerships Act, for example, was implemented in 2014, as a follow-up to the judgment of the Constitutional Court on successive adoption (see section 10.3.5.3 below).[144]

The following (sub)sections discuss in more detail four important fields of law in which full equalisation has long been no reality or was no reality at the time this research was concluded (i.e., 31 July 2014). These concern employment law (section 10.3.4.1), the legal position of civil servants (section 10.3.4.2), tax issues (section 10.3.4.3), and parental rights. Because of their centrality to the present case study, the latter are discussed separately in section 10.3.5.

137 Gesetz zur Überarbeitung des Lebenspartnerschaftsrechts [Civil Partnership Law (Revision) Act], Act of 15 December 2004, *BGBl. I* No. 69, p. 3396. The Act was passed on 12 October 2004 by the *Bundestag* [Parliament] and entered into force on 1 January 2005.

138 *BT-Drs.* 15/3445, p. 14.

139 Observation of the Bayerisches Verwaltungsgericht München, the referring Court in the case of *Maruko*, as discussed below, and as quoted in Case C-267/06 *Tadao Maruko* v. *Versorgungsanstalt der deutschen Bühnen* [2008] ECR I-1757, ECLI:EU:C:2008:179, para. 68.

140 See section 10.3.5.1 below.

141 *BT-Drs.* 16/497 and *BT-Drs.* 16/3423.

142 For example, *LT-Drs.* 14/2724.

143 For example, Plenarprotokoll 14/55 of the Landestag Nordrhein-Westfalen of 8 March 2007, p. 6199.

144 *BGBl. I*, p. 786.

10.3.4.1. Employment law

A prominent issue under employment law in respect of which *Lebenspartners* were, for a long time, treated differently from spouses concerns survivors' pensions. This difference in treatment resulted in various court proceedings and in one of these a preliminary reference to the Court of Justice of the European Union (CJEU) was made. The *Maruko* case concerned the occupational pension scheme managed by the German Theatre Pension Institution ('*Versorgungsanstalt der deutschen Bühnen*'), under which a civil partner – contrary to a spouse – did not receive a survivor's pension after the death of the partner. This was reason for the Bavarian Administrative Court to make a preliminary reference to the CJEU in June 2006.[145] The principal question of the referring court was whether Article 1, in conjunction with Article 2(2)(a) of Directive 2000/78/EC,[146] precluded regulations governing a supplementary pension scheme of the kind at issue in the case.

As discussed in more detail in Chapter 9, the CJEU ruled in its judgment of 1 April 2008 in the *Maruko* case[147] that an occupational pension scheme under which a civil partner did not receive a survivor's pension after the death of the partner like spouses did, was indeed precluded if, under national law, the civil partnership placed persons of the same sex in a situation comparable to that of spouses so far as that survivor's benefit was concerned. The CJEU left it up to the referring court to determine in a concrete case whether such comparability of situations could be found. In the CJEU judgment it was, however, already indicated that the referring court itself had acknowledged that in Germany a 'harmonization between marriage and life partnership' existed, which could be regarded as 'a gradual movement towards recognizing equivalence' and that therefore the registered civil partnership, while not identical to marriage, placed persons of the same sex in a situation comparable to that of spouses as far as the survivor's benefit was concerned.[148] Therefore it came not by surprise that the Bavarian Administrative Court subsequently decided in the plaintiff's favour.[149] It held that, as a surviving civil partner, Maruko was in a situation comparable to that of a spouse who was entitled to the survivor's benefit provided for under the occupational pension scheme managed by the '*Versorgungsanstalt der deutschen Bühnen*'.

A year later, the Federal Labour Court (*Bundes Arbeitsgericht*, BAG) confirmed that since the entry into force of the Civil Partnership (Revision) Act of January 2005, civil partners of the same sex were in a situation comparable to that of spouses,

145 VG München 1 June 2006 (dec.), Az. M 3 K 05.1595.

146 Council Directive 2000/78/EC of 27 November 2000 establishing a general framework for equal treatment in employment and occupation [2000] OJ L303/16.

147 Case C-267/06 *Tadao Maruko* v. *Versorgungsanstalt der deutschen Bühnen* [2008] ECR I-1757, ECLI:EU:C:2008:179. See M. Bruns, 'Die Maruko-Entscheidung im Spannungsfeld zwischen europäischer und nationaler Auslegung' ['The Maruko judgment in the area of tension between European and national reading'], *NJW* (2008) p. 1929 and S. Stüber, 'Was folgt aus "Maruko"?' ['What follows from "Maruko"?'], *NVwz* (2008) p. 750.

148 *Idem*, para. 69.

149 VG München 30 October 2008, Az. M 12 K 08.1484.

as far as survivors' benefits were concerned.[150] Referring to the BVerfG judgment of 2002 concerning the Civil Partnerships Act,[151] the Labour Court held that while Article 6(1) Basic Law prohibited the legislature from giving preferential treatment to other ways of life over marriage, there was no obligation on the legislature in the form of a '*Abstandsgebots*' (requirement of distance) to disadvantage other ways of life *vis-à-vis* marriage.[152]

10.3.4.2. The legal position of civil servants

As explained above, civil servants were not covered by the 2001 Civil Partnerships Act, nor by its 2004 revision. Subsequently, also in this area of law, court litigation eventually forced the legislature to take action.

In cases decided at the time when the *Maruko* case was pending before the CJEU,[153] and shortly after the CJEU judgment in that case was delivered,[154] both the Federal Administrative Court[155] and the Second Senate of the Constitutional Court held differences in treatment between civil servants in a civil partnership and married civil servants as regards social benefits to be compatible with the German Basic Law. The Constitutional Court held that the situation of civil partners and spouses in respect of child benefits was not comparable, because of the special role marriage played in the raising of children and because of the resultant connected loss of income.[156] Decisive importance was attached to the fact that the German legislature had not provided for full equalisation of civil servants in the Civil Partnerships Act, nor in its 2004 Revision Act.[157] In a judgment delivered soon thereafter, the Federal Administrative Court even held the situation of civil partners and spouses to be generally incomparable.[158]

---

150 BAG 15 September 2009, Az. 3 AZR 294/09, *NJW* 2010 p.1474. See A. Bissels and M. Lützeler, 'Aktuelle Rechtsprechung zum Allgemeinen Gleichbehandlungsgesetz 2009/2010 (Teil 2)' ['Recent case-law on the General Equal Treatment Act 2009–2010 (Part 2)'], *BB* (2010) p. 1725 at pp. 1728–1729 and U. Langohr-Plato, 'Hinterbliebenenversorgung für eingetragene Lebenspartner' ['Survivors' pensions for registered partners'], *juris Praxis Report -ArbR* 11/2010 Anm. 5. By judgment of 14 January 2009 the Federal Labour Court had yet held that in respect of company pensions ('betrieblichen Altersversorgung'), civil partners and spouses were in a comparable situation. BAG 14 January 2009, Az. 3 AZR 20/07. See also BAG 29 April 2004, Az. 6 AZR 101/03, where the BAG had held that civil partners were like spouses entitled to residence allowance ('*Ortszuschlag*').

151 See 10.3.3 above.

152 BAG 15 September 2009, Az. 3 AZR 294/09, *NJW* 2010 p.1474, para. 23.

153 BVerfG 20 September 2007 (dec.), Az. 2 BvR 855/06, *NJW* 2008 p. 209 and BVerfG 8 November 2007 (dec.), Az. 2 BvR 2466/06.

154 BVerfG 6 May 2008 (dec.), Az. 2 BvR 1830/06, *NJW* 2008 p. 2325.

155 BVerwG 15 November 2007, Az. 2 C 33/06, *NJW* 2008 p. 868. See D. Kugele, 'Kein Anspruch auf Familienzuschlag der Stufe 1 bei eingetragener Lebenspartnerschaft' ['No entitlement to family benefits in category 1 for civil partnerships'], *jurisPR-BVerwG* 10/2008 Anm. 3.

156 BVerfG 6 May 2008 (dec.), Az. 2 BvR 1830/06, *NJW* 2008 p. 2325, para. 17.

157 *Idem*, para. 13.

158 BVerwG 15 November 2007, Az. 2 C 33/06, *NJW* 2008 p. 868. See Wiemann 2010, *supra* n. 49, at p. 1427, footnote 7.

In 2009 – possibly under influence of the CJEU judgment in the *Maruko* case – the BVerfG departed from this line of case law. In a judgment of 7 July 2009, the First Senate of the BVerfG took a diametrically opposite position on the matter than the Second Senate had taken before, by holding that that the unequal treatment of married civil servants and civil servants in a civil partnership in respect of survivors' pensions was contrary to the general principle of equality of Article 3(1) Basic Law.[159] The First Senate held the unequal treatment of marriage and registered civil partnerships with regard to survivors' pensions under an occupational pension scheme, for civil service employees who had supplementary pensions insurance with the Supplementary Pensions Agency for Federal and State Employees ('*Versorgungsanstalt des Bundes und der Länder*'), to be incompatible with Article 3(1) of the Basic Law.[160] The Federal Court of Justice (BGH), against whose judgment this appeal with the BVerfG had been lodged, had held that personal or marital status constituted the differentiating criterion for the unequal treatment, and had considered that this status was available to the persons affected irrespective of their sexual orientation. The BVerfG considered that line of reasoning to be 'too formal' and not doing justice to reality.[161] The Constitutional Court stressed that the civil partnership was introduced with the explicit objective to terminate discrimination against same-sex couples. Therefrom it followed that 'provisions which govern[ed] the rights of registered civil partners [...] typically relate[d] to homosexual persons, and those which govern the rights of spouses typically relate[d] to heterosexual persons.'[162] On that ground the Court concluded that the difference in treatment between marriages and civil partnerships with regard to survivors' pensions, constituted unequal treatment on the basis of sexual orientation.[163] From established case law it followed that such unequal treatment was to be subjected to a strict review under Article 3(3) Basic Law.[164] The BVerfG considered that a mere reference to marriage and its protection under Article 6(1) of the Basic Law was not sufficient to justify the unequal treatment on the basis of sexual orientation. The Court held:

> 'If the privileged treatment of marriage is accompanied by unfavourable treatment of other ways of life, even where these are comparable to marriage with regard to the life situation provided for and the objectives pursued by the provisions, the mere reference

159 BVerfG 7 July 2009, 1 BvR 1164/07, *NJW* 2010 p. 1439. See M. Grunberger, 'Die Gleichbehandlung von Ehe und eingetragener Lebenspartnerschaft im Zusammenspiel von Unionsrecht und nationalem Verfassungsrecht. Das Urteil des BVerfG zur VBL-Hinterbliebenenrente' ['The equal treatment of marriage and civil partnership in interaction with Union law and national constitutional law'], *FPR* (2010) p. 203.

160 BVerfG 7 July 2009 (dec.), Az. 1 BvR 1164/07, *NJW* 2010 p. 1439. For an analysis of the retroactive effects of this finding, see T. Hoppe, 'Verpartnerte Beamte: Rückwirkender Anspruch auf Gleichstelling?', *ZBR Heft* (2010) p. 189 at pp. 189–191. This case concerning survivor's pensions also had a tax dimension. This limb of the case is discussed in further detail below (section 10.3.4.3).

161 Wiemann welcomed that the BVerfG took real life considerations into account, which reminded her of the reasoning by which the CJEU in the *Maruko* case came to the conclusion that there was indirect discrimination on the ground of sexual orientation. Wiemann 2010, *supra* n. 49, at p. 1428.

162 BVerfG 7 July 2009 (dec.), Az. 1 BvR 1164/07, *NJW* 2010 p. 1439, para. 92.

163 *Idem*. The wording of the judgment does not allow for a conclusion as to the question whether the BVerfG considered this to be direct or indirect discrimination.

164 *Idem*, para. 88. See, *inter alia*, BVerfG 26 January 1993, Az. 1 BvL 43/92, *NJW* 1933 p. 1517.

> to the requirement of protecting marriage does not justify such a differentiation. For the authority to give favourable treatment to marriage over other ways of life in fulfilment and further refining of the constitutional mandate to promote marriage does not give rise to a requirement contained in Article 6.1 of the Basic Law to disadvantage other ways of life in comparison to marriage. It cannot be constitutionally justified to derive from the special protection of marriage a rule that other partnerships are to be structured in a way different from marriage and to be given lesser rights [...]. Beyond the mere reference to Article 6.1 of the Basic Law, a sufficiently weighty factual reason is required here which, measured against the given subject and objective of regulation, justifies the unfavourable treatment of other ways of life.'[165]

The Court did not consider there to be any viable objective reasons for unequal treatment in the area of occupational survivors' pensions: such objections did not result from the objectives and the concrete structure of this pensions system, nor from a difference of the life situations of married couples and civil partners. The Court held both civil partnership and marriage to be of a permanent nature and to create a mutual obligation of support.[166] The BVerfG rejected the reasoning of the Federal Court of Justice that a reason for differentiating between marriage and civil partnership could be found in the fact that married couples typically had a different pension requirement than civil partners because of gaps in their working lives due to their care for children. Not only could the image of the 'breadwinner marriage' no longer be regarded as the yardstick for assigning survivors' benefits, but this argument also overlooked that just as in marriage, in civil partnerships the community of the partners could be structured in such a way that one partner had an increased need for provision. The Court ruled that 'insofar as privileged treatment of marriage is based on the fact that it produces children, the constitutionally permissible and constitutionally required promotion of parents is primarily the subject of the constitutional protection of the fundamental rights of the family, and as such it is not restricted to married parents'.[167] By thus holding that raising children was not a typical distinction between marriage and civil partnership, the Court disconnected the special protection of marriage from the special protection of the family (see also section 10.3.5, concerning parental issues).[168]

This judgment had implications for other areas of law in which civil partners and spouses were treated unequally, for instance concerning taxes (see section 10.3.4.3) and parental rights (see section 10.3.5).[169] However, the judgment did not solve all issues concerning the legal position of civil servants in civil partnerships,[170] nor did

---

165 *Idem*, para. 105. See also Bissels and Lützeler 2010, *supra* n. 150, at p. 1729.

166 *Idem*, para. 102.

167 *Idem*, para. 103.

168 Wiemann 2010, *supra* n. 49, at p. 1429 and Henkel 2011, *supra* n. 49, at p. 259.

169 See also K. Muscheler, 'Die Reform des Lebenspartnerschaftsrechts' ['The reform of the Civil Partnership Act'], *FPR* (2010), *supra* n. 49, at p. 1429.

170 It is therefore not without reason that Musscheler wrote in 2010 that 'chaos had broken out' in this area of law. Muscheler 2010, *supra* n. 169, at p. 233.

its implementation law of 2011.[171] Another step towards full equalisation was taken by the Constitutional Court in a judgment of June 2012, when it outlawed differences in treatment in respect of family benefits ('*Familienzuschlag*').[172] By the time this research was concluded (i.e., 31 July 2014), the position of federal civil servants in a registered partnership was equalised with civil servants who were married in basically all respects.[173]

10.3.4.3. Tax issues

Tax law has for a long time been another area of law in which civil partnerships and marriage have been treated differently. The Civil Partnerships Bill had originally foreseen some equalisation in this area, however this was included in the statute that required the approval of the *Bundesrat* and that subsequently did not make it into law.[174]

An example of such unequal treatment concerned income tax. Under the Income Tax Act (*Einkommensteuergesetzes* (EStG)) civil partners, contrary to spouses,[175] had no option of combining their incomes for the purpose of tax assessment ('*Zusammenveranlagung*'), which also implied that they had no entitlement to the financial benefit of income splitting ('*Ehegattensplitting*'), whereby the total income of a married couple was taxed on the basis of equal halves.[176] In 2004 and 2005 various financial district courts held this difference in treatment between civil partners and spouses to be compatible with the Constitution, because Article 6(1) Basic Law allowed for privileged treatment of marriage over other forms of cohabitation in respect of taxes.[177] The Federal Financial Court (BFG) confirmed this approach on various occasions.[178] It thereby underlined that the legislature had explicitly not opted for a full equalisation of civil partnership and marriage in respect of income taxes.

171 Gesetz zur Übertragung ehebezogener Regelungen im öffentlichen Dienstrecht auf Lebenspartnerschaften [Act on the application of marriage-related regulations in civil service law on civil partnerships], Act of 14 November 2011, *BGBl. I* 2011, No. 58, p. 2219.

172 BVerfG 19 June 2012 (dec.), Az. 2 BvR 1397/09, *NJW* 2012 p. 2790. As a result of this judgment the law was amended at Federal level. Gesetz zur Neuregelung der Professorenbesoldung und zur Änderung weiterer dienstrechtlicher Vorschriften, Professorenbesoldungsneuregelungsgesetz [Act introducing a new regulation on the pay of professors and on the amendment of other applicable regulations], Act of 20 June 2013. *BGBl. I* 2013, 1514. The Act entered into force on 1 August 2013.

173 On its website, the LSVD has provided a useful overview of the situation in the several States. See www.lsvd.de/recht/ratgeber-zum-lpartg/7-arbeiter-angestellte-und-beamte.html#c1372, visited June 2014.

174 See J. Selder, 'Das Bundesverfassungsgericht und die Homo-Ehe im Steuerrecht' ['The German Constitutional Court and same-sex marriage in the area of tax law'], *DStR* (2013) p. 1064 at p. 1065. See also section 10.3.1 above.

175 As provided for at the time under Arts. 26, 26b and 32a (5) EStG.

176 For a calculation example of the resulting differences of the tax assessment between civil partners and spouses, see M. Maurer, 'Die rechtliche Behandlung von Lebenspartnern im Steuernrecht' ['The legal treatment of civil partner in the area of tax law'], *FPR* (2010) p. 196 at pp. 196–197.

177 FG Saarland 21 January 2004, Az. 1 K 466/02, *NJW* 2004 p. 1268; FG Berlin 21 June 2004, Az. 9 K 9037/03; FG Hamburg 8 December 2004, Az. II 510/03; FG Niedersachsen 15 December 2004, Az. 2 K 292/03 and FG Niedersachsen 8 June 2005, Az. 2 K 267/03.

178 BFH 26 January 2006, Az. III R 51/05, *NJW* 2006 p. 1837. See also BFH 20 July 2006, Az III R 8/04, *NJW* 2006, 3310 and BFH 19 October 2006, Az. III R 29/06. By decision of 8 June 2011 the

The Constitutional Court in the end ruled differently in a judgment of May 2013. However, before that judgment is discussed, first its line of case law on another tax issue, namely inheritance tax, is set out. Under the Gift and Inheritance Tax Act of 1996 and the 1997 Annual Tax Reform Act,[179] registered civil partners were significantly more burdened than spouses in respect of inheritance tax: civil partners were placed in a different tax class from spouses and were consequently not granted the same personal exemptions.[180] Following the Inheritance Tax Reform Act (*Erbschaftsteuerreformgesetz, EStG*) of 24 December 2008,[181] the personal exemption and the exemption for retirement benefits were determined in the same way for both inheriting civil partners and spouses. Still, civil partners continued to be treated like distant relatives and unrelated persons and taxed at the highest tax rates. The lawsuits of two individuals, who were in a civil partnership and who were disadvantageously affected by these regulations, reached the BVerfG.

By order of 21 July 2010, the First Senate of the BVerfG ruled that the inheritance tax law discrimination against civil partners in comparison to spouses regarding the personal exemption and the tax rate, as well as their exclusion from the exemption for retirement benefits, was incompatible with the general principle of equality (Article 3(1) of the Basic Law).[182] The Court considered that there was no difference

---

Bundesfinanzhof rejected the claim that civil partners could claim change of their income tax category. BFH 8 June 2011 (dec.), Az. III B 210/10.

179 Erbschaftsteuer- und Schenkungsteuergesetz a.F., ErbStG a.F. [Gift and Inheritance Tax Act. old version], version dated 20 December 1996.

180 The BVerfG's press office described the relevant provisions as follows: 'While pursuant to §§ 15.1 and 19.1 ErbStG a.F. spouses were subject to the most beneficial Tax Class 1 and, depending upon the amount of the inheritance, were subject to a tax rate between 7 and 30%, civil partners were classified as "other recipients" and placed in Tax Class III, which provides for tax rates of between 17 and 50%. Moreover, § 16.1 no. 1 ErbStG a.F. granted spouses a personal exemption in the amount of DM 600,000/€ 307,000 and § 17.1 ErbStG a.F. granted a special exemption for retirement benefits in the amount of DM 500,000/€ 256,000. On the other hand, registered civil partners, because of their placement in Tax Class III, were only entitled to an exemption in the amount of DM 10,000/€ 5,200 (§ 16.1 no. 5, § 15.1 ErbStG a.F.). They were completely excluded from the benefit of the tax exemption for retirement benefits. In the Inheritance Tax Reform Act (*Erbschaftsteuerreformgesetz*) of 24 December 2008, the provisions described above in the Gift and Inheritance Tax Act were amended to the benefit of registered civil partners to the extent that the personal exemption and the exemption for retirement benefits are determined in the same way for both inheriting civil partners and spouses. Nevertheless, registered civil partners continue to be treated like distant relatives and unrelated persons and taxed at the highest tax rates. Pursuant to the Federal Government's draft legislation for the 2010 Annual Tax Reform Act of 22 June 2010, complete equality for civil partners and spouses in the gift and Inheritance tax law – also in regard to tax rates – is intended.' Press release of the Press Office of the Federal Constitutional Court of Germany, no. 63/2010 of 17 August 2010, online available at: www.bverfg.de/pressemitteilungen/bvg10-063en.html, visited July 2011.

181 Gesetz zur Reform des Erbschaftsteuer- und Bewertungsrechts (ErbStRG) [Inheritance Tax Reform Act] *BGBl. I* 2008 p. 3018. This Act was adopted following a judgment of the BVerfG of 2006 (BVerfG 7 November 2006 (dec.), Az. 1 BvL 10/02, *NJW* 2007 p. 573), in which the Constitutional Court held the Inheritance Tax Act to be partly incompatible with Art. 3(1) Basic Law, on grounds that were not related to the difference in treatment between civil partners and spouses.

182 BVerfG 21 July 2010 (dec.), Az. 1 BvR 2464/07, *NJW* 2010 p. 2783. See M. Messner, 'Lebenspartnerschaft – Steuerliche Konsequenzen des BVerfG-Beschlusses vom 21. 7. 2010' ['Civil partnership – implications of the decision of the German Constitutional Court of 21 July 2010 for tax law'], *DStR* (2010) p. 1875.

between civil partners in comparison to spouses that was of such weight that it could justify the disadvantage to civil partners in the Gift and Inheritance Tax Act in the version pursuant to the 1997 Annual Tax Reform Act.[183] Granting a privilege to spouses and not to civil partners under the law regarding the personal exemption could not be justified solely by reference to the State's special protection of marriage and the family (Article 6(1) Basic Law). Referring to its judgment concerning survivors' pensions for civil servants of July 2009 (see 10.3.4.2 above), the Court reiterated that if the promotion of marriage was accompanied by unfavourable treatment of other ways of living together – even where these were comparable to marriage with regard to the life situation provided for and the objectives pursued by the legislation – the mere reference to the requirement of protecting marriage under Article 6(1) of the Basic Law did not justify such a differentiation. The Court held that the authority of the State to be active in respect of marriage and the family in fulfilment of its duty of protection as set forth in Article 6(1) remained completely unaffected by the question of the extent to which others can assert claims for equal treatment.[184] Only the principle of equality (Article 3(1) Basic Law), in accordance with the relevant principles as developed by the Federal Constitutional Court, determined whether and to what extent others – in this case registered civil partners – had a claim for treatment equal to the statutory or actual promotion of married spouses and family members.[185] The Constitutional Court noted that marriage was fundamentally different from civil partnership in its suitability as 'starting point for the succession of generations'. For a civil partnership it was fundamentally impossible to produce joint children, because of its limitation to same-sex couples. Marriage, on the contrary, – as a union between different sex couples and despite the free choice of spouses for parenthood – was considered by the Court to be the privileged legal institute for family building.[186] The Court accepted that it could be argued that this suitability of marriage as a starting point for the succession of generations could justify higher personal allowances for spouses in tax law, with a view to the possible inheritance of the family property by joint children. However, now that the legislature had not made a distinction between marriages with children and childless marriages in setting the personal allowance rates, the Court rejected this argument.[187]

The Court gave the legislature until 31 December 2010 to enact a new rule for those old cases affected by the (former version of the) Gift and Inheritance Tax Act. These new rules were to remove the infringement on equality from the time period between the effective date of the Civil Partnerships Act of 16 February 2001 until the effective date of the Inheritance Tax Reform Act of 24 December 2008.[188] The legislature did not immediately take action, however, presumably because it was awaiting the judgment of the Second BVerfG in the pending cases in respect of income splitting.

---

183 The Court considered that this applied to the personal exemption pursuant to § 16 ErbStG a.F., to the exemption for retirement benefits pursuant to § 17 ErbStG a.F., and to the tax rate pursuant to § 19 ErbStG a.F.

184 BVerfG 21 July 2010 (dec.), Az. 1 BvR 2464/07, *NJW* 2010 p. 2783, para. 92.

185 *Idem*, para. 92.

186 *Idem*, para. 106.

187 *Idem*, para. 107.

188 See also Maurer 2010, *supra* n. 176.

Before the Constitutional Court issued that long-awaited ruling it firstly found, in another case, the unequal treatment of spouses and civil partners in respect of conveyance tax ('*Grunderwerbsteuerrecht*') incommensurable with Article 3 Basic Law and thus unconstitutional.[189]

This judgment of July 2012 was received as fitting in with a consistent line of case law of the BVerfG.[190] It therefore did not come as a surprise that in respect of income tax also, the BVerfG ruled that civil partners had to be treated equally with spouses. This was decided by the Second Senate of the BVerfG in May 2013, when it dealt with the tax dimension of the 2009 judgment of the First Senate of the BVerfG concerning survivors' pensions for civil servants, as discussed above.[191]

On 7 May 2013, the BVerfG ruled that the unequal treatment of registered partners when compared to spouses in respect of income splitting constituted indirect discrimination on grounds of sexual orientation.[192] This implied that a strict proportionality test applied. The Court reiterated that the special protection of marriage ex Article 6(1) Basic Law was in itself no sufficient justification.[193] Further, neither the aim of the income splitting for spouses, nor the legislature's competence to apply categorisation in tax law constituted a sufficiently weighty reason justifying the indirect discrimination. The Court underlined that the legislature had from the beginning structured civil partnership 'in a way comparable to marriage as a community of extensively shared responsibility'[194] and that it had continuously equalised civil partnership further with marriage.[195] Both marriage and civil partnership formed unions of economic production and consumption ('*Gemeinschaften des Verbrauchs und Erwerbs*').[196] Because the income splitting applied to spouses irrespective of whether they were raising children, any 'family-related intentions'[197] could not justify the indirect discrimination either. Supporting family-building was no justification for category-based preferential treatment of marriage over civil partnership. The fact that generally more children were raised within marriage when compared to civil partnership, did not alter this conclusion, as it could not be ignored that children were also raised in civil partnerships.[198]

189 BVerfG 18 July 2012 (dec.), Az. 1 BvL 16/11, *NJW* 2012 p. 2719. See F. Strohal, 'Verfassungswidrige Ungleichbehandlung von Ehegatten und eingetragenen Lebenspartnern im Grunderwerbsteuerrecht' ['Unconstitutional unequal treatment between spouses and registered partners in the area of conveyance tax law'], *FamFR* (2012) p. 432.

190 S. Muckel, 'Ungleichbehandlung von Ehe und eingetragener Lebenspartnerschaft – Grunderwerbsteuer' ['Unequal treatment of marriage and civil partnership – conveyance tax'], *JA* (2012) p. 877.

191 BVerfG 7 May 2013 (dec.), Az. 2 BvR 909/06 a.o., *NJW* 2013 p. 2257.

192 *Idem*, para. 78.

193 *Idem*, paras. 80–85.

194 Federal Consitutional Court Press Office, Press release no. 41/2013 of 6 June 2013, online available at: www.bundesverfassungsgericht.de/pressemitteilungen/bvg13-041en.html, visited August 2013.

195 BVerfG 7 May 2013 (dec.), Az. 2 BvR 909/06 a.o., *NJW* 2013 p. 2257, para. 90.

196 *Idem*, paras. 95 and 102.

197 Federal Consitutional Court Press Office, Press release no. 41/2013 of 6 June 2013, online available at: www.bundesverfassungsgericht.de/pressemitteilungen/bvg13-041en.html, visited August 2013.

198 BVerfG 7 May 2013 (dec.), Az. 2 BvR 909/06 a.o., *NJW* 2013 p. 2257, paras. 102–103.

The Court concluded that the legislature had to eliminate the established violation of Article 3(1) Basic Law, and it had to do so retroactively to the moment of the entry into force of the Civil Partnerships Act in August 2001.[199] Because the legislature could choose between different means in order to achieve this, the BVerfG issued a declaration of incompatibility of the relevant provisions of the Income Tax Act with the Basic Law.[200] Until the legislature had introduced new legislation, the relevant provisions had to be applied to civil partners and spouses equally.[201]

Two out of eight Judges disagreed with the majority finding and wrote a separate opinion. They disputed that the legislature had from the outset intended to structure civil partnership in a similar fashion as marriage. This could only be said from the moment the Civil Partnerships Revision Act had entered into force, hence from the year 2005. Since the facts of the cases before it originated from fiscal years 2001 and 2002, the preferential treatment of marriage during that period could be justified, exactly because civil partnership and marriage were not comparable. Justices Landau and Kessal-Wulf warned that the 'Senate [had replaced] the assessment of the legislature, which [was] the only legitimate authority, with its own.'[202]

This ruling was generally considered to be consistent with the existing line of BVerfG case law in respect of equal treatment of civil partners, which had been based on the legislature's own principled choices.[203] That the BVerfG accorded retroactive effect to its ruling to the moment of introduction of the civil partnership, may have come more as a surprise. The costs involved for the German State were estimated at approximately 175 million euro in 2013 and around 60 million annually from then on.[204]

This time the legislature acted quickly. On 19 July 2013, a new Article 2(8) in the Income Tax Act (*Einkommensteuergesetz*) entered into force, providing that those clauses that applied to spouses, equally applied to civil partners.[205] The legislature thus deliberately chose to equalise the position of civil partners with that of spouses in respect of the entire Income Tax Act, and not just the question of income splitting. Not

199 *Idem*, paras. 107–111.

200 *Idem*, para. 112.

201 *Idem*, para. 113.

202 Federal Consitutional Court Press Office, Press release no. 41/2013 of 6 June 2013, online available at: www.bundesverfassungsgericht.de/pressemitteilungen/bvg13-041en.html, visited August 2013.

203 E.g. S. Muckel, 'Ausschluss eingetragener Lebenspartner vom Ehegattensplitting verfassungswidrig' ['Exclusion of civil partners from income splitting unconstitutional'], *JA* (2013) p. 714. Brosius-Gersdorf regretted that the Court did not examine whether the income splitting in itself was constitutional. The author held that the measure constituted gender discrimination. F. Brosius-Gersdorf, 'Verfassungswidrigkeit der Ungleichbehandlung von Ehen und eingetragenen Lebenspartnerschaften beim Ehegattensplitting' ['Unconstitutionality of unequal treatment of marriage and civil partnership in respect of income splitting'], *FamFR* (2013) p. 312.

204 'Ehegattensplitting für eingetragene Lebenspartner: Koalitionsfraktionen bringen Gesetzentwurf ins Parlament ein', *Becklink* 1026983 (Verlag C.H. Beck 2011).

205 Art. 1(1) Gesetz vom 15. 7. 2013 zur Änderung des EStG in Umsetzung der Entscheidung des BVerfG vom 7. 5. 2013 [Act of 15 July 2013 on the Amendment of the EStG with a view to implementation of the judgment of the BVerfG of 7 May 2013], *BGBl. I*, p. 2397.

all related tax acts were simultaneously amended at the time, but some amendments followed suit.[206] Moreover, in April 2014 the Federal Government tabled a bill that provided for equal treatment of civil partners and spouses in all tax laws.[207] This Act entered into force on 24 July 2014.[208]

On the basis of the discussed line of BVerfG case law in tax matters, Selder concluded that the Constitutional Court had 'dismantled the constitutional position of marriage in tax law in a radical way'. According to the author the special protection of marriage under Article 6(1) Basic Law had become an empty shell that had developed over time from an obligation to privilege marriage to a prohibition on discrimination.[209]

10.3.5. Parental rights for same-sex couples

Parental rights for same-sex couples have been much debated in German politics and it is in this area that marriage and registered partnership have not (yet) been fully equalised under the law.

When civil partnership was introduced in 2001, the legislature held that same-sex civil partnerships were 'fundamentally' different from different-sex unions, because no common genetic children could be born within civil partnerships.[210] It was acknowledged that nonetheless in civil partnerships children could also be, and were, raised, and that their best interests required that certain measures were taken. Provision was therefore made for a right to parental access for civil partners.[211] The possibility was also introduced that in the case of death, an order could be given that the child remained with the person(s) to whom it related (so-called '*Verbleibensanordnungen*'). Civil partners were furthermore given the power to share in decisions on matters relating to the child's everyday life if he or she lived together with the parent (the so-called '*kleines Sorgerecht*').[212]

More far-reaching parental rights for civil partners were only granted gradually over the past decade, and the most principled amendments were commanded by rulings of the German Constitutional Court. The various subsections below contain a chronological and – mostly – thematical discussion of the (development of) the relevant laws.

206 E.g. Act of 18 July 2014, *BGBl. I* p. 1042, providing for the relevant amendment of the *Einkommensteuer-Durchführungsverordnung (EStDV)* [Income Tax Implementation Decree].

207 *BT-Drs.* 18/1306.

208 *BGBl. I* 2014, no. 32, p. 1042.

209 Selder 2013, *supra* n. 174, at p. 1067.

210 *BT-Drs.* 14/3751, p. 33.

211 Art. 2 no. 12 LPartG, now provided for in Art. 1685(2) BGB.

212 Art. 9(1) LPartG.

10.3.5.1. 2004: Introduction of second-parent adoption

When the Civil Partnerships Act was revised in 2004, it was felt that the best interests of the child had not been not sufficiently served by the 2001 Act.[213] Measures were considered necessary to strengthen the legal position of children raised in civil partnerships, as well as their parents. The 2004 Revision Act therefore made it possible for a civil partner to adopt the genetic child of the other civil partner, so-called *Stiefkindadoption* (step-child adoption), hereafter referred to as second-parent adoption.[214] The BVerfG later held such second-parent adoption to be compatible with the Basic Law.[215] In its judgment, the Court made clear that each parent individually enjoyed the constitutional parental rights of Article 6(2) Basic Law and not merely two parents as a union.[216]

The pre-existing option of single-parent adoption had not been affected by the Civil Partnerships Act of 2001. Since the 2004 revision it is, however, provided that if a person in a civil partnership wishes to adopt a child, the consent of one's civil partner is required. The 2004 Revision Act explicitly did not provide for successive adoption ('*Sukzessivadoption*') or joint adoption by civil partners.[217] While the latter is still[218] not possible for civil partners under German law (see 10.3.5.4 below), legislative change in respect of successive adoption was only achieved after court proceedings (see 10.3.5.3 below). Before the relevant BVerfG ruling of 2013 is discussed, first the relevant aspects of the Court's case law of the preceding years are set out.

10.3.5.2. 2009 and 2010: principled BVerfG rulings

As noted above, the rulings of the Constitutional Court on survivors' pensions and inheritance also had implications for parental rights for civil partners. For long it has been a controversial matter in German law and doctrine whether the close intertwining of marriage and the family in the wording of Article 6(1) of the Basic Law, implied that only the families of married partners enjoy constitutional protection.[219] In its ruling of July 2009 on survivors' pensions for civil partners (see 10.3.4.2 above) the Constitutional Court rejected this reading of Article 6(1) Basic Law. It held:

---

213 *BT-Drs.* 15/3445, p. 14.

214 Art. 9(7) LPartG, Art. 1755(1) and (3), Art. 1755(2) BGB, as introduced by the 2004 Revision Act.

215 BVerfG 10 August 2009 (dec.), Az. 1 BvL 15/09. See also AG Elmshorn 20 December 2010 (dec.), Az. 46 F 9/10, *NJW* 2011 p. 1085. The case concerned a lesbian couple in a civil partnership, one of whom had become pregnant with the use of anonymously donated sperm. The Elmshorn Court ruled that it was in the child's best interest for the civil partner of the biological mother not to have to comply with the year of caring for the child before adoption could take place ('*Adoptionspflegejahr*'), as had been requested by the competent child welfare office.

216 BVerfG 10 August 2009 (dec.), Az. 1 BvL 15/09, para. 15.

217 *BT-Drs.* 15/3445, p. 15.

218 State of affairs on 31 July 2014.

219 E.g. Grösschner 2004, *supra* n. 22, at p. 825; W. Heun, 'Art. 3', in H. Dreier (ed.), *Grundgesetz-Kommentar, Band 1, Präambel, Artikel 1–19* [German Basic Law Commentary, Volume 1, Preamble, Articles 1–19], 2nd edn. (Tübingen, Mohr Siebeck 2004) p. 399 at p. 482, Rn. 140.

'[...] the constitutionally permissible and constitutionally required promotion of parents is primarily the subject of the constitutional protection of the fundamental rights of the family, and as such it is not restricted to married parents [...].'[220]

With this ruling the Court disconnected the special protection of marriage from that of the family (see also 10.3.4.2 above). The Court furthermore took into account the reality that a growing number of children were raised outside marriage.[221] On the other hand, in its 2010 judgment on inheritance tax (see 10.4.4.2 above), the Court held that marriage differed in principle from civil partnership '[...] in its qualification as a starting point for a succession of generations'.[222] It therefore considered marriage a privileged area of law for family building. It has been concluded on the basis of this reasoning that the Court had thus '[...] stated cautiously that the reproductive abilities of a married couple may justify providing benefits for married couples that are not provided for civil partners.'[223] This has indeed proven true in respect of reimbursement for AHR treatment (see 10.4.5.6 below). However, the relevant case law of the Constitutional Court predates the judgment here discussed. In later case law of the Constitutional Court no such reasoning has been repeated. In fact, the Constitutional Court took a different approach in its ruling of 2013 on successive adoption by civil partners, by instead focusing on the right to equal treatment of the children concerned.

10.3.5.3. 2013: Successive adoption

As explained above, there has for long been a prohibition on successive adoption for civil partners ('*Verbot der Kettenadoption*') under German law.[224] Thus, for civil partners, it was not possible to adopt the minor adopted child[225] of the other civil partner.[226] A bill tabled by the Greens in 2007, aiming at the abolition of this difference in treatment, did not make it to the debate stage.[227]

220 BVerfG 7 July 2009 (dec.), Az. 1 BvR 1164/07, *NJW* 2010 p. 1439, paras. 102–103.

221 *Idem*, para. 113, where the Court refers to 'Rupp/Bergold, in: Rupp, *Die Lebenssituation von Kindern in gleichgeschlechtlichen Lebenspartnerschaften*, Staatsinstitut für Familienforschung an der Universität Bamberg 2009, p. 282', from which it followed that at that time an estimated number of approximately 2,200 children in Germany lived in 13,000 registered civil partnerships. See also Wiemann 2010, *supra* n. 49, at p. 1429 referring to a study of the Central Statistical Office of 2008, which showed that in 2006 in West Germany 23 per cent and in Eastern Germany 42 per cent of all children under 18 were raised in so-called alternative types of family situations. See www.destatis.de/jetspeed/portal/cms/Sites/destatis/Internet/DE/Content/Publikationen/Querschnittsveroeffentlichungen/Datenreport/Downloads/Datenreport2008Familie,property=file.pdf, p. 32ff.

222 BVerfG 21 July 2010 (dec.), Az. 1 BvR 2464/07, *NJW* 2010 p. 2783. English translation by Saunders in Saunders 2012, *supra* n. 20, p. 935.

223 Saunders 2012, *supra* n. 20, at p. 935.

224 Art. 1742 BGB and Art. 9(7) of the Civil Partnerships Act (LPartG).

225 In principle this adopted child was also the non-genetic child, although this could be different in surrogacy cases. See ch. 4, section 4.3.9.

226 Art. 1742 BGB read at the time: 'An adopted child may, as long as the adoption relationship exists, in the lifetime of an adoptive parent only be adopted by that parent's spouse'.

227 *BT-Drs.* 16/5596.

By judgment of 1 December 2009, the Court of Appeal (*Oberlandesgericht*, OLG) of Hamm held the prohibition on successive adoption by civil partners to be compatible with the Basic Law.[228] This Court held that while the emotional and social parentage of the civil partner of a parent enjoyed protection under Article 6(1) Basic Law, from this provision no imperative requirement for the legislature to provide for adoption by same-sex couples followed.[229] According to the OLG, the institutes of marriage and family within the meaning of Article 6 Basic Law were based on the view that the upbringing of children was the task of the family consisting of mother, father and child.[230] The judgment received considerable criticism in legal scholarship. Often, it was argued that the principled question of whether it would be contrary to the child's best interests to be raised by a same-sex couple, had already been answered by the legislature when the possibility of second-parent adoption was introduced in 2005.[231] Further, the critique was issued that primarily children raised by parents in a civil partnership were put in a disadvantaged position *vis-à-vis* children raised by married couples.[232] Other scholars agreed with the Court that the upbringing of children by same-sex couples would be contrary to the child's best interests.[233]

In April 2010 the Greens tabled another bill seeking full equalisation of civil partnership and marriage in respect of adoption rights.[234] Considering how the political parties were balanced in the German Parliament at the time, Henkel observed in 2011 that this bill had limited chances of making it into law.[235] This proved to be different, however, after the issue of successive adoption by civil partners had been put before the BVerfG.[236]

---

228 OLG Hamm 1 December 2009 (dec.), Az. 15 Wx 236/09, *NJW* 2010 p. 2065. Earlier decisions in this matter had been rendered LG Münster 16 March 2009 (dec.), Az. 05 T 775/08 and AG Münster 30 September 2008 (dec.), Az. 105 XVI 5/08.

229 The Court referred to BVerfG 17 July 2002, Az. 1 BvF 1/01, *NJW* 2002 p. 2543, in particular to para. 103.

230 The Court held that the at the time most recent judgment of the BVerfG on the matter – namely BVerfG 7 July 2009 (dec.), Az. 1 BvR 1164/07, *NJW* 2010 p. 1439 – did not alter this conclusion.

231 L. Milzer, 'Anmerkung zum OLG Hamm, Beschluss vom 01.12.2009 – 15 Wx 236/09' ['Case-note to OLG Hamm decision of 1 December 2009 – 15 Wx 236/09'], *FamFR* (2010) p. 47 and Henkel 2011, *supra* n. 49, at p. 263. See also H. Grziwotz, 'Anmerkung zum Urteil des OLG Hamm vom 01.12.2009 (I-15 Wx 236/09, FamRZ 2010, 1259) – Partner einer eingetragenen Lebenspartnerschaft kann Adoptivkind des anderen Partners nicht an Kindes statt annehmen' ['Commentary to the judgment of the OLG Hamm of 01.12.2009 (I-15 Wx 236/09, FamRZ 2010, 1259) – Civil partner cannot adopt adoptive child if his or her partner'], *Zeitschrift für das gesamte Familienrecht, FamRZ* (2010) p. 1261.

232 Muscheler 2010, *supra* n. 169, at p. 231; N. Dethloff, 'Adoption und Sorgerecht – Problembereiche für die eingetragenen Lebenspartner?' ['Adoption and parental authority – area of concern for the civil partner?'], *FPR* (2010) p. 208; W. Enders, 'Stiefkindadoption' ['Second-parent adoption'], *FPR* (2004) p. 60 and G. Müller, 'Anmerkung zu OLG Hamm: Sukzessivadoption eines Kindes durch den eingetragenen Lebenspartner' ['Case note to OLG Hamm: successive adoption of a child by a registered partner'], *DNotZ* (2010) p. 698.

233 Schüffner alleged that there was an increased risk of phaedophilic offences if a child was raised by a same-sex couple. Schüffner 2007, *supra* n. 74, at pp. 161–162.

234 *BT-Dr* 17/1429.

235 Henkel 2011, *supra* n. 49, at p. 259. Henkel, however, also refers in his comment to an opinion poll which showed wide public support for the introduction of joint adoption for civil partners. He refers to www.mingle-trend.respondi.com/de/28_06_2010/deutsche-befurworten-adoption-durch-gleichgeschlechtliche-paare (Opinion poll of 28 June 2010).

236 Request for constitutional review of 29 December 2009, Az. 1 BvR 3247/09.

Only a year after the OLG of Hamm had held the prohibition on successive adoption by civil partners in the German Civil Code to be compatible with the Basic Law, another OLG, namely the Hanseatic Court of Appeal (Hamburg) ruled to the contrary and held this prohibition to be in violation of the principle of equal treatment of Article 3(3) of the Basic Law.[237] This court therefore referred the constitutional issue at hand to the BVerfG.[238] The Hanseatic OLG acknowledged that the wording of Article 1742 BGB – following which '[...] an adopted child may, as long as the adoption relationship exists, in the lifetime of an adoptive parent only be adopted by that parent's spouse' – was unambiguous. The Hanseatic OLG also acknowledged that during the various revisions of the Civil Partnerships Act, the legislature had deliberately not introduced the option of a simultaneous or subsequent joint adoption by civil partners. The fact that the 2004 Revision Act provided for second-parent adoption by the civil partner, was considered a political compromise, at a time when no parliamentary majority could be formed for a full equalisation of civil partnership with marriage.[239] Nevertheless, the OLG ruled that there were no weighty reasons for this difference in treatment on grounds of sexual orientation. At the time when the Adoption law was drafted in the 1970s, a distinction between marriage and other types of partnerships was considered justified because only marriage enjoyed legal protection.[240] According to the OLG that justification ground was superseded in the meantime, since civil partnership and marriage had been equalised in terms of legally binding responsibilities for the partner.[241] The OLG did not, furthermore, accept that the difference in treatment could be justified on the basis of the child's best interests. As the OLG observed, the upbringing of children by a same-sex couple had yet been made possible under German law. The Court held as unconstitutional the assumption of the legislature that the best interests of a child who was adopted by one of the civil partners by whom it was raised would be harmed, while that would not be the case for a child that was genetically related to one of the civil partners by whom it was raised. On the contrary, the OLG reasoned that an adopted child was even more in need of legal protection. The OLG held the legal implications of the prohibition on joint adoption by civil partners for the inheritance and maintenance rights of the child adopted by one parent only to be harmful to the child's best interests. It also referred to a study of 2009 conducted by order of the Ministry of Justice,[242] which

237 OLG Hamburg 22 December 2010 (dec.), Az. 2 Wx 23/09, *NJW* 2011 p. 1104.

238 Art. 100(1) Basic Law in combination with Art. 13 No. 11, 80 ff. BVerfGG.

239 OLG Hamburg 22 December 2010 (dec.), Az. 2 Wx 23/09, *NJW* 2011 p. 1104, para. 12.

240 *BT-Drs.* 7/3061, p. 30.

241 The Court referred to, *inter alia*, BVerfG 7 July 2009 (dec.), Az. 1 BvR 1164/07, *NJW* 2010 p. 1439; C. Hillgruber, 'Über die Ungleichbehandlung von Ehe und eingetragener Lebenspartnerschaft im Bereich der betrieblichen Hinterbliebenenversorgung – Kritische Anmerkung zum Beschluss des Bundesverfassungsgerichts vom 07.07.2009 (AZ: 1 BvR 1164/07)' ['On the unequal treatment of marriage and registered civil partnership in respect of survivor's pensions – A critical note on the decision of the German Constitutional Court of 7 July 2009 (AZ: 1 BvR 1164/07)'], *JZ* (2010) p. 41 at p. 44 and to T. Hoppe, 'Die Verfassungswidrigkeit der Ungleichbehandlung von Ehe und eingetragener Lebenspartnerschaft im Bereich der betrieblichen Hinterbliebenenrente (VBL)' ['The unconstitutionality of the unequal treatment of marriage and civil partnership in respect of occupational survivor's pensions (VBL)'], *DVBl.* (2009) p. 1516 at p. 1517.

242 M. Rupp (ed.), *Lebenssituation von Kindern in gleichgeschlechtlichen Lebenspartnerschaften* [The social situation of children in same-sex partnerships] (Köln, Bundesanzeiger Verlag 2009).

had shown that for a sound development it was not necessary for a child to be raised by parents of different sex. Instead, the quality of the inner family ties was decisive. The report had concluded that full equalisation of civil partnership with marriage in respect of adoption would be in the child's best interests.[243] Under reference to the BVerfG decision of 7 July 2009,[244] the OLG Hamburg ruled that the special protection of marriage on the basis of Article 6(1) Basic Law could not justify the difference in treatment between civil partners and married partners in this respect.

While the case was pending before the BVerfG,[245] various bills aiming to lift the prohibition on successive adoption for civil partners were tabled.[246] The Federal Government announced in December 2011 that the issue was under consideration, but that it first wished to await the BVerfG judgment.[247] It asserted that successive adoption was prohibited under Article 6(2) of the European Convention on the Adoption of Children. At the time, Germany was investigating signing of the 2008 Revised European Convention on the Adoption of Children, which provides for an opt-in for adoption by same-sex (married or civil) partners.[248]

In February 2013, the First Senate of the BVerfG rendered its long awaited judgment in the case.[249] The Court unanimously ruled that the exclusion of registered partners from successive adoption was in violation of the right to equal treatment of both the children living in such a relationship and the respective civil partners under Article 3(1) of the German Basic Law. The Court held the exclusion of civil partners from successive adoption not to be in violation of certain rights under Article 6 of the German Basic Law, however, more precisely the right of children to be ensured parental care by the State under Article 2(1) in combination with Article 6(2) of the Basic Law; the natural right of parents to the care and upbringing of their children (Article 6(2)) and the special protection of the family under Article 6(1) Basic Law.

On the outset, the Court noted that the legislative proceedings did not provide any explanations as to why the legislature had not provided for successive adoption by civil partners, while in fact the bill for the 2004 Revision Act had – without distinguishing between genetic and non-genetic children – pointed at the beneficial consequences for both child and parents of an adoption by a civil partner.[250]

---

243 OLG Hamburg 22 December 2010 (dec.), Az. 2 Wx 23/09, *NJW* 2011 p. 1104, para. 30.

244 BVerfG 7 July 2009 (dec.), Az. 1 BvR 1164/07, *NJW* 2010 p. 1439, paras. 104–105.

245 Request for constitutional review of 29 December 2009, Az. 1 BvR 3247/09. See also Henkel 2011, *supra* n. 49, at p. (264) and the position paper ('*Stellungnahme*') of the *Lesben- und Schwulenverbandes in Deutschland* on case 1 BvR 3247/09 of 17 February 2010, online available at www.tmp.lsvd.de/fileadmin/pics/Dokumente/Adoption/Adoption-100217.pdf, visited July 2011.

246 For example, *BT-Drs.* 17/1429 and *BR-Drs.* 124/11.

247 *BT-Drs.*17/8248.

248 Germany finally signed the Revised European Convention on the Adoption of Children in May 2014. See also *BT-Drs.* 17/2329.

249 BVerfG 19 February 2013, Az. 1 BvL 1/11, 1 BvR 3247/09, *NJW* 2013 p. 847.

250 The Court referred to *BT-Drs.* 15/3445, p. 15.

As to the State's obligation under Article 6(2) Basic Law to watch over parents in the performance of their duty, the Court ruled that this did not include an obligation for the legislature to provide for successive adoption for civil partners.[251] The Court acknowledged that the prohibition on successive adoption implied in practice that the children concerned could only have one legal parent.[252] It held, however, that this in itself did not exceed the discretion that the legislature enjoyed as regards the manner in which it made constitutional rights effective, particularly not now that the child concerned was not parentless and that the civil partner of the adoptive parent could obtain the power to share in decisions on matters relating to the child's everyday life.[253] In the same vein, the Court held that the exclusion of civil partners from the option of successive adoption did not violate the right to special protection of the family under Article 6(1). Even though a family consisting of two civil partners and a biological or adopted child of one of them enjoyed protection under this provision, there was no obligation on the State under the Basic Law to create a possibility to adopt the non-biological child of the civil partner. While the legislature had an obligation to provide for a legal framework within which family relations could develop, it also enjoyed a certain discretion as to the family forms it provided for.[254]

The Constitutional Court further ruled that the 'parental constitutional right' ('*Elterngrundrecht*') ex Article 6(2) Basic Law was not violated. The Court reiterated that the best interests of the child are an essential element of this Article and that the rights of legal parents in the first place served the protection of children.[255] While legal parents of the same sex were included in the scope of this right and while each legal parent on his or her own was a bearer of this right,[256] 'mere' social parenthood did not come within the scope of this Article, the Court ruled. Because the civil partner of a person who adopted a child was not the legal parent of that child, he or she could not rely on the constitutional parental right under Article 6(2) of the Basic Law. Hence, civil partners could not claim any right to successive adoption on this ground.[257]

The Court also ruled, however, that the exclusion of civil partners of successive adoption violated the right to equal treatment of the children concerned (Article 3(1) Basic Law). It held that those children who had been adopted by a person in a registered partnership were denied possibilities for their personal development ('*Entwicklung und Lebensgestaltung*'), which children adopted by married persons and children born with a person in a civil partnership did enjoy.[258] In particular, the law excluded that these children would have a second legal parent, who could fully

251 The second paragraph of Art. 6 Basic Law provides that parents have a natural right to as well as a duty for the care and the upbringing of children, while the State watches over them in the performance of this duty.

252 BVerfG 19 February 2013, Az. 1 BvL 1/11, 1 BvR 3247/09, *NJW* 2013 p. 847, para. 44.

253 *Idem*, paras. 45–46.

254 *Idem*, para. 68.

255 *Idem*, para. 49.

256 *Idem*, paras. 49–50.

257 *Idem*, paras. 58–59.

258 *Idem*, para. 73.

take up the care and upbringing of the child, as envisaged in the Constitution.[259] This difference in treatment could not be justified, the Court held. The court examined no less than eight possible justifications, but rejected them all.

Principally the Court considered that the difference in treatment was not in the interests of the child. It could not be maintained that to grow up within a same-sex relationship or that the practice of successive adoption in itself harmed the child's interests. The Court noted that successive adoption had a stabilising effect on the child's developmental psychology and served the integration and consolidation of the adopted child in the new family. An equal legal position of the parents towards the child would have an equally stabilising effect and could strengthen the child's sense of belonging and the parents' sense of responsibility. The denial of legal recognition of such a family, on the other hand, could be experienced by the child as a rejection of its person and its family.[260] The Court also noted that successive adoption would improve the legal position of the children concerned in respect of parental authority, as well as succession and maintenance, in situations of separation or decease of (one of) the parents.

In respect of a general aim to restrict the practice of successive adoption, the Court held there to be no justification to distinguish in that regard between children adopted by persons in a civil partnership and children adopted by married persons. The Court also was not convinced by the argument that the exclusion served to prevent that the legal prohibition on joint adoption by civil partners was circumvented. The Court stressed that the case before it was not about the constitutionality of the prohibition on joint adoption by civil partners, but noted in this regard that the exclusion of civil partners from successive adoption could not prevent that an adopted child lived together with its adoptive parent and his or her civil partner. Justifications on grounds of protection of marriage and family or the constitutional parental rights, were equally rejected by the Court.

The Court further held that the unequal treatment of civil partners when compared with spouses in respect of successive adoption under Article 9(7) LPartG violated Article 3(1) Basic Law.[261] The same held for the unequal treatment of civil partners of parents with an adopted child, when compared to civil partners of genetic parents.[262] The Court left open the question of whether the unequal treatment of children who were adopted by a parent in a civil partnership when compared to children who were adopted by a married parent, violated the prohibition on unequal treatment between children born within marriage and children born out of wedlock.[263]

259 *Idem*, para. 73. In its oral submission to the Constitutional Court, *Bündnis 90/Die Grünen* had extensively set out the beneficial effects of successive adoption for the children concerned. For an account of their argument, see in particular para. 33 of the BVerfG judgment.

260 *Idem*, para. 83.

261 *Idem*, para. 104.

262 *Idem*, para. 105.

263 *Idem*, para. 103.

As a rule a violation of the Basic Law results in the nullity of the relevant legislative provision. In the present case, however, the Court merely declared Article 9(7) LPartG incompatible with the Basic Law, because, so the Court noted, the legislature had various options to remedy the unequal treatment, including a general non-discriminating restriction of the legal possibilities for adoption.

In academia this judgment was generally received as fitting in well with the existing case law of the BVerfG that eliminated unequal treatment of civil partners when compared to spouses.[264] However, the approach of the Court in this case was received differently. Some praised the Constitutional Court for its courage to base its reasoning on the best interests of the child.[265] Others, were (very) critical instead, and claimed that the Court had unjustifiably completely shunted off Article 6(1) Basic Law.[266] It was furthermore observed that marriage had now been completely untied of its historical connotation and was only seen from a functional perspective.[267] Again it was concluded that Article 6(1) Basic Law was now read as a prohibition on discrimination against other relationship forms ('*Lebensformen*').[268]

The question was also raised whether the judgment implied that the legislature now also had to legislate for joint adoption for same-sex couples.[269] The BVerfG judgment left this question open. Although a bill to that effect had been pending since 2010,[270] Parliament was divided over this matter and could not reach agreement on this point.[271] It therefore only legislated on successive adoption. On 27 June 2014 a new Article 9(7) LPartG entered into force, which reads: 'A civil partner may adopt the child of his civil partner alone.'[272] While the introduction of this provision thus brought an end to the debate on successive adoption for same-sex couples, the question of joint adoption for these couples remained open.

---

264 S. Muckel, 'Sukzessive Adoption – Ablehnung für eingetragene Lebenspartner verfassungswidrig' ['Successive adoption – nonadmission of civil partners unconstitutional'], *JA* (2013) p. 396 and W. Frenz, 'Eheschutz ade? BVerfG stärkt gleichgeschlechtliche Paare', *NVwZ* (2013) p. 1200.

265 E.g. Muckel 2013A, *supra* n. 264 and I. Kroppenberg, 'Unvereinbarkeit des Verbots der sukzessiven Stiefkindadoption durch eingetragene Lebenspartner mit dem Grundgesetz' ['The incompatibility of the prohibition of successive adoption by civil partners with the German Basic Law'], *NJW* (2013) p. 2161 at p. 2162.

266 E.g. Brosius-Gersdorf 2013A, *supra* n. 136, at p. 170 and P. Reimer and M. Jestaedt, *JZ* 2013, 468, at 469.

267 W. Frenz, 'Eheschutz ade? BVerfG stärkt gleichgeschlechtliche Paare' ['Protection of marriage, farewell? German Constitutional Court supports same-sex couples'], *NVwZ* (2013) p. 1200 at p. 1201.

268 *Idem*, at p. 1202.

269 Kroppenberg 2013, *supra* n. 265, at p. 2162.

270 *BT-Drs.* 17/1429.

271 Legal academia was also divided. For references see Kroppenberg 2013, *supra* n. 265, at p. 2162, footnote 19.

272 Gesetz zur Umsetzung der Entscheidung des Bundesverfassungsgerichts zur Sukzessivadoption durch Lebenspartner [Act on the implementation of the judgment of the German Constitutional Court on successive adoption by civil partners], Act of 20 June 2014, *BGBl. I* p. 786. The Article further reads: 'In this case, section 1743, first sentence, section 1751(2) and (4), second sentence, section 1755(1) and (3), section 1755(2), section 1756(2), section 1757(2), first sentence, and section 1772(1), first sentence, letter c of the Civil Code shall apply mutatis mutandis.'

10.3.5.4. Exclusion of civil partners from joint adoption

Same-sex couples are excluded from joint adoption.[273] The lifting of the successive adoption prohibition implies that same-sex civil partners can establish the same legal situation in two (albeit in principle time-consuming) steps.[274] Joint adoption of a child has nonetheless been considered a different matter. As Kroppenberg has explained, to allow for joint adoption by civil partners, would require the legislature to definitively depart from its traditional norm, underlying German adoption laws, of the 'core family', consisting of spouses and their natural children.[275] Kroppenberg has also questioned whether this norm is still consistent with the present day and whether it serves the best interests of the child.[276]

In March 2013 the Administrative Court (AG) of Schöneberg asked the Constitutional Court to rule on the constitutionality of the exclusion of civil partners from joint adoption,[277] but because the referring Court had not yet taken the recently issued judgment on successive adoption into account, this referral was declared inadmissible in January 2014 for insufficient motivation.[278]

In May 2014 the German government signed the Revised European Convention on the Adoption of Children in May 2014, which allows for – but does not impose on States – joint adoption by same-sex partners. Whether this was an indication that legislative change on this point was forthcoming was insufficiently clear at the time this research was concluded (i.e., 31 July 2014).

10.3.5.5. Legal parenthood by operation of the law

Under the present state of the law, German law does not provide for legal parenthood by operation of the law for same-sex couples. Under German law only the woman who gave birth can be registered on the birth certificate of the child as mother of the child (see also Chapter 4, section 4.3.9). If she is married, a rebuttable presumption that her husband is the child's father applies (Article 1592 Civil Code).[279] No such presumption applies between civil partners, as a case of 2010 has confirmed.

---

273 Art. 1741(2) Civil Code reads: 'A person who is not married may adopt a child only alone. A married couple may adopt a child only jointly. A spouse may adopt a child of his spouse alone. He may also adopt a child alone if the other spouse cannot adopt the child because he is incapable of contracting or has not yet reached the age of twenty-one.'

274 M. Zschiebsch, 'Nichtzulassung der Sukzessivadoption durch eingetragenen Lebenspartner verfassungswidrig' ['Non-admission of successive adoption by a civil partner unconstitutional'], *Juris Praxiz Report FamR* 22/2013, Anm. 6. The author further explains that parents who give up their child for adoption cannot require that the child is not placed with a same-sex couple. Increasingly more Courts, however, deal with both adoptions in one and the same sitting.

275 Kroppenberg 2013, *supra* n. 265, at p. 2163.

276 *Idem.*

277 AG Berlin-Schöneberg 8 March 2013, Az. 24 F 250/12.

278 BVerfG 23 January 2014 (dec.), Az. 1 BvL 2/13.

279 Art. 1592 BGB.

In 2009 two women in a civil partnership, one of whom had given birth to a child after heterologous insemination, applied to the Courts to have the child's birth certificate changed. They wished to be both registered on it as parents of the child and thus to have the blank space on the certificate filled with the name of the civil partner of the birth mother. The two women relied on Articles 3 and 6 of the Basic Law. They also claimed that the presumption of parenthood of Article 1592 was to be applied analogously in their case. As they explained, the legal father of a child was either the man who was married to the birth mother at the time of birth, or the man who recognised the child. Whether this man was also the genetic father of the child and whether he was its carer was irrelevant for the establishment of legal parenthood under German Law. The Hamburg District Court rejected this reasoning and ruled instead that the presumption of Article 1592 Civil Code was based on a presumption of descent and that such descent could be ruled out in the case at hand. The Court further noted that the legislature had already provided for a possibility to establish parental links between a child and the civil partner of that child's parent, by introducing second-parent adoption in 2005. The District Court accordingly dismissed the claim as being unfounded.[280]

The two women unsuccessfully appealed their case before the competent appeals courts.[281] Moreover, by judgment of 2 July 2010, the Constitutional Court rejected their constitutional complaint.[282] Because the complainants in this case subsequently (unsuccessfully) lodged a complaint with the ECtHR under Article 8 in conjunction with Article 14, the latter Court's summary of the findings of the Constitutional Court can be quoted here:

> 'The Constitutional Court observed, at the outset, that there was no indication that the lower courts had failed to take into account the requirements of the European Convention on Human Rights. It further considered that the refusal to insert the first applicant into the birth certificate prior to adoption did not violate the applicants' right to the enjoyment of their family life. Article 6 of the Basic Law protected the family as a union of parents and children. It did not matter in this respect whether the children descended from their parents and whether they were born in or out of wedlock. However, the entry of the name of a civil partner into the birth certificate did not concern the family life between the civil partners and the child. The birth certificate had the sole purpose of giving evidence of the child's descent. It did not interfere in any way with the child's living together with his or her parents within the family. […] The Constitutional Court further considered that the applicant had not been discriminated against. Civil partners did not have a right to be treated equally to legal or biological fathers with respect to their entry into the birth certificate. In this respect, the two groups were not comparable, as biological or legal paternity established a legal relationship comprising mutual rights and duties. Such a legal relationship did not exist between the civil partner and the child, as long as the child was

280 AG Hamburg 24 June 2009 (dec.), Az. 60 III 35/09.

281 On 4 November 2009 the Hamburg Regional Court rejected the applicants' appeal. LG Hamburg 4 November 2009 (dec.), Az. 301 T 596/09. On 26 January 2010 the Hanseatic Court of Appeal rejected the applicants' appeal on points of law. OLG Hamburg 26 January 2010 (dec.), Az. 2 Wx 125/09.

282 BVerfG 2 July 2010 (dec.), Az. 1 BvR 666/10, *NJW* 2010 p. 2783.

> not adopted. The fact that there was no legal presumption that the mother's civil partner was the child's second parent did not amount to discrimination vis-à-vis married couples, as the legal presumption was based on biological descent and did not have a basis in the case of civil partners.'[283]

In May 2013 the Strasbourg Court declared this complaint manifestly ill-founded and therefore inadmissible (see Chapter 8, section 8.2.4.2).[284]

10.3.5.6. Access to AHR treatment

As more extensively explained in Chapter 4, single women and women with a same-sex partner are in many German States excluded from access to AHR treatment with the use of donated gametes.[285] Further, only married couples are entitled to reimbursement for artificial insemination.[286] By judgment of 28 February 2007 the BVerfG upheld this regulation as compatible with the Basic Law.[287] The Court considered that by reason of the constitutional protection of marriage, the legislature was not, in principle, prevented from treating marriage more favourably than other ways of life. To give preferential treatment to marriage in the social law provisions on the financing of artificial insemination was at the time considered justified by the Court, in particular out of consideration for the legally protected status of marriage as a responsible relationship and a guarantee of stability.[288] Whether this reasoning is commensurable with the above-discussed later BVerfG case law in respect of equal treatment of registered partners and spouses in other realms of law, may, however, be questioned.

10.3.6. Towards access to marriage for same-sex couples?

From the moment civil partnership for same-sex partners was introduced in Germany in 2001, the question as to whether and to what extent it should be equalised with marriage has been on the table in politics, court proceedings and academia.[289] As the

---

283 ECtHR 7 May 2013 (dec.), *Boeckel and Gessner-Boeckel* v. *Germany*, no. 8017/11, paras. 13–14. A comparable line of reasoning was adopted by the Court of Appeals of Karlsruhe in a case concerning parental access after the separation of civil partners. In a 2010, this Court ruled that the female civil partner of a mother did not have a right to access to the child after separation of the civil partners. The Court noted that the legislature had deliberately not provided for parenthood by operation of the law for female civil partners and thus not for automatic parenthood of the social mother (the civil partner of a mother). In the case at hand the Court furthermore did not consider access by the social mother in the interests of the child. OLG Karlsruhe 16 November 2010 (dec.), Az. 5 UF 217/10, *NJW* 2011 p. 1012.

284 ECtHR 7 May 2013 (dec.), *Boeckel and Gessner-Boeckel* v. *Germany*, no. 8017/11.

285 Ch. 4, section 4.3.3.

286 Art. 27a (1)(3) SGB V.

287 See BVerfG 28 February 2007, Az. 1 BvL 5/03, *NJW* 2007 p. 1343, as referred to in BVerfG 21 July 2010 (dec.), Az. 1 BvR 2464/07, *NJW* 2010 p. 2783.

288 See BVerfG 28 February 2007, Az. 1 BvL 5/03, *NJW* 2007 p. 1343. See also BVerfG 7 July 2009 (dec.), Az. 1 BvR 1164/07, *NJW* 2010 p. 1439, paras. 102–103, where the BVerfG refers to its judgment of 28 February 2007.

289 An important question in academia has been what was left of the special protection of Art. 6 Basic Law. Wiemann answered this question in 2010 with 'not much'. Wiemann 2010, *supra* n. 49, at p. 1430.

discussion above has shown, the Federal Constitutional Court's case law has been a major driving force in indeed establishing further equalisation between these two institutions.

While many differences in areas such as tax law, social protection and the position of civil servants have thus been lifted over the course of time, certain differences still remain today. These mainly concern parental rights for same-sex civil partners (see 10.3.5 above). Legislative initiatives to achieve full equalisation of civil partnership and marriage have so far been unsuccessful.[290]

Over the years there have also been various bills tabled seeking the opening up of marriage to same-sex couples.[291] In a bill of 2010 it was held that public opinion on the institute of marriage had changed in German society and it was argued that there was therefore no longer a justification for different treatment between homosexual and heterosexual couples and to limit marriage to couples of different sex only.[292] The German debate about the opening up of marriage gained a particular momentum in 2013 when the two important Constitutional Courts rulings in respect of income splitting and successive adoption came out (see above). In that same year more than 3,000 prominent Germans petitioned the German Parliament for the equal access of same-sex couples to marriage.[293] Various bills seeking the opening up of marriage were also tabled in Parliament by left-wing parties.[294] In the Senate (*Bundesrat*) several States jointly tabled a bill seeking the opening up of marriage to same-sex couples.[295] The Senate consequently tabled a bill to that effect in Parliament.[296] The Explanatory Memorandum to the Bill explained, *inter alia*, that marriage was by then understood as a union in which partners supported each other and carried responsibilities for one another ('*Beistands- und Verantwortungsgemeinschaft*'), irrespective of whether they were also raising children. A new definition and understanding of the term 'marriage' in Article 6(1) of the Basic Law, to the effect of including same-sex spouses, was considered possible without amending the text of the Article. The Explanatory Memorandum also pointed out that civil partnership was perceived as marriage by the public and that research had shown that a clear majority of the population was in favour of opening up marriage to same-sex couples.[297] Finally, reference was made to the legislation of countries that had yet legislated for access to marriage for same-sex couples.

Henkel spoke of a 'fight' in German academia about the question what from a constitutional point of view was the difference between the institute of marriage and that of the registered civil partnership. Henkel 2011, *supra* n. 49, at p 259. Henkel did not explicitly refer to authors with different points of view on this matter. Concerning the terminology used, however, the author referred to Hillgruber 2010, *supra* n. 241, at p. 43. Saunders has held that the concept of marriage in Art. 6(1) had to include civil partnerships. Saunders 2012, *supra* n. 20, at p. 930.

290 *Inter alia BT-Drs.* 16/497; *BT-Drs.* 16/3423 and *BT-Drs.* 17/2113.

291 *Inter alia BT-Drs.* 16/13596; *BT-Drs.* 17/2023 and *BT-Drs.* 17/6343.

292 *BT-Drs.* 17/2113.

293 'Prominente fordern volle Gleichstellung der Homo-Ehe', *Becklink* 1026468 (Verlag C.H. Beck 2013).

294 *BT-Drs.* 17/12677; *BT-Drs.* 17/13912 and *BT-Drs.* 18/8.

295 *BR-Drs.* 196/13.

296 *Idem* and *BT-Drs.* 17/13426.

297 *BT-Drs.* 17/13426, p. 7.

In late 2011 a new government was formed, as a result of which the above discussed bill ceased to be pending.[298] The newly governing Christian parties, the CDU and CSU, openly opposed the opening up of marriage,[299] and the coalition agreement between the CDU, CSU and SPD (the Social Democrats) parties of November 2013 did not include the matter.[300] As a result, the opening up of marriage to same-sex couples had not materialised at the time this research was concluded (i.e., 31 July 2014) and it was uncertain if and, if so, when access to marriage for same-sex couples would become reality in Germany. It was further insufficiently clear to what extent the possible opening up of marriage would also provide for full equalisation between same-sex and different-sex spouses in respect of parental rights.

10.4. Same-sex relationships and cross-border movement

This section discusses the cross-border perspective of the German laws on legal recognition of same-sex relationships. Following the structure of the other chapters of this case study as set out in Chapter 1, section 1.5, the relevant German Private International Law regime, as well as implementation of the relevant EU Directives are discussed. It is furthermore noted here that in 2010 Germany and France concluded a bilateral agreement on optional matrimonial property regimes.[301] The agreement provides for a matrimonial property regime of the 'community of accrued gains' model, that all married couples whose matrimonial property regime is covered by the substantive law of one of the contracting states can choose. Also couples who have concluded a registered partnership under German law may opt for this regime.[302] The Agreement, that is open to other EU Member States,[303] was received as revolutionary and of 'European significance', because it was the first step in the direction of harmonisation of substantive family law in Europe.[304]

298 See www.dipbt.bundestag.de/extrakt/ba/WP17/517/51735.html, visited 18 April 2012.

299 G. Bohsem, 'Union verweigert volle Gleichstellung der Homo-Ehe', *Süddeutsche.de* 4 June 2014.

300 'Deutschlands Zukunft Gestalten, Koalitionsvertrag Zwischen CDU, CSU UND SPD' ['Giving shape to Germany's future. Coalition Agreement between CDU, CSU UND SPD'], 18th legislative period, online availabe at www.cdu.de/koalitionsvertrag, visited 2 February 2014.

301 Deutsch-französische Güterstand der Wahl-Zugewinngemeinschaft [Franco-German Agreement on the Optional Matrimonial Property Regime], adopted in January 2010. The Agreement and its implementation Act entered into force on 1 May 2013. See *BGBl.* 2013 II, 431 and *BGBl.* 2012 II, 178.

302 Art. 7 LPartG in combination with Art. 1519 German Civil Code. See T. Jäger, 'Der neue deutsch-französische Güterstand der Wahl-Zugewinngemeinschaft – Inhalt und seine ersten Folgen für die Gesetzgebung und Beratungspraxis' ['The new Franco-German Agreement on the Optional Matrimonial Property Regime – Content and ist first consequences for the legislative process and consulting practice'], *DNotZ* (2010) p. 804 at p. 822.

303 Art. 21 of the Franco-German Agreement, *supra* n. 301.

304 European Parliament, Directorate-General for Internal Policies Policy Department C: Citizens' Rights And Constitutional Affairs Legal And Parliamentary Affairs, 'The Franco-German agreement on an elective 'community of accrued gains'matrimonial property regime', Note PE 425.658. See also A. Fötschl, 'The COMPR of Germany and France: Epoch-Making in the Unification of Law', 18 *European Review of Private Law* (2010) p. 881.

10.4.1. Cross-border movement; some statistics

There are only limited statistics available in respect of Germany that are relevant for the present case study. According to the data provided by the German Federal Statistical Office, 32,000 civil partnerships had been concluded in Germany by the year 2012, while in total 72,000 same-sex couples were living together in a shared household.[305] The statistics did not provide for information about the nationality or country of residence of the civil partners. However, it was also clear that in that same year more than 7 million non-German citizens were living in Germany.[306] How many of them had concluded a civil partnership in Germany, or had yet entered into a registered partnership or marriage with a same-sex partner in a foreign country, can only be guessed. The case law below on cross-border cases shows that, in any case also, cross-border movement to from and Germany by same-sex couples and their families has taken and is taking place.

10.4.2. (Development of) the relevant German conflict-of-laws rules

As noted in Chapter 4,[307] German Private International Law is laid down in the Second Chapter of the Introductory Act to the Civil Code (*Einführungsgesetz zum Bürgerlichen Gesetzbuche*, EGBGB).[308] The Third Section of this Chapter sees at Family Law. Articles 13 to 17 EGBGB determine the applicable law on marriage and related issues. Guiding principles thereby are the nationality or citizenship ('*Staatsangehörigkeit*') and the habitual residence ('*domicile*') of the (future) spouses.[309]

The introduction of same-sex civil partnerships in other European states and in particular the opening up of marriage to same-sex couples in the Netherlands in 2001,[310] raised the question as to if, and if so, how, such partnerships and marriages were to be recognised. Until the entry into force of the Civil Partnerships Act in 2001, German law itself did not provide for any form of registered partnership for same-sex couples.[311] At the time, the prevailing view in legal scholarship was that a marriage between two persons of the same sex conflicted with the German

305 Statistisches Bundesamt, *Statistisches Jahrbuch 2013*, p. 56, online available at: www.destatis.de/DE/Publikationen/StatistischesJahrbuch/Bevoelkerung.pdf;jsessionid=A0654F39FB762DD168CF40CCABC19328.cae3?__blob=publicationFile, visited 2 February 2014.

306 *Idem*, p. 40.

307 Ch. 4, section 4.5.3.

308 Einführungsgesetz zum Bürgerlichen Gesetzbuche, EGBGB [Introductory Act to the Civil Code], promulgated on 21 September 1994, *BGBl. I* p. 2494.

309 Translation taken from www.gesetze-im-internet.de/englisch_bgbeg/index.html, visited June 2014.

310 See ch. 12, section 12.3.5.

311 Röthel therefore at the time pleaded for recognition of foreign same-sex partnerships under the marriage regime of Art. 13ff EGBGB. A. Röthel, 'Registrierte Partnerschaften im internationalen Privatrecht' ['Civil partnerships in international private law'], *IPRax* (2000) p. 74.

public order (Article 6 EGBGB)[312] and therefore had to be refused recognition under German law.[313]

The Civil Partnerships Act of 2001 provided for the incorporation of a new Article on registered partnerships in the Introductory Act to the Civil Code.[314] This new Article, now Article 17b EGBGB,[315] promised to put an end to the debate in German legal scholarship as to which German Private International Law regime was to be applied to foreign same-sex partnerships and marriages.[316] While it may have tentatively done so, soon new debates were evoked, as will become clear from the subsections below.

Foreign judgments in family matters are in principle recognised under German law,[317] unless such recognition is considered manifestly incompatible with fundamental principles of German law, in particular when it is incompatible with fundamental rights.[318]

10.4.3. Access to registered partnership for foreign same-sex couples

The German Civil Partnerships Act contains no requirements in respect of nationality or habitual residence of the future registered partners. In fact, Article 17b (1) EGBGB provides that '[t]he formation of a registered life partnership, its general effects and property regime, as well as its dissolution are governed by the substantive provisions of the country in which the life partnership is registered.'[319] This also

312 Art. 6 EGBGB provides that '[a] provision of the law of another country shall not be applied where its application would lead to a result which is manifestly incompatible with the fundamental principles of German law.' The Article adds to this that inapplicability ensues, in particular, if the application of foreign law 'would be incompatible with civil rights.'

313 See A. Röthel 2000, *supra* n. 311, at p. 78.

314 Art. 3 (25) LPartG.

315 Originally this Article was numbered Art. 17a EGBGB (Act of 16 February 2001, *BGBl. I* p. 266, entry into force 1 August 2001). This changed to Art. 17b EGBGB by Act of 11 December 2001, *BGBl. I* p. 3513, entry into force 1 January 2002.

316 See for example Röthel 2000, *supra* n. 311, at pp. 74–79, who pleaded for recognition of such foreign partnerships under the marriage regime of Art. 13ff EGBGB.

317 Art. 108 Gesetz über das Verfahren in Familiensachen und in den Angelegenheiten der freiwilligen Gerichtsbarkeit (FamFG) [Act on the Procedure in Family Matters and in Matters of Non-contentious Jurisdiction], Act of 7 December 2008, *BGBl. I* p. 2586.

318 Art. 109(4) FamFG.

319 The English translation of the first para. of Art. 17b reads: 'The formation of a registered life partnership, its general effects and property regime, as well as its dissolution are governed by the substantive provisions of the country in which the life partnership is registered. Matters related to maintenance and succession shall be governed by the law designated as applicable by the general rules; if under these rules, the life partnership fails to qualify for statutory rights to maintenance or succession, the first sentence of this Article shall apply mutatis mutandis. The balancing of future pensions is governed by the law applicable under sentence 1; it shall only be carried out if accordingly German law is applicable and if the law of one of the countries, whose nationals the life partners are at the time when the application for termination of the life partnership is filed, recognizes a balancing of future pensions of life partners. Otherwise, it shall be carried out pursuant to German law on application of a life partner if the other life partner has acquired during the subsistence of the life partnership an

goes for the balancing of future pensions (the so-called '*Versorgungsausgleich*').[320] Matters related to maintenance and succession on the other hand, are governed by 'the law designated as applicable by the general rules'.[321] Certain areas, including parental issues ('*Kindschaftsrecht*'), are not covered by Article 17b EGBGB;[322] here, the general conflict-of-laws rules of Articles 19–22 EGBGB apply.[323]

The fact that Article 17b EGBGB makes the law of the country of registration (and not the nationality or the habitual residence (domicile)) decisive in determining the applicable law, was new in German Private International Law[324] and unique in its inclusiveness when compared to the Private International Law regimes of other European states.[325] By making the law of the country of registration decisive in the determination of the applicable law, the German legislature deliberately enabled foreigners to enter into a registered civil partnership in Germany, even if that was not possible under the law of their state of nationality.[326] Moreover, the third paragraph of this Article enables couples who entered into a civil partnership abroad to re-register their partnership under the German civil partnership regime.[327] This also deviates from general international practice: more commonly previous registration abroad forms an obstacle to such re-registration.[328]

---

inland future pension right insofar as carrying it out would not be inconsistent with equity in light of the economic circumstances of both sides also during the time which was not spent within the country.' Translation taken from: www.gesetze-im-internet.de/englisch_bgbeg/englisch_bgbeg.html#p0099, visited June 2014.

320 There is considerable German case law on the balancing of future pensions in cross-border situations. This is not discussed in detail in this chapter. Refence is made to, *inter alia*, AG Stadtroda 3 April 2012, Az. 2 F 151/11 and BGH 16 October 2013 (dec.), Az. XII ZB 176/12, *NJW* 2014 p. 61.

321 Art. 17b (1)(2) EGBGB.

322 Apart from parental issues, also rent law is excluded. Coester claimed in this regard that the German legislature obviously did not consider parental issues relevant for same-sex couples. M. Coester, 'Art. 17b EGBGB Eingetragene Lebenspartnerschaft' ['Art. 17b EGBGB Civil Partnership'], in: F. Jürgen Säcker and R. Rixecker (eds.), *Münchener Kommentar zum BGB* [Münchener Commentary to the BGB], 5th edn. (München, Verlag C.H. Beck 2010) Rn. 76.

323 See Coester 2010, *supra* n. 322, Rn. 73 and V. Gärtner, 'Art. 17b EGBGB, Eingetragene Lebenspartnerschaft' ['Art. 17b EGBGB, civil partnership'], in: M. Herberger et al., *Juris Praxiskommentar BGB* [Juris Commentary on the BGB for legal practitioners], 7th edn. (Saarbrücken, juris GmbH 2014) Rn. 54–58.

324 A. Röthel, 'Art. 17b EGBGB', in: M. Würdinger, *Juris Praxiskommentar BGB, Band 6 – Internationales Privatrecht* [Juris Commentary on the BGB, Volume 6 – International Private Law], 5th edn. (Saarbrücken, juris GmbH 2010).

325 Coester 2010, *supra n.* 322, Rn. 9.

326 *BT-Drs.* 14/3751 p. 60 and *BT-Drs.* 17/8248, p. 3. See, *inter alia*, R. Süß, 'Notarieller Gestaltungsbedarf bei Eingetragenen Lebenspartnerschaften mit Ausländern' ['The need for notary guidance in civil partnerships with foreign partners'], *DNotZ* (2001) p. 168 at p. 169.

327 Art. 17b (3) provides that if a civil partnership between the same persons is registered in different countries, '[…] its effects shall, from the time of its registration on, be determined on the basis of the last life partnership entered into'.

328 Coester 2010, *supra n.* 322, Rn. 18. Coester observed in 2013 that the clause was becoming increasingly more redundant, because European Union law increasingly more covered the relevant areas, such as maintance and inheritance. M. Coester, 'Art. 17b EGBGB unter dem Einfluss des Europäischen Kollisionsrechts' ['Art. 17b EGBGB under the influence of European conflict-of-laws rules'], 22 *IPRax* (2013) pp. 114- 122 at p. 121.

The fact that the legislature thus accepted or even encouraged 'registration tourism',[329] received only limited criticism in legal scholarship.[330] As Coester explains, both the registration criterion and the possibility of re-registration fitted in with the central aim of the Civil Partnerships Act, which was the abolition of discrimination on grounds of sexual orientation. The German aspirations in this respect where clearly not limited to its own citizens and residents; the legislature explicitly permitted couples from foreign countries with no or with weaker same-sex partnership regimes to enter into the stronger German civil partnership.[331] There are, however, no statistics available on whether, and if so, the extent to which, this option was indeed also taken up by foreign couples (see 10.4.1 above). In other words, the scope of any possible 'registration tourism' is unknown.

10.4.4. Implementation of Directives 2004/38 and 2003/86 in German law

Regulation (EEC) 1612/68 was implemented in German law by means of the Residence Act of (*Aufenthaltsgesetz/EWG*) of 1969.[332] Its Article 7 provided for rights of entry and residence for the family members of workers. Family members were defined in line with the Regulation as the worker's spouse and their children who were under 21 years old or were dependants, as well dependent relatives in the ascending line of the worker and his spouse. The Aliens Act 1990[333] provided for rules in respect of family reunification, both to German nationals, as well as to foreigners legally resident in Germany. Spouses, children and dependent family members of foreigners with a residency permit, and those of Germans, could qualify for such family reunification.[334] The Act also provided for a hardship clause for other family members.[335] By way of the 2001 Civil Partnerships Act the group of qualifying family members for family reunification under the Aliens Act was extended to civil partners.[336] No provision was made at the time for any amendment

---

329 Röthel 2010, *supra* n. 324, Rn. 18, referring, *inter alia*, to D. Henrich, 'Kollisionsrechtliche Fragen der eingetragenen Lebenspartnerschaft' ['Conflict-of-laws questions on Civil Partnership'], *Zeitschrift für das gesamte Familienrecht, FamRZ* (2002) p. 137.

330 Röthel refers to T. Rauscher, *Internationales Privatrecht*, 3rd edn. 2009, p. 196.

331 Coester 2010, *supra* n. 322, Rn. 12 and 17–18. See also B. Heiderhoff, 'BeckOK EGBGB Art. 17b' ['Beck Online Commentary Art. 17b EGBGB'], in: H.G. Bamberger and H. Roth (eds.), *Beck'scher Online-Kommentar BGB* [Beck Online commentary to the BGB], 32nd edn. (München, Verlag C.H. Beck 2014) Rn. 2. Coester has observed that this fitted in with the general trend of 'materialisation' of Private international law. The author has explained that Art. 17(3) furthermore aimed to provide clarity and legal certainty as well as to provide a choice of law to registered partners. Coester 2013, *supra* n. 328, at pp. 115–116.

332 Gesetz über Einreise und Aufenthalt von Staatsangehörigen der Mitgliedstaaten der Europäischen Wirtschaftsgemeinschaft (AufenthG/EWG) [Act on the entry and residence of nationals of EC Member States], Act of 22 July 1969, *BGBl. I* p. 927, Revised by Act of 31 January 1980, *BGBl. I* p, 116, as well as by by the Ausländergesetz [Aliens Act], Act of 9 July 1990, *BGBl. I* p. 1354 at p. 1356 ff.

333 Gesetz über die Einreise und den Aufenthalt von Ausländern im Bundesgebiet (Ausländergesetz) [Act on the entry and residence of aliens in the Federal State (Aliens Act)], Act of 9 July 1990, *BGBl. I* p. 1354, at p. 1356.

334 Arts. 17 to 23 of the Aliens Act 1990 (*no longer in force*).

335 Art. 22 of the Aliens Act 1990 (*no longer in force*).

336 Art. 3 (11)(1) LPartG, inserting a new Art. 27a in the Ausländergesetz [Aliens Act].

to the Residence Act to provide for civil partners of workers within the meaning of Regulation 1612/68.

In September 2004 the Administrative Court of Karlsruhe delivered a judgment in a case in which a Chinese man who was married to a Dutchman appealed against the refusal of the German authorities to grant him an EU residence permit for spouses of EU citizens (at the time called a '*Aufenthaltserlaubnis-EG*') on the basis of Article 7 Aufenthaltsgesetz/EWG.[337] The Chinese citizen and his same-sex Dutch partner had married in the Netherlands in 2001. The Dutchman was employed in Germany and he therefore had a residence permit as a worker. His spouse had lived and studied in Germany since 1986 and had on that ground been repeatedly granted a student residence permit for a period of two years. Soon after the marriage, the student residence permit was going to expire, and the Chinese husband had submitted an application for the issuing of an EU residence permit for spouses of EU workers for a period of five years. The German authorities refused to issue such a permit, as recognition of the Dutch same-sex marriage as marriage for this purpose was held to conflict with German public order (Article 6 EGBGB).[338] The Chinese man could accordingly not be considered a 'spouse' within the meaning of Article 10(1)(a) Directive 1612/68 EEC.[339] The marriage of the couple was nevertheless recognised as a registered civil partnership. On that basis the Chinese man was granted a residence permit for a duration of two years.[340] The Chinese man appealed to the Administrative Court of Karlsruhe, which confirmed that a marriage between same-sex partners concluded under Dutch law was not a lawful German marriage. From CJEU case law it followed that 'spouse' within the meaning of the relevant Article 10(1)(a) of Directive 1612/68, related to traditional different-sex marriages only. This interpretation was confirmed by the newly enacted Directive 2004/38/EC which had not yet been transposed into German law, as well as by Article 9 of the – at the time non-binding – EU Charter of Fundamental Rights. Under reference to the CJEU judgment in the *Reed* case[341] the Court of Karlsruhe concluded that only a general, Europe-wide societal change could justify the extension of the term 'spouse' to include same-sex partners. In the Court's opinion the sole fact that the Netherlands and Belgium had opened up marriage to same-sex couples could not be regarded as such a societal change. Accordingly, the German court upheld the refusal to issue the five-year residence permit for spouses of EU citizens.

---

337 VG Karlsruhe 9 September 2004, Az. 2 K 1420/03, *IPrax* (2006) p. 284. See also A. Röthel, 'Anerkennung gleichgeschlechtlicher Ehen nach deutschem und europäischem Recht' ['Recognition of same-sex marriage under German and European law'], *IPrax* (2006) p. 250 and R. Koolhoven, 'Het Nederlandse opengestelde huwelijk in het Duitse IPR. De eerste rechterlijke uitspraak is daar!' ['The Dutch opened up marriage in German Private international law. The first court judgment has been issued!'], *NIPR* (2005) p. 138. The subsequent appeal lodged with the BVerwG in this case (Az. 1 C 26.04) was repealed.

338 See ch. 4, section 4.5.3.

339 Art. 7(1) AufenthG/EWG, as applicable at the time, was based on Art. 10 (1a) Directive 1612/68. The Act was lifted as of 1 January 2005, and replaced by the Gesetz über die allgemeine Freizügigkeit von Unionsbürgern (Freizügigkeitsgesetz/EU – FreizügG/EU) [Act on the Free movement of EU-citizens (Free movement Act EU)], Act of 30 April 2004, *BGBl. I*, p. 1950.

340 Art. 27a in combination with Art. 18 I No. 1 AuslG and Art. 15 AufenthG/EWG.

341 Case 59/85 *Netherlands* v. *Reed* [1986] ECR 1283, ECLI:EU:C:1986:157. See ch. 9, section 9.6.1.

The subsequent Free Movement Directive (2004/38), as well as the EU Family Reunification Directive (2003/86) were implemented in German law by means of the Immigration Act ('*Zuwanderungsgesetz*') that entered into force on 1 January 2005.[342] This Act contained both the Residence Act (AufenthG)[343] and the Free Movement Act (FreizügG/EU),[344] as well as amendments to several other acts.

The Free Movement Act of 2004 provided that spouses of EU citizens, being family members within the meaning of the Directive, had a right to entry and residence. It was not clarified in this Act, however, whether this included same-sex spouses. As explained in more detail below (sections 10.4.5 and 10.4.6) later case law has confirmed the above discussed ruling of the Karslruhe Administrative Court holding that same-sex spouses of EU citizens are not recognised as 'spouses' and thus not as 'family members' within the meaning of the Free Movement Act.[345] They have nonetheless been granted entry and residence rights, because – as explained more elaborately below[346] – spouses have been, and still are, recognised as civil partners ('*Lebenspartners*') under German law. The latter group was, as noted above, not included in the definition of 'family member' under the relevant Article 3(2) of the Free Movement Act.[347] Instead, in respect of the entry and residence of civil partners of EU citizens, who did not have a free movement right of their own, those provisions of the Residence Act (AufenthG) that applied to civil partners ('*Lebenspartners*') of German nationals, applied in these cases.[348] As illustrated by the ruling of the Administrative Court of Karlsruhe discussed above, this meant that the residency permits issued to civil partners could be shorter in duration than those of spouses who were granted derived rights under the Free Movement Act.

Some authors wondered whether the relevant provisions of the Free Movement Act were in conformity with Article 2(2) of the Free Movement Directive, which provides that registered partners are recognised as 'family members' if the legislation of

---

342 Gesetz zur Steuerung und Begrenzung der Zuwanderung und zur Regelung des Aufenthalts und der Integration von Unionsbürgern und Ausländern (Zuwanderungsgesetz) [Act on the regulation and limitation of immigration and regulating the residence and integration of EU-citizens and aliens (Immigration Act)], Act of 30 July 2004, *BGBl. I* p. 1950. This Act revoked the Aufenthaltsgesetz/EWG.

343 Gesetz über den Aufenthalt, die Erwerbstätigkeit und die Integration von Ausländern im Bundesgebiet (Aufenthaltgesetz, AufenthG) [Act on the residence, access to the labour market and integration of aliens in the Federal State (Residence Act)], Act of 30 April 2004, *BGBl. I*, p. 1950.

344 Gesetz über die allgemeine Freizügigkeit von Unionsbürgern (Freizügigkeitsgesetz/EU – FreizügG/EU) [Act on the Free movement of EU-citizens (Free movement Act EU)], Act of 30 April 2004, *BGBl. I*, p. 1950.

345 In 2008, in a case concerning a Brazilian national who had concluded a marriage under Spanish law with a same-sex Spanish national, the Administrative Court of Darmstadt left open the question of whether the Brazilian national was entitled to free movement as the spouse or as the civil partner of an EU citizen. VG Darmstadt 5 June 2008 (dec.), Az. 5 L 277/08.

346 See section 10.4.6.

347 This Art. 3(2) FreizügG/EU only concerned spouses, the direct descendants who were under the age of 21 or were dependants and those of the spouse, as well as at the dependent direct relatives in the ascending line and those of the spouse.

348 Art. 3(6) FreizügG/EU.

the host Member State treats registered partnerships as equivalent to marriage.[349] Particularly as civil partnership and marriage were increasingly more equalised under German law, it was claimed that same-sex registered partners of EU citizens[350] had to be granted entry and residence as family members under the Free Movement Directive.[351] In 2013, the legislature indeed amended the Free Movement Act, so as to provide expressly that in respect of entry and residence, civil partners and spouses were treated equally under this Act.[352] This also implied that same-sex spouses of migrating EU citizens, who were, and are, recognised as civil partners under the Free Movement Act, were from then on effectively treated equally with different-sex spouses in respect of entry and residence.

The Residence Act (AufenthG) of 2005 contains rules in respect of family reunification, including for third-country nationals. The relevant Articles 27 to 31 of the Act provide family reunification rights for spouses, as well as for minor relatives in the direct descending line, and for carers of these children. It has not been made explicit in the Act whether the term 'spouses' includes same-sex spouses. Generally, however, same-sex spouses have instead been recognised as civil partners ('*Lebenspartners*') under German law, as noted above and explained more elaborately below. In respect of family reunification that does not make any difference, since Article 27(2) of the Residence Act provides that the rules regarding family reunification also apply to partners in a 'partnership-like relationship' ('*lebenspartnerschaftlichen Gemeinschaft*'). It has been held that this category concerns same-sex partners only, as the term would refer to civil partners within the meaning of the German Civil Partnership Act (see more elaborately below).[353] In any case, it follows from this Article 27(2) that both same-sex spouses and same-sex registered partners of third-country nationals may qualify for family reunification on an equal footing with different-sex spouses.

The following subsections explain how foreign same-sex marriages and registered partnerships are recognised under German Private International Law. As will become clear, marriages between partners of the same sex are recognised under German law as civil partnerships, not as marriages. The question has come before a German Court whether such 'downgrading' is commensurable with EU free movement law. This matter is discussed in subsection 10.4.7.

---

349 H. Hoffmann, 'FreizügG/EU § 3' ['§ 3 FreizügG/EU'], in R. Hofmann and H. Hoffmann, *Ausländerrecht* [Aliens law], 1st edn. (Baden-Baden, Nomos 2008)Rn. 19; H. Tewocht, 'Die Neuregelung des Freizügigkeitsgesetzes/EU' ['The new regulation of the EU freedom of movement Act'], *ZAR* (2013) p. 221 at p. 225. See also G. Brinkmann, 'Zehn Jahre Freizügigkeitsgesetz' ['Ten years Free Movement Act'], *ZAR* (2014) p. 213 at p. 217.

350 As explained in section 10.4.5 below, under German law only same-sex partners may be recognised as registered partners within the meaning of the Civil Partnerships Act.

351 Tewocht 2013, *supra* n. 349, at p. 225.

352 *Gesetz zur Anderung des Freizugigkeitsgesetzes/EU* [Act amending the Free Movement EU Act], Act of 21 January 2013, *BGBl. I* p. 86, entry into force on 29 January 2013.

353 R. Göbel-Zimmermann, 'Gleichgeschlechtliche Lebenspartnerschaften (§ 27 Abs 2)' ['Same-sex civil partnerships (§ 27 para. 2)'], in: B. Huber, *Aufenthaltsgesetz* [Residence Act], 1st edn. (München, Verlag C.H. Beck 2010) Rn. 45.

10.4.5. Recognition of foreign same-sex registered partnerships under German law

As noted above, Article 17b EGBGB provides for conflict-of-laws rules in respect of registered partnerships. The German civil partnership sets the standard for the functional qualification of partnerships registered abroad. Constitutive for this qualification is the formal establishment of a relationship in a foreign country, resulting in a certain civil status with legal effects.[354] Whether it is required that both partners are of the same sex is a controversial matter. While some answer this question in the negative,[355] other scholars have held this to be a constitutive element for the German civil partnership.[356]

The fourth paragraph of Article 17b limits the effects of civil partnerships registered abroad. This so-called '*Sperrklausel*' or '*Kappungsgrenze*'[357] reads:

> 'The effects of a life partnerships registered abroad shall not exceed those arising under the provisions of the German Civil Code and the Registered Partnerships Act.'[358]

Article 17b (4) is considered to be a *lex specialis* of the general public order clause of Article 6 EGBGB (see Chapter 4, section 4.5.3).[359] It limits the effects of more advanced civil partnership regimes to those of the German civil partnership. The effects of more limited foreign partnership regimes are however not lifted to the German standard.[360] Effectively, in all situations the 'weakest' regime is applied.[361]

While most scholars agree that the clause should be broadly interpreted,[362] it is unclear what the term 'effects' covers exactly[363] and when such effects can be considered to 'exceed' those of the German civil partnership.[364] There is wide agreement that

---

354 Coester 2010, *supra* n. 322, Rn. 10.

355 *Idem*, Rn. 11 and Heiderhoff 2014B, *supra* n. 331, Rn. 13–14.

356 Röthel 2010, *supra* n. 324, Rn. 6.

357 *Idem*, Rn. 2.

358 Translation of the Introductory Act to the Civil Code (in the version promulgated on 21 September 1994, *BGBl. I* p. 2494, last amended by law of 25 June 2009, *BGBl. I* p. 1574) provided by Dr. Juliana Mörsdorf-Schulte LL.M. (Univ. of California, Berkeley), online available at: www.gesetze-im-internet.de/englisch_bgbeg/englisch_bgbeg.html, visited June 2014.

359 Art. 17b (4) EGBGB is perceived as not to rule out application of Art. 6 EGBGB entirely; the general public order clause forms the fall-back option. Forkert 2003, *supra* n. 42, at p. 296; Röthel 2010, *supra* n. 324, Rn. 50 and 55; P. Kiel, `Hk-LpartR' ['Hk-LpartR'], in: M. Bruns and R. Kemper, *Lebenspartnerschaftsrecht, Handkommentar* [Civil Partnership Commentary], 2nd edn. (Baden-Baden, Nomos Verlagsgesellschaft 2006) at pp. 427–428.

360 As noted above, partners instead have the option of re-registering their partnership under the German law (Art. 17b (3)). See Coester 2010, *supra* n. 322, Rn. 84 and Röthel 2010, *supra* n. 324, Rn. 50.

361 Kiel 2006, *supra* n. 359, at p. 427.

362 M. Gebauer and A. Staudinger, 'Registrierte Lebenspartnerschaften und die Kappungsregel des Art. 17b Abs. 4 EGBGB' ['Civil partnerships and the limitation clause of Art. 17b para. 4 EGBGB'], *IPRax* (2002) p. 275 at p. 276 and Coester 2010, *supra* n. 322, Rn. 10.

363 *Inter alia*, Gebauer and Staudinger 2002, *supra* n. 362, at p. 276; Forkert 2003, *supra* n. 42, at p. 297 and Kiel 2006, *supra* n. 359, at p. 427.

364 Wagner 2001, *supra* n. 358, as referred to by Coester 2010, *supra* n. 322, Rn. 87. Coester has furthermore pointed out that since Art 17(4) EGBG was introduced, increasingly more matters have been regulated

effects in respect of parental rights, in any case fall under the '*Kappungsgrenze*', as these are expressly excluded from the scope of Article 17b (1) EGBGB.[365]

Legal scholarship has furthermore been divided over the question of whether a tie with Germany is required for the application of Article 17b (4). In other words, it is debated whether Article 17b (4) contains a so-called '*Inlandsbezug*', as is the case in respect of the general public order clause of Article 6 EGBGB. Strictly following its wording, Article 17b (4) seems to apply even in cases where the partners have no (strong) ties with Germany.[366] Many scholars have therefore held the existence or the intensity of such ties not to be required or relevant for the application this provision.[367] Others are critical,[368] while some even argue that the '*Inlandsbezug*' is an implied constitutive element of Article 17b (4).[369]

From the moment of its introduction, the '*Kappungsgrenze*' of Article 17b (4) received considerable criticism in legal scholarship.[370] A fundamental line of criticism concerns the aims pursued by the legislature with the provision.[371] The Explanatory Memorandum to the Article explained that this provision was intended as a compromise between the protection of the good faith of interested parties ('*Vertrauensschutz für die Beteiligten*') on the one hand and legal certainty and the guarantee and facilitation of national judicial matters ('*Sicherheit und Leichtigkeit des Rechtsverkehrs im Inland*') on the other.[372] In legal scholarship, it has been questioned whether this aim was indeed achieved with this clause.[373] A general consensus consists that the fourth paragraph was additionally – or perhaps even primarily – inspired by the legislature's wish to give material protection to the institution of marriage,[374] as well as by the national legal discussion about the constitutionality of the Civil Partnerships Act.[375] The clause was held to implement the requirement of distance ('*Abstandsgebot*'), which the legislature at that time considered to be required by

by EU law, such as maintenance and inheritance, as a result of which these effects no longer fall under this 'Kappungsgrenze'. Coester 2013, *supra* n. 328, at p. 121.

365 Forkert 2003, *supra* n. 42, at p. 301; Röthel 2010, *supra* n. 324, Rn. 52. See also Coester 2013, *supra* n. 328, at p. 121.

366 Kiel 2006, *supra* n. 359, at p. 427.

367 Wagner 2001, *supra* n. 358, at p. 292; Süß 2001 *supra* n. 326, at p. 171; Röthel 2010, *supra* n. 324, Rn. 53, P. Mankowski, *J. von Staudingers Kommentar zum Bürgerlichen Gesetzbuch mit Einführungsgesetz und Nebengestezen* [J. von Staudinger's Commentary to the Civil Code, with the Introductory Act and anciliary acts] (Sellier, Berlin 2011) p. 863, Rn. 86.

368 Gebauer and Staudinger 2002, *supra* n. 362, pp. 280–281.

369 Coester 2010, *supra* n. 322, Rn. 96. The author holds that the aims of 'guaranty and facilitation of national judicial matters' and the special protection of marriage can only be pursued in cases with a clear link with the German jurisdiction (see below).

370 Kiel 2006, *supra* n. 359, at p. 427. For an example of such criticism see D. Jakob, *Die eingetragene Lebenspartnerschaft im internationalen Privatrecht* [Civil partnership in International Private Law] (Köln, Schmidt 2002) p. 183 ff and 232 ff.

371 E.g. Süß 2001, *supra* n. 326.

372 *BT-Drs.* 14/3751, p. 61.

373 *Inter alia* Kiel 2006, *supra* n. 359, at pp. 427–428.

374 Coester 2010, *supra* n. 322, Rn. 87.

375 *Idem*, Rn. 84.

Article 6(1) Basic Law.[376] The tenability of this aim became, however, questionable[377] after the BVerfG had ruled in 2002 that from this Article no such *'Abstandsgebot'* followed (see also 10.3.3 above).[378] In search for an alternative legitimate aim that could justify the maintenance in force of Article 17b (4) EGBGB after the 2002 BVerfG judgment, Coester observed that this judgment could be interpreted such that from Article 6(1) Basic Law a prohibition of disfavouring of marriage *vis-à-vis* civil partnership followed. If the special protection of marriage was interpreted in that manner, the author considered, the function of the fourth paragraph would be to ensure that foreign law concerning same-sex partnerships did not negatively affect the legal position of spouses in Germany.[379] Kiel thought the legislature had primarily aimed to ward off foreign regulations concerning the effects of same-sex partnerships in respect of parental rights.[380] The author maintained, however, that parental rights established under foreign law could not be undone by Article 17b (4). Nevertheless, the clause prevents that partners who entered into a civil partnership under the law of a foreign country, can in respect of their parental rights rely on that foreign partnership regime in Germany.

Various scholars further have questioned why the legislature felt the need to create a special reservation clause (*'Vorbehaltsklausel'*), instead of trusting the general public order clause of Article 6 EGBGB to be sufficient to deal with 'dubious' foreign institutions.[381] Also the criticism was issued that the *'Kappungsgrenze'* scaled down or even contradicted the openness towards foreign law of the registration criterion of the first paragraph of Article 17 EGBGB.[382] The *'Kappungsgrenze'* was furthermore held to be difficult to reconcile with the EU law principle of mutual recognition, to the extent that this could be held to apply in cross-border family law matters.[383] Coester observed that the combination of paragraphs 3 and 4 of Article 17b EGBGB showed the – what he called the – 'questionable' and 'disproportional' tendency of the German legislature to impose the German civil partnership model at the

376 *Idem*, Rn. 85. See also Gebauer and Staudinger 2002, *supra* n. 362, at p. 282; Henrich 2002, *supra* n. 329, at p. 144), Süß 2001, *supra* n. 326, at p. 172 and K. Thorn, 'Entwicklungen des Internationalen Privatrechts 2000–2001' ['Developments in International Private Law 2000–2001'], *IPRax* (2002) p. 349 at p. 355.

377 Röthel 2010, *supra* n. 324, Rn. 51.

378 BVerfG 17 July 2002, Az. 1 BvF 1/01, *NJW* 2002 p. 2543.

379 Coester 2010, *supra n.* 322, Rn. 87.

380 Kiel 2006, *supra* n. 359, at p. 428.

381 Coester 2010, *supra* n. 322, Rn. 84 and A. Röthel, jurisPK-BGB, Article 17b EGBGB, 5th edn. 2010, Rn. 51.

382 Jakob 2002, *supra* n. 370, at p. 183ff; Coester 2010, *supra* n. 322, Rn. 84 and 88; Röthel 2010, *supra* n. 324, Rn. 50 and B. Heiderhoff, 'BeckOK EGBGB Art. 17b' ['Beck Online Commentary Art. 17b EGBGB'], in: H.G. Bamberger and H. Roth (eds.), *Beck'scher Online-Kommentar BGB* [Beck Online commentary to the BGB], 19th edn. (München, Verlag C.H. Beck 2011) Rn. 45.

383 Coester 2010, *supra* n. 322, Rn. 88. See also R. Baratta, 'Problematic elements of an implicit rule providing for mutual recognition of personal and family status in the EC', *IPRax (*2007) pp. 4–7.

international level as far as possible.[384] Gebauer and Staudinger argued that the rule led to contradictory values ('*Wertungswidersprüchen*') and to discrimination.[385]

With a view to all these points of criticism it has been suggested in legal scholarship from the moment of its introduction that Article 17b (4) EGBGB had to be abolished.[386] The ongoing process of equalisation of the German registered civil partnership with marriage, provided even more ground for such appeals.[387] By way of alternative, a case has been made for a reasonable teleological interpretation and application of the clause.[388] By the time this research was concluded, however, i.e., by 31 July 2014, the provision was still in force, and being applied by the German courts.

10.4.6. Recognition of foreign same-sex marriages under German law

As explained above, the opening up of marriage to same-sex couples in other European states, starting with the Netherlands in 2001, raised the question as to which German Private International Law regime had to be applied to these marriages: Articles 13–17 EGBGB concerning marriage, or Article 17b EGBGB concerning civil partnerships?

German legal scholarship was divided on the matter. Firstly there were legal scholars who argued that a same-sex marriage registered abroad between two spouses of the nationality of a country in which such a marriage was provided for, had to be qualified and recognised as a marriage within the meaning of Article 13ff EGBGB under German law.[389] They mostly stressed that habitual residence (domicile) and nationality were the criteria on the basis of which the applicable law was to be determined. In their view there only would be an obstacle to recognition of a foreign same-sex marriage as marriage if one of the spouses was a national from a country which law did not provide for a same-sex marriage – as was the case if one of the spouses was German. Such an obstacle to marriage would result in the nullity of the marriage (a so-called '*Nichtehe*',[390] a void marriage). Others opined that since the entry into force of the German Civil Partnerships Act, when the German legislature expressly awarded legal recognition and protection to formal partnerships between

384 Institutions with less far-reaching legal effects than the German registered civil partnership can be lifted to the German level through re-registration (Art. 17b (3) EGBGB). At the same time more advanced institutions are levelled down to the German standard (Art. 17b (4) EGBGB), in order to maintain the difference between marriage and partnership also at the international level. Coester 2010, *supra* n. 322, Rn. 18. See also Röthel 2010, *supra* n. 324, Rn. 50.

385 Gebauer and Staudinger 2002, *supra* n. 362, at p. 276.

386 *Idem*, at pp. 275–282.

387 Coester 2010, *supra* n. 322, Rn. 88.

388 *Idem*, Rn. 88 ff. See also Kiel 2006, *supra* n. 359, at p. 428.

389 *Inter alia* Kiel 2006, *supra* n. 359, at pp. 427–428. See also a 2006 Bill of the Greens (*BT-Dr* 16/3423), which proposed to recognise foreign same-sex marriages as marriage, instead of a registered civil partnerships. For a critical note to this proposal, see Muscheler 2010, *supra* n. 169, at p. 227.

390 For marriage, a relevant factor is the nationality of the spouses. So if a German national is involved, a same-sex marriage is for certain a '*Nichtehe*' (void marriage). It can only be recognised as a registered civil partnership. Compare VG Berlin 15 June 2010, 23 A 242/08.

two persons of the same sex, it could no longer be maintained that a same-sex marriage was manifestly incompatible with the fundamental principles of German law. These authors therefore argued that a foreign same-sex marriage could no longer be refused recognition on the basis of public order arguments.[391] They contended that the mere fact that the foreign legislature had moved further forward in the process of equal treatment of same-sex couples and different-sex couples than the German legislature had, could not form a justification for the warding off of foreign law.[392]

Yet other scholars opined that a foreign same-sex marriage could be registered in Germany as a civil partnership only.[393] This view has been confirmed by case law. The first relevant case dates from June 2002, when the Financial Court of Niedersaksen ruled that a marriage between two Dutch women, concluded in conformity with Dutch law, could not be recognised as a marriage within the meaning of German law. The applicant could therefore not claim child benefits for the children of her lesbian partner, as were granted to spouses under German law.[394] By judgment of 30 November 2004, the Federal Financial Court (‘*Bundesfinanzhof*’ (BFH)) confirmed that on the basis of Article 17b (4) EGBGB a marriage between a couple of the same sex that was concluded abroad could under German law only be recognised as a civil partnership, as from Article 17b (4) EGBGB it followed that the effects of a civil partnership registered abroad did not exceed those arising under the German civil partnership.[395] Hence, as confirmed in various judgments of a later date,[396] a same-sex marriage concluded under foreign law can only be registered in Germany as civil partnership (‘*Lebenspartnerschaft*’).[397] This is not different if the spouses are German nationals.[398]

---

391 Kiel 2006, *supra* n. 359, at p. 429, under reference to, *inter alia*, A. Röthel, ‘Gleichgeschlechtliche Ehe und ordre public’ [Same-sex marriage and *ordre public*], *IPRax* (2002) p. 496 at p. 498f and Gebauer and Staudinger 2002, *supra* n. 362, at p. 277.

392 Kiel 2006, *supra* n. 359, at p. 429.

393 E.g. Coester 2010, *supra* n. 322, Rn. 144–148 and Gärtner 2014, *supra* n. 323, Rn. 11. As Martiny explained in 2012: ‘From the point of view of the existing German law, it is not a same-sex relationship as such, but only the exceeding effect which is offensive. It would be inconsistent if a foreign life partnership in Germany were recognised, whereas an exceeding relationship would find no recognition at all. This is an argument for the recognition of the same-sex marriage at least as a life partnership in the sense of Art. 17b Introductory Law.’ D. Martiny, ‘Private International Law Aspects of Same-Sex couples under German Law’, in: K. Boele-Woelki and A. Fuchs (eds*), Legal recognition of same-sex Relationships in Europe, National, cross-border and European perspectives*, 2nd edn. (Cambridge, Intersentia 2012) p. 189 at p. 198.

394 FG Niedersachsen 4 June 2002, Az. 6 K 525/98 Ki. See also FG Niedersachsen 10 June 2004, Az. 5 K 156/03.

395 BFH 30 November 2004, Az. VIII R 61/04 (NV).

396 E.g. VG Münster 13 December 2007, Az. 3 K 1845/05, in which the Court held that the legal effects of a Dutch same-sex marriage could not extend further than those of a registered civil partnership under German law (i.e. the BGB and the LPartG). See also VG Köln 19 March 2009, Az. 13 K 1841/07 and VG Berlin 15 June 2010, Az. 23 A 242/08; OLG Zweibrücken 21 March 2011 (dec.), Az. 3 W 170/10, *NJW-RR* 2011 p. 1156; AG München 4 January 2011 (dec.), Az. 721 UR III 193/10; OLG Zweibrücken 21 March 2011 (dec.), Az. 3 W 170/10, *NJW-RR* 2011 p. 1156 and OLG München 6 July 2011 (dec.), Az. 31 Wx 103/11.

397 Art. 35 *Personenstandsgesetz* (*PStG*) [Civil Status Act].

398 OLG Köln 5 July 2010 (dec.), Az. 16 Wx 64/10 and KG 3 March 2011 (dec.), Az. 1 W 74/17.

Interestingly, however, the Court of Appeal ('*Kammergericht*' (KG)) of Berlin has been willing to apply Dutch law to a request for a divorce between a couple who had concluded same-sex marriage under Dutch law.[399] The Court held that the Dutch same-sex marriage was valid on the basis of Article 13(1), as its conclusion was governed by Dutch law.[400] Further, from Article 15(1)(17)(1) first sentence EGBGB it followed that Dutch law applied to the dissolution of a marriage between two persons of the same sex that had been concluded under Dutch law. The Court held that the application of Dutch law did not lead to a result that was manifestly incompatible with the fundamental principles of German law, precisely because its result was that a same-sex marriage was no longer existent.[401] Other courts have reportedly instead applied the conflict-of-laws rule for registered partnerships to the dissolution of foreign marriages.[402]

10.4.7. 'Downgrading' and free movement law according to the German Courts

The previous subsections have shown that 'downgrading' may take place under German law. Consequently the question has been raised before the German Courts as to whether this 'downgrading' constituted a violation of EU free movement rights.

The Administrative Court ('*Verwaltungsgericht*' (VG)) of Berlin ruled in 2010 that the fact that a same-sex marriage concluded between two EU citizens under foreign law was registered as a civil partnership in the German register ('*Lebenspartnerschaftsregister*'), did not impede the free movement rights of Articles 21(1) and 22(1) TFEU of the EU citizens concerned.[403] The fact that the same-sex marriage was registered as marriage in the register of another EU Member State did not alter this conclusion.

The case was brought by a German national who had entered into a marriage with a Spanish same-sex partner in Canada, hence under Canadian law. While their marriage had been registered in the Spanish marriage register, in Germany their marriage was registered as a civil partnership ('*Lebenspartnerschaft*'). The plaintiff requested this to be changed into 'marriage' ('*Ehe*'), but the authorities instead changed his civil status into 'unmarried' ('*ledig*'), because a marriage between same-sex partners was considered void ('*Nichtehe*'). The plaintiff asked the Administrative Court of Berlin

---

399 KG 19 June 2008 (dec.), Az. 16 WF 163/08.

400 Art. 13(1) EGBGB reads: 'The conditions for the conclusion of marriage are, as regards each person engaged to be married, governed by the law of the country of which he or she is a national.'

401 KG 19 June 2008 (dec.), Az. 16 WF 163/08.

402 D. Martiny, 'Workshop: cross-border recognition (and refusal of recognition) of registered partnerships and marriages with a focus on their financial aspects and the consequences for divorce, maintenance and succession', in: K. Boele-Woelki and A. Fuchs (eds.), *Legal recognition of same-sex Relationships in Europe, National, cross-border and European perspectives*, 2nd edn. (Cambridge, Intersentia 2012) p. 225 at p. 241, referring in footnote 39 to AG Münster 20 January 2010, Az. 56 F 79/09, *NJW-RR* 2010 p. 1308.

403 VG Berlin 15 June 2010, Az. 23 A 242/08. See B. Heiderhoff 2011, supra n. 382, Rn. 46.

to have the entry in the German register changed into 'married', or, alternatively, into '*Lebenspartnerschaft*'. He argued that the EGBGB was not applicable as it only dealt with private law matters, while here a public law matter was concerned. He furthermore claimed that from EU law an obligation followed to recognise his same-sex marriage.[404] The Berlin Court rejected this reasoning. It ruled that the entry had to be changed into '*Lebenspartnerschaft*', but that an entry as 'married' was not required. Because of a lack of an interstate element, the Court held that the case before it fell outside the scope of EU law.[405]

Even if EU law was applicable, the Court held, there was no interference with EU law, as the entry of the plaintiff's marriage into the register as '*Lebenspartnerschaft*' did not have any serious disadvantages of a professional or a private character.[406] Further, the record in the register was not legally binding.[407] Even if there were an interference with free movement law, the Court held this to be justified on grounds of the special protection of marriage ex Article 6(1) Basic Law.[408] The Court considered that – other than name, which is part of a person's identity[409] – civil status was not of great importance in judicial matters. The general prohibition on discrimination ex Article 18 TFEU was not violated, as the entry into the register affected all citizens equally. Besides, the entry into the register was not in violation of Directive 2000/78 as the lack of a Union competence in respect of the question of whether a marriage is concerned, prevented the matter from falling within the scope of this Directive. Lastly, on the basis of Article 2 (2b) of the Free Movement Directive (Directive 2004/38) the Court concluded that there was no obligation under EU law to recognise the same-sex marriage of the plaintiff.[410] The Court saw no reason to make a preliminary reference to the CJEU as it held there to be no uncertainty about the interpretation of Union Law in the matter before it.[411] In addition and conclusion, the VG Berlin held the ECHR not to be violated as its Article 12 did not require the recognition of same-sex marriages.[412]

It is noted that this judgment of the Administrative Court of Berlin – as far as the present author is aware, so far the only judgment of a German Court on the

---

404 *Idem*, para. 3.

405 The Court held that there was no interstate element because the plaintiff was a German national who lived in Germany and because the question at issue concerned only the legal relationship between him and the State. See para. 18 of the judgment, in which the Court referred to Joined Cases C-64/96 and C-65/96 *Ücker/Jacquet* [1997] ECR I-3171, ECLI:EU:C:1997:285.

406 VG Berlin 15 June 2010, Az. 23 A 242/08, para. 19.

407 *Idem*, para. 19.

408 *Idem*, para. 20.

409 *Idem*, para. 20. The Court referred to Case C-148/02 *Garcia Avello* [2003] ECR I-11613, ECLI:EU:C:2003:539 and Case C-353/06 *Grunkin* [2008] ECR I-7639, ECLI:EU:C:2008:559.

410 Following Art. 2(2)(b) of Directive 2004/38 a 'family member' is '[...] the partner with whom the Union citizen has contracted a registered partnership, on the basis of the legislation of a Member State, if the legislation of the host Member State treats registered partnerships as equivalent to marriage and in accordance with the conditions laid down in the relevant legislation of the host Member State.' See more elaborately Ch. 9, section 9.6.2.

411 VG Berlin 15 June 2010, Az. 23 A 242/08, para. 24.

412 *Idem*, para. 25.

matter – dates from 2010. Since that time, the German civil partnership has only been more equalised with marriage. That fact may render it less likely that a German Court would rule otherwise on the question of the commensurability of this type of downgrading with EU free movement rules.

10.4.8. Cross-border parental issues

There have also been several cross-border cases relating to parental rights of same-sex couples before the German courts. Generally, the parental rights established by couples under foreign law, have been recognised by the courts, including in cases where such rights could not have been established under German law.

In cross-border cases concerning second-parent adoption by same-sex partners, German courts have applied German law. For example, in 2010 the District Court (*'Amtsgericht'* (AG)) of Nürnberg decided a case that concerned an American from California who lived in Germany and who wanted to adopt the biological child of his Italian same-sex spouse, with whom he was married under Belgian law. The child had Russian and Italian citizenship.[413] While in principle the relevant Californian adoption was to apply, because the adopter had American nationality,[414] the Court applied German law instead. It did so under Article 4(2)(1) EGBGB (*renvoi*, *'Rückverweisung'*), because for application of the relevant Californian law it was required that the adoptive parent and child had been living in California for at least six uninterrupted months, a criterion that was not fulfilled in the case at hand. The adoption was approved by the Court on the basis of Article 9(7) of the Civil Partnership Act, which allows for second-parent adoption by civil partners, in combination with Articles 1755(1) and 1755(2) of the German Civil Code (BGB). In another case of 2010,[415] the District Court (AG) of Stuttgart applied German law to a case involving a foreign national who wanted to adopt the biological child of her German civil partner, with whom she had concluded a civil partnership under German law.[416]

There are also examples of recognition by German Courts of foreign court orders concerning joint adoptions by same-sex partners. As noted, above, foreign judgments in family matters are in principle recognised under German law,[417] unless such recognition is considered manifestly incompatible with fundamental principles of

---

413 AG Nürnberg 25 September 2010 (dec.), Az. XVI 57/09.

414 As explained in Ch. 4, section 4.5.3, Art. 22 EGBGB provides that the adoption of a child is governed by the law of the country of which the adopter is a national at the time of the adoption. Art. 23 EGBGB further provides that '[t]he necessity and the granting of the consent of the child, and of a person who is related to the child under family law, to a declaration of descent, to conferring a name, or to an adoption are additionally governed by the law of the country of which the child is a national.' However, where the best interest of the child so requires, German law is applied instead.

415 AG Stuttgart 25 October 2010 (dec.), Az. 29 F 2062/09.

416 The Court held Art. 22(1) second sentence EGBGB applicable, following which adoption by (one or both) spouses is subject to the law governing the general effects of marriage.

417 Art. 108 FamFG.

German law.[418] In a judgment of 2012, the Berlin Court of Appeal ('*Kammergericht*' (KG)) held that it could not be maintained that the recognition of a foreign adoption order, concerning a joint adoption by a same-sex couple, would be contrary to the foundations of the German legal order, to such an extent that it would lift the fundamental rule that foreign adoption orders could not be challenged.[419] The Court noted that this was particularly so since the question of the validity of a same-sex joint adoption under German law was much debated. The obligation to observe German law could not be pursued by trampling upon the interests of the children concerned. Instead, holding on to the fundamental rule that adoption orders could not be challenged, served the best interests of the child to a much greater extent, the Court ruled.[420]

A similar line of reasoning was adopted by the Appeals Court (*Oberlandesgericht* (OLG)) of Schleswig-Holstein in a judgment of March 2014.[421] The case concerned a joint adoption by a German national and her same-sex US-national partner under US law. At the time the adoption order was issued, the relationship of the two women was not legally recognised in any way. This was ground for the competent German administrative court of first instance to refuse to recognise the American adoption order.[422] While that judgment was appealed, the two women got married in California (USA). In its judgment of March 2014, the Appeals Court ruled that in view of the increasing extension of adoption rights to same-sex partners under German law, it could not be maintained that recognition of the contested adoption order was manifestly incompatible with the foundations of German law. The Court therefore recognised the adoption.

All these judgments date from recent years, and the German courts evidently grounded their reasoning in recent developments in the area of adoption rights for same-sex couples under German law. That fact may also explain that same-sex couples have been less successful in claiming legal parenthood by operation of the law in cross-border situations. As explained in section 10.4.5 above it is not possible under German law for so-called 'co-mothers' to be recognised by operation of the law as legal parent of the child of their same-sex partner who is the biological parent. On the basis of Article 1592(1) German Civil Code (BGB) the father of a child is the man who is married to the mother of the child at the date of birth, but there is no such presumption of parenthood for same-sex registered partners. In March 2011, the OLG of Celle ruled that the presumption of paternity did not analogously apply to a

418 Art. 109(4) FamFG.

419 KG 11 December 2012 (dec.), Az. 1 W 404/12; See also F. Strohal, jurisPR-FamR 3/2013 Anm. 4 and B. Heiderhoff, 'BeckOK EGBGB Art. 22' ['Beck Online Commentary Art. 22 EGBGB'], in: H.G. Bamberger and H. Roth (eds.), *Beck'scher Online-Kommentar BGB* [Beck Online commentary to the BGB], 32nd edn. (München, Verlag C.H. Beck 2014) Rn. 64–65. The case concerned an adoption order by a South-African Court.

420 KG 11 December 2012 (dec.), Az. 1 W 404/12, para. 20. This case was subsequently appealed to the Federal Court (BGH), which case was still pending (Az. XII ZB 730/12) at the time this research was concluded (i.e. 31 July 2014).

421 OLG Schleswig 14 March 2014 (dec.), Az. 12 UF 14/13.

422 AG Schleswig 4 January 2013 (dec.), Az. 91 F 276/11.

situation involving two women, one German national and the other Italian, who had concluded marriage under Spanish law.[423] The so-called 'co-mother', who had been recognised as such under Spanish law, could not be registered on the German birth register as (co-)mother of the child, because German filiation law did not allow for the granting of paternity to two same-sex partners, except for in adoption situations.[424]

10.4.9. Recognition of German civil partnerships in other Member States

The present author has not become aware of any report of couples in a German civil partnership having particular difficulties with having that civil status recognised in other EU Member States. These couples presumably encounter refusals of such recognition in those Member States that do not provide for any form of legal recognition of same-sex relationships. Because of the fact that the German civil partnership has been extensively equalised with marriage, it is unlikely that Member States that have themselves introduced a registered partnership for same-sex partners, will refuse the German partnership recognition under their national law. Countries that have refrained from introducing a separate regime, but have instead opened up marriage to same-sex couples, may possibly be willing to recognise the German civil partnership as marriage under their national law, now that it has been equalised with this institute to such a great extent.

10.5. Conclusions

The German debate and standard-setting on legal recognition of same-sex couples has pre-eminently been a step-by-step process. The first concrete step by means of the introduction of the German civil partnership in 2001, was followed by numerous legislative amendments over the subsequent 13 years. With a view to further equalising the legal position of civil partners with that of spouses, amendments were introduced in areas of law varying from tax law to parental rights. Such change was frequently imposed by a Court judgment, in many cases by the Constitutional Court.

This phased process can be explained by a long existing tensed relation between the special protection of marriage under Article 6 of the German Basic Law and the right to equality before the law under Article 3 Basic Law. While initially the former was seen as a *lex specialis* of the latter, and thus as having precedence, over time this relationship has been reversed. The most recent line of case law of the Constitutional Court in relation to same-sex relationships is no longer about the special protection of marriage, so it has been observed, but about the protection of civil partnership

[423] OLG Celle 10 March 2011 (dec.), Az. 17 W 48/10, *NJW-RR* 2011 p. 1157. See also AG Hannover 3 November 2010 (dec.), Az. 85 III 103/10 and B. Heiderhoff, 'Der gewönliche Aufenthalt von Säuglingen' ['The habitual residence of infants'], *IPRax* (2012) p. 523.

[424] *Idem.*

against discrimination.[425] The special protection of marriage under Article 6(1) Basic Law has consequently been qualified by some as 'an empty shell'.[426]

In particular in relation to parental matters, the equal treatment argument provided for an important new perspective, as it was directly related to the rights of the child. In the ground-breaking 2013 judgment of the Constitutional Court on successive adoption, it was the *child's* right to equal treatment on the basis of which the Court ruled that the prohibition on successive adoption by civil partners could not be justified.

Regardless of these developments, the opening up of marriage to same-sex couples, while debated at various occasions, has proven a bridge too far. It is possible that the far-reaching equalisation of civil partnership with marriage has taken the sting out of this debate. On the other hand, there are still clear differences between civil partners and spouses in the sphere of parental rights, namely in respect of joint adoption and legal parenthood by operation of the law. For some, these differences may be reason for finding the opening up of marriage even more important, yet others may hold these differences justified because of the special status of marriage and the biological differences between different-sex and same-sex couples.

In cross-border situations, change has been brought about at the same fairly slow, perhaps even slower, pace. For example, it took until 2013, before the legislature amended the Free Movement Act, so as to provide expressly that in respect of entry and residence, civil partners and spouses were treated equally under this Act. Further, in cross-border situations, a clear domination of the German standard is visible. On the one hand, the German Civil Partnership is unique in its openness to foreign same-sex couples, exactly because the German legislature wished to broaden its aspirations for equal treatment to couples from outside Germany. On the other hand, the special protection of marriage as a bond between a man and a woman under Article 6(1) Basic Law has also found expression in German Private International Law. Under the so-called '*Kappungsgrenze*', foreign same-sex marriages are downgraded to the standard of the German Partnership. Such downgrading has been held unproblematic under EU free movement rules, by German courts. Serious criticism has also been issued, however, on the German conflict-of-laws rules in this context, particularly because of the increased equalisation of civil partnership with marriage. Interestingly, in cross-border parental matters, such developments under German law have – together with the best interests of the child – been grounds for German courts to recognise parental links that same-sex couples had established abroad.

[425] Coester 2013, *supra* n. 328, at p. 121.
[426] Selder 2013, *supra* n. 174, at p. 1067. See section 10.3.4.4 above.

Chapter 11
Ireland

11.1. Constitutional framework

The Irish Constitution, as enacted in 1937, makes no express provision for the right to respect for private life. This right is covered by Article 40.3, which protects more generally the 'personal rights' (see Chapter 5, section 5.1). Two other Articles that are highly relevant in the context of the present case study are Article 40.1 (equality before the law) and Article 41 (protection of marriage and the family).

11.1.1. Equality before the law

Article 40.1 of the Irish Constitution provides that '[a]ll citizens shall, as human persons, be held equal before the law.' While this Article does not specify any discrimination grounds, under statutory law sexual orientation has constituted a prohibited ground of discrimination in employment[1] and access to goods and services since the late 1990s.[2] These statutory norms have proven a more common and more successful avenue for complaints about discrimination on grounds of sexual orientation than Article 40.1 of the Constitution.

11.1.2. The right to marry and the protection of family under the Irish Constitution

Even though the Irish Constitution (1937) does not contain an express right to marry, the institution of marriage is strongly embedded in it. Article 41.1.1° recognises the family as 'the natural primary and fundamental unit group of society, and as a moral institution possessing inalienable and imprescriptible rights, antecedent and superior to all positive law.' The third paragraph of this Article furthermore reads:

> 'The State pledges itself to guard with special care the institution of Marriage, on which the Family is founded, and to protect it against attack.'[3]

---

1 Art. 6(2)(d) Unfair Dismissals (Amendment) Act 1993 and Employment Equality Act 1998, No. 21/1998.

2 Art. 3(2)(d) Equal Status Act 2000, No. 8/2000.

3 Art. 41.3.1° Constitution of Ireland.

In *Donovan* v. *Minister for Justice* (1951) the High Court found for the first time that a right to marry was implied in the Irish Constitution.[4] This right was subsequently recognised by Justice Kenny in *Ryan* (1965)[5] as an example of the personal rights latent in Article 40.3.1°.[6] The constitutional right to marry was confirmed in later case law on various occasions.[7]

Marriage and family are intrinsically linked in Article 41 of the Irish Constitution. Consequently, the constitutional protection of the family is confined to families based on marriage, as the Court held in *the State (Nicolaou)* v. *An Bord Uchtála* (1966)[8] and since then this has repeatedly been confirmed.[9] In other words, non-marital families do not enjoy protection under the Irish Constitution. As Ryan has explained, this implies that '[...] somewhat counter-intuitively [...], children do not necessarily make a constitutional "family". Everything depends on the marital status of their parents.'[10] The marital family unit is thus afforded 'robust protection'.[11] As a consequence, as observed in 2010 '[i]n practice in Irish law the marital status of a child's parents will often have a significant, if not decisive, bearing on the nature and extent of the rights of the child and his or her parents.'[12] Such concerns have been addressed in both the envisaged Thirty-first Amendment to the Constitution (see Chapter 5, section 5.1.3) as well as in the Children and Family Relationships Bill (see section 11.3.5.3 below).

At the same time, childless married couples also enjoy protection under this constitutional provision;[13] procreation is not essential in the context of the Irish

4 *Donovan* v. *Minister for Justice* [1951] 85 ILTR 134. See also A. O'Sullivan, 'Same-sex marriage and the Irish Constitution', 13 *The International Journal of Human Rights* (2009) p. 477 at pp. 480 and 487, who explains that '[a]s a personal right, it is not absolute and its exercise may be restricted by the state within constitutionally permissible limits, namely, protection of other constitutional rights and maintenance of the "common good".'

5 *Ryan* v. *Attorney General* [1965] IESC 1; [1965] IR 294.

6 See G. Hogan and G. Whyte, *J.M. Kelly, The Irish Constitution* (Dublin, LexisNexis Butterworths 2003) p. 1468.

7 E.g. *O'Shea* v. *Ireland* [2007] 2 IR 313. See F. Ryan, 'Out of the shadow of the Constitution: civil partnership, cohabitation and the constitutional family', 48 *The Irish Jurist* (2012) p. 201 at p. 209. See also C. Power, 'The right to Marry', 9 *Irish Journal of Family Law* (2006) p. 3.

8 *The State (Nicolaou)* v. *An Bord Uchtála* [1966] IR 567. See also Ryan 2012, *supra* n. 7, at p. 210.

9 E.g. in *WO'R* v. *EH* [1996] IESC 4; [1996] 2 IR 248. See Ryan 2012, *supra* n. 7, at pp. 211–212.

10 Ryan 2012, *supra* n. 7, at p. 208.

11 N. O'Shea, 'Can Ireland's Constitution Remain Premised on the "Inalienable" Protection of the Marital Family Unit Without Continuing to Fail its International Obligations on the Rights of the Child?', *Irish Journal of Family Law* (2012) p. 87 at pp. 92–93. The author observed: 'While the referendum's positive result may have symbolic value for the rights of the Irish child, any practical changes brought about by the referendum are likely to be minimal, particularly as Art. 41 remains unchanged.'

12 Joint Committee on the Constitutional Amendment on Children, *Third Report. Twenty-eighth Amendment of the Constitution Bill 2007 Proposal for a constitutional amendment to strengthen children's rights. Final Report*, February 2010, p. 19, online available at www.oireachtas.ie/parliament/media/housesoftheoireachtas/contentassets/documents/JC-Constitutional-Amendment-on-Children-Final-Report.pdf, visited September 2010. In *The State (Nicolaou)* v. *An Bord Uchtála* (1966) the Supreme Court held that that while all children had the same natural and imprescriptible rights regardless of the marital status of their parents at birth, children with unmarried parents did 'not necessarily' have the same legal rights. Walsh J. in *The State (Nicolaou)* v. *An Bord Uchtála* [1966] IR 567.

13 *Murray* v. *Ireland* [1985] IR 532.

constitutional protection of marriage.[14] Indeed, also the Irish courts accepted in 1985 that the inability to procreate does not remove the right to marry.[15]

The exclusion of non-marital relationships and families from constitutional protection does not mean that protection by the law of these relationships and families is precluded. As long as they are not treated more favourably than married couples and marriage-based families,[16] legal recognition of non-marital couples and families is not unconstitutional.[17]

The text of Article 41 of the Irish Constitution is neutral as regards gender of the spouses, but the reference to the role of women and mothers in that same provision is a first indication that only traditional families, based on a marriage between one man and one woman, have been legally recognised in Ireland. This reading has indeed been repeatedly confirmed in case law. In *Murphy* v. *Attorney General* (1982), Hamilton J. spoke of marriage as a 'permanent, indissoluble union of man and woman'.[18] In *Murray* (1985), it was noted that '[t]he concept and nature of marriage, was derived from the Christian notion of a partnership based on an irrevocable personal consent given by both spouses which establishes a unique and very special life-long relationship'.[19] In *B.* v. *R.* (1995)[20] Judge Costello held marriage to be '[...] the voluntary and permanent union of one man and one woman to the exclusion of all others for life'.[21] In *Foy -v- An t-Ard Chláraitheoir & Ors* (2002), a case involving a transsexual, High Court Judge McKechnie held that 'marriage as understood by the Constitution, by statute and by case law' referred to 'the union of a biological man with a biological woman'. The Judge considered it to be 'crucial for legal purposes' in the Irish jurisdiction that the parties were of different sexes and concluded that Article 12 ECHR was 'equally so predicated'.[22] The Judge ruled in conclusion:

> '[...] in my view there is no sustainable basis for the applicant's submission that the existing law, which carries the impugned provision which prohibits the applicant from marrying a party who is of the same biological sex as herself, is a violation of her constitutional right to marry. Finally and in any event, as with the other rights as asserted, this right to marry is not absolute and has to be evaluated in the context of several other rights including the

---

14 B. Tobin, 'Law, politics and the child-centric approach to marriage in Ireland', 48 *The Irish Jurist* (2012) p. 210.

15 Tobin has held that as a result of *Murray* v. *Ireland* '[...] procreation is not an essential element of a valid subsisting marriage under Irish law'. B. Tobin, 'Gay marriage – a bridge too far?', 15 *Irish Student Law Review* (2007) p. 175 at p. 176 and *Murray* v. *Ireland* [1985] IR 532, 537.

16 C. Power, 'Family law', 12 *Irish Journal of Family Law* (2009) p. 22, referring to *Murphy* v. *Attorney General* [1982] IR 241 and *Zappone* v. *Revenue Commissioners* [2006] IEHC 404. See also Ryan 2012, *supra* n. 7, at p. 231.

17 See also Ryan 2012, *supra* n. 7, at pp. 211–212.

18 *Murphy* v. *Attorney General* [1982] IR 241. Compare the judgment of Costello J. in *Murray* v. *Ireland*, [1985] IR 532.

19 *Murray* v. *Ireland* [1985] ILRM 536.

20 *B* v. *R* [1995] 1 ILRM 491.

21 *Idem*, at 495.

22 *Foy* v. *An t-Ard Chláraitheoir & Ors* [2002] IEHC 116, at 175.

> rights of society. When so looked at I believe that for the purposes of marriage the State can legitimately hold the view which is espoused by and is evident from its laws.'[23]

The position that the Irish constitutional right to marry only concerns marriage between parties of different sexes was confirmed in subsequent case law. In *D.T.* v. *C.T.* (2002)[24] Justice Murray defined marriage as 'a solemn contract of partnership entered into between a man and a woman with a special status recognised by the Constitution.' Another judgment to this effect is *Zappone & Anor* v. *Revenue Commissioners & Ors* (2006),[25] which is discussed in more detail below.[26] An even more recent confirmation that only different-sex spouses enjoy a constitutional right to marry dates from 2010.[27]

11.2. (De-)criminalisation of homosexual activities

Until the 1990s, certain homosexual activities between consenting adult men were punishable under Irish law.[28] Section 11 of the Criminal Law Amendment Act 1885 provided that:

> 'Any male person who, in public or in private, commits [...] any act of gross indecency with another male person, shall be guilty of a misdemeanour, and being convicted thereof shall be liable at the discretion of the court to be imprisoned for any term not exceeding two years, with or without hard labour.'[29]

What particular acts in any given case could be held to amount to gross indecency was a matter which was not statutorily defined and was therefore for the courts to decide on the basis of the particular facts of each case. Although in practice hardly any prosecutions were brought on this basis, Irish courts were unwilling to declare

---

23 *Idem.* After the ECtHR judgment in the case of *Christine Goodwin* (2002, see Ch. 8, section 8.2.1), a new case was brought by Dr. Foy, however, this time the High Court did not make any finding on the applicant's complaint under Art. 12 ECHR and accordingly did not address the question whether of the Irish constitutional right to marry concerns different-sex spouses only. *Foy -v- An t-Ard Chláraitheoir & Ors* [2007] IEHC 470.

24 *D.T.* v. *C.T.* [2003] 1 ILRM 321.

25 *Zappone & Anor* v. *Revenue Commissioners & Ors* [2006] IEHC 404.

26 Section 11.3.2.

27 *HAH* v. *SAA*, unreported, High Court, November 4, 2010, as referred to in B. Tobin, 'Same-Sex Marriage in Ireland: The Rocky Road to Recognition', *Irish Journal of Family Law* (2012) p. 102 at p. 104.

28 Sections 61 and 62 of the Offences against the Person Act, 1861 and Section 11 of the Criminal Law Amendment Act, 1885.

29 This section of the 1885 Act is also known as the *Labouchere Amendment*, named after the Member of Parliament who introduced it. Section 61 of the Offences against the Person Act, 1861 provided: 'Whosoever shall be convicted of the abominable crime of buggery, committed either with mankind or with any animal, shall be liable to be kept in penal servitude for life.' Section 62 of the same Act read: 'Whosoever shall attempt to commit the said abominable crime, or shall be guilty of any assault with intent to commit the same, or of any indecent assault upon a male person, shall be guilty of a misdemeanour, and being convicted thereof shall be liable to be kept in penal servitude for any term not exceeding ten years.'

the relevant provisions unconstitutional. It took a judgment by the ECtHR for this effect to be reached.

In November 1977 Mr. Norris, an active homosexual and campaigner for homosexual rights in Ireland, instituted proceedings in the High Court. Although he himself had not been prosecuted for gross indecency with another male person, he claimed before the High Court that these laws were no longer in force by reason of the effect of Article 50 of the Constitution of Ireland, which declared that laws passed before the enactment of the Constitution but which were inconsistent with it, did not continue to be in force. The High Court dismissed Mr. Norris's action on legal grounds.[30] On appeal, the Supreme Court, by a three to two majority in its decision of 22 April 1983, upheld the judgment of the High Court. Chief Justice O'Higgins, who was in the majority, held:

> 'On the ground of the Christian nature of our State and on the grounds that the deliberate practice of homosexuality is morally wrong, that it is damaging to the health both of individuals and the public and, finally, that it is potentially harmful to the institution of marriage, I can find no inconsistency with the Constitution in the laws which make such conduct criminal. It follows, in my view, that no right of privacy, as claimed by the plaintiff, can prevail against the operation of such criminal sanctions.'[31]

According to the majority the State had an interest in the general moral well-being of the community and was entitled to discourage conduct which was 'morally wrong and harmful to a way of life and to values which the State wishes to protect'. Hamilton remarked that the three-of-two majority was heavily influenced by the Christian ethos of the Constitution itself, that was particularly prevalent in the Preamble.[32] O'Connell observed that the majority relied 'on a perfectionist theory of morality to limit the right to sexual freedom of gay men and others wishing to have anal intercourse'. Thereby the majority accepted that the conventional morality of society defined the limits of individual freedom.[33] O'Connell contrasted this approach with that of the majority in *McGee* (1973),[34] a case on contraceptives, where the judges paid 'great respect to the principles of autonomy and pluralism'.[35]

---

30 *Norris* v. *Attorney General* [1983] IESC 3; [1984] IR 36.

31 *Idem*, judgment by O'Higgins CJ. In its majority decision, the Supreme Court based itself, furthermore, and, *inter alia*, on the following considerations: '(1) Homosexuality has always been condemned in Christian teaching as being morally wrong. It has equally been regarded by society for many centuries as an offence against nature and a very serious crime; (2) Exclusive homosexuality, whether the condition be congenital or acquired, can result in great distress and unhappiness for the individual and can lead to depression, despair and suicide; (3) The homosexually oriented can be importuned into a homosexual lifestyle which can become habitual; (4) Male homosexual conduct has resulted, in other countries, in the spread of all forms of venereal disease and this has now become a significant public health problem in England; (5) Homosexual conduct can be inimical to marriage and is per se harmful to it as an institution.'

32 L. Hamilton, 'Matters of life and death', 65 *Fordham Law Review* (1996) p. 543 at p. 547.

33 R. O'Connell 2010, *supra* n. 3, at p. 598.

34 See Ch. 5, section 5.1.1.

35 R. O'Connell 2010, *supra* n. 3, at p. 599.

Before the Supreme Court Mr. Norris contended unsuccessfully that the ECtHR judgment in the case of *Dudgeon* (1981) had to be followed,[36] as the ECtHR had ruled in that case that the very same statutory provisions as had been in force until that time in the United Kingdom constituted a violation of Article 8 ECHR. Chief Justice O'Higgins, in the majority judgment, held that the Convention, being an international agreement, did not, and could not, form part of Ireland's domestic law, nor affect in any way questions which arose thereunder.

Norris lodged a complaint with the European Commission for Human Rights (ECmHR), which referred the case to the ECtHR. In its judgment of October 1988, the Court, under reference to the 'indistinguishable' case of *Dudgeon*, held the relevant Irish statutory provisions to be in violation of Article 8 ECHR.[37] The Court delivered its judgment in 1988, but the criminal law in Ireland remained unchanged until the Criminal Justice (Sexual Offences) Act of 1993 entered into force,[38] which made consensual sexual activity between all persons above 17 years of age lawful.[39] It has been submitted that the Convention played a relatively minor role in this change of the law; by that time other legislative measures, making sexual orientation a protected status in various fields, had already been adopted or were to be adopted.[40]

The abolishment of the criminalisation of homosexual activities as late as 1993, formed the starting point for dramatic changes in respect of legal recognition of same-sex relationships in a time frame of two decades only. Less than 20 years later, in 2011, a civil partnership for same-sex couples was introduced, as will now be discussed.

11.3. Legal recognition of same-sex relationships under Irish law

As noted in section 11.1.2 above, the family holds a very prominent place in the Irish Constitution. It is recognised as 'the natural primary and fundamental unit group of Society'. The Constitution only protects the family based on marriage and consequently Irish family laws for long also only employed this restrictive definition of the family (see 11.3.5 below).[41] Very traditional family laws have been in force for a longtime, for example:

36 ECtHR [GC] 22 October 1981, *Dudgeon* v. *the United Kingdom*, no. 7525/76. See Ch. 8, section 8.1.1.

37 ECtHR 26 October 1988, *Norris* v. *Ireland*, no. 10581/83.

38 Criminal Justice (Sexual Offences) Act, 1993, No. 20/1993.

39 See D. O'Connell, 'Ireland', in: R. Blackburn and J. Polakiewicz (eds.), *Fundamental Rights in Europe. The ECHR and its Member States 1950–2000* (Oxford: Oxford University Press 2001) p. 423 at p. 467.

40 See L. Flynn, 'From individual Protection to Recognition of Relationships? Same-Sex Couples and the Irish Experience of Sexual Orientation Law Reform', in: R. Wintemute and M. Andenæs (eds.), *The legal recognition of same-sex partnerships? A study of national, European and international law* (Oxford: Hart 2001) p. 591 at pp. 594–595.

41 F. Ryan, The Civil Partnership and Certain Rights and Obligations of Cohabitants Act 2010 (Round Hall, Dublin 2011) p. 8.

> 'Only in 1973 was a ban on married women working in the civil service lifted. Women were not allowed to sit on juries before this date either. Nor were single mothers entitled to social assistance. Contraceptives became available to everyone only in 1984. Divorce – limited – arrived in 1986. In 1991, it became illegal for a man to rape his wife. Two years later homosexuality was decriminalised.'[42]

Until a decade into the second millennium, there was hardly any recognition of non-marital relationships in general, including those of different-sex couples. As Ryan explains, to the extent that non-martial relationships enjoyed legal protection, same-sex couples were generally excluded as the relevant provisions applied to couples 'living together as husband and wife'.[43] Once the first steps were made, however, change was brought about at a relatively fast pace: in 2011 the civil partnership was introduced for same-sex couples; in 2013 legislation was drafted which would allow for joint adoption by same-sex couples; and even a referendum on same-sex marriage has been planned for 2015. This section 11.3 describes and analyses the various developments over time under Irish law in the direction of legal recognition of relationships between same-sex partners.

11.3.1. Early developments towards legal recognition

At the beginning of the new millennium the Irish Equality Authority[44] published various reports that were of direct relevance to the rights of same-sex partners. The first report dealt with partnership rights of same-sex couples.[45] Its authors recognised a need for action in this area but did not make specific recommendations. The report served as a basis for the work of the Advisory Committee established to report to the Equality Authority on the equality agenda for lesbian, gay and bisexual people, which issued a report in 2002.[46] One of the recommendations made by the latter Committee read:

> 'The Department [of Justice, Equality and Law Reform] should ensure that same-sex couples are treated in an equal manner by extending the right to nominate a partner with legal rights to same-sex couples, comparable with those recognised for a spouse.'[47]

---

42 Wording ascribed to S.-A. Buckley, a social historian at National University of Ireland in Galway, as quoted in H. Mahoney, 'Same-sex marriage underlines social change in Ireland', *euobserver.com* 7 May 2013, www.euobserver.com/lgbti/119963, visited July 2013.

43 Ryan 2011, *supra* n. 41, at pp. 8–9. This was, for instance, the case in respect of social assistance. See Ryan 2011, *supra* n. 41, at p. 20.

44 The Irish Equality Authority is an independent body set up under the Employment Equality Act 1998. It was established on 18th October 1999.

45 J. Mee and K. Ronayne, *Partnership rights of same sex couples* (Dublin, The Equality Authority 2000).

46 The Equality Authority, *Implementing Equality for Lesbians, Gays and Bisexuals*, 2002, online available www.equality.ie, visited September 2002.

47 *Idem*, at p. 29.

This was the first time that a statutory organisation publicly made such statements in support of legal recognition of same-sex relationships.[48] In April 2004 the Irish Law Reform Commission (LRC)[49] issued a consultation paper on the rights and obligations of cohabitants.[50] The Commission proposed a presumptive scheme, imposing certain legal rights and duties on 'qualified cohabitants',[51] who had been living together in a marriage-like relationship for three years.[52] The LRC took the view that such a scheme should be extended to different-sex as well as same-sex cohabitants.[53] The option of civil registration of same-sex relationships was not addressed in the consultation paper.[54]

The recommendations of the LRC were not immediately followed up. Instead, in 2004 a new Act on Civil Registration entered into force, which provided that there was an impediment to a marriage if both parties are of the same sex.[55] The inclusion of this explicit provision at a time when the first European countries had opened up marriage to same-sex couples was criticised by equality groups for being discriminatory.[56]

Further, in that same year the Civil Partnership Act was introduced in the United Kingdom, including in Northern Ireland, which provided for civil partnership for same-sex couples.[57] Various authorities and authors claimed that this entailed a need for action for the Irish legislature, as under the Good Friday agreement, the Republic

---

48 Center for Evaluation Innovation, *Civil Partnership and Ireland: How a Minority Achieved a Majority. A case study of the gay and lesbian equality network*, Center for Evaluation Innovation November 2012, p. 2, online available at www.glen.ie/attachments/Case_Study_-_How_a_minority.PDF, visited July 2014.

49 The Law Reform Commission was established on 20 October 1975, pursuant to section 3 of the Law Reform Commission Act 1975. It is an independent statutory body whose main aim is to keep the law under review and to make practical proposals for its reform, 'so that the law reflects the changing needs of Irish society'. See www. lawreform.ie, visited October 2010.

50 Law Reform Commission, *Consultation Paper on the Rights and Duties of Cohabitants*, Law Reform Commission: April 2004 CP 32–2004.

51 The Commission defined 'qualified cohabitees' as persons who, although they are not married to one another, live together in a 'marriage like' relationship for a continuous period of three years, or where there is a child of the relationship, for two years. Law Reform Commission 2004, *supra* n. 50, at pp. 1 and 4.

52 Presumptive meant that the scheme only applied once the cohabitation had ended. See B. Tobin, 'Relationship Recognition for Same-Sex Couples in Ireland: The Proposed Models Critiqued', 11 *Irish Journal of Family Law* (2008) p. 10.

53 Law Reform Commission 2004, *supra* n. 50, at p. 14.

54 Critical in this regard was Mee. J. Mee, 'A critique of the Law Reform Commission's consultation paper on the rights and duties of cohabitees', 39 *The Irish Jurist* (2004) p. 74. In 2006 the paper was followed up by a report in which the LRC also pleaded for the development of a legal framework concerning cohabitants, either different-sex or same-sex, who live together in an intimate relationship. Again, the option of civil partnership was not discussed. Law Reform Commission, *Report, Rights and Duties of Cohabitants* (Law Reform Commission December 2006, LRC 82-2006).

55 Section 2(2)(e) Civil Registration Act 2004. Tobin has noted that this impediment to same-sex marriage was not discussed during the Committee's debate. Tobin 2012B, *supra* n. 27, at p. 103.

56 See C. Power, 'The benefits of marriage', 7 *Irish Journal of Family Law* (2004) p. 29.

57 Civil Partnership Act 2004, Act of 18 November 2004, 2004 ch. 33.

of Ireland was under an obligation to provide for an 'at least an equivalent level of human rights protection' as prevalent in Northern Ireland.[58]

It was also in 2004 that Senator Norris – who had also been a successful plaintiff in various legal proceedings on the prohibition on homosexual conduct (see 11.3 above) – presented his Civil Partnership Bill.[59] According to its Explanatory Memorandum the purpose of the Bill was:

> '[...] to make provision for and in connection with civil partnership, that is a conjugal relationship entered into and registered in accordance with the Act between two persons aged 18 and upwards of either the same or different gender or sex, who are cohabiting, and who are not already married or in another civil partnership, and are not within certain prohibited degrees of relationship with each other.'[60]

The Bill was the first legislative initiative for introducing legal recognition of same-sex relationships. It provided that civil partners were to be regarded in law '[...] as having the same rights and entitlements as parties to a marriage'.[61]

When the Norris Bill was debated in the Senate ('*Seanad*') in February 2005, the Minister for Justice acknowledged that the position before the law of same-sex couples and the possible extension of State recognition to civil partnerships between such persons, needed to be addressed. Two aspects of this Bill were nevertheless considered problematic: (1) the fact that the Bill provided a status for cohabitants which attracted the same rights and entitlements as conventional marriage; and (2) the fact that the proposed legislation was restricted to so-called 'conjugal relations'. The first issue was even held to be contrary to the Constitution. Consequently the debate on the Bill was adjourned[62] and ultimately (on 11 October 2007) this Bill was withdrawn. This delay and withdrawal had much to do with other ongoing issues, such as the issuing of the tenth progress report of the *Oireachtas* Committee on the Constitution in 2006. In this report the Committee held that:

> 'Provision for same-sex marriage would bring practical benefits. But it would require a constitutional amendment to extend the definition of the family. However, legislation could extend to such couples a broad range of marriage-like privileges without any need to amend the Constitution (as has been suggested in the case of cohabiting heterosexual couples).'[63]

---

58 See Irish Council for Civil Liberties, *Equality for all families*, April 2006, pp. 49 and 60, online available at: www.iccl.ie/equality-for-all-families-.html, visited 19 June 2014, p. 60; B. Tobin, 'Same-Sex Couples and the Law: Recent Developments in the British Isles', 23 *International Journal of Law, Policy and the Family* (2009) p. 309 at p. 318 and Ryan 2011, *supra* n. 41, at p. 12.

59 Bill Number 54 of 2004.

60 Explanatory memorandum to Bill Number 54 of 2004.

61 Section 6 of the Bill Number 54 of 2004.

62 Seanad Éireann Debates [Senate debates], Vol. 179, 16 February 2005.

63 The All-party Oireachtas Committee on the Constitution, *Tenth progress report, The Family* (Stationery Office, Dublin 2006), p. 87, online available at www.constitution.ie/Documents/Oireachtas%20 10th-Report-Family%202006.pdf, visited June 2014.

The Committee furthermore held that '[...] an amendment to extend the definition of the family would cause deep and long-lasting division in our society and would not necessarily be passed by a majority.'[64] Still, it recommended the introduction of the civil partnership for both same-sex and different-sex couples.[65] Other authoritative pleas for the introduction of legal recognition of same-sex relationships were simultaneously made. A 2006 report of the Irish Human Rights Commission (IHRC) on *de facto* couples concluded that from an international human rights point of view there was a compelling case to be made for the State to provide some formal level of legal recognition to same-sex couples, if not to *de facto* couples generally.[66] The Irish Council for Civil Liberties, for its part, made a plea for the opening up of marriage to same-sex couples.[67]

In March 2006 the Minister for Justice, Equality and Law Reform established a Working Group on Domestic Partnership.[68] The Group's task was

> '[...] to consider the categories of partnerships and relationships outside of marriage to which legal effect and recognition might be accorded, consistent with Constitutional provisions and to identify options as to how and to what extent legal recognition could be given to those alternative forms of partnership, including partnerships entered into outside the State.'[69]

For this purpose the Working Group was to take into account models in place in other countries.[70] By the end of November 2006 the working group published an options paper,[71] which examined various options for unmarried cohabiting couples, namely: contractual arrangements; a presumptive scheme; limited civil partnership; full civil partnership; and legislative review and reform. The introduction of partnership for different-sex couples which would be equivalent or closely analogous to marriage was considered to be '[...] vulnerable to constitutional challenge on the ground that it constitute[d] an attack on the institution of marriage by providing a competing institution'.[72] In addition the Working Group was '[...] not convinced that there [were] many cohabiting opposite-sex couples who [were] unwilling to marry but [would] be willing to enter a registration scheme which ha[d] all the attendant obligations of

---

64 *Idem*, at p. 122.

65 Tobin argued that a civil partnership for different-sex couples would be unconstitutional, as it would amount to a state-sponsored institution competing with marriage. Tobin 2008, *supra* n. 52.

66 J. Walsh and F. Ryan, *The Rights of De Facto Couples* (Dublin, Irish Human Rights Commission 2006) p. 130, online available at www.ihrc.ie/download/pdf/report_defactocouples.pdf, visited June 2014.

67 Irish Council for Civil Liberties, *Equality for all families*, April 2006, p. 60, online available at www.iccl.ie/equality-for-all-families-.html, visited June 2014.

68 See www.justice.ie/en/JELR/Pages/PR07000328, visited June 2014.

69 Www.justice.ie/en/JELR/Pages/PR07000947, visited June 2014.

70 See the Group's Terms of reference as reproduced on www.justice.ie/en/JELR/Pages/PR07000328, visited June 2014.

71 Options Paper presented by the Working Group on Domestic Partnership to the Tánaiste and Minister for Justice, Equality and Law Reform, Mr. Michael McDowell, T.D., November 2006, online available at www.justice.ie/en/JELR/OptionsPaper.pdf/Files/OptionsPaper.pdf, visited July 2014.

72 *Idem*, at p. 45.

marriage'.[73] By contrast, the Group believed that full civil partnership for same-sex couples was recommendable. Such a partnership was seen as a distinct institution separate from, and not competing with, marriage, and thus not suffering the same constitutional vulnerability as full civil partnership for different-sex couples.[74] The opening up of marriage to same-sex couples was nevertheless held to be vulnerable to constitutional challenge, '[...] given the special position marriage [was] afforded in the Constitution and the interpretation of the definition of marriage in constitutional actions before the Courts'.[75] In this respect the options paper also noted that a High Court judgment was pending in the *Zappone & Anor* case, concerning the recognition of a foreign same-sex marriage.[76] Even though this concerned a cross-border case, and would thus fit in best under section 11.4 below, it is discussed most extensively in this section, as the case has proven highly important for Ireland's national debate and standard-setting on legal recognition of same-sex couples.

11.3.2. The *Zappone & Anor* judgment (2006)

In *Zappone & Anor* v. *Revenue Commissioners & Ors* (2006),[77] two women who had concluded a marriage in Canada unsuccessfully claimed they should be allowed to profit from certain tax benefits that were afforded exclusively to married couples under the Taxes Consolidation Act 1997. The Revenue Commissioner refused to recognise their marriage certificate from British Columbia, Canada. When the case came before the Irish High Court in 2006, Justice Dunne was confronted with the question of whether the right to marry inherent in the Constitution encompassed the right to same-sex marriage, and if not, whether the traditional right as interpreted in the impugned provisions was incompatible with the provisions of the ECHR. Justice Dunne ruled that the refusal to recognise the Canadian marriage certificate had not breached any of the plaintiffs' rights as marriage as defined in the Irish Constitution was between a man and a woman. The Justice did not accept the arguments of the plaintiffs to the effect that the definition of marriage as understood in 1937, when the Constitution was enacted, required to be reconsidered in the light of standards and conditions prevailing in 2010.

Justice Dunne first observed that there was no consensus around the world that supported a widespread move towards same-sex marriage. She then continued:

> 'Marriage was understood under the 1937 Constitution to be confined to persons of the opposite sex. That has been reiterated in a number of [...] decisions [...], notably the decision of Costello J. in *Murray* v. *Ireland*, the Supreme Court decision in *T.F.* v. *Ireland* and the judgment of Murray J. in *T.* v. *T.* [...] Judgment in the *T.* v. *T.* case was given as

[73] *Idem*, at p. 45.
[74] *Idem*, at p. 51.
[75] *Idem*, at pp. 50–51.
[76] *Idem*, at p. 51.
[77] *Zappone & Anor* v. *Revenue Commissioners & Ors* [2006] IEHC 404.

recently as 2003. Thus it cannot be said that this is some kind of fossilised understanding of marriage.'[78]

Justice Dunne furthermore pointed out that in Ireland 'as recently as 2004' Section 2(2)(e) of the Civil Registration Act had been enacted, an Act which was entitled to a presumption of constitutionality and which had to be considered 'an expression of the prevailing view as to the basis for capacity to marry'. Reading Articles 41 and 42 of the Constitution together,[79] Justice Dunne found it '[...] very difficult to see how the definition of marriage could, having regard to the ordinary and natural meaning of the words used, relate to a same sex couple.'

The High Court Justice furthermore found that the plaintiffs were not treated in law any differently from any other non-married different-sex couple. And even if there was in fact any form of discriminatory distinction between same-sex couples and different-sex couples by reason of the exclusion of same-sex couples from the right to marry, 'then Article 41 in its clear terms as to guarding' and 'the issue as to the welfare of children' provided the necessary justification.[80] In conclusion Justice Dunne held that the plaintiffs' claim for recognition of their Canadian marriage and the challenge to the relevant provisions of the Tax Code failed.

The strong adherence by Justice Dunne to the historical approach, instead of interpreting the Constitution contemporaneously as a living instrument, was criticised for not being consistent with previous case law.[81] O'Sullivan furthermore wondered whether '[...] in dealing with capacity to exercise a right constituting a traditional constitutional value, recently enacted legislation or regulation [could] suffice.'[82]

As regards the claims made under the ECHR, Justice Dunne referred to the judgment of the English High Court in the case of *Wilkinson and Kitzenger*.[83] She found that judgment 'compelling' in setting out '[...] the position in relation to the right of marriage as identified by the European Court of Human Rights in [*Christine*] *Goodwin*.'[84] *Christine Goodwin* had concerned a post-operative transsexual who was refused an alteration of her sex on the birth register and could therefore not marry someone from the post-operative different sex. The English High Court had held that the breach of Article 12 found in *Christine Goodwin* was based on the

78 *Idem*. The *T.* v. *T* case to which the Judge refers concerns *D.T.* v. *C.T.*, 1 ILRM 321.

79 Art. 42 of the Constitution of Ireland provides for a right to education and refers to 'parents' in this regards.

80 For a critique on this reasoning see B. Tobin, 'Recognition of Canadian Same-sex Marriage: Zappone and Gilligan v Revenue Commissioners and Others', 1 *Irish Human Rights Law Review* (2010) p. 217 at p. 222.

81 O'Sullivan for example argues that the contemporaneous interpretation as adopted by the Court in *Sinnott* v. *Minister for Education* [2001] 2 IR 505 should have been applied. O'Sullivan 2009, *supra* n. 4, at p. 488.

82 *Idem*, at p. 485.

83 *Wilkinson and Kitzinger* v. *Attorney General*, a decision of the High Court (Unreported, 31st July, 2006) by Potter J.

84 On *Christine Goodwin* (2002), see Ch. 8, section 8.2.1.

ECtHR's finding that gender could be determined by criteria other than simply biological factors. Thus, from *Christine Goodwin* no right to same-sex marriage could be deduced. The English High Court held that '[...] the wording of Article 12 refer[red] to the right to "marry" in the traditional sense (namely as a marriage between a man and a woman)' and noted that there were clear limitations to the 'living instrument' doctrine. Because there was no Europe-wide consensus on the subject, the Convention could not be treated as having evolved and as having expanded its scope to encompass same-sex relationships within the concept of marriage, the English Court concluded. Justice Dunne saw no reason for reaching any conclusion different from that which the English High Court had reached in the *Wilkinson and Kitzenger* case.

Justice Dunne nevertheless explicitly invited the Irish legislature to take further action in this field. She acknowledged that undoubtedly people in the position of the plaintiffs, whether they were same-sex couples or different-sex couples, could '[...] suffer great difficulty or hardship in the event of the death or serious illness of their partners.' Therefore she held that it was 'to be hoped that the legislative changes to ameliorate these difficulties' would not be 'long in coming.' The Justice did not consider this a matter up to the courts though; ultimately, it was for the legislature to determine the extent to which such changes had to be made, she held. This invitation did not go unheard, but the legislative process proved time consuming.[85]

11.3.3. Towards a Civil Partnership Act

In December 2006 – the same month in which the High Court judgment in *Zappone & Anor* was delivered – the Irish Labour Party tabled its Civil Unions Bill.[86] In line with the abovementioned options paper on domestic partnership, the Bill proposed a civil registration scheme extending the full range of rights and duties of marriage to same-sex couples.[87] The second stage of the debate on the Bill was delayed after the approval of a government amendment to that effect. The amendment noted that terms of the Civil Unions Bill 2006, as presented, appeared to be 'inconsistent with the provisions of the Constitution', in particular 'the State's constitutional duty to protect with special care the institution of marriage'. Also, it was regarded as prudent to await the Supreme Court decision in the *Zappone & Anor* case as that case had been appealed in the meantime.[88]

Late April 2007 the *Dáil Éireann* was dissolved. After the elections of May 24, 2007 the Bill was put before the new parliament, but again the debate was adjourned.

---

85 As explained further in section 11.3.6 below, the *Zappone* case was subsequently appealed to the Supreme Court.

86 Bill Number 68 of 2006.

87 Explanatory Memorandum to Bill Number 68 of 2006, p. 3.

88 Dáil Éireann – Volume 632 – 21 February, 2007, Civil Unions Bill 2006: Second Stage (Resumed), online available at www.historical-debates.oireachtas.ie/D/0632/D.0632.200702210028.html, visited 9 July 2014.

Reportedly the Minister for Justice Equality and Law Reform, opposed the Bill after having been '[...] advised by the Attorney General that it was contrary to the explicit recognition given to the family based on marriage in the Constitution.'[89] The legislative programme of the newly appointed Irish government, however, contained the commitment to legislate for civil partnership at the earliest possible date in the lifetime of the government.[90] Subsequently in June 2008, the General Scheme of the Civil Partnership Bill was published[91] and a year later, in June 2009, the government presented its Civil Partnership Bill 2009 to the Houses of the Oireachtas.[92] According to its Explanatory Memorandum the purpose of the Bill was the following:

> 'The purpose of the Bill is to establish a statutory civil partnership registration scheme for same-sex couples together with a range of rights, obligations and protections consequent on registration, and to set out the manner in which civil partnerships may be dissolved and with what conditions.'[93]

By limiting access to civil partnership to same-sex couples, the new institution would not rival marriage (which was open to different-sex couples only) and would thus not be subject to constitutional challenge on this point.[94] It was presumably because of the same constitutional concerns that the complex and lengthy Bill stated in detail which rights and obligations applied to civil partners. Ryan observed in this regard at the time:

> 'The earlier bills simply stated that civil partnership would be equivalent to marriage in most respects. The Government Bill, by contrast, seeks to enumerate one by one the various rights and responsibilities that will apply to civil partners. While far more laborious, it appears this approach was preferred for constitutional reasons, the logic being that a direct equation with marriage is more likely to provoke constitutional concerns. The Government thus preferred to list explicitly the various consequences of civil partnership without seeking to compare it directly with marriage. A review of the proposal, however, reveals a union that (with some important exceptions) is substantially

---

89 Y. Moynihan, "God has given you one face and you give yourself another": The implications of transsexual recognition in matters of marriage: Dr Lydia Foy's laudable victory spawns reform in terms of same-sex unions', 11 *Irish Journal of Family Law* (2008) p. 38.

90 Programme for Government 2007–2012, www.taoiseach.gov.ie/eng/.../ProgforGovEng.rtf, visited June 2014. At p. 87 of this Programme it was held: 'This Government is committed to full equality for all in our society. Taking account of the options paper prepared by the Colley Group and the pending Supreme Court case, we will legislate for Civil Partnerships at the earliest possible date in the lifetime of the Government.'

91 Ryan referred to the publication of this scheme as marking 'a watershed in modern Irish law'. F. Ryan, 'The General Scheme of the Civil Partnership Bill 2008: Brave New Dawn or Missed Opportunity?', 11 *Irish Journal of Family Law* (2008) p. 51.

92 Civil Partnership Bill 2009, Bill No. 44 of 2009.

93 Explanatory Memorandum to the Civil Partnership Bill 2009, p. 1.

94 Ryan 2012, *supra* n. 7, at pp. 233–234, referring (in footnote 182) to J. Mee, 'Cohabitation, Civil Partnership and the Constitution' in Doyle and Binchy (eds.), *Committed Relationships and the Law* (Dublin, Four Courts Press 2007), pp. 201–207.

> equivalent to marriage. In fact, it is clear from the heavy borrowing from current marriage legislation, that civil partnership is based largely on the same blueprint.'[95]

This approach thus removed most constitutional concerns and the Bill passed through the *Dáil* 'relatively smooth and speedy'.[96] In the *Senead* it met with more concerns, mainly, as Ryan has explained, in relation to conscientious objections.[97] Still, in July 2010, both Houses of the Oireachtas passed the Bill; in the *Dáil* it was passed without a vote, while the *Senead* adopted the Bill with a 48-4 vote.[98] Soon thereafter, on 19 July, the President signed the Bill, without a reference to the Supreme Court for a review of its constitutionality.[99] The Civil Partnership and Certain Rights and Obligations of Cohabitants Act 2010[100] (hereafter referred to as 'Civil Partnership Act' or 'the 2010 Act') entered into force in January 2011. The Act introduced two new schemes, namely civil partnership and (qualified) cohabitation.[101] The latter scheme, that applies automatically to cohabiting partners in an 'intimate and committed relationship' – whether of different or the same sex – who meet certain criteria, is not extensively discussed here. Instead, the focus lies on the civil partnership.

11.3.4. The Civil Partnership Act 2010

Civil partnership as introduced by the 2010 Act is open to same-sex partners only. In other words, only same-sex couples have the option of entering into a civil partnership, while different-sex couples only have the option of concluding a civil marriage. Other impediments to the registration of a civil partnership occur, *inter alia*, when the parties to the intended civil partnership are married, already in a civil partnership or are under the age of 18 years.[102]

The prospective civil partners must give three months' written notice of their intention to enter into the partnership. While marriage can be celebrated by religious solemnisers, this does not hold for civil partnership; the ceremony for registering the partnership is wholly secular.[103] A civil partnership can be dissolved through a court order, after the partners have lived apart for two out of the three preceding years.[104]

---

95 Ryan 2008, *supra* n. 91, at pp. 51- 57. See also Ryan 2012, *supra* n. 7, at p. 247.

96 See Ryan 2011, *supra* n. 41, at p. 13.

97 *Idem.* This concern was no longer very visible in the debate once the Act was adopted.

98 See Center for Evaluation Innovation, *Civil Partnership and Ireland: How a Minority Achieved a Majority. A case study of the gay and lesbian equality network* (Center for Evaluation Innovation, November 2012) p. 13, online available at www.glen.ie/attachments/Case_Study_-_How_a_minority.PDF, visited 9 July 2014.

99 Art. 26 Constitution of Ireland.

100 Civil Partnership and Certain Rights and Obligations of Cohabitants Act 2010, No. 24/2010, online available at www.irishstatutebook.ie/2010/en/act/pub/0024/print.html, visited 9 July 2014.

101 Ryan 2011, *supra* n. 41, at p. 8.

102 Section 2(2)(A) Civil Registration Act 2004, as amended by Section 7(3) of the Civil Partnership and Certain Rights and Obligations of Cohabitants Act 2010.

103 See Ryan 2011, *supra* n. 41, at p. 13.

104 Section 12 of the Civil Partnership and Certain Rights and Obligations of Cohabitants Act 2010.

Again, there is a difference with marriage in this regard, as spouses must have been living apart for four out of the five preceding years before they can divorce.[105]

Despite these differences of a more procedural nature, civil partnership has substantially generally been put on a par with marriage. The rights and obligations of civil partners are in many respects 'largely identical' to those of spouses, for example in respect of maintenance, property and succession.[106] The Civil Partnership Act does not deal with taxes and social assistance, but simultaneous and subsequent amendments of the relevant legislation established that, also in respect of these matters, civil partners were treated the same as spouses.[107] Still, a 2011 study by LGBT advocacy organisation *Marriage Equality* found 169 differences in treatment between civil partners and spouses under Irish legislation, concerning mainly '[...] family law, immigration, housing, court procedure, inheritance, taxation and freedom of information [...].'[108]

The most prominent – and much debated – exception to the general equalisation of civil partnership with marriage indeed concerned parental rights and various other situations involving children. As discussed more extensively in the following subsection, the 2010 Civil Partnership Act did not provide for anything in this regard. As this was heavily criticised, in the years that followed, new proposals for legislation were drafted which aimed to protect the position of children born with civil partners and cohabiting (same-sex) partners (see section 11.3.5 below).

While the Civil Partnership Act was generally welcomed as a great improvement for the protection of the rights of same-sex couples, the 'separate but equal' approach at the bottom of the introduction of this new regime for same-sex couples only, has been criticised.[109] As Ryan has pointed out, an important implication thereof is that there is no constitutional protection of the civil partnership. As a consequence, 'civil partnership could be abolished without constitutional difficulty'.[110] This lack of constitutional protection was further confirmed by the Supreme Court, which ruled in a 2009 judgment that the constitutional protection of the family did not extend to *de facto* families, as further explained hereafter in section 11.3.5.1.[111]

105 Art. 41.3.2° of the Constitution of Ireland.

106 Ryan 2011, *supra* n. 41, at p. 14.

107 Finance (No. 3) Act 2011, No. 18/2011 and Social Welfare and Pensions Act 2010, No. 37/2010.

108 P. Faugan, *Missing pieces. A comparison of the rights and responsibilities gained from civil partnership compared to the rights and responsibilities gained through civil marriage in Ireland* (Marriage Equality 2011) p. 6, online available at www.marriagequality.ie/download/pdf/missing_pieces.pdf, visited July 2014.

109 Ryan 2008, *supra* n. 91, referring (in footnote 4) to the arguments put forward by *Marriag Equality*. See www.marriagequality.ie, visited July 2014.

110 Ryan 2012, *supra* n. 7, at p. 242.

111 *McD* v. *L. & Anor* [2009] IESC 81, [2010] 2 IR 199. See 11.3.5.1 below.

11.3.5. Parental rights for same-sex couples under Irish law

As the previous sections have made clear, for a long time same-sex relationships did not enjoy any legal protection under Irish law. This was even more so for so-called rainbow families – families built by same-sex partners. In fact, *de facto* families in general – including unmarried different-sex couples – have long had to do without any legal protection.[112] The Irish constitutional reading and protection of the family is limited to the family based on marriage (as explained above) and the legislation long showed a strong adherence to biological parenthood. As O'Connell noted in 2010, '[a]part from adoption and guardianship situations, there is no recognition of non-biological parenthood in Irish law.'[113] In that same year McLoone observed that there seemed to be '[...] a reluctance to recognise the position of same-sex couples as parents'.[114] Reddington noted that '[...] perhaps it [was] time that Ireland's own historic interpretation of the family under the Constitution [was] revisited and amended to suit the needs of the citizens it serve[d] in a more modern, diverse and increasingly secular society.'[115] As explained in the following subsections, change may indeed be underway.

Access to reproductive services is in principle guaranteed for same-sex couples and lesbian and gay individuals under equality legislation that has been in place in Ireland since the year 2000. Nonetheless, as explained in Chapter 5, section 5.3.3, same-sex couples may encounter refusals when they try to get access to AHR treatment.

Yet before the introduction of civil partnership for same-sex couples in 2011, incidental High Court rulings showed an increased recognition of parenting by same-sex couples. In *Zappone & Anor* (2006) Justice Dunne held that further studies were necessary before a firm conclusion as to the consequences of same-sex marriage for the welfare of children could be reached,[116] but she also held that there was

> '[...] no evidence of any kind tendered to the court to demonstrate that children brought up by a same sex couple or a single homosexual parent [were] adversely affected by the family structure in which they are raised.'[117]

---

112 The lack of legal rights for non-biological parents was also 'one of the key themes' running through a 2013 study on LGBT parents in Ireland. J. Pillinger and P. Fagan, *LGBT parents in Ireland. A study into the experiences of Lesbian, Gay, Bisexual and Transgender People in Ireland who are parents or who are planning parenthood*, Report commissioned by LGBT Diversity, February 2013, p. 113, online available at www.marriagequality.ie/download/pdf/lgbt_parents_in_ireland_full_report.pdf, visited July 2014.

113 D. O'Connell, *Legal Study on Homophobia and Discrimination on Grounds of Sexual Orientation and Gender Identity, Thematic Study Ireland* (Galway 2010) p. 12, online available at http://fra.europa.eu/en/national-contribution/2012/country-thematic-studies-homophobia-transphobia-and-discrimination, visited June 2014.

114 C. McLoone, 'Civil Partnership and Certain Rights and Obligations of Cohabitants Act 2010: A Practitioner's Guide', 14 *Irish Journal of Family Law* (2011) p. 58.

115 D. Reddington, 'Civil Partnership vs Marriage – the Approach of the European Court of Human Rights', 14 *Irish Journal of Family Law* (2011) p. 15.

116 *Zappone & Anor* v. *Revenue Commissioners & Ors* [2006] IEHC 404.

117 *Idem*, at 118.

In 2008, the High Court in *McD* v. *L & Anor* even went as far as to grant legal protection to same-sex *de facto* families. This ground-breaking ruling was, however, overruled by the Supreme Court a year later.

11.3.5.1. McD v. L & Anor (2009): no constitutional protection of same-sex de facto family life

In December 2009 the Supreme Court rendered its judgment in the *McD* v. *L & Anor* case. The facts of this case about a sperm donor who wished to have access to his biological child, born to a lesbian couple, have been set out in Case Study I (see Chapter 5, section 5.3.4). In *McD* v. *L & Anor*, the High Court had initially – and for the first time – ruled that the two lesbian women and their child enjoyed protection as a *de facto* family under Article 8 ECHR. Judge Hedigan had acknowledged that the Irish Constitution did not recognise 'the concept of a same-sex de facto family', but had noted that this did not preclude the recognition of the '*de facto* heterosexual family' by the courts.[118] The High Court Judge based this protection on the right to respect for family life ex Article 8 ECHR, even though the ECtHR had at the time not yet brought same-sex relationships within the scope of that Article. The Judge concluded:

> '[...] where a lesbian couple live together in a long term committed relationship of mutual support involving close ties of a personal nature which, were it a heterosexual relationship, would be regarded as a de facto family, they must be regarded as themselves constituting a de facto family enjoying rights as such under article 8 of the European Convention on Human Rights. Moreover, where a child is born into such a family unit and is cared for and nurtured therein, then the child itself is a part of such a de facto family unit. Applying this to the case here it seems clear that between the respondents and the infant there exist such personal ties as give rise to family rights under article 8 of the ECHR.'[119]

On this basis the High Court denied the applicant, the sperm donor, access to his biological child that was being raised by its biological and genetic mother and her lesbian partner. The case was, however, appealed and consequently the ruling of the Irish High Court was overturned by a unanimous Supreme Court judgment of 10 December 2009.[120] The Supreme Court judges felt that the High Court had gone too far and exceeded its jurisdiction by 'outpacing' the ECtHR and so developing 'previously non-existent rights by reference to the ECHR'.[121] In the words of Judge Fennelly:

---

118 C. Power and G. Shannon, 'Practice and Procedure, Sperm donors and the legal recognition for same-sex couples', 11 *Irish Journal of Family Law* (2008) p. 44.

119 *McD* v. *L. & Anor* [2009] IESC 81, [2010] 2 IR 199 at 235–236, as quoted in Ryan 2012, *supra* n. 7, at p. 216.

120 C. Hogan,'JMcD v PL and BM Sperm Donor Fathers and De Facto Families', 13 *Irish Journal of Family Law* (2010) p. 83.

121 C. Murray, 'Recognising the Modern Family: Extending Legislative Guardianship Rights in Ireland', 15 *Irish Journal of Family Law* (2012) p. 39.

> 'The existing case-law of the European Court seems clearly to be to the effect that a de facto family of the sort claimed does not come within the scope of Article 8. [...] It is important that the Convention be interpreted consistently. The courts of the individual states should not adopt interpretations of the Convention at variance with the current Strasbourg jurisprudence.'

The Supreme Court reiterated that the protection of the family under the Irish Constitution only saw at the family based on marriage and in addition held that there was no Irish law in place that recognised *de facto* same-sex families. Judge Fennelly explained that '[...] [n]either the Constitution nor the law in force in Ireland recognise[d] persons in the position of the respondents as constituting a family with the natural child of one of them'.[122] Judge Geoghegan observed that there was '[...] nothing wrong with the rather useful expression 'de facto family' provided it [was] not regarded as a legal term or given a legal connotation'.[123] Judge Denham was as firm as to hold that '[t]here is no institution in Ireland of a de facto family.'[124]

The Supreme Court made clear that this finding did not mean that the *de facto* situation of the parties to the case should not be taken into consideration. However, in assessing the matter, so the Supreme Court ruled, the child's welfare was a primary consideration. It was 'the kernel of the issue' in questions concerning guardianship, custody and access.[125] On the basis of the welfare of the child central to this case, the Supreme Court requested the High Court to make access arrangements for the applicant to the child.[126]

This Supreme Court judgment thus once again confirmed the 'narrow conception of the family in the Constitution'.[127] Hogan observed that the judgment was 'in keeping with the trend in favour of biological truth and contact with natural parents' and 'clearly' represented 'a blow for so called "non-traditional families"'.[128] Daly held it conceivable that the decision would be challenged in the future 'on the basis that it is no longer in conformity with the Convention.'[129] Ryan observed, on the other hand, that the judgment made clear that, '[...] to the extent that the definition of family in the Convention would bring the Convention into conflict with the Constitution, the Constitution would, as a matter of domestic law, prevail.'[130] With a view to the later judgment of the ECtHR in the case of *Schalk and Kopf* v. *Austria* to the effect that same-sex couples enjoy protection of the right to respect for family life under Article 8 ECHR,[131] this is an even more interesting finding.

122 *McD* v. *L & Anor* [2010]1 ILRM 461, Fennelly J.
123 *McD* v. *L & Anor* [2010]1 ILRM 461 at 495, Geoghegan J.
124 *McD* v. *L & Anor* [2010]1 ILRM 461, Denham J.
125 *Idem*, at 63.
126 O'Shea 2012, *supra* n. 11, at p. 90.
127 Murray 2012, *supra* n. 121.
128 Hogan 2010, *supra* n. 120.
129 A. Daly, 'Ignoring Reality: Children and the Civil Partnership Act in Ireland', 14 *Irish Journal of Family Law* (2011) p. 82.
130 Ryan 2008, *supra* n. 91, p. 218.
131 See Ch. 8, section 8.2.2.

The Supreme Court's ruling thus denied the legal protection that High Court Judge Hedigan had granted to rainbow families. Supreme Court Judge Fennelly expressly noted that the absence of any provisions in Irish law securing the rights of these families seemed something that called 'for urgent consideration by the legislature.'[132] By the time the *McD* v. *L & Anor* judgment came out, the Civil Partnership Act and a revision of the Adoption Act were yet under debate in Parliament. However, both Acts failed to provide for the identified need for legal protection of rainbow families.

11.3.5.2. Limited change brought about by the 2010 Adoption Act and the 2010 Civil Partnership Act

In 2010 a new Adoption Act entered into force which was still in force when this research was concluded (i.e., 31 July 2014). While until that time only married couples who were living together could adopt a child,[133] the new Act introduced single-parent adoption, rendering it possible for lesbian and gays to become parents of a non-genetic child. A single person or one partner of a couple – irrespective of his or her sexual orientation – may adopt if the Adoption Authority considers it desirable. The Authority must regard the welfare of the child as its first and paramount consideration.[134] The civil partner or cohabiting partner of an adoptive parent may seek access to the child, but cannot establish any parental links with the child.[135]

While the Ombudsman for Children had at the time advised to also enable both different-sex and same-sex unmarried couples to jointly adopt a child, no such option was introduced by the Adoption Act 2010.[136] Same-sex couples only have the option of submitting a joint application to foster children.[137] The Children's Ombudsman considered the State's policy in this regard inconsistent and 'arbitrary from the child's point of view'.[138] She wondered what the purpose was of barring these couples from applying to adopt and observed in this respect:

> 'It cannot logically arise from a concern on the part of the State regarding the capacity of unmarried opposite-sex and same sex couples to care for children, given that the State already entrusts young people to their care – potentially for many years – and has already provided in law for a situation in which they can effectively occupy the role of guardians. Indeed, during the debates in the Seanad regarding the Adoption Bill, the Minister for

132 *McD. v. L. & Anor* [2008] IEHC 96, Hedigan J.

133 E.g. Section 10 Adoption Act 1991, No. 14/1991.

134 Section 33 Adoption Act 2010, No. 21/2010.

135 See also www.citizensinformation.ie/en/birth_family_relationships/cohabiting_couples/adoption_and_unmarried_couples.html, visited July 2014.

136 Ombudsman for Children, *Advice of the Ombudsman for Children on the Adoption Bill 2009*, 2009, p. 27, online available at www.oco.ie/wp-content/uploads/2014/03/Adviceonadoption.pdf, visited July 2014.

137 Murray 2012, *supra* n. 121.

138 Ombudsman for Children 2009, *supra* n. 136, at p. 23.

> Children and Youth Affairs clarified that, based on the experience of the foster services, the State has no difficulty with same-sex couples being parents or minding children.'[139]

The Civil Partnership Act that entered into force a few months after the 2010 Adoption Act did not bring any further protection for rainbow families. In fact, the Act did simply not address the question of parental rights for civil partners.[140] As Ryan observed, 'a studious effort' had been made '[...] generally to avoid the use of the term "family" as a description for civil partners'. The author was of the view that this was 'undoubtedly a consequence of the confinement of family in the Constitution to the family based on marriage.'[141] Daly explained that the 2010 Civil Partnership Act contained many provisions that were taken from laws relating to marriage and noted that while '[...] in many of the original provisions, references were made to the need to provide for the interests of children of the family', such references had not been included in the Civil Partnership Act 2010, 'intentionally removing children from the legislative picture.'[142]

That the matter had simply not been unforeseen, was also illustrated by the fact that during the debates on the Civil Partnership Bill in the *Seanad* an amendment to provide for step-parenthood for civil partners had been rejected.[143] Also, the Ombudsman for Children had been critical of the Civil Partnership Bill:

> 'Although the situation of children was clearly considered in the drafting of the Civil Partnership Bill, the approach adopted was not one which placed the rights of the children who will be affected by the Bill to the forefront. Indeed, provisions from other areas of the law that acted as templates for the Civil Partnership Bill and which included references to the need to provide for dependent children of the family were adapted for the Civil Partnership Bill in a manner which effectively removed the protections afforded to children of marital families from children with same-sex parents in a civil partnership.'[144]

As a result of the approach chosen, children of parents in civil partnerships were not granted the same protection as children of married parents. For example, as explained

139 *Idem*, p. 24, referring (in footnote 36) to Seanad Éireann, Parliamentary Debates, Vol. 194 No. 6, p. 361, online available at www.oco.ie/wp-content/uploads/2014/03/Adviceonadoption.pdf, visited July 2014. See also GLEN – Gay and Lesbian Equality Network, *Submission to Joint Oireachtas Committee on Justice, Defence and Equality on the Heads of the Children and Family Relationships Bill*, February 2014, p. 3, online available at www.glen.ie/attachments/GLEN_Submission_to_Oireachtas_Committee_on_the_Heads_of_Children__Family_Relationships_Bill.pdf, visited July 2014.

140 As Ryan explains, the Act was not 'entirely oblivious to the existence of children'. For example, in granting maintenance in case of dissolution of a civil partnership, the Court must take into account the civil partner's obligations to his or her biological and adopted child(ren). Ryan 2011, *supra* n. 41, at p. 27.

141 Ryan 2012, *supra* n. 7, at pp. 236–237.

142 Daly 2011A, *supra* n. 133.

143 Amendment 37. See also Law Reform Commission, *Report on the Legal Aspects of Family Relationships*, December 2010, LRC 101–2010, p. 39, online available on www.lawreform.ie/_fileupload/Reports/r101Family(1).pdf, visited July 2014.

144 Ombudsman for Children, *Advice of the Ombudsman for Children on the Civil Partnership Bill 2009*, July 2010, online available at www.oco.ie/wp-content/uploads/2014/03/Advice-OCO-Civil-Partnership-Bill-2009.pdf, visited July 2014.

by Ryan, '[...] civil partnership dissolution [...] may be granted without reference to the needs of children' and no mechanism is in place '[...] allowing the biological parent to share guardianship rights with his or her civil partner.'[145] Other differences between the legal position of children raised by spouses and those growing up with civil partners relate to maintenance upon relationship breakdown, shared home protection and succession to the tenancy of a deceased parent.[146]

The Law Reform Commission urged the legislature in December 2010, thus right before the entry into force of the Civil Partnership Act, to introduce legislation to facilitate the extension of parental responsibility to civil partners and step-parents.[147] This did not go unheard, although it would take the Minister until January 2014 to introduce draft legislation.

11.3.5.3. The Children and Family Relationships Bill (2014)

The Irish government announced in 2011 that it intended to amend the 2010 Civil Partnership Act, in order 'to address any anomalies or omissions, including those relating to children'.[148] It took until 2014, however, for the Children and Family Relationships Bill (as also discussed in Chapter 5, section 5.3.2) to be drafted, in which (some of) these matters were indeed addressed.

A first important change that was to be brought about by the Children and Family Relationships Bill concerned joint adoption by civil partners,[149] something which the Ombudsman for Children had pleaded for years earlier.[150] The Bill envisaged that civil partners would be able to jointly adopt a child, including in intercountry situations. In a revised version of the Bill this was extended to cohabiting couples who had been living together for at least three years.[151] The Bill did not explicitly provide for second-parent or successive adoption, but it seems unlikely that this would be outlawed now that joint adoption is to be introduced.

---

145 Ryan 2012, *supra* n. 7, at p. 239.

146 Daly 2011A, *supra* n. 129, at pp. 82–86.

147 The Commission recommended that where parental responsibility was extended by court order the court would have regard 'to, among other factors, the wishes and best interests of the child and the views of other parties with parental responsibility.' Law Reform Commission 2010, *supra* n. 143, at p. 41.

148 Government for National Recovery 2011–2016, online available at www.taoiseach.gov.ie/eng/Work_Of_The_Department/Programme_for_Government/Programme_for_Government_2011–2016.pdf, visited June 2014.

149 Children and Family Relationships Bill 2014, Head 77.

150 See note 136 above. This development was welcomed by the Ombudsman for Children. Ombudsman for Children, *Advice on the General Scheme of the Children and Family Relationships Bill 2014*, May 2014, p. 57, online available at www.oco.ie/wp-content/uploads/2014/06/OCOAdviceonChildandFamilyRelBill2014.pdf, visited June 2014.

151 General Scheme of the Children and Family Relationships Bill, Summary of Provisions, online available at www.justice.ie/en/JELR/Note%20on%20the%20General%20Scheme%20of%20the%20Children%20and%20Family%20Relationships%20Bill.pdf/Files/Note%20on%20the%20General%20Scheme%20of%20the%20Children%20and%20Family%20Relationships%20Bill.pdf, visited July 2014.

Secondly, the Bill provided for detailed rules on the establishment of parental links in situations involving AHR treatment and/or surrogacy. As explained in Chapter 5,[152] the relevant provisions of the Bill were based on the rule that the birth mother was always considered the child's mother, and thus, as the parent. Importantly, provision was made for legal parenthood by operation of the law for female civil partners. Under the Bill it was made possible for the civil or cohabiting partner of the mother to become the parent, and thus guardian, of the child.[153] As explained in the General Scheme, '[t]he husband, civil partner or cohabitant of the mother [was] considered to be the other parent of the child if he or she ha[d] given a consent which remain[ed] valid at the time the procedure leading to implantation [took] place.'[154] Also, there was a rebuttable presumption of consent on the part of the mother's spouse, partner or cohabitant to becoming a child's parent.[155]

Further, disputes between parents were not solved on the basis of a genetic link only; in order to protect the rights of the child '[...] a genetic parent [could not] exclude the other parent by obtaining a declaration that s/he [was] not a parent of the child, nor [could] a parent repudiate her or his responsibilities to a child on the grounds that they [were] not genetically connected.'[156] These rules thus implied a correction of the *McD* v. *L & Anor* case (see 11.3.5.1 above).

The described rules thus envisaged the granting of strong protection to the families of same-sex couples consisting of two women. This protection was not extended to male same-sex couples. The proposed rules concerning parentage in cases involving surrogacy would have enabled same-sex couples consisting of two men to both establish parental links with a child born with a surrogate mother that was genetically related to one of them.[157] Following the proposed Bill this could be done through assignment of parentage by the Court. The consent of the birth mother would have been decisive; if she did not consent, she would be the legal mother. This would also hold in situations where a lesbian couple resorted to a surrogacy agreement, including where one of them provided the ovum for the creation of an embryo that was to be implanted in the surrogate mother's womb.[158] As explained in Chapter 5,[159] the provisions on surrogacy were, however, removed from the revised version of the Bill that was published in September 2014.

152 See section 5.3.2.

153 Heads 10 and 38 Children and Family Relationships Bill 2014.

154 Explanation to Head 10, General Scheme, p. 22. Following Head 10(8) it is for the Minister to make regulations on the form that such consent must take.

155 Head 10(6) Children and Family Relationships Bill 2014.

156 Explanation to Head 10, General Scheme, p. 23. As acknowledged in the Explanatory Memorandum, these rules [...] could limit the rights of a "known donor" who wishes to establish a legal connection with a child.'. 'However', it is held, '[...] there is a balance of rights to be achieved and the best interests of the child are likely to be served by having legal certainty and security in his or her family unit.'

157 Head 12(1) Children and Family Relationships Bill 2014.

158 Head 12(2) Children and Family Relationships Bill 2014.

159 See section 5.3.9.

The Bill furthermore provided for the equalisation of the legal position of children whose parents were in a civil partnership with that of children whose parents were spouses, in respect of maintenance, shared home protection and responsibilities towards the children in situation of a dissolution.[160] The Minister for Justice affirmed in April 2014 that the Bill would not 'downgrade or devalue' the traditional marital family but [would] ensure all children are treated equally'.[161]

11.3.6. Towards access to marriage for same-sex couples?

Already before civil partnership was introduced in Ireland, voices were heard that the creation of a new institution only for same-sex couples, instead of opening up marriage to these couples was discriminatory and treated this group as second-class citizens. The Irish Council for Civil Liberties (ICCL), for example, held such in 2006. The ICCL noted 'the inherent paradox in the adage "separate but equal"' and was of the view that the marriage ban compromised same-sex couples' right to dignity and equality.[162] In legal scholarship it was also observed that full equality for same-sex couples 'undoubtedly' demanded equal access to civil marriage.[163]

It has been much debated in legal academia and in politics whether the opening up of marriage to same-sex couples would require constitutional amendment, and thus whether a referendum on the matter would be mandatory. While the Constitution refers to the marriage institution in neutral terms, the Supreme Court in its case law defined marriage as between a man and a woman only.[164] As Ryan explained in 2011:

> '[...] it remains somewhat unclear whether the Constitution precludes same-sex marriage. Article 41.3 does not define marriage and on its face does not appear to prevent same-sex marriage from being enacted. On the other hand, to interpret Article 41.3 as potentially applying to same-sex as well as opposite-sex marriage would involve a significant departure from the historical meaning of marriage.'[165]

The strong reliance on this historical and static constitutional understanding of marriage by High Court Justice Dunne in *Zappone*, could be held to support the conclusion that the opening up of marriage to same-sex couples would require a

---

160 Heads 72–74 of the Children and Family Relationships Bill 2014 (Revised version September 2014). See also GLEN – Gay and Lesbian Equality Network, *Submission to Joint Oireachtas Committee on Justice, Defence and Equality on the Heads of the Children and Family Relationships Bill*, February 2014, p. 8, online available at www.glen.ie/attachments/GLEN_Submission_to_Oireachtas_Committee_on_the_Heads_of_Children__Family_Relationships_Bill.pdf, visited June 2014.

161 P. Duncan, 'New Bill 'won't devalue' traditional marital families', *Irishtimes.com* 10 April 2014, www.irishtimes.com/news/social-affairs/new-bill-won-t-devalue-traditional-marital-families-1.1757969, visited July 2014.

162 Faugan 2011, *supra* n. 108, at p. 8.

163 Ryan 2008, *supra* n. 91.

164 See 11.1.2 above. O'Sullivan held in 2009 that there was '[...] no textual exclusion in the Constitution precluding a same-sex couple from exercising a personal right to marry each other.' O'Sullivan 2009, *supra* n. 4, at p. 487.

165 Ryan 2011, *supra* n. 41, at p. 36.

referendum.[166] Others expressed the view that there was no constitutional impediment to the opening up of marriage.[167] Tobin grounded this conclusion in the clear judicial deference of the Court in this matter and in other sensitive social matters, as displayed by Justice Dunne in *Zappone*.[168] At the same, the author took into account the option that the judiciary would instead 'slam the door firmly shut on same-sex marriage', if a Bill opening up marriage to same-sex couples would be referred to the Supreme Court by the President under Article 26 of the Irish Constitution.[169]

When the Irish government prepared the Civil Partnership Act, some authors wondered whether the government planned 'on it being the last word on the same-sex marriage debate'.[170] This turned out not to be the case, however, for long, an argument against the undertaking of any legislative action on the matter was the pending appeal in the *Zappone & Anor* case (see 11.3.2 above) before the Supreme Court.[171] Many authors at the time thought that the Supreme Court was likely to defer to the legislature, just like the High Court had.[172] The case remained pending for several years, however, and in the meantime, the legislature took the initiative in the matter.

In 2011 the government announced the establishment of a Constitutional Convention, a forum of 100 representatives from Irish society and politics, to make recommendations on possible Constitutional reform. Amongst the topics to be covered by the Convention was 'provision for same-sex marriage'.[173]

While the Convention was in progress, a hearing in the *Zappone* case was scheduled for June 2012. Reportedly, the plaintiffs dropped the case just a few weeks before that, and lodged a fresh application with the High Court instead. As Tobin explained:

---

166 Ryan 2012, *supra* n. 7, at pp. 222–223.

167 *Idem*, at p. 223, referring (in footnotes 120 and 121) to E. Carolan, 'Committed Non-Marital Couples and the Irish Constitution', in Doyle and Binchy (eds.), *Committed Relationships and the Law* (Dublin, Four Courts Press 2007); Tobin 2012A, *supra* n. 14; C. O'Mahony, 'Constitution is not an obstacle to legalising gay marriage', *Irish Times*, July 16, 2012, online available at www.irishtimes.com/newspaper/opinion/2012/0716/1224320203659.html and E. Daly, "Same sex marriage doesn't need a referendum", 15 July 2012, online available at www.humanrights.ie/index.php/2012/07/15/same-sex-marriage-doesnt-need-a-referendum.

168 Tobin 2012A, *supra* n. 14.

169 *Idem*. See also *supra* n. 99.

170 *Idem*, at p. 321. Tobin later opined that the enactment of Civil Partnership legislation '[...] could sound the death knell for the recognition of a right to same-sex marriage under Art. 41 of the Constitution.' He explained that that was '[...] because the High Court could display the same legislative deference as Dunne J. in 2006 and consequently refuse to expand the current constitutional understanding that marriage is heterosexual in nature by finding that the 2010 Act represents the prevailing social consensus on the appropriate form of legal recognition for same-sex relationships.' Tobin 2012B, *supra* n. 27, at p.104.

171 The appeal to the Supreme Court was lodged in 2007. See also Tobin 2007, *supra* n. 15, at p. 175.

172 *Inter alia*, O'Sullivan, *supra* n. 4, at p. 488 and Tobin 2010, *supra* n. 80, at p. 221.

173 The task that the Constitutional Convention has been given is set out in the Resolution of the Houses of the Oireachtas of July, 2012, online available at www.constitution.ie/Documents/Terms_of_Reference.pdf, visited 8 July 2014.

> 'In the new High Court proceedings, the plaintiffs are seeking to impugn s. 2(2)(e) of the Civil Registration Act 2004 [...], the first Irish statutory provision to define marriage as between a man and a woman. This provision went unchallenged in the original High Court proceedings in 2006. The plaintiffs also claimed that they would mount a challenge to the Civil Partnership and Certain Rights and Obligations of Cohabitants Act 2010 [...].'[174]

The latter application was still pending at the time of conclusion of this research (i.e., 31 July 2014). As a result of rapid developments in the meantime, however, the opening up of marriage to same-sex couples in Ireland has become increasingly more realistic. In July 2012 the Deputy Prime Minister, the *Tánaiste*, declared his support for marriage equality.[175] In April 2013 the Constitutional Convention favoured a Constitutional amendment requiring the legislature to legislate for same-sex marriage, by a clear majority of 79 per cent.[176] The Convention also supported the introduction of legislation '[...] to address the parentage, guardianship and upbringing of children in families headed by same-sex married parents.'[177] In early 2014 the government announced that a referendum on same-sex marriage would be held in spring 2015. It was furthermore announced that the Minister for Justice and Equality would bring legislative proposals to government in 2014.[178] By the time this research was concluded (i.e., 31 July 2014), no such Bill had been published.

11.4. Same-sex relationships and cross-border movement

11.4.1. Cross-border movement; some statistics

The Central Statistics Office (CSO) of Ireland keeps statistics on the number of civil partnerships registered per year. For example, there were 536 civil partnerships registered in 2011[179] and 429 in 2012.[180] These statistics do not give any details on matters like the nationality of the partners concerned.

---

174 Tobin 2012B, *supra* n. 27, at p. 102.

175 See www.humanrights.ie/index.php/2012/07/01/marriage-equality-and-the-weight-to-be-borne-by-the-constitutional-convention, visited July 2014.

176 This outcome was in line with opinion polls of 2012 which showed that at the time 74 per cent of the Irish people was in favour of marriage equality for same-sex couples. See *Marriage Equality*'s submission to the 2013 Constitutional Convention, pp. 4–5, online available at www.marriageequality.ie/getinformed/me_publications/marriage-equality-constitutional-convention-submission, visited July 2014.

177 *Third Report of the Convention on the Constitution. Amending the Constitution to provide for same-sex marriage*, June 2013, online available at www.constitution.ie/AttachmentDownload.ashx?mid=c90ab08b-ece2-e211-a5a0-005056a32ee4, visited July 2014.

178 *Programme for Government: Annual Report 2014, Government for National Recovery 2011–2016*, March 2014, p. 70, online available at: www.taoiseach.gov.ie/eng/Work_Of_The_Department/Programme_for_Government/Programme_for_Government_Annual_Report_20141.pdf, visited June 2014.

179 These concerned 335 male unions and 201 female unions. See www.cso.ie/en/newsandevents/pressreleases/2013pressreleases/pressreleasemarriagesandcivilpartnerships2011, visited June 2014.

180 These concerned 263 male unions and 166 female unions. See www.cso.ie/en/newsandevents/pressreleases/2014pressreleases/pressreleasemarriagesandcivilpartnerships2012, visited June 2014.

This is different for statistics that Gay and Lesbian Equality Network GLEN has published, on the basis of figures provided by the General Registrar Office.[181] These statistics show that by August 2014, in total 2,934 people entered Civil Partnerships in Ireland since they first became available in 2011. It was thereby noted that '[t]hese figures [did] not account for the hundreds of Irish lesbian and gay people who were married or entered a civil partnership abroad.'[182]

Of the 2,934 people that entered Civil Partnerships in Ireland since 2011, no less than 25 per cent (714 persons) had another nationality than Irish. Almost half of them (300 persons) were EU citizens, with UK nationals and Polish nationals being the biggest groups represented (136 and 53 respectively). At the same time, it was noted that '[...] most of the couples who entered a Civil Partnership in Ireland intended to live in Ireland after their civil partnership.' Only 64 out of 1,467 couples – hence 9.6 per cent – intended to live in another country. Out of these 64, 22 intended to live in another EU Member State. This may be an indication of the scale at which so-called 'registration tourism' takes place, however, because these statistics are not accompanied by any interpretation, no firm conclusions can be drawn in this regard.

11.4.2. Access to civil partnership for foreign same-sex couples

Before civil partnership was introduced in the Irish jurisdiction, foreign same-sex couples had, just as Irish same-sex couples, no access to any form of legal recognition in Ireland. This changed with the entry into force of the Civil Partnership Act 2010. Under this Act there is no requirement of residence, domicile or nationality of the (future) civil partners.[183] This implies that foreign same-sex couples can enter into a civil partnership in Ireland, so long as they – like residents and nationals of Ireland – fulfil the criteria under the 2010 Act[184] and meet the general requirements set out by the General Register Office (GRO).[185] The statistics referred to above show that this opportunity has indeed been seized upon by same-sex couples consisting of one or two foreign partners.

---

181 GLEN – Gay and Lesbian Equality Network, *Civil Partnerships in Ireland: Figures from April 2011 to 30th June 2014* Released: 17th August 2014, online available at www.glen.ie/attachments/Civil_Partnership_Statistics_to_June_2014.pdf, visited June 2014.

182 *Idem* .

183 A domicile requirement has only been set for special court orders, for instance for court orders declaring '[...] that the civil partnership was at its inception a valid civil partnership'. Art. 4(1) Civil Partnership Act.

184 Article 7A Civil Partnership Act.

185 General Register Office (GRO) of Ireland, 'Information note on Civil Partnership', www.welfare.ie/en/Pages/Civil_Partnership.aspx, visited July 2014.

11.4.3. Implementation of Directives 2004/38 and 2003/86 in Irish law

The Free Movement Directive (2004/38) was implemented in Ireland by means of a statutory instrument of 2006 ('the 2006 Regulations').[186] This instrument makes a distinction between 'qualifying family members' of Union citizens and 'permitted family members'. The first group includes the spouse of the EU citizen and their minor or dependant children.[187] Qualifying family members may not be refused entry, unless there is a clear and individualised health or public security risk.[188] The category of 'permitted family members' includes other members of the EU citizen's household, as well as 'the partner with whom the Union citizen has a durable relationship, duly attested'.[189] Whether someone is indeed a 'permitted family member' within the meaning of this instrument, is established on the basis of 'an extensive examination of the personal circumstances of the person concerned'.[190] Unless the Minister is not satisfied that the person concerned is a permitted family member, entry may, again, only be refused if such entry would pose a clear and individualised health or public security risk.[191]

The Family Reunification Directive (2003/86/EC) has not been transposed into Irish law.[192] Only for persons with refugee status has provision been made for family reunification. Under Article 18 of the Refugee Act 1996,[193] spouses, minor children and – in exceptional cases – other dependent family members[194] of refugees can apply for family reunification. This excludes same-sex partners, whether they are spouses, civil partners or stable partners. As pointed out by O'Connell in 2010, the existence of such formal relationships could, however, '[...] impact positively on the assessment of a relationship for the purpose of dealing with a family reunification claim [...].'[195] On an *ad hoc* discretionary basis exceptional leave to enter for the

---

186 European Communities (Free Movement of Persons) (No. 2) Regulations 2006, S.I. No. 656 of 2006, amended in 2008 by European Communities (Free Movement Of Persons) (Amendment) Regulations 2008, S.I. No. 310 of 2008.

187 Art. 2(1) S.I. No. 656 of 2006 reads: '[...] "qualifying family member", in relation to a Union citizen, means – (a) the Union citizen's spouse; (b) a direct descendant of the Union citizen who is – (i) under the age of 21, or (ii) a dependant of the Union citizen; (c) a direct descendant of the spouse of the Union citizen who is – (i) under the age of 21, or (ii) a dependant of the spouse of the Union citizen; (d) a dependent direct relative of the Union citizen in the ascending line, or (e) a dependent direct relative of the spouse of the Union citizen in the ascending line.'

188 Art. 4(2) S.I. No. 656 of 2006.

189 Art. 2(1) S.I. No. 656 of 2006.

190 Art. 5(2) S.I. No. 656 of 2006.

191 Art. 5(4) S.I. No. 656 of 2006.

192 D. O'Connell 2010, *supra* n. 113, at p. 13.

193 Refugee Act 1996, No. 17/1996.

194 This excluded life partners, as 'dependent member of the family', in relation to a refugee, is defined as '[...] any grandparent, parent, brother, sister, child, grandchild, ward or guardian of the refugee who is dependent on the refugee or is suffering from a mental or physical disability to such extent that it is not reasonable for him or her to maintain himself or herself fully.' Art. 18(4)(b) Refugee Act 1996.

195 D. O'Connell 2010, *supra* n. 113, at p. 13.

purpose of reunifying same-sex partners had been granted by the Minister for Justice, Equality and Law Reform.[196]

When Civil Partnership was introduced in Ireland in 2011, neither the 2006 Regulations, nor the Refugee Act were amended. The immigration authorities, however, adopted an official policy of treating a civil partnership in the same way as marriage for immigration purposes.[197] In other words, both same-sex registered partners and same-sex spouses of EU citizens are – in principle – granted entry as 'qualifying family members' under the 2006 Regulations, and same-sex civil partners and same-sex spouses of refugees qualify for family reunification under the Refugee Act. Couples in partnerships that are not recognised under Irish law as civil partnership,[198] may be recognised as *de facto* couples (hence as 'permitted family members') under the 2006 Regulations. There is also a policy of treating same-sex stable partners and different-sex stable partners in the same way.[199] These policies were only made publicly available through the website of the Irish Naturalisation and Immigration Service.

LGBT advocacy organisation *Marriage Equality* reported in 2011 that there was a gap between the official policy and the legislative reality. It was held:

> 'Differences include, civil partners not being included under the definition of 'qualifying family members' in regulations which transposed EU free movement provisions. This may mean the Irish Government are in breach of their obligations under this EU directive. As a result of the approach taken to deal with civil partnership through immigration policy rather than by amending immigration legislation [...] civil partners are left without the protection and certainty of the law. Rather they are reliant on measures of policy that may change in a way that does not apply to legislation.'[200]

When this research was concluded (i.e., 31 July 2014) no legislative amendments had been made in this respect, except for that in 2011 it was established that civil partners are treated equally with and married couples in legislation on acquiring Irish citizenship.[201]

---

196 O'Connell underlined that there was only anecdotal evidence to this effect and that in the absence of statistical evidence of this granting of exceptional leave, it was 'impossible to analyse the manner in which this discretion [had been or was being] exercised.' D. O'Connell 2010, *supra* n. 113, at p. 13.

197 Website of the Irish Naturalisation and Immigration Service, www.inis.gov.ie/en/INIS/Pages/Civil%20 Partnership, visited June 2014.

198 On recognition, see section 11.4.4 below.

199 Website of the Irish Naturalisation and Immigration Service, www.inis.gov.ie/en/INIS/Pages/Civil%20 Partnership, visited June 2014. It is there held that: 'There is no change in the manner in which partners who are neither civil partners [...] nor married persons are dealt with. The existing arrangements continue to apply and the gender mix in such partnerships is not material to the immigration decision.'

200 Faugan 2011, *supra* n. 108, at p. 7.

201 Section 33 of the Civil Law (Miscellaneous Provisions) Act 2011, No. 23/2011.

11.4.4. Recognition of foreign partnerships and marriages under Irish law

Before the introduction of civil partnership in Ireland, foreign same-sex civil partnerships and marriages were not recognised under Irish law. This practice was confirmed by the High Court judgment in *Zappone & Anor*, where the High Court held that under Irish law 'marriage' saw at different-sex marriage only (see 11.3.2 above).

The situation changed with the entry into force of the Civil Partnership Act in 2011. Following its Section 5, foreign legal relationships can be recognised as civil partnerships under Irish law, provided certain requirements are met. The relationship must be exclusive in nature under the law of the jurisdiction in which the legal relationship was entered into. Also, it must be registered under the law of that jurisdiction and it must be permanent, unless the parties dissolve it through the courts. Lastly, the rights and obligations attendant on the relationship must be, in the opinion of the Irish Minister for Justice, Equality and Law Reform, '[...] sufficient to indicate that the relationship would be treated comparably to a civil partnership'.[202] If the same-sex partners to a relationship legally recognised in another country are within the prohibited degrees of relationship, as set out in the Irish Civil Registration Act, they are not treated as civil partners under Irish law.[203] This means, *inter alia*, that foreign different-sex partnerships are not recognised as civil partnership in Ireland, as there is an impediment to enter into a civil partnership in Ireland if the partners are not of the same sex.

The Minister for Justice, Equality and Law Reform has the power to recognise classes of foreign civil partnerships by order, which must be laid before the Houses of the Oireachtas.[204] Since the entry into force of the 2010 Act, three such orders have been adopted.[205] The lists of recognised partnerships includes the UK Registered Partnership and the German *Eigetragene Lebenspartnerschaft*, but the French PACS and the Dutch registered partnership – which can both be dissolved without court order – are not on the list and thus not recognised as civil partnerships under Irish law.

Foreign same-sex marriages are only recognised as civil partnerships in Ireland, not as marriages. Same-sex marriages from countries like the Netherlands, Belgium, Spain and Portugal are included in the relevant orders. Consequently, 'downgrading' takes place in the Irish context. The present author is not aware of any case law

---

202 Art. 5(1) S.I. No. 656 of 2006.

203 Art. 5(3) S.I. No. 656 of 2006.

204 Art. 5(1) and (5) S.I. No. 656 of 2006.

205 State of affairs on 31 July 2104. These concern: S.I. No. 649 of 2010 Civil Partnership (Recognition of Registered Foreign Relationships) Order 2010; S.I. No. 642 of 2011 Civil Partnership (Recognition of Registered Foreign Relationships) Order 2011 and S.I. No. 505 of 2012 Civil Partnership (Recognition of Registered Foreign Relationships) Order 2012. These are online available on the website of the Irish Naturalisation and Immigration Service, www.inis.gov.ie/en/INIS/Pages/Civil%20Partnership, visited July 2014.

from the Irish courts in which this has been challenged on the basis of the EU free movement provisions.

11.4.5. Parental issues

The present author has not become aware of any court proceedings following difficulties that foreign same-sex couples have had in having their parental links recognised in Ireland. A 2008 study by O'Connell implied that such difficulties could, nonetheless, occur. He noted:

> 'Because of the privilege attaching to biological parenthood in Irish law the family reunification rights of children and their biological parents are stronger. Obviously, this may have a further disproportionate adverse impact on LGBT parents where only one or neither party is the biological parent of the child or children in question.'[206]

Same-sex couples who have resorted to surrogacy in another country, may, moreover, experience difficulties in establishing their legal parenthood in Ireland, as set out in Chapter 5, section 5.5.4.

The 2014 Family Relationships Bill provided for various amendments to the Adoption Act as a result of which adoptive parents from other countries moving to Ireland would have their adoptions recognised in Ireland.[207] Gay and Lesbian Equality Network GLEN observed in this regard:

> 'This is an important provision for lesbian and gay couples who may have adopted jointly in other countries, for example the UK and who subsequently move to live and work Ireland, to be recognised as the parents of the child here.'[208]

11.4.6. Recognition of Irish civil partnerships in other Member States

There is little reason to think that people who concluded a civil partnership in Ireland will experience difficulties in having their partnership recognised in other EU Member States that also provide for a civil partnership for same-sex couples. Obviously this may be different in States that do not provide for any such form of recognition.

---

206 D. O'Connell, *Legal Study on Homophobia and Discrimination on Grounds of Sexual Orientation and Gender Identity, Thematic Study Ireland* (Galway 2008), p. 10, online available at http://fra.europa.eu/en/country-report/2012/country-reports-homophobia-and-discrimination-grounds-sexual-orientation-part-1, visited June 2014, as confirmed in D. O'Connell 2010, *supra* n. 113, at p. 13.

207 Part 12 of Children and Family Relationships Bill 2014 (version September 2014).

208 GLEN – Gay and Lesbian Equality Network, *Submission to the Justice, Defence and Equality Committee on the Heads of the Children & Family Relationships Bill*, February 2014, pp. 8–9, online available at www.glen.ie/attachments/GLEN_Submission_to_Oireachtas_Committee_on_the_Heads_of_Children__Family_Relationships_Bill.pdf, visited June 2014.

11.5. Conclusions

The development of the Irish law on legal recognition of same-sex couples demonstrates how much Ireland has changed in over one generation.[209] While homosexual conduct was criminalised until 1993, because it was considered 'morally wrong' and 'damaging to the health both of individuals and the public',[210] in 2013 the Constitutional Convention, by a clear majority, favoured a Constitutional amendment requiring the legislature to legislate for same-sex marriage. These progressive legal changes have been attributed to a series of factors, such as '[...] joining the EU in 1973, an increasingly vocal feminist movement, the economic boom of the 1990s and the weakening grip of the Catholic Church, largely due to sex abuse scandals.'[211]

The Irish Courts have been firm in defining marriage as protected under the Irish Constitution as between man and woman only. They explicitly deferred to the legislature in respect of the introduction of any form of legal recognition of same-sex relationships. The High Court *Zappone* judgment (2006) thus formed an impetus for legislative change, together with the introduction of civil unions in the UK in 2004 combined with Ireland's obligations under the Good Friday agreement (section 11.3).

While the first civil partnership Bill was already on the table in 2004, it took until 2011 before the introduction of civil partnership for same-sex couples was a reality. Various debates were adjourned and bills withdrawn. Also, there were constitutional concerns that the new institute would be too similar to marriage. This was reason for the legislature to take a 'separate but equal' approach (section 11.3.4). Parental matters have proven most controversial in this context. This is, again, explained by the traditional understanding of family that dominated the Irish laws for centuries. At the time of conclusion of this research (i.e., 31 July 2014), there was no second-parent adoption, no successive adoption, no joint adoption and no legal parenthood by operation of the law for same-sex couples. This could all change at once if the Children and Family Relationships Bill is adopted. The guiding principle for this fundamental change has been the rights of the child.[212]

Moreover, by 2014 the opening up of marriage to same-sex couple had become a realistic option. Because a constitutional amendment was considered necessary, a referendum was announced for spring 2015. All in all, because of these significant changes, Ireland is '[...] less likely to be seen as an anomalous case among Western developed nations.'[213]

---

209 Ryan noted in 2011 that '[...] in many respects the [Civil Partnerships] Act demonstrate[d] just how much Ireland [had] changed in less than a generation.' Ryan 2011, *supra* n. 41, at p. v.

210 *Norris* v. *Attorney General* [1983] IESC 3; [1984] IR 36.

211 Wording ascribed to S.-A. Buckley, a social historian at National University of Ireland in Galway, by H. Mahoney, 'Same-sex marriage underlines social change in Ireland', *euobserver.com* 7 May 2013, www.euobserver.com/lgbti/119963, visited July 2014.

212 As noted by Canavan in 2012, 'Ireland has been part of the global shift in the position of children, primarily facilitated by an increasing emphasis on children's rights [...]'. J. Canavan, 'Family and Family Change in Ireland: An Overview', 33 *Journal of Family Issues* (2012) p. 10 at p. 24.

213 *Idem*, at p. 23.

Religion played a fairly modest role in the Irish debates and standard-setting in respect of legal recognition of same-sex relationships. While in early cases like *Norris* (1983) and *Murray* (1985) references were made to Christianity, in later cases in this area, no such references were repeated. When civil partnership was introduced in 2010, religion was explicitly left out of the equation, as it was provided that religious solemnisers could not celebrate civil partnership.

The case law of the ECtHR has played a twofold role in the Irish context. On the one hand it has been an important (although presumably not the only) factor in abolishing the criminalisation of homosexual conduct in the early 1990s. On the other hand, it has been referred by Irish courts as a ground for not extending certain rights to same-sex couples.[214]

In cross-border cases the Irish standard is upheld. Foreign same-sex civil partnerships and marriages are only recognised in Ireland if they meet the criteria of the Irish civil partnership. This means that partnerships that can be dissolved outside the courts and different-sex partnerships are not recognised. Most relevant rules in this regard are laid down in Ministerial orders and policy documents, instead of in statutory legislation. In respect of cross-border cases involving parental matters, much may change when the foreseen changes of Family Relationships Bill may take effect. Also, if marriage is indeed opened up, this will inevitably mean that foreign same-sex marriages are also recognised as such under Irish law

Because Irish law sets no domicile or nationality requirements, the Irish civil partnership is very accessible to foreign same-sex couples. Statistics show that the Irish civil partnership indeed has an international character (section 11.4.1), yet as these statistics are not accompanied by any further interpretation, one has to be careful in inferring any conclusions from these numbers.

214 In *Zappone & Anor* v. *Revenue Commissioners & Ors* (2006) the Court (indirectly) referred to the ECtHR's judgment in *Christine Goodwin* (2002) as justification for holding on to the traditional marriage concept, while in *McD* v. *L & Anor* (2009) the Supreme Court referred to the ECtHR caselaw when it ruled that *de facto* same-sex family life enjoyed no protection under the Convention or Irish law. The Court explicitly held in the latter case that the Irish Courts were not to 'outpace' the ECtHR (see section 11.3.5.1 above).

Chapter 12
The Netherlands

12.1. Constitutional framework

The number of provisions in the Dutch Constitution that are of direct relevance for the present case study on legal recognition of same-sex couples is fairly limited. The Dutch Constitution does not contain a right to respect for family life, nor is the right to marry constitutionally protected. Article 10(1) of the Constitution protects the right to respect for private life, and it may be said to also cover a right to establish personal and intimate relationships with other persons of one's choosing.[1] However, as pointed out by Boele-Woelki et al. in 2006, this right has not been invoked in any legal procedures, presumably because Dutch legislation sufficiently protected this right,[2] as this chapter will confirm. Also of importance are the rights of the child, which are not expressly protected by the Constitution either; the protection of these rights was further explained in Chapter 6, section 6.1.2. By contrast, an important provision of the Dutch Constitution for the present case study is its Article 1, which protects the right to equal treatment.

As stressed before, because the Netherlands' constitutional system adheres to a relatively 'monist theory' of International Law, international guarantees binding upon the Netherlands such as the ECHR, directly filter into the national legal system. Therefore, the ECHR as interpreted and applied in the ECtHR's case law, and as set out in Chapter 8, basically makes up for an important part of the Dutch constitutional framework in respect of legal recognition of same-sex couples.

12.1.1. Equal treatment (Article 1)

Since 1983 the Dutch Constitution has contained a non-discrimination clause which prohibits '[d]iscrimination on grounds of religion, belief, political opinion,

---

1 See W.C.J. Robert and J.M.A. Waaijer (eds.), *Relatievrijheid en recht: inleidingen en verslag van de Leidse Conferentie van 25 en 26 mei 1982* [Relationship freedom and the law: introductory remarks to and report of the Leiden Conference of 25 and 26 May 1982] (Deventer, Kluwer 1983) p. XI.

2 K. Boele-Woelki et al., *Huwelijk of geregistreerd partnerschap? Een evaluatie van de Wet openstelling huwelijk en de Wet geregistreerd partnerschap in opdracht van het Ministerie van Justitie* [Marriage or registered partnership? An evaulation of the Act opening up marriage and the Registered Partnership Act by order of the Ministry of Justice] (The Hague, WODC, Ministerie van Justitie 2006, Annex to *Kamerstukken II* 30800-VI no. 32), p. 13, referring (in footnote 60) to W. Schrama, *De niet-huwelijkse samenleving in het Nederlandse en Duitse recht* [Non-marital cohabitation in Dutch and German law] (Amsterdam, Ars Notariatus Kluwer 2004) pp. 233–234.

race or sex or on any other grounds whatsoever'.[3] The wording 'or any other grounds whatsoever' was inserted first of all because Parliament explicitly wished to also cover discrimination against lesbians and gays.[4] This was accompanied by discussions in Parliament about the introduction of equal treatment legislation. In 1994 the *Algemene Wet Gelijke Behandeling* (General Equal Treatment Act (GETA)) entered into force. It outlaws discrimination on grounds of sexual orientation in the area of employment and the provision of services.[5] Further, under Article 429*quater* of the Criminal Code it is a criminal offence to 'discriminate against persons on the grounds of their race, religion, beliefs, sex or heterosexual or homosexual orientation', in the execution of a 'profession, business or official capacity'.[6]

Over the past decade in particular, the Dutch government has taken an active stance against discrimination on grounds of sexual orientation, for example by means of a national action plan to improve the social acceptance and empowerment of LGBT citizens.[7]

12.2. (De-)criminalisation of homosexual activities

When the Netherlands were under French rule after the French Revolution, in 1791, the criminalisation of homosexual acts was abolished. This was confirmed in the *Code Pénal* of 1811.[8] A century later, however, in the year 1911, as part of the Legislation on Public Morals (*'Zedelijkheidswetgeving'*) a new Article 248*bis* was included in the Criminal Code, which criminalised 'lewd acts' (*'ontuchtige handelingen'*) between an adult and a consenting minor of the same sex who had not reached the age of 21 years.[9] Fundamental societal changes during the 1960s

3 *Stb.* 1983, 70.

4 See C. Waaldijk, 'Constitutional Protection Against Discrimination of Homosexuals', 13 *Journal of Homosexuality* (1986/1987) p. 57 at pp. 59–60.

5 *Stb.* 1994, 230.

6 For the purposes of this provision, Art. 90 quater Sr defines discrimination as '[...] any form of distinction or any act of exclusion, restriction or preference that intends or may result in the destruction or infringement of the equal exercise, enjoyment or recognition of human rights and fundamental freedoms in the political, economic, social or cultural field, or in any other area of society'.

7 For example, during the period 2008–2011, a comprehensive LGBT national action plan entitled 'Simply Gay', was in implemented, which encompassed 60 different measures, including 24 projects sponsored by various government departments to improve the social acceptance and empowerment of LGBT citizens. Dutch Ministry of Education, Culture and Science (2007), *Gewoon homo zijn; Lesbisch en homoemancipatiebeleid 2008–2011* [Simply gay; Dutch Government LGBT Policy document 2008–2011], Netherlands: Ministry of Education, Culture and Science, online available (in Dutch) at www.rijksoverheid.nl/documenten-en-publicaties/notas/2007/11/14/notalesbisch-en-homo-emancipatiebeleid-2008–2011-gewoon-homo-zijn.html, visited April 2011.

8 G. Hekma, *Homoseksualiteit in Nederland van 1730 tot de moderne tijd* [Homosexuality in the Netherlands from 1730 to the modern age] (Amsterdam, Meulenhoff 2004) p. 40.

9 Act adopted on 20 May 1911, *Stb.* 1911, 130, entry into force 15 June 1911, *Stb.* 1911, 135. The present author is not aware of any official statistics on the number of prosecutions based on this provision in the Dutch Criminal Code. Historian Hekma has reported (without references) that in the period 1911–1971 a total number of approximately 5,000 persons were prosecuted on the basis of Art. 248*bis* Sr (*old*), of which approximately 2,800 were convicted, while 1,500 cases were dismissed. Hekma 2004, *supra* n. 8, at p. 70. Hekma notes (at p. 96) that the number of criminal convictions on the basis of Art. 248*bis*

resulted in the crossing out of Article 248*bis* of the Criminal Code in the year 1971.[10] Since that time, the minimum age of 16 years for consensual intercourse also applies to acts between persons of the same sex.[11]

12.3. Legal recognition of same-sex relationships under Dutch law

The question of legal recognition of same-sex relationships was briefly discussed in parliament in 1970, in the context of the abolition of the criminal prohibition on homosexual acts (see 12.2 above).[12] In the early 1990s it became the subject of several court proceedings, but in most of these cases, the applicants were unsuccessful. For instance, the Court of Appeal of The Hague ruled in 1981 that under Dutch law same-sex marriage could not exist.[13] While this ruling triggered discussion on same-sex marriage in legal scholarship,[14] eventually the issue only really got political attention after a judgment of the Supreme Court of 1990.[15]

12.3.1 The 1990 Supreme Court judgment on same-sex marriage

In 1988 a woman appealed to the District Court of Rotterdam against the refusal of a registrar of the municipality of Ridderkerk to conclude a marriage between her and

---

did not increase considerably during the Second World War. He claims (at p. 100) that the factual persecution of gay men even increased after the War. The author furthermore notes (at p. 234) that is it very probable that under the Act on Public Morals many gay men were prosecuted and convicted of public indecency/outrage to public decency, which concerned another provision in the Criminal Code. Hekma refers in this context to P. Koenders, *Tussen christelijk Réveil en seksuele revolutie. Bestrijding van zedeloosheid in Nederland, met nadruk op de repressie van homoseksualiteit* (IISG Amsterdam 1996) pp. 830–831.

10 Amendment of 12 May 1971, *Stb.* 1971, 212. For the Explanatory memorandum, see *Kamerstukken II* 1969/70, 10347 no. 3. See also Boele-Woelki et al. 2006, *supra* n. 2, at p. 3.

11 Art. 245 Sr.

12 *Kamerstukken II* 1969/70, 10 347, no. 5, p. 2. See C. Waaldijk, 'Partnerschapsregistratie en huwelijk: toenemende rechtsgelijkheid voor geslachtsgelijke partners en hun kinderen' [Partnership registration and marriage: increasing equality before the law for same-sex partners and their children'], in: H. Lenters et al., *De familie geregeld?* [The family taken care of?] (Lelystad, Koninklijke Vermande 2000) p. 121 at p. 126.

13 Hof 's-Gravenhage 18 June 1981, *NJ* 1983 No. 94, ECLI:NL:GHSGR:1981:AC7248. Waaldijk has explained that [...] 'the exclusion of same same-sex couples from marriage and from certain marriage-related rights and duties, led to several test cases in the 1980s and 1990s. Some of these focused on particular privileges of marriage, such as joint parental authority, adoption, partner immigration, widow's pensions, or specific tax benefits. These cases were generally unsuccessful.' C. Waaldijk, 'Small change; how the road to same-sex marriage got paved in the Netherlands', in: R. Wintemute and M. Andenaes (eds.), *Legal Recognition of Same-Sex Partnerships – A Study of National, European and International Law* (Oxford, Hart Publishing 2001) p. 437 at p. 443. See also Waaldijk 2000, *supra* n. 12, at p. 128, where the author, *inter alia*, referred (in footnote 30) to Hof Amsterdam 6 May 1993, *NJ* 1994 No. 681, ECLI:NL:GHAMS:1993:AB9423.

14 E.g. C. Waaldijk, 'Beantwoording rechtsvraag (170). Gelijkheidsbeginsel. Homohuwelijk' ['Answer to legal question (170). The principle of equal treatment. Same-sex marriage'], 36 *Ars Aequi* (1987) p. 644.

15 E.g. I. Stroosnijder, 'Aandacht fracties gewekt. Beweging in landelijke politiek over homohuwelijk', *NG* no. 41, 12 October 1990, p. 8.

another woman. The District Court held that to rule, as the plaintiff petitioned, that Book 1 of the Dutch Civil Code allowed same-sex partners to enter into marriage, would be to go beyond an acceptable interpretation of the law. Since such a decision would conflict with the system of the law, it would in fact be tantamount to creating a new right.[16] The Court held this to be a matter for the legislature, not the judiciary, even more so because a ruling to that effect would have far-reaching consequences for legislation on matters like parentage, inheritance and adoption. Because of the Dutch prohibition on constitutional review of acts of parliament (‘*toetsingsverbod*’),[17] the Court did not examine the law in the light of the principle of equality ex Article 1 of the Dutch Constitution. Referring to the *Rees* judgment, where the ECtHR had ruled that Article 12 ECHR (the right to marry) pertained to the traditional marriage between persons of opposite biological sex (see Chapter 8, section 8.2.1), the District Court furthermore held that the relevant Dutch legislation was not in violation of this provision. Because of this interpretation of Article 12 ECHR, it also found no discrimination in violation of Article 14 ECHR. On largely similar grounds, the District Court dismissed the claims based on Articles 23 and 2 ICCPR, protecting the right to marry and the prohibition of discrimination.

The District Court's ruling was confirmed on appeal.[18] The Court of Appeal of The Hague held that the laws on marriage primarily served to legitimate reproduction between man and woman. Because same-sex couples did not have such a possibility of procreation, they did not come within the scope of the (existing) marriage laws. The Appeals Court endorsed the finding of the District Court that it was for the legislature to decide upon lifting the ban on access to marriage for same-sex couples. It held that if the Court were to rule to that effect, the result would be a definitive amendment of the law, which would be done entirely outside the democratic decision-making process, and which related to a complex subject-matter. Moreover, the present legislation was based on the notion that marriage was open to man and woman only, an idea that was firmly embedded in the entire western world, which had existed for many centuries and which many at the time still considered entirely natural. The plaintiff subsequently lodged a cassation appeal with the Supreme Court.

A few months before the Supreme Court gave a final ruling in this case, the District Court of Amsterdam issued a judgment in a similar case brought by two men who appealed against a refusal by a civil servant to register their same-sex marriage.[19] On the basis of teleological and systematic interpretation, the District Court ruled that a same-sex marriage did not exist under Dutch law. In line with the judgments of the Rotterdam District Court and the Court of Appeal, the District Court refused to

[16] Rb. Rotterdam 5 December 1988, NJ 1989 No. 871, as referred to by C. Waaldijk, ‘De heteroseksuele exclusiviteit van het huwelijk na Hoge Raad 19 oktober 1990’ [‘The heterosexual exclusivity of marriage after Supreme Court 19 October 1990’], 40 *Ars Aequi* (1991) p. 47 at p. 47.

[17] Article 120 Gw.

[18] Hof 's-Gravenhage 2 June 1989, *NJ* 1989 No. 871, ECLI:NL:GHSGR:1989:AB8024.

[19] Rb. Amsterdam 13 February 1990, *Rekest no.* 89.2072 H. See also K. Boele-Woelki and P.C. Tange, ‘Geen huwelijk tussen personen van hetzelfde geslacht’ [‘No marriage between partners of the same sex’], *NJCM-Bulletin* 1990, p. 456.

review the matter on the basis of International treaty law. It held that even if the refusal were in violation of a Treaty provision, it was not for the judiciary to determine the manner in which the equal treatment of same-sex couples and different-sex couples was to be established.[20]

In cassation, the Supreme Court ('*Hoge Raad*') ruled, on the basis of grammatical and teleological interpretation of the relevant section of the Dutch Civil Code,[21] that same-sex couples could not enter into marriage.[22] Even if developments in society supported the view that it was no longer justified that civil marriage was not open to same-sex couples, this could not justify an interpretation of the law which unmistakably deviated from the spirit of the law. This was even more so, since a matter was at stake which concerned public order and in relation to which legal certainty played an important role. The view that the law had to be interpreted in conformity with the principle of equality (Article 1 of the Constitution) could not alter this conclusion. The Supreme Court furthermore agreed with the Court of Appeal that Articles 12 ECHR and 23 ICCPR concerned the traditional marriage between man and woman and that the case disclosed no discrimination in violation of Article 14 ECHR or Article 2 ICCPR. The Supreme Court considered that there was no ground for interpreting Article 12 ECHR in conjunction with Articles 8 and 14 ECHR 'more dynamically' than the ECtHR had done so far in its case law.[23] According to the Supreme Court, civil marriage was traditionally defined as a durable civil union between a man and a woman, to which a series of legal effects were given which partly related to the difference in sex between the spouses and the thereto related legal consequences in respect of their future children. The fact remained, the Supreme Court considered, that it was possibly insufficiently justifiable to exclude certain legal effects that follow from marriage from the durable cohabitation of two partners of the same sex. The Supreme Court held, however, that such an issue – which could generally only be decided by the legislature anyway – was not under discussion in the case at hand. Accordingly, it dismissed the appeal.

The Supreme Court's ruling met with both approval and criticism in legal scholarship. Most scholars considered the Court's interpretation of the national and international law reasonable,[24] but some claimed that the 'heterosexual exclusiveness' of marriage as defined by the Supreme Court was in violation of the relevant ECHR and ICCPR provisions.[25] It was the *obiter dictum* in the Court's judgment – where the Court

20 *Idem*, para. 4. The Court furthermore considered the matter not to be that urgent that it could not be left to the legislature.

21 The relevant Art. 1:30 BW (*old*) read at the time: 'The law only sees at the civil aspects of marriage' ('De wet beschouwt het huwelijk alleen in zijn burgerlijke betrekkingen'). It thus did not refer to the combined gender of the future spouses.

22 HR 19 October 1990, *NJ* 1992 No. 129, ECLI:NL:HR:1990:AD1260. See also L. Mulder, 'Té gelijk voor de wet: het 'homo-huwelijk' als heet hangijzer' ['Too equal for the law: same-sex marriage as controversial issue'], 46 *Tijdschrift voor Bestuurswetenschappen en Publiekrecht* (1991) p. 307 and Waaldijk 1991, *supra* n. 16, at p. 47.

23 Critical on this point was E. Alkema in his case note to this judgment in *NJ* 1992 No. 129. The author found this exercise of judicial restraint by the Supreme Court striking.

24 *Inter alia*, the case note by E.A.A. Luijten to the ruling in *NJ* 1992 No. 129.

25 Waaldijk 1991, *supra* n. 16, at p. 54.

held that it was possibly insufficiently justifiable to exclude certain legal effects that follow from marriage from the durable cohabitation of two partners of the same sex – that laid the foundations for legislative change in the field.[26]

12.3.2. The first legislative initiatives towards legal recognition of same-sex relationships

Very soon after the Supreme Court judgment, most political parties embraced the idea of the introduction of a registered partnership for partners with a marriage impediment.[27] In the early 1990s a special commission, the Kortmann Commission, was installed by the government to investigate whether legal effects could be given to other forms of durable relationships than marriage.[28]

In its report entitled 'Ways of living together' ('*Leefvormen*'),[29] the Kortmann Commission observed that over the years a complex web of laws regulating forms of *de facto* cohabitation had come into existence which lacked coherence. The Commission therefore suggested creating three forms of registration of relationships: (1) marriage, open to different-sex couples only; (2) a life partnership ('*levensgezelschap*') which resembled marriage, but was also open to couples with marriage impediments, such as same-sex couples and relatives; and (3) a 'light' registered partnership ('*partnerschap*') which formalised *de facto* cohabitation, but with legal effects which were more limited than marriage. The report was generally positively received in the political arena.[30] The government agreed with the finding of the report that everyone had to have the possibility to have his or her durable union with another person formally registered and recognised by public law. The government also agreed that cohabiting partners who, because of an impediment to marriage, could not marry, should be enabled to officially register their durable relationship in the Registry of Births, Deaths and Marriages. Such registration was not to have any effect in regard to parental links, but the government held that it

---

26 Boele-Woelki et al. 2006, *supra* n. 2, at p. 4.

27 Waaldijk 1991, *supra* n.16, at p. 56 and Waaldijk 2001A, *supra* n. 13, at p. 443.

28 In practice, various municipalities began to register same-sex relationships in special registers. These registrations had no legal effect. According to Curry-Sumner about 130 municipalities established such registers in the early 1990s. I. Curry Sumner, *All's well that ends registered?: the substantive and private international law aspects of non-marital registered relationships in Europe: a comparison of the laws of Belgium, France, The Netherlands, Switzerland and the United Kingdom* (Antwerp, Intersentia 2005) pp. 119–120. See also P.P.M. Hoevenaars, 'Het wetsvoorstel partnerschapsregistratie' ['The bill on partnership registration'], 128 *WPNR* (1997) p. 226 at p. 227.

29 Kortmann I Commission, *Leefvormen* [Ways of living together], Annex to *Kamerstukken II* 1991/92, 22 300 VI, no. 36. *Handelingen II* 1990–91, 18, pp. 907–908. See also. C. Waaldijk, 'Vrij samen. Over het advies van de commissie-Kortmann inzake de vrijwillige registratie van leefvormen' ['Free together. On the Advice of the Kortmann Commission in respect of voluntary registration of ways of living together'], *Regelmaat* (1992) p. 43.

30 *Kamerstukken II* 1991/92, 22 700, no. 1 and *Kamerstukken II* 1992/93, 22 700, no. 3.

should be possible for a registered partner to share in the partner's parental authority (see also 12.3.6 below).[31]

In 1994 the government tabled a bill for the introduction of a registered partnership, with legal effects which were very similar to those of marriage.[32] There was one principled exception: the registered partnership would have no legal effects in respect of parental rights. Matters relating to (joint) parental authority were covered by another bill (see 12.3.6 below).[33] The original partnership bill introduced registration only for couples who were prevented from marrying because of kinship or because they were of the same sex.[34] It was held that because marriage was reserved for man and woman, an alternative form of registration for same-sex couples was desirable.[35] During the deliberations this was, however, soon amended. The registration for close relatives was rejected and the registered partnership was also opened to couples of different sexes who were not prevented from marrying, as this was considered to meet a need of different-sex couples.[36]

The (amended) registered partnership bill was adopted with a majority vote in the Lower House of Parliament ('*Tweede Kamer*') in December 1996.[37] The Senate ('*Eerste Kamer*') adopted the bill without voting in July 1997.[38] The *Wet Geregistreerd Partnerschap* (Act Introducing Registered Partnerships) entered into force on 1 January 1998.[39] It was evaluated for the first time in 2006, together with the 2001 Act which opened up marriage (see 12.3.5 below).[40]

12.3.3. The Act Introducing Registered Partnerships (1998)

With the Act Introducing Registered Partnerships, two objectives were pursued: (1) to ensure equal treatment for same-sex couples who wished to formalise their

---

31 *Kamerstukken II* 1993/94, 23 714, nos. 1–3. The intention to draft this bill was yet announced in a Government Memorandum of 1993. *Kamerstukken II* 1992/93, 22700, no. 3.

32 *Kamerstukken II* 1993/94, 23 761, no. 3, p. 2. As Hekma rightly points out the 1994 so-called 'purple' government was the first in many decades in which no Christian political party was represented. Hekma 2004, *supra* n. 8, at p. 174. For an analysis of the bill see L. Schutte-Heide-Jorgensen, 'Recht op homohuwelijk?' ['A right to same-sex marriage?'], 47 *Ars Aequi* (1997) p. 86.

33 *Kamerstukken II* 1993/94, 23 714, nos. 1–3.

34 *Kamerstukken II* 1993/94, 23 761, no. 3, p. 2.

35 *Idem,* at p. 3.

36 *Kamerstukken II* 1994/95, 23 761, no. 5. See also S.F.M. Wortmann, 'Zo zijn we niet getrouwd. De openstelling van het huwelijk voor personen van hetzelfde geslacht' ['That was not what we agreed on. The opening up of marriage for same-sex couples'], 49 *Ars Aequi* (2000) p. 82 at p. 83. Critical was M.J.A. van Mourik, 'Privaatrecht Aktueel. Geregistreerd partnerschap!' ['Topical issues of private law. Registered partnership!'], 128 *WPNR* (1997) p. 225.

37 *Handelingen II* 1996/97, 14, pp. 3374–3375. The Christian Democrats (CDA), who voted against the bill, critically noted that precision and legal certainty suffered from the haste with which this bill had been drafted. This political party, *inter alia,* felt that insufficient attention had been paid to the legal effects of this partnership in other countries. *Handelingen II* 1996/97,14, p. 3375.

38 *Handelingen I* 1996/97, 33, p. 1963.

39 Act of 5 July 1997, *Stb.* 1997, 324. The Act entered into force on 1 January 1998.

40 Boele-Woelki et al. 2006, *supra* n. 2.

relationships; and (2) to provide an alternative to different-sex couples who preferred registering a partnership over getting married.[41] To a certain extent, these objectives were difficult to reconcile: while the first objective implied that registered partnerships had to be equalised with marriage as much as possible, the second implied that the two institutions had to be 'clearly distinguishable'.[42] The result was that, while the institution of the registered partnership was sculpted 'as far as possible according to the marital model', a 'number of exceptions to this overall resemblance' were created.[43] These concerned primarily parental rights (see section 12.3.6 below).

The rights and duties of registered partners are generally equal to those of married partners.[44] The legal effects of the registered partnership are for the most part also similar to those of marriage. This in any case holds for legislation concerning property, name, inheritance, taxes, social security, criminal procedure and nationality.[45]

A registered partnership can be entered into by two persons, either of different or the same sex.[46] The partners may not be married at the time they enter into the registered partnership. The conditions for establishment of a registered partnership are broadly similar to those for marriage. The future partners must give notice of their intention to enter into a partnership to the Registry of a Dutch municipality at least two weeks before the registry ceremony.[47] The ceremony takes place in the presence of a Registrar, who draws up a certificate of registration, which is archived in the Registry of Registered Partnerships.[48] Also with regard to termination, the legislation on the registered partnership is broadly similar to that in respect of marriage.[49] A registered partnership may be dissolved by a court order at the request of one of the registered partners or of both of them.[50] If both partners consent to the termination of their partnership, they can have their partnership terminated by registration through the Registrar of Civil Status of a dated declaration, signed by both registered partners and one or more solicitors or notaries, which confirms that the registered partners have made an agreement with regard to the termination of their registered partnership.[51] Hence, while court intervention is always required for

41 *Idem, supra* n. 2, at p. 246. The Evaluation Report furthermore concluded (at p. 247) that '[f]rom the sociological research it would appear that registered partnership is regarded by both same-sex and different-sex couples as an alternative to marriage. Registered partnerships is regarded more a business arrangement, whilst the reasons for choosing to marry lie more embedded in the symbolic and emotional sphere.'

42 *Idem.*

43 *Idem*, at pp. 246–247.

44 Art. 1:80b BW. The exception is what is provided for in regard of a legal separation of married partners.

45 Boele-Woelki et al. 2006, *supra* n. 2, at p. 219.

46 Art. 1:80a (1) BW.

47 Art. 1:80a (4) BW. Where both prospective registered partners, of whom at least one has the Dutch nationality, have their domicile outside the Netherlands, but intend to enter into a registered partnership with each other in a Dutch municipality, the formal notice of registered partnership must be given to the Registrar of Civil Status of the municipality of The Hague.

48 Art. 1:17(1) BW.

49 Boele-Woelki et al. 2006, *supra* n. 2, at p. 247.

50 Art. 1:80c (1)(d) BW.

51 Art. 1:80c (1)(c) BW. Translation taken from www.dutchcivilcode.com, visited June 2014. See also Art. 1:80d BW.

dissolution of a marriage, a registered partnership can be terminated without court proceedings. Further, a registered partnership may be converted into marriage.[52]

Over the years, the legislation regulating the registered partnership has been amended several times, with the main result that the differences regarding parental rights have levelled out and the institution of registered partnerships is now even more similar to marriage than it was before. This increased equalisation of registered partnerships with marriage is discussed hereafter. First, for reasons of chronology, the opening up of marriage to same-sex partners is discussed. It has been held to be '[...] plausible that the discussion enveloping the introduction of registered partnership paved the way for or, at the very least, contributed to the opening of civil marriage to same-sex couples.'[53]

12.3.4. Towards the opening up of marriage

The entry into force of the Act Introducing Registered Partnerships did not end the debate about equal treatment of same-sex couples. In fact, even before the adoption of this Act, there was much debate in Parliament on whether marriage should be opened up to same-sex couples.[54] The above-discussed 1990 Supreme Court judgment played an important role in this debate. In 1996, i.e., before adoption of the Registered Partnerships Act, a motion was adopted in Parliament which held that marriage had to be opened up to same-sex couples.[55] In response to the motion, the Secretary of State for Justice asked the Kortmann Commission – the same Commission that had published a report on ways of living together in 1990 – to map out the advantages and disadvantages, both at the national and the international level, of the opening up of marriage to same-sex couples.[56] When the report of this 'Kortmann II Commission' was published in 1997,[57] it was clear that the Commission was divided on the matter. Controversial issues were the implications of the principle of equal treatment, the (symbolic) meaning of marriage and the effects of opening up marriage at the international level, as well as the desirability of those effects.[58] It was

52 Art. 1:80g BW. For same-sex registered partners this has only been possible since the opening up of marriage in 2001. Until 1 March 2009 it was also possible to convert a marriage into a registered partnership, but the relevant Art. 1:77(a) BW (*old*) was repealed by the Wet bevordering voortgezet ouderschap en zorgvuldige scheiding [Act advancement of continued parenthood and divorce with care] Act of 27 November 2008, *Stb.* 2008, 500, entry into force per 1 March 2009.

53 Boele-Woelki et al. 2006, *supra* n. 2, at p. 247.

54 *Idem*, at, p. 7.

55 *Kamerstukken II* 1995/96, 22 700, no. 18. It has been pointed out that this suggestion was already made in 1990 by the political party D66. Boele-Woelki et al. 2006, *supra* n. 2, at p. 7, referring to *Handelingen II* 1990/91, 18, p. 926.

56 *Kamerstukken II* 1997/98, 22 700, no. 20. The Commission was installed following two motions adopted by Parliament. *Kamerstukken II* 1995/96, 22 700, nos. 14 and 18. See also P. Vlaardingerbroek, *GS Personen- en Familierecht, titel 5A Boek 1 BW, aant. 2*, update of 1 April 2011.

57 S.C.J.J. Kortmann, *Commissie inzake openstelling van het burgerlijk huwelijk voor twee personen van hetzelfde geslacht*, Den Haag Ministerie van Justitie, October 1997. The report was presented to the Secretary of State of Justice on 28 October 1997.

58 See Boele-Woelki et al. 2006, *supra* n. 2, at p. 8.

noted that the different views within the Commission reflected the different views within society on the matter.[59] A small majority of five out of eight Commission members was of the opinion that marriage had to be opened up to same-sex couples, the decisive argument being that the existing discriminating and grievous exclusion of this group had to be ended.[60] The minority was of the view that same-sex couples and different-sex couples were equally worthy of protection, but they were not in an identical position because of same-sex couples' inability to reproduce. The minority considered reproduction an essential element of marriage.[61] These three members of the Commission furthermore attached considerable weight to the international perspective of opening up marriage and warned that the problematic consequences of the creation of so-called 'limping relationships' – relationships that were legally recognised in one State, but not in another – were not to be underestimated.[62] The majority had held that those couples concerned had to consciously accept the legal phenomenon of limping relationships.

The government agreed with the minority of the Kortmann II Commission. It held that the aim of equal treatment of same-sex and different-sex couples could also be achieved through further development of the institution of registered partnership.[63] An important argument for the government was that various other countries had introduced registered partnerships for same-sex couples or were in the course of introducing such registered partnerships, while no other country in the world had opened up marriage to same-sex couples. It subscribed to the warning of the minority of the Kortmann II Commission that opening up marriage would result in limping relationships. It furthermore felt that a 'relatively small jurisdiction like the Netherlands' was not to deviate from international practice.[64]

Parliament disagreed with the position taken by the government and, by a relatively small majority (81 to 60 votes), adopted a motion requesting the government to draft a bill for the opening up of marriage.[65] This time, albeit with some delay, the government acted accordingly[66] and a bill for an act opening up marriage was tabled in July 1999.[67] Just before the tabling of this bill the Advisory Department

---

59 *Idem*, at p. 9.

60 See also the Article by of one of the Commission-members A.W.M. Willems, 'Het homohuwelijk: een te hoge prijs?' ['Same-sex marriage: a too high a price?'], 21 *Tijdschrift voor Familie- en Jeugdrecht* (1999) p. 217.

61 F. van Vliet, 'Van achterdeur naar zij-ingang: Commissie Kortmann en gelijkgeslachtelijke leefvormen' ['From backdoor to side entrance: the Kortmann Commission and ways of living together by same-sex couples'], 14 *Nemesis* (1998) p. 13 at p. 20.

62 *Idem.*

63 *Kamerstukken II* 1997/98, 22 700, no. 23, pp. 7–8. The government was, however, prepared to introduce adoption for persons of the same sex. See 12.3.6 below. See also S.F.M. Wortmann, 'Zo zijn we niet getrouwd. De openstelling van het huwelijk voor personen van hetzelfde geslacht' ['That was not what we agreed on. The opening up of marriage for same-sex couples'], 49 *Ars Aequi* (2000) pp. 82, at p. 84.

64 See *Kamerstukken II* 1998/99, 26 672, no. 3, p. 3.

65 *Kamerstukken II* 1997/98, 22 700, no. 26 and *Handelingen II* 1997/98, 49, pp. 5642–5643.

66 See the Coalition Agreement of 1998, *Kamerstukken II* 1997/98, 26 024, no. 9. p. 68.

67 *Kamerstukken II* 1998/99, 26 672, nos. 1–2.

of the Dutch Council of State issued a negative opinion on the matter.[68] Given that no other country in the world had at the time opened up marriage to same-sex couples, the Council of State was particularly concerned about the non-recognition of marriages between same-sex spouses in other countries, which would result in limping relationships.[69] The Council felt that as long as no special rules of Private International Law were drafted on the matter, the time was not ripe for the opening up of marriage to same-sex couples.[70] The government nonetheless proceeded with the bill and postponed regulation of the Private International Law aspects to a later date (see section 12.4 below).[71] The Deputy Prime Minister even held that she wanted to try and convince other States also to open up marriage to same-sex couples.[72] The Secretary of State for Justice later explained to Parliament that this would primarily take the form of initiating consultation at the international level on registered partnerships and similar institutions, in which the opening up of marriage would be included.[73] The government first of all intended to raise awareness of and understanding for recognition issues. Subsequently it could be explored if the drafting of an international instrument was feasible, it was held.[74] The government expected it to take considerable time before these discussions would pay off.[75] The government found it difficult to predict to what extent the Dutch opening up of marriage would meet with understanding within the Council of Europe, the International Commission on Civil Status and the Hague Conference on Private International Law. From the fact that support had been expressed by these organisations for international consultation on the Private International Law aspects of new forms of unmarried cohabitation, the government concluded that in other States also views were changing. The government was therefore not afraid that the Netherlands would not be taken seriously at the international level.[76] In response to the argument made by some parties in Parliament that from an international perspective the Netherlands isolated itself by opening up marriage to same-sex couples, the government held that the legislation was drafted 'in full awareness' of the fact that for the time being, the Dutch legislation would be relatively exceptional.[77]

---

68 Advisory Department of the Council of State, Opinion of 23 March 1999, no. WO3.98.0593–19I, *Kamerstukken II* 1998/99, 26 672, no. B.

69 *Idem*, at p. 2.

70 The Explanatory Memorandum had acknowledged this legal issue and had therefore proposed to ask the State Commission on Private International Law for advice, after the bill had been adopted by Parliament. The Council of State held that conflict rules had to be drafted before the bill was sent to Parliament. This advice was, however, not followed-up. See also section 12.4 below.

71 *Kamerstukken II* 27 762 no. 3, p. 5. The Senate (*Eerste Kamer*) adopted the Bill on 23 January 2001. *Handelingen I* 2000/01, 15, pp. 687–688.

72 'Homohuwelijk exporteren', *Algemeen Dagblad* 12 December 1998, p. 3. See also *Kamerstukken II* 1999/00, 26 672, no. 4, p.16.

73 *Kamerstukken II* 1999/00, 26 672, no. 4, p. 21.

74 *Kamerstukken II* 1999/00, 26 672, no. 5, pp. 14 and 20–21.

75 *Idem*, at p. 12.

76 *Idem*, at p. 24.

77 *Idem*, at pp. 23–24.

On 7 September 2000 the Act opening civil marriage to same-sex couples was adopted in the Lower House by a large majority.[78] The Preamble of the Act did not express the legislature's motivation for introducing the Act, but in an accompanying press release of the Ministry of Justice it was stated that, against the background of the principle of equal treatment, there was no objective justification for the exclusion of same-sex couples from marriage.[79] As explained by the authors of the 2006 Evaluation of the Act:

> 'The creation of registered partnership was, in the eyes of the legislature, not sufficient to satisfy the requirements imposed by the principle of equality, as laid down in the Dutch Constitution. This principle necessitated that exactly the same institution be open to same-sex and different couples.'[80]

The government showed full awareness that, by opening up marriage, it broke with a long tradition of Western civilisation. It acknowledged that the departure of what had long been an essential characteristic of marriage, namely that marriage was between man and woman only, implied an essential change of the meaning of marriage, which was no longer linked to religious views. The government also held, however, that the opening up of marriage by no means 'denatured' marriage between different-sex couples.[81]

The new Act was both endorsed and criticised in legal scholarship. Some scholars held the opening up of marriage to same-sex couples to be against the *essentiale* of marriage.[82] Others were critical of the haste with which the legislature had proceeded and the choice it had made to postpone regulation of the Private International Law aspects.[83] Various authors pointed out that, from a legal perspective, there was no need for opening up marriage, because a registered partnership had yet been introduced.[84] Some received the Act as primarily symbolic and 'a matter of ideology'.[85] Others, however, stressed the importance of the signal that the new Act gave that full equality before the law was desirable and possible.[86]

---

78 The Act was adopted with 109 votes in favour and 33 votes against. *Handelingen II* 1999/00, 100, pp. 6468.

79 C. Waaldijk, 'De voorgestelde Wet openstelling huwelijk en de daarmee samenhangende wijzigingen inzake adoptie en geregistreerd partnerschap' ['The proposed Act opening up marriage and the related amendments of the law on adoption and registered partnership'], 21 *Tijdschrift voor Familie- en Jeugdrecht* (1999) p. 198 at p. 199.

80 Boele-Woelki et al. 2006, *supra* n. 2, at p. 246.

81 *Kamerstukken II* 1999/2000, 26 672, no. 5, p. 7.

82 L. Westerhof, 'Is het huwelijk tussen personen van hetzelfde geslacht een fictie en, zo ja, kan op deze fictie de wettelijke regeling van dit huwelijk worden gebaseerd?' ['Is same-sex marriage a fiction, and if so, can the legal regulation of this marriage be based on this fiction?'], 75 *Nederlands Juristenblad* (2000) p. 1021.

83 K. Boele-Woelki, 'De prijs van het homohuwelijk' ['The price of gay marriage'], *Tijdschrift voor Familie- en Jeugdrecht* (1999) p. 113.

84 *Inter alia*, Wortmann 2000, *supra* n. 63, at p. 84.

85 *Idem*.

86 Waaldijk 1999, *supra* n. 79, at p. 208.

12.3.5. The Act opening civil marriage to same-sex couples (2001)

Since the entry into force of the Act opening civil marriage to same-sex couples in 2001,[87] Article 1:30(1) Civil Code provides that '[a] marriage may be entered into by two persons of a different or of the same sex.' The conditions for the conclusion of a marriage, for instance in respect of age of the marriage candidates, are the same for both same-sex and different-sex couples and there are no differences in regard to interruption of an intended marriage or annulment of a marriage.[88] The legal effects of marriage are also generally the same. For example, both same-sex and different-sex spouses have marital community of property, unless they have provided otherwise by nuptial agreement and they can use each others' family name.[89] There are, however, two important differences in legal effects between same-sex spouses and different-sex spouses. These concern parental rights and the recognition and effects of their marriages abroad.[90] Both these issues will be discussed separately in this Chapter. The gradual awarding of parental rights to same-sex couples – either registered partners or married – is discussed in section 12.3.6 below. The development of the relevant Dutch rules of Private International Law is discussed in section 12.4.

At the time when marriage was opened up to same-sex couples in the Netherlands, there was discussion if registered partnership should be abolished.[91] After all, the primary aim of the introduction of registered partnership had been to provide legal recognition to same-sex relationships and with the opening up of marriage even more equal treatment was established. Both institutes were maintained, however, and still exist today, because there was and is a considerable group of different-sex and same-sex couples that prefer the less value-laden registered partnership over marriage.[92] Over the years the differences between the legal regimes and effects of marriage and registered partnership have been increasingly more levelled out.[93]

A thorny issue in the Dutch debate on the opening up of marriage that has been debated for many years concerns the question of civil registrars with conscientious objections. The government initially held that this was a matter for the municipalities

---

87 *Wet openstelling huwelijk* [Act on the Opening Up of Civil Marriage] of 21 December 2000, *Stb.* 2001, 9, entry into force on 1 April 2001.

88 Arts. 1:50–1:57 and 1:69–1:77 BW.

89 Arts. 1:9; 1:93 and 1:94 BW.

90 *Kamerstukken II* 1998/99, 26 672, no. 3, p. 4.

91 Some even suggested that civil marriage had to be abolished, leaving religious marriage and civil registered partnership as only choices. Wortmann 2000, *supra* n. 63, at pp. 84–85. Nuytinck regretted the choice not to abolish registered partnership. A.J.M. Nuytinck, 'Het geregistreerd partnerschap wordt niet afgeschaft. Jammer, een gemiste kans!' ['The registered partnership will not be abolished. Shame, a missed opportunity!'], 139 *WPNR* (2008) p. 306.

92 Boele-Woelki et al. 2006, *supra* n. 2, at p. 10. See also *Kamerstukken II* 1999/00, 26 672, no. 5, p. 15 and Waaldijk 2000, *supra* n. 12, at pp. 180–181.

93 A.J.M. Nuytinck, 'Huwelijk en geregistreerd partnerschap groeien steeds verder naar elkaar toe' ['Marriage and registered partnership are growing towards one another'], 142 *WPNR* (2011) p. 1001. As Curry-Sumner explained in 2005, '[t]he two institutions are treated exactly the same with respect to public law (e.g. taxation and social security) and are effectively treated the same for private law issues as well.' Curry-Sumner 2005A, *supra* n. 28, at p. 127.

to find practical solutions to, as long as it was guaranteed that same-sex couples could conclude a marriage in every Dutch municipality.[94] The issue remained controversial for a number of years; it was debated in Parliament on various occasions,[95] it was the subject of various court proceedings,[96] and bodies like the Equal Treatment Commission (now the Human Rights Institute)[97] and the Council of State[98] issued opinions on the question. Only in July 2014, a bill was adopted into law, marking the end of a long debate on this topic. It provided that civil servants with conscientious objections to the conclusion of marriage and/or a registered partnership between to persons of the same sex could no longer be appointed as registrars. It was left to the municipalities to decide on how to deal with already employed registrars with conscientious objections.[99]

12.3.6. Parental rights for same-sex couples

Parental rights for same-sex couples have long been, and still are, a rather debated topic in Dutch politics and society. Although the legislature has consistently tried to stay as close as possible to biological reality in its laws on parentage, it has increasingly departed from that basic principle. Parental rights have gradually been strengthened over the years, particularly for couples consisting of two women. As will be explained below, for reasons of differences in biological reality, the parental rights of gay couples are not as strong as those of lesbian couples.

Before the gradual development of parental rights for same-sex couples is set out, it is important to clarify the distinction between legal parenthood (*'juridisch*

---

94 *Kamerstukken II* 1998/99, 26 672, no. 12.

95 See also Boele-Woelki et al. 2006, *supra* n. 2, at pp. 15–16.

96 Rb. Leeuwarden 24 June 2003, ECLI:NL:RBLEE:2003:AH8543. In October 2013 District Court 's-Gravenhage upheld the dismissal by the Municipality of 's-Gravenhage of a registrar who refused to conclude marriages between same-sex couples. The Court dismissed the registrar's claim that his freedom of religion had been violated. Rb. 's-Gravenhage 23 October 2013, ECLI:NL:RBDHA:2013:14133.

97 In an Opinion of 2008, the Equal Treatment Commission (ETC) held that municipalities were under an obligation to enforce the law; that they had to refrain from discrimination on grounds of sexual orientation and that they had to see to it that their civil servants carried out their tasks in conformity with these obligations. Only in cases where a civil servant had more tasks than the conclusion of marriages only, there was limited room to give in to such objections. Following the Opinion of the ETC the government asked the Advisory Department of the Council of State to issue an Opinion on the matter. Equal Treatment Commission (now College voor de Rechten van de Mens), *Trouwen? Geen bezwaar!* ['To marry? No objections!'], ECT, Advisory Opinion, No. 2008/04. See also the ECT's earlier Opinions Nos. 2008/40 and 2002/25.

98 The Council of State took the view that while all municipalities were under a legal obligation to guarantee access to marriage for same-sex couples, in individual cases of conscientious objections individual arrangements could be made in order to protect the registrar's right to respect for religion. The Council saw no ground for separate, national legislation on the matter. Advisory Division of the Council of State, Opinion of 9 May 2012, *Kamerstukken II* 2011/12, 33 344, no. 5.

99 Wet van 4 juli 2014 tot wijziging van het Burgerlijk Wetboek en de Algemene wet gelijke behandeling met betrekking tot ambtenaren van de burgerlijke stand die onderscheid maken als bedoeld in de Algemene wet gelijke behandeling [Act of 4 July 2014 amending the General Equal Treatment Act as regards civil servants who make a difference in treatment in the meaning of the General Equal Treatment Act]], *Stb.* 2014, 260.

ouderschap') and parental authority ('*ouderlijk gezag*') under Dutch law. Legal parenthood forms part of the law on lineage ('*afstammingsrecht*') and has, *inter alia*, effect for the name and nationality of the child, as well as for succession.[100] Legal parenthood may be established by operation of the law (i.e., through birth), through the act of recognition or adoption of the child, or through judicial determination of legal parenthood.[101] Under Dutch law, the woman who gives birth to a child is always the legal mother of that child (*mater semper certa est*).[102] The man who is married to the woman who gives birth, is legal parent of the child by operation of the law. In 2014 this was extended to the female spouse and the (male or female) registered partner of the woman who gives birth (see section 12.3.6.4 below).[103] If an unmarried woman gives birth to a child, another person – usually her partner – may become legal parent through adoption, recognition or determination of parenthood by a court.

Parental authority creates rights and duties which are relevant for the upbringing of, and care for, the child.[104] A person who has been vested with parental authority may, for instance, hold the child's property under trust. A person endowed with parental authority is not necessarily also the legal parent of the child. For instance, a person may have parental authority over his or her partner's child, without being the child's legal parent.[105] On the other hand, although the legal parent mostly has parental authority over the child, sometimes a special act may be required to obtain such authority, as in the case of recognition of a natural child by the father.

Dutch society changed considerably in the 1960s. Next to the traditional family, consisting of husband and wife and their children, other forms of family became more common practice and were increasingly socially accepted. These new forms of family life were accorded protection by the ECtHR under Article 8 ECHR, as well as by the Dutch Supreme Court.[106] This was different, however, in respect of parental rights for same-sex couples; with regard to this sensitive issue, the Dutch courts deferred to the legislature.[107] For example, in a judgment of 1989 the Supreme

---

100 *Kamerstukken II* 2011/12, 33 032, no. 3, p. 1.

101 Arts. 1:198–199 BW.

102 Art. 1:198 BW.

103 As will be explained below (in section 12.3.7.4), this does not apply to same-sex couples consisting of two men.

104 Arts. 1:251–253y BW.

105 Art. 1:245 and 1:253sa BW. The notion 'authority' under Dutch law, covers both parental authority ('*ouderlijk gezag*') and guardianship ('*voogdij*'). Parental authority is exercised by one parent or two parents jointly. Guardianship is exercised by a third person.

106 As acknowledged in a Government Memorandum on 'ways of living together' ('*Notitie leefvormen*'), *Kamerstukken II* 1994/95, 22 700, no. 5, p. 8. The memorandum referred to ECtHR 13 June 1979, *Marckx* v. *Belgium*, no. 6833/74; ECtHR 18 December 1986, *Johnston a.o.* v. *Ireland*, no. 9697/82; ECtHR 26 May 1995, *Keegan* v. *Ireland*, no. 16969/90; HR 6 November 1987, *NJ* 1988 No. 829, ECLI:NL:HR:1987:AB9568; HR 10 March 1989, *NJ* 1990 No. 24, ECLI:NL:1989:AC1343 and HR 23 March 1990, *NJ* 1991 Nos. 149 and 150, ECLI:NL:HR:1990:AD1066.

107 The 1995 government Memorandum on ways of living together held that the case law of the European Court of Human Rights had not – to date – given any indications that it was plausible that the relationship of two persons who were not or who could biologically not be the parents of a child could be qualified as 'family life' within the meaning of Art. 8 ECHR. *Kamerstukken II* 1994/95, 22 700, no. 5, p. 8.

Court ruled that, other than different-sex couples, same-sex couples were not entitled to parental authority, because they could not both establish parental links with the child, mainly because same-sex couples could not conclude a marriage.[108] In 1997 the Supreme Court furthermore rejected a request by a woman who wished to adopt the children born with her female partner within their stable relationship.[109] The Supreme Court held that it was not for the Court to set aside the existing requirement in the Civil Code that only married (hence different-sex) couples could adopt a child.[110]

In the legislative debate on legal recognition of same-sex relationships during the 1990s, parental rights for same-sex couples proved to be a controversial issue.[111] It was clear from the outset that the Registered Partnership Act would not regulate parental rights.[112] The legislature acknowledged, however, that increasingly more children were raised by same-sex couples. While it expressly wished to refrain from giving 'a moral or pedagogical/psychological judgment on the general issue of whether it was in the interest of the child to be cared for by a couple of the same sex', the legislature felt that the interests of the child required that some form of legal protection was given to these forms of *de facto* family life.[113] At the same time it wished to hold on to the principle that the laws on lineage were in line with biological descent.[114] For that reason, the government at the time rejected joint adoption by two persons of the same sex. It furthermore pragmatically held that such an adoption

108 HR 24 February 1989, *NJ* 1989 No. 741, ECLI:NL:HR:1989:AD0648 (with a case note by EAA en EAAL). For an early plea for the right to acknowledge a child as hers for female partners of mothers, see F. van Vliet, 'Erkenning: mensenrecht of mannenrecht?' ['Recognition: human right or men's right?'], 63 *Nederlands Juristenblad* (1988) p. 1263.

109 The two petitioners had been in a stable and committed relationship for many years when one of them conceived a child with the use of sperm from an anonymous donor. The woman subsequently gave birth to two more children. The two women jointly cared for the children and after several years the partner of the mother wished to adopt the children.

110 Even if it were accepted that partnerships between same-sex couples and their relationships with children raised within these relationships deserved greater protection, the way in which to provide for this would still require a political choice, the Court considered. HR 5 September 1997, *NJ* 1998 No. 686, ECLI:NL:HR:1997:ZC2420.

111 For instance, the Emancipatieraad [Emancipation Council], a government-appointed advisory body, held in 1991 (as paraphrased in *Kamerstukken II* 1994/95, 22700, no. 5, p. 6) that it was time to depart from the general principle that laws on lineage had to be in line with biological descent. It advised introducing joint adoption for same-sex couples.

112 Boele-Woelki et al. hold that registered partnership was originally intended to provide for legal regulation of the relationship between partners and not of their relation to children who would be raised within that relationship. According to the authors, this was so because registered partnership was not intended for couples with children. Boele-Woelki et al. 2006, *supra* n. 2, at p. 6. It must also be noted, however, that the Kortmann Commission had yet proposed in 1997 to introduce second-parent adoption and joint adoption for same-sex couples and that, as Vlaardingerbroek pointed out, the government had not rejected this suggestion in its Memorandum on ways of living together of 1998. *Kamerstukken II* 1997/98, 22700 no. 23 and P. Vlaardingerbroek, 'Adoptie door paren van gelijk geslacht' ['Adoption by same-sex couples'], 22 *Tijdschrift voor Familie- en Jeugdrecht* (2000) p. 198.

113 *Kamerstukken II* 1992/93, 22 700, no. 3, p. 18.

114 *Kamerstukken II* 1994/95, 22 700, no. 5, pp. 9–10.

would in all probability not be recognised by foreign countries.[115] The government was considering, however, the introduction of single-parent adoption.[116]

The first actual step on the path to recognition of parental rights for same-sex couples was the granting of parental authority. In the beginning of the 1990s a bill was drafted following which (same-sex) registered partners could apply for parental authority over their partner's child.[117] The Act on joint parental authority for registered partners entered into force on 1 January 1998, the same date as the Act Introducing Registered Partnerships.[118]

12.3.6.1. Early developments; single-parent adoption

In 1998, single-parent adoption was introduced in Dutch law.[119] Because no discrimination on grounds of sexual orientation was permitted, persons with a homosexual orientation or in a same-sex relationship were also enabled adopt a child.[120] If the adoptive parent had a (same-sex) partner, he or she could subsequently apply for parental authority over the child. It was furthermore provided that unmarried different-sex couples could jointly adopt a child from the Netherlands.[121] Adoption by the same-sex partner of a child's legal parent (second-parent adoption (in Dutch: '*partneradoptie*')) and joint adoption by same-sex couples were not introduced at the time, because to establish such parental links between a child and two persons of the same sex was considered to be too big an abstraction from biological reality.[122]

In the meantime, however, support for greater legal protection of the links between children and the same-sex couples caring for them, was rapidly growing.[123] In 1996 Parliament had adopted two motions which held that joint adoption by same-sex

115 *Idem*, at p. 10.

116 *Idem*, at p. 1.

117 *Kamerstukken II* 1993/94, 23 714, nos. 1–3. Because parental authority had no effect on the laws on lineage, this approach was considered to fit in with two basic principles underlying the Dutch family laws, namely that the laws on lineage in essence reflected the biological parentage and that parental authority, safe a few exceptions, belonged to those from whom the child was descended. *Kamerstukken II* 1992/93, 22 700, no. 3, p. 17.

118 Wet van 30 oktober 1997 tot wijziging van, onder meer, Boek 1 van het Burgerlijk Wetboek in verband met invoering van gezamenlijk gezag voor een ouder en zijn partner en van gezamenlijke voogdij [Act of 30 October 1997 amending, *inter alia*, Volume 1 of the Civil Code with a view to introduction of joint authority for a parent and his partner and of joint guardianship], *Stb.* 1997, 506, entry into force per 1 January 1998.

119 Wet van 24 december 1997 tot herziening van het afstammingsrecht alsmede van de regeling van adoptie [Act of 24 December 1997 amending the law on descent as well as the adoption regulations] *Stb.* 1997, 772, entry into force per 1 April 1998. See also Vliet, van 1998, *supra* n. 61, at p. 17.

120 Vlaardingerbroek 2000, *supra* n. 112, at p. 200. Second-parent adoption had been possible for different-sex couples since 1979.

121 Art. 1:227 BW (old). For a clarification that the couple had to be of different sex, see also *Kamerstukken II* 1995/96, 24 649, no. 3, p. 14. Interstate adoption was the only possible for married couples or for individuals. Art. 1 Wet opneming buitenlandse kinderen ter adoptie (Wobka) [Act on the fostering of children from foreign countries with the purpose of adoption].

122 See also Curry-Sumner 2005A, *supra* n. 28, at pp. 120–121 and Vlaardingerbroek 2000, *supra* n. 112, at p. 202.

123 For a plea for greater protection of these links see Waaldijk 2000, *supra* n. 12, at pp. 177–179.

couples had to introduced,[124] and the subsequently appointed Kortmann II Commission (see above) had taken the same view.[125] The government also endorsed the viewpoint that any child raised and cared for by a same-sex couple in a durable relationship was entitled to legal protection of the links between this couple and the child[126] and a bill introducing adoption by same-sex couples was tabled in 1999.[127]

When the opening up of marriage to same-sex couples was debated in Parliament, however, the debate on parental issues was separated from the debate on the actual opening of marriage. Following the advice of the Kortmann Commission II, the Explanatory Memorandum to the Act opening up marriage expressly mentioned that a marriage between same-sex partners would not establish any parental links by operation of the law.[128] Measures to enforce the protection of the links between the child and the same-sex couple caring for it, were introduced separately, but simultaneously.

12.3.6.2. 2001: Joint adoption of children from the Netherlands; second-parent and successive adoption and joint parental authority

By Act of 2001, same-sex couples (either married, registered or in a stable relationship) were enabled to jointly adopt a child from the Netherlands.[129] Because annually only 50 to 100 children from the Netherlands were given up for adoption,[130] in practice only a limited number of same-sex couples could establish a family through this newly introduced institute of joint adoption. The simultaneous introduction of second-parent and successive adoption for same-sex couples,[131] following which a same-sex married, registered or stable partner was able to adopt the (genetic or adopted) child of his or her partner, was of greater practical relevance.[132]

---

124 *Kamerstukken II* 1995/96, 22 700, nos. 14 and 18.

125 Rapport Commissie inzake openstelling van het burgerlijk huwelijk voor personen van hetzelfde geslacht [Report of the Commission on opening up of civil marriage to couples of the same sex] (The Hague, Ministry of Justice, October 1997) pp. 9–10. The Commission furthermore recommended providing for parental authority by operation of the law when a child was born within a registered partnership and to provide that this form of joint authority had effect for the laws on inheritance. See *Kamerstukken II* 1997/98, 22 700, nos. 23 and *Kamerstukken II* 1999/00, 22 700, no. 31.

126 *Kamerstukken II* 1998/99, 26673, no. 3, p. 2.

127 *Kamerstukken II* 1998/99, 26 673, nos. 1–3. See also *Kamerstukken II* 1997/98, 22 700, no. 23, p. 3 and F. van Vliet, 'Door de zij-ingang naar niemandsland?' ['Through the side entrance into no man's land?'], 16 *Nemesis* (2000) p. 41. The coalition agreement of 1997 yet provided that a bill to this effect was to be tabled by the end of 1998 and this was done accordingly. *Kamerstukken II* 1997/98, 26 024, no. 9, p. 68. See also *Kamerstukken II* 1997/98, 22 700, no. 23.

128 *Kamerstukken II* 2001/02, 27 762 no. 3, p. 4. See also *Kamerstukken II* 1997/98, 22 700, no. 23, p. 2.

129 Wet adoptie door personen van hetzelfde geslacht [Act on adoption by persons of the same sex] Act of 21 December 2000, *Stb.* 2001, 10. The Act entered into force 1 April 2001, the same date on which the Act Opening up Marriage entered into force. See also Vlaardingerbroek 2000, *supra* n. 112 and A.W.M. Willems, 'Adoptie door homo-ouders en de positie van de spermadonor' ['Adoption by gay parents and the position of the sperm donor'], 22 *Tijdschrift voor Familie- en Jeugdrecht* (2000) p. 226.

130 *Kamerstukken II* 1994/95, 22 700, no. 5, p. 13. See also Vlaardingerbroek 2000, *supra* n. 112, at p. 200.

131 Act on adoption by persons of the same-sex (Wet adoptie door personen van hetzelfde geslacht), Act of 21 December 2000, *Stb.* 2001, 10. Entry into force 1 April 2001.

132 Vlaardingerbroek 2000, *supra* n. 112, at pp. 200–201.

Following the new adoption laws, any couple or any partner of a legal parent could petition to the Court for a joint adoption, a second-parent adoption or a successive adoption, if the partners had lived together uninterruptedly for a period of at least three years and had jointly cared for the child for a period of at least one uninterrupted year immediately preceding the adoption request.[133] Next to the yet existing requirement that any adoption had to be in the best interests of the child,[134] a new requirement was introduced that an adoption could only be approved if the child could not expect anything from its 'original parent(s)' ('*oorspronkelijke ouder(s)*').[135] This could concern both a legal and a genetic parent.[136]

International (interstate) adoption was not (yet) introduced for same-sex couples, as the legislature considered that 'not appropriate' given existing international relations.[137] In fact, the Act on interstate adoption was explicitly amended to clarify that the term 'spouses' in this context referred to different-sex spouses only.[138] According to the government, this was 'no principled position', but concerned a practical measure which was required not to imperil the relations with countries of origin of adoptees and not to create false expectations with adoptive parents.[139] The State Commission for Private International Law criticised the discriminating character of this rule in its report on the Act opening civil marriage to same-sex couples.[140]

In addition to the adoption laws, the laws on parental authority were amended in 2001. Same-sex spouses and registered partners were vested with joint parental authority, by operation of law, over a child born during their marriage or registered

133 Art. 1:227(3) and Art. 1:228(1)(f) BW.

134 Art. 1:227(2) BW.

135 Art. 1:227(3) BW. See also *Kamerstukken II* 1998/99, 26 673, no. 3, p. 1. For an example of a judgment in which this condition was applied see Hof Amsterdam 4 May 2010, ECLI:NL:GHAMS:2010:BM3903.

136 See also M.J. Vonk, *Commentaar op Burgerlijk Wetboek Boek 1 art. 227 (en 228) (artikeltekst geldig vanaf 01-01-2009)* [Commentary on the Civil Code, Book 1 (art. 227 (and 228) (version valid as of 01-01-2009)] (Sdu Opmaat (online) 2011) para. C.3.1.

137 Reference was made to a survey by the Ministry of Justice into six countries of origin and six countries of destination in the adoption context of 1997, which had shown a strong preference for married couples for interstate adoption. *Kamerstukken II* 1998/99, 26 673, no. 3, p. 3 and *Kamerstukken II* 1996/97, 22 700, no. 22. Critical on this point: Waaldijk 1999, *supra* n. 79, at pp. 202–203. The author considered it 'unnecessary' to codify other countries' policies in the Dutch law.

138 Art. II Wet van 8 maart 2001 tot aanpassing van wetgeving in verband met de openstelling van het huwelijk en de invoering van adoptie door personen van hetzelfde geslacht [Act of 8 March 2001 amending legislation with a view to the opening up of marriage and the introduction of adoption by couples of the same sex], *Stb.* 2001, 128.

139 *Kamerstukken II* 1999/00, 27 256, no. 4, pp. 10–11.

140 Staatscommissie voor het Internationaal Privaatrecht, *Advies inzake het internationaal privaatrecht in verband met de openstelling van het huwelijk voor personen van hetzelfde geslacht* [Advice concerning Private International Law in relation to the opening up of marriage for persons of the same sex], December 2001, pp. 26–27, online available at www.rijksoverheid.nl/bestanden/documenten-en-publicaties/rapporten/2001/12/01/internationaal-privaatrecht-in-verband-met-de-openstelling-van-het-huwelijk-voor-personen-van-hetzelfde-geslacht/internationaalprivaatrechtinverbandmetdeopenstellingvanhethuwelijkvoorpersonenvanhetzelfdegeslacht.pdf, visited May 2010, as well as at www.justitie.nl/themas/wetgeving/rapporten_en_notas/privaatrecht/Staatscommissie_IPR.asp, visited May 2010.

partnership, provided the child had no other legal parent.[141] Because of the latter restriction, the new provision was primarily relevant for couples consisting of two women, who could now exercise joint parental authority in situations where there was no father, for instance because the child had been conceived with the use of anonymously donated sperm.[142] The newly introduced Article 1:253 (sa) Civil Code did and does not apply to couples consisting of two men (whether married or registered) because in that situation there is in principle always another legal parent, namely the mother of the child.[143]

The 2001 amendments did not end the debate on parental rights for same-sex couples. Various parties insisted on a further equalisation of the parental rights of same-sex couples – in particular couples consisting of two women – with those of different-sex couples. During the deliberations on the opening up of marriage, Parliament had adopted a motion requesting the government to explore the legal options, including recognition, which could achieve the greatest (as reasonably) possible equalisation of the legal position of children born within a relationship of two women with that of children born within a different-sex relationship.[144] In response, the government maintained that full equalisation of the position of same-sex couples with that of different-sex couples in respect of parental links and the laws on lineage, would be too far removed from the basic principle underpinning Dutch family laws that legal parenthood in principle corresponded with genetic parenthood.[145] The government furthermore felt that such equalisation paid too little attention to the fact that a third party could be involved and that it fell out of pace with international standards.[146]

141 Art. 1: 253 BW, introduced by Wet tot wijziging van Boek 1 van het Burgerlijk Wetboek in verband met het gezamenlijk gezag van rechtswege bij geboorte tijdens een geregistreerd partnerschap [Act Amending Volume 1 of the Civil Code with a view to joint authority by operation of the law after birth in a registered partnership], Act of 4 October 2001, *Stb.* 2001, 468 entry into force on 1 January 2002, *Stb.* 2001, 544.

142 As Curry-Sumner and Vonk point out, lesbian couples were the primary addressees of the new Act. I. Curry-Sumner and M.J. Vonk, 'Adoptie door paren van hetzelfde geslacht: wie probeert de wet te beschermen?', 28 *Tijdschrift voor Familie- en Jeugdrecht* (2006) p. 39 at p. 39. The authors refer to *Kamerstukken II* 1998/99, 26 673, no. 3, p. 3.

143 This follows from the above discussed *mater semper certa est* rule. In those situations Art. 1:253 (t) BW applies, which provides that the partner of a parent endowed with parental authority may apply for parental authority, even in situations where another person has established parental links with the child. For such a request for joint parental authority to be granted, the couple must have jointly taken care of the child for a period of at least one year immediately preceding the request for parental authority by the partner and the parent must have exercised parental authority for a period of at least three years immediately preceding his/her partner's request for parental authority. The granting of joint parental authority is refused if, in the light of the interests of the other parent, there is a reasonable fear that the awarding of such joint parental authority would neglect the child's interests (Art. 253t (2) and (3) BW).

144 *Kamerstukken II* 1999/00, 26 672 and 26 673, no. 9.

145 Boele-Woelki et al. 2006, *supra* n. 2, at p. 21, referring (in footnote 140) to: *Kamerstukken II* 2003/04, 26 672 and 26 673, no. 14, pp. 3–5 and *Kamerstukken II* 2004/05, 26 672 and 26 673, no. 15. The Explanatory Memorandum to the Act Opening up marriage had also yet held that to assume that a child born within the relationship of two women descended from both women, would unacceptably stretch reality and would create too big a distance between biological truth and law. *Kamerstukken II* 1998/99, 26 672, no. 3, pp. 4–5.

146 *Idem.*

Because of these considerations the improvement of the legal position of children born within lesbian relationships was initially established through further amendment of the adoption laws. While the first legislative initiatives to this effect were taken in 2005, it took until 2009 before a new Act entered into force.[147]

12.3.6.3. 2009: Interstate adoption by same-sex spouses and simplification of second-parent adoption

An important change brought about by the 2009 Act was that interstate adoption was made possible for same-sex spouses.[148] In 2012, the Netherlands furthermore ratified the Revised CoE Adoption Convention[149] which provides for the possibility of joint adoption by same-sex couples.[150] In practice, however, the practical effect of this change so far has been limited. Not many same-sex spouses are able to jointly adopt a child from abroad, as many foreign countries do not want to collaborate in such an interstate adoption.

Moreover, the 2009 amendments simplified the procedures for second-parent adoption, especially for couples consisting of two women.[151] The three year cohabitation condition (see above),[152] was lifted for situations where the child was born 'within the relationship' of the parent and the adoptive parent.[153] For the situation where a child was born within the relationship of two female life partners, the condition was lifted that they had to have jointly taken care of the child for a

---

147 Wijziging van Boek 1 van het Burgerlijk Wetboek in verband met verkorting van de adoptieprocedure en wijziging van de Wet opneming buitenlandse kinderen ter adoptie (Wobka) in verband met adoptie door echtgenoten van gelijk geslacht tezamen. Act of 24 October 2008 [Act amending Volume 1 of the Civil Code with a view to shortening of the adoption procedure and amendment of the Act on the fostering of children from foreign countries with the purpose of adoption, in relation to joint adoption by same-sex spouses], *Stb.* 2008, 425, entry into force per 1 January 2009. See also L. van Hoppe, 'Wijziging van Boek 1 van het Burgerlijk Wetboek in verband met verkorting van de adoptieprocedure en wijziging van de Wet opneming buitenlandse pleegkinderen ter adoptie in verband met adoptie door echtgenoten van gelijk geslacht tezamen' ['Amendment of Book 1 of the Civil Code in relation to the adoption procedure and amendment of the Act placement of foreign foster children for adoption in relation to joint adoption by same-sex spouses'], 48 *Ars Aequi* (2009) p. 191.

148 Art. III Wet van 24 oktober 2008 tot wijziging van Boek 1 van het Burgerlijk Wetboek in verband met verkorting van de adoptie-procedure en wijziging van de Wet opneming buitenlandse kinderen ter adoptie in verband met adoptie door echtgenoten van gelijk geslacht tezamen [Act amending Chapter 1 of the Civil Code concerning the shortening of the adoption procedure and amendment of the Act on the fostering of children from foreign countries with the purpose of adoption as regards joint adoption by couples of the same sex], Act of 24 October 2008, *Stb.* 2008, 425, entry into force per 1 January 2009.

149 European Convention on the Adoption of Children (Revised) CETS No.202 (Strasbourg 2008).

150 Art. 7(2) European Convention on the Adoption of Children (Revised).

151 Wet van 24 oktober 2008 tot wijziging van Boek 1 van het Burgerlijk Wetboek in verband met verkorting van de adoptie-procedure en wijziging van de Wet opneming buitenlandse kinderen ter adoptie in verband met adoptie door echtgenoten van gelijk geslacht tezamen [Act amending Chapter 1 of the Civil Code concerning the shortening of the adoption procedure and amendment of the Act on the fostering of children from foreign countries with the purpose of adoption as regards joint adoption by couples of the same sex], Act of 24 October 2008, *Stb.* 2008, 425, entry into force per 1 January 2009.

152 The cohabitation condition set the rule that the legal parent and his or her partner had to have lived together for a period of at least three uninterrupted years, immediately preceding the adoption request.

153 The new Art. 1:227(2) BW.

period of at least a year.[154] Further, it was provided that a request for second-parent adoption was as a rule granted, where the child was born in a relationship of two women and was conceived with the use of donated gametes in correspondence with the Act Donor Information Artificial Reproduction.[155] Lastly, the 2009 Act stipulated that the procedure for second-parent adoption could be initiated before the child's birth and would have effect from the date of birth, provided no existing parental links were severed by the adoption.[156] Because of the latter condition, this rule did and does not apply to couples consisting of two men, as in that situation the parental links between the mother and the child stand in the way of an immediately effective second-parent adoption.

Some Dutch scholars have concluded that, as a result of these amendments to the adoption laws, the legal position of a child born in a relationship between two women was as much as possible equalised with that of a child born within a different-sex relationship.[157] Others felt that full equalisation required something more than amendments to the adoption laws only. In their view, after all, adoption procedures were time consuming and the law as it stood provided no solution to the deadlock situation where a mother and the genetic father of a child disagreed on who should be the second legal parent of the child, the female partner of the mother or the genetic father of the child.[158]

12.3.6.4. 2014: Legal parenthood by operation of the law for female couples

In 2007, when the bill on interstate and second-parent adoption for same-sex couples was under debate, Parliament adopted a motion which called for the introduction of recognition and legal parenthood by operation of the law for situations where a child was born within the relationship of two women.[159] The government subsequently appointed an advisory expert commission, the Kalsbeek Commission, which was

154 The new Art. 1:228(3) BW. See *Kamerstukken II* 1999/00, 26 673, no. 15.

155 The new Art. 1:227(4) BW. This would only be different if such adoption would be evidently not in the child's interests or if the conditions of Art. 1:228 BW were not met. For a case where a Court granted an adoption request to the same-sex former spouse of the mother (the original 'co-mother') instead of the new same-sex partner of the mother (as desired by the mother), see Rb. Breda 27 July 2011, ECLI:NL:RBBRE:2011:BR2383.

156 New Art. 1:230(2) BW. See also M.J.C. Koens, *Groene Serie Personen- en Familierecht, 2.4 Adoptie door personen van gelijk geslacht bij: Burgerlijk Wetboek Boek 1, Artikel 227 [Verzoek tot adoptie]* [Green Series Family Law, 2.4 Adoption by persons of the same sex: Civil Code Book 1, Article 227 [Adoption reguest]] (Kluwer, update 12 December 2011) and P. Vlaardingerbroek, *Groene Serie Personen- en Familierecht, 1 Geregistreerd partnerschap; algemeen bij: Burgerlijk Wetboek Boek 1, Titel 5A Het geregistreerd partnerschap* [Green Series Family Law, 1 Registered Partnership, general: Civil Code Book 1, Title 5A, The registered partnership] (Kluwer, update 1 April 2011). In 2011 the Central Appeals Tibunal ruled in a case originating from 2006 (hence before the possibility of prenatal adoption was introduced for same-sex couples) that there were no particularly serious reasons which could justify a difference in treatment between a child born within a same-sex marriage and a child born within a different-sex marriage with respect to half orphan's benefits. CRvB 24 June 2011 (dec.), ECLI:NL:CRVB:2011:BQ9855.

157 Vlaardingerbroek 2011, *supra* n. 156.

158 *Kamerstukken II* 2011/12, 33 032, no. 3.

159 *Kamerstukken II* 2006/07, 30 800 VI, no. 60.

asked to explore the legal options, other than adoption, to establish legal parenthood for a so-called 'co-mother'.[160] Taking the interests of the child and the principle of equal treatment as a point of departure, the Kalsbeek Commission was of the opinion that legal protection of social parenthood had to prevail over holding on to (the presumption of) biological parenthood.[161] It recommended enabling co-mothers to establish parental links with their partner's child through recognition and advised making judicial determination of parenthood possible for co-mothers under the same conditions as applied to male partners of mothers. The Commission held it a matter for the legislature, however, to decide upon legal parenthood for the co-mother by operation of the law in situations where a child was born within a marriage between two women.[162]

The legislature followed the advice of the Kalsbeek Commission in a bill tabled in 2011.[163] Taking the interests of the child as primary consideration, the bill provided for legal parenthood for the co-mother by operation of the law, where a child was born within marriage between two women and where it was established that the genetic father of the child would play no role in the child's upbringing. This would be the case where the child was conceived with the use of sperm from a sperm bank, situation in which the donor was not known to the two women. In all other situations, so it was proposed, the co-mother could recognise the child as her child. Further, the legal parenthood of a co-mother could be judicially established if, as life partner of a mother, she had agreed with an act which could have resulted in the begetting of the child.[164] At the same time, some improvement of the legal position of the sperm donor who maintained close ties with the child, was proposed. In situations where the mother refused to give permission to this donor to recognise the child as his, the donor could petition to the court for substitute permission.[165]

---

160 *Kamerstukken II* 2006/07, 30 551, no. 8. The term 'co-mother' (in Dutch 'duomoeder' or 'meemoeder') refers to the woman in a lesbian relationship who is not the birth mother but cares for the child that was born in or grows up in their relationship.

161 Commissie lesbisch ouderschap en interlandelijke adoptie (Commissie Kalsbeek) [Commission on lesbian parenthood and interstate adoption (Kalsbeek Commission)], *Lesbisch ouderschap* [Lesbian parenthood], Report of October 2007, online available at www.aoo.nl/downloads/2007-10-31-MvJ.pdf, visited March 2010.

162 *Kamerstukken II* 2011/12, 33 032, no. 3.

163 *Kamerstukken II* 2011/12, 33 032, no. 2. The bill was generally positively received by interest groups during the internet consultation by the Ministry of Justice, as well as in academia. See M.J. Vonk, 'Het conceptwetsvoorstel lesbisch ouderschap onder de loep' ['A closer look at the bill on lesbian parenthood'], 141 *WPNR* (2010) p. 348 and www.internetconsultatie.nl/ouderschapduomoeder, visited January 2011. See also A.J.M. Nuytinck, 'Concept-wetsvoorstel lesbisch ouderschap: meemoeder wordt juridisch moeder van rechtswege of door erkenning' [Draft bill lesbian parenthood: co-mother becomes legal mother by operation of the law or by recognition'], 141 *WPNR* (2010) p. 343. Forder and Bakker argued that the Bill paid too little attention to the rights of the child. C.J. Forder and R. Bakker, 'Kroniek van personen- en familierecht' ['Chronicle of family law legislation'], 85 *Nederlands Juristenblad* (2010) p. 1796.

164 This entailed, *inter alia*, that the co-mother could be subjected to a maintenance order on the basis of Arts. 11:394 and 11:395(b) BW.

165 *Kamerstukken II* 2011/12, 33 032, no. 3, p. 5.

This bill meant a change in the existing family laws because – next to genetic parenthood – social parenthood was firmly introduced as ground for the establishment of legal parenthood.[166] It was particularly in respect of this 'fundamental' change that the Council of State was very critical in its Advisory Opinion on the bill.[167] The Council failed to see a justification for the proposed departure of the basic principle underpinning Dutch family laws that legal parenthood in principle corresponded with genetic parenthood.

The Council of State furthermore warned that the forms of legal parenthood for co-mothers as proposed in the bill would not be recognised in other countries. The Kalsbeek Commission had been of the opinion that such risks should not prevent the Dutch legislature from once again taking the role of a 'model country', as it also had done by the opening up of marriage and the introduction of joint adoption for same-sex couples.[168] During the debate in Parliament on the bill possible legal problems that co-mothers could encounter abroad were also a point of discussion, but this risk was generally accepted and it was hoped that this could be remedied as much as possible through informing the public and other countries on this point.[169]

Parliament ('*Tweede Kamer*') adopted the bill on lesbian parenthood in October 2012.[170] It was adopted by the Senate ('*Eerste Kamer*') on 12 November 2013.[171] On that same date the Senate adopted another bill that had been tabled by the government in the meantime. This bill provided for rules extending the co-mothers regime to female registered partners.[172] The government regarded this as the tailpiece of the existing (or soon to be introduced) legislation, which provided for legal parenthood for the male spouse, the female spouse and the male registered partner of a woman who gives birth to a child.[173] The bill did not focus on legal parenthood by operation of the law in respect of relationships between two men, as it was held that a child 'cannot be born in a relationship of two men'.[174]

Both Acts entered into force on 1 April 2014.[175] Since that time Article 1:198 of the Civil Code provides that the mother of a child is the woman (a) who gave birth to the

166 *Idem*, p. 4.

167 Advisory Division of the Council of State, Opinion of 15 April 2011, W03.11.0034/II, *Kamerstukken II* 2011/12, 33 032, no. 4.

168 A.J.M. Nuytinck, 'Lesbisch ouderschap. Bespreking van het rapport van de Commissie lesbisch ouderschap en interlandelijke adoptie (commissie-Kalsbeek)' ['Lesbian parenthood. Review of the Report lesbian parenthood and interstate adoption (Kalsbeek Commission)'] 139 *WPNR* (2008) p. 44.

169 The Secretary of State for Justice acknowledged that if a lesbian couple moved to another State, the best solution could be that the co-mother could adopt the child, as that form of legal parenthood was most likely to be recognised by the other State. *Handelingen II* 2011/12, 13, pp. 13, 18 and 68.

170 *Kamerstukken II* 2012/13, 33 032, no. 16.

171 *Handelingen I* 2013/14, pp. 9–7.

172 *Kamerstukken II* 2012/13, 33 526, no. 2.

173 *Kamerstukken II* 2012/13, 33 526, no. 3, p. 2.

174 *Kamerstukken II* 2011/12, 33 032, no. 3, p. 2 and *Kamerstukken II* 2012/13, 33 526, nos. 2–3.

175 Wet van 25 november 2013 tot wijziging van Boek 1 van het Burgerlijk Wetboek in verband met het juridisch ouderschap van de vrouwelijke partner van de moeder anders dan door adoptie [Act of 25 November amending Volume 1 of the Civil Code, with a view to legal parenthood of the female partner of the mother other than by means of adoption], *Stb.* 2013, 480 and Wet van 27 november 2013

child; or (b) who is at the moment of birth the spouse or the registered partner of the woman who gives birth to the child, if this child was conceived as a result of IVF with the use of a donor not known to the woman and in accordance with the Donor Information Act; (c) who has recognised the child; (d) whose parenthood has been judicially established; or (e) who has adopted the child.

During the parliamentary debates on the bills on lesbian parenthood the question was raised if the law was also to provide for parental authority for multiple parents. The Secretary of State for Justice promised to have a research conducted on this issue.[176] In February 2014 the '*Wetenschappelijk Onderzoek- en Documentatiecentrum*' (WODC), the Research and Documentation Centre of the Ministry of Security and Justice, published a report,[177] that, *inter alia*, addressed the situation where a child is born in a relationship between two women with the use of a sperm donor who is known to the women. The authors of the report held that any action undertaken by the legislature had to put the best interests of the child first. However, as these interests required different approaches, they could not recommend one particular approach. Also, the report questioned whether any legislative action in respect of parental authority was at all necessary in these situations, as only few problems had been reported by the families concerned in a survey conducted by the researchers. The relations between these parties were generally good. The researchers considered a more inclusive approach, addressing both parental authority and legal parenthood for multiple parents, fruitful, and they therefore welcomed the appointment of the State Commission on Legal Parenthood ('*Staatscommissie Herijking Ouderschap*'). This Commission has the mandate to advise on possible amendments of the Civil Code in respect of: (a) legal parenthood, (b) multiple parenthood and parental authority by multiple parents, and (c) surrogate motherhood.[178]

12.3.6.5. Access to AHR treatment

As explained in Chapter 6, section 6.3.2, the standard applied in decision-making around reproduction in the Netherlands is the reasonable well-being of the child. While IVF clinics have a considerable discretion when it comes to access to treatment,[179] the categorical exclusion of certain groups in society is not allowed.[180] This certainly entails that exclusion of all same-sex couples or individuals with

---

tot wijziging van het Burgerlijk Wetboek en het Wetboek van Burgerlijke Rechtsvordering mede in verband met de evaluatie van de Wet openstelling huwelijk en de Wet geregistreerd partnerschap [Act of 27 November 2013 amending the Civil Code and the Civil Proceedings Act, *inter alia*, with a view to the evaluation of the Act opening up marriage and the Registered Partnership Act], *Stb.* 2013, 486.

176 *Handelingen II* 2012/13, pp.13–18.

177 M.V. Antokolskaia et al., *Meeroudergezag: een oplossing voor kinderen met meer dan twee ouders? Een empirisch en rechtsvergelijkend onderzoek* [Parental authority by multiple parents: a solution for children who have more than two parents? An empirical and comparative legal study] (Den Haag, Boom Juridische uitgevers 2014).

178 As discussed more extensively in Ch. 6, section 6.3.8.

179 See Ch. 6., section 6.3.2. See also Rb. 's-Gravenhage (pres.) 17 July 1990, ECLI:NL:RBSGR:1990:AD1197.

180 NVOG, *Modelprotocol Mogelijke morele contra-indicaties bij vruchtbaarheidsbehandelingen* [Model Protocol concerning possible moral counter-indications for fertility treatment], p. 3, online

a homosexual orientation is prohibited and the present author is not aware of any cases where access was nonetheless refused to same-sex couples. Still, in practice their access to AHR treatment may be more limited when compared to different-sex couples. This may, for instance, be so because not all clinics cooperate with a sperm bank.[181]

12.4. Same-sex relationships and cross-border movement

12.4.1. Cross-border movement: some statistics

Statistics Netherlands keeps statistics on the number of registered partnerships and marriages concluded by same-sex couples on an annual basis in the Netherlands. On average two per cent of the total number of marriages annually concluded concerns same-sex spouses.[182] In respect of registered partnerships this percentage was much higher in the first years after registered partnerships were introduced (65 per cent in 1998; 53 per cent in 1999 and 55 per cent in 2000), but after the opening up of marriage in 2001, this number decreased to a steady 5 to 6 per cent of the total number of partnerships annually registered in the Netherlands.[183] For marriages a (detailed) breakdown in country of birth of the spouses is available.[184] For example, in 2001, 437 same-sex marriages were concluded whereby at least one partner was born outside the Netherlands. In 2013, this number had dropped to 305. The numbers do not make clear whether these partners have Dutch nationality and/or how long they had been resident in the Netherlands by the time they got married. There are no statistics available in respect of the country of birth, nationality or country of residence of persons entering into a registered partnership under Dutch law. On the basis of statistics of the Civil Registry of the Municipality of Amsterdam, Jessurun d'Oliveira estimated in 1999 that approximately 5 per cent of the total number of

available at www.nvog.nl/Sites/Files/0000000935_NVOG%20Modelprotocol%20Mogelijke%20Morele%20Contraindicaties%20Vruchtbaarheidsbehandelingen%202010.pdf, visited June 2014.

181 As explained in Ch. 6, section 6.3.2, the Dutch government has held this to be acceptable. *Kamerstukken II* 32 500 XVI, no. 112, p. 3. See also Dutch Equal Treatment Commission, Decision 2009-31.

182 Data of *Centraal Bureau voor de Statistiek* [*Statistics Netherlands*] of 28 October 2011 give the following numbers per year. The number between brackets is the total number of marriages concluded in the Netherlands in the relevant year: 2001: 2,414 (73,190); 2002: 1,838 (76,393); 2003: 1,499 (72243); 2004: 1,210 (66,847); 2005: 1,150 (65,859); 2006: 1,212 (60,102); 2007: 1,341 (67,152); 2008: 1,408 (69,971); 2009: 1,385 (67,663); 2010: 1,354 (67,051). Online available at www.statline.cbs.nl/StatWeb/publication/?DM=SLNL&PA=60036NED&D1=1-2,4-16,74,128&D2=a&HDR=G1&STB=T&VW=T, visited February 2013. Hence, only in the year 2001, when marriage was opened up, was the percentage of same-sex marriages slightly higher, namely 3 per cent.

183 Data of *Statistics Netherlands* of 27 June 2012 give the following numbers per year. The number between brackets is the total number of partnerships registered in the Netherlands in the relevant year: 1998: 3,010 (4,626); 1999: 1,757 (3,257); 2000: 1,600 (2,922); 2001: 530 (3,377); 2002: 547 (8,321); 2003: 542 (10,119); 2004: 583 (11,156); 2005: 608 (11,307); 2006: 619 (10,801); 2007: 605 (10,550); 2008: 611 (10,842); 2009: 495 (9,497); 2010: 487 (9,571); 2011: 481 (9,945). Online available at www.statline.cbs.nl/StatWeb/publication/?VW=T&DM=SLNL&PA=37772ned&D1=35-47&D2=48-l&HD=120104-1452&HDR=G1&STB=T, visited 21 February 2013.

184 See www.statline.cbs.nl/StatWeb/publication/?DM=SLNL&PA=60036NED&D1=107-127,161-181,213&D2=5-17&HDR=G1&STB=T&VW=T, visited September 2014.

partnerships that were annually registered in the Netherlands involved non-Dutch nationals.[185]

In respect of (im)migration there are only very few relevant statistics available. The present author is not aware of any Dutch statistics on the number of Dutch same-sex married and registered couples that migrate to other (EU Member) States. There are furthermore no detailed statistics available on the number of same-sex couples or partners from other (EU) countries that are annually granted (or refused) residence rights in the Netherlands. On the basis of the data available it may be very tentatively estimated that annually approximately 50 same-sex partners are admitted to the Netherlands under Directive 2004/38/EC,[186] while approximately 2 per cent of the requests for family reunification under Directive 2003/86/EC concern same-sex partners.[187]

---

185 H.U. Jessurun d'Oliveira, 'Het geregistreerd partnerschap, het 'homohuwelijk' en het IPR' ['Registered partnership, 'gay marriage' and Private International Law'], 74 *Nederlands Juristenblad* (1999) p. 305 at p. 305.

186 These estimations are based on K. Waaldijk et al., *Homophobia, transphobia and discrimination on grounds of sexual orientation and gender identity, Comparative legal analysis, Thematic study Netherlands, 2010 Update*, European Union Agency for Fundamental Rights 2010, online available at www.fra.europa.eu/sites/default/files/fra_uploads/1363-LGBT-2010_thematic-study_NL.pdf, visited February 2013. The authors hold on p. 25: '[…] for a recent study a sample of 336 cases were examined involving successful applications of non-EU citizens claiming residence in the Netherlands on the basis of EU law, because their spouse/partner was a EU (or EEA or Swiss) citizen. It was found that 15 of these cases involved a same-sex partner. The sample of 336 represented around 10 per cent of all such cases having been decided in the years 2005–2008. It should be noted however that only for two thirds of all honoured applications of that period the study could establish both the citizenship of the sponsor and the type of (family) relationship between applicant and sponsor. Furthermore, the number of successful applications increased from around 900 in 2005 to around 2,500 in 2008, while the annual number of rejected applications increased similarly from around 100 to around 300 during that period. Taking all that into account, it could be estimated – very tentatively – that in these four years perhaps over 200 same-sex partners were admitted to the Netherlands under Directive 2004/38/EC.' The report refers in (in footnote 96) to: A. Schreijenberg et al., *Gemeenschapsrecht en gezinsmigratie. Het gebruik van het gemeenschapsrecht door gezinsmigranten uit derde landen* [Community law and family migration. The use of Community law by third-country migrants for family migration] (The Hague Ministry of Justice 2009), pp. 11, 16, 29, 31 and 83, online available at www.wodc.nl/onderzoeksdatabase/neveneffecten-van-toepassing-van-het-europese-gemeenschaps-recht-bij-gezinsmigratie.aspx?cp=44&cs=6796, visited June 2014.

187 Waaldijk et al. 2010, *supra* n. 187, have noted (at p. 30): 'Not many figures are available on the number of same-sex partners that have successfully applied for family reunification/formation. However, a recent study of the period July 2003 to February 2006 yielded some figures. Over that period of 32 months there were 23,407 successful applications for a provisional residence permit for a spouse or partner. The study found that 461 of these cases involved same-sex partners, i.e. two per cent. Same-sex partners were much more often involved in the 8,296 cases where the sponsor was a Dutch citizen (3.4 per cent or 282 permits) than in the 15,111 cases where the sponsor was a foreigner (1.2 per cent or 179 permits). It should be noted however that the total number of successful applications between 01.07.2003 and 01.11.2004 was more than 50 per cent higher than that between 01.11.2004 and 01.03.2006. This is probably due to the increased income and age requirements for family formation that took effect on 1.11.2004. Since then the sponsor needs to be at least 21 years of age, and needs to have an income equal to at least 120 per cent of the minimum wage.' In footnote 119 this report refers to: H. Muermans and J. Liu, 'Gezinsvorming in cijfers' [Family formation in numbers'], in: *Internationale gezinsvorming begrensd? Een evaluatie van de verhoging van de inkomens- en leeftijdseis bij migratie van buitenlandse partners naar Nederland* [International family formation restricted? An evaluation of the raised income and age requirements with regard to the migration of foreign partners to the

12.4.2. (Development of) the relevant Dutch conflict-of-laws rules

Dutch Private International Law is firmly rooted in international Treaty law. In respect of marriage, for instance, the applicable law was, for 70 years, the Hague Convention relating to the settlement of the conflict of the laws concerning marriage of 1902.[188] When this Treaty was annulled in the late 1970s,[189] the Netherlands subsequently ratified the Hague Convention of 14 March 1978 on Celebration and Recognition of the Validity of Marriages.[190] The latter Convention entered into force in the Netherlands in 1991.[191] However, because it was for a long time uncertain whether there would be enough ratifications for this Convention to enter into force,[192] the Dutch legislature soon after ratification drafted national conflict-of-laws rules in respect of marriage.[193] This Private International Law (Marriages) Act (*Wet conflictenrecht huwelijk*) implemented and supplemented the Hague Convention.[194] Other relevant instruments of the Hague Conference on Private International Law, to which the Netherlands is a Contracting Party, are the 1970 Convention on the Recognition of Divorces and Legal Separations[195] and the 1978 Convention on the Law Applicable to Matrimonial Property Regimes.[196] The Netherlands neither signed nor ratified the – not (yet) in force – Convention on the recognition of registered partnerships of the International Commission on Civil Status (ICCS).[197]

Netherlands] (The Hague: Ministry of Justice 2009), pp. 25, 29, 31 and 175, online available at www.wodc.nl/onderzoeksdatabase/de-gevolgen-van-de-aanscherping-van-het-gezinsvormingsbeleid.aspx?cp=44&cs=6799, visited June 2014.

188 Convention of 12 June 1902 relating to the settlement of the conflict of the laws concerning marriage, *Stb.* 1904, 121.

189 Wet van 10 februari 1977, houdende goedkeuring van het voornemen tot opzegging van het Verdrag van 's-Gravenhage van 12 juni 1902 [Act of 10 February 1977 approving of the intention to revoke the Hague Concention of 12 June 1902], *Stb.* 1977, 61. The Treaty was revoked as of 1 June 1979 (*Trb.* 1977, 57), because it was considered to no longer conform to modern standards. A.P.M.J. Vonken, *GS Personen- en Familierecht, regeling WCH, aant. 1*, Kluwer (last update 01-05-2004).

190 Convention of 14 March 1978 on Celebration and Recognition of the Validity of Marriages, no. 26, entry into force 1 May 1991.

191 *Stb.* 1989, 391.

192 A.P.M.J. Vonken, *GS Personen- en Familierecht, regeling WCH, aant. 1*, Kluwer (last update 1 May 2004). In the end only two other States, Luxembourg and Australia, ratified the Convention. Three other States (Egypt, Finland and Portugal) have signed the Convention but not (yet) ratified it.

193 *Kamerstukken II* 1987/88, 20 507 and *Kamerstukken I* 1988/89, 20 507.

194 Private International Law (Marriages) Act) of 7 September 1989 (Wet conflictenrecht huwelijk) *Stb.* 1989, 392, entry into force 1 January 1990.

195 Convention of 1 June 1970 on the Recognition of Divorces and Legal Separations, entry into force on 24 August 1975. In the Netherlands the Convention entered into force on 22 August 1981. Next to the Netherlands, 18 other States are Contracting Parties to this Convention.

196 Convention of 14 March 1978 on the Law Applicable to Matrimonial Property Regimes (entry into force 1 September 1992). In the Netherlands the Convention also entered into force on 1 September 1992. Only the Netherlands, France and Luxembourg are Contracting Parties to this Convention.

197 Convention on the recognition of registered partnership, ICCS Convention no. 32, opened for signature at Munich on 5 September 2007. Following its Art. 19, the Convention will enter into force after two member States of the ICCS have ratified, accepted or approved it. Following the chart of signatures and ratifications as published on the website of the ICCS (update 15 June 2014) only Spain ratified this Convention, while Portugal signed the Convention.

When registered partnerships were introduced in the Netherlands, and later when marriage was opened up to same-sex couples, a recurring theme in the debate was the applicability of these International Treaties – and the Dutch laws implementing them – to these 'new' institutions. This will therefore also be a recurring theme in the subsections below, which set out the relevant Dutch conflict-of-laws rules. First a brief introduction to the development of these rules is given.

The 'international aspects' of the introduction of the registered partnership and the opening up of marriage to same-sex couples have been much debated. In both cases, although heavily criticised by some, the legislature postponed the drafting and adoption of conflict-of-laws rules until well after the entry into force of the new legal regime.[198] Neither the Act Introducing Registered Partnerships nor the Act Opening Up Marriage contained any provisions on recognition or the applicable law in international cases. When the Registered Partnerships Bill was under debate in Parliament in the mid-1990s, the Secretary of State for Justice felt that as long as the (details of the) substantive law had not yet been decided upon, there was little use in endeavouring to draft conflict-of-laws rules, or in asking the State Commission on Private International Law for advice on the matter.[199] Just before the entry into force of the Act Introducing Registered Partnerships, the latter Commission was indeed asked to give an advice on the Private International Law aspects of the Act and to make a proposal for conflict-of-laws rules, which could then for the time being function as 'policy measures' (*'beleidsregels'*).[200] Actual implementation of the advice and the accompanying proposal for legislation was, however, postponed. On the one hand, the government wanted to wait to see if the rapid legislative developments in respect of registered partnerships in other countries would perhaps result in the drafting of a Treaty instrument. On the other hand, legislation for the opening up of marriage was already in preparation at the time and the government wished to capture all Private International Law issues in one piece of legislation.[201] By 2001, the year when the Act Opening Up Marriage entered into force, the government – acknowledging that it was not very likely that an international treaty on the matter would be drafted and adopted in the foreseeable future – felt that it was time to draft legislation.[202]

---

198 Very critical of this choice for postponement was H.U. Jessurun d'Oliveira, 'Het raadselachtige buitenland, de partnerregistratie en het burgerlijk huwelijk voor homo's en lesbo's' ['The mysterious other countries, partner registration and civil marriage for gays and lesbians'], 71 *Nederlands Juristenblad* (1996) p. 755.

199 *Kamerstukken II* 1995/96, 22700 no. 7, p. 1.

200 The advice of the State Commission on Private International Law (Staatscommissie voor het Internationaal Privaatrecht) of 8 May 1998 was published in 20 *Tijdschrift voor Familie- en Jeugdrecht* (1998), pp. 146–159 and in 131 *WPNR* (2000) p. 375. See also I.S. Joppe, 'Het geregistreerd partnerschap in het Nederlands IPR (I)' ['Registered partnership in Dutch Private International Law (I)'], 131 *WPNR* (2000) p. 371 and I.S. Joppe, 'Het geregistreerd partnerschap in het Nederlands IPR (II)' ['Registered partnership in Dutch Private International Law (II)', 131 *WPNR* (2000) p. 391. Critical of the fact that the advice was published in legal journals only was H.U. Jessurun d'Oliveira 1999, *supra* n. 186, at p. 306.

201 *Kamerstukken II* 2002/03, 28 924, no. 3, p. 2. See also Joppe 2000A, *supra* n. 200.

202 *Idem.* Earlier intentions to draft legislation on this matter had been expressed in *Kamerstukken I* 1996/97, 23 761, no. 157b, p. 4 and *Kamerstukken II* 1999/00, 26 672, no. 5, p. 18.

A much debated issue was (and is) whether any of the existing Private International Law Treaty instruments – in particular the Hague Convention on the Celebration and Recognition of the Validity of Marriages of 1978[203] – and the Dutch laws implementing them, applied to (same-sex) registered partnership and to same-sex marriage. The government took the view that none of the international Treaties did, as they were drafted at a time when the institutes of registered partnerships and same-sex marriage did not yet exist.[204] It therefore concluded that the Netherlands was free to adjust its national legislation to changed views in society and to draft its own conflict-of-laws rules on the issue.[205]

This approach has been criticised. Boele-Woelki, for example, held that from a Private International Law perspective, the price for the introduction of same-sex marriage was too high.[206] The opening up of marriage would imply that the Netherlands would unilaterally breach the silent consensus on the definition of marriage that underpinned the relevant international Treaties, she held.[207] Boele-Woelki warned that Dutch family law was 'no isolated practice ground' but had to operate in the wider European context. Following this publication, concerns were expressed in Parliament that the Netherlands no longer would be taken seriously internationally.[208]

Because the government was of the opinion that the Hague Treaties did not apply to same-sex marriages, however, it saw no need – as suggested by some members in Dutch Parliament following Boele-Woelki's critique – to revoke these Treaties, nor to ask other States for permission to employ a different interpretation of 'marriage'. For the sake of clarity and to increase the chances of recognition by other States, the government nonetheless wished to bring the Dutch rules of Private International Law as much as possible in line with the Treaties to which it was a party.[209] The government held that the responsibility of the Netherlands *vis-à-vis* other States did

[203] Convention of 14 March 1978 on Celebration and Recognition of the Validity of Marriages, The Hague, entry into force per 1 May 1991.

[204] In respect of registered partnerships: *Kamerstukken II* 2002/03, 28 924, no. 3, p. 3, in respect of same-sex marriage: *Kamerstukken II* 1998/99, 27 762 no. 3, p. 5 and *Kamerstukken II* 1999/00, 26 672 no. 5, p. 19.

[205] *Kamerstukken II* 1998/99, 27 762 no. 3, p. 5 and *Kamerstukken II* 1999/00, 26 672, no. 5, p. 23.

[206] Boele-Woelki 1999, *supra* n. 83, at p. 113.

[207] *Idem.* See also Bogdan who held in respect of the 1970 Convention on the Recognition of Divorces and Legal Separations and the 1978 Convention on the Law Applicable to Matrimonial Property Regimes: 'At the time of the conclusion of [...] [these] legal instruments, the concept of same-sex marriages was unheard of and it was certainly not taken into consideration by the parties. The introduction, by one contracting state, of a new dimension to a traditional legal term cannot reasonably obligate the other contracting states. It is therefore submitted that it would be contrary to the principle of good faith to consider the contracting states bound by the rules of the said conventions as far as Dutch same-sex marriages are concerned.' M. Bogdan, 'Some Reflections on the Treatment of Dutch Same-sex Marriages in European and Private International Law', in: T. Einhorn and K. Siehr (eds.), *Intercontinental cooperation through private international law: essays in memory of Peter E. Nygh* (The Hague, T.M.C. Asser Press 2004) p. 25 at p. 29.

[208] *Kamerstukken II* 1998/99, 26 672, no. 4, pp. 14–18. For the government response to this concern, see section 12.3.6 below.

[209] *Kamerstukken II* 1999/2000, 26 672, no. 5, pp. 19–20.

not go any further than to provide for clear information.[210] It had no intentions to assist same-sex couples in individual cases in explaining the status of their marriage to foreign authorities, but planned to issue a brochure which briefly explained the main features of the new Dutch legislation in various languages.[211] This brochure could also be used by official representations of the Netherlands in other States.[212] The government held it to be impossible to predict what legal effects would be given to the Dutch same-sex marriage by other States, but it expressed the hope that foreign legal practice would be 'innovative' in finding solutions.[213]

The State Commission on Private International Law held in December 2001 that there was no use (then) in drafting rules on the recognition of foreign same-sex marriages, because no other country had (then) introduced legislation to that effect.[214] It furthermore noted that such recognition would most probably not be problematic in the Dutch legal order.[215] The Commission did not consider the question of the recognition of Dutch same-sex marriages by other States, as that matter did not come within the competences of the Dutch legislature anyway.[216]

The State Commission was divided on the question of whether the Dutch 'opened up marriage' fell within the scope of the Hague Convention on the Celebration and Recognition of the Validity of Marriages of 1978.[217] As the report explained, if the Convention indeed applied to same-sex marriages, the other Contracting States to this Convention were, in principle, under the obligation to recognise a Dutch same-sex marriage,[218] as well as to celebrate a same-sex marriage if its choice of law rules designated Dutch law as the applicable law.[219] In both situations, however, so it was explained, the States could invoke a public policy exception.[220] One part of the Commission agreed with the government that the Convention did not apply

210 *Idem*, at p. 23.

211 *Idem*, at p. 18.

212 *Idem*, at p. 23.

213 *Idem*, at p. 17.

214 Staatscommissie voor het Internationaal Privaatrecht 2001, *supra* n. 140, at p. 4. The Commission had examined to what extent the relevant existing Private International Law Treaties relating to family law left room for the Dutch legislature to provide for specific conflict-of-laws rules concerning the Dutch opened up marriage and concerning adoption by same-sex couples. Joppe 2000A, *supra* n. 200, at p. 371.

215 Staatscommissie voor het Internationaal Privaatrecht 2001, *supra* n. 140, at p. 6.

216 *Idem*, at p. 4. The government was also well aware that any Dutch Private International Law legislation could not guarantee that a same-sex marriage concluded under Dutch law would be recognised abroad, as this was wholly dependent upon the rules of Private International Law of the State where recognition was sought. *Kamerstukken II* 1999/2000, 26 672, no. 5, p. 22.

217 Staatscommissie voor het Internationaal Privaatrecht 2001, *supra* n. 140, at p. 7.

218 Art. 9 (first sentence) of the 1978 Hague Convention on the Celebration and Recognition of the Validity of Marriages reads: 'A marriage validly entered into under the law of the State of celebration or which subsequently becomes valid under that law shall be considered as such in all Contracting States, subject to the provisions of this Chapter.' It must be noted that in fact the only other Contracting States to this Convention next to the Netherlands are Luxembourg and Australia.

219 Art. 3(2) of the 1978 Hague Convention on the Celebration and Recognition of the Validity of Marriages. See also Staatscommissie voor het Internationaal Privaatrecht 2001, *supra* n. 140, at p. 6.

220 Arts. 5 and 14 of the 1978 Hague Convention on the Celebration and Recognition of the Validity of Marriages.

and that therefore the Dutch government was free to draft its own conflict-of-laws rules.[221] On the basis of a historic interpretation, other members of the Commission came to a different conclusion. These members pointed out that same-sex marriage was indeed discussed during the drafting of the Convention and that – partly for that reason – the drafters had deliberately not provided for a definition of 'marriage' in the Convention.[222] In any case, so the full Commission concluded, the Dutch Private International Law (marriages) Act, which implemented the Convention, also applied to same-sex marriages and no amendment to this Act was required.[223]

The Commission also held that the 1978 Convention on the Law Applicable to Matrimonial Property Regimes[224] adopted the same definition of marriage as the Hague Convention on the Celebration and Recognition of the Validity of Marriages and that it could therefore possibly be held to be applicable to same-sex marriage.[225] The Commission was furthermore of the opinion that the *Brussels II* Regulation also applied to the Dutch (opened up) marriage, and that there was therefore only limited room for the Dutch legislature to make use of its residual competence to draft rules on jurisdiction.[226] Further, the Commission held that there were strong (historic) arguments that the Hague Adoption Convention of 1993[227] excluded adoption by same-sex couples.[228] The Commission therefore recommended that the government conclude bilateral or multilateral agreements with (Contracting) States that had no principled objections to adoption by same-sex couples.[229]

Following the advice of the Commission, the government continued the drafting of conflict-of-laws rules for registered partnerships. It acknowledged that the existing rules of Private International Law concerning marriage could not be fully analogously applied to registered partnerships as they were distinct institutes after all.[230] However, because the underlying principle of the Act Introducing Registered

221 These members of the Commission referred to the Explanatory Report to the Convention according to which marriage was to be defined 'in its broadest, international sense'.

222 These members of the Commission referred to the *Actes et Documents de la Treizième Session Tome III, Mariage* (1978). Support for this vision can be found in L. Pellis, 'Het homohuwelijk: een bijzonder nationaal product' ['Same-sex marriage: a special national product'] 24 *Tijdschrift voor Familie- en Jeugdrecht* (2002) p. 162 and A.P.M.J. Vonken, *Asser/Vonken, Asser 10-II Het internationale personen-, familie- en erfrecht, 69 Huwelijk personen gelijk geslacht*, update of 23 July 2012.

223 In one necessary amendment was yet foreseen in the Act of 8 March 2001 amending legislation with a view to the opening up of marriage and the introduction of adoption by couples of the same sex (Wet van 8 maart 2001 tot aanpassing wetgeving in verband met openstelling van het huwelijk en de invoering van personen van hetzelfde geslacht, *Stb.* 2001,128. This concerned the prohibition on polygamy in Art. 3(1)(d), which provided that one man could be married to one woman only and one woman to one man only. This wording was changed to the more neutral 'person'.

224 Convention of 14 March 1978 on the Law Applicable to Matrimonial Property Regimes, entry into force 1 September 1992.

225 Staatscommissie voor het Internationaal Privaatrecht 2001, *supra* n. 140, at p. 13.

226 *Idem*, at p. 34.

227 Convention of 29 May 1993 on Protection of Children and Co-operation in Respect of Intercountry Adoption, The Hague, entry into force 1 May 1995.

228 Staatscommissie voor het Internationaal Privaatrecht 2001, *supra* n. 140, at p. 24.

229 *Idem*, at, p. 34.

230 As Frohn explained, analogous application of the conflict-of-laws rules in relation to marriage to registered partnership, could have resulted in a reference to the laws of a country which did not provide

Partnerships had been to equalise registered partnerships as much as possible with marriage, the legislature also applied the conflict-of-laws rules for marriage as analogously as possible.[231] For partnerships registered in the Netherlands, unilateral conflict-of-laws rules were adopted, which determined in what situations Dutch law applied to these registered partnerships entered into under Dutch law.[232] For foreign partnerships, the *lex loci celebrationis* was applied (see below).[233]

After the Private International Law (registered partnership) Act (*Wet conflictenrecht geregistreerd partnerschap*) had entered into force in 2004,[234] in 2012 all Dutch Private International Law rules, including those relating to marriage and registered partnership, were brought together in a new tenth chapter in the Dutch Civil Code.[235] This was mainly a 'cosmetic' operation; substantively very little changed.[236] The following subsections set out the relevant substantive rules of Dutch Private International Law for various situations involving same-sex registered partnerships and marriages, starting with the situation where foreign same-sex couples wish to enter into a marriage or partnership in the Netherlands.

12.4.3. Access to marriage and registered partnerships for foreign same-sex couples

Since the Netherlands was of the first countries in the world which provided for a form of legal recognition of same-sex relationships, there was, when the registered partnership was introduced, a certain fear of 'registration tourism' and sham registrations.[237] Until 2001, when marriage was opened up, the rules concerning access to registered partnerships were more stringent when compared to the rules on

---

for registered partnership. E.N. Frohn, 'Geregistreerd Partnerschap' ['Registered Partnership'], in: Th. M. de Boer and F. Ibili (eds.), *Nederlands internationaal personen- en familierecht: wegwijzer voor de rechtspraktijk* [Dutch international family law: guidance for legal practice] (Deventer, Kluwer 2012) p. 281 at p. 281.

231 *Kamerstukken II* 2002/03, 28 924, no. 3, p. 3.

232 As Bell explained: '[...] the Dutch legislation governing registered partnership sought to depart from normal rules of private international law in order to ensure that Dutch law would remain the applicable jurisdiction in most disputes surrounding Dutch registered partners.' M. Bell, 'Holding Back the Tide? Cross-Border Recognition of Same-Sex Partnerships within the European Union', 12 *European Review of Private Law* (2004) p. 613 at p. 627. At the time of drafting of the Act, the legislature accepted that it could prove desirable in the future to amend the law on this point. See *Kamerstukken II* 2002/03, 28 924, no. 3, p. 3.

233 Art. 10:61(5)(a) and (b) BW. See also *Kamerstukken II* 2002/03, 28 924, no. 3, p. 3 and Frohn 2012, *supra* n. 231, at p. 281.

234 Wet conflictenrecht geregistreerd partnerschap [Act conflict-of-laws rules registered partnership], Act of 6 July 2004, *Stb.* 2004, 334. This Act was revoked per 1 January 2012 by Art. IV of *Vaststellings- en Invoeringswet Boek 10 BW* [Implementation Act Volume 10 of the Civil Code].

235 *Stb.* 2011, 272.

236 As Heijning explains, the new Arts. 10:60 to 10:90 BW were an 'almost literal copy' of the Private Internatinal Law (Registered Partnership) Act. S.H. Heijning, 'Boek 10 BW: IPR-regels geregistreerd partnerschap (art. 10:60 t/m 10:91 BW)' ['Book 10 BW: PIL-rules registered partnership (Art. 10:60 to 10:91 BW)'], 141 *WPNR* (2010) p. 311.

237 *Kamerstukken II* 1996/97, 23 761, no. 3, p. 5; no. 7, p. 15; no. 11, pp. 7–8. See also Curry-Sumner 2005A, *supra* n. 28, at pp. 123–124 and Boele-Woelki et al. 2006, *supra* n. 2, at pp. 13–14.

access to marriage.[238] While a marriage could also be celebrated in the Netherlands if one of the future spouses had neither Dutch nationality, nor a valid residence title,[239] for registered partnerships *both* partners had to be either Dutch nationals or nationals of an EU/EEA country or legal residents in the Netherlands.[240] Following the advice by the Kortmann II Commission (see section 12.3.4 above) this difference was lifted in 2001,[241] when the laws on marriages of convenience and registered partnerships of convenience were equated.[242] Another amendment concerned the repeal of a provision in the conflict-of-laws marriages Act according to which a marriage involving one or two non-Dutch nationals, on public order grounds, could not be celebrated in the Netherlands if the future spouses were of the same sex.[243]

Under the present legislation, two partners – whether of the same or different sex – can celebrate a marriage or enter into a registered partnership in the Netherlands if at least one of the partners is legally resident in the Netherlands *or* has Dutch nationality.[244] In this regard it is irrelevant whether the law of the country of which the non-Dutch partner(s) is or are (a) national(s), recognises same-sex marriage.[245]

One remaining difference between the registered partnership and marriage relates particularly to cross-border situations and concerns choice of law. Non-Dutch nationals residing in the Netherlands, who meet the conditions of Dutch law for concluding a marriage, may also decide to celebrate the marriage under the law of their country of nationality.[246] For partners who wish to enter into a registered partnership, this option is not open. Article 10:60(2) Civil Code provides that the

238 See also Waaldijk 1999, *supra* n. 79, at p. 207.

239 Art. 1:43(1) BW (*old*).

240 Art. 1:80a (1) and (2) BW (*old*). See also *Kamerstukken II* 1992/93, 22 700, no. 3, p. 6 and *Kamerstukken II* 1993/94, 23 761, no. 3, p. 4, as well as H.U. Jessurun d'Oliveira, 'Geregistreerd partnerschap en de Europese Unie, kanttekeningen over de internationale reikwijdte van het wetsvoorstel' ['Registered partnership and the European Union: comments on the international scope of the bill'], 70 *Nederlands Juristenblad* (1995), p. 1569 and Jessurun d'Oliveira 1996, *supra* n. 199.

241 *Kamerstukken II* 1999/00, 26 0862, no. 3, p. 5. Wet van 13 december 2000 tot wijziging van de regeling in Boek 1 van het Burgerlijk Wetboek met betrekking tot het naamrecht, de voorkoming van schijnhuwelijken en het tijdstip van de totstandkoming van de scheiding van tafel en bed alsmede van enige andere wetten [Act of 13 December 2000 amending Book One of the Civil Code concerning the right of the name, the prevention of marriages of convenience and legal separation as well as several others Acts], *Stb.* 2001, 11.

242 Following Arts. 1:50 and 1:80a (5) BW an intended marriage or registered partnership may be interrupted when the objective of the prospective spouses or registered partners of one of them is not the fulfillment of the duties which the law connects to a marriage or registered partnership, but to obtain access to the Netherlands.

243 Art. 3(1)(d) Wet Conflictenrecht Huwelijk (*old*). See *Kamerstukken II* 1998/99, 26 672, no. 3, p. 7.

244 Arts. 1:43(1) and 1:80a (4) BW. As explained by the Ministry of Foreign Affairs, if neither partner is a Dutch national while they both live abroad, they may not marry in the Netherlands. If neither partner is a Dutch national, they may marry in the Netherlands provided one of them is resident there. If both partners live outside the Netherlands, they may marry in the Netherlands provided one of them is a Dutch national. Partners who both live in the Netherlands may marry even if neither of them is a Dutch national. Netherlands Ministry of Foreign Affairs, *FAQ Same-sex marriage 2010*, p. 7, online available at www.minbuza.nl/binaries/content/assets/minbuza/en/import/en/you_and_the_netherlands/about_the_netherlands/ethical_issues/qa-homohuwelijk-2011-en---def.pdf, visited June 2012.

245 *Idem*, at p. 6.

246 Art. 10:28 BW.

question of whether the partners qualify for entering into a registered partnership with each other in the Netherlands, is governed by Dutch law.[247] Application of foreign law may be rejected for being manifestly incompatible with Dutch public order.[248] The wording 'manifestly incompatible' makes clear that this exception must be applied restrictively.[249] For marriages, the public order notion is given further interpretation in Article 10:29 Civil Code. Issues such as too young in age, too close in kinship, and disturbed mental capacity of the future spouses, as well as non-exclusiveness of the marriage, may justify a refusal to apply foreign law.[250] On the other hand, the celebration of a marriage cannot be refused on the ground that there is an impediment to this marriage under the law of the State of nationality of the future spouses, if that impediment itself is contrary to Dutch public order.[251] Hence, the fact that the future spouses are of the same sex cannot be accepted as impediment to the celebration of a marriage in the Netherlands, for to accept such unequal treatment would be against Dutch public order.

12.4.4. Implementation of Directives 2004/38 and 2003/86 in Dutch Law

Unmarried different-sex and same-sex partners have been recognised for purposes of immigration to the Netherlands since 1975.[252] Under Dutch law both same-sex and different-sex spouses or registered partners of EU citizens are considered 'family members' within the meaning of Directive 2004/38.[253] A right to residence is also provided for the partner with whom the EU citizen is in a duly attested, stable, long-term relationship, as well as for the minor children of this partner.[254]

---

247 Art. 10:60(2) BW. See also M. Gordijn, 'Geregistreerd Partnerschap' ['Registered partnership'], in: A. Baptiste and E.W.M. Gubbels, *Burgerzaken & Boek 10 BW* [Civil matters and Book 10 BW] (Zoetermeer, NVVB 2012) p. 92 at pp. 94–95. The Minister for Justice held that it constituted no unacceptable restriction if non-Dutch national partners who did not meet the conditions of Dutch law, were not allowed to enter into a registered partnership under Dutch law. *Kamerstukken II* 2002/03, 28 924, no. 3, p. 9.

248 Art. 10:6 BW.

249 A.P.M.J. Vonken, *Asser/Vonken 10-II 2012/114* (update 23 July 2012).

250 Following Article 10:29(1) BW the celebration of a marriage in the Netherlands is against public policy, if (a) the future spouses have not reached the age of 15 years; (b) if the future spouses are siblings or related to each other in the direct line by blood or by adoption; (c) if the free consent of one of the future spouses is missing or the mental capacity of one of them is so disturbed that he is unable to determine his own will or to understand the significance of his declarations; (d) if the marriage would be in conflict with the rule that a person may only be united in marriage with one other person at the same time and (e) if the marriage would be in conflict with the rule that a person who wishes to conclude a marriage may not simultaneously be registered as a partner in a registered partnership.

251 Art. 10:29(2) BW.

252 Waaldijk et al. 2010, supra n. 188, at p. 24. The report refers (in footnote 91) to K. Waaldijk, *More or less together: levels of legal consequences of marriage, cohabitation and registered partnership for different-sex and same-sex partners. A comparative study of nine European countries* (Paris, Institut National d'Études Démographiques 2005) p. 147, online available at www.hdl.handle.net/1887/12585, visited June 2010.

253 Art. 8.7 Vreemdelingenbesluit [Aliens Decree], implementing Directive 2004/38/EC.

254 Art. 8.7(4) Vreemdelingenbesluit [Aliens Decree]. Until 2009 the relationship could be attested by the partners signing a *relatieverklaring* ['declaration of relationship']. *Vreemdelingencirculaire* [Aliens Circular] B10/5.2.2. As of 31 January 2009 the partners should normally also produce evidence either

Also in respect of family reunification[255] Dutch law makes no distinction between same-sex and different-sex partners or between their family members.[256] In 2012 family reunification was limited to – what was called – the 'core family' (*'kerngezin'*), i.e. spouses, registered partners and minor children only.[257] In other words, unmarried stable partners no longer qualified for family reunification. Provision was made for same-sex couples who had no access to marriage in their home countries. They could apply for a 'marriage visa' for the duration of six months, enabling them to enter the Netherlands to conclude a marriage or a registered partnership. These amendments were repealed in 2013.[258]

12.4.5. Recognition of foreign registered partnerships and marriages under Dutch law

Because a foreign same-sex marriage will always be of later date than the entry into force of the Dutch opening up of marriage Act, it has never been an issue whether foreign same-sex marriages would be recognised as such under Dutch law.[259] They are indeed recognised as marriage under Dutch law.[260] In the words of Vonken, the principle of equal treatment as provided for in Article 1 of the Dutch Constitution and Article 26 ICCPR also has effect in Dutch Private International Law.[261]

With respect to registered partnerships the situation is somewhat different. At the time when the Dutch legislature drafted conflict-of-laws rules, registered partnership legislation was introduced in a limited number of countries only and the various regimes varied significantly. Therefore, the Dutch legislature set certain standards which foreign registered partnerships have to meet in order to be recognised as registered partnership under Dutch law.[262]

---

that they have or recently had a joint household for at least six months, or that they have a child together. Aliens Circular A2/6.2.2.2.

255 Under Dutch law the term 'family reunification' includes family formation.

256 Arts. 3.13 to 3.15 Vreemdelingenbesluit [Aliens Decree]. Family members are: (a) the adult who is, according to Dutch Private International Law, legitimately married to the foreigner or who is, according to Dutch law, the registered partner of the foreigner; (b) the adult who has a lasting and exclusive relationship with the foreigner, provided that certain requirements are met; and (c) the minor natural or legitimate child of the foreigner who, in the Minister's opinion, is actually a family member of that foreigner and already was so in the country of origin and who comes under the legitimate authority of the foreigner. For each of the three categories a requirement is that the partners actually live together and have a joint household (Art. 3.17, Aliens Decree).

257 Decree of 27th March 2012 amending the Aliens Decree 2000, *Stb.* 2012, 148.

258 *Stb.* 2013, 184.

259 Compare Staatscommissie voor het Internationaal Privaatrecht 2001, *supra* n. 140, at p. 6.

260 Following Art. 10:31(1) BW '[a] marriage that is contracted outside the Netherlands and that is valid under the law of the State where it took place or that has become valid afterwards according to the law of that State, is recognised in the Netherlands as a valid marriage.' Translation taken from www.dutchcivillaw.com/civilcodebook01010.htm, visited June 2014.

261 A.P.M.J. Vonken, *Asser/Vonken, Asser 10-II Het internationale personen-, familie- en erfrecht, 69 Huwelijk personen gelijk geslacht*, update of 23 July 2012.

262 *Kamerstukken II* 2002/03, 28 924, no. 3, pp. 2–3. These requirements were included in the bill, following advice of the Council of State. *Kamerstukken II* 28 924, no. B, pp. 2–3.

As a rule a registered partnership that is entered into outside the Netherlands and that is valid under the (Private International) law of the State where it is entered into or that has become valid afterwards according to the law of that State, is recognised in the Netherlands as a valid registered partnership.[263] However, only partnerships that have '*Standesfolge*' (i.e., excluding purely contractual partnerships) and which are open to two persons in a close personal and effective relationship only, qualify for recognition as registered partnership under Dutch law.[264] The partnership must be registered with a competent public authority and the partnership must be exclusive in the sense that the partners cannot at the same time be in a marriage or any comparable institution.[265] Furthermore, the rights and obligations of the registered partners to each other must be equal to or in essence corresponding to those of spouses.[266] This includes the obligation to support one another and to provide each other with 'what is needed' ('*het nodige*').[267] Other relevant indications that the partnership corresponds to marriage, are an obligation to have a reasonable share in the costs of the household and several liability for the debts of the common household.[268]

The Civil Code also provides for two corresponding public policy exceptions for registered partnerships and marriage in recognition cases.[269] However, these exceptions can (again) only be successfully invoked in cases of a manifest conflict with Dutch public order and must be applied (very) restrictively.[270] In a situation where mere recognition is requested of a marriage or registered partnership that has been celebrated or registered in another State, the connection with the Dutch legal order will be looser, than in a situation where a request is made to have marriage or partnership celebrated in the Netherlands. This is even more so, if considerable time has elapsed since the celebration of the marriage or registration of the partnership in the other State. These factors render invocation and application of the public order exception in recognition cases even less appropriate.[271] In any case, it is obvious that the mere fact that the future spouses or registered partners are of the same sex can

---

263 Art. 10:61(1) and (2) BW. Following the fourth paragraph of this Article, '[...] a registered partnership is presumed to be valid if a certificate of registered partnership has been issued by a competent authority'. See also Heijning 2010, *supra* n. 237.

264 *Kamerstukken II* 2002/03, 28 924, no. 3, p. 10 and *Kamerstukken II* 2002/03, 28 924, no. 3, pp. 2–3.

265 Art. 10:61(5)(a) and (b) BW.

266 Art. 10:61(5)(c) BW.

267 *Kamerstukken II* 2002/03, 28 924, no. 3, pp. 2–3.

268 *Idem*. In the Explanatory Memorandum to the Private International Law (registered partnership) Act, the Dutch legislature held that the Belgian legal cohabitation ('wettelijke samenwoning'), the French 'pacte civil de solidarité' and the legally recognised forms of cohabitation in the laws of Catalonia and Aragon met these criteria.

269 Arts. 10:21 and 10:62 BW. See also *Kamerstukken II* 2009/10, 32137, no. 3, p. 47.

270 Gordijn 2012, *supra* n. 248, at pp. 100–101 and Frohn 2012, *supra* n. 231, at, pp. 286–287. Possible examples the authors mention are if one of the partners or both partners was yet in a registered partnership or marriage at the time of entering into the partnership; if one of the partners or both partners were younger than 15 years of age at the time of the registration; if one of the partners or both partners were at the time of entering into the partnership incapable of his or her free will, or of understanding the meaning of his or her declaration to enter into the partnership. As Frohn has pointed out, application of the public order exception must be in line with the principle of proportionality: the lesser close the partnership is related to Dutch law, the lesser reasonable it is to apply the exception.

271 A.P.M.J. Vonken, *Asser/Vonken 10-II 2012/92*, update of 23 July 2012.

never constitute ground for application of the public order exception under Dutch law.

12.4.6. Parental issues

Under the present state of Dutch law,[272] the recognition of parental links established in another country is not to be expected problematic on the mere ground that the couple is of the same sex.[273] This may possibly only be different in the – as yet hypothetical – case that a foreign State allows for the establishment of parental links for couples consisting of two men through operation of the law.

Same-sex couples from the Netherlands may, however, experience problems if they wish to have their parental links recognised in another country. Very few other States provide for as far-reaching parental rights for same-sex couples as the Netherlands. It is generally accepted that parental links of same-sex couples or partners have a higher chance of being recognised abroad if they are established through adoption, than if they are established through recognition or by operation of the law, because adoption involves an examination by a court.[274]

12.4.7. Recognition of Dutch partnerships and marriages in other Member States

From the first moment registered partnership was considered in the Netherlands, and later when the opening up of marriage to same-sex couples was under debate, concerns have been expressed that recognition abroad could be (very) problematic.[275] After all, the new Dutch regimes represented 'a challenge to the Private International Law of other countries.'[276]

The Kortmann II Commission conducted a questionnaire amongst the Council of Europe Member States, which showed that only very few countries would recognise a Dutch same-sex marriage.[277] The government acknowledged that same-sex spouses

272 It is recalled that this research was concluded on 31 July 2014.

273 In the past this was, however, different. For instance in 2003 – before joint interstate adoption was introduced for same-sex couples – a District Court refused to recognise a joint adoption by a same-sex couple under American law. Rb. Zwolle 30 June 2003, ECLI:NL:RBZWO:2003:AI0668. See also Curry-Sumner and Vonk 2006, *supra* n. 142. The authors hold that a week earlier in a similar case another District Court, however, recognised the adoption.

274 The Commission on lesbian parenthood and interstate adoption (also referred to as Kalsbeek Commission) had therefore proposed to issue a declaratory decision in situations where a co-mother had established parental links with a child through recognition or by operation of the law. So far, this has not been followed up, but the adoption option for co-mothers was deliberately upheld. Commissie lesbisch ouderschap en interlandelijke adoptie 2007, *supra* n. 161, at p. 44. See Nuytinck 2010, *supra* n. 169, at pp. 343–348.

275 E.g. *Kamerstukken II* 1998/99, 26 672, no. 4, pp. 14–18.

276 Bogdan 2004, *supra* n. 208, at p. 25.

277 *Kamerstukken II* 1998/99, 26 672, no. 3, pp. 7–8.

could encounter 'several practical and legal problems' abroad, but also held that this was 'one aspect' the future same-sex spouses had to be aware of.[278] The fact that same-sex spouses may possibly not be awarded any rights as 'family members' of migrating EU citizens was acknowledged by the government to be 'a practical problem which should not be underestimated'. The government also held, however, that this did not constitute a decisive argument against opening up marriage. It was for the individuals concerned to consider the pros and cons, the government held.[279] It stressed that the legislation was initiated with the express consideration that the risk of limping relationships was no reason to refrain from opening up marriage to same-sex couples. The government intended to inform the public through a brochure (see above).[280] The State Commission on Private International Law agreed with the government that it was important to inform same-sex couples who wished to enter into a marriage, about the risk that their marriage would not be recognised as such in other countries, even though it also considered it very well possible that certain legal effects would be given to it.[281]

It indeed proved to be the case that same-sex couples experience 'substantial problems' in other countries.[282] Obviously the (level of) recognition depends on the national regime of the host Member State. As Boele-Woelki et al. explain:

> 'In those countries to have opened civil marriage to same-sex couples, the recognition of Dutch same-sex marriages is generally not problematic. In those countries where a domestic form of registered partnership has been created, same-sex marriages celebrated abroad are often afforded recognition as this domestic form of registered partnership. In those jurisdictions were no substantive law regime is available for same-sex couples to formalise their relationship, the chances are great that a Dutch same-sex marriage will not be recognised.'[283]

Hence, even if some form of recognition is afforded, this may entail the downgrading of a civil status as spouses to registered partners with considerably more limited legal

---

278 *Kamerstukken II* 1998/99, 26 672, no. 3, p. 8. Waaldijk has translated the relevant paragraph in the Explanatory Memorandum as follows: 'The question relating to the completely new legal phenomenon of marriage between persons of the same sex concerns the interpretation of the notion of public order to be expected in other countries. Such interpretation relates to social opinion about homosexuality. As a result of this, spouses of the same sex may encounter various practical and legal problems abroad. This is something for future spouses of the same sex to take into account.' C. Waaldijk, 'Others may follow: the introduction of marriage, quasi-marriage, and semi-marriage for same-sex couples in European countries', 38 *New England Law Review* (2004) p. 569 at p. 577.

279 *Kamerstukken II* 1999/00, 26 672, no. 5, p. 11. On this question see also H.U. Jessurun d'Oliveira, 'Vrijheid van verkeer voor geregistreerde partners in de Europese Unie. Hoog tijd!' ['Free movement for registered partners in the European Union. High time!'], 76 *Nederlands Juristenblad* (2001) p. 205.

280 *Kamerstukken II* 1999/00, 26 672, no. 5, p. 6.

281 Staatscommissie voor het Internationaal Privaatrecht 2001, *supra* n. 140, at p. 11. Pellis held that the State Commission should have urged the government more to raise the issue of 'limping relationships' at European and international level. Pellis 2002, *supra* n. 223, at p. 167.

282 Boele-Woelki et al. 2006, *supra* n. 2, at p. 246.

283 *Idem*, at p. 247.

effects,[284] as many States do not recognise the Dutch distinction between marriage and registered partnership.[285] Other States do not recognise the Dutch registered partnership as registered partnership under their national laws because it is open to both same-sex and different-sex couples. Yet other States refuse to give Dutch same-sex marriages and partnerships any recognition on public order grounds.[286] Further, the fact that same-sex spouses and registered partners cannot obtain an international (marriage) certificate under the ICCS Convention on the issue of multilingual extracts from civil status records,[287] may cause practical problems when these couples go abroad.[288]

12.5. Conclusions

When it comes to legal recognition of same-sex relationships, the Netherlands is, and always has been, in the vanguard. Firmly based on the principle of equal treatment, the legal recognition of same-sex relationships has gradually increased since the 1990s towards a strong level of protection nowadays. Same-sex couples now have access to the institutions of marriage and registered partnerships on the same footing as different-sex couples. After various amendments to the law over the past decades, these institutions now generally have the same legal effects and there are almost no differences between same-sex couples and different-sex couples in this regard. Parentage has proven to be the most controversial issue, however, and it is in this area that same-sex marriages and registered partnerships are still not entirely equal to different-sex marriages and registered partnerships. On grounds of biological differences, this holds especially for couples consisting of two men. This difference has so far been upheld on the ground that from a biological perspective, couples of two men are not in the same position as couples of two women. Nonetheless, it is

---

284 For example, it was reported that in Germany, the United Kingdom, the Czech Republic, Denmark, Finland, Luxembourg, Slovenia and Switzerland, Dutch same-sex marriages were not recognised as a marriage, but as registered or civil partnerships. It was unclear if Dutch same-sex marriage and registered partnerships would be recognised at all in France and Italy. Boele-Woelki et al. 2006, *supra* n. 2, at pp. 190 and 247 and K. Boele-Woelki et al., 'The evaluation of same-sex marriages and registered partnerships in the Netherlands', 8 *Yearbook of Private International Law* (2007) p. 27 at p. 31. See also Bell 2004, *supra* n. 233, at p. 629.

285 Boele-Woelki et al. 2006, *supra* n. 2, at p. 224.

286 See Waaldijk 2004, *supra* n. 279, at p. 577, referring (in footnote 41) to K. McKnorrie, 'Would Scots Law Recognise a Dutch Same-Sex Marriage?', 7 *Edinburgh L. Rev* (2003) p. 147.

287 ICCS Convention on the issue of multilingual extracts from civil status records, Vienna 8 September 1976, ICCS Convention no. 16.

288 Boele-Woelki et al. 2006, *supra* n. 2, at p. 80. In response to Parliamentary Questions on this issue, the Minister for Justice informed Parliament in 2010 that the ICCS was in the progress of adapting its model certificate accordingly. He furthermore held that in the meantime there were various other means through which the Civil Registry could issue a translated civil status record to same-sex spouses. *Aanhangsel Handelingen II* 2010/11, 95. As to date (i.e. 31 July 2014) the ICCS certificate as available on the website of the ICCS (www.ciecl.org/Conventions/Conv16.pdf, visited 31 July 2014) has not been amended on this point. In this regard it is furthermore interesting to note that the original bill for the Act Opening Up Marriage provided that an official declaration of no impediment to marriage would only be issued to a Dutch national who wished to conclude a marriage abroad under (then) Art. 1:49a BW, if the person intended to conclude a marriage with a person of different sex. This provision was not included in the final Act.

not inconceivable that gay couples will challenge this difference in treatment in the future.[289]

Legal recognition of same-sex relationships has primarily been introduced in the form of legislation and on the initiative of the Dutch Parliament and government, although court judgments sometimes functioned as a trigger. In general the courts have, however, shown strong deference towards the legislature, both in respect of legal recognition of same-sex relationships and in respect of parental rights for same-sex couples. In this respect, Waaldijk has described the Dutch process as 'an extremely gradual and almost perversely nuanced (but highly successful) process of legislative recognition of same-sex partnership'. The author finds this a 'prime example' of the operation of what he calls the 'law of small change'.[290] It is indeed true that the Dutch process is an incremental one, with every step taken raising the question why another step should not be taken as well. In the words of Waaldijk, '[...] the debate could focus on whether there were any acceptable arguments against reducing the legal distinctions between same-sex and different-sex partners *a little further*.'[291] At the same time, it cannot go unnoticed that certain steps were taken rather quickly. For instance, as Boele-Woelki et al. hold:

> 'At the start of the 1990s it was almost impossible to foresee that within ten years it would have been possible to open civil marriage to same-sex couples. Changes in the political composition of the government and unremitting social change both contributed to the rapid legal developments in this field.'[292]

The 'foreign countries' argument has played an ambiguous role in the whole process. On the one hand the clear wish to be a pioneer in Europe, or even in the world, prompted the Dutch legislature to (rapidly) introduce legislation.[293] At the same time, fear that other countries would not accept or recognise the Dutch legislative choices, was presented as an argument against legislative change. In this way, the 'foreign countries' argument functioned almost as an 'excuse'.[294] This was the main reason why the Dutch government initially did not want to risk opening up marriage, and

---

289 See Nuytinck 2010, *supra* n. 275. Earlier see Hoevenaars 1997, *supra* n. 28, at p. 232.

290 Waaldijk describes the 'law of the small change' as follows: 'Any legislative change advancing the recognition and acceptance of homosexuality will only be enacted, if that change is either perceived as small, or if that change is sufficiently reduced in impact by some accompanying legislative 'small change' that reinforces the condemnation of homosexuality'. Waaldijk 2001A, *supra* n. 13, at pp. 440–441.

291 *Idem*, at p. 453.

292 Boele-Woelki et al. 2006, *supra* n. 2, at p. 249.

293 The Deputy Prime Minister of the Netherlands held in 1998 that in ethical issues, the Netherlands was often the first, while often other States followed after some time. 'Homohuwelijk exporteren', *Algemeen Dagblad* 12 December 1998, p. 3.

294 See for example C. Waaldijk, 'Naar een gelijkgeslachtelijk huwelijk. Waarom het buitenland, het afstammingsrecht en de invoering van geregistreerde partnerschap geen argumenten zijn voor handhaving van de heteroseksuele exclusiviteit van het huwelijk' ['Towards a same-sex marriage. Why other countries, the law on descent and the introduction of registered partnership are no arguments for maintaining the heterosexual exclusivity of marriage'], 17 *Tijdschrift voor Familie- en Jeugdrecht* (1995) p. 223.

the argument also played an important role in the debates about parental rights for same-sex couples. In the end, although heavily criticised for it, the legislature was prepared to put up with the risk of 'limping relationships' as it – once again – felt that the principle of equal treatment had to prevail.

The development of Private International Law rules has been a considerably less smooth process than the introduction of registered partnership and same-sex marriage in the first place. While there remains, today, debate about the applicability of International Treaties, the application of the Dutch conflict-of-laws rules to foreign same-sex relationships, has not proven very problematic (see section 12.4.5), and Dutch law makes no distinction between same-sex couples and different-sex couples in respect of free movement of EU citizens and family reunification (section 12.4.4). This is different for the recognition of Dutch same-sex marriages and same-sex registered partnerships, as well as parental links established by same-sex couples under Dutch law, by other States (section 12.4.7). Although limited statistical data is available in this respect (see section 12.4.1), it is clear that migrating same-sex couples have encountered various legal and practical problems when seeking recognition of their civil status in other countries.

Chapter 13
Conclusions Case Study II

13.1. The internal picture – What do the various jurisdictions provide in respect of legal recognition of same-sex relationships?

13.1.1. Different paths, different paces, but similar direction

From the present case study a picture has emerged of different jurisdictions moving at different paces, a movement which nonetheless generally seems to be going in a similar direction. Whether the legislature or the judiciary is taking the lead, this direction consists of awarding increasingly more protection to same-sex couples and rainbow families. Nevertheless, the difference in pace of the three States studied in this research is striking. Moreover, not only are there differences in the speed of their movement, but the case studies have also shown that the States have followed different paths.[1] The paths chosen have been very determinative for the nature of the debates at the national level and for the ensuing (judicial) balancing exercises. For example, where a separate civil partnership was created for same-sex couples, as was the case in Germany and Ireland, the debates in essence related to a (presumed) tension between traditional notions of marriage and – initially – family on the one hand, and the principle of equal treatment on the other.[2] This also implied that for the assessment of whether there was discrimination on grounds of sexual orientation, civil partnership was compared with marriage. In the Netherlands, on the other hand, a registered partnership was introduced that was open to different-sex couples and same-sex couples, while marriage was soon thereafter opened up to same-sex couples as well. Consequently, civil status has played a less prominent role in debates on differences in treatment between same-sex and different-sex couples in the Netherlands.

---

1 Curry-Sumner has divided formalised registration schemes for same-sex couples into five different models, namely: monistic, dualistic with weak registration; dualistic with strong registration; pluralistic with weak registration and pluralistic with strong registration. I. Curry Sumner, *All's well that ends registered?: the substantive and private international law aspects of non-marital registered relationships in Europe: a comparison of the laws of Belgium, France, The Netherlands, Switzerland and the United Kingdom* (Antwerp, Intersentia 2005).

2 Other considerations in debates on legal recognition of same-sex relationships have been legal certainty and coherence of legislation. For instance, one of the reasons in the Netherlands to consider the introduction of a registered partnership, was the fact that in the Netherlands over the years a complex web of laws regulating forms of *de facto* cohabitation had come into existence which lacked coherence. The ECtHR has also at times held that States must ensure that their legislative framework in the area is coherent. See ch. 12, section 12.3.2 and ch. 8, section 8.2.4.1.2.

As set out in the various subsections below, European law has so far had only minimal impact on national standard-setting in respect of legal recognition of same-sex relationships. This first section of this concluding Chapter will firstly address the balancing of equal treatment and traditional notions of marriage and the family in section 13.1.2. Subsequently, the question of when same-sex couples and different-sex couples are in a comparable situation and require equalisation of their position, is addressed (section 13.1.3). Section 13.1.4 discusses how the various jurisdictions studied for this research have dealt with parental rights for same-sex couples and how this developed over time. The diversity in legislative and judicial processes is set out in section 13.1.5. Section 13.2 addresses the cross-border picture and discusses the various legal responses to cross-border movement that can be identified in the present case study.

13.1.2. Equal treatment *vs.* traditional notions of marriage and the family

In all jurisdictions studied for this case study, equal treatment has been an important and often decisive argument in the debates on legal recognition of same-sex relationships. A desire to abolish discrimination on grounds of sexual orientation has been at the basis of a gradual but generally steady development towards increased protection of LGBT rights and, correspondingly, legal recognition of same-sex relationships in the three States studied. Still, other (general) interests have at times been considered weightier. Traditional notions of marriage and (marriage-based) family have been the most prominent and most often accepted counter-interests in this regard.

Because of its long history and tradition, marriage has a special place in the national legal orders of the three States studied for this case study. As elaborately set out in Chapters 10 and 11, this particularly holds for Germany and Ireland, whose Constitutions provide for special protection of marriage. Marriage is thereby understood as between man and woman only. Initially, the protection of traditional marriage and family was put forward in national legislative debates as an argument against any legal recognition of same-sex relationships. Later, in Germany and Ireland, the special protection of marriage was ground for creating a separate institution for same-sex relationships, while reserving marriage for different-sex couples only (see also 13.1.3 below). Both EU law and the ECtHR have respected such national choices. In the case law of the ECtHR, traditional marriage has generally enjoyed strong protection. As set out in Chapter 8, the ECtHR has held that marriage is 'singled out for special treatment' under Article 12 ECHR, and that it confers a special status on those who enter into it.[3] The ECtHR has repeatedly ruled that 'marriage' under Article 12 ECHR concerns traditional marriage between man and woman only and the Court has recognised a State interest in maintaining 'the traditional institution of marriage intact'.[4] States enjoy a wide margin of appreciation

---

3 See Ch. 8, section 8.1.3.
4 See Ch. 8, section 8.2.5.

when it comes to access to marriage and protection of traditional marriage has been accepted as justification ground for a distinction between (different-sex) spouses and (same-sex) stable partners, whether registered partners or unmarried partners (see also section 13.1.3 below).[5]

These debates have been, and are, however, in flux. Support for protection of traditional marriage has been or is eroding in all three States studied for this case study. The Dutch legislature deliberately gave precedence to the principle of equal treatment over tradition in 2001 when it opened up marriage to same-sex couples. In Ireland, the opening up of marriage to same-sex couples is presently being contemplated. In Germany this is not (yet) the case, but clear changes are also visible there. As observed in Chapter 10, the most recent line of case law of the German Constitutional Court in relation to same-sex relationships is no longer about the special protection of marriage, but about the protection of civil partnership against discrimination.[6] A similar development can be seen partly in the case law of the CJEU. The CJEU has also implicitly begun to tamper with the protection of traditional marriage by finding same-sex registered partners in a legal and factual situation comparable to that of spouses as regards certain employment benefit (see also 13.1.3 below).[7] The Luxembourg Court thereby gave a neutral reading of marriage as 'a form of civil union', without referring to any special status of marriage. Even the ECtHR has made the (though so far only symbolic) steps of finding that same-sex couples come within the scope of Article 12 (the right to marry).

In the same vein, views on traditional family have also developed over time. In particular, there is a trend emerging towards increased protection of the interests of the child in this context. This development has been visible both at the national level and in the case law of the Strasbourg Court, and it has had clear implications for the development of parental rights for same-sex couples, as is further discussed in section 13.1.4 below.

Moreover, outside the sphere of marriage, in fact, the protection of LGBT rights and same-sex relationships has grown increasingly stronger, including at the European level. Within the EU, equal treatment has been very strongly pursued in the field of employment, but even in areas of law where the EU has no competences, Member States must comply with the principle of non-discrimination as protected under EU law.[8] Under the ECHR, discrimination on grounds of sexual orientation requires particularly serious reasons by way of justification. In cases where no difference in civil status was concerned (see 13.1.3 below), this rule has resulted in stronger protection of same sex relationships. The ECtHR has furthermore held that same-sex

5 In cases where same-sex couples claimed that they were treated differently from different-sex couples, the special status of marriage has often been a ground for not even finding comparability of the situations of same-sex couples and those of different-sex couples, or in any case for justifying a difference in treatment between these groups.

6 See Ch. 10, section 10.5.

7 See Ch. 9, section 9.3.3.2.

8 See Ch. 9, section 9.3.

relationships enjoy the protection of both private and family life under Article 8 ECHR and has explicitly recognised that same-sex couples – just like different-sex couples – have a need for legal recognition and protection of their relationships. Although – as yet – no full consequences were given to these findings, there are, as observed in Chapter 8, hints that the Strasbourg Court may move in the direction of the definition of a positive obligation for the States to provide for some form of legal recognition of same-sex relationships.

The notion of protection of morals has not, as such, appeared explicitly in debates and decision-making on legal recognition of same-sex relationships. It was underlying the initial criminalisation of homosexual acts in all three States studied for this case study and was in that context in itself accepted as a legitimate state interest by the ECtHR.[9] The protection of morals has, however, scarcely been relied upon in respect of legal recognition of same-sex relationships, nor has the ECtHR accepted the protection of morals as a legitimate aim to justify reserving marriage for man and woman only.[10]

13.1.3. The comparability issue and the equalisation imperative

Courts and legislatures in the various jurisdictions studied in this research have dealt differently with discrimination complaints, in particular with the question of whether same-sex couples and different-sex couples were in a comparable situation if their civil status was different. This accordingly has had implications for the question of whether these groups should be treated equally.

As observed in Chapter 8, in the case law of the ECtHR, the special status of marriage has often been a ground for the ECtHR for not even finding comparability of the situations of unmarried same-sex couples and married different-sex couples, or in any case for justifying a difference in treatment between these groups. The fact that marriage was not open to same-sex couples under the law of the respective State had no bearing on these findings. In other words, the Court did not find indirect discrimination in these cases. The ECtHR has extended this formal equality based approach to cases involving other forms of a 'special legal status', such as registered partnerships.[11] The Strasbourg Court has thus only held couples with the same civil status to be in comparable situations; where different-sex couples had a 'special legal status', this status distinguished their situation from that of same-sex couples who did not have this status, irrespective of whether same-sex couples had access to that

---

[9] See Ch. 8, section 8.1.1.

[10] In *Schalk and Kopf* (2010), the wide margin was justified because general measures of economic or social strategy were concerned. Only in *Hämäläinen* (2013) – which case concerned the marriage of a post-operative transsexual – did the Court note that the case raised 'sensitive moral or ethical issues'. ECtHR 24 June 2010, *Schalk and Kopf* v. *Austria*, no. 30141/04, para. 98 and ECtHR [GC] 16 July 2014, *Hämäläinen* v. *Finland*, no. 37359/09, para. 75. See also Ch. 8, section 8.2.2.

[11] As more elaborately discussed in Ch. 8, section 8.2.3.2, this has been defined in the Court's case law as 'a public undertaking, carrying with it a body of rights and obligations of a contractual nature'. ECtHR [GC] 29 April 2008, *Burden* v. *the United Kingdom*, no. 13378/05, para. 65.

special legal status or not. This approach of the Strasbourg Court also implies that States are under no obligation to equalise alternative registration forms with marriage. In fact, the ECtHR has held that States enjoy a certain margin of appreciation as regards the exact status conferred by alternative means of recognition.[12]

The CJEU, on the other hand, has taken a different approach. In older case law the CJEU had been as evasive as the ECtHR by holding that a special legal status was decisive in cases where discrimination on grounds of sexual orientation was claimed.[13] However, more recently the CJEU has held in various cases that there is direct discrimination on grounds of sexual orientation where at the national level certain employment benefits are reserved to spouses, while marriage is reserved to different-sex couples only and under national law, same-sex registered partners are in a legal and factual situation comparable to that of spouses as regards that benefit. The Luxembourg Court has thus imposed on States the obligation to equalise alternative registration forms with marriage, where marriage is open to different-sex couples only. This obligation only applies, however, where that alternative registration form is comparable to marriage under the national law, and only in respect of certain employment related benefits. While initially the CJEU left it to the national courts to assess the issue of comparability of situations, more recently, the Court instead assessed this issue itself. It held that even the French PACS met the requirement of comparability, while that partnership form is not as close to marriage as, for example, the German civil partnership, which was central to earlier case law of the CJEU in the area.[14] The Luxembourg Court has thus over time become more instructive in this area and has correspondingly left less room for national courts to decide such cases.

Both Ireland and Germany have chosen a 'separate but equal' approach, by creating a separate institute for same-sex couples that nonetheless granted equivalent rights. In Germany this was first introduced in 2001 and over time the German civil partnership was increasingly more equalised with marriage on the basis of the principle of equal treatment. German courts thus did not hesitate to compare the position of (same-sex) civil partners with that of (different-sex) spouses and found indirect discrimination on grounds of sexual orientation where they were treated differently without sufficient justification. In Ireland, the comparison with marriage was generally avoided by the legislature when introducing civil partnerships, and the fact that the opening up of marriage was explored the very same year that civil partnerships were introduced, rendered such comparison and any equalisation of civil partnership increasingly more redundant. As noted above, in the Netherlands, differences in legal status have been even less relevant in debates over equal rights for same-sex couples. Instead, for instance in the context of parental rights, biological differences have been at times accepted as justification for a difference in treatment between same-sex couples and different-sex couples.

---

[12] See Ch. 8, sections 8.2.2.2 and 8.2.6.

[13] Joined Cases C-122/99 P and C-125/99 P *D and Kingdom of Sweden* v. *Council* [2001] ECR I-4319, ECLI:EU:C:2001:304, as discussed in section 9.2 of Ch. 9.

[14] See Ch. 9, section 9.3.3.

When it comes to the examination of discrimination cases, more precisely the question of whether situations are comparable, there are thus clear differences in approach between the various jurisdictions. This is a matter in respect of which not only do the national jurisdictions diverge, but also under the two European systems (EU law and the ECHR), different approaches to these questions have been taken.

13.1.4. Parental rights for same-sex couples: gradual shift to best interests of the child

Clear developments towards stronger protection of parental rights of lesbians and gays and of same-sex couples have been visible in all national jurisdictions studied for this case study, as well as under the ECHR. Where initially the interests of the child were perceived as an argument against the granting of parental rights to same-sex couples or single lesbians and gays, it is nowadays generally no longer accepted that to be born and/or raised in a same-sex relationship is not in the interests of the child.[15] On the contrary, it has been increasingly accepted by legislatures and courts that it is in the interests of these children that legal protection is given to the family they are born and/or raised in. Also, the view that equal treatment of same-sex parents is in fact in the interest of the child has received increasingly more support. There has thus been, as also noted in 13.1.2 above, a discernible shift from more traditional notions of the family to more child-centred approaches.

The ECtHR's contribution to these developments has consisted first of all of its insistence on the importance of granting legal recognition to *de facto* family life.[16] Further, this Court has ruled that sexual orientation may not be the decisive factor in decisions on parental rights for individuals.[17] Moreover, while the Strasbourg Court has accepted the protection of the interests of the child and protection of the traditional family as weighty and legitimate reasons which may justify a difference in treatment between same-sex and different-sex couples in relevantly similar situations, it has been increasingly stricter in its examination of the proportionality of limitations on parental rights for same-sex couples.[18] In its most recent case law in the area, the Strasbourg Court noted that it was in fact in the interest of the child that unmarried same-sex couples and unmarried different-sex couples were not treated differently in parental matters.

---

15 For example, in *X. a.o.* v. *Austria* (2013), the ECtHR implicity found that generally no evidence existed '[...] to show that a family with two parents of the same sex could in no circumstances adequately provide for a child's needs'. ECtHR [GC] 19 February 2013, *X. a.o.* v. *Austria*, no. 19010/07, para. 142. See also Ch. 8, section 8.2.4.1.2.

16 Ch. 8.1.2. See also Ch. 2, section 2.1.1.

17 Ch. 8, section 8.2.4.

18 As concluded in Ch. 8, section 8.2.4.1.2, in choosing means to protect the family, States must take into account developments in society and changes in the perception of social and civil status and relational issues. Also, an examination of each individual case must be made possible, as that is most in keeping with the best interests of the child.

The German Constitutional Court recently adopted a similar line of reasoning in a case on successive adoption for same-sex couples of 2013 and took it further in two respects. Firstly, while the relevant ECtHR judgment concerned a case in which no 'special legal status' was involved (see 13.1.3 above), in the German case such a status was involved, but the German Court nonetheless found that (same-sex) civil partners were in a comparable situation to (different-sex) spouses.[19] Moreover, and more importantly, the German Constitutional Court found that the difference in treatment of (same-sex) civil partners and (different-sex) spouses, violated the right to equal treatment of the child. The child's rights were thus made central to the assessment of the parents' claim to be treated equally with different-sex partners.

Still, in Germany, and this also holds for Ireland, the protection of the parental rights of same-sex couples is lagging behind when compared to those of different-sex couples. Joint adoption and legal parenthood by operation of the law are prime examples of such differences.[20] In respect of Ireland it has in fact been observed that the rights, interests and needs of children living in rainbow families were 'largely ignored',[21] although some fundamental changes in this regard have been anticipated recently.

It seems that not all such differences in protection of parental rights for same-sex couples and different-sex couples are necessarily ruled out under the ECHR. The ECtHR has accepted differences in treatment if a difference in legal status is also concerned (see 13.1.3 above) and in recent case law the Court once again confirmed that alternative registration forms do not have to exhaustively regulate on parental matters.[22] The ECtHR has, moreover, accepted that biological differences between different-sex couples and same-sex couples, decisively distinguish these groups in respect of parental matters.[23] Such biological differences have also been a consideration in debates on parental rights for same-sex couples at the national level. In the Netherlands this debate has, over the years, moved from biological differences between same-sex couples when compared to different-sex couples to the biological differences between male and female same-sex couples. Under Dutch law, as it presently stands, the parental rights of couples consisting of two men stay behind when compared to two women and this has been justified on grounds of biological differences between these groups.[24]

Parental rights for same-sex couples have thus enjoyed increasingly more protection, both at the national level and under the ECHR, but parental rights of (male) same-sex couples generally still enjoy less protection when compared to different-sex couples.

---

19 See Ch. 10, section 10.3.5.3.

20 See Ch. 10, sections 10.3.5.4 and 10.3.5.5, and Ch. 11, section 11.3.5.

21 A. Daly, 'Ignoring Reality: Children and the Civil Partnership Act in Ireland', 14 *Irish Journal of Family Law* (2011) p. 82.

22 See Ch. 8, section 8.2.6.

23 See Ch. 8, section 8.2.4.2.

24 See Ch. 12, sections 12.3.6.4 and 12.5.

13.1.5. How was change brought about? Typification of (legislative and judicial) processes

As noted above in 13.1.1, the legislative and judicial processes in the various national jurisdictions studied for the present case study have differed. Amongst them, the Netherlands have proven the most progressive and most proactive. In a way the Netherlands can be said to belong to those States who have set the tone within the European Union – or even the world – in respect of legal recognition of same-sex relationships. Being a pioneer in this area, the Netherlands set and followed its own pace. After the initial impetus came from the judiciary, the legislature took the lead by introducing a few fundamental changes in a relatively short period of time. Subsequently, as observed in Chapter 12, a legislative process commenced that has been described as 'the law of the small change'.[25]

In Germany a step-by-step approach has been taken as well, although the German point of departure has been different and the Courts have played a much more prominent role in the process. Here, the initial impetus came from the legislature who introduced a civil partnership for same-sex couples in 2001. It has been mainly court decisions that have subsequently prompted the legislature to remove differences between (same-sex) registered partners and (different-sex) spouses, in respect of all sorts of matters, ranging from taxes, to pensions, to parental rights (see 13.1.3 above).[26] The German process can thus well be described as an incremental one.[27] Perhaps, it may even be qualified as 'disjointed incrementalism', because this kind of decision-making could be held to have led 'to a less desirable outcome than radical action at the outset would have achieved.'[28]

In Ireland, the process had different phases, each with a different pace. Overall, however, it is striking that fundamental change was introduced in a relatively short period of time. Ireland was comparatively late with the abolition of the criminalisation of homosexual conduct, and the build-up to the introduction of a civil partnership for same-sex couples took some time, namely from 2004 to 2011. The impetus for the introduction of this civil partnership came from the judiciary and was reinforced by the introduction of a civil union for same-sex couples in the UK in 2004.[29] The Civil Partnership Act was in the end adopted following a remarkably smooth legislative process, however, and without any review of constitutionality by the Irish Supreme

25 See Ch. 12, section 12.5.

26 See ch. 10, section 10.5.

27 Incrementalism has been defined as '[t]he political or administrative practice of making small changes to existing policy rather than undertaking radical or ambitious plans'. C. Calhoun (ed.), *Dictionary of the Social Sciences* (Oxford, Oxford University Press, published online: 2002, eISBN: 9780199891184). In some definitions of incrementalism, the decision-making process is started 'not with some ideal goal in mind but from current policies.' I. McLean and A. McMillan, *The Concise Oxford Dictionary of Politics*, 3rd edn. (Oxford, Oxford University Press, Published online: 2009, eISBN: 9780191727191).

28 Calhoun 2002, *supra* n. 28.

29 As explained in Ch. 11, section 11.3.1, the Republic of Ireland was under an obligation to provide for an 'at least an equivalent level of human rights protection' as prevalent in Northern-Ireland, under the so-called Good Friday agreement.

Court. It was, moreover, followed by rapid developments as a result of which a strong increase in parental rights for same-sex couples and the opening up of marriage to same-sex couples were being contemplated in Ireland at the time this research was concluded.[30]

Compared to the action taken at national level, the European jurisdictions generally have taken a rather reactive, pragmatic and incremental approach.[31] The EU legislature as well as the CJEU and the ECtHR generally follow the pace set by national legislatures and courts and (the absence of) European consensus in the area has played a primordial role in the case law of both European Courts.[32] While the decriminalisation of homosexual conduct was expressly demanded by the ECtHR, fundamental choices in respect of legal recognition of same-sex relationships have been left to the States. They enjoy a margin of appreciation in the timing of the introduction of legislative changes and the Strasbourg Court has never 'reproached' a State for not introducing legislative change in respect of legal recognition of same-sex relationships any sooner than it did. In a way, the ECtHR could therefore be said to have provided States with an 'excuse' to delay or postpone the introduction of (fundamental) change in the area. Its case law has in any case enabled, or perhaps even stimulated, States to take an incremental approach in these matters.

While the ECtHR has thus been primarily reactive in the area, case law has at the same time been continually developing. Slowly and carefully, the Strasbourg Court has increasingly defined its position in respect of legal recognition of same-sex relationships. As noted above and as elaborately discussed in Chapter 8, there are hints in the case law of the ECtHR that this Court may be taking more firm stances in future case law, for example by defining a positive obligation for States to provide for an alternative registration form. At the same time it must be noted that the ECtHR has made clear that isolated positions in this area are not necessarily incompatible with the Convention.[33]

---

30 That is 31 July 2014.

31 Incrementalism has been explicitly advocated by the EU Justice Commissioner, who has held the following during a meeting of the European Parliament in 2010: 'I am sure you understand that this is, for some Member States, a very delicate political and social question, because the way of looking at things is not the same all across Europe. [...] We have to advance step by step. We must, most of all on the basis of our guidelines, bring the Member States to accept these rules. For many, this is very new and very unusual. For some, it is very shocking. We have to advance cautiously, because what we do not want [...] is [...] to be too harsh. In saying this, I am not speaking about the basic values, which are not in question, but we have to bring resisting Member States, step by step, to accept the general rules. What we do not want is to have people starting to oppose same-sex marriages, the recognition of rights and non-discrimination. [...]. I do not want there to be any doubts about the fundamentals, about the rights of free movement, irrespective of sexual orientation or ethnicity. These we are going to apply step by step.' Tuesday, 7 September 2010 – Strasbourg, PV 07/09/2010 – 17 CRE 07/09/2010 – 17, online available at www.europarl.europa.eu/sides/getDoc.do?pubRef=-//EP//TEXT+CRE+20100907+ITEM-017+DOC+XML+V0//EN&language=EN, visited 24 June 2014.

32 See Ch. 8 and Ch. 9, in particular section 9.2.

33 In *Vallianatos* (2013), the ECtHR held: 'The fact that, at the end of a gradual evolution, a country finds itself in an isolated position as regards one aspect of its legislation does not necessarily imply that that aspect offends the Convention, particularly in a field – matrimony – which is so closely bound up with the cultural and historical traditions of each society and its deep-rooted ideas about the family unit.'

13.1.6. Resumé and outlook

The present case study has made clear that when it comes to legal recognition of same-sex relationships across the European Union, States have taken the lead, rather than the European institutions. National legislatures, courts and administrative bodies set the tone and pace and the European level generally only follows. The European Courts have at times given some subtle nudges to the national legislature or judiciary, but this has generally only been in situations where first (principled) steps towards legal recognition had yet been taken at the national level. In the case law of the ECtHR, civil status has often functioned as a vehicle for unequal treatment of same-sex couples and different-sex couples. Only in cases where no 'special legal status' was involved, the ECtHR has applied a strict scrutiny test.

Traditional notions of marriage and the family have toned down in all three States studied in this research, although they have not been completely abandoned in all States. Also, under the ECHR marriage still enjoys strong protection. Moreover, the increased acknowledgement and legal protection of *de facto* family life has been paired with the acceptance of biological differences between different-sex couples and same-sex couples, and between lesbian couples and gay couples, as justification for certain differences in treatment between these groups in respect of parental matters. Unequal treatment of same-sex couples does thus still exist, but there has been a shift in the justification grounds from more morally charged grounds to more value-neutral grounds.

Generally a steady development towards increased protection of LGBT rights, and correspondingly, legal recognition of same-sex relationships has been discernible. Such change has been in most cases brought about gradually and at a slow pace, with some exceptions of much quicker developments. These developments are likely to continue in the future. Possibly the European level will take a more proactive stance in some respects. In any case it is likely that the European Courts will continue to nudge national legislatures and courts in this process of increased equalisation of the legal position of same-sex couples with that of different-sex couples.

13.2. The cross-border picture – Legal responses to cross-border movement

As set out in the various Chapters of this case study, cross-border movement within the context of the present case study is taking place in the sense that, naturally, same-sex couples and rainbow families have been, and are, moving around the EU.[34] From a legal perspective a distinction can be made between two types of cross-border movement. The first concerns situations where same-sex couples move to another State with the express purpose of having their relationship legally recognised under

ECtHR [GC] 7 November 2013, *Vallianatos a.o.* v. *Greece*, nos. 29381/09 and 32684/09, para. 92. See Ch. 8, section 8.2.6.

34 See Ch. 9, section 9.5, Ch. 10, section 10.4.1, Ch. 11, section 11.4.1 and Ch. 12, section 12.4.1.

the more permissive regime of that other State. This type of cross-border movement has been referred to as 'registration tourism' and 'marriage tourism'. Secondly, there are cross-border situations where same-sex couples or rainbow families move to other States, or desire to do so, for other purposes, such as work.

Following the approach taken in Chapter 7, this section identifies categories of legal responses of States to these two types of cross-border movement by same-sex couples and rainbow families. Based on the findings of this case study two such categories can be distinguished. The first consists of warding off (the effects of) cross-border movement. As further explained in section 13.2.1, States may (try to) deter same-sex couples and rainbow families from going to other States or from moving to their State. Secondly, as a mirror of the 'warding off' approach, States may choose to accommodate (the effects of) cross-border movement of same-sex couples and rainbow families, as is discussed in section 13.2.2 below. For both these categories it is assessed in this section what interests, considerations, perspectives or values have inspired or dictated these legal responses.[35] Also, this section discusses the extent to which European law (both EU law and the ECHR) leaves room for the respective legal responses at national level or in fact even encourages or dictates them. Lastly, it is examined what the implications of these legal responses are or may be for the States concerned, as well as for the same-sex couples and rainbow families involved in the cross-border movement.

Section 13.2.3 explains that two categories of legal responses that were identified in Case Study I on reproductive matters have not been very visible in the present case study. These are outsourcing, whereby foreign options (partly) justify a restrictive regime at domestic level, and adaptation, entailing the adjustment of national standard-setting in the area to that of another State or other States to which cross-border movement takes place. Instead, as further explained in section 13.2.3, the present case study has shown that the troubles that same-sex couples and rainbow families may encounter when moving abroad may be a reason for States to 'back out' from introducing legal recognition of same-sex relationships at national level.

The final section, section 2.4, assesses how the various legal responses to cross-border movement as identified in the present case study relate to one another.

13.2.1. Warding off

Two types of warding off can be discerned in the present case study, which correspond with the two types of cross-border situations set out above. States may firstly desire to prevent cross-border movement for registration or marriage purposes (section 13.2.1.1). Also, they may obstruct cross-border movement by same-sex couples and rainbow families for other purposes than registration or

35 As also noted in Ch. 7, one of course needs to take care not to ascribe more intentions or underlying motives to the various State measures discussed than can be derived from the type of legal research conducted in this case study.

marriage (section 13.2.1.2). In the latter situation, the warding off by States is not necessarily directed against the cross-border movement of the same-sex couples and rainbow families concerned as such, but rather against certain legal effects of their relationship, such as their civil status or their parental links.

13.2.1.1. Restrictions on access to marriage and civil partnership

The present case study has made clear that some States with relatively permissive regimes in respect of legal recognition of same-sex relationships have warded off cross-border movement by same-sex couples towards their countries for the purpose of concluding a marriage or a civil partnership. For example, when the Netherlands introduced registered partnership and later opened up marriage to same-sex couples, it wished to prevent so-called marriage and registration 'tourism' towards the Netherlands. Presumably, the Netherlands did not wish to upset its diplomatic relations with States which did not (yet) provide for legal recognition of same-sex relationships. There was also a fear of sham registrations. As discussed in Chapter 12, this initially resulted in setting particularly strict conditions for access to registered partnerships.[36] While these requirements have been relaxed over time, at least one of the future spouses or future partners still must be legally resident in the Netherlands or have Dutch nationality in order to register a partnership or enter into a marriage under Dutch law.[37] This thus renders it impossible for foreign couples to go to the Netherlands with the mere purpose of having their relationship legally recognised under Dutch law. Whether such limitations are acceptable under EU (free movement) law, is a matter that has not been discussed extensively in Chapter 9, although it was noted that they are probably not problematic.[38]

States that function as home States in this type of cross-border situations, may for their part try to restrict travel by same-sex couples to other States for registration and marriage purposes. They may do so in order to uphold certain national standards, such as the special protection of traditional marriage. While none of the three States studied in this research appears to have taken such warding off measures, they have nonetheless been identified in this case study. As noted in Chapter 9, reports have been made to the European Commission about refusals by national authorities to issue civil status records to same-sex couples who requested such documents for the purpose of marrying or registering their partnerships in another Member State.[39] The intervention by the European Commission in these cases showed that such warding off measures may be problematic under EU law. The Commission held the national practices incompatible with the right to respect for private and family life (Article 7 CFR), the prohibition of non-discrimination on the basis of sexual orientation (Article 21 CFR) and EU rules guaranteeing free movement and residence.

---

36 See Ch. 12, section 12.4.3.
37 *Idem.*
38 See Ch. 9, section 9.6, footnote 205.
39 See Ch. 9, section 9.6.3.

13.2.1.2. Non-recognition or downgrading of foreign civil status and parental links

States that function as host States in cross-border situations – or States to which couples return (see above) – may take a warding off approach by refusing to recognise the civil status of a same-sex couple whose relationship was legally recognised in another State by means of registered partnership or marriage. Warding off by the host State may also consist of downgrading such a civil status or by non-recognition of parental links of rainbow families established abroad.

This type of warding off may first of all have implications for decisions on entry and residence of same-sex couples. As explained in Chapter 9, here a distinction can be made between migrating EU citizens and third-country nationals (TCNs) with same-sex partners. Warding off in this context may consist of refusals to authorise entry and residence of same-sex partners of EU citizens or of family reunification applications of same-sex partners of TCNs. It may also consist of the subjecting of such authorisation to stricter conditions, when compared to different-sex partners.

For example, as explained in Chapter 10, in Germany until 2005, same-sex spouses and registered partners of workers (EU citizens) were not recognised as qualifying family members under the Residence Act and could thus be refused entry and residence. Between 2005 and 2013 residency permits for same-sex spouses and same-sex civil partners of migrating EU citizens could be of shorter duration when compared to those of different-sex spouses.[40] Also, until 2005 same-sex spouses and same-sex registered partners of third-country nationals could not qualify for family reunification on an equal footing with different-sex spouses.[41] In Ireland it was only in 2011, when civil partnership was introduced in Ireland, that same-sex spouses and same-sex registered partners of EU citizens were granted entry and residence as 'qualifying family members'. Until that time, their formal relationship status could positively impact the authorities' assessment of whether they were 'permitted family members'. Also for family reunification purposes was a marriage or civil partnership status of a same-sex couple until 2011 only an element in the authorities' assessment, but not a qualifying status per se.

As elaborately discussed in Chapter 9, there are as yet various open questions as to whether this kind of warding off is compatible with EU free movement law. It has been shown that it cannot be ruled out that same-sex spouses of EU citizens may be refused recognition as spouses and thus as family members within the meaning of the Free Movement Directive, and the same holds for registered partners of EU citizens where the host State does not provide for a partnership status under the national law. In those cases there is nonetheless a duty to facilitate entry and residence of these same-sex stable partners of EU citizens.[42] Such a fallback option does not exist under

40 In 2013 these differences were abolished. See Ch. 10, section 10.4.4 and see section 13.2.2.2 below.

41 Since 2005 both same-sex spouses and same-sex registered partners of third-country nationals may qualify for family reunification on an equal footing with different-sex spouses. See Ch. 10, section 10.4.4 and see section 13.2.2.2 below.

42 See Ch. 9, section 9.6.2.3.

the Family Reunification Directive, however, and Member States have discretion in respect of reunification applications by registered and unmarried partners of TCNs, although States may thereby not discriminate on grounds of sexual orientation.[43] There is thus particular room for warding off in the context of family reunification by same-sex partners of TCNs.

Further, even if entry and residence have been granted to the same-sex partner of a migrating EU citizen or a third-country national, there are other realms of the law in which warding off may take shape. Same-sex couples may encounter difficulties in their daily lives if their civil status is not recognised or is downgraded in the host Member State.

Before Germany and Ireland introduced civil partnerships for same-sex couples in 2001 and 2010 respectively, foreign same-sex marriages were not recognised at all in these States. Since that time marriages between same-sex couples that were celebrated abroad have been recognised as civil partnerships and thus downgraded. As explained in Chapter 10, the so-called '*Kappungsgrenze*' has been held to have been inspired by the German legislature's wish to give material protection to the institution of marriage. Out of the three States studied in this research, only in the Netherlands are foreign same-sex marriages recognised as marriage, and this has been so from the outset since this country was the first to open up marriage to same-sex couples. Chapter 12 has shown that there are also EU Member States where same-sex marriages are not at all recognised under the law.[44]

When it comes to registered partnerships of same-sex couples that were entered into abroad, the situation is somewhat different. In Ireland and Germany, these are recognised, but only those that resemble the national registered partnerships. Also in the Netherlands foreign registered partnerships must meet certain requirements in order to be recognised as registered partnerships. The setting of such requirements may result in downgrading or even the non-recognition of the foreign registered partnership. For instance in Ireland, foreign same-sex civil partnerships that can be dissolved outside the courts – such as the Dutch registered partnership – are not recognised.

Lastly, while not numerous, there have been cases where one of the three States studied in this research has not recognised parental links of same-sex couples that had been established under the law of another State. For example, in a Dutch case of 2003 – before joint interstate adoption was introduced for same-sex couples in the Netherlands – a District Court refused to recognise a joint adoption by a same-sex couple under American law.[45] In Germany in 2011 a so-called 'co-mother', who had been recognised as such under Spanish law, could not be registered in the German

[43] It has also been shown that if a long-term resident has entered into a (same-sex) registered partnership in one of the Member States and wishes to move to another Member State, it is at the discretion of the second Member State whether he or she is allowed to bring his or her registered partner.

[44] See Ch. 12, section 12.4.7.

[45] See Ch. 12, section 12.4.6.

birth register as (co-)mother of the child of her and her female partner, because German filiation law did not allow for the granting of paternity to two same-sex partners, except for in adoption situations.[46] As discussed in Chapter 9, it has been reported more broadly in respect of the situation within the EU that parental links may be stripped away from children in rainbow families upon movement to another Member State.[47]

As explained in depth in Chapter 9, there remain many open questions as to whether EU law allows for warding off by means of non-recognition or downgrading of civil status and/or parental rights of migrating same-sex couples. German Courts have held the downgrading of a marriage of a same-sex couple involving an EU citizen into a civil partnership unproblematic under EU free movement rules,[48] but as the CJEU has never ruled on the question, it is not certain whether it would follow this reasoning. As also discussed in Chapter 9, it may in fact be problematic under primary EU law, as it may hinder the free movement of the EU citizen concerned.[49] The ECtHR has so far not given guidance in this area, except for its rulings in international adoption and surrogacy cases, which provide clear clues that warding off by means of non-recognition of parental links legally established in another State may be incompatible with the best interests of the child (see also 13.2.2.2 below).[50]

13.2.1.3. Observations

Warding off measures may be perceived by States with less permissive regimes as enabling them to prevent the 'import' of undesired partnership or marriage forms. By subjecting couples with a foreign civil status to their national standards, States can uphold these standards, such as the special protection of marriage. Also, by doing so, States can prevent that migrating same-sex couples are treated more favourably than same-sex couples within their own jurisdiction. Such reverse discrimination might, after all, put pressure on States to treat the latter group as favourably as the former. States with more permissive regimes may, for their part, ensure, with warding off measures such as those described under section 13.2.1.1, that they cannot be reproached for 'exporting' their regimes and thus for imposing their standards on other States. Warding off, in other words prevents any 'spill-over effects' and confirms jurisdictions along State borders.

Clearly, same-sex couples and individuals carry the burden of warding off measures as they restrict their cross-border movement. This is particularly so where the entry and residence of a same-sex partner is refused and couples can thus not move as couple to another State. While entry and residence of a same-sex stable partner of an

46 See Ch. 10, section 10.4.8.

47 See ILGA Europe, *ILGA Europe's contribution to the Green Paper* (ILGA-Europe 2011) p. 20, online available at www.ilga-europe.org/home/publications/policy_papers/green_paper_april_2011, visited June 2014. See also Ch. 9, section 9.7.3.

48 See Ch. 10, section 10.4.7.

49 Ch. 9, section 9.6.3.

50 Ch. 8, section 8.3.3. See also Ch. 7, section 7.2.2.1.

EU citizen will in principle be facilitated under EU law, this is different for same-sex partners of third-country nationals, regardless of whether or not they are registered partners, and possibly even regardless of whether they are spouses.[51] Moreover, as noted above, same-sex couples may meet obstacles in their daily lives as a result of warding off measures. Both non-recognition and downgrading of their civil status by a host State may imply for same-sex couples that upon moving to another State certain or all legal effects of their relationship status are no longer recognised. Hence, they carry the risk of so-called 'limping relationships', which, for example, may have implications for their property or their pensions. Also, the rights and entitlements that the couples concerned enjoy in the host State, for example in respect of tax benefits or parental rights, depend on the regime of the host State. In cases where families no longer enjoy legal recognition upon crossing a border, because parental links are not recognised, this inevitably also has (serious) implications for children involved.

13.2.2. Accommodation

Instead of warding them off, States may also opt for an entirely different approach towards (the effects of) cross-border movement, which is to accommodate them. Again, a distinction can be made between two types of accommodating responses, which correspond to the two kinds of cross-border movement that were described above.

13.2.2.1. Providing access to marriage and registered partnership

Both the German and the Irish legislature have deliberately enabled foreign same-sex couples to enter into registered civil partnerships under their domestic regimes. No nationality or domicile (or habitual residence) requirements are set for having access to civil partnerships in these States.[52] German law also gives couples who entered into civil partnerships abroad the option to re-register their partnerships under the German civil partnership regime.[53] A need to prevent 'registration tourism' (see 13.2.1.1 above) was thus apparently not felt in Ireland and Germany. Indeed, as explained in Chapter 10, the German Civil Partnership is so open to foreign same-sex couples because the German legislature wished to extend its aspirations to abolish discrimination on grounds of sexual orientation outside Germany. The Netherlands, even though it had a clear wish to be a pioneer in Europe, or even in the world, in respect of the legal recognition of same-sex relationships, has – as discussed above – not made marriage and registered partnerships so easily accessible to foreign couples. As discussed in Chapter 12, only in 2012, and only for a period of little over a year, did the Netherlands actively accommodate cross-border movement

[51] See Ch. 9, section 9.6.4.

[52] Ch. 10, section 10.4.3 and Ch. 11, section 11.4.2.

[53] Ch. 10, section 10.4.3.

towards it for registration purposes, by enabling same-sex couples from abroad to apply for a 'marriage visa'.[54]

13.2.2.2. Recognition of foreign civil status and parental links

As briefly noted in section 13.2.1.2, and as extensively discussed in Chapter 9, as matters stand today there are still a few open questions regarding the application of EU (free movement) law to cross-border movement by same-sex couples. Some accommodation obligations can nonetheless be identified. A clear accommodation obligation exists in respect of the entry and residence of registered partners of migrating EU citizens under the Free Movement Directive. This is only a conditional accommodation obligation, however, as States are only obliged to grant registered partners entry and residence as family members within the meaning of the Directive, if their legislation treats registered partnerships as equivalent to marriage. In that regard, as noted in Chapter 9, it is unclear what 'equivalent to marriage' means exactly. In any case, Article 3(2) Free Movement Directive sets a clear minimum accommodation obligation, as States must facilitate the entry and residence of same-sex stable partners of EU citizens. As noted above, States have more discretion when it comes to family members of third-country nationals. The only firm accommodation obligation in respect of TCNs concerns their spouses, but it is as yet not sufficiently clear whether this includes same-sex spouses.[55]

The EU Commission, for its part, has strongly advocated an accommodating approach, as voiced by former Commissioner Reding, who has held that EU Member States must recognise any marriage or registered partnership legally concluded in another State.[56] The Commission has, moreover, explored the options for, or initiated, legislation that imposes certain accommodation obligations on States or could potentially do so, in respect of matters that concern the daily life of migrating same-sex couples, such as their property regimes.[57]

There may furthermore be a positive accommodation obligation by means of recognition under ECHR. The Strasbourg case law gives the strongest indication that this may be so in respect of parental links. As discussed in Chapters 2 and 7, the Court's case law in international adoption and surrogacy cases is a strong indication that the best interests of the child, in particular its right to personal identity, indeed require an accommodating approach in cross-border cases concerning rainbow families.[58]

---

54 As explained in Ch. 12, section 12.4.4, this measure was introduced to alleviate the effects of a newly introduced rule that unmarried stable partners no longer qualified for family reunification. When the latter rule was lifted, so was the marriage visa measure.

55 See Ch. 9, section 9.6.4.

56 See Ch. 9, section 9.6.2.1.

57 See Ch. 9, section 9.7.2.

58 See also Ch. 7, section 7.2.2.1.

Turning to the national level, in the Netherlands, the granting of entry and residence to same-sex partners of EU citizens, or the approving of family reunification applications by same-sex partners of third-country nationals, has never been an issue. In Ireland explicit accommodation of the cross-border movement of same-sex couples (whether or not it involved EU citizens) was introduced in 2011, albeit that these changes were only laid down in policy, not in law.[59] In Germany, same-sex partners of EU citizens have only been recognised on a fully equal basis with different-sex partners of EU citizens since 2013, while same-sex spouses and same-sex registered partners of third-country nationals have qualified for family reunification on an equal footing with different-sex spouses since 2005.

The picture in respect of the legal position of same-sex couples after entry and residence, is equally diverse. In the Netherlands, foreign same-sex registered partnerships and marriages have been recognised as such and it is therefore unlikely that foreign same-sex couples will lose certain rights upon moving to the Netherlands. In Ireland and Germany same-sex marriages are downgraded, while foreign same-sex registered partnerships are recognised only if they meet certain standards (see 13.2.1.2 above). This could be perceived as partial, conditional accommodation. Same-sex couples that migrate to Germany or Ireland (may) thus enjoy protection under the law of these States, but the level of protection may be lower when compared to the home State. Boosting or upgrading of the same-sex couple's civil status has been explicitly ruled out in Germany.[60]

When it comes to parental links, there have been clear examples of an accommodating approach being taken by national courts. For instance, various German courts have, in more recent years, recognised parental links that same-sex couples had established abroad, including – with some exceptions[61] – in cases where such links could not have been established under German law. The best interests of the child as well as developments in German law towards the greater equalisation of civil partnership with marriage in respect of parental matters, have been express grounds for such accommodation. In that regard it has been expressly held by some courts that children were not to be the victim of their parents' cross-border movement; the obligation to observe German law could not be pursued by trampling upon the children concerned.[62] In Ireland a similar approach has been adopted in the 2014 Family Relationships Bill.[63] In the Netherlands, apart from a few early exceptions,[64] generally an accommodating approach has been taken in respect of cross-border cases involving parental matters. This is unsurprising, since the Netherlands has also been in the vanguard when it comes to granting parental rights to same-sex couples.

59 Ch. 11, section 11.4.3.
60 Ch. 10, section 10.4.5.
61 See the situation involving a so-called co-mother, as discussed in section 13.2.1.2 above.
62 See Ch. 10, section 10.4.8.
63 See Ch. 11, section 11.4.5.
64 See the example referred to in section 13.2.1.2 above.

13.2.2.3. Observations

Accommodation in the context of the present case study, may take either more (pro-) active or more passive forms, which may each have different implications for the States concerned. Firstly, the kind of measures as discussed in section 13.2.2.1 above, may be perceived as active promotion of national standards at the international level, possibly even as 'exportation' of national standards to other States. This may have implications for the diplomatic relations of the State concerned.[65]

Accommodation by means of recognition of civil status or parental links established abroad generally takes a more passive form, as in most cases States only recognise these to the level they provide for them at national level, and do not actively have to provide for anything under their national law in this regard. This clearly holds for the forms of partial and conditional accommodation that Ireland and Germany employ in respect of foreign same-sex marriages and partnerships (see above). The recognition of foreign same-sex marriages and partnerships, as well as parental links, by the Netherlands is also mainly passive, as it comes down to recognising something foreign that meets the national standard.

Accommodation by means of recognition takes a more active form where a civil status is recognised that is not at all provided for at national level, or where parental links are recognised that could not have been established under the national law of the host state in the first place. Recognition in such circumstances may imply reverse discrimination and this may put pressure, perhaps even 'serious pressure',[66] on host States to amend their national family laws and to adapt them to the standard of the State of origin.

For individuals, accommodation is evidently much more beneficial than warding off, as it optimises their free movement. Accommodation enables same-sex couples to move to (other) EU Member States and to continue to enjoy their family lives there. Moreover, it reduces or takes away the risk of limping relationships and of parental links not being recognised in the daily lives of the rainbow families in the host States. Same-sex couples may also profit from access to registration forms abroad, although the positive effect may be diminished if this status is not recognised upon return to the home State or upon movement to another State with a less permissive regimes.

---

65 As noted above, the Dutch legislature feared being accused of imposing their national standards upon other States through the claiming of recognition of a civil status acquired under their national law. Within the confines of the present legal research no backlash implications have, however, been identified.

66 M. Melcher, 'Private international law and registered relationships: an EU perspective', 20 *European Review of Private Law* (2012) p. 1075 at p. 1085.

13.2.3. Outsourcing, adaptation and backing out

Different from in Case Study I on reproductive rights, in the present case study on legal recognition of same-sex relationships, an outsourcing approach has not been seen to have been employed by the ECtHR. In other words, this Court has not accepted foreign registration options as (part of a) justification of restrictive national regimes in respect of legal recognition of same-sex couples. States have also not claimed an interest in such an outsourcing option. This may be explained by the fact that in many cases, there is no true 'safety valve' or 'outsourcing option' for States in the context of the present case study, as various States subject access to marriage or partnership registration to conditions relating to residency and/or nationality (see 13.2.1.1 above).[67] Also, the possible existence of an 'outsourcing' option does not exclude that, upon return to their States of origin, the couples concerned may claim recognition of their newly acquired civil status. The pressure on the national law that ensues from such claims, may considerably diminish the desired effects of the 'outsourcing' option.

It is very likely that States may also respond to cross-border movement in the context of the present case study by adjusting their national standard-setting in the area to that of another State or other States to which cross-border movement takes place. In the present case study no such express adaptation measures can be identified, however. The fact that cross-border movement is taking place, has not, as such, been put forward as a reason for introducing forms of legal recognition of same-sex relationships at the national level. What has been visible, however, is that developments in other European countries and at the European and international levels have had some impact at the national level in all three national jurisdictions studied in this case study. Some States did not want to lag behind other (European) States or in European integration in a broader sense. For instance, the German Civil Partnership Act aimed to adopt and transpose two European calls for the creation of legal options for the registration of same-sex unions.[68]

The present case study has also revealed another response to cross-border movement by same-sex couples which is perhaps best described as 'backing out'. As discussed in Chapter 12, in the Netherlands fear that other countries would not accept or recognise the Dutch legislative choices, was presented as an argument against the granting of certain rights to same-sex couples. It was the main reason why the Dutch government initially did not want to risk opening up marriage or to introduce joint international adoption for same-sex couples. Hence, although in the end the fears did not materialise in the Netherlands, cross-border movement potentially has a chilling effect on the development of national standard-setting in respect of legal recognition of same-sex relationships. This is of course most likely to occur where States are in the vanguard and this chilling effect may diminish the more other States grant legal recognition to same-sex relationships.

---

[67] See Ch. 12, section 12.4.3.

[68] See Ch. 10, section 10.3.2.

13.2.4. Resumé and outlook

In the present case study in essence two categories of legal responses to cross-border movement have been identified: warding off and accommodation. In their most extreme form these are, in the context of the present case study, mutually exclusive. However, it has turned out that different degrees of warding off and of accommodation are possible. For example, in some cases States, like Ireland and Germany have resorted to partial or conditional accommodation in their dealing with cross-border movement in the context of the present case study (see 13.2.2.3 above). It has furthermore been shown that States have generally maintained their national standards in cross-border cases, which implies that they have either warded off or resorted to passive forms of accommodation only. Generally only if, or to the extent that, a certain level of legal recognition of same-sex relationships and rainbow families was provided for at national level, have States recognised foreign civil status and parental links. In other words, these legal responses have been in most cases a perfect reflection of what has been provided for at domestic level and have developed as progressively as national standards. This has only differed exceptionally, with cross-border cases involving parental matters being the clearest example. Here, sometimes – and increasingly – the best interests of the child have been considered to require such recognition. However, in these cases generally reference has also been made to the family law standards of the host State and at times this has implied that recognition is not provided for.[69]

Because all three States studied in this research have introduced some form of legal recognition of same-sex relationships and have granted some parental rights to these couples, the implications for individual couples and families moving to these States may be not so severe when compared to States that do not provide for any form of legal recognition under their national law. Still, the effects on individuals of for example downgrading should not be underestimated (see 13.2.1.3 above).

Standard-setting at the European level for cross-border cases in the context of the present case study has so far been fairly minimal. Some minimum accommodation obligations in respect of the entry and residence of same-sex partners of EU citizens follow from the relevant Free Movement Directive, but particularly as regards the legal position of these couples once entry and residence have been granted, there remain various open questions. Here, case law of the CJEU or further guidance of the EU legislature on the discretion that States either have or do not have in these matters, is much desired. The ECtHR has given the clearest guidance in this regard in respect of cases concerning parental matters, but under the ECHR also, not all issues arising in cross-border cases have crystallised. This also implies that, as goes for Case Study I,[70] there is room and potential for (further) bilateral or coordinated legal responses to develop, for example, by means of the harmonisation of Private International Law.

---

69 See the German case concerning a co-mother as discussed in section 13.2.1.2 above.

70 See Ch. 7, section 7.2.5.

Other categories of – and in fact also different types of – legal responses to cross-border movement in the context of the present case study that have been visible, albeit to a limited extent only, are adaptation and 'backing out'. These concern not so much the responses of States to individual cross-border cases, but their reaction to (potential) incidences of such movement at a more abstract level. They are in fact opposites, or in any case communicating vessels, as the greater the number of States that provide for legal recognition of same-sex relationships, the more likely it is that adaptation instead of 'backing out' takes place.

Conclusions

Chapter 14
Conclusions

14.1. Morally sensitive issues and cross-border movement in the EU

This concluding chapter firstly sketches the overall picture that arises from the two case studies on reproductive matters and legal recognition of same-sex relationships respectively. Parallels are drawn and trends are discerned in respect of balancing exercises and legislative and judicial processes in these morally sensitive issues (sections 14.1.1 and 14.1.2 respectively). Section 14.1.3 focuses on the case law of the two European Courts in these matters. Legal responses to cross-border movement in morally sensitive issues are subsequently discussed in section 14.1.4. The concluding section, section 14.2, reflects upon this overall picture by means of a number of observations.

14.1.1. Balancing exercises in morally sensitive issues

Given that both case studies concern morally sensitive issues, they have also addressed complex balancing exercises. The interests included in such balancing exercises differ in number and (sometimes) in nature between the case studies. In Case Study I on reproductive matters, a broader range of interests is involved when compared to Case Study II on the legal recognition of same-sex relationships. The spectrum of interests involved in reproductive issues ranges from interests like personal autonomy to human dignity and protection of the (unborn) child. In Case Study II on the legal recognition of same-sex relationships, by contrast, most balancing exercises concern, or at least have concerned in the past, equal treatment on the one hand and traditional notions of marriage and the family on the other.[1] This difference in the number of interests may first of all be explained by the fact that Case Study I on reproductive matters covers a wide(r) variety of issues, ranging from abortion to various types of assisted human reproduction (e.g. donation of gametes and preimplantation genetic diagnosis), to surrogacy. The subject-matter of Case Study II on the other hand, is more straightforward, as it is about access to civil status and parental rights for same-sex couples. Moreover, with each reproductive issue discussed in Case Study I, generally a broader range of interests is involved, when compared to the subject-matter of Case Study II. This may be explained by the fact that in reproductive matters generally more parties are concerned (e.g.

[1] This was different in respect of parental rights for same-sex couples, however, as there also the interests of the child came in (see below). See more elaborately Ch. 13, section 13.1.4.

the (unborn or future) child, gamete donors or surrogate mothers) whose interests the State may also intend to protect. In Case Study II any conflict is between the interests of same-sex couples and those of the State, or the general interest. This is only different in respect of parental matters, as there are also the rights of the child to consider (see below).

The present research has shown that the jurisdictions studied generally recognise the same interests in the relevant case studies, but the weight that is, or has been, accorded to these interests differs between the various jurisdictions. The ECtHR has recognised most of the relevant individual interests and has held that these fall within the scope of the ECHR. The actual protection of such interests has, however, sometimes lagged behind. Striking examples are *Schalk and Kopf*, where the Strasbourg Court held that same-sex couples come within the scope of Article 12 ECHR (the right to marry), but nonetheless considered a complete barrier on access to marriage for same-sex couples compatible with the ECHR; and *A, B and C*, where the Court held that abortion on social and medical grounds fell within scope of the right to private life (Article 8 ECHR), but nonetheless held that an absolute prohibition on this practice could be upheld.[2]

The interests of the child have prevailed in both case studies, and can thus be said to be a connecting factor between the two case studies. In Case Study I, it has been demonstrated that the rights of the (future) child have been put forward in legislative debates and in judicial proceedings, and at times they have been accepted by legislatures and courts as an argument against certain forms of reproductive treatment. In Case Study II this interest has been – increasingly – prominent in the context of parental rights for same-sex couples. Both case studies have shown that involvement of the interests of the (future) child makes a crucial difference to balancing exercises and in both case studies developments towards a more child-centred approach have been visible. Even more so once a child is born, its rights and interests are accepted to be the primordial consideration in all legal systems studied. This has proven of particular relevance in cross-border cases, such as cross-border surrogacy cases.[3]

This great focus on the interests of the child also reveals, at a more general level, a shift in the nature of interests. Both case studies point to an emerging trend of granting more protection to relatively concrete interests such as the best interests of the child, over rather abstract interests like 'the traditional institution of marriage'. This development can also be regarded as a shift from values deeply entrenched in the society and law of a specific State, to less value-charged values that are (more) commonly shared and transnational. Put differently, an erosion of the typical national is taking place. For example, 'the best interests of the child' can be regarded a value-neutral interest, to which not many would object and that is not unique to one specific State. That the ECtHR has been focusing increasingly on similarly value-neutral principles like legal certainty and information in the context

2 See Ch. 8, section 8.2.2; and Ch. 2, section 2.2.3, respectively.

3 See, *inter alia*, Ch. 2, section 2.4.2.

of reproductive matters, reveals a similar trend. That is not to say that tradition has completely dissolved as a relevant interest in the national and European debates and standard-setting. For example, the ECtHR accepts the special status of traditional marriage as a justification for reserving access to marriage to different-sex couples. Also, traditional notions of the family can be held to have indirectly played a role where importance has been attached to biological reality, as has been the case in the context of both case studies.[4] While the ECtHR will presumably not reduce the protection of traditional marriage so long as a majority of States strongly holds on to it, it is to be expected that the trend of focusing on value-neutral interests in the ECtHR case law will continue in the future, which may also have implications for traditional notions of the family.

When it comes to the actual balancing exercises, another trend is a greater legal recognition of *de facto* situations, such as *de facto* family life (see also 14.2.3 below). Over time, legislatures and courts have come to acknowledge that those in relationship forms and family forms that were not as such recognised under the law also required protection. The ECtHR in particular has given important impetus to this development that has clearly had implications for national standard-setting in these areas. Next to this, there appears to be increased focus on balancing in individual cases. Although Case Study I has made clear that there has been room under the ECHR for bright line rules in reproductive matters, generally there has been increasing attention paid to careful balancing in individual cases, with due regard for the individual circumstances of the case concerned. This holds expressly for situations where a child is involved, and it also applies in abortion cases, for example. Both these developments have proven relevant in both internal and cross-border situations.

These trends regarding the nature of interests and regarding balancing exercises have brought about concrete changes at the national level in standard-setting in these areas and there is reason to assume that further changes will be brought about in the (near) future. In both case studies there have been hints or even clear signs that change is, or may be, forthcoming in the relevant standard-setting on reproductive matters and/or legal recognition of same-sex relationships. Presumably because the balancing exercises are more straightforward, in Case Study II the direction and possible end point of debates and standard-setting in the area are clearer and more well-defined than in Case Study I. In Case Study II, generally developments towards greater protection of LGBT rights and increased legal recognition of same-sex relationships have been discernible in the various jurisdictions, and there is reason to assume that these developments will continue in the five jurisdictions included in this research.[5] In Case Study I, on the other hand, because of the advancement of medical science there is more (potential) for new scientific developments and thus new (ethical) challenges for the legislature and the judiciary whereby it is not so clear from the outset which direction they will take. For instance, recently a technique has

---

4 See, *inter alia*, Ch. 2, section 2.4.1 and Ch. 8, section 8.2.4.2.
5 See Ch. 13, section 13.1.1.

been developed as a result of which children may have three genetic parents, which also raises questions regarding multiple parenthood.[6] In a State like the Netherlands, this may possibly trigger the 'repeating break' process, as set out in Chapter 6, whereby such a new medical technological development will meet with concerns about its ethical acceptability, but will nonetheless been regulated for, by subjecting it to certain limitations.

14.1.2. Legislative and judicial processes in morally sensitive issues

The European jurisdictions generally have taken a rather reactive, pragmatic and incremental approach to morally sensitive issues. There has been little to no substantive standard-setting at the EU level on these matters, but the relevance of the vast body of EU law in areas like cross-border health care, the free movement of persons, and equal treatment for the two case studies, must not be underestimated. Where a case was brought before the CJEU that related to either reproductive matters or legal recognition of same-sex relationships more substantively, this Court has generally taken a very careful and reactive approach (see also 14.3.1 and 14.3.2 below). The Strasbourg Court has also generally been reluctant to intervene in these matters. States have been left much room to introduce change at their own pace, as long as the competing interests were weighed in the national legislative process, and as long as they kept the area under review. The ECtHR has never reproached States for delays in the adoption of legislation in these areas; only where States had taken a first step, has the ECtHR sometimes found violations of the ECHR (see 14.3.2 below). The ECtHR has thus enabled, or perhaps even stimulated, States to take an incremental approach in these matters.

When it comes to the legislative and judicial processes at the national level studied in the two case studies, some general trends can be discerned, although these have often been accompanied by evident exceptions. In both case studies change was generally brought about at a slow pace, often step-by-step, and in both case studies there has often been a certain or even considerable reluctance on the side of the legislature to regulate the relevant area. At times faster developments were also discernible, however, for instance in Ireland in the context of Case Study II.[7] Reluctance on the side of the legislature has also proven no ironclad rule, as, for instance, the Dutch legislature showed, with its eagerness to legislate for the legal recognition of same-sex relationships.

Presumably because a broader range of interests appears to be involved in reproductive matters (see 14.1.1 above) and because the issues discussed in Case Study I are more diverse, so the legislative and judicial processes have been broader and more diverse. In the context of Case Study I, setbacks have been identified more often when

---

[6] C. Pritchard, 'The girl with three biological parents', *bbc.com* 31 August 2014, www.bbc.com/news/magazine-28986843, visited February 2015 and J. Callagher, 'MPs say yes to three-person babies', *bbc.com* 3 February 2015, www.bbc.com/news/health-31069173, visited February 2015.

[7] See Ch. 13, section 13.1.1.

compared to Case Study II, where the developments appeared to take a more steady course, namely towards increasing recognition of same-sex relationships (see above). In Case Study II the pace at which such change was brought about has differed much though, both between the national jurisdictions studied, as within State jurisdictions.[8] As explained in Chapter 13, this difference in pace may be related to a difference in the path chosen by States. For instance, in Germany fairly early (in 2001) a separate civil partnership for same-sex couples was introduced, which was, over the years, slowly but steadily increasingly equalised with marriage. Ireland, on the other hand, for long provided for no form of legal recognition of same-sex relationships, but once it introduced civil partnerships in 2011, developments happened very fast, as that very same year the initial steps towards the opening up of marriage were taken.[9]

The interplay between the legislature and the judiciary, as well as between the European and the national levels has differed in and between the case studies. Generally, when compared to the Netherlands, in Ireland and Germany the judiciary has played a more important role in standard-setting in morally sensitive matters. The German Constitutional Court has impacted much of the national standard-setting in both case studies, while in the case of Ireland some issues were in the end decided by the ECtHR, most profoundly in the context of abortion.

14.1.3. Morally sensitive issues before the European Courts

A number of things are striking if one takes a closer look at how the CJEU and the ECtHR have dealt with cases concerning morally sensitive issues. As also noted above, these Courts have generally taken a very prudent approach to such matters, leaving ample room to States to decide on these issues at the national level. This section observes, first of all, that the approach of both Courts could at times even be described as 'evasive'. In addition, both European Courts have applied a similar kind of reasoning that is – in subsection 14.1.3.2 below – typified as the 'in for a penny, in for a pound' approach. Lastly, in the case law of the ECtHR, for both case studies variations on the margin of appreciation doctrine can be identified, as discussed in subsection 14.1.3.3.

14.1.3.1. Very careful, at times evasive, Courts

Both the CJEU and the ECtHR have repeatedly emphasised in cases concerning morally sensitive issues that their judgment applied only in the case at hand and that they were 'not called upon',[10] or that it was not their 'task'[11] to answer 'general

8 *Idem.*

9 See Ch. 11, section 11.3.6.

10 *Inter alia*, Case C-506/06 *Sabine Mayr* [2008] ECR I-1017, ECLI:EU:C:2008:119 and Case C-34/10 *Oliver Brüstle* v. *Greenpeace eV* [2011] ECR I-9821, ECLI:EU:C:2011:669. See Ch. 3, sections 3.1.1.

11 *Inter alia*, ECtHR 24 June 2010, *Schalk and Kopf* v. *Austria*, no. 30141/04 and ECtHR [GC] 3 November 2011, *S.H. a.o.* v. *Austria*, no. 57813/00. See Ch. 8, section 8.2.2 and Ch.2, section 2.3.3 respectively.

questions'[12] or 'broach'[13] ethical questions. Both Courts have at times gone to great lengths to explain what the case before them was *not* about, and what their judgment did not implicate.[14] They thus explicitly delineated the scope of the cases before them and correspondingly the effects of their rulings. While this is inherent in case law and the role of the judiciary in general, the explicitness of such statements in the relevant judgments discussed in this research have caught the eye. Moreover, although one has to be careful not to become suggestive, at times it proves difficult to avoid the impression that these Courts have been eager to find a 'way out' in such cases, in order to avoid the need to address the respective thorny issues. In any case, some of the rulings in these areas deviated from standing case law. For example, the finding of the CJEU in *Grogan*, that the link between the activity of the defendant student associations and medical terminations of pregnancies carried out in clinics in another Member State was 'too tenuous' for there to be a restriction of free movement,[15] has been received as at variance with the then existing line of case law.[16] Another example are the surrogacy cases *C.D.* and *Z.*, where the CJEU was fairly rigid in holding that the cases did not come within the scope of any of the Directives invoked by the plaintiffs.[17] One of the rulings of the ECtHR with a semblance of evasiveness, is its inadmissibility decision in abortion case *D.* v. *Ireland*. The ECtHR accepted that the exhaustion of domestic remedies criterion was fulfilled because it found it 'unlikely' that the Irish courts would interpret the Irish abortion prohibition 'with remorseless logic', a finding from which the ECtHR itself later deviated.[18] The ECtHR seems, further at times, to have been 'hiding behind' what already had been introduced at the national level. In *Schalk and Kopf*, for example, the Court noted that a civil partnership for same-sex couples had been introduced in Austria in the meantime, and therefore considered it 'not its task' to establish whether the lack of any means of legal recognition for same-sex couples would have constituted a violation of Article 14 taken in conjunction with Article 8 if this situation had persisted at the time the Court decided the case.[19] Also, the ECtHR's formal equality approach in respect of complaints about discrimination on grounds of sexual orientation, whereby the Court held that same-sex partners were not in a comparable situation to different-sex spouses,[20] can be perceived in some cases as a 'way out', especially where the Court did not take into account

---

12 *Inter alia*, ECtHR [GC] 19 February 2013, *X. a.o.* v. *Austria*, no. 19010/07 and ECtHR [GC] 7 November 2013, *Vallianatos a.o.* v. *Greece*, nos. 29381/09 and 32684/09. See Ch. 8, sections 8.2.4.1.2 and 8.2.3.4.

13 *Inter alia*, Case C-506/06 *Sabine Mayr* [2008] ECR I-1017, ECLI:EU:C:2008:119 and Case C-34/10 *Oliver Brüstle* v. *Greenpeace eV* [2011] ECR I-9821, ECLI:EU:C:2011:669. See Ch. 3, section 3.1.1.

14 *Idem*; ECtHR 26 June 2014, *Mennesson* v. *France*, no. 65192/11 and ECtHR [GC] 7 November 2013, *Vallianatos a.o.* v. *Greece*, nos. 29381/09 and 32684/09. See Ch. 3, section 3.1.1; Ch. 2, section 2.4.2; and Ch. 8, section 8.2.3.4 respectively.

15 See Ch. 3, section 3.5.2.1.

16 *Idem*.

17 See Ch. 3, section 3.3.4.

18 See Ch. 2, sections 2.2.1 and 2.2.3.

19 See Ch. 8, section 8.2.2.2. See also N.R. Koffeman, 'Case note to ECtHR 24 June 2010, *Schalk and Kopf* v. *Austria*, no. 30141/04', 11 *European Human Rights Cases* 2010/92 (in Dutch).

20 See Ch. 13, section 13.1.3.

that marriage was not open to same-sex couples.[21] The latter brings us to a specific approach that both European Courts have taken on morally sensitive issues.

14.1.3.2. The 'in for a penny, in for a pound' approach

In both case studies both the CJEU and the ECtHR have taken a specific approach that has been referred to as 'in for a penny, in for a pound'.[22] It entails the idea that States may decide whether or not to grant a certain right or entitlement at the national level, but once they do indeed grant that right or entitlement and they thereby act within the scope of European law, they must do so in a way which meets European standards. In other words, the European Courts respect national decisions in these areas in their most fundamental and principled forms, but subject national measures that give effect to such principled choices to their scrutiny as soon as they have a connection with European law.

In the case law of the CJEU, the 'in for a penny, in for a pound' approach has been visible in particular in the employment cases discussed in the context of Case Study II. The Luxembourg Court there has held that *if* States introduce legislation which puts (same-sex) civil partners and (different-sex) spouses in a comparable situation in respect of a certain employment benefit, while marriage is under the law of that State open to different-sex couples only, they must then extend the employment benefit concerned to civil partners.[23] Hence, it is up to States to decide on the legal recognition of same-sex relationships, but once they have introduced a partnership form for these couples, they must ensure their equal treatment in the context of employment as provided for under EU law.

The ECtHR has employed the 'in for a penny, in for a pound' approach in more diverse settings and correspondingly in more diverse fashions. It has held, firstly, and following similar lines as are visible in the CJEU case law, in the context of Case Study II that States must grant rights and entitlements that come within the scope of the Convention in a non-discriminatory manner.[24] However, as noted in Chapter 13,

21 See Ch. 8, section 8.2.5.

22 J. Gerards, 'Judicial Minimalism and 'Dependency'', in: M. van Roosmalen et al. (eds.), *Fundamental Rights and Principles. Liber Amicorum Pieter van Dijk* (Cambridge, Intersentia 2013) p. 73 at p. 81 and J. Gerards, 'The European Court of Human Rights and the national courts: giving shape to the notion of 'shared responsibility'', in: J. Gerards and J. Fleuren, *Implementation of the European Convention on Human Rights and of the judgments of the ECtHR in national case law. A comparative analysis* (Cambridge, Intersentia 2014) pp. 13–94. In Dutch academia the approach has also been referred to as '*vastklikmethode*', which is most literally translated as 'pinning down method'. See, *inter alia*, J.H. Gerards, *EVRM – algemene beginselen* [ECHR – general principles] (Den Haag Sdu 2011) pp. 58–62 and N.R. Koffeman, 'Het Ierse abortusverbod en het EVRM; is uitbesteding de nieuwe norm?' ['The Irish abortion ban and the ECHR: is outsourcing the new standard?'], 36 *NTM/NJCM-Bulletin* (2011) p. 372 at pp. 374–375.

23 See Ch. 3 section 9.3.

24 In Case Study I the non-discrimination requirement has not been so visible in the case law of the ECtHR. It was applied by the Chamber in the *S.H. and Others* case concerning gamete donation, but this was later overruled by the Grand Chamber. In fact, the Strasbourg Court has – without explaining this further – held a same-sex couple, not to be in a similar situation to infertile heterosexual couples. See Ch. 2, section 2.3.3.

when compared to the CJEU, the ECtHR has taken a more formal equality approach in the relevant cases by accepting civil status as a vehicle for a difference in treatment.[25] The ECtHR has thus only applied the 'in for a penny, in for a pound' approach in cases where different-sex couples and same-sex couples with the same legal status were treated differently. In other words, the reach of the approach has been narrower in the case law of the ECtHR, when compared to that of the CJEU. On the other hand, the CJEU's application of the approach in the context of Case Study II has been – given the division of competences within the EU – confined to employment cases, while the ECtHR's case law extends to all matters that fall within the scope of a material Convention right, such as the right to respect for private life (Article 8 ECHR). In the context of Case Study I the 'in for a penny, in for a pound' approach in the case law of the ECtHR has entailed that *if* States decide to legalise abortion on certain grounds, they must ensure that there are sufficient procedural safeguards in place to make that right effective.[26] States must furthermore shape their legal frameworks in the area of reproductive matters '[…] in a coherent manner which allows the different legitimate interests involved to be adequately taken into account.'[27] Also, in respect of both case studies, the ECtHR has made clear that States must ensure that their legislation in these areas is consistent,[28] and thus that principled choices are continued on in various realms of the law.[29]

That both European Courts have employed the 'in for a penny, in for a pound' can be explained in different ways. Firstly, in respect of the CJEU it must be noted that when it comes to civil status, an area is concerned in which the EU has no competence. The CJEU can accordingly not give any ruling in respect of the question of whether States must introduce a civil partnership for same-sex couples, but it can rule upon the implications of such a choice in the field of employment, as that is an area in respect of which the EU is competent. Under the Convention, the rationale for the 'in for a penny, in for a pound' reasoning is not so much a matter of a classic division of competences, but it nonetheless has everything to do with the relationship between the ECtHR and the States. When it comes to the ECtHR, the 'in for a penny, in for a pound' approach can be perceived as a means of steering a middle course between respect for States' sovereignty and national (democratically justified) decision-making on the one hand, and protection of the rights of individuals on the other. By pressing for relatively value-neutral aspects such as consistency, the ECtHR can impose certain common standards on States without touching upon the true difficulties (see more elaborately 14.2.1 below).

---

25 See Ch. 13, section 13.1.6.

26 See more elaborately Ch. 2, sections 2.2.3.5 and 2.2.4.

27 E.g. ECtHR [GC] 3 November 2011, *S.H. a.o.* v. *Austria*, no. 57813/00, para. 100. See Ch. 2, section 2.3.3.

28 *Inter alia*, ECtHR 28 August 2012, *Costa and Pavan* v. *Italy*, no. 54270/10 and ECtHR [GC] 19 February 2013, *X. a.o.* v. *Austria*, no. 19010/07. See Ch. 2, section 2.3.4 and Ch. 8, section 8.2.3.1.

29 It has been noted in this regard that one may wonder if it is indeed feasible to be entirely coherent in regulation in these fields. Plus, there is a risk that 'coherence' is interpreted in a rather subjective manner. N.R. Koffeman, 'Case-note to ECtHR 28 August 2012, *Costa and Pavan* v. *Italy*, no. 54270/10', 13 *European Human Rights Cases* 2012/222 (in Dutch).

14.1.3.3. Variations on the margin of appreciation in the ECtHR's case law

What is also striking, if one studies the case law of the ECtHR in both case studies, is that this Court has introduced some unprecedented variations on its well-established margin of appreciation in these morally sensitive areas. This especially holds for the ECtHR's case law in reproductive matters,[30] but it can also be noted in the context of Case Study II. These variations mainly concern the use of consensus based arguments for determining the width of the margin. Firstly, in some cases the Court has set a higher barrier, by holding that for a common ground to decisively narrow the margin, it had to be 'based on settled and long-standing principles established in the law of the member States'.[31] Also, incidentally the lack of consensus on a broadly defined issue could trump an existing consensus on a more specific issue.[32] A third variation has featured only in Case Study II so far and concerns the limiting of the number of States that were taken into account in the determination of the consensus. As discussed in Chapter 8, in the Austrian *X. and Others* case concerning second-parent adoption for same-sex couples, the ECtHR held that it could only compare the Austrian choice to limit second-parent adoption for unmarried couples to different-sex couples with that of those States that allowed for second-parent adoption in unmarried couples. The Court consequently found the relevant group of ten States to be too narrow a sample to draw a conclusion as to the existence of a possible European consensus on this issue.[33]

While in the first two variations the established absence of consensus resulted in the granting of a wide margin and thus in more discretion for the States, in the latter case, consensus was sidelined as a factor influencing the width of the margin of appreciation. The margin in the *X. and Others* case was narrow(ed) because discrimination on grounds of sexual orientation was concerned. While the former variations thus stood in the way of finding any violation, in the latter case it in fact 'enabled' the Court to find a violation. It is noted that the Court's determination of the width of the margin in the *X. and Others* case also fits in with the 'in for a penny, in for a pound' approach as described above, that it had taken in that case. After all, the Court ruled that States were under no obligation under the Convention to introduce second-parent adoption for unmarried couples, but once they had, they could not discriminate between same-sex and different-sex couples in this respect. That the Court in those circumstances also only compared with those States that had introduced second-parent adoption for unmarried couples, thus logically followed from the approach it had taken.

---

30 As observed in Ch. 2, section 2.5.

31 ECtHR [GC] 3 November 2011, *S.H. a.o.* v. *Austria*, no. 57813/00, para. 96.

32 It is recalled that in the abortion case, *A, B and C* v. *Ireland* (2010) an existing consensus towards allowing abortion for abortion on social and medical grounds was outweighed by a lack of European consensus in respect of the right to life of the unborn. Ch. 2, section 2.2.3.4.

33 ECtHR [GC] 19 February 2013, *X. a.o.* v. *Austria*, no. 19010/07, para. 149.

14.1.3.4. Resumé and outlook

The European Courts have thus taken a careful, at times evasive, approach in morally sensitive matters, but have nonetheless held States to take the consequences of their choices in these matters. The wide margin of appreciation that the ECtHR generally accords in these matters and the above discussed variations on the determination of the width of the margin of appreciation resulting in an (even) wide(r) margin being accorded, fit in with the picture of a careful (or even evasive) Court. The 'in for a penny, in for a pound' approach, and – in the case of the ECtHR – the tailoring of the margin of appreciation to that approach, on the other hand, illustrate that both European Courts have in certain circumstances and to some extent intervened in these morally sensitive matters. Both these developments are likely to be continued in the (near) future, with possibly the latter taking the overhand over the former.

14.1.4. Legal responses to cross-border movement in respect of morally sensitive matters

On the basis of the research in the case studies, a range of legal responses to cross-border movement in morally sensitive issues has been identified in Chapters 7 and 13. In both case studies 'warding off' (the effects of) cross-border movement, that is the deterring of people from going to other States or from coming to their State, and the opposite, 'accommodation' of (the effects of) cross-border movement, have turned out to be taking place, with the latter gaining ground. A gradual converting of warding off into accommodation is visible for both case studies, and it also has been found that increasing numbers of accommodation obligations have been formulated at the European level. Concrete accommodation obligations that have been demanded from the European level are first of all that in cross-border abortion cases and cross-border reproductive care (CBRC) cases, information about foreign treatment options and – in any case in cross-border abortion cases – follow-up care must be provided.[34] Accommodation by means of recognition of the legal effects of foreign options, is obligatory in cross-border surrogacy cases, as parental links established abroad must be recognised, in any case if the intended father is also the genetic father. In the context of Case Study II, the accommodation obligation can be mentioned that States must 'facilitate' the entrance of stable same-sex partners of migrating EU citizens. Also, States that have a registered partnership at national level that is equivalent to marriage, must authorise the entry and residence of registered partners of migrating EU citizens.

The present research has furthermore revealed that there are different forms of accommodation. In both case studies, but particularly in Case Study II on legal recognition of same-sex relationships, there have been cases of partial accommodation or conditional accommodation, which means that accommodation is made dependent upon the national (internal) standards. For instance, none of the States studied have

34 See Ch. 7, section 7.2.2.

recognised a civil status of same-sex couples that was not provided for at the national level,[35] while in Germany and Ireland foreign marriages of same-sex couples are downgraded to a civil partnership. An example of conditional accommodation in the context of Case Study I is that under EU law, States only have to reimburse treatment obtained abroad if their national scheme provides for reimbursement for that kind of treatment.[36] Such conditional accommodation is thus fairly passive, as it does not require any extra effort from the State concerned. There have also been more active forms of accommodation by means of recognition that were taken by States or even imposed on them by the European level. For instance, in cross-border cases involving parental rights of same-sex couples, exceptionally but recently increasingly more often, domestic courts have recognised parental links established abroad,[37] while such recognition is, under certain circumstances, obligatory under the ECHR in cross-border surrogacy cases (see above).

That accommodation is gaining ground may be explained by an increased acknowledgement of the fact that in cross-border situations different interests are at stake, or in any case that these interests are weighted differently in cross-border situations. While the relevant individual and general interests do not cease to exist at the border,[38] other interests may become weightier once a cross-border situation is concerned. This holds true particularly in cross-border situations where individual burdens exist, and even more so when a child is involved whose interests must prevail. For instance, in the cross-border surrogacy case *Mennesson*, the ECtHR understood that the respondent State in international surrogacy cases aimed to protect children and surrogate mothers by refusing recognition of parental links established abroad and acknowledged that it had an interest 'in ensuring that its members conform[ed] to the choice made democratically within that community'. Still, a fair balance had to be struck between this interest of the State and individual interests, the best interests of the child concerned being paramount.[39] In this international surrogacy case, this finding resulted in an obligation to recognise parental links legally established in another State.

While accommodation may alleviate or remove individual burdens that are involved in cross-border movement, certainly not all individual burdens involved in cross-border movement have been addressed at State level. From the analysis in both Chapters 7 and 13 it can be concluded that sometimes States have appeared unwilling to alleviate individual burdens, taking the stance that these are the responsibility of the individuals. It must also be noted in this regard that some individual burdens may prove very difficult to protect unilaterally, as for the protection of certain interests, States are dependent upon other States. For example, if a State wants to protect the right of children to know their genetic origins, it must make arrangements with

---

35 See Ch. 13, section 13.2.2.3.

36 See Ch. 3, section 3.6.2.1 and Ch. 7, section 7.2.2.2.

37 See Ch. 13, section 13.2.2.2.

38 Compare the dissenters to ECtHR [GC] 3 November 2011, *S.H. a.o.* v. *Austria*, no. 57813/00, para. 13 and ECtHR 26 June 2014, *Mennesson* v. *France*, no. 65192/11.

39 See Ch. 2, section 2.4.2.

another State in situations where the children have been conceived with the use of gametes donated in that other State.

Legal responses at a more abstract level to the phenomenon of cross-border movement in morally sensitive issues have been: 'outsourcing' as identified in Case Study I; 'backing out' as identified in Case Study II; and 'adaptation' as has been visible in both case studies, albeit in Case Study I more expressly than in Case Study II. As explained in Chapter 13, the fact that 'outsourcing' – whereby foreign options contribute to the justification of restrictive regimes at domestic level – has not occurred in the context of Case Study II, may be partly explained by the fact that foreign registration and marriage options are not always easily accessible.[40] In 'backing out', fear that other countries may not accept or recognise the domestic legislative choices has been a ground for not introducing certain change. That this particular response has not been so expressly visible in the context of Case Study I may be explained in different ways. For Germany and the Netherlands it is possibly explained by the fact these States have not contemplated introducing a reproductive method that included a risk that its legal effects would not be recognised in other States. In Ireland, by contrast, there were plans on the table to legalise surrogacy, but these were withdrawn. Whether 'backing out' was part of the motivation behind this decision, is insufficiently clear.

Chapters 7 and 13 have pointed out that the various legal responses also have implications for the individual. Although foreign options in principle contribute to the range of options that individuals have, cross-border movement inherently brings with it burdens for individuals, which, in fact, may be considerable, particularly in outsourcing situations.[41] The warding off of cross-border movement may add to such burdens, while accommodation may alleviate some of them. Burdens for individuals that can only be removed by means of adaptation, are burdens involved in the travelling itself and burdens that occur in the daily lives of families living in a State that does not legally recognise their civil status or their parental links.

14.2. OBSERVATIONS

14.2.1. Limited substantive European standard-setting, but nonetheless...

Despite limited competences at EU level and the granting of a wide margin of appreciation by the ECtHR in many of the morally sensitive issues addressed in this research, it cannot be denied that there is increasingly more (indirect) European standard-setting in these areas, both in internal and cross-border situations.

As noted in section 14.1.4 above, the present research has made clear that there is a growing set of European standards for cross-border situations. States' legal responses

40 As noted in Ch. 13, section 13.2.1.1, various States subject access to marriage or partnership registration to conditions relating to residency and/or nationality.

41 See Ch. 7, section 7.2.4.

to cross-border situations are increasingly more dictated by European law. However, the (potential for) (indirect) impact of European law on internal situations can also not be overlooked. This may first of all be the consequence of the 'in for a penny, in for a pound' approach, as described in section 14.1.3.2 above. This rather pragmatic approach of the European Courts has created obligations for States that cannot be ignored. In other words, while not encroaching upon the most fundamental moral choices of States, there is European standard-setting in these areas, albeit in a more implicit manner. After all, *if* States recognise the existence of a right at the national level, they are also obliged to set up sufficient preconditions for the effective and non-discriminatory enjoyment of that right.[42] They furthermore have to ensure that their legal framework in the area is coherent and consistent. While this is not harmonisation *per se*, such reasoning may nonetheless have a harmonising impact. States can only escape such European influence by not making a first step at all (see also 14.2.1 below), but whether that is a realistic scenario, can be questioned. Particularly where other (non-European) States are taking steps in these areas, and where medical scientific developments keep progressing, States may desire to make their regimes more permissive, at least to some extent.

It has furthermore proven increasingly difficult to separate the 'European' from the 'national' in these areas, since terminology is employed at the European level that is, in principle, defined at the national level. EU law texts contain terms such as 'spouse', 'embryo' and 'pregnant worker', which concern or relate to matters in respect of which the Member States are exclusively competent. Even though the relevant documents generally refer to national legislation in this regard, it can be difficult to keep these two levels of jurisdiction apart. The CJEU has repeatedly stressed in the relevant cases that its definition of such terms is a legal definition concerning the relevant Directive only (see also 14.1.3.1 above), but it remains very difficult to rule out any radiating effect of any such definition adopted by the CJEU. It may affect standard-setting at the national level, and/or may influence other realms of EU law. For example, in academia often references have been made to the CJEU case law in staff cases and employment cases to substantiate an argument on the approach the CJEU should take in free movement cases involving same-sex couples.[43] The Court may be indeed inclined to take that case law into account if such a case should come before it. This effect may be reinforced by non-binding standard-setting in the EU, in particular in the area of LGBT rights.[44] Related hereto is that obligations of States under EU equal treatment legislation may also have a radiating effect on national standard-setting in other fields of law. For instance, the more States are required to equalise the position of same-sex couples with that of different-sex couples in the area of employment, the more likely it seems that they will also do so in other areas, possibly including parental matters.

---

42 Heringa and Van Hoof speak in this regard of 'the socialising effect of Article 14'. Heringa and Van Hoof, 'Prohibition of discrimination (Article 14)', in: P. van Dijk et al. (eds.), *Theory and Practice of the European Convention on Human Rights* (Antwerpen, Intersentia 2006) p. 1051.

43 See Ch. 9, section 9.6.

44 See Ch. 9, section 9.4.

On the basis of the above one could conclude that EU law, as well as the ECHR, are spreading like oil in these areas. The 'European' and the 'national' are thus becoming increasingly interwoven. This may also have implications for (variety in) national moral choices.

14.2.2. Implications for (the variety in) national moral choices

The present research has confirmed the premise that there is (a wide) diversity in national standard-setting in morally sensitive issues in the European Union. At the same time, it can be observed that various factors have or may have implications for (the variety in) national moral choices throughout the European Union. This holds, firstly, for the increased indirect impact of European law on national standard-setting in morally sensitive issues, as described above. Further, cross-border movement in itself, as well legal responses thereto – whether deliberately chosen by States or imposed on them by European law – have an impact in this respect.

When it comes to internal situations, it can be observed that the implicit or indirect harmonising effect of the 'in for a penny, in for a pound' approach of the European Courts as described above, is a particular one. It namely risks becoming an 'all or nothing' approach, and may in this way drive a wedge between the European States. States may either choose not to recognise a certain right or to grant a certain entitlement at all – a principled approach for which the European level leaves room – or they recognise the existence of a right at the national level, but are also obliged to set up the above-mentioned sufficient preconditions for the enjoyment of that right. This effectively limits States' room for manoeuvre; either they take no steps at all or they take the first step, which often, although not necessarily, results in an obligation to take even more steps or many steps at once. The latter implication is reinforced by the fact that States must provide for a coherent framework in these areas, which entails that any principled choice made must be followed up on in all realms of the law. Also, the principle will keep applying to each new step that States make. The States' range of options has thus become rather black-and-white; either they take a very traditional approach to these matters,[45] or they join the States in the vanguard. There is not much middle ground left, as intermediary and partly discriminatory or partly ineffective approaches to these morally sensitive issues cannot be easily justified. This particularly holds true in the context of Case Study II where the range of options is more black-and-white to begin with, but also applies in respect of Case Study I. All in all, the variety in moral choices may be delimited by the 'in for a penny, in for a pound' approach.

Turning to the cross-border picture, it has been observed that in some circumstances cross-border movement can provide a means to uphold national standards for internal situations, and thus (a variety in) moral choices. This may hold particularly true in

45 *Cf.* F. de Londras and K. Dzehtsiarou, 'Grand Chamber of the European Court of Human Rights, A, B & C v Ireland', 62 *International and Comparative Law Quarterly* (2013) p. 250 at p. 262.

the context of Case Study I, and academic literature has been especially elaborate in respect of such an effect of cross-border reproductive care (CBRC). Pennings has opined, for example, that CBRC should be seen as '[...] a safety valve that avoids moral conflict, and as such, contributes to a peaceful coexistence of different ethical and religious views in Europe.'[46] The present research has shown that any such effect of cross-border movement in morally sensitive issues may, however, be diminished if the discretion of States to react to such cross-border movement is restricted by European standard-setting. Whether this is indeed the case, depends on the type of legal response that is imposed on States by the European level. Where States are required to recognise the legal effects of cross-border movement, this is more likely to have an impact on their standard-setting at the national level in the area.[47] Hence, in those situations cross-border movement may not function as a safety valve. Where no such recognition of legal effects is involved, however, as is the case in respect of some of the types of reproductive treatment discussed in Case Study I, this may be different. The 'mere' accommodating of such cross-border movement by means of arranging practicalities such as information and follow-up care, may put less pressure on national standard-setting and may thus may enable States to uphold less permissive regimes. Here, outsourcing – whereby foreign options contribute to the justification of restrictive regimes – becomes more realistic.[48] Storrow has observed in respect of CBRC that '[...] the opportunity for patients to go abroad for treatment tempers organized resistance to the law and allows government to pass stricter regulations than it otherwise might.'[49] In other words, where the ECtHR applies an outsourcing approach and combines it with accommodation obligations of a limited impact, as it has done in the context of Case Study I,[50] States with less permissive regimes may be less inclined to move towards the more permissive side of the moral spectrum. They may instead remain on the less permissive side.

Where there are no realistic outsourcing options, however, cross-border movement and legal responses thereto may instead impact national standard-setting for internal situations and lead to the dominance of more permissive regimes in this regard. Firstly, it has appeared in the context of Case Study I that cross-border movement may in itself be a trigger for adaptation of the national standard to those of States functioning as countries of destination in these situations. For instance, in the context of CBRC, quality and safety concerns about foreign treatment options have been put forward as grounds for such adaptation.[51] In addition, in both case studies

46 G. Pennings, 'Legal harmonization and reproductive tourism in Europe', 19 *Human Reproduction* (2004) p. 2689 at p. 2694. See also A.P. Ferraretti et al., 'Cross-border reproductive care: a phenomenon expressing the controversial aspects of reproductive technologies', 20 *Reproductive BioMedicine Online* (2010) p. 261 at p. 262.

47 See Ch. 7, section 7.2.2.3 and Ch. 13, section 13.2.2.3.

48 See Ch. 7, section 7.2.4.

49 R.F. Storrow, 'The pluralism problem in cross-border reproductive care', 25 *Human Reproduction* (2010) p. 2939 at p. 2941.

50 See Ch. 7, section 7.2.4.

51 See Ch. 7, section 7.2.3. Concerns about 'deleterious extra-territorial effects' (Storrow 2010, *supra* n. 50, at p. 2941) of such cross-border movement could potentially be another ground for adaptation. Here one may think of concerns about risks of exploitation of gamete donors or surrogate mothers in foreign countries.

(potential for) more implicit impact on national standard-setting by means of legal responses to cross-border movement has been identified. As also noted above, accommodation consisting of the recognition of the legal effects of such cross-border movement – a civil status or parental links established in another country – may affect national standard-setting for internal situations. Possibly even more so when such accommodation is imposed upon them by European law, States acting as host States or countries of origin in such cross-border situations may feel pressurised to adapt their national standard-setting in these areas to the standard that they (must) apply in cross-border situations.[52] This may hold particularly true in situations where States are required under European law to recognise a civil status or forms of parental links that their national law does not even provide for. There is thus reason to assume that, in certain circumstances, because of cross-border movement and because legal responses to such movement are required, States are inclined to move in the direction of more progressive regimes. Whether this also inherently implies a move to the most progressive regime, cannot be firmly concluded on the basis of the present research, but requires further (sociological) research. It seems a probable conclusion, since so long as more progressive regimes exist, adaptation or implicit pressure of accommodation may occur. In other words, cross-border movement may imply that also States that are yet on the fairly progressive side, (feel pressurised to) move towards the most progressive regime. This is further confirmed by the fact that while 'backing out' has been visible as well, this has been only incidentally and only occurred when a State was considering being very first to take a step towards a more progressive side of the moral spectrum.[53]

There are thus simultaneous dynamics in opposite directions taking place, that all may have implications for (the variety in) national choices in morally sensitive issues in the European Union. Where an outsourcing approach is applied, it may be more likely that States with less permissive regimes remain on that side of the moral spectrum, while accommodation obligations and concerns about implications of cross-border movement, may prompt States to move to or towards the other side of this spectrum. These dynamics not only have implications for individuals involved in cross-border movement in these matters (see also 14.1.4 above), but – as national standard-setting for internal situations may be affected by these dynamics – also for the nationals of the States concerned that do not cross borders.

14.2.3. Reality outpaces and dictates the law, particularly in cross-border cases

The present research has, furthermore, shown that in many situations complex balancing exercises and ethical objections to certain practices were outpaced by real time developments. This applies in internal situations, but even more so in cross-border situations. Even if national legislatures desired so on ethical or moral

52 See Ch. 7, section 7.2.2.3 and Ch. 13, section 13.2.2.3.
53 See Ch. 13, section 13.2.3.

grounds, they have not been able to prevent certain matters from becoming reality and correspondingly from becoming facts of law. Particularly relevant for Case Study II has been the reality that States cannot prevent that *de facto* family life is being formed. Particularly in the ECtHR case law, increasingly more protection has been granted to *de facto* family life.[54]

States may ban or limit certain practices deemed undesirable within their own jurisdictions, but to prevent people from going abroad for such practices has proven much harder. As a result it has been even more so in cross-border situations that reality has outpaced and dictated the law. The *faits accomplis* of a born child and of parental links having been established abroad in cross-border surrogacy cases, with which States have been confronted in cross-border situations, have proven forceful arguments for narrowing the room for manoeuvre for States in such situations. Although so far not confirmed in any European case law, in the future this also may hold for the *fait accompli* of an established civil status in the context of Case Study II.

This time the dynamic of cross-border movement has thus had clear implications for legal responses to cross-border movement. Accommodation obligations have most often been dictated by reality. The reality of cross-border movement as such has furthermore at times been the ground for pragmatic responses like adaptation, as also observed above.

14.2.4. The cross-border dimension of multilevel jurisdictions

Lastly, the present research has provided the insight that in cross-border situations in fact a unique realm of law applies. Those who cross borders (within the EU), enter a special dimension of law. EU free movement law and Private International Law are the readiest and most established areas of law that set standards for cross-border situations, but the present research has revealed that standard-setting for cross-border situations in morally sensitive issues is more comprehensive than those two realms of law alone. It encompasses the aforementioned areas of law, but also includes others, most profoundly human rights law. This shows all the more that the cross-border dimension is not confined to one level of jurisdiction in the European multilevel jurisdiction. Cross-border situations cut diagonally through horizontal and vertical interaction of legal systems and form the trigger, the legal stepping stone, for such interaction. Moreover, apart from such interaction between legal systems, cross-border movement may establish an interrelation or interdependency between legal systems, in the sense that foreign options can contribute to the justification of domestic restrictions. This makes it even more likely that cross-border situations concern a distinct realm of law.

---

54 ECtHR 19 February 2013, *X. a.o.* v. *Austria*, no. 19010/07, para. 145, under reference to ECtHR 28 June 2007, *Wagner and J.M.W.L.* v. *Luxembourg*, no. 76240/01, para. 119; ECtHR 25 January 2007, *Eski* v. *Austria*, no. 21949/03, para. 39 and ECtHR 13 December 2007, *Emonet a.o. v. Switzerland*, no. 39051/03, paras. 63–64.

For individuals involved in cross-border movement this generally implies that they have more legal means to have their interests protected. For States it implies that their decision-making in cross-border situations is encroached upon. This may, as observed above, indirectly affect national standard-setting in morally sensitive issues and thus have implications for (the variety of) moral choices in the European Union.

Executive Summary

Morally sensitive issues and cross-border movement in the EU

The cases of reproductive matters and legal recognition of same-sex relationships

Within the European Union (EU) considerable diversity exists in respect of morally sensitive issues like abortion, assisted human reproduction (AHR), surrogacy and legal recognition of same-sex relationships. While the 20th century has witnessed an increased intergovernmental cooperation between States as well as an increased transferral of State powers to supranational organisations such as the EU, certain competences have traditionally remained with the States. The aforementioned morally sensitive issues are areas of law *par excellence* where standards are primarily set at State level. It is usually considered that it should be left to each State to decide whether, for example, abortion is available on social grounds, whether couples can become parents with the involvement of a surrogate mother and whether same-sex couples can marry and/or adopt children.

While there is no strong degree of European regulation in these areas, and diversity is generally respected at European level, there is nonetheless a certain potential for European regulation in these fields. The EU has competences in respect of issues that are strongly related to, and at times intertwined with, reproductive matters and legal recognition of same-sex relationships. Here, one may think of competences in the areas of health and equal treatment. In addition, several of these morally sensitive issues come within the scope of the European Convention on Human Rights (ECHR), for instance by means of the right to respect for private life under Article 8 ECHR. There is thus (potential for) (indirect) European influence in these areas.

Cross-border movement within the EU furthermore adds a new dimension to this complex picture. Cross-border movement is a given within the EU; people move around for various reasons and purposes, not uncommonly pursuing economic objectives. Such mobility is enabled and stimulated by the EU free movement rules that, *inter alia*, protect the free movement of persons and the freedom to receive services in another EU Member State. Diverging regimes in the aforementioned morally sensitive matters may create obstacles to such cross-border movement; they may hinder or deter persons from making use of their free movement rights. For instance, same-sex couples may be discouraged from moving to an EU Member State where they have no possibility to have their relationship legally recognised by means of a civil partnership or marriage. Differences in regimes in morally sensitive issues may, by contrast, also be the direct impetus for cross-border movement within the EU, as people from Member States with less permissive regimes may wish to enjoy the possibilities, rights and benefits of more permissive regimes of other States. For example, in Member States with restrictive abortion regimes, women who wish to have their pregnancies terminated may want to travel to Member States with more liberal regimes.

Such cross-border movement and the existing obstacles thereto do not only highlight existing diversity in morally sensitive issues, they also imply, among other things, that States are increasingly confronted with (the consequences and effects of) other States' regimes. For example, same-sex couples residing in one EU Member State may claim recognition of their marriage concluded in another Member State, while women or couples who had a certain type of AHR treatment in another State that is outlawed under the law of their own State, may claim reimbursement of the costs involved in that treatment under the national health system of their State. Such confrontation may require a reaction from the States involved, whether they function as country of origin or as country of destination or both.

The present research explores this cross-border dimension of morally sensitive issues within the European Union. It provides an overview of trends and developments in national and European law in morally sensitive issues and gives insight into the interests that are at stake and the dynamics that apply both in internal and in cross-border situations.

Two thematic case studies and five jurisdictions

The backbone of the present research consists of two thematic case studies – one on reproductive matters (Case Study I) and one on legal recognition of same-sex relationships (Case Study II) – which focus on five jurisdictions. The latter encompass three national jurisdictions – Ireland, Germany and the Netherlands – and two European jurisdictions or systems, namely the EU and the ECHR. The case studies have been chosen because they concern pre-eminently morally sensitive issues and, consequently, politically controversial matters, in respect of which EU Member States have long taken different positions and still did so at the time this research was commenced (i.e., in 2009), as well as when it was concluded (i.e. July 2014). Moreover, the issues covered by the two case studies are not 'just' morally sensitive issues, they also concern areas in which fundamental rights claims can be made and – importantly, given the focus of this research – that have a demonstrable cross-border dimension. The three national jurisdictions have been selected, *inter alia*, because they cover a certain range in approaches in respect of reproductive matters and legal recognition of same-sex relationships and have different (constitutional) profiles.

Both case studies follow the same structure. Each one consists of six chapters, five describing the standard-setting in the five selected jurisdictions (the ECHR, the EU,

Germany, Ireland and the Netherlands respectively), and one drawing conclusions for the respective case study.

Case Study I – Reproductive matters

Case Study I on reproductive matters covers three subjects, namely abortion, assisted human reproduction (AHR) and surrogacy. For each of these topics, the five substantive chapters in Case Study I (i.e. Chapters 2 to 6) investigate, for the relevant European and national jurisdictions, what – if any – standard-setting is in place, and how this developed over time. For a better understanding of the relevant standard-setting and – where relevant – the debates in politics and legal scholarship concerning these often controversial matters, a general (constitutional) framework is sketched first. A brief introduction is given to very prominent rights in the relevant jurisdiction (e.g. the protection of the unborn on the Irish jurisdiction), as well as to a selection of themes and – in the case of the EU – competences that are key in the case study. It is subsequently set out if the relevant reproductive services are at all legalised and if so, under what conditions access to these services is provided for. Also, the financing of abortion and AHR treatment under each State's national health system is briefly addressed. In the discussion of national regulation of surrogacy, the possibilities – if they exist at all – for intended parents to establish parental links with a child born following a surrogacy arrangement are also discussed. The discussion of regulation of AHR addresses a number of issues that may occur in the course of AHR treatment, namely, the donation of gametes and embryos, preimplantation genetic diagnosis (PGD), gender selection and vitrification of egg cells.

The analysis of the internal picture for each of the jurisdictions provides insight into what considerations and interests play, or have played, a role in legislative debates and case law and how change was or may be brought about. It also provides the basis for the subsequent analysis of the cross-border picture that is enclosed in each substantive chapter. The latter analysis starts – where available – with some statistics on the scale of cross-border movement in the context of the case study in the respective jurisdiction. Subsequently each of the substantive chapters examines for the respective jurisdiction how it has dealt and deals with cross-border situations in reproductive matters and how the jurisdictions interact in this regard. Thereby, *inter alia*, Private International Law regimes and (national implementation of) the EU free movement rules are studied, in order to answer questions like whether foreign birth certificates are recognised in cross-border surrogacy cases or whether women who wish to have an abortion in another country have a right to access to information about such foreign abortion services, as well as a right to follow-up treatment upon return.

Chapter 7 draws conclusions on Case Study I. It discerns trends in standard-setting and in judicial and legislative processes regarding reproductive matters. It is, for instance, observed in Chapter 7 that balancing of interests related to reproductive matters has often had different outcomes in the three States studied and that the legislative and judicial processes in the States have taken different shapes. Also, European law (both EU law and the ECHR) explicitly allows for such diversity between legal regimes in reproductive matters. States are left room to make their own principled choices in these moral and ethical issues and they are free to prohibit reproductive practices, as long as the relevant interests have been balanced in the decision-making and as long as their principled choices are consistent. However, once they decide to regulate in the area, they must also provide for the effective enjoyment of rights and entitlements, which entails that they must ensure that the applicable procedures enable careful decision-making. There are, at the same time, also similarities in the ways in which reproductive matters have been dealt with in the various jurisdictions. Generally, over time more reproductive practices have been legalised and regulated for, or at least initiatives to that effect have been taken. Also, a gradual development towards a central role for the best interests of the child is clearly visible, although the views on what these require exactly have in some cases changed over time. Furthermore, a development has been visible towards assessment of reproductive matters with due regard to the individual circumstances of the case. Both at European and national levels, there has been increased attention focused on the introduction of procedures allowing for careful decision-making in reproductive matters.

On the basis of the analysis of Chapters 2 to 6, Chapter 7 continues to identify four types of legal responses to cross-border movement for reproductive matters. The first is 'warding off' (the effects of) cross-border movement, that is the deterring of people from going to other States or from coming to their state. Such warding off may take different shapes, ranging from travel bans to non-recognition of legal parenthood established in another State in an international surrogacy situation. Secondly, as a mirror to the 'warding off' approach, States may choose to accommodate (the effects of) cross-border movement in reproductive matters, for example by providing for information and follow-up care in case of cross-border abortion. A third type of response is 'adaptation', which means the adjustment of national standard-setting in the area to that of another State or other States to which cross-border movement takes place. Lastly, cross-border movement has in some situations enabled States to 'outsource' the protection of certain interests in reproductive matters to other States. The ECtHR has in some cases namely held that foreign treatment options contributed to the justification of restrictive regimes.

For each of these legal responses, Chapter 7 assesses the extent to which the respective response is commensurable with or even dictated by European law. For example, it is concluded that warding off by means of non-recognition of legal effects of foreign options or by means of bans on information on foreign treatment options has generally proven not easily justified under European law, and refusing follow-up care may also be problematic. It is furthermore assessed how these legal responses relate to one another and what the implications of each respective category of legal responses are, or may be, for the States concerned, as well as for the individuals involved in the cross-border movement.

Case Study II – Legal recognition of same-sex relationships

Chapters 8 to 12 of Case Study II explore what the five selected jurisdictions provide for in respect of legal recognition of same-sex relationships. Thereby a first focal point is whether same-sex couples have (a right to) access to a registration form – civil partnership or marriage – under the relevant jurisdictions and, if so, what these entail. Secondly, the case study covers the question of parental rights for same-sex couples. Thereby various forms of adoption are discussed, namely second-parent adoption (adoption of a child by the partner of the child's legal and genetic parent), successive adoption (the situation where a partner adopts the child of an adoptive parent) and joint adoption. Also, legal parenthood by operation of the law and access to AHR treatment for same-sex couples are addressed.

The five substantive chapters of this case study follow the same basic structure as Chapters 2 to 6 of Case Study I (see above). They thus start with a general (constitutional) framework, followed by a discussion of the internal and the cross-border picture respectively. As in Case Study I, the debates in politics and legal scholarship are – where relevant – included in those discussions.

Chapter 13 concludes for Case Study II that when it comes to legal recognition of same-sex relationships across the European Union, States have taken the lead, rather than the European institutions. National legislatures, courts and administrative bodies set the tone and pace and the European level generally only follows. The European Courts have at times given some subtle nudges to the national legislature or judiciary, but this was generally only in situations where first (principled) steps towards legal recognition had already been taken at the national level. In the case law of the ECtHR, civil status has often functioned as a vehicle for unequal treatment of same-sex couples and different-sex couples. Only in cases where no 'special legal status' was involved, has the ECtHR applied strict scrutiny.

Traditional notions of marriage and the family have toned down in all three States studied, although they have not been completely abandoned in all States. Also, under the ECHR marriage does still enjoy strong protection. Moreover, the increased acknowledgement and legal protection of *de facto* family life has been paired with the acceptance of biological differences between different-sex couples and same-sex couples, and between lesbian couples and gay couples, as justification for certain differences in treatment between these groups in respect of parental matters. Unequal treatment of same-sex couples does thus still exist, but there has been a shift in the justification grounds from more morally charged grounds to more value-neutral grounds.

Generally a steady development towards increased protection of LGBT rights and correspondingly legal recognition of same-sex relationships has been discernible. Such change has been in most cases brought about gradually and at a slow pace, with some exceptions of much quicker developments. These developments are likely to continue in the future. Possibly the European level will take a more proactive stance in some respects. In any case it is likely that the European Courts will continue to nudge national legislatures and courts in this process of increased equalisation of the legal position of same-sex couples with that of different-sex couples.

In respect of cross-border situations, Chapter 13 concludes that in essence two categories of legal responses to cross-border movement can be identified in Case Study II: 'warding off' and 'accommodation'. In their most extreme form these are, in the context of the case study at hand, mutually exclusive. However, it has turned out that different degrees of 'warding off' and of 'accommodation' are possible. In some cases States have resorted to partial or conditional accommodation in their dealing with cross-border movement in the context of Case Study II. For example, in Ireland and Germany same-sex marriages have been 'downgraded' to the level of civil partnership, while foreign same-sex registered partnerships are recognised only if they meet certain standards. Other categories of legal responses to cross-border movement in the context of Case Study II that have been visible – albeit to a limited extent only – are 'adaptation' and 'backing out'. The latter implies the situation where fear that other countries will not accept or recognise the national legislative choices, is presented as an argument against the granting of certain rights to same-sex couples. Following the lines of Chapter 7, it is assessed subsequently in Chapter 13 how the various legal responses relate to one another and what the implications of each respective category of legal responses are, or may be, for the States concerned, as well as for the individuals involved in the cross-border movement. Chapter 13 furthermore concludes that standard-setting at the European level for cross-border cases in the context of Case Study II has so far been fairly minimal. Some minimum accommodation obligations in respect of the entry and residence of same-sex partners of EU citizens follow from the relevant Free Movement Directive, but particularly as regards the legal position of these couples once entry and residence have been granted, there remain various open questions. Here, case law of the CJEU or further guidance of the EU legislature as to the discretion that States either have or not do not have in these matters is much desired.

Conclusions

The concluding chapter, Chapter 14, provides a synthesis of the relevant findings of Chapters 7 and 13, as well as a number of observations about morally sensitive issues and cross-border movement within the EU more generally. It draws parallels and discerns trends in respect of balancing exercises and legislative and judicial processes in morally sensitive issues. For example, while the jurisdictions studied for this research generally recognise the same interests in the relevant case studies, the weight that is, or has been, accorded to these interests differs or has differed between the various jurisdictions. The interests of the child have prevailed in both case studies, and both case studies have shown that involvement of the interests of the (future) child, makes a crucial difference to balancing exercises, especially in cross-border cases, such as cross-border surrogacy cases. The two case studies furthermore point to an emerging trend of granting more protection to relatively concrete interests such as the best interests of the child, over rather abstract interests like 'the traditional marriage institute'. This development can also be regarded as a shift from values deeply entrenched in the society and law of a specific State, to less value-charged values that are (more) commonly shared and transnational. When it comes to the actual balancing exercises, another trend is a greater legal recognition of *de facto* situations, such as *de facto* family life. Next to this, there appears to be increased attention for balancing in individual cases.

European jurisdictions generally have taken a rather reactive, pragmatic and incremental approach in morally sensitive issues. Particularly the approach of both European Courts (the CJEU and the ECtHR) at times could even be described as evasive. Nevertheless, both European Courts have applied a similar kind of reasoning that is typified as the 'in for a penny, in for a pound' approach. This entails the idea that States may decide whether or not to grant a certain right or entitlement at national level, but once they do indeed grant that right or entitlement and they thereby act within the scope of European law, they must do so in a way which meets European standards. States have thus been held to take the consequences of their choices in morally sensitive matters. Further, in the case law of the ECtHR, for both case studies variations on the margin of appreciation doctrine can be identified, which mainly concern the use of consensus based arguments for determining the width of the margin.

In respect of the legal responses to cross-border movement in respect of morally sensitive matters, Chapter 14 concludes, *inter alia*, that a gradual converting of 'warding off' in 'accommodation' is visible for both case studies, while increasingly more accommodation obligations have been formulated at the European level. For example, in cross-border abortion cases and cross-border reproductive care (CBRC) cases, information about foreign treatment options and – in any case in cross-border abortion cases – follow-up care must be provided and States must 'facilitate' the entry and residence of stable same-sex partners of migrating EU citizens. That accommodation is gaining ground may be explained by an increased acknowledgement of the fact that in cross-border situations different interests are at stake, or in any case that these interests are weighted differently in cross-border situations. This holds particularly true in cross-border situations where individual burdens exist, and even more so when a child is involved whose interests must prevail.

One of the general observations made in Chapter 14, is that despite limited competences at EU level and the granting of a wide margin of appreciation by the ECtHR in many of the morally sensitive issues addressed in the research, it cannot be denied that there is increasing (indirect) European standard-setting in these areas, both in internal and cross-border situations. This also has implications for (the variety in) national moral choices throughout the European Union. The 'in for a penny, in for a pound' approach of the European Courts as described above, (potentially) has particular implications. It namely risks becoming an 'all or nothing' approach, and may in this way drive a wedge between the European States. Further, cross-border movement in itself, as well legal responses thereto – whether deliberately chosen by States or imposed on them by European law – also has implications for (the variety in) national choices in morally sensitive issues in the European Union. On the one hand, cross-border movement may in principle provide a means to uphold national standards for internal situations and thus (a variety in) moral choices. This especially holds true if an outsourcing approach is taken under European law. However, where other legal responses to such cross-border movement are dictated by European law, such an effect of cross-border movement may be diminished. This applies in particular where States are, under European law required to recognise legal effects of, and thus accommodate, cross-border movement. As a consequence thereof, they may feel pressurised to adapt their national standard-setting in these areas to the standards they are bound to apply in cross-border situations. This also implies that where an outsourcing approach is applied, it is likely that States with less permissive regimes remain on their side of the moral spectrum, while accommodation obligations and concerns about implications of cross-border movement, may prompt States to move to or towards the more permissive of this spectrum.

Chapter 14 furthermore observes that in many situations complex balancing exercises and ethical objections to certain practices have been outpaced by real time developments. Even if national legislatures desired so on ethical or moral grounds, they have not been able to prevent certain matters from becoming reality and, correspondingly, from becoming facts of law. States may ban or limit certain practices deemed undesirable within their own jurisdictions, but to prevent people from going abroad for such practices has proven much harder. As a result it has been even more so in cross-border situations that reality has outpaced and dictated the law.

The final chapter is concluded with the observation that in cross-border situations in fact a unique realm of law applies. Those who cross borders (within the EU) enter a special dimension of law that encompasses, apart from EU free movement law and Private International Law, also other areas of law, most profoundly human rights law.

Executive Summary (in Dutch)

Moreel gevoelige onderwerpen en grensoverschrijdend verkeer in de EU

Voortplantingsvraagstukken en wettelijke erkenning van relaties tussen personen van gelijk geslacht

Binnen de Europese Unie (EU) bestaat aanzienlijke verscheidenheid ten aanzien van moreel gevoelige onderwerpen als abortus, kunstmatige voortplanting, draagmoederschap en wettelijke erkenning van relaties tussen personen van gelijk geslacht. Terwijl in de twintigste eeuw steeds meer bevoegdheden zijn overgedragen naar supranationale organisaties zoals de EU, is een aantal bevoegdheden van oudsher bij de staten gebleven. Voornoemde moreel gevoelige onderwerpen betreffen bij uitstek rechtsgebieden waarbinnen normstelling eerst en vooral op het nationale niveau plaatsvindt. Het wordt veelal geacht aan staten te zijn om te beslissen of zij – bijvoorbeeld – abortus op niet-medische gronden of draagmoederschap toestaan en of koppels van gelijk geslacht kunnen trouwen of kinderen kunnen adopteren.

Hoewel er geen sterke mate van Europese regulering op deze terreinen bestaat en bovendien de bestaande diversiteit over het algemeen op Europees niveau wordt erkend, is er niettemin een zeker potentieel voor Europese regulering. De EU heeft namelijk bevoegdheden op terreinen die dicht raken aan en soms zelfs nauw verbonden zijn met voorplantingskwesties en wettelijke erkenning van relaties tussen personen van gelijk geslacht. Bovendien vallen diverse van deze moreel gevoelige onderwerpen binnen de reikwijdte van het Europees Verdrag voor de Rechten van de Mens (EVRM), bijvoorbeeld onder het recht op respect voor privéleven van artikel 8 EVRM. Er is dus (potentieel voor) (indirecte) Europese invloed op deze terreinen.

Grensoverschrijdend verkeer binnen de EU voegt bovendien een nieuwe dimensie toe aan dit in zichzelf al complexe beeld. Grensoverschrijdend verkeer is een gegeven binnen de EU: mensen bewegen zich door de EU om diverse redenen, niet zelden economische redenen. Dergelijke mobiliteit wordt mogelijk gemaakt en gestimuleerd door de EU vrij verkeersregels, die onder meer het vrij verkeer van personen en de vrijheid diensten te ontvangen in andere EU lidstaten omvatten. Onderling afwijkende regimes in bovengenoemde moreel gevoelige onderwerpen kunnen dergelijk verkeer hinderen; zij kunnen mensen beperken in hun mobiliteit of hen afschrikken gebruik te maken van hun vrij verkeersrechten. Koppels van gelijk geslacht kunnen bijvoorbeeld ontmoedigd zijn om naar een andere lidstaat te verhuizen als zij daar geen mogelijkheid hebben tot wettelijke erkenning van hun relatie. Tegelijkertijd kunnen verschillen tussen de regimes van landen op deze terreinen ook juist de directe aanleiding zijn voor grensoverschrijdend verkeer, omdat mensen uit staten met restrictievere regimes de mogelijkheden, rechten en aanspraken van lidstaten met meer liberale regimes wensen te genieten. Hier kan bijvoorbeeld gedacht worden aan vrouwen uit lidstaten met strenge abortuswetgeving die voor een abortus naar een lidstaat met liberalere regelgeving gaan.

Dergelijk grensoverschrijdend verkeer en de bestaande beperkingen daarop maken niet alleen de verschillen tussen de staten op deze terreinen zichtbaar, zij impliceren onder meer ook dat staten in toenemende mate geconfronteerd worden met (de gevolgen en effecten van) de regimes van andere staten. Dit gebeurt bijvoorbeeld omdat koppels van gelijk geslacht die in de ene EU lidstaat wonen, om erkenning vragen van hun in een andere staat gesloten huwelijk, of omdat vrouwen of koppels die een bepaalde reproductieve behandeling hebben ondergaan in een andere lidstaat, terwijl die behandeling in eigen land wettelijk niet is toegestaan, bij thuiskomst om vergoeding vragen van de kosten van die behandeling onder de ziektekostenverzekering. Dergelijke confrontaties vragen doorgaans om een (juridisch) antwoord van de betrokken staten, of ze nu als thuisland of als gastland of beide fungeren.

Dit proefschrift verkent deze grensoverschrijdend verkeersdimensie van moreel gevoelige onderwerpen in de Europese Unie. Het geeft een overzicht van trends en ontwikkelingen in nationaal en Europees recht in moreel gevoelige kwesties en geeft inzicht in de belangen die daarbij spelen en de dynamieken die zich in zowel interne als grensoverschrijdende situaties voordoen.

Twee thematische casestudy's en vijf rechtsstelsels

De basis van dit onderzoek bestaat uit twee thematische casestudy's: één over voortplantingsvraagstukken (Casestudy I) en één over wettelijke erkenning van relaties tussen personen van gelijk geslacht (Casestudy II). Deze casestudy's concentreren zich op vijf rechtsstelsels; drie nationale stelsels – Ierland, Duitsland en Nederland – en twee Europese stelsels of systemen, namelijk de EU en het EVRM. De casestudy's zijn gekozen omdat zij bij uitstek moreel gevoelige onderwerpen en dus politiek gevoelige kwesties betreffen, ten aanzien waarvan de EU lidstaten lange tijd verschillende posities hebben ingenomen en dat nog steeds deden toen dit onderzoek werd aangevangen in 2009 en (gedeeltelijk) tevens toen het werd afgesloten in juli 2014. Bovendien gaat het niet 'slechts' om moreel gevoelige kwesties, het betreffen ook terreinen ten aanzien waarvan mensenrechtelijke aanspraken kunnen worden gemaakt en die – belangrijk gelet op de focus van dit onderzoek – een evidente grensoverschrijdend verkeersdimensie hebben. De keuze voor de drie nationale rechtstelsels is onder meer ingegeven door het feit dat zij een zekere spreiding vertegenwoordigen in benaderingen ten aanzien van voortplantingsvraagstukken en wettelijke erkenning van relaties tussen personen van gelijk geslacht en omdat deze landen verschillende (constitutionele) profielen hebben.

De twee casestudy's hebben dezelfde opbouw. Elk bestaat uit zes hoofdstukken: vijf die de regelgeving in de vijf geselecteerde jurisdicties beschrijven (het EVRM, de EU, Duitsland, Ierland en Nederland respectievelijk) en één met conclusies voor de casestudy.

Casestudy I – Voortplantingsvraagstukken

Casestudy I over voortplantingsvraagstukken omvat drie onderwerpen: abortus, medische geassisteerde voortplanting en draagmoederschap. Voor ieder van deze onderwerpen onderzoeken de vijf basishoofdstukken van Casestudy I (hoofdstukken 2 tot en met 6) voor de betreffende Europese en nationale stelsels welke regelgeving er al dan niet bestaat en hoe deze zich over de tijd ontwikkeld heeft. Ter vergroting van het begrip van deze regelgeving en – waar relevant – de debatten in politiek en de rechtswetenschap over deze vaak controversiële onderwerpen, wordt allereerst een algemeen (constitutioneel) kader geschetst. Een korte inleiding wordt gegeven op prominente rechten in de relevante rechtsstelsels (bijvoorbeeld de bescherming van het ongeboren kind in het Ierse recht), alsook op een selectie van thema's en – in het geval van de EU – bevoegdheden die van centraal belang zijn in de casestudy. Vervolgens zet ieder van deze hoofdstukken uiteen of de relevante voortplantingsbehandelingen wettelijk zijn toegestaan en gereguleerd en zo ja, onder welke voorwaarden er een recht op toegang tot deze behandelingen bestaat. Bij de bespreking van de nationale regelgeving ten aanzien van draagmoederschap wordt ook besproken of en in hoeverre wensouders ouderschapsrechten kunnen krijgen over een kind dat in het kader van een draagmoederschapsovereenkomst is geboren. De bespreking van regulering van medische geassisteerde voortplantingsbehandelingen in de vijf rechtsstelsels omvat een viertal onderwerpen: donatie van voortplantingscellen en embryo's, preïmplantatie genetische diagnostiek (PGD), geslachtsselectie en vitrificatie van eicellen.

De analyse van de interne situatie voor ieder van de rechtstelsels biedt inzicht in het soort belangen en overwegingen dat in parlementaire debatten en rechtspraak speelt of heeft gespeeld en in de wijze waarop verandering is of zou kunnen worden doorgevoerd. Het legt ook de basis voor de analyse van de grensoverschrijdende situatie, die vervolgens in ieder van deze hoofdstukken wordt uitgevoerd. Laatstgenoemde analyse begint – waar voorhanden – met enige cijfers over de omvang van het relevante grensoverschrijdend verkeer in de betreffende jurisdictie. Vervolgens onderzoekt ieder van de vijf basishoofdstukken voor het betreffende rechtsstelsel hoe is en wordt omgegaan met grensoverschrijdende situaties in voortplantingsvraagstukken en hoe de stelsels zich in dit opzicht tot elkaar verhouden. Daarbij worden, onder meer, de internationaalprivaatrechtelijke regimes en de (nationale implementatie van) de EU vrij verkeersregels bestudeerd, teneinde vragen te beantwoorden als de vraag of buitenlandse geboorteakten worden erkend in internationale draagmoederschapszaken en of vrouwen die in een andere lidstaat een abortus wensen te ondergaan recht hebben op informatie over dergelijke abortusdiensten, alsook een recht op vervolgbehandeling na terugkeer naar hun eigen staat.

Hoofdstuk 7 formuleert conclusies voor Casestudy I. Het ontwaart trends in regulering van voortplantingsvraagstukken en in wetgevingsprocessen en rechtspraak. Zo wordt in hoofdstuk 7 vastgesteld dat belangenafwegingen bij voortplantingsvraagstukken vaak uiteenlopende uitkomsten hebben gehad in de drie bestudeerde staten en dat de processen in wetgeving en rechtspraak in de staten op verschillende wijze vorm hebben gekregen. Daarnaast laat Europees recht (EU-recht en het EVRM) uitdrukkelijk ruimte voor dergelijke diversiteit in de regulering van voortplantingsvraagstukken. Staten wordt ruimte gelaten om eigen principiële keuzes te maken in deze moreel gevoelige en ethische kwesties en ze zijn vrij om bepaalde praktijken te verbieden zolang ze de relevante belangen hebben meegewogen in hun besluitvorming en zolang hun principiële keuzes consistent zijn. Zodra een staat echter besluit op dit gebied te gaan reguleren, dan moet hij ook een effectieve bescherming van de relevante rechten en aanspraken waarborgen. Dit betekent dat staten moeten garanderen dat de toepasselijke procedures een zorgvuldige besluitvorming mogelijk maken. Behalve dergelijke verschillen zijn er ook overeenkomsten in de wijze waarop met voorplantingsvraagstukken is en wordt omgegaan in de verschillende rechtsstelsels. Over het algemeen zijn over de tijd steeds meer praktijken en behandelingen gelegaliseerd en gereguleerd, of zijn daartoe in ieder geval initiatieven genomen. Tevens is een geleidelijke ontwikkeling naar een (meer) centrale rol voor het belang van het kind duidelijk zichtbaar, hoewel in sommige gevallen de opvattingen over wat dit belang precies vereist over de tijd zijn gewijzigd. Bovendien is een ontwikkeling zichtbaar waarbij voortplantingsvraagstukken worden beoordeeld met veel aandacht voor de bijzondere omstandigheden van het geval. Zowel op Europees als nationaal niveau is er in toenemende mate aandacht voor procedures die zorgvuldige belangenafwegingen in voortplantingskwesties mogelijk maken.

Op basis van de analyse van hoofdstukken 2 tot en met 6 identificeert hoofdstuk 7 vervolgens vier categorieën 'legal responses' op grensoverschrijdend verkeer in voortplantingsvraagstukken. De eerste is het 'afweren' ('warding off') van de (gevolgen van) grensoverschrijdend verkeer, waarbij staten mensen ontmoedigen naar een andere staat te gaan of naar het eigen land te komen. Dergelijk afweren kan verschillende vormen aannemen, variërend van reisverboden tot – in internationale draagmoederschapszaken – het niet-erkennen van het in een ander land gevestigde juridisch ouderschap van wensouders. Een tweede 'legal response', accommodatie ('accommodation'), vormt het spiegelbeeld van afweren. Deze doet zich bijvoorbeeld voor als staten ervoor kiezen informatie over buitenlandse abortusdiensten te verschaffen en medische vervolgbehandeling aan te bieden. Ten derde kunnen staten hun eigen op interne situaties toepasselijke regelgeving ook aanpassen aan die van een andere staat of andere staten waarnaartoe grensoverschrijdend verkeer plaatsvindt ('adaptation'). Tot slot heeft grensoverschrijdend verkeer in voortplantingszaken in bepaalde gevallen ertoe geleid dat staten de bescherming van belangen die bij voortplantingsvraagstukken spelen, kunnen uitbesteden naar andere staten ('outsourcing'). Het EHRM heeft in enkele zaken namelijk geoordeeld dat buitenlandse behandelmogelijkheden bijdroegen aan de rechtvaardiging van de strenge regelgeving van een land.

Voor ieder van deze 'legal responses' analyseert hoofdstuk 7 in welke mate zij verenigbaar zijn met Europees recht of daar zelfs door worden voorgeschreven. Er is bijvoorbeeld gebleken dat het afweren van grensoverschrijdend verkeer door middel van het niet-erkennen van de juridische gevolgen van buitenlandse behandelopties of door middel van het verbieden van informatie over buitenlandse behandelmogelijkheden niet gemakkelijk gerechtvaardigd kan worden onder Europees recht, terwijl weigering van vervolgbehandeling bij terugkomst ook problematisch kan zijn. Tevens onderzoekt hoofdstuk 7 hoe de verschillend 'legal responses' zich tot elkaar verhouden en wat de implicaties van elke categorie van 'legal responses' zijn of zouden kunnen zijn voor de betrokken staten, alsmede voor de betrokken individuen.

Casestudy II – Wettelijke erkenning van relaties tussen personen van gelijk geslacht

Hoofdstukken 8 tot en met 12 van Casestudy II brengen in kaart wat de vijf bestudeerde rechtsstelsels bepalen ten aanzien van wettelijke erkenning van relaties tussen personen van gelijk geslacht. Daarbij is een eerste centrale vraag of koppels van gelijk geslacht (een recht op) toegang tot een vorm van wettelijke erkenning van hun relatie hebben (huwelijk of geregistreerd partnerschap) en zo ja, wat dit behelst. Ten tweede gaat de casestudy in op de ouderschapsrechten van koppels van gelijk geslacht. Daarbij worden verschillende adoptievormen behandeld, namelijk stiefouderadoptie (adoptie door de partner van de juridische en genetische ouder van een kind), 'successieve adoptie' (waarbij een adoptiekind wordt geadopteerd door de partner van de adoptieouder) en gezamenlijke adoptie. Tevens worden ouderschap van rechtswege en toegang tot medische geassisteerde voortplanting voor koppels van gelijk geslacht besproken.

De vijf basishoofdstukken van deze casestudy hebben dezelfde opbouw als hoofdstukken 2 tot en met 6 van Casestudy I (zie hierboven). Zij beginnen dus met een algemeen (constitutioneel) kader, gevolgd door een bespreking van het interne, respectievelijk het grensoverschrijdende plaatje. Net als in Casestudy I worden daarbij – waar relevant – ook de debatten in politiek en rechtswetenschap betrokken.

Hoofdstuk 13 concludeert voor Casestudy II dat ten aanzien van wettelijke erkenning van relaties tussen personen van gelijk geslacht binnen de Europese Unie de staten het voortouw hebben genomen en niet zozeer Europese instanties. Nationale wetgevers en bestuursorganen hebben de toon gezet en 'Europa' heeft over het algemeen slechts gevolgd. De Europese Hoven (het EU HvJ en het EHRM) hebben soms wel prikjes uitgedeeld naar de nationale wetgever of rechter, maar dit was over het algemeen enkel het geval in situaties waar de eerste (principiële) stappen in de richting van wettelijke erkenning reeds op nationaal niveau waren gezet. In de rechtspraak van het EHRM heeft burgerlijke status vaak als vehikel gefungeerd voor ongelijke behandeling van koppels van gelijk geslacht en koppels van verschillend geslacht. Slechts in gevallen waar geen sprake was van een 'speciale wettelijke status', heeft het EHRM een strenge toets toegepast.

Traditionele noties van het huwelijk en het gezin hebben in alle drie de staten aan gewicht ingeboet, hoewel ze niet geheel zijn verlaten. Bovendien geniet het huwelijk onder het EVRM nog altijd sterke bescherming. Daarnaast is de toegenomen erkenning en juridische bescherming van *de facto* gezinsleven gepaard gegaan met het aanvaarden van biologische verschillen tussen koppels van verschillend geslacht en koppels van gelijk geslacht en tussen koppels bestaande uit twee vrouwen en koppels bestaande uit twee mannen als rechtvaardiging voor bepaalde verschillen in behandeling van deze groepen ten aanzien van ouderschapsrechten. Ongelijke behandeling van koppels van gelijk geslacht komt dus nog steeds voor, maar er heeft een verschuiving plaatsgevonden van meer moreel beladen rechtvaardigingsgronden naar meer moreel neutrale gronden.

Over het algemeen is een gestage ontwikkeling zichtbaar naar toenemende bescherming van LHBT-rechten en zodoende ook naar toenemende wettelijke erkenning van relaties tussen personen van gelijk geslacht. Dergelijke verandering is in de meeste gevallen langzaam en geleidelijk doorgevoerd, al zijn er ook uitzonderingen van veel snellere ontwikkelingen. Het valt te verwachten dat deze lijn in de toekomst wordt doorgezet. Mogelijk neemt 'Europa' in sommige opzichten een meer proactieve houding. In ieder geval ligt het in de lijn der verwachtingen dat de Europese Hoven prikjes zullen blijven uitdelen aan nationale rechters en wetgevers in dit proces van toenemende gelijkstelling van de wettelijke positie van koppels van gelijk geslacht met die van koppels van verschillend geslacht.

Ten aanzien van grensoverschrijdende situaties concludeert hoofdstuk 13 dat zich in wezen twee categorieën van 'legal responses' op grensoverschrijdend verkeer voordoen in Casestudy II, namelijk 'afweren' en 'accommodatie'. In hun uiterste vorm zijn deze in de context van deze casestudy onverenigbaar. Echter, uit de casestudy blijkt dat verschillende niveaus van afweren en van accommodatie mogelijk zijn. In sommige gevallen hebben staten gekozen voor gedeeltelijke of voorwaardelijke accommodatie in hun omgang met grensoverschrijdend verkeer in de context van Casestudy II. Zo erkennen Ierland en Duitsland huwelijken tussen personen van gelijk geslacht enkel tot op het niveau van geregistreerde partnerschappen ('downgrading'), terwijl buitenlandse geregistreerde partnerschappen alleen worden erkend indien ze aan bepaalde criteria voldoen. Andere categorieën van 'legal responses' op grensoverschrijdend verkeer die zich – hoewel slechts in beperkte mate – in deze casestudy hebben voorgedaan zijn aanpassing en terugtrekking ('backing out'). Met terugtrekking wordt gedoeld op de situatie waarbij vrees dat andere landen de keuzes van de nationale wetgever niet zullen aanvaarden of erkennen, wordt gepresenteerd als argument tegen het toekennen van bepaalde rechten aan koppels van gelijk geslacht.

Op vergelijkbare wijze als in hoofdstuk 7, onderzoekt hoofdstuk 13 vervolgens hoe de verschillende 'legal responses' zich tot elkaar verhouden en wat de implicaties van iedere categorie van 'legal responses' zijn of zouden kunnen zijn voor de betrokken staten en individuen. Hoofdstuk 13 concludeert dat regelgeving op Europees niveau voor grensoverschrijdend verkeer in de context van deze casestudy tot dusver redelijk beperkt is gebleven. Uit de EU Vrij verkeersrichtlijn volgen wel enkele minimumverplichtingen ten aanzien van toegang en verblijf van partners van gelijk geslacht van EU-burgers, maar in het bijzonder ten aanzien van de wettelijke positie van deze koppels nadat toegang en verblijf zijn toegekend, bestaan er vooralsnog diverse open vragen. Hierbij zijn rechtspraak van het EU HvJ en/of verdere handreikingen van de EU-wetgever over de beoordelingsruimte die staten al dan niet genieten in deze kwesties, zeer gewenst.

Conclusies

Het afsluitende hoofdstuk, hoofdstuk 14, bevat een synthese van de bevindingen van hoofdstukken 7 en 13, alsmede een aantal observaties over moreel gevoelige onderwerpen en grensoverschrijdend verkeer binnen de EU meer in het algemeen. Er worden parallellen getrokken en trends onderscheiden ten aanzien van belangenafwegingen en processen in wetgeving en rechtspraak in deze moreel gevoelige onderwerpen. Bijvoorbeeld, terwijl in de vijf rechtsstelsels die in dit onderzoek zijn bestudeerd, over het algemeen dezelfde belangen zijn erkend in de betreffende casestudy's, zit er verschil in het gewicht dat daaraan wordt of is toegekend in de verschillende stelsels. Het belang van het kind heeft in beide casestudy's een (prominente) rol gespeeld en uit beide casestudy's is gebleken dat betrokkenheid van het belang van het (toekomstige) kind een cruciaal verschil maakt voor belangenafwegingen, met name in grensoverschrijdende situaties, zoals bij internationaal draagmoedershap. Uit beide casestudy's komt bovendien een beginnende trend naar voren tot sterkere bescherming van relatief concrete belangen zoals het belang van het kind, in vergelijking met meer abstracte belangen als 'het traditionele huwelijksinstituut'. Deze ontwikkeling kan ook worden geduid als een verschuiving van waarden die sterk in de maatschappij en het recht van een specifieke staat zijn verankerd naar minder beladen waarden die (meer) algemeen gedeeld en transnationaal zijn. Ten aanzien van de daadwerkelijke belangenafwegingen is een andere trend dat *de facto* situaties, bijvoorbeeld *de facto* gezinsleven, meer erkenning krijgen. Daarnaast lijkt er in toenemende mate aandacht te zijn voor belangenafwegingen in concrete, individuele gevallen.

De Europese jurisdicties hebben over het algemeen een behoorlijk reactieve, pragmatische en incrementalistische benadering gekozen in moreel gevoelige onderwerpen. Met name de benadering van beide Europese Hoven kan in sommige gevallen zelfs omschreven worden als 'ontwijkend'. Niettemin hebben beide Hoven een vergelijkbare redeneringswijze toegepast, die ook wel wordt geduid met de term 'vastklikmethode' ('in for a penny, in for a pound approach'). Dit komt erop neer dat staten mogen beslissen of ze op deze terreinen een bepaald recht of een bepaalde aanspraak op nationaal niveau toekennen, maar zodra ze inderdaad besluiten dat recht of die aanspraak toe te kennen en ze daarbij handelen binnen de reikwijdte van het Europees recht, moeten ze dat ook doen op een wijze die aan Europese standaarden voldoet. Staten worden dus gehouden de gevolgen van hun keuzes in moreel gevoelige onderwerpen te dragen. Daarnaast komen in de rechtspraak van het EHRM ten aanzien van beide casestudy's variaties op de 'margin of appreciation' doctrine voor. Zij betreffen met name het gebruik van op consensus gebaseerde overwegingen bij bepaling van de omvang van deze beoordelingsruimte.

Eén van de algemene observaties van hoofdstuk 14 is dat ondanks dat de EU beperkte bevoegdheden heeft en het EHRM een wijde 'margin of appreciation' toekent in veel van de moreel gevoelige onderwerpen die in dit onderzoek centraal staan, niet kan worden ontkend dat er in toenemende mate (indirecte) Europese regulering bestaat op deze terreinen, zowel voor interne als voor grensoverschrijdende situaties. Dit heeft ook gevolgen voor de verscheidenheid aan nationale morele keuzes binnen de Europese Unie. De vastklikmethode van de Europese Hoven, zoals hierboven omschreven, heeft (potentieel) in het bijzonder gevolgen voor die verscheidenheid. Deze draagt namelijk het risico met zich een 'alles of niets' benadering te worden en kan op die manier een wig drijven tussen de Europese staten. Bovendien hebben grensoverschrijdend verkeer en de 'legal responses' daarop – of ze nu bewust door staten gekozen zijn of aan hen zijn opgelegd door Europees recht – ook gevolgen voor de (verscheidenheid in) morele keuzes. In beginsel kan grensoverschrijdend verkeer ertoe bijdragen dat nationale regelgeving voor interne situaties – en daarmee dus (een verscheidenheid in) morele keuzes – gehandhaafd kunnen worden. Dit geldt met name indien op Europees niveau een uitbestedingsbenadering (zie hierboven) is gekozen. Waar Europees recht daarentegen andere 'legal responses' voorschrijft, kan een dergelijk effect van grensoverschrijdend verkeer worden afgezwakt. Dit gaat met name op indien staten onder Europees recht verplicht worden de juridische implicaties van grensoverschrijdend verkeer te erkennen en dus dat verkeer te accommoderen. In dat geval kunnen zij zich namelijk gedwongen voelen hun nationale regelgeving voor interne situaties aan te passen aan de normen die zij onder Europees recht op grensoverschrijdende situaties moeten toepassen. Dit impliceert tevens dat waar een uitbestedingsbenadering wordt toegepast, staten aan de restrictievere kant van het morele spectrum geneigd te zijn daar te blijven, terwijl accommodatieverplichtingen en zorgen over de juridische gevolgen van grensoverschrijdend verkeer staten ertoe kunnen aanzetten te verschuiven naar de liberalere kant van dit spectrum.

Hoofdstuk 14 concludeert verder dat in veel situaties complexe belangenafwegingen en ethische bezwaren tegen bepaalde praktijken zijn of worden ingehaald door de realiteit. Zelfs waar nationale wetgevers dat wensten op ethische of morele gronden, zijn zij niet in staat gebleken te voorkomen dat sommige zaken realiteit en dientengevolge rechtsfeiten werden. Staten kunnen sommige praktijken die zij ongewenst achten wel verbieden of beperken binnen de eigen rechtsorde, maar voorkomen dat mensen daarvoor naar het buitenland gaan is veel moeilijker gebleken.

Daardoor geldt des te meer in grensoverschrijdende situaties dat de realiteit het recht heeft ingehaald en voorgeschreven.

Het slothoofdstuk rondt af met de observatie dat in grensoverschrijdende situaties in feite een uniek rechtsdomein van toepassing is. Zij die grenzen oversteken (binnen de EU), betreden een speciale dimensie van het recht die, behalve de EU vrij verkeersregels en Internationaal privaatrecht ook andere rechtsgebieden omvat, eerst en vooral de mensenrechten.

Bibliography

Antokolskaia et al. 2014: M.V. Antokolskaia et al., *Meeroudergezag: een oplossing voor kinderen met meer dan twee ouders? Een empirisch en rechtsvergelijkend onderzoek* [Parental authority by multiple parents: a solution for children who have more than two parents? An empirical and comparative legal study] (Den Haag, Boom Juridische uitgevers 2014)

Antoni 2010: M. Antoni, 'Art 6 [Schutz von Ehe und Familie, nichteheliche Kinder]' ['Art. 6 [Protection of marriage and family, children born out of wedlock]'], in: D. Hömig (ed.) *Grundgesetz für die Bundesrepublik Deutschland* [Constitution for the Federal Republic of Germany], 9th edn. (Baden-Baden, Nomos Verlagsgesellschaft 2010) pp. 110–120

Asscher and Koops 2010: E. Asscher and B.-J. Koops, 'The right not to know and preimplantation genetic diagnosis for Huntington's disease', 36 *J Med Ethics* (2010) pp. 30–33

Bacik 1997: I. Bacik, 'Guest Editorial', 3 *Medico-Legal Journal of Ireland* (1997) pp. 1–2

Badura 2014: P. Badura 'GG Art 6' ['Art. 6 Basic Law'] in: R. Herzorg et al. (eds.), *Maunz und Dürig Grundgesetz-Kommentar* [Maunz and Dürig Commentary to the Basic Law], 71st edn. (München, Verlag Beck 2014)

Bamforth 2011: N. Bamforth, 'Families But Not (Yet) Marriages? Same-Sex Partners and the Developing European Convention 'Margin of Appreciation', 23 *Child and Family Law Quarterly* (2011) pp. 128–143

Baratta 2007: R. Baratta, 'Problematic elements of an implicit rule providing for mutual recognition of personal and family status in the EC', *IPRax* (2007) pp. 4–7

Barnard 2007: C. Barnard, *The substantive law of the EU. The four freedoms*, 2nd ed (Oxford, Oxford University Press 2007)

Beckhove 2009: E. Beckhove, 'Die Kostenübernahme für künstliche Befruchtungen – Fallgruppen' ['Reimbursement of artificial insemination – categories of cases'], *NJOZ* (2009) pp. 1465–1473

Beckmann 1998: R. Beckmann, 'Der "Wegfall" der embryopathischen Indikation' ['The "abolition" of de embryopatic indication'], *MedR* (1998) pp. 155–161

Beckmann 2009: R. Beckman 'Präimplantationsdiagnostik und Embryonenschutzgesetz, Zugleich Besprechung von LG Berlin' ['Preimplantation genetic diagnosis and the Embryo Protection Act, as well as case-note to LG Berlin'], *ZfL* (2009) pp. 125–131

Beers, van 2010: B.C. van Beers, *Persoon en lichaam in het recht. Menselijke waardigheid en zelfbeschikking in het tijdperk van biotechnologie* [Person and body under the law. Human dignity and personal autonomy in the era of biotechnology] (Den Haag, Boom 2009)

Beers, van 2012A: B. van Beers, 'Het Europese Hof van Justitie over de vermarkting van menselijke embryo's. Van economische naar ook bio-ethische integratie binnen de EU?' ['The European Court of Justice on the commercialisation of human embryos. From economic to also bio-ethical integration in the EU?'], 37 *NTM/NJCM-Bull.* (2012) pp. 242–256

Beers, van 2012B: B. van Beers, 'Case-note to ECtHR 3 November 2011, *S.H. a.o v. Austria*, no. 57813/00', 13 *European Human Rights Cases* 2012/38 (in Dutch)

Belew 2003–2004: K.L. Belew, 'Stem Cell Division: Abortion Law and Its Influence on the Adoption of Radically Different Embryonic Stem Cell Legislation in the United States, the United Kingdom and Germany', 39 *Texas international Law Journal* (2003–2004) pp. 479–520

Bell 2001: M. Bell, 'Sexual Orientation Discrimination in Employment; An Evolving Role for the European Union', in: R. Wintemute and M. Andenæs, *Legal Recognition of Same-Sex Partnerships, A Study of National, European and International Law*, Oxford-Portland Oregon: Hart Publishing 2001, pp. 653–676

Bell 2004: M. Bell, 'Holding Back the Tide? Cross-Border Recognition of Same-Sex Partnerships within the European Union', 12 *European Review of Private Law* (2004) pp. 613–632

Bell 2011: M. Bell, 'The Principle of Equal Treatment; widening and deepening', in: P. Craig and G. De Búrca, *The evolution of EU Law*, 2nd edn. (Oxford, Oxford University Press 2011) pp. 611–639

Benicke 2013: C. Benicke, 'Kollisionsrechtliche Fragen der Leihmutterschaft' ['Conflict-of-laws questions in respect of surrogacy'], *StAZ* (2013) pp. 101–114

Ben-Naf'tali and Canor 2008: O. Ben-Naf'tali and I. Canor, 'Case note to Evans v. United Kingdom (2007)', *American Journal of International Law* (2008) pp. 102–132

Berg, van den and Buijssen 2004: M.F.M. van den Berg and C. Buijssen, 'Hoogtechnologisch draagmoederschap', ['High-technological surrogacy'] 79 *Nederlands Juristenblad* (2004) pp. 724–728

Berer 2013: M. Berer, 'Termination of pregnancy as emergency obstetric care: the interpretation of Catholic health policy and the consequences for pregnant women. An analysis of the death of Savita Halappanavar in Ireland and similar cases', 41 *Reproductive Health Matters* (2013) pp. 9–17

Besselink 2012: L. Besselink, 'Case C-208/09, Ilonka Sayn-Wittgenstein v. Landeshauptmann von Wien, judgment of the Court (second chamber) of 22 December 2010', 49 *CMLRev* (2012) pp. 671–693

Besson 2008: S. Besson, 'The Reception Process in Ireland and the United Kingdom', in: H. Keller and A. Stone Sweet (eds.), *A Europe of Rights. The impact of the ECHR on National Legal Systems* (Oxford, Oxford University Press) pp. 31–106

Bissels and Lützeler 2010: See A. Bissels and M. Lützeler, 'Aktuelle Rechtsprechung zum Allgemeinen Gleichbehandlungsgesetz 2009/2010 (Teil 2)' ['Recent case-law on the General Equal Treatment Act 2009–2010 (Part 2)'], *BB* (2010) pp. 1725–1733

Blair 2000: M. Blair, 'Unveiling Our Heritage: A Comparative Examination of Access by Adopted Persons and Their Families to Identifying and Non–identifying Information', 3 *Irish Journal of Family Law* (2000) pp. 10–23

Blekxtoon and Ballegooij, van 2005: R. Blekxtoon and W. van Ballegooij, *Handbook on the European Arrest Warrant* (The Hague, T.M.C. Asser Press 2005)

Blyth 2010: E. Blyth, 'Fertility patients' experiences of cross-border reproductive care', 94 *Fertility and Sterility* (2010) pp. e11-e14

Bockel, van and Wattel 2013: W.B. van Bockel and P.J. Wattel, 'New Wine into Old Wineskins: the Scope of the Charter of Fundamental Rights of the EU after Åkerberg Fransson', 38 *European Law Review* (2013) pp. 866–883

Boele-Woelki 1999: K. Boele-Woelki, 'De prijs van het homohuwelijk' ['The price of gay marriage'], *Tijdschrift voor Familie- en Jeugdrecht* (1999) p. 113

Boele-Woelki et al. 2006: K. Boele-Woelki et al., *Huwelijk of geregistreerd partnerschap? Een evaluatie van de Wet openstelling huwelijk en de Wet geregistreerd partnerschap in opdracht van het Ministerie van Justitie* [Marriage or registered partnership? An evaulation of the Act opening up marriage and the Registered Partnership Act by order of the Ministry of Justice] (The Hague, WODC, Ministerie van Justitie 2006)

Boele-Woelki et al. 2007, K. Boele-Woelki et al., 'The evaluation of same-sex marriages and registered partnerships in the Netherlands', 8 *Yearbook of Private International Law* (2007) pp. 27–35

Boele-Woelki et al. 2011: K. Boele-Woelki et al., *Draagmoederschap en illegale opneming van kinderen* [Surrogacy and unlawful placement of children] (Utrecht, Utrecht Centre for European research into Family Law 2011), online available at: www.wodc.nl/onderzoeksdatabase/draagmoederschap.aspx?cp=44&cs=6837, visited June 2014

Boele-Woelki and Tang, van der 1990: K. Boele-Woelki and P.C. Tange, 'Geen huwelijk tussen personen van hetzelfde geslacht' ['No marriage between partners of the same sex'], *NJCM-Bulletin* 1990, pp. 456–460

Bogdan 2003: M. Bogdan, 'Registered Partnerships and EC law', in: K. Boele-Woelki and A. Fuchs (eds.), *Legal recognition of same-sex couples in Europe* (Antwerp, Intersentia 2003) pp. 171–177

Bogdan 2004: M. Bogdan, 'Some Reflections on the Treatment of Dutch Same-sex Marriages in European and Private International Law', in: T. Einhorn and K. Siehr (eds.), *Intercontinental cooperation through private international law: essays in memory of Peter E. Nygh* (The Hague, T.M.C. Asser Press 2004) pp. 25–35

Bogdan 2009: M. Bogdan, 'Private International Law Aspects of the Introduction of Same-Sex Marriages in Sweden', 78 *Nordic Journal of International Law* (2009) pp. 253–261

Bokelmann and Bokelmann 2003: V. Bokelmann and M. Bokelmann, *Zur Lage der für andere übernommen Mutterschaft in Deutschland, Rechtsvergleich mit Reformvorschlägen* [On the situation of surrogate motherhood in Germany, Comparitive legal research with proposals for reform] (Frankfurt am Main, Peter Lang 2003)

Bonini-Baraldi 2006: M. Bonini-Baraldi, 'The Employment Equality Directive and other aspects of European Law', in: C. Waaldijk and M. Bonini-Baraldi, *Sexual orientation discrimination in the European Union, National laws and the Employment Equality Directive* (The Hague, TMC Asser Press 2006) pp. 5–59

Bonnet 2004: V. Bonnet, 'L'accouchement sous X et la Cour Européenne des Droits de l'Homme (à propos de l'arrêt *Odièvre c. la France* du 13 février 2003)', 58 *Revue trimestrielle des droits de l'homme* (2004) pp. 406–421

Borg-Barthet 2012: J. Borg-Barthet, 'The principled imperative to recognise same-sex unions in the EU', 8 *Journal of Private International Law* (2012) pp. 359–388

Böse 2010: M. Böse 'StGB § 5 Auslandstaten gegen inländische Rechtsgüter' ['Criminal Code § 5 Acts committed abroad against domestic legal interests'] in: U. Kindhauser, *Strafgesetzbuch: Lehr- und Praxiskommentar* [Criminal Code: Commentary for studies and legal practice] (Baden-Baden, Nomos 2010)

Braake, te 1995: Th.A.M. te Braake, 'De juridische status van het embryo: een stevig aangemeerde leer' ['The legal status of the embryo, a firmly anchored doctrine'], 19 *Tijdschrift voor Gezondheidsrecht* (1995) pp. 32–35

Braake, te 2004: T.A.M. te Braake, 'The Dutch 2002 Embryos Act and the Convention on Human Rights and Biomedicine: Some Issues', 11 *European Journal of Health Law* (2004) pp. 139–151

Braake, te 2008: Th.A.M. te Braake, 'Preïmplantatie genetische diagnostiek: een stand van zaken' ['Preimplantation genetic diagnosis: a state of affairs'], 32 *Tijdschrift voor Gezondheidsrecht* (2008) pp. 174–186

Brandts 2011: R. Brandts, 'Artikel 27a SGB V' ['Article 27a Social Law Act part V'] in: S. Leitherer, *Kasseler Kommentar zum Socialversicherungsrecht* [Kasseler Commentary to Social security law], 69st edn. (München Verlag H.C. Beck 2011)

Braun 2003: J. Braun, 'Das Lebenspartnerschaftsgesetz auf dem Prüfstand' ['The Civil Partnership Act in trial phase'], *Juristische Schulung, JuS* (2002) pp. 21–26

Brems 2006: E. Brems, 'Case note to *Evans* v. *the United Kingdom* (2006)', 7 *European Human Rights Cases* 2006/47 (in Dutch)

Brinkmann 2014: G. Brinkmann, 'Zehn Jahre Freizügigkeitsgesetz' ['Ten years Free Movement Act'], *ZAR* (2014) pp. 213–220

Broekhuijsen-Molenaar 1991: A.M.L. Broekhuijsen-Molenaar, *Civielrechtelijke aspecten van kunstmatige inseminatie en draagmoederschap* [Civil law aspects of artificial insemination and surrogacy] (Deventer, Kluwer 1991)

Brosius-Gersdorf 2013A: F. Brosius-Gersdorf: 'Gleichstellung von Ehe und Lebenspartnerschaft' ['Equalistation of marriage and civil partnership'], *FamFR* (2013) pp. 169–172

Brosius-Gersdorf 2013B: F. Brosius-Gersdorf, 'Verfassungswidrigkeit der Ungleichbehandlung von Ehen und eingetragenen Lebenspartnerschaften beim Ehegattensplitting' ['Unconstitutionality of unequal treatment of marriage and civil partnership in respect of income splitting'], *FamFR* (2013) p. 312

Brugger 1986: W. Brugger, 'Abtreibung – ein Grundrecht oder ein Verbrechen? Ein Vergleich der Urteile des United States Supreme Court und des BVerfG' ['Abortion – a fundamental right or a criminal act? A comparison of the case law of the United States Supreme Court and the German Constitutional Court'], *NJW* (1986) pp. 896–901

Bruijn, de 1979: J. de Bruijn, *Geschiedenis van de abortus in Nederland: een analyse van opvattingen en discussies 1600–1979* [History of abortion in the Netherlands; an analysis of views and debates 1600–1979] (Amsterdam, Van Gennep 1979)

Brunet et al. 2013: L. Brunet et al., *A Comparative Study on the Regime of Surrogacy in EU Member States*, 2013, PE 474.403, p. 157 and 194, online available at www.europarl.europa.eu/RegData/etudes/etudes/join/2013/474403/IPOL-JURI_ET(2013)474403_EN.pdf, visited March 2014

Bruns 2008: M. Bruns, 'Die Maruko-Entscheidung im Spannungsfeld zwischen europäischer und nationaler Auslegung' ['The Maruko judgment in the area of tension between European and national reading'], *NJW* (2008) pp. 1929–1931

Bubsby et al. 2008: H. Bubsby et al., 'Ethical EU law? The influence of the European Group on Ethics in Science and New Technologies', 33 *European Law Review* (2008) pp. 803–842

Buckley 1998: A.M. Buckley, 'The primacy of democracy over natural law in Irish abortion law: an examination of the C case', 9 *Duke Journal of Comparative & International Law* (1998) p. 275–309

Bundesminister für Forschung und Technologie 1985: Bundesminister für Forschung und Technologie (ed.) [Federal Minister for Research and Technology], *In-vitro-Fertilisation, Genomanalyse und Gentherapie, Bericht der gemeinsamen Arbeitsgruppe des Bundesministers für Forschung und Technologie und des Bundesministers für Justiz ('Benda-Bericht')* [In vitro fertilisation, genome anlysis and gene therapy, report of the joint working group of the Federal Minister for Research and Technology and the Federal Minister of Justice] No. 6 in the series *Gentechnologie – Chancen und Risiken* [Gene technology – Opportunities and Risks] (München, Schweitzer 1985)

Búrca, de 1993: G. de Búrca, 'Fundamental Human Rights and the Reach of EC law', 13 *Oxford Journal of Legal Studies* (1993) pp. 283–319

Burg, van der 1994: W. van der Burg, 'De juridische 'status' van het embryo: een op drift geraakte fictie' ['The legal 'status' of the embryo: a drifting fiction'], 18 *Tijdschrift voor Gezondheidsrecht* (1994) pp. 129–140

Cabral 2004: P. Cabral, 'The internal market and the right to cross border medical care', 29 *European Law Review* (2004) pp. 673–686

Caffrey 2013: A. Caffrey, 'Surrogacy-Genetics v Gestation: The Determination of "Mother" in Irish Law', 19 *Medico-Legal Journal of Ireland* (2013) pp. 34–36

Calhoun 2002: C. Calhoun (ed.), *Dictionary of the Social Sciences* (Oxford, Oxford University Press, published online: 2002, eISBN: 9780199891184)

Canavan 2012: J. Canavan, 'Family and Family Change in Ireland: An Overview', 33 *Journal of Family Issues* (2012) pp. 10–28

Case 2009: M.A. Case 2009, 'Perfectionism and Fundamentalism in the Application of the German Abortion Laws', in S. H. Williams, *Constituting equality: gender equality and comparative constitutional rights* (New York, Cambridge University Press 2009) pp. 93–106

Classen 2010: C.D. Classen, 'Die Lebenspartnerschaft im Beamtenrecht' ['The registered partnership in civil servants law'], *FPR* (2010) pp. 200–203

Clifford 2002: A.M. Clifford, 'Abortion in International waters off the coast of Ireland: avoiding a collision between Irish moral sovereignty and the European Community', 14 *Pace International Law Review* (2002) pp. 385–433

Clissman and Barrett 2012: I. Clissmann and J. Barrett, 'The Embryo in vitro after Roche v Roche: What Protection is Now Offered?', 18 *Medico-Legal Journal of Ireland* (2012) pp. 13–20

Coester 2010: M. Coester, 'Art. 17b EGBGB Eingetragene Lebenspartnerschaft' ['Art. 17b EGBGB Civil Partnership'], in: F. Jürgen Säcker and R. Rixecker (eds.), *Münchener Kommentar zum BGB* [Münchener Commentary to the BGB], 5th edn. (München, Verlag C.H. Beck 2010)

Coester 2013: M. Coester, 'Art. 17b EGBGB unter dem Einfluss des Europäischen Kollisionsrechts' ['Art. 17b EGBGB under the influence of European conflict-of-laws rules'], 22 *IPRax* (2013) pp. 114–122

Cohen 2012: I.G. Cohen, 'S.H. and Others v. Austria and circumvention tourism', 25 *Reproductive BioMedicine Online* (2012) pp. 660–662

Cole 1993–1994: D. Cole, '"Going to England": Irish Abortion Law and the European Community', 17 *Hastings Int'l & Comp. L. Rev.* (1993–1994) pp. 113–142

Colvin 1992: C.M. Colvin, 'Society for the Protection of unborn children (Ireland) Ltd v Grogan: Irish abortion law and the free movement of services in the European Community', 15 *Fordham International Law Journal* (1992) pp. 476–526

Cooper 2011: S.L. Cooper, 'Marriage, Family, Discrimination & Contradiction: An Evaluation of the Legacy and Future of the European Court of Human Rights' Jurisprudence on LGBT Rights', 12 *German Law Journal* (2011) pp. 1743–1763, online available at: www.germanlawjournal.com/pdfs/Vol12-No10/PDF_Vol_12_No_10_1746-1763_Articles_Cooper.pdf, visited June 2014

Cornides 2012: J. Cornides, 'Three Case Studies on Anti-Discrimination', *European Journal of International Law*, 23 *Eur. J. Int'l L.* (2012) pp. 517–542

Costello 2009: C. Costello, 'Metock: free movement and "normal family life" in the Union', 46 *CMLRev* (2009) pp. 587–662

Coveney 2005: H. Coveney, 'A Brave New World: Family Law Implications of Assisted Reproductive Technologies', 8 *Irish Journal of Family Law* (2005) pp. 12–18

Coveney 2007: H. Coveney, 'Assisted Reproductive Technologies and the Status of the Embryo', 13 *Medico-Legal Journal of Ireland* (2007) pp. 14–19

Coverleyn et al. 2007: A. Coverleyn et al., *Pre-implantation Genetic Diagnosis in Europe* (Joint Research Centre of the European Commission, January 2007), online available at www.ftp.jrc.es/EURdoc/eur22764en.pdf, visited July 2014

Craig and De Búrca 2011: P. Craig and G. De Búrca, EU law, *Text, cases and materials*, 5th edn. (Oxford, Oxford University Press 2011)

Curry-Sumner 2005A: I. Curry Sumner, *All's well that ends registered?: the substantive and private international law aspects of non-marital registered relationships in Europe: a comparison of the laws of Belgium, France, The Netherlands, Switzerland and the United Kingdom* (Antwerp, Intersentia 2005)

Curry-Sumner 2005B: I. Curry-Sumner, 'General Patterns in Registration Schemes for Unmarried Couples and the Implications for Ireland', 8 *Irish Journal of Family Law* (2005) pp. 9–14

Curry-Sumner and Vonk 2006: I. Curry-Sumner and M.J. Vonk, 'Adoptie door paren van hetzelfde geslacht: wie probeert de wet te beschermen?' ['Adoption by couples of the same sex: who is the law trying to protect?'], 28 *Tijdschrift voor Familie- en Jeugdrecht* (2006) pp. 39–44

Curtin 1992: D. Curtin, 'Case note to ECJ C-159/90', 29 *CML Rev* (1992) pp. 585- 603

Cusack 1997: D.A. Cusack, 'Abortion – Conflicting Rights, Duties and Arguments', 3 *Medico-Legal Journal of Ireland* (1997) pp. 82–83

Czerner 2009: F. Czerner, 'Reform der Reform: Wiedereinführung der embryopathischen Indikation bei Spätabtreibungen?' ['Reform of the reform: reintroduction of the embryopathic indication for late abortions?'], *ZRP* (2009) pp. 233–236

Daly 2011A: A. Daly, 'Ignoring Reality: Children and the Civil Partnership Act in Ireland', 14 *Irish Journal of Family Law* (2011) pp. 82–86

Daly 2011B: B. Daly, '"Braxton Hick's" or the Birth of a New Era? Tracing the Development of Ireland's Abortion Laws in Respect of European Court of Human Rights Jurisprudence', *European Journal of Health Law* 18 (2011) pp. 375–395

Darby 1977: J.J. Darby, *Alternative Draft of a Penal Code for The Federal Republic of Germany* (New York, South Hackensack 1977)

Davies 2011: G. Davies, 'Legislating for Patients' Rights', in: J.W. van de Gronden et al. (eds.), *Health care and EU law* (The Hague, T.M.C. Asser Press 2011) pp. 191–210

De la Rosa 2012: S. De la Rosa, 'The Directive on cross-border healthcare or the art of codifying complex case law', 49 *CML Rev.* (2012) pp. 15–46

Dederer 2010: H.-G Dederer,' Zur Straflosigkeit der Präimplantationsdiagnostik, Anmerkungen zu BGH, Urt. v. 6.7.2010 – 5 StR 386/09' ['To the impunity of preimplantation genetic diagnosis, Commentary to the BGH judgment of 6.7.2010 – 5 StR 386/09'], *MedR* (2010) pp. 819–822

Denys 1999: C. Denys, 'Homosexuality: a non-issue in Community law?', 24 *European Law Review* (1999) pp. 419–425

Derksen and Staal 2012: J.T.M. Derksen and P.C. Staal, *Rapport Een leeftijdsgrens voor vruchtbaarheidsbehandelingen* [Report an age limit for fertility treatment] (Diemen, CVZ 2012)

Dermout 2001: S.M. Dermout, *De eerste logeerpartij, hoogtechnologisch draagmoederschap in Nederland* [The first time staying over, high technological surrogacy in the Netherlands] (Groningen, s.n. 2001)

Dermout et al. 2010: S. Dermout et al., 'Non-commercial surrogacy: an account of patient management in the first Dutch Centre for IVF Surrogacy, from 1997 to 2004', 25 *Human Reproduction* (2010) pp. 443–449

Dethloff 2010: N. Dethloff, 'Adoption und Sorgerecht – Problembereiche für die eingetragenen Lebenspartner?' ['Adoption and parental authority – area of concern for the civil partner?'], *FPR* (2010) pp. 208–210

Deutsch 1986: E. Deutsch, 'Des Menschen Vater und Mutter. Die künstliche Befruchtung beim Menschen – Zulässigkeit und zivilrechtliche Folgen' ['A man's father and mother. Artificial insemination with human beings – Permissibility and civil law effects'], *NJW* (1986) pp. 1971–1975

Deutsch 1993: E. Deutsch, 'Neues Verfassungszivilrecht: Rechtswidriger Abtreibungsvertrag gültig – Unterhaltspflicht aber kein Schaden' ['New Constitutional civil law: unlawful abortion convention in force – Maintenance obligation but no damages'], *NJW* (1993) pp. 2361–2363

Deutsch 2003: E. Deutsch, 'Die Spätabtreibung als juristisches Problem' ['Late abortions as a legal problem'], *ZRP* (2003) pp. 332–336

Deutscher Anwaltverein 2011: *Stellungnahme des Deutschen Anwaltvereins durch den Medizinrechtsausschuss zu den Gesetzentwürfen zur Präimplantationsdiagsnostik* [Position

paper of the working group on medical law of the German bar association on the draft bill on preimplantation genetic diagnosis], No. 12/2011, March 2011, online available at www.anwaltverein.de, visited June 2014
Deutscher Ethikrat 2011: Deutscher Ethikrat, *Präimplantationsdiagnostik Stellungnahme* [Preimplantation genetic diagnosis, position paper], Berlin, 8 March 2011, online available at www.ethikrat.org/dateien/pdf/stellungnahme-praeimplantations diagnostik.pdf, visited June 2014
Dewitz, von 2009: C. von Dewitz, 'Diskriminierung ungeborener Kinder mit Behinderungen durch die gesetzliche Regelung zum Schwangerschaftsabbruch' ['Discrimination of unborn children with disabilities by way of the regulation on termination of pregnancy'], *Zfl* (2009) pp. 74–87
Dickens 2010: B. Dickens, 'Cross-border reproductive services', 111 *International Journal of Gynecology and Obstetrics* (2010) pp. 190–191
Diederichsen 2000: U. Diederichsen, 'Homosexuelle – von Gesetzes wegen?' ['Homosexual – by law?'], *NJW* (2000) pp. 1841–1844
Di Fabio 2014: U. Di Fabio, 'GG Art. 2' ['Art. 2 German Basic Law'], in: R. Herzorg et al. (eds.) *Maunz und Dürig Grundgesetz-Kommentar* [Maunz and Dürig Commentary to the Basic Law], 71st edn. (München, Verlag Beck 2014)
Dijk, van et al. 2006: P. van Dijk et al. (eds.), *Theory and Practice of the European Convention on Human Rights* (Antwerpen, Intersentia 2006)
Dondorp et al. 2012: W. Dondorp et al., 'Oocyte cryopreservation for age-related fertility loss', 27 *Human Reproduction* (2012) pp. 1231–1237
Dondorp and Wert, de 2012A: W. Dondorp and G. de Wert, *Reageerbuisdebat. Over de maakbaarheid van de voortplanting* [Test tube debate. On the manipulability of human reproduction] (Den Haag, ZonMw 2012), online available at www.zonmw.nl/uploads/tx_vipublicaties/ZonMw_E_G_Reageerbuisdebat170x240.pdf, visited June 2014
Dondorp and Wert, de 2012B: W.J. Dondorp and G.M.W.R. de Wert, 'Postmortale eiceldonatie: wat is er tegen?' ['Postmortal egg cell donation; what to object against it?'], 156 *Nederlands Tijdschrift voor Geneeskunde* (2012) pp. 564–570
Donnelly 2011: S. Donnelly, 'A, B and C v Ireland: A Commentary', 17 *Medico-Legal Journal of Ireland* (2011) pp. 43–48
Donoghue and Smyth 2013: S. Donoghue and C.-M. Smyth, 'Abortion for Foetal Abnormalities in Ireland; The Limited Scope of the Irish Government's Response to the A, B and C Judgment', 20 *European Journal of Health Law* (2013) pp. 117–143
Dooley 1999: D. Dooley, 'Assisted Reproduction: the pursuit of consensus?', 5 *Medico-Legal Journal of Ireland* (1999) pp. 65–69
Doty 2009: K.A. Doty, 'From *Fretté* to *E.B.*: The European Court of Human Rights on Gay and Lesbian Adoption', 18 *Law and Sexuality Rev. Lesbian Gay Bisexual & Legal Issues* (2009) pp. 121–141
Douglas-Scott 2004: S. Douglas-Scott, 'The rule of law in the European Union – putting the security into the area of freedom, security and justice', 29 *European Law Review* (2004) pp. 219–242
Dreier 2004: H. Dreier, 'Art. 1', in: H. Dreier (ed.), *Grundgesetz-Kommentar, Band 1, Präambel, Artikel 1–19* [Commentary to the Basic Law, Volume 2, Preamble, Articles 1–19], 2nd edn. (Tübingen, Mohr Siebeck 2004) pp. 39–231
Eggert and Rolston 1994: A. Eggert and B. Rolston, 'Ireland', in: B. Rolston and A. Eggert (eds.), *Abortion in the new Europe, A comparative handbook*, Westport (etc.): Greenwood Press 1994, pp. 157–172

Eijkholt 2007: M. Eijkholt, 'Het recht op procreatie: voldragen of in statu nascendi?' ['The right to procreate: carried to term or in *statu nascendi*?'], 31 *Tijdschrift voor Gezondheidsrecht* (2007) pp. 2–13

Eijkholt 2010: M. Eijkholt, 'The right to found a family as a stillborn right to procreate?', 18 *Medical Law Review* (2010) pp. 127–151

Ellis 2002: E. Ellis, 'Case note to Joined Cases C-122 & 125/99P, D and Sweden v. Council. Judgment of the European Court of Justice of 31 May 2001, Full Court,' 39 *CMLRev* 39 (2002) pp. 151–157

Enders 2004: W. Enders, 'Stiefkindadoption' ['second-parent adoption'], *FPR* (2004) pp. 60–64

Enschedé 1966: Ch.J. Enschedé, 'Abortus op medische indicatie en strafrecht' ['Abortion on the basis of a medical indication and criminal law'], 41 *Nederlands juristenblad, Njb* (1966) pp. 1109–1118

Ensig Sørensen 2011: K. Ensig Sørensen, 'Reconciling secondary legislation and the treaty rights of free movement', 17 *European Law Review* (2011) pp. 339–361

Eriksson 2009: A. Eriksson, 'European Court of Justice: Broadening the Scope of European Nondiscrimination Law [notes]', 7 *International Journal of Constitutional Law* (2009) pp. 731–753

Eschelbach 2011: R. Eschelbach, 'BeckOK StGB § 218' ['Beck online Commentary to StGB § 218'], in: B. von Heintschel-Heinegg (ed.), *Beck'scher Online-Kommentar StGB* [Beck Online Commentary to the StGB], 15th ed (München, Beck Verlag 2011)

Eser 1986: A. Eser, 'Reform of German abortion law: first experiences', 34 *The American Journal of Comparative Law* (1986) pp. 369–383

Eser 1994: A. Eser, 'Schwangerschaftsabbruch: Reformversuche im Umsetzung des BVErfG-Urteils' ['Termination of pregnancy: reform efforts in the implementation of the judgment of the German Constitutional Court'], *JZ* (1994) pp. 503–510

Esser 1983: W. Esser, 'Die Rechtswidrigkeit des Aborts' ['The unlawfulness of abortions'], *MedR* (1983) pp. 57–60

European Commission 2012: European Commission – Directorate-General for Justice, *2011 Report on the Application of the EU Charter of Fundamental Rights* (Luxembourg, Publications Office of the European Union 2012), online available www.ec.europa.eu/justice/fundamental-rights/files/charter_report_en.pdf, visited June 2014

European Union Agency for Fundamental Rights 2008: European Union Agency for Fundamental Rights, *Homophobia, transphobia and discrimination on grounds of sexual orientation and gender identity. Comparative legal analysis* (Luxembourg, Publications Office of the European Union 2008), online available at www.fra.europa.eu/en/publication/2010/homophobia-and-discrimination-grounds-sexual-orientation-eu-member-states-part-i, visited June 2014

European Union Agency for Fundamental Rights 2010: European Union Agency for Fundamental Rights, *Homophobia, transphobia and discrimination on grounds of sexual orientation and gender identity. Comparative legal analysis. 2010 update* (Luxembourg, Publications Office of the European Union 2010), online available at www.fra.europa.eu/en/publication/2012/homophobia-transphobia-and-discrimination-grounds-sexual-orientation-and-gender, visited June 2014

European Union Agency for Fundamental Rights 2011A: European Union Agency for Fundamental Rights, *Annual Report 2011; Fundamental rights: challenges and achievements in 2011* (Luxembourg, Publications Office of the European Union 2012), online available at www.fra.europa.eu/en/publication/2012/fundamental-rights-challenges-and-achievements-2011, visited June 2014

European Union Agency for Fundamental Rights 2011B: European Union Agency for Fundamental Rights, *Homophobia, transphobia and discrimination on grounds of sexual orientation and gender identity in the EU Member States. Summary of findings, trends, challenges and promising practices* (Luxembourg, Publications Office of the European Union 2011), online available at www.fra.europa.eu/en/publication/2011/homophobia-transphobia-and-discrimination-grounds-sexual-orientation-and-gender, visited June 2014

European Union Agency for Fundamental Rights 2013A: European Union Agency for Fundamental Rights, *Fundamental rights: challenges and achievements in 2012, Annual report 2012* (Luxembourg, Publications Office of the European Union 2013), online available at www.fra.europa.eu/sites/default/files/annual-report-2012_en.pdf, visited June 2014

European Union Agency for Fundamental Rights 2013B: European Union Agency for Fundamental Rights, *EU LGBT survey, European Union lesbian, gay, bisexual and transgender survey, Results at a glance* (Luxembourg, Publications Office of the European Union 2013) online available at www.fra.europa.eu/sites/default/files/eu-lgbt-survey-results-at-a-glance_en.pdf, visited June 2014

Exter, den 2005: A. den Exter, 'Access to Health Care in the Netherlands: The Influence of (European) Treaty Law', 33 *Journal of Law, Medicine & Ethics* (2005) pp. 698–710

Fabbrini 2011: F. Fabbrini, 'The European Court of Human Rights, the EU Charter of Fundamental Rights, and the right to abortion: Roe v. Wade on the other side of the Atlantic?', 18 *Columbia Journal of European Law* (2011/12) pp. 1–54

Fabbrini 2012: F. Fabbrini, *Fundamental rights in Europe, Challenges and Transformations of a Multilevel System in Comparative Perspective* (© Federico Fabbrini 2012)

Fallon 2007: M. Fallon, 'Constraints of internal market law on family law', in: J. Meeusen et al. (eds.), *International family law for the European Union* (Antwerpen, Intersentia 2007) pp. 149–181

Faugan 2011: P. Faugan, *Missing pieces. A comparison of the rights and responsibilities gained from civil partnership compared to the rights and responsibilities gained through civil marriage in Ireland* (Marriage Equality 2011), online available at www.marriagequality.ie/download/pdf/missing_pieces.pdf, visited July 2014

Ferdinand 2010: P. Ferdinand, *Pränatal- und Präimplantationsdiagnistik aus verfassungsrechtlicher Sicht* [Prenatal and preimplantation genetic diagnosis from a constitutional perspective] (Frankfurt am Main, Peter Lang 2010)

Fernhout 1992: D.M. Fernhout, *Rechtsvragen rond in vitro fertilisatie en embryo-transfer* [Questions of law on *in vitro* fertilisation and embryo transfer] (Arnhem, Gouda Quint 1992)

Ferraretti et al. 2010: A.P. Ferraretti et al., 'Cross-border reproductive care: a phenomenon expressing the controversial aspects of reproductive technologies', 20 *Reproductive BioMedicine Online* (2010) pp. 261–266

Findlay 1980: M.J. Findlay, 'Criminal Liability For Complicity In Abortions Committed Outside Ireland', 15 *The Irish Jurist* (1980) pp. 88–98

Finlay 1992: T.A. Finlay, 'The Constitution of Ireland in a Changing Society', in: D. Curtin and D. O'Keeffe (eds.), *Constitutional Adjudication in European Community and National Law – Essays for the Hon. Mr. Justice T.F. O'Higgin* (Dublin, Butterworth 1992)

Fitzmaurice 2001: P. Fitzmaurice, '*Attorney General v X*: A lost opportunity to examine the limits of European integration', 26 *Brooklyn Journal of International Law* (2001) pp. 1723–1754

Fletcher 2000: R. Fletcher, 'National crisis, *supra*national opportunity: the Irish construction of abortion as a European service', 8 *Reproductive Health Matters* (2000) pp. 35–44

Fleurke 2012: F.M. Fleurke, 'Case note to Case C-34/10 (*Brüstle*)', 13 *European Human Rights Cases* 2012/54 (in Dutch)

Flynn 1999: L. Flynn, 'The implications of article 13 EC – after Amsterdam, will some forms of discrimination be more equal than others?', 36 *CMLRev* (1999) pp. 117–1152

Flynn 2001: L. Flynn, 'From individual Protection to Recognition of Relationships? Same-Sex Couples and the Irish Experience of Sexual Orientation Law Reform', in: R. Wintemute and M. Andenæs (eds.), *The legal recognition of same-sex partnerships? A study of national, European and international law* (Oxford: Hart 2001) pp. 591–604

Forkert 2003: M. Forkert, *Eingetragene Lebenspartnerschaften im deutschen IPR: Art. 17b EGBGB* [Civil partnerships in German Private International Law: Art. 17b EGBGB] (Tübingen, Mohr Siebeck 2003)

Fötschl 2010: A. Fötschl, 'The COMPR of Germany and France: Epoch-Making in the Unification of Law', 18 *European Review of Private Law* (2010) pp. 881–889

Forder 1994: C. Forder, 'Abortion: A Constitutional Problem in European Perspective', 1 *Maastricht Journal of European and Comparative Law* (1994) pp. 56–100

Forder and Bakker 2010: C.J. Forder and R. Bakker, 'Kroniek van personen- en familierecht' ['Chronicle of family law legislation'], 85 *Nederlands Juristenblad* (2010) p. 1796

Fox and Murhpy 1992: M. Fox and T. Murphy, 'Irish Abortion: Seeking Refuge in a Jurisprudence of Doubt and Delegation', 19 *Journal of Law and Society* (1992) pp. 454–466

Frenz 2013: W. Frenz, 'Eheschutz ade? BVerfG stärkt gleichgeschlechtliche Paare' ['Protection of marriage, farewell? German Constitutional Court supports same-sex couples'], *NVwZ* (2013) pp. 1200–1202

Friederici 2011: P. Friederici, 'Unzulässigkeit der Adoption auf Grund eines Leimuttervertrags' ['Inadmissibility of adoption on the basis of a surrogacy agreement'], *FamFR* (2011) p. 551

Frohn 2012: E.N. Frohn, 'Geregistreerd Partnerschap' ['Registered Partnership'], in: Th.M. de Boer and F. Ibili (eds.), *Nederlands internationaal personen- en familierecht: wegwijzer voor de rechtspraktijk* [Dutch international family law: guidance for legal practice] (Deventer, Kluwer 2012) pp. 281–299

Fuchs 2005: M. Fuchs, *National ethics councils. Their backgrounds, functions and modes of operation compared* (Berlin, German National Ethics Council 2005) online available at: www.ethikrat.org/_english/publications/Fuchs_International_Ethics_Councils.pdf, visited March 2011

Gade and Thiele 2013: G.D. Gade and C. Thiele, 'Ehe und eingetragene Lebenspartnerschaft: Zwei namensverschiedene Rechtsinstitute gleichen Inhalts?' ['Marriage and civil partnership: Two legal institutions with a different name but the same content?'], *DÖV* (2013) pp. 142–151

Gärtner 2014: V. Gärtner, 'Art. 17b EGBGB, Eingetragene Lebenspartnerschaft' ['Art. 17b EGBGB, civil partnership'], in: M. Herberger et al., *Juris Praxiskommentar BGB* [Juris Commentary on the BGB for legal practitioners], 7th edn. (Saarbrücken, juris GmbH 2014)

Gebauer and Staudinger 2002: M. Gebauer and A. Staudinger, 'Registrierte Lebenspartnerschaften und die Kappungsregel des Art. 17b Abs. 4 EGBGB' ['Civil partnerships and the limitation clause of Art. 17b para. 4 EGBGB'], *IPRax* (2002) pp. 275–282

Geesink and Steegers: I. Geesink and C. Steegers, *Nier te koop, baarmoeder te huur: wereldwijde handel in lichaamsmateriaal* [Kidney for sale, uterus to let: worldwide trade in human body material] (Amsterdam, Bakker 2011)

Gerards 2007: J. Gerards, 'Discrimination grounds', in: D. Schiek et al. (eds), *Cases, materials and text on national, supranational and international non-discrimination law* (Oxford, Hart Publishing 2007) pp. 33–184

Gerards 2011A: J.H. Gerards, 'Case note to ECtHR [GC] 16 December 2010, *A, B and C* v. *Ireland*, no. 25579/05', 12 *European Human Rights Cases* 2011/40 (in Dutch)

Gerards 2011B: J.H. Gerards, *EVRM – algemene beginselen* [ECHR – general principles] (Den Haag Sdu 2011)

Gerards and Claes 2012: J.H. Gerards and M. Claes, 'National report – The Netherlands', in: J. Laffranque (ed.), *The Protection of Fundamental Rights Post-Lisbon: The Interaction between the Charter of Fundamental Rights of the European Union, the European Convention on Human Rights and National Constitutions*, Reports of the XXV FIDE Congress Tallinn, Vol. 1 (Tartu, Tartu University Press 2012) pp. 613–677

Gerards 2013: J. Gerards, 'Judicial Minimalism and 'Dependency'', in: M. van Roosmalen et al. (eds.), *Fundamental Rights and Principles. Liber Amicorum Pieter van Dijk* (Cambridge, Intersentia 2013) pp. 73–92

Gerards et al. 2013: J. Gerards et al., 'Zelfbeschikking in de Nederlandse Grondwet' ['Personal autonomy in the Dutch Constitution'], in: *Achtergrondstudies Zelfbeschikking in de zorg* [Backgroundstudies on Personal autonomy in health care], Reeks evaluatie regelgeving: deel 35 (Den Haag, ZonMw 2013)

Gerards 2014: J. Gerards, 'The European Court of Human Rights and the national courts: giving shape to the notion of 'shared responsibility'', in: J. Gerards and J. Fleuren, *Implementation of the European Convention on Human Rights and of the judgments of the ECtHR in national case law. A comparative analysis* (Cambridge, Intersentia 2014) pp. 13–94

Gerhard 2009: K.S. Gerhard, *Die eingetragene Lebensparterschaft – Eine historisch-dogmatische Bestandsaufnahme zur Frage nach einem neuen familienrechtlichen Institut* [The German Civil partnership – a historic-dogmatic inventory of the question for a new family law institute] (Göttingen, Sierke Verlag 2009)

Gilmartin and White 2011: M. Gilmartin and A. White, 'Comparative Perspectives Symposium: Gender and Medical Tourism. Interrogating Medical Tourism: Ireland, Abortion, and Mobility Rights', 36 *Signs* (2011) pp. 275–280

Gissler et al. 2011: M. Gissler et al., 'Terminations of pregnancy in the European Union', 119 *BJOG An International Journal of Obstetrics and Gynaecology*, 2011, pp. 324–332

Giwer 2002: E. Giwer, *Rechtsfragen der Präimplantationsdiagnostik: eine Studie zum rechtlichen Schutz des Embryos im Zusammenhang mit der Präimplantationsdiagnostik unter besonderer Berücksichtigung grundrechtlicher Schutzpflichten* [Legal questions on preimplantation genetic diagnosis: a study into the protection of embryos in relation to preimplantation genetic diagnosis taking particular account of constitutional obligations to protect] (Berlin, Duncker & Humblot 2001)

Göbel-Zimmermann 2010: R. Göbel-Zimmermann, 'Gleichgeschlechtliche Lebenspartnerschaften (§ 27 Abs 2)' ['Same-sex civil partnerships (§ 27 para. 2)'], in: B. Huber, *Aufenthaltsgesetz* [Residence Act], 1st edn. (München, Verlag C.H. Beck 2010)

Gomperts 2002: R. Gomperts, 'Women on Waves: Where Next for the Abortion Boat?', 19 *Reproductive Health Matters* (2002) pp. 180–183

Gordijn 2012: M. Gordijn, 'Geregistreerd Partnerschap' ['Registered partnership'], in: A. Baptiste and E.W.M Gubbels, *Burgerzaken & Boek 10 BW* [Civil matters and Book 10 BW] (Zoetermeer, NVVB 2012) pp. 92–109

Graupner 2012: H. Graupner, 'Comparing people or institutions? Sexual Orientation Discrimination and the Court of Justice of the European Union', in K. Boele-Woelki and A. Fuchs (eds.), *Legal recognition of same-sex Relationships in Europe, National, cross-border and European perspectives*, 2nd edn. (Cambridge, Intersentia 2012) pp. 271–282

Groh 2011: T. Groh, 'Anmerkung zu C-34/10 (*Brüstle*)' ['Case note to Case C-34/10 (*Brüstle*)'], 23 *Europäische Zeitschrift für Wirtschaftsrecht* (2011) pp. 910–912

Gronden, van de 2011: J.W. van de Gronden, 'Richtlijn rechten van patiënten bij grensoverschrijdende gezondheidszorg: veel huiswerk voor de Nederlandse zorgwetgever?' ['Directive on rights of patients in cross-border health care: too much homework for the Dutch legislature on health?'], 59 *Tijdschrift voor Europees en economisch recht, SEW* (2001) pp. 373–387

Gronden, van de and Szyszcak 2011: J. van de Gronden and E. Szyszczak, 'Conclusions: Constructing a 'Solid' Multi-Layered Health Care Edifice', in: J.W. van de Gronden et al. (eds.), *Health care and EU law* (The Hague, T.M.C. Asser Press 2011) pp. 481–495

Gronden, van de et al. 2011: J.W. van de Gronden et al. (eds.), *Health care and EU law* (The Hague, T.M.C. Asser Press 2011)

Groot, de and Kuipers 2008: G.-R. de Groot and J.-J. Kuipers, 'The New provisions on Private International Law in the Treaty of Lisbon', 15 *Maastricht Journal of European and Comparative Law* (2008) pp. 109–114

Gropp 2012: W. Gropp, 'StGB § 218 Schwangerschaftsabbruch' ['§ 218 StGB Termination of pregnancy'], in W. Joeks and K. Miebach (eds.), *Münchener Kommentar zum StGB* [*Münchener Commentary to the StGB*], 2nd edn. (München, Verlag C.H. Beck 2012)

Grösschner 2004: R. Grösschner, 'Art. 6' ['Art. 6'], in H. Dreier (ed.), *Grundgesetz-Kommentar, Band 1, Präambel, Artikel 1–19* [German Basic Law Commentary, Volume 1, Preamble, Articles 1–19], 2nd edn. (Tübingen, Mohr Siebeck 2004) pp. 748–825

Grube 2007: F. Grube, 'Aufwendungen einer unverheirateten Frau für künstliche Befruchtung als außergewöhnliche Belastung' ['Expenses of an unmarried woman for artificial insemination as extraordinary financial burden'], *juris Praxis Report SteuerRecht* 45 (2007) Anm. 5

Grunberger 2010: M. Grunberger, 'Die Gleichbehandlung von Ehe und eingetragener Lebenspartnerschaft im Zusammenspiel von Unionsrecht und nationalem Verfassungsrecht. Das Urteil des BVerfG zur VBL-Hinterbliebenenrente' ['The equal treatment of marriage and civil partnership in interaction with Union law and national constitutional law'], *FPR* (2010) pp. 203–208

Grziwotz 2010: H. Grziwotz, 'Anmerkung zum Urteil des OLG Hamm vom 01.12.2009 (I-15 Wx 236/09, FamRZ 2010, 1259) – Partner einer eingetragenen Lebenspartnerschaft kann Adoptivkind des anderen Partners nicht an Kindes statt annehmen' ['Commentary to the judgment of the OLG Hamm of 01.12.2009 (I-15 Wx 236/09, FamRZ 2010, 1259) – Civil partner cannot adopt adoptive child if his or her partner'], *Zeitschrift für das gesamte Familienrecht, FamRZ* (2010) pp. 1260–1261

Guild 2001: E. Guild, 'Free Movement and Same-Sex Relationships', in: R. Wintemute and M. Andenæs (ed.), *Legal Recognition of Same-Sex Partnerships, A Study of National, European and International Law* (Oxford, Hart Publishing 2001) pp. 677–689

Halliday 2003: S. Halliday, 'A comparative analysis of some of the legal parameters of the right to life and the right to privacy in the regulation of abortion', in: J. MacEldowney and G. Weick, *Human rights in transition* (Frankfurt am Main, Peter Lang 2003) pp. 85–105

Hamilton 1996: L. Hamilton, 'Matters of life and death', 65 *Fordham Law Review* (1996) pp. 543–559

Hamilton 2013: F. Hamilton, 'Why the margin of appreciation is not the answer to the gay marriage debate', 13 *European Human Rights Law Review* (2013) pp. 47–55

Hancher and Sauter 2010: L. Hancher and W. Sauter, 'One step beyond? From Sodemare to Docmorris: The EU's freedom of establishment case law concerning healthcare', 47 *CMLRev* (2010) pp. 117–146.

Harris et al. 2009: Harris et al., *Law of the European Convention on Human Rights* (Oxford, Oxford University Press 2009)

Hatzopoulos 2002: V. Hatzopoulos, 'Killing National Health and Insurance Systems but Healing Patients? The European Market for Health Care after the Judgments of the ECJ in Vanbraekel and Peerbooms', 39 *CMLRev.* (2002) pp. 705–720

Heiderhoff 2011; B. Heiderhoff, 'BeckOK EGBGB Art. 17b' ['Beck Online Commentary Art. 17b EGBGB'], in: H.G. Bamberger and H. Roth (eds.), *Beck'scher Online-Kommentar BGB* [Beck Online commentary to the BGB], 19th edn. (München, Verlag C.H. Beck 2011)

Heiderhoff 2012: B. Heiderhoff, 'Der gewönliche Aufenthalt von Säuglingen' ['The habitual residence of infants'], *IPRax* (2012) pp. 523–526

Heiderhoff 2014A: B. Heiderhoff, 'Rechtliche Abstammung im Ausland geborener Leihmutterkinder' ['The legal descent of surrogate children born abroad'], *NJW* (2014) pp. 2673–2678

Heiderhoff 2014B: B. Heiderhoff, 'BeckOK EGBGB Art. 17b' ['Beck Online Commentary Art. 17b EGBGB'], in: H.G. Bamberger and H. Roth (eds.), *Beck'scher Online-Kommentar BGB* [Beck Online commentary to the BGB], 32nd edn. (München, Verlag C.H. Beck 2014)

Heiderhoff 2014C: B. Heiderhoff, 'BeckOK EGBGB Art. 22' ['Beck Online Commentary Art. 22 EGBGB'], in: H.G. Bamberger and H. Roth (eds.), *Beck'scher Online-Kommentar BGB* [Beck Online commentary to the BGB], 32nd edn. (München, Verlag C.H. Beck 2014)

Heijden, van der 1976: P.F. van der Heijden, 'Juridisch voorspel tot de abortus ontwerpen' ['Legal prelude to the abortion plans'], 13 *Nederlands jurstenblad* (1976) pp. 425–437

Heijning 2010: S.H. Heijning, 'Boek 10 BW: IPR-regels geregistreerd partnerschap (art. 10:60 t/m 10:91 BW)' ['Book 10 BW: PIL-rules registered partnership (Art. 10:60 to 10:91 BW)'], 141 *WPNR* (2010) pp. 311–317

Hekma 2004: G. Hekma, *Homoseksualiteit in Nederland van 1730 tot de moderne tijd* [Homosexuality in the Netherlands from 1730 to the modern age] (Amsterdam, Meulenhoff 2004)

Hendriks 2011: A.C. Hendriks, 'Case note to ECtHR [GC] 16 December 2010, *A, B and C* v. *Ireland*, no. 25579/05', 12 *European Human Rights Cases* 2011/40 (in Dutch)

Hendriks 2012A: A.C. Hendriks, 'Het recht op voortplanting en zijn grenzen. Redactioneel' ['The right to procreate and its limitations. Editorial'], 36 *Tijdschrift voor Gezondheidsrecht* (2012) p. 279

Hendriks 2012B: A. Hendriks, 'Case-note to ECtHR 2 October 2012, *Daniela Knecht* v. *Romania*, no. 10048/10', 13 *European Human Rights Cases* 2012/228 (in Dutch)

Henette-Vauchez 2012: S. Henette-Vauchez, 'L'embryon de l'Union', 48 *RTD eur.* (2012) pp. 355–368

Henkel 2011: J. Henkel, `Fällt nun auch das "Fremdkindadoptionsverbot"?' ['Is the 'ban on international abortion' now also being dropped?'], *NJW* (2011) pp. 259–264

Henking 2010: T. Henking, *Wertungswidersprüche zwischen Embryonenschutzgesetz und den Regelungen des Schwangerschaftsabbruchs? Am Beispiel des Verbots der Präimplantationsdiagnostik* [Contradictory values between the Emrbyo Protection Act and the Regulations on termination of pregnancy. The prohibition on preimplantation genetic diagnosis as an example] (Baden-Baden, Nomos Verlagsgesellschaft 2010)

Henrich 2002: D. Henrich, 'Kollisionsrechtliche Fragen der eingetragenen Lebenspartnerschaft' ['Conflict-of-laws questions on Civil Partnership'], *Zeitschrift für das gesamte Familienrecht, FamRZ* (2002) pp. 137–144

Herdegen 2011: M. Herdegen, 'GG Art. 1 Abs 1' ['Art. 1 para. 1 GG'], in: R. Herzorg et al. (eds.), *Maunz und Dürig Grundgesetz-Kommentar* [Maunz and Dürig Commentary to the Basic Law], 55th ed (München, Verlag Beck 2011)

Hermes and Walther 1993: G. Hermes and S. Walther, 'Schwangerschaftsabbruch zwischen Recht und Unrecht – Das zweite Abtreibungsurteil des BVerfG und seine Folge' ['Pregnancy termination between right and wrong – The second judgment on abortion of the German Constitutional Court and its consequences'], *NJW* (1993) pp. 2337–2347

Hervey 2003: T.K. Hervey, 'The right to health in European Union law', in: T. Hervey and J. Kenner (eds.), *Economic and social rights under the EU Charter of Fundamental Rights: a legal perspective* (Oxford, Hart 2003) pp. 193–222

Hervey 2005: T.K. Hervey, 'We don't see a Connection: the "Right to Health" in the EU Charter and European Social Charter', in: G. De Búrca et al. (eds.), *Social rights in Europe* (Oxford, Oxford University Press 2005) pp. 305–335

Hervey 2007: T.K. Hervey, 'The Current Legal Framework on the Right to Seek Health Care Abroad in the European Union', 9 *The Cambridge Yearbook of European Legal Studies* (2007) pp. 261–286

Hervey 2011: T.K. Hervey, 'Cooperation between health care authorities in the proposed Directive', in: J.W. van de Gronden et al. (eds.), *Health care and EU law* (The Hague, T.M.C. Asser Press 2011) pp. 161–190

Hervey and McHale 2004: T.K. Hervey and J.V. McHale, *Health Law and the European Union*, (Cambridge: Cambridge University Press 2004)

Heun 2004: W. Heun, 'Art. 3' ['Art. 3'], in H. Dreier (ed.), *Grundgesetz-Kommentar, Band 1, Präambel, Artikel 1–19* [German Basic Law Commentary, Volume 1, Preamble, Articles 1–19], 2nd edn. (Tübingen, Mohr Siebeck 2004) pp. 399–483

Hewson 2007: B. Hewson, 'Ireland's Miss D: a 'bizarre dispute'', *Bpas Reproductive Review* (2007), online available at www.reproductivereview.org/index.php/rr/article/186, visited June 2014

Hilbert 1994: A.M. Hilbert, 'Notes, The Irish Abortion Debate: Substantive Rights and Affecting Commerce Jurisprudential Models', 26 *VanderBilt Journal of Transnational Law* (1994) pp. 1117–1162

Hillgruber 2010: C. Hillgruber, 'Über die Ungleichbehandlung von Ehe und eingetragener Lebenspartnerschaft im Bereich der betrieblichen Hinterbliebenenversorgung – Kritische Anmerkung zum Beschluss des Bundesverfassungsgerichts vom 07.07.2009 (AZ: 1 BvR 1164/07)' ['On the unequal treatment of marriage and registered civil partnership in respect of survivor's pensions – A critical note on the decision of the German Constitutional Court of 7 July 2009 (AZ: 1 BvR 1164/07)'], *JZ* (2010) pp. 41–44

Hilson 2008: C. Hilson, 'The Unpatriotism of the Economic Constitution? Rights to Free Movement and their Impact on National and European Identity', 14 *European Law Journal* (2008) pp. 186–202

Hodson 2011: L. Hodson, 'A Marriage by any other Name? Schalk and Kopf v. Austria,' 11 *Human Rights Law Review* (2011) pp. 170–179

Hoevenaars 1997: P.P.M. Hoevenaars, 'Het wetsvoorstel partnerschapsregistratie' ['The bill on partnership registration'], 128 *WPNR* (1997) pp. 226–232

Hoffmann 2008: H. Hoffmann, 'FreizügG/EU § 3' ['§ 3 FreizügG/EU'], in R. Hofmann and H. Hoffmann, *Ausländerrecht* [Aliens law], 1st edn. (Baden-Baden, Nomos 2008)

Hofmann 2011: H. Hofmann, 'Art 6' ['Art. 6'], in: B. Smidt-Bleibtreu et al., *GG Komentar* [GG Commentary], 11th edn. (Berlin, Carl Heymanns Verlag 2011) pp. 268–302

Hoffmann-Klein 2010: F. Hoffmann-Klein, 'Zur Verfassungsmäßigkeit der Abtreibungsfinanzierung' ['On the constitutionality of the financing of abortion'], *ZfL* (2010) pp. 82–85

Höfler 2011: K. Höfler, 'SGB V § 24b Schwangerschaftsabbruch und Sterilisation' ['§ 24b SGB V Pregnancy Termination and Sterilisation'], in: S. Leitherer (ed.), *Kasseler Kommentar, Sozialversicherungsrecht* [Kasseler Commentary social insurance law], 69th ed (München, Verlag Beck 2011)

Hogan 2010: C. Hogan, 'JMcD v PL and BM Sperm Donor Fathers and De Facto Families', 13 *Irish Journal of Family Law* (2010) pp. 83–93

Hogan and Whyte 2003: G. Hogan and G. Whyte, *J.M. Kelly, The Irish Constitution* (Dublin, LexisNexis Butterworths 2003)

Hooff, van et al 2010: M.H. Van Hooff et al., 'O-199 Cross-border reproductive care for egg-donation in Dutch women', 25 *Human Reproduction* (2010) p. i79, online available at www.humrep.oxfordjournals.org/content/25/suppl_1/i77.abstract3, visited May 2014

Hoppe 2009: T. Hoppe, 'Die Verfassungswidrigkeit der Ungleichbehandlung von Ehe und eingetragener Lebenspartnerschaft im Bereich der betrieblichen Hinterbliebenenrente

(VBL)' ['The unconstitutionality of the unequal treatment of marriage and civil partnership in respect of occupational survivor's pensions (VBL)'], *DVBl.* (2009) pp. 1516–1519

Hoppe, van 2009: L. van Hoppe, 'Wijziging van Boek 1 van het Burgerlijk Wetboek in verband met verkorting van de adoptieprocedure en wijziging van de Wet opneming buitenlandse pleegkinderen ter adoptie in verband met adoptie door echtgenoten van gelijk geslacht tezamen' ['Amendment of Book 1 of the Civil Code in relation to the adoption procedure and amendment of the Act placement of foreign foster children for adoption in relation to joint adoption by same-sex spouses'], 48 *Ars Aequi* (2009) pp. 191–195

Hoppe 2010: T. Hoppe, 'Verpartnerte Beamte: Rückwirkender Anspruch auf Gleichstellung?' ['Civil servants in civil partnerships: retroactive right to equal treatment?'], *ZBR Heft* (2010) pp. 189–216

Human Rights Watch 2010: Human Rights Watch, *A State of Isolation, Access to Abortion for Women in Ireland* (New York, Human Rights Watch 2010), www.hrw.org/node/87910, visited 3 June 2010

Huster 2009: S. Huster, `Die Leistungspflicht der GKV für Maßnahmen der künstlichen Befruchtung und der Krankheitsbegriff' ['The obligation of the GKV to reimburse artificial insemination and the definition of illness'], *NJW* (2009) pp. 1713–1716

ILGA-Europe 2011: ILGA-Europe, *ILGA-Europe's contribution to the Green Paper* (ILGA-Europe 2011), www.ilga-europe.org/home/publications/policy_papers/green_paper_april_2011, visited June 2014

Isensee 1986: J. Isensee, 'Abtreibung als Leistungstatbestand der Sozialversicherung und der grundgesetzliche Schutz des ungeborenen Lebens' ['Abortion as an element of offence under social insurance law and the constitutional protection of the life of the unborn child'], *NJW* (1986) pp. 1645–1651

Jäger 2010: T. Jäger, 'Der neue deutsch-französische Güterstand der Wahl-Zugewinngemeinschaft – Inhalt und seine ersten Folgen für die Gesetzgebung und Beratungspraxis' ['The new Franco-German Agreement on the Optional Matrimonial Property Regime – Content and ist first consequences for the legislative process and consulting practice'] , *DNotZ* (2010) pp. 804–826

Jakob 2002: D. Jakob, *Die eingetragene Lebenspartnerschaft im internationalen Privatrecht* [Civil partnership in International Private Law] (Köln, Schmidt 2002)

Janssen 2013: H.L. Janssen, 'Commentaar op art. 12 EVRM, para. C.1.8', ['Commentary to Art. 12 ECHR, para. C.1.8'], in: *Sdu Commentaar EVRM, Deel 1 – Materiele* bepalingen ['Sdu Commentary to the ECHR, Part 1 – Material provisions'] (Den Haag, Sdu Uitgevers 2013)

Janssens et al. 2005: P.M.W. Janssens et al., 'Wet Donorgegevens Kunstmatige Bevruchting: inhoud en gevolgen' ['Act Donor Information Artificial Reproduction: content and consequences'], 149 *Nederlands Tijdschrift voor Geneeskunde* (2005) pp. 1412–1416

Jessurun d'Oliveira 1995: H.U. Jessurun d'Oliveira, 'Geregistreerd partnerschap en de Europese Unie, kanttekeningen over de internationale reikwijdte van het wetsvoorstel' ['Registered partnership and the European Union: comments on the international scope of the bill'], 70 *Nederlands Juristenblad* (1995) p. 1569

Jessurun d'Oliveira 1996: H.U. Jessurun d'Oliveira, 'Het raadselachtige buitenland, de partnerregistratie en het burgerlijk huwelijk voor homo's en lesbo's' ['The mysterious other countries, partner registration and civil marriage for gays and lesbians'], 71 *Nederlands Juristenblad* (1996) pp. 755–756

Jessurun d'Oliveira 1999: H.U. Jessurun d'Oliveira, 'Het geregistreerd partnerschap, het 'homohuwelijk' en het IPR' ['Registered partnership, 'gay marriage' and Private International Law'], 74 *Nederlands Juristenblad* (1999) pp. 305–306

Jessurun d'Oliveira 2000: H.U. Jessurun d'Oliveira, 'Freedom of movement of spouses and registered partners in the European Union', in: J. Basedow et al. (eds), *Private Law in the international arena – From national conflict rules towards harmonization and unification, Liber amicorum Kurt Siehr* (The Hague, TCM Asser Press 2000) pp. 527–543

Jessurun d'Oliveira 2001: H.U. Jessurun d'Oliveira, 'Vrijheid van verkeer voor geregistreerde partners in de Europese Unie. Hoog tijd!' ['Free movement for registered partners in the European Union. High time!'], 76 *Nederlands Juristenblad* (2001) pp. 205–210

Johansen 2003: S.J. Johansen, 'Clearly Ambiguous: A Visitor's View of the Irish Abortion Referendum of 2002', 25 *Loyola of Los Angeles International & Comparative Law Review* (2003) pp. 205–241

Johnson 2004: K.J. Johnson, '"New thinking about an old issue;" the abortion controversy continues in Russia and Ireland – *Could Roe* v. *Wade* have been the better solution?', 15 *Indiana International and Comparative Law Review* (2004) pp. 183–213

Joppe 2000A: I.S. Joppe, 'Het geregistreerd partnerschap in het Nederlands IPR (I)' ['Registered partnership in Dutch Private International Law (I)'], 131 *WPNR* (2000) pp. 371–375

Joppe 2000B: I.S. Joppe, 'Het geregistreerd partnerschap in het Nederlands IPR (II)' ['Registered partnership in Dutch Private International Law (II)', 131 *WPNR* (2000) pp. 391–395

Jorzig 2013: A. Jorzig, 'Anspruch auf Kenntnis der genetischen Abstammung eines durch eine heterologe Insemination gezeugten Kindes' ['The right to information on the genetic descent of a child born through heterologous insemination'], *jurisPR-MedizinR* (2013) Anm. 1

Kalkman-Bogerd 1999: L.E. Kalkman-Bogerd, 'Het nieuwe Planningsbesluit in-vitrofertilisatie. Enkele kanttekeningen' ['The new planning decree *in vitro* fertilisation. Some comments'], 23 *Tijdschrift voor Gezondheidsrecht* (1999) pp. 56–65

Karakosta 2013: C. Karakosta, 'Portability of same-sex marriages and registered partnerships within the EU', 2 *Cyprus Human Rights Law Review* (2013) pp.53–82

Keller et al. 1992: R. Keller et al., *Embryonenschutsgesetz, Kommentar zum Embryonenschutzgesetz* [Embryo Protection Act, Commentary to the Embryo Protection Act] (Stuttgart, W. Kolhammer GmbH 1992)

Kemper 2003: R. Kemper, `Die Lebenspartnerschaft in der Entwicklung – Perspektiven für die Weiterentwicklung des Lebenspartnerschaftsrechts nach dem Urteil des BVerfG vom 17. 7. 2002' ['The civil partnership in development – Prospects for the further development of the law on civil partnership after the judgment of the German Constitutional Court of 17 July 2002'], *FPR* (2003) pp. 1–5

Kentenich and Pietzer 2010: H. Kentenich and K. Pietzer, 'Überlegungen zur gesetzlichen Nachbesserung in der Reproduktionsmedizin' ['Thoughts on legislative improvements in the field of reproduction medicine'], in: H. Frister and D. Olzen, *Reproduktionsmedizin, Rechtliche Fragestellungen. Dokumentation der Tagung zum 10-jährigen Bestehen des Instituts für Rechtsfragen der Medizin Düsseldorf* [Reproduction medicine, legal questions. Proceedings of the Conference for the 10 year anniversary of the Düsseldorf institute for medical legal issues] (Düsseldorf, Düsseldorf University Press 2010) pp. 59–74

Ketting and Van Praag: E. Ketting and P. van Praag, *Schwangerschaftsabbruch, Gesetz und Praxis im internationalen Vergleich* [Termination of pregnancy, law and practice in international comparison] (Tübingen, DGVT 1985)

Kiel 2006: P. Kiel, 'Hk-LpartR' ['Hk-LpartR'], in: M. Bruns and R. Kemper, *Lebenspartnerschaftsrecht, Handkommentar* [Civil Partnership Commentary], 2nd edn. (Baden-Baden, Nomos Verlagsgesellschaft 2006)

Kirchof 2001: P. Kirchhof, 'Lebenspartnerschaftsgesetze und Grundgesetz' ['Law on civil partnerships and the Constitution'], *FPR* (2001) pp. 436–439

Kischel 2014: U. Kischel, 'BeckOK GG Art. 3–2. Sexuelle Orienterung' ['BeckOK GG Art. 3–2. Sexual Orientation'], in: V. Epping and C. Hillgruber (eds.), *Beck'scher Online-Kommentar*

GG [Beck Online Commentary to the German Basic Law], 21st edn. (München, Verlag Beck 2014)
Klashtorny 1996: N. Klashtorny, 'Ireland's abortion law: an abuse of international law', 10 *Temple International & Comparative Law Journal* (1996) pp. 419–443
Klinkhammer 2007: F. Klinkhammer, 'Der Scheinvater und sein Kind – Das Urteil des BVerfG vom 13.2.2007 und seine gesetzlichen Folgen' ['The ostensible father and his child – The judgment of the German Constitutional Court of 12 February 2007 and its legal consequences'], *Forum Familienrecht* 4/2007, pp. 128–131, online available at www.forum-familienrecht.de/neu/dateien/0407/128-131.pdf, visited March 2011
Koch 1998: H.-G. Koch, 'Bundersrepublik Deutschland' ['Federal Republic of Germany'], in: A. Eser and H.-G. Koch, *Schwangerschaftsabbruch im internationalen Vergleich, Rechtlichen Regelungen – Soziale Rahmenbedingungen – Empirische Grunddaten, Teil 1: Europa* [Abortion in international comparison, legal regulation – social framework – empirial basic data, Part 1: Europe] (Baden-Baden, Nomos Verlagsgesellschaft 1988) pp. 17–324
Kochenov 2009: D. Kochenov, 'On options of citizens and moral choices of states: gays and European federalism', 33 *Fordham International Law Journal* (2009) pp. 156–205
Koegler 1996: S. Koegler, 'Ireland's Abortion Information Act of 1995', 29 *Vanderbilt Journal of Transnational Law* (1996) pp. 1117–1150
Koffeman 2010: N.R. Koffeman, 'Case note to ECtHR 24 June 2010, *Schalk and Kopf* v. *Austria*, no. 30141/04', 11 *European Human Rights Cases* 2010/92 (in Dutch)
Koffeman 2011A: N.R. Koffeman, 'Case note to ECtHR 21 September 2010 (dec.), *Manenc* v. *France*, no. 66686/09', 12 *European Human Rights Cases* 2011/28 (in Dutch)
Koffeman 2011B: N.R. Koffeman, 'Het Ierse abortusverbod en het EVRM; is uitbesteding de nieuwe norm?' ['The Irish abortion ban and the ECHR: is outsourcing the new standard?'], 36 *NTM/NJCM-Bulletin* (2011) pp. 372–374 (in Dutch)
Koffeman 2012A: N.R. Koffeman, 'Case-note to ECtHR 15 March 2012, *Gas and Dubois* v. *France*, no. 25951/07', 13 *European Human Rights Cases* 2012/114 (in Dutch)
Koffeman 2012B: N.R. Koffeman, 'Case-note to ECtHR 28 August 2012, *Costa and Pavan* v. *Italy*, no. 54270/10', 13 *European Human Rights Cases* 2012/222 (in Dutch)
Koffeman 2013: N.R. Koffeman, 'Case-note to ECtHR [GC] 19 February 2013, *X. a.o.* v. *Austria*, no. 19010/07', 14 *European Human Rights Cases* 2013/104 (in Dutch)
Koffeman 2014A: N.R. Koffeman, 'Case-note to ECtHR [GC] 7 November 2013, *Vallianatos a.o.* v. *Greece*, nos. 29381/09 and 32684/09', 15 *European Human Rights Cases* 2014/34 (in Dutch)
Koffeman 2014B: N.R. Koffeman, 'Case-note to ECtHR 26 June 2014, *Mennesson* v. *France*, no. 65192/11 and ECtHR 26 June 2014, *Labassee* v. *France*, no. 65941/11', 15 *European Human Rights Cases* 2014/222 (in Dutch)
Koffeman 2014C: N.R. Koffeman, 'Case-note to ECtHR 8 July 2014 (dec.), *D. a.o.* v. *Belgium*, no. 29176/13', 15 *European Human Rights Cases* 2014/269 (in Dutch)
Koolhoven 2005: R. Koolhoven, 'Het Nederlandse opengestelde huwelijk in het Duitse IPR. De eerste rechterlijke uitspraak is daar!' ['The Dutch opened up marriage in German Private International Law. The first court judgment has been issued!'], *NIPR* (2005) pp. 138–142
Kreimer 1993: S.F. Kreimer, 'But Whoever Treasures Freedom ...: The Right to Travel and Extraterritorial Abortions', 91 *Michigan Law Review* (1993) pp. 907–938
Kremer et al. 2007: J. Kremer et al., 'Zorg over de grens. Geen grip op kwaliteit van buitenlandse fertiliteitsbehandelingen' ['Care across the border. No grip on the quality of foreign fertily treatment'], 62 *Medisch Contact* (2007) pp. 1343–1346
Kreß 2010: H. Kreß, 'Präimplantationsdiagnostik und Fortpflanzungsmedizin angesichts des ethischen Pluralismus. Rechtspolitische Gesichtspunkte nach dem Urteil des BGH' ['Preimplantation genetic diagnosis in the light of ethical pluralism. Legal political

considerations after the judgment of the German Federal Court of Justice'], *ZRP* (2010) pp. 201–205

Kreß 2013: H. Kreß. 'Samenspende und Leihmutterschaft – Problemstand, Rechtsunsicherheiten, Regelungsansätze' ['Sperm donation and surrogacy – Problems, legal uncertainty, regulatory approaches'], *FPR* (2013) pp. 240–243

Kroppenberg 2013: I. Kroppenberg, 'Unvereinbarkeit des Verbots der sukzessiven Stiefkindadoption durch eingetragene Lebenspartner mit dem Grundgesetz' ['The incompatibility of the prohibition of successive adoption by civil partners with the German Basic Law'], *NJW* (2013) pp. 2161–2164

Kruijer et al. 2010: H. Kruijer et al., *Landelijke abortusregistratie 2008* [National abortion registration 2008] (Utrecht, Rutgers Nisso Groep 2010), online available at www.rng.nl/productenendiensten/onderzoekspublicaties/downloadbare-publicaties-in-pdf, visited June 2010

Kugele 2008: D. Kugele, 'Kein Anspruch auf Familienzuschlag der Stufe 1 bei eingetragener Lebenspartnerschaft' [No entitlement to family benefits in category 1 for civil partnerships'], *jurisPR-BVerwG* 10/2008

Kunz-Schmidt 2011: S. Kunz-Schmidt, 'Präimplantationsdiagnostik (PID) – der Stand des Gesetzgebungsverfahrens und der aktuellen Diskussion' ['Preimplantation genetic diagnosis (PGD) – the current legislative procedure and debate'], *NJ* (2011) pp. 231–239

Küppers 1988: W. Küppers, *Die zivilrechtlichen Folgen der entgeltlichen Tragemutterschaft* [The civil consequences of commercial surrogacy] (Frankfurt am Main, Peter Lang 1988)

Lammich 1988: S. Lammich, 'Landesbericht Deutsche Demokratische Republik' ['National report German Democratic Republic'], in A. Eser and H.-G. Koch, *Schwangerschaftsabbruch im internationalen Vergleich, Rechtlichen Regelungen – Soziale Rahmenbedingungen – Empirische Grunddaten, Teil 1: Europa* [Abortion in international comparison, legal regulation – social framework – empirial basic data, part 1: Europe] (Baden-Baden, Nomos Verlagsgesellschaft 1988) pp. 326–382

Lang 2014: H. Lang, 'BeckOK GG Art. 2' ['Beck online Commentary to Art. 2 GG'], in: V. Epping and C. Hillgruber (eds.), *Beck'scher Online-Kommentar GG* [Beck Online Commentary to the German Basic Law], 22nd edn. (München, Verlag Beck 2014)

Langohr-Plato 2010: U. Langohr-Plato, 'Hinterbliebenenversorgung für eingetragene Lebenspartner' ['Survivor's pensions for registered partners'], *juris Praxis Report -ArbR* 11/2010 Anm. 5

Lanz-Zumstein 1986: M. Lanz-Zumstein (ed.), *Embryonenschutz und Befruchtungstechnik, Seminarbericht*
und Stellungnahmen aus der Arbeitsgruppe "Gentechnologie" des deutschen Juristinnenbundes [Protection of embryos and fertilisation techniques, Seminar report and statements of the working group "Genetic Engineering" of the German Women Lawyers' Association], (München, J. Schweitzer Verlag 1986)

Laufs 2009: A. Laufs, 'Schwangerschaftsabbruch' ['Termination of pregnancy'], in A. Laufs et al., *Arztrecht* [Medical law], 6th edn. (München, Verlag Beck 2009)

Laufs 2010: A. Laufs, '§ 129 Fortpflanzungs- und Genmedizin' ['§ 129 Reproduction and gene medicine'] in: A. Laufs and B.R. Kern (eds.), *Handbuch des Arztrechts* [Handbook of medical law] 4th edn. (München, Verlag C.H. Beck 2010)

Lawson 1994: R.A. Lawson, 'The Irish Abortion Cases: European Limits to National Sovereignty?', 1 *European Journal of Health Law* (1994) pp. 167–186

Lee, van and Wijsen 2008: L. van Lee and C. Wijsen, *Landelijke abortusregistratie 2007* [National abortion registration 2007] (Utrecht, Rutgers Nisso Groep 2008), online available at www.rng.nl/productenendiensten/onderzoekspublicaties/downloadbare-publicaties-in-pdf, visited 2 June 2010

Leenen 1986: H.J.J. Leenen, 'De gezondheidsrechtelijke status van het embryo' ['The status of the embryo in medical law'], in J.K.M. Gevers and H.J.J. Leenen (eds.), *Rechtsvragen rond voortplanting en erfelijkheid* [Legal questions surrounding human reproduction and heredity] (Deventer, Kluwer 1986)

Leenen 1988: H.J.J. Leenen, *Handboek Gezondheidsrecht* [Handbook Medical Law], 2nd edn. (Alphen aan de Rijn, Samson 1988)

Lenaerts 2009–2010: K. Lenaerts, 'Federalism and the rule of law: perspectives from the European Court of Justice', 33 *Fordham International Law Journal* (2009–2010) pp. 1338–1387

Lenaerts 2013: K. Lenaerts, 'The EU Charter of Fundamental Rights: Scope of Application and Methods of Interpretation', in: V. Kronenberger et al. (eds), *De Rome à Lisbonne: les juridictions de l'Union européenne à la croisée des chemins: mélanges en l'honneur de Paolo Mengozzi* (Bruxelles, Bruylant 2013) pp. 107–143

Lenaerts and Gutierrez-Fons 2010: K. Lenaerts and J.A. Gutiérrez-Fons, 'The constitutional allocation of powers and general principles of EU law', 46 *CMLRev* (2010) pp. 1629–1699

Deutsche Akademie der Naturforscher Leopoldina et al. 2011: Deutsche Akademie der Naturforscher Leopoldina et al., *Ad-hoc statement Preimplantation genetic diagnosis (PGD). The effects of limited approval in Germany*, January 2011, online available at: www.leopoldina.org/fileadmin/user_upload/Politik/Empfehlungen/Nationale_Empfehlungen/stellungnahme_PID_2011_final_a4ansicht_EN.pdf, visited June 2011

Liermann 1991: S. Liermann, 'Der Begriff 'Ersatzmutter' im Embryonenschutzgesetz' ['The notion of 'surrogate mother' in the Embryo Protecion Act'], *Zeitschrift für das gesamte Familienrecht, FamRZ* (1991) p. 1403

Lind 1997: C. Lind, 'Perceptions of sex in the legal determination of fatherhood – X, Y and Z v UK', 9 *Child & Fam. L. Q.* (1997) pp. 401–498

Loenen 2013: T. Loenen, 'Gelijk recht op tweede-ouderadoptie voor ongehuwde homoseksuele en heteroseksuele paren. X e.a. tegen Oostenrijk' ['Equal right to joint adoption for unmarried homosexual and heterosexual couples. X. a.o. v. Austria'], 38 *NJCM-Bull/NTM* (2013) pp. 627–643

Londras, de 2013: F. de Londras, 'Suicide and Abortion: Analysing the Legislative Options in Ireland', 19 *Medico-Legal Journal of Ireland* 2013, pp. 4–10

Londras, de and Dzehtsiarou 2013: F. de Londras and K. Dzehtsiarou, 'Grand Chamber of the European Court of Human Rights, A, B & C v Ireland', 62 *International and Comparative Law Quarterly* (2013) pp. 250–262

Londras, de and Graham 2013: F. de Londras and L. Graham, 'Impossible Floodgates and Unworkable Analogies in the Irish Abortion Debate', 3 *Irish Journal of Legal Studies* (2013) pp. 54–75

Lüderitz 1990: A. Lüderitz, 'Verbot von Kinderhandel und Ersatzmuttervermittlung durch Änderung des Adoptionsvermittlungsgesetzes' ['Prohibition of child trafficking and of surrogacy mediation by means of amendment of the German adoption Act'], *NJW* (1990) pp.1633–1637

Lungstras 2010: A.B. Lungstras, 'Die Präimplantationsdiagnostik verbieten oder erlauben?' ['To allow or not to allow preimplantation genetic diagnosis'], *NJ* (2010) pp. 485–492

MacLean 1999: D.A. MacLean, 'Can the EC kill the Irish unborn?; An investigation of the European Community's ability to impinge on the moral sovereignty of Member States', 28 *Hofstra Law Review* (1999) pp. 527–571

Madden 1995: D. Madden, 'Medico-Legal Aspects of In Vitro Fertilisation and Related Infertility Treatments', 1 *Medico-Legal Journal of Ireland* (1995) pp. 13–17

Madden 1996: D. Madden, 'Legal Issues in Artificial Insemination', 2 *Medico-Legal Journal of Ireland* (1996) pp. 11–18

Madden 1997: D. Madden, 'In Vitro Fertilisation: The Moral and Legal Status of the Human Pre-Embryo', *Medico-Legal Journal of Ireland* (1997) pp. 12–20

Madden 2001: D. Madden, 'Recent Developments in Assisted Human Reproduction: Legal and Ethical Issues', 7 *Medico-Legal Journal of Ireland* (2001) pp. 53–62

Madden 2011: D. Madden, 'Guest Editorial: Assisted Reproduction in Ireland – Time to Legislate', 17 *Medico-Legal Journal of Ireland* (2011) pp. 3–5

Magli et al. 2008: M.C. Magli et al., 'Revised guidelines for good practice in IVF laboratories', 23 *Human Reproduction* (2008) pp. 1253–1262

Malenstein, van 1986: G. van Malestein, 'In vitro fertilisatie in het ziekenfondspakket! Afwijzend besluit Van der Reijden juridisch niet meer houdbaar' ['In vitro fertilisation in the National Health Scheme! Refusal Van der Reijden no longer legally tenable'], 41 *Medisch Contact* (1986) pp. 722–724

Mankowski 2011: P. Mankowski, *J. von Staudingers Kommentar zum Bürgerlichen Gesetzbuch mit Einführungsgesetz und Nebengestezen* [J. von Staudinger's Commentary to the Civil Code, with the Introductory Act and anciliary acts] (Sellier, Berlin 2011)

Manners 1996: P. Manners, 'Can governmental policy trump the freedom of speech? Access to information about abortion services in Ireland and the United States', 20 *Suffolk Transnational Law Review* (1996) pp. 289–301

Martiny 2012A: D. Martiny, 'Private International Law Aspects of Same-Sex couples under German Law', in: K. Boele-Woelki and A. Fuchs (eds.), *Legal recognition of same-sex Relationships in Europe, National, cross-border and European perspectives*, 2nd edn. (Cambridge, Intersentia 2012) pp. 189–223

Martiny 2012B: D. Martiny, 'Workshop: cross-border recognition (and refusal of recognition) of registered partnerships and marriages with a focus on their financial aspects and the consequences for divorce, maintenance and succession', in: K. Boele-Woelki and A. Fuchs (eds.), *Legal recognition of same-sex Relationships in Europe, National, cross-border and European perspectives*, 2nd edn. (Cambridge, Intersentia 2012) pp. 225–252

Mattern 1991: M.G. Mattern, 'German Abortion Law: The Unwanted Child of Reunification', 13 *Loyola of Los Angeles International and Comparative Law Review* (1990–1991) pp. 643–694

Maurer 2001A: A. Maurer, 'Federal Constitutional Court To Decide Whether to Issue a Temporary Injunction Against Germany's New Lifetime Partnerships Law for Homosexual Couples', 2 *German Law Journal* (2001), available at www.germanlawjournal.com/index.php?pageID=11&artID=42, visited June 2014

Maurer 2001B: A. Maurer, 'Federal Constitutional Court Does Not Issue Temporary Injunction to Block the Entry Into Force of the Lifetime Partnership Law', 2 *German Law Journal* (2001), available at www.germanlawjournal.com/index.php?pageID=11&artID=73, visited June 2014

Maurer 2010: M. Maurer, 'Die rechtliche Behandlung von Lebenspartnern im Steuernrecht' ['The legal treatment of civil partner in the area of tax law'], *FPR* (2010) pp. 196–199

Mayer 2014: C. Mayer, 'Sachwidrige Differenzierungen in internationalen Leihmutterschaftsfällen' ['Improper differentiations in international surrogacy cases'], *IPRax* (2014) pp. 57–62

McBrien 2002: M.C. McBrien, 'Ireland: balancing traditional domestic abortion law with modern reality and international influence', 26 *Suffolk Transnational Law Review* (2002) pp. 195–222

McCracken 2001: B. McCracken, 'The Irish Constitution – an overview', in: J. Sarkin and W. Binchy (eds.), *Human Rights, the Citizen and the State. South African and Irish Approaches* (Dublin, Round Hall Sweet & Maxwell, 2001) pp. 52–62

Mcguinnes and Uí Chonnachtaigh 2011: S. Mcguinness and S. Uí Chonnachtaigh, 'Implications of Recent Developments in Ireland for the Status of the Embryo, Special Section: Bioethics beyond Borders 2011', 20 *Cambridge Quarterly of Healthcare Ethics* (2011) pp. 396–408

McGuinness 2011: S. McGuinness, 'Commentary. A, B, and C leads to D (for Delegation!)', 19 *Medical Law Review* (2011) pp. 476–491

McHale 2010: J. McHale, 'Fundamental rights and health care', in: E. Mossialos et al. (eds.), *Health Systems Governance in Europe: The Role of European Union Law and Policy* (Cambridge, Cambridge University Press 2010) pp. 282–314, online available at www.euro.who.int/en/who-we-are/partners/observatory/studies/health-systems-governance-in-europe-the-role-of-eu-law-and-policy, visited June 2014

McInnes 1999: J. McInnes, 'Case note to Case C249/ 96, Lisa Jacqueline Grant v. South West Trains Ltd, Judgment of the Full Court of 17 February 1998, [1998] ECR I636', 36 *CMLRev* (1999) pp. 1043–1058

McKnorrie 2003: K. McKnorrie, 'Would Scots Law Recognise a Dutch Same-Sex Marriage?', 7 *Edinburgh L. Rev* (2003) pp. 147–173

McLean and McMillan 2009: I. McLean and A. McMillan, *The Concise Oxford Dictionary of Politics*, 3rd edn. (Oxford, Oxford University Press, Published online: 2009, eISBN: 9780191727191)

McLoone 2011: C. McLoone, 'Civil Partnership and Certain Rights and Obligations of Cohabitants Act 2010: A Practitioner's Guide', 14 *Irish Journal of Family Law* (2011) pp. 58–63

McMahon 2011: A. McMahon, 'The Legal Status of Embryos In Vitro in Ireland – A "Precarious" Position', 17 *Medico-Legal Journal of Ireland* (2011) pp. 33–42

Mee 2004: J. Mee, 'A critique of the Law Reform Commission's consultation paper on the rights and duties of cohabitees', 39 *The Irish Jurist* (2004) pp. 74–110

Mee and Ronayne 2000: J. Mee and K. Ronayne, *Partnership rights of same sex couples* (Dublin, The Equality Authority 2000)

Meer-Noort, van der et al. 2011: I. van der Meer-Noort et al., 'Cross border reproductive care; gebruik van eiceldonatie in het buitenland door Nederlandse vrouwen' ['Cross border reproductive care; use of egg cell donation by Dutch women in foreign countries'], 128 *Nederlands Tijdschrift voor Obstetrie & Gynaecologie* (2011) pp. 98–103

Meeusen et al. 2007: J. Meeusen et al., 'General Report', in J. Meeusen et al. (eds.), *International family law for the European Union* (Antwerpen, Intersentia 2007) pp. 1–24

Mei, van der 2006: A.P. van der Mei, 'Zorg over de grens' ['Care across the border'], in: M. Faure and M. Peeters (eds.), *Grensoverschrijdend recht* [Cross-border law] (Antwerpen, Intersentia 2006) pp. 49–71

Mei, van der 2011: A.P. van der Mei, 'Cross-border access to healthcare and entitlement to complementary "Vanbraekel reimbursement"', 36 *European Law Review* (2011) pp. 431–439

Melcher 2012: M. Melcher, 'Private international law and registered relationships: an EU perspective', 20 *European Review of Private Law* (2012) pp. 1075–1096

Mercurio 2003: B. Mercurio, 'Abortion in Ireland: An analysis of the Legal Transformation Resulting from Membership in the European Union', 11 *Tulane Journal of International & Comparative Law* (2003) pp. 141–180

Mertes et al. 2012: H. Mertes et al., 'Implications of oocyte cryostorage for the practice of oocyte donation', 27 *Human Reproduction* (2012) pp. 2886–2893

Messner 2010: M. Messner, 'Lebenspartnerschaft – Steuerliche Konsequenzen des BVerfG-Beschlusses vom 21. 7. 2010' ['Civil partnership – implications of the decision of the German Constitutional Court of 21 July 2010 for tax law'], *DStR* (2010) pp. 1875–1879

Millns 2002: S. Millns, 'Reproducing inequalities; assisted conception and the challenge of legal pluralism', 24 *Journal of Social Welfare and Family Law* (2002) pp. 19–36

Milzer 2010: L. Milzer, 'Anmerkung zum OLG Hamm, Beschluss vom 01.12.2009 – 15 Wx 236/09' ['Case-note to OLG Hamm decision of 1 December 2009 – 15 Wx 236/09'], *FamFR* (2010) p. 47

Moriarty and Mooney Cottter 2004: B. Moriarty and A.-M. Mooney Cotter (eds.), *Human rights law* (Oxford, Oxford University Press 2004)

Moschel 2009: M. Moschel, 'Germany's Life Partnerships: Separate and Unequal', 16 *Colum. J. Eur. L.* (2009–2010) pp. 37–66

Mourik, van 1997: M.J.A. van Mourik, 'Privaatrecht Aktueel. Geregistreerd partnerschap!' ['Topical issues of private law. Registered partnership!'], 128 *WPNR* (1997) pp. 225–226

Moynihan 2008: Y. Moynihan, "God has given you one face and you give yourself another": The implications of transsexual recognition in matters of marriage: Dr Lydia Foy's laudable victory spawns reform in terms of same-sex unions', 11 *Irish Journal of Family Law* (2008) pp. 38–43

Muckel 2012: S. Muckel, 'Ungleichbehandlung von Ehe und eingetragener Lebenspartnerschaft – Grunderwerbsteuer' ['Unequal treatment of marriage and civil partnership – conveyance tax'], *JA* (2012) pp. 877–879

Muckel 2013A: S. Muckel, 'Sukzessive Adoption – Ablehnung für eingetragene Lebenspartner verfassungswidrig' ['Successive adoption – nonadmission of civil partners unconstitutional'], *JA* (2013) pp. 396–398

Muckel 2013B: S. Muckel, 'Ausschluss eingetragener Lebenspartner vom Ehegattensplitting verfassungswidrig' ['Exclusion of civil partners from income splitting unconstitutional'], *JA* (2013) pp. 714–717

Muermans and Liu 2009: H. Muermans and J. Liu, 'Gezinsvorming in cijfers' [Family formation in numbers'], in: *Internationale gezinsvorming begrensd? Een evaluatie van de verhoging van de inkomens- en leeftijdseis bij migratie van buitenlandse partners naar Nederland* [International family formation restricted? An evaluation of the raised income and age requirements with regard to the migration of foreign partners to the Netherlands] (The Hague: Ministry of Justice 2009), online available at www.wodc.nl/onderzoeksdatabase/de-gevolgen-van-de-aanscherping-van-het-gezins vormingsbeleid.aspx?cp=44&cs=6799, visited June 2014

Mulder 1991: L. Mulder, 'Té gelijk voor de wet: het 'homo-huwelijk' als heet hangijzer' ['Too equal for the law: same-sex marriage as controversial issue'], 46 *Tijdschrift voor Bestuurswetenschappen en Publiekrecht* (1991) pp. 307–312

Mulder 2012: J. Mulder, 'Some More Equal than Others? Matrimonial Benefits and the CJEU's Case Law on Discrimination on the Grounds of Sexual Orientation', 19 *Maastricht Journal of European and Comparative Law* (2012) pp. 505–523

Mullally 2006: S. Mullally, 'Debating Reproductive Rights in Ireland', in: B. Lockwood (ed.), *Women's Rights, A Human Rights Quarterly Reader* (Baltimore, Johns Hopkins University Press 2006) pp. 613–638

Mulligan 2011: A. Mulligan, 'Frozen Embryo Disposition In Ireland After *Roche v Roche*', 46 *The Irish Jurist* (2011) pp. 202–210

Mulligan 2013: A. Mulligan, 'Surrogacy in the Courts: The Definition of Motherhood', guest post at *humanrights.ie* of 30 January 2013, www.humanrights.ie/index.php/2013/01/30/surrogacy-in-the-courts-the-definition-of-motherhood, visited May 2014

Müller 2010: G. Müller, 'Anmerkung zu OLG Hamm: Sukzessivadoption eines Kindes durch den eingetragenen Lebenspartner' ['Case note to OLG Hamm: successive adoption of a child by a registered partner'], *DNotZ* (2010) pp. 698–703

Müller-Terpitz 2010: R. Müller-Terpitz, 'Das Recht auf Fortpflanzung – Vorgaben der Verfassung und der EMRK' ['The right to procreate – guidelines of the German Constitution and the ECHR'], in: H. Frister and D. Olzen (eds.), *Reproduktionsmedizin, Rechtliche Fragestellungen. Dokumentation der Tagung zum 10-jährigen Bestehen des Instituts für Rechtsfragen der Medizin Düsseldorf* [Reproduction medicine, legal questions. Proceedings of the Conference for the 10 year anniversary of the Düsseldorf institute for medical legal issues] (Düsseldorf, Düsseldorf University Press 2010) pp. 9–26

Müller-Terpitz 2011: R. Müller-Terpitz, 'Gesetz zum Schutz von Embryonen (Embryonenschutzgesetz – ESchG)' [Act on the protection of embryos (Embryo Protection Act – ESchG)'], in: A. Spickhoff, *Medizinrecht* [Medical Law], 1st edn. (München, Verlag Beck 2011)

Müller-Terpitz 2014A: R. Müller-Terpitz, 'GG Art. 6 [Ehe, Familie, nicht eheliche Kinder]' ['Marriage, family, children born out of wedlock'], in: A. Spickhoff, *Medizinrecht* [Medical Law], 2nd edn. (München, Verlag Beck 2014)

Müller-Terpitz 2014B: R. Müller-Terpitz, 'Gesetz zum Schutz von Embryonen (Embryonenschutzgesetz – ESchG)' [Act on the protection of embryos (Embryo Protection Act – ESchG)'], in: A. Spickhoff, *Medizinrecht* [Medical Law], 2nd edn. (München, Verlag Beck 2014)

Münch, von 1999: I. von Münch, 'Antidiskriminierungsgesetz – notwendig oder überflüssig?' ['Anti-discrimination Act – necessary or superfluous? '] *NJW* (1999) pp. 260–262

Murphy 1994: F. Murphy, 'Maastricht: implementation in Ireland', 19 *European Law Review* (1994) pp. 94–104

Murray 2012: C. Murray, 'Recognising the Modern Family: Extending Legislative Guardianship Rights in Ireland', 15 *Irish Journal of Family Law* (2012) pp. 39–48

Muscheler 2010: K. Muscheler, 'Die Reform des Lebenspartnerschaftsrechts' ['The reform of the Civil Partnership Act'], *FPR* (2010) pp. 227–236

Nationalen Ethikrat 2003: Nationalen Ethikrat (German Ethics Council), *Stellungnahme Genetische Diagnostik vor und während der Schwangerschaft* [Position paper genetic diagnosis before and during pregnancy], 2003 Nationalen Ethikrat (German Ethics Council), *Stellungnahme Genetische Diagnostik vor und wahrend der Schwangerschaft* [Position paper genetic diagnosis before and during pregnancy] (Nationaler Ethikrat, Berlin 2003) online available at: www.ethikrat.org/dateien/pdf/Stellungnahme_Genetische-Diagnostik.pdf, visited June 2014

National Rapporteur on Trafficking in Human Beings 2012: National Rapporteur on Trafficking in Human Beings, *Human trafficking for the purpose of the removal of organs and forced commercial surrogacy* (The Hague, BNRM 2012), online available at www.bnrm.nl/publicaties/orgaanverwijdering-draagmoederschap/index.aspx, visited June 2014

Neidert 2002: R. Neidert, 'Das überschätzte Embryonenschutzgesetz – was es verbietet und nicht verbietet' ['The overestimated law Embryo Protection Act – what it prohibits and does not prohibit'], *ZRP* (2002) pp. 467–471

Nelken 2009: D. Nelken, *Beyond law in context: developing a sociological understanding of law* (London, Ashgate 2009)

Nekkebroeck et al. 2010: J. Nekkebroeck et al., 'A preliminary profile of women opting for oocyte cryopreservation for non-medical reasons', 25 *Human Reproduction* (2010) pp. i15–i16

Ní Shúilleabháin 2010A: M. Ní Shuilleabhan, *Cross-Border Divorce Law. Brussels II bis* (Oxford, Oxford University Press 2010)

Ní Shúilleabháin 2010B: M. Ní Shúilleabháin, 'Ten years of European family law: Retrospective reflections from a common law perspective', 59 *International and Comparative Law Quarterly* (2010) pp. 1021–1053

Nuytinck 2008A: A.J.M. Nuytinck, 'Lesbisch ouderschap. Bespreking van het rapport van de Commissie lesbisch ouderschap en interlandelijke adoptie (commissie-Kalsbeek)' ['Lesbian parenthood. Review of the Report lesbian parenthood and interstate adoption (Kalsbeek Commission)'] 139 *WPNR* (2008) pp. 44–48

Nuytinck 2008B: A.J.M. Nuytinck, 'Het geregistreerd partnerschap wordt niet afgeschaft. Jammer, een gemiste kans!' ['The registered partnership will not be abolished. Shame, a missed opportunity!'], 139 *WPNR* (2008) pp. 306–312

Nuytinck 2010: A.J.M. Nuytinck, 'Concept-wetsvoorstel lesbisch ouderschap: meemoeder wordt juridisch moeder van rechtswege of door erkenning' [Draft bill lesbian parenthood: co-mother becomes legal mother by operation of the law or by recognition'], 141 *WPNR* (2010) pp. 343–348

Nuytinck 2011: A.J.M. Nuytinck, 'Huwelijk en geregistreerd partnerschap groeien steeds verder naar elkaar toe' ['Marriage and registered partnership are growing towards one another'], 142 *WPNR* (2011) pp. 1001–1007

O'Connell 2001: D. O'Connell, 'Ireland', in: R. Blackburn and J. Polakiewicz (eds.), *Fundamental Rights in Europe. The ECHR and its Member States 1950–2000* (Oxford: Oxford University Press 2001) pp. 423–474

O'Connell 2008: D. O'Connell, *Legal Study on Homophobia and Discrimination on Grounds of Sexual Orientation and Gender Identity, Thematic Study Ireland* (Galway 2008), online available at http://fra.europa.eu/en/country-report/2012/country-reports-homophobia-and-discrimination-grounds-sexual-orientation-part-1, visited June 2014

D. O'Connell 2010: D. O'Connell, *Legal Study on Homophobia and Discrimination on Grounds of Sexual Orientation and Gender Identity, Thematic Study Ireland* (Galway 2010), online available at www.fra.europa.eu/en/national-contribution/2012/country-thematic-studies-homophobia-transphobia-and-discrimination, visited June 2014

R. O'Connell 2010: R. O'Connell, 'Natural Law: Alive and Kicking?: a Look at the Constitutional Morality of Sexual Privacy in Ireland', in: L. May, and J. Brown (eds), *Philosophy of law: classic and contemporary readings* (Chichester, Wiley-Blackwell 2010) pp. 585–601

O'Connor 1997: D. O'Connor, 'Limiting "public morality" exceptions to free movement in Europe: Ireland's role in a changing European Union', 22 *Brooklyn Journal of International Law* (1997) pp. 695–733

O'Leary 1992: S. O'Leary, 'The Court of Justice as reluctant constitutional adjudicator: an examination of the abortion information case', 17 *European Law Review* (1992), pp. 138–157

O'Leary 2011: S. O'Leary, 'Free movement of persons and services', in: P. Graig and G. de Búrca, *The Evolution of EU law* (Oxford: Oxford University Press 2011) pp. 499–545

Olsthoorn-Heim et al. 2006: E.T.M. Olsthoorn-Heim et al., *Evaluatie Embryowet* [Evaluation Embryo Act], Reeks evaluatie regelgeving deel 20 (Den Haag: ZonMw 2006)

O'Shea 2012: N. O'Shea, 'Can Ireland's Constitution Remain Premised on the "Inalienable" Protection of the Marital Family Unit Without Continuing to Fail its International Obligations on the Rights of the Child?', 4 *Irish Journal of Family Law* (2012) pp. 87–94

O'Sullivan 2009: A. O'Sullivan, 'Same-sex marriage and the Irish Constitution', 13 *The International Journal of Human Rights* (2009) pp. 477–492

O'Sullivan et al. 2013: C. O'Sullivan et al., 'Article 40.3.3 and the Protection of Life During Pregnancy Bill 2013: The Impetus for, and Process of, Legislative Change', 3 *Irish Journal of Legal Studies* (2013) pp. 1–17

Oort, van 2012: C. van Oort, *Commentaar op Wetboek van Strafrecht, art. 296* [Commentary to the Criminal Code, Article 296] (Den Haag: OpMaat Sdu 2012)

Oudhof 2000: G.T. Oudhof, 'Het wetsvoorstel 'Wet donorgegevens kunstmatige inseminatie' en de (tegengestelde) belangen van het kind' [The Bill 'Act Donor Information Artificial Insemination' and the (conflicting) interests of the child'], *Tijdschrift voor Familie en Jeugdrecht* (2000) pp. 229–237

Oudhof 2002: T. Oudhof, 'Het belang van het kind bij kunstmatige voortplanting na overlijden: What's in the name' ['The interests of the child in artificial reproduction after decease: Whats in the name'], *Tijdschrift voor Familie- en Jeugdrecht* (2002) pp. 288–298

Outshoorn 1986: J. Outshoorn, *De politieke strijd rondom de abortuswetgeving in Nederland 1964–1984* [The political fight surrounding abortion legislation in the Netherlands 1964–1984] ('s-Gravenhage, VUGA 1986)

Papadopoulou 2002: L. Papadopoulou, 'In(di)visible Citizens(hip): Same-sex Partners in European Immigration Law', 21 *Yearbook of European Law* (2002) pp. 229–262

Palm and Baeten 2011: W. Palm and R. Baeten, 'The quality and safety paradox in the patients' rights Directive', 21 *European Journal of Public Health* (2011) pp. 272–274

Palm and Glinos 2010: W. Palm and I.A. Glinos, 'Enabling patient mobility in the EU: between free movement and coordination', in: E. Mossialos et al. (eds.), *Health Systems Governance in Europe: The Role of European Union Law and Policy* (Cambridge, Cambridge University Press 2010) pp. 509–560, online available at www.euro.who.int/en/who-we-are/partners/observatory/studies/health-systems-governance-in-europe-the-role-of-eu-law-and-policy, visited June 2014

Pauly 1997: W. Pauly, 'Sperrwirkungen des verfassungsrechtlichen Ehebegriffs' ['Barrier effects of the constitutional concept of marriage'], *NJW* (1997) pp. 1955–1957

Pelchen and Häberle 2011: G. Pelchen and P. Häberle, 'E 100. Gesetz zum Schutz von Embryonen (Embryonenschutzgesetz – ESchG) – § 2 Missbräuchliche Verwendung menschlicher Embryonen' Embryonen' [E.100. Act on the protection of embryos (Embryo Protection Act) – § 2 Abusive use of human embryos], in: G. Erbs and M. Kohlhaas, *Strafrechtliche Nebengesetze* [Ancillary criminal laws] (München: Verlag C.H. Beck 2011)

Pellis 2002: L. Pellis, 'Het homohuwelijk: een bijzonder nationaal product' ['Same-sex marriage: a special national product'] 24 *Tijdschrift voor Familie- en Jeugdrecht* (2002) pp. 162–168

Pennings 2004: G. Pennings, 'Legal harmonization and reproductive tourism in Europe', 19 *Human Reproduction* (2004) pp. 2689–2694

Pennings et al. 2008: G. Pennings et al., 'Cross-border reproductive care', 23 *Human Reproduction* (2008) pp. 2182–2184

Pennings et al. 2009: G. Pennings et al., 'Cross-border reproductive care in Belgium', 24 *Human Reproduction* (2009) pp. 3108–3118

Pennings 2010: G. Pennings, 'The rough guide to insemination: cross-border travelling for donor semen due to different regulations', *Facts, Views and Vision in ObGyn, Monograph* (2010) pp. 55–60, online available at www.fvvo.eu/assets/103/21-Pennings.pdf, visited May 2014

Pennings and Heidi 2010: G. Pennings and M. Heidi, 'The state and the infertile patient looking for treatment abroad: a difficult relationship', in: A. Tupasela (ed.), *Consumer Medicine* (TemaNord 2010) No. 530, pp. 99–114

Power 2004: C. Power, 'The benefits of marriage', 7 *Irish Journal of Family Law* (2004) pp. 29–31

Power 2006: C. Power, 'The Right to Marry', 9 *Irish Journal of Family Law* (2006) pp. 31–32

Power 2009: C. Power, 'Family law', 12 *Irish Journal of Family Law* (2009) pp. 22–24

Power and Shannon 2008: C. Power and G. Shannon, 'Practice and Procedure, Sperm donors and the legal recognition for same-sex couples', 11 *Irish Journal of Family Law* (2008) pp. 44–48

Power and Shannon 2009: C. Power and G. Shannon, 'Practice and Procedure, Assisted reproduction in Ireland', 12 *Irish Journal of Family Law* (2009) pp. 45–48

Prehn 2011: A. Prehn, 'Die Strafbarkeit der post-mortem-Befruchtung nach dem Embryonenschutzgesetz' ['The punishability of post-mortem fertilization under the Embryo Protection Act'], *MedR* (2011) pp. 559–568

Prütting and Höfling 2010: D. Prütting and W. Höfling, *Fachanwaltskommentar Medizinrecht* [Lawyers' commentary to medical law], 1st edn. 2010

Quaas et al. 2008: M. Quaas et al., '§ 68 Einzelfelder der Biomedizin, b) Kryokonservierung' ['§ 68 Individual areas of Biomedicine, b) cryopreservation'], in: M. Quaas et al., *Medizinrecht* [Medical law] 2nd edn. (München, Verlag C.H. Beck 2008)

Rademakers 2002: J. Rademakers, *Abortus in Nederland 1993–2000. Jaarverslag van de landelijke abortusregistratie* [Abortion the the Netherlands 1993–2000. Annual report of the national abortion registration] (Heemstede, StiSAN 2002)

Ratzel 2010: R. Ratzel 'Beschränkung des Rechts auf Fortpflanzung durch das ärztliche Berufsrecht' ['Limitation of the right to procreate by means of the law on the medical profession'], in: H. Frister and D. Olzen (eds.), *Reproduktionsmedizin, Rechtliche Fragestellungen. Dokumentation der Tagung zum 10-jährigen Bestehen des Instituts für Rechtsfragen der Medizin Düsseldorf* [Reproduction medicine, legal questions. Proceedings of the Conference for the 10 year anniversary of the Düsseldorf institute for medical legal issues] (Düsseldorf, Düsseldorf University Press 2010) pp. 43–58

Rauscher 2011: T. Rauscher, '§ 1591 Mutterschaft' ['§ 1591 Maternity'] in: *J. von Staudingers Kommentar zum Bürgerlichen Gezetzbuch mit Einführungsgesetz und Nebengesetzen. Buch 4. Familienrecht, §§ 1589, 1600d (Abstammung)* [J. von Staudinger's Commentary to the Civil Code, with the Introductory Act and anciliary acts, Volume 4, Family law, §§ 1589, 1600d (descent)] (Berlin, Sellier 2011)

Rayar and Wadsworth 1997: L. Rayar and S. Wadsworth, *The Dutch Penal Code* (Colorado, Fred B. Rothman &Co Littleton 1997)

Reddington 2011: D. Reddington, 'Civil Partnership vs Marriage – the Approach of the European Court of Human Rights', 14 *Irish Journal of Family Law* (2011) pp. 15–17

Reid and Caracciolo Di Torella 2002: E. Reid and E. Caracciolo Di Torella, 'The changing shape of the "European family" and fundamental rights', 27 *European Law Review* (2002) pp. 80–90

Reinke 2008: M. Reinke, *Fortpflanzungsfreiheit und das Verbot der Fremdeizellspende* [Freedom of reproduction and the prohibition of egg cell donation] (Berlin, Duncker & Humblot 2008)

Rijpma and Koffeman 2014: J. Rijpma and N. Koffeman, 'Free Movement Rights for Same-Sex Couples Under EU Law; What Role to Play for the CJEU?', in: D. Gallo et al. (eds.), *Same-Sex Couples before National, Supranational and International Jurisdictions* (Berlin, Springer 2014) pp. 455–491

Rhinehart 2013: M.A. Rhinehart, 'Abortions in Ireland: Reconciling a History of Restrictive Abortion Practices with the European Court of Human Rights' Ruling in *A., B. & C.* v. *Ireland*', 117 *Penn State Law Review* (2012–2013) pp. 959–978

Robbers 2010: G. Robbers, 'Artikel 6' ['Article 6'], in: C. Starck et al., *Kommentar zum Grundgesetz* [Commentary to the Basic Law] (München, Verlag Franz Vahlen 2010) pp. 683–755

Robert and Waaijer 1983: W.C.J. Robert and J.M.A. Waaijer (eds.), *Relatievrijheid en recht: inleidingen en verslag van de Leidse Conferentie van 25 en 26 mei 1982* [Relationship freedom and the law: introductory remarks to and report of the Leiden Conference of 25 and 26 May 1982] (Deventer, Kluwer 1983)

Röthel 2000: A. Röthel, 'Registrierte Partnerschaften im internationalen Privatrecht' ['Civil partnerships in international private law'], *IPRax* (2000) pp. 74–79

Röthel 2002: A. Röthel, 'Gleichgeschlechtliche Ehe und ordre public' [Same-sex marriage and *ordre public*], *IPRax* (2002) pp. 495–500

Röthel 2006: A. Röthel, 'Anerkennung gleichgeschlechtlicher Ehen nach deutschem und europäischem Recht' ['Recognition of same-sex marriage under German and European law'], *IPrax* (2006) pp. 250–253

Röthel 2010: A. Röthel, 'Art. 17b EGBGB', in: M. Würdinger, *Juris Praxiskommentar BGB, Band 6 – Internationales Privatrecht* [Juris Commentary on the BGB, Volume 6 – International Private Law], 5th edn. (Saarbrücken, juris GmbH 2010)

Rott 2005: P. Rott, 'What is the Role of the ECJ in EC Private Law? – A Comment on the ECJ judgments in Océano Grupo, Freiburger Kommunalbauten, Leitner and Veedfald', 1 *Hanse Law Review* (2005) pp. 7–9

Rupp 2009: M. Rupp (ed.), *Lebenssituation von Kindern in gleichgeschlechtlichen Lebenspartnerschaften* [The social situation of children in same-sex partnerships] (Köln, Bundesanzeiger Verlag 2009)

Ruso and Thöni 2010: B. Ruso and M. Thöni, 'Quo vadis Präimplantationsdiagnostik?' ['Quo vadis preimplantation genetic diagnosis?'], *MedR* (2010) pp. 74–78

Ryan 2008: F. Ryan, 'The General Scheme of the Civil Partnership Bill 2008: Brave New Dawn or Missed Opportunity', 11 *Irish Journal of Family Law* (2008) pp. 51–57

Ryan 2011: F. Ryan, *The Civil Partnership and Certain Rights and Obligations of Cohabitants Act 2010* (Round Hall, Dublin 2011)

Ryan 2012: F. Ryan, 'Out of the shadow of the Constitution: civil partnership, cohabitation and the constitutional family', 48 *The Irish Jurist* (2012) pp. 201–248

Ryan et al. 2012: S. Ryan et al., *Report of the expert group on the judgment in A, B and C v Ireland*, (Department of Health and Children, November 2012)

Saarloos 2010: K. Saarloos, *European private international law on legal parentage? Thoughts on a European instrument implementing the principle of mutual recognition in legal parentage* (Maastricht, s.n. 2010)

Satzger et al. 2009: H. Satzger et al. (eds.), *StGB, Strafgesetzbuch Kommentar* [StGB, Commentary to the Criminal Code] (Köln, Heymann 2009)

Saunders 2012: A. Saunders, 'Marriage, Same-Sex Partnership, and the German Constitution', 13 *German Law Journal* pp. 911–940 (2012), available at www.germanlawjournal.com/index.php?pageID=11&artID=1448, visited June 2014

Scannell 2007: B. Scannell, 'Brave New World? The Ethics of Pre-implantation Genetic Diagnosis in Ireland', 13 *Medico-Legal Journal of Ireland* (2007) pp. 27–35

Schafhausen 2010: M. Schafhausen, 'Herausgabe von imprägnierten Eizellen nach dem Tode des Mannes' [Release of fertilised egg cells after decease of the man'], *jurisPR-MedizinR* (9/2010)

Schmeilzl and Kruger 2006: B. Schmeilzl and M. Krüger, `Künstliche Befruchtung: Wer trägt die Kosten? Eine Übersicht nach Fallgruppen' ['Artificial insemination: who bears the costs? An overview according to categories of cases'], *NZS* (2006) p. 630

Schmitt-Kammler and von Coelln 2009: A. Schmitt-Kammler and C. von Coelln, 'Art. 6 [Ehe und Familie]' ['Art 6 [Marriage and Family'], in M. Sachs, *Grundgesetz Kommentar* [Basic Law Commentary], 5th edn. (München Verlag C.H. Beck 2009) pp. 348 ff

Scholz and Uhle 2001: R. Scholz and A. Uhle, 'Eingetragene Lebenspartnerschaft' und 'Grundgesetz' ['Civil partnership' and 'Basic Law'], *NJW* (2001) p. 393–400

Schrama 2004: W. Schrama, *De niet-huwelijkse samenleving in het Nederlandse en Duitse recht* [Non-marital cohabitation in Dutch and German law] (Amsterdam, Ars Notariatus Kluwer 2004)

Schreijenberg et al. 2009: A. Schreijenberg et al., *Gemeenschapsrecht en gezinsmigratie. Het gebruik van het gemeenschapsrecht door gezinsmigranten uit derde landen* [Community law and family migration. The use of Community law by third-country migrants for family migration] (The Hague Ministry of Justice 2009), online available at www.wodc.nl/onderzoeksdatabase/neveneffecten-van-toepassing-van-het-europese-gemeenschaps-recht-bij-gezinsmigratie.aspx?cp=44&cs=6796, visited June 2014

Schroth 2010: U. Schroth, 'Präimplantationsdiagnostik zur Feststellung genetischer Schäden eines extrakorporal erzeugten Embryos' ['Preimplantation genetic diagnosis to determine genetic disorders of *in vitro* embryos'], *NJW* (2010) pp. 2676–2677

Schüffner 2007: M. Schüffner, *Eheschutz und Lebenspartnerschaft, Eine verfassungsrechtliche Untersuchung des Lebenspartnerschaftsrechts im Lichte des Art. 6 GG* [Marriage protection and civil partnership, a constitutional examination of the law on civil partnership in light of Art. 6 of the German Basic Law] (Berlin, Duncker & Humblot 2007)

Schutte-Heide-Jørgensen 1997: L. Schutte-Heide-Jørgensen, 'Recht op homohuwelijk?' ['A right to same-sex marriage?'], 47 *Ars Aequi* (1997) pp. 86–92

Schweppe 2001: J. Schweppe, 'Mothers, Fathers, Children and the Unborn – Abortion and the Twenty-Fifth Amendment to the Constitution Bill', 9 *Irish Student Law Review* (2001) pp. 136–162

Schweppe 2011: J. Schweppe, 'Taking Responsibility for the "Abortion Issue": Some Thoughts on Legislative Reform in the Aftermath of A, B and C', 14 *Irish Journal of Family Law* (2011) pp. 50–56

Schyff, van der 2012: G. van der Schyff, 'The constitutional relationship between the European Union and its member states: the role of national identity in article 4(2) TEU', 37 *European Law Review* (2012) pp. 563–583

Seibert 1986: H. Seibert, 'Gesetzgebungskompetenz und Regelungsbefugnis im Bereich der Befruchtungstechniken' ['Legislative power and regulatory power in the area of fertilization techniques'], in: M. Lanz-Zumstein, *Embryonenschutz und Befruchtungstechnik, Seminarbericht und Stellungnahmen aus der Arbeitsgruppe "Gentechnologie" des deutschen Juristinnenbundes* [Protection of embryos and fertilisation techniques, seminar report and statements from the working group "Genetic Engineering" of the German Women Lawyers Association] (München, J Schweitzer Verlag 1986) pp. 142–150

Selder 2013: J. Selder, 'Das Bundesverfassungsgericht und die Homo-Ehe im Steuerrecht' ['The German Constitutional Court and same-sex marriage in the area of tax law'], *DStR* (2013) pp. 1064–1068

Sheikh 2010: A.A. Sheikh, 'The Latest Medical Council Guidelines: New and Improved', 16 *Medico-Legal Journal of Ireland* (2010) pp. 62–63

Sheikh 2012: A.A. Sheikh, 'Medico-Legal Aspects of the Savita Halappanavar Case', 18 *Medico-Legal Journal of Ireland* (2012) pp. 58–61

Shenfield et al. 2010: F. Shenfield et al., 'Cross border reproductive care in six European countries', 25 *Human Reproduction* (2010) pp. 1361–1368

Sherlock 1989: A. Sherlock, 'The right to life of the unborn and the Irish Constitution', 24 *Irish Jurist* (1989) pp. 13–50

Siehr 2003: K. Siehr, 'Family unions in private international law', 50 *Netherlands International Law Review* (2003) pp. 419–435

Sills and Healy 2008: E.S. Sills and C.M. Healy, 'Building Irish families through surrogacy: medical and judicial issues for the advanced reproductive technologies', 5 *Reproductive Health* (2008), online available at www.reproductive-health-journal.com/content/5/1/9, visited September 2011

Smits 2012: J.M. Smits, *The Mind and Method of the Legal Academic* (Cheltenham, Elgar 2012)

Somsen 2012: H. Somsen, 'Brüstle: embryonale fout met grote gevolgen' ['Brüstle: embroynic mistake with major consequences'], *Nederlands Tijdschrift voor Europees Recht* (2012) pp. 33–39

Spranger 2012: T.M. Spranger, 'Case C-34/10, Oliver Brüstle v. Greenpeace e.V., Judgment of the Court (Grand Chamber) of 18 October 2011', 49 *CLMRev.* (2012) pp. 1197–1209

Staunton 2011: C. Staunton, 'As Easy as A, B and C: Will A, B and C v. Ireland Be Ireland's Wake-up Call for Abortion Rights?', 18 *European Journal of Health Law* (2011) pp. 205–219

Steinbeis 2012: M. Steinbeis, 'Mater überhaupt nicht semper certa est' ['*Mater semper certa est* does not hold at all'], blog of 2 November 2012, www.verfassungsblog.de/mater-uberhaupt-nicht-semper-certa-est/#.VGDYgxYeDCF, visited November 2014

Steinkamp et al. 2012: N. Steinkamp et al., *Evaluatie Regeling Preïmplantatie Genetische Diagnostiek (PGD). Besliskader – behoefteraming – ethisch debat* [Evaluation of the Regulation preimplantation genetic diagnosis (PGD). Framework for decision-making – assesment of needs – ethical debate] (Nijmegen, IQ healthcare 2012) online available at www.zonmw.nl/nl/projecten/project-detail/evaluatie-van-het-beslissingskader-pgd-ervaringen-van-professionals-en-paren-met-kinderwens/rapport, visited June 2014

Sterling 1997: A.-M.E.W. Sterling, 'The European Union and Abortion Tourism: Liberalizing Ireland's Abortion Law', 20 *Boston College International & Comparative Law Review* (1997) pp. 385–406

Storrow 2010: R. Storrow, 'The pluralism problem in cross-border reproductive care', 25 *Human Reproduction* (2010) pp. 2939–2943

Storrow 2011: R.F. Storrow, 'Assisted Reproduction on treacherous terrain: the legal hazards of cross-border reproductive travel', 23 *Reproductive BioMedicine Online* (2011) pp. 538–545

Storrow 2012: R.F. Storrow, 'Judicial review of restrictions on gamete donation in Europe', 25 *Reproductive BioMedicine Online* (2012) pp. 655–659

Storskrubb 2011: E. Storskrubb, 'Civil Jusitice – A newcomer and an unstoppable wave?', in: P. Graig and G. De Búrca, *The evolution of EU Law*, 2nd edn. (Oxford, Oxford University Press 2011) pp. 299–321

Strick 2002: K. Strick, 'Gleichgeschlechtliche Partnerschaft – Vom Straftatbestand zum Status?' ['Same-sex partnership – from criminal offence to legal status?'], *Deutsches und Europaisches FamilenRecht, DEuFamR* (2002) pp. 82–94

Strohal 2012: See F. Strohal, 'Verfassungswidrige Ungleichbehandlung von Ehegatten und eingetragenen Lebenspartnern im Grunderwerbsteuerrecht' ['Unconstitutional unequal treatment between spouses and registered partners in the area of conveyance tax law'], *FamFR* (2012) p. 432

Stüber 2003: S. Stüber, `Lebenspartnerschaft – viele offene Fragen' ['Civil partnership – many open questions'], *NJW* (2003) pp. 2721–2724

Stüber 2008: S. Stüber, 'Was folgt aus "Maruko"?' ['What follows from "Maruko"?'], *NVwz* (2008) pp. 750–752

Süß 2001: R. Süß, 'Notarieller Gestaltungsbedarf bei Eingetragenen Lebenspartnerschaften mit Ausländern' ['The need for notary guidance in civil partnerships with foreign partners'], *DNotZ* (2001) pp. 168–176

Tanca 1993: A. Tanca, 'European Citizenship and the Rights of Lesbians and Gay Men', in: K. Waaldijk and A. Clapham, *Homosexuality: a European Community issue, Essays on Lesbian and gay rights in European Law and Policy* (Dordrecht, Martinus Nijhoff Publishers 1993) pp. 271–288

Tann, von der 2012: C. von der Tann, 'Entwicklungen in der Rechtsstellung eingetragener Lebenspartnerschaften' ['Developments in the legal position of civil partnerships'], *FamFR* (2012) pp. 195–199

Tewocht 2013: H. Tewocht, 'Die Neuregelung des Freizügigkeitsgesetzes/EU' ['The new regulation of the EU freedom of movement Act'], *ZAR* (2013) pp. 221–229

Thompson 1994: A. Thompson, 'International protection of women's rights: an analysis of *Open Door Counselling Ltd. and Dublin Well woman Centre v Ireland*', 12 *Boston University International Law Journal* (1994) pp. 371–406

Thorn 2002: K. Thorn, 'Entwicklungen des Internationalen Privatrechts 2000–2001' ['Developments in International Private Law 2000–2001'], *IPRax* (2002) pp. 349–364

Tobin 2007: B. Tobin, 'Gay marriage – a bridge too far?', 15 *Irish Student Law Review* (2007) pp. 175–196

Tobin 2008: B. Tobin, 'Relationship Recognition for Same-sex Couples in Ireland: The Proposed Models Critiqued', 11 *Irish Journal of Family Law* (2008) pp. 10–15

Tobin 2009: B. Tobin, 'Same-Sex Couples and the Law: Recent Developments in the British Isles', 23 *International Journal of Law, Policy and the Family* (2009) pp. 309–330

Tobin 2010: B. Tobin, 'Recognition of Canadian Same-sex Marriage: Zappone and Gilligan v Revenue Commissioners and Others', 1 *Irish Human Rights Law Review* (2010) pp. 217–225

Tobin 2012A: B. Tobin, 'Law, politics and the child-centric approach to marriage in Ireland', 48 *The Irish Jurist* (2012) pp. 210–224

Tobin 2012B: B. Tobin, 'Same- Sex Marriage in Ireland: The Rocky Road to Recognition', 15 *Irish Journal of Family Law* (2012) pp. 102–108

Tobler and Waaldijk 2009: C. Tobler and K. Waaldijk, 'Case note to Case C-267/06, Tadao Maruko v. Versorgungsanstalt der deutschen Bühnen, Judgment of the Grand Chamber of the Court of Justice of 1 April 2008', 46 *CMLRev* (2009) pp. 723–746

Toner 2003: H. Toner, 'Immigration Rights of Same-Sex Couples in EC-law', in K. Boele-Woelki and A. Fuchs (eds.), *Legal recognition of same-sex couples in Europe* (Antwerp, Intersentia 2003) pp. 178–193

Toner 2012: H. Toner, 'Migration rights and same-sex couples in EU law: a case study', in: K. Boele-Woelki and A. Fuchs (eds.), *Legal recognition of same-sex Relationships in Europe, National, cross-border and European perspectives*, 2nd edn. (Cambridge, Intersentia 2012) pp. 285–308

Tridimas 2006: T. Tridimas, *The General Principles of EU law*, 2nd edn. (Oxford, Oxford University Press 2006)

Tröndle 1995: H. Tröndle, 'Das Schwangeren- und Familienhilfeänderungsgesetz' [The Pregnancy and Family Assistance Revision Act'], *NJW* (1995) pp. 3009–3019

Turkmendag et al. 2008: I. Turkmendag et al., 'The removal of donor anonymity in the UK: the silencing of claims by would-be parents', 22 *International Journal of Law, Policy and Family* (2008) pp. 283–310

Twining 1997: W. Twining, *Law in context, enlarging a discipline* (Oxford: Clarendon Press 1997)

Ulsenheimer 2010: K. Ulsenheimer, 'Schwangerschaftsabbruch' ['Termination of pregnancy'], in: A. Laufs and B.R. Kern (eds.), *Handbuch des Arztrechts* [Handbook of medical law], 4th edn. (München, Verlag Beck 2010)

Van Rij et al. 2012: M.C. Van Rij et al., 'Preimplantation genetic diagnosis (PGD) for Huntington's disease: the experience of three European centres', 20 *European Journal of Human Genetics* (2012) pp. 368–375

Veerman and Hendriks 1996: T. Veerman and A. Hendriks, 'Recht op toegang tot IVF. IVF bij alleenstaande, lesbische en oudere vrouwen' ['A right to access to IVF treatment. IVF treatment for single, lesbian women and women of age'], 12 *Nemesis* (1996) pp. 136–145

Verschraegen 2012: B. Verschraegen, 'The Right to Private and Family Life, the Right to Marry and to Found a Family, and the Prohibition of Discrimination', in: K. Boele-Woelki and A. Fuchs (eds.), *Legal recognition of same-sex Relationships in Europe, National, cross-border and European perspectives*, 2nd edn. (Cambridge, Intersentia 2012) pp. 255–270

Vlaardingerbroek 2000: P. Vlaardingerbroek, 'Adoptie door paren van gelijk geslacht' ['Adoption by same-sex couples'], 22 *Tijdschrift voor Familie- en Jeugdrecht* (2000) pp. 198–202

Vliet, van 1988: F. van Vliet, 'Erkenning: mensenrecht of mannenrecht?' ['Recognition: human right or men's right?'], 63 *Nederlands Juristenblad* (1988) pp. 1263–1267

Vliet, van 1998: F. van Vliet, 'Van achterdeur naar zij-ingang: Commissie Kortmann en gelijkgeslachtelijke leefvormen' ['From backdoor to side entrance: the Kortmann Commission and ways of living together by same-sex couples'], 14 *Nemesis* (1998) pp. 13–22

Vliet, van 2000: F. van Vliet, 'Door de zij-ingang naar niemandsland?' ['Through the side entrance into no man's land?'], 16 *Nemesis* (2000) pp. 41–50

Vlijmen, van and Tol, van der 2012: S.C.A. van Vlijmen and J.H. van der Tol, 'Draagmoederschap in opkomst: specifieke wet- en regelgeving noodzakelijk?' ['Surrogacy booming: specific regulation necessary?'], *Tijdschrift voor Familie- en Jeugdrecht* (2012) pp. 160–166

Vollaard 2007: H. Vollaard, 'Patiëntenmobiliteit in een Europese zorgruimte' ['Patient mobility in the European area of care'], in: A.C. Hendriks and H.-M. Th. D. ten Napel, *Volksgezondheid in een veellalige rechtsorde. Eenheid en verscheidenheid van norm en praktijk* [Public health in a multilevel jurisdiction. Unity and diversity in standards and practice] (Alphen aan de Rijn, Kluwer 2007) pp. 291–305

Von Dannecker 2010: G. von Dannecker, 'Können europäische Vorgaben ein Tätigwerden des nationalen Strafgesetzgebers auf dem Gebiet des Biostrafrechts erzwingen?' ['Can European guidelines exact action of national criminal law legislatures in the area of bio criminal law?'], in: E. Hilgendorf and S. Beck, *Biomedizinische Forschung in Europa* [Biomedical research in Europe], IUS Europaeum 49 (Baden-Baden, Nomos 2010) pp. 161 ff

Vonk 2011: M.J. Vonk, *Commentaar op Burgerlijk Wetboek Boek 1 art. 227 (en 228)(artikeltekst geldig vanaf 01-01-2009)* [Commentary on the Civil Code, Book 1 (art. 227 (and 228) (version valid as of 01-01-2009)] (Sdu Opmaat (online) 2011)

Vonk 2010: M.J. Vonk, 'Het conceptwetsvoorstel lesbisch ouderschap onder de loep' ['A closer look at the bill on lesbian parenthood'], 141 *WPNR* (2010) pp. 348–351

Waaldijk 1986/1987: C. Waaldijk, 'Constitutional Protection Against Discrimination of Homosexuals', 13 *Journal of Homosexuality* (1986/1987) pp. 57–68

Waaldijk 1987: C. Waaldijk, 'Beantwoording rechtsvraag (170). Gelijkheidsbeginsel. Homohuwelijk' ['Answer to legal question (170). The principle of equal treatment. Same-sex marriage'], 36 *Ars Aequi* (1987) pp. 644–650

Waaldijk 1991: C. Waaldijk, 'De heteroseksuele exclusiviteit van het huwelijk na Hoge Raad 19 oktober 1990' ['The heterosexual exclusivity of marriage after Supreme Court 19 October 1990'], 40 *Ars Aequi* (1991) pp. 47–56

Waaldijk 1992: C. Waaldijk, 'Vrij samen. Over het advies van de commissie-Kortmann inzake de vrijwillige registratie van leefvormen' ['Free together. On the Advice of the Kortmann Commission in respect of voluntary registration of ways of living together'], *Regelmaat* (1992) pp. 43–49

Waaldijk 1995: C. Waaldijk, 'Naar een gelijkgeslachtelijk huwelijk. Waarom het buitenland, het afstammingsrecht en de invoering van geregistreerde partnerschap geen argumenten zijn voor handhaving van de heteroseksuele exclusiviteit van het huwelijk' ['Towards a same-sex marriage. Why other countries, the law on descent and the introduction of registered partnership are no arguments for maintaining the heterosexual exclusivity of marriage'], 17 *Tijdschrift voor Familie- en Jeugdrecht* (1995) pp. 223–228

Waaldijk 1999: C. Waaldijk, 'De voorgestelde Wet openstelling huwelijk en de daarmee samenhangende wijzigingen inzake adoptie en geregistreerd partnerschap' ['The proposed Act opening up marriage and the related amendments of the law on adoption and registered partnership'], 21 *Tijdschrift voor Familie- en Jeugdrecht* (1999) pp. 198–208

Waaldijk 2000: C. Waaldijk, 'Partnerschapsregistratie en huwelijk: toenemende rechtsgelijkheid voor geslachtsgelijke partners en hun kinderen' [Partnership registration and marriage: increasing equality before the law for same-sex partners and their children'], in: H. Lenters et al., *De familie geregeld?* [The family taken care of?] (Lelystad, Koninklijke Vermande 2000) pp. 121–183

Waaldijk 2001A: C. Waaldijk, 'Small change; how the road to same-sex marriage got paved in the Netherlands', in: R. Wintemute and M. Andenaes (eds.), *Legal Recognition of Same-Sex Partnerships – A Study of National, European and International Law* (Oxford, Hart Publishing 2001) pp. 437–464

Waaldijk 2001B: K. Waaldijk, 'Towards the Recognition of Same-Sex Partners in EU law', in: R. Wintemute and M. Andenæs (eds.), *Legal Recognition of Same-Sex Partnerships, A Study of National, European and International Law* (Oxford, Hart Publishing 2001) pp. 635–651

Waaldijk 2004: C. Waaldijk, 'Others may follow: the introduction of marriage, quasi-marriage, and semi-marriage for same-sex couples in European countries', 38 *New England Law Review* (2004) pp. 569–589

Waaldijk 2005: K. Waaldijk, *More or less together: levels of legal consequences of marriage, cohabitation and registered partnership for different-sex and same-sex partners. A comparative study of nine European countries* (Paris, Institut National d'Études Démographiques 2005), online available at www.hdl.handle.net/1887/12585, visited June 2010

Waaldijk and Bonini-Baraldi 2006: C. Waaldijk and M. Bonini-Baraldi, *Sexual orientation discrimination in the European Union, National laws and the Employment Equality Directive* (The Hague, TMC Asser Press 2006)

Waaldijk et al. 2010: K. Waaldijk, *Homophobia, transphobia and discrimination on grounds of sexual orientation and gender identity, Comparative legal analysis, Thematic study Netherlands, 2010 Update*, European Union Agency for Fundamental Rights 2010, online available at: www.fra.europa.eu/sites/default/files/fra_uploads/1363-LGBT-2010_thematic-study_NL.pdf, visited February 2013

Wache 2011: V. Wache, '§ 13a AdVermiG nr. 1' ['§ 13a AdVermiG no. 1'], in: G. Erbs and M. Kohlhaas (eds.), *Strafrechtliche Nebengesetze* [Ancillary criminal laws] (München, Verlag C.H. Beck 2011)

Waddington 2011: L.B. Waddington, 'Future Prospects for EU Equality Law. Lessons to be Learnt from the Proposed Equal Treatment Directive', 17 *European Law Review* (2011) pp. 163–184

Waele, de and Vleuten, van der 2011: H. de Waele and A. van der Vleuten, 'Judicial Activism in the European Court of Justice – The Case of LGBT Rights', 19 *Mich. St. U. Coll. L. J. Int'l L.* (2010–2011) pp. 639–666

Wagner 2001: R. Wagner, 'Das neue Internationale Privat- und Verfahrens- recht zur eingetragenen Lebenspartnerschaft' ['The new international private and procedural law on civil partnerships'], 21 *IPRax* (2001) pp. 281–293

Walsh and Ryan 2006: J. Walsh and F. Ryan, *The Rights of De Facto Couples* (Dublin, Irish Human Rights Commission 2006)

Ward 1994: P. Ward, 'Ireland: Abortion: X + Y = ?!', 33 *University of Louisville Journal of Family Law* (1994) pp. 385–407

Wautelet 2012: P. Wautelet, 'Private International Law aspects of same-sex marriages and partnerships in Europe – Divided we stand?', in: K. Boele-Woelki and A. Fuchs (eds.), *Legal recognition of same-sex Relationships in Europe, National, cross-border and European perspectives*, 2nd edn. (Cambridge, Intersentia 2012) pp. 143–188

Weinstein 1993: J.A. Weinstein, '"An Irish solution to an Irish problem": Ireland's struggle with abortion law', 10 *Arizona Journal of International & Comparative Law* (1993) pp. 165–200

Wellenhoffer 2013: M. Wellenhoffer, 'Die Samenspende und ihre (späten) Rechtsfolgen' ['Sperm donation and its (late) legal consequences'], *Zeitschrift für das gesamte Familienrecht, FamRZ* (2013) pp. 825- 830

Werle and Jeßberger 2007: G. Werle and F. Jeßberger, 'Rn 132' ['Rn. 132'], in: H.W. Laufhütte et al., *Leipziger Kommentar, Großkommentar zum Strafgesetzbuch* [Leipziger Commentary, Commentary to the Criminal Code] (Berlin, De Gruyter Recht 2007)

Westerhof 2000: L. Westerhof, 'Is het huwelijk tussen personen van hetzelfde geslacht een fictie en, zo ja, kan op deze fictie de wettelijke regeling van dit huwelijk worden gebaseerd?' ['Is same-sex marriage a fiction, and if so, can the legal regulation of this marriage be based on this fiction?'], 75 *Nederlands Juristenblad* (2000) p. 1021

White and Ovey 2010: C.A. White and C. Ovey, *Jacobs, White and Ovey, The European Convention on Human Rights* (Oxford, Oxford University Press 2010)

Whyte 2006: G. Whyte, 'The Moral Status of the Embryo', 12 *Medico-Legal Journal of Ireland* (2006) pp. 77–82

Wicks 2011: E. Wicks, '*A, B, C v Ireland*: Abortion Law under the European Convention on Human Rights', 11 *HRLR* (2011) pp. 556–566

Wiemann 2010: R. Wiemann, 'Rosige Aussichten für die Gleichstellung gleichgeschlechtlicher Lebenspartner mit Ehegatten?' ['A rosy future for the equal treatment of registered partners and spouses?'] *NJW* (2010) pp. 1427–1430

Willems 1999: A.W.M. Willems, 'Het homohuwelijk: een te hoge prijs?' ['Same-sex marriage: a too high a price?'], 21 *Tijdschrift voor Familie- en Jeugdrecht* (1999) p. 217

Willems 2000: A.W.M. Willems, 'Adoptie door homo-ouders en de positie van de spermadonor' ['Adoption by gay parents and the position of the sperm donor'], 22 *Tijdschrift voor Familie- en Jeugdrecht* (2000) pp. 226–229

Winkel et al. 2010: E. Winkel et al., 'Draagmoederschap na ivf in het buitenland. Dilemma's bij de begeleiding' ['Surrogacy after IVF treatment in a foreign country. Dillemas in the counselling'], 154 *Nederlands Tijdschrijft voor Geneeskunde* (2010) p. A1777

Wintemute 2001: R. Wintemute, 'Conclusion', in: R. Wintemute and M. Andenæs (eds.), *Legal Recognition of Same-Sex Partnerships, A Study of National, European and International Law* (Oxford, Hart Publishing 2001) pp. 759–773

Winter et al. 2012: H.B. Winter et al., *Evaluatie Embryowet en Wet donorgegevens kunstmatige bevruchting* [Evaluation Embryo Act and the Act Donor Information Artificial Reproduction] (Den Haag, ZonMw 2012)

Wladimiroff and Christiaens 1998: J.W. Wladimiroff and G.C.M.L. Christiaens, 'Het rapport 'Late zwangerschapsafbreking: zorgvuldigheid en toetsing' van de overleggroep Late Zwangerschapsafbreking' ['The Report 'Late pregnancy termination: care and examination' of the consultation group Late pregnancy termination'], 142 *Nederlands Tijdschrijft voor Geneeskunde* (1998) pp. 2627–2629

Wortmann 2000: S.F.M. Wortmann, 'Zo zijn we niet getrouwd. De openstelling van het huwelijk voor personen van hetzelfde geslacht' ['That was not what we agreed on. The opening up of marriage for same-sex couples'], 49 *Ars Aequi* (2000) pp. 82–87

Young 2005: A.L. Young, 'The Charter, Constitution and Human Rights: is this the Beginning or the End for Human Rights Protections by Community Law?', 11 *European Public Law* (2005) pp. 219–240

Young Lee 1996: J. Young Lee, *Unterhaltsverpflichtungen bei Leihmutterschaft* [Maintenance obligations in the case of surrogacy] (Baden-Baden, Nomos Verlagsgesellschaft 1996)

Zeeman et al. 2008: G.G. Zeeman et al., 'Toetsing van late zwangerschapsafbreking, 2004–2007' ['Review of late pregnancy terminations, 2004–2007'], 152 *Nederlands Tijdschrift voor Geneeskunde* (2008) pp. 2632–2635

Zimmerman 1993: A. Zimmerman, 'Verbreitung von Informationen über Schwangerschafts-unterbrechungen und Europäische Menschenrechtskonvention' ['Dissemination of information on the termination of pregnancies and the European Convention on Human Rights'], *NJW* 1993, pp. 2966–2969

Zschiebsch 2013: M. Zschiebsch, 'Nichtzulassung der Sukzessivadoption durch eingetragenen Lebenspartner verfassungswidrig' ['Non-admission of successive adoption by a civil partner unconstitutional'], *Juris Praxiz Report FamR* 22/2013, Anm. 6

Župan 2013: M. Župan, 'Registered partnership in cross-border situations – where invisibility to law lies?', in: N. Bodigora-Vukubrat et al. (eds), *Invisible Minorities in Law* (Hamburg, Verlag Dr. Kovac 2013) pp. 95–113

Table of Cases

European Court of Human Rights

ECtHR 25 April 1978, *Tyrer* v. *the United Kingdom*, no. 5856/72
ECtHR 13 June 1979, *Marckx* v. *Belgium*, no. 6833/74
ECtHR 9 October 1979, *Airey* v. *Ireland*, no. 6289/73
ECtHR [GC] 6 November 1980, *Van Oosterwijck* v. *Belgium*, no. 7654/76
ECtHR [GC] 22 October 1981, *Dudgeon* v. *the United Kingdom*, no. 7525/76
ECtHR 28 November 1984, *Rasmussen* v. *Denmark*, no. 8777/79
ECtHR 28 May 1985, *Abdulaziz, Cabales and Balkandali* v. *the United Kingdom*, nos. 9214/80 a.o.
ECtHR [GC] 17 October 1986, *Rees* v. *the United Kingdom*, no. 9532/81
ECtHR 26 October 1986, *Norris* v. *Ireland*, no. 10581/83
ECtHR 18 December 1986, *Johnston a.o.* v. *Ireland*, no. 9697/82
ECtHR 8 July 1987, *W.* v. *the United Kingdom*, no. 9749/82
ECtHR 18 December 1987, *F.* v. *Switzerland*, no. 11329/85
ECtHR 26 October 1988, *Norris* v. *Ireland*, no. 10581/83
ECtHR [GC] 7 July 1989, *Gaskin* v. *the United Kingdom*, no. 10454/83
ECtHR [GC] 27 September 1990, *Cossey* v. *the United Kingdom*, no. 10843/84
ECtHR 29 October 1992, *Open Door and Dublin Well Woman* v. *Ireland*, nos. 14234/88 and 14235/88
ECtHR 22 April 1993, *Modinos* v. *Cyprus*, no. 15070/89
ECtHR 27 October 1994, *Kroon a.o.* v. *the Netherlands*, no. 18535/91
ECtHR 26 May 1995, *Keegan* v. *Ireland*, no. 16969/90
ECtHR 7 August 1996, *Johansen* v. *Norway*, no. 17383/90
ECtHR 19 February 1997, *Laskey, Jaggard and Brown* v. *the United Kingdom*, nos. 21627/93 a.o.
ECtHR 22 April 1997, *X, Y and Z* v. *the United Kingdom*, no. 21830/93
ECtHR 27 March 1998, *Petrovic* v. *Austria*, no. 20458/92
ECtHR 27 September 1999, *Smith and Grady* v. *the United Kingdom*, nos. 33985/96 and 33986/96
ECtHR 16 November 1999, *E.P.* v. *Italy*, no. 31127/96
ECtHR 21 December 1999, *Salgueiro da Silva Mouta* v. *Portugal*, no. 33290/96
ECtHR 27 April 2000 (dec.), *Shackell* v. *the United Kingdom*, no. 45851/99
ECtHR [GC] 13 July 2000, *Scozzari and Giunta* v. *Italy*, nos. 39221/98 and 41963/98
ECtHR 10 May 2001 (dec.), *Mata Estevez* v. *Spain*, no. 56501/00
ECtHR 18 September 2001 (dec.), *Kalashnikov* v. *Russia*, no. 47095/99
ECtHR 26 February 2002, *Fretté* v. *France*, no. 36515/97
ECtHR 4 June 2002, *Wessels-Bergervoet* v. *the Netherlands*, no. 34462/97
ECtHR 11 July 2002, *Christine Goodwin* v. *the United Kingdom*, no. 28657/95
ECtHR 4 September 2002, *Mikulic* v. *Croatia*, no. 53176/99
ECtHR 5 September 2002 (dec.), *Boso* v. *Italy*, no. 50490/99
ECtHR 5 November 2002, *Yousef* v. *the Netherlands*, no. 33711/96
ECtHR 9 January 2003, *L. and V.* v. *Austria*, nos. 39392/98 and 39829/98
ECtHR 9 January 2003, *S.L.* v. *Austria*, no. 45330/99
ECtHR [GC] 13 February 2003, *Odièvre* v. *France*, no. 42326/98

ECtHR 6 March 2003 (dec.), *Sijakova and others* v. *"The former Yugoslav Republic of Macedonia"*, no. 67914/01
ECtHR 29 April 2003, *Aliev* v. *Ukraine*, no. 41220/98
ECtHR 26 June 2003, *Maire* v. *Portugal*, no. 48206/99
ECtHR 24 July 2003, *Karner* v. *Austria*, no. 40016/98
ECtHR [GC] 8 July 2004, *Vo* v. *France*, no. 53924/00
ECtHR [GC] 4 February 2005, *Mamatkulov and Askarov* v. *Turkey*, nos. 46827/99 and 46951/99
ECtHR 13 September 2005, *B. and L.* v. *the United Kingdom*, no. 36536/02
ECtHR [GC] 6 October 2005, *Hirst (no. 2)* v. *the United Kingdom*, no. 74025/01
ECtHR 16 October 2005, *Maurice* v. *France*, no. 11810/03
ECtHR 24 November 2005, *Shofman* v. *Russia*, no. 74826/01
ECtHR 7 March 2006, *Evans* v. *the United Kingdom*, no. 6339/05
ECtHR [GC] 12 April 2006, *Stec a.o.* v. *the United Kingdom*, no. 65731/01
ECtHR 18 May 2006, *Różański* v. *Poland*, no. 55339/00
ECtHR 10 June 2006, *Schwizgebel* v. *Switzerland*, no. 25762/07
ECtHR 27 June 2006 (dec.), *D.* v. *Ireland*, no. 26499/02
ECtHR 13 July 2006, *Jäggi* v. *Switzerland*, no. 58757/00
ECtHR [GC] 18 October 2006, *Üner* v. *the Netherlands*, no. 46410/99
ECtHR 28 November 2006 (dec.), *R. and F.* v. *the United Kingdom*, no. 35748/05
ECtHR 28 November 2006 (dec.), *Parry* v. *the United Kingdom*, no. 42971/05
ECtHR 25 January 2007, *Eski* v. *Austria*, no. 21949/03
ECtHR 20 March 2007, *Tysiąc* v. *Poland*, no. 5410/03
ECtHR [GC] 10 April 2007, *Evans* v. *the United Kingdom*, no. 6339/05
ECtHR 3 May 2007, *Baczkowski a.o.* v. *Poland*, no. 1543/06
ECtHR 28 June 2007, *Wagner and J.M.W.L.* v. *Luxembourg*, no. 76240/01
ECtHR [GC] 30 July 2007, *Sheffield and Horsham* v. *the United Kingdom*, nos. 22985/93 and 23390/94
ECtHR 6 September 2007, *Chapin and Charpentier* v. *France*, no. 40183/07
ECtHR 15 November 2007 (dec.), *S.H. and others* v. *Austria*, no. 57813/00
ECtHR [GC] 4 December 2007, *Dickson* v. *the United Kingdom*, no. 44362/04
ECtHR 13 December 2007, *Emonet a.o.* v. *Switzerland*, no. 39051/03
ECtHR [GC] 22 January 2008, *E.B.* v. *France*, no. 43546/02
ECtHR [GC] 29 April 2008, *Burden* v. *the United Kingdom*, no. 13378/05
ECtHR 22 May 2008, *Petrov* v. *Bulgaria*, no. 15197/02
ECtHR 23 June 2008, *Maslov* v *Bulgaria*, no. 1638/03
ECtHR 4 November 2008 (dec.), *Courten* v. *the United Kingdom*, no. 4479/06
ECtHR 1 May 2009, *Kalacheva* v. *Russia*, no. 3451/05
ECtHR 12 May 2009, *Korelc* v. *Slovenia*, no. 28456/03
ECtHR 23 June 2009 (dec.), *M.W.* v. *the United Kingdom*, no. 11313/02
ECtHR 5 January 2010, *Frasik* v. *Poland*, no. 22933/02
ECtHR 5 January 2010, *Jaremowicz* v. *Poland*, no. 24023/03
ECtHR 2 March 2010, *Kozak* v. *Poland*, no. 13102/02
ECtHR [GC] 16 March 2010, *Carson a.o.* v. *the United Kingdom*, no. 42184/05
ECtHR 4 April 2010, *S.H. a.o.* v. *Austria*, no. 57813/00
ECtHR 24 June 2010, *Schalk and Kopf* v. *Austria*, no. 30141/04
ECtHR [GC] 6 July 2010, *Neulinger and Shuruk* v. *Switzerland*, no. 41615/07
ECtHR 22 July 2010, *P.B. and J.S.* v. *Austria*, no. 18984/02
ECtHR 21 September 2010 (dec.), *Manenc* v. *France*, no. 66686/09
ECtHR 28 September 2010, *J.M.* v. *the United Kingdom*, no. 37060/06
ECtHR 21 October 2010, *Alekseyev v. Russia*, nos. 4916/07 a.o.

ECtHR [GC] 11 November 2010, *Şerife Yiğit* v. *Turkey*, no. 3976/05
ECtHR 14 December 2010, *Ternovsky* v. *Hungary*, no. 67545/09
ECtHR [GC] 16 December 2010, *A, B and C* v. *Ireland*, no. 25579/05
ECtHR 21 December 2010, *Anayo* v. *Germany*, no. 20578/07
ECtHR 3 May 2011, *Negrepontis-Giannisis* v. *Greece*, no. 56759/08
ECtHR 26 May 2011, *R. R.* v. *Poland*, no. 27617/04
ECtHR [GC] 3 November 2011, *S.H. a.o.* v. *Austria*, no. 57813/00
ECtHR 8 November 2011, *V.C.* v. *Slowakia*, no. 18968/07
ECtHR 15 March 2012, *Gas and Dubois* v. *France*, no. 25951/07
ECtHR 22 March 2012, *Ahrens* v. *Germany*, no. 45071/99
ECtHR 3 April 2012, *Van der Heijden* v. *The Netherlands*, no. 42857/05
ECtHR 12 June 2012, *Genderdoc-M* v. *Moldova*, no. 9106/06
ECtHR 28 August 2012, *Costa and Pavan* v. *Italy*, no. 54270/10
ECtHR 25 September 2012, *Godelli* v. *Italy*, no. 33783/09
ECtHR 2 October 2012, *Daniela Knecht* v. *Romania*, no. 10048/10
ECtHR 30 October 2012, *P. and S.* v. *Poland*, no. 57375/08
ECtHR 12 November 2012, *H.* v. *Finland*, no. 37359/09
ECtHR 15 January 2013, *Eweida and Others v. the United Kingdom*, nos. 48420/10 a.o.
ECtHR [GC] 19 February 2013, *X. a.o.* v. *Austria*, no. 19010/07
ECtHR 7 May 2013 (dec.), *Sabine Boeckel and Anja Gessner-Boeckel* v. *Germany*, no. 8017/11
ECtHR 28 May 2013 (dec.), *Parrillo* v. *Italy*, no. 46470/11
ECtHR [GC] 7 November 2013, *Vallianatos a.o.* v. *Greece*, nos. 29381/09 and 32684/09
ECtHR [GC] 26 November 2013, *X* v. *Latvia*, no. 27853/09
ECtHR 5 June 2014, *I.S.* v. *Germany*, no. 31021/08
ECtHR 24 June 2014, *A.K.* v. *Latvia*, no. 33011/08
ECtHR 26 June 2014, *Labassee* v. *France*, no. 65941/11
ECtHR 26 June 2014, *Mennesson* v. *France*, no. 65192/11
ECtHR 8 July 2014 (dec.), *D. a.o.* v. *Belgium*, no. 29176/13
ECtHR [GC] 16 July 2014, *Hämäläinen* v. *Finland*, no. 37359/09

European Commission of Human Rights

ECmHR 21 May 1975 (dec.), *X.* v. *the United Kingdom*, no. 6564/74
ECmHR 19 May 1976 (dec.), *Brüggeman and Scheuten* v. *Germany*, no. 6959/75
ECmHR 1 March 1979 (report), *Van Oosterwijck* v. *Belgium*, no. 7654/76
ECmHR 13 December 1979 (report), *Hamer* v. *the United Kingdom*, no. 7114/75
ECmHR 13 March 1980 (report), *Dudgeon* v. *the United Kingdom*, no. 7525/76
ECmHR 10 July 1980 (report), *Draper* v. *the United Kingdom*, no. 8186/78
ECmHR 3 May 1983 (dec.), *X. and Y* v. *the United Kingdom*, no. 9369/81
ECmHR 14 May 1986 (dec.), *S.* v. *the United Kingdom*, no. 11718/85
ECmHR 11 November 1986 (dec.), *Lindsay* v. *the United Kingdom*, no. 11089/84
ECmHR 15 December 1988 (dec.), *Paula James* v. *the United Kingdom*, no. 10622/83
ECmHR 17 March 1989 (report), *W.* v. *the United Kingdom*, no. 11095/84
ECmHR 9 October 1989 (dec.), *C. and L.M.* v. *the United Kingdom*, no. 14753/89
ECmHR 10 February 1990 (dec.), *B.* v. *the United Kingdom*, no. 16106/90
ECmHR 7 March 1991 (report), *Open Door and Dublin Well Woman* v. *Ireland*, nos. 14234/88 and 14235/88
ECmHR 19 May 1992 (dec.), *Kerkhoven and Hinke* v. *the Netherlands*, no. 15666/89
ECmHR 19 May 1992 (dec.), *Hercz* v. *Norway*, no. 17004/90

ECmHR 8 February 1993 (dec.), *J.R.M.* v. *the Netherlands*, no. 16944/90
ECmHR 16 October 1996 (dec.), *Sanders* v. *France*, no. 31401/96
ECmHR 22 October 1997 (dec.), *E.L.H. and P.B.H.* v. *the United Kingdom*, no. 32568/96

European Court of Justice

Case 26/62 *NV Algemene Transport- en Expeditie Onderneming van Gend & Loos* v. *Netherlands Inland Revenue Administration* [1963] ECR 0001, ECLI:EU:C:1963:1
Case 6/64 *Flaminio Costa* v. *E.N.E.L.* [1964] ECR 585, ECLI:EU:C:1964:66
Case 11-70 *International Handelsgesellschaft mbH* v. *Einfuhr- und Vorratsstelle für Getreide und Futtermittel* [1970] ECR 1125, ECLI:EU:C:1970:114
Case 41/74 *Yvonne van Duyn* v. *Home Office* [1974] ECR 1337, ECLI:EU:C:1974:133
Case 5/77 *Carlo Tedeschi* v. *Denkavit Commerciale s.r.l.* [1977] ECR 1555, ECLI:EU:C:1977:144
Case 30-77 *Régina* v. *Pierre Bouchereau* [1977] ECR 1999, ECLI:EU:C:1977:172
Case 117/77 *Bestuur van het Algemeen Ziekenfonds Drenthe-Platteland* v. *G. Pierik* [1978] ECR 825, ECLI:EU:C:1978:72
Case 182/78 *Pierik (No. 2)* [1979] ECR 1977, ECLI:EU:C:1979:142
Case 110/79 *Una Coonan* v. *Insurance Officer* [1980] ECR 1445, ECLI:EU:C:1980:112
Case 15/81 *Gaston Schul Douane Epediteur BV* v. *Inspecteur der Invoerrechten en Accijnzen, Roosendaal* [1982] ECR 1409, ECLI:EU:C:1982:135
Case 238/82 *Duphar BV and others* v. *The Netherlands State* [1984] ECR 523, ECLI:EU:C:1984:45
Joined Cases 286/82 and 26/83 *Graziana Luisi and Giuseppe Carbone* v. *Ministero del Tesoro* [1984] ECR 377, ECLI:EU:C:1984:35
Case 327/82 *Ekro BV Vee- en Vleeshandel* v. *Produktschap voor Vee en Vlees* [1984] ECR 107, ECLI:EU:C:1984:11
Case 59/85 *State of the Netherlands* v. *Ann Florence Reed* [1986] ECR 1283, ECLI:EU:C:1986:157
Case 121/85 *Conegate Limited* v. *HM Customs & Excise* [1986] ECR 1007, ECLI:EU:C:1986:114
Case 352/85 *Bond van Adverteerders and others* v. *The Netherlands State* [1988] ECR 2085, ECLI:EU:C:1988:196
Case 249/86 *Commission of the European Communities* v. *Federal Republic of Germany* [1989] ECR 1263, ECLI:EU:C:1989:204
Case C-349/87 *Elissavet Paraschi* v. *Landesversicherungsanstalt Württemberg* [1991] ECR I-4501, ECLI:EU:C:1991:372
Case C-177/88 *Elisabeth Johanna Pacifica Dekker* v. *Stichting Vormingscentrum voor Jong Volwassenen (VJV-Centrum) Plus* [1990] ECR I-3941, ECLI:EU:C:1990:383
Case C-159/90 *The Society for the Protection of Unborn Children Ireland Ltd* v. *Stephen Grogan and others* [1991] ECR I-4685, ECLI:EU:C:1991:378
Case C-370/90 *The Queen* v. *Immigration Appeal Tribunal and Surinder Singh, ex parte Secretary of State for Home Department* [1992] ECR I-4265, ECLI:EU:C:1992:296
Case C-168/91 *Christos Konstantinidis* v. *Stadt Altensteig – Standesamt und Landratsamt Calw – Ordnungsamt* [1993] ECR I-1191, ECLI:EU:C:1993:115
Case C-415/93 *Union royale belge des sociétés de football association ASBL* v. *Jean-Marc Bosman, Royal club liégeois SA* v. *Jean-Marc Bosman and others and Union des associations européennes de football (UEFA)* v. *Jean-Marc Bosman* [1995] ECR I-4921, ECLI:EU:C:1995:463
Case C-55/94 *Reinhard Gebhard* v. *Consiglio dell'Ordine degli Avvocati e Procuratori di Milano* [1995] ECR I-4165, ECLI:EU:C:1995:411
Case C-336/94 *Eftalia Dafeki* v. *Landesversicherungsanstalt Württemberg* [1997] ECR I-6761, ECLI:EU:C:1997:579

Joined Cases C-4/95 and C-5/95 *Fritz Stöber and José Manuel Piosa Pereira* v. *Bundesanstalt für Arbeit* [1997] ECR I-511, ECLI:EU:C:1997:44
Case C-70/95 *Sodemare SA, Anni Azzurri Holding SpA and Anni Azzurri Rezzato Srl* v. *Regione Lombardia* [1997] ECR I-3395, ECLI:EU:C:1997:301
Joined Cases C-64/96 and C-65/96 *Land Nordrhein-Westfalen* v. *Kari Ücker and Vera Jacquet* [1997] ECR I-3171, ECLI:EU:C:1997:285
Case C-158/96 *Raymond Kohll* v. *Union des caisses de maladie* [1998] ECR I-1931, ECLI:EU:C:1998:171
Case C-249/96 *Lisa Jacqueline Grant* v. *South-West Trains Ltd* [1998] ECR I-621, ECLI:EU:C:1998:63
Case C-212/97 *Centros Ltd* v. *Erhvervs- og Selskabsstyrelsen* [1999] ECR I-1459, ECLI:EU:C:1999:126
Case C-287/98 *Grand Duchy of Luxemburg* v. *Berthe Linster, Aloyse Linster and Yvonne Linster* [2000] ECR I-6917, ECLI:EU:C:2000:468
Case C-368/98 *Abdon Vanbraekel and Others* v. *Alliance nationale des mutualités chrétiennes (ANMC)* [2001] ECR I-5363, ECLI:EU:C:2001:400
Case C-377/98 *Kingdom of Netherlands* v. *European Parliament and Council of the European Union* [2001] ECR I-7079, ECLI:EU:C:2001:523
Joined Cases C-122/99 P and C-125/99 P *D and Kingdom of Sweden* v. *Council of the European Union* [2001] ECR I-4319, ECLI:EU:C:2001:304
Case C-157/99 *B.S.M. Geraets-Smits* v. *Stichting Ziekenfonds VGZ* and *H.T.M. Peerbooms* v. *Stichting CZ Groep Zorgverzekeringen* [2001] ECR I-5473, ECLI:EU:C:2001:404
Case C-385/99 *V.G. Müller-Fauré* v. *Onderlinge Waarborgmaatschappij OZ Zorgverzekeringen UA* and *E.E.M. van Riet* v. *Onderlinge Waarborgmaatschappij ZAO Zorgverzekeringen* [2003] ECR I-4509, ECLI:EU:C:2003:270
Case C-413/99 *Baumbast and R* v. *Secretary of State for the Home Department* [2002] ECR I-7091, ECLI:EU:C:2002:493
Case C-208/00 *Überseering BV* v. *Nordic Construction Company Baumanagement GmbH (NCC)* [2002] ECR I-9919, ECLI:EU:C:2002:632
Case C-56/01 *Patricia Inizan* v. *Caisse primaire d'assurance maladie des Hauts-de-Seine* [2003] ECR I-12403, ECLI:EU:C:2003:578
Case C-322/01 *Deutscher Apothekerverband eV* v. *0800 DocMorris NV and Jacquel Waterval* [2003] ECR I-14887, ECLI:EU:C:2003:664
Case C-8/02 *Ludwig Leichtle* v. *Bundesanstalt für Arbeit* [2004] ECR I-2641, ECLI:EU:C:2004:161
Case C-36/02 *Omega Spielhallen- und Automatenaufstellungs-GmbH* v. *Oberbürgermeisterin der Bundesstadt Bonn* [2004] ECR I-9609, ECLI:EU:C:2004:614
Case C-148/02 *Carlos Garcia Avello* v. *Belgian State* [2003] ECR I-11613, ECLI:EU:C:2003:539
Case C-145/03 *Heirs of Annette Keller* v. *Instituto Nacional de la Seguridad Social (INSS) and de Gestión Sanitaria (Ingesa)* [2005] ECR I-2529, ECLI:EU:C:2005:211
Case C-540/03 *European Parliament* v. *Council of the European Union* [2006] ECR I-5769, ECLI:EU:C:2006:429
Case C-372/04 *The Queen, on the application of Yvonne Watts* v. *Bedford Primary Care Trust and Secretary of State for Health* [2006] ECR I-4325, ECLI:EU:C:2006:325
Case C-110/05 *Commission of the European Communities* v. *Italian Republic* [2009] ECR I-519, ECLI:EU:C:2009:66
Case C-444/05 *Aikaterini Stamatelaki* v. *NPDD Organismos Asfaliseos Eleftheron Epangelmation (OAEE)* [2007] ECR I-3185, ECLI:EU:C:2007:231
Case C-267/06 *Tadao Maruko* v. *Versorgungsanstalt der deutschen Bühnen* [2008] ECR I-1757, ECLI:EU:C:2008:179
Case C-353/06 *Stefan Grunkin and Dorothee Regina Paul* [2008] ECR I-7639, ECLI:EU:C:2008:559

Case C-506/06 *Sabine Mayr* v. *Bäckerei und Konditorei Gerhard Flöckner OHG* [2008] ECR I-1017, ECLI:EU:C:2008:119

Case C-33/07 *Ministerul Administraţiei şi Internelor – Direcţia Generală de Paşapoarte Bucureşti* v. *Gheorghe Jipa* [2008] ECR I-5157, ECLI:EU:C:2008:396

Case C-141/07 *Commission of the European Communities* v. *Federal Republic of Germany* [2008] ECR I-6935, ECLI:EU:C:2008:492

Case C-169/07 *Hartlauer Handelsgesellschaft mbG* v. *Wiener Landesregierung und Oberösterreichische Landesregierung* [2009] ECR I-1721, ECLI:EU:C:2009:141

Joined Cases C-171/07 and C-172/07 *Apothekerkammer des Saarlandes and Others and Helga Neumann-Seiwert* v. *Saarland and Ministerium für Justiz, Gesundheit und Soziales* [2009] ECR I-4171, ECLI:EU:C:2009:316

Case C-5/08 *Infopaq International A/S* v. *Danske Dagblades Forening* [2009] ECR I-6569, ECLI:EU:C:2009:465

Case C-19/08 *Migrationsverket* v. *Edgar Petrosian and Others* [2009] ECR I-495, ECLI:EU:C:2009:41

Case C-73/08 *Nicolas Bressol and Others and Céline Chaverot and Others* v. *Gouvernement de la Communauté française* [2010] ECR I-2735, ECLI:EU:C:2010:181

Case C-127/08 *Blaise Baheten Metock and Others* v. *Minister for Justice, Equality and Law Reform* [2008] ECR I-6241, ECLI:EU:C:2008:449

Case C-147/08 *Jürgen Römer* v. *Freie und Hansestadt Hamburg* [2011] ECR I-3591, ECLI:EU:C:2011:286

Case C-211/08 *European Commission* v. *Kingdom of Spain* [2010] ECR I-5267, ECLI:EU:C:2010:340

Case C-467/08 *Padawan SL* v. *Sociedad General de Autores y Editores de España (SGAE)* [2010] ECR I-10055, ECLI:EU:C:2010:620

Case C-512/08 *European Commission* v. *French Republic* [2010] ECR I-8833, ECLI:EU:C:2010:579

Case C-137/09 *Marc Michel Josemans* v. *Burgemeester van Maastricht* [2010] ECR I-13019, ECLI:EU:C:2010:774

Case C-173/09 *Georgi Ivanov Elchinov* v. *Natsionalna zdravnoosiguritelna kasa* [2010] ECR I-8889, ECLI:EU:C:2010:581

Case C-255/09 *European Commission* v. *Portuguese Republic* [2011] ECR I-10547, ECLI:EU:C:2011:695

Case C-391/09 *Malgožata Runevič-Vardyn and Łukasz Paweł Wardyn* v. *Vilniaus miesto savivaldybės administracija and Others* [2011] ECR I-3787, ECLI:EU:C:2011:291

Case C-403/09 *Jasna Detiček* v. *Maurizio Sgueglia* [2009] ECR I-12193, ECLI:EU:C:2009:810

Case C-34/10 *Oliver Brüstle* v. *Greenpeace eV* [2011] ECR I-9821, ECLI:EU:C:2011:669

Case C-393/10 *Dermod Patrick O'Brien* v. *Ministry of Justice* [2012] ECR 0000, ECLI:EU:C:2012:110

Joined Cases C-411/10 and C-493/10 *N.S.* v. *Secretary of State for the Home Department* and *M.E. and Others* v. *Refugee Applications Commissioner and Minister for Justice, Equality and Law Reform* [2011] ECR I-13905, ECLI:EU:C:2011:865

Case C-617/10 *Åklagaren* v. *Hans Åkerberg Fransson* [2013] ECR 0000, ECLI:EU:C:2013:105

Case C-83/11 *Secretary of State for the Home Department* v. *Muhammad Sazzadur Rahman and Others* [2012] ECR 0000, ECLI:EU:C:2012:519

Case C-399/11 *Stefano Melloni* v. *Ministerio Fiscal* [2013] ECR 0000, ECLI:EU:C:2013:107

Case C-648/11 *The Queen, on the application of MA and Others* v. *Secretary of State for the Home Department* [2013] ECR 0000, ECLI:EU:C:2013:367

Case C-167/12 *C.D.* v. *S.T.*, *nyr*, ECLI:EU:C:2014:169

Case C-267/12 *Frédéric Hay* v. *Crédit agricole mutuel de Charente-Maritime et des Deux-Sèvres* [2013 ECR 0000, ECLI:EU:C:2013:823

Case C-363/12 *Z.* v. *A Government department and The Board of management of a community school*, *nyr*, ECLI:EU:C:2014:159
Joined Cases C-58/13 and C-59/13 *Angelo Alberto Torresi en Pierfrancesco Torresi* v. *Consiglio dell'Ordine degli Avvocati di Macerata*, *nyr*, ECLI:EU:C:2014:2088

General Court

Case T-43/90 *José Miguel Díaz García* v. *European Parliament* [1992] ECR II-2619, ECLI:EU:T:1992:120
Case T-85/91 *Lilian R. Khouri* v. *Commission of the European Communities* [1992] ECR II-2637, ECLI:EU:T:1992:121
Case T-65/92 *Monique Arauxo-Dumay* v. *Commission of the European Communities* [1993] ECR II-597, ECLI:EU:T:1993:47
Case T-264/97 *D* v. *Council of the European Union* [1999] ECR FP-I-A-00001, ECLI:EU:T:1999:13
Case T-58/08 *Commission of the European Communities* v. *Anton Pieter Roodhuijzen* [2009] ECR II-3797, ECLI:EU:T:2009:385

Civil Service Tribunal

Case F-86/09 *W* v. *European Commission* [2010] ECR 0000, ECLI:EU:F:2010:125

England

R. v. *Bourne* [1939] 1 KB 687, [1938] 3 All ER 615
Wilkinson and Kitzinger v. *Attorney General*, unreported (31 July 2006)

Germany

Bundesverfassungsgericht (German Constitutional Court)

BVerfG 16 January 1957, Az. 1 BvR 253/56, *NJW* 1957 p. 297
BVerfG 17 January 1957 (dec.), Az. 1 BvL 4/54, *NJW* 1957 p. 417
BVerfG 10 May 1957, Az. 1 BvR 550/52, *NJW* 1957 p. 865
BVerfG 29 July 1959, Az. 1 BvR 205/58 a.o, *NJW* 1959 p. 1483
BVerfG 16 July 1969, Az. 1 BvL 19/63, *NJW* 1969 p. 1707
BVerfG 4 May 1971, Az 1 BvR 636/68, *NJW* 1971 p. 1509
BVerfG 2 October 1973, Az. 1 BvL 7/72, *NJW* 1973 p. 2195
BVerfG 14 November 1973 (dec.), Az. 1 BvR 719/69, *NJW* 1974 p. 545
BVerfG 29 May 1974, Az. 2 BvL 52/71, *NJW* 1974 p. 1697
BVerfG 25 February 1975, Az. 1 BvF 2/74 a.o., *NJW* 1975 p. 573
BVerfG 11 October 1978, Az. 1 BvR 16/72, *NJW* 1979 p. 595
BVerfG 28 February 1980, Az. 1 BvL 136/78
BVerfG 30 November 1982, Az. 1 BvR 818/81, *NJW* 1983 p. 511
BVerfG 18 April 1984 (dec.), Az. 1 BvL 43/81, *NJW* 1984 p. 1805
BVerfG, 14 November 1984 (dec.), Az. 1 BvR 14/82 and 1642/82

BVerfG 22 October 1986, Az. 2 BvR 197/83, *NJW* 1987 p. 577
BVerfG 18 January 1988 (dec.), Az. 1 BvR 1589/87, *NJW* 1988 p. 3010
BVerfG 31 January 1989, Az. 1 BvL 17/87, *NJW* 1989 p. 891
BVerfG 17 November 1992, Az. 1 BvL 8/87, *NJW* 1993 p. 643
BVerfG 26 January 1993, Az. 1 BvL 43/92, *NJW* 1933 p. 1517
BVerfG 28 May 1993, Az. 2 BvF 2/90 a.o., *NJW* 1993 p. 1751
BVerfG 4 October 1993 (dec.), Az. 1 BvR 640/93, *NJW* 1993 p. 3058
BVerfG 10 October 1995, Az. 1 BvR 1476/91 a.o., *NJW* 1995 p. 3303
BVerfG 16 February 2000, Az. 1 BvR 420/97, *NJW* 2000 p. 857
BVerfG 18 July 2001 (dec.), Az. 1 BvQ 23/01, *NJW* 2001 p. 2457
BVerfG 5 February 2002 (dec.), Az. 1 BvR 105/95 a.o., *NJW* 2002 p. 1185
BVerfG 17 July 2002, Az. 1 BvF 1/01, *NJW* 2002 p. 2543
BVerfG 11 March 2003 (dec.), Az. 1 BvR 426, *NJW* 2003 p. 1303
BVerfG 14 October 2004, Az. 2 BvR 1481/04, *NJW* 2004 p. 3407
BVerfG 9 November 2004, Az.1 BvR 684/98, *NJW* 2005 p. 1413
BVerfG 7 November 2006 (dec.), Az. 1 BvL 10/02, *NJW* 2007 p. 573
BVerfG 13 February 2007, Az. 1 BvR 421/05, *NJW* 2007 p. 753
BVerfG 28 February 2007, Az. 1 BvL 5/03, *NJW* 2007 p. 1343
BVerfG 20 September 2007 (dec.), Az. 2 BvR 855/06, *NJW* 2008 p. 209
BVerfG 8 November 2007 (dec.), Az. 2 BvR 2466/06
BVerfG 6 May 2008 (dec.), Az. 2 BvR 1830/06, *NJW* 2008 p. 2325
BVerfG 27 May 2008 (dec.), Az. 1 BvL 10/05, *NJW* 2008 p. 3117
BVerfG 13 October 2008 (dec.), Az. 1 BvR 1548/03, *NJW* 2009 p. 423
BVerfG 27 February 2009 (dec.), Az. 1 BvR 2982/07, *NJW* 2009 p. 1733
BVerfG 30 June 2009, Az. 2 BvE 2/08 a.o., *NJW* 2009 p. 2267
BVerfG 7 July 2009 (dec.), Az. 1 BvR 1164/07, *NJW* 2010 p. 1439
BVerfG 10 August 2009 (dec.), Az. 1 BvL 15/09
BVerfG 2 July 2010 (dec.), Az. 1 BvR 666/10, *NJW* 2011 p. 988
BVerfG 21 July 2010 (dec.), Az. 1 BvR 2464/07, *NJW* 2010 p. 2783
BVerfG 19 June 2012 (dec.), Az. 2 BvR 1397/09, *NJW* 2012 p. 2790
BVerfG 18 July 2012 (dec.), Az. 1 BvL 16/11, *NJW* 2012 p. 2719
BVerfG 22 August 2012 (dec.), Az. 1 BvR 573/12, *NJW-RR* 2013 p. 1
BVerfG 19 February 2013, Az. 1 BvL 1/11, 1 BvR 3247/09, *NJW* 2013 p. 847
BVerfG 7 May 2013 (dec.), Az. 2 BvR 909/06 a.o., *NJW* 2013 p. 2257
BVerfG 23 January 2014 (dec.), Az. 1 BvL 2/13

Bundesverwaltungsgericht (Federal Administrative Court)

BVerwG 27 February 1996, Az. 1 C 41/93, *NJW* 1997 p. 956
BVerwG 15 November 2007, Az. 2 C 33/06, *NJW* 2008 p. 868

Bundesgerichtshof (Supreme Court)

BGH 25 June 2008 (dec.), Az. XII ZB 163/06, *NJW* 2008 p. 3429
BGH 6 July 2010, Az. 5 StR 386/09, *NJW* 2010 p. 2672
BGH 16 October 2013 (dec.), Az. XII ZB 176/12, *NJW* 2014 p. 61

Bundesarbeitsgericht (Federal Labour Court)

BAG 29 April 2004, Az. 6 AZR 101/03
BAG 14 January 2009, Az. 3 AZR 20/07
BAG 15 September 2009, Az. 3 AZR 294/09, *NJW* 2010 p. 1474

Bundesfinanzhof (Federal Financial Court)

BFH 18 May 1999, Az. III R 46/97, *NJW* 1999 p. 2767
BFH 30 November 2004, Az. VIII R 61/04 (NV)
BFH 28 July 2005, Az. III R 30/03, *NJW* 2005 p. 3517
BFH 26 January 2006, Az. III R 51/05, *NJW* 2006 p. 1837
BFH 19 October 2006, Az. III R 29/06
BFH 10 May 2007, Az. III R 47/05, *NJW* 2007 p. 3596
BFH 16 December 2010, Az. VI R 43/10, *NJW* 2011 p. 2077
BFH 8 June 2011 (dec.), Az. III B 210/10

Bundessocialgericht (Federal Social Court)

BSG 3 April 2001, Az. B 1 KR 40/00 R, *NJW* 2002 p. 1598
BSG 9 October 2001, Az. B 1 KR 33/00 R, *NJW* 2002 p. 1517
BSG 22 March 2005, Az. B 1 KR 11/03 R, *NJW* 2005 p. 2476
BSG 19 September 2007, Az. B 1 KR 6/07 R
BSG 3 March 2009, Az. B 1 KR 7/08 R
BSG 17 February 2010, Az. B 1 KR 10/09 R

Kammergericht (Court of Appeal of Berlin)

KG 19 June 2008 (dec.), Az. 16 WF 163/08
KG 9 October 2008 (dec.), Az. 3 Ws 139/08
KG 3 March 2011 (dec.), Az. 1 W 74/17
KG 11 December 2012 (dec.), Az. 1 W 404/12
KG 1 August 2013, Az. 1 W 413/12, *NJW* 2015 p. 479

Socialgericht (Social Court)

SG Berlin 23 March 2007, Az. S 86 KR 660/04

Oberverwaltungsgericht (Administrative Court of Appeal)

OVG Münster 15 January 2014 (dec.), Az. 12 A 2078/13

Oberlandesgericht (Court of Appeal)

OLG Hamm 7 April 1983 (dec.), Az. 3 Ss OWi 2007/82, *NJW* 1985 p. 2205

OLG Hamm 2 December 1985 (dec.), Az. 11 W 18/85, *NJW* 1986 p. 781
OLG Hamm 1 December 2009 (dec.), Az. 15 Wx 236/09, *NJW* 2010 p. 2065
OLG Hamburg 26 January 2010 (dec.), Az. 2 Wx 125/09
OLG Rostock 7 May 2010, Az. 7 U 67/09
OLG Köln 5 July 2010 (dec.), Az. 16 Wx 64/10
OLG Karlsruhe 16 November 2010 (dec.), Az. 5 UF 217/10, *NJW* 2011 p. 1012
OLG Hamburg 22 December 2010 (dec.), Az. 2 Wx 23/09, *NJW* 2011 p. 1104
OLG Celle 10 March 2011 (dec.), Az. 17 W 48/10, *NJW-RR* 2011 p. 1157
OLG Zweibrücken 21 March 2011 (dec.), Az. 3 W 170/10, *NJW-RR* 2011 p. 1156
OLG München 6 July 2011 (dec.), Az. 31 Wx 103/11
OLG Stuttgart 7 February 2012 (dec.), Az. 8 W 46/12, *NJW-RR* 2012 p. 389
OLG Hamm 6 February 2013, Az. I-14 U 7/12, *NJW* 2013 p. 1167
OLG Düsseldorf 26 April 2013 (dec.), Az. I-3 Wx 211/12
OLG Karlsruhe 7 February 2014 (dec.), Az. 16 UF 274/13, *NJW* 2014 p. 2050
OLG Schleswig 14 March 2014 (dec.), Az. 12 UF 14/13

Landesgericht (State Court)

LG Freiburg 25 March 1987, Az. 8 O 556/86, *NJW* 1987 p. 1486
LG Frankfurt 22 March 1993 (dec.), Az. 2/9 T 17/93, *NJW* 1993 p. 1998
LG Dortmund 13 August 2007 (dec.), Az. 15 T 87/07
LG Münster 16 March 2009 (dec.), Az. 05 T 775/08
LG Berlin 14 May 2009, Az. (512) 1 Kap Js 1424-06 KLs (26/08), *NJW* 2010 p. 2672
LG Hamburg 4 November 2009 (dec.), Az. 301 T 596/09
LG Frankfurt a.M. 3 August 2012 (dec.), Az. 2-09 T 51/11

Verwaltungsgericht (Administrative Court)

VG Karlsruhe 9 September 2004, Az. 2 K 1420/03
VG München 1 June 2006 (dec.), Az. M 3 K 05.1595
VG Münster 13 December 2007, Az. 3 K 1845/05
VG Darmstadt 5 June 2008 (dec.), Az. 5 L 277/08
VG München 30 October 2008, Az. M 12 K 08.1484
VG Köln 19 March 2009, Az. 13 K 1841/07
VG Berlin 26 November 2009 (dec.), Az. 11 L 396/09
VG Berlin 15 June 2010, Az. 23 A 242/08
VG Berlin 15 April 2011 (dec.), Az. 23 L 79/11
VG Berlin 5 September 2012 (dec.), Az. 23 L 283/12
VG Köln 13 November 2013, Az. 10 K 2043/12

Finanzgericht (Financial Court)

FG München 21 February 2000 (dec.), Az. 16 V 5568/99
FG Niedersachsen 4 June 2002, Az. 6 K 525/98 Ki
FG Düsseldorf 9 May 2003, Az. 18 K 7931/00 E
FG Saarland 21 January 2004, Az. 1 K 466/02, *NJW* 2004 p. 1268
FG Niedersachsen 10 June 2004, Az. 5 K 156/03

FG Berlin 21 June 2004, Az. 9 K 9037/03
FG Hamburg 8 December 2004, Az. II 510/03
FG Niedersachsen 15 December 2004, Az. 2 K 292/03
FG Niedersachsen 8 June 2005, Az. 2 K 267/03
FG Niedersachsen 14 March 2013, Az. 5 K 9/11

Amtsgericht (District Court)

AG Gütersloh 17 December 1985, Az. 5 XVI 7/85
AG Frankfurt a.M. 21 December 1992 (dec.), Az. 40 UR III E 166/92, *NJW* 1993 p. 940
AG Hamm 19 March 2007 (dec.), Az. XVI 23/06
AG Münster 30 September 2008 (dec.), Az. 105 XVI 5/08
AG Hamburg 24 June 2009 (dec.), Az. 60 III 35/09
AG Nürnberg 14 December 2009 (dec.), Az. UR III 0264/09
AG Münster 20 January 2010, Az. 56 F 79/09, *NJW-RR* 2010 p. 1308
AG Nürnberg 25 September 2010 (dec.), Az. XVI 57/09
AG Stuttgart 25 October 2010 (dec.), Az. 29 F 2062/09
AG Hannover 3 November 2010 (dec.), Az. 85 III 103/10
AG Elmshorn 20 December 2010 (dec.), Az. 46 F 9/10, *NJW* 2011 p. 1085
AG München 4 January 2011 (dec.), Az. 721 UR III 193/10
AG Hamm 22 February 2011 (dec.), Az. XVI 192/08
AG Stadtroda 3 April 2012, Az. 2 F 151/11
AG Schleswig 4 January 2013 (dec.), Az. 91 F 276/11
AG Berlin-Schöneberg 8 March 2013, Az. 24 F 250/12
AG Frankfurt a.M. 7 May 2013 (dec.), Az. 464 F 10402/12
AG Neuss 13 May 2013 (dec.), Az. 45 F 74/13

Ireland

Supreme Court of Ireland

Ryan v. *Attorney General* [1965] IESC 1; [1965] IR 294
The State (Nicolaou) v. *An Bord Uchtála* [1966] IR 567
McGee v. *Attorney General & Anor* [1973] IESC 2; [1974] IR 284
G. v. *An Bord Uchtála* [1980] IR 32
Murphy v. *Attorney General* [1982] IR 241
Campus Oil v. *Minister for Industry* [1983] IESC 2; [1983] IR 82
Norris v. *Attorney General* [1983] IESC 3; [1984] IR 36
The Attorney General (Society for the Protection of the Unborn Children (Ireland Ltd) v. *Open Door Counselling Ltd* [1988] IR 593; [1987] ILRM 477
The Society for the Protection of Unborn Children (Ireland) Ltd v. *Grogan* [1989] IR 753; [1990] ILRM 350
Murray v. *Ireland* [1991] ILRM 465
Attorney General v. *X* [1992] 1 IR 1; [1992] ILRM 401
Attorney General ex rel Society for the Protection of Unborn Children (Ireland) Ltd. v. *Open Door Counselling & Dublin Well Woman Centre Ltd.* [1994] 1 ILRM 256
B. v. *R* [1995] 1 ILRM 491

Article 26 and the Regulation of Information (Services outside the State for the Termination of Pregnancies) Bill 1995, In Re [1995] IESC 9; [1995] 1 IR 1
WO'R v. *EH* [1996] IESC 4; [1996] 2 IR 248
.O'T. v. *B., The Rotunda Girls Aid Society & Father Doyle, and M. H.* v. *Father Doyle and The Rotunda Girls Aid Society* [1998] 2 IR 321
Sinnott v. *Minister for Education* [2001] IESC 63; [2001] 2 IR 545
Baby O. v. *Minister for Justice, Equality and Law Reform* [2002] IESC 44; [2002] 2 IR 169
ID.T. v. *C.T.* [2003] 1 ILRM 321
O'Shea v. *Ireland* [2007] 2 IR 313
Roche v. *Roche & ors* [2009] IESC 82
McD v. *L. & Anor* [2009] IESC 81; [2010] 2 IR 199

High Court of Ireland

Donovan v. *Minister for Justice* [1951] 85 ILTR 134
Murray v. *Ireland* [1985] IR 532
SPUC v. *Grogan and others* [1993] 1 CMLR 197
A. and B. v. *Eastern Health Board & C.* [1997] IEHC 176; [1998] 1 IR 464; [1998] 1 ILRM 460
Foy v. *An t-Ard Chláraitheoir & Ors* [2002] IEHC 116
Zappone & Anor v. *Revenue Commissioners & Ors* [2006] IEHC 404
R. v. *R. & Ors* [2006] IEHC 221
M. R. v. *T. R. & Ors* [2006] IEHC 359
D (A Minor) v. *District Judge Brennan, the Health Services Executive, Ireland and the Attorney General,* unreported (9 May 2007)
Foy v. *An t-Ard Chláraitheoir & Ors* [2007] IEHC 470
McD v. *L. & Anor* [2008] IEHC 96
Ugbelese & Ors v. *The Minister for Justice Equality and Law Reform* [2009] IEHC 598
McD v. *L & Anor* [2010] IEHC 120
HAH v. *SAA*, unreported (4 November 2010)
M.R. & Another v. *An t Ard Chláraitheoir* [2013] IEHC 91
High Court 5 March 2013, 2011 No. 68 CAF, *unreported*

The Netherlands

Hoge Raad (Supreme Court)

HR 24 May 1897, W 6978
HR 6 November 1987, *NJ* 1988 No. 829, ECLI:NL:HR:1987:AB9568
HR 24 February 1989, *NJ* 1989 No. 741, ECLI:NL:HR:1989:AD0648
HR 10 March 1989, *NJ* 1990 No. 24, ECLI:NL:1989:AC1343
HR 23 March 1990, *NJ* 1991 Nos. 149 and 150, ECLI:NL:HR:1990:AD1066
HR 29 May 1990, *NJ* 1991 No. 217, ECLI:NL:HR:1990:ZC8539
HR 19 October 1990, *NJ* 1992 No. 129, ECLI:NL:HR:1990:AD1260
HR 15 April 1994, *NJ* 1994 No. 608, ECLI:NL:HR:1994:ZC1337
HR 16 June 1995, *NJ* 1997 No. 131, ECLI:NL:HR:1995:ZC1757
HR 5 September 1997, *NJ* 1998 No. 686, ECLI:NL:HR:1997:ZC2420
HR 22 April 2005, ECLI:NL:HR:2005:AT4486

Afdeling Bestuursrechtspraak Raad van State (Administrative Jurisdiction Division of the Council of State)

ABRvS 3 May 2006, ECLI:NL:RVS:2006:AW7365

Centrale Raad van Beroep (Central Appeals Tribunal)

CRvB 19 November 1985, ECLI:NL:CRVB:1985:AK2681
CRvB 11 July 2000, ECLI:NL:CRVB:2000:ZB8921
CRvB 31 January 2007, ECLI:NL:CRVB:2007:AZ8510
CRvB 14 February 2007, ECLI:NL:CRVB:2007:AZ9694
CRvB 14 February 2007, ECLI:NL:CRVB:2007:AZ9700
CRvB 24 June 2011 (dec.), ECLI:NL:CRVB:2011:BQ9855

Gerechtshof (Court of Appeal)

Hof 's-Gravenhage 18 June 1981, *NJ* 1983 No. 94, ECLI:NL:GHSGR:1981:AC7248
Hof 's-Gravenhage 2 June 1989, *NJ* 1989 No. 871, ECLI:NL:GHSGR:1989:AB8024
Hof Amsterdam 6 May 1993, *NJ* 1994, 681, ECLI:NL:GHAMS:1993:AB9423
Hof 's-Gravenhage 21 August 1998, ECLI:NL:GHSGR:1998:AD2927
Hof Arnhem 16 April 2002, ECLI:NL:GHARN:2002:AE1479
Hof Amsterdam 25 November 2008, ECLI:NL:GHAMS:2008:BG5157
Hof 's-Gravenhage 10 February 2010, ECLI:NL:GHSGR:2010:BL8563
Hof Amsterdam 4 May 2010, ECLI:NL:GHAMS:2010:BM3903
Hof 's-Gravenhage 1 December 2010, ECLI:NL:GHSGR:2010:BO7387

Rechtbank (District Court)

Rb. Amsterdam 5 February 1942, *NJ* 1942 No. 244
Rb. Amsterdam 20 January 1949, *NJ* 1949 No. 586
Rb. Amsterdam 26 March 1953, *NJ* 1953 No. 377
Rb. Amsterdam 8 July 1976, *NJ* 1977 No. 477, ECLI:NL:RBAMS:1976:AC0431
Rb. Rotterdam 5 December 1988, *NJ* 1989 No. 871
Rb. 's-Gravenhage (pres.) 9 March 1989, ECLI:NL:RBSGR:1989:AH2615
Rb. Amsterdam 13 February 1990, *Rekest no.* 89.2072 H
Rb. 's-Gravenhage (pres.) 17 July 1990, ECLI:NL:RBSGR:1990:AD1197
Rb. Utrecht 26 March 1997 and 10 December 1997, *NJ* 1999 No. 462, ECLI:NL:RBUTR:1997:AC1768
Rb. Utrecht 24 May 2002, ECLI:NL:RBUTR:2002:AE3518
Rb. Leeuwarden 24 June 2003, ECLI:NL:RBLEE:2003:AH8543
Rb. Zwolle 30 June 2003, ECLI:NL:RBZWO:2003:AI0668
Rb. Amsterdam 7 October 2003, ECLI:NL:RBAMS:2003:AN9605
Rb. Amsterdam 7 October 2003, ECLI:NL:RBAMS:2003:AN9606
Rb. Almelo 13 November 2003, ECLI:NL:RBALM:2003:BM5834
Rb. 's-Gravenhage 12 February 2004, ECLI:NL:RBSGR:2004:AO3791
Rb. Amsterdam 1 June 2004, ECLI:NL:RBAMS:2004:AP1251
Rb. Maastricht 28 June 2004, ECLI:NL:RBMAA:2004:AP8808

Rb. Utrecht 13 July 2004, case no. SBR03/1073, *unpublished*
Rb. Amsterdam 28 February 2005, AWB 04/3469, *unpublished*
Rb. Rotterdam 9 May 2006, ECLI:NL:RBROT:2006:AX2185
Rb. Utrecht 24 October 2007, ECLI:NL:RBUTR:2007:BB6360
Rb. 's-Gravenhage 11 December 2007, ECLI:NL:RBSGR:2007:BB9844
Rb. Arnhem 20 February 2008, ECLI:NL:RBARN:2008:BC8012
Rb. 's-Gravenhage 7 October 2008, ECLI:NL:RBSGR:2008:BG0849
Rb. Roermond 29 June 2009, ECLI:NL:RBROE:2009:BJ0644
Rb. 's-Gravenhage 14 September 2009, ECLI:NL:RBSGR:2009:BK1197
Rb. Groningen 27 April 2010, ECLI:NL:RBGRO:2010:BM3904
Rb. 's-Gravenhage (vrzr.) 9 November 2010, ECLI:NL:RBSGR:2010:BP3764
Rb. Haarlem (vrzr.) 10 January 2011, ECLI:NL:RBHAA:2011:BP0426
Rb. 's-Hertogenbosch 18 August 2011, ECLI:NL:RBSHE:2011:BR5334
Rb. 's-Gravenhage 24 October 2011, ECLI:NL:RBSGR:2011:BU3627
Rb. 's-Gravenhage 18 January 2012, ECLI:NL:RBSGR:2012:BV2597
Rb. Dordrecht 7 February 2012, ECLI:NL:RBDOR:2012:BV6246
Rb. Haarlem 6 November 2012, ECLI:NL:RBHAA:2012:5285
Rb. 's-Gravenhage 8 January 2013, ECLI:NL:RBDHA:2013:18948
Rb. 's-Gravenhage 13 August 2013, ECLI:NL:RBDHA:2013:12313
Rb. 's-Gravenhage 23 October 2013, ECLI:NL:RBDHA:2013:14133
Rb. Noord-Holland 18 December 2013, ECLI:NL:RBNHO:2013:12578

United States of America

US Supreme Court

Griswold v. *Connecticut*, 381 US 479 (1965)
Eisenstadt v. *Baird*, 405 US 438 (1972)
Roe v. *Wade* 410 US 113 (1973)

INDEX*

* Terms followed by section. Section numbers with an asterisk include the subsections of that respective section.

N

O

P

R

S

Curriculum Vitae

Nelleke Koffeman was born in 1984 in Oss, the Netherlands. After completing the gymnasium at the Corderius College in Amersfoort in 2002, she chose to study law at Leiden University. Four years later, in 2006, she obtained her Master's Diploma in Constitutional and Administrative Law from this university. During her studies she worked, *inter alia*, as a student assistant at the Europa Institute of the Leiden Law School. Also, she did internships with the Permanent Representation of the Netherlands to the Council of Europe in Strasbourg and with the human rights department of the Dutch Ministry of Justice in The Hague.

In 2007 Koffeman lectured the Moot Court course for undergraduate students at Leiden Law School. Subsequently, in 2008, she was appointed by the E.M. Meijers Institute of the Leiden Law School as a PhD candidate at the Leiden Europa Institute. In 2008, she contributed, in that position, to the so-called Fundamental Rights Agency Group of Legal Experts (FRALEX) and, *inter alia*, co-authored a comparative study on child trafficking in Europe for the Fundamental Rights Agency of the European Union. She also lectured and coordinated several courses on European (human rights) law at Leiden Law School both at undergraduate and graduate level.

In the course of her PhD research Nelleke Koffeman has visited NUI Galway in Ireland twice, in 2009 and 2013. She has further been a visiting researcher at the Humboldt Universität zu Berlin (in 2011) and at Fordham Law School in New York (in 2013). For the latter two research visits she was awarded research grants of the German Academic Exchange Service (DAAD) and the Dr. H.A. van Beuningen fund of the Leiden University Fund respectively.

Koffeman has regularly participated in (international) conferences, has published in various (Dutch) legal journals and books and has been involved in several research projects, including a study on personal autonomy in medical care for the Netherlands Organisation for Health Research and Development in 2013. In 2015 Koffeman was appointed Assistant Professor in European law at the Europa Institute of Leiden University.

School of Human Rights Research Series

The School of Human Rights Research is a joint effort by human rights researchers in the Netherlands. Its central research theme is the nature and meaning of international standards in the field of human rights, their application and promotion in the national legal order, their interplay with national standards, and the international supervision of such application. The School of Human Rights Research Series only includes English titles that contribute to a better understanding of the different aspects of human rights.

For previous volumes in the series, please visit http://shr.intersentia.com.

Published titles within the Series:

65. Gustavo Arosemena, *Rights, Scarcity and Justice. An Analytical Inquiry into the Adjudication of the Welfare Aspects of Human Rights*
    ISBN 978-1-78068-275-4
66. Etienne Ruvebana, *Prevention of Genocide under International Law. An analysis of the obligations of states and the United Nations to prevent genocide at the primary, secondary and tertiary levels*
    ISBN 978-1-78068-273-0
67. Evgeni Moyakine, *The Privatized Art of War. Private Military and Security Companies and State Responsibility for Their Unlawful Conduct in Conflict Areas*
    ISBN 978-1-78068-281-5
68. Esther Janssen, *Faith in Public Debate. On Freedom of Expression, Hate Speech and Religion in France and The Netherlands*
    ISBN 978-1-78068-309-6
69. Stefanie Jansen-Wilhelm, *Accepting Assistance in the Aftermath of Disasters*
    ISBN 978-1-78068-329-4
70. Helen Beckmann-Hamzei, *The Child in ICC Proceedings*
    ISBN 978-1-78068-339-3
71. Karel De Meester, *The Investigation Phase in International Criminal Procedure: In Search of Common Rules*
    ISBN 978-1-78068-305-8